KT-569-715

Neuropsychology for Clinical Practice

Neuropsychology for Clinical Practice

Etiology, Assessment, and Treatment of Common Neurological Disorders

Russell L. Adams
Oscar A. Parsons
Jan L. Culbertson
Sara Jo Nixon

American Psychological Association • Washington, DC

Published by
American Psychological Association
750 First Street, NE
Washington, DC 20002

Copies may be ordered from
APA Order Department
P.O. Box 2710
Hyattsville, MD 20784

In the UK and Europe, copies may be ordered from
American Psychological Association
3 Henrietta Street
Covent Garden, London
WC2E 8LU England

Typeset in Berkeley by University Graphics, York, PA

Printer: Edwards Brothers, Inc., Ann Arbor, MI
Cover Designer: Berg Design, Albany, NY
Technical/Production Editor: Molly R. Flickinger

Library of Congress Cataloging-in-Publication Data
Neuropsychology for clinical practice : etiology, assessment, and
treatment of common neurological disorders / edited by Russell L.
Adams . . . [et al.].
p. cm.
Includes bibliographical references and indexes.
ISBN 1-55798-298-8 (acid-free paper)
1. Neuropsychiatry. 2. Clinical neuropsychology. I. Adams,
Russell L., 1941–
[DNLM: 1. Central Nervous System Diseases. 2. Child Development
Disorders. WL 300 N49384 1996]
RC341.N4356 1996
616.8—dc20
DNLM/DLC
for Library of Congress 95-49944
CIP

British Library Cataloguing-in-Publication Data
A CIP record is available from the British Library

Printed in the United States of America
First edition

This book is dedicated to Scott Russell Adams, who died on August 5, 1990, of complications surrounding a head injury. He was a third-year religion major at Baylor University when injured in an accident while volunteering his time cleaning up after a special universitywide event.

Contents

Contributors

Russell L. Adams, *Director of the Adult Neuropsychological Laboratory, of Postdoctoral Training in Clinical Neuropsychology, and of the Clinical Psychology Internship Program, Department of Psychiatry and Behavioral Sciences, University of Oklahoma Health Sciences Center*

William W. Beatty, *Director, Graduate Studies in Biopsychology, Department of Psychiatry and Behavioral Sciences, University of Oklahoma Health Sciences Center*

Jan L. Culbertson, *Director, Neuropsychology Services, Child Study Center, University of Oklahoma Health Sciences Center*

Jane E. Edmonds, *Intern, Child Study Center, University of Oklahoma Health Sciences Center and Mental Health Consortium*

Michelle R. Jenkins, *Phoenix, Arizona (formerly, Postdoctoral Clinical Neuropsychology Fellow, University of Oklahoma Health Sciences Center)*

Herman E. Jones, *Neuropsychologist, Comprehensive Oklahoma Program for Epilepsy, Epilepsy Center, Department of Neurology, University of Oklahoma Health Sciences Center*

Kevin R. Krull, *University of Chicago Medical School, Chicago, Illinois (formerly, Postdoctoral Clinical Neuropsychology Fellow, University of Oklahoma Health Sciences Center)*

William R. Leber, *Director of Neuropsychology, Veterans Affairs Medical Clinic, University of Oklahoma Health Sciences Center*

Sara Jo Nixon, *Director of Cognitive Studies Laboratory, Department of Psychiatry and Behavioral Sciences, University of Oklahoma Health Sciences Center*

Oscar A. Parsons, *George Lynn Cross Research Professor Emeritus, Department of Psychiatry and Behavioral Sciences, University of Oklahoma Health Sciences Center*

Eugene J. Rankin, *Immanuel Rehabilitation Center, Omaha, Nebraska (formerly, Postdoctoral Clinical Neuropsychology Fellow, University of Oklahoma Health Sciences Center)*

James G. Scott, *Director of Pediatric Neuropsychology Laboratory, University of Oklahoma Health Sciences Center*

Vicki M. Soukup, *Department of Neurology, University of Texas Medical Branch, Galveston (formerly, Clinical Psychology Intern, University of Oklahoma Health Sciences Center)*

David J. G. Williamson, *Neuropsychological Services, Columbus, Georgia (formerly, Postdoctoral Clinical Neuropsychology Fellow, University of Oklahoma Health Sciences Center)*

Preface

This book was developed in response to the need for mental health practitioners (e.g., clinical psychologists, clinical neuropsychologists, psychiatrists, social workers, and family counselors) to have a practical, hands-on resource describing the etiology, assessment, and treatment of the most common neuropsychological disorders.[1] As the first draft of the book was reviewed by experts in the field, it became clear that the book would serve a much broader audience, including graduate students taking courses in neuropsychology or in a neuropsychology rotation as part of a clinical internship; postdoctoral students in neuropsychology; and others who work with people who have neuropsychological disorders, such as rehabilitation counselors and attorneys.

A number of books today provide a compendium of specific neuropsychological tests or a list of syndromes and their associated neuropsychological correlates. Still others are specialized texts on specific neurological disorders—such as head injury, dementia, or seizures—presenting a sometimes overwhelming amount of information to the practitioner or neuropsychologist. My coeditors and I felt that what was missing was a practical clinical book that could integrate information on neuropsychological assessment and test selection with descriptions of symptom presentation, etiology, epidemiology, genetics, pathophysiology, prognosis, and treatment of the most common neurological disorders.

The authors of individual chapters are (or were) all associated in some fashion with the University of Oklahoma Health Sciences Center. Many chapters were written by combining the knowledge and experience of a faculty neuropsychologist with that of a second-year postdoctoral neuropsychological fellow. This combination was engineered to provide the dual advantages of depth of experience and the freshness, inquisitiveness, and practicality of bright young neuropsychologists of the future.

Because of the common association of the chapter authors, a description of the neuropsychological program at the University of Oklahoma Health Sciences Center is in order. The Adult Oklahoma Neuropsychology Laboratory at the University Hospital was one of the first in the country, established in 1962 by Oscar A. Parsons. Since 1978, it has been under my direction. Three other laboratories are also part of the neuropsychology program at the University of Oklahoma Health Sciences Center: One is located at the Veterans Affairs Medical Center, under the direction of William R. Leber. Another child neuropsychology laboratory is housed at the Oklahoma Children's Hospital Pediatric Department (Child Study Center) and directed by Jan L. Culbertson. A third child neuropsychology laboratory is directed by James G. Scott in the Department of Psychiatry and Behavioral Sciences.

The staff at the Health Sciences Center is composed of six clinical neuropsychologists and two

[1]In fact, the book had its genesis in the Clinical Psychology Division (Division 12) of the American Psychological Association.

experimental neuropsychologists. There is also a clinical psychology internship program with approximately eight interns. Two of these interns are in the specialized neuropsychology training program. There are also from two to five postdoctoral neuropsychology fellows in the program each year. One staff member who specializes in biological psychology trains a number of students specializing in experimental neuropsychology.

Oscar A. Parsons, who remains senior mentor for the program staff, also developed the Biological Psychology Program, Psychology Internship, and Neuropsychology Postdoctoral Training Program. Herman E. Jones, a neuropsychologist at the epilepsy center, works with the Neurology Department and is actively involved in the training program. Each chapter in this book is authored or coauthored by a staff neuropsychologist writing in his or her specific area of specialty.

This book is certainly not meant to be a cookbook. It will not enable the reader to proceed immediately to testing a given patient after reviewing a single chapter. Although many specific guidelines and suggestions are provided throughout, the contributors do not mean to imply that the way in which staff at the University of Oklahoma Health Sciences Center evaluate patients is the only way or necessarily the best way. It is simply a way that staff have found most useful over the years. Readers, especially attorneys, are advised that the guidance given is presented only as suggestions and recommendations; fully trained and competent neuropsychologists can and do deviate markedly from information presented in this book and still perform excellent evaluations.

This book is dedicated to my son, Scott Russell Adams, who suffered a head injury and later died while a student at Baylor University. This book is also dedicated to Sue Adams, my wife, and my son David. Recognition is also given to the meritorious Karen Dean, who has been the psychometrician at the University of Oklahoma laboratory for over 25 years. Special thanks are extended to Thomas Boll for his review of a draft of the book, as well as to Eddie Schoelen and Holly Stokes for their word-processing skills and for providing other assistance needed to bring this book to completion. Both Peggy Schlegel and Molly Flickinger of APA Books have been very helpful while moving this book through its development and production stages, respectively. The volume editors also thank our students, who have taught us, and our many patients, who through their suffering and moral courage have taught us even more.

Russell L. Adams

CHAPTER 1

INTRODUCTION

Russell L. Adams

As a profession, clinical neuropsychology is relatively new in comparison with other areas of psychology. However, the field has grown rapidly, from a small group of scientists and practitioners in the early 1960s to one of the largest specialty groups within psychology today. As one example of this growth, although the American Psychological Association's (APA's) Division of Neuropsychology was established in the late 1970s, it is now one of the largest divisions in the APA.

Although the profession of clinical neuropsychology is fairly new, the term *neuropsychology* was used occasionally in the 1930s and 1940s. Hans Lukas Teuber used the term in the title of his presentation at the APA convention in 1948. Also in his presentation, Teuber stated that "neuropsychological" test methods should be used in assessing lesion locations in clinical practice (Benton, 1986).

WHAT IS NEUROPSYCHOLOGY?

To put it succinctly, neuropsychology as a science is the study of brain–behavior relationships. Clinical neuropsychology as a practice is the application of these brain–behavior relationship principles to the individual patient for assessment, treatment, and rehabilitative purposes.

APA's Division of Clinical Neuropsychology (Division 40) has formally defined a clinical neuropsychologist as "a professional psychologist who applies principles of assessment and intervention based on the scientific study of human behavior as it relates to normal and abnormal functioning of the central nervous system" (Adams & Rourke, 1992, p. 5).[1] Division 40 has also specified the training required by these neuropsychologists in order to practice. This training has as a prerequisite a doctorate in psychology and involves 2 years of additional formal postdoctoral training in clinical neuropsychology, as well as completion of a 1-year specialized neuropsychology internship.

The types of referral questions asked of clinical neuropsychologists by physicians vary a great deal. They may include diagnostic questions, such as "Does this elderly patient have dementia, or does he have pseudodementia?" Or they may be prognostic questions concerning future performance: "What can be expected in the future of this patient, who has had a severe head injury?" Vocational and placement questions—such as "Will this patient be able to return to work, and, if so, what jobs might be suitable for her?"—are also common.

WHO THIS BOOK CAN INFORM

This book is intended for several audiences, each of whom may find the book useful in a slightly different way. The first audience consists of clinical psychologists and other mental health professionals (e.g., social workers, psychiatrists, and family counselors) who provide therapy and other services to individuals with neurological problems and their fami-

[1]Hereinafter, and throughout the book, clinical neuropsychologists may be referred to simply as *neuropsychologists*, because in the chapters that follow, the applied clinical context is assumed.

lies. This audience will benefit by gaining an understanding of the nature of various disorders, including typical symptom presentation and how these symptoms affect functioning, both in the therapy setting and in the patient's everyday life. These professionals will also learn about the process of neuropsychological diagnosis, which will allow them to communicate better with neuropsychologists and other specialists and make better use of the reports and feedback they may receive about their patients. Finally, this audience will benefit from the specific guidance that is provided with regard to treatment and the limitations that are often involved in treating individuals struggling with neuropsychological disorders.

The second audience for this book consists of graduate students in psychology who are either taking a class in neuropsychology or participating in a neuropsychology rotation in a clinical internship. All of the chapters in the book have been developed to provide information in the most accessible way possible. Basic concepts are explained and information is organized in such a way as to make the practice of neuropsychology with patients having specific disorders concrete and comprehensive. Because of these same features, postdoctoral neuropsychology fellows will also find the book useful as they begin their formal training.

The third audience for this book comprises physicians who refer patients for neuropsychological assessment; additional medical personnel, such as nurses, physical therapists, occupational therapists, vocational rehabilitation counselors; and others who use the results of neuropsychological assessments in their respective areas of practice. Attorneys and judges will find much to help them put neuropsychological assessment findings in context. In legal contexts, however, one should keep in mind that the guidance given in this book represents authors' particular approaches to practice. As mentioned in the preface, fully trained and competent neuropsychologists can and do deviate markedly from information presented in this book and still perform excellent evaluations.

COMMON NEUROPSYCHOLOGICAL DISORDERS

This book describes the etiology, symptom presentation, neuropsychological evaluation, and treatment of some of the most common neurological–neurosurgical disorders coming to the attention of the clinical neuropsychologist today. To determine the most common disorders, we consulted the 1990 survey by Putnam and DeLuca. Conducted with 872 neuropsychologists, this survey asked participants questions concerning the amount of time that they spend seeing patients of different diagnostic groups. The percentages presented below are approximations obtained by averaging the responses of neuropsychologists in private practice with those who work in other settings (e.g., university hospitals, medical schools, or medical group practices). Patients with traumatic brain injury occupied the highest percentage of neuropsychologists' time (22%). Omitting psychiatric patients, the next most common diagnostic group of patients seen were those with learning disabilities (11.5%), followed by patients with dementia (9%). In descending order, the other diagnostic groups occupying significant amounts of neuropsychologists' time were as follows: forensic referrals (8%); cerebral vascular accidents (7%); other geriatric diagnoses, including Parkinson's disease (5%); seizures (4%); substance abuse (4%); brain tumors (3%); pain syndrome (2%); toxic encephalography (2%); demyelinating disorders, such as multiple sclerosis (1%); and AIDS (1%).

ORGANIZATION OF THE BOOK

This book is divided into three major sections, addressing adult neuropsychology, child and life-span neuropsychology, and forensic and treatment issues. What follows is a brief description of the chapters in each section, including the referral questions that are frequently posed for patients with these conditions.

Section I: Adult Neuropsychology

The problems discussed in this first section were chosen for inclusion in this book because they are generally among the most common neuropsychological problems referred to neuropsychologists. Patients with traumatic brain injury, which is described in chapter 2, compose the most frequently referred group. Head injuries by and large occur mostly in younger patients. Frequently, referral questions involve prognosis and vocational evaluations: What type of job can this patient do now that he or she has had a head injury? Does it make sense for him or her to return to college, and, if so, when? What can be done to help this patient's anger problem and marked personality change? Do you think he or she will ever go back to work? Head-injured patients differ much in severity, ranging from patients in chronic vegetative states to those who can return or go on to college. This chapter emphasizes that neuropsychological tests chosen to assess patients who have traumatic brain injuries must be able to measure a wide spectrum of disorders.

Chapters 3 and 4 cover dementia, the second most common reason for referrals of adult patients. These patients may have Alzheimer's disease, vascular dementia, pseudodementia, or reversible dementia. Referral questions are frequently along the following lines: "Does this 60-year-old patient have early dementia or are her problems in memory the result of normal aging?" "Please evaluate and provide a baseline for the neuropsychological status of this patient with vascular dementia." Alternatively, a treating physician may ask: "Please assist with this patient's refusal to accept restriction on her driving." "Help the family understand what to expect from this patient in the future" or "Does this patient have early dementia or depression? Her memory is terrible."

Patients who have reversible dementia are most frequently seen in a hospital setting. The elderly patient taking a long list of prescription medications may suddenly show confusion, memory problems, and disorientation and may experience visual hallucinations. Neuropsychologists working in hospitals may be called on to help decide if the problem is an acute delirium, a dementia, or some combination of the two.

Chapter 5 discusses not only epilepsy but also nonepileptic seizure disorders. The latter were formally referred to in the past as *pseudoseizures*. Epilepsy is the second most common neurological disorder, affecting some 5 out of every 1,000 persons. As the chapter points out, between 10% and 40% of patients who are evaluated in comprehensive epileptic centers suffer not from epilepsy but from nonepileptic attack disorders. A *nonepileptic attack disorder* is defined as a paroxysmal episode of behavioral alterations that, in many respects, resembles an epileptic attack but is not associated with electrographic features. Referral questions for neuropsychological evaluation of epileptic patients thus cover a wide range. Frequently, questions center around requests for help in the differential diagnosis between epilepsy and nonepileptic attack disorder. Associated psychological problems may also be assessed, along with treatment recommendations. Assistance is frequently requested in predicting success following temporal lobe resection for patients who have had partial complex seizures. In addition, neuropsychologists often are asked to assist with or to conduct intracarotid amytal tests for lateralized language and memory functions. Finally, a neuropsychologist is often asked to help patients and their families understand epilepsy and adapt their lifestyles, including driving and vocational concerns. Vocational implications of having epilepsy can be devastating to the patient who works around dangerous equipment or who must drive.

The problem of alcoholism, discussed in chapter 6, affects about 10% of the U.S. population. Major brain changes have been identified in patients with alcoholism, including lower brain weights and significantly greater ventricular size, among other anatomical changes. Only about 10% of these patients meet the criteria in the fourth edition of the *Diagnostic and Statistical Manual of Mental Disorders* (American Psychiatric Association, 1994) for an organic mental disorder or an amnestic syndrome. As stated in this chapter, the remaining 90% have brain changes that are less severe but can nevertheless significantly affect their day-to-day living.

Referral questions for alcoholic patients with suspected brain impairment frequently are directed toward quantifying the degree of cognitive, memory, and other deficits in higher cortical function that are present. Neuropsychologists may be asked to describe how alcohol brain-related cognitive problems might affect daily life. Frequently, the treating practitioner wants to know what impact cognitive deficits might have on treatment and discharge planning. Questions regarding prediction of resumption of drinking on the basis of neuropsychological test performance are also occasionally asked, especially by staff of inpatient alcohol treatment programs.

Chapter 7 discusses human immunodeficiency virus (HIV-1), the disease that can develop into AIDS. As this chapter points out, HIV infection is the third leading cause of death in the United States among 25- to 44-year-olds and the ninth leading killer of people overall. The most common referral question by physicians has to do with quantifying any cognitive deficits that may exist, thus providing a baseline for possible future changes. Neuropsychologists may also be asked to assess depression and provide treatment.

As cognitive and other changes occur in some HIV–AIDS patients, neuropsychologists may be asked to quantify these changes. Severity of cognitive deficits can range from no cognitive deficits in HIV-positive patents to the severe dementia seen in some patients who have AIDS dementia complex.

In chapter 8, on multiple sclerosis (MS), the author points out that from 250,000 to 700,000 persons live with multiple sclerosis in the United States. An interesting fact is that the prevalence of this disorder is not uniform throughout the country. Residents of the northern United States (i.e., above 40° N latitude) are 3 times more likely to contract MS than those of more southern states. MS involves an inflammatory demyelination anywhere in the central nervous system. Clinical neuropsychologists are usually not involved in diagnosing MS but, instead, are asked to assess the extent of cognitive problems that a given patient with the disorder may have. MS can progress downward over time, and neuropsychological tests can provide a baseline of functioning. Because some cases of MS have a bleak prognosis, neuropsychologists may be asked to help certain MS patients and their families adjust psychologically to this potentially devastating illness. Depression is common, and psychotherapy is sometimes needed. Sexual problems, particularly impotency in men, are also a concern.

Parkinson's disease, discussed in chapter 9, is a common neurological disorder affecting 1% of the population over 50 years of age. This disease is characterized by a resting tremor, postural reflex impairment, cogwheel rigidity, and slowness in movement (bradykinesia). Neuropsychologists are asked to evaluate patients with Parkinson's disease because of concerns about depression, dementia, or both. Evaluations frequently concern the operation of motor vehicles and handling of personal financial affairs.

Section II: Child and Life-Span Developmental Neuropsychology

In this section, chapter authors discuss neuropsychological problems that often come to the attention of child neuropsychologists, although two of these disorders—attention deficit/hyperactivity disorder (ADHD) and learning disabilities—are sometimes not diagnosed until adolescence or adulthood.

Approximately 3%–5% of the population is affected by ADHD (American Psychiatric Association, 1994). Neuropsychologists as well as clinical psychologists are asked to assist in the differential diagnosis of ADHD; to make treatment recommendations, including suggested pharmacotherapy and psychotherapy; and to help with patient education. As pointed out in chapter 10, many ADHD disorders are not recognized until the patient reaches adulthood. Therefore, this chapter focuses not only on ADHD in children but also on how this disorder affects adolescents and adults. The authors suggest specific tests to use in evaluating patients with ADHD across the developmental spectrum.

The same developmental approach is taken with learning disabilities in chapter 11. Learning disabilities are also found in young and older adults as well as young children and adolescents. Approximately 4% of all school-age children have some type of learning disability, according to some estimates (Chalfant, 1989). In addition, there are wide variations in definitions of disabilities among states and school districts, which obviously result in variation in the number of children diagnosed with learning disabilities. Referral questions for such children center largely around diagnostic treatment and school placement issues. Educational suggestions for dealing with a particular child who has learning disabilities are often requested. With such knowledge, teachers of students with learning disabilities can better understand the strengths and problems of a given child. For adults, accurate diagnoses of learning disabilities are frequently a challenge. Issues for this population may include how to cope with the disorder and how to compensate for problems on the job. Often, associated psychological problems (e.g., depression or low self-esteem) need to be assessed as well.

Chapter 12, on fetal alcohol syndrome, points out that the problem occurs at the rate of about 1.9 cases per 100,000 lives. In comparison, the rate for fetal alcohol effects is much more common (3.25 per 10,000 live births). Fetal alcohol effects are diagnosed when all the criteria for fetal alcohol syndrome are not met. Referral questions for these children frequently center around quantification of the degree of deficit, assessing associated behavioral problems, and obtaining assistance in treatment and educational placement.

Section III: Issues in Forensic Neuropsychology and Psychotherapy

This last section of the book is devoted to applications of neuropsychology in two specific settings: forensic and psychotherapeutic. The chapter on forensic neuropsychology and expert testimony (chap. 13) presents a practical guide to the clinical neuropsychologist in working in civil proceedings. Nuts-and-bolts information is presented, such as how to relate to attorneys and important ethical behavior in the courtroom. Certain parts of the APA ethical guidelines as they relate specifically to neuropsychological examination and testimonies are discussed. Unfortunately, in a court situation, some patients are known to malinger to obtain larger settlements, and the neuropsychologist must be alert to this possibility. Therefore, several ways to detect malingering are discussed.

Chapter 14, the last chapter of the book, presents suggestions on how clinical neuropsychologists and other practitioners can approach psychotherapy with brain-injured patients, the most commonly referred group of patients and typically the youngest. Many patients with brain injuries have definite cognitive, personality, and motivational deficits that are often superimposed on personality traits or troublesome relationships that developed prior to their injuries. Psychotherapy is a difficult enterprise in and of itself, but it can be especially challenging with these patients. For example, many brain-injured patients have memory deficits that hamper recall of what went on from session to session. This chapter describes some of these dilemmas as well as strategies for addressing them.

References

Adams, K. M., & Rourke, B. P. (Eds.). (1992). *TCN guide to professional practice in clinical neuropsychology.* Berwyn, PA: Swets-Zeitlinger.

American Psychiatric Association. (1994). *Diagnostic and statistical manual of mental disorders* (4th ed.). Washington, DC: Author.

Benton, A. (1986, August). *Evolution of a clinical specialty.* Paper presented at the Annual Convention of the American Board of Professional Psychology, Washington, DC.

Chalfant, J. C. (1989). Learning disabilities: Policy issues and promising approaches. *American Psychologist, 44,* 392–398.

Putnam, S. H., & DeLuca, J. W. (1990). The TCN professional practice survey: I. General practices of neuropsychologists in primary employment and private practice settings. *The Clinical Neuropsychologist, 4,* 199–243.

Teuber, H. L. (1948). *Neuropsychology.* Paper presented at the 56th Annual Convention of the American Psychological Association, Boston, MA.

SECTION I

ADULT NEUROPSYCHOLOGY

CHAPTER 2

TRAUMATIC BRAIN INJURY

David J. G. Williamson, James G. Scott, and Russell L. Adams

According to a recent survey (Putnam & DeLuca, 1990), clinical neuropsychologists devote a greater proportion of their clinical time to patients who have suffered head trauma than to any other single group. Survivors of traumatic brain injury (TBI) have therefore received a great deal of empirical attention from neuropsychologists and affiliated professionals. These research efforts have had mixed results in terms of guiding the assessment and treatment of patients who have suffered a brain injury. Conflicting theories and results abound, leaving the clinician at something of a loss when a patient or a patient's family member asks exactly what has happened and what is going to happen as a result of an injury. This chapter is essentially an attempt to answer those questions as specifically as the current body of knowledge allows. In this attempt, we try to provide a description of the changes engendered by TBI, an account of how these changes evolve over time, an overview of interventions that may help to maximize recovery from these changes, and suggestions about ways in which these changes may best be quantified. Given the breadth of material that has been written about these issues, this review is necessarily incomplete, and references are provided as supplemental information for the interested reader.

Each year, 190 of every 100,000 people will be admitted to a hospital with a closed head injury (CHI), and 12 of every 100,000 will be admitted for a penetrating head injury (PHI; Schwab, Grafman, Salazar, & Kraft, 1993). Given this discrepancy in incidence rates, as well the substantial overlap between key pathological and clinical outcome features between patients receiving PHIs versus CHIs (Schwab et al., 1993), we focus primarily on the results of studies examining TBI attributable to CHI. For the purposes of this discussion, "neuropsychological function" is subdivided into the realms of arousal, attention, orientation, memory, language, visuospatial functions, executive functions, and psychological–personality functions. This categorization is done solely to structure the discussion; we clearly acknowledge that these subdivisions are extensively interdependent. Attention is given primarily to the assessment of individuals who have recovered enough from their injuries to receive a full neuropsychological test battery; however, because clinical neuropsychologists are becoming increasingly involved in the neuropsychological assessment and behavioral management of patients in acute rehabilitation settings, the unique demands of this population are addressed as well. Also in this chapter, we briefly address the role of the neuropsychologist in dealing with the psychological and family issues that are inevitably affected by these injuries, particularly with regard to the subacute setting. Finally, we present two case studies to illustrate assessment and treatment issues in the subacute and outpatient settings, respectively.

DEFINITIONS

A number of terms have been used to describe a traumatic injury to the brain. The three terms used most commonly (and, at times, interchangeably) are *CHI*, *PHI*, and *TBI*. We use *TBI* to broadly encompass any injury to the head that engenders a change

TABLE 1

Classification of Severity of Traumatic Brain Injury

	Traumatic brain injury		
Measure	**Mild**	**Moderate**	**Severe**
Glasgow Coma Scale	13–15	9–12	3–8
Loss of consciousness	< 20 min	20 min–36 hr	> 36 hr
Posttraumatic amnesia	< 24 hr	1–7 days	> 7 days

in consciousness, however brief. The criteria used to classify the severity of a TBI are presented in Table 1. Of those TBIs requiring hospitalization for more than 24 hr, approximately 75% are classified as mild, 15% as moderate, and 10% as severe (B. Jennett & MacMillan, 1981; Kraus et al., 1984; Kraus & Nourjah, 1988).

EPIDEMIOLOGY OF TBI

Approximately 2 million people suffer TBIs each year (National Institute of Neurological Disorders and Stroke [NINDS], 1989). Of these, between 75,000 and 100,000 will die, whereas another 70,000 to 90,000 will remain permanently disabled (NINDS, 1989). Of patients who go to the hospital, 500,000 will require hospitalization for greater than 24 hr. The resulting economic impact of TBI is enormous, with an estimated $25 billion spent each year on acute care alone (NINDS, 1989). Furthermore, the lifetime cost of treatment for a survivor of a severe TBI has been estimated to exceed $4 million, over half of which is paid for by public agencies (NINDS, 1989).

There are a few notable trends in the demographic pattern of TBI incidence. Even limiting oneself to the cases of TBI requiring more than 24 hr of hospitalization, the incidence of TBI is comparable to that of dementia of the Alzheimer's type (DAT) and cerebrovascular accidents (CVAs, or strokes). Unlike DAT and CVAs, however, TBI is primarily a condition of the young, with peak rates of incidence occurring between the ages of 15 and 24 years of age. For people under the age of 35 years, TBI accounts for greater rates of death and disability than all other causes combined (NINDS, 1989). In general, males are twice as likely as females to suffer a TBI, and the injuries suffered by males tend to be more severe (Dikmen, Machamer, Winn, & Temkin, 1995). In adulthood, TBI is typically an injury suffered in a motor vehicle accident. Recent data have suggested that alcohol is involved with two thirds of all TBIs, with as many as 50% of TBI victims having blood alcohol levels that exceed legal limits (Dikmen, Donovan, Løberg, Machamer, & Temkin, 1993). Falls are the primary etiology of TBI in children and elderly people, whereas it is estimated that 64% of TBIs suffered by infants are a direct result of child abuse (NINDS, 1989).

NEUROPATHOLOGY OF TBI

CHI

The neuropathological changes that occur most frequently secondary to TBI suffered as a result of CHI follow logically from the physics of the injury. In the typical CHI, the skull makes contact with a relatively immovable surface at a high rate of speed. As the skull comes to an abrupt stop, the velocity of movement is then imparted to the brain, along with whatever rotational forces were present. As a result of these forces, the brain itself may be stretched and rotated within the skull. An obvious consequence of these dynamics is impact of the brain against the interior of the skull. A less obvious consequence is shear strain, that is, the pulling apart of axons and disruption of cell bodies that occurs as a result of the momentary distortion of the brain's shape and density (Holbourn, 1943; Levin, Benton, & Grossman, 1982). These dynamics are the primary contributors to the three crucial processes that determine the neurological impact of TBI secondary to CHI: diffuse axonal injury, focal cortical contusion, and hypoxic–ischemic injury (Alexander, 1987).

Diffuse axonal injury results from the shear strain induced by CHI and is typically accompanied by loss of consciousness (J. H. Adams, Mitchell, Murray, & Scott, 1982; Katz & Alexander, 1994). This injury may be mild enough to affect only scattered regions of the parasagittal white matter or severe enough to cause widespread axonal disruption in both hemispheres as well as focal softenings in the corpus callosum and dorsolateral tegmentum of the midbrain (Alexander, 1987; Gale, Johnson, Bigler, & Blatter, 1995). The disruption of consciousness following TBI seems to be preferentially related to the extent of diffuse axonal injury. Clinically, patients with diffuse axonal injury are lucid less frequently, typically suffer less severe focal contusion, and are less likely to have skull fractures, increased intracerebral pressure, or intracranial hematoma (Alexander, 1987). The typical parasagittal distribution of damage often leads to motor impairment that is more severe in the legs than the arms, whereas the neuropsychological functions that are largely mediated by perisylvian cortices (e.g., language and praxis) remain largely unaffected. The relationship between amount of damage and eventual outcome in some psychosocial and cognitive measures is more predictable in patients that have suffered diffuse axonal injury than in those whose injuries are limited to focal cortical contusion or hypoxic–ischemic injury (Gale et al., 1995).

Focal cortical contusions are local abrasions on the brain's surface resulting directly from the impact of the brain against the interior of the skull. They involve neurons, axons, and blood vessels. This impact may occur as a result of either the linear force of the impact, the rotational force of the impact, or both. The linear forces may cause abrasions at the point of contact (coup), directly across the skull from the point of contact (contrecoup), or both. In contrast, the rotational forces may induce cortical abrasions at any location at which the brain was moved along the interior of the skull (Alexander, 1987). Both postmortem and radiological studies have confirmed that focal contusions are most likely to occur in the inferior (orbital) frontal regions and the inferior anterior temporal lobes (R. D. Adams & Victor, 1993; Alexander, 1987). The preferential vulnerability of these sites is a simple result of cranial morphology and the typical vectors of force occurring in CHI:

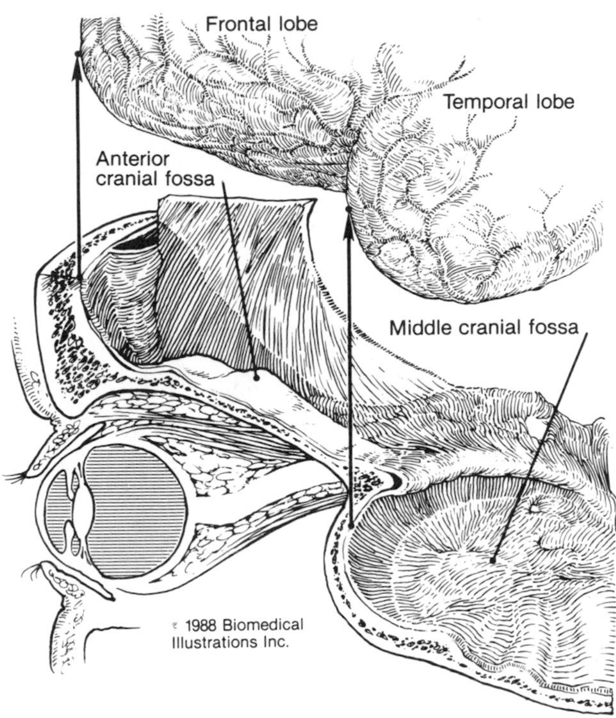

FIGURE 1. Anatomical sites commonly involved in closed head injury. Copyright 1988 by Biomedical Illustrations, Seattle, WA. Reprinted with permission.

Abrasion of the inferior frontal cortex occurs along the orbital plate of the frontal bone and cribriform plate of the ethmoid bone, whereas abrasion of anterior temporal cortices occurs along the raised sphenoid wing just anterior to the temporal lobes (see Figure 1). Focal cortical contusions need not be associated with any coma, and clinical manifestation is similar to that of any similar focal lesion in terms of time course, lesion topography, and neuropsychological sequelae. In general, it is much more difficult to predict outcome in patients with focal cortical contusions in the absence of diffuse axonal injury because of the greater amount of neuropathological heterogeneity inherent in the population (Katz & Alexander, 1994).

Changes resulting from hypoxic–ischemic injury include frank infarction in the distribution of one cerebral vessel, patchy small areas of infarction in the distribution of one or more arterial border zones, and erratic neuronal dropout. These changes are relatively uncommon after TBI (Katz & Alexander, 1994), but when they do occur, they are usually secondary to periods of increased intracranial pressure or reduced arterial pressure. These changes may appear in isolation or in combination with each other. As a result of the tentorial herniation that may occur during periods of increased intracranial pressure, the most frequent site of infarction secondary to this sort of injury is the territory of the posterior cerebral artery, and infarction is often bilateral in nature (Alexander, 1987). Although the data quantifying the neuropsychological sequelae of hypoxic–ischemic injury are relatively sparse, one can reason on the basis of current knowledge of clinicoanatomical associations that such an injury may engender cortical visual disturbances (occipitotemporal regions fed by the posterior cerebral arteries), dementia (bilateral diffuse border zone damage), amnestic syndrome (hippocampal damage), or a vegetative state (diffuse pseudolaminar necrosis). Because the radiological quantification of hypoxic–ischemic injury remains relatively undeveloped, these postulated deficits await empirical validation (Alexander, 1987).

PHI

Although the focus of this chapter is on TBI secondary to CHI, we provide a brief overview of the differences between CHI and PHI. The interested reader is referred to Grafman and Salazar (1987) for a more thorough discussion. The essential feature of PHIs is a focal lesion penetrating the skull and dura that is frequently caused by gunshot wounds or severe depressed skull fractures. Because of the impact-absorbent nature of the penetration of the skull, the morphological changes produced in these injuries are restricted more narrowly to the path of the projectile or the area directly under the depressed fracture. This is particularly true of wounds inflicted by relatively low-velocity projectiles (e.g., gunshot wounds inflicted by handguns). However, as the caliber and velocity of the projectile increase, the likelihood that effects will occur farther away from the site of impact or path of the projectile increases significantly (Swan & Swan, 1980).

Acutely, PHI differs from CHI in a number of ways. Most notably, coma is uncommon after PHI. This finding may reflect the fact that diffuse axonal injury is far less common after PHI than after CHI (Allen, Scott, & Tanner, 1982). In contrast, because of the invasive nature of PHI, infection in PHI is a far more common complication than in CHI. In terms of neuropsychological sequelae, posttraumatic amnesia occurs far less frequently after PHI. Salazar and colleagues (1986) found that 47% of a sample of Vietnam veterans who had suffered PHIs had no anterograde amnesia, whereas 87% had no retrograde amnesia. Chronically, PHI is distinguished from CHI by the increased frequency of posttraumatic epilepsy. Estimates suggest that up to 53% of survivors of PHI may develop a seizure disorder, in comparison with only 5% of survivors of CHI (or up to 25%, in the presence of severe CHI with subdural hematoma; Grafman & Salazar, 1987). Chronic neuropsychological effects of PHI are characterized by greater focal neurobehavioral deficits, especially after PHI secondary to a low-velocity missile wound. As with the focal cortical contusions described above, the specific deficits that one observes may vary widely according to the regions involved in the injury. Although the data directly comparing neurocognitive outcomes of CHI and PHI are sparse, there has been some suggestion that survivors of PHI fare better overall (Grafman & Salazar, 1987), possibly because of the relatively more limited extent of neuropathology after PHI. The ways in which lesion site and size affect this relationship have yet to be fully explored, however.

RADIOLOGICAL AND BIOMEDICAL TESTS

Clinical neuropsychologists often find that knowledge of the various medical and radiological diagnostic techniques used in assessing and treating TBI is a valuable aid, both for understanding the nature of the injury and for communicating with other health care professionals. The emergency room evaluation of a TBI almost invariably includes a computed tomography (CT) scan, primarily to rule out the possibility of intracranial bleeding. It is important for the clinician to remember that, although an emergency room CT scan does a very competent job of ruling out the possibility of intracranial bleeding, it does not provide conclusive evidence about which regions of the brain have been injured (Cope, Date, & Mar, 1993). Broadly speaking, the goal of the CT scan is to examine the relative densities of neighboring regions. Acutely, the density of an infarcted region of tissue may not differ enough from the surrounding tissue to appear abnormal on a CT scan. It is for this reason that most laboratories requiring specific definition of lesions (in terms of location and size) wait a minimum of 7 to 10 days to acquire the CT scans with which to make these determinations (Levin, Williams, et al., 1988).

As one would expect, the number of structural abnormalities seen in the brain increases with the severity of injury. Ninety-five percent of individuals who have suffered a severe TBI show abnormalities in CT scans, in comparison with 25% of individuals with moderate injuries (Levin, Amparo, et al., 1987). Mild head injuries are only rarely associated with abnormal CT scan findings. As indicated above, however, initial CT scan findings may be limited in terms of providing meaningful information to the neuropsychologist. Magnetic resonance (MR) imaging improves on this to some degree, in that this technique is generally superior to CT scans in defining the number, location, and depth of lesions across all levels of injury severity. In the acute phase, MR imaging has been shown to be superior to CT scanning in detecting nonhemorrhagic contusions, nonhemorrhagic white-matter lesions, some subdural collections, and brainstem lesions (D. G. Daniel, Zigon, & Weinberger, 1992; Gandy, Snow, Zimmerman, & Deck, 1984; Gentry, Godersky, Thompson, & Dunn, 1988; Hadley et al., 1988; Hesselink et al., 1988; Levin, Amparo, et al., 1987; Zimmerman, Bilaniuk, Hackney, Goldberg, & Grossman, 1986). In the subacute and chronic stages after TBI, MR imaging is superior to CT scanning in detecting intracerebral hemorrhage, white-matter changes, and subcortical and temporal lobe abnormalities (Han et al., 1984; Hesselink et al., 1988; Levin, Handel, Goldman, Eisenberg, & Guinto, 1985; Snow, Zimmerman, Gandy, & Deck, 1986; Zimmerman et al., 1986). Even this information may not be helpful to the clinician in terms of helping the family form expectations for recovery, however: Although the number, depth, and location of lesions found through MR imaging have been found to be significantly correlated with both the severity of TBI and neuropsychological test performance in the early stages of recovery (Jenkins, Teasdale, Hadley, MacPherson, & Rowan, 1986; Levin, Amparo, et al., 1987; Levin, Williams, et al., 1988), the relationship of CT and MR findings to chronic neuropsychological recovery is not as strong (J. T. L. Wilson et al., 1988).

Technologies examining the metabolic activity of the brain may also prove valuable to the clinician in developing an understanding of exactly what is going on neurologically after TBI. Data suggest that the area of the "functional lesion" in the brain after a CVA likely exceeds the boundaries of the actual structural lesion as shown on MR imaging; that is, the area that is receiving significantly less cerebral blood flow or metabolizing significantly less glucose than normal extends beyond the tissue that was directly damaged by the CVA (Metter et al., 1989). Recent findings have suggested that this dynamic is at work after TBI as well (Langfitt et al., 1987). Because these images reflect the amount of activity occurring in the dendritic fields of different regions (Collins, 1991), this widespread effect is likely substantially influenced by the lack of neural transmissions emanating from the damaged region. The functional significance of these findings has yet to be firmly established, but they may prove important to eventual understanding of the pathophysiology of TBI.

Electroencephalograms (EEGs) have been shown to have moderate predictive ability for survival after TBI (Synek, 1988). Acute EEG after TBI is usually characterized by overall slowing of brain-wave activity with intermittent spontaneous high-frequency waves. Generally speaking, lower frequency and amplitude EEG readings following TBI predict poor prognoses. Failure to show EEG changes in response to external stimuli is the characteristic most predictive of mortality (Bricolo, 1976). The use of EEG in acute assessment of TBI is hindered by the usual administration of pharmacological agents with known electrophysiological slowing effects, interference from other electrical equipment in the emergency room setting, and the frequent agitation and uncooperativeness of patients. Likewise, the use of quantitative EEG (e.g., "brainmapping") in the clinical diagnosis of TBI remains controversial (American Academy of Neurology, 1989).

The use of evoked potentials to measure changes in the resting electrophysiological or homeostatic potential of brain tissue has been examined by several investigators. These studies typically examine changes in the resting or homeostatic potential that are induced by presentation of a particular somatic, visual, or auditory stimulus. These efforts have produced results that appear promising for both diagnosis and prediction. Somatosensory evoked potentials (SEPs) have been considered to be of less value in assessing TBI because they require integrity of the somatosensory system. More recently, research has focused on visual evoked potentials (VEPs) and auditory evoked potentials (AEPs). Although still preliminary, results from studies examining VEPs have shown that these methods may be used to detect pathophysiological disturbance along the visual pathway. In addition, studies have also demonstrated pragmatic value in differentiating mild-TBI patients who have posttraumatic cognitive deficits from those who do not have posttraumatic deficits (Gupta, Verma, & Guidice, 1986; Rappaport, Hopkins, & Hall, 1977). Similarly, AEPs have been studied to assess brainstem integrity in TBI patients. These evoked potentials assess the pathway beginning at the eighth cranial nerve, progressing through auditory brainstem nuclei and terminating in the contralateral Heschel's gyrus. Abnormalities in various components along this pathway suggest dysfunction in distinct brainstem nuclei (Ropper & Miller, 1985; Stockard & Rossiter, 1977). As with EEG data, results currently suggest that AEP data are better at predicting morbidity in TBI than in accurately predicting functional outcome (Lindsey, Pasaoglu, & Hirst, 1990; Shin, Ehrenberg, & Wythe, 1989).

PROGNOSIS

From 70% to 75% of deaths from TBI occur within the first 3 days after the injury (Clifton, Grossman, Makela, & Minor, 1980; Clifton, McCormick, & Grossman, 1981). For survivors, the vast majority of neurobehavioral recovery is made in the first year after the injury (Jones, 1992). This recovery typically proceeds in a curvilinear fashion, with the most rapid recovery occurring within the first 3–6 months and the plateau typically occurring at approximately 2 years (Jones, 1992). Within this framework, specific abilities recover at different rates than others, and some data suggest that survivors of severe TBI may continue to make additional recovery past the 2-year plateau (Jones, 1992). The prediction of each individual's recovery from TBI is as heterogeneous as the pathophysiology of TBI itself. Much of the disparity in the literature on outcomes is due to the variables assessed at outcome. For example, outcome may be measured in terms of cognitive functioning, occupational functioning, social functioning, physical functioning, or degree of independence in activities of daily living. Nevertheless, attempts to predict outcome from TBI have had some success in identifying important variables in prognosis. For pragmatic purposes, prognostic indicators can be grouped into premorbid variables and neurological variables.

Premorbid Variables

Several characteristics have been identified as important variables in predicting outcome from TBI. Age at the time of injury is among the most important predictors of eventual recovery (Katz & Alexander, 1994; Levati, Farina, Vecchi, Rossanda, & Marrubini, 1982; Narayan, Greenberg, Miller, & Enas, 1981). As adults get older, mortality increases and chances for a good recovery decrease. Age effects appear to become more pronounced around 40 years (Katz & Alexander, 1994). Acutely, length of coma appears to be independent of age, whereas duration of posttraumatic amnesia lengthens with age (Katz & Alexander, 1994). Long-term recovery in particular is mediated by age. For instance, Katz and Alexander (1994) found that among older patients (i.e., over 60 years old) who had suffered mild diffuse axonal injury secondary to TBI, 30% were severely disabled 12 months after the injury; the analogous rate for patients under 60 was 0%. Similarly, when more severe injuries were examined, 54.5% of older patients were severely disabled at 12 months, whereas only 7.4% of patients under 20 remained severely disabled.

The prognosis for children under 5 years of age is more uncertain. Although there has been some suggestion in the literature that this age group has a higher mortality rate than children between the ages of 5 and 20 (Braakman, Gelpke, Habbema, Maas, & Minderhoud, 1980), there are also data suggesting lower mortality in this age group (Bruce, Schut, Bruno, Wood, & Sutton, 1978; Carlsson, Von Essen,

EXHIBIT 1

Psychosocial Predictors of Recovery From Traumatic Brain Injury

Positive prognosis	Negative prognosis
Younger than 35 years old	Older than 45 years old
No previous brain injury	Previous brain injury
No history of substance abuse	History of substance abuse
Good academic achievement	Poor academic achievement
Stable work history	Erratic work history
Strong social support networks	Poor social support networks
No history of legal difficulties	Criminal history
Premorbidly independent financially and geographically	No history of independence

& Lofgren, 1968; Langfitt & Gennarelli, 1982). Likewise, the commonly held belief that children will recover more completely than an adult with a similar brain injury has yet to receive consistent empirical support (Leurssen, 1991; Rutter, Chadwick, & Schaffer, 1983).

Several indexes of adequate premorbid psychosocial function, such as educational functioning, adequacy of interpersonal and social relationships, occupational history, and preexisting history of substance abuse or criminal behavior, have been related to outcome (Sbordone & Howard, 1989). Likewise, the existence of a previous head injury is a negative prognostic sign; however, the precise relationship between number of TBIs and decrements in neuropsychological function has yet to be firmly established (Gronwall, 1987). Exhibit 1 shows premorbid characteristics that should be considered in evaluating prognosis after TBI.

Finally, an accurate estimate of the TBI victim's premorbid intellectual ability is critical to understanding the severity of the person's deficits and to setting reasonable expectations for recovery and treatment. The most common estimate of this in the general population is the IQ. Some researchers (Barona, Reynolds, & Chastain, 1984; R. S. Wilson et al., 1978) have used demographic variables (e.g., education or occupation) to provide a rough index of intellectual function. Others (Bryan, Wiens, & Crossen, 1992) have based estimates on tests of abilities that are relatively resistant to the effects of TBI, such as the ability to read words that do not conform to standard rules of spelling in English (e.g., *yacht*). Some attempts at combining demographic information and irregular reading tasks appear promising (Corrigan & Berry, 1991; Grober & Sliwinski, 1991; Willshire, Kinsella, & Prior, 1991), but these results await replication.

Recent work has attempted to improve on the accuracy of these estimates by combining demographic variables and performances on tests of "resistant" abilities. Specifically, the Oklahoma Premorbid Intelligence Estimate uses empirically derived linear combinations of age, education, occupation, race, and either Vocabulary or Picture Completion tests from the Wechsler Adult Intelligence Scale–Revised (WAIS-R; depending on patient performance) to estimate premorbid IQ. This technique has the dual advantages of (a) using a combination of performance and demographic variables and (b) being linked to either a language or relatively nonverbal task, thus limiting the potential impact of focal (particularly left-hemisphere) deficits on estimation accuracy. Results have suggested that this algorithm performs extremely well for individuals without other complicating conditions as well as for patients with TBI, dementia, cerebrovascular disease, or neoplastic processes (Krull, Scott, & Sherer, 1995; Williamson, Scott, Krull, & Adams, 1994). The algorithm for calculating this measure may be found in Exhibit 2.

Neurological Variables

Neurological variables that predict prognosis in TBI are summarized in Exhibit 3. Although extensive discussion of these variables is beyond the scope of this chapter, brief description and explanation of many of

EXHIBIT 2

The Oklahoma Premorbid Intelligence Estimate

Administer the Vocabulary and Picture Completion tests of the Wechsler Adult Intelligence Scale–Revised (WAIS-R). Compare the raw scaled scores. If the scores are equal or the score on Vocabulary is higher, use Equation 1 to estimate premorbid IQ. If the Picture Completion score is higher, use Equation 2.

$$\text{Full-Scale IQ} = 69.43 - 2.68(\text{Race}) + 0.85(\text{Education}) - 0.66(\text{Occupation}) + 0.76(\text{Vocabulary Raw Score}) \quad (1)$$

$$\text{Full-Scale IQ} = 52.76 + 0.24(\text{Age}) - 3.73(\text{Race}) + 3.10(\text{Education}) - 0.71(\text{Occupation}) + 2.30(\text{Picture Completion Raw Score}) \quad (2)$$

Coding of variables

Age: In years

Race: 1 = Caucasian; 2 = other

Education:
1 = 0–7 years
2 = 8 years
3 = 9–11 years
4 = 12 years
5 = 13–15 years
6 = 16+ years

Occupation:
1 = Professional/technical
2 = Manager/administrator/clerical/sales
3 = Craftsman/foreman
4 = Operators/service/domestic/farmers
5 = Laborers
6 = Not in the labor force (including students[a] and homemakers)

These codings are based on those found in the WAIS-R manual (Wechsler, 1981), pp. 16–18.
[a]*For all subjects ages 16–19, use the occupation of the head of the subject's household. For all retirees, code the highest level of occupational achievement before retirement.*

these predictors may prove instructive for their appropriate interpretation.

The ability of neurological information obtained in the acute-care setting to accurately predict eventual outcome remains a matter of some debate (B. Jennett, Teasdale, Murray, & Murray, 1992). Two commonly used indexes of injury severity are the depth and duration of coma. The depth of coma is most often quantified by using the Glasgow Coma Scale (GCS), an observational scale based on ratings of the patient's best visual, verbal, and motor responses (Teasdale & Jennett, 1974). Although the predictive validity of GCS ratings taken within the first 6 hr after injury is not without question, sequential ratings of the patient's status over the first 48 hr have proven to be predictive of many aspects of functional outcome (Bricolo, Turazzi, & Feriotti, 1980). Almost without exception, prognosis worsens as the depth and duration of coma increase.

Posttraumatic amnesia (PTA) has also gained acceptance as a measure of injury severity (Katz & Alexander, 1994; Levin, Lilly, Papanicolaou, & Eisenberg, 1992). PTA is the period of time after a TBI during which the patient is confused, disoriented, and has a great deal of difficulty acquiring and retrieving new information (Baddeley, Sunderland, Watts, & Wilson, 1987). Although the duration of PTA is highly related to that of coma, the relationship is quite variable and suggests that the two indexes measure different (though likely) overlapping neurological phenomena (Levin et al., 1992). Katz and Alexander (1994) have provided a gross numerical description of the relationship between length of coma and duration of PTA on the basis of their rehabilitation sample: Duration of PTA (in weeks) = (0.4 × Length of Coma [in days]) + 3.6. They noted that this relationship becomes much more variable as coma duration extends past 7 days. Katz and Alexander also found that PTA was the strongest predictor of outcome at 12 months in patients with diffuse axonal injury. In the more general TBI population, the duration of PTA has been related to aspects of neurocognitive recovery 6 months (Levin, Papanicolaou, & Eisenberg, 1984) and 2–5 years after injury.

The prognostic utility of a number of individual neurological signs has been examined as well. The

EXHIBIT 3

Neurological Predictors of Recovery From Traumatic Brain Injury

Positive prognosis	Negative prognosis
Initial Glasgow Coma Scale score > 9	Initial Glasgow Coma Scale score < 9
Posttraumatic amnesia < 24 hr	Posttraumatic amnesia > 24 hr
Loss of consciousness < 6 hr	Loss of consciousness > 24 hr
CT scan and MR imaging abnormalities restricted to cortex	Subcortical CT scan and MR imaging abnormalities
No dural penetration	Dural penetration
No posturing	Decorticate or decerebrate posturing
Diffuse or focal contusion only	Subdural hematoma
ICP < 20 mmHg	ICP > 20 mmHg
No multimodal evoked-potential abnormalities	Multimodal evoked-potential abnormalities
No pupillary response abnormalities	Pupillary response abnormalities
No hypoxia	Hypoxia
No ocular motor abnormalities	Ocular motor abnormalities
No complications in other systems (e.g., renal or cardiac)	Secondary systemic complications

CT = computed tomography; MR = magnetic resonance; ICP = increased intracranial pressure.

development of increased intracranial pressure signals a negative prognosis (Becker, Miller, & Greenberg, 1982; Miller et al., 1977). Likewise, physically observable signs, such as decorticate or decerebrate posturing, are negatively prognostic. Any suggestion of brainstem involvement (e.g., asymmetrical, enlarged, or sluggishly responsive pupils) does not bode well for eventual outcome, nor do abnormal extraocular movements, such as medial or lateral deviations of the eye (Braakman et al., 1980). The impact of specific complications has been examined as well. The mortality rate of CHI may increase to as high as 60% in the presence of acute subdural hematoma (Bowers & Marshall, 1980; Gennarelli et al., 1982). A number of variables may improve this statistic, however. For instance, if the hematoma is evacuated within 4 hr of the injury, outcome improves significantly (Seelig et al., 1981). Mortality rates decrease as hematoma becomes more subacute. Epidural hematomas are associated with better outcomes than are subdural or intracerebral hematomas (Gennarelli et al., 1982).

In contrast with the signs that have established prognostic value, there are a few readily observable behaviors that have no significant relationship to eventual outcome. For instance, the presence of acute hemiparesis has little prognostic value. Acute hemiparesis tends to resolve spontaneously, and it does not appear to be related to long-term outcome (Jennett, Teasdale, Braakman, Minderhoud, & Knill-Jones, 1976). Likewise, the ability of the patient to talk does not bear a strong relationship to eventual outcome: Data have shown that approximately one third of all fatally injured patients talk at some point after injury (Reilly, Graham, Adams, & Jennett, 1975; Rose, Valtonen, & Jennett, 1977).

THE ROLE OF THE NEUROPSYCHOLOGIST

The neuropsychologist plays a variety of roles in the care of the patient who has had a TBI. These roles vary substantially depending on the setting in which the neuropsychologist is employed, the stage of recovery of the patient, and the assessment questions and treatment goals that are being addressed. Exhibit 4 shows a number of the questions that are asked of neuropsychologists by different parties.

Here and in other parts of this chapter dealing with the assessment of neuropsychological constructs, we are quick to acknowledge that there are alternative ways of conceptualizing and measuring neuropsychological phenomena. An exhaustive review of these is impossible within the context of this discussion. Instead of attempting such a review, we try to highlight the constructs of interest and provide examples of measures that we have found helpful in quantifying these constructs. Virtually all performances on neuropsychological measures are multifactorially determined; thus, classification of the cognitive domains that are tapped by each test are somewhat arbitrary. The results of each test must therefore be viewed in the larger context of the body of all test results and background information.

NEUROPSYCHOLOGICAL EFFECTS OF CHI

Arousal and Attention

Definitions. Arousal and attention play fundamental roles in most cognitive tasks. In the presence of intact sensory modalities, it is the combination of arousal and attention that enables the registration, awareness, and cognitive processing of one's environment. Although these terms are frequently used interchangeably, they are conceptually distinct. *Arousal* may be conceptualized in terms of both the wakefulness of a person from one time of day to another (tonic arousal) and the sudden increase in preparedness to respond that immediately follows a stimulus signaling the impending need for a quick response (phasic arousal; Posner & Rafal, 1987).

EXHIBIT 4

Questions Commonly Asked of Neuropsychologists

Family or survivor of a traumatic brain injury

When and how much will the individual recover?

- Cognitive (i.e., memory, information-processing speed, and language)
- Emotional (i.e., personality changes)

Will he or she be able to live independently?

- Transportation (i.e., when can he or she start driving again?)
- Self-care and organizational skills

Will he or she be able to return to work?

Medical and rehabilitation staff

Does the individual have any cognitive deficits that affect his or her ability to participate in the rehabilitative process?

- Orientation to situation and surroundings
- Comprehension of aural and written language
- Adequate levels of arousal, attention, and concentration
- Ability to learn, remember, and implement new skills

Does the individual have any emotional or motivational deficits that affect his or her ability to participate in the rehabilitative process?

- Awareness of deficits
- Depression or anxiety
- Premorbid personality pathology

Vocational rehabilitators and employers

Will the individual be able to resume his or her original duties or return to school?

- What is the time course and prognosis for recovery of vocationally or educationally related skills?

What strengths and weaknesses should be taken into account if an alternative placement must be sought?

In contrast, *attention* is a diverse, multifaceted construct that broadly refers to "a hypothetical state of the brain that determines what stimuli or aspects of stimuli will influence behavior" (Hebb, 1949, as cited by Buchtel, 1987). The term *attentional deficit* is typically used to describe two distinct but related phenomena: (a) neglect, in which the patient does not appear to recognize an area of space, despite intact primary sensory modalities; and (b) impairments in the ability to assimilate the important features of one's environment in a rapid or sustained fashion. Attentional neglect is relatively rare after TBI; however, impairments in the ability to process one's environment flexibly and efficiently are common (Gronwall, 1987). Because of its typical clinical manifestation, we address attentional neglect in the context of visuospatial disorders, whereas we examine difficulties with processing efficiency in this section.

Impairments in one's ability to efficiently process the environment are broken down arbitrarily into four types (Sohlberg & Mateer, 1989): (a) difficulty in maintaining high levels of concentration (sustained attention), (b) difficulty in maintaining attentional focus on a single stimulus in the presence of distractors (selective attention), (c) difficulty in dividing attention between numerous salient stimuli (divided attention), and (d) difficulty in shifting appropriately between stimuli (attentional control). Obviously, these deficits do not reflect mutually exclusive conceptual entities, and alternative frameworks have been proposed (Moscovitch, 1981; Stuss, 1991; Van Zomeren & Brouwer, 1987). However, these categories adequately capture the symptomatology that is often seen in the clinical setting.

Deficits. Because of the common disruption in connections between the brainstem reticular formation and the cortex caused by diffuse axonal injury, marked changes in arousal levels are common after TBI. Acutely, this is often manifested in varying stages of coma. Although the Glasgow Coma Scale does an adequate job of quantifying these changes, obvious changes in tonic and phasic arousal patterns often persist after emergence from coma. In the subacute setting, one frequently sees alternating periods of hypoarousal and agitation. As neuropsychologists continue to make inroads to rehabilitation settings, behavioral management of the agitated subacute patient is a responsibility that is falling on the clinician with increasing frequency. Even beyond the subacute setting, however, changes in arousal may be evident. Typically, these are not the gross deficits in arousal that one sees in the acute or subacute care settings; rather, these changes are subtle in nature, although they may present a significant obstacle to the survivor's return to his or her premorbid level of functioning. Such changes are manifested most commonly as increased fatigability and disruptions in diurnal arousal patterns (Guilleminault, Faull, Miles, & Van der Hoad, 1983). In addition, some researchers have posited that the disruption of arousal mechanisms is a primary contributor to the changes commonly observed in reaction time, information-processing speed, and the different aspects of attention among TBI patients (Gronwall, 1987).

Sustained attention may be viewed in terms of attention to externally as well as internally generated stimuli. *Externally generated stimuli* include any stimulus whose content is largely independent of an individual's behavior or state of mind (e.g., television program, flashing lights, a series of tones, or someone else's speech). *Internally generated stimuli* are those that an individual is responsible for generating (e.g., a line of conversation) or internal representations that an individual must recall, reproduce, or manipulate (e.g., the alphabet or a number line). *Vigilance* is the term commonly used to describe sustained maintenance of attention for the purpose of detecting critical but infrequent external stimuli (Parasuraman, Mutter, & Molloy, 1991). Normal performance on experimental vigilance tasks is marked by an initially high rate of detection of critical events that declines gradually over time (Davies & Parasuraman, 1982). This decline occurs more rapidly for visual events than for auditory events and is accelerated by increasing the frequency of critical events (Parasuraman et al., 1991). The decline of vigilance is mitigated to some extent if the critical event follows a predictable pattern or if it is signaled in some way. Vigilance is important in such activities as driving, where the majority of time is spent performing relatively overlearned behaviors and attentional demand is relatively low, until an infrequent but critical event (e.g., brake lights ahead or a careless pedestrian) occurs. Typically, vigilance has been quantified in the laboratory setting by measuring the speed with which subjects make a motor response to a predefined, infrequently occurring stimulus. When vigilance is quantified in this way, one finds that the rate at which vigilance declines in survivors of TBI does not differ significantly from the rate of decline shown in healthy individuals. Rather, differences between the two populations may be attributed largely to the generalized decrease in reaction time (Parasuraman et al., 1991; Ponsford & Kinsella, 1992).

Whereas sustained attention is maintenance of concentration over time, selective attention is concerned with the ability to focus on a particular stimulus in the presence of distractors. Examples include attending to a conversation while the television is on in the background or attempting to read a book while the kids are playing in the next room. Impairment in this ability is typically termed "distractibility." Although the empirical study of selective attention deficits in TBI survivors has met with mixed results, a consistent theme seems to emerge when one compares the different sorts of tasks that have been used in the research. In general, survivors of TBI are not impaired in their ability to attend to one of a number of competing aspects of a single stimulus, such as attending to color rather than word in the Stroop Color and Word Test (Stroop, 1935; Van Zomeren & Brouwer, 1987). Instead, the decrement of performance by TBI patients in these tasks seems to be related primarily to the generalized decrease in response time. In contrast, TBI survivors are impaired on tasks that require inhibition of a motor response to a distracting separate stimulus (Hicks & Birren, 1970; Van Zomeren & Brouwer, 1987). For example, when required to make a rapid motor response to a signal that occurs in conjunction with a similar, distracting signal, TBI survivors show more impairment than can be explained on the basis of a decrease in reaction time alone (Van Zomeren & Brouwer, 1987). This deficit remits gradually over a period of several months after injury, such that there are no significant differences between the performance of survivors of minor head injuries and healthy individuals 6 months after injury (Van Zomeren & Brouwer, 1987). However, these difficulties may persist for years in survivors of severe head injury (Levin, Benton, & Grossman, 1982). Given the neuropathology of TBI, this result is not surprising, because increases in distractibility have been linked preferentially to lesions in the orbitofrontal regions (Stuss et al., 1982).

Whereas selective attention tasks assess the ability of the patient to "screen out" extraneous stimuli, tasks assessing divided attention examine the patient's ability either to make use of information presented from simultaneously occurring but separate sources or to maintain adequate levels of performance of an ongoing task while having to process incoming information that may or may not be related to the task. Tasks assessing divided attention may be similar to tasks assessing selective attention, in that both types of tasks require the presence of multiple stimuli. However, in divided attention tasks, integration of the information provided by the multiple stimuli is necessary for optimal performance (e.g., driving in Manhattan at midday), whereas in selective attention tasks, integration of multiple stimuli is detrimental to performance (e.g., carrying on a conversation at a crowded party).

It is often difficult to distinguish a deficit in the ability to simultaneously process multiple stimuli from reductions in information-processing speed or attentional capacity (Gronwall, 1987; Posner & Rafal, 1987; Van Zomeren & Brouwer, 1987). Clinically, however, complaints such as "I can't listen to the radio when I drive anymore because it's too distracting" or "I can only concentrate on one thing at a time now" are among the most common complaints that neuropsychologists hear from TBI survivors. Patients with brain injuries have consistently shown significant deficits in these sorts of tasks (Van Zomeren & Brouwer, 1987).

Finally, deficiency in attentional control may be viewed as a supraordinate construct that accounts for the difficulties in selective and divided attention that have been observed for survivors of TBIs. When attentional control is intact, one "shuts out" extraneous stimuli or switches appropriately between competing simultaneous stimuli as well as the average person does. The notion of a "central executive" has been proposed and explored by a number of researchers (Baddeley & Hitch, 1974; Posner, 1987; Shallice, 1982; Shallice & Burgess, 1991b). Conceptually, the central executive is responsible for weighing the various internal and external demands of any given situation and allocating cognitive and emotional resources in the manner best suited to meet the needs of the organism at any given moment. Such determinations likely involve widespread cortical–subcortical networks that include thalamic nuclei in addition to parietal, limbic, and prefrontal cortices (Desimone, Wessinger, Thomas, & Schneider, 1990; Posner, 1987; Posner & Rafal, 1987). With regard to attention, this central executive is thought to play a key role in several processes: (a) determining the informational or survival valence of all stimuli in the attentional field, (b) disengaging attention from less valent stimuli, (c) moving to valent stimuli, (d) engaging attention to valent stimuli, and (e) inhibiting movement to less valent stimuli (Posner & Rafal, 1987). These processes have been shown to break down in different ways, depending on the neural substrates that have been disrupted (Posner & Rafal, 1987). The line between classification of these processes as attentional versus executive is not sharply drawn (see our discussion below on executive functions); rather, it is left arbitrary for the purposes of our discussion. Given the deficits in selective and divided attention that have been shown to exist in the TBI population, one would presume that the processes laid out above are disrupted. However, careful studies of these phenomena have not yet been performed with TBI populations, and it remains to be seen if one or more typical patterns of breakdown exist in this sequence of cognitive steps.

Investigations of the specific stages of information processing that may be differentially impaired after TBI have been performed. For more information about these issues as well as a more comprehensive overview of the theoretical background of the area, readers should consult these specific studies (Schmitter-Edgecombe, Marks, Fahy, & Long, 1992; Shum, McFarland, Bain, & Humphreys, 1990). In communication with survivors, families, and staff, presenting the attentional changes incurred as a result of TBI in terms of decreases in information-processing speed or attentional capacity seems to provide a relatively solid framework from which these changes can be viewed.

Assessment. Although systematic study of patterns of arousal is relatively sparse, methods for quantifying levels of arousal are relatively well standardized. Specifically, the GCS and the Levels of Cognitive Functioning Scale (more commonly referred to as the *Rancho Los Amigos Scale*) are used widely across centers treating acute and subacute TBI survivors (see Tables 2 and 3). Despite the lack of careful empirical investigations into the reliability and validity of the Rancho scale, widespread use and practical utility make familiarity with these scales a necessity for the clinician involved with care in acute or subacute settings.

Systematic quantification of attentional deficits has, conversely, been more elusive. When broadly defined, "attention" is a construct that is demanded by virtually all neuropsychological tests, yet is specifically tested by virtually none. Furthermore, attention is a multifaceted construct, and a deficit in one of the attentional components outlined above does not necessarily imply a similar deficit in the other components. As such, formal tests of attention and concentration tend to combine a number of cognitive operations. Perhaps the most common operation demanded in these sorts of tasks is the ability to maintain information in rote memory (e.g., Digit Span—Forward from the WAIS-R); however, nearly as ubiquitous is maintaining this information in rote memory while manipulating it either sequentially or arithmetically (e.g., Digit Span—Backward from the WAIS-R, Arithmetic from the WAIS-R, Paced Auditory Serial Addition Task], spelling *WORLD* backward). Another component often added to these tasks is the ability to think or move rapidly (i.e., psychomotor speed) in response to test items (e.g., Digit Symbol from the WAIS-R, Digit Symbol Modalities Test, and Trail-Making Test).

Perhaps the most commonly used index of attention is the Freedom From Distractibility (FD) index from the WAIS-R (J. Cohen, 1957; Leckliter, Matarazzo, & Silverstein, 1986; Smith et al., 1992; Waller & Waldman, 1990). Derived from the Arithmetic and Digit Span tests, this index is one of the three consistently used in studies of normal individuals (along with Verbal Comprehension and Perceptual Organization indexes). Conceptually, the two tests making up this index require participants to maintain aurally presented information in rote memory while manipulating that information, either

TABLE 2

The Glasgow Coma Scale

Response	Score	Characteristic
		Eye opening
None	1	Not attributable to ocular swelling
To pain	2	Pain stimulus is applied to chest or limbs
To speech	3	Nonspecific response to speech or shout, but this does not imply that the patient obeys command to open eyes
Spontaneous	4	Eyes are open, but this does not imply intact awareness
		Motor response
No response	1	Flaccid
Extension	2	"Decerebrate"; adduction, internal rotation of shoulder, and pronation of the forearm
Abnormal flexion	3	"Decorticate"; abnormal flexion and adduction of the shoulder
Withdrawal	4	Normal flexor response; withdraws from pain stimulus with adduction of the shoulder
Localizes pain	5	Pain stimulus applied to supraocular region or fingertip causes limb to move so as to attempt to remove it
Obeys commands	6	Follows simple commands
		Verbal response
No response	1	(Self-explanatory)
Incomprehensible	2	Moaning and groaning, but no recognizable words
Inappropriate	3	Intelligible speech (e.g., shouting or swearing), but no sustained or coherent conversation
Confused	4	Responds to questions in a conversational manner, but responses indicate varying degrees of disorientation and confusion
Oriented	5	Normal orientation to time, place, and person

Note: Summed Glasgow Coma Scale score = Eye + Motor + Verbal; range = 3–15. From *Neurobehavioral Consequences of Closed Head Injury* (2nd ed., p. 34), by H. Levin, A. L. Benton, and R. G. Grossman, 1982, New York: Oxford University Press. Copyright 1982 by Oxford University Press. Reprinted with permission.

by reversing the order in which it was presented or by carrying out calculations using the material. In addition, the Arithmetic test places a premium on performing these manipulations rapidly. Thus, the FD index might be most appropriately viewed as an index that is strongly weighted by information-processing speed and that combines sustained attention to an internal representation with divided attention. Although this index is useful in discriminating those who have heterogeneous types of brain pathology from normal individuals (Scott, Sherer, & Adams, 1995), studies directed specifically at examining the abilities of TBI survivors have yet to be performed. Likewise, the degree to which the sensitivity of the FD index varies over the various stages of recovery from TBI has not been explored. Thus, although the clinical utility of the FD index is intuitively appealing, the current lack of empirical validation with survivors of TBI suggests that clinicians should use caution in interpreting the index in isolation.

In contrast to the FD index, the Paced Auditory Serial Addition Task was developed by Gronwall and her colleagues (Brittain, LaMarche, Reeder, Roth, & Boll, 1991; Gronwall & Sampson, 1974; Gronwall & Wrightson, 1981; O'Shaughnessy, Fowler, & Reid, 1984) specifically to quantify the decrement of information-processing speed caused by TBI. Like the FD index, this task places a premium on sustained attention, internal representations, divided attention, and information-processing speed; however, it incorporates a stronger interference component than do either of the tasks composing the FD index. Advantages of the test include its extensive use in the literature, demonstrated predictive validity, and relatively brief administration time (Gronwall & Wrightson, 1981). In addition, normative information stratified by Shipley IQ and years of education have been published (Brittain et al., 1991).

Another frequently used test of attention is the Trail-Making Test. This measure has been widely written about and is a standard component of most neuropsychological test batteries (Jarvis & Barth, 1984; Lezak, 1983; Parsons, 1986; Reitan, 1958). In the context of the framework presented above, the first part of this measure (Trails A) may be viewed as a measure of sustained attention to an internally generated, overlearned sequence combined with visual scanning and motor speed. The second component of the task (Trails B) may be viewed as combining the demands of Trails A with the ability to alternate between internal representations. This test is particularly valuable to the clinician because of its simplicity, its short administration time, its extensive use in the literature, and its demonstrated prognostic utility (Lezak, 1983; Spreen & Strauss, 1991). A variety of other measures have been used in the assessment of attention; a selective summary of these is given in Exhibit 5.

The clinical interview with the TBI survivor and family is perhaps the most valuable tool available to

TABLE 3

Rancho Los Amigos Scale of Cognitive Levels and Expected Behavior

Level	Response	Characteristic
I	Response	Unresponsive to all stimuli
II	Generalized	Inconsistent, nonpurposeful, nonspecific reactions to stimuli; responds to pain, but response may be delayed
III	Localized response	Inconsistent reaction directly related to type of stimulus presented; responds to some commands; may respond to discomfort
IV	Confused, agitated	Disoriented and unaware of present events, with frequent bizarre and inappropriate behavior; attention span is short and ability to process information is impaired
V	Confused, inappropriate, nonagitated response	Nonpurposeful random or fragmented responses when task complexity exceeds abilities; patient appears alert and responds to simple commands; performs previously learned tasks but is unable to learn new ones
VI	Confused, appropriate response	Behavior is goal directed; responses are appropriate to the situation, with incorrect responses because of memory difficulties
VII	Automatic, appropriate response	Correct routine responses that are robotlike; appears oriented to setting, but insight, judgment, and problem solving are poor
VIII	Purposeful, appropriate response	Correct responding is a carryover of new learning; no required supervision, poor tolerance for stress, and some abstract reasoning difficulties

Note: Data are from *Intervention Strategies for Language Disorders Secondary to Head Trauma*, by C. Hagen and D. Malkmus, 1979, paper presented at the American Speech, Language, and Hearing Association Convention, Short Course, Atlanta, Georgia (as cited in Sohlberg & Mateer, 1989). Adapted with permission.

EXHIBIT 5

Measures Commonly Used in the Clinical Assessment of Attention

Tests of sustained attention, rote memory, and sequential manipulation

- Wechsler Adult Intelligence Scale–Revised (WAIS-R), Digit Span test
- Knox Cubes
- Corsi Cubes
- Spelling words backward (such as *world*)

Tests of sustained attention, divided attention, arithmetic manipulation, and information-processing speed

- Paced Auditory Serial Addition Task
- WAIS-R, Arithmetic test
- Serial subtraction from 100 by 7s (Serial 7s)
- Peterson–Peterson Auditory Consonant Trigrams

Tests of rote memory, information-processing speed, and psychomotor speed

- WAIS-R, Digit Symbol test
- Symbol Digit Modalities Test

Tests of attentional control and psychomotor speed

- Trail-Making Test
- Stroop Color and Word Test

the clinician to determine which aspects of attention may have been affected by the injury. A number of the stereotypical presentations of TBI attentional deficits have been provided in the descriptions above, and it is important that the clinician make careful note of these when they occur.

Treatment and recovery. Behavioral treatments of the alternating levels of arousal seen during emergence from coma are primarily directed at structuring the patient's environment. If the patient is becoming agitated frequently, then family and staff should be instructed to minimize stimulation in the patient's room by closing window shades, turning the television down or off, and interacting with the patient in a measured, nonthreatening manner. People interacting with agitated patients often tend to mirror the patient's agitation by becoming louder or speaking more rapidly. Given that the hyperactivity seen in animals with prefrontal lesions increases in conditions of high surrounding activity (Fuster, 1989), such mirroring of the patient is likely to exacerbate rather than limit further agitation. In addition, the patient should be given orientation information frequently, because he or she is unlikely to retain it. The patient's behavior may also be modified by increasing attention during calm periods in an attempt to positively reinforce this behavior. A variety of other strategies directed toward modifying agitation behaviorally have been discussed in the literature; the interested reader should consult the more comprehensive review of these strategies (as well as behavioral interventions across the spectrum of neuropsychological deficits) provided by McGlynn (1990). Finally, pharmacological intervention directed at markedly reducing the patient's level of agitation should not be ruled out if the patient represents a danger to himself or herself or to others and resists behavioral interventions (Mapou, 1992).

Detailed accounts of interventions aimed at improving the attentional capacities of patients have been presented by a number of authors (Ben-Yishay, Piasetsky, & Rattok, 1987; Sohlberg & Mateer, 1986, 1987, 1989). Rather than recount these strategies in a detailed fashion, we focus on common themes between the strategies and refer readers to the source articles for specifics on implementation. In general, these strategies conceptualize attention as a multifactorial construct, with some aspects more fundamental than others. The overall strategy is one of attempting to improve the different aspects of attention in a hierarchical fashion, beginning with the more basic, ubiquitous aspects and progressing to more complex and demanding tasks. For instance, fundamental components to initially address include the patient's ability to maintain an appropriate level of wakefulness and the ability to establish an attentional focus. At the highest levels of the hierarchy, the patient might be asked to maintain a high level of concentration on tasks in which input from both external stimuli and internal calculations would be required for successful task performance. Although somewhat different in terms of fundamental conceptualization, both Ben-Yishay et al. and Sohlberg and Mateer have provided evidence that their respective strategies for improving attentional deficits are effective when appropriately applied, although the methodological compromises often necessary in the clinical setting have precluded carefully controlled group studies documenting the effectiveness of the programs (Ben-Yishay et al., 1987; Sohlberg & Mateer, 1987). A related benefit from improvements in attention is concomitant improvement in memory, and Sohlberg and Mateer (1987) have provided data suggesting that such improvement does occur in some patients.

Orientation

Definition. *Orientation* may be briefly defined as knowledge about one's self and surroundings. Informal assessment of orientation is a common component of even the most elementary mental status examination. The aspects of orientation most frequently assessed are (a) personal information (name, age, birthdate, address, and family information), (b) location (city, state, building, and floor of building), (c) time (date, month, year, and time of day), and (d) situation (realization of what has happened and why the examination is taking place).

Deficits. Transient loss of orientation is a common consequence of a global disruption of brain function (W. F. Daniel, Crovitz, & Weiner, 1987; High, Levin, & Gary, 1990). However, despite the ubiquity of this phenomenon, there have been very few systematic studies describing how orientation is disrupted following TBI. High et al. studied 84 patients who had been admitted to a neurosurgery unit after sustaining CHIs of varying severity. Patients were studied from the time they were able to follow simple verbal commands (end of coma) until their scores on the Galveston Orientation and Amnesia Test (GOAT) were in the normal range for 2 consecutive days (end of PTA). Orientation to person was considered intact if the person was able to identify himself or herself and give a correct birthdate on 2 consecutive days. Orientation to place was considered intact when the person was aware of being in a hospital and could correctly identify the city in which the hospital was located for 2 consecutive days. Finally, the person was considered to be oriented to time if the date he or she gave was within 5 days of the actual date for 2 consecutive days.

Not surprisingly, the timetable for recovery of orientation closely paralleled severity of injury. The average numbers of days before recovery of orientation (coma + PTA) were 48.1, 34.6, 14.1, and 14.0 for severe injuries, moderate injuries, mild injuries with other medical complications, and mild injuries without complications, respectively. When compared with patients who had no lesions visualized on CT scans and those whose lesions spared the frontal and temporal regions, patients with focal frontal lobe lesions took significantly longer to recover their orientation. Patients with temporal or frontotemporal lesions fell between the two extremes, differing from neither significantly. Because the median GCS did not vary according to location of primary lesion, this finding suggests that frontal and, possibly, temporal regions may play an important role in maintaining orientation independent of the severity of neurological insult. Age also appears to be important, because despite a lack of correlation between age and severity of injury (as indexed by GCS score) in the studied sample, older patients had longer periods of impaired orientation (High et al., 1990).

In addition to the timetable of recovery of orientation, High et al.'s (1990) data also helped to characterize the pattern of recovery of orientation. The majority of patients, regardless of the severity of injury or the laterality of the lesion, regained orientation first to person, then to place, and finally to time. The majority also displaced the date backward in time, with older patients and patients with frontotemporal lesions showing greater backward displacement than those from other groups. Typically, this backward displacement in time shrank gradually as the patient's recovery progressed. This pattern is consistent with the notion that, because of their organization and repetition, older memories are less susceptible to disruption by cerebral insult than more recent memories (Levin, 1989; Ribot, 1882). A competing hypothesis, pointed out by Sohlberg and Mateer (1989), is that orientation is most easily recovered for those aspects of knowledge for which the most cues exist. So, for instance, "person" remains constant, and knowledge of person requires no new learning on the part of the patient, but depends entirely on recall. In contrast, orientation to both place and time require some new learning, with time requiring continual updating for accuracy.

Assessment. Although the assessment of orientation is typically done informally, formal measures are available. The standard among these measures is the aforementioned GOAT (Levin, O'Donnell, & Grossman, 1979). This test has been used extensively with TBI populations in both clinical and research settings (see Exhibit 6). In addition, Levin et al. (1984) found that PTA as defined by the GOAT relates strongly to both the severity of initial neurological impairment as measured by the GCS and to overall recovery at 6 months. A potential limitation of the GOAT is its requirement of a moderate degree of competence with expressive language and speech. This requirement can be mitigated to a large extent by using the Good Samaritan Hospital Orientation Test (Exhibit 7; Sohlberg & Mateer, 1989). This instrument, based on the GOAT, requires only that the patient be able to signal yes or no responses in some fashion. Although this measure is less widely used than the GOAT and is necessarily less comprehensive, it does provide a standard measure of orientation when use of the GOAT is impractical because of the patient's limitations. Given the potential prognostic value of the length of PTA, the patient's orientation status should be noted in the medical record on a daily basis whenever possible. Should one be interested in determining the duration of PTA retrospectively in the absence of formal assessment of orientation, the criteria of High et al. (1990) outlined above for recovery of orientation to person, place, and date (each for 2 consecutive days) can serve as a relatively accurate means of defining the end of PTA.

Treatment and recovery. The ability of behavioral interventions to accelerate the recovery of orientation beyond that which would occur spontaneously has yet to be conclusively shown (Sohlberg & Mateer, 1989). Particularly in the acute phase, then, intervention aimed at accelerating recovery of orientation should have a relatively low priority in relationship to other treatment goals. However, given that a number of cognitive treatment modalities require awareness of self and surroundings as well as a sense of temporal contiguity as a foundation, the continued assessment of orientation status provides useful signposts for guiding the timing of treatment initiation.

Some types of learning are relatively preserved during PTA. Ewart, Levin, Watson, and Kalisky (1989) have shown that survivors of TBI who remain in PTA are able to acquire new motor skills that generalize to the post-PTA period (i.e., "procedural learning"). This finding mirrors those for other amnestic populations (N. J. Cohen & Squire, 1980). It also raises the possibility that other aspects of memory that have been shown to be relatively preserved in some amnestic populations (e.g., "implicit memory," or material that was encoded at a preconscious level) may also be intact in TBI survivors. The preservation of these abilities and their applicability to rehabilitation interventions remains an area open to empirical exploration.

A small subset of survivors of severe TBI never return to full orientation. These patients remain chronically confused, and so their home environment and daily activity schedule should be structured with this in mind. Williams (1987, as cited in Sohlberg & Mateer, 1989) has compiled a number of helpful suggestions that may aid in this goal (see Exhibit 8).

Memory

Definitions. *Memory* may be broadly defined as the process by which previous experience influences an organism's current cognitive, emotional, or behavioral state. The breadth of the construct, however, is such that one must look at specific aspects of memory to gain a full understanding of its workings in the individual case. Cognitive psychologists and neuroscientists have put a great deal of effort into defining the cognitive, neuroanatomical, and physiological parameters of memory; thus, models of these functions abound (Squire & Butters, 1992). A taxonomy of these models is shown in Figure 2, in which memory is broken down into declarative memory (i.e., "explicit memory," or the kind of information that is ordinarily available as conscious recollections) and nondeclarative memory (i.e., "implicit memory,"

EXHIBIT 6

The Galveston Orientation and Amnesia Test

Name ____________________ Date of test _____/_____/_____

Age: __________ Sex: M F Day of the week: s m t w t f s

Date of birth _____/_____/_____ Time __________ am pm

Diagnosis: _________________________ Date of injury: _____/_____/_____

Galveston Orientation and Amnesia Test Error/Points

1. What is your name? (2) ______________ _____/_____
   When were you born? (4) ______________ _____/_____
   Where do you live? (4) ______________ _____/_____
2. Where are you now? (5) city ______________ _____/_____
   (5) hospital ______________ _____/_____
3. On what date were you admitted to this hospital? (5) _____/_____
   How did you get here? (5) ______________ _____/_____
4. What is the first event you can remember after the injury?
   (5) ______________________________ _____/_____
   Can you describe in detail (e.g., date, time, and companions) the first event you can recall after the injury?
   (5) ______________________________ _____/_____
5. Can you describe the last event you recall before the accident?
   (5) ______________________________ _____/_____
   Can you describe in detail (e.g., date, time, and companions) the first event you can recall before the injury?
   (5) ______________________________ _____/_____
6. What time is it now? ______________________________
   (−1 for each 30 min removed from correct time, to maximum of −5) _____/_____
7. What day of the week is it? ______________
   (−1 for each day removed from the correct one) _____/_____
8. What day of the month is it? ______________
   (−1 for each day removed from correct date, to maximum of −5) _____/_____
9. What is the month? ______________________________
   (−5 for each month removed from the correct one to maximum of −15) _____/_____
10. What is the year? ______________________________
    (−10 for each year removed from correct one to maximum of −30) _____/_____

Total error points _____/_____

Total score (100 points − total error points) _____/_____

Scoring and interpretation: If an item is answered incorrectly, then the number of error points scored is indicated in parentheses. A score less than 65 is considered significantly impaired, whereas scores from 66 to 75 are considered borderline.

From "The Galveston Orientation and Amnesia Test: A Practical Scale to Assess Cognition After Head Injury," by H. S. Levin, V. M. O'Donnell, and R. G. Grossman, 1979, Journal of Nervous and Mental Diseases, *167, p. 677. Copyright 1979 by Williams and Wilkins. Adapted with permission.*

EXHIBIT 7

The Good Samaritan Hospital Orientation Test (Yes–No Responses)

Administer this version of the orientation test to patients who cannot respond verbally more than yes or no or have a reliable way to indicate yes or no (e.g., pointing, writing, eyeblink, thumbs up or down). Vary the order in which correct and incorrect answers are presented for responses. Also, vary the incorrect answer (i.e., use a variety of incorrect names instead of the same one each time).

Date:

Personal information:

1. Is your name (first only) ______________? (incorrect)
2. Is your name (first only) ______________? (correct)
3. Are you ______________ years old? (incorrect)
4. Are you ______________ years old? (correct)
5. Do you live in ______________? (incorrect)
6. Do you live in ______________? (correct)

Orientation to place:

7. Is this place a school?
8. Is this place a hospital?

Orientation to time:

9. Is it the month of ______________ now? (incorrect)
10. Is it the month of ______________ now? (correct)

From Introduction to Cognitive Rehabilitation: Theory and Practice *(p. 101), by M. M. Sohlberg and C. A. Mateer, 1989, New York: Guilford Press. Copyright 1989 by Guilford Press. Reprinted with permission.*

or information that has been learned but typically does not afford access to the original experience or to any memory content; Squire et al., 1990). Investigations based on such models have been able to move beyond the simple quantitative aspects of memory to examine how information is remembered. Thus, information is available describing both the quantitative effects of TBI on memory (such as number of elements recalled or rate of forgetting) and some of its qualitative aspects, such as sensitivity to interference, ability to make use of semantic organization, and sensitivity to contextual cues. This breakdown of the process of memory and the ways in which this process is disrupted by TBI is important for the meaningful design of treatments aimed at improving the memory performance of TBI survivors.

Deficits. Memory problems are the most common complaint mentioned by survivors of TBI and their families up to 7 years after a severe head injury (Oddy, Coughlan, Tyerman, & Jenkins, 1985). These deficits play a major role in shaping the life of the TBI survivor. For instance, Brooks, McKinlay, Symington, Beattie, and Campsie (1987) found that, along with slowed information processing, impairment in verbal memory was one of the strongest predictors of unemployment 7 years after injury. Further darkening the picture is the fact that the preferential impact of TBI on medial temporal and ventral frontal regions has a more detrimental effect on memory than on overall cognitive function (J. H. Adams, Graham, Scott, Parker, & Doyle, 1980; Levin, 1989; Levin, Goldstein, High, & Eisenberg, 1988). In addition, the effect of severe TBI on memory appears to be independent of its effect on information-processing speed (Gronwall & Wrightson, 1981). The magnitude of deficits seems to be related to the severity of the initial injury, although lasting memory deficits have been reported in a small percentage of patients who have suffered mild TBI (Levin, 1989).

The impairment of memory function after moderate to severe TBI seems to follow a relatively characteristic pattern. After the patient regains consciousness, one observes the posttraumatic amnesic state described above. Following the end of PTA, the memory performance of TBI survivors may be differentiated from that of normal individuals by an increased rate of forgetting and an increased susceptibility to interference (Jetter, Poser, Freeman, & Markowitsch, 1986; Levin, 1989). Although the

EXHIBIT 8

Guidelines for Home Management of the Chronically Confused Person

The goal is to provide a home environment that is structured, predictable, and as unthreatening as possible. Some of these suggestions may help, some may not—it is important to find out the best fit for the individual and the family environment.

- Maintain the individual in familiar surroundings. Trips and visits to new places, although entertaining to others, might produce anxiety.
- Avoid ambiguity, and do not present unnecessary choices or decisions. Use statements such as the following: "Now we must go to the store." "Now it is time to take a shower." "Brian is coming to visit after supper."
- Be aware that mental tasks beyond the individual's capacity produce anxiety. Although this does not mean that new things should not be tried, be sensitive to when they are not going well and backtrack when necessary (maybe to try again later). Avoid confronting the individual with tasks that stress areas of weakness. Therapies should be delivered routinely by the same therapist.
- Try to maintain a daily routine that features well-established landmarks, such as regular meals. Make life predictable. Avoid breaks in routine. Extend necessary changes in routine over time instead of making changes abruptly.
- Understand that fatigue will be poorly tolerated. Schedule visits to doctors after a period of sleep. Encourage very frequent periods of rest. Do not schedule several hours of unbroken activity.
- Limit coffee and tea, because stimulant effects may be amplified. Be alert for adverse side effects of other prescription and nonprescription medications.
- Provide adequate lighting in all areas. Consider fluorescent fixtures in hallways, on stairs, and in bathrooms.
- Limit confusion and confusing stimulation. Family gatherings may be overwhelming. Recreational activities may not be well tolerated, even if they involve previously favorite places or activities.
- Be alert for indications of change in physical or mental status (e.g., prolonged agitation, escalated combativeness, or changes in sleep or eating patterns).
- It may help to have a radio tuned to a station playing familiar tunes. Television may contribute to the confusion of the environment.
- Anticipate the possibility of the individual wandering off and getting lost. Sew labels into clothing so that others will know who he or she is; provide a telephone number and an address.
- Make sure that caregivers take time to do things for themselves. Caregivers who are "burned out" do not take care of their relatives as well as those who take some time to look after themselves every once in a while.

From "Management of the Patient With Chronic Confusion," by D. Williams, 1987, as cited in Sohlberg and Mateer (1989). Copyright 1989 by Guilford Press. Adapted with permission.

deficits are typically generalized, material-specific (i.e., verbal or visuospatial) deficits have been noted; however, these are more common following head injuries that are complicated by subdural hematoma (Levin, 1989). These memory difficulties may be missed on gross examination, because the ability of TBI survivors to remember material in a rote fashion or for very short intervals without the presence of strong distractors may be relatively unimpaired (Jetter et al., 1986).

Over the past decade, more attention has been paid to the ways in which TBI disrupts more qualitative aspects of memory. Two aspects in particular appear to be affected by TBI: (a) reduced implementation of organizational mnemonic strategies and (b) impaired memory for contextual factors.

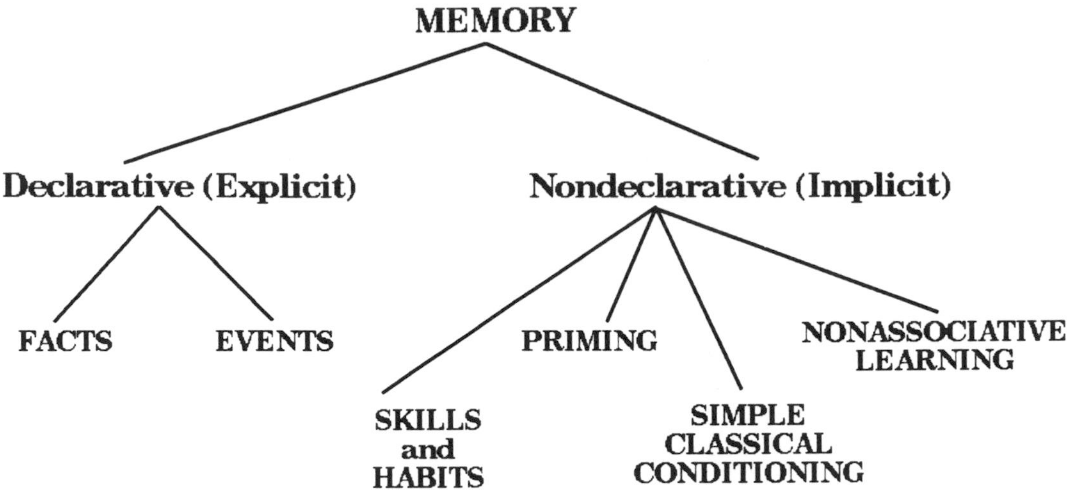

FIGURE 2. A tentative memory taxonomy. From "Memory, Hippocampus, and Brain Systems (p. 826)," by L.R. Squire and B. J. Knowlton. In *The Cognitive Neurosciences,* edited by M. Gazzaniga, 1994, Cambridge, MA: MIT Press. Copyright 1994 by MIT Press. Adapted with permission.

Organizational mnemonic strategies are used to "chunk" information into fewer, more manageable pieces. TBI survivors are less likely to spontaneously organize information semantically than are controls (Crosson, Novack, Trenerry, & Craig, 1988; Levin & Goldstein, 1986; Novack, Kofoed, & Crosson, 1995). However, unlike a number of other amnesic populations, the memory performance of TBI survivors shows clear gains when this sort of organization is externally imposed on the material to be learned, although the benefit they derive is less than that derived by uninjured individuals (Goldstein, Levin, Boake, & Lohrey, 1990; Levin, 1989; Novack et al., 1995). Although TBI survivors are able to better their performance through the use of semantic strategies, their ability to discriminate the correct response from among semantically related alternatives during free-recall tasks is impaired; thus, they produce significantly more "semantic intrusions" (e.g., recalling "apples" instead of "grapes") than do normal individuals (Crosson, Sartor, Jenny, Nabors, & Moberg, 1993; Novack et al., 1995). Likewise, TBI survivors are more likely to incorrectly identify semantically related words as having been presented to them in yes–no recognition tasks (Levin, 1989).

Contextual factors in memory consist of information about the material to be remembered, such as the time, frequency, and source of the material. For example, one might forget the content of a phone message but remember that the message was received between two other messages from other companies at approximately 2 p.m. In this case, despite an inability to explicitly recall the informational content of the memory, one can describe the context in which the information was received. These variables are felt by some (e.g., Hirst, 1982) to be encoded relatively "automatically" in normal performance. In general, TBI survivors are poorer at these sorts of discriminations than healthy individuals. These findings are consistent with a pattern commonly seen in patients that have suffered frontal lobe damage (Milner, Petrides, & Smith, 1985) and have been variously attributed to impairments in a specific system specialized for spatiotemporal information (Schacter, 1987), disconnection between "fact memory" and "context memory" (Shimamura & Squire, 1987), deficient strategies of retrieval (Moscovitch, 1989), and attentional problems (Dywan, Segalowitz, Henderson, & Jacoby, 1993). Tweedy and Vakil (1988) provided data suggesting that TBI survivors are relatively impaired in their judgment of temporal order, spatial location, and frequency of occurrence relative to control participants. However, further data provided by Vakil, Blachstein, and Hoofien (1991) have suggested that these deficits may be evident only in tasks that explicitly require recall of contextual factors and not in tasks in which the encoding and retrieval of contextual factors remains implicit. Dywan et al. (1993) have provided data suggesting that TBI survivors are impaired in their ability to establish stable links between names and faces over a series of trials, which they interpret as an impairment in "memory for source." Whether the memory for source problems identified by Dywan et al. and the semantic intrusion–false-positive problems discussed above reflect a common underlying cognitive deficit remains an open question.

Assessment. Because of the interest that psychologists have had in memory function over the years, a broad selection of instruments is available for assessment. Because measures are available for assessing many aspects of memory, we recommend that clinicians take a close look at both the quantitative and qualitative aspects of the TBI survivor's memory performance. The results of these measures may provide valuable information to help maximize rehabilitative efforts. A summary of important constructs to assess is presented in Table 4 along with some suggested tests. Because few, if any, "pure" memory tests are available (Moscovitch, 1992), the clinician should always keep an eye open for commonalities across tests that may reflect impairments in abilities secondarily addressed by each measure, particularly those related to deficits in "executive function" (discussed in some detail later in this chapter).

Another important commonality to bear in mind is the effect that language disturbances may have on tests of verbal memory. Crosson, Cooper, Lincoln, Bauer, and Velozo (1993) have shown that even relatively mild language disturbances seen after blunt head injury may affect an individual's ability to efficiently process verbal information at the input or output stage of a memory task. Their results showed that the contribution of language deficits to scores on recall measures of such tests as the California Verbal Learning Test (CVLT) may be minimized by examining the percentage of items remembered correctly from the best performance during the initial learning trials rather than by examination of the absolute number of items correctly recalled (Crosson, Cooper, et al., 1993).

A metacognitive aspect of memory that is often very important to assess is the patient's assessment of his or her own performance on the memory tests or his or her memory in general. Studies examining awareness of memory deficit after TBI suggest that survivors may significantly underestimate the magnitude of their memory deficits as measured by experimental tests (Baddeley et al., 1987). The knowledge of whether the patient is relatively accurate in evaluating his or her performance or consistently errs in one direction or the other may be very helpful in de-

TABLE 4

Neuropsychological Assessment of Memory

Construct of interest	Measure
Verbal memory	
Immediate span	Digit Span (WAIS-R, WMS-R) List A (CVLT) Logical Memory (WMS-R) Paired Associates (WMS-R)
Free recall, short delay	CVLT
Cued recall, short delay	CVLT
Free recall, long delay	CVLT Logical Memory (WMS-R)
Cued recall, long delay	CVLT Paired Associates (WMS-R)
Learning over repeated trials (quantitative performance and qualitative style)	Approach to learning on CVLT Ability to learn "easy" and "hard" word pairs
Recognition memory	True–false identification of correct items and foils
Visuoperceptual memory	
Immediate span	Visual Reproduction (WMS-R) Corsi Blocks ROCF copy
Free recall, long delay	Visual Reproduction (WMS-R) ROCF long delay
Learning over repeated trials (quantitative performance and qualitative style)	Tactual Performance Test (spatial rather than visual memory)

Note: WAIS-R = Wechsler Adult Intelligence Scale–Revised; CVLT = California Verbal Learning Test; WMS-R = Wechsler Memory Scale–Revised; ROCF = Rey–Osterreith Complex Figure.

vising strategies to help him or her compensate for any lingering memory problems in the most effective way possible. It is also diagnostically valuable to distinguish the typical overestimation of memory performance resulting from an awareness deficit from the typical underestimation of performance attributable to depression.

Treatment and recovery. A great deal of optimistic effort has gone into the investigation of memory rehabilitation. Unfortunately, the results, by and large, have not been good. Put simply, it is extremely difficult to make a clinically meaningful difference in the ability of a memory-disordered patient to recall information (O'Connor & Cermak, 1987; B. A. Wilson, 1992). There are a number of obstacles that seem to impede the progress of memory rehabilitation. The first obstacle deals with the nature of the mnemonic strategies themselves. In general, mnemonic strategies attempt to elaborate or strengthen the way in which to-be-remembered information is encoded. Although such strategies may partially address the decreased ability of TBI survivors to spontaneously organize information to be remembered, they do little to address an accelerated rate of forgetting. Another problem with mnemonic strategies is that they inevitably place a burden on other functions that may also be impaired (e.g., concentration, semantic elaboration, and planning). Thus, although these strategies may work with non-brain-injured individuals or in controlled situations, they are usually ineffective in the TBI population because of their reliance on cognitive abilities that have become impaired. Instead, a more fruitful strategy might be to work around the identified deficits by using and emphasizing those cognitive functions that remain relatively unimpaired. Finally, there is a major pragmatic problem with mnemonics: Survivors of TBI make relatively little use of these learned strategies outside of the training setting. The relative contributions of deficits in planning, problem solving, initiative, and motivation probably vary from person to person, but the bottom line is simply that, even if the strategies appear to be effective in a carefully controlled setting, they are of little value if they do not generalize to the TBI survivor's "real life."

Given these obstacles, current work in memory rehabilitation is focused in two directions. First, cognitive neuroscientists continue to define the parameters of normal and impaired learning and memory performance, so that scientists and clinicians alike will have a clearer picture of the strengths and weaknesses characteristic of TBI survivors in devising strategies to improve memory performance. Such work has revealed that abilities such as procedural memory and semantic priming remain relatively unimpaired in amnesic populations (Ewart et al., 1989; Schmitter-Edgecombe, Marks, & Fahy, 1993), and some strategies have begun to incorporate these spared abilities into intervention programs (Glisky, Schacter, & Tulving, 1986). Likewise, recent work by Sohlberg, White, Evans, and Mateer (1992a, 1992b) has explored the ways in which prospective memory (or "remembering to remember" to do things such as pay bills and go to appointments) is affected by TBI, and initial results suggest that these deficits may respond favorably to treatment. The other major thrust has been toward maximizing the patient's comprehension and ability to apply compensatory strategies in an effort to maximize the generalizability of the techniques. Such an approach has been used successfully by a number of groups with "memory books." It is vital to tailor the approach to the needs and abilities of each patient (Sohlberg & Mateer, 1989). A suggested structure for such a memory book is provided in Exhibit 9.

Language

Definitions. In the context of this discussion, *language* is narrowly defined as one's ability to comprehend and implement the use of symbolic information for the purpose of communicating concepts. At a gross level, language may be conceptualized as consisting of comprehension, fluency, repetition, and naming (Benson, 1993). *Comprehension* refers to the ability of an individual to accurately perceive auditory or visual symbolic information and translate this information into meaningful concepts. *Fluency* refers to the ability of an individual to produce language at will, both spontaneously and in response to a prompt. Fluency may be further divided into (a) the ability to generate grammatically correct language at an ideational level (i.e., before vocalization) and (b) the ability to smoothly vocalize (or write) an in-

EXHIBIT 9

List of Possible Memory Notebook Sections

Orientation	Autobiographical information concerning personal information (age, phone number, address, etc.) as well as information about the brain injury (what happened, when it happened, etc.)
Memory log	For keeping track of what has been done daily; charts for hour-by-hour listings are often helpful
Calendar	A calendar with dates and times, which allows the scheduling of appointments and dates
Things to do	List of things that need to be accomplished in a given day; include a place to mark when each needs to be completed and when it has been accomplished
Transportation	Contains maps or bus information to frequented areas such as malls, banks, and stores
Feelings log	Contains charts for recording feelings relative to specific instances or times
Names	Important for recording names and identifying information about new people

From Introduction to Cognitive Rehabilitation: Theory and Practice *(p. 161), by M. M. Sohlberg and C. A. Mateer, 1989, New York: Guilford Press. Copyright 1989 by Guilford Press. Reprinted with permission.*

tended message (Alexander, Benson, & Stuss, 1989). *Naming* typically refers to the ability to correctly label objects when asked to do so, and *repetition* is the ability to reproduce a sequence of aurally presented words.

Deficits. Although historical documents have suggested that posttraumatic aphasia has been noted for centuries (Benton & Joynt, 1960; Ebbell, 1937; Levin et al., 1982), the systematic study of language disturbance after head injury is a relatively recent phenomenon. As a result of these efforts, it is known that classical syndromes of aphasia occur in only about 2% of patients admitted to hospitals with CHIs (Heilman, Safran, & Geschwind, 1971; Levin et al., 1982). This rate is higher for those who have suffered PHI or mass lesions (e.g., hematomas) affecting the regions typically implicated in language function. In these latter cases, the pattern of language disturbance is consistent with the pattern observed after vascular lesions in the same regions (Levin et al., 1982). Despite the rarity of classical aphasic syndromes, however, varying degrees of less pervasive language disturbance are common after TBI (Crosson, Cooper, et al., 1993; Levin et al., 1982).

As with all neuropsychological sequelae of TBI, the pattern of deficits varies according to the areas of the brain injured. In general, however, the aspects of language most consistently affected after TBI are language comprehension, naming, spontaneous word finding, and the ability to generate words that begin with specific letters (Levin, Grossman, & Kelly, 1976; Sarno, 1980). Long-term follow-up studies have suggested that comprehension recovers relatively quickly, whereas the naming, word-finding, and word-generation deficits are more likely to be chronic but relatively subtle in nature (Levin et al., 1982). A significant minority of severe TBI survivors remain aphasic; these patients typically have longer durations of coma and show a pervasive pattern of global cognitive impairment (Levin, Grossman, Sarwar, & Meyers, 1981). Dysarthria is also seen in conjunction with posttraumatic language disturbance. *Dysarthria* may be grossly defined as problems with the motor speech system that impair the pronunciation or production of words despite normal formulation on the part of the speaker. It is important to not confuse aphasia and dysarthria, for the two phenomena may be caused by entirely dissociable injuries, and the presence of one is not necessarily indicative of the other (Sarno, 1980). Furthermore, dysarthria often persists long past the time that language difficulties are largely overcome (Sarno, 1980).

TBI may also affect the way in which language is used (i.e., the discourse style of an individual). *Narrative discourse* is the use of language to communicate a complex event, such as a story, or narrative, to another person. *Conversational discourse* is the manner in which one communicates during the interactive course of a conversation. TBI may affect both of these discourse styles, in that information content, cohesive ties, and communicative efficiency are reduced whereas hesitational phenomena are increased in comparison with uninjured individuals (Chapman et al., 1992; Ehrlich, 1988; Mentis & Prutting, 1987; Wyckoff, 1984). Currently, the extent to which these phenomena can be distinguished from the manifestation of the above-noted word-finding and generative difficulties observed at the discourse level remains unclear.

Assessment. The neuropsychologist's role in assessing language depends on the nature of the setting and the referral question. In the acute setting, the question is usually one of defining gross deficits in expressive and receptive language so that treatment staff may know how to communicate with the patient most effectively. It is in an assessment of this sort that awareness of the relationship between orientation and language recovery becomes extremely important. As noted earlier, the indexes most typically used to measure the end of coma and the end of PTA assume at least minimal competence with receptive and expressive language. Therefore, a patient with a receptive or expressive language disturbance that is selective may appear to be at a lower functional level than is actually the case; likewise, a confused, disoriented patient may appear to exhibit a greater degree of language pathology than is actually the case. Thus, it is important to note both the level of orientation and the level of language recovery before drawing firm conclusions about either one (Levin et al., 1982).

Formal language evaluation of the subacute or chronic survivor of TBI for the purposes of designing and evaluating a program of speech therapy is typically performed by speech and language therapists. In contrast, the neuropsychologist's role in such evaluations is to establish the extent to which language deficits affect other neuropsychological abilities of the individual and the ways in which these deficits may affect other aspects of psychological, vocational, or social function. Assessment of language in these patients typically involves screening their ability to comprehend simple and complex commands, name objects, repeat words and phrases, and generate words in a fluent manner (both in spontaneous conversation and when prompted by a stimulus letter or semantic category). Reading and writing are also typically screened. A number of tests incorporating these components are commercially available, or one may get a rough idea about the integrity of these functions through an informal, bedside exam (Benson, 1993). A sample of the tests commonly used to screen these functions is given in Table 5. The weight given to each component depends on the nature of the referral question. Because the study of discourse changes in survivors of TBI is relatively new, formal instruments for the assessment of these changes are not commercially available; this

TABLE 5

Neuropsychological Screening of Language Function

Construct of interest	Measure
Spontaneous word finding	Spontaneous conversation
Word or sound substitutions (paraphasias)	Spontaneous conversation
Effort required to produce output	Spontaneous conversation
Complexity of grammar	Spontaneous conversation
Naming objects	Boston Naming Test, Visual Naming Test (MAE)
Single-word generation ("verbal fluency")	FAS, Controlled Oral Word Association Test (MAE)
Repetition	Sentence Repetition (MAE, NCCEA)
Comprehension	Token Test (MAE)

Note: MAE = Multilingual Aphasia Examination; NCCEA = Neurosensory Center Comprehensive Examination for Aphasia.

is not likely to change until researchers delineate exactly which deficits are present and how amenable these deficits are to remediation.

Treatment and recovery. Fortunately, aphasia following TBI typically carries a better prognosis than aphasia secondary to vascular lesions (Levin et al., 1982). Barring extensive damage to the areas directly involved in language, even patients with moderate acute language difficulties may reasonably expect to recover to a much more functional level, with perhaps some residual difficulties with naming and spontaneous word finding (Levin et al., 1981). When aphasia does occur secondary to TBI, the treatment approaches do not differ significantly from those used to treat aphasia secondary to other etiologies. Such strategies have been reviewed in detail elsewhere (Basso, 1987; Goodglass, 1987). Rehabilitation of the impairments in discourse style remains at the theoretical level, with very little empirical data supporting any particular approach to the problem. Sohlberg and Mateer (1989) gave a number of logically reasoned suggestions about methods of assessment and treatment of these problems; however, the jury remains out on the amenability of these deficits to intervention. Treatment remains largely in the realm of the speech and language pathologist familiar with neurogenic language disturbance. The neuropsychologist's primary roles in these sorts of cases are most often (a) to screen for the approximate level of language pathology and (b) to help the family, physicians, rehabilitation personnel, and nursing staff by serving as a liaison who is familiar with the principles of language pathology, the likely resolution of these deficits, and their potential impact on the individual patient and his or her family system.

Visuoperceptual Function

Definitions. Perceptual deficits secondary to TBI are relatively uncommon. The most commonly discussed deficits in the literature are those of visual perception. Although less common than many other types of neuropsychological deficits following TBI, visuoperceptual deficits have the potential to be extremely disruptive in the survivor's rehabilitation and subsequent readjustment. Visuoperceptual disturbances may occur at all levels of the perceptual system following TBI, from basic deficits in extraocular movements to impairments in visuospatial organization (Gianutsos & Matheson, 1987; Ratcliff, 1987). The breadth of knowledge needed to adequately assess and treat visual function strongly encourages an interdisciplinary approach, and some have made the suggestion that ophthalmological screening should be a standard component of initial evaluations before designing rehabilitation strategies for individual patients (Gianutsos & Matheson, 1987). In any case, the clinician should be aware that disturbances may occur at any point in this process and should not hesitate to consult appropriate professionals when disturbance is suspected. Given the nature of neuropsychological training, it is usually the "higher" disturbances of visuoperceptual function (i.e., those that rely on processes demanding the involvement of association cortices) that neuropsychologists are called on to assess and remediate; therefore, it is these processes with which we deal most closely.

At a basic level, there are two relatively distinct visual systems, relying primarily on cortical and subcortical mechanisms, respectively (Schneider, 1969). The first, known as the *retinogeniculostriate system*, provides the sensory basis for conscious visual experience. Damage at any point along this system results in defects of the visual field (see Figure 3). The primarily subcortical retinotectal system, in contrast, functions at a preconscious level and plays an important role in detection of stimuli in the visual environment and shifting gaze so that stimuli are in the center of the visual field. Damage to this system may result in difficulties with visual orientation, detection of critical elements in the visual field, and difficulties with upward gaze (Ratcliff, 1987).

After a visual image is received by the primary visual cortex, secondary and tertiary occipital cortices refine the image in terms of contours, colors, features, and motion. Visual information is sent to at least two parallel systems—one for elaborating on the identity of the stimuli and one for elaborating on the position of the stimuli in space (Desimone et al., 1990; Mishkin, Ungerleider, & Macko, 1983). The former, "what is it" system is represented primarily in temporo-occipital association cortices, whereas the "where is it" system is represented primarily in the parietal cortices.

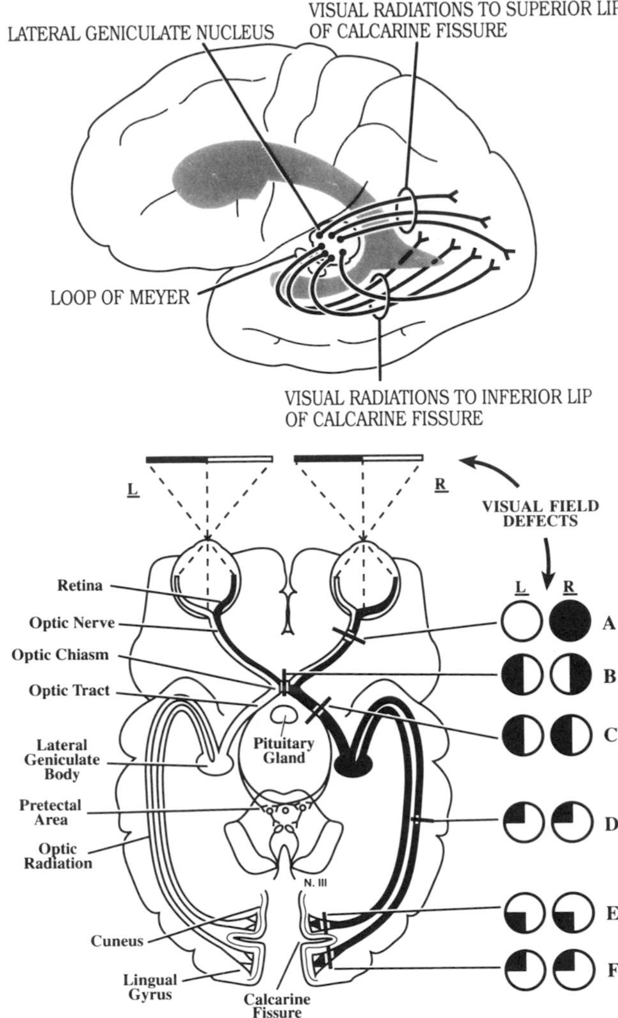

FIGURE 3. Location and effects of lesions on the retinogeniculostriate system.

Two sorts of disorders are commonly mentioned in discussions of visuoperceptual dysfunction: visuoperceptive disorders and neglect syndromes. Visuoperceptive disorders are those that involve disruption of the "what is it" system and are defined by impairment in the ability to "make visual sense" of stimuli or impairments in the ability to match the visual image to knowledge about the stimulus. Neglect syndromes, in contrast, are defined by the failure to report, respond, or orient to novel or meaningful stimuli across modalities presented in a particular region of space, most commonly to the side opposite the brain lesion (Heilman, Watson, & Valenstein, 1993). These syndromes are the most commonly seen disruptions of the "where is it" system. Although neglect syndromes are not visuoperceptual deficits per se (and, in fact, are distinguished by generalization beyond visual function), the clinical manifestations of neglect syndromes are more similar to visuoperceptual deficits than to the other sorts of deficits reviewed in this chapter. Clinically, visuoperceptive disorders and neglect may overlap, but for the purposes of simplicity, we discuss the two as separate from each other. For more in-depth consideration of the theoretical and neurological underpinnings of these deficits, readers should refer to more comprehensive reviews devoted to these topics (Benton & Tranel, 1993; Heilman et al., 1993).

Deficits. TBI may impair a number of basic sensory and motor functions that affect vision. Impairments in extraocular movements secondary to cranial nerve trauma or decreases in visual acuity secondary to traumatic compression of the optic nerve occur relatively frequently after TBI (Gianutsos & Matheson, 1987). However, disruption of higher order visual processing is relatively uncommon. Thus, relatively little research has gone into quantifying incidence rates or qualitative aspects of visuoperceptive disturbances following TBI. Recent neurophysiological reports (Heinze, Münte, Gobiet, Niemann, & Ruff, 1992) have suggested that a substantial number of CHI survivors may have deficits in early feature recognition, such that they do not process small visual details as efficiently or as accurately as age-matched control subjects. It has been suggested that this deficit may occur across modalities and that it may contribute to the global reduction in information-processing efficiency commonly seen after CHI (Gronwall, 1987; Heinze et al., 1992). Aside from this deficit, the visuoperceptual problems seen in survivors of TBI are more a function of focal deficits suffered in individual injuries rather than deficits seen across the population in general.

A broad array of visuospatial–constructional deficits may occur after TBI, including alexia (inability to read), agnosia (inability to recognize the identity of objects), and difficulties with visuospatial concept formation. Again, these deficits typically result from PHIs or mass lesions preferentially affecting specific cortical or subcortical regions and are uncommon sequelae of CHI. When these deficits do occur, their manifestation is consistent with that seen after CVA or other focal insults, as has been described in detail elsewhere (Benton & Tranel, 1993; Heilman et al., 1993; Sohlberg & Mateer, 1989).

In attentional neglect, the clinical picture with which the clinician will most likely be confronted is a patient who fails to respond to stimuli on his or her left side. Right neglect is observed less frequently, whereas neglect of vertical space or depth is rarely reported (Heilman et al., 1993). Given intact visual fields, the patient's failure to respond may be due to one of a number of syndromes, all of which are generally subsumed under the umbrella of attentional neglect. Given the number of conceptually distinct deficits that may fall under this umbrella, it is important that the clinician delineate the specific deficit, for this may have important implications for rehabilitation or compensatory strategies. As a rough conceptual guideline, the clinician must ascertain whether the deficit is at the attentional level (i.e., in the ability to cognitively attend to the stimuli on one side of space) or at the intentional level (i.e., in the ability to interact with a side of space). Although this distinction has yet to be fully explored among TBI survivors, it has been shown to hold up at the behavioral and neurological levels, both in ablation studies with monkeys and experimentally with humans who have suffered CVAs (Heilman & Watson, 1991).

Assessment. If one does not have the benefit of an ophthalmological examination, then it is helpful to at least get a general idea of the patient's basic visual function. The clinician may make use of a number of simple tools to roughly assess visual acuity, extraocular movements, and visual fields. A rough index of visual acuity may be obtained by using conventional letter eye charts or contrast sensitivity plates (Gianutsos & Matheson, 1987). Extraocular movements and smooth visual pursuit may be examined by having the patient fixate his or her head position and follow the clinician's finger horizontally and vertically, as depicted in Figure 4. Visual fields may be tested by having the patient fixate on the clinician's face (nose) and indicate when he or she first sees a peripherally approaching stimulus in each of the four visual quadrants (usually a pen or finger). Again, this type of assessment is intended only for screening purposes, and it is not as accurate as more formal evaluations (Trobe, Acosta, Krischer, & Trick, 1981). It is offered here as a rough guideline for clinicians to use for screening purposes when more formal evaluation is impractical. If abnormalities become apparent or the patient complains of visual disturbance in the face of what appears to be a normal exam, the clinician should refer the patient for more complete neuro-ophthalmological evaluation.

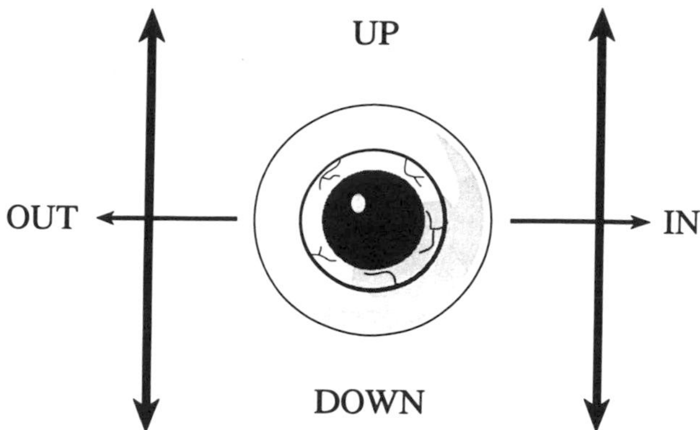

FIGURE 4. Examination of extraocular movements.

In addition to the basic visual sensory examination, it is important to screen for neglect. At bedside, at least three modalities should be tested for clear differentiation from sensory abnormalities (Heilman et al., 1993). Fingers are often used as somesthetic stimuli, but one may also use cotton applicators or pins. Auditory stimuli may be provided by rubbing or snapping fingers. Visual stimuli may be provided by finger movements. These stimuli should be presented unilaterally to both sides of the body in random order. If the patient responds normally to unilateral stimulation, then the clinician should intersperse the unilateral trials with bilateral stimulation to check for extinction of simultaneous stimuli. Although healthy individuals may sometimes report only unilateral stimuli if different regions are stimulated simultaneously (e.g., left face and right hand), they do not extinguish simultaneous stimuli to symmetrical regions (e.g., to both hands; Heilman et al., 1993).

If an expressive language or speech deficit exists that precludes verbal response by the patient, then the examiner may have the patient move the hand on the side that was stimulated. Should this modality of response be chosen, it is also important to examine for directional akinesia, or difficulty in moving in one area of space despite intact motor strength and coordination (Heilman et al., 1993). Examination for such a deficit may be performed by having the patient move the hand opposite to the stimulated side after a set of trials in which the patient moves the hand of the stimulated side. If the hand that does not move remains constant between sets of trials, then directional akinesia rather than attentional neglect is present. Unilateral akinesia may also be manifested in tasks that demand sustained bilateral action, such as raising both arms and holding them out.

In formal neuropsychological testing, a variety of tests have been used to assess visual inattention, most of which involve some degree of motor production (Lezak, 1983). Perhaps the most commonly used measures are line bisection, in which patients are required to vertically bisect horizontal lines of various lengths occurring at various places on the page, and letter cancellation, in which the patient is required to scan an array of letters and draw a line through each instance of a given letter. Other tasks involving more complex motor production include copying addresses or relatively simple designs (such as a flower, clock, or cross). Results of these screening measures are not equivalent, and dissociations between them may have implications about the specific neurological and cognitive underpinnings of a given patient's deficit (Binder, Marshall, Lazar, Benjamin, & Mohr, 1992; Halligan & Marshall, 1992; Ishiai, Sugishita, Ichikawa, Gono, & Watabiki, 1993). Patients have also been required to read a passage of text or describe a scene with which both the patient and the examiner are familiar from two specific viewing points directly opposite to each other. Some patients with hemispatial neglect will describe only one side of the scene in each description, but both descriptions together encompass the entire scene (Bisiach & Luzatti, 1978). When using text, the examiner must be sure to use a sample that crosses the midline of the visual field (i.e., a newspaper, with its short columns, may be too narrow).

In addition to assessing attentional neglect, the neuropsychologist may also choose to examine visuoperceptual analysis at higher levels. There are a wide variety of measures available for this purpose (Gianutsos & Matheson, 1987; Lezak, 1983), ranging from relatively simple matching tasks to complex tests requiring mental assembly and rotation. A relatively comprehensive list of the various measures has been compiled by Gianutsos and Matheson (1987). The level of analysis chosen by the clinician depends in large part on the status of the patient and the goals of the assessment. In Table 6, we recommend a number of instruments to be used in assessing various aspects of visuoperceptual function.

An important ability that relies heavily on visuospatial skills is the ability to drive. Although obviously demanding a number of other skills—such as judgment, attention, and adequate reaction time—intact visuospatial skills are a prerequisite for competent driving. As neuropsychologists continue to make inroads into medical and rehabilitation settings, they are increasingly called on to make often difficult decisions about the competence of TBI survivors to drive. This is an extremely important decision to the individual who has made a relatively good recovery, because the ability to freely use an automobile is a major determinant of a person's functional independence once he or she has left the rehabilitation setting. State law often preempts the decision if the person suffers from seizures; most states have specific guidelines about the amount of time that must have elapsed since the last seizure before a person may drive again. It is the patient who has subtle to moderate neuropsychological deficits but not seizures who presents the greatest challenge in determining driving competence.

Unfortunately, results of studies examining neuropsychologists' ability to predict driving competence have been mixed at best (Gouvier et al., 1989; Hopewell & Van Zomeren, 1990; Van Zomeren, Brouwer, Rothengatter, & Snoek, 1988; Wedding, 1992). Two of the fundamental difficulties facing this area of inquiry are (a) lack of an empirical or legal definition of "a competent driver" and (b) the relatively poor generalization of results across laboratories. Although there has been support for the predictive validity of performance on some measures (e.g., oral version of the Symbol Digit Modalities Test and Picture Completion and Picture Arrangement from the WAIS-R), the replicability of these results has been poor (Gouvier et al., 1989; Van Zomeren et al., 1988; Wedding, 1992).

TABLE 6

Neuropsychological Screening of Visuoperceptual Function

Construct of interest	Measure
Integrity of visual and attentional–intentional fields	Confrontation; crossed-response; extinction to simultaneous bilateral stimulation
Right–left orientation	Confrontation
Ability to match to sample	Judgment of Line Orientation, Benton Facial Recognition Task
Ability to copy sample	Copy of Rey–Osterreith Complex Figure
Ability to manipulate elements to form copy of sample	Block Design test (WAIS-R)
Ability to recognize incongruous detail	Picture Completion test (WAIS-R)
Ability to generalize from detail to concept	Object Assembly test (WAIS-R)
Ability to form and make use of abstract visual concept	Benton Facial Recognition Task
Ability to form and make use of abstract spatial concept	Tactual Performance Test

Note: WAIS-R = Wechsler Adult Intelligence Scale–Revised.

Although a number of statistical and methodological issues contribute to this lack of generalization, the bottom line is that neuropsychologists have very little "hard data" on which to base decisions about a patient's competence to drive. In the absence of consistent empirical data, Hopewell and Van Zomeren (1990) have suggested the following factors, in decreasing order of importance, as valuable to the determination of driving competence:

1. Previous driving and accident or violation history, adjusted for driving experience;
2. General personality and attitudinal factors;
3. Pattern and severity of alcohol or substance abuse;
4. Nature and extent of psychiatric disturbance;
5. Basic psychomotor abilities (assuming no disqualifying conditions, such as blindness).

In addition, one should give serious consideration to practical examinations of driving skill whenever possible. These may be performed in simulators or on closed traffic courses, on which a number of different traffic conditions may be simulated (Gouvier et al., 1988), potentially with small-scale vehicles that minimize cost but not predictive validity (Gouvier et al., 1989). Although the available data do not uniformly support the predictive validity of observations of driving behavior on closed courses (Sivak, Olson, Kewman, Won, & Henson, 1981), some investigators have achieved success with programs using small-scale vehicles (Kewman et al., 1985).

Treatment and recovery. Little information is available on the long-term prognosis of visual field cuts. In terms of rehabilitation strategies, however, there is little difference between those directed at field cuts and those directed at hemispatial neglect. Most studies of rehabilitation strategies for visuoperceptual disorders have focused on hemispatial neglect. Perhaps the most consistent finding among these studies has been that the majority of patients with hemispatial neglect spontaneously recover to functional limits within 6 months of injury (Gianutsos & Matheson, 1987; Heilman et al., 1993). A variety of intervention programs have been designed to maximize this recovery (Gouvier, Webster, & Warner, 1986). Diller and Weinberg (1977, cited in Gianutsos & Matheson, 1987) identified the organizing tenets of these interventions as (a) compelling the patient to turn into the affected field; (b) providing an anchoring stimulus (e.g., a vertical line at the margin); (c) decreasing the density of stimuli (e.g., isolating lines of print); and (d) pacing so as to slow the patient's scanning.

In addition to the central tenets outlined above, other researchers (Gouvier et al., 1986; Sohlberg & Mateer, 1989; Weinberg et al., 1979) have implemented supplemental strategies directed toward improving visual organization and nonvisual sensory awareness. Although the available data do not uniformly support positive gains beyond those expected from spontaneous recovery (Taylor, Schaeffer, Blumenthal, & Grisell, 1971), the majority of studies have suggested that there is certainly potential for enhanced recovery with the aid of intervention strategies (Gouvier et al., 1986; Sohlberg & Mateer, 1989). The consistency with which these gains may be made across a wide range of patients (or the role that the site, type, and extent of neuropathology plays in determining the likelihood that these strategies will be effective) remains an open empirical question.

Executive Function

Definition. Over the past decade, conceptualization of the way in which the brain processes new information has evolved significantly. One of the major paradigmatic shifts that has occurred is in the conceptualization of "basic" versus "executive" systems. In various ways, a number of researchers (Damasio, 1991; Damasio & Anderson, 1993; Fuster, 1989; Shallice & Burgess, 1991a; Stuss, 1987; Stuss & Benson, 1986) have described the brain as an organized, integrated network of fixed functional systems that are specialized to deal with specific types of information (language, visuospatial relationships, etc.). These systems are located primarily in the posterior-basal regions of the brain, with each having extensive interconnections with the prefrontal cortex. Although functioning in an integrated environment, each functional system may be viewed as relatively independent; indeed, when working in routine, overlearned ways, each system can competently handle the information for which it is specialized. However, when presented with a novel task, these systems have no preexisting "program," and they will operate in a very inefficient manner unless the task is analyzed and an appropriate program is designed. This process of task definition and program design is the realm of the executive functions, which are generally acknowledged to be mediated primarily in the prefrontal cortex (Damasio, 1991; Stuss, 1987). Stuss (1987) has more precisely defined executive functioning as the ability "to extract and use information from the posterior brain systems, and to anticipate, select, plan, experiment, modify, and act on such information in novel situations" (p. 175).

Deficits. For years, clinicians have acknowledged the existence of a subgroup of TBI survivors for whom readjustment to premorbid levels of functioning is markedly worse than would be predicted from their apparently good cognitive and emotional recovery (Luria & Homskaya, 1964). As cited in Goldstein and Levin (1987), Luria and Homskaya characterized this clinical picture as one of patients

> *without marked disturbances of motor activity or sensitivity, gnosis, or praxis, or defects of speech or even "formal intellectual functions," but at the same time meaningful, directed behavior can be severely disturbed as a whole. (p. 331).*

This pattern is most typically ascribed to injuries of the frontal lobes. Although most careful analyses of such cases describe patients that have had very well-localized focal neuropathology (Eslinger & Damasio, 1985), such deficits may also be seen after TBI (Shallice & Burgess, 1991b).

In the clinical setting, disorders of executive function are most typically described as personality changes. These changes may take various forms. Deficits in the ability to anticipate consequences may manifest themselves in increased impulsivity on the part of the individual. Deficits in the ability to derive and implement a plan may manifest themselves in marked overreliance on previously used plans of action. For example, the individual may become much more inflexible, insisting that actions be performed in a certain way (e.g., setting the table in a specific sequence or moving through the grocery store by a specific path) and becoming very anxious or irritated if deviations from this pattern are required. Alternatively, the patient may take a very concrete, rigid approach to problem solving. When this is combined with an inability to constructively incorporate feedback, individuals often find themselves in situations that are extremely frustrating to both themselves and others. For instance, in a vocational position requiring the ability to deal with unanticipated events (i.e., requiring the patient to "think on his or her feet"), the TBI survivor with deficits in executive functions may think of only one way to solve a problem and will be much more likely to persist in using that strategy despite convincing evidence that the strategy is not working.

Some of the deficits in executive functioning noted in survivors of TBI reinforce the often-repeated maxim that, in neuropsychology, it is difficult to interpret isolated findings meaningfully; rather, one must examine findings "in the company they keep." As previously noted, an aspect of executive functioning that is often impaired following TBI is the ability to effectively organize or plan actions. These deficits have been noted not only in and of themselves—such as when TBI patients have significant difficulty allocating resources to accomplish a given number of goals in a given amount of time (Shallice & Burgess, 1991b)—but also in the qualitative ways in which other cognitive functions break down after TBI. For example, the diminished use of organizational mnemonic strategies and the diminished organization of conversational discourse may both be seen as impairments emanating from impaired executive functioning rather than as specific impairments of memory or language functions per se.

Assessment. The assessment of executive function presents a unique challenge to the clinical neuropsychologist, in that such assessment runs contrary to what psychologists often intuitively seek in constructing assessment techniques. For decades, neuropsychologists have prided themselves on their ability to construct standardized tests by which valid information could be gained about the cognitive abilities of an individual in a relatively short amount of time. These tasks are typically relatively short in duration, very structured in terms of task demands, and clearly defined in terms of correct responses. It is these sorts of tasks that demand the least of one's ability to anticipate, select, plan, experiment, modify, and act on information in novel situations. Although the situation is typically novel, the demands for organization, planning, and making use of feedback in altering behavior are usually minimal. An awareness of this limitation is important to clinicians, because a number of cases in which the patient looked "clean" on neuropsychological testing yet remained impaired in everyday life (without obvious secondary gain issues) have been reported (Eslinger & Damasio, 1985).

An important component to any neuropsychological evaluation, then, is some sort of assessment of the patient's ability to anticipate, select, plan, experiment, modify, and act on information in novel situations. The most useful assessment of these abilities is the clinical interview. A number of telling signs may indicate difficulties with executive functions. A difficulty that obviously flows from the above discussion is a noticeable decrement in the individual's ability to plan multistep activities, such as the preparation of meals or social events. At times, sequences as simple as following a recipe become difficult for survivors of severe TBI. One needs to ascertain that there are no motor or sensory difficulties that account for decrements in performance on these tasks. In addition, one needs to ascertain that the deficits are not primarily attributable to deficits in other cognitive abilities, such as memory, language, or praxis. Finally, it is important to determine the contribution of "psychological" factors (i.e., behavioral changes typically seen secondary to depression or anxiety) to the manifestation of executive dysfunctions (see below for more details).

In addition to the clinical interview, attempts have been made to develop and standardize instruments targeted specifically at executive functioning. These tests fall into two general clusters: (a) those that assess the ability to establish, maintain, and switch between abstract cognitive sets on the basis of feedback from the examiner and (b) those meant to assess the ability to plan and implement a strategy to accomplish a complex task. The first category of tests is far more established than the latter in terms of psychometric assessment techniques. Indeed, one of the earliest neuropsychological assessment devices, Halstead's Category Test (Reitan & Wolfson, 1985), is the prototype of this sort of test, and its direct descendant, the Booklet Category Test, continues to be widely used today. The other widely used test for assessing these abilities is the Wisconsin Card Sorting Test (Heaton, 1981). Although there are other tests that can assess these functions, these two are the most commonly used, and both have the advantage of widespread use in both research and clinical settings. These tests are not identical in the abilities they measure, and they are affected by deficits in abilities other than executive functioning (Donders & Kirsch, 1991; Perrine, 1993). Likewise, despite their reputation as "frontal lobe tests," data have shown that it is impossible to interpret results of these measures as pure indexes of frontal lobe functioning (Anderson, Damasio, Jones, & Tranel, 1991; Mountain & Snow, 1993; Reitan & Wolfson, 1995).

There are very few standardized tests of a person's ability to formulate and carry out a plan of action. A number of different approaches have been used to assess this. One of the primary approaches has been to assess the patient's visuospatial planning ability. This is done by having patients solve mazes (Porteus, 1965), construct structures from Tinkertoys (Lezak, 1983), and determine the fewest number of moves that would result in a specific construction given a specific set of preconditions (i.e., variations on the Tower of Hanoi task; Shallice, 1982). Unfortunately, none of these measures have been systematically normed on a TBI population. Thus, interpretation again relies on careful observation of patient performance combined with consideration of results of other testing. Another approach has been to assess patients' ability to prioritize, organize, and carry out a plan of action to accomplish a number of tasks in a given amount of time (Shallice & Burgess, 1991b). Shallice and Burgess presented evidence suggesting that survivors of severe TBI are chronically impaired on their performance of these sorts of activities, although the pattern of deficit varies. To date, this is the only study to carefully examine performance on such tasks, and given the small number of participants and relatively superficial description of the lesions identified on CT scans and MR imaging, these findings should certainly be replicated before firm conclusions are drawn. However, the patterns described by Shallice and Burgess are seen commonly in the clinical setting, and the described deficits in planning can clearly be differentiated from the learning-and-set-shifting deficits quantified by such traditional tasks as the Booklet Category Test or the Wisconsin Card Sorting Test.

Treatment and recovery. Unfortunately, the study of the rehabilitation of executive functions is still in its infancy, and to date there is little more on which to base intervention strategies than theoretical models and a few case studies. Thus, only tentative observations and suggestions are available to the clinician confronted with a patient and family wanting help with these problems. As stated by Sohlberg and Mateer (1989), "the guiding principle in the rehabilitation of executive functions involves structure" (p. 240). The formulation, modification, and implementation of cognitive sets serves to structure the person's world. If these abilities are impaired, then so is the level of organization with which one can interact with the world. Consequently, those models of executive-function rehabilitation that have been most clearly articulated focus on ways in which the TBI survivor may learn new strategies for structuring the environment and approaching new situations more explicitly (Ben-Yishay & Diller, 1983a, 1983b; Cicerone & Wood, 1987; Craine, 1982; Sohlberg & Mateer, 1989; Zec, Parks, Gambach, & Vicari, 1992). Rehabilitative strategies spawned by these perspectives include memorization and practice of routine daily schedules (Craine, 1982), external cuing and work with repetitive structured tasks (Sohlberg & Mateer, 1989; Zec et al., 1992), and incorporation of cognitive–behavioral techniques of behavioral modification (Zec et al., 1992). The paucity of research on the success of these treatment programs across patients makes it impossible to recommend one approach over the other; rather, at the current time, we recommend that those in search of interventions take a look at each program and decide which fits best with the resources and patients at hand.

Personality and Psychological Function

Definitions. Changes in the behavior of TBI survivors are common from the moment of injury onward. Although acute changes in behavior may distress the family and challenge the staff of a TBI unit, it is the chronic changes in personality that are often the most debilitating sequelae of TBI (Brooks et al., 1987). A related but dissociated component of these changes is the extent to which the patient is unaware of the cognitive and emotional changes induced primarily or secondarily by the brain injury. Given the importance of changes in personality and disrupted levels of awareness to the psychological, social, and vocational adjustment of both the TBI survivor and the family, as well as the central role that the clinician often plays in helping the respective parties deal with these issues, these areas are discussed at length in chapter 14 of this book. The following discussion focuses more specifically on the role of the neuropsychologist in the acute and subacute settings: specifically, on the behavioral management of the TBI survivor and the education and counseling of relatives of the survivor.

Deficits. Most of the behavioral difficulties experienced with TBI survivors in the acute and subacute settings are related to the previously discussed unstable levels of arousal, orientation, and attention. It is important to inform the family at this point in the patient's recovery about the timetable of symptom development, because the changes seen at one point in recovery may be quite different from those seen at a later point. Acutely, agitation may manifest itself as anger, combativeness, or both (Chandler, Barnhill, & Gualtieri, 1988). Although commonly seen in the acute TBI patient, the prognostic significance of agitation is unclear, as are the neuropathological mechanisms associated with it. A conceptual distinction has been made by Reyes, Bhattacharyya, and Heller (1981) between agitated patients (who exhibit constant uninhibited movement) and restless patients (who are able to temporarily inhibit their level of movement). This distinction may prove useful, because data have suggested that early posttraumatic restlessness is associated with return to work, whereas agitation is not. Agitated patients are also more likely to require supervision after discharge. Although these findings provide a foundation from which to work in examining these issues in the future, more studies are needed before statements concerning the natural course or predictive value of posttraumatic agitation may be made with confidence.

Increased levels of irritability, on the other hand, appear to be a common and much more chronic change for TBI survivors. Indeed, irritability after TBI is the most common complaint identified by both patients and spouses (Prigitano, 1992). These increases in irritability appear to be independent of the severity of initial injury (Dikmen, Temkin, & Armsden, 1989; McKinlay, Brooks, Bond, Martinage, & Marshall, 1981; Van Zomeren & Van Den Burg, 1985). Hinkeldey and Corrigan (1990) found that irritability was related more strongly to two variables—tiring more easily around people and having trouble following conversations—than to simply tiring more easily, suggesting that interpersonal situations in particular become more difficult for the TBI survivor. The relative stability of these changes may be maintained in part by the psychosocial consequences of some of the neuropsychological deficits commonly seen after TBI (Prigitano et al., 1986). For instance, decreases in speed of information processing, ability to shift rapidly between cognitive sets, ability to quickly and accurately identify the source of a given bit of information in memory, and ability to habituate to noxious stimuli may all affect a TBI survivor's ability to successfully negotiate his or her social environment—in effect, lowering the frustration threshold for these sorts of situations.

A deficit related to personality change that may be particularly disabling over time is impairment of the TBI survivor's awareness of his or her deficits. Data have shown that TBI survivors consistently underestimate their degree of impairment in comparison with the ratings of family members and staff, especially with regard to changes in personality functioning (Prigitano, 1991). In the rehabilitation setting, such deficits have profound impact not only on the initial presentation of the TBI survivor but also on subsequent remediation or behavioral compensation for neurobehavioral deficits (Crosson et al., 1989). Obviously, if a survivor feels that there are no problems, then he or she will be less likely to participate in interventions directed at ameliorating these deficits. Likewise, persistence in relying on impaired abilities in tasks that require intact memory or social skills likely will place the TBI survivor at increased risk for vocational disability or social isolation (Prigitano, 1991).

The way in which the TBI survivor's family handles the injury may have a powerful effect on his or her eventual adjustment. Although the way that each family copes with the changes engendered by TBI varies considerably, there do seem to be a few relatively consistent patterns. Over the long term, changes in personality are more burdensome to the family than either cognitive or physical changes (Kreutzer, Marwitz, & Kepler, 1992; Lezak, 1988). There are also common, though far from universal, stages of adjustment that families of TBI survivors experience. Acutely, the family's primary concern is survival. As survival becomes assured, the family is often concerned about any permanent changes in the survivor's physical status, such as hemiplegia or dysarthria. During the first few months, there is typically a period of initial hope as the patient's survival becomes assured and rapid gains are seen. As the rate of recovery slows, however, the initial optimism recedes, and it is at this point that concern about the survivor's long-term prognosis for recovery of cognitive function and resolution of personality changes often begins to emerge the most strongly. This stage is often followed by a period of uncertainty or denial of the functional and psychosocial implications of the injury. Because of the importance of these issues to the long-term recovery of both the TBI survivor and the family, they are discussed in detail by Leber and Jenkins elsewhere in this book (chap. 14).

Assessment. The most important instrument in the assessment of personality change is the clinical interview of the patient and those who interact with him or her on a regular basis. The importance of informant report is particularly great after TBI for several reasons. First, survivors of TBI are often involved in legal action related to their injuries and, thus, may emphasize certain aspects of their deficits or recovery at the expense of others (regardless of the intentionality of this emphasis). Conversely, an impairment in the survivor's self-awareness may lead to an underestimation of deficits (Prigitano, 1992; Prigitano & Schacter, 1991). In either circumstance, it is especially important in these cases to gain as many relatively independent sources of information about the survivor as possible. An instrument that may prove helpful in quantifying the views of various sources is the Patient Competency Rating Scale (Prigitano et al., 1986). This instrument has been used successfully to quantify different opinions of the TBI survivor's capabilities as perceived by the family, rehabilitation staff, and the survivors themselves. In general, survivors present the most optimistic picture, staff present the least optimistic picture, and family fall somewhere in between (Fordyce & Rouche, 1986). Another instrument geared toward assessing those aspects of personality and executive function that are commonly affected by TBI is the Iowa Collateral Head Injury Interview (Varney & Menefee, 1993). Because of the novelty of this scale, there are relatively few data describing its characteristics across a wide population; however, early indications have suggested that it provides valuable information about the survivor's and his or her family's view of these types of deficits. When considering the information obtained from these measures, it is important to ascertain the extent to which these behaviors represent a change from the individual's premorbid behavior, in terms of intensity and frequency of behavior.

An important distinction to make when assessing TBI survivors is between psychological symptoms secondary to psychopathology and similar symptoms related more closely to neurological damage. The disorder of greatest overlap is depression. In non-TBI groups, depression has been linked to difficulties with concentration, mildly impaired short-term memory, irritability, increased emotional lability, and loss of interest in one's environment. These same deficits may be present in the TBI population purely as a function of neurological impairment, although the more typical picture is likely one that confounds neurological and psychological phenomena with each other. These issues become particularly important when one is interpreting standard measures of personality, such as the MMPI-2. A number of items on such tests are consistent with expected sequelae of neurological damage, which elevate clinical scales if endorsed honestly. For instance, Gass (1991) found that endorsement of items corresponding to potentially genuine neurological complaints could significantly elevate Scales 1 (Hypochondriasis), 2 (Depression), 3 (Hysteria), 7 (Psychasthenia), and 8 (Schizophrenia) on the MMPI-2. On the other hand, endorsement of such items by a neurologically impaired patient does not imply that the more common clinical psychological interpretations should not apply. Rather, the clinician must remain cognizant of the confounds inherent in such test interpretation and be sure to integrate all available information from interviews, behavioral observations, and careful analysis of the specific items endorsed before interpreting such measures for neurologically impaired populations. Given the importance of the clinical interview to such interpretations, a rough outline sketching the basic areas to be covered in an interview is included in Exhibit 10.

Finally, the clinical neuropsychologist is often asked about how the changes brought about by the individual's injuries will affect his or her ability to return to work. These requests come from both family and vocational counselors alike. Such questions are typically answered by conducting a formal neuropsychological assessment. There are a number of factors to keep in mind in such an evaluation. First, it is important to refrain from being rushed into such an evaluation before appropriate to the individual's level of recovery. The results of any evaluation of a survivor of moderate-to-severe TBI done before 6 months postinjury must be considered tenuous, because this is the period of most rapid recovery. Likewise, it is important to schedule a follow-up evaluation for any individual seen within the first year after injury. Such a follow-up gives the clinician some appreciation for the substantial variability seen in recovery after moderate-to-severe TBI and also allows monitoring of any attempts to return to work over the intervening period. Such attempts are helpful to analyze in terms of the remaining strengths and weaknesses of the individual that, although subtle in terms of neuropsychological test results, may have major implications in the vocational setting.

EXHIBIT 10

Important Questions to Ask When Interviewing a Patient With a Traumatic Brain Injury and His or Her Family

Chief complaint

1. What problems are currently being experienced?
   - Memory
   - Attention and speed of information processing
   - Personality
     Irritability
     Depression
     Anxiety
   - Language (problems finding words or following conversations)
   - Executive functions (amenability to change and ability to plan)
2. What was the time course of the development of these problems?
   - How long after the injury did the problems emerge?
   - How have the problems changed since the injury?
     Are the problems getting better, worse, or staying the same?
   - Could these be exacerbations of premorbid problems?
3. Is there any injury-related litigation pending?

Information about injury

1. When did the injury occur?
2. Are there records of medical diagnoses and care given secondary to the injury?
   - Time after injury that scan was performed
   - Presence and location of tissue damage

(continues)

EXHIBIT 10 (*Continued*)

- Accident report filed by emergency medical technicians and police
- Emergency room records

3. Does the patient remember the injury?
4. What is the last thing remembered before the injury?
5. What is the first thing remembered after the injury?
   - When did the patient begin to track ongoing events after the injury (i.e., "wake up")?

Prior medical history

1. Illnesses and injuries
   - Head injuries, multiple sclerosis, diabetes, cardiovascular disease, and substance abuse
   - Psychiatric disorder and treatment
2. Surgeries
3. Allergies
4. Current medications
   - Might any of these affect results of testing?

Social history

1. Vocational history
2. Educational history
   - Highest grade completed
   - General level of academic performance
   - History of learning problems or learning disability?
3. Family environment
   - Changes since the injury
4. Goals: What does the patient plan to be doing a year from now?

It is also important to have an idea of the specific vocational competencies that an individual needs. In general, the clinician must attempt to mentally place the person in the midst of the workplace as much as possible. Must the individual be able to "think on his or her feet?" Does work take place in a very distracting environment? Must the individual be able to learn new information and master new skills rapidly? How much and what type of interpersonal interactions will be required? These are the sorts of questions that the clinician must consider in the context of the results of a neuropsychological evaluation before drawing conclusions about the potential of a given individual to return to work. An identical pattern of neuropsychological deficits and recovery may place no limitations on returning to work as an assembly-line worker (where one's tasks may be entirely predetermined and overlearned) but may completely rule out working as an independent electrician (where rapid, novel problem solving is required every day). Whenever possible, it may prove valuable for the clinical neuropsychologist—with the individual's permission—to obtain descriptions of job requirements from referring vocational counselors or employers. Finally, job trials may prove enormously helpful in determining exactly the aspects of the vocational environment that may demand special compensatory measures or that may need to be avoided (Thomas, 1990). Thomas has suggested a conceptual guideline to categorizing vocational potential once all of the above factors have been considered (see Exhibit 11).

Treatment and recovery. Measures that may be taken to minimize agitation in TBI survivors in the postacute setting have been discussed above with re-

EXHIBIT 11

Conceptual Categories of Vocational Limitations

No limitations apparent	The person can perform the job without assistance, at a competitive rate and quality, and demonstrates potential to be flexible in work assignments.
Mild limitations	Few or no limitations. Job performance is generally adequate; however, changes in work assignments are likely to cause problems. Problems in work speed or quality may be noted. Selective placement may be required.
Moderate limitations	Vocational limitations are such that the person is likely to be successful only under prescribed circumstances of work environment, supervision, or work-hour restrictions. Quality or quantity of work is likely to be below industry standards. Job placement will require supported or transitional employment for initial instruction and an extended follow-up period.
Severe limitations	Long-term supported employment will likely be necessary. Because of productivity or quality of work, a special wage certificate may be needed or an assistant at the workplace may be necessary. Intensive job support and intervention will be required, or sheltered employment will be necessary.
Profound limitations	Work, either sheltered or supported, is unlikely in the forseeable future.

Data are from "Vocational Evaluation of Persons With Traumatic Head Injury," by D.F. Thomas. In Traumatic Brain Injury and Vocational Rehabilitation *(p. 121), edited by D. Corthell, 1990, Menomonie, WI: Research and Training Center, University of Wisconsin—Stout. Copyright 1990 by Research and Training Center, University of Wisconsin—Stout. Adapted with permission.*

gard to arousal and attentional deficits. In those cases in which PTA has resolved but self-awareness remains impaired, the initial treatment phase must be aimed first at increasing the TBI survivor's awareness of cognitive and emotional deficits and subsequently at defining mutual treatment goals. A number of holistic programs have been developed that combine individual and small-group treatment activities "to help patients achieve a realistic perception of their impact upon others and the need to compensate for permanent residual neurobehavioral disorders" (Prigitano, 1991, p. 123).

An important dynamic for the neuropsychologist to follow in the recovery of a TBI survivor is the attributions made concerning personality changes after the injury and the reactions to the survivor's behavior as a result of those attributions. In other words, it is important to see if the survivor, family, and staff view the behavior as being influenced by the injury (i.e., "organic") or independent of the injury (i.e., "functional"). This attribution may be critical in the adjustment of the TBI survivor and his or her family. For both parties, changes that are more attributable to pathophysiological factors are commonly seen as "beyond the patient's control" and, consequently, tend to be viewed in a different (usually more forgiving) light. Alternatively, it is not uncommon for TBI survivors to overattribute deficits or difficulties in living to pathophysiological consequences of the brain injury, thereby completely absolving themselves of responsibility for their behavior and reducing the expectation for active participation in the rehabilitation process. This deferment of responsibility frequently impedes recovery and is difficult to change when expectations, attributions, and reinforcement schedules have been predicated on such a premise. Although there are few data specifically addressing this question, we have found that a cognitive–behavioral approach of challenging the survivor's hopeless thoughts or overattributions from within the context of a supportive relationship may prove to be effective.

One of the most important roles that the neuropsychologist plays in the acute and subacute care settings is that of educator. Patients and families alike often have no idea of what to expect in terms of cognitive, behavioral, and emotional recovery from their injuries. The clinical neuropsychologist is in a unique position in terms of training and experience to help the patient and family understand the likely time course, pattern, and outcome of recovery. Although absolute levels of recovery are impossible to predict, the well-trained neuropsychologist can combine knowledge from the areas of behavioral neurology, neuropsychology, neuropathology, cognitive science, and clinical psychology to construct an integrated picture of the current neuropsychological status of the patient, of how the course of recovery is likely (but certainly not guaranteed) to proceed, and of the probable hurdles that the patient and family will have to face in returning the patient to his or her optimum level of physical, psychological, social, and vocational well-being (McLellan, 1991).

CASE STUDIES

Two case studies are presented below; each is meant to highlight different aspects of the potential sequelae of TBI. Rather than merely presenting formal reports or progress notes for each patient, we present information in a form meant to simulate the gradual building of a conceptual model for each patient in terms of what specific processes are occurring, how these processes are likely to manifest themselves, and what implications these processes have for the patient's prognosis. The first case demonstrates a relatively typical survivor of TBI who has been referred to a subacute rehabilitation setting. The second case demonstrates the potential long-term consequences of TBI on cognitive, personality, and vocational function.

The Case of SB

SB is a 25-year-old White male involved in a single-car accident in the early morning hours. He was driving home from a late-night party while intoxicated, swerved off the road, and flipped his pickup truck so many times that the cab was separated from the body of the truck. He was found under the dashboard of the cab and admitted to an emergency room approximately 2–3 hr after the injury. On admission, he was noted to have suffered a number of orthopedic injuries, none of which were life threatening or contributed to his mental status changes. He was unconscious and responsive only to pain. He had no signs suggestive of a focal cortical lesion, and his pupils were equal in size. Initial CT scans showed a right posterior temporal contusion and a suboccipital subdural hematoma on top of the tentorium in the intrahemispheric space. The orthopedic injuries were addressed surgically without change of mental status. He was intubated and admitted to the intensive care unit.

SB's stay in intensive care was marked by slow but steady neurological improvement. His intracerebral pressure never rose beyond normal limits. After 2 weeks, SB was verbalizing, moving all extremities, and able to follow one-step commands. However, he remained disoriented to his own age, birthdate, location, and the circumstances that brought him into the hospital. Follow-up CT scans showed improvement in the right temporal contusion and little change in the subdural hematoma. Information from interviewing SB's family (all of whom lived in the area) revealed that SB had been employed as a plumber since graduating from high school. He'd had no significant medical history before his accident. SB's family described him as a generally happy young man who drank more often than they preferred, although they did not consider him to be an alcoholic.

At this point, the clinician already has some valuable information about the current status and range of likely outcomes for SB. In terms of premorbid status, his academic and vocational history suggest that he likely was functioning in the average range of intelligence premorbidly. There is no suggestion of significant premorbid mood or thought disorder. SB was intoxicated at the time of the injury, although the existence or extent of a significant substance abuse problem remained in question at this point. In terms of medical and neuropsychological factors, SB had emerged from coma but not from PTA at 2 weeks postinjury. Although CT scans showed a subdural hematoma, this was not of sufficient size or instability to evacuate, and it resolved spontaneously. The presence of 2 weeks of coma in the absence of frank brainstem pathology suggested that some diffuse axonal injury occurred, and there was radiological evidence for a focal cortical contusion in the right posterior temporal region. On the basis of the information already at hand, one might predict a number of the common sequelae of TBI, particularly those associated with diffuse axonal injury (e.g., slowed information-processing speed).

> *At 4 weeks postinjury, SB was transferred to a subacute rehabilitation hospital with the goal of improving functional deficits related to both his orthopedic injuries and his cognitive deficits. On admission, SB was oriented to person, place, and time. He was restless and easily distracted, but he was easily redirected to the task at hand. It was noted that he answered slowly in conversation but spoke in a somewhat rapid, "pressured" manner. Although he had no apparent difficulties with expressive or receptive language, he spoke in a manner that was often tangential and circumlocutious. He had difficulty with tasks that demanded a great deal of concentration, such as counting backward from 100 by 7s (Serial 7s). He also had difficulty inhibiting inappropriate responses on tasks requiring him to make a motor movement different from the examiner when prompted (i.e., holding up one finger when the examiner holds up two, and vice versa). His short-term memory was very poor, in that he could remember only one of three words in 5 min and zero of three words at 20 min. However, SB was able to recognize the correct words at each time interval when they were presented in a multiple-choice format. SB was very concrete in his interpretation of proverbs, and he had a great deal of difficulty attempting to solve problems in more than one way. Despite obvious changes in his neuropsychological status (which were confirmed as readily noticeable by his family), SB reported that there had been no changes in his cognitive status since the accident. At the initial assessment, SB's family members reported that he was progressing well, but they still saw significant deficits in his memory and general demeanor. They reported that since the accident, he had been much more outgoing and, at times, too talkative. Fortunately, he seemed genuinely contrite about being involved in an automobile accident while intoxicated, and his family remained hopeful that this would result in a lasting change in the frequency of his drinking.*

It is at this point in a patient's recovery that the neuropsychologist takes a more active role. First, the responsibility for the recognition, description, and quantification of the above deficits often falls to the neuropsychologist. Likewise, communication with staff and family of the implications of these deficits for the patient's rehabilitation and eventual recovery is often the responsibility of the neuropsychologist. At this point, SB was showing a number of the deficits commonly found after TBI. His speed of information processing was slowed, his discourse was tangential, and he had difficulty inhibiting inappropriate responses. His short-term memory was poor, but his ability to accurately recognize the presented words suggested that the deficits may be due more to a retrieval deficit than to an inability to register, encode, and store the information. Importantly, SB showed no awareness of his cognitive deficits. In terms of implications for rehabilitation, the neuropsychologist must stress to staff that SB cannot be relied on to remember important information without external aids and that interventions predicated on his desire to "get back to normal" in terms of his cognitive capacity are unlikely to be effective without first convincing SB that these deficits do indeed exist. Specific interventions directed at increasing awareness of deficits as well as remediating more specific cognitive deficits in such cases may be chosen as appropriate from the types of strategies discussed above.

SB continued to progress during his stay at the rehabilitation hospital. At the time of discharge (approximately 2 months postinjury), SB continued to have mild cognitive deficits, particularly in terms of decreased information-processing speed and impaired memory (especially on delayed-recall tasks). Although his discourse was still somewhat tangential, his ability to remain focused on one topic or task had improved considerably since his admission to the rehabilitation hospital. Likewise, he remained more talkative than he had been premorbidly, but his ability to inhibit both motor and verbal responses had improved significantly. Given the extent of his recovery at 2 months, it was felt that his long-term prognosis for recovery was good. To assist with more precise quantification of SB's remaining deficits, it was recommended that he undergo formal neuropsychological evaluation at 6 months postinjury, at which time his recovery should have stabilized to a greater degree. In addition to describing his likely pattern of neuropsychological recovery, 6-month follow-up would also provide information about SB's success in changing his drinking behavior.

In contrast with Patient SB, Patient MJ illustrates some of the potential long-term sequelae of moderate-to-severe TBI.

The Case of MJ

MJ is a 38-year-old woman referred for neuropsychological testing by her neurologist for quantification of cognitive and emotional changes secondary to TBI. As is sometimes the case in outpatient referrals, no medical records were available at the time of the evaluation. According to her report, MJ was injured approximately 7 months before neuropsychological evaluation when the car in which she was sitting was struck from behind by a drunk driver moving at a high rate of speed. She was comatose for 2–4 days after the injury, and she reportedly remembered nothing from slightly before the accident until the time she "woke up" in the hospital approximately 5 days later. She reported that she had made a relatively rapid recovery in the weeks following the injury, but that this rate of recovery had slowed considerably over the previous month. The man who had struck her car had been convicted of driving under the influence of alcohol, and there was no litigation pending at the time of the evaluation.

MJ reported having a number of difficulties since her injury. She stated that, although she had no gross motor abnormalities such as hemiparesis, she was no longer capable of carrying out activities demanding large-motor coordination, such as bicycling or swimming, because of an inability to "get everything moving in the right direction at the same time." She also reported difficulties with maintaining concentration, recall of material she had just read, simultaneous performance of two tasks, decreased tolerance for frustration, fatigue, speech articulation (particularly when tired), and recall of computer routines at her workplace that she had once trained others to use. She also reported that, although she had once used her left hand for most activities other than writing, she now used her right hand exclusively. Since her injury, she had frequent headaches that were moderate to severe and did not seem amenable to over-the-counter medications.

She stated that she had a difficult time carrying through with any activity involving a number of discrete steps; for instance, she was unable to follow a recipe to completion because she would become confused or lose her place. She stated that she took an inordinately long time to shop for groceries, because if she did not follow a specific route from one end of the store to the other, she would become confused and would simply leave. Finally, she reported an enormous increase in the time it took her to make decisions, however trivial; for instance, another factor contributing to her increased grocery-shopping time was that, once she found the types of items she was looking for, she could not decide between the various brands. As an extreme example of this, MJ reported that her father had become very frustrated with her at a local mall because she had taken 2 hr to decide which one of four new irons she was going to purchase.

Before being injured, MJ had been employed as an assistant administrator for a large firm. In addition, she had been taking night classes in pursuit of a doctoral degree from a large southern university, with her long-term goal being a teaching position in a university setting. According to her report, she had received excellent evaluations in both her job and classes, and she enjoyed both of them a great deal. She held a bachelor's degree and reported that she had always found academics enjoyable and relatively easy. In contrast to her professional life, MJ's personal life had been somewhat difficult. Although she had a number of acquaintances and reportedly made friends easily, she had not been happily married and, in fact, reported that she had been planning to get divorced before the injury. She had been seen for psychiatric treatment both individually and with her husband to resolve their marital difficulties. During individual treatment, she was reportedly diagnosed with major depression, which she attributed primarily to her marital difficulties. She denied any history of substance abuse. Since the injury, she and her husband had reconciled, although she remained ambivalent about the relationship.

On the basis of MJ's history and presenting complaints, the clinician may already begin to form a number of hypotheses. First, it appears that MJ was functioning at a relatively high intellectual level premorbidly. Alcohol abuse does not appear to be a problem in terms of her premorbid function or recovery. She did have a clinically significant history of depression, and although this did not appear to affect her ability to function vocationally, the setting that reportedly contributed most heavily to the depression's etiology (i.e., her ambivalent relationship with her husband) was an ongoing concern. The cognitive complaints with which she presented could all be reasonably accounted for on the basis of the typical neuropsychological profile of TBI. She described difficulties with sustained and divided attention (which may be framed in terms of increased limitations in information-processing speed and capacity), memory, fatigue, periodic dysarthria emerging when she was very tired, and increased irritability. She clearly had major deficits in her ability to formulate and carry out a complex plan of action. Likewise, when she was following a plan, she had extreme difficulty if forced to deviate from it.

MJ was extremely cooperative during all phases of the neuropsychological evaluation. She appeared to be highly motivated to perform well on all assessment tasks. She worked at a steady but sometimes moderately slow pace. During the interview, MJ was soft-spoken and had sporadic word-finding difficulties. She exhibited excellent insight into the existence and likely origin of her cognitive difficulties, and she became tearful when describing her frustration over her perceived loss of abilities.

The results of MJ's neuropsychological testing are shown in Exhibit 12. A number of findings are notable. Most strikingly, MJ's overall level of intellectual functioning remained in the superior range, with a Verbal IQ in the very superior range and Performance IQ in the high average range. Similarly, her memory for the short passages of the revised edition of the Wechsler Memory Scale remained strong, whereas a more demanding task of supraspan learning and memory (California Verbal Learning Test) was impaired relative to expectations based on her Verbal IQ. Delayed memory for visual information was likewise impaired, as evidenced by her poor recall of

EXHIBIT 12

Results of MJ's Neuropsychological Evaluation

Intellectual

Wechsler Adult Intelligence Scale–Revised

Full-Scale IQ: 126
Verbal IQ: 130
Performance IQ: 111
Age-scaled subtest scores:

Information:	13
Digit Span:	10
Vocabulary:	17
Arithmetic:	15
Comprehension:	18
Similarities:	15
Picture Completion:	13
Picture Arrangement:	14
Block Design:	8
Object Assembly:	12
Digit Symbol:	10

Memory and concentration

Peterson–Peterson Auditory Consonant Trigrams

0 s: 15/15
3 s: 8/15
9 s: 9/15
18 s: 4/15

Wechsler Memory Scale–Revised

Logical Memory

Immediate Recall:	82nd percentile
Delayed Recall:	86th percentile

Visual Reproduction

Immediate Recall:	79th percentile
Delayed Recall:	33rd percentile

EXHIBIT 12 (*Continued*)

California Verbal Learning Test

	Score	z score
Monday list (Trial 1)	8	−1
Monday list (Trial 5)	12	−2
Tuesday list	8	0
Short delay, free recall	11	−1
Short delay, cued recall	11	−1
Long delay, free recall	10	−2
Long delay, cued recall	10	−2
Recognition hits	12	−3
Recognition false positive	1	*

Rey–Osterreith Complex Figure	
Immediate recall	< 10th percentile
Delayed recall (20 min)	< 10th percentile
Tactual Performance Test	
Memory	7 items recalled
Localization	4 items correctly localized

Language

Multilingual Aphasia Examination	
Visual Naming	75th percentile
Controlled Oral Word Association	15th percentile
Sentence Repetition	98th percentile
Token Test	82nd percentile
Category Fluency	
Animals	15 words
Fruits and Vegetables	19 words

Visuoperceptual functioning

Judgment of line orientation	75th percentile
Rey–Osterreith Complex Figure (copy)	No errors
Tactual Perceptual Test	
Right	7′ 47″
Left	10′ 20″
Both	5′ 48″

Motor function

Finger Oscillation Test	
Right	31.8 (< 2nd percentile)
Left	28.4 (< 2nd percentile)
Grooved Pegboard Test	
Right	78″ (< 2nd percentile)
Left	75″ (14th percentile)

(*continues*)

EXHIBIT 12 (*Continued*)

Executive functioning

Trail-Making Test	
Part A	36″
Part B	46″
Wisconsin Card Sorting Task	
Categories achieved	6
Perseverative errors	9
Total errors	15
Total correct	72

Personality functioning

Minnesota Multiphasic Personality Inventory

44	62	46	80	88	86	79	49	76	86	101	91	64	71	46	32	40
L	F	K	1	2	3	4	5	6	7	8	9	0	A	R	Es	MAC

both the Wechsler Memory Scale–Revised figures and the Rey–Osterreith Complex Figure after delays. Although language was grossly normal in conversation, deficits were apparent in her ability to generate words beginning with the letters C, F, or L. Discourse patterns were not examined formally. Visuospatial abilities appeared to be within normal limits. Motor speed and dexterity were significantly impaired bilaterally. Executive functions were formally evaluated with the Trail-Making Test and Wisconsin Card Sorting Test. Interestingly, MJ's performance on both of these measures was well within normal limits. Finally, interview and personality testing both suggested that MJ was undergoing a great deal of psychological distress, primarily related to the emotional, social, and vocational implications of her injuries as well as to preexisting relationship issues with her husband.

Rather than providing a comprehensive review of all potential interpretations of the test data, we presented the summary above to highlight a few salient points. The results are consistent with a number of the features that one would expect after TBI, especially when interpreted in light of MJ's high level of overall intellectual functioning. Both verbal and visual memory were preferentially impaired, and this impairment was greater on tasks incorporating a delay. Tasks preferentially tapping attention and concentration were relatively impaired as well, although they fell within the normal range. Perhaps most interestingly, however, was MJ's performance on measures of executive function. Although her clinical presentation would suggest that these difficulties may indeed be the most pervasive problems affecting her everyday functioning, a blind interpretation of the test data would suggest that MJ has no difficulty establishing, maintaining, and alternating between abstract cognitive sets. Although this conclusion is certainly accurate in describing her performance on the Wisconsin Card Sorting Test, it clearly fails to generalize to the executive functions of her everyday life, in which she has severe difficulty. Such a schism has been noted by others (Eslinger & Damasio, 1985), and this case serves to reinforce the point that a careful clinical history is essential for gaining a holistic view of a patient's real-life deficits. Whether other tests of executive function, such as those described by Shallice and Burgess (1991a), may provide a more valid result in these sorts of cases remains an open empirical question.

Other results of note include MJ's MMPI profile, which suggested that she was in acute emotional distress, with prominent features of disorganization, psychomotor acceleration, depression, and anxiety. There was no evidence of thought disorder. Of great clinical concern was the high level of psychomotor acceleration combined with both psychodiagnostic and self-report evidence of obsessiveness and passive suicidal ideation.

On the basis of the results of MJ's evaluation, it was recommended that MJ become involved in a psychotherapeutic relationship with two primary goals: (a) adjustment to and compensation for cognitive changes that had occurred secondary to her brain injury and (b) psychotherapy to address her high levels of psychological distress. The neuropsychologist recommended that MJ return to her job in a gradual fashion, so that areas of difficulty could be identified early and dealt with efficiently. The clinician also recommended that MJ resume a number of social activities that she had discontinued after the accident. The recommended therapeutic relationship was initiated and maintained for approximately 18 months following the evaluation. As her recovery progressed, MJ's ability to sequence behaviors improved to some extent, as did her ability to analyze the demands of situations and plan appropriate strategies for accomplishing a given set of goals (particularly with regard to grocery shopping). Eventually, MJ attempted to return to both her original job and to graduate-level classes.

Her job required a great deal of rapid creative problem solving while interacting with clients who were sometimes angry, as well as the ability to formalize the solutions she created and teach them to others. The job was also relatively inflexible in terms of work hours, in that all activity occurred between 9:30 a.m. and 4:30 p.m. each day. As MJ tried to return to work, she found that she could not think as quickly as she once did, and she was far more distractible and irritable. Likewise, she became fatigued much more quickly, and she found that if she went more than 1 day without a daytime nap of at least 2 hr, she would become clumsy and dysarthric by the end of the day.

MJ's return to academic work was marked by other kinds of difficulties. She had trouble remembering material that she had read. She addressed this difficulty with some success by taking notes on notecards as she read the required material. However, the classes in which MJ was enrolled also required a great deal of writing. MJ felt that she had no difficulty understanding the concepts that her professor was trying to communicate in lectures or writing small sections of papers to address individual ideas. However, she was completely unable to tie the disparate elements of a writing project together into a cohesive whole. She reported that this difficulty had never existed before her brain injury, and she was unable to figure out a satisfactory compensatory strategy.

As the therapeutic relationship progressed, and MJ became more aware of the extent of her limitations and comfortable with a number of compensatory strategies that aided her in daily life, the focus of the relationship shifted from education and experimentation to adaptation and coping. Whereas MJ's ability had been high enough premorbidly that she could literally "fix anything if [she] tried hard enough," she began to accept that she would not be able to return to her high premorbid level of function. Although she maintained expectations of continued recovery over the next few years, these expectations were narrowed considerably from their original extent, and she began to plan with a more conservative estimate of her abilities in mind.

Although MJ's case is not the most typical presentation of the sequelae of TBI, a number of elements are commonly found. Survivors of TBI must often come to grips with a reduced set of capabilities. When the alteration hits at the heart of the survivor's livelihood (such as in MJ's case, where the abilities of rapid, creative problem solving and high-level conceptual organization were—in all likelihood—irreparably damaged), the changes in the survivor's life can be particularly difficult. Also contributing to difficulty in cases such as MJ's is the relative preservation of basic cognitive functions (other than memory) with a pervasive deficit in the ability to use these functions to deal with the dilemmas, decisions, and novel problems of everyday life in an efficient manner. Thus, although MJ was undoubtedly functioning at a very high level intellectually, and she had been able to learn effective means of managing her memory deficits and decreased tolerance for frustration, her inability to organize her available cognitive resources figured significantly in the degree of disability she suffered as a result of her injury.

CONCLUSIONS

The clinician who works with survivors of TBI is able to draw on an increasingly broad and sophisticated body of research to help conceptualize the nature and remediability of neurobehavioral deficits incurred as a result of such an injury. As it now stands, the relatively common occurrence of attentional difficulties, memory impairments, personality changes, and awareness deficits after TBI has been well established. Work remains to be done on defining the exact parameters of these deficits, as well as the most effective means of remediating them. Likewise, research continues to explore the parameters of the organizational deficits sometimes seen after TBI, which may cut across memory, language, and executive functioning in the form of poorly organized discourse patterns, inefficient mnemonic strategies, and impaired ability to plan a sequence of actions, respectively. Finally, the past decade has seen greater attention devoted to the social and vocational impact of TBI on both patients and their families. Undoubtedly, researchers will continue to advance understanding of the neurobehavioral sequelae of TBI. Because such research represents the clinical front line, it is imperative that neuropsychologists pay careful attention to these advances to gain greater insight into the experiential world of the people we treat, so that we can maximize patients' return to physical, psychological, social, and vocational well-being.

References

Adams, J. H., Graham, D., Scott, G., Parker, L. S., & Doyle, D. (1980). Brain damage in fatal nonmissile head injury. *Journal of Clinical Pathology*, *33*, 1132–1145.

Adams, J. H., Mitchell, D. E., Murray, L. S., & Scott, G. (1982). Diffuse axonal injury due to nonmissile head injury: Analysis of 45 cases. *Annals of Neurology*, *12*, 557.

Adams, R. D., & Victor, M. (1993). Craniocerebral trauma. In R. D. Adams & M. Victor (Eds.), *Principles of neurology* (5th ed., pp. 749–775). New York: McGraw-Hill.

Alexander, M. P. (1987). The role of neurobehavioral syndromes in the rehabilitation and outcome of closed head injury. In H. S. Levin, J. Grafman, & H. M. Eisenberg (Eds.), *Neurobehavioral recovery from head injury* (pp. 191–205). New York: Oxford University Press.

Alexander, M. P., Benson, D. F., & Stuss, D. T. (1989). Frontal lobes and language. *Brain and Language*, *37*, 656–691.

Allen, I. V., Scott, R., & Tanner, J. A. (1982). Experimental high velocity missile head injury. *Injury*, *14*, 183–193.

American Academy of Neurology, Therapeutics and Technology Assessment Subcommittee. (1989). Assessment: EEG brain mapping. *Neurology*, *39*, 1100–1101.

Anderson, S. W., Damasio, H., Jones, R. D., & Tranel, D. (1991). Wisconsin Card Sorting Test performance as a measure of frontal lobe damage. *Journal of Clinical and Experimental Neuropsychology*, *13*, 909–922.

Baddeley, A., & Hitch, G. (1974). Working memory. *Psychology of Learning and Motivation*, *8*, 47–89.

Baddeley, A., Sunderland, A., Watts, K. P., & Wilson, B. A. (1987). Closed head injury and memory. In H. S. Levin, J. Grafman, & H. M. Eisenberg (Eds.), *Neurobehavioral recovery from head injury* (pp. 295–317). New York: Oxford University Press.

Barona, A., Reynolds, C. R., & Chastain, R. (1984). A demographically based index of premorbid intelligence for the WAIS-R. *Journal of Consulting and Clinical Psychology*, *52*, 885–887.

Basso, A. (1987). Approaches to neuropsychological rehabilitation: Language disorders. In M. Meier, A. Benton, & L. Diller (Eds.), *Neuropsychological rehabilitation* (pp. 294–314). New York: Guilford Press.

Becker, D. P., Miller, J. D., & Greenberg, R. P. (1982). Prognosis after head injury. In J. R. Youmans (Ed.), *Neurological surgery* (pp. 21–42). Philadelphia: W. B. Saunders.

Benson, D. F. (1993). Aphasia. In K. M. Heilman & E. Valenstein (Eds.), *Clinical neuropsychology* (pp. 17–36). New York: Oxford University Press.

Benton, A. L., & Joynt, R. J. (1960). Early descriptions of aphasia. *Archives of Neurology*, *3*, 205–221.

Benton, A. L., & Tranel, D. (1993). Visuoperceptual, visuospatial, and visuoconstructive disorders. In K. M. Heilman & E. Valenstein (Eds.), *Clinical neuropsychology* (pp. 165–214). New York: Oxford University Press.

Ben-Yishay, Y., & Diller, L. (1983a). Cognitive deficits. In E. A. Griffith, M. Bond, & J. Miller (Eds.), *Rehabilitation of the head injured adult* (pp. 167–183). Philadelphia: Davis.

Ben-Yishay, Y., & Diller, L. (1983b). Cognitive remediation. In E. A. Griffith, M. Bond, & J. Miller (Eds.), *Rehabilitation of the head injured adult* (pp. 367–380). Philadelphia: Davis.

Ben-Yishay, Y., Piasetsky, E. B., & Rattok, J. (1987). A systematic method for ameliorating disorders in basic attention. In M. Meier, A. Benton, & L. Diller (Eds.), *Neuropsychological rehabilitation* (pp. 165–181). New York: Guilford Press.

Binder, J., Marshall, R., Lazar, R., Benjamin, J., & Mohr, J. P. (1992). Distinct syndromes of hemineglect. *Archives of Neurology*, *49*, 1187–1194.

Bisiach, E., & Luzatti, C. (1978). Unilateral neglect of representational space. *Cortex*, *14*, 129–133.

Bowers, S. A., & Marshall, L. F. (1980). Outcome in 200 consecutive cases of severe head injury treated in San Diego county: A prospective analysis. *Neurosurgery*, *6*, 237–242.

Braakman, R., Gelpke, G. J., Habbema, J. D. F., Maas, A. I. R., & Minderhoud, J. M. (1980). Systematic selection of prognostic features in patients with severe head injury. *Neurosurgery*, *6*, 362–370.

Bricolo, A. (1976). Electroencephalography in neurotraumatology. *Clinical Electroencephalogy*, *7*, 184–197.

Bricolo, A., Turazzi, S., & Feriotti, G. (1980). Prolonged posttraumatic unconsciousness. *Journal of Neurosurgery*, *52*, 625–634.

Brittain, J. L., LaMarche, J. A., Reeder, K. P., Roth, D. L., & Boll, T. J. (1991). Effects of age and IQ on Paced Auditory Serial Addition Task (PASAT) performance. *The Clinical Neuropsychologist*, *5*, 163–175.

Brooks, N., McKinlay, W., Symington, C., Beattie, A., & Campsie, L. (1987). Return to work within the first seven years of severe head injury. *Brain Injury*, *1*, 5–19.

Bruce, D. A., Schut, L., Bruno, L. A., Wood, J. H., & Sutton, L. N. (1978). Outcome following severe head injuries in children. *Journal of Neurosurgery*, *48*, 679–688.

Bryan, J. E., Wiens, A. N., & Crossen, J. R. (1992). Estimating WAIS-R IQ scores from the National Adult Reading Test–Revised among normal adults. *Journal of Clinical and Experimental Neuropsychology*, *14*, 64.

Buchtel, H. A. (1987). Attention and vigilance after head trauma. In H. S. Levin, J. Grafman, & H. M. Eisenberg (Eds.), *Neurobehavioral recovery from head injury* (pp. 372–378). New York: Oxford University Press.

Carlsson, C. A., von Essen, C., & Lofgren, J. (1968). Factors affecting the clinical course of patients with severe head injuries. *Journal of Neurosurgery*, *29*, 242–251.

Chandler, M. C., Barnhill, J. L., & Gualtieri, C. T. (1988). Amantadine for the agitated head-injury patient. *Brain Injury*, *2*, 309–311.

Chapman, S. B., Culhane, K. A., Levin, H. S., Harward, H., Mendelsohn, D., Ewing-Cobbs, L., Fletcher, J. M., & Bruce, D. (1992). Narrative discourse after closed head injury in children and adolescents. *Brain and Language*, *43*, 42–65.

Cicerone, K. D., & Wood, J. C. (1987). Planning disorder after closed head injury: A case study. *Archives of Physical Medicine and Rehabilitation*, *68*, 111–115.

Clifton, G. L., Grossman, R. G., Makela, M., & Minor, M. E. (1980). Neurological course and correlated computerized tomography findings after severe closed head injury. *Journal of Neurosurgery*, *52*, 611–624.

Clifton, G. L., McCormick, W. F., & Grossman, R. G. (1981). Neuropathology of early and late deaths after head injury. *Neurosurgery*, *8*, 309–314.

Cohen, J. (1957). The factorial structure of the WAIS between early adulthood and old age. *Journal of Consulting Psychology*, *21*, 283–290.

Cohen, N. J., & Squire, L. R. (1980). Preserved learning and retention of pattern analyzing skills in amnesia: Dissociation of knowing how and knowing that. *Science*, *210*, 207–209.

Collins, R. C. (1991). Basic aspects of functional brain metabolism. In D. J. Chadwick & J. Whelan (Eds.), *Exploring brain functional anatomy with positron tomography* (pp. 6–22). New York: Wiley.

Cope, D. N., Date, E. S., & Mar, E. Y. (1993). Serial computerized tomographic evaluations in traumatic brain injury. *Archives of Physical Medicine and Rehabilitation, 69*, 483–486.

Corrigan, S. K., & Berry, D. T. R. (1991). Prediction of IQ in normal older persons: A comparison of two methods. *Archives of Clinical Neuropsychology, 17*, 323–324.

Craine, S. F. (1982). The retraining of frontal lobe dysfunction. In L. E. Trexler (Ed.), *Cognitive rehabilitation: Conceptualization and intervention* (pp. 239–262). New York: Plenum.

Crosson, B., Barco, P. P., Velozo, C. A., Bolesta, M. M., Werts, D., & Brobeck, T. (1989). Awareness and compensation in post-acute head injury rehabilitation. *Journal of Head Trauma Rehabilitation, 4*, 46–54.

Crosson, B., Cooper, P. V., Lincoln, R. K., Bauer, R. M., & Velozo, C. A. (1993). Relationship between verbal memory and language performance after blunt head injury. *The Clinical Neuropsychologist, 7*, 250–267.

Crosson, B., Novack, T. A., Trenerry, M. R., & Craig, P. L. (1988). California Verbal Learning Test performance in severely head-injured and neurologically normal adult males. *Journal of Clinical and Experimental Neuropsychology, 10*, 754–768.

Crosson, B., Sartor, K. J., Jenny, A. B., Nabors, N. A., & Moberg, P. J. (1993). Increased intrusions during verbal recall in traumatic and nontraumatic lesions of the temporal lobe. *Neuropsychology, 7*, 193–208.

Damasio, A. R. (1991). Concluding comments. In H. S. Levin, H. M. Eisenberg, & A. L. Benton (Eds.), *Frontal lobe function and dysfunction* (pp. 401–407). New York: Oxford University Press.

Damasio, A. R., & Anderson, S. W. (1993). The frontal lobes. In K. M. Heilman & E. Valenstein (Eds.), *Clinical neuropsychology* (pp. 409–460). New York: Oxford University Press.

Daniel, D. G., Zigon, J. R., & Weinberger, D. R. (1992). Brain imaging in neuropsychiatry. In S. Yudofsky & R. Hales (Eds.), *Textbook of neuropsychiatry* (2nd ed., pp. 165–186). Washington, DC: American Psychiatric Press.

Daniel, W. F., Crovitz, H. F., & Weiner, R. D. (1987). Neuropsychological aspects of disorientation. *Cortex, 23*, 169–187.

Davies, D. R., & Parasuraman, R. (1982). *The psychology of vigilance.* San Diego, CA: Academic Press.

Desimone, R., Wessinger, M., Thomas, L., & Schneider, W. (1990). Attentional control of visual perception: Cortical and subcortical mechanisms. In *Cold Spring Harbor symposia of quantitative biology, Vol. LV: The brain* (pp. 1007–1023). New York: Cold Spring Harbor Laboratory Press.

Dikmen, S. S., Donovan, D. M., Løberg, T., Machamer, J. E., & Temkin, N. R. (1993). Alcohol use and its effects on neuropsychological outcome in head injury. *Neuropsychology, 7*, 296–305.

Dikmen, S. S., Machamer, J. E., Winn, H. R., & Temkin, N. R. (1995). Neuropsychological outcome at 1-year post head injury. *Neuropsychology, 9*, 80–90.

Dikmen, S. S., Temkin, N., & Armsden, G. (1989). Neuropsychological recovery: Relationship to psychosocial functioning and postconcussional complaints. In H. S. Levin, H. M. Eisenberg, & A. L. Benton (Eds.), *Mild head injury* (pp. 229–241). New York: Oxford University Press.

Diller, L., & Weinberg, J. (1977). Hemi-inattention in rehabilitation: The evolution of a rational remediation program. In E. Weinstein & R. Friedland (Eds.), *Advances in neurology* (Vol. 18, pp. 63–82). New York: Raven Press.

Donders, J., & Kirsch, N. (1991). Nature and implications of selective impairment on the Booklet Category Test and Wisconsin Card Sorting Test. *The Clinical Neuropsychologist, 5*, 78–82.

Dywan, J., Segalowitz, S. J., Henderson, D., & Jacoby, L. (1993). Memory for source after traumatic brain injury. *Brain and Cognition, 21*, 20–43.

Ebbell, B. (1937). *The papyrus ebers.* Copenhagen, The Netherlands: Levin and Munksgaard.

Ehrlich, J. S. (1988). Selective characteristics of narrative discourse in head-injured and normal adults. *Journal of Communication Disorders, 21*, 1–9.

Eslinger, P. J., & Damasio, A. R. (1985). Severe disturbance of higher cognition after bilateral frontal lobe ablation: Patient EVR. *Neurology, 35*, 1731–1741.

Ewart, J., Levin, H. S., Watson, M. G., & Kalisky, Z. (1989). Procedural memory during posttraumatic amnesia in survivors of severe closed head injury: Implications for rehabilitation. *Archives of Neurology, 46*, 911–916.

Fordyce, D. J., & Rouche, J. R. (1986). Changes in perspectives of disability among patients, staff, and relatives during rehabilitation of brain injury. *Rehabilitation Psychology, 31*, 217–229.

Fuster, J. M. (1989). *The prefrontal cortex* (2nd ed.). New York: Raven Press.

Gale, S. D., Johnson, S. C., Bigler, E. D., & Blatter, D. D. (1995). Nonspecific white matter degeneration following traumatic brain injury. *Journal of the International Neuropsychological Society, 1*, 17–28.

Gandy, S. E., Snow, R. B., Zimmerman, R. D., & Deck, M. D. F. (1984). Cranial nuclear magnetic resonance imaging in head trauma. *Annals of Neurology, 16*, 254–257.

Gass, C. S. (1991). MMPI-2 interpretation and closed head injury: A correction factor. *Psychological Assessment, 3*, 27–31.

Gennarelli, T. A., Spielman, G. M., Langfitt, T. W., Gildenberg, P. L., Harrington, T., Jane, J. A., Marshall, L. F., Miller, J. D., & Pitts, L. H. (1982). Influence of the type of intracranial lesion on outcome from severe head injury. *Journal of Neurosurgery, 56*, 26–33.

Gentry, L. R., Godersky, J. C., Thompson, B., & Dunn, V. D. (1988). Prospective comparative study of intermediate-field MR and CT in the evaluation of closed head trauma. *Journal of Neuroradiology, 9*, 91–100.

Gianutsos, R., & Matheson, P. (1987). The rehabilitation of visual perceptual disorders attributable to brain injury. In M. J. Meier, A. Benton, & L. Diller (Eds.), *Neuropsychological rehabilitation* (pp. 202–241). New York: Guilford Press.

Glisky, E. L., Schacter, D. L., & Tulving, E. (1986). Learning and retention of computer-related vocabulary in memory-impaired patients: Method of vanishing cues. *Journal of Clinical and Experimental Neuropsychology, 8*, 292–312.

Goldstein, F. C., & Levin, H. S. (1987). Disorders of reasoning and problem-solving ability. In M. Meier, A. Benton, & L. Diller (Eds.), *Neuropsychological rehabilitation* (pp. 327–354). New York: Guilford Press.

Goldstein, F. C., Levin, H., Boake, C., & Lohrey, J. H. (1990). Facilitation of memory performance through induced semantic processing in survivors of severe closed head injury. *Journal of Clinical and Experimental Neuropsychology, 12*, 286–300.

Goodglass, H. (1987). Neurolinguistic principles and aphasia therapy. In M. Meier, A. Benton, & L. Diller (Eds.), *Neuropsychological rehabilitation* (pp. 315–326). New York: Guilford Press.

Gouvier, W. D., Maxfield, M. W., Schweitzer, J. R., Horton, C. R., Shipp, M., Neilson, K., & Hale, P. (1989). Psychometric prediction of driving performance among the disabled. *Archives of Physical Medicine and Rehabilitation, 70*, 745–750.

Gouvier, W. D., Schweitzer, J. R., Horton, C. R., Maxfield, M. W., Shipp, M., Seaman, R. L., & Hale, P. N. (1988). A systems approach to assessing driving skills among TBI and other severely disabled individuals. *Rehabilitation Education, 2*, 197–204.

Gouvier, W. D., Webster, J. S., & Warner, M. S. (1986). Treatment of acquired visuoperceptual and hemiattentional disorder. *Annals of Behavioral Medicine, 8*, 1–20.

Grafman, J., & Salazar, A. (1987). Methodological considerations relevant to the comparison of recovery from penetrating and closed head injuries. In H. S. Levin, J. Grafman, & H. M. Eisenberg (Eds.), *Neurobehavioral recovery from head injury* (pp. 372–378). New York: Oxford University Press.

Grober, E., & Sliwinski, M. (1991). Development and validation of a model for estimating premorbid verbal intelligence in the elderly. *Journal of Clinical and Experimental Neuropsychology, 13*, 933–949.

Gronwall, D. (1987). Advances in the assessment of attention and information processing after head injury. In H. S. Levin, J. Grafman, & H. M. Eisenberg (Eds.), *Neurobehavioral recovery from head injury* (pp. 355–371). New York: Oxford University Press.

Gronwall, D., & Sampson, H. (1974). *The psychological effects of concussion*. New York: Oxford University Press.

Gronwall, D., & Wrightson, P. (1981). Memory and information processing capacity after closed head injury. *Journal of Neurology, Neurosurgery, and Psychiatry, 44*, 889–895.

Guilleminault, C., Faull, K. F., Miles, L., & Van der Hoad, J. (1983). Posttraumatic excessive daytime sleepiness: A review of 20 patients. *Neurology, 33*, 1584–1589

Gupta, N. K., Verma, N. P., & Guidice, M. A. (1986). Visual evoked response in head trauma: Pattern-shift stimulus. *Neurology, 36*, 578–581.

Hadley, D. M., Teasdale, G. M., Jenkins, A., Condon, B., MacPherson, P., Patterson, J., & Rowan, J. O. (1988). Magnetic resonance imaging in acute head injury. *Clinical Radiology, 39*, 131–139.

Hagen, C., & Malkmus, D. (1979, November). *Intervention strategies for language disorders secondary to head trauma*. Paper presented at the American Speech, Language, and Hearing Association Convention, Short Course, Atlanta, Georgia.

Halligan, P. W., & Marshall, J. C. (1992). Left visuospatial neglect: A meaningless entity? *Cortex, 28*, 525–535.

Han, J. S., Kaufman, B., Alfidi, R. J., Heung, H. N., Benson, J. E., Haaga, J. R., El Yousef, S. J., Clampitt, M. E., Bonstelle, C. T., & Huss, R. (1984). Head trauma evaluated by magnetic resonance and computed tomography: A comparison. *Radiology, 150*, 71–77.

Heaton, R. K. (1981). *A manual for the Wisconsin Card Sorting Test*. Odessa, FL: Psychological Assessment Resources.

Hebb, D. O. (1949). *The organization of behavior*. New York: Wiley.

Heilman, K. M., Safran, A., & Geschwind, N. (1971). Closed head trauma and aphasia. *Journal of Neurology, Neurosurgery, and Psychiatry, 34*, 265–269.

Heilman, K. M., & Watson, R. T. (1991). Intentional motor disorders. In H. S. Levin, H. M. Eisenberg, & A. L. Benton (Eds.), *Frontal lobe function and dysfunction* (pp. 199–213). New York: Oxford University Press.

Heilman, K. M., Watson, R. T., & Valenstein, E. (1993). Neglect and related disorders. In K. M. Heilman & E. Valenstein (Eds.), *Clinical neuropsychology* (pp. 279–336). New York: Oxford University Press.

Heinze, H.-J., Münte, T. F., Gobiet, W., Niemann, H., & Ruff, R. M. (1992). Parallel and serial search after closed head injury: Electrophysiological evidence for perceptual dysfunctions. *Neuropsychologia, 30*, 495–514.

Hesselink, J. R., Dowd, C. F., Healy, M. E., Hajek, P., Baker, L. L., & Luerssen, T. G. (1988). MR imaging of brain contusions: A comparative study with CT. *American Journal of Neuroradiology, 9*, 269–278.

Hicks, L., & Birren, J. E. (1970). Aging, brain damage, and psychomotor slowing. *Psychological Bulletin, 74*, 377–396.

High, W. M., Levin, H. S., & Gary, H. E. (1990). Recovery of orientation following closed-head injury. *Journal of Clinical and Experimental Neuropsychology, 12*, 703–714.

Hinkeldey, N. S., & Corrigan, J. D. (1990). The structure of head-injured patients' neurobehavioral complaints: A preliminary study. *Brain Injury, 4*, 115–133.

Hirst, W. (1982). The amnesic syndrome: Descriptions and explanations. *Psychological Bulletin*, 91, 435–460.

Holbourn, A. H. S. (1943). Mechanics of head injury. *Lancet*, 2, 438–441.

Hopewell, C. A., & Van Zomeren, A. H. (1990). Neuropsychological aspects of motor vehicle operation. In D. E. Tupper & K. D. Cicerone (Eds.), *The neuropsychology of everyday life*. Norwell, MA: Kluwer Academic.

Ishiai, S., Sugishita, M., Ichikawa, T., Gono, S., & Watabiki, S. (1993). Clock-drawing test and unilateral spatial neglect. *Neurology, 43*, 106–110.

Jarvis, P. E., & Barth, J. T. (1984). *Halstead-Reitan test battery: An interpretive guide*. Odessa, FL: Psychological Assessment Resources.

Jenkins, A., Teasdale, G., Hadley, M. D., MacPherson, P., & Rowan, J. O. (1986). Brain lesions detected by magnetic resonance imaging in mild and severe head injuries. *Lancet*, 2, 445–446.

Jennett, B., Teasdale, G., Braakman, R., Minderhoud, J., & Knill-Jones, R. (1976). Predicting outcome in individual patients after severe head injury. *Lancet, 1*, 1031–1034.

Jennett, B., Teasdale, G., Murray, G., & Murray, L. (1992). Head injury. In R. W. Evans, D. S. Baskin, & F. M. Yatsu (Eds.), *Prognosis of neurological disorders* (pp. 85–96). New York: Oxford University Press.

Jetter, W., Poser, U., Freeman, R. B., Jr., & Markowitsch, H. J. (1986). A verbal long-term memory deficit in frontal lobe damaged patients. *Cortex*, 22, 229–242.

Jones, C. L. (1992). Recovery from head trauma: A curvilinear process? In C. J. Long & L. K. Ross (Eds.), *Handbook of head trauma: Acute care to recovery* (pp. 247–270). New York: Plenum.

Katz, D. I., & Alexander, M. P. (1994). Traumatic brain injury: Predicting course of recovery and outcome for patients admitted to rehabilitation. *Archives of Neurology, 51*, 661–670.

Kewman, D., Siergerman, C., Kinter, H., Chu, S., Henson, D., & Reeder, C. (1985). Simulation training of psychomotor skills: Teaching the brain-injured patient to drive. *Rehabilitation Psychology, 30*, 11–27.

Kraus, J. F., Black, M. A., Hessol, N., Ley, P., Rokaw, W., Sullivan, C., Bowers, S., Knowlton, S., & Marshall, L. (1984). The incidence of acute brain injury and serious impairment in a defined population. *American Journal of Epidemiology, 119*, 186–201.

Kraus, J. F., & Nourjah, P. (1988). The epidemiology of mild uncomplicated head injury. *Journal of Trauma, 29*, 1637–1643.

Kreutzer, J. S., Marwitz, J. H., & Kepler, K. (1992). Traumatic brain injury: Family response and outcome. *Archives of Physical Medicine and Rehabilitation, 73*, 771–778.

Krull, K. R., Scott, J. G., & Sherer, M. (1995). Estimation of premorbid intelligence from combined performance and demographic variables. *The Clinical Neuropsychologist, 9*, 83–88.

Langfitt, T. W., & Gennarelli, T. A. (1982). Can the outcome from head injury be improved? *Journal of Neurosurgery, 56*, 19–25.

Langfitt, T. W., Obrist, W. D., Alavi, A., Grossman, R., Zimmerman, R., Jaggi, J., Uzzell, B., Reivich, M., & Patton, D. (1987). Regional structure and function in head-injured patients: Correlation of CT, MRI, PET, CBF, and neuropsychological assessment. In H. S. Levin, J. Grafman, & H. M. Eisenberg (Eds.), *Neurobehavioral recovery from head injury* (pp. 30–42). New York: Oxford University Press.

Leckliter, I. N., Matarazzo, J. D., & Silverstein, A. B. (1986). A literature review of factor analytic studies of the WAIS-R. *Journal of Clinical Psychology, 42*, 332–342.

Leurssen, T. G. (1991). Head injuries in children. In H. M. Eisenberg & E. F. Aldrich (Eds.), *Neurosurgery clinics of North America: Management of head injury* (Vol. 2, pp. 309–410). Philadelphia: W. B. Saunders.

Levati, A., Farina, M. L., Vecchi, G., Rossanda, M., & Marrubini, M. B. (1982). Prognosis of severe head injuries. *Journal of Neurosurgery, 57*, 779–783.

Levin, H. (1989). Memory deficit after closed-head injury. *Journal of Clinical and Experimental Neuropsychology, 12*, 129–153.

Levin, H., Benton, A. L., & Grossman, R. G. (1982). *Neurobehavioral consequences of closed head injury* (2nd ed.). New York: Oxford University Press.

Levin, H. S., Amparo, E. G., Eisenberg, H. M., Williams, D. H., High, W. M., McArdle, C. B., & Weiner, R. L., (1987). Magnetic resonance imaging and computerized tomography in relation to neurobehavioral sequelae at mild and moderate head injury. *Journal of Neurosurgery, 66*, 706–713.

Levin, H. S., & Goldstein, F. C. (1986). Organization of verbal memory after severe closed head injury. *Journal of Clinical and Experimental Neuropsychology, 8*, 643–656.

Levin, H. S., Goldstein, F. C., High, W. M., Jr., & Eisenberg, H. M. (1988). Automatic and effortful processing after severe closed head injury. *Brain and Cognition, 7*, 283–297.

Levin, H. S., Grossman, R. G., & Kelly, P. J. (1976). Aphasic disorder in patients with closed head injury. *Journal of Neurology, Neurosurgery, and Psychiatry, 39*, 1062–1070.

Levin, H. S., Grossman, R. G., Sarwar, M., & Meyers, C. A. (1981). Linguistic recovery after closed head injury. *Brain and Language, 12*, 360–374.

Levin, H. S., Handel, S. F., Goldman, A. M., Eisenberg, H. M., & Guinto, F. C. (1985). Magnetic resonance imaging after "diffuse" nonmissile head injury. *Archives of Neurology, 42*, 963–968.

Levin, H. S., Lilly, M. A., Papanicolaou, A., & Eisenberg, H. M. (1992). Posttraumatic and retrograde amnesia after closed head injury. In L. R. Squire & N. Butters (Eds.), *Neuropsychology of memory* (pp. 290–308). New York: Guilford Press.

Levin, H. S., O'Donnell, V. M., & Grossman, R. G., (1979). The Galveston Orientation and Amnesia Test: A practical scale to assess cognition after head injury. *Journal of Nervous and Mental Disorders, 167*, 675–684.

Levin, H. S., Papanicolaou, A., & Eisenberg, H. M. (1984). Observations on amnesia after nonmissile head injury. In L. R. Squire & N. Butters (Eds.), *Neuropsychology of memory* (pp. 247–257). New York: Guilford Press.

Levin, H. S., Williams, D. H., Crofford, M. J., High, W., Eisenberg, H. M., Amparo, E. G., Guinto, F. C., Kalisky, Z., Handel, S. F., Goldman, A. M. (1988). Relationship of depth of brain lesion to consciousness and outcome after closed head injury. *Journal of Neurosurgery, 69*, 861–866.

Lezak, M. D. (1983). *Neuropsychological assessment* (2nd ed.). New York: Oxford University Press.

Lezak, M. D. (1988). Brain damage is a family affair. *Journal of Clinical and Experimental Psychology, 10*, 111–123.

Lindsey, K., Pasaoglu, A., & Hirst, D. (1990). Somatosensory and auditory brain stem conduction after head injury: A comparison with clinical features in prediction of outcome. *Neurosurgery, 26*, 278–285.

Luria, A. R., & Homskaya, E. D. (1964). Disturbances in the regulative role of speech with frontal lobe lesions. In J. M. Warren & K. A. Ahert (Eds.), *The frontal granular cortex and behavior*. New York: McGraw-Hill.

Mapou, R. L. (1992). Neuropathology and neuropsychology of behavioral disturbances following traumatic brain injury. In C. J. Long & L. K. Ross (Eds.), *Handbook of head trauma: Acute care to recovery* (pp. 75–87). New York: Plenum.

McGlynn, S. M. (1990). Behavioral approaches to neuropsychological rehabilitation. *Psychological Bulletin, 108*, 420–441.

McKinlay, W. W., Brooks, D. N., Bond, M. R., Martinage, D. P., & Marshall, M. M. (1981). The short-term outcome of severe blunt head injury as reported by relatives of the injured persons. *Journal of Neurology, Neurosurgery, and Psychiatry, 48*, 527–533.

McLellan, D. L. (1991). Functional recovery and the principles of disability medicine. In M. Swash & J. Oxbury (Eds.), *Clinical neurology* (pp. 768–790). Edinburgh, Scotland: Churchill Livingstone.

Mentis, M., & Prutting, C. A. (1987). Cohesion in the discourse of normal and head-injured adults. *Journal of Speech and Hearing Research, 30*, 88–98.

Metter, E. J., Kempler, D., Jackson, C., Hanson, W. R., Maziotta, J. C., & Phelps, M. E. (1989). Cerebral glucose metabolism in Wernicke's, Broca's, and conduction aphasia. *Archives of Neurology, 46*, 27–34.

Miller, J. D., Becker, D. P., Ward, J. D., Sullivan, H. G., Adams, W. E., & Rosner, M. J. (1977). Significance of intracerebral pressure in severe head injury. *Journal of Neurosurgery, 47*, 503–516.

Milner, B., Petrides, M., & Smith, M. L. (1985). Frontal lobes and the temporal organization of memory. *Human Neurobiology, 4*, 137–142.

Mishkin, M., Ungerleider, L., & Macko, K. A. (1983). Object vision and spatial vision: Two cortical pathways. *Trends in the Neurosciences, 6*, 414–417.

Moscovitch, M. (1981). Multiple dissociations of function in the amnesic syndrome. In L. Cermak (Ed.), *Human memory and amnesia* (pp. 337–370). Hillsdale, NJ: Erlbaum.

Moscovitch, M. (1989). Confabulation and the frontal systems: Strategic versus associative retrieval in neuropsychological theories of memory. In H. L. Roediger III, & F. I. M. Craik (Eds.), *Varieties of memory and consciousness: Essays in honour of Endel Tulving* (pp. 133–160). Hillsdale, NJ: Erlbaum.

Moscovitch, M. (1992). A neuropsychological model of memory and consciousness. In L. R. Squire & N. Butters (Eds.), *Neuropsychology of memory* (pp. 5–22). New York: Guilford Press.

Mountain, M. A., & Snow, W. G. (1993). Wisconsin Card Sorting Test as a measure of frontal pathology: A review. *The Clinical Neuropsychologist*, *7*, 108–118.

Narayan, R. K., Greenberg, R. P., Miller, J. D., & Enas, G. G. (1981). Improved confidence of outcome in severe head injury. *Journal of Neurosurgery*, *54*, 751–762.

National Institute of Neurological Disorders and Stroke. (1989). *Interagency head-injury task force report*. Bethesda, MD: National Institutes of Health.

Novack, T. A., Kofoed, B. A., & Crosson, B. (1995). Sequential performance on the California Verbal Learning Test following traumatic brain injury. *The Clinical Neuropsychologist*, *9*, 38–43.

O'Connor, M., & Cermak, L. S. (1987). Rehabilitation of organic memory disorder. In M. Meier, A. Benton, & L. Diller (Eds.), *Neuropsychological rehabilitation* (pp. 260–279). New York: Guilford Press.

Oddy, M., Coughlan, T., Tyerman, A., & Jenkins, D. (1985). Social adjustment after closed head injury: A further follow-up seven years after injury. *Journal of Neurology, Neurosurgery, and Psychiatry*, *48*, 564–568.

O'Shaughnessy, E. J., Fowler, R. S., & Reid, V. (1984). Sequelae of mild closed head injuries. *Journal of Family Practice*, *18*, 391–394.

Parasuraman, R., Mutter, S. A., & Molloy, R. (1991). Sustained attention following mild closed-head injury. *Journal of Clinical and Experimental Neuropsychology*, *13*, 789–811.

Parsons, O. A. (1986). Overview of the Halstead–Reitan battery. In T. Incagnoli (Ed.), *The clinical application of neuropsychological test batteries* (pp. 155–233). New York: Plenum.

Perrine, K. (1993). Differential aspects of conceptual processing in the Category Test and Wisconsin Card Sorting Test. *Journal of Clinical and Experimental Neuropsychology*, *15*, 461–473.

Ponsford, J., & Kinsella, G. (1992). Attentional deficits following closed-head injury. *Journal of Clinical and Experimental Neuropsychology*, *14*, 822–838.

Porteus, S. D. (1965). *Porteus Maze Test. Fifty years' application*. New York: Psychological Corporation.

Posner, M. I. (1987). Selective attention in head injury. In H. S. Levin, J. Grafman, & H. M. Eisenberg (Eds.), *Neurobehavioral recovery from head injury* (pp. 390–397). New York: Oxford University Press.

Posner, M. I., & Rafal, R. D. (1987). Cognitive theories of attention and the rehabilitation of attentional deficits. In M. Meier, A. Benton, & L. Diller (Eds.), *Neuropsychological rehabilitation* (pp. 182–201). New York: Guilford Press.

Prigitano, G. P. (1991). Disturbances of self-awareness of deficit after traumatic brain injury. In G. P. Prigitano & D. L. Schacter (Eds.), *Awareness of deficit after brain injury: Theoretical and clinical implications* (pp. 111–126). New York: Oxford University Press.

Prigitano, G. P. (1992). Personality disturbances associated with traumatic brain injury. *Journal of Consulting and Clinical Psychology*, *60*, 360–368.

Prigitano, G. P., Fordyce, D., Zeiner, H., Roueche, J., Pepping, M., & Wood, B. (1986). *Neuropsychological rehabilitation after brain injury*. Baltimore: Johns Hopkins University Press.

Prigitano, G. P., & Schacter, D. (1991). *Awareness of deficit after brain injury: Theoretical and clinical implications*. New York: Oxford University Press.

Putnam, S. H., & DeLuca, J. W. (1990). The TCN professional practice survey: I. General practices of neuropsychologists in primary employment and private practice settings. *The Clinical Neuropsychologist*, *4*, 199–243.

Rappaport, M., Hopkins, R., & Hall, K. (1977). Evoked brain potentials and disability in brain damaged patients. *Archives of Physical Medicine amd Rehabilitation*, *58*, 333–338.

Ratcliff, G. (1987). Perception and complex visual processes. In M. Meier, A. Benton, & L. Diller (Eds.), *Neuropsychological rehabilitation* (pp. 242–259). New York: Guilford Press.

Reilly, P. L., Graham, D. I., Adams, J. H., & Jennett, B. (1975). Patients with head injuries who talk and die. *Lancet*, *2*, 375–377.

Reitan, R. M. (1958). Validity of the Trail-Making Test as an indication of organic brain damage. *Perceptual Motor Skills*, *8*, 271–276.

Reitan, R. M., & Wolfson, D. (1985). *The Halstead–Reitan neuropsychological test battery: Theory and clinical interpretation*. Tucson, AZ: Neuropsychology Press.

Reitan, R. M., & Wolfson, D. (1995). Category Test and Trail-Making Test as measures of frontal lobe functions. *The Clinical Neuropsychologist*, *9*, 50–56.

Reyes, R. L., Bhattacharyya, A. K., & Heller, D. (1981). Traumatic head injury: Restlessness and agitation as prognosticators of physical and psychologic improvement in patients. *Archives of Physical Medicine and Rehabilitation*, *62*, 20–23.

Ribot, T. (1882). *Diseases of memory: An essay in the positive psychology*. New York: Appleton-Century-Crofts.

Ropper, R. H., & Miller, D. C. (1985). Acute traumatic midbrain hemorrhage. *Annals of Neurology*, *18*, 80–86.

Rose, J., Valtonen, S., & Jennett, B. (1977). Avoidable factors contributing to death after head injury. *British Medical Journal*, *2*, 615–618.

Rutter, M., Chadwick, O., & Schaffer, D. (1983). Head injury. In M. Rutter (Ed.), *Developmental neuropsychiatry* (pp. 83–111). New York: Guilford Press.

Salazar, A. M., Grafman, J. H., Vance, S. C., Weingartner, H., Dillon, J. D., & Ludlow, C. (1986). Consciousness and amnesia after penetrating head injury: Neurology and neuroanatomy. *Neurology*, *36*, 178–187.

Sarno, M. T. (1980). The nature of verbal impairment after closed head injury. *Journal of Nervous and Mental Disorders, 168*, 685–692.

Sbordone, R. J., & Howard, M. (1989). *Predictors of rehabilitation potential and outcome from head trauma.* Unpublished manuscript.

Schacter, D. L. (1987). Memory, amnesia, and frontal lobe dysfunction. *Psychobiology*, 15, 21–36.

Schmitter-Edgecombe, M. E., Marks, W., & Fahy, J. F. (1993). Semantic priming after severe closed head trauma: Automatic and attentional processes. *Neuropsychology*, 7, 136–148.

Schmitter-Edgecombe, M. E., Marks, W., Fahy, J. F., & Long, C. J. (1992). Effects of severe closed-head injury on three stages of information processing. *Journal of Clinical and Experimental Neuropsychology*, 5, 717–737.

Schneider, G. E. (1969). Two visual systems. *Science*, *163*, 895–902.

Schwab, K., Grafman, J., Salazar, A. M., & Kraft, J. (1993). Residual impairments and work status 15 years after penetrating head injury: Report from the Vietnam Head Injury Study. *Neurology*, *43*, 95–103.

Scott, J., Sherer, M., & Adams, R. L. (1995). Clinical utility of the WAIS-R factor-derived standard scores in assessing brain injury. *The Clinical Neuropsychologist*, *9*, 93–97.

Seelig, J. M., Becker, D. P., Miller, J. D., Greenberg, R. P., Ward, J. D., & Choi, S. C. (1981). Traumatic acute subdural hematoma. Major mortality reduction in comatose patients treated within four hours. *New England Journal of Medicine*, *304*, 1511–1512.

Shallice, T. (1982). Specific impairments of planning. *Philosophical Transactions of the Royal Society of London (Biology)*, *298*, 199–209.

Shallice, T., & Burgess, P. W. (1991a). Deficits in strategy application following frontal lobe lesions in man. *Brain*, 114, 727–741.

Shallice, T., & Burgess, P. W. (1991b). Higher order cognitive impairments and frontal lobe lesions in man. In H. S. Levin, H. M. Eisenberg, & A. L. Benton (Eds.), *Frontal lobe function and dysfunction* (pp. 125–138). New York: Oxford University Press.

Shimamura, A. P., & Squire, L. R. (1987). A neuropsychological study of fact memory and source amnesia. *Journal of Experimental Psychology: Learning, Memory, and Cognition*, *13*, 464–473.

Shin, D. Y., Ehrenberg, B., & Wythe, J. (1989). Evoked potential assessment: Utility in prognosis of chronic head injury. *Archives of Physical Medicine and Rehabilitation*, *70*, 189–193.

Shum, D. H. K., McFarland, K., Bain, J. D., & Humphreys, M. S. (1990). Effects of closed-head injury on attentional processes: An information-processing stage analysis. *Journal of Clinical and Experimental Neuropsychology*, *12*, 247–264.

Sivak, M., Olson, P. L., Kewman, D. G., Won, H., & Henson, D. L. (1981). Driving and perceptual/cognitive skills: Behavioral consequences of brain damage. *Archives of Physical Medicine and Rehabilitation*, *62*, 476–483.

Smith, G. E., Ivnik, R. J., Malec, J. F., Kokmen, E., Tangalos, E. G., & Kurland, L. T. (1992). Mayo's Older Americans Normative Studies (MOANS): Factor structure of a core battery. *Psychological Assessment*, *4*, 382–390.

Snow, R. B., Zimmerman, R. D., Gandy, S. E., & Deck, M. D. F. (1986). Comparison of magnetic resonance imaging and computed tomography in the evaluation of head injury. *Neurosurgery*, *18*, 45–52.

Sohlberg, M. M., & Mateer, C. A. (1986). *Attention process training (APT)*. Puyallup, WA: Association for Neuropsychological Research and Development.

Sohlberg, M. M., & Mateer, C. A. (1987). Effectiveness of an attention training program. *Journal of Clinical and Experimental Neuropsychology*, *9*, 117–130.

Sohlberg, M. M., & Mateer, C. A. (1989). *Introduction to cognitive rehabilitation: Theory and practice*. New York: Guilford Press.

Sohlberg, M. M., White, O., Evans, E., & Mateer, C. (1992a). Background and initial case studies into the effects of prospective memory training. *Brain Injury*, 6, 129–138.

Sohlberg, M. M., White, O., Evans, E., & Mateer, C. (1992b). An investigation of the effects of prospective memory training. *Brain Injury*, *6*, 139–154.

Spreen, O., & Strauss, E. (1991). *A compendium of neuropsychological tests: Administration, norms, and commentary*. New York: Oxford University Press.

Squire, L. R., & Butters, N. (1992). *Neuropsychology of memory*. New York: Guilford Press.

Squire, L. R., Zola-Morgan, S., Cave, C. B., Haist, F., Musen, G., & Suzuki, W. A. (1990). Memory: Organization of brain systems and cognition. In *Cold Spring Harbor symposia of quantitative biology, Vol. LV: The brain* (pp. 1007–1023). New York: Cold Spring Harbor Laboratory Press.

Stockard, J., & Rossiter, V. (1977). Clinical and pathological correlates of brainstem auditory evoked response abnormalities. *Neurology*, *27*, 316–325.

Stroop, J. R. (1935). Studies of interference in serial verbal reactions. *Journal of Experimental Psychology*, *18*, 643–662.

Stuss, D. T. (1987). Contribution of frontal lobe injury to cognitive impairment after closed head injury: Methods of assessment and recent findings. In H. S. Levin, J. Grafman, & H. M. Eisenberg (Eds.), *Neurobehavioral recovery from head injury* (pp. 166–177). New York: Oxford University Press.

Stuss, D. T. (1991). Interference effects of memory function in postleukotomy patients: An attentional perspective. In H. S. Levin, H. M. Eisenberg, & A. L.

Benton (Eds.), *Frontal lobe function and dysfunction* (pp. 157–172). New York: Oxford University Press.

Stuss, D. T., & Benson, D. F. (1986). *The frontal lobes.* New York: Raven Press.

Stuss, D. T., Kaplan, E. F., Benson, D. F., Weir, W. S., Chiulli, S., & Sarazin, F. F. (1982). Evidence for the involvement of orbito-frontal cortex in memory functions: An interference effect. *Journal of Comparative Physiological Psychiatry, 96,* 913–925.

Swan, K. G., & Swan, R. C. (1980). *Gunshot wounds: Pathophysiology management.* Littlejohn, MA: PSG Publishing.

Synek, V. M. (1988). Prognostically important EEG coma patterns in diffuse axonic and traumatic encephalopathies in adults. *Journal of Clinical Neurophysiology, 5,* 161–174.

Taylor, M. M., Schaeffer, J. N., Blumenthal, F. S., & Grisell, J. L. (1971). Perceptual training in patients with left hemiplegia. *Archives of Physical Medicine and Rehabilitation, 52,* 163–169.

Teasdale, G., & Jennett, B. (1974). Assessment of coma and impaired consciousness: A practical scale. *Lancet, 2,* 81–83.

Thomas, D. F. (1990). Vocational evaluation of persons with traumatic head injury. In D. Corthell (Ed.), *Traumatic brain injury and vocational rehabilitation* (pp. 111–139). Menomonie, WI: Research and Training Center, University of Wisconsin—Stout.

Trobe, J. D., Acosta, P. C., Krischer, J. P., & Trick, G. L. (1981). Confrontation visual field techniques in detection of anterior visual pathway lesions. *Annals of Neurology,* 10, 28–34.

Tweedy, J. R., & Vakil, E. (1988). Evaluating evidence for automaticity in frequency of occurrence judgements: A bias for bias? *Journal of Clinical and Experimental Neuropsychology, 10,* 664–674.

Vakil, E., Blachstein, H., & Hoofien, D. (1991). Automatic temporal order judgement: The effect of intentionality of retrieval on closed-head-injured patients. *Journal of Clinical and Experimental Neuropsychology, 13,* 291–298.

Van Zomeren, A. H., & Brouwer, W. H. (1987). Head injury and concepts of attention. In H. S. Levin, J. Grafman, & H. M. Eisenberg (Eds.), *Neurobehavioral recovery from head injury* (pp. 191–205). New York: Oxford University Press.

Van Zomeren, A. H., Brouwer, W. H., Rothengatter, J. A., & Snoek, J. W. (1988). Fitness to drive a car after recovery from severe head injury. *Archives of Physical Medicine and Rehabilitation, 69,* 90–96.

Van Zomeren, A. H., & Van Den Burg, W. (1985). Residual complaints of patients two years after severe head injury. *Journal of Neurology, Neurosurgery, and Psychiatry, 48,* 21–28.

Varney, N. R., & Menefee, L. (1993). Psychosocial and executive deficits following closed head injury: Implications for orbital frontal cortex. *Journal of Head Trauma Rehabilitation, 8,* 32–44.

Waller, N. G., & Waldman, I. D. (1990). A reexamination of the WAIS-R factor structure. *Psychological Assessment, 2,* 139–144.

Wechsler, D. (1981). *Wechsler Adult Intelligence Scale–Revised.* New York: Psychological Corporation.

Wedding, D. (1992). Neurological impairment and driving ability. In C. J. Long & L. K. Ross (Eds.), *Handbook of head trauma: Acute care to recovery* (pp. 417–422). New York: Plenum.

Weinberg, J., Diller, L., Gordon, W. A., Gerstman, L. J., Lieberman, A., Lakin, P., Hodges, G., & Ezrachi, O. (1979). Training sensory awareness and spatial organization in people with right brain damage. *Archives of Physical Medicine and Rehabilitation, 60,* 491–496.

Williams, D. (1987). *Management of the patient with chronic confusion.* Unpublished manuscript.

Williamson, D., Scott, J., Krull, K., & Adams, R. L. (1994, February). *The Oklahoma premorbid intelligence estimate (OPIE): Validation on clinical samples.* Poster presented at the Annual Meetings of the International Neuropsychological Society, Cincinnati, Ohio.

Willshire, D., Kinsella, G., & Prior, M. (1991). Estimating WAIS-R IQ from the National Adult Reading Test: A cross-validation. *Journal of Clinical and Experimental Neuropsychology, 13,* 204–216.

Wilson, B. A. (1992). Rehabilitation and memory disorders. In L. R. Squire & N. Butters (Eds.), *Neuropsychology of memory* (pp. 315–321). New York: Guilford Press.

Wilson, J. T. L., Wied FD. M., Condon, B., Teasdale, G., & Brooks, D. N. (1988). Early and late magnetic resonance imaging and neuropsychological outcome after head injury. *Journal of Neurology, Neurosurgery, and Psychiatry, 51,* 391–396.

Wilson, R. S., Rosenbaum, G., Brown, G., Rourke, D., Whitman, D., & Grisell, J. (1978). An index of premorbid intelligence. *Journal of Consulting and Clinical Psychology, 46,* 1554–1555.

Wyckoff, L. H. (1984). *Narrative and procedural discourse following closed head injury.* Doctoral dissertation, University of Florida, Gainesville.

Zec, R. F., Parks, R. W., Gambach, J., & Vicari, S. (1992). The executive board system: An innovative approach to cognitive–behavioral rehabilitation in patients with traumatic brain injury. In C. J. Long & L. K. Ross (Eds.), *Handbook of head trauma: Acute care to recovery* (pp. 219–230). New York: Plenum.

Zimmerman, R. A., Bilaniuk, L., Hackney, D. B., Goldberg, H. I., & Grossman, R. I. (1986). Head injury: Early results of comparing CT and high-field MRI. *American Journal of Neuroradiology, 7,* 757–764.

CHAPTER 3

ALZHEIMER'S DISEASE AND VASCULAR DEMENTIA

Sara Jo Nixon

It is estimated that 20% of the U.S. population will be over 65 years of age by 2030 (P. C. Albert & Albert, 1984). The increasing number of older adults creates a growing need to examine mental health issues of specific concern to this group. Of particular concern to older people as well as their families are the etiology, clinical symptomatology, treatment, and prognosis of cognitive and intellectual decline often associated with aging. It has been estimated that as many as 10% to 20% of people over the age of 65 may be affected by chronic brain syndromes (Ban, 1978; Brody, 1982). This estimate rises to 25% when individuals over the age of 80 are considered separately (Hooper, 1992). Given the difficulty in identifying and examining such patients, this estimate may be quite conservative. Terry and Katzman (1983) reported that as many as 4 million Americans have an intellectual impairment severe enough to meet the criteria for dementia.

In this chapter, I address many aspects of dementia. First, I present general information relevant to the topic. This is formatted as a general overview, discussing criteria and types of dementia, and is followed by a brief discussion of epidemiology and survival rates. Next, I detail genetic and other proposed etiological factors of dementia. This is followed by a discussion addressing clinical symptomatology across a variety of neuropsychological and behavioral domains. I then turn to a discussion of pathophysiology and outline treatment and family support issues, respectively, in the next two parts of the chapter. Next, I detail diagnostic and assessment issues, presenting several exhibits and tables that outline this process as well as representative instruments that are used. I conclude with two case histories and a brief summary.

OVERVIEW

It is important to note that "dementia" is a syndrome consisting of disturbances in distinct intellectual functions. The cardinal symptom of dementia is memory loss, but other functions are also affected. Other affected areas include orientation, abstraction and problem solving, judgment, visual–spatial performance, and language, as well as changes in personality and emotionality.

There are several diseases that produce primary degenerative dementias. These include Pick's disease, Wilson's disease, Creutzfeldt–Jakob disease, and dementia of the Alzheimer's type (DAT). It has been estimated that at least 50% of all dementia cases can be accounted for by DAT (Alexopoulos & Mattis, 1991; Chui, 1989; Mesulam, 1985; Van Dijk, Dippel, & Habbema, 1991).

The earlier literature attempted to subtype DAT on the basis of age of symptom onset, *presenile* cases being those cases presenting prior to the age of 65 and *senile* cases being those presenting after age 65. Recent work has suggested that these subtypes do not constitute separate disease entities; that is, they may not represent differential etiologies or outcomes. However, some data suggest that age of onset (early vs. late) may be associated with differential heritability risk and rapidity of disease progression (Friedland, 1988; Lishman, 1987) as well as differential loss of specific neurotransmitter function

(Sparks et al., 1992). I examine these potential differences later in the discussion on genetics and subtypes. Except where specific differences are being examined, *DAT* is used throughout this chapter to refer to both late and early onset cases.

Multi-infarct dementia (MID) constitutes the second most common source of dementia. MID is generally assumed to account for approximately 4%–23% of observed dementia (Alexopoulos & Mattis, 1991; Katzman, Lasker, & Bernstein, 1988; Larson, Reifler, Featherstone, & English, 1984). However, Kase (1991) has suggested that MID is frequently overestimated and proposed that a more accurate estimate may be 10%. Furthermore, Hachinski (1991) has recently suggested that MID may not be the "only or even the most important form of vascular dementia" (p. 64).

Because of its vascular origin, MID has been referred to as *vascular* or *arteriosclerotic dementia*. The underlying assumption of this is that the dementia is produced by a generalized atherosclerosis of all cerebral vessels. However, some neuropathological studies have revealed specific multiple infarcts (Hachinski, 1991; Sadock, 1980). This controversy regarding appropriate terminology was apparently resolved in the fourth edition of the *Diagnostic and Statistical Manual of Mental Disorders* (*DSM-IV*; American Psychiatric Association [APA], 1994) with the adoption of the term *vascular dementia* (VD). Therefore, I have used this term in the current chapter.

Some researchers have suggested that a useful subtyping of VD might be made on the basis of location of the infarcts. For instance, dementia accompanying cortical insult might be referred to as *cortical atherosclerotic dementia* (CAD), whereas dementia associated with subcortical insult would be called *subcortical arteriosclerotic dementia* (SAD; Chui, 1989). These subtypes are not yet widely used. However, they do provide a framework for future research.

Much of the research on dementia has used combined samples of DAT, VD, and mixed (VD–DAT) patients. No doubt some of this mixing has occurred as a result of the difficulty of appropriately diagnosing the two types of dementia until death (Mendez, Mastri, Sung, & Frey, 1992). Studies have suggested that, despite differences in etiology, there are considerable similarities in the two disease states. Therefore, in this chapter, I discuss the two types of dementia together, making distinctions where appropriate.

Criteria for the diagnosis of DAT and VD, as they are depicted in the *DSM-IV*, are outlined in Exhibit 1.

EXHIBIT 1

Diagnostic Criteria for Dementia of the Alzheimer's Type and Vascular Dementias

Common characteristics

I. The development of multiple cognitive deficits manifested by
   - A. memory impairment (an inability both to learn new information and to recall old information) and
   - B. at least one of the following:
     1. aphasia
     2. apraxia
     3. agnosia
     4. disturbances in executive functioning.

II. The cognitive deficits must
   - A. cause significant impairment in social or occupational functioning and
   - B. represent a significant decline from previous levels.

III. Deficits do not occur exclusively during the course of delerium.

Differentiating characteristics

Dementia of the Alzheimer's type:

- gradual onset
- continuing decline

Vascular dementias:

- evidence of focal signs or symptoms or laboratory evidence of cerebral vascular disease.

From Diagnostic and Statistical Manual of Mental Disorders *(4th ed., pp. 142–144), by the American Psychiatric Association, 1994, Washington, DC: Author. Copyright 1994 by the American Psychiatric Association. Adapted with permission.*

The common criteria are presented first, followed by those criteria that apply differentially to each. It should be noted that, in both cases, other suspected confounding conditions must be assessed and treated. This process results in DAT being a diagnosis made by elimination.

EPIDEMIOLOGY AND SURVIVAL

As noted above, it has been estimated that at least 10% of people over the age of 65 have significant intellectual decline (Brody, 1982). More than 50% of these dementias are believed to be of the Alzheimer type, and as many as approximately 20% are VD (Mahendra, 1987), although some believe this estimate is too high (Kase, 1991). The remaining are mixed or are the result of other disease processes.

In a recent prevalence study, prevalence rates for dementia were 30.5 in 1,000 for men and 48.2 in 1,000 for women. The increased risk for women was significant in the older age range (over 75 years), with the odds ratio being 1:8 (Bachman et al., 1992). Other studies have failed to find this sex difference (Farrer, O'Sullivan, Cupples, Growdon, & Myers, 1989; Schoenberg, Anderson, & Haerer, 1985). When sex differences are observed, they may be due to differences in the constituencies of the samples. Specifically, the differential sex ratio is higher if only DAT cases are considered (Bachman et al., 1992). Whereas some researchers have indicated that equal numbers of men and women are affected by VD (Lishman, 1987), others have suggested a male predominance (see Kase, 1991). Estimates of life expectancy after diagnosis range from 2 to 15 years (Barclay, Zemcov, Blass, & Sansone, 1985; Lishman, 1987). It is generally assumed that disease progression is slower in VD than in DAT (Lishman, 1987). However, some research suggests either equal or shorter survival rates for those with VD (Barclay et al., 1985; Hier, Warach, Gorelick, & Thomas, 1989; D. C. Martin, Miller, Kapoor, Arena, & Baller, 1987).

Van Dijk and colleagues (1991) reviewed 41 articles on survival in dementia. Summarizing 2-year survival data, they found that survival rates for DAT and VD were quite similar. Perhaps not surprisingly, survival rates were quite different for outpatients than for nursing home residents. Seventy-five percent (range = 60%–95%) of the outpatients were still living at the 2-year assessment, whereas only 50% (range = 30%–65%) of the nursing home residents had survived. In nursing homes, women, with an average survival rate of 60%, had better prognoses than did men, who had an average survival rate of only 40%. These studies also revealed that patients with dementia have reduced survival rates in comparison with age- and sex-matched populations. Interestingly, Van Dijk et al.'s review did not suggest increased survival rates in recent decades for patients who have dementia.

GENETICS AND OTHER ETIOLOGIES

Genetics

Sporadic cases are the most frequently occurring type of DAT (Hardy & Higgins, 1992). It is difficult to separate the sporadic from the familial late-onset cases because of the unavailability of family members, so researchers often combine epidemiological data of the two groups, using the age of onset as the criterion variable. Using this method, sporadic and familial late-onset cases constitute at least 70% of the cases of dementia (Hooper, 1992).

Genetic-familial influences are, however, strongly indicated in DAT (Heyman et al., 1984; Hofman et al., 1989; R. L. Martin, Gerteis, & Gabrielli, 1988). In fact, in a recent report on risk factors for DAT, Mendez and colleagues (Mendez, Underwood, et al., 1992) found that 33% of DAT patients had a first-degree relative with dementia, in comparison with only 21% of non-DAT patients with dementia and 12% of unaffected older people. Risk appears to increase to approximately 40 times control values when a person has two or more relatives affected by dementia (Hofman et al., 1989).

Although some studies have suggested that early onset DAT may be more likely to be determined by genetic factors than late-onset DAT, other studies have not supported this conclusion. Recent studies on relative risk in first-degree relatives of patients with DAT have indicated significant risk increases across a wide range of onset ages (Hofman et al., 1989; R. L. Martin et al., 1988; Mendez, Underwood, et al., 1992; Mohs, Breitner, Silverman, & Davis, 1987).

Consistent with an autosomal dominant inheritance, risk is reportedly greater for first-degree relatives in comparison with second-degree relatives and for siblings as opposed to other first-degree relatives (Amaducci et al., 1986). However, a recent study of twins failed to support this hypothesis. This study found that the concordance rate for DAT was approximately 40% for both monozygotic and dizygotic twins (Nee et al., 1987). Thus, it is likely that DAT is not a homogeneous disorder arising from an autosomal dominant allele. More likely, there are several contributing factors that may form the basis of meaningful subtypes (Hooper, 1992).

Subtypes

There is continued interest in defining DAT subtypes. It is assumed that the development of meaningful subtypes may lead to differential treatment as well as to preventive regimens. As mentioned above, one of the first DAT typologies considered was based on the age of symptom onset. Researchers have found early onset cases to be associated with (a) increased reductions in choline acetyltransferase and acetylcholinesterase (Arai, Ichimiya, Kosaka, Moroji, & Iizuka, 1992; Sparks et al., 1992); (b) increased reductions in serotonin and norepinephrine (Arai et al., 1992); (c) increased aluminum absorption (Taylor et al., 1992); (d) differential involvement of white matter (Scheltens et al., 1992); and (e) differential clinical presentation and progression (Blennow, Wallin, Uhlemann, & Gottfries, 1991; Burns, Jacoby, & Levy, 1990).

It has also been observed that the genetic loci for late and early onset may be dissimilar (Roses et al., 1990). Recent research suggests that three genes—one located on Chromosome 21, one on Chromosome 14, and another unmapped—are closely associated with early onset familial DAT. Late-onset and sporadic cases appear to be linked to a location on Chromosome 19 (Hooper, 1992).

Other Subtypes

Friedland (1988) outlined five possible systems of classification for DAT subtypes: (a) inheritance (familial vs. sporadic), (b) age of onset and progression, (c) dosage (aberration) of Chromosome 21, (d) the presence or absence of motor signs, and (e) behavioral features (predominantly right or left or symmetrical impairment). Because items A and B were discussed above, the following discussion is limited to Items C–E.

Dosage of Chromosome 21. There is a considerable literature examining the relationship of DAT and Chromosome 21. Some of this work has shown an increased incidence of Down's syndrome in the families of patients with DAT (Heyman et al., 1983, 1984). Furthermore, it has been shown that virtually all people with Down's syndrome that are 35–40 years of age and older develop the pathological evidence of DAT. However, they do not necessarily develop the behavioral concomitants (Ball, Schapiro, & Rapoport, 1986; Wisniewski, Wisniewski, & Wen, 1985). Chromosomal analyses have suggested that a restriction-fragment polymorphism from Chromosome 21 may segregate with DAT in some cases (St. George-Hyslop et al., 1987, 1990). Lishman (1987) reviewed literature suggesting that a dysfunction of microtubules may be the unitary defect resulting in the meitotic nondisjunction producing Down's syndrome as well as in the immunoproliferative disorders that are more common in families with a history of DAT.

Recent studies, however, have produced contradictory evidence regarding the role of Chromosome 21 (Roses et al., 1990; Schellenberg et al., 1988). It is now established that beta-amyloid, its protein precursor, or both are involved in DAT. Interestingly, the genetic coding for its precursor protein is located on Chromosome 21 (Tanzi et al., 1987). I discuss beta-amyloid below in my examination of biological changes.

Presence or absence of motor signs. A substantial number of patients who have DAT experience problems in motoric functioning relatively early in the disease process. Patients with extrapyramidal or myoclonus symptomatology have been shown to have reduced homovanillic acid and reduced biopterin when compared with DAT patients without motor-functioning problems (Kaye, 1988). This change suggests dopamine-function disruption in certain DAT groups. Given the evidence about age of onset, it is notable that patients with myoclonus, but no extrapyramidal signs, had younger ages of onset than other DAT patients. DAT patients with both myoclonus and extrapyramidal signs also had reduced levels of 5-HIAA, the primary metabolite of serotonin. It has been suggested that the presence versus absence of motor signs might be useful not only in predicting disease progression but also in identifying useful treatment interventions (Kaye, 1988).

Behavioral features. Behavioral features in DAT patients may be used to divide patients into groups exhibiting primarily visuospatial defects, primarily verbal–linguistic deficits, or deficiencies in both areas (Friedland, 1988). However, these behavioral distinctions are probably not independent of other variables. Specifically, verbal–linguistic deficits have been associated with younger onset and greater heritability (Breitner & Folstein, 1984; McDonald, 1969). Thus, it is unlikely that behavioral features per se will serve as the underlying factor in the development of meaningful subtypes.

Other Etiologies

There has been considerable research on factors other than genetics that may increase risk for DAT. A wide range of variables—including history of alcoholism, viral exposure, aluminum levels, head trauma, use of analgesics, levels of physical activity, cigarette smoking, animal contacts, and nose picking—have been examined (Hebert et al., 1992; Henderson et al., 1992; Heyman et al., 1984; Van Duijn et al., 1992). Few have proven very useful.

Occasionally, there have been data suggesting the viral transmission of DAT (Crapper-McLachlan & DeBoni, 1980). However, most research has failed to support this hypothesis (Goudsmit et al., 1980; Lishman, 1987).

Aluminum levels are often elevated in DAT patients (Candy et al., 1986; Lishman, 1987). Whereas earliest studies suggested a relationship between these levels and degree of cognitive compromise (Crapper, Krishman, & Quittkat, 1976), later studies failed to support this finding (McDermott, Smith, Iqbul, & Wisniewski, 1979). However, there is an apparent renewed interest in the possible role of cerebral aluminum in specific subtypes of DAT (Martyn et al., 1989; Taylor et al., 1992).

Iron levels are also increased in DAT patients, particularly in parietal areas (Drayer, 1985, 1987). Currently, it is presumed that this accumulation is the result of the disease process rather than its cause.

Some data suggest that female patients with DAT are more likely to have had thyroid disease than are women without DAT (25% vs. 7.1%; Heyman et al., 1984). There are also data that suggest an increased risk for DAT in individuals who have head injuries, particularly if the event occurred recently (Heyman et al., 1984; Van Duijn et al., 1992). However, these findings have not been consistently observed. Mendez and colleagues (Mendez, Underwood, et al., 1992) reported no greater incidence of alcoholism, psychiatric illness, electroconvulsive shock therapy, heart disease, cerebrovascular disease, hypertension, diabetes, thyroid disease, familial Down's syndrome, or head trauma in DAT patients in comparison with non-DAT patients.

CLINICAL SYMPTOMATOLOGY

It has been accurately stated that behavioral heterogeneity is the hallmark of DAT (Koss, 1988). Patients present with a variety of signs and symptoms. The most consistently observed deficit in DAT is the gradual deterioration in all aspects of psychological functioning, including failure in memory function (particularly the failure to register information), deterioration in intellectual functioning (most evident in nonroutine activities), and emotional and personality changes (Chui, 1989; Lishman, 1987).

Certain studies have indicated visuospatial dysfunction early in the disease (Crystal, Horoupian, Katzman, & Jotkowitz, 1982; Teng, Chui, Schneider, & Metzger, 1987). Linguistic problems unaccompanied by significant memory problems have also been reported (Kirshner, Webb, Kelly, & Wells, 1984). Significant problems involving aphasia, apraxia, or agnosia, however, generally appear later in the process (Chui, 1989).

Extrapyramidal, parkinsonian motor signs are observed in approximately 30% of DAT patients (Chui, Teng, Henderson, & Moy, 1985; Mayeux, Stern, & Spanton, 1985). Myoclonus is reported in about 10% of DAT patients (Hauser, Morris, Heston, & Anderson, 1986). These motor symptoms may coexist (Kaye, 1988). Epileptic seizures may also be reported (Lishman, 1987).

One of the primary clinical features for distinguishing between VD and DAT is assumed to be the nature of symptom onset. In contrast to DAT, VD is generally assumed to proceed in an abrupt, stepwise fashion. Progression of VD is often characterized by a fluctuating course, a history of hypertension and stroke, evidence of associated arteriosclerosis, and focal neurological signs and symptoms (Chui, 1989; Hachinski et al., 1975). Furthermore, VD patients may be noted as suffering less global impairment and demonstrating differential involvement of language skills (Kontiola, Laaksonen, Sulkava, & Erkinjuntti, 1990; Roberts, McGeorge, & Caird, 1978).

Recent studies have suggested that some of these clinical assumptions must be reconsidered. Zubenko (1990) found that stepwise progression was observed in only 6 of the 40 dementia patients (15%) who experienced multiple cerebral infarctions. Similarly, Fischer and colleagues (Fischer, Gatterer, Marterer, Simanyi, & Danielczyk, 1990) found that, although abrupt onset and stepwise deterioration could be used to exclude the clinical diagnosis of DAT, VD could not be excluded on the basis of the absence of these characteristics. Interestingly, approximately 50% of their VD patients failed to show the "typical" abrupt onset and stepwise deterioration. They concluded that the stepwise course may be more useful when considering late as opposed to early VD patients.

Cognitive and Neuropsychological Changes

Although general intellectual deterioration is the cognitive hallmark of DAT, nonverbal measures appear to be affected to a greater extent than are verbal measures. This differential effect is particularly evident in mildly and moderately affected cases (Chui, 1989; Eisdorfer & Cohen, 1980; Friedland, 1989; Jacoby & Levy, 1980).

The literature suggests that one of the aspects of cognitive performance useful in distinguishing between VD and DAT patients involves language and speech (Heindel, Salmon, & Butters, 1993). Specifically, Powell, Cummings, Hill, and Benson (1988) found that VD patients were more impaired than DAT patients in the mechanics of speech (i.e., pitch, rate, articulation, and melody). However, patients who had DAT were more impaired on the linguistic features of speech: the information content of spontaneous speech and confrontation naming. Fischer, Marterer, and Danielcyzk (1990) found that right–left disorientation was related to language and visual–spatial dysfunction depending on the location of the lesion for patients with VD, but that this was unrelated to such measures for patients with DAT.

In a recent study, Kontiola et al. (1990) compared the performance of 33 DAT patients, 52 VD patients, and 86 elderly community residents. All participants completed a test battery that was based on Luria's Neuropsychological Investigation (Christensen, 1975). The results indicated several conclusions. First, mild dementia was accompanied by small changes in abstract naming, fluency, understanding of complex structures, and verbal amnestic and conceptual processes. Second, patients with mild DAT were slightly superior to those with mild VD on understanding of phrases and grammatical structures and completion of a sentence. Third, patients with VD were superior to patients with DAT on understanding of temporal relations, complex grammatical structures, repetition of sentences, repetition of dissociative sentences and stories, and word span. Finally, factor analysis of the different stages of dementia indicated different patterns for the mild and severe groups. That is, the solution for the mild group was similar to that for the control participants, whereas the factor solution for the severe patients reflected the frequently observed diffuse language impairment associated with dementia.

Fuld (1984) developed a profile from the Wechsler Adult Intelligence Scale–Revised (WAIS-R; Wechsler, 1981) to differentiate VD and DAT patients. According to her data, the profile presented below was observed in approximately 50% of the DAT patients but only 7% of the VD patients.

> A (mean of Information and Vocabulary subtests) > B (mean of Similarities and Digit Span subtest scores) > C (mean of Digit Symbol and Block Design subtests) ≤ D (Object Assembly subtest score)
>
> A > D

Later work has produced mixed, but primarily negative results (Brinkman & Braun, 1984; Logsdon, Teri, Williams, Vitiello, & Prinz, 1989). In a recent study, Gfeller and Rankin (1991) found that the Fuld profile was neither sensitive nor specific to DAT. Fifteen percent of the DAT patients and 12% of the VD patients demonstrated the profile. Gfeller and Rankin suggested that neuropsychological batteries are best used to identify the severity and extent of patients' deficits rather than as tools of differential diagnosis.

Mendez and Ashla-Mendez (1991) also examined differences between DAT and VD patients on a battery of neuropsychological tests. However, rather than including only the standard structured tests, they added two unstructured tests: the Cookie Theft Picture (Goodglass & Kaplan, 1972) and the Lezak Tinker Toy Test (Lezak, 1982). Consistent with much of the previous literature, the structured tasks revealed that the only significant difference between the groups was poorer memory performance by the patients with DAT on certain memory tasks. The unstructured tasks, however, revealed potential differences in the involvement of underlying processes. Specifically, these tests indicated fewer words per minute and fewer constructional assemblages by the group with VD. These data are consistent with the assumption that spontaneous behavior and behavioral initiation may be particularly impaired in patients who have VD (Ishii, Nishihara, & Imamura, 1986; Wolfe, Linn, Babikian, Knoefel, & Albert, 1990).

Task demands and dementia severity of participants contribute to the variability obtained across and within studies. For example, Duchek, Cheney, Ferraro, and Storandt (1991) administered the Associate Learning task from the Wechsler Memory Scale (WMS) to elderly control participants and DAT patients. Using the Clinical Dementia Rating Scale, Berg (1988) identified three subgroups of patients who had DAT: very early, mildly, and moderately impaired. Subjects were presented with the 10 pairs (6 related pairs and 4 unrelated pairs) under standard instructions and procedures. The results indicated that only the moderately impaired group failed to demonstrate any learning on the easy (related) pairs. On the difficult pairs, however, only the elderly control participants and the very early DAT group exhibited learning. This study was one of the first to demonstrate that repetitive presentation of material may enhance explicit memory function in milder stages of DAT.

Whereas most studies of explicit memory function reveal some level of impairment, studies of implicit memory, specifically priming, have produced mixed results (Heindel et al., 1993). *Priming* refers to the temporary and unconscious enhancement of performance through prior exposure to stimuli (Shimamura, 1986). For example, if shown the word *motel* in a likability task, subjects are more likely to complete the word stem *mot_* with the word *motel* during a later task. This enhancement occurs even though the subject is unaware of the relationship between the tasks (Graf, Squire, & Mandler, 1984; Warrington & Weiskrantz, 1968, 1970).

Two recent studies using patients with DAT have shown that they are less likely to complete word stems with previously presented words (Salmon, Shimamura, Butters, & Smith, 1988; Shimamura, Salmon, Squire, & Butters, 1987). Two other studies, using a lexical decision task rather than a word completion task, have also failed to show priming in patients who have DAT (Bondi & Kaszniak, 1991; Heindel, Salmon, Shults, Walicke, & Butters, 1989). Other forms of priming are also affected by DAT. Recent studies have shown that DAT patients perform inferiorly on semantic priming tasks (Salmon et al., 1988) and priming tasks using pictorial stimuli (Heindel, Salmon, & Butters, 1990).

On the other hand, Hartman (1991) and Nebes and colleagues (Nebes, Boller, & Holland, 1986; Nebes, Brady, & Huff, 1989; Nebes, Martin, & Horn, 1984) found that patients with DAT exhibit intact semantic priming, at least early in the disease process or in constrained contexts. It should be noted that patients with DAT in Hartman's study failed to use semantic information to generate expectations on the semantic priming task and only inconsistently used categorical information. Hartman has suggested that these impairments resulted from underlying attentional deficits.

Friedman, Hamberger, Stern, and Marder (1992) examined brain electrophysiology in DAT and control groups, using a repetitive priming technique. In this protocol, participants typically showed a larger positive response to the second presentation of words within a list in comparison with the first presentation (i.e., a "repetition effect"). Friedman et al.'s group data indicated that DAT and control participants showed similar patterns of electrophysiological responses in this paradigm; that is, as a group, the DAT patients showed the repetition effect. However, the effect was markedly reduced in the patients with DAT. Given the performance variability evidenced in this study and reported by others using related paradigms (e.g., M. Albert & Milberg, 1989; Knopman & Nissen, 1987), Friedman et al. suggested that a potential area for future research would be to identify characteristics of those people with DAT who demonstrate the repetition effect versus those who do not.

Procedural or skill learning and performance does not appear to be substantially affected by DAT, at least in earlier stages. For example, DAT patients have been found to exhibit essentially normal motor-skill learning (Eslinger & Damasio, 1986; Heindel et al., 1989). Finally, in some patients who have DAT, specific skills are preserved despite extensive losses in other areas (Beatty et al., 1988). A case study depicting this situation is provided at the end of this chapter.

Emotional and Personality Changes

Before marked intellectual deterioration is obvious in dementia, significant emotional changes often occur. These include depression, anxiety, irritability, agitation, loss of interest, withdrawal, and somatic complaints (Lishman, 1987). Some of these changes accompany aging as well as other disorders, including pseudodementia, and increase the difficulty in making an accurate diagnosis of dementia versus affective disorders.

Depression is frequently reported in studies of VD. It has been estimated that as many as 66% of patients with VD demonstrate depressive symptoms. Another 25% meet the criteria for major depressive disorder (Cummings, 1988, 1989). Results of studies on the relationship between lesion location and depression in VD have been somewhat inconsistent (House, Dennis, Warlow, Hawton, & Molyneux, 1990; Robinson, Kubos, Starr, Rao, & Price, 1984).

Studies of depression in DAT patients are even less consistent. Cross-sectional studies have indicated that the frequency of major depressive episodes may range from 0% to 88% in DAT populations (Cummings, 1989; Cummings, Miller, Hill, & Nesnkes, 1987; Merriam, Aronson, Gaston, Wey, & Katz, 1988). Depressive symptomatology reportedly decreases with increasing severity of DAT (Fischer, Simanyi, & Danielczyk, 1990). It is thought that the cognitive devastation accompanying DAT may account for the reduced depression in later stages (Lishman, 1987).

Petry, Cummings, Hill, and Shapiro (1988) conducted a study of personality traits in 30 male patients with DAT and 30 male healthy older controls. They asked wives to complete the personality inventory developed by Brooks and McKinlay (1983) assessing personality change since symptom onset (for DAT patients) or retirement (for control participants). The inventory consisted of 18 adjective pairs describing a wide range of personality traits (e.g., down to earth vs. out of touch, relies on others vs. does things himself, energetic vs. lifeless, and cruel vs. kind). Brooks and McKinlay found that DAT patients showed significant changes on 12 of the 18 items, whereas control participants showed none. Specifically, patients were described as being less self-reliant, mature, enthusiastic, stable, kind, and generous; they were more out of touch, unreasonable, lifeless, unhappy, and irritable. The Mini-Mental State Exam (MMSE) was administered to assess severity. The only personality trait that correlated with MMSE scores was excitability; the more severely affected patients were more excitable. A stepwise discriminate analysis using a jackknifed classification indicated that two measures of change correctly assigned 96.7% of the participants to their groups (retirees vs. patients with DAT). These measures were self-reliance and down to earth. These findings are consistent with previous reports (Cummings & Benson, 1986; Rubin, Morris, & Berg, 1987) indicating widespread personality changes relatively early in the disease process.

Using the same instrument, Dian, Cummings, Petry, and Hill (1990) conducted a study of personality alterations in 20 male patients with VD. Comparisons between VD and control participants indicated significant differences on 12 of the 18 items. VD patients, as reported by spouses or daughter caretakers, were less energetic, practical, mature, enthusiastic, happy, self-reliant, generous, stable, mature, and talkative. Instead, they were more cruel and unreasonable. Control participants and VD patients did not differ on caution, irritability, excitability, temper, fondness of company, or affectionateness. Two of the measures were correlated with MMSE scores for the patients. As MMSE scores declined, they were seen as being less kind and less generous. These studies suggest considerable similarity between the personality alterations of those who have VD and those who have DAT.

Swearer, Drachman, O'Donnell, and Mitchell (1988) investigated the number and type of troublesome and disruptive behaviors in DAT, VD, and VD–DAT patients. Their analysis revealed three behavioral clusters: aggressive, ideational, and vegetative. Consistent with early work by Gustafson (1975), they found that aggressive behaviors were the most frequent. The three groups did not differ in these behaviors. The degree to which they were observed, however, correlated positively with the severity of the dementia. Emotional disturbances, primarily depression and anxiety, were observed in more than 60% of the patients. The degree of emotional disturbance was not correlated with severity of dementia. This pattern suggests that these emotional disturbances may exist as primary rather than secondary aspects of dementia. The absence of a significant correlation between emotional disturbance and severity of dementia has been reported by other researchers as well (Kaszniak, Wilson, Lazarus, Lesser, & Fox, 1981).

Psychotic symptomatology is highly variable in the dementias. In some reports, psychotic features such as delusions and hallucinations are very infrequent (Coblentz, Mattis, & Zingesser, 1973; Liston, 1979), whereas others report psychotic symptomatology in the majority of their patients (Goodman, 1953). These symptoms are not frequently reported in the early stages of dementia (Lishman, 1987). However, delusions and paranoid ideations have been noted as initial symptoms (Goodman, 1953; Ziegler, 1954).

DeBettigies, Mahurin, and Pirozzolo (1990) studied perception of daily living skills in VD and DAT patients. They found that DAT patients had significantly less insight than did VD patients regarding their impairment. This lack of insight was not related to age, education, mental status, or depression. Rather, it was positively related to the caregiver's perception of burden. These findings suggest an important interaction between patient and caregiver skill and capacity.

Prognosis

There have been many attempts to identify predictors of the progression of cognitive and functional dysfunction in patients with dementia. The list of factors that have been linked to faster progression includes age of onset (Huff, Growdon, Corkin, & Rosen, 1987), alcohol abuse (Teri, Hughes, & Larson, 1990), disease severity at first exam (Drachman, O'Donnell, Lew, & Swearer, 1990), hearing impairment (Uhlmann, Larson, & Koepsell, 1986), language impairment (Kaszniak et al., 1978; Knesevich, LaBarge, & Edwards, 1986), myoclonus (Mayeux et al., 1985), presence of motor signs (Mayeux et al., 1985), and psychoses (Stern, Mayeux, Sano, Hauser, & Bush, 1987). Unfortunately, the data regarding these variables are not entirely consistent.

In a recent study, Welsh, Butters, Hughes, Mohs, and Heyman (1992) tried to determine whether neuropsychological measures might be useful in detecting the presence of mild DAT and staging the dementia. They studied 147 DAT patients and 49 control participants, using the neuropsychological measures developed for the Consortium to Establish a Registry for Alzheimer's Disease. These data were consistent with data from their earlier work (Welsh, Butters, Hughes, Mohs, & Heyman, 1991), indicating that the most sensitive measure for detecting mild DAT was delayed recall. The only other measure that enhanced identification of mild DAT was confrontational naming. However, confrontational naming, by itself, had little predictive power. For staging the disease, they found a combination of variables to be most effective. This combination included measures of fluency, praxis, and recognition memory. These data are consistent with the clinical experience of finding early symptoms focusing on memory function and later symptoms involving lexical–semantic and visual–spatial processes.

Mortimer, Ebbitt, Jun, and Finch (1992) have also examined potential predictors of decline. They studied 65 patients with DAT, to varying degrees of severity, for up to 4 years. Their results indicated considerable variability in rates of cognitive and functional decline across patients and suggested the absence of a single pattern of progression for DAT. Although functional and cognitive decline were significantly correlated, 60% of the variance was unshared, suggesting that these areas may be subject to parallel, yet distinct, disease progression. Initial linear regression analyses indicated that some factors were related to both types of decline whereas others were differentially related to functional and cognitive progression. Functional decline was most strongly predicted ($p < .001$) by paranoid behavior, hallucinations, and activity disturbances during the first year of study. The presence of extrapyramidal signs and lower scores on nonverbal neuropsychological tests at the time of entry in the study also predicted faster functional decline ($p < .001$). Cognitive decline, on the other hand, was predicted most strongly by lower scores on verbal neuropsychological tests at first exam, more aggressive behavior, and sleep disturbances during the first year of study ($p < .001$). Follow-up stepwise multiple linear regressions indicated that lower scores on the verbal cognitive factor at entry, higher MMSE scores at entry, and younger age predicted increased rates of cognitive progression. This analysis, when applied to functional progression, indicated that higher scores on hallucinations, lower scores on the nonverbal cognitive factor at entry, and sex (i.e., being female) predicted faster decline. Mortimer et al. suggested that because hallucinations were unrelated to cognitive severity, patients who had hallucinations may have represented a subgroup of DAT with precipitous functional decline.

In the review conducted by Van Dijk et al. (1991), several indicators of poor prognosis in DAT and VD were noted. These predictors include physical problems and dependency, incontinence, electroencephalogram (EEG) abnormalities, lower scores on observational scales or tests, and hypertension.

Sleep disturbances may be particularly important in predicting progression (Aharon-Peretz et al., 1991; Bliwise, 1989; Bliwise, Tinklenberg, & Yesavage, 1992). In fact, sleep disturbances have been identified as a major factor in the institutionalization of patients with dementia (Pollak, Perlick, Linsner, Wenston, & Hsieh, 1990).

PATHOPHYSIOLOGICAL AND BIOLOGICAL ASSESSMENTS

DAT is associated with significant changes in the structure and function of the brain. The critical features for the histopathological diagnosis of DAT are the presence of neuritic plaques and neurofibrillary tangles. DAT is also accompanied by granulovacular change, atrophy, cell loss, and ventricular dilation. A patient's total brain volume may be reduced by 15% to 20% (Drayer, 1988). Among the more distinguishing features of DAT are the neurofibrillary changes throughout the cortex and the differential involvement of the temporal, hippocampal, and amygdala regions (Zimmerman, Fleming, Lee, St.-Louis, & Deck, 1986). Some researchers have, however, reported a differential involvement of the parieto-occipital lobes (Terry & Katzman, 1983). There remains considerable argument concerning whether the brain changes observed in DAT are qualitatively or only quantitatively different than those accompanying normal aging (Arriagada, Marzloff, & Hyman, 1992; Blessed, Tomlinson, & Roth, 1968; Winblad, Hardy, Backman, & Nilsson, 1985).

Neurotransmitter and Neurophysiological Function

Although the bulk of the early literature focused on the cholinergic system, it is now well recognized that DAT is a multiple neurotransmitter system disorder (Arai et al., 1992; Iizuka & Arai, 1990). There is a large literature addressing this issue, much of which is beyond the scope of this chapter. I therefore present only a brief summary of current research.

As noted above, loss of cholinergic function in patients who have DAT is well documented (Arai et al., 1992; Sparks et al., 1992; Sunderland et al., 1987; Winblad et al., 1985). There are significant reductions in both choline acetyltransferase and acetylcholinesterase in DAT patients relative to control subjects without dementia and VD patients (Perry, Gibson, Blessed, Perry, & Tomlinson, 1977; Wilcock, Esiri, Bowen, & Smith, 1982). It may be of some importance that recent data suggest a differential loss associated with age of onset. Specifically, earlier ages of onset are reportedly accompanied by greater loss of choline acetyltransferase (Arai et al., 1992; Sparks et al., 1992) and acetylcholinesterase (Sparks et al., 1992).

Loss of cholinergic function is largely consistent with what is known about the relationship among cholinergic function, cognitive performance, and neuroanatomy (see Bartus, Dean, Beer, & Lippa, 1982). However, some data are inconsistent with this presumed relationship. Specifically, Kish et al. (1988) examined patients with dominantly inherited olivopontocerebellar atrophy—a disease that produces cerebral cortical reduction in cholinergic function—and DAT. Members of both groups had equivalent levels of cholinergic function, yet those in the former group demonstrated little, if any, cognitive impairment. They also demonstrated no aphasia, apraxia, or agnosia. This finding, in combination with those indicating limited therapeutic effects of cholinergic agents (Bartus et al., 1982; Brinkman, Pomara, Goodnick, Barnett, & Domino, 1982; Mohs et al., 1985), raises critical questions concerning the role of cholinergic function in DAT.

Other systems compromised by DAT are serotonin (Arai et al., 1992; Tariot et al., 1987), dopamine (Sparks, Markesbery, & Slevin, 1986), norepinephrine (Arai et al., 1992; Bondareff et al., 1987), gamma-aminobutyric acid (McGeer, McGeer, & Suzuki, 1977), and the neuropeptide somatostatin (Crystal & Davies, 1982; Perry et al., 1981). Less consistently, alterations in substance P and glutamate, particularly N-methyl-D-aspartate (NMDA) function, have been observed (Maragos, Chu, Young, D'Amato, & Young, 1987; Meldrum & Garthwaite, 1990; Pomara et al., 1992; Porter, Cowburn, Alasuzoff, Briggs, & Roberts, 1992). The relationship between these changes and the cognitive decline accompanying DAT have not yet been defined.

Other neurophysiological changes have also been noted and merit further study. These findings include alterations in vasopressin-associated human neurophysin and oxytocin-associated human neurophysin (North, Harbaugh, & Reeder, 1992). Certain subgroups of DAT patients have also been found to have differentially higher concentrations of GM1 gangliosides (Blennow, Davidsson, et al., 1991). These findings could be predicted because DAT is characterized by progressive neuronal degeneration, and, therefore, one would expect a greater degree of cell turnover that, in turn, is accompanied by release of gangliosides (Doljanski & Kapeller, 1976).

Finally, alterations in levels of steroid hormones and cortisol have also been reported (Näsman et al., 1991; Rudman, Shetty, & Mattson, 1990) in both DAT and VD patients. It has been suggested that abnormal ratios of cortisol to certain adrenal androgens may differentially damage hippocampal cells (Sapolsky, Packan, & Vale, 1988).

VD is not associated with the same degree of neurophysiological alteration as DAT (Mann, Lincoln, Yates, Stamp, & Toper, 1980). Some studies have found decreases in choline acetyltransferase in VD patients (Crystal & Davies, 1982; Perry et al., 1981; Sakurada, Alufuzoff, Winblad, & Nordberg, 1990). Yet, other studies have failed to support this finding (Rinne, Säkö, Päljarvi, Molsa, & Rinne, 1988).

Other Changes

As reported previously, dementia patients also experience changes in the brain's electrophysiological responses (Friedman et al., 1992). Buchwald, Erwin, Read, Van Lancher, and Cummings (1989) found that the P1 component (a positivity that occurs approximately 100 ms after stimulus presentation) in auditory-evoked potentials was missing in patients with DAT. They suggested that P1 may be related to cholinergic innervation of the thalamus. Polich, Ladish, and Bloom (1990) observed longer latencies and reduced amplitudes for the P300 component (a positivity that occurs approximately 300 ms after stimulus presentation) in DAT patients in comparison with control participants. Studies of DAT patients have indicated that P300 may be modulated by the serotonergic system (Ito, Yamao, Fukuda, Mimori, & Nakanura, 1990).

Zubenko, Huff, Becker, Beyer, and Teply (1988) found that approximately 50% of the DAT patients they tested exhibited increased systemic platelet-membrane fluidity. Furthermore, those patients with increased fluidity demonstrated greater dissociation of dysfunction on tasks related to left–right parietal function. Increases in platelet fluidity were not observed for either depressed patients (Zubenko et al., 1987) or those with VD (Hicks, Brammer, Hymas, & Levy, 1987). In a later study, conducted by Kaakkola and colleagues (1990), significant increases in membrane fluidity were again observed in DAT patients. However, in this study, similar increases were also seen in VD patients. These later data suggest that membrane fluidity cannot be used as a specific biological marker for DAT.

Recently, considerable attention has been directed to the role of beta-amyloid and its protein precursor (APP) in DAT. It is well known that beta-amyloid is the primary constituent of the neuritic plaques and neurofibrillary tangles characteristic of DAT. What is unclear is whether beta-amyloid is a causative or a correlative agent in DAT (Hardy & Higgins, 1992; Hooper, 1992; Terry et al., 1991; Yanker et al., 1989).

There are also other alterations in protein function in DAT (Wolozin, Pruchnicki, Dickson, & Davies, 1986). Ghanbari and colleagues (1990) examined the concentration of Alzheimer disease-associated protein (ADAP), using the monoclonal antibody ALZ-50. Using this immunoassay, they were able to correctly classify 87.5% of the DAT patients, reporting no false positives. Increased levels of ADAP were not associated with age, severity of dementia, or the number of plaques. Later work by this same group confirmed the general findings (Bissette et al., 1991). Perhaps ALZ-50 or a related antibody will prove useful as a diagnostic tool or biological marker of dementia (Bissette et al., 1991; Selkoe, 1990).

In addition to the chromosomal abnormalities mentioned previously, there may be other changes in patients with dementia. For example, some researchers have observed chromosomal loss in DAT, but not VD patients (Jarvik, Altshuler, Kato, & Blumner, 1971; Nielsen, 1970). Some research has suggested a sex difference in this chromosomal loss, with women being particularly affected (Jarvik, Yen, & Moralishuili, 1974; Nielsen, 1968, 1970).

A host of biomedical tests have been used to examine DAT and VD. The list includes EEGs, tests of regional cerebral blood flow (rCBF), computed tomography (CT) scans, positron emission tomography (PET) scans, and magnetic resonance imaging (MR imaging) analyses.

EEG studies have shown generalized slowing in both VD and DAT patients. Patients with DAT show reductions in quantity of alpha, even early in the disease. This change is followed by alterations in the theta and delta frequencies (Lishman, 1987). Not surprisingly, focal abnormalities are more frequently observed for patients who have VD (Harrison, Thomas, DuBoulay, & Marshall, 1979; Lishman, 1987). The site of the abnormality tends to correlate with focal neurological signs (Lishman, 1987; Roberts et al., 1978). Martin-Loeches and colleagues (1991), using brain electrical activity mapping, found that alterations in the theta band may be useful in differentiating VD from DAT patients. Interestingly, they found no significant alterations in alpha waveforms for either VD or DAT patients.

PET studies, measuring cerebral metabolism, have indicated that VD is characterized by focal asymmetrical areas of abnormality. DAT, conversely, is characterized by hypometabolism throughout the brain, with the exception of primary sensory and motor areas (Benson et al., 1983). Particularly susceptible areas in patients with DAT appear to be posterior-temporal and inferior-parietal regions, and frontal areas also affected (Friedland, 1989). Data suggest that the frequently observed behavioral heterogeneity of DAT may be related to the differential involvement of specific brain areas (Friedland, 1989; Grady, 1988). Reports indicating relatively greater involvement of verbal and linguistic functions in DAT patients with left-parietal involvement and relatively greater visuospatial dysfunction in those with right-parietal involvement offer support for this hypothesis (Friedland, 1989). Some research suggests that the cortical abnormalities may antedate the observance of nonmemory neuropsychological deficits (Grady, 1988; Haxby, 1988).

Given the relative expense of PET, many researchers have made note of the fact that cerebral metabolism is typically coupled with cerebral blood flow and are using the less expensive single photon emission computed tomography (SPECT) scan to study brain function. Most of these studies have also observed reduced function (i.e., blood flow) in the temporoparietal regions of DAT patients, with more variable abnormalities in patients with VD (Hunter et al., 1989; Weinstein et al., 1991). Although some researchers have suggested that SPECT scanning be used to differentially diagnose VD and DAT (Sharp et al., 1986), other investigators do not currently support that application (Weinstein et al., 1991).

Earlier studies of rCBF using Xenon^{133} inhalation methods also noted significant decreases in DAT patients but less consistent results with VD patients (Lishman, 1987).

CT scans have revealed consistent cerebral atrophy with secondary enlargement of cortical sulci and ventricles. Hypodensity in the medial temporal lobe is often observed and is presumably related to hippocampal atrophy (Drayer, 1988). CT scans of patients with VD often reveal cerebral atrophy, with specific areas of low attenuations. Medial cortical atrophy may be evidenced as ventricular dilation, with small lacunar infarcts remaining undetected (Drayer, 1988).

Two types of white-matter changes have been noted. The first involves an examination of periventricular white-matter changes. The second refers to white-matter changes distant from the ventricles. Some investigators have referred to the latter changes as *leukaraiosis* (e.g., Lopez et al., 1992). Other researchers use leukaraiosis to refer to either type of change (Mirsen et al., 1991). This inconsistency complicates interpretation of results. However, it is evident that both types of alterations are frequently observed in VD and DAT populations. Mirsen and colleagues (1991) cited data indicating that 10% to 16% of healthy age-matched control participants exhibited leukaraiosis in comparison with 30%–33% of DAT patients. Percentages of VD patients showing white-matter changes ranged from 20% to 97%. Thus, it is obvious that results are highly variable and should be interpreted cautiously. Some studies have suggested that the degree of white-matter changes may be related to the degree of cognitive impairment (Diaz et al., 1991; Kato, Sugawara, Ito, & Kogure, 1990). Other studies, such as that conducted by Lopez and colleagues (1992), have found no relation between white-matter lucencies and cognitive function.

MR imaging studies have shown cerebral atrophy resulting in widened cortical sulci, the lateral and third ventricles (Drayer, 1988; Fazekas, Chawluk, Alavi, Hurtig, & Zimmerman, 1987). Although some studies have found that proton relaxation times are related to severity of dementia, other research has not supported this conclusion (Besson et al., 1985; Bondareff, Raval, Coletti, & Hauser, 1988; Christie, et al., 1988). The capacity of MR imaging to serve as a diagnostic tool is also not yet well established (Besson, Best, & Skinner, 1992; Davis et al., 1992; Drayer, 1988).

TREATMENT

The development of pharmacological treatments for DAT has received increasing attention over the past 15–20 years. Most of the focus has been directed to the role of the cholinergic system. Early studies examined the possibility that administering cholinergic precursors, agonists or antagonists, would affect performance (Bartus et al., 1982; Sunderland et al., 1987). Unfortunately, this work produced largely negative results (Bartus et al., 1982; Tariot et al., 1987).

More recent studies have examined the possibility of slowing cholinergic neuronal death through the administration of the calcium antagonist nimodipine (Ban et al., 1990; Branconnier, Branconnier, Walshe, McCarthy, & Morse, 1992; Scriabine, Schuurman, & Traber, 1989). Examining 178 patients with dementia, Ban and colleagues (1990) found that nimodipine-treated patients were significantly improved relative to those treated with a placebo on measures of memory, mental status, depression, severity of illness, social behavior, and overall impression. Although these data require replication, they suggest an important possibility for treatment development.

Other researchers have examined the possibility that drugs that stimulate use of acetylcholine (Villardita, Grioli, Lomeo, Cattaneo, & Parini, 1992) or inhibit its metabolism may enhance function (i.e., tetrahydroaminoacridine, or tacrine; Cohen et al., 1992; Eagger, Morant, Levy, & Sahakian, 1992). Generally, the findings have been mixed (Cohen et al., 1992; Eagger et al., 1992). However, the Federal Drug Administration approved the use of tacrine in spring 1993.

Other work has examined the role of serotonergic agents. Nyth and Gottfries (1990) found that citalopram, a serotonergic reuptake inhibitor, reduced emotional disturbances in patients with DAT but failed to elicit a positive response from those with VD. Neither group showed improvement in cognitive or motor functions. Olafsson et al. (1992) studied the effects of the serotonin reuptake inhibitor fluvoxamine. Contrary to their earlier findings, they found no significant benefit for either DAT or VD patients. However, there were trends favoring fluvoxamine on measures of emotional function.

Other researchers are examining the potential benefit of acidic phospholipids (Crook, Petrie, Wells, & Massari, 1992), monoamine oxidase-B inhibitors (Tariot et al., 1987), and nerve-growth factors (Everall & Kerwin, 1990; Saffran, 1992).

Some work on VD has suggested that cytidine, a naturally occurring pyridine-containing nucleotide, may improve cerebral function by enhancing cerebral metabolism (Gallai, Mazzotta, Firenze, Montesi, & Del Gatto, 1991). This study, however, focused only on brain electrophysiology and did not use neuropsychological testing. Black and colleagues (1992) studied the effectiveness of pentoxifylline, a methylxanthine used in the treatment of peripheral vascular disease. Their findings suggested that this drug may slow the progression of dementia in VD patients if there is "relatively clear-cut evidence of a cerebrovascular etiology, but not for those for whom the evidence of a vascular etiology is relatively vague" (pp. 241–242). Wade (1991)—in a brief review of VD and drug treatment—stated that there is no effective drug therapy, concluding that rational treatment must be centered on simply preventing recurrent ischemic episodes.

In summary, there are no established pharmacological interventions that consistently improve or maintain the cognitive function of patients who have DAT or VD. However, there are a number of potential compounds that may prove useful after additional research and with particular cases. Currently, effective pharmacological treatment is limited to the use of antidepressants, anxiolytics, and neuroleptics to address the psychiatric symptoms; antihypertensives and related medications to address the cardiovascular components; and tacrine to address cognitive impairment in some subgroups.

Because patients who have dementia may be compromised in their ability to report illness or discomfort, an important component of treatment is having family and support systems that are alert to such signs. Furthermore, patients need a balance of activities within a safe, structured environment.

Directly related to the decision regarding institutionalization of patients with dementia is the primary caregiver's capacity to continue in the caretaking role. Appropriate social agencies and physicians are critical components of the necessary support for caregivers, extended family, and friends (Powell-Proctor & Miller, 1982). Being aware of the burden created by serving as a caregiver is important in determining the need for additional support. Table 1, developed by Edwards (pp. 164–165; 1994), illustrates many of the factors that may affect perceived burden. Caregiving individuals with multiple risk factors for high perceived burden might be encouraged to participate in support groups, to identify back-up caregivers for time-out, and to develop coping strategies very early in their caregiving role.

In addition to assessing perceived burden, it is important that family and professional caregivers develop effective means of communicating with the patient. Table 2, adapted from the Alzheimer's Association's (1988) booklet and presented by Edwards (1994), provides specific suggestions regarding this issue. One of the primary messages conveyed throughout these suggestions is the need to focus on the individual, not the increasing disability, and to provide the opportunity for individual choice for as long as possible.

DIAGNOSIS AND ASSESSMENT

It should be reiterated that a clinical diagnosis of DAT is a diagnosis by exclusion. Technically, DAT can be diagnosed only at autopsy through the identification of neuritic plaques and neurofibrillary tangles. It is hoped that neurobiological tests will soon be available to provide accurate data for use in clinical diagnoses. In the interim, an accurate diagnosis of either VD or DAT requires a careful, thorough physical examination, including a complete medical history, with particular attention to substance use and abuse, head trauma, and head injury. Blood and urine tests should be included to assess the possibility of metabolic imbalances and infection.

The number of cognitive and behavioral assessment instruments being used by clinicians and re-

TABLE 1

Factors Affecting Burden in Caregiving for the Patient Who Has Dementia

Sources of burden	Possible reactions	Ways to handle
Roles played by caregiver:		
Directly related to giving care	Usually tolerated, although involves some stress	Analyze ability of patient and allow patient to use ability. Survey actual needs for patient's well-being and meet only these. Seek respite when overburdened.
Additional roles	Source of greater burden, and more difficult to accept if patient needs high level of assistance	Consider actual need for the role: Must it be done? Can someone else do it? Delegate to others when possible. Seek respite.
Age of caregiver	Younger persons find greater burden	Reduce number of multiple roles. Learn and use problem-solving skills. Do not give up all of one's own time. Seek and use respite.
Demands from patient:		
Disorientation Antisocial behavior	Burden created by conflict of past behaviors and present ones	Seek education about behavior changes. Use problem-solving techniques. Deal with pertinent behavior. Use respite.
Number of negative events during some time period, say, a week Undesirable nature of such events	Burden greater when perceived as "too many" and "too undesirable"	Examine nature of such events. Determine need for care. Concentrate on essential events. Determine why some tasks are so undesirable. Seek help. Use respite.
Sex of caregiver	Women may be more at risk of perceived burden than men.	Do not try to do everything for the patient. Arrange to get relief every day. Analyze tasks for essential needs of the patient. Meet essential needs. Use respite.

Note: From *When Memory Fails: Helping the Alzheimer's and Dementia Patient* (pp. 164–165), by A. J. Edwards, 1994, New York: Plenum. Copyright 1994 by Plenum. Reprinted with permission.

searchers is too large to review in this chapter. Therefore, only a brief description of the more frequently used tools and their primary references are provided in Table 3. The list is categorized on the basis of the major focuses of the instruments: global assessment of dementia and staging, cognitive functions, and behavioral skills and affect. Interested readers are encouraged to consult publications by Kluger and Ferris (1991) or by McDougall (1990) for more complete evaluations of the major instruments.

The primary scale for assessing VD is the ischemic score derived from the scale developed by Hachinski et al. (1975). This scale includes 13 items that are scored as either 1 or 2 (absence or presence, respectively); Table 4 shows this scale. Higher scores are associated with a greater probability of a dementia of vascular origin. Several revisions of the scoring criteria have been attempted (see Fischer, Jellinger, Gatterer, & Danielczyk, 1991). However, the most frequently used criteria assume that scores of 7 and above are associated with VD, scores of 4 and below are associated with DAT, and scores of 5 and 6 reflect mixed etiology. Given the number of mixed etiologies, the Hachinski scale's ability to discriminate between DAT, VD, and VD–DAT is an important issue. Fischer et al. (1991) concluded that this scale

TABLE 2

Techniques for Communicating With a Patient Who Has Dementia

Technique	Patient behavior	Caregiver response
Consistency	Reacts adversely to stimulation	Reduce or remove source
	Eats only a bite or two	Allow patient to stop, but bring back to table after a few minutes
	Reacts poorly to change in routine	Maintain regular schedule for as many activities as possible
	Unsure of time or place	Practice reality orientation
Calmness	Questions many statements	Repeat quietly and firmly
	Reacts with anger to some request	Keep voice low and calm; be rational but understanding
	Seems unsure and insecure	Talk in warm and encouraging manner
Reassuring gesture	Patient seems insecure and at a loss	Touch patient, holding hand or arm around shoulder
		Talk gently and calmly, smile, be relaxed
Keeping eye contact	Patient is disoriented	Look directly into patient's eyes while talking; smile to offer feeling of security
Use of voice	Needs understanding and communication	Use normal voice tone; do not be condescending; talk in a quiet place without distraction; show respect and acceptance
Keeping message simple	Patient does not understand	Use reality method with orienting information first; speak naturally, without hurrying
	Patient to be given instructions of some kind	Use one sentence for each idea; check understanding before proceeding
	Involvement to assure understanding	Have patient explain ideas; present this in a way that shows a need for help in understanding
Active listening	Patient is agitated, wants to express feelings or needs	Do not interrupt; signal acceptance of message by nods, or smiles when appropriate; repeat what patient has said when message is completed
Using distracters	Patient is demanding, unhappy, perhaps abusive	Listen and accept message, but offer some activity or distracter when message is completed
	Patient is bored, restless, overly dependent	Offer some favored activity or option; if necessary, try several
	Refuses to eat, or eats only sweets	Offer reward of sweets as meal is eaten, or with meal as option
	Refuses to bathe	Offer option of tub or shower; set routine time for bath, with reward to follow
Being punctual	Patient will not delay or wait	Keep routine in a consistent manner
	Patient left alone for period of time	Arrange for someone to keep contact
	Unfamiliar place, such as an office	Keep waiting time to a minimum; ensure that person has contact during wait

Note: From *When Memory Fails: Helping the Alzheimer's and Dementia Patient* (pp. 220–222), by A. J. Edwards, 1994, New York: Plenum. Copyright 1994 by Plenum. Reprinted with permission.

might be most useful as an exclusionary tool. It is sufficiently sensitive to vascular pathogenesis to warrant its administration to individuals being considered for DAT studies (e.g., those scoring above 7 would not be included). However, it is insufficiently sensitive to warrant its use to differentially diagnose. In fact, Fischer et al.'s data indicated that 21% of the DAT patients were falsely diagnosed as having VD. Perhaps not surprisingly, the most powerful discriminator on the scale was the "history of stroke" item. These data, as well as those summarized in the clinical symptomatology section, suggest the need for continued research regarding the development of a sensitive, yet specific tool for clinical administration.

To aid clinicians in selecting testing instruments, I present a list of the more frequently administered assessment instruments used at the University of Oklahoma Neuropsychology Laboratory in Exhibit 2.

TABLE 3

Instruments Frequently Used to Assess Dementia

Category	Instrument and characteristics	Selected reference
Comprehensive dementia and staging	Blessed Rating Scales:[a] One of the most frequently used scales. Has major subscales examining dementia and information, memory and concentration. The Dementia scale includes assessment of daily living skills, personal habits, and personality.	Blessed, Tomlinson, & Roth, 1968
	Brief Cognitive Rating Scale. A multiaxial instrument assessing concentration, recent memory, past memory, orientation, and daily functioning and self-care. It excludes measures of mood changes and psychosis.	Reisberg & Ferris, 1988
	Clinical Dementia Rating. Describes five degrees of impairment within six categories of cognitive function: memory orientation, judgment–problem solving, community affairs, home and hobbies, and personal care.	Hughes, Berg, Danziger, Coben, & Martin, 1982
	Global Deterioration Scales. Assesses seven broad stages of cognitive functional decline. Stages range from 1 (*no impairment*) to 7 (*very severe cognitive and functional decline*). Particularly useful in discriminating normal to early impairment and delineating within severe range of impairment.	Reisberg & Ferris, 1985; Reisberg, Ferris, de Leon, & Crook, 1982
Cognitive	Cognitive Capacity Screening Examination. A 30-item questionnaire to ascertain presence of organic mental syndrome. It is not specific enough to differentiate etiology of dementia. Although frequently used, it is most useful as a measure of identifying intact subjects.	McCartney & Palmateer, 1985
	Dementia of the Alzheimer Type (DAT) Inventory. Assesses clinical signs and symptoms common in DAT, such as amnesia, aphasia, abnormal cognitive, motor, and visuospatial skills. Developed to distinguish DAT from other dementias.	Cummings & Benson, 1986
	Mattis Dementia Rating Scale. Assesses a wide range of cognitive abilities, including both verbal and motor perseveration and verbal and nonverbal abstraction and recent memory.	Mattis, 1976, 1988
	Mini-Mental State Examination.[a] Scores less than 23 are generally assumed to reflect dementia, unless patient has 8 or fewer years of education. Scores are subject to floor effect relatively early in DAT.	Folstein, Folstein, & McHugh, 1975
Affect and behavioral skills		
Affect	Beck Depression Inventory. Self-report questionnaire with 21 items assessing vegetative, behavioral, and cognitive components of depression.	Beck, Steer, & Garbin, 1988
	Cornell Scale for Depression. Nineteen-item scale covering five areas: mood-related signs, behavioral disturbances, physical signs, cyclic functions, and ideational disturbances. Information is gathered by clinician after interview with patient and caregiver.	Alexopoulos, Abrams, Young, & Shamoian, 1988
	Dementia Mood Assessment Scale. Interview with 24 items developed in conjunction with the National Institute of Mental Health to assess mood in cognitively impaired patients. Intended for use at baseline and throughout drug treatment. Two subsections: Items 1–17 assess severity of depression; Items 18–24 assess severity of dementia. Information is collected from patient, caregiver, and staff.	Sunderland, Alterman, et al., 1988; Sunderland, Hill, Lawlor, & Molchan, 1988

(*continues*)

TABLE 3 (*Continued*)

Instruments Frequently Used to Assess Dementia

Category	Instrument and characteristics	Selected reference
Affect	Geriatric Depression Scale. Fifteen- and 30-item forms are available. It is an observer-rated scale developed specifically for evaluating depression in elderly people. It does not exclude vegetative or somatic symptomatology.	Yesavage, 1988; Yesavage, Brink, Rose, & Adey, 1983
	Hamilton Depression Rating Scale. Interview instrument (17 items) assessing severity of symptoms (both vegetative and somatic symptoms). Although often considered the "gold standard" for assessing depression, some studies have suggested it is relatively insensitive or is subject to inflated scores.	Hamilton, 1960, 1967; Lichtenberg, Marcopulos, Steiner, & Tabscott, 1992
Behavioral	Behavioral Pathology in Alzheimer's Disease. Completed by mental health professionals, the instrument charts behavioral symptoms in seven categories: paranoid and delusion ideation, hallucinations, activity disturbances, aggressive behavior, sleep disturbances, affective symptoms and anxiety, and phobic disturbances.	Reisberg et al., 1987
	Dementia Behavior Disturbance Scale. Assesses only observable behaviors, with emphasis on those related to caregiver burden. Includes eight items rated on 5-point scale, from 0 (*occurs never*) to 5 (*occurs all the time*). Examples include screaming for no reason, inappropriate sexual advances, and making unwarranted accusations.	Baumgarten, Becker, & Gauthier, 1990
	Neurobehavioral Rating Scale. Relatively new: A 27-item multidimensional observer-rated scale assessing severity of cognitive, psychiatric, and behavioral disturbances. It is not sensitive to disease etiology and is not a diagnostic tool. Initial research suggests it has reasonable construct validity and convergent validity. Comprehensive coverage plus easy administration and acceptable reliability may support its increased use.	Sultzer, Levin, Mahler, High, & Cummings, 1992
Daily living skills	Instrumental Activities of Daily Living Scale. Evaluates abilities in eight areas, such as preparing food, shopping, and taking medications. Available in both observer-rated and self-rated versions.	Lawton & Brody, 1969, 1988a, 1988b
	Katz Activities of Daily Living Scale. Evaluates physical activities of daily living. The six activities examined represent landmarks in self-care development (e.g., bathing, dressing, toileting, continence, feeding, and moving in and out of bed or chair).	Katz, 1983
	Physical Self-Maintenance Scale. Examines functioning in six physical areas: toileting, feeding, dressing, grooming, physical ambulation, and bathing. Available in both observer- and self-rated versions. It is the counterpart to the instrumental activities evaluated by the Instrumental Activities of Daily Living Scale.	Lawton & Brody, 1969, 1988c, 1988d

[a]Recognized by the National Institute of Neurological and Communicative Disorders and Stroke and by the Alzheimer's Disease and Related Disorders Associative Work Group as a useful aid in examination of dementia of the Alzheimer's type.

Of course, these instruments may be supplemented with others, as deemed appropriate by professional personnel. However, those listed provide a broad-based assessment of patient function as determined by both family and self-report while requiring minimal assessment time. It should also be noted that estimates of premorbid IQ may be used. Procedures for estimating premorbid IQ on the basis of demographic variables are outlined by Williamson, Scott, and Adams in chapter 2 of this book.

Exhibits 3–5 provide scoring information for each of the instruments listed in Exhibit 2. Few studies

TABLE 4

Hachinski Ischemic Scale

Feature	Score
Abrupt onset	2
Stepwise deterioration	1
Fluctuating course	2
Nocturnal confusion	1
Relative preservation of personality	1
Depression	1
Somatic complaints	1
Emotional incontinence	1
History of hypertension	1
History of strokes	2
Evidence of associated atherosclerosis	1
Focal neurological symptoms	2
Focal neurological signs	2

Note: From "Cerebral Blood Flow in Dementia," by Hachinski et al., 1975, *Archives of Neurology*, *32*, pp. 632–637. Copyright 1975 by the American Medical Association. Reprinted with permission.

EXHIBIT 2

Basic Assessment and Interview Instruments Used at the University of Oklahoma Neuropsychology Laboratory

Individual assessment

Memory function:

Wechsler Memory Scale or
Wechsler Memory Scale–Revised (Wechsler, 1945, 1987)
- Logical Memory
- Visual Reproduction
- Both immediate and 30-minute-delayed testing

Dementia assessment:

Dementia Rating Scale (Mattis, 1988)

Affective assessment:

Geriatric Depression Scale (Parmelee, Lawton, & Katz, 1989; Yesavage, Brink, Rose, & Adey, 1983; Yesavage, Brink, Rose, Lum, et al., 1983)

Familial assessment

General functioning:

Functional Rating Scale (Hutton, 1985)

Cognitive assessment:

Cognitive Behavior Rating Scales (Williams, 1987)

Interview instruments

Cardiovascular effects:

Ischemia Rating Scale (Hachinski et al., 1975)

Overall dysfunction:

Global Deterioration Scale (modified; Reisberg & Ferris, 1985)

have published data on individuals over the age of 74 from the revised WMS; exceptions include the work of Ivnik et al. (1992a, 1992b) and Cullum, Butters, Tröster, and Salmon (1990). The scores provided in Exhibit 3 were obtained from the work of Cullum et al. These data were selected because they were divided by subtest, with both mean raw scores and standard deviations provided. Having these subtest scores available facilitates interpretation, particularly if only the indicated subtests are administered. If the entire battery is given, examiners might consult Ivnik et al.'s (1992a, 1992b) articles for discussions of indices. Only the scores from individuals over the age of 74 are presented in the Exhibits; standard norms may be used for younger subjects. The mean age of individuals in this sample was 79.8 years (*SD* = 4.3 years; range = 75–95). Their mean level of education was 14.6 years (*SD* = 3.0 years).

Before presenting the case histories, I provide a summary of some relevant clinical issues regarding DAT and VD on the next few pages. Exhibit 6 outlines the general areas of inquiry for the family or caretaker of the patient who has dementia. In investigating symptom onset and progression, it is also useful to ask the family to identify some important events in the past year, 6 months, 1 month, and 1 week. These events may serve as time benchmarks and prompts for an assessment of memory impairment in later interviews with the patient, providing a gross index of current general memory. It is also important to determine to what extent the family be-

EXHIBIT 3

Scoring Criteria for Basic Assessment Battery, Individual Assessment Instruments: University of Oklahoma Neuropsychology Laboratory

Wechsler Memory Scale–Revised:[a]

	Raw score	
	M	*SD*
Logical Memory		
Immediate Recall	25.0	7.5
Delayed Recall	20.9	8.4
Forgetting–Savings	83%	18%
Visual Reproduction		
Immediate Recall	29.1	7.3
Delayed Recall	20.1	9.1
Forgetting–Savings	68%	25%

Geriatric Depression Scale:

Possible major depression: scores of 17 or above
Possible minor depression: scores between 11 and 16.9
Scores < 11 are not deemed clinically significant

Dementia Rating Scale:

Consists of five subscales with a total of 144 points
Normal elderly $M = 137.3$, $SD = 6.9$
2 standard deviations below mean = 123
Only initiation–perseveration scale differentiates mild dementia from normals: 2 standard deviations below mean = 29

[a]*Age range = 75–95 years.*

lieves that a patient's everyday activities, personal care, and social activities have been compromised. This information is relevant in determining an appropriate treatment plan and identifying support services for the family.

The chart described in the third part of the section on symptom onset may play an important role in eliminating minimization by the family as well as in clarifying contributing factors. Furthermore, the process of identifying the last period of "normal" functioning and tracing the decline until the present may be important in determining the family's awareness of the process and provide insight regarding their ability to provide support.

Table 5 provides a quick reference regarding emergency situations for patients with dementia. As the patient's ability to successfully complete daily living activities declines, these issues become increasingly salient. Making this information available in the form of a handout may be useful for family reference and discussion.

Progressive dementia's insult on the body and brain produces a need for increasing daily care. As the patient's cognitive functioning declines without initial decline in physical and motor skills, the opportunity for adverse consequences increases. Eventually, even if not initially so, the family is confronted with considering residential care. A number of factors influence this important decision: the availability and quality of in-home nursing care, the mental and physical health of available caretakers, and the availability of support persons and services for the caretaker. Some patients are maintained in family homes rather far into the disease process. Others are placed in residential facilities earlier in the process.

It is important that the process of residential facility selection be initiated early enough to provide the family with time to process the decision and make the selection without the burden of severe time demands. As the selection process is initiated, there are a number of issues that must be considered. Many of these issues are outlined in Exhibit 7 (taken from Gwyther, 1988). Although the patient's safety and well-being are the primary considerations, there are other factors reflecting the values of the family that will also influence the final decision.

A summary of general clinical issues relevant to both DAT and VD is provided in Exhibit 8. Details regarding these summary statements are provided in the text and in other tables or exhibits. Furthermore,

EXHIBIT 4

Scoring Criteria for Basic Assessment Battery, Familial Assessment: University of Oklahoma Neuropsychology Laboratory

Functional Rating Scale

Sum the scores (0–3) for each of 14 categories.
Total scores range from 0 to 42. Higher scores indicate greater dysfunction. Scale may be most useful as qualitative assessment of patient's relative strength and weaknesses.

Cognitive–Behavioral Rating Scale

Nine subscales with a total of 116 points.
Higher raw scores reflect greater impairment. Tabled scores are transformed *T* scores (*M* = 100, *SD* = 15).
Lower *T* scores reflect greater impairment. Raw score means and standard deviations for each of the subscales for persons between the ages of 60–69 years and 70–79 years are presented below.

	Age			
	60–69 years		70–79 years	
Subscale	*M*	*SD*	*M*	*SD*
Language Disorder	11.86	2.93	12.26	2.93
Agitation	10.14	3.02	10.63	3.06
Need for Routine	10.33	3.07	10.51	3.40
Depression	33.09	6.34	35.44	7.55
Higher Cognitive Deficits	16.80	4.30	17.78	4.00
Memory Disorder	28.43	7.63	31.57	7.77
Dementia	31.13	5.93	32.42	7.89
Apraxia	5.58	1.20	5.54	1.48
Disorientation	5.32	1.30	5.47	1.35

many of these issues are illustrated in the case histories given below.

Case Study: DAT

Demographics and background. Mrs. J is a right-handed, 72-year-old, White woman referred for neuropsychological testing at the request of a psychiatrist. She had completed 14 years of education (high school plus 2 years of college). Before retiring, she had worked as a part-time bookkeeper in the family business.

Mrs. J was accompanied by her son and daughter-in-law to the interview with the clinical neuropsychologist. She was cooperative and alert during the interview and test session. She was oriented to person, place, and time, although she was unsure of the date. Her mood was primarily serious, although she showed an ability to appreciate humor. She displayed mood-congruent affect.

Although admitting to recent problems with memory (over the past year), she denied a need for evaluation. She reported frustration with the memory

EXHIBIT 5

Scoring Criteria for Basic Assessment Battery, Interview Instruments: University of Oklahoma Neuropsychology Laboratory

Ischemia Rating Scale

Scores range from 0 to 18.
Scores ≤ 4 are generally judged to indicate nonvascular dementia.
Scores ≥ 7 are judged to likely reflect vascular dementia.
Scores of 4–7 indicate a clinical need for further assessment.

Global Deterioration Scale

Identifies seven stages of dementia; stages are progressive, ranging from no subjective or objective indicators of impairment to virtually complete absence of interactive and self-care behaviors.
Stage 1: No subjective or objective impairment.
Stage 2: Subjective reports of memory problems; no significant indicators on objective tests.
Stage 3: Early confusion—impairment may be limited largely to memory and concentration functions.
Stage 4: Late confusion—difficulty in complex tasks, denial of impairment, and social withdrawal.
Stage 5: Early dementia—some daily living skills compromised; emotionally labile.
Stage 6: Middle dementia—significant memory impairment (e.g., forgets name of spouse or children); daily living skills compromised; significant agitation and paranoia.
Stage 7: Late dementia—significant verbal and motor impairment (incontinence and absence of speech); eventual loss of all communicative (verbal and nonverbal) skills; loss of appetite.

problems, but used notes and lists to compensate. She indicated that she sometimes forgets where she places things, people's names, and why she went into a room. She reported no suicidal, homicidal, or paranoid ideations of hallucinations. She did indicate that she was lonely and more irritable and anxious than she had been in the past. She reported that she was not having problems with sleep or appetite.

Reports from her family indicated increasing problems with memory over the past 5 years. They estimated that her current level of functioning was 65% to 70% lower than it had been 5 years before. They reported that she repeats herself frequently, becomes easily confused, and has gotten lost at least once when driving. They noted that she has difficulty following conversations if there are distractions (e.g., television), loses her train of thought, confuses words, and experiences difficulty in remembering names. They confirmed that the primary change in affect was an increased irritability over the previous 5 years.

Mrs. J's son reported that in the previous 2 years she had occasionally worked as a cashier in retail stores. However, she had experienced difficulty in these jobs because of memory problems, such as leaving jewelry unlocked and placing unpurchased items in customers' bags. At one job, she had continued to return to work, forgetting that she had been fired.

Mrs. J's medical history was uneventful. She was taking estrogen replacement therapy and denied the use of other prescriptions or illicit drugs. She reported drinking approximately 4 oz. of vodka daily.

Neuropsychological assessment. Mrs. J was tested over the course of 1 day (for approximately 8 hr). The test battery included the WAIS-R (Wechsler, 1981), the WMS (Russell, 1975, 1988), the Wisconsin Card Sorting Test (Heaton, 1981), the Boston Naming Test (Kaplan, Goodglass, & Weintraub, 1983), and the Rey Auditory Verbal Learning Test (Rey, 1964), as well as others. Her performance on the WAIS-R indicated a Full-Scale IQ of 88, with a Verbal IQ of 87 and a Performance IQ of 93. In light of her educational achievements, this level probably indicates a lowered level of functioning. No significant depression or anxiety were observed with the Beck Depression Inventory and Geriatric Depression Scale. Her attention, concentration, and verbal and nonverbal memory abilities were moderately to severely impaired. Similarly, her performance on tests of new learning was impaired. Her conceptual shifting skills and nonverbal problem-solving and abstraction skills were also impaired. Her performance on visual–motor, visual–spatial, constructional, verbal abstract reasoning, and receptive and expressive language tasks were within normal limits. Her confrontational naming ability was in the borderline range. Her numerical reasoning and mental computational skills were below average.

These results are consistent with a diagnosis of DAT. Clinical recommendations included (a) attempting to reduce the reported loneliness through involvement in appropriate community activities and

EXHIBIT 6

Suggested Outline for Family and Caretaker Interview

A. Information regarding symptom onset and progression
   1. Specific changes. What changes have been observed in the patient? Are there specific areas of functioning that appear to be more affected than others (e.g., memory vs. language vs. motor function)? When were these changes first observed? How has the patient responded to these changes (e.g., denial, depression, or use of memory aids)?
   2. Possible contributing factors. Was the onset of symptomatology preceded by any illness, physical or psychological trauma (including falls, death of a friend or family member, and viral infections)? If so, what and when? Has the patient experienced any of these events in the past few months? If so, what and when? What medications does the patient take?
   3. Charting the pattern. Ask the family to indicate the most recent year in which the patient was functioning at 100%, then ask them to identify the current level of functioning (portion of 100%). Inquire about the pattern of decline over the time between 100% to the current level (steady decline, periods of stability, periods of recovery of function, etc.). Finally, identify any significant events that may have occurred during this period.

B. Family history

   Collect information regarding dementia symptomatology, cardiovascular disease, and psychiatric illness in primary and secondary relatives. Although knowledge of formal clinical diagnoses is important, observed patterns of symptomatology in close relatives who have not received such diagnoses may also be useful in clarifying confounding factors.

C. Support structure and general information
   1. Medical examination. A complete medical examination is essential. If it has not yet been conducted, its importance should be emphasized to the family. The need for coordinated efforts between mental health and general medical personnel should also be discussed.
   2. Family support. Lists of area support groups, assistance groups, and so on should also be made available to the family. Specific concerns may focus on dealing with emergency situations and eventual residential placement. Well-written, accurate resource books should also be identified (e.g., *Understanding Alzheimer's Disease*; Aronson, 1988). Exhibit 5 and Table 4 provide quick references for some of these issues.

TABLE 5

Emergency Situations for Patients Who Have Alzheimer's and Their Caregivers

Problem	Disposition	Preventive measure
	Patient emergencies	
Patient gets sick—fever, convulsions, heart attack, or stroke—or becomes injured.	Medical: family doctor, rescue squad, or hospital emergency room.	Have emergency numbers available. Have knowledge of first-aid measures. Make sure patient has regular medical care. Check environment for potential hazards.
Patient gets violent or uncontrollably agitated.	Medical: family doctor or hospital emergency room; may require police assistance.	Have emergency numbers available. Consult physician for medication and have it available. Keep environment calm.
Patient ingests poison or foreign object.	Medical: family doctor, poison control center, or hospital emergency room.	Have emergency numbers available. Keep poisonous substances in a locked cabinet.
Patient is abused by caregiver; patient gets hurt.	Medical: family doctor, hospital emergency room, or counseling for caregiver.	Have emergency numbers available. Seek counseling before this happens: professional or support groups.
Patient gets lost.	Social: family, friends, neighbors, social supports, police; use chapter, radio, TV, newspaper.	Have emergency numbers available. Get patient an ID bracelet. Put locks and alarms on doors. Do not leave patient alone.
Patient is victimized.	Social–legal: family, police, and legal intervention may be needed; conservatorship or guardianship; may need to involve protective services.	Have emergency numbers available. Consult an attorney regarding protecting patient's interests. Do not leave patient unsupervised. Do not allow patient to carry large sums of money, checks, or credit cards.
Patient gets arrested or accused of a crime.	Educational and legal intervention may be needed.	Have emergency numbers available. Close supervision of patient in public places.
	Caregiver emergencies	
Caregiver gets sick suddenly and cannot care for patient.	Family–social support: family, friends, neighbors to be contacted. Family doctor may arrange temporary hospitalization or nursing-home placement. Other respite services may be available.	Have important and emergency numbers available. Make arrangements in advance with friends and relatives. Check out temporary respite care available.
Caregiver is suicidal.	Medical: family doctor, hospital emergency room, or mental-health-crisis team. Arrange care for patient.	Have important and emergency numbers available. Seek professional counseling or support groups.
Caregiver dies suddenly.	Social: family, friend, neighbor, respite care. Arrange care for patient.	Have important and emergency numbers posted by telephone. Discuss emergency plans with relatives or friends. Have all information—people to call, or respite services—clearly outlined.
Nursing home tries to discharge patient for unmanageable behavior.	Social–medical: family doctor, counseling services for caregiver, ombudsman	Choose the proper long-term-care facility for the patient. Facility should be experienced in working with Alzheimer patients. Keep in contact with the staff—physicians, nurses, aides.

TABLE 5 (*Continued*)

Problem	Disposition	Preventive measures
	Urgent, but not emergency, situations	
Caregiver reports that patient has stopped eating and drinking.	Medical: family doctor or other source of medical care.	Have important and emergency numbers available.
Caregiver reports that patient has been having repeated falls.	Medical: family doctor or other source of medical care.	Have important and emergency numbers available.
Caregiver reports adverse drug reaction in patient.	Medical: family doctor or other source of medical care.	Have important and emergency numbers available. Know about possible side effects of medications.
Caregiver is at "wit's end."	Social–medical: family doctor, chapter, one-on-one support group, respite.	Seek professional counseling or support groups. Use respite services to give caregiver personal time.
Caregiver unsuccessful in leaving patient at hospital emergency room.	Social: planning and counseling with assistance of family doctor and counseling services. Temporary placement may help.	Use respite services regularly. Seek professional counseling or support groups.
Caregiver requires elective surgery or elective hospital admission.	Social: planning, temporary placement, or in-home respite to care for patient.	Make arrangements in advance for temporary placement.
Patient dies, and caregiver wants autopsy.	Medical: family doctor; refer to local support group representatives and ADRDA Autopsy Network.	Advance planning: Discuss with family members and contact ADRDA for more information.

Note: From "Emergency Situations for Patients and Caregivers," by E. S. Yatzkan. In *Understanding Alzheimer's Disease* (pp. 157–161), edited by M. K. Aronson, 1988, New York: Macmillan.

(b) reducing the amount of alcohol consumed. Although it was unlikely that reducing the alcohol consumption would significantly enhance the client's cognitive state, it might serve to protect her from alcohol-related trauma and accidents (head injury, etc.). Additional clinical recommendations included advising the family of support services, including adult day-care facilities and in-home support.

Case Study: Preserved Musical Skill in DAT

Demographics and background. Mr. T is a right-handed, 71-year-old, White man who was referred by a psychiatrist for neuropsychological evaluation. He had completed 15 years of education and was self-employed as a successful insurance executive. Information was obtained in interviews with Mr. T and his spouse. Medical records were also reviewed. Presenting complaints included memory problems, confusion, and irritability.

In addition to his spouse, Mr. T was also accompanied by his two adult daughters. He was well groomed, cooperative, and friendly. He was alert and oriented. His mood was predominately serious, and he reported some feelings of depression and sadness. He displayed mood-congruent affect and was able to appreciate humor. No suicidal, homicidal, or paranoid ideation was noted. He denied any history of special education or learning difficulties. It was noted that Mr. T's mother had dementia prior to her death.

Mr. T's medical history was positive for high blood pressure, heart murmur, occasional headaches, chronic hearing loss in the left ear, and sharp chest pains. He had undergone four major surgeries within the previous 3 years, exhibiting postsurgical delirium following the most recent surgery. Mr. T's recent EEG had been normal. MR imaging demonstrated mild cerebral atrophy, with some very subtle small-vessel change consistent with his age. No evidence of VD-related changes was noted.

EXHIBIT 7

Nursing Home Evaluation Checklist

General

	Yes	No
1. Does the home have a current license from the state?	___	___
2. Does the administrator have a current license from the state?	___	___
3. If you need and are eligible for financial assistance, is the home certified to participate in government or other programs that provide it?	___	___
4. Does the home provide special services, such as a specific diet or therapy that the patient needs?	___	___

Physical considerations

	Yes	No
5. Location		
a. Pleasing to the patient?	___	___
b. Convenient for patient's personal doctor?	___	___
c. Convenient for frequent visits?	___	___
d. Near a hospital?	___	___
6. Accident prevention		
a. Well lighted inside?	___	___
b. Free of hazards underfoot?	___	___
c. Chairs sturdy and not easily tipped?	___	___
d. Warning signs posted around freshly waxed floors?	___	___
e. Handrails in hallways and grab bars in bathroom?	___	___
7. Fire safety		
a. Meets federal and state codes?	___	___
b. Exits clearly marked and unobstructed?	___	___
c. Written emergency-evacuation plan?	___	___
d. Frequent fire drills?	___	___
e. Exit doors unlocked on the inside?	___	___
f. Stairways enclosed and doors to stairways kept closed?	___	___
8. Bedrooms		
a. Open on to hall?	___	___
b. Window?	___	___
c. No more than four beds per room?	___	___
d. Easy access to each bed?	___	___
e. Drapery for each bed?	___	___
f. Nurse call bell by each bed?	___	___
g. Fresh drinking water at each bed?	___	___
h. At least one comfortable chair per patient?	___	___
i. Reading lights?	___	___
j. Clothes closet and drawers?	___	___
k. Room for a wheelchair to maneuver?	___	___
l. Care used in selecting roommates?	___	___
9. Cleanliness		
a. Generally clean, even though it may have a lived-in look?	___	___
b. Free of unpleasant odors?	___	___
c. Incontinent patients given prompt attention?	___	___
10. Lobby		
a. Is the atmosphere welcoming?	___	___
b. If also a lounge, is it being used by residents?	___	___

EXHIBIT 7 (*Continued*)

	Yes	No
c. Furniture attractive and comfortable?	___	___
d. Plants and flowers?	___	___
e. Certificates and licenses displayed?	___	___
11. Hallways		
a. Large enough for two wheelchairs to pass with ease?	___	___
b. Hand-grip railing on the sides?	___	___
12. Dining room		
a. Attractive and inviting?	___	___
b. Comfortable chairs and table?	___	___
c. Easy to move around in?	___	___
d. Tables convenient for those in wheelchairs?	___	___
e. Food tasty and attractively served?	___	___
f. Meals match posted menu?	___	___
g. Those needing help receiving it?	___	___
13. Kitchen		
a. Food preparation, dishwashing, and garbage areas separated?	___	___
b. Food needing refrigeration not standing on counters?	___	___
c. Kitchen help observing sanitation rules?	___	___
14. Activity rooms		
a. Rooms available for patients' activities?	___	___
b. Equipment (games, easels, yarn, kiln, etc.) available?	___	___
c. Residents using equipment?	___	___
15. Special-purpose rooms		
a. Rooms set aside for physical examinations or therapy?	___	___
b. Rooms being used for stated purposes?	___	___
16. Isolation room		
a. At least one bed and bathroom available for patients with contagious illness?	___	___
17. Toilet facilities		
a. Convenient to bedrooms?	___	___
b. Easy for a wheelchair patient to use?	___	___
c. Sink?	___	___
d. Nurse call bell?	___	___
e. Hand grips on or near toilets?	___	___
f. Bathtubs and showers with nonslip surfaces?	___	___
18. Grounds		
a. Can residents get fresh air?	___	___
b. Ramps to help handicapped?	___	___
Services		
19. Medical		
a. Physician available in emergency?	___	___
b. Private physician allowed?	___	___
c. Regular medical attention assured?	___	___
d. Thorough physical immediately before or upon admission?	___	___
e. Medical records and plan of care kept?	___	___
f. Patient involved in developing plans for treatment?	___	___
g. Other medical services (dentists, optometrists, etc.) available regularly?	___	___
h. Freedom to purchase medicines outside home?	___	___

(*continues*)

EXHIBIT 7 (*Continued*)

	Yes	No
20. Hospitalization		
a. Arrangement for nearby hospital for transfer, when necessary?	___	___
21. Nursing services		
a. Is a registered nurse responsible for nursing staff (in a skilled nursing home)?	___	___
b. Is a licensed practical nurse on duty day and night in a skilled nursing home?	___	___
c. Trained nurse's aids and orderlies on duty in homes providing some nursing care?	___	___
22. Rehabilitation		
a. Specialists in various therapies available when needed?	___	___
23. Activities program		
a. Individual patient preferences observed?	___	___
b. Group and individual activities?	___	___
c. Residents encouraged (but not forced) to participate?	___	___
d. Outside trips for those who can go?	___	___
e. Do volunteers from the community work with patients?	___	___
24. Religious observances		
a. Arrangements made for patient to worship as he or she pleases?	___	___
b. Religious observances a matter of choice?	___	___
25. Social services		
a. Social worker available to help residents and families?	___	___
26. Food		
a. Dietitian plans menus for patients on special diets?	___	___
b. Variety from meal to meal?	___	___
c. Meals served at normal times?	___	___
d. Plenty of time for each meal?	___	___
e. Snacks?	___	___
f. Food delivered to patients' rooms?	___	___
g. Help with eating given when needed?	___	___
27. Grooming		
a. Barbers and beauticians available for men and women?	___	___
Attitudes and atmosphere		
28. General atmosphere friendly and supportive?	___	___
29. Residents retain human rights?		
a. May participate in planning treatment?	___	___
b. Medical records are held confidential?	___	___
c. Can patients veto experimental research?	___	___
d. Patients have freedom and privacy to attend to personal needs?	___	___
e. Can married couples share a room?	___	___
f. All have opportunities to socialize?	___	___
g. May manage own finances if capable or obtain accounting if not?	___	___
h. May decorate their own bedrooms?	___	___

EXHIBIT 7 (*Continued*)

	Yes	No
i. May wear their own clothes?	___	___
j. May communicate with anyone without censorship?	___	___
k. Are not transferred or discharged arbitrarily?	___	___
30. Administrator and staff available to discuss problems?		
a. Patients and relatives can discuss complaints without fear of reprisal?	___	___
b. Staff responds to calls quickly and courteously?	___	___
31. Residents appear alert, unless very ill?	___	___
32. Visiting hours accommodate residents and relatives?	___	___
33. Civil rights regulations observed?	___	___
34. Visitors and volunteers pleased with home?	___	___

Scoring

Generally, the best home is the one for which you check the most "yes" answers. However, different homes offer different services. You must decide which services are most important to you. If the answer to any of the first 4 questions is "no," do not use the home.

From "Nursing-Home-Care Issues," by L. P. Gwyther. In Understanding Alzheimer's Disease *(pp. 257–262), edited by M. K. Aronson, 1988, New York: Macmillan. Copyright 1988 by Alzheimer's Disease and Related Disorders Association. Reprinted with permission of MacMillan General Reference USA, a Division of Simon & Schuster, Inc.*

Mr. T reported that memory problems had begun 3 years before and had gradually worsened. He indicated that he had difficulty remembering names and details at work, but denied other work-related problems. Mr. T reported that he was still driving and that he considered himself a "good driver." However, he stated that he no longer played golf.

Mr. T's spouse reported that he had difficulty remembering to turn off appliances. She stated that he had poor memory for geographic directions, addresses, and frequently used telephone numbers. She also reported that he experienced word-choice problems and was having difficulty reading and completing household chores (e.g., setting the table). She indicated that he was easily distracted and confused, irritable, and slower in movement and thought. Mrs. T also reported that her husband frequently repeated himself. In contrast to his report, Mrs. T reported that Mr. T was a much slower driver and sometimes missed turns. She also explained that he had had difficulty tying his shoes and neckties.

At the time of interview, Mr. T was socially withdrawn and sleeping more. He reported frustration with his memory problems and sadness and worry about life. His main source of enjoyment was playing trombone. Mr. T has played with a jazz band for 28 years. He continues to play on a weekly basis. Objective assessments substantiated his wife's reports that he remains an excellent musician (Beatty et al., 1994).

Neuropsychological assessment. Mr. T's overall level of cognitive functioning was in the low average range, with a WAIS-R Full-Scale IQ of 81 (10th percentile), a Verbal IQ of 90 (25th percentile), and Performance IQ of 72 (3rd percentile). The difference between his verbal and nonverbal cognitive performance was significant. Given Mr. T's educational and occupational history, it appeared that there had been a general lowering of both verbal and perceptual motor skills, with particular loss in the area of nonverbal cognitive skills. Mr. T's overall cognitive performance on the Dementia Rating Scale was consistent with a diagnosis of dementia. He scored at the 82nd percentile in comparison with a sample of dementia patients his age. In short, Mr. T exhibited a pattern of performance consistent with a diagnosis of DAT across a wide variety of neuropsychological

EXHIBIT 8

Clinical Summary Notes: Assessing Individuals Who Have Dementia

Complete medical examinations and medical histories are essential aspects of the overall assessment. Histories of hypertension, treated or untreated, or other medical conditions should be carefully noted. Imaging techniques often indicate more focal abnormalities in patients with vascular dementia (VD). However, in isolation, these may not provide a clear distinction between those with VD and those with dementia of the Alzheimer's type (DAT).

The stepwise course of deterioration frequently associated with VD may not be accurate. Many patients with VD do not exhibit this pattern. Thus, the Hachinski Ischemic Scale may not be useful in discriminating a large number of DAT patients from VD patients.

Both VD and DAT patients exhibit significant personality change. However, insight and concern regarding cognitive and psychosocial problems is greater in the patient who has VD.

Depressive symptomatology is very common in VD and early stage DAT patients. Appropriate pharmacotherapy may be useful in reducing this depression. Both patient and family must be educated regarding potential side effects and drug interactions. The clinician must work carefully with the family to ensure compliance.

There is a substantial genetic-familial factor with DAT. Reports of dementia in primary relatives, particularly if multiple relatives or siblings are reported, should indicate the possibility of DAT.

The clinician should be open to the possibility of comorbid conditions. Specifically, mixed diagnoses of VD–DAT may be possible. Other conditions that affect cognitive function may, of course, also exist (e.g., hypothyroidism). Communicating with appropriate medical personnel is an important part of quality patient care.

The clinical neuropsychologist plays a critical role in the continuing care of patients who have dementia. This role includes helping the patient and family identify existing strengths, providing support and referrals, and helping the patient and family manage the psychological stressors accompanying DAT and VD.

tests, including the Luria three-step test (Christensen, 1975).

In Mr. T's situation, the more intriguing data were not those assessing his cognitive deficits. Rather, the more interesting findings were those indicating preserved function in musical abilities. As a part of Dr. William Beatty's ongoing work in preserved functions in DAT, Mr. T's playing ability and memory for musical information were assessed through the use of videotaping, audio taping, and memory tests (Beatty et al., 1994). One of the immediately notable observations was that Mr. T did not use sheet music or other memory aids during performances.

Evaluation of the quality of Mr. T's previous and present playing by laypersons and professional musicians revealed only very subtle changes in his playing over the past 25 years. Given the amount of time that had elapsed from the earlier recordings to the time of interview, it was impossible to determine whether these subtle changes are age related (e.g., unwillingness or inability to play notes at the upper ranges of the instrument) or the result of dementia.

Mr. T's memory for musical information was also remarkably intact. He was able to recall 16 of 20 well-known Christian songs and to recognize the titles of the 4 he could not recall. He was asked to name the titles of 12 well-known Dixieland jazz compositions while listening to tape-recorded versions of each piece. He correctly named 6 selections and stated that all 12 were familiar. Three other jazz musicians (other members of Mr. T's band) named an average of 10.3 selections. It might be noted that individuals without dementia and musical skill who were tested were able to name only 4 selections, judging that an average of 7.7 were familiar.

This case illustrates the potential for preserved functions, even in people who have severe dementia. The presence of these preserved areas indicates that certain memories may be relatively intact but inaccessible for some patients with DAT.

SUMMARY

DAT and VD have profound effects on patients, families, friends, and the larger society. With the numbers of older Americans expected to continue to increase, the significance of these issues will become more pressing. The psychosocial and cognitive devastation of these diseases, particularly DAT, is complete. Unfortunately, there are no pharmacological or medical interventions that can reverse the cognitive decline. Certain medications, such as antidepressants and anxiolytics, may serve to reduce affective and behavioral disturbances. Newer medications such as tacrine may serve to improve cognitive performance. Appropriate use of antihypertensives with patients who have VD may slow the progression of the disease. Currently, the most effective treatment for the patient involves providing a supportive, safe environment with a balance of activities that do not produce frustration. Support for family and close friends is also an important aspect of treatment planning. Caregivers need to be informed about support services, including home nursing and respite care.

Research on the role of the neurotransmitters, neuropeptides, and nerve growth factor will produce new treatment possibilities. Current work on the roles of specific genes also offers significant hope for effective intervention and prevention in the future. It is unlikely, however, that one gene combination will account for all cases of DAT. Therefore, it is imperative, for both VD and DAT patients, that research considering a wide range of possible contributing factors be continued.

References

Aharon-Peretz, J., Masiah, A., Pillar, T., Epstein, R., Tzischinsky, O., & Lavie, P. (1991). Sleep–wake cycles in multi-infarct dementia and dementia of the Alzheimer's type. *Neurology*, *41*, 1616–1619.

Albert, P. C., & Albert, M. L. (1984). History and scope of geriatric neurology. In M. L. Albert (Ed.), *Clinical neurology of aging* (pp. 3–9). New York: Oxford University Press.

Albert, M., & Milberg, W. (1989). Semantic processing in patients with Alzheimer's disease. *Brain and Language*, *37*, 163–171.

Alexopoulos, G. S., Abrams, R. C., Young, R. C., & Shamoian, C. A. (1988). Cornell scale for depression in dementia. *Biological Psychiatry*, *23*, 271–284.

Alexopoulos, G. S., & Mattis, S. (1991). Diagnosing cognitive dysfunction in the elderly: Primary screening tests. *Geriatrics*, *46*, 33–44.

Alzheimer's Association. (1988). *Special care for Alzheimer's patients*. Chicago: Author.

Amaducci, L. A., Fratiglioni, L., Rocca, W. A., Fieschi, C., Livrea, P., Pedone, D., Bracco, L., Lippi, A., Gandolfo, C., Bino, G., Massimiliano, P., Bonatti, M. L., Girotti, F., Francesco, C., Tavolato, B., Ferla, S., Lenzi, G. L., Carolei, A., Gambi, A., Grigoletto, F., & Schoenberg, B. S. (1986). Risk factors for clinically diagnosed Alzheimer's disease: A case-control study of an Italian population. *Neurology*, *36*, 922–931.

American Psychiatric Association. (1994). *Diagnostic and statistical manual of mental disorders* (4th ed.). Washington, DC: Author.

Arai, H., Ichimiya, Y., Kosaka, K., Moroji, T., & Iizuka, R. (1992). Neurotransmitter changes in early- and late-onset Alzheimer-type dementia. *Progressive Neuro-Psychopharmacology and Biological Psychiatry*, *16*, 883–890.

Aronson, M. K. (Ed.). (1988). *Understanding Alzheimer's disease*. New York: Macmillan.

Arriagada, P. V., Marzloff, K., & Hyman, B. T. (1992). Distribution of Alzheimer-type pathologic changes in nondemented elderly individuals matches the pattern in Alzheimer's disease. *Neurology*, *42*, 1681–1688.

Bachman, D. L., Wolf, P. A., Linn, R., Knoefel, J. E., Cobb, J., Belanger, A., D'Agostino, R. B., & White, L. R. (1992). Prevalence of dementia and probable senile dementia of the Alzheimer type in the Framingham Study. *Neurology*, *42*, 115–119.

Ball, M. J., Schapiro, M. B., & Rapoport, S. I. (1986). Neuropathological relationships between Down syndrome and senile dementia of the Alzheimer type. In C. J. Epstein (Ed.), *Neurobiology of Down syndrome* (pp. 45–58). New York: Raven Press.

Ban, T. A. (1978). Organic problems in the aged: Brain syndrome and alcoholism. Psychiatric aspects of the organic brain syndrome and pharmacological approaches to treatment. *Journal of Geriatric Psychiatry*, *11*, 135–159.

Ban, T. A., Morey, L., Aguglia, E., Azzarelli, O., Balsano, F., Marigliano, V., Caglieris, N., Sterlicchio, M., Capurso, A., Tomasi, N. A., Crepaldi, G., Volpe, D., Palmieri, G., Ambrosi, G., Polli, E., Cortellaro, M., Zanussi, C., & Froldi, M. (1990). Nimodipine in the treatment of old age dementias. *Neuro-*

Psychopharmacology and Biological Psychiatry, 14, 525–551.

Barclay, C. C., Zemcov, A., Blass, J. P., & Sansone, J. (1985). Survival in Alzheimer's disease and vascular dementias. *Neurology, 35,* 834–840.

Bartus, R. T., Dean, R. L., III, Beer, B., & Lippa, A. S. (1982). The cholinergic hypothesis of geriatric memory dysfunction. *Science, 217,* 408–417.

Baumgarten, M., Becker, R., & Gauthier, S. (1990). Validity and reliability of the Dementia Behavior Disturbance Scale. *Journal of the American Geriatrics Society, 38,* 221–226.

Beatty, W. W., Winn, P., Adams, R. L., Allen, E. W., Wilson, D. A., Prince, J. R., Olson, K. A., Dean, K., & Littleford, D. (1994). Preserved cognitive skills in dementia of the Alzheimer type. *Archives of Neurology, 51,* 1040–1046.

Beatty, W. W., Zavadil, K. D., Bailly, R. C., Rixen, G. J., Zavadil, L. E., Farnham, N., & Fisher, L. (1988). Preserved musical skill in a severely demented patient. *International Journal of Clinical Neuropsychology, 10,* 158–164.

Beck, A. T., Steer, R. A., & Garbin, M. G. (1988). Psychometric properties of the Beck Depression Inventory: Twenty-five years of evaluation. *Clinical Psychology Review, 8,* 77–100.

Benson, D. F., Kuhl, D. E., Hawkins, R. A., Phelps, M. E., Cummings, J. L., & Tsai, S. Y. (1983). The flurodeoxyglucose 18F scan in Alzheimer's disease and multi-infarct dementia. *Archives of Neurology, 40,* 711–714.

Berg, L. (1988). Clinical dementia rating (CDR). *Psychopharmacology Bulletin, 24,* 637–639.

Besson, J. A. O., Best, P. V., & Skinner, E. R. (1992). Post-mortem proton magnetic resonance spectrometric measures of brain regions in patients with a pathological diagnosis of Alzheimer's disease and multi-infarct dementia. *British Journal of Psychiatry, 160,* 187–190.

Besson, J. A. O., Corrigan, F. M., Foreman, E. I., Eastwood, L. M., Smith, F. W., & Ashcroft, G. W. (1985). Nuclear magnetic resonance (NMR), II. Imaging in dementia. *British Journal of Psychiatry, 146,* 31–35.

Bissette, G., Smith, W. H., Dole, K. C., Crain, B., Ghanbari, H., Miller, B., & Nemeroff, C. B. (1991). Alterations in Alzheimer's disease-associated protein in Alzheimer's disease frontal and temporal cortex. *Archives of General Psychiatry, 48,* 1009–1012.

Black, R. S., Barclay, L. L., Nolan, K. A., Thaler, H. T., Hardiman, S. T., & Blass, J. P. (1992). Pentoxifylline in cerebrovascular dementia. *Journal of the American Geriatrics Society, 40,* 237–244.

Blennow, K., Davidsson, P., Wallin, A., Fredman, P., Gottfries, C.-G., Karlsson, I., Månsson, J.-E., & Svennerholm, L. (1991). Gangliosides in cerebrospinal fluid in probable Alzheimer's disease. *Archives of Neurology, 48,* 1032–1035.

Blennow, K., Wallin, B. K., Uhlemann, C., & Gottfries, C. G. (1991). White-matter lesions on CT in Alzheimer's patients: Relation to clinical symptomatology and vascular factors. *Acta Neurologica Scandinavica, 83,* 187–193.

Blessed, G., Tomlinson, B. E., & Roth, M. (1968). The association between quantitative measures of dementia and of senile change in the cerebral grey matter of elderly subjects. *British Journal of Psychiatry, 114,* 797–811.

Bliwise, D. L. (1989). Dementia. In M. H. Kryger, T. Roth, & W. C. Dement (Eds.), *Principles and practice of sleep medicine* (pp. 358–363). Philadelphia: W. B. Saunders.

Bliwise, D. L., Tinklenberg, J. R., & Yesavage, J. A. (1992). Timing of sleep and wakefulness in Alzheimer's disease patients residing at home. *Biological Psychiatry, 31,* 1163–1165.

Bondareff, W., Mountjoy, C. Q., Roth, M., Rosso, M. N., Iversen, L. L., & Reynolds, G. P. (1987). Age and histopathologic heterogeneity in Alzheimer's disease: Evidence for subtypes. *Archives of General Psychiatry, 44,* 412–417.

Bondareff, W., Raval, J., Coletti, P. M., & Hauser, D. L. (1988). Quantitative magnetic resonance imaging and the severity of dementia in Alzheimer's disease. *American Journal of Psychiatry, 145,* 853–856.

Bondi, M. W., & Kaszniak, A. W. (1991). Implicit and explicit memory in Alzheimer's disease and Parkinson's disease. *Journal of Clinical and Experimental Neuropsychology, 13,* 339–358.

Branconnier, R. J., Branconnier, M. E., Walshe, T. M., McCarthy, C., & Morse, P.-A. (1992). Blocking the $CA^{2\pm}$ activated cytotoxic mechanisms of cholinergic neuronal death: A novel treatment strategy for Alzheimer's disease. *Psychopharmacology Bulletin, 28,* 175–181.

Breitner, J. C. S., & Folstein, M. F. (1984). Familial Alzheimer dementia: A prevalent disorder with specific clinical features. *Psychological Medicine, 14,* 63–80.

Brinkman, S. D., & Braun, P. (1984). Classification of dementia patients by a WAIS profile related to central cholinergic deficiencies. *Journal of Clinical Neuropsychology, 6,* 393–400.

Brinkman, S. D., Pomara, N., Goodnick, P. J., Barnett, M. A., & Domino, E. F. (1982). A dose-ranging study of lecithin in the treatment of primary degenerative dementia Alzheimer's disease. *Journal of Clinical Psychopharmacology, 2,* 281–285.

Brody, J. A. (1982). An epidemiologist views senile dementia: Facts and fragments. *American Journal of Epidemiology, 115,* 155.

Brooks, D. N., & McKinlay, W. (1983). Personality and behavioural change after severe blunt head injury: A relative's view. *Journal of Neurology, Neurosurgery, and Psychiatry, 16,* 336–344.

Buchwald, J., Erwin, R., Read, S., Van Lancher, D., & Cummings, J. (1989). Midlatency auditory evoked responses: Differential abnormality PI in Alzheimer's disease. *Electroencephalography and Clinical Neurophysiology, 74,* 378–384.

Burns, A., Jacoby, R., & Levy, R. (1990). Psychiatric phenomena in Alzheimer's disease. I: Disorders of thought content. *British Journal of Psychiatry, 157,* 72–76.

Candy, J. M., Oakley, A. E., Klinowski, J., Carpenter, T. A., Perry, R. H., Atark, J. R., Perry, E. K., Blessed, G., Fairbairn, A., & Edwardson, J. A. (1986). Aluminosilicates and senile plaque formation in Alzheimer's disease. *Lancet, 1,* 354–357.

Christensen, A. L. (1975). *Luria's neuropsychological investigation manual.* New York: Spectrum Publications.

Christie, J. E., Kean, D. M., Douglas, R. H. B., Engleman, H. M., St. Clair, D., & Blackburn, I. M. (1988). Magnetic resonance imaging in pre-senile dementia of Alzheimer-type, multi-infarct dementia and Korsakoff's syndrome. *Psychological Medicine, 18,* 319–329.

Chui, H. C. (1989). Dementia: A review emphasizing clinicopathologic correlation and brain–behavior relationships. *Archives of Neurology, 46,* 806–814.

Chui, H. C., Teng, E. L., Henderson, V. W., & Moy, A. C. (1985). Clinical subtypes of dementia of the Alzheimer type. *Neurology, 35,* 1544–1550.

Coblentz, J. M., Mattis, S., & Zingesser, L. H. (1973). Presenile dementia: Clinical aspects and evaluation of cerebrospinal fluid dynamics. *Archives of Neurology, 29,* 299–308.

Cohen, M. B., Fitten, L. J., Lake, R. R., Perryman, K. M., Graham, L. S., & Sevrin, R. (1992). SPECT brain imaging in Alzheimer's disease during treatment with oral tetrahydroaminoacridine and lecithin. *Clinical Nuclear Medicine, 17,* 312–315.

Crapper, D. R., Krishman, S. S., & Quittkat, S. (1976). Aluminum neurofibillary degeneration and Alzheimer's disease. *Brain, 99,* 67–80.

Crapper-McLachlan, D. R., & DeBoni, U. (1980). Etiologic factors in senile dementias of the Alzheimer's type. In L. Amaducci, A. Davison, & P. Antvono (Eds.), *Aging of the brain and dementia* (Vol. 13, pp. 173–181). New York: Raven Press.

Crook, T., Petrie, W., Wells, C., & Massari, D. C. (1992). Effects of phosphatidylserine in Alzheimer's disease. *Psychopharmacology Bulletin, 28,* 61–66.

Crystal, H. A., & Davies, P. (1982). Cortical substance P-like immunoreactivity in cases of Alzheimer's disease and senile dementia of the Alzheimer type. *Journal of Neurochemistry, 38,* 1781–1784.

Crystal, H. A., Horoupian, D. S., Katzman, R., & Jotkowitz, S. (1982). Biopsy-proved Alzheimer's disease presenting as right parietal lobe syndrome. *Annals of Neurology, 12,* 186–188.

Cullum, C. M., Butters, N., Tröster, A. I., & Salmon, D. P. (1990). Normal aging and forgetting rates on the Wechsler Memory Scale–Revised. *Archives of Clinical Neuropsychology, 5,* 23–30.

Cummings, J. L. (1988). The dementias of Parkinson's disease: Prevalence, characteristics, neurobiology, and comparison with dementia of the Alzheimer type. *Annals of Neurology, 28*(Suppl. 11), 15–23.

Cummings, J. L. (1989). Dementia and depression: An evolving enigma. *Journal of Neuropsychiatry, 1,* 236–242.

Cummings, J. L., & Benson, D. F. (1986). Dementia of the Alzheimer type: An inventory of diagnostic clinical features. *Journal of the American Geriatrics Society, 34,* 12–19.

Cummings, J. L., Miller, B., Hill, M. A., & Nesnkes, R. (1987). Neuropsychiatric aspects of multi-infarct dementia and dementia of the Alzheimer type. *Archives of Neurology, 44,* 389–393.

Davis, P. C., Gray, L., Albert, M., Wilkinson, W., Hughes, J., Heyman, A., Gado, M., Kumar, A. J., Destian, S., Lee, C., Duvall, E., Kido, D., Nelson, M. J., Bello, J., Weathers, S., Jolesz, F., Kikinis, R., & Brooks, M. (1992). The Consortium to Establish a Registry for Alzheimer's Disease (CERAD): Part III. Reliability of a standardized MRI evaluation of Alzheimer's disease. *Neurology, 42,* 1676–1680.

DeBettigies, B. H., Mahurin, R. K., & Pirozzolo, F. J. (1990). Insight for impairment in independent living skills in Alzheimer's disease and multi-infarct dementia. *Journal of Clinical and Experimental Neuropsychology, 12,* 355–363.

Dian, L., Cummings, J. L., Petry, S., & Hill, M. A. (1990). Personality alterations in multi-infarct dementia. *Psychosomatic, 31,* 415–419.

Diaz, J. F., Merskey, H., Hachinski, V. C., Lee, D. H., Boniferro, M., Wong, C. J., Mirsen, T. R., & Fox, H. (1991). Improved recognition of leukoaraiosis and cognitive impairment in Alzheimer's disease. *Archives of Neurology, 48,* 1022–1025.

Doljanski, F., & Kapeller, M. (1976). Cell surface shedding: The phenomenon and its possible significance. *Journal of Theoretical Biology, 62,* 253–270.

Drachman, D. A., O'Donnell, B. F., Lew, R. A., & Swearer, J. M. (1990). The prognosis of Alzheimer's disease. "How far" rather than "how fast" best predicts the course. *Archives of Neurology*, *47*, 851–856.

Drayer, B. P. (1985). Neurometabolic applications of magnetic resonance. In *Categorical course on magnetic resonance syllabus* (pp. 185–211). Bethesda, MD: American College of Radiology.

Drayer, B. P. (1987). Magnetic resonance imaging and brain: Implications in the diagnosis and pathochemistry of movement disorders and dementia. *BNI Quarterly*, *3*, 15–30.

Drayer, B. P. (1988). Imaging of the aging brain: Part II. Pathologic conditions. *Radiology*, *166*, 797–806.

Duchek, J. M., Cheney, M., Ferraro, F. R., & Storandt, M. (1991). Paired associate learning in senile dementia of the Alzheimer type. *Archives of Neurology*, *48*, 1038–1040.

Eagger, S., Morant, N., Levy, R., & Sahakian, B. (1992). Tacrine in Alzheimer's disease: Time course of changes in cognitive function and practice effects. *British Journal of Psychiatry*, *160*, 36–40.

Edwards, A. J. (1994). *When memory fails: Helping the Alzheimer's and dementia patient*. New York: Plenum.

Eisdorfer, C., & Cohen, D. (1980). Serum immunoglobulins and cognitive status in the elderly: II. An immunological–behavioral relationship? *British Journal of Psychiatry*, *136*, 40–45.

Eslinger, P. J., & Damasio, A. R. (1986). Preserved motor learning in Alzheimer's disease: Implications for anatomy and behavior. *Journal of Neuroscience*, *6*, 3006–3009.

Everall, I. P., & Kerwin, R. (1990). The role of nerve growth factor in Alzheimer's disease. *Psychological Medicine*, *20*, 249–251.

Farrer, L. A., O'Sullivan, D. M., Cupples, L. A., Growdon, J. H., & Myers, R. H. (1989). Assessment of genetic risk for Alzheimer's disease among first degree relatives. *Annals of Neurology*, *25*, 485–493.

Fazekas, E., Chawluk, J. B., Alavi, A., Hurtig, H. I., & Zimmerman, R. A. (1987). MR signal abnormalities at 1–5T in Alzheimer's dementia and normal aging. *American Journal of Neuroradiology*, *8*, 421–426.

Fischer, P., Gatterer, G., Marterer, A., Simanyi, M., & Danielczyk, W. (1990). Course characteristics in the differentiation of dementia of the Alzheimer type and multi-infarct dementia. *Acta Psychiatrica Scandinavia*, *81*, 551–553.

Fischer, P., Jellinger, K., Gatterer, G., & Danielczyk, W. (1991). Prospective neuropathological validation of Hachinski's Ischaemic Score in dementias. *Journal of Neurology, Neurosurgery, and Psychiatry*, *54*, 580–583.

Fischer, P., Marterer, A. & Danielczyk, W. (1990). Right–left disorientation in dementia of the Alzheimer type. *Neurology*, *40*, 1619–1620.

Fischer, P., Simanyi, M., & Danielczyk, W. (1990). Depression in dementia of the Alzheimer type and in multi-infarct dementia. *American Journal of Psychiatry*, *147*, 1484–1487.

Folstein, M. F., Folstein, S. E., & McHugh, P. R. (1975). Mini-Mental State: A practical method for grading the cognitive state of patients for the clinician. *Journal of Psychiatric Research*, *12*, 189–198.

Friedland, R. P. (1988). Variability of clinical manifestations. *Annals of International Medicine*, *109*, 298–311.

Friedland, R. P. (1989). Positron imaging in dementing illness. *Journal of Neuropsychiatry*, *1*, 556–560.

Friedman, D., Hamberger, M., Stern, Y., & Marder, K. (1992). Event-related potentials (ERPs) during repetition priming in Alzheimer's patients and young and older controls. *Journal of Clinical and Experimental Neuropsychology*, *14*, 448–462.

Fuld, P. A. (1984). Test profile of cholinergic dysfunction and of Alzheimer-type dementia. *Journal of Clinical Neuropsychology*, *6*, 380–392.

Gallai, V., Mazzotta, G., Firenze, C., Montesi, S., & Del Gatto, F. (1991). Study of the P300 and cerebral maps in subjects with multi-infarct dementia treated with cytidine. *Psychopharmacology*, *103*, 1–5.

Gfeller, J. D., & Rankin, E. J. (1991). The WAIS-R profile as a cognitive marker of Alzheimer's disease: A misguided venture? *Journal of Clinical and Experimental Neuropsychology*, *13*, 629–636.

Ghanbari, H. A., Miller, B. E., Haigler, H. J., Arato, M., Bissette, G., Davies, P., Nemeroff, C. B., Perry, E. K., Perry, R., Ravid, R., Swaab, D. F., Whetsell, W. O., & Zemlan, F. P. (1990). Biochemical assay of Alzheimer's disease-associated protein(s) in human brain tissue: A clinical study. *Journal of the American Medical Association*, *263*, 2907–2910.

Goodglass, H., & Kaplan, E. (1972). *Assessment of aphasia and related disorders*. Philadephia: Lea and Febiger.

Goodman, L. (1953). Alzheimer's disease: A clinical–pathologic analysis of cases with a theory on pathogenesis. *Journal of Nervous and Mental Diseases*, *118*, 129–133.

Goudsmit, J., Morrow, C. H., Asher, D. M., Yanagihara, R. T., Masters, C. L., Gibbs, C. J., & Gajdusek, D. C. (1980). Evidence for and against the transmissibility of Alzheimer's disease. *Neurology*, *30*, 945–950.

Grady, C. L. (1988). Longitudinal changes in brain metabolism. *Annals of International Medicine*, *109*, 302–304.

Graf, P., Squire, L. R., & Mandler, G. (1984) The information that amnesic patients do not forget. *Journal of*

Experimental Psychology: Learning, Memory, and Cognition, *10*, 164–178.

Gustafson, L. (1975). Dementia with onset in the presenile period. *Acta Psychiatrica Scandinavica*, *257*, 9–35.

Gwyther, L. P. (1988). Nursing-home-care issues. In M. K. Aronson (Ed.), *Understanding Alzheimer's disease* (pp. 238–262). New York: Macmillan.

Hachinski, V. C. (1991). Multi-infarct dementia: A reappraisal. *Alzheimer Disease and Associated Disorders*, *5*(4), 64–68.

Hachinski, V. C., Iliff, L. D., Zilhka, E., DuBoulay, G. H., McAllister, V. L., Marshall, J., Russell, R., & Symon, L. (1975). Cerebral blood flow in dementia. *Archives of Neurology*, *32*, 632–637.

Hamilton, M. (1960). A rating scale for depression. *Journal of Neurology, Neurosurgery, and Psychiatry*, *23*, 56–62.

Hamilton, M. (1967). Development of a rating scale for primary depressive illness. *British Journal of Social and Clinical Psychology*, *6*, 278–296.

Hardy, J. A., & Higgins, G. A. (1992). Alzheimer's disease: The amyloid cascade hypothesis. *Science*, *256*, 184–185.

Harrison, M. J. G., Thomas, D. J., DuBoulay, G. H., & Marshall, J. (1979). Multiinfarct dementia. *Journal of the Neurological Sciences*, *40*, 97–103.

Hartman, M. (1991). The use of semantic knowledge in Alzheimer's disease: Evidence for impairments of attention. *Neuropsychologia*, *29*, 213–228.

Hauser, W. A., Morris, M. L., Heston, L. L., & Anderson, V. E. (1986). Seizures and myoclonus in patients with Alzheimer's disease. *Neurology*, *36*, 1226–1230.

Haxby, J. (1988). Heterogeneous patterns of regional cerebral glucose use. *Annals of International Medicine*, *109*, 300–302.

Heaton, R. K. (1981). *Wisconsin Card Sorting Test manual*. Odessa, FL: Psychological Assessment Resources.

Hebert, D. E., Scherr, P. A., Beckett, L. A., Funkenstein, H. H., Albert, M. S., Chown, M. J., & Evans, D. A. (1992). Relation of smoking and alcohol consumption to incident Alzheimer's disease. *American Journal of Epidemiology*, *135*, 347–355.

Heindel, W. C., Salmon, D. P., & Butters, N. (1990). Pictorial priming and cued recall in Alzheimer's and Huntington's disease. *Brain and Cognition*, *13*, 282–295.

Heindel, W. C., Salmon, D. P., & Butters, N. (1993). Cognitive approaches to the memory disorders of demented patients. In P. B. Sutker & H. E. Adams (Eds.), *Comprehensive handbook of psychopathology* (2nd ed., pp. 735–761). New York: Plenum.

Heindel, W. C., Salmon, D. P., Shults, C. W., Walicke, P. A., & Butters, N. (1989). Neuropsychological evidence for multiple implicit memory systems: A comparison of Alzheimer's, Huntington's, and Parkinson's disease patients. *Journal of Neuroscience*, *9*, 582–587.

Henderson, A. S., Jorn, A. F., Korten, A. E., Creasey, H., McCusker, E., Broe, G. A., Longley, W., & Anthony, J. C. (1992). Environmental risk factors for Alzheimer's disease: Their relationship to age of onset and to familial or sporadic types. *Psychological Medicine*, *22*, 429–436.

Heyman, A., Wilkinson, W. E., Hurwitz, B. J., Schmechel, D., Sigmon, A. H., Weinberg, T., Helms, M. J., & Swift, M. (1983). Alzheimer's disease: Genetic aspects and associated clinical disorders. *Annals of Neurology*, *14*, 507–515.

Heyman, A., Wilkinson, W. E., Stafford, J. A., Helms, M. J., Sigmon, A. H., & Weinberg, T. (1984). Alzheimer's disease: A study of epidemiology aspects. *Annals of Neurology*, *15*, 335–341.

Hicks, N., Brammer, M. J., Hymas, N., & Levy, R. (1987). Platelet membrane properties in Alzheimer and multi-infarct dementias. *Alzheimer Disease and Associate Disorders*, *1*, 90–97.

Hier, D. B., Warach, J. D., Gorelick, P. B., & Thomas, J. (1989). Predictors of survival in clinically diagnosed Alzheimer's disease and multi-infarct dementia. *Archives of Neurology*, *46*, 1213–1216.

Hofman, A., Schulte, W., Tanja, T. A., Van Duijn, C. M., Haaxma, R., Lameris, A. J., Otten, V. M., & Saan, R. J. (1989). History of dementia and Parkinson's disease in 1st degree relatives of patients with Alzheimer's disease. *Neurology*, *39*, 1589–1592.

Hooper, C. (1992). Encircling a mechanism in Alzheimer's disease. *Journal of NIH Research*, *4*, 48–54.

House, A., Dennis, M., Warlow, C., Hawton, K., & Molyneux, A. (1990). The relationship between intellectual impairment and mood disorder in the first year after stroke. *Psychological Medicine*, *20*, 805–814.

Huff, F. J., Growdon, J. H., Corkin, S., & Rosen, T. J. (1987). Age at onset and rate of progression of Alzheimer's disease. *Journal of the American Geriatrics Society*, *35*, 27–30.

Hughes, C. P., Berg, L., Danziger, W. L., Coben, L. A., & Martin, R. L. (1982). A new clinical scale for the staging of dementia. *British Journal of Psychiatry*, *140*, 566–572.

Hunter, R., McLuskie, R., Wyper, D., Patterson, J., Christie, J. E., Brooks, D. N., McCulloch, J., Fink, G., & Goodwin, G. M. (1989). The pattern of function-related regional cerebral blood flow investigated by single photon emission tomography with Tc-HMPAO in patients with presenile Alzheimer's disease and Korsakoff's psychosis. *Psychological Medicine*, *19*, 847–855.

Hutton, J. T. (1985). Predictors of nursing placement of patients with Alzheimer's disease. *Texas Medicine, 81*, 41.

Iizuka, R., & Arai, H. (1990). Neurotransmitter changes in Alzheimer-type dementia. In T. Nagatsu & M. Yoshida (Eds.), *Basic, clinical, and therapeutic aspects of Alzheimer's and Parkinson's diseases* (pp. 459–464). New York: Plenum.

Ishii, N., Nishihara, Y., & Imamura, T. (1986). Why do frontal lobe symptoms predominate in vascular dementia with lacunes? *Neurology, 36*, 340–345.

Ito, J., Yamao, S., Fukuda, H., Mimori, Y., & Nakanura, S. (1990). The P300 event-related potentials in dementia of the Alzheimer type: Correlations between P300 and monoamine metabolites. *Electroencephalography and Clinical Neurophysiology, 77*, 174–178.

Ivnik, R. J., Malec, J. F., Smith, G. E., Tangalos, E. G., Petersen, R. C., Kokmen, E., & Kurland, L. T. (1992a). Mayo's older Americans normative studies: WAIS-R norms of ages 56 to 97. *Clinical Neuropsychologist, 6*(Suppl.), 1–30.

Ivnik, R. J., Malec, J. F., Smith, G. E., Tangalos, E. G., Petersen, R. C., Kokmen, E., & Kurland, L. T. (1992b). Mayo's older Americans normative studies: WMS-R norms for ages 56 to 94. *Clinical Neuropsychologist, 6*(Suppl.), 49–82.

Jacoby, R. J., & Levy, R. (1980). Computed tomography in the elderly: II. Senile dementia: Diagnosis and functional impairment. *British Journal of Psychiatry, 136*, 256–269.

Jarvik, L. F., Altshuler, K. Z., Kato, T., & Blumner, B. (1971). Organic brain syndrome and chromosome loss in aged twins. *Diseases of the Nervous System, 32*, 159–170.

Jarvik, L. F., Yen, F. S., & Moralishuili, E. (1974). Chromosome examinations in aging institutionalized women. *Journal of Gerontology, 29*, 269–276.

Kaakkola, S., Rosenberg, P. H., Alila, A., Erkinjuntti, T., Sulkava, R., & Palo, J. (1990). Platelet membrane fluidity in Alzheimer's disease and multi-infarct dementia: A spin label study. *Acta Neurologica Scandinavia, 84*, 18–21.

Kaplan, E., Goodglass, H., & Weintraub, S. (1983). *Boston Naming Test.* Philadelphia: Lea and Febiger.

Kase, C. S. (1991). Epidemiology of multi-infarct dementia. *Alzheimer Disease and Associated Disorders, 5*(2), 71–76.

Kaszniak, A. W., Fox, J., Gandell, D. L., Garron, D. C., Huckman, M. S., & Ramsey, R. G. (1978). Predictors of mortality in presenile and senile dementia. *Annals of Neurology, 3*, 246–252.

Kaszniak, A. W., Wilson, R., Lazarus, L., Lesser, J., & Fox, J. H. (1981, February). *Memory and depression in dementia.* Paper presented at the Ninth Annual Meeting of the International Neuropsychological Society, Atlanta, GA.

Kato, H., Sugawara, Y., Ito, H., & Kogure, K. (1990). White-matter lucencies in multi-infarct dementia: A somatosensory evoked potentials and CT study. *Acta Neurologica Scandinavica, 81*, 181–183.

Katz, S. (1983). Assessing self-maintenance: Activities of daily living, mobility, and instrumental activities of daily living. *Journal of the American Geriatrics Society, 31*, 721–727.

Katzman, R., Lasker, B., & Bernstein, N. (1988). Advances in the diagnosis of dementia: Accuracy of diagnosis and consequences of misdiagnosis of disorders causing dementias. In R. D. Terry (Ed.), *Aging and the brain* (pp. 17–62). New York: Raven Press.

Kaye, J. (1988). Neurochemical aspects of motor impairment. In R. P. Friedland (Moderator), Alzheimer's disease: Clinical and biological heterogeneity. *Annals of International Medicine, 109*, 307–308.

Kirshner, H. S., Webb, W. G., Kelly, M. P., & Wells, C. E. (1984). Language disturbance: An initial symptom of cortical degeneration and dementia. *Archives of Neurology, 41*, 491–496.

Kish, S. J., El-Awar, M., Schut, L., Leach, L., Oscar-Berman, M., & Freedman, M. (1988). Cognitive deficit in olivopontocerebellar atrophy: Implications for the cholinergic hypothesis of Alzheimer's dementia. *Annals of Neurology, 24*, 200–206.

Kluger, A., & Ferris, S. H. (1991). Scales for the assessment of Alzheimer's disease. *Alzheimer's Disease, 14*, 309–326.

Knesevich, J. W., LaBarge, E., & Edwards, D. (1986). Predictive value of the Boston Naming Test in mild senile dementia of the Alzheimer type. *Psychiatry Research, 19*, 155–161.

Knopman, D. S., & Nissen, M. J. (1987). Implicit learning in patients with probable Alzheimer's disease. *Neurology, 37*, 784–788.

Kontiola, P., Laaksonen, R., Sulkava, R., & Erkinjuntti, T. (1990). Pattern of language impairment is different in Alzheimer's disease and multi-infarct dementia. *Brain and Language, 38*, 364–383.

Koss, E. (1988). Behavioral heterogeneity. In R. P. Friedland (Moderator), Alzheimer's disease: Clinical and biological heterogeneity. *Annals of International Medicine, 109*, 298–311.

Larson, E. B., Reifler, B., Featherstone, H. J., & English, D. R. (1984). Dementia in elderly outpatients: A prospective study. *Annals of International Medicine, 100*, 417–423.

Lawton, M. P., & Brody, E. M. (1969). Assessment of older people: Self-maintaining and instrumental activities of daily living. *Gerontologist, 9*, 179–186.

Lawton, M. P., & Brody, E. M. (1988a). Instrumental Activities of Daily Living (IADL) Scale: Original observer-rated version. *Psychopharmacology Bulletin, 24*, 785–787.

Lawton, M. P., & Brody, E. M. (1988b). Instrumental Activities of Daily Living (IADL) Scale: Self-rated version. *Psychopharmacology Bulletin, 24*, 789–791.

Lawton, M. P., & Brody, E. M. (1988c). Physical Self-Maintenance Scale (PSMS): Original observer-rated version. *Psychopharmacology Bulletin, 24*, 793–794.

Lawton, M. P., & Brody, E. M. (1988d). Physical Self-Maintenance Scale (PSMS): Self-rated version. *Psychopharmacology Bulletin, 24*, 795–797.

Lezak, M. D. (1982). The problem of assessing executive functions. *International Journal of Psychology, 17*, 281–297.

Lichtenberg, P. A., Marcopulos, B. A., Steiner, D. A., & Tabscott, J. A. (1992). Comparison of the Hamilton Depression Rating Scale and the Geriatric Depression Scale: Detection of depression in dementia patients. *Psychological Reports, 70*, 515–521.

Lishman, W. A. (1987). *Organic psychiatry: The Psychological consequences of cerebral disorder* (2nd ed.). Oxford, England: Blackwell Scientific.

Liston, E. H. (1979). Clinical findings in presenile dementia. *Journal of Nervous and Mental Disease, 167*, 337–342.

Logsdon, R. G., Teri, L., Williams, D. E., Vitiello, M. V., & Prinz, P. N. (1989). The WAIS-R profile: A diagnostic tool for Alzheimer's disease? *Journal of Clinical and Experimental Neuropsychology, 11*, 892–898.

Lopez, O. L., Becker, J. T., Rezek, D., Wess, J., Boller, F., Reynolds, C. F., III, & Panisset, M. (1992). Neuropsychiatric correlates of cerebral white-matter radiolucencies in probable Alzheimer's disease. *Archives of Neurology, 49*, 828–834.

Mahendra, B. (1987). *Dementia: A survey of the syndrome of dementia* (2nd ed.). Lancaster: MTP Press.

Mann, D. M. A., Lincoln, J., Yates, P. O., Stamp, J. E., & Toper, S. (1980). Changes in the monoamine containing neurones of the human CNS in senile dementia. *British Journal of Psychiatry, 136*, 533–541.

Maragos, W. F., Chu, D. C. M., Young, A. B., D'Amato, C. J., & Young, J. B. (1987). Loss of hippocampal [3H] TCP binding in Alzheimer's disease. *Neuroscience Letters, 93*, 225.

Martin, D. C., Miller, J. K., Kapoor, W., Arena, V. C., & Baller, F. (1987). A controlled study of survival with dementia. *Archives of Neurology, 44*, 1122–1126.

Martin, R. L., Gerteis, G., & Gabrielli, W. F. (1988). A family-genetic study of dementia of Alzheimer's type. *Archives of General Psychiatry, 45*, 894–900.

Martin-Loeches, M., Gil, P., Jimenez, F., Exposito, F. J., Miguel, F., Cacabelos, R., & Rubia, F. J. (1991). Topographic maps of brain electrical activity in primary degenerative dementia of the Alzheimer type and multi-infarct dementia. *Biological Psychiatry, 29*, 211–223.

Martyn, C. N., Barker, D. J. P., Osmond, C., Harris, E. C., Edwardson, J. A., & Lacey, R. F. (1989). Geographical relation between Alzheimer's disease and aluminium in drinking water. *Lancet*, 59–65.

Mattis, S. (1976). Mental status examination for organic mental syndrome in the elderly patient. In R. Bellack & B. Karasu (Eds.), *Geriatric psychiatry* (pp. 77–121). New York: Grune & Stratton.

Mattis, S. (1988). *DRS: Dementia Rating Scale manual.* Odessa, FL: Psychological Assessment Resources.

Mayeux, R., Stern, Y., & Spanton, S. (1985). Heterogeneity in dementia of the Alzheimer's type: Evidence for subgroups. *Neurology, 35*, 453–461.

McCartney, J. R., & Palmateer, L. M. (1985). Assessment of cognitive deficit in geriatrics patients: A study of physician behavior. *Journal of the American Geriatrics Society, 33*, 467–471.

McDermott, J. R., Smith, A. I., Iqbul, K., & Wisniewski, H. M. (1979). Brain aluminum in aging and Alzheimer's disease. *Neurology, 29*, 309–314.

McDonald, C. (1969). Clinical heterogeneity in senile dementia. *British Journal of Psychiatry, 115*, 267–271.

McDougall, G. J. (1990). A review of screening instruments for assessing cognition and mental status in older adults. *Nurse Practitioner, 15*, 18–28.

McGeer, P. L., McGeer, E. G., & Suzuki, J. S. (1977). Aging and extra pyramidal function. *Archives of Neurology, 84*, 33–35.

Meldrum, B. S., & Garthwaite, J. (1990). Excitatory amino acid neurotoxicity and neurodegenerative disease. *Trends in Pharmacological Sciences, 11*, 379.

Mendez, M. F., & Ashla-Mendez, M. (1991). Differences between multi-infarct dementia and Alzheimer's disease on unstructured neuropsychological tasks. *Journal of Clinical and Experimental Neuropsychology, 13*, 923–932.

Mendez, M. F., Mastri, A. R., Sung, J. H., & Frey, W. H., II. (1992). Clinically diagnosed Alzheimer disease: Neuropathologic findings in 650 cases. *Alzheimer Disease and Associated Disorders, 6*(1), 35–43.

Mendez, M. F., Underwood, K. L., Zander, B. A., Mastri, A. R., Sung, J. H., & Frey, W. H., II. (1992). Risk factors in Alzheimer's disease: A clinicopathologic study. *Neurology, 42*, 770–775.

Merriam, A. E., Aronson, M. K., Gaston, P., Wey, S. L., & Katz, I. (1988). The psychiatric symptoms of Alzheimer's disease. *Journal of the American Geriatrics Society, 36*, 7–12.

Mesulam, M. M. (1985). Dementia: Its definition, differential diagnosis, and subtypes. *Journal of the American Medical Association*, *253*, 2559–2561.

Mirsen, T. R., Lee, D. H., Wong, C. J., Diaz, J. F., Fox, A. J., Hachinski, V. C., & Merskey, H. (1991). Clinical correlates of white-matter changes on magnetic resonance imaging scans of the brain. *Archives of Neurology*, *48*, 1015–1021.

Mohs, R. C., Breitner, J. C. S., Silverman, J. M., & Davis, K. L. (1987). Alzheimer's disease. *Archives of General Psychiatry*, *44*, 405–408.

Mohs, R. C., Davis, B. M., Johns, C. A., Matne, A. A., Greenwald, B. S., Horvath, T. B., & Davis, K. L. (1985). Oral physostigmine treatment of patients with Alzheimer's disease. *American Journal of Psychiatry*, *142*, 28–33.

Mortimer, J. A., Ebbitt, B., Jun, S., & Finch, M. D. (1992). Predictors of cognitive and functional progression in patients with probable Alzheimer's disease. *Neurology*, *42*, 1689–1696.

Näsman, B., Olsson, T., Bäckström, T., Eriksson, S., Grankvist, K., Viitanen, M., & Bucht, G. (1991). Serum dehydroepiandrosterone sulfate in Alzheimer's disease and in multi-infarct dementia. *Biological Psychiatry*, *30*, 684–690.

Nebes, R. D., Boller, F., & Holland, A. (1986). Use of semantic context by patients with Alzheimer's disease. *Psychology of Aging*, *1*, 261–269.

Nebes, R. D., Brady, C. B., & Huff, F. J. (1989). Automatic and attentional mechanisms of semantic priming in Alzheimer's disease. *Journal of Clinical and Experimental Neuropsychology*, *11*, 219–230.

Nebes, R. D., Martin, D. C., & Horn, L. C. (1984). Sparing of semantic memory in Alzheimer's disease. *Journal of Abnormal Psychology*, *93*, 321–330.

Nee, L. E., Eldridge, R., Sunderland, T., Thomas, C. B., Katz, D., Thompson, K. E., Weingartner, H., Weiss, H., Julian, C., & Cohen, R. (1987). Dementia of the Alzheimer type: Clinical and family study of 22 twin pairs. *Neurology*, *37*, 359–363.

Nielsen, J. (1968). Chromosomes in senile dementia. *British Journal of Psychiatry*, *114*, 303–309.

Nielsen, J. (1970). Chromosomes in senile, presenile, and arteriosclerotic dementia. *Journal of Gerontology*, *25*, 312–315.

North, W. G., Harbaugh, R., & Reeder, T. (1992). An evaluation of human neurophysin production in Alzheimer's disease: Preliminary observations. *Neurobiology of Aging*, *13*, 261–265.

Nyth, A. L., & Gottfries, C. G. (1990). The clinical efficacy of citalopram in treatment of emotional disturbances in dementia disorders: A nordic multicentre study. *British Journal of Psychiatry*, *157*, 894–901.

Olafsson, K., Jfrgensen, S., Jensen, H. V., Bille, A., Arup, P., & Andersen, J. (1992). Fluvoxamine in the treatment of demented elderly patients: A double-blind, placebo-controlled study. *Acta Psychiatrica Scandinavica*, *85*, 453–456.

Parmelee, P. A., Katz, I. R., & Lawton, M. P. (1989). Depression among institutionalized aged: Assessment and prevalence estimation. *Journal of Gerontology*, *44*, 22–29.

Perry, E. K., Blessed, G., Tomlinson, B. E., Perry, R. H., Crow, T. J., Cross, A. J., Dockray, G. J., Dimline, R., & Arregui, A. (1981). Neurochemical activities in human temporal lobe related to aging and Alzheimer type changes. *Neurobiology of Aging*, *2*, 251–256.

Perry, E. K., Gibson, P. H., Blessed, G., Perry, R. H., & Tomlinson, B. E. (1977). Neurotransmitter enzyme abnormalities in senile dementia. *Journal of the Neurological Sciences*, *34*, 247–265.

Petry, S., Cummings, J. L., Hill, M. A., & Shapiro, J. (1988). Personality alterations in dementia of the Alzheimer's type. *Archives of Neurology*, *45*, 1187–1190.

Polich, J., Ladish, C., & Bloom, F. (1990). P300 assessment of early Alzheimer's disease. *Electroencephalography and Clinical Neurophysiology*, *77*, 179–189.

Pollak, C. P., Perlick, D., Linsner, J. P., Wenston, J., & Hsieh, F. (1990). Sleep problems in the community elderly as predictors of death and nursing home placement. *Journal of Community Health*, *15*, 123–135.

Pomara, N., Singh, R., Deptula, D., Chou, J. C.-Y., Schwartz, M. B., & LeWitt, P. A. (1992). Glutamate and other CSF amino acids in Alzheimer's disease. *American Journal of Psychiatry*, *149*, 251–254.

Porter, R. H. P., Cowburn, R. F., Alasuzoff, I., Briggs, R. S. J., & Roberts, P. J. (1992). Heterogeneity of NMDA receptors labelled with [3H]3-((+)-2-carboxypiperazin-4-y1) propyl-1-phosphonic acid ([3H] CPP): Receptor status in Alzheimer's disease brains. *European Journal of Pharmacology: Molecular Pharmacology Section*, *225*, 195–201.

Powell, A. L., Cummings, J. L., Hill, M. A., & Benson, D. F. (1988). Speech and language alterations in multi-infarct dementia. *Neurology*, *38*, 717–719.

Powell-Proctor, L., & Miller, E. (1982). Reality orientation: A critical appraisal. *British Journal of Psychiatry*, *140*, 457–463.

Reisberg, B., Borenstein, J., Salob, S. P., Ferris, S. H., Franssen, E., & Georgotas, A. (1987). Behavioral symptoms in Alzheimer's disease: Phenomenology and treatment. *Journal of Clinical Psychiatry*, *48*(5), 9–15.

Reisberg, B., & Ferris, S. H. (1985). A clinical rating scale for symptoms of psychosis in Alzheimer's disease. *Psychopharmacology Bulletin, 21*, 101–104.

Reisberg, B., & Ferris, S. H. (1988). The Brief Cognitive Rating Scale (BCRS). *Psychopharmocology Bulletin, 24*, 629–636.

Reisberg, B., Ferris, S. H., de Leon, M. J., & Crook, T. (1982). The Global Deterioration Scale (GDS) for assessment of primary degenerative dementia. *American Journal of Psychiatry, 139*, 1136–1139.

Rey, A. (1964). *L'examen clinique en psychologie* [The clinical examination in psychology]. Paris: Presses Universitaires de France.

Rinne, J. O., Säkö, E., Päljarvi, L., Molsa, P. K., & Rinne, U. K. (1988). A comparison of brain choline acetyltransferase activity in Alzheimer's disease, multiinfarct dementia and combined dementia. *Brain Research, 73*, 121–128.

Roberts, M. A., McGeorge, A. P., & Caird, F. I. (1978). Electroencephalography and computerized tomography in vascular and non-vascular dementia in old age. *Journal of Neurology, Neurosurgery, and Psychiatry, 48*, 903–906.

Robinson, R., Kubos, K., Starr, L. B., Rao, K., & Price, T. R. (1984). Mood disorders in stroke patients: Importance of location of lesion. *Brain, 107*, 81–93.

Roses, A. D., Peviceak-Vance, M. A., Clark, C. M., Gilbert, J. R., Yamaoka, L. H., Haynes, C. S., Speer, M. C., Gaskell, P. C., Hung, W., Trofatter, J. A., Earl, N. L., Lee, J. E., Alberto, M. J., Dawson, D. V., Bartlett, R. J., Siddique, T., Vance, J. M., Conneally, P. M., & Heyman, A. L. (1990). Linkage studies of late onset familial Alzheimer's disease. In R. J. Wurtman, S. Corkin, J. H. Growdon, & E. Ritter-Walker (Eds.), *Advances in neurology: Vol. 51. Alzheimer's disease* (pp. 185–196). New York: Raven Press.

Rubin, E. H., Morris, J. C., & Berg, L. (1987). The progression of personality changes in patients with mild senile dementia of the Alzheimer type. *Journal of the American Geriatrics Society, 35*, 721–725.

Rudman, D., Shetty, K. R., & Mattson, D. E. (1990). Plasma dehydroepiandrosterone sulfate in nursing home men. *Journal of the American Geriatrics Society, 38*, 421–427.

Russell, E. W. (1975). A multiple scoring method of assessment of complex memory factors. *Journal of Consulting and Clinical Psychology, 43*, 800–809.

Russell, E. W. (1988). Renorming Russell's version of the Wechsler Memory Scale. *Journal of Clinical and Experimental Neuropsychology, 10*, 235–249.

Sadock, B. J. (1980). Organic mental disorders associated with circulatory disturbances (including multi-infarct dementia). In H. I. Kaplan, A. M. Freedman, & B. J. Sadock (Eds.), *Comprehensive textbook of psychiatry, 2 (3rd ed.*, pp. 1329–1404). Baltimore: Williams & Wilkins.

Saffran, B. N. (1992). Should intracerebroventricular nerve growth factor be used to treat Alzheimer's disease? *Perspectives in Biology and Medicine, 35*, 471–486.

Sakurada, T., Alufuzoff, I., Winblad, B., & Nordberg, A. (1990). Substance P-like immunoreactivity, choline acetyltransferase activity and cholinergic muscarinic receptors in Alzheimer's disease and multi-infarct dementia. *Brain Research, 521*, 329–332.

Salmon, D. P., Shimamura, A. P., Butters, N., & Smith, S. (1988). Lexical and semantic priming deficits in patients with Alzheimer's disease. *Journal of Clinical and Experimental Neuropsychology, 10*, 477–494.

Sapolsky, R. M., Packan, D. R., & Vale, W. (1988). Glucocorticoid toxicity in the hippocampus: In vitro demonstration. *Brain Research, 453*, 367–371.

Schellenberg, G. D., Bird, T. D., Wijsman, E. M., Moore, D. K., Boehnke, M., Bryant, E. M., Lampe, T. H., Nochlin, D., Sermi, S. M., Deeb, S. S., Beyreuther, K., & Martin, G. M. (1988). Absence of linkage of chromosome 21q21 markers to familial Alzheimer's disease. *Science, 241*, 1507–1510.

Scheltens, P. H., Barkhof, F., Valk, J., Algra, P. R., Van Der Hoop, R. G., Nauta, J., & Wolters, E. C. H. (1992). White-matter lesions on magnetic resonance imaging in clinically diagnosed Alzheimer's disease: Evidence for heterogeneity. *Brain, 115*, 735–748.

Schoenberg, B. J., Anderson, D. W., & Haerer, A. F. (1985). Severe dementia prevalence and clinical features in a biracial U.S. population. *Archives of Neurology, 42*, 740–743.

Scriabine, A., Schuurman, T., & Traber, J. (1989). Pharmacological basis for the use of nimodipine in central nervous system disorders. *FASEB Journal, 3*, 1799–1806.

Selkoe, D. J. (1990). Deciphering Alzheimer's disease: The amyloid precursor yields new clues. *Science, 248*, 1058–1060.

Sharp, P., Gemmel, H., Cherryman, G., Besson, J., Crawford, J., & Smith, F. (1986). Application of Iodine-123-Labeled Isopropylamphetamine imaging to the study of dementia. *Journal of Nuclear Medicine, 27*, 761–768.

Shimamura, A. (1986). Priming effects in amnesia: Evidence for a dissociable memory function. *Quarterly Journal of Experimental Psychology*, 619–644.

Shimamura, A. P., Salmon, D. P., Squire, L. R., & Butters, N. (1987). Memory dysfunction and word priming in dementia and amnesia. *Behavioral Neuroscience, 101*, 347–351.

Sparks, D. L., Hunsaker, J. C., III, Slevin, J. T., DeKosky, S. T., Kryscio, R. J., & Markesbery, W. R. (1992). Monoaminergic and cholinergic synaptic markers in the nucleus basalis of meynert (nbM): Normal age-related changes and the effect of heart disease and Alzheimer's disease. *Annals of Neurology, 31,* 611–620.

Sparks, D. L., Markesbery, W. R., & Slevin, J. T. (1986). Alzheimer's disease: Monoamines and spiperone binding reduced in nucleus basalis. *Annals of Neurology, 18,* 562–565.

St. George-Hyslop, P. H., Haines, J. L., Farrer, L. A., Polinsky, R., Van Broeckhoven, C., Goate, A., Crapper-McLachlan, D. R., Orr, H., Bruni, A. C., Sorbi, S., Rainero, I., Foncin, J.-F., Pollen, D., Cantu, J.-M., Tupler, R., Voskresenskaya, N., Mayeux, R., Growdon, J., Fried, V. A., Myers, R. H., Nee, L., Backhovens, H., Martin, J.-J., Rossor, M., Owen, M. J., Mullan, M., Percy, M. E., Karlinsky, H., Rich, S., Heston, L., Montes, M., Mortillai, M., Nacmias, N., Gusella, J. F., Hardy, J. A., & other members of the FAD collaborative study group. (1990). Genetic linkage studies suggest that Alzheimer's disease is not a single homogeneous disorder. *Nature, 347,* 194–197.

St. George-Hyslop, P. H., Tanzi, R. E., Polinsky, R. J., Haines, J. L., Nee, L., Watkins, P. C., Myers, R. H., Feldman, R. G., Pollen, D., & Drachman, D. (1987). The genetic deficit causing familial Alzheimer's disease maps on chromosome 21. *Science, 35,* 885–890.

Stern, Y., Mayeux, R., Sano, M., Hauser, W. A., & Bush, T. (1987). Predictors of disease course in patients with probable Alzheimer's disease. *Neurology, 37,* 1649–1653.

Sultzer, D. L., Levin, H. S., Mahler, M. E., High, W. M., & Cummings, J. L. (1992). Assessment of cognitive, psychiatric, and behavioral disturbances in patients with dementia: The Neurobehavioral Rating Scale. *Journal of the American Geriatrics Society, 40,* 549–555.

Sunderland, T., Alterman, I., Yount, D., Hill, J. L., Tariot, P. N., Newhouse, P. A., Mueller, E. A., Mellow, A. M., & Cohen, R. M. (1988). A new scale for the assessment of depressed mood in dementia subjects. *American Journal of Psychiatry, 145,* 955–959.

Sunderland, T., Hill, J. L., Lawlor, B. A., & Molchan, S. E. (1988). NIMH dementia mood assessment scale (DMAS). *Psychopharmacology Bulletin, 24,* 747–753.

Sunderland, T., Tariot, P. N., Cohen, R. M., Weingartner, H., Mueller, E. A., & Murphy, D. L. (1987). Anticholinergic sensitivity in patients with dementia of the Alzheimer type and age-matched controls: A dose-response study. *Archives of General Psychiatry, 441,* 418–426.

Swearer, J. M., Drachman, D. A., O'Donnell, B. F., & Mitchell, A. L. (1988). Troublesome and disruptive behaviors in dementia. *Journal of the American Geriatrics Society, 36,* 784–790.

Tanzi, R. E., Gusella, J. F., Watkins, P. C., Bruns, G. A., St. George-Hyslop, P., Van Keuren, M. L., Patterson, D., Pagan, S., Kurnit, D. M., & Neve, R. L. (1987). Amyloid beta protein gene: CDNA, MRNA distribution, and genetic linkage near the Alzheimer locus. *Science, 235,* 880–884.

Tariot, P. N., Cohen, R. M., Sunderland, T., Newhouse, P. A., Yount, D., Mellow, A. M., Weingartner, H., Mueller, E. A., & Murphy, D. L. (1987). L-deprenyl in Alzheimer's disease. *Archives of General Psychiatry, 49,* 427–433.

Taylor, G. A., Ferrier, I. N., McLoughlin, I. J., Fairbairn, A. F., McKeith, I. G., Lett, D., & Edwardson, J. A. (1992). Gastrointestinal absorption of aluminium in Alzheimer's disease: Response to aluminium cirtrate. *Age and Aging, 21,* 81–90.

Teng, E. L., Chui, H. C., Schneider, L. S., & Metzger, L. E. (1987). Alzheimer's dementia: Performance on the Mini-Mental State Examination. *Journal of Consulting and Clinical Psychology, 55,* 96–100.

Teri, L., Hughes, J. P., & Larson, E. B. (1990). Cognitive deterioration in Alzheimer's disease: Behavioral and health factors. *Journal of Gerontology, 45,* 58–63.

Terry, R. D., & Katzman, R. (1983). Senile dementia of the Alzheimer type. *Annals of Neurology, 14,* 497–506.

Terry, R. D., Masliah, E., Salmon, D. P., Butters, N., DeTeresa, R., Hill, R., Hansen, L. A., & Katzman, R. (1991). Physical basis of cognitive alterations in Alzheimer's disease: Synapse loss is the major correlate of cognitive impairment. *Annals of Neurology, 30,* 572–580.

Uhlmann, R. F., Larson, E. B., & Koepsell, T. D. (1986). Hearing impairment and cognitive decline in senile dementia of the Alzheimer's type. *Journal of the American Geriatrics Society, 34,* 207–210.

Van Dijk, P. T. M., Dippel, D. W. J., & Habbema, J. D. F. (1991). Survival of patients with dementia. *Journal of the American Geriatrics Society, 39,* 603–610.

Van Duijn, C. M., Tanja, T. A., Haaxma, R., Schulte, W., Saan, R. J., Lameris, A. J., Antonides-Hendriks, G., & Hofman, A. (1992). Head trauma and the risk of Alzheimer's disease. *American Journal of Epidemiology, 135,* 775–782.

Villardita, C., Grioli, S., Lomeo, C., Cattaneo, C., & Parini, J. (1992). Clinical studies with oxiracetam in patients with dementia of Alzheimer type and multi-infarct dementia of mild to moderate degree. *Neuropsychobiology, 25,* 24–28.

Wade, J. P. H. (1991). Multi-infarct dementia: Prevention and treatment. *Alzheimer Disease and Associated Disorders,* 5(2), 144–148.

Warrington, E. K., & Weiskrantz, L. (1968). New method of testing long-term retention with special reference to amnesic patients. *Nature, 217,* 972–974.

Warrington, E. K., & Weiskrantz, L. (1970). Amnesic syndrome: Consolidation or retrieval? *Nature, 228,* 628–630.

Wechsler, D. (1945). A standardized memory scale for clinical use. *Journal of Psychology, 19,* 87–95.

Wechsler, D. (1981). *Wechsler Adult Intelligence Scale–Revised.* New York: Psychological Corporation.

Wechsler, D. (1987). *Wechsler Memory Scale–Revised manual.* New York: Psychological Corporation.

Weinstein, H. C., Haan, J., Van Royen, E. O., Derix, M. M. A., Lanser, J. B. K., Van der Zant, F., Dunnewold, R. J. W., Van Kroonenburgh, M. J. P. G., Pauwels, E. K. J., Van der Velde, E. A., Hijdra, A., & Buruma, O. J. S. (1991). SPECT in the diagnosis of Alzheimer's disease and multi-infarct-dementia. *Clinical Neurology and Neurosurgery, 93*(1), 39–43.

Welsh, K. A., Butters, N., Hughes, J., Mohs, R., & Heyman, A. (1991). Detection of abnormal memory decline in mild cases of Alzheimer's disease using CERAD neuropsychological measures. *Archives of Neurology, 48,* 278–281.

Welsh, K. A., Butters, N., Hughes, J. P., Mohs, R. C., & Heyman, A. (1992). Detection and staging of dementia in Alzheimer's disease: Use of the neuropsychological measures developed for the consortium to establish a registry for Alzheimer's disease. *Archives of Neurology, 49,* 448–452.

Wilcock, G. K., Esiri, M. M., Bowen, D. M., & Smith, C. C. T. (1982). Alzheimer's disease: Correlations of cortical choline acety transference activity under the severity of dementia and histological abnormalities. *Journal of the Neurological Sciences, 57,* 407–417.

Williams, J. M. (1987). *Cognitive Behavior Rating Scales manual.* Odessa, FL: Psychological Assessment Resources.

Winblad, B., Hardy, J., Backman, L., & Nilsson, L. (1985). Memory function and brain biochemistry in normal aging and in senile dementia. In *Annals of the New York Academy of Sciences* (pp. 255–268). New York: New York Academy of Sciences.

Wisniewski, K. E., Wisniewski, H. M., & Wen, G. Y. (1985). Occurrence of neuropathological changes and dementia of Alzheimer's disease in Down's syndrome. *Annals of Neurology, 17,* 278–282.

Wolfe, N., Linn, R., Babikian, V. L., Knoefel, J. E., & Albert, M. L. (1990). Frontal systems impairment following multiple lacunar infarcts. *Archives of Neurology, 47,* 129–132.

Wolozin, B. I., Pruchnicki, A., Dickson, D. W., & Davies, P. (1986). A neuronal antigen in the brains of Alzheimer patients. *Science, 232,* 648–650.

Yanker, B. A., Dawes, L. R., Fisher, S., Villa-Komaroff, L., Oster-Granite, M. L., & Neve, R. L. (1989). Neurotoxicity of a fragment of the amyloid precursor associated with Alzheimer's disease. *Science, 245,* 417–420.

Yatzkan, E. S. (1988). Emergency situations for patients and caregivers. In M. K. Aronson (Ed.), *Understanding Alzheimer's disease* (pp. 146–162). New York: Macmillan.

Yesavage, J. A. (1988). Geriatric Depression Scale. *Psychopharmacology Bulletin, 24,* 709–711.

Yesavage, J. A., Brink, T. L., Rose, T., & Adey, M. (1983). The Geriatric Depression Rating Scale: Comparisons with other self-report and psychiatric scales. In T. Crook, S. Ferns, & R. Barks (Eds.), *Assessments in geriatrics psychopharmacology* (pp. 153–167). New Canaan, CT: Mark Pouley Associates.

Yesavage, J. A., Brink, T. L., Rose, T. L., Lum, O., Huang, V., Adey, M., & Leirer, V. O. (1983). Development and validation of a geriatric depression scale. *Journal of Psychiatric Research, 17,* 31–49.

Ziegler, D. K. (1954). Cerebral atrophy in psychiatric patients. *American Journal of Psychiatry, 111,* 454–458.

Zimmerman, R. D., Fleming, C. A., Lee, B. C., Saint-Louis, L. A., & Deck, M. B. (1986). Periventricular hyperintensity as seen by magnetic resonance: Prevalence and significance. *American Journal of Roentgenology, 146,* 443–450.

Zubenko, G. S. (1990). Progression of illness in the differential diagnosis of primary dementia. *American Journal of Psychiatry, 147,* 435–438.

Zubenko, G. S., Cohen, B. M., Reynolds, C. F., Boller, F., Malinakova, I., & Keefe, N. (1987). Platelet membrane fluidity in Alzheimer's disease and major depression. *American Journal of Psychiatry, 144,* 860–868.

Zubenko, G. S., Huff, F. J., Becker, J., Beyer, J., & Teply, I. (1988). Cognitive and platelet membrane fluidity in Alzheimer's disease. *Biological Psychiatry, 24,* 925–936.

CHAPTER 4

SECONDARY DEMENTIAS: REVERSIBLE DEMENTIAS AND PSEUDODEMENTIA

Sara Jo Nixon

In chapter 3, I addressed the more common causes of cognitive decline in older adults, such as dementia of the Alzheimer's type (DAT) and vascular dementia. However, there are a host of other disorders that may lead to cognitive dysfunction in older adults. These disorders include psychiatric disorders such as Ganser's syndrome and depression; disorders attributable to medications; and neurologic and metabolic disorders such as B6 deficiency, basal ganglia disorders, head injuries, and viral infections (Cunha, 1990; Feher, Inbody, Nolan, & Pirozzolo, 1988; Lishman, 1987; Rosenthal & Goodwin, 1985; Taylor, 1990).

In the current chapter, I review dementias in elderly people that are not the result of *primary* loss of cortical or subcortical function but, rather, result as *secondary* outcomes from other disease processes. The literature is somewhat inconsistent in the precise terminology used (Kramer & Reifler, 1992; Maletta, 1990; McAllister, 1983). In most cases, however, *reversible dementia* is the more general term, referring to those cases of dementia that are believed to be due to an underlying pathological process that is potentially reversible with proper treatment (Maletta, 1990). Reversible dementias include those attributable to vitamin deficiencies, medications, and coexisting psychiatric disorders. Cunha (1990) cited studies indicating that as many as 10% to 30% of those patients presenting with dementia symptomatology may have a treatable or partly reversible pathologic process.

Pseudodementia is a more specific term, referring to "behavioral changes that resemble those of the progressive degenerative dementias, but which are attributable to so-called functional causes" (Jones, Tranel, Benton, & Paulsen, 1992, p. 13). That is, *pseudodementia* is typically used to refer to the coexistence of a psychiatric disorder and dementia. The literature suggests that the most common pseudodementia and the most easily misdiagnosed is that associated with depression (Alexopoulos & Mattis, 1991; desRosiers, 1992; Haggerty, Golden, Evans, & Janowsky, 1988; Jones et al., 1992; Lishman, 1987; McAllister, 1983).

In the current chapter, I focus on four general areas: (a) potential causes of secondary dementias; (b) general clinical differentiations between pseudodementia and primary degenerative dementia (PDD), particularly DAT; (c) differential diagnosis and assessment; and (d) treatment and prognosis. In keeping with other chapters in this book, I present case studies at the conclusion of the chapter.

ETIOLOGIES OF SECONDARY DEMENTIAS

Describing the etiology of secondary dementias is extremely difficult for two reasons. First, frequently more than one biopsychological system is compromised in individuals evidencing cognitive decline (Kramer & Reifler, 1992; Larson, Reifler, Sumi, Canfield, & Chinn, 1985). Second, a large number of factors have been shown to contribute to cognitive decline.

Etiological factors can be roughly divided into four categories: chemical, environmental, physical, and psychiatric. Chemical factors include intoxication by anesthesia, alcohol, and heavy metals and use of a wide range of medications. Overstimulation, major lifestyle changes, and sensory deprivation are examples of environmental factors. Physical disorders that are known to produce cognitive decline include thyroid and other endocrine-system disorders; metabolic disorders, such as hepatic encephalopathy; and vitamin deficiency disorders, such as anemia and Wernicke–Korsakoff syndrome. Psychiatric factors include chronic schizophrenia and depression. Milder associations between cognitive decline and a variety of other conditions and disorders—including subdural hematoma, cerebral tumor, anoxia or hypoxia, cerebrovascular accidents, normal pressure hydrocephalus, brain abscesses, cardiac disorders, and pulmonary failure—have also been suggested. Clearly, a detailed discussion of all of the potential etiological factors is beyond the scope of this chapter. (See Exhibit 1 for an outline of these variables.) Readers are referred to Thompson's (1987) excellent review and to Lishman (1987), Feher et al. (1988), Rosenthal and Goodwin (1985), and Taylor (1990).

Given the large number of factors that have been identified as potential contributors to cognitive decline, and given the fact that many secondary dementias are caused by more than one factor, it is important that diagnosis and assessment for secondary dementias include a thorough, comprehensive medical history that examines etiological factors in all four categories. For example, clinicians should be especially alert to a patient's use of medications.

EXHIBIT 1

Variables and Conditions Associated With Secondary Dementia

Chemical intoxication

- Anesthesia
- Exogenous or industrial agents (including alcohol)
- Heavy metals

Endocrinopathies

- Hyperadrenalism[a]
- Hyperadrenalism and exogenous steroids[a]
- Hypoglycemia[a]
- Hypopituitarism[a]
- Parathyroid disease
- Thyroid abnormalities

Environmental sources

- Overstimulation or change
- Sensory deprivation or impairment (paraphrenia)

Medications

- Anticholinergics
- Anticonvulsants
- Antihypertensives
- Anxiolytics

Metabolic electrolyte disorders

- Hepatic encephalopathy
- Hypercalcemia
- Hypoatremia
- Uremic encephalopathy
- Volume depletion

Nutritional deficiencies

- Anemia (folate [B_{12}])
- Pellagra (niacin)
- Wernicke–Korsakoff syndrome (thiamine [B_1])

Psychiatric disorders

- Chronic schizophrenia
- Depression (pseudodementia)
- Hypomania
- Neurotic reaction[b]
- Repeated electroconvulsive therapy

[a]Usually associated with affective symptoms but should be considered in differential diagnosis. [b]It may be argued, as does Thompson (1987), that emotional stresses or conflicts are, by definition, not the underlying cause of dementia. However, they may be seen as "releasing factors for certain symptomatology."

EXHIBIT 2

Commonly Used Medications That May Cause Cognitive or Affective Change in Elderly Patients

Beta-blockers, especially propranolol (Inderal)

Antihypertensive agents

- Beta-blockers (see above)
- Methyldopa
- Reserpine
- Clonidine
- Diuretics

Neuroleptics

- Haloperidol (Haldol)
- Chlorpromazine (Thorazine)
- Thioridazine (Mellaril)
- Fluphenazine (Prolixin)
- Perphenazine (Trilafon)
- Loxapine (Loxitane)
- Molindone (Moban)
- Thiothixene (Navane)
- Trifluoperazine (Stelazine)

Benzodiazepines

- Diazepam (Valium)
- Flurazepam (Dalmane)
- Clorazepate (Tranxene)
- Chlordiazepoxide (Librium)
- Prazepam (Centrax)
- Alprazolam (Xanax)
- Halazepam (Paxipam)
- Triazolam (Halcion)
- Temazepam (Restoril)
- Oxazepam (Serax)
- Lorazepam (Ativan)

Antiseizure medications

- Barbiturates
- Carbamazepine (Tegretol)
- Phenytoin (Dilantin)
- Phenobarbital

Antihistamines

- Cimetidine (Tagamet)

Anticholinergic agents

- Atropine
- Benztropine
- Diphenhydramine
- Trihexyphenidyl

Antiarrythmic agents

- Procainamide
- Disopyramide
- Quinidine

Steroids

From "Depression and Other Psychiatric Disorders," by M. A. Jenike. In Geriatric Neuropsychology *(p. 127), edited by M. S. Albert and M. Moss, 1988, New York: Guilford Press. Copyright 1988 by Guilford Press. Reprinted with permission.*

Geriatric patients are major consumers of prescription and over-the-counter drugs, and studies have revealed that a host of these medications produce effects symptomatic of cognitive decline. Readers should consult Jenike (1988) in regard to cognitive decline and affective change. Exhibit 2 provides a list of some of the results found by researchers who have studied the adverse effects of medications on elderly people. Some specific areas of concern are discussed in the following paragraphs.

Neuroleptics are frequently prescribed for agitation in elderly patients. However, these drugs may create a drug-induced parkinsonism (Hollister, 1988b, with symptoms such as stooped posture, halting slow gait, and drooling. As one might expect, spontaneity and normal facial expressions may also be lost (Taylor, 1990).

Benzodiazepines are an anxiolytic drug class frequently administered to elderly people. Metabolism of benzodiazepines is significantly slowed in such patients (Greenblatt, Shader, & Harmatz, 1989), resulting in higher plasma levels. Some studies suggest that older people may be more sensitive to benzodiazepines, regardless of dose level. That is, their response to this type of drug, at any level, has been shown to be greater than that in younger persons

(Greenblatt et al., 1989; Pomara et al., 1985). It has been suggested that the adjusted odds ratio for developing an adverse drug effect in elderly patients is 5.89, and most of the increased risk is associated with long-acting benzodiazepines (Kramer & Reifler, 1992).

Greenblatt et al. (1991) examined the *pharmacokinetics* and *pharmacodynamics* of triazolam (Halcion), a common benzodiazepine, using healthy elderly people (mean age = 69 years, *SD* = 1.1) and young people (mean age = 30 years, *SD* = 1.2). Their data revealed enhanced sedation and greater impairment in psychomotor performance in elderly than in younger subjects at the same dosage. This increased sensitivity appears to be related to increased plasma levels (i.e., pharmacokinetics) rather than stemming from an intrinsic sensitivity to the drug (i.e., pharmacodynamics). These authors suggested that dosage of triazolam for elderly people should be reduced, on average, by 50%.

Elderly people are particularly sensitive to the side effects of anticholinergics, including antidepressants with cholinergic action (i.e., tricyclics; Taylor, 1990). Peripheral effects include dry mouth, urinary hesitancy, and loss of visual accommodation (Hollister, 1988a). Central effects include anxiety, delirium, disorientation, hallucinations, hyperactivity, and seizures (Hollister, 1988a).

Digitalis, a drug used to control cardiac disorders, may also be dangerous. Therapeutic ranges are, unfortunately, close to toxic doses. Furthermore, even in blood levels within the therapeutic level, changes in cognitive and psychological function may be noted (Taylor, 1990). Exhibit 2 lists common medications that may produce adverse cognitive or affective changes in older patients. Of course, other substances, such as alcohol and illicit drugs, may also affect cognitive and affective functions (see next section).

Hypothyroidism is estimated to occur in 0.9% to 14.4% of elderly people (Robuschi, Safran, Braverman, Gnudi, & Toti, 1987). *Hypothyroidism* constitutes a descriptor, rather than a diagnosis, and refers to an inadequate supply of thyroid hormone to body tissues. It results either from loss or atrophy of the thyroid tissue *(primary hypothyroidism)* or from dysfunction in the hypothalamic or pituitary systems *(secondary hypothyroidism)*. It is estimated that primary hypothyroidism accounts for 95% of the cases (Inbar, 1985). Note that the use of certain drugs, such as lithium, iodide, and amiodarone, may create a drug-induced hypothyroidism (Hamburger & Kaplan, 1989).

Hypothyroidism is accompanied by a variety of signs and symptoms. Included are delayed relaxation of the myotatic stretch reflex at the ankle, eyelid edema, fatigue, constipation, weight gain, feelings of coldness, slow speech, and memory impairment (Smith & Granger, 1992). The most common cause of hypothyroidism in the elderly is believed to be autoimmune hypothyroiditis (Marsh & Burns, 1986; Robuschi et al., 1987).

Of those vitamins associated with cognitive decline, deficiencies in vitamin B_{12} (cyanocobalamin) have received the most attention (Rosenthal & Goodwin, 1985). Vitamin B_{12} deficiencies are seldom caused by dietary restrictions. More frequently they are due to specific disease processes, often the loss of a necessary intrinsic factor. The initial signs are typically physiological, that is, distal parasthesias due to posterior and lateral spinal column degeneration (Rosenthal & Goodwin, 1985; Thompson, 1987). Megaloblastic hematologic changes are prevalent. In B_{12}-deficient individuals, the tissue folate stores are depleted, although serum levels of folate may be normal. Prolonged deficiencies in B_{12} produce pernicious anemia. Treatment with folate improves the megaloblastic changes, but neurologic changes persist. In fact, administration of folate in B_{12}-deficient patients may precipitate psychiatric symptomatology (Chanarin, 1979; Conley & Krevans, 1951; Lishman, 1987; Rosenthal & Goodwin, 1985).

The mental signs of B_{12} deficiency proceed from irritability to apathy to somnolence to marked paranoid states with emotional lability to psychosis and, ultimately, to encephalopathic states and dementia. Delusions, hallucinations, seizures, optic atrophy, and incontinence are also observed (Lishman, 1987; Rosenthal & Goodwin, 1985).

Electroencephalogram (EEG) abnormalities are also noted in these patients. In an older study (Walton, Kiloh, Osselton, & Farrall, 1954), these abnormalities were observed in 64% (51/80) of patients with untreated pernicious anemia. After treatment, 47 patients were reevaluated. Seventy-four percent (31/47) produced normal EEGs, and 11 others showed substantial improvement. A later study conducted by Wallace and Westmoreland (1976) also indicated EEG abnormalities in approximately 60% of untreated pernicious anemia patients.

Nicotinic acid deficiency is also associated with mental changes (Lishman, 1987). Specifically, it can produce *pellagra,* which is characterized by "the classic triad (three Ds)" (Thompson, 1987, pp. 119–120) of dementia, dermatitis, and diarrhea. Initial symptoms include insomnia, fatigue, nervousness, irritability, and depression with memory loss (Rosenthal & Goodwin, 1985). The acute confusional state observed in pellagra is corrected with niacin therapy. Note that deficiencies in other substances—such as thiamine (B_1), pyroxidine (B_6), and tryptophan—may interact with the niacin deficiency and contribute to some of the observed changes (Rosenthal & Goodwin, 1985).

Deficiencies in thiamine are associated with an acute confusional state known as *Wernicke's encephalopathy* (Lishman, 1987). It is frequently associated with chronic alcohol abuse in nutritionally deficient individuals (Lishman, 1987). However, it may result from other sources of severe thiamine insufficiency (Lishman, 1987). Contributing factors probably include a genetic susceptibility to thiamine deficiency (Martin, McCool, & Singleton, 1993).

Wernicke's encephalopathy is characterized by ocular abnormalities, ataxia, and mental confusion (Lishman, 1987). If untreated, it may lead to coma and death. These symptoms may appear abruptly and are reversible with timely administration of thiamine. Unfortunately, after the acute dementia is alleviated, patients may exhibit an amnestic syndrome known as *Korsakoff's psychosis* (Martin et al., 1993; Parsons & Nixon, 1993).

As noted previously, however, these metabolic processes are not the only source of secondary dementia symptomatology. Certain psychiatric disorders, particularly depression, may also be associated with dementia symptomatology. This issue is discussed at length in the Differential Diagnosis and Assessment section. As shown in Exhibit 1, environmental factors such as overstimulation and sensory deprivation may also be associated with cognitive decline and symptoms of dementia. If left undetected and untreated, the older adult is increasingly isolated, confused, and frustrated and may be eventually subject to psychotic symptomatology.

In summary, the factors associated with secondary dementia are many. They may be relatively subtle, and they are often interactive. Thus, accurate diagnosis and treatment planning are complicated. Thorough medical and psychosocial evaluations are imperative. Difficulty in determining an accurate diagnosis may produce additional frustration and confusion for patients and their families. Thus, it is important that families be prepared for and supported through the essential evaluation and assessment process. Some issues related to family support are discussed in chapter 3, Alzheimer's Disease and Vascular Dementia.

DIFFERENTIATING PSEUDODEMENTIA FROM PDD

Given the potential treatability of certain of the pseudodementias, it is important that they be distinguished from DAT and MID, in which the treatment is largely support and maintenance. Unfortunately, much of the presenting symptomatology in pseudodementia is similar, if not identical, to that associated with PDD. This similarity in signs and symptoms creates a difficult discrimination task for clinicians (Reynolds, Hoch, et al., 1988). Pseudodementia associated with depression (DD) is the most frequently occurring (Lishman, 1987) and most easily misdiagnosed. The review of desRosiers (1992) suggested that as many as 10% to 20% of patients are misdiagnosed, either as depression mistaken as organic dementia or vice versa. Given the prevalence and clinical importance of depression in elderly people (Emery & Oxman, 1992; McCullough, 1991), this section focuses on distinguishing DD from PDD, usually DAT.

Cognitive and behavioral impairment in PDD is assessed with essentially the same instruments as those used in suspected DD. Therefore, no separate lists of assessment materials are provided here. Interested readers might refer to chapter 3 in this

TABLE 1

Diagnostic Aspects of Dementia and Pseudodementia

Variable	Pseudodementia	Organic dementia[a]
History and course		
Onset	More precise, usually in terms of days or weeks	Insidious
Course	Rapid, uneven	Slow, worse at night
Past history	Depression or mania frequently	Uncertain relation
Family history	Depression or mania frequently	Positive family history for dementia in ≈ 50% DAT
Affect and general behavior		
Mood	Depressed; little or no response to sad or funny situations; behavior and affect inconsistent with degree of cognitive impairment	Shallow or labile; exaggerated or normal response to sad or funny situations; consistent with degree of cognitive deficit
Cooperation	Poor; little effort to perform well; responds often with "I don't know"; apathetic, emphasizes failures	Good; frustrated by inability to do well; response to queries approximate confabricated or perseverated; emphasizes trivial accomplishment
Neuropsychological and biomedical		
Memory	Emphasizes memory loss; greater impairment of personality features (e.g., confidence, drive, interests, and attention)	Denies or minimizes impairment; greater impairment in cognitive features (e.g., recent memory and orientation to time and date)
MMSE	Variable on repeated exams	Consistent on repeated exams
Symptoms	Increased psychologic symptoms: sadness, anxiety, somatic symptoms	Increased neurologic symptoms: dysphasia, dyspraxia, agnosia, incontinence
CT and EEG	Typically normal for age	Often abnormal

Note: DAT = dementia of the Alzheimer's type; MMSE = Mini-Mental State Exam (Folstein, Folstein, & McHugh, 1975); CT = computed tomography; EEG = electroencephalogram.
[a]A detailed description of dementia, primarily DAT and multi-infarct dementia, is included in chapter 3.

volume for lists and descriptions of relevant instruments. The next section illustrates the ways in which the two groups may differ from each other on some of these tests.

Before turning to these comparisons, however, note that with any of the suspected secondary dementias, it is particularly important that a careful alcohol and other drug-use assessment be conducted. Exemplars for such interviews are presented in chapter 7, on HIV-1 infection (drug-use interview) and chapter 6, on alcohol use and negative consequences.

Several of the clinical variables that may be useful in differentially diagnosing DD are outlined in Table 1. Although these distinctions may serve as a framework for clinical diagnosis, note that the overlap in categories may be considerable.

DIFFERENTIAL DIAGNOSIS AND ASSESSMENT

Neurocognitive Performance

A number of studies examining potential differences in self-report measures, traditional neuropsychological assessments, and biopsychological measures have been conducted. One of the more frequently cited studies was conducted by Reynolds, Hoch, et al. (1988). They conducted a comparison of 14 DD patients and 28 patients who met criteria for PDD with depressive symptomatology. Before receiving treatment for the depressive symptomatology, subjects completed the Mini-Mental State Exam (MMSE; Folstein, Folstein, & McHugh, 1975), the Blessed Dementia Rating Scale (Blessed, Tomlinson, & Roth, 1968), and the Hamilton Rating Scale for Depression (Hamilton, 1960).

Analyses on group differences on these tests revealed that DD patients achieved higher (better) global MMSE scores, as well as higher scores on (a) orientation to time and place; (b) registration; and (c) performance of calculations, naming, reading, writing, and copying. Interestingly, the groups did not differ on measures of short-term recall, repetition, or completing a three-stage command.

DD patients were also *less* impaired on the Blessed scale. Items that were particularly sensitive to differences between DD and PDD were (a) inability of patients to find their way about indoors, (b) inability to find their way about familiar streets, and (c) difficulty in dressing.

Finally, DD patients indicated *greater* depression on the Hamilton. Specifically, they reported more severe delayed insomnia (early morning wakings), more psychological anxiety, more somatic anxiety, and greater loss of libido.

Overall, these findings are in keeping with previous cross-sectional work with these populations (Folstein et al., 1975; Folstein & McHugh, 1978; Lazarus, Newton, Cohler, Lesser, & Schweon, 1987; Rabins, Merchant, & Nestadt, 1984).

To determine the predictive utility of the three tests, Reynolds, Hoch, et al. (1988) subjected the MMSE, the Blessed, and the Hamilton to a forced discriminant function analysis. The results indicated that 78.6% of the participants could be correctly identified. Two of the 14 (14.3%) DD patients and 7 of the 28 (25%) of the PDD patients were misclassified.

To improve the prognostic utility of the tests, the forced discriminant function was rerun using only seven of the individual variables: orientation to time (MMSE), psychological anxiety (Hamilton), inability to find one's way about familiar streets (Blessed), difficulty with dressing (Blessed), delayed insomnia (Hamilton), loss of libido (Hamilton), and inability to find one's way about indoors (Blessed). This analysis indicated that 90.5% of the patients were correctly classified. Almost 93% (92.9%) of the DD and 89.3% of the PDD patients were correctly identified. A backward elimination procedure on the model indicated that the more predictive items were the first four listed above. These items accounted for 85.7% of the variance in the model. Thus, these findings suggest that PDD patients show greater disorientation to time, more difficulty with dressing, and more difficulty in finding their way around familiar surroundings. DD patients, on the other hand, express more psychological anxiety.

This latter finding regarding psychological anxiety is in keeping with literature suggesting that DD patients are more likely to give "I don't know" answers and express concern about their poor memory than are PDD patients (O'Connor, Pollitt, Roth, Brook, & Reiss, 1990; C. E. Wells, 1979). McGlone et al. (1990) examined the relation between self-reported memory function, relatives' report of patients' memory function, depression, and objective memory scores. They found that patients' reports of poor memory function were correlated with depressive symptomatology, whereas relatives' reports were related to objective measures of memory dysfunction. Interestingly, objective memory testing improved the specificity, but not the sensitivity, of the self-report measure alone. These findings suggest that self-report measures of memory function, although not substituting for performance measures, may provide important first-stage assessment information and indicate a need for careful evaluation for concomitant depression.

Jones et al. (1992) conducted a longitudinal study of 37 patients referred for differential diagnoses of dementia of an organic origin versus pseudodementia. Their primary objective was to determine to what extent clinical diagnoses made on the basis of neuropsychological performance were related to clinical outcome. Participants were rated on a scale of 1 to 5 (1 = *dementia of organic origin*, 3 = *dementia of unsure etiology*, and 5 = *dementia due to "nonorganic" origin [i.e., pseudodementia]*), on the basis of a neuropsychological test battery. They were retested not less than 6 months later. The average time between assessments was 19 months.

The test battery included the Information, Digit Span, and Block Design subtests of the Wechsler Adult Intelligence Scale–Revised (WAIS-R; Wechsler, 1981); the Controlled Oral Work Association (COWA; Benton, Hamsher, Varney, & Spreen, 1983); the Logical Memory and Paired Associate Learning subtests from the Wechsler Memory Scale (WMS; Wechsler, 1945); the Revised Visual Retention Test (RVRT; Benton, 1974); the Facial Recognition Test (FRT; Benton et al., 1983); and the Temporal Orientation Questionnaire (TOQ; Benton et al., 1983). Whenever possible, alternative forms were used in the two test sessions.

Analyses indicated that most participants (73%) initially diagnosed with either organic dementia or pseudodementia retained that classification at retest. A substantial number, however, were reclassified at retest. Specifically, 8 participants who were originally classified with pseudodementia were reclassified as having dementia, and 2 who were first diagnosed with dementia were reclassified as having pseudodementia.

Correlations between testing at Time 1 and eventual clinical diagnosis indicated that several tests appeared to be differentially sensitive to early organic dementia. These tests included the TOQ, WAIS-R Block Design, and the RVRT. Whereas the patients with dementia performed relatively poorly on these tests, the patients with pseudodementia performed relatively well.

Shuttleworth and Huber (1989) conducted a frequently cited study examining the use of the Picture Absurdities Test (F. L. Wells & Ruesch, 1972) to distinguish DD, DAT, and vascular dementia. They recruited 55 participants meeting criteria for DAT, 13 with DD, and 9 with vascular dementia. They found that the performance of patients with DAT was significantly inferior to the other groups but that the quality of the other groups' performance did not differ. Failure to obtain differences between vascular dementia and DD groups may be due to the small cell sizes. Even with this limitation, however, this finding is important because it was obtained although the groups were equated for factors known to influence performance on this test: age, education, and severity of dementia. Unfortunately, no healthy elderly control group was used. Thus, although it can be concluded that DD patients are superior to DAT patients on this test, it is not possible to compare their performance to normal elderly subjects by means of this study.

Chaves and Izquierdo (1992) examined cognitive function in participants with dementia, participants with depression, and controls. Participants completed tests of immediate, recent, and remote memory; the MMSE; a screening for language disorders; and tests of abstraction, calculation, judgment, praxis, and gnostic functions. Analyses indicated significant differences among the groups on memory function, with depressed participants performing significantly better than patients with dementia. The performance of depressed participants was inferior, but not significantly so, to controls on these tests.

Tests of association using scores on the language, praxis, gnosis, abstraction, and calculation tests indicated that patients indicating deficits in abstraction, calculation, praxis, and language were 16 times more likely to have dementia rather than depression (relative frequency of gnosis disturbances was very low in all groups). On the other hand, impairment in calculation without accompanying impairment in praxis or abstraction was associated with a diagnosis of depression.

It has been hypothesized that the memory deficits observed in DAT and DD patients are not due to a common process (Hart, Kwentus, Harkins, Taylor, & Rybarczyk, 1985). Specifically, it has been proposed that motivational and attentional deficits in DD subjects produce an impairment primarily in learning efficiency with essentially normal memory retention of well-learned material. DAT patients, on the other hand, fail to consolidate information effectively and, thus, experience greater forgetting over time. To test this hypothesis, Hart, Kwentus, Taylor, and Harkins (1987) conducted a comparison of DAT, DD, and normal control participants on a battery of neuropsychological tests and a rate-of-forgetting test. The rate-of-forgetting test consisted of the individual presentation of 130 slides of line drawings of common objects followed by a yes–no recognition test (16 slides, 8 old, and 8 new). Level of learning was equated across the groups by requiring a 13/16 correct-response criterion on the recognition test. Participants who failed to meet this criterion were given a second recognition test; all participants achieved criterion on this second test.

In keeping with data indicating considerable overlap in DAT and DD patients, the results indicated that these groups performed similarly on tests of general intelligence, reasoning, verbal fluency, and concentration. DAT patients' performance was inferior to DD patients on tests of temporal orientation and verbal memory.

The rate-of-forgetting test appeared to be useful in distinguishing the two groups. In keeping with the hypothesis, DAT participants showed differential forgetting, even at the shortest time interval (10 min). However, DD patients showed essentially normal forgetting at this interval, although they required more time than controls to achieve learning criterion. Thus, these data suggest that memory impairment in DD may be due to deficits in encoding and initial acquisition, as opposed to consolidation and retrieval processes. Tests dissociating the acquisition process and the consolidation and retrieval processes may be particularly useful in distinguishing DD and DAT.

Cognitive slowing has been of considerable interest in the study of dementia and depression (Gordon & Carson, 1990; Hart & Kwentus, 1987; Nelson & Charney, 1981; Pirozzolo, Mahurin, Loring, Appel, & Maletta, 1985; Vrtunski, Patterson, Mack, & Hill, 1983; Williams, Jones, Briscoe, Thomas, & Cronin, 1991). A classic task for assessment of cognitive slowing and memory function is the Sternberg (1975) task. In this task, participants are typically given a varying number of items to retain in memory (memory set). A probe stimulus is presented, and the participant is asked to determine whether the probe is a part of the memory set. Generally, the reaction time increases linearly as a function of the number of items in the memory set. Given the fact that the motor response is the same regardless of the size of the memory set, the slope of the reaction time function is presumed to reflect the time required to perform a single memory comparison. The intercept is presumed to reflect the time required in perceptual encoding of the stimulus, motor initiation, and execution.

Certain participant groups, including DAT patients, find the task extremely difficult and provide uninterpretable data (Hilbert, Niederehe, & Kahn, 1976). Therefore, Nebes, Brady, and Reynolds (1992) modified the task in their study of response slowing in DAT (mean age = 76.9 years, *SD* = 8.6), elderly depressed (mean age = 66.5 years, *SD* = 6.0), normal elderly (mean age = 76.4 years, *SD* = 5.4), and normal young (mean age = 23.9 years, *SD* = 3.4) participants. Specifically, Nebes et al. asked participants to simply enumerate, using a voice-activated response key, the number of dots (1 to 4) presented by means of a tachistoscope, and then they determined participants' response times to the various stimulus sets. (Control tasks for the time required to produce each word—*one, two, three,* or *four*—were also conducted.)

There were several important findings from this study. First, response times increased with the number of dots in the array, for all groups. Second, the magnitude of the slope differed for the groups. Slopes of between 30 and 40 ms were observed for both normal groups and the elderly depressed. However, the slope for participants with DAT was substantially greater (between 66% and 134% greater). These findings are in keeping with the hypothesis that elderly depressed people do not suffer from a cognitive slowing per se. However, there are limitations to generalizing from this study. Specifically, unlike previous work (Hart & Kwentus, 1987; Hilbert et al., 1976), the intercepts for the elderly depressed people and normal elderly people did not differ (i.e., elderly people who were depressed showed no psychomotor slowing). This outcome may be related to the selection process, which eliminated elderly depressed participants who demonstrated cognitive impairment.

Hart and Kwentus (1987), on the other hand, included such participants in their study. Their work indicated psychomotor, but no central cognitive, slowing in depressed and cognitively impaired elderly people. Including a group of DD patients in the current study would have provided important information regarding the underlying processes compromised in pseudodementia.

Abas, Sahakian, and Levy (1990) also investigated neuropsychological functioning in DD participants. Similar to the previous study, they selected elderly depressed participants who did not exhibit dementia ($n = 20$; mean age = 70.4, $SD = 6.1$) and compared their cognitive performance to both normal elderly controls ($n = 20$; mean age = 68.3 years, $SD = 5.6$) and DAT participants ($n = 19$; mean age = 70.9 years, $SD = 6.3$). In addition to initial assessment, testing was conducted after recovery in the depressed participants. (These data are discussed in the Prognosis section.)

Participants completed a series of tests, including the Kendrick Cognitive Tests for the Elderly (Kendrick, 1985) and a computerized battery that emphasizes visual memory. Specific tests measured pattern recognition, spatial recognition, simultaneous matching to sample, delayed matching to sample, and conditional associative learning.

Interestingly, these participants' performance on the pattern- and spatial-recognition tasks was almost identical to that of the DAT subjects. Their accuracy scores and latencies were significantly inferior to controls, but not different from the DAT group. Thus, in contrast to the Nebes et al. (1992) work, this study did show significant slowing in the elderly depressed group.

The matching-to-sample task failed to differentiate the groups. However, the delayed-matching-to-sample task revealed that DAT and depressed participants were essentially equivalent in their level of performance, both being significantly inferior to control participants. Both groups also showed a significant delay-dependent deficit in accuracy, with impairment being positively correlated with delay.

Latencies were also delayed in the DAT and depressed groups in relation to the controls. However, DAT and depressed participants did not differ from each other. Analysis of the Group × Delay interaction on latencies of correct responses revealed that although DAT and control participants showed a pattern of increasing latencies with increasing difficulty (e.g., length of delay), depressed participants showed increased delays *regardless* of difficulty.

The conditional learning test requires participants to learn the location or locations of specific patterns. The test has four levels of difficulty. In the simplest level, participants are required to learn the location of only one pattern. The more difficult sets require learning the correct location of either three, six, or eight individual patterns. Participants have 10 trials in which to learn the position of each set of patterns. If participants fail to learn a set of patterns within 10 trials, they are automatically terminated from the test.

Of the control participants, 100% attained criterion across all sets. Only 30% of the depressed and 16% of the DAT participants completed all sets. At the most difficult level, depressed participants performed as poorly as did the DAT participants. In fact, the data indicated that depressed participants performed as well as controls only up to completion of the first set of three items.

The Kendrick tests also revealed significant deficits by depressed and DAT participants. Although depressed participants' performance lay between the control and DAT participants' on the object-learning test, they performed no better than the DAT participants on the digit-copying test.

Note that current medication and a history of electroconvulsive therapy were not associated with differential performance in the depressed group. That is, regardless of current pharmacological treatment (present vs. absent) and electroconvulsive therapy history, depressed participants indicated significant deficits in learning and memory functions. Furthermore, these deficits were not related to severity of current depression.

Despite the similarity in depressed and DAT participants, there were some data suggesting qualitative differences between the groups. Specifically, patterns of errors in the two groups differed. Depressed participants made significantly fewer random errors on the delayed-matching-to-sample task than did DAT participants. DAT participants, on the other hand, made proportionately fewer shape-distractor errors than color-distractor errors, whereas depressed participants showed approximately equal proportions of shape- and color-distractor errors. Abas et al. (1990) concluded that this pattern indicated that DAT patients are less able to memorize shape, a more difficult concept than color.

Additionally, DAT participants showed a delay-dependent increase in latencies on the delayed-matching-to-sample task, which was not paralleled by depressed participants. Depressed participants indicated slower latencies, regardless of delay. That is, depressed participants did not show a sensitivity to the increased cognitive load created by the increased delays. This finding is in keeping with the hypothesis that at least a part of the cognitive dysfunction associated with depression is produced by faulty effortful processing (Cohen, Weingartner, Smallberg, Pickar, & Murphy, 1982; Henry, Weingartner, & Murphy, 1973; Reus, Silberman, Post, & Weingartner, 1979).

Finally, depressed participants performed better than DAT patients on the conditional-associative-learning task, although their performance was inferior to controls. Note that this task has an inherent bias in reducing error in subsequent responses once a correct location is learned. Using this inherent organizational structure provides a cue for correct responding. It appears that depressed elderly persons are more able to use this strategy than are DAT patients.

Antisaccadic eye movements (deliberate eye movements opposite from the visual stimulus) have also been studied in cognitively impaired patients (Fletcher & Sharpe, 1986; Fukushima et al., 1988; Lasker, Zee, Hain, Folstein, & Singer, 1987; Pierrot-Deseilligny, Rivaud, Pillon, Fournier, & Agid, 1989). Currie, Ramsden, McArthur, and Maruff (1991) studied 30 DAT, 5 Huntington's chorea, and 12 DD patients using a clinical antisaccadic test. This test consisted of asking patients to first look at the examiner's nose until one of the examiner's index fingers moved, and then to move their eyes in the direction of the finger movement (saccadic movement). The saccades were continued until the patient could correctly perform the task. Next, patients were asked to move their eyes in the direction opposite from the examiner's finger movement (antisaccadic movement). Once patients indicated understanding of the task, 25 trials (5 practice and 20 test trials) were administered with random determination of laterality. A percentage error rate was determined (number of antisaccadic errors out of 20) × 100.

In addition to correlating well with laboratory measures of eye movement, the task discriminated among participant groups. When compared with normative data, 83% of the DAT participants produced error rates in the impaired range (>30% error rate), and error rates correlated well with severity of dementia. Those participants with Huntington's disease produced error rates even higher than the DAT patients, with all participants having error rates in the impaired range (all >32%). On the other hand, all DD patients produced error rates within normal bounds. Thus, a simple and relatively effective assessment for PDD versus DD might include this clinical antisaccadic test.

In summary, discriminating DD from DAT patients on the basis of neuropsychological assessment remains difficult; consistent differential response patterns have yet to be identified. A potentially useful test may be the antisaccadic test described above. However, additional studies are needed to support these early, promising results. Difficulty in determining a diagnosis solely from neuropsychological data reinforces the earlier call for thorough medical evaluations to accompany neuropsychological examinations. Despite this noted limitation, a neuropsychological examination, identifying preserved as well as impaired areas, is a critical aspect of diagnosis and treatment planning.

Neurophysiologic Assessment

Event-related potentials have also been used to examine potential differences in a variety of clinical and developmental studies regarding, for example, aging, psychiatric disorders, and dementia (e.g., Chiappa, 1990; Iragui, Kutas, Mitchiner, & Hillyard, 1993; Ollo, Johnson, & Grafman, 1991). One of the primary components of the event-related potential study is the P300, a positivity in the brain electrophysiological response occurring with maximum amplitude at approximately 300 ms after stimulus presentation (see Oken, 1989, and Rohrbaugh, Parasuraman, & Johnson, 1990, for discussions).

Several studies have been conducted using event-related potentials to examine differences between patients with dementia and patients with pseudodementia. Whereas some studies have observed significant differences between these groups (Brown, Marsh, & Larue, 1982; Goodin, Keneth, & Starr, 1978; Lai, Brown, Marsh, & Larue, 1983; Pfefferbaum, Wenegrat, Ford, Roth, & Kopel, 1984;

Polich, Ehlers, Otis, Mandell, & Bloom, 1986), others have failed to find such differences (Slaets & Fortgens, 1984; St. Clair, Blackwood, & Christe, 1985). Gottlieb, Wertman, and Bentin (1991) examined the possibility that some of the inconsistency in the literature might be attributable to the difference(s) between active and passive tasks. To address this question, 25 patients with organic dementia (80% DAT), 14 DD patients, and 24 controls participated in an *auditory oddball paradigm,* under both active and passive conditions.

The auditory oddball paradigm is a procedure in which a P300 is produced after presentation of rarely occurring odd tones, if they are task relevant (e.g., must be tallied or counted). In the present protocol, the rare tones were lower in pitch than the frequent tones and occurred only 15% of the time. Brain electrical activity was measured from midline scalp electrodes.

In the passive-listening condition, participants were presented with a series of 120 stimuli and instructed to simply listen to the tones. This is a condition unlikely to produce a very large or consistent P300, although P300-like forms may be observed. In the active-listening condition, participants were instructed to silently count the number of rarely occurring tones. Appropriate assistance was provided in counting for those participants who had difficulty in remembering the counts.

The data were analyzed using two models. The first measured amplitude on a peak-to-peak basis (N2 to P3) and the latency as the latency of the P300 peak. The second assessed amplitude as the mean of peak-to-peak amplitudes between N2–P3 and P3–N4 and the latency as the mean between initial and final latency of the P300 wave. Results indicated no significant group differences in either amplitude or latency for the P300-like waveform in the passive-listening condition. However, there were significant differences in the active condition. P300 amplitudes were reduced for both clinical groups, regardless of measurement technique. The latency was significantly longer in the group with dementia as opposed to the other groups, but only in the second, mean measurement procedure.

Research suggests that P300 amplitude, as opposed to latency, is associated with memory functions (Donchin & Coles, 1988). If this is true, these data suggest that patients with pseudodementia may suffer from an organic but potentially reversible memory dysfunction (Gottlieb et al., 1991). They also suggest that latency measures may be more sensitive to subtle differences between patients with dementia and patients with pseudodementia.

Electroencephalographic data obtained during sleep have also been used to study differences between these groups. Reynolds, Kupfer, et al. (1988) conducted a large-scale study of EEG in sleep with elderly participants. They studied a total of 235 participants; 77 healthy elderly controls (mean age = 69.3 years, SD = 6.4), 67 depressed patients (mean age = 70.3 years, SD = 5.7), 49 patients having dementia (mean age = 72.8 years, SD = 8.0), and 42 patients with mixed clinical pres-entations of dementia and depression. Fourteen of this last group were classified as DD (mean age = 75.1 years, SD = 5.6), and 28 were diagnosed with PDD with depressive features (mean age = 71.4 years, SD = 8.0).

Analysis of the sleep data indicated that four predictor variables could correctly classify 80% of the participants in the larger patient groups (having depression vs. having dementia). These variables were REM sleep latency (lower in depressives), REM sleep percentage (higher in depressives), indeterminate non-REM sleep percentage (higher in patients with dementia), and early morning awakening (more marked in depressives).

Additional analyses were conducted on the group of 42 mixed-symptom participants. These analyses supported the previous findings; 64% of the participants were correctly classified (PDD vs. DD). These findings are also consistent with these investigators' previous work (Reynolds et al., 1986), which suggested that greater sleep disturbance in terms of greater sleep continuity disturbance and early morning awakening in patients with pseudodementia may be reliable indicators of disease progression over 2 years.

Using a much smaller group of participants (N = 26), this group studied the effects of sleep deprivation on EEG patterns in 18 PDD with depressive features (mean age = 71.9 years, SD = 6.3) and 8 DD (mean age = 73.3 years, SD = 8.8) participants

(Buysse et al., 1988). Participants provided baseline data as well as data on 2 nights after sleep deprivation. Patients with pseudodementia were found to have (a) less severe symptoms of dementia at baseline, (b) decreased depression ratings after sleep deprivation, (c) higher REM sleep percentage and phasic REM activity and intensity at baseline, and (d) longer first REM period on Recovery Night 2. Interestingly, the REM rebound was not initiated until the third REM period on the first night but was evident across all REM periods in Recovery Night 2. The group having dementia showed essentially constant amounts of REM across both baseline and recovery nights.

Brenner, Reynolds, and Ulrich (1989) examined EEG patterns in 33 patients with mixed symptoms of depression and dementia. Two groups, those with PDD and depressive features (Group 1: $n = 23$; mean age = 72.4 years, $SD = 6.9$) and those with DD (Group 2: $n = 10$; mean age = 75.8 years, $SD = 5.7$), were defined. For comparison, 35 DAT participants without depression (Group 3: mean age = 67.4 years, $SD = 8.9$), 23 participants with depression but no cognitive impairment (Group 4: mean = 69.8 years, $SD = 7.9$), and 61 healthy elderly control participants (mean = 66.9 years, $SD = 6.8$) were also studied. Subjects were free of psychoactive medication for at least 10 days, with the exception of 1 depressed subject who had 2 mg of haloperidol 7 days before testing.

EEG records were analyzed across four domains: incidence of normal EEGs; comparisons of abnormalities; comparison of DD, depressed, and control participants; and comparison of participants with dementia (with or without concurrent depression) to controls. Analyses on incidence of normal EEGs revealed that whereas 80% of the DD participants produced normal EEGs, only 35% of the PDD-with-depressive-features participants did. Thirty-one percent of the DAT patients and 70% of the depressed patients had normal EEGs.

Differences were obtained between Groups 1 and 2 and between Groups 3 and 4 on EEG grade location and on quantitative EEG scores. Only patients with dementia, with or without depressive symptoms, showed moderately or severely abnormal EEGs. There were no significant differences between Groups 1 and 2 or between Groups 3 and 4 on the dominant posterior rhythm. However, this rhythm was significantly slowed for Groups 2 and 4 (those with depression) when compared with controls. These data indicate that there are significant differences between subgroups of patients with mixed symptomatology and that the patterns for these subgroups are similar to the "pure" groups (i.e., patients with pseudodementia resemble patients with depression, and patients with dementia and depression resemble patients with dementia only). These differences may be clinically useful in differentiating the groups.

Other investigators have considered structural brain changes in these groups. Pearlson et al. (1989) examined the computer tomography (CT) scans and neuropsychological assessments of elderly participants (age >60 years) who suffered from either major depression or DAT or were healthy. A substantial percentage (58%) of the depressed group demonstrated cognitive impairment on the MMSE before treatment for depression. These cognitively impaired, depressed participants constituted the DD group. Note that the groups did not differ in terms of age or sex distribution.

CT scans were evaluated for both ventricular dilation and attenuation. Neuropsychological testing consisted of the Boston Naming Test (Kaplan, Goodglass, & Weintraub, 1978), a 10-word adaptation of the Rey Auditory Verbal Learning Test (Rey, 1964). An added dependent variable was the maximum number of words recalled 30 min after the Rey words were presented. Approximately 2 years after initial assessment, participants were readministered the MMSE.

The data indicated that the performance of the depressed-without-dementia participants was insignificantly inferior to the controls on initial cognitive testing. However, the performance of DD and DAT patients was significantly worse. Immediate word recall on the Rey was particularly difficult for the DD and DAT subjects. The controls recalled an average of 6.4 ($SD = 1.3$); the depressed recalled an average of 5.9 ($SD = 1.2$). DD participants recalled only 4.5 ($SD = 2.1$), and DAT participants recalled 3.2 ($SD = 1.8$).

Initial assessment of ventricular dilation differences also indicated significant group differences.

Individual comparison procedures indicated that both DAT and DD patients were significantly different from the controls. The depressed but not cognitively impaired participants were not significantly different from any other group. Attentuation scores revealed an identical pattern, with both DAT and DD participants having lower scores than controls.

Significant correlations between neuropsychological tests and CT measures were also obtained. Inferior performance on the immediate verbal recall was associated with increased ventricular dilation for both the DD and DAT groups. However, scores on the MMSE and Boston Naming Test were related to CT scanning measures only for the DAT group.

Follow-up testing revealed (a) no significant change in MMSE scores for the depressed group, (b) increases in the MMSE scores for the DD group, (c) reduced depression scores for both depressed subgroups, and (d) lower MMSE scores in the DAT group. These data suggest that DD may be associated with structural brain changes but that these changes are not necessarily associated with cognitive decline over a 2-year period. However, note that measures of cognitive function other than the MMSE apparently were not assessed at Time 2. A more complete assessment might have produced more distinguishing data. It also appears that the CT scans were not readministered at Time 2. Follow-up CT scans would have been useful in evaluating cerebral recovery and its relation to cognitive functioning in these groups.

CT measures were also obtained in the study by Abas et al. (1990), described earlier. They do not discuss the findings in regard to their DAT subjects. Comparisons between the control and depressed participants indicated that mean values for ventricular brain ratio and for gross cortical atrophy were higher, but not significantly so, for the depressed participants. Correlations between these CT measures and cognitive measures revealed that ventricular brain ratio correlated with two measures of speed, delayed-matching-to-sample latency, and Kendrick Digit Copying Test time. Gross cortical atrophy was not related to any cognitive measure. For depressed subjects, age also correlated with delayed-matching-to-sample latency, but not to ventricular brain ratio. Age was not related to any variables for controls. In depressed participants, earlier age of onset was associated with greater cognitive impairment. This finding lends support to the hypothesis that the effects of age on cognitive performance may be increased in depressed patients.

Using positron emission tomography techniques, Dolan et al. (1992) examined regional cerebral blood flow in depressed patients. Subjects were divided on the basis of MMSE scores. Those scoring at or below 25 were classified as depressed/impaired (n = 10). Those with scores above 29 were classified as unimpaired (n = 10). These subjects were younger than those studied in previously cited work: The mean age for the depressed/impaired group was 60.9 years (SD = 7.8), and the mean age for the unimpaired group was 53.2 years (SD = 14.8). The age difference was not significant for the groups. The groups also did not differ in terms of the proportion of unipolar versus bipolar subjects, the proportion of subjects on medication, severity of depression, or the sex distribution.

Analyses indicated a pattern of a significant reduction in regional cerebral blood flow (rCBF) in the left anterior medial prefrontal cortex accompanied by an increase in rCBF in the cerebellar vermis in the depressed/impaired group, in relation to the unimpaired group. Thus, these data suggest functional changes associated with impairment, different from those observed in depression alone (i.e., regional decreases in the association areas). Dolan et al. (1992) pointed out that the decrease in rCBF in the medial frontal pole was probably the more critical finding in regard to cognitive function. The frontal pole has reciprocal connections with higher order association areas and thus plays an important role in determining global cognitive function. Dolan et al. hypothesized that the unexpected increase in rCBF, the cerebellar vermis, may have been the result of generalized arousal. However, they had no data to either support or refute the hypothesis.

Another explanation offered by Dolan et al. (1992) was that this cerebellar increase is directly related to cognitive impairment. The cerebellum has been implicated in higher cognitive functioning (i.e., motor planning, learning, and associative learning).

Thus, a functional reciprocity may exist between these two areas of observed abnormalities.

Overall Summary

In summary, a wide range of neurophysiologic methods have been used in the study of DD. Similar to the neuropsychological findings described earlier, the literature reflects considerable inconsistency. That is, in some studies, these measures may successfully differentiate DD from PDD and DAT; in other studies, they do not. Measurement issues, as well as unaccounted for participant variables, may contribute to the lack of consistency.

Pseudodementia patients demonstrate a wide array of cognitive impairments, including problems in learning, memory, and psychomotor performance. A substantial number of these patients also show abnormalities in brain structure and function as evidenced in CT scanning, positron emission tomography, and event-related potential studies. The overlap in cognitive and neuropsychological dysfunction is considerable between DD and PDD patients, making differential diagnoses difficult—particularly if early stage DAT is suspected. The groups appear to differ in the severity of their impairment and in the quality of their responses. Behaviorally, DD patients are generally more concerned about their cognitive loss and express greater depressive symptomatology. However, as noted in chapter 3, depression frequently accompanies DAT, particularly in the earlier stages. From a clinical perspective, the data from a simple test of antisaccadic movements may be useful in distinguishing between DD and PDD patients. On this test, DD patients performed normally, whereas PDD patients made significantly more errors.

TREATMENT AND PROGNOSIS

Treatment

In those cases where metabolic imbalances or psychiatric disorders are suspected or identified, appropriate medical treatment should be applied. This treatment might involve a wide range of possibilities, including vitamin supplements and antidepressant medication. Ideally, this treatment is provided by a physician working in close association with the therapist or psychologist. Such an arrangement facilitates treatment planning and evaluation and provides additional support for the patient and family.

Furthermore, to assess treatment success, it is important that periodic evaluations be conducted. This follow-up will be most useful if the physician and psychologist communicate regularly regarding medication, metabolic status, general health, and cognitive status. Failure to obtain improvements in cognitive functioning despite achieving normal metabolic status, a decrease in depressive symptomatology, and so on, suggest that a PDD must be considered. If improvement is obtained and medical treatment is discontinued, follow-up neuropsychological assessment may be designed to ensure that cognitive functions are maintained.

Prognosis

As noted previously, the term *reversible* implies that with proper treatment, cognitive decline can be reversed. Thus, there are important implications for patients, families, and health care professionals when the term is used. To offer the diagnosis of "reversible dementia" establishes an atmosphere of hope for a return to normalcy. However, to what extent do cognitive abilities actually recover after the source of the dementia (e.g., vitamin deficiency or hypothyroidism) is corrected? Furthermore, does an episode of depression with or without accompanying dementia increase risk for PDD? I address this second question first.

Alexopoulos and Chester (1992) published a review regarding outcomes of depression in elderly patients. They cited data that indicated that cognitively intact elderly people with depression develop degenerative (irreversible) dementia at the rate of approximately 4% per year (Baldwin & Jolley, 1986; Kay, Roth, & Hopkins, 1955; Murphy, 1983). This percentage is in keeping with the rate for the general elderly population.

However, subjects who have been diagnosed with depression with reversible dementia develop degenerative dementia at rates 2.5 to 6 times higher than the general elderly population. That is, they develop degenerative or irreversible dementia at a rate of between 9% and 25% per year (Alexopoulos, 1990;

Alexopoulos & Abrams, 1991; Reding, Haycox, & Blass, 1985). Interestingly, the literature suggests that patients with initial diagnoses of depression with dementia have later ages of onset for depression than did those patients without dementia (Alexopoulos, 1990).

From their review of the literature, Alexopoulos and Chester (1992) concluded that given the high comorbidity of depression and dementia, it is reasonable to assume that elderly depressives with some degree of cognitive dysfunction may be at increased risk for developing degenerative dementia. That is, perhaps it is not depression, per se, but rather the pseudodementia that occurs in some cases that is associated with an increased vulnerability for degenerative dementia. Other investigators have failed to support this hypothesis (Sachdev, Smith, Angus-Lepan, & Rodriguez, 1990).

The remaining question addresses the extent of recovery in so-called reversible dementias. Cunha (1990) reviewed the recovery patterns of 26 patients between the ages of 60 and 92 given diagnoses of reversible dementia. Two patients in the sample had normal pressure hydrocephalus, 1 had a cerebral tumor, 4 had hypothyroidism, 13 had vitamin B_{12} deficiency, 2 had hyperthyroidism, and 4 had DD. Patients were interviewed and administered the MMSE. One normal pressure hydrocephalus patient, 3 DD patients, and the patient with the cerebral tumor failed to return for the follow-up, which occurred between 6 and 24 months after assessment. At follow-up, participants were readministered the MMSE. Assessment of the MMSE scores indicated that return to normal function had occurred in only 2 participants: 1 normal pressure hydrocephalus participant and 1 case of DD. Note, however, that Cunha reported that the 3 other DD participants improved over the study period but failed to return for follow-up.

The participants with hyper- or hypothyroidism or vitamin B_{12} deficiency failed to improve. Contrary to expectations regarding reversible dementias, these patients indicated continued cognitive decline despite medical intervention.

Copeland et al. (1992) also reported poor outcomes in reversible dementias. They studied the prognosis in 21 DD participants, age 65 and over, over a 3-year period. They found that only 1 participant had recovered. Six retained their classification, 4 exhibited subclinical levels of depression, 2 were no longer depressed but exhibited symptoms of dementia, 5 had developed dementia, 1 had developed a paranoid illness, 1 a hypochondriacal illness, and the last an anxiety state.

Kral and Emery (1989) examined the cognitive function of 44 DD patients (mean age = 76.5 years) after treatment for depression. In all cases, treatment for depression was effective and resulted in a return to premorbid levels of intellectual function. However, later assessments conducted at an average of 8 years after treatment revealed that 89% (39 of 44) had developed DAT. This finding is in keeping with prior work by Kral (1982) in which it was found that 20 of 22 patients initially treated for DD eventually developed DAT.

Abas et al. (1990), in the study detailed earlier, conducted follow-up cognitive assessments on subjects after recovery from depression. (It might be useful to reiterate that their sample of depressed and cognitively impaired participants were not clinically demented.) They found significant improvement in this group across several tests. However, they also observed substantial continued inferiority. Specifically, recovered depressives were inferior to controls on latency measures for pattern and spatial recognition, accuracy on spatial recognition, and accuracy and latencies on the delayed-matching-to-sample test. Additionally, only 60% of the recovered depressives successfully completed all sets of the conditional visuospatial associative learning test. Finally, this group performed no more quickly on the Kendrick Digit Copying test than did the DAT participants. Recovered depressives were equivalent to controls on the matching-to-sample task, the Kendrick Object Learning test (Kendrick, 1985), and the pattern recognition test. Contrary to the pattern with controls, age correlated with performance on a number of the tests. Ventricular brain ratio correlated with performance for this group only on those tests that failed to show recovery.

In general, these data suggest that the terms *reversible* and *pseudodementia* must be used with care. Concern regarding the application and implication of the terms continues (Abas et al., 1990; Alexopoulos

EXHIBIT 3

Diagnostic and Treatment Caveats Regarding Pseudodementia

- A complete medical examination, including assessment of substance abuse, head injury, and metabolic dysfunction, is imperative. The most competent neuropsychological exam is inadequate in the absence of this information. Having complete information is essential in developing the therapeutic relationship with both the patient and family.
- DD patients show less cognitive impairment than do PDD patients, overall. However, these differences are generally obtained when *groups* are compared. To date, there are no standard cutoff scores that will readily separate DD and PDD patients. Some work suggests that consistency in performance across testing (e.g., MMSE scores at two times) may be indicative of DD.
- DD patients report considerable concern regarding their perceived mental decline, memory loss, and overall functioning. Appropriate pharmacological intervention (e.g., antidepressants) may produce significant improvement in cognitive and psychosocial functioning.
- The use of such therapies requires the education of patient and family regarding possible side effects. Because many elderly people are on multiple medications, potential drug interactions must be carefully evaluated and discussed with the family.
- One of the keys to successful treatment of DD patients is follow-up. Assessment of improvement in mood and cognitive status after psychotherapy or pharmacotherapy may serve to validate the initial diagnosis. Lack of improvement in cognitive status suggests that other processes such as PDD may be involved. It is important to consider the possibility that multiple processes may be contributing to the patient's poor status.
- Long-term follow-up is also merited. Current data suggest that a substantial number of patients with secondary dementias fail to improve or may develop PDD. This information must be shared carefully with the family. Maintaining the quality of life for patient and family may be facilitated by continued, although perhaps intermittent (e.g., yearly), interaction.

DD = pseudodementia associated with depression; PDD = primary degenerative dementia; MMSE = Mini-Mental State Examination.

& Chester, 1992; Maletta, 1990). It is obvious that reversible dementias, generally, and DD, specifically, may be only partially, and in some cases not at all, reversible. The outcome for individual patients remains unclear.

That is not to say that these dementias are not treatable, even if they are not always curable. Appropriate medical intervention, psychological and emotional support, and referral to community resources are important aspects of enhancing the quality of life, regardless of the diagnosis. Maletta (1990) proposed the perspective that "all patients with cognitive/functional decline, no matter how defined or what the cause, are eminently treatable individuals" (p. 136).

As noted earlier, many of the differences in DD and PDD are outlined in Table 1. Exhibit 3 summarizes some of the important issues of diagnosis and treatment of pseudodementia for the clinical psychologist. Many of these issues are illustrated in the case histories that follow.

CASE HISTORIES

Two case histories are presented below. The first has been reprinted with permission from Lishman (1987). The second is a case taken from the file of the Neuropsychological Assessment Laboratory directed by Russell Adams at the University of Oklahoma Health Sciences Center. The second case illustrates the more typical case observed in clinical settings. Specifically, there are several potentially contributing factors, which complicate diagnosis.

Ms. L

A 43-year-old woman of good previous intelligence and stable personality was referred to hospital with a 6-month history of insomnia, difficulty in thinking clearly, forgetfulness when shopping and difficulty in managing her home. Three weeks before admission, she had developed an acute episode of agitation with incoherent and muddled speech, and from that time she had become progressively out of touch with those around her. On examination, she was perplexed and anxious but showed no noteworthy evidence of depression. Her talk was incoherent, she was disoriented for time, and psychometric examination revealed a full scale IQ of 60 (Verbal scale = 68, Performance scale = 59). The electroencephalogram showed some reduction of activity over the right central area and slow waves in the posterior temporal regions. The air encephalogram showed dilation of the right lateral ventricle with some cortical atrophy over the surface. A diagnosis of presenile dementia was made, and after an unsuccessful trial at home, she was transferred to a mental hospital in another part of the country. There she could be visited by her sisters while her husband continued to rear the children alone.

Some six years later she was re-referred for assessment at the request of her relatives. They had noted great variability in her condition, and, although most of the time she had continued to be incoherent and perplexed, she had not deteriorated further as expected. On weekend leaves from hospital in recent months, she had even shown short-lived spells of near normal behavior.

Examination now showed her to be slow, incoherent and perplexed as before, often losing the thread in simple sentences and with obvious difficulty in assembling her thoughts. Now, however, she was correctly oriented and showed definite evidence of mild depression. Her level of performance fluctuated remarkably from day to day, and sometimes she proved capable of answering questions and holding brief conversations on simple matters. The air encephalogram showed persistent cortical atrophy on the right and the ventricles were slightly larger than before, but repeated psychometric testing showed considerably better scores (Full-Scale IQ = 91; Verbal IQ = 97; Performance IQ = 84). However, tests of new learning ability remained firmly in the organic range.

She was started on imipramine and this was followed by slow improvement. Later, six ECTs were given with further improvement still. Lucid intervals became increasingly prolonged and she began for the first time to take some interest in her affairs and predicament. Unfortunately it emerged that in the intervening years, her husband had established a liaison with his housekeeper and he now refused to have her home, but despite the distress of this discovery, she achieved a job as a typist and eventually left hospital to live in a hostel nearby. She remained well during the next 12 months, apart from occasional brief relapses to her former incoherent state after particularly distressing episodes in relation to her family situation. She then died suddenly of a subarachnoid hemorrhage and autopsy was not obtained.[1]

This case, reported by Lishman (1987), is a classic example of secondary dementia, specifically DD. A misdiagnosis of "presenile dementia" was originally made and institutionalization was required. Not until a follow-up evaluation was conducted years later was another disorder apparently considered and an alternative treatment instituted. Substantial improvement followed. However, it should be noted that this improvement was not immediate. Rather, improvement was progressive and followed a combination treatment of both ECT and antidepressant medication. This case illustrates the clinical importance of (a) follow-up evaluations and (b) the use of combination therapies, particularly in difficult or only partially responsive cases.

Mrs. D

Demographics and background. Mrs. D is a 68-year-old, White, married female. She was referred for neuropsychological evaluation because of family concerns regarding memory and personality changes

[1]From *Organic Psychiatry: The Psychological Consequences of Cerebral Disorder* (p. 412), by W. A. Lishman, 1987, Oxford, England: Blackwell Scientific. Copyright 1987 by Blackwell Scientific. Reprinted with permission.

over the previous few months. She had completed high school and worked for brief periods of time outside the home. However, her primary occupation had been that of a homemaker.

Mrs. D was accompanied by her spouse and adult daughter. She was cooperative and alert during the assessment. She was oriented to person, place, time, day, and month and was free from homicidal, paranoid, or suicidal ideation. Mrs. D denied being depressed, but reported occasionally "feeling down," especially when experiencing a headache. Mrs. D displayed mood congruent affect and showed an appreciation for humor.

Mrs. D's primary complaint was in regard to the pain in her feet resulting from diabetes. At one point in the interview, she indicated that she was hoping this assessment might identify ways to eliminate the pain. Mrs. D did endorse some difficulty in concentrating because she reported becoming "overheated" while working in her garden approximately 6 months earlier. She denied any problems in completing household chores, shopping, or handling money. She admitted that she sometimes forgot to turn off the stove, but denied having memory problems. She was aware that her spouse and daughter believed that she suffered from memory dysfunction.

Reports from family members indicated substantial problems in the areas of memory and daily living skills. Specifically, they reported that Mrs. D had difficulty reading the newspaper, forgot to turn off lights and appliances, had difficulty sewing, was unable to coordinate activities (e.g., meal preparation), lost and misplaced items, and became confused. They also indicated that she had trouble recalling names, was unable to perform arithmetic or maintain the checkbook, and was no longer able to retain verbal information regarding geographic locations. This last disability was significant in light of the fact that Mrs. D had served as the family "navigator." Other areas of reported disability included difficulties in following conversations, word-finding problems, and with speed in planning and executing motor sequences.

The family reported considerable fluctuation in Mrs. D's level of functioning. Some days she was at near-normal levels of functioning. On other days, she was significantly impaired. All parties listed the "overheating" incident in the garden, occurring approximately 6 months prior to evaluation, as an important point of change in Mrs. D's functioning.

Mrs. D reported that after this event, control of her blood sugar became more difficult. Family members reported that after this event the right side of Mrs. D's mouth drooped, her speech was slurred, and her memory was significantly impaired for several days. They also associated increased anxiety with this event. The family believed she was functioning at approximately 60% of her previous level of functioning at the time of evaluation.

Mrs. D's medical history was positive for diabetes and high blood pressure. She also had been treated for "heart problems" and continued to experience periodic chest pains. She had had five surgeries (hysterectomy, colostomy, appendectomy, lobe removal from left breast, and gallbladder surgery). She reportedly suffered oxygen deprivation as a child and had experienced severe headaches throughout adulthood. There was no family history of psychiatric disorders. Mrs. D had a brother who reportedly suffered from dementialike symptomatology.

A review of the patient's current medications revealed at least eight prescriptive or over the counter drugs. These drugs included a nonsteroidal anti-inflammatory drug, four drugs related to cardiovascular functioning (one medication for angina pectoris, and three for hypertension), one for control of blood sugar, one thyroid replacement, a vasoconstrictor for control of migraines, and a tricyclic antidepressant. Consultation with the *Physicians' Desk Reference* manual indicated that several of these drugs could potentiate each other, adversely interact with Mrs. D's several medical conditions, or adversely affect cognitive functioning.

Neuropsychological assessment. Mrs. D was tested over the course of 1 day (approximately 8 hr). The test battery included the WAIS-R (Wechsler, 1981), the WMS (Wechsler, 1987), the Dementia Rating Scale (DRS; Mattis, 1976), the Geriatric Depression Scale (Yesavage, 1988) and the Minnesota Multiphasic Personality Inventory (MMPI), as well as other learning tests.

Her test performance was variable. Her auditory attention and concentration scores were in the low average range. Her performance on the attention subtest of the DRS was above cutoff for a diagnosis of dementia.

Her verbal memory abilities were within the normal range. However, her nonverbal abilities were in the impaired range. For example, her immediate recall on the WMS—Logical Memory was at the 84th percentile and her delayed recall at the 58th percentile. Similarly, her performance on the verbal learning and memory tests was within the expected range on trials to criterion, on recall at both short and long delays, and on recognition memory. In contrast, her immediate recall for figural material was at the 30th percentile and the delayed recall for figures dropped to the 9th percentile. Her performance on the DRS memory subtest was at the 98th percentile for individuals of her age with dementia.

Mrs. D's vocabulary, verbal comprehension, verbal fluency, and computation and mathematical reasoning skills were within normal range. Similarly, her performance on the Perceptual–Spatial/Constructional subtest of the WAIS-R was in the average range. Her performance on her time scores on the Tactual Performance Test was moderately to severely impaired. Her ability to copy the Rey–Osterreith Complex Figure was also impaired, being below the 10th percentile.

Her performance on tests such as the Wisconsin Card Sorting Test and the Initiation–Perseveration scale of the DRS indicated an inability to plan and initiate behavior, an inability to change cognitive sets, and a preponderance of perseverative responses. Thus, although her verbal learning and memory processes were within the normal range, her nonverbal abstract reasoning and abstract abilities, nonverbal learning and conceptual set shifting skills were impaired.

Mrs. D did not achieve clinically significant levels of depression or anxiety. However, consideration of Mrs. D's MMPI revealed a tendency to deny underlying feelings of insecurity, anxiety, and depression, and that she used excessive repression. Furthermore, it suggested that she was introverted, lacked self-confidence, overcontrolled, and not likely to display her emotions directly. There were no significant elevations on the clinical scales. However, Mrs. D appeared dissatisfied and had depressive trends.

This pattern of neuropsychological performance, personality traits, and current medications suggests a need for careful evaluation of the possible interaction of these variables. Additional neurologic workups may be useful in facilitating an accurate diagnosis. At this point, a diagnosis of early dementia appears inappropriate. A more fitting approach would be to attempt changes in her medication regimen, obtain appropriate psychological counseling for her depressive tendencies, and continue careful observation. Even if later assessments indicate the presence of DAT or are consistent with change to vascular dementia, appropriate pharmacological and psychologic treatment at this time may enhance her quality of life.

CONCLUSION

By definition, secondary or reversible dementias occur as a result of some pathological process that is theoretically reversible with appropriate treatment. It is estimated that between 10% and 30% of patients presenting with dementia symptomatology may have at least a partially treatable process (Cunha, 1990). The variables and conditions associated with reversible dementia include chemical intoxication, medications, nutritional deficiencies, metabolic imbalances, environmental factors, and psychiatric disorders. There are known medical treatments for most of these conditions. Therefore, it is important that appropriate assessment and subsequent medical intervention be applied.

Differentiating reversible dementias, particularly dementia associated with depression, from the primary degenerative dementias, such as DAT, is a difficult task. However, it is one that psychologists are often requested to do. Neuropsychological and neurophysiological assessments do not clearly discriminate the two. The clinical importance of being able to provide a differential diagnosis is obvious. In the case of the dementias, specific medical intervention that may improve functioning can be identified. On the other hand, with DAT, treatment is largely limited to support and maintenance. Appropriate diagnosis and treatment require thorough medical and neuropsychological assessments. Furthermore, follow-up assessment may also be important for appropriate patient care.

Current data raise important questions regarding the reversibility of reversible dementias. These data reinforce the need for follow-up evaluation and continued support for the family and patient.

References

Abas, M. A., Sahakian, B. J., & Levy, R. (1990). Neuropsychological deficits and CT scan changes in elderly depressives. *Psychological Medicine, 20,* 507–520.

Alexopoulos, G. S. (1990). Clinical and biological findings in late-onset depression. In A. Tasman, S. M. Goldfinger, & C. A. Kaufman (Eds.), *American Psychiatric Press review of psychiatry* (Vol. 9, 249–262). Washington, DC: American Psychiatric Press.

Alexopoulos, G. S., & Abrams, R. C. (1991). Depression in Alzheimer's disease. *Psychiatric Clinics of North America, 14,* 327–340.

Alexopoulos, G. S., & Chester, J. G. (1992). Outcomes of geriatric depression. *Clinics in Geriatric Medicine, 8,* 363–376.

Alexopoulos, G. S., & Mattis, S. (1991). Diagnosing cognitive dysfunction in the elderly: Primary screening tests. *Geriatrics, 46*(12), 33–44.

Baldwin, R. C., & Jolley, D. J. (1986). The prognosis of depression in old age. *British Journal of Psychiatry, 149,* 574–583.

Benton, A. L. (1974). *The Revised Visual Retention Test: Clinical and experimental application* (4th ed.). New York: Psychological Corporation.

Benton, A. L., Hamsher, K., Varney, N. R., & Spreen, O. (1983). *Contributions to neuropsychological assessment.* New York: Oxford University Press.

Blessed, G., Tomlinson, B. E., & Roth, M. (1968). The association between quantitative measures of dementia and of senile change in the cerebral grey matter of elderly subjects. *British Journal of Psychiatry, 114,* 797–811.

Brenner, R. P., Reynolds, C. F., III, & Ulrich, R. F. (1989). EEG findings in depressive pseudodementia and dementia with secondary depression. *Electroencephalography and Clinical Neurophysiology, 72,* 298–304.

Brown, W. S., Marsh, J. T., & Larue, A. (1982). Event-related potentials in psychiatry: Differentiating depression and dementia in the elderly. *Bulletin of the Los Angeles Neurological Societies, 47,* 92–107.

Buysse, D. J., Reynolds, C. F., III, Kupfer, D. J., Houck, P. R., Hoch, C. C., Stack, J. A., & Berman, S. R. (1988). Electroencephalographic sleep in depressive pseudodementia. *Archives of General Psychiatry, 45,* 568–575.

Chanarin, I. (1979). *The megaloblastic anaemias.* Oxford, England: Blackwell Scientific.

Chaves, M. L. F., & Izquierdo, I. (1992). Differential diagnosis between dementia and depression: A study of efficiency increment. *Acta Neurologica Scandinavica, 85,* 378–382.

Chiappa, K. H. (1990). *Evoked potentials in clinical medicine* (2nd ed.). New York: Raven Press.

Cohen, R. M., Weingartner, H., Smallberg, S. A., Pickar, D., & Murphy, D. L. (1982). Effort and cognition in depression. *Archives of General Psychiatry, 39,* 593–597.

Conley, C. L., & Krevans, J. R. (1951). Development of neurologic manifestations of pernicious anemia during multivitamin therapy. *New England Journal of Medicine, 245,* 529.

Copeland, J. R. M., Davidson, I. A., Dewey, M. E., Gilmore, C., Larkin, B. A., McWilliam, C., Saunders, P. A., Scott, A., Sharma, V., & Sullivan, C. (1992). Alzheimer's disease, other dementias, depression and pseudodementia: Prevalence, incidence and three-year outcome in Liverpool. *British Journal of Psychiatry, 161,* 230–239.

Cunha, U. G. V. (1990). An investigation of dementia among elderly outpatients. *Acta Psychiatrica Scandinavica, 82,* 261–263.

Currie, J., Ramsden, B., McArthur, C., & Maruff, P. (1991). Validation of a clinical antisaccadic eye movement test in the assessment of dementia. *Archives of Neurology, 48,* 644–648.

desRosiers, G. (1992). Primary or depressive dementia: Psychometric assessment. *Clinical Psychology Review, 12,* 307–343.

Dolan, R. J., Bench, C. J., Brown, R. G., Scott, L. C., Friston, K. J., & Frackowiak, R. S. J. (1992). Regional cerebral blood flow abnormalities in depressed patients with cognitive impairment. *Journal of Neurology, Neurosurgery, and Psychiatry, 55,* 768–773.

Donchin, E., & Coles, M. G. H. (1988). Is the P300 component a manifestation of context updating? *Behavioral and Brain Sciences, 11,* 357–374.

Emery, V. O., & Oxman, T. E. (1992). Update on the dementia spectrum of depression. *American Journal of Psychiatry, 149,* 305–317.

Feher, E. P., Inbody, S. B., Nolan, B., & Pirozzolo, F. J. (1988). Other neurologic diseases with dementia as a sequela. *Clinics in Geriatric Medicine, 4,* 799–814.

Fletcher, W. A., & Sharpe, J. A. (1986). Saccadic eye movement dysfunction in Alzheimer's disease. *Annals of Neurology, 20,* 464–471.

Folstein, M. F., Folstein, S. E., & McHugh, P. R. (1975). "Mini-Mental State": A practical method for grading the cognitive state of patients for the clinician. *Journal of Psychiatry Research, 12,* 189–198.

Folstein, M. F., & McHugh, P. R. (1978). Dementia syndrome of depression. In R. Katzman, R. D. Terry, & K. L. Beck (Eds.), *Aging, 7: Alzheimer's disease, senile dementia and related disorders* (pp. 87–93). New York: Raven Press.

Fukushima, J., Fukushima, K., Chiba, T., Tanaka, S., Yamashita, I., & Kato, M. (1988). Disturbances of voluntary control of saccadic eye movements in schizophrenic patients. *Biological Psychiatry, 23,* 670–677.

Goodin, D. S., Keneth, C. S., & Starr, A. (1978). Long event related component of the auditory evoked potential in dementia. *Brain, 101,* 635–646.

Gordon, B., & Carson, K. (1990). The basis for choice reaction time slowing in Alzheimer's disease. *Brain and Cognition, 13,* 148–166.

Gottlieb, D., Wertman, E., & Bentin, S. (1991). Passive listening and task-related P300 measurement for the evaluation of dementia and pseudodementia. *Clinical Electroencephalography, 22*(2), 102–107.

Greenblatt, D. J., Harmatz, J. S., Shapiro, L., Engelhardt, N., Gouthro, T. A., & Shader, R. I. (1991). Sensitivity to triazolam in the elderly. *New England Journal of Medicine, 324,* 1691–1698.

Greenblatt, D. J., Shader, R. I., & Harmatz, J. S. (1989). Implications of altered drug disposition in the elderly: Studies of benzodiazepines. *Journal of Clinical Pharmacology, 29,* 866–872.

Haggerty, J. J., Golden, R. N., Evans, D. L., & Janowsky, D. S. (1988). Differential diagnosis of pseudodementia in the elderly. *Geriatrics, 43*(3), 61–74.

Hamburger, J. I., & Kaplan, M. M. (1989). Hypothyroidism: Don't treat patients who don't have it. *Postgraduate Medicine, 86,* 67–74.

Hamilton, M. (1960). A rating scale for depression. *Journal of Neurology, Neurosurgery, and Psychiatry, 23,* 56–62.

Hart, R. P., & Kwentus, J. A. (1987). Psychomotor slowing and subcortical-type dysfunction in depression. *Journal of Neurology, Neurosurgery, and Psychiatry, 50,* 1263–1266.

Hart, R. P., Kwentus, J. A., Harkins, S. W., Taylor, J. R., & Rybarczyk, B. D. (1985, August). *Rate of forgetting in mild Alzheimer-type dementia.* Paper presented at the 93rd Annual Convention of the American Psychological Association, Los Angeles.

Hart, R. P., Kwentus, J. A., Taylor, J. R., & Harkins, S. W. (1987). Rate of forgetting in dementia and depression. *Journal of Consulting and Clinical Psychology, 55,* 101–105.

Henry, G. M., Weingartner, H., & Murphy, G. L. (1973). Influence of affective states and psychoactive drugs on verbal learning and memory. *American Journal of Psychiatry, 130,* 966–971.

Hilbert, T. N. M., Niederehe, G., & Kahn, R. L. (1976). Accuracy and speed of memory in depressed and organic aged. *Educational Gerontology, 1,* 131–146.

Hollister, L. E. (1988a). Antidepressants. In Howard H. Goldman (Ed.), *Review of general psychiatry* (2nd ed., pp. 592–599). Norwalk, CT: Appleton & Lange.

Hollister, L. E. (1988b). Antipsychotics and mood stabilizers. In Howard H. Goldman (Ed.), *Review of general psychiatry* (2nd ed., pp. 580–591). Norwalk, CT: Appleton & Lange.

Inbar, S. H. (1985). The thyroid gland. In J. Wilson & D. Foster (Eds.), *Textbook of endocrinology* (7th ed., pp. 775–793). Philadelphia: W. B. Saunders.

Iragui, V. J., Kutas, M., Mitchiner, M. R., & Hillyard, S. A. (1993). Effects of aging on event-related brain potentials and reaction times in an auditory oddball task. *Psychophysiology, 30,* 10–22.

Jenike, M. A. (1988). Depression and other psychiatric disorders. In M. S. Albert & M. Moss (Eds.), *Geriatric neuropsychology* (pp. 115–144). New York: Guilford Press.

Jones, R. D., Tranel, D., Benton, A., & Paulsen, J. (1992). Differentiating dementia from "pseudodementia" early in the clinical course: Utility of neuropsychological tests. *Neuropsychology, 6,* 13–21.

Kaplan, E. F., Goodglass, H., & Weintraub, S. (1978). *The Boston Naming Test.* Boston: Author.

Kay, D. W. K., Roth, M., & Hopkins, B. (1955). Affective disorders arising in the senium. *Journal of Mental Science, 101,* 302–316.

Kendrick, D. C. (1985). *Kendrick Cognitive Tests for the elderly.* Windsor: NFER-Nelson.

Kral, V. A. (1982). Depressive pseudodemenz und senile demenz vom Alzheimer type. *Eine Pilotstudie DerNervenarzt, 53,* 284–286.

Kral, V. A., & Emery, O. B. (1989). Long-term follow-up of depressive pseudodementia of the aged. *Canadian Journal of Psychiatry, 34,* 445–446.

Kramer, S. I., & Reifler, B. V. (1992). Depression, dementia, and reversible dementia. *Clinics in Geriatric Medicine, 8,* 289–297.

Lai, J. A., Brown, J. S., Marsh, J. T., & Larue, A. (1983). Covariation of P3 latency and mini-mental state scores in geriatric patients. *Psychophysiology, 20,* 455–460.

Larson, E. B., Reifler, B. V., Sumi, S. M., Canfield, C. G., & Chinn, N. M. (1985). Diagnostic evaluation of 200 elderly outpatients with suspected dementia. *Journal of Gerontology, 40,* 536–543.

Lasker, A. G., Zee, D. S., Hain, T. C., Folstein, S. E., & Singer, H. S. (1987). Saccades in Huntington's disease: Initiation defects and distractibility. *Neurology, 37,* 364–370.

Lazarus, L. W., Newton, N., Cohler, B., Lesser, J., & Schweon, C. (1987). Frequency and presentation of depressive symptoms in patients with primary degenerative dementia. *American Journal of Psychiatry, 144,* 41–45.

Lishman, W. A. (1987). The senile dementias, presenile dementias, and pseudodementias. *Organic psychiatry: The psychological consequences of cerebral disorder* (2nd ed., pp. 370–427). Oxford, England: Blackwell Scientific.

Maletta, G. J. (1990). The concept of "reversible" dementia: How nonreliable terminology may impair effective treatment. *American Geriatrics Society, 38,* 136–140.

Marsh, A., & Burns, A. (1986). Thyroid stimulating hormone (TSH) measurements in dementing patients [Letter]. *Medical Laboratory Sciences, 43,* 294–296.

Martin, P. R., McCool, B. A., & Singleton, C. K. (1993). Genetic sensitivity to thiamine deficiency and development of alcoholic organic brain disease. *Alcoholism: Clinical and Experimental Research, 17,* 31–37.

Mattis, S. (1976). Mental status examination for organic mental syndrome in the elderly patient. In R. Bellack & B. Karasu (Eds.), *Geriatric psychiatry* (pp. 77–121). New York: Grune and Stratton.

McAllister, T. W. (1983). Overview: Pseudodementia. *American Journal of Psychiatry, 140,* 528–533.

McCullough, P. K. (1991). Geriatric depression: Atypical presentations, hidden meanings. *Geriatrics, 46*(10), 72–76.

McGlone, J., Gupta, S., Humphrey, D., Oppenheimer, S., Mirsen, T., & Evans, D. R. (1990). Screening for early dementia using memory complaints from patients and relatives. *Archives of Neurology, 47,* 1189–1193.

Murphy, E. (1983). The prognosis of depression in old age. *British Journal of Psychiatry, 142,* 111–119.

Nebes, R. D., Brady, C. B., & Reynolds, C. F., III (1992). Cognitive slowing in Azheimer's disease and geriatric depression. *Journal of Gerontology: Psychological Sciences, 47,* 331–336.

Nelson, J. C., & Charney, D. S. (1981). The symptoms of major depressive illness. *American Journal of Psychiatry, 138,* 1–3.

O'Connor, D. W., Pollitt, P. A., Roth, M., Brook, C. P. B., & Reiss, B. B. (1990). Memory complaints and impairment in normal, depressed, and demented elderly persons identified in a community survey. *Archives of General Psychiatry, 47,* 224–227.

Oken, B. S. (1989). Endogenous event-related potentials. In Keith H. Chiappa (Ed.), *Evoked potentials in clinical medicine* (2nd ed., pp. 563–592). New York: Raven Press.

Ollo, C., Johnson, R., Jr., & Grafman, J. (1991). Signs of cognitive change in HIV disease: An event-related brain potential study. *Neurology, 41,* 209–215.

Parsons, O. A., & Nixon, S. J. (1993). Neurobehavioral sequelae of alcoholism. *Neurologic Clinics, 11,* 205–218.

Pearlson, G. D., Rabins, P. V., Kim, W. S., Speedie, L. J., Moberg, L. J., Burns, A., & Bascom, M. J. (1989). Structural brain CT changes and cognitive deficits in elderly depressives with and without reversible dementia ("pseudodementia"). *Psychological Medicine, 19,* 573–584.

Pfefferbaum, A., Wenegrat, B. G., Ford, J. M., Roth, W. T., & Kopel, B. S. (1984). Clinical application of the P3 component of event related potentials, II. Dementia, depression and schizophrenia. *Electroencephalography and Clinical Neurophysiology, 59,* 104–124.

Pierrot-Deseilligny, C. H., Rivaud, S., Pillon, B., Fournier, E., & Agid, Y. (1989). Lateral visually guided saccades in progressive supranuclear palsy. *Brain, 112,* 471–487.

Pirozzolo, F. J., Mahurin, R. K., Loring, D. W., Appel, S. H., & Maletta, G. J. (1985). Choice reaction time modifiability in dementia and depression. *International Journal of Neuroscience, 26,* 1–7.

Polich, J., Ehlers, C. L., Otis, S., Mandell, A. J., & Bloom, F. E. (1986). P300 latency reflects the degree of cognitive decline in dementing illness. *Electroencephalography and Clinical Neurophysiology, 63,* 138–144.

Pomara, N., Stanley, B., Block, R., Berchou, R. C., Stanley, M., Greenblatt, D. J., Newton, R. E., & Gershon, S. (1985). Increased sensitivity of the elderly to the central depressant effects of diazepam. *Journal of Clinical Psychiatry, 46*(5), 185–187.

Rabins, P. V., Merchant, A., & Nestadt, G. (1984). Criteria for diagnosing reversible dementia caused by depression: Validation by two-year follow-up. *British Journal of Psychiatry, 144,* 488–492.

Reding, M., Haycox, J., & Blass, J. (1985). Depression in patients referred to a dementia clinic: A 3-year prospective study. *Archives of Neurology, 42,* 894–896.

Reus, V. I., Silberman, E., Post, R. M., & Weingartner, H. (1979). D-Amphetamine: Effects on memory in a depressed population. *Biological Psychiatry, 14,* 345–356.

Rey, A. (1964). *L'examen clinique en psychologie* [The clinical examination in psychology]. Paris: Presses Universitaires de France.

Reynolds, C. F., III, Hoch, C. C., Kupfer, D. J., Buysse, D. J., Houck, P. R., Stack, J. A., & Campbell, D. W.

(1988). Bedside differentiation of depressive pseudodementia from dementia. *American Journal of Psychiatry, 145,* 1099–1103.

Reynolds, C. F., III, Kupfer, D. J., Hoch, C. C., Stack, J. A., Houck, P. R., & Sewitch, D. (1986). Two-year follow-up of elderly patients with mixed depression and dementia: Clinical and EEG sleep findings. *Journal of the American Geriatrics Society, 34,* 793–799.

Reynolds, C. F., III, Kupfer, D. J., Houck, P. R., Hoch, C. C., Stack, J. A., Berman, S. R., & Zimmer, B. (1988). Reliable discrimination of elderly depressed and demented patients by electroencephalographic sleep data. *Archives of General Psychiatry, 45,* 258–264.

Robuschi, G., Safran, M., Braverman, L. E., Gnudi, A., & Toti, E. (1987). Hypothyroidism in the elderly. *Endocrine Reviews, 8,* 142–153.

Rohrbaugh, J. W., Parasuraman, R., & Johnson, R., Jr. (1990). *Event-related brain potentials: Basic issues and applications.* New York: Oxford University Press.

Rosenthal, M. J., & Goodwin, J. S. (1985). Cognitive effects of nutritional deficiency. *Advanced Nutrition, 7,* 71–100.

Sachdev, P. S., Smith, J. S., Angus-Lepan, H., & Rodriguez, P. (1990). Pseudodementia twelve years on. *Journal of Neurology, Neurosurgery, and Psychiatry, 53,* 254–259.

Shuttleworth, E. C., & Huber, S. J. (1989). The picture absurdities test in the evaluation of dementia. *Brain and Cognition, 11,* 50–59.

Slaets, J. P., & Fortgens, G. (1984). On the value of P300 event related potentials in the differential diagnosis of dementia. *British Journal of Psychiatry, 145,* 652–656.

Smith, C. L., & Granger, C. V. (1992). Hypothyroidism producing reversible dementia. *American Journal of Physical Medicine and Rehabilitation, 71,* 28–30.

St. Clair, D. M., Blackwood, D. H. R., & Christe, J. E. (1985). P3 and other long latency auditory evoked potentials in possible dementia Alzheimer-type and alcoholic Korsakof syndrome. *British Journal of Psychiatry, 147,* 702–708.

Sternberg, S. (1975). Memory scanning: New findings and current controversies. *Quarterly Journal of Experimental Psychology, 27,* 1–32.

Taylor, R. L. (1990). *The old and the young. Distinguishing psychological from organic disorders: Screening for psychological masquerade.* New York: Springer.

Thompson, T. L. (1987). Dementia. In R. E. Hales & S. C. Yudofsky (Eds.), *Textbook of neuropsychiatry* (pp. 107–124). Washington, DC: American Psychiatric Press.

Vrtunski, P. B., Patterson, N. B., Mack, J. L., & Hill, G. O. (1983). Microbehavioural analysis on the choice reaction time response in senile dementia. *Brain, 106,* 927–947.

Wallace, P. W., & Westmoreland, B. F. (1976). The electroencephalogram in pernicious anemia. *Mayo Clinic Proceedings, 51,* 281.

Walton, J. N., Kiloh, L. G., Osselton, J. W., & Farrall, J. (1954). The electroencephalogram in pernicious anaemia and subacute combined degeneration of the cord. *Electroencephalography and Clinical Neurophysiology, 6,* 45.

Wechsler, D. (1945). A standardized memory scale for clinical use. *Journal of Psychology, 19,* 87–95.

Wechsler, D. (1981). *Manual for the Wechsler Adult Intelligence Scale–Revised.* New York: Psychological Corporation.

Wechsler, D. (1987). *WMS-R: Wechsler Memory Scale–Revised.* New York: Psychological Corporation.

Wells, C. E. (1979). Pseudodementia. *American Journal of Psychiatry, 136,* 895–900.

Wells, F. L., & Ruesch, J. (1972). *Mental examiner's handbook.* New York: Psychological Corporation.

Williams, P. A., Jones, G. H., Briscoe, M., Thomas, R., & Cronin, P. (1991). P300 and reaction-time measures in senile dementia of the Alzheimer type. *British Journal of Psychiatry, 159,* 410–414.

Yesavage, J. A. (1988). Geriatric Depression Scale. *Psychopharmacology Bulletin, 24,* 709–711.

CHAPTER 5

EPILEPSY AND NONEPILEPTIC ATTACK DISORDER

Eugene J. Rankin, Russell L. Adams, and Herman E. Jones

Epilepsy is a very common disorder. Estimates are that approximately 5 out of 1,000 people suffer from epilepsy (McIntosh, 1992), which makes epilepsy the second most common neurological disorder (Adams & Victor, 1993). Despite the large number of cases, epilepsy is one of the most neglected areas of psychology. Although profound behavioral changes occur during epileptic seizures, many training programs in psychology devote little time to this subject. This may be because of the vast amount and interdisciplinary nature of the information available. A brief review of the references in this chapter, for example, reveals that information on epilepsy is often found in the neurology, neurosurgery, psychiatry, and neuropsychology literature as well as in clinical psychology journals.

The overall goal of this chapter is to provide basic information to students and practitioners on the diagnosis, assessment, and treatment of adults who have epileptic disorders and to address pertinent issues for which practitioners could assist in the evaluation and treatment of such individuals. In addition, relevant assessment and treatment information is provided on adults who have disorders that resemble epilepsy. When appropriate, we provide clinical examples taken from the Neuropsychological Assessment Laboratory at the University of Oklahoma Health Sciences Center to illustrate.

This chapter is divided into five sections. In the first section we define complex terms used in epileptology and discuss the etiology, epidemiology, genetics, and neuroanatomical substrates for epilepsy. We next discuss the diagnostic methods used to identify epilepsy as well as various treatment approaches. We also review various psychological and behavioral issues associated with epilepsy, such as the epileptic personality and ictal and interictal violence in individuals with epilepsy. The diagnosis, classification, and treatment of nonepileptic attack disorders (NEADs) are then reviewed. Finally, we present two neuropsychological cases to illustrate points made throughout the chapter.

DEFINITIONS

The terms *epilepsy* and *seizure* are often confused. On the one hand, a seizure is the resulting behavior or set of behaviors, characterized by an apparent alteration of responsiveness and motor, sensory, or autonomic dysfunction, caused by excessive neuronal discharges in the brain (Gastaut, 1973; Porter, 1991). A seizure is a single event. On the other hand, epilepsy is recurrent seizure activity resulting from a primary discharge of aberrant neurons within the brain. Epileptic seizures are classified into one of two types: partial or generalized (Gastaut, 1970).

Classification of Epileptic Seizures

To assist in classification, the Commission on Classification and Terminology of the International League Against Epilepsy (CCTILAE) developed the International Classification of Epileptic Seizures (ICES) in 1981, reproduced in Exhibit 1.

We would like to express our sincere appreciation to Bruce P. Hermann for his thoughtful comments and suggestions on earlier versions of this chapter.

EXHIBIT 1

International Classification of Epileptic Seizures

I. Partial, or focal, seizures (seizures beginning locally)
  A. Simple (without loss of consciousness)
    1. Motor (focal motor without march, Jacksonian, versive, postural, phonatory)
    2. Somatosensory or special sensory (visual, auditory, olfactory, gustatory, vertiginous)
    3. Autonomic
    4. Psychic (dysphasic, dysmnesic, cognitive, affective, illusions, structured hallucinations)
  B. Complex (with impaired consciousness)
    1. Beginning as simple partial seizures and progressing to impairment of consciousness
      a. With simple partial features
      b. With automatisms
    2. With impairment of consciousness at onset
      a. With impairment of consciousness only
      b. With automatisms
  C. Partial seizures evolving to secondarily generalized seizures
    1. Simple partial seizures evolving to generalized seizures
    2. Complex partial seizures evolving to generalized seizures
    3. Simple partial seizures evolving to complex partial seizures evolving to generalized seizures

II. Generalized seizures (bilaterally symmetrical and without local onset)
  A. Absence seizures
    1. Absence (petit mal)
      a. Impairment of consciousness only
      b. With mild clonic components
      c. With atonic components
      d. With tonic components
      e. With automatisms
      f. With autonomic components
      (b through f used alone or in combination)
    2. Atypical absence
  B. Myoclonic seizures
  C. Clonic seizures
  D. Tonic seizures
  E. Tonic–clonic seizures
  F. Atonic seizures (astatic; combinations of the above may occur, such as B and F, B and D)

III. Unclassified epileptic seizures (because of inadequate data)

From "Proposal for Revised Clinical and Electroencephalographic Classification of Epileptic Seizures," by the Commission on Classification and Terminology of the International League Against Epilepsy, 1981, Epilepsia, 22, *pp. 493–495. Copyright 1981 by Raven Press. Adapted with permission.*

The ICES is a classification system that is based on the behavioral and clinical features of epileptic seizures. Classification is made without reference to anatomical substrate, etiology, or age of onset. The ICES subdivides epileptic seizures into partial seizures (i.e., seizures presumably of a focal origin) and generalized seizures (i.e., seizures presumably of a generalized origin).

Partial seizures are subdivided into simple partial seizures, complex partial seizures, and partial seizures that secondarily generalize into generalized seizures. A simple partial seizure implies no altering of consciousness, whereas a complex partial seizure implies altered cognition and altered consciousness (CCTILAE, 1981). Generalized seizures are characterized by an immediate loss of consciousness with symmetrical cortical electrical discharges (Stevenson & King, 1987). Primary generalized seizures lack an aura, lateralized sensory or motor disturbances, and focal electroencephalographic (EEG) abnormalities (CCTILAE, 1981). Generalized seizures are classified into several categories, which include the nonconvulsive type, absence seizures (also known as petit mal), or the convulsive (also known as grand mal) type, such as myoclonic, clonic, tonic, tonic–clonic, and atonic seizures (CCTILAE, 1981). The major seizure types commonly encountered in clinical practice are described next.

Partial seizures. ***Simple partial seizures.*** Simple partial seizures are seizures that have a focal onset and no alterations in consciousness (CCTILAE, 1981, Porter, 1984). There are four types of simple partial seizures: focal motor, somatosensory (special sensory), autonomic, and psychic. Motor varieties of simple partial seizures include those that remain cortically focal and those that spread along the motor cortex. The former appears behaviorally as an involuntary movement of a body part (e.g., head turning to one side) or paralysis of a body part (e.g., speech arrest). The latter variety may begin as a movement in a finger that then extends to the entire arm and face, which is called a "Jacksonian seizure" (CCTILAE, 1981). Sensory varieties of simple partial seizures can be either positive somatosensory types (i.e., tingling sensations, etc.) or negative somatosensory types (i.e., sensory loss, numbness, etc.), or they can manifest with "special sensory symptoms" consisting of specific but simple auditory, visual, or olfactory sensations. Autonomic varieties of simple partial seizures are characterized by vomiting, pallor, sweating, piloerection, among other phenomena (CCTILAE, 1981). A final type involves simple partial seizures that present with psychic phenomena, such as dysphasia, dysmnesia, or affective symptomatology (CCTILAE, 1981).

An example of a simple partial seizure is as follows: A 25-year-old woman reports experiencing olfactory hallucinations of a burning smell that last no more than 30 s for any given episode. She reports that she has never lost consciousness during these episodes and that she experiences approximately 10 such episodes per month.

Complex partial seizures. A complex partial seizure is a seizure of focal cortical onset characterized by a loss of consciousness (CCTILAE, 1981). Typically, the only physical manifestations of complex partial seizures are automatisms, which present in more than 90% of complex seizures (Theodore, Porter, & Penry, 1981). Briefly, automatisms are simple, repetitive, and purposeless face or hand movements, such as swallowing, kissing, and lip smacking or fumbling, scratching, and rubbing the abdomen, and they are usually followed by amnesia of the event (Gastaut, 1973). Automatisms also can present as complex behaviors that are out of context to the situation and can include walking, running, and other complex activities. The amnesia for the event and disruption of consciousness differentiates the automatism from the motor variety of simple partial seizures (Porter, 1984).

An example of a partial complex seizure is as follows: A 23-year-old man reports a period of unconsciousness in which he stares off into space, picks at his clothing, and lip smacks. These events resolve over a period of 2 min with a gradual return of consciousness. Following this event, the man reports feeling confused, feeling sleepy, and having a severe headache.

Partial seizures that secondarily generalize. A partial seizure also may "secondarily generalize" into a generalized seizure. This is true of both simple partial and complex partial seizure types. A person may experience only a simple complex seizure, a simple partial seizure that progresses into a complex partial seizure, a simple partial seizure that generalizes into a generalized tonic–clonic seizure, or a simple partial seizure that progresses into a complex partial seizure that then generalizes into a generalized tonic–clonic seizure (Porter, 1984).

An example of a secondary generalization of a complex partial seizure is as follows: A 34-year-old woman describes her seizures as beginning with a feeling of déjà vu, lip smacking, and picking at her clothes, followed by generalized tonic–clonic movements. She reports that these events last 15 s to 2 min, after which she feels nauseated, is fatigued, and has severe headaches.

Generalized seizures. ***Absence seizures.*** Absence seizures, a type of generalized epileptic seizure, are 1- to 10-s lapses in attention that are accompanied in many cases by automatisms, subtle clonic limb movements, and blinking or upward rotation of the eyes (CCTILAE, 1981). It is noteworthy that the probability of automatisms during absence seizures increases with the duration of the seizure (Penry & Dreifuss, 1969). During the absence, the patient is usually able to maintain muscle tone and bladder control, but mental and physical activity are disrupted. After the seizure, there is no postictal confusion, agitation, or sleepiness, nor does the patient experience retrograde amnesia. Absence seizures typically begin between the ages of 4 and 12 years (Penry, Porter, & Dreifuss, 1975). Many individuals with absence seizures experience a remission in early adulthood, although in many patients, generalized tonic–clonic seizures completely replace the absence seizures (Adams & Victor, 1993).

An example of an absence seizure is as follows: An 8-year-old girl of normal intelligence experiences 30 or more events each day; the events come without warning and consist of staring, rapid, upgoing eyes, blinking of the eyelids, lip smacking, a quick end of the seizure, and a rapid return to a normal level of consciousness. The events last for approximately 15 s each, without postictal confusion or sleepiness. Her EEG reveals 3-Hz generalized spike-and-wave discharges during the ictal events, in contrast to her normal background activity.

Generalized convulsive seizures. There are several forms of generalized convulsive seizures, including myoclonic, tonic, clonic, tonic–clonic, and atonic. In the past, these types of seizures were collectively called *grand mal* (Stevenson & King, 1987). Myoclonic seizures are characterized by brusque, brief muscular contractions occurring intermittently and unpredictably, and they are often causally related to hypoxia (Adams & Victor, 1993). Clonic seizures are characterized by a repetitive jerking of the entire body (CCTILAE, 1981). Tonic seizures are characterized by rigid muscular contractions, accompanied by eye and head deviations (CCTILAE, 1981). Tonic–clonic seizures are the most frequently encountered of the generalized seizures (CCTILAE, 1981) and are characterized by a loss of consciousness, with muscle flexion, then extension, and a 4- to 8-s tremor that turns into a clonic phase (Gastaut & Broughton, 1972). Atonic seizures are characterized by a sudden loss of muscle tone and have been described as "drop attacks" (CCTILAE, 1981).

Postictally, the patient who experiences generalized seizure activity reports confusion, amnesia, and disorientation for the seizure and any immediate events preceding it (Stevenson & King, 1987). EEGs taken immediately after the seizure show decreased cortical activity. This is called *postictal depression* (Sato & Rose, 1986). In addition, serum prolactin levels elevate for 15–30 min after the seizure (Trimble, 1978).

An example of a myoclonic seizure is the following: A 25-year-old woman reports a warningless loss of consciousness followed by muscle jerking in her extremities, rarely lasting more than 2 min. An example of a tonic–clonic seizure is as follows: A 26-year-old man reports a warningless loss of consciousness. Witnesses to the man's seizures describe a sudden muscle stiffening (tonic phase), followed by symmetrical involuntary jerking of all extremities (clonic phase). These events rarely last more than 2 min. When the man regains consciousness, he reports having a severe headache. Finally, an example of an atonic seizure is as follows: A 13-year-old girl experiences a warningless loss of consciousness and falls to the ground, lying motionless with decreased muscle tone. The duration of the seizure rarely lasts for more than 2 min.

Status epilepticus. A person with status epilepticus experiences one seizure after another before fully recovering from the preceding seizure (Porter, 1984). There are several types of status epilepticus, both partial and generalized varieties. Partial varieties of status epilepticus include epilepsia partialis continua (also referred to as simple partial status) and complex partial status (also referred to as psychomotor status). Generalized varieties of status epilepticus include absence status (also referred to as petit mal status or spike-wave stupor), primary generalized tonic–clonic status, and secondary generalized tonic–clonic status following a partial onset (Porter, 1984). Note that the convulsive generalized varieties of status epilepticus are medical emergencies because of the prolonged nature of the attack, resulting hypoxic injury, and excitotoxic effects to the brain (Porter, 1984).

Specific epileptic syndromes. The CCTILAE released a supplement to the ICES, the International Classification of Epilepsies and Epileptic Syndromes, in 1989. This supplement facilitates communication among health care professionals. It subdivides seizures into two major classes: focal versus generalized seizures, and idiopathic (i.e., no underlying cause) versus cryptogenic (i.e., the cause is hidden but presumed known) versus symptomatic (i.e., known cause) seizures. Because of limited space, we mention this only briefly. The reader can find more information in the supplement (CCTILAE, 1989).

Causes of Epilepsy

The causes of epileptic seizures are numerous, the majority of which are unknown and remain undetected. Table 1 shows various causes of epileptic seizures as manifested in different age groups (Adams & Victor, 1993).

Epidemiology of Epilepsy

Determining the prevalence and incidence of epilepsy has been problematic for many reasons, including difficulties in defining seizure types, the lack of accurate information in reporting epileptic seizures, and the age of onset and duration of the disorder. Hence, most epidemiological rates for epilepsy are underestimates (Engel, 1989). In the past, issues of definition were particularly important because detailed diagnostic studies (including multiple EEG tracings and concurrent videotaping) were not completed in many patients who presented with epilepsy.

Using current definitions, McIntosh (1992) reported that 5 out of every 1,000 people are afflicted with chronic epileptic seizures. A further statistical breakdown of those individuals experiencing epileptic attacks reveals the following prevalence rates as cited by Lechtenberg (1990): Sixty-two percent of seizures are of partial onset, with roughly 10% being of the simple partial variety, 40% being of the complex partial variety, and 12% progressing from partial to secondary generalized seizures. Thirty-eight percent of seizures are of primary generalized onset,

TABLE 1

Causes of Recurrent Seizures in Different Age Groups

Age of onset	Probable cause
Neonatal	Congenital maldevelopment, birth injury, anoxia, metabolic disorders (hypocalcemia, hypoglycemia, vitamin B_6 deficiency, phenylketonuria, and others)
Infancy (1–6 months)	As above, plus infantile spasms
Early childhood (6 months to 3 years)	Infantile spasms, febrile convulsions, birth injury and anoxia, infections, trauma, metabolic disorders
Childhood (3–10 years)	Perinatal anoxia, injury at birth or later, infections, thrombosis of cerebral arteries or veins, metabolic disorders, or indeterminate cause ("idiopathic" epilepsy)
Adolescence (10–18 years)	Idiopathic epilepsy, including genetically transmitted types, trauma, drugs
Early adulthood (18–25 years)	Idiopathic epilepsy, trauma, neoplasm, withdrawal from alcohol or other sedative–hypnotic drugs
Middle age (35–60 years)	Trauma, neoplasm, vascular disease, alcohol, or other drug withdrawal
Late life (over 60 years)	Vascular disease, tumor, degenerative disease, trauma

Note: Meningitis and its complications may be a cause of seizures at any age. This is also true of severe metabolic disturbances. In tropical and subtropical countries, parasitic infection of the central nervous system is a common cause. From *Principles of Neurology* (5th ed., p. 289), by R. D. Adams and M. Victor, 1993, New York: McGraw-Hill. Copyright 1993 by McGraw-Hill. Reprinted with permission.

with roughly 11% being tonic–clonic seizures, 10% being absence seizures, and the remaining 17% taking other generalized seizure forms. The incidence of epilepsy also varies with age. As can be seen in Table 1, the greatest number of new cases of epilepsy occurs during the first and later years of life.

Genetic Characteristics of Epilepsy

The role of genetics in epilepsy has been investigated extensively, although the results are far from conclusive. This lack of clarity is not surprising when one considers the numerous etiologies that make up the various epileptic disorders. For example, epilepsy can result from a tumor, head injury, stroke, metabolic disturbance, and a variety of idiopathic conditions. In this section we attempt to introduce the topic of genetic characteristics of epilepsy but do not provide a comprehensive review.

Genetic characteristics of epilepsy are conceptualized in terms of primary and secondary syndromes. The primary syndromes are epileptic seizures that are principal expressions of the genetic defect. The secondary syndromes are epileptic seizures that are incidentally associated with another neurological or systemic disorder (Engel, 1989).

Primary epileptic syndromes are considered age dependent (i.e., their phenotypic expression is manifested at certain developmental periods) and, in some cases, gender influenced (i.e., their expression is unequally represented among either male or female patients). One common primary epileptic syndrome is the classic "absence attack," which is thought to be transmitted through an incompletely penetrant autosomal dominant mode of inheritance (Metrakos & Metrakos, 1961). The onset age of this syndrome is typically between 3 and 13 years, and girls are overrepresented (Loiseau, 1985). An autosomal dominant mode of inheritance also is found in various other primary epileptic syndromes of childhood (e.g., benign neonatal familial convulsions, benign childhood epilepsy with centrotemporal spikes). Other primary epileptic syndromes include myoclonic absence epilepsy, juvenile absence epilepsy, and juvenile myoclonic epilepsy. The genetic bases of these syndromes are not known.

Secondary epileptic syndromes are not directly the result of a primary genetic defect and do not co-occur in each case. There are a variety of inherited disorders with which epilepsy may co-occur, including myelin disorders, vitamin disorders, electrolytic disorders, endocrine metabolism disorders, and disorders of lipid metabolism (Engel, 1989).

Neuroanatomical Substrate for Epilepsy

Epileptic seizures can originate from anywhere in the brain, both cortically and subcortically (Stevenson & King, 1987). To assist in locating epileptogenic foci, EEGs and various other neuroimaging techniques are used (described later). However, the behavioral manifestations of the resulting seizure can be wholly unrelated to its origin and are affected by the location of onset, pattern, and speed of the epileptogenic spread to adjacent brain structures. Because of this complex situation, the sequential onset of the behavioral manifestation of seizures becomes important in assisting confirmation of the neuroanatomical location of the epileptogenic foci. Like in the previous sections, here we attempt to present a simplified account of a complex correlation of findings. Some of the more frequently observed behavioral manifestations of seizures that arise from cortical regions include memory impairment with seizures arising from mesial temporal regions; language impairment arising from lateral temporal regions; speech arrest, forced thinking, or Jacksonian march seizures arising from frontal regions; somatosensory disturbances arising from parietal regions; and visual disturbances arising from occipital regions (CCTILAE, 1989).

Neurochemically, seizures are believed to result from an inhibition or blockade of the neurotransmitter gamma-aminobutyric acid (GABA), the major inhibitory neurotransmitter in the brain; GABA blockade results in an excessive excitation at the cellular level (Adams & Victor, 1993; Stevenson & King, 1987). Most medications with anticonvulsant properties tend to facilitate this inhibitory process by increasing cortical levels of GABA (Stevenson & King, 1987).

DIAGNOSIS AND TREATMENT OF EPILEPSY

Diagnosis

Electroencephalogram. EEG is a device that records the electrical activity of the brain. Electrical brain activity is recorded by placing electrodes on

TABLE 2

Four Common Electroencephalographic Patterns in Normal Individuals

Activity	Hz (cycles/second)	Typical cortical location	Cognitive state
Alpha	8–13	Posterior (occipital)	Relaxation
Beta	>13	Anterior (frontal)	Focused attention
Theta	4–7	Generalized	Deep sleep
Delta	1–3	Generalized	Deep sleep

Note: From *Clinical Neurology for Psychiatrists* (p. 195), by D. M. Kaufman, 1990, Philadelphia: W. B. Saunders. Copyright 1990 by W. B. Saunders. Adapted with permission.

the scalp (i.e., scalp electrodes). In candidates for epilepsy surgery, the electrodes are placed on the surface of the brain (i.e., subdural strip electrodes) or within the substance of the brain (i.e., depth electrodes). The EEG is a measure of electrical brain function, unlike a computed tomography (CT) scan or a magnetic resonance (MR) image, which is a measure of brain structure. Overall, the EEG represents the most sensitive clinical test for diagnosing epileptic seizures. However, abnormalities seen on an EEG are not necessarily proof that a person has epilepsy. Even if abnormal electrical events are present interictally, the events suggest a predisposition for epilepsy but are not proof of epilepsy. In fact, abnormal EEG patterns are observed in approximately 3% of normal (i.e., seizure-free) individuals (Fenton, 1982). In addition, approximately 20% of epilepsy patients have completely normal interictal EEG patterns (Kaufman, 1990). Even when an actual seizure event is captured by an EEG, the seizure activity can be obscured by motion artifact if the person is having a convulsion.

The EEG records four distinct brain waves in the normal individual. Table 2 shows this information. When an epileptic seizure occurs, the EEG records specific abnormal electrical events that consist of electrical spikes, slow waves, or complexes of both. The various types of epileptic seizures have distinctive EEG patterns and are summarized in Table 3. For example, partial seizures will present with focal or localized onset. Generalized seizures have a bilateral onset on an EEG suggestive of widespread cerebral involvement. In many cases, the seizure focus is subcortical in both primary generalized seizures and

TABLE 3

Typical Electroencephalogram (EEG) Patterns Associated With Several Types of Epileptic Seizures

Seizure	Typical EEG pattern
Absence	Generalized 2.5–3.5 Hz spike-wave discharges with abrupt onset and termination
Generalized tonic–clonic	Sudden reduction of background amplitude followed by diffuse fast activity of 10 Hz, which increases in amplitude and shifts into spike-wave or polyspike-wave pattern of gradually decreasing frequency
Simple partial	Focal epileptogenic activity with associated spikes or sharp wave EEG abnormality
Complex partial	No stereotyped ictal EEG pattern, although there is initial suppression of background activity with replacement by rhythmical slow theta wave frequency and ictal discharges characterized either by unilateral, bisynchronously or independently bilateral, or spreading from one side to the other

Note: From "The Electroencephalogram in the Evaluation of the Patient With Epilepsy," by S. Sato and D. F. Rose, 1986, *Neurologic Clinics*, *4*, pp. 509–529. Copyright 1986 by W. B. Saunders. Adapted with permission.

partial complex seizures (e.g., the hippocampus). If the patient does not demonstrate specific abnormalities or actual seizure activity during standard EEG placement, there are several methods that may induce seizure activity. These methods include hyperventilation (Miley & Forster, 1977), stroboscopic light (Bickford, 1979), pedaling a stationary bicycle, and sleep deprivation (Ellingson, Wilken, & Bennett, 1984).

Individuals for whom these methods fail to elicit epileptiform activity occasionally undergo additional electrode placement consisting of nasopharyngeal, sphenoidal, or subdural strips. An additional enhancement to the process of recording epileptiform activity includes the use of simultaneous video–EEG telemetry. Simultaneous video–EEG telemetry allows for the correlation of videotape recording of the behavioral features of a person's seizure with the electrical seizure activity as measured by an EEG. The use of this technology has been particularly helpful in making differential diagnoses between individuals with epilepsy and those with nonepileptiform disorders (Desai, Porter, & Penry, 1982).

Neuroimaging. There are four methods of neuroimaging used in the diagnosis of epilepsy, two of which involve brain structure (CT scanning and MR imaging), and two of which involve brain function (positron emission tomography [PET] and single photon emission computed tomography [SPECT]). CT scanning and MR imaging assist in the diagnostic process by identifying structural abnormalities in the brain. However, although abnormalities may be identified on either CT scans or MR images, the degree to which the abnormalities are epileptogenic must be further correlated with both clinical and electro-physiological investigations (Kuzniecky et al., 1993).

CT scanning works by using exogenous X-ray penetration that identifies tissue density changes, particularly at the interface between tissue and fluid or tissue and bone. One advantage of CT scanning with individuals suffering from intractable epilepsy includes its ability to detect vascular malformations or tumors (Kuzniecky et al., 1993). The disadvantages of CT scanning include its ability to image temporal lobe structures lying deep within the middle fossa, sensitivities some patients have to contrast material, and exposure to radiation (Blom et al., 1984).

MR imaging works by detecting radiofrequency energy absorbed by brain tissue after the tissue is subjected to a strong magnetic field. More specifically, the magnetic field orients the protons, causing the protons to align themselves in the same direction as the magnetic field. Once accomplished, a radio frequency is introduced, which vibrates the protons and changes their alignment. The radio frequency is then switched off, allowing the protons to return to their original position. The energy absorbed by the protons are then computer analyzed and an image is subsequently constructed. The advantages of MR imaging include its crisp visual detail of neuroanatomical structures, its increased sensitivity to the identification of mesial temporal lobe sclerosis (i.e., damage), and the lack of radiation exposure.

In determining the etiology of a seizure disorder, an abnormal CT scan or MR image is a helpful adjunct. For example, the identification of asymmetric hippocampal volumes by MR imaging is often helpful in elucidating the site of partial complex seizures of temporal lobe onset. However, a normal CT scan or MR image is not as useful as one might imagine because abnormalities may still exist but are not detectable by these methods.

In contrast to structural neuroimaging approaches, PET and SPECT examine changes in cellular metabolism in the brain. It is particularly helpful in diagnosing partial seizure disorders, in which focal hypometabolic activity can be observed interictally and hypermetabolic activity can be observed during a seizure (Engel, Kuhl, Phelps, & Crandall, 1982; Newmark et al., 1982). These technologies also appear helpful in the differential diagnoses of primary generalized tonic–clonic and absence seizures, typically demonstrating generalized increases in metabolism (Henry, Chugani, Abou-Khalil, Theodore, & Swartz, 1993). By contrast, interictal SPECT imaging does not appear to be as reliable as interictal PET, and further research is needed to validate the procedure (Berkovic, Newton, Chiron, & Dulac, 1993). Finally, the uses of PET and SPECT in diagnosing epileptic states continue to be limited by their lack of availability in most epilepsy centers (Adams & Victor, 1993).

Neuropsychological assessment. ***Clinical interview.*** One of the most important aspects of evaluating someone with epilepsy is to conduct a thorough clinical interview that reviews the presenting problem in detail. This includes interviewing significant others who know the patient well. The questions provided in Exhibit 2 were designed to assist the clinician in obtaining a detailed and accurate clinical history. It is unlikely that the patient or significant other will have all of this information available to him or her if not notified beforehand. We have found it helpful to notify the patient before the appointment to ask him or her to gather as much information as possible about his or her disorder, including initial seizure onset, seizure frequency and types, and seizure course, as well as all the various medications he or she has taken both in the past and now. We also ask that someone who knows the patient well accompany him or her to the evaluation.

During the clinical interview, it is important to be attentive to the nonspecific aspects of the patient's self-report of his or her seizure disorder. Is the patient's self-report vague, or is it specific and stereotyped? Does the patient seem to remember the event or have a general awareness of activities occurring around him or her during the event, or does the patient report an abrupt loss of consciousness with absolutely no recall for activities preceding and during the event?

Neuropsychological Battery for Epilepsy. The first standardized test battery for patients with epilepsy was the Neuropsychological Battery for Epilepsy (NBE; Dodrill, 1978). According to Dodrill (personal communication, October 4, 1989), there are "no universal patterns of cognitive test performance" among individuals with epilepsy. Given this situation, the NBE was developed by using a renormed version of the Halstead–Reitan Neuropsychological Test Battery, along with other specific measures. This NBE is sensitive to the detection of cognitive deficits in patients with epilepsy. Research using the NBE has demonstrated that the battery is sensitive to the effects of EEG epileptiform (Wilkus & Dodrill, 1976) and nonepileptiform abnormalities (Dodrill & Wilkus, 1978), antiepileptic medication (Dodrill & Temkin, 1989), and psychosocial adjustment (Dodrill & Clemmons, 1984).

The development of the NBE progressed in three parts. First, 100 measures were administered to a heterogeneous group of patients with epilepsy and nonneurological control subjects who were matched on age, education, gender, occupation, and race. All measures were evaluated for their ability to discriminate between patients with epilepsy and normal control subjects at a predetermined alpha level of .01. The measures that were not able to discriminate at this level were dropped from further evaluation. The second step was to reduce measurement redundancy by evaluating the degree of test overlap. A test was eliminated if it correlated more than .66 with any other measure. The degree of discriminability and overlap with other measures also were considered in the elimination of a measure. Finally, the resulting battery was cross-validated with a new patient sample. The result was 16 measures that met all the criteria of discriminability, test overlap, and cross-validation. Following this, cutoff scores were established for each measure based on the original sample of subjects. Table 4 shows the 16 measures, their cutoff scores, and the percentage of correct classifications.

Criticisms of the NBE include its neglect of important emotional and psychosocial issues and a lack of flexibility necessary to address a wider variety of referral questions. Because of these criticisms, many neuropsychologists add additional tests to increase diagnostic sensitivity, or they use completely different groups of tests other than those measures used with the NBE. The NBE is discussed here because we usually use it in our neuropsychological evaluations.

Supplemental neuropsychological measures. Several additional measures to supplement the NBE include the Wechsler Adult Intelligence Scale (WAIS; Wechsler, 1955) or its revision (WAIS-R; Wechsler, 1981), the Wechsler Memory Scale (WMS; Wechsler, 1945) or its revision (WMS-R; Wechsler, 1987), the

EXHIBIT 2

Epilepsy History Questions

Onset of ictus

1. How many different seizure types do you have?
2. For each seizure type, what is the first thing that happens in a typical seizure?
   a. Is there an aura (somatosensory, special sensory, motor, or psychic)?
   b. Is there an abrupt loss of consciousness?
   c. Is there a gradual loss of consciousness or was there a hazy state in which you have some memory for voices around you or movements? (psychogenic NEADs)
   d. Do you fall during your events and, if so, have you ever hurt yourself?

Ictally

1. What do other people observe during your seizure?
   a. Have a witness describe the patient's seizures
   b. Were the observed behaviors complicated, organized, and prolonged but not recalled?
   c. Is the event continuous in its progression or does it speed up and slow down?
   d. Were the observed behaviors directed toward persons or objects?
   e. Were the observed behaviors characterized by a pronounced decrease of behavioral functioning?
   f. Were the observed behaviors bizarre and purposeless?
   g. What happened to the person's eyes during the seizure event?
      1) Did they dilate?
      2) Did they turn in one direction?
   h. What happened to the person's head during the seizure event?
      1) Did it turn in one direction?
   i. Was there any period of either urinary or fecal incontinence during any of your seizures?
   j. What is your skin color during your seizure (pale, flesh, blue, natural, etc.)?
   k. Was one side of the body affected more than the other?
2. What is happening around you when you have a seizure (check for stressful events such as arguments, prolonged lack of food, sleep deprivation, etc.)?
3. How long does the seizure last?
   a. No more than 10 s for the absence seizure
   b. No more than 180 s for the partial or generalized seizures
   c. Often several minutes for the psychogenic NEADs
4. Are the seizures exactly the same each time or do they vary?

Postictally

1. How do you feel after the seizure?
   a. Postictally, patients experiencing partial complex and generalized tonic–clonic seizures report feeling nausea, tiredness, and headache
   b. Postictally, patients with absence seizures and patients with NEADs will report no postictal confusion but a return of normal awareness
2. Has one side of your body ever been paralyzed or weak following a seizure?
   a. If so, how long (should be 24 hr or less)?

EXHIBIT 2 (*Continued*)

General

1. At what age did your seizures start?
2. Have you ever had one seizure right after the other without stop?
3. If so, what did you do? (With convulsive status epilepticus, this is medical emergency and the patient would have been transported to the nearest hospital; often with NEADs, the events will remit by themselves, after which the patient resumes normal functioning.)
4. For women, do you experience an increase of seizures around menses or ovulation (catamenial epilepsy)?
5. Had you recently used alcohol or drugs and/or stopped taking alcohol or drugs after prolonged use?
6. Anticonvulsant medications:
   a. What anticonvulsants have you been put on?
   b. For each medication, in what amounts?
   c. For each medication, for how long?
   d. For each medication, what was the effect on your seizure disorder?

Biomedical studies (obtained from medical records)

1. Is there evidence of abnormal interictal EEG activity?
2. Does CT scanning or MR imaging suggest structural abnormalities?
3. Do laboratory values suggest abnormal chemical levels?
   a. Check glucose, BUN, calcium, sodium, and serum prolactin levels
4. If lumbar puncture was performed, were the values within normal limits?

Individual medical history

1. Birth and early childhood history
   a. Were you born on time?
   b. Were there any complications during your birth (anoxia, jaundice, etc.)?
   c. Did you sustain any injuries before, during, or after your birth (i.e., head trauma)?
   d. Did you contract the usual childhood illnesses without sequelae?
   e. Did you meet developmental milestones on time (sit at 6 months, walk at 12 months, talk at 18 months, etc.)?
2. Do you have any sort of heart problem (hypertension, mitral valve prolapse, aortic stenosis, etc.)?
3. Have you ever fainted?
4. What other medications are you taking now?
5. Have you ever sustained a head injury?
6. What toxic substances have you been exposed to?

Individual psychiatric history

1. Have you ever seen a psychiatrist, psychologist, social worker, minister, or any other type of mental health professional for any mental or emotional problem?
2. Have you ever attempted suicide? (If so, how?)
3. What is your earliest memory of childhood? (Look for gaps in memory or poor recall of events in general, which may be suggestive of sexual abuse)

(continues)

EXHIBIT 2 (*Continued*)

4. Have you ever been sexually abused?
5. What recreational drugs do you use (alcohol, marijuana, etc.).

Family medical and psychiatric history

1. Does anyone else in your family have seizures?
2. Has anyone in your family ever seen a psychiatrist, psychologist, social worker, minister, or any other type of mental health professional for any mental or emotional problem?
3. Does anyone in your family take medication for nerves?

NEADs = nonepileptic attack disorders; EEG = electroencephalographic; CT = computed tomography; MR = magnetic resonance; BUN = blood urea nitrogen.

Wisconsin Card Sorting Test (WCST; Heaton, 1981), and the Washington Psychosocial Seizure Inventory (WPSI; Dodrill, Batzel, Queisser, & Temkin, 1980).

The WAIS and WAIS-R have been used extensively in evaluations of people with epilepsy (Jones-Gotman, Smith, & Zatorre, 1993). Overall, the WAIS and WAIS-R appear to be best used to derive an estimate of intellectual functioning rather than as a tool for lateralizing or localizing epileptogenic foci, given recent research by Hermann et al. (1995), who

TABLE 4

Neuropsychological Battery for Epilepsy: Test Variables, Cutoff Scores, and Percentage of Correct Classifications

Measure	Cutoff (inside/outside)	Correct classification (%)
Category test	53/54	63
Tactual Performance Test		
Total time	16.2/16.3 min	74
Memory score	8/7 blocks recalled	67
Localization score	4/3 blocks correct	65
Seashore Rhythm Test	26/25 correct	66
Finger Tapping total		
Male	101/100 taps (mean)	84
Female	92/91 taps (mean)	80
Trail Making Test, Part B	81/82 s	71
Aphasia Screening Test errors	2/3 errors	64
Constructional dyspraxia	Questionable/mild	65
Perceptual exam	6/7 errors	66
Seashore Tonal Memory	22/21 correct	67
Stroop, Part 1	93/94 s	68
Stroop, Part 2 − Part 1	150/151 s	70
Name Writing (total time)	0.85/0.84 letters per s	72
Wechsler Memory Scale		
Logical Memory	19/18 total memory bits	68
Visual Reproduction	11/10 total memory bits	78
Summary score: Total tests impaired	6/7 outside normal limits	81

Note: From "A Neuropsychological Battery for Epilepsy," by C. B. Dodrill, 1978, *Epilepsia*, *19*, p. 619. Copyright 1978 by Raven Press. Adapted with permission.

showed that the WAIS-R is not good at identifying the laterality of epileptogenic lesions. In previous attempts at lateralizing or localizing lesions in people with known epilepsy, various investigators have proposed that patients with known epileptic lesions of the left temporal lobe have specific language-related memory deficits that can be demonstrated by examining WAIS Information and Vocabulary subtest performance and contrasting this performance with performance on the WAIS Similarities subtest (Bolter, Veneklasen, & Long, 1981; Dobbins & Russell, 1990; Milberg, Greiffenstein, Lewis, & Rourke, 1980; Russell, 1987). Using an index score of (Information + Vocabulary)/2 − Similarities, in which a negative index score indicates greater temporal lobe pathology, Milberg et al. (1980) was able to reliably discriminate 80% of patients with generalized or partial complex seizures of temporal lobe origin, although a replication of that study by Bolter et al. (1981) was not as favorable. For differential diagnostic purposes, using WAIS or WAIS-R scores have met with considerable failure, particularly when comparing the WAIS performance of people with and without epilepsy (Sackellares et al., 1985).

The WMS and the WMS-R can provide important information about the presence of memory deficits as well as the possible existence of lateralizing signs (Chelune & Bornstein, 1988; Jones-Gotman et al., 1993; Russell, 1975). Memory capacity is often affected in people with epilepsy because of the location of the epileptogenic foci within mesial temporal lobe structures. In particular, double dissociations of memory functioning have been found among individuals with unilateral epileptogenic foci using the WMS (Delaney, Rosen, Mattson, & Novelly, 1980) and the WMS-R (Chelune & Bornstein, 1988): Verbal memory impairment was strongly associated with left temporal lobe foci, and visual memory impairment was strongly associated with right temporal lobe foci.

The WCST is a test of abstraction and shift of mental set that provides important information about problem-solving strategies typically ascribed to frontal lobe functioning. Previous research using SPECT with a Xenon^{133} inhalation technique with healthy individuals has suggested that the nondominant dorsolateral prefrontal cortex becomes activated during WCST performance (Weinberger, Berman, & Zec, 1986). Before the Weinberger et al. investigation, a study conducted by Milner (1963) revealed that in comparison with nonneurological control subjects, patients with dorsolateral frontal epilepsy had significantly more perseverative errors and total errors, but they did not have a significant amount of nonperseverative errors. Later, Hermann, Wyler, and Richey (1988) investigated the effect of dominant versus nondominant temporal lobe epileptogenic foci on rates of WCST perseverative responses and discovered that patients with nondominant foci had more total errors and perseverative errors than did patients with dominant temporal foci. They postulated a "neural noise" hypothesis for this result, suggesting that frontal cortices were activated secondary to temporal lobe activity through the various white matter pathways connecting these structures. Notably, after temporal lobe resection surgery in 17 of these patients, not only were the patients' seizures controlled significantly, but when the WCST was readministered, the amount of total and perseverative errors declined at a level greater than could be attributable to practice effects. In addition, there appears to be an association between laterality of epileptogenic activity, perseverative responding on the WCST, and dysphoric mood state (Hermann, Seidenberg, Haltiner, & Wyler, 1991). Specifically, greater levels of depression are associated with perseverative response scores on the WCST among patients with complex partial seizures of left temporal origin. However, it is important to consider that poor performance is not always specific to frontal lobe lesions: Previous research has shown that poor performance cannot be considered to be solely indicative of frontal lobe dysfunction (Anderson, Damasio, Jones, & Tranel, 1991).

For emotional functioning, the WPSI is a good, objective measure of psychosocial phenomena frequently associated with epilepsy. This 132-item inventory is composed of three validity scales and eight clinical scales. The clinical scales are as follows: Family Background, Emotional Adjustment, Interpersonal Adjustment, Vocational Adjustment, Financial Status, Adjustment to Seizures, Medicine and Medical Management, and Overall Psychosocial Functioning. In total, the WPSI requires approximately 20 min to complete and can be quickly hand-scored with stencils. Clinical inferences can be derived quickly by way of profile analysis. The WPSI shows remarkable profile consistencies with problem areas identified among divergent groups of patients with epilepsy (Dodrill, Breyer, Diamond, Dubinsky, & Geary, 1984).

Treatment

Pharmacotherapy. Treatment of epileptic seizures follows seizure diagnosis and classification. Consequently, it is important that the practitioner working with a patient with epilepsy have at least a basic understanding of the various antiepileptic medications in general as well as the specific antiepileptic medication the patient is taking. Next, we review the general pharmacokinetic properties of antiepileptic medications, toxicity, and current therapeutic approaches.

***Pharmacokinetic properties*.** Antiepileptic medications work by circulating in the bloodstream at an optimal and steady therapeutic level to provide maximum seizure control (Porter, 1984). This therapeutic level is called the *plasma drug level*. This level is routinely measured from an assay of the patient's blood. Therapeutic levels vary from patient to patient and must be adjusted over time to achieve optimal seizure control and to minimize toxic side effects. The optimal therapeutic level depends on several factors, including the medication's half-life. The term *half-life* refers to the time it takes a drug to reach half of its initial level in the bloodstream. Therefore, if a medication taken at 6:00 a.m. has a plasma blood level of 20 μg/ml and at noon the plasma blood level reaches 10 μg/ml, that medication has a half-life of 6 hr. Half-lives differ for the various antiepileptic medications. For example, carbamazepine (Tegretol) has a short half-life, and phenobarbital has a long half-life. Half-lives also differ depending on what other antiepileptic medications or other medications (e.g., hypertensive medications) are being used simultaneously. The second important factor of antiepileptic medication is that of achieving a steady plasma drug level throughout the day (Porter, 1984). This can be affected by if and when the medication is taken. Steady plasma drug levels are best achieved by taking the antiepileptic medication as prescribed. This can be enhanced by taking the medication after meals, which will not only decrease the medication's absorption rate into the bloodstream (and thereby ensuring a more steady level) but also will reduce any gastric discomfort caused by taking it on an empty stomach (Porter, 1984).

To ensure a steady plasma drug level, patients must be compliant with their medication regime as prescribed by their physician. An example of noncompliance is a patient who forgets to take his or her antiepileptic medications and then takes too many pills before his or her visit to his or her physician and becomes sick. Another example of noncompliance is the patient who simply forgets to take his or her medications and experiences generalized tonic–clonic status epilepticus, a potentially life-threatening condition, as described earlier.

There are many antiepileptic medications currently on the market. Table 5 lists the major antiepileptic medications according to their generic and trade names, usual daily dosages, serum half-lives, effective plasma drug levels, and recommended seizure types. Just before we finished writing this chapter, Felbamate was taken off the market because of reports of several serious medical complications associated with its use. One must be aware that the association between certain antiepileptic medications and types of seizures the medication is used to treat is only a guide. Antiepileptic medications may be used differently, in different amounts, and in different combinations to achieve adequate seizure control balanced by minimal toxic side effects. Overall, these medications are what the neurologist or other treating physician uses to treat epileptic seizures.

Some medications, including other antiepileptic medications, can either increase or decrease the patient's ability to achieve a steady plasma drug level. Table 6 lists other medications that may either increase or decrease plasma blood levels of the first-line antiepileptic medication.

Toxicity. The term *toxicity* refers to cognitive, neurological, and other physical side effects caused by taking antiepileptic medications. These side effects can be acute or chronic. Table 7 lists the acute

TABLE 5

Major Antiepileptic Medications Currently Available

Generic name	Typical dosage: Children (mg/kg)	Typical dosage: Adults (mg)	Serum half-life (hr)	Plasma blood level (μg/ml)	Principal therapeutic indications
		Standard antiepileptic medications[a]			
Phenobarbital (Luminal)	3–5	60–200	96 ± 12	10–40	Tonic–clonic, simple and complex partial, absence
Phenytoin (Dilantin)	4–7	300–400	24 ± 12	10–20	Tonic–clonic, simple and complex partial seizures
Carbamazepine (Tegretol)	20–30	600–1,200	12 ± 3	4–10	Tonic–clonic, complex partial seizures
Primidone (Mysoline)	10–25	750–1,500	12 ± 6	5–15	Tonic–clonic, simple and complex partial seizures
Ethosuximide (Zarontin)	20–40	750–2,000	40 ± 6	50–100	Absence seizures
Methsuximide (Celontin)	10–20	500–1,000	40 ± 6	40–100	Absence
Diazepam Valium	0.15–2	10–150			Status epilepticus
Lorazepam (Ativan)	0.03–0.22				Status epilepticus
ACTH	40–60[b]				Infantile spasms
Valproic acid (Depakote)	30–60	1,000–3,000	8 ± 2	50–100	Absence and myoclonic seizures, adjunctive drug in tonic–clonic and complex partial seizures
Clonazepam (Klonopin)	0.01–0.2	1.5–20	18–50	0.01–0.07	Absence, myoclonus
		Recently developed antiepileptic medications[c]			
Gabapentin (Neurontin)	NA	600–2,400	5–7	>2.0	Partial seizures that secondarily generalize and secondarily generalized seizures
Felbamate (Felbatol)	NA	2,400–3,600	18–24	20–60	Partial seizures, generalized seizures, Lennox-Gastaut syndrome
Lamotrigine (Lamictal)	NA	100–700	24 ± 6	1–3	Partial seizures

Note: Trade names are in parentheses. ACTH = adrenocorticotropic hormone. NA = not applicable (no information available).
[a]From *Principles of Neurology* (5th ed., p. 294), by R. D. Adams and M. Victor, 1993, New York: McGraw-Hill. Copyright 1993 by McGraw-Hill. Reprinted with permission.
[b]Dosage is in units per day.
[c]Data are from the manufacturers' prescribing information.

and chronic side effects of the major antiepileptic medications. Practitioners working with patients on antiepileptic medication should familiarize themselves with the manifestation of the acute side effects of antiepileptic medication toxicity and, on the basis of a clinical assessment, inform the patient's treating physician of the findings if toxicity is suspected.

The acute findings of antiepileptic medication toxicity are important to identify and can usually be detected during a clinical interview. The acute effects

TABLE 6

Other Pharmacotherapeutic Agents That May Raise or Lower Plasma Blood Levels When Taken With Major Antiepileptic Medications

Anticonvulsant medication	Drugs that raise plasma blood levels	Drugs that lower plasma blood levels
Dilantin	Coumadin Valium Ritalin Librium Darvon Zarontin Estrogen Thorazine Compazine Depakene, Depakote Phenobarbital	Tegretol Folic acid Depakene, Depakote Alcohol Phenobarbital Antacids Diazoxide
Tegretol		Dilantin Phenobarbital Mysoline
Phenobarbital	Depakene	
Depakote		Tegretol Phenobarbital Primidone Dilantin
Lamictal	Depakene, Depakote	Tegretol Dilantin

Note: Data are from the manufacturers' prescribing information.

may be manifested either with abnormal eye movements (i.e., nystagmus, inability to fix gaze on objects, dyscongugate gaze, diplopia), incoordination (i.e., cerebellar ataxia), vestibular dysfunction (i.e., vertigo, dizziness), or cognitive impairment (i.e., sedation, attention–concentration difficulties, agitation, irritability) (Porter, 1984). These findings should be communicated to the patient's physician.

Current pharmacotherapeutic approaches. The current therapeutic approach to treating epileptic seizures involves using one drug as a method of control, and, if this drug proves ineffective, changing to another drug. This approach, referred to as *monotherapy*, replaces previous combined-medication (i.e., "polytherapy") approaches (Reynolds & Shorvan, 1981). Monotherapy is believed to be safer because there are fewer cognitive and physical side effects. It also is easier for patients to be compliant. Changing antiepileptic medications typically involves beginning the new medication concurrently with the original medication, such that adequate plasma drug levels are achieved with the new medication. After this point, the first medication is slowly tapered off. If monotherapy fails to control the seizures, the physician may decide to use a combined antiepileptic medication regimen. If this approach is chosen, dosage levels of the medications may be raised or lowered accordingly if medication interaction effects are known to occur (i.e., one medication inadvertently raises or lowers the plasma drug level of the other medication).

Epilepsy surgery and related procedures. Here, we briefly review surgical procedures used in treating epileptic seizure disorders and issues involved in identifying appropriate surgical candidates. We also discuss the intracarotid amytal test (ICAT), which is often given first before deciding to perform epilepsy surgery. We do not comprehensively review the various surgical procedures or the ICAT; rather, we provide an introduction to this area of treatment.

Surgical interventions. In recent years, considerable attention has been devoted to surgical interventions as an alternative treatment to medication for intractable epileptic seizure disorders. For patients with medication-resistant intractable epilepsy, surgical removal of the epileptogenic foci is a way to significantly reduce or even eliminate the individual's seizure disorder. The use of epilepsy surgery has grown tremendously, as documented in a recent survey of comprehensive epilepsy centers demonstrating that approximately 8,300 surgical procedures took place between 1986 and 1990, in comparison with the approximately 3,400 procedures recorded before 1985 (Engel & Shewmon, 1993). For approximately 80–90% of patients with medically intractable seizure disorders, epilepsy surgery can offer improved seizure control (Delgado-Escueta & Walsh, 1985; Engel, 1987; Walczak et al., 1990). The defin-

TABLE 7

Frequent Acute and Chronic Side Effects of Major Antiepileptic Medications

Medication	Side effects: Acute	Side effects: Chronic
Phenobarbital	Sedation, nystagmus, ataxia confusion (especially in elderly)	Encephalopathy, cognitive impairment, megaloblastic anemia
Dilantin	GI distress, dizziness, nystagmus, ataxia, sedation	Gingival hyperplasia, skin thickening, hirsutism, encephalopathy, pigmentation or rash
Tegretol	GI distress, vertigo, diplopia, drowsiness, hyponatremia	Thrombocytopenia, anorexia
Mysoline	Sedation, vertigo, diplopia, ataxia, nystagmus, nausea	Megaloblastic anemia
Zarontin	GI distress, sedation, dizziness, agitation, nausea, vomiting, ataxia	Anorexia, lupuslike reactions
Depakene and Depakote	GI distress, sedation, tremor, reversible amenorrhea, acute hepatotoxicity, ataxia	Anorexia, tremor, weight gain, increase in appetite, liver dysfunction, hair loss, thrombocytopenia, pancreatitis
Klonopin	Sedation, slurred speech, abnormal eye movements, tremor	Psychiatric changes, anorexia, weight change
Neurontin	Fatigue, dizziness, drowsiness, ataxia	Weight gain
Felbatol	Decreased food consumption, mild nausea or GI discomfort, ataxia, dizziness, diplopia, headache, agitation, insomnia	Weight loss, rashes
Lamictal	Dizziness, diplopia, blurred vision, somnolence, nausea, ataxia	

Note: Data are from the manufacturers' prescribing information. GI = gastrointestinal.

ition of the term *medically intractable* differs in minor ways from comprehensive center to comprehensive center, but most centers include the following criteria in its definition: seizure frequency, type of epileptic syndrome, age of onset of epilepsy, course of the disorder, type of medication side effects, and tolerance of the medication side effects (Engel & Shewmon, 1993).

There are several types of surgical procedures currently offered depending on the type of syndrome. These procedures include anterior temporal lobectomy, amygdalohippocampectomy, extratemporal resection, lesionectomy, hemispherectomy, and corpus callosotomy. The most frequently done procedure is the anterior temporal lobectomy, which accounts for approximately 60% of all epilepsy surgical procedures (Engel & Shewmon, 1993).

For anterior temporal lobe resections and amygdalohippocampectomy, predictive signs for favorable surgical outcome include a temporal lobe lesion in general (and hippocampal sclerosis in particular that is identifiable on clinical, EEG, neuropsychological, and radiographic testing), a limited duration of the disorder, and material-specific memory deficits (Wieser, 1991). Extratemporal surgical procedures involve surgical removal of epileptogenic foci outside of the temporal lobe (Williamson, Van Ness, Wieser, & Quesney, 1993). One variety of this procedure includes lesionectomy and is used when the source of the epileptogenesis is known (i.e., structural lesions, tumors, and other foreign-body pathology; Cascino, Boon, & Fish, 1993). Hemispherectomies are an infrequently used procedure because there are resulting medical complications. However, there are several disorders (i.e., vascular occlusions, tuberous sclerosis, and Sturge-Weber syndrome) that may benefit from a modified hemispherectomy to reduce seizure frequency (Andermann, Freeman, Vigevano, & Hwang, 1993). Finally, corpus callosotomies are surgical procedures that interrupt the spread of electrical discharges between the cerebral hemispheres.

This procedure is typically used in individuals experiencing generalized seizures.

Intracarotid amytal test (ICAT). Before surgery, candidates routinely undergo an ICAT, which is also known as the *Wada test*. This procedure was recently recommended by the National Institutes of Health Consensus Development Conference in 1990 for all individuals undergoing cortical resection surgery for intractable seizures. The purpose of the ICAT procedure is to separately evaluate each hemisphere for speech dominance and memory capacity before surgery. If problems are encountered, brain mapping using cortical stimulation is often instituted to avoid hemiparesis and language deficits (Ojemann et al., 1993). Frequently, neuropsychologists perform the cognitive portion of this procedure. In addition to the information gleaned from practical applications, the results of this procedure are important for the theoretical understanding of the cortical mediation of language and memory.

Administration procedures. There are two basic components of the ICAT administration—anesthetizing and psychometric—both of which occur simultaneously and neither of which have been standardized across epilepsy centers (Rausch et al., 1993; Snyder, Novelly, & Harris, 1990). In essence, there are as many procedures as there are epilepsy centers performing the procedure. Amytal dosages routinely differ across centers because of the preferences of the physicians administering the drug and patient differences. Typically, injections of 100–200 mg in 10 ml of sterile water are administered as a bolus through the carotid artery. The psychometric component also routinely differs across centers, as do the criteria used to determine language and memory dominance.

The following is a description of the ICAT procedure that is based on the work of Blume, Grabow, Darley, and Aronson (1973). (See also Table 8.) As noted earlier, there are other ICAT assessment procedures currently in use (e.g., Loring, Meador, & Lee, 1992), and the procedure discussed here (Blume et al., 1973) represents one basic approach. To provide some background on the basic assumptions for the procedure, if the unanesthetized, damaged hemisphere has a lesion involving the hippocampal formation, the sodium amytal injection to the anesthetized, undamaged hemisphere should produce a temporary memory disturbance (Milner, Branch, & Rasmussen, 1962). Conversely, anesthetizing the nonfunctional (i.e., damaged) hippocampus should result in an absence of memory disturbance.

Throughout the procedure, the patient's brain waves are monitored and recorded by an EEG, and split-screen video telemetry is frequently used to evaluate the procedure. The radiologist inserts a catheter into the femoral artery near the groin and positions the catheter in the internal carotid artery on either the left or right side, immediately past the artery's bifurcation with the external carotid artery. An arteriogram is performed to ensure that abnormal vasculature does not exist and that the catheter is positioned properly. At this point, the patient is shown a number and a color by the examiner and is asked to remember them. The patient is then instructed to flex his or her legs, wiggle his or her fingers, and hold both arms above his or her head; the patient also is asked to begin counting backward.

Sodium amytal is then released as a bolus through the catheter within 3 s. The amytal perfuses and anesthetizes the cerebral hemisphere of interest, and the effect of the anesthesia is confirmed by EEG depression. If the left hemisphere is perfused, a profound contralateral (right-sided) flaccid hemiparesis (i.e., the patient's right arm drops) and hemianopsia (i.e., the patient becomes blind in his or her right visual field) results; if the patient is left-hemisphere dominant for language, he or she also becomes globally aphasic (i.e., the patient will cease counting). Frequently, the patient becomes obtunded, although this should abate within 30 s, and when he or she awakens, testing proceeds.

After the injection and when testable, the examiner asks the patient to perform several tasks to evaluate auditory comprehension, verbal expression, and recognition memory. The quality of the patient's language is evaluated for paraphasic and dysnomic errors. During this portion of the procedure, it is important to present material to the patient's visual field that was not affected by the amytal because of the iatrogenically produced hemianopsia. After approximately 30 min, the contralateral hemisphere is perfused and cognitively tested in a similar fashion.

TABLE 8

Protocol for Intracarotid Amobarbital Test of Language and Memory

Section	Time	Task	Example
1	3 min	Shown	Number
	2 min	Shown	Color
	30 s	Request	Flex legs, raise arms, wiggle fingers, begin counting
Amytal injection			
2	When testable	Request	Continue counting
		Follow spoken commands	Stick out tongue, wiggle tongue, and blow
		Recognize printed words	Horse, tree, and sleep
	90 s	Recognize design	Cross and clock
		Repeat spoken words	Snowman, gingerbread, artillery, impossibility, and please sit down
	2 min	Exhibit limb strength	Raise arms, grip, and foot dorsiflex
	2.5 min	Describe	Three pictures
		Define	Island and motor
	3.5 min	Recall or recognition	Number and color
	4 min	Exhibit limb strength	Raise arm, grip, and foot dorsiflex
	Every 2 min after		Limb strength until normal for patient
3	12 min	Recall	Spontaneous or multiple choice

Note: From "Intracarotid Amobarbital Test of Language and Memory Before Temporal Lobectomy for Seizure Control," by W. T. Blume, J. D. Grabow, F. L. Darley, and A. E. Aronson, 1973, *Neurology*, *23*, p. 815. Copyright 1973 by Advanstar Communications. Adapted with permission.

Criticisms. There are a number of criticisms that are important to consider regarding the use of the ICAT procedure. These criticisms revolve primarily around the standardized administration of amytal, determination of hemispheric memory capacity, and criteria for speech production.

One problem involving the ICAT procedure is the lack of agreement across centers regarding appropriate amytal dosage levels. Snyder et al. (1990) reported that 25% of the 55 epilepsy centers surveyed increase the administered dosage according to the weight of the patient. This change across patients can affect the results of cognitive testing, given that brain–body weight correlations are presumably low (Holloway, 1980). An equally problematic situation involves underanesthetizing the right and left hemispheres.

A second problem concerns whether the ICAT is reasonably able to discern hemispheric capacity for memory functioning. The answer to this problem appears to lie in the sensitivity of the ICAT procedure being used (Rausch et al., 1993), although it is generally accepted that the procedure can identify patients at risk for postoperative amnestic syndrome. However, what constitutes a "memory pass" is largely unclear in most protocols. The lack of standardized amytal dosages across centers may pose one threat to the procedure's ability to predict memory patency, as it has regarding the prediction of language laterality as described earlier. For example, Novelly and Williamson (1989) reported that repeating the ICAT procedure at a lower dosage in 21 patients who previously failed the procedure subsequently yielded passing scores in all 21 patients. Subsequent surgical resections did not result in amnesia, as had been predicted at the higher dosages.

A third problem with the ICAT procedure is the criterion used to determine speech production (Snyder et al., 1990). This issue relates directly to the reported prevalence rates of mixed speech dominance (MSD). The investigation by Snyder et al. demonstrated that the wide fluctuation of rates of MSD among epilepsy centers was related to the criteria used to determine speech production. Higher rates of MSD were associated with centers using partial phoneme vocalization, serial rote speech, and vocalizations of familiar words as speech production criteria. It is unclear to what degree these criteria represented actual speech or were simply overlearned expressions. If they represent the latter, then MSD rates would have been inflated.

Despite these criticisms, the ICAT procedure has made it possible to investigate several clinically important concepts in the field of neuropsychology. Among them is the issue of the effects of early cerebral injury on language lateralization. In a large series of patients, Branch, Milner, and Rasmussen (1964) determined that, on the basis of ICAT findings, patients who sustained left cerebral injuries before the age of 5 had a greater prevalence of right-hemisphere (67%) and bilateral (11%) language representation than expected. In a control sample of patients who did not sustain left-hemisphere injury, Branch et al. (1964) found that a comparable group of patients had prevalence rates of 64% for left-hemisphere dominance, 20% for right-hemisphere dominance, and 16% for bilateral dominance. These findings suggest that the nervous system demonstrates plasticity of language functions up to a certain age.

Psychotherapy and social support. Important psychosocial consequences of epilepsy encompass the interaction between personality (conceptualized as both biological and behavioral) and environmental variables. For example, the patient with epilepsy has many concerns about his or her disorder that include physical, cognitive, psychological, financial, occupational, social, and lifestyle restrictions. In addition, these concerns are different depending on the age of seizure onset. For example, a child with epilepsy may have adjusted to life with seizures compared with an adult who developed a seizure disorder, who may react with depression and withdrawal. One of the most important aspects of psychotherapy with individuals who have a chronic disease such as epilepsy is the provision of accurate and understandable information. In addition to the clinical information that the practitioner can provide, the practitioner can also provide the patient with the address of the Epilepsy Foundation of America.[1] The foundation provides free information to patients and parents of children and adolescents with epilepsy, assists the patient with locating medical specialists in his or her community for treatment, and provides the telephone numbers of local affiliate organizations offering support services, such as support groups.

Perception of social competency. The patient with epilepsy experiences numerous psychosocial consequences as a result of his or her chronic illness. Some of these consequences are specific and unique to epilepsy, including the random nature of the events, occupational limitations, and driving restrictions. Other consequences are more general and pertain to anyone with a stigmatizing chronic illness. These consequences both directly and indirectly affect the perception of social competence in patients with epilepsy.

Unlike individuals with other chronic illnesses, people with epilepsy experience their illness in an unpredictable and random manner, and this unpredictability reduces their perceptions of having control over their own life. This process may become debilitating in its own right and may markedly interfere with normal social activities and interpersonal relationships. In addition, people with epilepsy are unable to work in certain settings because they may injure themselves or others if they have a seizure. Employment restrictions as well as job discrimination make employability difficult, and these factors likely contribute to the underemployment of people with epilepsy. Individuals with epilepsy also must abide by certain driving restrictions, which vary from state to state. These restrictions place added burdens on others who must transport the patient to appointments or employment settings. Even so, many people with epilepsy are noncompliant with driving restrictions, and this noncompliance adds further stigma to one's self-identity, in that the person feels badly about breaking the law (Andermann, Remillard, Zifkin, Trottier, & Drouin, 1988). A consideration of these psychosocial issues is important in understanding the person with epilepsy.

Restrictions. As described earlier, people with seizure disorders should not operate dangerous machinery, work in high places, or work around open

[1]The address of the Epilepsy Foundation of America is 4351 Garden City Dr., Ste. 406, Landover, MD 20785; (301) 459-3700.

flames or with flammable material given the high cost of injury to self or others if he or she had a seizure while engaged in such an activity. Ensuring compliance with certain restrictions can be particularly relevant for the patient who wants to get a job or return to work. For example, the practitioner may be asked to write a letter stating that the patient is able to return to work after a traumatic brain injury with a seizure disorder as a secondary complication, although such duties are best handled by the patient's treating physician.

Limiting employment does not mean that a person with a seizure disorder is unemployable. To assist the person with a seizure disorder in obtaining employment, a referral to vocational rehabilitation may be one way to increase his or her chances.

Similar restrictions apply to leisure activities and other non-work-related activities. Individuals with epilepsy should not swim alone, nor should they operate heavy machinery at home. Driving restrictions are a frequent cause for concern. Laws regarding the operation of a motor vehicle differ from state to state, but most states require that the patient be seizure free for a year before driving privileges are reinstated. State laws pertaining to epilepsy are available from the Epilepsy Foundation of America. Motor vehicle insurance rates are not usually higher for those with epilepsy. However, the person must inform his or her insurance company of the seizure disorder. The patient with epilepsy also should not combine alcohol and antiepileptic medications. Alcohol should be avoided by the person taking antiepileptic medications because it lowers the plasma drug levels of the medicine (Porter, 1984). If a patient on antiepileptic medication does drink alcohol, a seizure may occur during the time when he or she is becoming sober as opposed to having a seizure while drinking.

Need for emotional support. Another important aspect of psychotherapy is to provide the person with epilepsy emotional support. Individuals with epilepsy often feel vulnerable given the uncontrollability and unpredictability of the disorder. One way to empower the patient is to provide the patient with pertinent information and to assist him or her with compliance with their anticonvulsant medication regime. Another way to help the patient is to encourage him or her to teach others about his or her condition, which will also help to dispel the numerous myths about the disorder. Teaching others will also reduce fears many people (i.e., teachers and coworkers) have about the patient and epilepsy.

Contact with physicians. An additional way practitioners can render assistance is by working closely with the treating physician. One method involves helping to improve the patient's compliance with his or her antiepileptic medication regimen. Because of the high frequency of memory problems, helping the patient with epilepsy learn to use a chart to track medication use provides the patient with a high degree of structure as well as a visual reminder. This works well with both adults and children because it reinforces compliance behaviors. With children, this approach can be integrated easily into a token economy system or some other behavioral management system. A second method includes reducing the patient's confusion about his or her medications. This may involve consulting with the physician about the patient's compliance problems if this is an issue and, if not medically contraindicated, recommending that the physician simplify the patient's medication intake. A third approach is educational and involves explaining the importance of taking antiepileptic medication as prescribed to ensure a steady plasma blood level. With all these approaches, it is important to enlist the participation of the patient, preferably as part of the treatment team. Doing so helps to empower the patient with the notion that he or she is able to provide some control over his or her medical condition.

PSYCHOLOGICAL AND BEHAVIORAL ISSUES ASSOCIATED WITH EPILEPSY

Practitioners are often asked to render an opinion about a person who either has epilepsy or has a disorder resembling epilepsy. Areas they are asked about include an understanding of the alleged epileptic personality, the concept of ictal and interictal violence in individuals with epilepsy, increased levels of psychopathology among people with epilepsy, and increased levels of depression among those with epilepsy. We review these points next.

The Epileptic Personality

In 1975, an article by Waxman and Geschwind was published in which they described a particular personality profile among patients with partial complex seizures of temporal lobe origin. Waxman and Geschwind described these patients as having interictal personality features of hypergraphia, hyperreligiosity, preoccupation with philosophical matters, and deepened emotionality. This personality profile was later investigated by Bear and Fedio (1977), who compared groups of patients with epilepsy with right and left EEG-confirmed foci with two control groups (one healthy control group and a second control group comprising people with neuromuscular disorders) on an inventory designed to measure various traits previously associated with this personality style. Bear and Fedio discovered significant differences between patients with epilepsy and control subjects. On the basis of these findings, they concluded that these specific changes related to epileptic abnormalities.

Since these investigations, there have been numerous investigations that cast significant doubt on the idea of a unique personality style among patients who have partial complex epilepsy (Mungas, 1982; Rodin & Schmaltz, 1984; Stevens, 1988). More specifically, these later investigations suggest the presence of underlying nonspecific psychopathology that is more likely to be environmentally related than organically related. There were no differences among patients with other neurological conditions or among patients with other types of epilepsy when compared with patients with partial complex seizures of temporal lobe origin (Dodrill & Batzel, 1986; Rodin & Schmaltz, 1984).

Ictal and Interictal Violence

According to Delgado-Escueta et al. (1981), the rate of ictal violence is approximately less than 0.1% (the term *ictal violence* refers to directed violent attacks that occur during a seizure). This figure is based on an evaluation of 7 out of 5,400 patients with epilepsy who were surveyed from 16 epilepsy centers worldwide and who were judged by a panel of epileptologists to have directed aggressive acts during their seizure. The results of this survey strongly suggest that individuals experiencing seizures do not have directed ictal violent episodes and that in the minority who had ictal violent episodes, the aggressive acts were stereotyped, simple, and short-lived. On the other hand, individuals who are having a seizure and who are being restrained may become combative, but their combativeness is not typically directed at anyone or anything.

An increased incidence of interictal violence among people with partial complex seizures of temporal lobe origin also has been investigated. There is extensive literature examining this issue. Devinsky and Bear (1984) asserted that such a relationship does exist. For example, they described several cases of patients who were alert and attentive during the aggressive act, and those acts typically followed some sort of provocation. Those authors suggested that repetitive subthreshhold electrochemical stimulation of limbic system structures may account for interictal aggressive acts, with associated impairment of frontal lobe mechanisms being responsible for failure to inhibit the acts. Although such a relationship is suggested in anecdotally related clinical cases, it has not been satisfactorily demonstrated in controlled investigations.

The relationship between interictal violence and epilepsy of temporal lobe origin is not yet clear, and this lack of clarity is likely attributable to inadequate conceptualizations of personality, inadequate measures of personality, diagnostic heterogeneity, and failure to consider the myriad of psychosocial factors affecting the individual with epilepsy.

Psychopathology and Epilepsy

Overall, the majority of people with epilepsy are free from significant psychopathology. However, in an investigation by Blumer (1975), approximately 25% of people with epilepsy may experience major psychopathology. In particular, an increased incidence of psychotic episodes was reported among people with epilepsy (Pincus & Tucker, 1985). However, this relationship may be artifactual because of selection biases. People with more severe forms of epilepsy are usually treated at university-based medical centers, where a majority of these types of investigations are conducted. An investigation by Currie, Heathfield, Henson, and Scott (1970) revealed that psychiatric hospitalizations varied considerably whether the epileptic patient was treated at a university-based clinic (25%) as opposed to being treated by private physicians (5–9%).

Increased Levels of Depression

Clinically, people with epilepsy have increased levels of depression, although empirically, a significant relationship has not been confirmed (Stevens, 1988). Part of the difficulty in establishing a relationship between epilepsy and depression lies in the heterogeneity of the epileptic condition. For example, there are numerous inconsistencies in the literature regarding the contribution of interictal left temporal lobe foci in the manifestation of depression, with some researchers discovering a positive relationship (Altshuler, Devinsky, Post, & Theodore, 1990; Mendez, Cummings, & Benson, 1986) and others being unable to confirm this relationship (Hermann & Whitman, 1989). However, Hermann et al. (1991) suggested that depression in patients with complex partial seizures may be moderated not only by laterality of epileptogenic foci but also by the intact nature of the frontal cortices. In patients with complex partial epilepsy of left temporal lobe origin, there was a significant relationship between increased perseverative responding on the WCST and dysphoria, suggesting a relationship between depression and left frontal lobe dysfunction.

Psychosocial issues also have been investigated as contributing to the development of depression among patients with epilepsy. People with epilepsy endure numerous stressors associated with their illness that include psychological and social stressors as well as biological and medication stressors. Hermann, Whitman, and Anton (1992) tested a multietiological model of psychosocial dysfunction in people with epilepsy and discovered that a majority of the variance associated with increased levels of depression was related to psychosocial factors. In particular, Hermann et al. discovered that an increased number of stressful life events as measured by the Life Experiences Survey (Sarason, Johnson, & Siegel, 1978), poor adjustment to epilepsy as measured by the Adjustment to Seizures scale of the WPSI (Dodrill et al., 1980), less adequate financial status as measured by the Financial Status scale of the WPSI, and being female were significantly related to increased levels of depression among people with epilepsy. Interestingly, biological factors such as age of seizure onset, laterality of seizure onset, seizure type, or etiology were not correlated with increased levels of depression.

NONEPILEPTIC ATTACK DISORDERS

NEADs, also referred to as nonepileptic seizures, are paroxysmal episodes of altered behavior that superficially resemble epileptic attacks, yet they lack the associated clinical or electrographic features (Liske & Forster, 1964). NEADs are therefore not neurogenic seizures because the electrical functioning of the brain remains normal throughout the attack. Using this definition, it is estimated that the prevalence of NEADs among comprehensive epilepsy centers range from 10% to 40% of evaluated patients (Jeavons, 1977; Mattson, 1980; Volvow, 1986). NEADs occur in patients with and without epilepsy, although diagnostically it should be demonstrated before it is assumed (Lesser, 1986). One benefit of using the term *NEAD* is that it does not carry the same stigmata that other historical definitions hold (e.g., use of the term *pseudoseizure*), in that the patient and family experience the events as "real." Likewise, the term *psychogenic seizure* is inadequate to describe these events. Although occasionally used by practitioners to describe nonneurogenic events, the term *psychogenic seizure* should be restricted to occasions in which a psychological event (i.e., a particular mood or idea) elicits a neurogenic event.

Here, we review current methods of differential diagnosis, classification, and treatment of NEADs, beginning first with a conceptualization of NEADs as a homogeneous entity distinct from epilepsy. We then attempt to reduce the homogeneity of the NEAD diagnosis through currently available methods of psychiatric classification.

Differentiating Between NEADs and Epileptic Seizures

Laboratory approaches to differential diagnosis. Occasionally, surface EEG recordings are not abnormal during epileptic seizures; this is often the case with seizures originating from frontal cortices or deep subcortical structures. In addition, EEGs are frequently difficult to interpret because of muscle movement during the seizures (referred to as a "movement artifact"). However, examining postictal EEGs (which are typically abnormal after an epileptic seizure but normal after a NEAD) and comparing this with ictal EEGs may be an important adjunct to ascertaining differential diagnoses between NEADs and epilepsy, as Desai et al. (1982) reported.

Another important adjunct to differential diagnoses is to examine changes in serum prolactin levels following a seizure event. Trimble (1978) reasoned that patients experiencing seizures would also overstimulate their hypothalamus. This stimulation would then result in abnormal prolactin release into the bloodstream. This hormone then could be easily measured and would provide proof of abnormal brain activity. Using three groups of patients (patients with NEADs, patients undergoing electroconvulsive shock therapy, and patients with generalized tonic–clonic seizures), Trimble discovered that the patients with NEADs did not show an increase of serum prolactin after their events, whereas the other two groups showed significant elevations. These elevations reached their peak in these two groups 20 min after the seizure. Subsequent investigations (Dana-Haeri, Trimble, & Oxley, 1983; Pritchard, Wannamaker, Sagel, & Daniel, 1985) confirmed these initial findings.

However, there are difficulties with this approach because rises in serum prolactin depend on the length and type of seizure activity. For example, absence seizures and seizures of unilateral onset will not show such elevations (Trimble, 1986). In addition, patients without epilepsy who experience syncope may show concomitant elevations in serum prolactin. In one study (Berkovic, 1984), a patient who did not have epileptic seizures but who did experience a convulsive syncopal episode had an abnormal rise in serum prolactin levels.

Clinical approaches to differential diagnosis. An absolute diagnosis of a NEAD based on clinical approaches cannot be made for several reasons. What can be said with some degree of certainty is that a particular seizure event is likely to be nonepileptic in origin. One reason is that a person may have epilepsy and a NEAD. Attempting to differentiate a NEAD from epilepsy is difficult, and there are no fixed rules to go by in attempting such a differential diagnosis. However, practitioners are frequently asked about the psychological contributions to a person's seizure disorder and are occasionally asked to assist in making a differential diagnosis. Previous research has shown that the most useful criteria in arriving at an accurate differential diagnosis include simultaneous video–EEG monitoring, ictal and postictal EEG recordings, and discerning the relationship between antiepileptic medication and seizure frequency (Desai et al., 1982). Such procedures have been shown to be useful and well tolerated among children and adults (Desai et al., 1982; Holmes, Sackellares, McKiernan, Ragland, & Dreifuss, 1980). However, diagnostic efforts are frequently confounded by those individuals who present with epilepsy and NEADs.

In attempting to behaviorally differentiate between an epileptic seizure and a NEAD, there are numerous descriptive features of the event that can be examined when attempting to infer whether a particular event is epileptic or nonepileptic in origin. These features, summarized by Desai et al. (1982), are presented in Table 9. However, note that the information in Table 9 describes "typical" events and that there are numerous atypical presentations of both NEADs and neurogenic events. Since the publication of the article by Desai et al. (1982), additional experience and technology have provided better methods with which to examine psychiatric conditions and NEADs. This information, presented in Table 9, has further blurred the distinction and distinct classification between NEADs and epilepsy, in that many episodes thought to have been NEADs were atypical epileptic events (i.e., frontal lobe seizures).

Gates, Ramani, Whalen, and Loewenson (1985) attempted to refine the ictal behavioral features of patients with telemetry-confirmed NEADs to patients having generalized tonic–clonic epileptic events. Statistical analyses revealed that the presence of out-of-phase upper and lower extremity movement, the presence of forward pelvic thrusting, and the absence of whole-body rigidity significantly separated the patients with NEADs from the patients with epilepsy, yielding a correct classification rate of 96%. However, Gates et al. emphasized that these "bedside

TABLE 9

Differential Clinical Features of Nonepileptic Attack Disorder (NEAD) and Generalized Tonic–Clonic Seizures

Variable	NEAD	Epilepsy
	Major criteria	
Comparison of event with known seizure type	Extremely wide range of events with bizarre and unusual behavior	Relatively little variation in events
EEG during seizure	Usually normal and unchanged from preictal	Abnormal and changed from preictal
EEG immediately after seizure	Usually normal and unchanged from preictal	Almost always abnormal and changed from preictal
Relation of attacks to medication regimen	Usually unrelated	Prominent, especially in severely affected patients
	Minor criteria	
Onset	Often gradual, prolonged nonspecific warning period may occur	Usually paroxysmal, but may be preceded by seizure of different type
Primary or secondary gain	Common	Rare, a few patients use seizures for secondary gain
Postictal confusion, lethargy, sleepiness	Often conspicuously absent; patient may be normal immediately after attack	Prominent
Postictal subjective complaints	May be smiling or laughing after seizure	Prominent if aroused
Suggestibility	Occasionally	None
Recollection of events during attack	Sometimes detailed	None
Violent behavior	Rare, but may be highly directed	None
Age	Usually older child or adult	Any, past infancy
Gross tonic–clonic motor phenomena	None, but resemblance is related to sophistication of mimicry	Always
Tongue biting	Rare	Frequent
Urinary incontinence	Rare	Frequent
Abnormal neurologic signs during seizure	None	May be present
Nocturnal occurrence	Rare	Common
Injuries sustained as a result of event	Rare, but occasionally occur	Common
Stereotypy of attacks	Attacks may or may not be varied, patterns may occasionally be widely divergent	Relatively little variation

Note: EEG = electroencephalogram. From "Psychogenic Seizures: A Study of 42 Attacks in Six Patients, With Intensive Monitoring," by B. T. Desai, R. J. Porter, and J. K. Penry, 1982, *Archives of Neurology*, *39*, pp. 207–208. In the public domain.

clinical criteria" are no substitute for definitive diagnostic testing but instead serve as an adjunct for further therapeutic directions.

Psychometric approaches to differential diagnosis. Psychometric differentiation of individuals with NEADs from individuals with epileptic seizures has been attempted, with limited success. For the practitioner asked to make a differential diagnosis instead of attempting to differentiate between epilepsy and NEADs, it would be more helpful to educate the referral source on the limits of psychometrics in answering this question. A more fruitful question would be whether a given patient has a psychological or psychiatric disorder that potentially manifests itself in NEADs.

Overall, two psychometric approaches have been undertaken: neuropsychological assessment and personality assessment. Neither approach in isolation from other biomedical procedures reliably differentiates between these two groups of patients (Hermann & Connell, 1992). The limited success of psychometrics appears to lie in the variability of the population of patients with NEADs. More specifically, patients with NEADs are a heterogeneous group, and their personality functioning, as measured by traditional psychometrics, overlaps considerably with patients known to have epilepsy. In addition, many patients with NEADs demonstrate neuropsychological impairment that is often similar to impairment demonstrated by patients with telemetry-verified epilepsy. These findings led Hermann and Connell (1992) to conclude that the use of psychometrics to differentiate NEADs from epilepsy is a "tenuous and risky business at best," due specifically to the potentially dangerous risk of patient misclassification. For example, patients without epilepsy may be treated with potentially toxic anticonvulsants or even surgical procedures if misclassified, or patients with epileptic seizures may go medically untreated due to misclassification.

Personality test performance. In the majority of research on using personality test variables to differentiate between patients with NEADs, the Minnesota Multiphasic Personality Inventory (MMPI; Hathaway & McKinley, 1951) has been used. Specifically, three methods of inquiry were used in these investigations: the Pseudoneurologic (Pn) scale, the conversion profile, and a modification of the conversion profile using specific decision rules.

The Pn scale was first used by Shaw and Matthews (1965) and later by Henrichs, Tucker, Farha, and Novelly (1988) to differentiate patients with NEADs from patients with epileptic seizures. The Pn scale was developed from a combination of 17 MMPI items that loaded on Scales 1, 3, and 4. Initial results appeared promising, although later investigations showed that the hit rate of this scale fell to near-chance levels (Henrichs et al., 1988).

Matthews, Shaw, and Klove (1966) initially investigated the conversion profile approach. To review, an individual having a conversion profile has substantial elevations on Scales 1 (Hypochondriasis) and 3 (Hysteria) relative to Scale 2 (Depression). Individuals with this MMPI profile tend to prefer medical explanations for psychological problems and tend to deny emotional difficulties. Wilkus and Dodrill (1989) demonstrated that when patients are grouped according to their NEAD behavior, the conversion approach shows some ability to separate certain select groups of patients with NEADs from patients with epileptic seizures.

The third approach is a modification of the conversion profile approach by using decision rules to differentiate patients with NEADs from patients with epileptic seizures (Wilkus, Dodrill, & Thompson, 1984). The rules of Wilkus et al. (1984) for using the MMPI are as follows: (a) Scale 1 or 3 is 70 or higher and is one of the two highest points disregarding Scales 5 and 0; (b) Scale 1 or 3 is 80 or higher, even though it is not one of the two highest points, and (c) Scales 1 and 3 are both higher than 59, and both are at least 10 points higher than Scale 2. With this approach, a patient is categorized as a patient with NEADs if he or she meets one of these three decision rules. In this investigation, Wilkus et al. (1984) reported a hit-rate accuracy of 81% for patients with NEADs and 87% for patients with epileptic seizures. However, a subsequent investigation by Vanderzant, Giordani, Berent, Dreifuss, and Sackellares (1986) failed to replicate the Wilkus et al. (1984) original findings.

Besides the MMPI, the WPSI (Dodrill et al., 1980) was used to attempt differential diagnoses. Overall, the results suggest that patients with NEADs report more problems with their family background, seizure adjustment, and concern over their relationship with their physician. However, it is important to consider that these difficulties do not appear to be unique to the patient with NEADs.

As indicated by the Wilkus et al. (1984) data on the MMPI and the WPSI, particular forms of psychological stressors may play a key role in the pathogenesis of NEADs. In particular, child sexual abuse of girls has been reported in several studies of female patients presenting with NEADs (Blumer, 1991; Goodwin, Simms, & Bergman, 1979; Gross, 1970; LaBarbera & Dozier, 1980). In the Wilkus et al. (1984) sample, 35% of the female patients had elevations on the Family Background scale of the WPSI, suggesting disturbed family backgrounds. However, this may represent a nonspecific finding that is true of a number of diagnostic entities (Hendler, 1984). Therefore, the clinical utility of this finding is limited.

Neuropsychological test performance. There are relatively few studies that have investigated the cognitive functioning of patients with NEADs. Overall, these investigations demonstrate that patients with NEADs present with impairment on neuropsychological tests, which suggest the presence of abnormal brain functioning, psychiatric problems, or both. Two of the more important investigations were conducted at the University of Virginia (Sackellares et al., 1985) and the University of Washington (Wilkus & Dodrill, 1989; Wilkus et al., 1984).

Sackellares et al. (1985) examined three groups of patients (patients with NEADs, patients with NEADs and epileptic seizures, and patients with generalized tonic–clonic epileptic seizures), all of whom had been administered the Halstead–Reitan Neuropsychological Test Battery, the WAIS (Wechsler, 1955), and other cognitive measures. Overall, the results demonstrated that the patients with NEADs performed better than either of the other groups on both intellectual and neuropsychological measures. Specifically, compared with the other two groups, the patients with NEADs performed significantly better on the Tactual Performance Test, the Category Test, the Seashore Rhythm Test, and the Speech–Sounds Perception Test, and they had significantly higher Verbal, Performance, and Full-Scale WAIS IQ scores. However, the overall performance of the patients with NEADs fell within the borderline range of impairment on the neuropsychological measures, suggesting that they either had neuropsychological impairment (in contrast to their relatively average scores on the WAIS) or psychiatric problems. For example, borderline neuropsychological performance was found among patients with significant psychiatric problems (Gray, Dean, Rattan, & Cramer, 1987). However, the findings of Sackellares et al. (1985) may be the result of methodological problems because the matching procedures used resulted in a significant 2-year difference on the education variable. Patients tended to be better educated in the patient group with generalized seizures.

Despite these methodological difficulties, similar results were obtained in investigations conducted by the University of Washington group. In their first investigation (Wilkus et al., 1984), two groups of patients (patients with NEADs and patients with epilepsy) were matched on age, education, and gender. Scores on the WAIS and the NBE were compared. Overall, the percentages of impaired scores were similar (46% among the patients with NEADs and 51% among the patients with epilepsy). Wilkus and Dodrill (1989) conducted a follow-up study of patients with partial seizures and patients with generalized seizures who were matched on age, sex, and education with patients diagnosed with NEADs. Overall, the results were again similar to the investigations of Wilkus et al. (1984) and Sackellares et al. (1985), in that although the performance of the patients with NEADs was less impaired as a whole, their performance still fell within a borderline impaired range. These results suggest that patients with epilepsy and patients with NEADs have some degree of cognitive impairment. It is unknown, however, whether the borderline performance of the patients with NEADs represents true brain-related deficits, psychiatric problems, or both.

Classification of nonepileptic attack disorders. The basic premise underlying the phenomena of NEADs is that the resulting behavior is an expression of differing underlying psychopathologies. Exhibit 3 presents a system by which to conceptualize the NEADs according to the degree of appreciation the person has regarding the psychological contribution to his or her behavior (conscious awareness) and the degree of intentionality the person has regarding symptom production (conscious control). The diagnostic categories are based on those of the fourth edition of the *Diagnostic and Statistical Manual of Mental Disorders* (*DSM–IV*; American Psychiatric Association, 1994). This approach, and approaches similar to it, allows for an accepted method of communication among health care providers (Gates, Luciano, & Devinsky, 1991) and for more accurate and appropriate treatment planning.

The discussion that follows classifies NEADs in which there is conscious awareness and conscious control over the behavior (e.g., factitious disorder with predominantly physical signs and symptoms, malingering), conscious awareness but a lack of conscious control over the behavior (e.g., anxiety disorders, mood disorders, somatoform disorders, intermittent explosive disorder), and neither conscious

EXHIBIT 3

Psychiatric Considerations for Individuals Presenting With Nonepileptic Attack Disorder

I. Patient is both consciously aware and able to exert conscious control over symptom production
   A. Factitious disorder with predominantly physical signs and symptoms
      1. Munchausen's syndrome
      2. Munchausen's syndrome by proxy
   B. Malingering

II. Patient may be consciously aware but lack conscious control over symptom production
   A. Anxiety disorder
      1. Panic disorder
         a. With agoraphobia
         b. Without agoraphobia
      2. Acute stress disorder
      3. Posttraumatic stress disorder
   B. Mood disorder
      1. Major depressive episode/major depressive disorder
      2. Mood disorder not otherwise specified
   C. Somatoform disorders
      1. Somatization disorder
      2. Conversion disorder
      3. Hypochondriasis
      4. Undifferentiated somatoform disorder
   D. Intermittent explosive disorder

III. Patient is both unconsciously aware and is unable to exert conscious control over symptom production
   A. Schizophrenia and other psychotic disorders
      1. Schizophrenia
      2. Delusional disorder
      3. Brief psychotic disorder
      4. Schizophreniform disorder
      5. Schizoaffective disorder
      6. Psychotic disorder not otherwise specified
   B. Dissociative disorders
      1. Depersonalization disorder
      2. Dissociative identity disorder
      3. Dissociative fugue
      4. Dissociative amnesia
      5. Dissociative disorder not otherwise specified

IV. Patients who present with both epilepsy and nonepileptic attack disorder

awareness nor conscious control over the behavior (e.g., schizophrenic and other psychotic disorders, dissociative disorders). This system of classification represents one method of classification of NEADs, developed from the clinical work of Herman E. Jones.

Factitious disorder with predominantly physical signs and symptoms. With factitious disorder with predominantly physical signs and symptoms, there is an intentional element inherent in the manifestation of physical symptomatology judged both by direct evidence and without external incentives (American Psychiatric Association, 1994). However, this diagnosis does not rule out the coexistence of an actual physical disorder. To diagnose it, clinicians should evaluate patients' motivation to maintain their NEAD behavior, paying attention to the diagnostic issue of patients' needs to assume a sick role. Patients may describe their clinical history with zeal and dramatic flair, yet be unable to answer more detailed questions consistently, or they may simply lie about their history in an intriguing way. Two serious forms of this disorder include Munchausen's syndrome and Munchausen's syndrome by proxy. The former category includes patients whose lives revolve around being sick and, in more severe forms, involves patients who intentionally cause their illness. Meadow (1982) described the latter diagnosis of Munchausen's syndrome by proxy as a form of child abuse, whereby the mother causes the child's illness and submits the child to unnecessary medical evaluations because of her claim that the child is sick. The parent also may present to the child's physician with the complaint that the child is ill (i.e., is having seizurelike episodes), yet no one other than the parent has witnessed these events.

Malingering. This condition involves the intentional production of physical or psychological symptoms motivated by primary gain (i.e., financial gain or avoidance of some undesirable state). Although malingering may be adaptive in some situations, this is rarely the case in individuals presenting with NEADs. Clinicians working with such patients need to closely evaluate patients' social and financial environment, looking for incentives that maintain the behavior. The diagnostic entity of malingering is discussed in further detail in chapter 13 in this book.

Anxiety disorders. Anxiety disorders may manifest as a NEAD, particularly panic disorder, acute stress disorder, and posttraumatic stress disorder (PTSD). Panic disorder can present with or without agoraphobia. The patient and the health care provider can often misinterpret these disorders as an epileptic aura, given the symptom complex of dizziness, tachycardia, depersonalization, and derealization, among other symptoms (Gates et al., 1991). Notably, however, Harper and Roth (1962) found that derealization phenomena were more common among individuals experiencing a panic attack than they were among people with epilepsy. What exacerbates the problem is that these attacks are recurrent, are not always associated with specific events, and may instill a fear of serious physical illness.

Acute stress disorder involves the experience of a traumatic event that is associated with a variety of dissociative responses, including decreased awareness of one's surroundings, derealization, depersonalization, and dissociative amnesia, among other symptoms. The event is persistently reexperienced by the person, and the disturbance lasts a minimum of 2 days and a maximum of 4 weeks (American Psychiatric Association, 1994). Similar to that of panic disorder, the symptomatology of acute stress disorder may be confused for an epileptic aura or partial complex seizure phenomenon (e.g., periods of unawareness, exaggerated startle response). If the patient reports periods of unawareness, it is important to talk with significant others to determine how complex the person's behavior was during the reported dissociative periods.

PTSD is a more chronic form of acute stress disorder; in our clinical experience it may be applicable to patients with NEADs who report amnestic episodes for important aspects of the trauma or anger outbursts. Again, it is important to determine the degree of complexity of the person's behavior during either the dissociative period or the anger outbursts.

Mood disorders. Mood disorders, particularly the depressive disorders, are included as possible causes of NEADs because the person's decreased ability to think or concentrate may be misinterpreted as an epileptic aura. The clinician must consider other symptomatology associated with major depression when contemplating this diagnosis as a cause of NEADs. In addition, major depression may be a secondary complication of one of the other diagnoses listed in this section, thereby contributing but not causing the NEAD behavior. Roy (1979) and others

(Gates et al., 1991) noted that depression is particularly common in patients with NEADs.

Somatoform disorders. Somatoform disorders are a class of disorders in which a physical symptom exists that suggests a physical disorder, yet no readily identifiable organic cause can be found (American Psychiatric Association, 1994). The production of symptoms is not intentional, yet the patient may show some appreciation for contributing psychological factors if asked. Therefore, there may or may not be some degree of conscious awareness. However, by definition, there is no conscious control over symptom production. This class of disorders is important to consider when contemplating a diagnosis of NEADs because of the tendency for inadequate coping strategies used by such individuals, the tendency for misinterpretation of physical symptoms, and the significant degree of emotional conflict that is often present. This class of disorders includes somatization disorder, undifferentiated somatoform disorder, conversion disorder, and hypochondriasis.

The diagnosis of somatization disorder (formerly known as hysteria or Briquet's syndrome) is applicable for individuals who present with numerous physical and pseudoneurological complaints or the persistent belief that they are ill, both of which result in medical treatment. The onset of this disorder is before the age of 30, and frequently it has occurred over several years (American Psychiatric Association, 1994). Undifferentiated somatoform disorder is one for which there is a lack of organic basis for one or more physical complaints or complaints that are greater than expected on the basis of medical findings (American Psychiatric Association, 1994). Essentially, undifferentiated somatoform disorder is a residual category for presentations that do not meet criteria for another somatoform disorder.

Conversion disorder is of particular interest to clinicians when searching for causes of NEADs. More specifically, conversion disorder involves a loss of motor or sensory functioning that suggests a physical disorder for which psychological factors are assumed to play a causative role (American Psychiatric Association, 1994). Notably, the *DSM-IV* has a specific subtype of conversion disorder denoting seizures or convulsions with voluntary motor or sensory components. Conversion disorder has traditionally been described for the mechanisms believed to be responsible for symptom production (i.e., primary gain and secondary gain). In conversion disorders in which primary gain is believed to be prominent, symptom production should be considered because of an unconscious conflict that is kept from awareness. For example, a seizurelike event occurs in reaction to a disagreement a female patient has with her mother over her father, who had sexually abused the patient when she was a child. Here, the conflict has to do with the unconscious feelings the patient has toward her father. On the other hand, in conversion disorders in which secondary gain is believed to be prominent, symptom production occurs to prevent some event from occurring. For example, a person may develop a seizurelike event to avoid desertion by his or her spouse. In both cases, the person may or may not be consciously aware of his or her symptoms, but he or she cannot exert conscious control over the production of his or her symptoms. In our clinical experience, this lack of conscious control over symptom production is one key characteristic that separates the diagnosis of conversion disorder from malingering.

Hypochondriasis is a preoccupation with or belief that one has a serious medical disorder based on the misinterpretation of physical symptomatology and despite medical evidence to the contrary (American Psychiatric Association, 1994). Such individuals would be likely to misperceive bodily sensations as epileptic auras and present their misperceptions to health care professionals for reassurance that they are not physically ill.

Intermittent explosive disorder. Intermittent explosive disorder is categorized among the impulse control disorders not classified elsewhere in the *DSM-IV* (American Psychiatric Association, 1994). It is characterized by discrete episodes of dyscontrol over aggressive impulses. This loss of control may result in physical assault or property destruction. Such aggressiveness is incongruent with any psychosocial stressor that may precede it. Although previous researchers have theorized that this disorder involves limbic or frontal epileptic foci (Mullan & Penfield, 1959), controlled investigations validating this theory have not been forthcoming. In our clinical experience, the person with NEADs secondary to intermittent explosive disorder may have awareness of the act but initially cannot exert any degree of conscious control over the behavior.

Schizophrenia and other psychotic disorders. Psychotic disorders may be confused with partial seizures secondary to a misinterpretation of the hallucinations as auras by the patient, health care workers, or both. Disorders that may be confused with seizure behavior and that need to be considered during a differential diagnosis include schizophrenia, delusional disorder, brief psychotic disorder, schizophreniform disorder, schizoaffective disorder, and psychotic disorder not otherwise specified.

Dissociative disorders. One of several disorders under this classification may accurately describe an individual presenting with NEADs. Briefly, a dissociative disorder is a disturbance or alteration in the normal integrative functions of identity, memory, consciousness, or the perception of the environment. Specific classifications include depersonalization disorder and dissociative identity disorder (formerly known as multiple personality disorder). In depersonalization disorder, patients' reactions may be confused with a simple partial seizure, given their experience of being detached from their mental processes (American Psychiatric Association, 1994). Individuals' inability to cope with psychosocial stressors also may manifest in dissociative identity disorder, exemplified by patients' reports of unaccounted periods of lost time and an inability to recall important information greater than would be expected by ordinary forgetfulness. Here, the presumed change from one personality to the other may be interpreted as the onset of a seizure. Another diagnostic category includes dissociative amnesia, in which individuals are unable to recall important personal information. People with dissociative amnesia may present with memory gaps for important personal information and can be differentiated from memory impairment seen with epilepsy in terms of the duration of memory loss (i.e., one's entire life or specific stressful periods in one's life). Dissociative fugue (formerly known as psychogenic fugue) also may be a diagnostic possibility, in that there is sudden, unexpected travel and confusion about personal identity (American Psychiatric Association, 1994). Dissociative fugue may be confused with automatisms seen with complex partial seizures or absence attacks, although important diagnostic differences include the duration of the behavior (usually brief with epileptic automatisms) and the complexity of the behavior (usually simple or semipurposeful with epileptic automatisms).

Treatment of Patients Who Present With NEADs

Treatment of patients with NEADs progresses from differential psychological diagnosis. As described earlier, it has been our experience that patients with NEADs can be classified according to their degree of conscious awareness and conscious control over symptoms. This requires a careful assessment of factors that may be contributing to the symptom presentation. Treatment also includes identifying the psychological sequelae associated with the manifestation of the NEADs. This involves obtaining a detailed psychological history, identifying potential sources of current emotional stress, identifying maladaptive coping strategies patients use to handle stress, and any systemic factor (i.e., identifying reinforcers, antecedents, and consequences of behavior) that helps to maintain patients' dysfunctional pattern of responding to stress. Data on the prognosis for patients with NEADs suggest an improvement rate of 55%–70% after psychological or psychiatric intervention (Krumholz & Niedermeyer, 1983; Trimble, 1986; Williams, Gold, Shrout, Shaffer, & Adams, 1979). Greater improvement was found in patients with an acute onset, higher intelligence, normal EEGs, hypnotizability, and reduction of antiepileptic medication. Lack of improvement was associated with greater psychosocial difficulty (Trimble, 1986).

For individuals whom a diagnosis of factitious disorder with physical symptoms, intermittent explosive disorder, or malingering may apply, it has been our experience that they may have an active awareness of their psychological issues with either primary or secondary gain as a mitigating factor, but they may staunchly deny that such a relationship exists. For examiners, this is often a good indicator of patients' degree of defensiveness. These patients may consciously change symptom presentation from examiner to examiner (i.e., presentation of one type of seizure disorder with one examiner and another type with another examiner); they may have an "evolving condition" that progresses from a "seizure disorder" to severe headache to a gait disturbance, or they may abruptly drop out of treatment. These patients are best treated in a supportive therapeutic environment with careful pacing of their improvement.

Individuals diagnosed with anxiety, mood, or somatoform disorders who have some awareness of the psychological contribution to their problem will likely be consciously aware that a relationship exists between their psychological level of stress and their symptom presentation. These individuals are best treated through a combination of pharmacotherapy and behavioral interventions designed to facilitate adaptive coping responses, including but not limited to assertiveness training, social skills training, and stress inoculation training (Gates et al., 1991).

In our experience, individuals diagnosed with dissociative or psychotic disorders will neither confirm nor deny any conscious element to their event. Such people are best treated with a combination of a supportive psychotherapeutic environment and pharmacotherapy. With psychotherapeutic interventions, it is often helpful to suggest to patients that they may be able to gain control of their attacks. Psychiatric consultation is also helpful.

A critical issue in working with patients who have NEADs is the presentation of the diagnosis to patients and their families. It has been our experience that discussions by the practitioner of a non-neurogenic etiology for the events can be tantamount to a challenge that patients are "faking" unless care is exercised. In individuals who have a conscious awareness of the psychological contribution to the events, this can often provoke more exaggerated and potentially harmful behavior. Individuals who have no conscious awareness of a psychological etiology will often strongly deny such a link and subsequently believe that the diagnosis (and the practitioner) is wrong. The presentation of the diagnosis should reflect the sophistication of the patients and their families, as well as consideration of the underlying psychopathology producing the events.

Another beneficial consideration is having patients and their families reconsider the events as "spells" or "attacks" and to refer to them in such a manner. We have found that these terms more clearly communicate with other practitioners the true nature of the event and allow the identified patient to have an alternative conceptualization for the behavior.

Once the diagnosis has been communicated, further conceptualization, treatment planning, and delivery can be accomplished. Typically, the practitioner will be the primary caregiver in this situation, with frequent consultation from the referring physician. Involvement with the spouse or family, when appropriate, will frequently be necessary to address the relevant issues.

CASE STUDIES

We present two neuropsychological case studies to facilitate the practitioner's understanding of the neuropsychological aspects of epilepsy and nonepileptic events. The first case is of a patient with epilepsy, and the second case is a patient diagnosed with NEADs.

The Case of AB

History. AB is a 40-year-old right-handed White woman with 12 years of education. She was referred for testing to determine her current levels of cognitive and emotional functioning, to assess her capacity for vocational rehabilitation, and to provide information with which to compare postoperative results if epilepsy surgery were indicated.

The patient reported a history of seizure disorder since the age of 18 months after experiencing a high fever. She described two different types of seizures. In the first, she gasped for breath, was slightly out of conscious contact, and dropped objects. She was unable to communicate during these events. She reported that these events lasted 60–90 s and occurred several times a day. After beginning Tegretol therapy, AB experienced only one of these seizures. In the second type of seizure, AB became rigid, yet there were no repetitive jerking movements after this period of rigidity. These seizures had occurred only at night. Collectively, her seizures all occurred around the time of menstruation. She reported never having experienced status epilepticus. Medications at the time of the assessment included Tegretol (200 mg by mouth [po], four times a day) and Dilantin (200 mg po, four times a day).

Data from previous diagnostic workups included a CT scan, which was normal. The patient also underwent EEG recordings that included nasopharyngeal leads, which revealed abnormal activity within the left anterior–left frontal area.

The patient completed high school on time without academic difficulties. She felt as if she had not been accepted by others in school. AB is currently unemployed. She had previously worked at a phone repair company for approximately 10 years, but was laid off because of lack of work. At the time of the evaluation, the patient had been married for 7 years and she and her husband had a 3-year-old daughter.

This brief history provides pertinent information regarding AB's premorbid status, the nature of her seizure disorder, associated biomedical test results, effects of antiepileptic medications, and psychosocial complications. Concerning her premorbid status, we inferred an average range of intellectual abilities because she was able to attend regular school without complications. Her seizures began when she was a toddler and, as a result, we could not be confident about being able to localize language functions as we would have liked to had her seizures begun after 5 years of age. The descriptions of her seizures were highly stereotypic and were correlated with abnormal electrical activity on the EEG. From CT scan results we were able to rule out structural abnormalities as causes for her seizures. On the basis of these clinical and biomedical test results, AB's seizures were consistent with complex partial seizures and generalized tonic seizures (nocturnal events). Given this information, we now consider her neuropsychological test results, presented in Exhibit 4.

Neuropsychological data. During testing, AB was cooperative, demonstrating adequate task persistence and performance motivation. She engaged in spontaneous speech, characterized by adequate prosody, grammar, volume, and rate. Mild articulation errors were observed in her speech. Her mood and affect were euthymic. Her thought content was free from suicidal, homicidal, or paranoid ideation, and her thought processes were logical and goal directed. Several measures frequently administered to individuals with known seizure disorders were not administered to this patient because of time limitations. In general, the results of this evaluation were considered to be a valid assessment of her current neuropsychological and personality functioning.

On the NBE, the patient scored in the impaired range on 9 of the 13 administered measures (i.e., the criterion for dysfunction equals or exceeds impairment on 7 of the individual measures). Given that these measures are sensitive to the presence of neuropathology in people with epilepsy, the current test results suggest a mild-to-moderate level of neuropsychological impairment. Information on specific aspects of the patient's neuropsychological test performance is presented next.

In terms of attentional skills, AB was able to maintain at least adequate attention and concentration during testing, as demonstrated by her low average scores on the WAIS-R's Freedom From Distractibility factor score. On the basis of her WAIS-R data, we observed that AB was functioning within the borderline range of overall intellectual abilities, with a nonsignificant difference between her Verbal IQ of 80 and her Performance IQ of 77. A similar nonsignificant trend was observed between the Verbal Comprehension and Perceptual Organization factor scores. These scores were not consistent with estimates of her premorbid level of intelligence.

In terms of memory functioning, the WMS data provided evidence of memory impairment, with immediate figural memory being relatively more impaired than immediate verbal memory. Similar poor performance was observed in an assessment of her incidental tactual memory.

However, her long-term retrieval of information suggested that verbal retrieval skills were somewhat more impaired relative to her intact figural skills. In terms of language abilities, no demonstrable impairment was observed during her conversational speech, except for mild articulation errors. AB's visual–spatial skills were evaluated, and her overall performance was mildly impaired on tasks of constructional skills (i.e., Block Design), visual sequencing (i.e., Picture Arrangement), and visual integration (i.e., Object Assembly).

EXHIBIT 4

Neuropsychological Test Results of Patient AB

Neuropsychological Battery for Epilepsy

Test variable	Score
Category test	94 errors[a]
Tactual Performance Test	
Total time	30.0 min[a]
Memory performance	4 blocks recalled[a]
Localization score	1 block correct[a]
Seashore Rhythm Test	21 correct[a]
Finger Tapping total	83 taps[a]
Trail Making Test (Part B)	115 s[a]
Aphasia Screening Test (errors)	3 errors
Constructional Dyspraxia	Questionable
Perceptual exam (errors)	3 errors
Name Writing (total time)	1.4 letters per s
Wechsler Memory Scale	
Logical Memory	15 total memory bits[a]
Visual Reproduction	2 total memory bits[a]
Summary score: Total tests impaired	9 of 13 tests administered outside normal limits

[a]Impaired

Intellectual Measures

Wechsler Adult Intelligence Scale–Revised

	Score	
Subtest	Standard	Age corrected
Information	6	6
Digit Span	6	7
Vocabulary	6	6
Arithmetic	7	8
Comprehension	5	5
Similarities	7	8
Picture Completion	5	6
Picture Arrangement	7	8
Block Design	5	6
Object Assembly	5	5
Digit Symbol	4	5

Verbal IQ = 80 (9th percentile)
Performance IQ = 77 (6th percentile)
Full-Scale IQ = 78 (7th percentile)
Verbal Comprehension factor score = 79 (8th percentile)
Perceptual Organizational factor score = 75 (5th percentile)
Freedom From Distractibility factor score = 85 (16th percentile)

Memory Measures

Wechsler Memory Scale

Test	Raw score	Interpretation
Logical Memory I	15	Mild–moderate impairment
Logical Memory II	9	Mild–moderate impairment
Logical Memory % retained	60	Mild–moderate impairment
Visual Reproduction I	2	Moderate–severe impairment
Visual Reproduction II	3	Moderate–severe impairment
Visual Reproduction % retained	100	Average

Visuospatial Measures

Test	Standard score	Age-corrected score
Picture Arrangement	7	8
Block Design	5	6
Object Assembly	5	5

Problem-Solving Measures

Tactual Performance Test

Right-hand total time (min)/blocks	10.0/8
Left-hand total time (min)/blocks	10.0/5
Both hands total time (min)/blocks	10.0/6
Total time (min)/total blocks	30.0/19
Memory score	4 blocks recalled
Location score	1 block correct

EXHIBIT 4 (*Continued*)

Trail-Making Test

Test	Time (s)	Total errors
Trails A	60	1
Trails B	115	1

Personality Measures

Minnesota Multiphasic Personality Inventory (T scores):

? = 2	*Pd* = 64
L = 66	*Mf* = 55
F = 62	*Pa* = 47
K = 55	*Pt* = 68
Hs = 70	*Sc* = 66
D = 82	*Ma* = 53
Hy = 66	*Si* = 69

Washington Psychosocial Seizure Inventory

Measure	Raw score	Scaled score	Severity
Family Background	5	3.0	Definite
Emotional Adjustment	20	3.7	Definite
Interpersonal Adjustment	16	4.0	Severe
Vocational Adjustment	11	4.2	Severe
Financial Status	6	4.0	Severe
Adjustment to Seizures	10	3.5	Definite
Medicine and Medical Management	5	3.5	Definite
Overall Psychosocial Functioning	42	4.0	Severe
Lie scale	1		
Rare Item scale	2		
Unanswered items	0		

Mild levels of impairment were observed on both the Category Test and the Trail Making Test. Her ability to abstract shared characteristics of objects and concepts (i.e., Similarities subtest) fell within the low average range. On the Tactual Performance Test, AB's performance was mildly to moderately impaired for the time she required to solve the task.

In terms of personality functioning, the patient did not attempt to overreport or underreport symptomatology on the MMPI. On the clinical scales of the MMPI, she obtained significant elevations on scales assessing feelings of depression and somatic preoccupation. Further examination of these issues on the WPSI revealed that AB reported severe difficulties with emotional, interpersonal, and vocational adjustment, which were compounded by concerns regarding her financial status. AB also reported problems regarding her adjustment to her seizure disorder and difficulties with the medical management of her seizure disorder.

Summary. AB is a 40-year-old woman who presented with seizures consisting of partial complex and generalized tonic types. Her seizure disorder had been present since childhood, yet she reported some problems with the medical management of her seizures. Neuropsychological test results revealed borderline intellectual abilities, memory impairment with deficiencies in verbal memory and figural memory, mild impairment of skills requiring visual–spatial integrity, and mild deficits on several problem-solving tasks. These findings are not of lateralizing or localizing value. Personality test results suggested emotional difficulties characterized by mild depression and somatic preoccupation. Concerning her adjustment to her seizure disorder, she appeared to have difficulties with emotional, interpersonal, and vocational adjustment.

Recommendations for this patient included the following: (a) Her cognitive performance on testing suggested limited occupational opportunities. (b) She was experiencing mild depression, which was partly related to her emotional, interpersonal, and vocational situations. She would probably benefit from brief problem-oriented psychotherapy designed to increase her level of coping skills by instructing her in alternative methods of problem resolution.

The Case of CD

History. CD is a 35-year-old right-handed White man with 10 years of education. He was referred to our service to determine his current level of neuropsychological and emotional functioning and to assist the referral source in determining the extent to which psychological factors contributed to his neurological complaints.

CD stated that his events began at the age of 1 year, with causes unknown. Initially, phenobarbital controlled these events, but it was discontinued when he was 10 years old. CD did not experience another event until 1987, when he sustained a head laceration that reportedly caused these events to recur.

CD reported that his events varied by intensity, duration, and characteristics. Some events lasted for minutes and other events lasted for hours. During these events, CD reportedly stared off into space, was unresponsive, and was disoriented. Shaking in all extremities often accompanied these events. He reported that stress typically caused these events and that the events had never occurred randomly. Following these events, the patient reportedly had headaches and felt "like a car that ran out of gas." In addition, CD's wife described an incident in which he did not recognize her for several weeks. Specifically, he "lost his identity" and did not know his own name or recognize his wife or children. CD's wife reported that he crawled around the house during his events. Medications at the time of the assessment included Dilantin (200 mg three times a day).

Data from previous diagnostic workups included CT scans and MR images, both of which were normal. In 1990, an EEG was conducted during wakefulness, hyperventilation, photic stimulation, drowsiness, and sleep, and the results were all within normal limits. The patient was later referred for video–EEG telemetry in March 1992. Several events were recorded during his 3-day stay, and all were nonepileptiform. During one event, CD was told that he would experience an event when a tuning fork was applied, and, following physical contact with the tuning fork, CD experienced an event. During another event, CD stood up in his bed, gathered his sheets and pillow, and jumped off the bed onto the floor.

CD's social history was remarkable for significant disability in his family of origin. He had a brother with a congenital birth defect and three other siblings who also reportedly experienced seizures. CD reported that he was always a poor student. He eventually left school after the 10th grade. His work history was sporadic. He was last employed at a freight company. During this employment, a box struck him on the head and his events returned. He has not been gainfully employed since then and has applied for Social Security Disability assistance. The patient is married and has three children. Both the patient and his wife describe family conflict, particularly about differences of opinion on parenting and financial issues.

This brief history provides important information that contributes to an accurate understanding of CD's presenting condition. On the basis of this information, we observed that CD was functioning in the low average range of abilities based on his educational and occupational history and that he was the product of a family whose existence was surrounded by disability. CD's description of his events did not coincide with any known pattern of epileptic seizure disorder. CD reported that some of his events lasted for hours and that they were always preceded by psychosocial stressors. One event in particular sounded as though the patient experienced a dissociative episode. Biomedical test results did not uncover any epileptiform activity on an EEG even when he was exposed to adverse conditions. He did experience one event on command and experienced another event in his hospital room that was characterized by directed, purposeful movements. Notably, both of those events were not accompanied by abnormal EEG activity. Given this clinical history, we discuss his neuropsychological test data, which are presented in Exhibit 5.

Neuropsychological data. Throughout testing, CD was cooperative and displayed adequate task persistence and performance motivation. His mood and affect were dysphoric. He engaged in spontaneous speech that was characterized by adequate prosody, articulation, volume, and rate. Mild educationally related errors were noted in his speech. His thought content was free from suicidal, homicidal, and paranoid ideation, and his thought processes were logical and goal directed. Several measures frequently administered to individuals with known or suspected seizure disorders were not administered to this patient because of time limitations. In general, the results of the evaluation were believed to be a valid assessment of his current neuropsychological and emotional functioning.

On the NBE, the patient scored in the impaired range on 6 of the 11 administered measures (i.e., the criterion for dysfunction equals or exceeds impairment on 7 of the individual measures). Overall, these test results suggest the possibility of the pres-

EXHIBIT 5

Neuropsychological Test Results of Patient CD

Neuropsychological Battery for Epilepsy

Test variable	Score
Category test	55 errors[a]
Tactual Performance Test	
Total time	14.8 min
Memory score	8 blocks recalled
Localization score	5 blocks correct
Finger Tapping total	94 taps[a]
Trail-Making Test (Part B)	83 s[a]
Aphasia Screening Test (errors)	5 errors[a]
Constructional Dyspraxia	Within normal limits
Perceptual exam	4 errors
Name Writing (total time)	1.6 letters per second
Wechsler Memory Scale	
Logical Memory	11.5 total memory bits[a]
Visual Reproduction	4 total memory bits[a]
Summary score: Total tests impaired	6 tests of 11 administered outside normal limit

[a]Impaired.

Intellectual Measures

Wechsler Adult Intelligence Scale–Revised

Subtest	Score	
	Standard	Age corrected
Information	5	4
Digit Span	7	7
Vocabulary	6	7
Arithmetic	8	9
Comprehension	8	8
Similarities	7	8
Picture Completion	9	10
Picture Arrangement	10	11
Block Design	9	10
Object Assembly	9	10
Digit Symbol	6	7

Verbal IQ = 83 (13th percentile)
Performance IQ = 95 (37th percentile)
Full-Scale IQ = 88 (21st percentile)
Verbal Comprehension factor score = 82 (12th percentile)
Perceptual Organizational factor score = 101 (53rd percentile)
Freedom From Distractibility factor score = 88 (21st percentile)

Memory Measures

Wechsler Memory Scale

Test	Raw score	Interpretation
Logical Memory I	11.5	Moderate–severe
Logical Memory II	9.5	Mild–moderate
Logical Memory % retained	82	Borderline
Visual Reproduction I	4	Moderate–severe
Visual Reproduction II	4	Mild–moderate
Visual Reproduction % retained	100	Average

Visuospatial Measures

Test	Standard score	Age-corrected score
Picture Arrangement	10	11
Block Design	9	10
Object Assembly	9	10

Problem-Solving Measures

Tactual Performance Test

Right-hand total time (min)/blocks	7.3/10
Left-hand total time (min)/blocks	4.8/10

(*continues*)

EXHIBIT 5 (*Continued*)

Both hands total time (min)/blocks	2.8/10
Total time (min)/total blocks	14.8/30
Memory score	8 blocks recalled
Location score	5 blocks correct

Trail-Making Test

Test	Time (s)	Total errors
Trails A	32	1
Trails B	83	0

Personality Measures

Minnesota Multiphasic Personality Inventory (T scores)

?	5	*Pd*	74
L	56	*Mf*	50
F	101	*Pa*	116
K	30	*Pt*	62
Hs	48	*Sc*	74
D	72	*Ma*	59
Hy	61	*Si*	68

ence of a neuropsychological deficit had all 16 measures been administered.

CD displayed adequate attentional skills, as demonstrated not only by his ability to remain on task and remember basic and complex verbal instructions, but also by his WAIS-R Freedom From Distractibility score, which placed his performance at the upper end of the low average range.

In terms of intellectual functioning, CD's general level of intellectual functioning fell within the low average range, with verbal abilities falling within the low average range and performance abilities falling within the average range. His academic skills were commensurate with his measured level of intelligence.

In terms of memory functioning, CD's performance was generally adequate when compared with premorbid estimates of his abilities. In particular, an examination of his percentage-retained scores for verbal and figural information on the WMS suggested adequate retrieval of information from long-term memory stores. His incidental tactual memory for geometric shapes also was adequate. CD's language skills during conversational speech were essentially adequate and suggested no evidence of pathology. His performance on several visuospatial and constructional tasks (i.e., Picture Arrangement, Block Design, and Object Assembly) was adequate.

CD's problem-solving skills were essentially adequate. He demonstrated adequate mental flexibility on the Trail Making Test, and his logical abstract reasoning skills on the Similarities subtest of the WAIS-R also were adequate. Although his Category Test score fell beyond the cutoff, his performance was still considered adequate when we took into account his premorbid history. On the Tactual Performance Test, CD's performance was adequate, and he demonstrated slow but steady improvement across trials.

In terms of personality functioning, CD tended to overreport emotional symptomatology. On the clinical scales, CD obtained substantial elevations on several of the scales, suggesting that he was highly suspicious of others and felt that others had malicious and self-serving motivations. He reported moderate levels of anger and depression, as well as bizarre sensory experiences.

Summary. CD presented with a long-standing history of behavioral events for which the manifestation of the events was inconsistent with any known pattern of epileptic seizure disorder. Neuropsychological test results were generally consistent with premorbid estimates of his abilities, falling within the low average range, and the results did not suggest either a focal or generalized pattern of neuropsychological deficit. Personality test results suggested significant psychopathology, consistent with his clinical history. Overall, his constellation of psychometric test results and clinical history suggested a *DSM–IV* diagnosis of factitious disorder with predominantly physical signs and symptoms. There was an intentional element to the patient's symptom production (e.g., his ability to experience an event on command) that suggested both conscious awareness and conscious control over many of these events. The patient was also from a family in which physical disability was prominent, and it is likely that one way he was able to solicit attention from family members was to assume a "sick role." Overall, although these test results cannot rule out the possibility of a true seizure disorder, psychological factors are a strong component in the manifestation of his presenting symptomatology.

Recommendations for the patient included the following: (a) This patient was intellectually capable of being productively employed. However, his psychiatric disorder was a significant impediment to his employability. (b) This patient would likely benefit from supportive psychotherapy designed to assist him with relinquishing the use of his events as a way of handling stressful situations.

SUMMARY

Throughout this chapter we have attempted to identify and describe the salient aspects in the understanding of both epilepsy and NEADs in terms of the various biomedical, cognitive, and personality means of evaluation, assessment, and diagnosis, as well as the various pharmacological and psychotherapeutic forms of treatment. Our goals were to provide students and practitioners with a practical reference for their work with patients with both epilepsy and events resembling epilepsy and to provide some direction for evaluation and treatment. Our theme throughout has been that these disorders are multifaceted and require a thorough understanding of neuroanatomical, neurochemical, and neuropsychological aspects, as well as psychological and social aspects.

To review, the first part of the chapter was concerned with the definition of what epilepsy is and how this definition distinguishes epilepsy from a single seizure. The ICES was presented as the current method used in classification of the epilepsies, which roughly divides epileptic seizures into partial seizures (i.e., those seizures presumably of a focal origin) and generalized seizures (i.e., those seizures presumably of a generalized origin). The second part of the chapter was concerned with the various measures used in the diagnosis of epilepsy, which included the EEG, various neuroimaging techniques, and neuropsychological assessment. Various treatment approaches also were discussed, including both pharmacological and psychotherapeutic approaches.

There are several areas in which practitioners are likely to be asked to assist in both the diagnosis and treatment of individuals with epilepsy or disorders resembling epilepsy, and these areas were reviewed. One of the more important points of contact for the practitioner includes the diagnosis and treatment of individuals with NEADs. Current research efforts suggest that NEADs are a heterogeneous constellation of psychiatric disorders rather than one particular diagnostic entity, given the lack of consistency among various neuropsychological, personality, and laboratory investigations. A framework was presented to assist practitioners in conceptualizing individuals who present with NEADs in terms of their degree of conscious awareness and conscious control over their symptom production.

References

Adams, R. D., & Victor, M. (1993). Epilepsy and other seizure disorders. In R. D. Adams & M. Victor (Eds.), *Principles of neurology* (5th ed., pp. 273–299). New York: McGraw-Hill.

Altshuler, L. L., Devinsky, O., Post, R. M., & Theodore, W. (1990). Depression, anxiety, and temporal lobe epilepsy: Laterality of focus and symptoms. *Archives of Neurology, 47,* 284–288.

American Psychiatric Association. (1994). *Diagnostic and statistical manual of mental disorders* (4th ed.). Washington, DC: Author.

Andermann, F., Freeman, J. M., Vigevano, F., & Hwang, P. A. L. S. (1993). Surgically remediable diffuse hemispheric syndromes. In J. Engel, Jr. (Ed.), *Surgical treatment of the epilepsies* (2nd ed., pp. 87–102). New York: Raven Press.

Andermann, F., Remillard, G. M., Zifkin, B. G., Trottier, R. G., & Drouin, P. (1988). Epilepsy and driving. *Canadian Journal of Neurological Sciences, 15,* 371–377.

Anderson, S. W., Damasio, H., Jones, R. D., & Tranel, D. (1991). Wisconsin Card Sorting Test performance as a measure of frontal lobe damage. *Journal of Clinical and Experimental Neuropsychology, 13,* 909–922.

Bear, D. M., & Fedio, P. (1977). Quantitative analysis of interictal behavior in temporal lobe epilepsy. *Archives of Neurology, 34,* 454–467.

Berkovic, S. (1984). *Clinical and experimental aspects of complex partial seizures.* Unpublished doctoral dissertation, University of Melbourne, Australia.

Berkovic, S. F., Newton, M. R., Chiron, C., & Dulac, O. (1993). Single photon emission tomography. In J.

Engel, Jr. (Ed.), *Surgical treatment of the epilepsies* (2nd ed., pp. 233–243). New York: Raven Press.

Bickford, R. G. (1979). Activation procedures and special electrodes. In D. W. Klass & D. D. Daly (Eds.), *Current practice of clinical electroencephalography* (pp. 269–305). New York: Raven Press.

Blom, R. J., Vinuela, F., Fox, A. J., Blume, W. T., Girvin, J., & Kaufmann, F. C. E. (1984). Computed tomography in temporal lobe epilepsy. *Journal of Computer Assisted Tomography, 8,* 401–405.

Blume, W. T., Grabow, J. D., Darley, F. L., & Aronson, A. E. (1973). Intracarotid amobarbital test of language and memory before temporal lobectomy for seizure control. *Neurology, 23,* 812–819.

Blumer, D. (1975). Temporal lobe epilepsy and its psychiatric significance. In F. D. Benson & D. Blumer (Eds.), *Psychiatric aspects of neurological disease* (pp. 171–198). New York: Grune & Stratton.

Blumer, D. (1991, September). *Pseudoseizures.* Paper presented at the University of Tennessee Psychiatric Grand Rounds, Memphis, TN.

Bolter, J., Veneklasen, J., & Long, C. J. (1981). Investigation of WAIS effectiveness in discriminating between temporal and generalized seizure patients. *Journal of Consulting and Clinical Psychology, 49,* 549–553.

Branch, C., Milner, B., & Rasmussen, T. (1964). Intracarotid sodium amytal for the lateralization of cerebral speech dominance: Observations in 123 patients. *Journal of Neurosurgery, 21,* 399–405.

Cascino, G. D., Boon, P. A. J. M., & Fish, D. R. (1993). Surgically remediable lesional syndromes. In J. Engel, Jr. (Ed.), *Surgical treatment of the epilepsies* (2nd ed., pp. 77–86). New York: Raven Press.

Chelune, G. J., & Bornstein, R. A. (1988). WMS-R patterns among patients with lateralized brain lesions. *The Clinical Neuropsychologist, 2,* 121–132.

Commission on Classification and Terminology of the International League Against Epilepsy. (1981). Proposal for revised clinical and electroencephalographic classification of epileptic seizures. *Epilepsia, 22,* 489–501.

Commission on Classification and Terminology of the International League Against Epilepsy. (1989). Proposal for revised classification of epilepsies and epileptic syndromes. *Epilepsia, 30,* 389–399.

Currie, S., Heathfield, R. W. G., Henson, R. A., & Scott, D. F. (1970). Clinical course and prognosis of temporal lobe epilepsy: A survey of 666 patients. *Brain, 94,* 173–190.

Dana-Haeri, J., Trimble, M. R., & Oxley, J. (1983). Prolactin and gonadotrophin changes following generalized and partial seizures. *Journal of Neurology, Neurosurgery, and Psychiatry, 46,* 331–335.

Delaney, R. C., Rosen, A. J., Mattson, R. H., & Novelly, R. A. (1980). Memory function in focal epilepsy: A comparison of non-surgical, unilateral temporal lobe and frontal lobe samples. *Cortex, 16,* 103–117.

Delgado-Escueta, A. V., Mattson, R. H., King, L., Goldensohn, E. S., Spiegel, H., Madsen, J., Crandall, P., Dreifuss, F., & Porter, R. J. (1981). The nature of aggression during epileptic seizures. *New England Journal of Medicine, 305,* 711.

Delgado-Escueta, A. V., & Walsh, G. O. (1985). Type I complex partial seizures of hippocampal origin: Excellent results of anterior temporal lobectomy. *Neurology, 35,* 143–154.

Desai, B. T., Porter, R. J., & Penry, J. K. (1982). Psychogenic seizures: A study of 42 attacks in six patients, with intensive monitoring. *Archives of Neurology, 39,* 202–209.

Devinsky, O., & Bear, D. (1984). Varieties of aggressive behavior in temporal lobe epilepsy. *American Journal of Psychiatry, 141,* 651–656.

Dobbins, C., & Russell, E. (1990). Left temporal lobe brain damage pattern on the Wechsler Adult Intelligence Scale. *Journal of Clinical Psychology, 46,* 863–868.

Dodrill, C. B. (1978). A neuropsychological battery for epilepsy. *Epilepsia, 19,* 611–623.

Dodrill, C. B., & Batzel, L. W. (1986). Interictal behavioral features of patients with epilepsy. *Epilepsia, 27* (Suppl. 2), S64–S76.

Dodrill, C. B., Batzel, L. W., Queisser, H. R., & Temkin, N. R. (1980). An objective method for the assessment of psychological and social problems among epileptics. *Epilepsia, 21,* 123–135.

Dodrill, C. B., Breyer, D. N., Diamond, M. B., Dubinsky, B. L., & Geary, B. B. (1984). Psychosocial problems among adults with epilepsy. *Epilepsia, 25,* 168–175.

Dodrill, C. B., & Clemmons, D. (1984). Use of neuropsychological tests to identify high school students with epilepsy who later demonstrate inadequate performances in life. *Journal of Consulting and Clinical Psychology, 52,* 520–527.

Dodrill, C. B., & Temkin, N. R. (1989). Motor speed is a contaminating variable in the measurement of the "cognitive" effects of phenytoin. *Epilepsia, 30,* 453–457.

Dodrill, C. B., & Wilkus, R. J. (1978). Neuropsychological correlates of the electroencephalogram in epileptics: III. Generalized nonepileptiform abnormalities. *Epilepsia, 19,* 453–462.

Ellingson, R. J., Wilken, K., & Bennett, D. R. (1984). Efficacy of sleep deprivation procedure in epileptic patients. *Journal of Clinical Neurophysiology, 1,* 83–101.

Engel, J. (1987). Approaches to localization of the epileptogenic lesions. In J. Engel, Jr. (Ed.), *Surgical treatment of the epilepsies* (2nd ed., pp. 75–95). New York: Raven Press.

Engel, J. (1989). *Seizures and epilepsy*. Philadelphia: F. A. Davis.

Engel, J., Kuhl, D. E., Phelps, M. E., & Crandall, P. H. (1982). Comparative localization of epileptic foci in partial epilepsy by PET and EEG. *Annals of Neurology, 12,* 529–537.

Engel, J., & Shewmon, D. A. (1993). Overview: Who should be considered a surgical candidate. In J. Engel, Jr. (Ed.), *Surgical treatment of the epilepsies* (2nd ed., pp. 23–34). New York: Raven Press.

Fenton, G. W. (1982). Hysterical alterations of consciousness. In A. Roy (Ed.), *Hysteria* (pp. 229–246). New York: Wiley.

Gastaut, H. (1970). Clinical and electroencephalographical classifications of epileptic seizures. *Epilepsia, 11,* 102–113.

Gastaut, H. (1973). *Dictionary of epilepsy* (Pt. 1). Geneva, Switzerland: World Health Organization.

Gastaut, H., & Broughton, R. (1972). *Epileptic seizures: Clinical and electrographic features, diagnosis and treatment*. Springfield, IL: Charles C Thomas.

Gates, J. R., Luciano, D., & Devinsky, O. (1991). The classification and treatment of nonepileptic events. In O. Devinsky & W. H. Theodore (Eds.), *Epilepsy and behavior* (pp. 251–263). New York: Wiley-Liss.

Gates, J. R., Ramani, V., Whalen, S., & Loewenson, R. (1985). Ictal characteristics of pseudoseizures. *Archives of Neurology, 42,* 1183–1187.

Goodwin, J., Simms, J., & Bergman, R. (1979). Hysterical seizures: A sequel to incest. *American Journal of Orthopsychiatry, 49,* 698–703.

Gray, J. W., Dean, R. S., Rattan, G., & Cramer, K. M. (1987). Neuropsychological aspects of primary affective depression. *International Journal of Neuroscience, 32,* 911–918.

Gross, M. (1970). Incestuous rape: A cause for hysterical seizures in four adolescent girls. *American Journal of Orthopsychiatry, 49,* 704–708.

Harper, M., & Roth, M. (1962). Temporal lobe epilepsy and the phobic anxiety-depersonalization syndrome: I. A comparative study. *Comprehensive Psychiatry, 3,* 129–151.

Hathaway, S. R., & McKinley, J. C. (1951). *Minnesota Multiphasic Personality Inventory: Manual*. New York: Psychological Corporation.

Heaton, R. K. (1981). *Wisconsin Card Sorting Test manual*. Odessa, FL: Psychological Assessment Resources.

Hendler, N. (1984). Depression caused by chronic pain. *Journal of Clinical Psychiatry, 45,* 30–36.

Henrichs, T. F., Tucker, D. M., Farha, J., & Novelly, R. A. (1988). MMPI indices in the identification of patients evidencing pseudoseizures. *Epilepsia, 29,* 184–187.

Henry, T. R., Chugani, H. T., Abou-Khalil, B. W., Theodore, W. H., & Swartz, B. E. (1993). Positron emission tomography. In J. Engel, Jr. (Ed.), *Surgical treatment of the epilepsies* (2nd ed., pp. 211–232). New York: Raven Press.

Hermann, B. P., & Connell, B. E. (1992). Neuropsychological assessment in the diagnosis of nonepileptic seizures. In T. L. Bennett (Ed.), *The neuropsychology of epilepsy* (pp. 59–70). New York: Plenum.

Hermann, B. P., Gold, J., Pusakulich, R., Wyler, A. R., Randolph, C., Rankin, E. J., & Hoye, W. (1995). Wechsler Adult Intelligence Scale–Revised in the evaluation of anterior temporal lobectomy candidates. *Epilepsia, 36,* 480–487.

Hermann, B. P., Seidenberg, M., Haltiner, A., & Wyler, A. R. (1991). Mood state in unilateral temporal lobe epilepsy. *Biological Psychiatry, 30,* 1205–1218.

Hermann, B. P., & Whitman, S. (1989). Psychosocial predictors of interictal depression. *Journal of Epilepsy, 2,* 231–237.

Hermann, B. P., Whitman, S., & Anton, M. (1992). A multietiological model of psychological and social dysfunction in epilepsy. In T. L. Bennett (Ed.), *The neuropsychology of epilepsy* (pp. 39–57). New York: Plenum.

Hermann, B. P., Wyler, A. R., & Richey, E. T. (1988). Wisconsin Card Sorting Test performance in patients with complex partial seizures of temporal-lobe origin. *Journal of Clinical and Experimental Neuropsychology, 10,* 467–476.

Holloway, R. L. (1980). Within-species brain-body weight variability: A reexamination of the Danish data and other primate species. *American Journal of Physical Anthropology, 53,* 109–121.

Holmes, G. L., Sackellares, J. C., McKiernan, J., Ragland, M., & Dreifuss, F. E. (1980). Evolution of childhood pseudoseizures using EEG telemetry and video tape monitoring. *Journal of Pediatrics, 97,* 554–558.

Jeavons, P. M. (1977). Choice of drug therapy in epilepsy. *Practitioner, 219,* 542–546.

Jones-Gotman, M., Smith, M., & Zatorre, R. J. (1993). Neuropsychological testing for localizing and lateralizing the epileptogenic region. In J. Engel, Jr. (Ed.), *Surgical treatment of the epilepsies* (2nd ed., pp. 245–261). New York: Raven Press.

Kaufman, D. M. (1990). *Clinical neurology for psychiatrists*. Philadelphia: Harcourt Brace Jovanovich.

Krumholz, A., & Niedermeyer, E. (1983). Psychogenic seizures: A clinical study with follow-up data. *Neurology, 33,* 498–502.

Kuzniecky, R. I., Cascino, G. D., Palmini, A., Jack, C. R., Berkovic, S. F., Jackson, G. D., & McCarthy, G. (1993). Structural neuroimaging. In J. Engel, Jr. (Ed.), *Surgical treatment of the epilepsies* (2nd ed., pp. 197–209). New York: Raven Press.

LaBarbera, J. D., & Dozier, J. E. (1980). Hysterical seizures: The role of sexual exploitation. *Psychosomatics, 21,* 897–903.

Lechtenberg, R. (1990). *Seizure recognition and treatment.* New York: Churchill Livingstone.

Lesser, R. P. (1986). Psychogenic seizures. *Psychosomatics, 27,* 823–829.

Liske, E., & Forster, F. M. (1964). Pseudoseizures: A problem in the diagnosis and management of epileptic patient. *Neurology, 14,* 41–49.

Loiseau, P. (1985). Childhood absence epilepsy. In J. Roger, C. Dravet, M. Bureau, F. E. Dreifuss, & P. Wolf (Eds.), *Epileptic syndromes in infancy, childhood, and adolescence* (pp. 106–120). London: Libbey.

Loring, D. W., Meador, K. J., & Lee, G. P. (1992). Criteria and validity issues in Wada assessment. In T. L. Bennett (Ed.), *The neuropsychology of epilepsy* (pp. 233–245). New York: Plenum.

Matthews, C. G., Shaw, D. J., & Klove, H. (1966). Psychological test performance in neurologic and "pseudo-neurologic" subjects. *Cortex, 2,* 244–253.

Mattson, R. H. (1980). Value of intensive monitoring. In J. A. Wada & J. K. Penry (Eds.), *Advances in epileptology: The 10th Epilepsy International Symposium* (pp. 43–51). New York: Raven Press.

McIntosh, G. C. (1992). Neurological conceptualizations of epilepsy. In T. L. Bennett (Ed.), *The neuropsychology of epilepsy* (pp. 17–37). New York: Plenum.

Meadow, R. (1982). Munchausen syndrome by proxy. *Archives of the Diseases of the Child, 57,* 92–98.

Mendez, M. F., Cummings, J. L., & Benson, D. R. (1986). Depression in epilepsy: Significance and phenomenology. *Archives of Neurology, 43,* 766–770.

Metrakos, K., & Metrakos, J. D. (1961). Genetics of convulsive disorders: II. Genetics and electroencephalographic studies in centrencephalic epilepsy. *Neurology, 11,* 474–483.

Milberg, W., Greiffenstein, M., Lewis, R., & Rourke, D. (1980). Differentiation of temporal lobe and generalized seizure patients with the WAIS. *Journal of Consulting and Clinical Psychology, 48,* 39–42.

Miley, C. E., & Forster, F. M. (1977). Activation of partial complex seizures by hyperventilation. *Archives of Neurology, 34,* 371–373.

Milner, B. (1963). Effects of different brain lesions on card sorting. *Archives of Neurology, 9,* 90–100.

Milner, B., Branch, C., & Rasmussen, T. (1962). Study of short term memory after intracarotid injection of sodium amytal. *Transactions of the American Neurological Association, 87,* 224–226.

Mullan, S., & Penfield, W. (1959). Illusions of comparative interpretation and emotion. *Archives of Neurology and Psychiatry, 81,* 269–284.

Mungas, D. (1982). Interictal behavior abnormality in temporal lobe epilepsy: A specific syndrome or nonspecific psychopathology? *Archives of General Psychiatry, 39,* 108–111.

National Institutes of Health Consensus Development Conference Statement: Surgery for epilepsy. (1990). *Epilepsia, 31,* 806–812.

Newmark, M. E., Theodore, W., DeLaPaz, R., Sato, S., DiChiro, G., Brooks, R. A., Kessler, R. M., & Porter, R. J. (1982). Positron emission computed tomography (PECT) in refractory complex partial seizures. *Transactions of the American Neurological Association, 106,* 34–37.

Novelly, R. A., & Williamson, P. D. (1989). Incidence of false-positive memory impairment in the intracarotid amytal procedure. *Epilepsia, 30,* 711.

Ojemann, G. A., Sutherling, W. W., Lesser, R. P., Dinner, D. S., Jayakar, P., & Saint-Hilaire, J. M. (1993). Cortical stimulation. In J. Engel, Jr. (Ed.), *Surgical treatment of the epilepsies* (2nd ed., pp. 399–414). New York: Raven Press.

Penry, J. K., & Dreifuss, F. E. (1969). Automatisms associated with the absence of petit mal epilepsy. *Archives of Neurology, 21,* 142–149.

Penry, J. K., Porter, R. J., & Dreifuss, F. E. (1975). Simultaneous recording of absence seizures with video tape and electroencephalography: A study of 374 seizures in 48 patients. *Brain, 98,* 427–440.

Pincus, J. H., & Tucker, G. J. (1985). *Behavioral neurology* (3rd ed.). New York: Oxford University Press.

Porter, R. J. (1984). *Epilepsy: 100 elementary principles.* Philadelphia: W. B. Saunders.

Porter, R. J. (1991). Diagnosis of psychogenic and other nonepileptic seizures in adults. In O. Devinsky & W. H. Theodore (Eds.), *Epilepsy and behavior* (pp. 237–249). New York: Wiley-Liss.

Pritchard, P. B., Wannamaker, B. B., Sagel, J., & Daniel, C. M. (1985). Serum prolactin and cortisol levels in evaluation of pseudoepileptic seizures. *Annals of Neurology, 18,* 87–89.

Rausch, R., Silfvenius, H., Wieser, H. G., Dodrill, C. B., Meador, K. J., & Jones-Gotman, M. (1993). In J. Engel, Jr. (Ed.), *Surgical treatment of the epilepsies* (2nd ed., pp. 341–357). New York: Raven Press.

Reynolds, E. H., & Shorvan, S. D. (1981). Monotherapy or polytherapy for epilepsy. *Epilepsia, 22,* 1–10.

Rodin, E., & Schmaltz, S. (1984). The Bear-Fedio Personality Inventory and temporal lobe epilepsy. *Neurology, 34,* 591.

Roy, A. (1979). Hysterical seizures. *Archives of Neurology, 36,* 447.

Russell, E. W. (1975). A multiple scoring method for assessment of complex memory functions. *Journal of Consulting and Clinical Psychology, 43,* 800–809.

Russell, E. W. (1987). Neuropsychological interpretation of the WAIS. *Neuropsychology, 1,* 2–6.

Sackellares, J. C., Giordani, B., Berent, S., Seidenberg, M., Dreifuss, F., Vanderzant, C. W., & Boll, T. J. (1985). Patients with pseudoseizures: Intellectual and cognitive performance. *Neurology, 35,* 116–119.

Sarason, I. G., Johnson, J. H., & Siegel, J. M. (1978). Assessing the impact of life changes: Development of the Life Experience Survey. *Journal of Consulting and Clinical Psychology, 46,* 932–946.

Sato, S., & Rose, D. F. (1986). The electroencephalogram in the evaluation of the patient with epilepsy. *Neurologic Clinics, 4,* 509–529.

Shaw, D. J., & Matthews, C. G. (1965). Differential MMPI performance of brain-damaged versus pseudoneurologic groups. *Journal of Clinical Psychology, 21,* 405–408.

Snyder, P. J., Novelly, R. A., & Harris, L. J. (1990). Mixed speech dominance in the intracarotid sodium amytal procedure: Validity and criteria isues. *Journal of Clinical and Experimental Neuropsychology, 12,* 629–643.

Stevens, J. R. (1988). Psychiatric aspects of epilepsy. *Journal of Clinical Psychiatry, 49,* 49–57.

Stevenson, J. M., & King, J. H. (1987). Neuropsychiatric aspects of epilepsy and epileptic seizures. In R. E. Hales & S. C. Yudofsky (Eds.), *Textbook of neuropsychiatry* (pp. 209–224). Washington, DC: American Psychiatric Press.

Theodore, W. H., Porter, R. J., & Penry, J. K. (1981). Complex partial seizures: A videotape analysis of 108 seizures in 25 patients. *Neurology, 31,* 108.

Trimble, M. R. (1978). Serum prolactin in epilepsy and hysteria. *British Medical Journal, 2,* 1682.

Trimble, M. R. (1986). Pseudoseizures. *Neurologic Clinics, 4,* 531–548.

Vanderzant, C. W., Giordani, B., Berent, S., Dreifuss, F. E., & Sackellares, J. C. (1986). Personality of patients with pseudoseizures. *Neurology, 36,* 664–668.

Volvow, M. R. (1986). Pseudoseizures: An overview. *Southern Medical Journal, 79,* 600–607.

Walczak, T. S., Radtke, R. A., McNamara, J. O., Lewis, D. V., Luther, J. S., Thompson, E., Wilson, W. P., Friedman, A. H., & Nashold, B. S. (1990). Anterior temporal lobectomy for complex partial seizures: Evaluation, results, and long-term follow-up in 100 cases. *Neurology, 40,* 413–418.

Waxman, S. G., & Geschwind, N. (1975). The interictal behavior syndrome of temporal lobe epilepsy. *Archives of General Psychiatry, 32,* 1580–1586.

Wechsler, D. (1945). A standardized memory scale for clinical use. *Journal of Psychology, 19,* 87–95.

Wechsler, D. (1955). *Manual for the Wechsler Adult Intelligence Scale.* New York: Psychological Corporation.

Wechsler, D. (1981). *WAIS-R manual: Wechsler Adult Intelligence Scale–Revised.* New York: Psychological Corporation.

Wechsler, D. (1987). *Wechsler Memory Scale–Revised.* New York: Psychological Corporation.

Weinberger, D. R., Berman, K., & Zec, R. F. (1986). Physiologic dysfunction of dorsolateral prefrontal cortex in schizophrenia. *Archives of General Psychiatry, 43,* 114–124.

Wieser, H. G. (1991). Selective amygdalohippocampectomy: Indications and follow-up. *Canadian Journal of Neurological Sciences, 18,* 617–627.

Wilkus, R. J., & Dodrill, C. B. (1976). Neuropsychological correlates of the electroencephalogram in epileptics: I. Topographic distribution and average rate of epileptiform activity. *Epilepsia, 17,* 89–100.

Wilkus, R. J., & Dodrill, C. B. (1989). Factors affecting the outcome of MMPI and neuropsychological assessments of psychogenic and epileptic seizure patients. *Epilepsia, 30,* 339–347.

Wilkus, R. J., Dodrill, C. B., & Thompson, P. M. (1984). Intensive EEG monitoring and psychological studies of patients with pseudoepileptic seizures. *Epilepsia, 25,* 100–107.

Williams, D. T., Gold, A. P., Shrout, P., Shaffer, D., & Adams, D. (1979). The impact of psychiatric intervention on patients with uncontrolled seizures. *Journal of Nervous and Mental Disease, 167,* 626–631.

Williamson, P. D., Van Ness, P. C., Wieser, H. G., & Quesney, L. F. (1993). Surgically remediable extratemporal syndromes. In J. Engel, Jr. (Ed.), *Surgical treatment of the epilepsies* (2nd ed., pp. 65–76). New York: Raven Press.

CHAPTER 6

ALCOHOL ABUSE AND ALCOHOLISM

Oscar A. Parsons

Alcohol and drug abuse are major problems in contemporary American society. Several decades ago, the U.S. Congress established the National Institute on Alcohol Abuse and Alcoholism and the National Institute on Drug Abuse to stimulate research on these public health problem areas. As a result, there has been an outpouring of new knowledge of the effects of alcohol and drug use on physical and mental functioning. In this chapter, the emphasis is on the assessment of neuropsychological functions in alcohol abusers. I chose alcohol abuse as a paradigm for drug abuse for several reasons. First, it is the most abused drug in American society. Second, there is consistent evidence for residual neuropsychological impairment in sober alcoholic individuals; such impairment in comparable individuals using other recreational drugs is sparse and infrequent. Third, when neuropsychological deficits are found in former drug abusers, they resemble those found in alcoholic patients (Golonbok, Moodley, & Lader, 1988; I. Grant & Judd, 1976; Hoff, Riordan, Alpert, & Volkow, 1991).

In this chapter, I discuss the epidemiology and genetic aspects of alcoholism, clinical symptomatology and diagnostic categories, brain changes associated with alcoholism, neuropsychological functioning of patients with alcoholic organic mental disorders and intermediate-stage alcoholic individuals, the determination of the degree of impairment in the latter, neuropsychological and cognitive models of the deficits, recovery of neuropsychological functions in alcoholic individuals, prediction of resumption of drinking, the neuropsychological assessment of alcoholic individuals, a recommended battery of tests, and illustrative cases.

EPIDEMIOLOGY

According to numerous estimates, about 10% of the U.S. adult population suffers from alcoholism. Approximately 4% fall into the category of alcohol abusers and 6% into the alcohol-dependent category (Institute of Medicine, 1987). The sex ratio of alcoholic males to females ranges from 3:1 to 5:1, depending on the populations sampled. White individuals have a significantly higher prevalence than do people of color (B. F. Grant, Harford, Hasin, Chou, & Pickering, 1992). According to the 1985 U.S. National Hospital Survey, of the 528,000 patients discharged from hospitals with a primary diagnosis of substance abuse, 427,680 (81%) were for alcoholism. These patients had a total of 4,345,000 days of hospital care (Institute of Medicine, 1987). In another national study, it was estimated that 3.4 million persons with a substance use disorder were seen during one year in ambulatory settings (professional and nonprofessional) for mental health or addiction-related reasons, which accounted for a total of 56.3 million visits (Narrow, Regier, Rae, Manderscheid, & Locke, 1993). One alarming indication of increased use of alcohol is that a comparison of male college students over a 12-year period (1980–1992), using similar procedures, indicated that the consumption of alcohol and the number of alcohol-related problems increased significantly during that period (Schuckit, Klein, Twitchell, & Springer, 1994).

In 1987, more than 1.4 million persons were treated in the United States for alcohol abuse and dependence; about 75% were male and 58% were aged 25–44 years (U.S. Department of Health and Human Services [USDHHS], 1990). Approximately 66% of those in treatment for alcohol or drug problems also had a current psychiatric disorder. Patients in treatment for alcoholism had somewhat higher lifetime prevalence rates for other psychiatric disorders (dual diagnoses); the latter were mainly diagnoses of antisocial personality, phobias, and depressive disorders (Ross, Glaser, & Germanson, 1989). It is obvious that alcoholism is a pervasive and important problem that neuropsychologists may encounter in many different patient contexts.

GENETICS

The etiology of alcoholism is multiply determined; genetic, neurochemical, neurophysiological, psychological, sociocultural, and economic factors all have been found to play a role (USDHHS, 1990, 1993). Recently, the role of genetics in alcoholism has received wide attention. Molecular genetics, animal research, and human studies of twins, adoptions, and family concordance have provided some of the strongest evidence (Blum et al., 1990; Cadoret, 1990; Cloninger, 1987; Kendler, Heath, Neale, Kessler, & Eaves, 1992). However, a critique of the studies of humans by Searles (1990) suggested that environmental factors might have been underemphasized as significant factors in alcoholism. In a study of the probands of alcohol-dependent male and female monozygotic and dizygotic twins, McGue, Pickens, and Svikis (1992) posited that the genetic influence may be more modest and age and gender specific (i.e., early onset men have the higher heritability index) "than is currently and widely believed" (p. 15).

Kendler et al. (1992) reported that the results of their study of female twins suggest that the genetic vulnerability to alcoholism in women is just as great as in men. The limitations of the molecular genetic approach with respect to alcoholism have been pointed out by Worton (1991). In summary, although there is little doubt that genetic factors do play an etiological role in alcohol abuse and alcoholism, the extent to which this genetic influence is expressed may depend on numerous other factors, as discussed earlier.

CLINICAL SYMPTOMATOLOGY AND DIAGNOSTIC CATEGORIES

As a drug, alcohol is classed with the barbiturate–sedatives, benzodiazepines (minor tranquilizers), and morphine (with its derivatives) as a central nervous system depressant (Winger, Hofman, & Woods, 1992). Similar to other drugs and poisons, when alcohol is ingested to excess it leads to intoxication. The acute stages of intoxication are well known and are not of concern here; however, the practitioner should always look for the behavioral signs of drug intoxication when conducting assessment or treatment procedures. Rather, the focus here is on the residual effects of repeated and prolonged ingestion of alcohol on the sober recovering alcoholic person's psychological functioning.

Alcoholism, as defined in the revised third edition of the *Diagnostic and Statistical Manual of Mental Disorders (DSM-III-R*; American Psychiatric Association, 1987, is divided into two categories: alcohol abuse and alcohol dependence. These categories, with minor changes in definition, are continued in the fourth edition of the *DSM* (*DSM-IV*; American Psychiatric Association, 1994). The identification of alcohol abuse and dependence in the same sample of patients using *DSM-III-R* versus proposed *DSM-IV* criteria was compared in a large representative national sample; the identifications were found to be highly correlated, with kappas exceeding .94 for both abuse and dependence (B. F. Grant et al., 1992). In a second study comparing the *DSM-III-R* and final *DSM-IV* criteria in a smaller and more diverse sample, Hasin and Grant (1994) reported kappas in the mid-.80s for agreement on the diagnosis of alcohol abuse or dependence. For practical purposes, either of the two editions may be used as a guide for diagnosis, although the more recent *DSM-IV* obviously is preferred.

There are four major categories of organic mental disorders associated with chronic alcohol abuse (as well as other psychoactive substances): withdrawal syndrome, delirium, dementia, and the amnestic syndrome (American Psychiatric Association, 1987, 1994). The first two categories are essentially medical problems that require immediate medical treatment. The majority of alcoholic individuals have clinically manifested withdrawal symptoms (e.g., tremors, weakness, irritability, sweating, sleep disturbances, etc.) ranging from mild to severe, which gradually subside and disappear in 5–7 days. A relatively small percentage of patients develop d.t.'s, but it is a life-threatening disorder with an estimated morbidity of 5%–15%. Neuropsychological assessment of the patients with d.t.'s or in the withdrawal state is not usually requested. However, practitioners should know that subclinical withdrawal changes may persist for several weeks in some patients (Begleiter & Porjesz, 1979).

After the withdrawal syndrome has cleared, as many as 10% of other detoxified patients may exhibit cognitive changes typical of dementia or the amnestic disorder (Horvath, 1975), both of which are diagnosable organic mental disorders. The remaining 90% do not meet the clinical criteria for an organic mental disorder, but 50–85% of them will manifest some mild-to-moderate impairment on neurocognitive tests compared with nonalcoholic peers (Parsons, 1986). Clinical researchers have long recognized the existence of this group of patients. Bennett, Mowery, and Fort (1960) suggested that these patients fall in an intermediate stage of alcoholic brain disease. I. Grant, Adams, and Reed (1987) proposed that a new diagnostic category be added for such patients: the intermediate duration (subacute) organic mental disorder of alcoholism. Regardless of whether this proposed diagnostic category is ever formally adopted, it does call attention to a majority of detoxified and abstinent alcoholic individuals. I refer to this group as "intermediate-stage" alcoholics.

BRAIN CHANGES ASSOCIATED WITH ALCOHOLISM

Although it is well-known that protracted alcohol abuse may affect any body organ deleteriously (USDHHS, 1990, 1993), the effects on the brain are of the greatest interest to neuropsychologists and other practitioners. Evidence of changes in brain structure and function has come from studies ranging from gross morphology to those at the molecular level. Perhaps the most directly relevant studies are those in neuropathology, electrophysiology, computed tomography (CT), magnetic resonance (MR) imaging, positron emission tomography (PET), and cerebral blood flow (CB).

The most systematic investigations of the brain changes in alcoholic amnestic disorder and alcoholic dementia were conducted by Victor, Adams, and Collins (1971). They found that the autopsy results of individuals with either diagnosis showed lesions of the Wernicke–Korsakoff type (i.e., neuropathological changes in the mammillary and dorsal–medial nucleus of the thalamus). Butters and Salmon (1986) suggested that changes in the basal frontal cortex, particularly in the nucleus basalis of Meynert, one of the primary sites for the production of cortical acetylcholine, also may be present. Thus, these two organic mental disorders in detoxified alcoholic patients have a clear neuropathological basis.

Brain changes in intermediate-stage alcoholics have been summarized recently by Harper and Kril (1993). Autopsy results showed that the brains of such alcoholic individuals, when compared with nonalcoholic peers, had a lower brain weight, lower white-matter volume, a reduction in the basal dendritic arbor of Layer III pyramidal neurons in the superior frontal and motor cortices, and significantly greater ventricular size.

Results of numerous CT scans of the brain have confirmed the presence of enlarged ventricles and sulci in the brains of alcoholic patients compared with nonalcoholic peers (Bergman, 1987; USDHHS, 1990; Wilkinson, 1987; Zakhari & Witt, 1992). MR imaging studies of chronic alcoholic patients also confirm these findings and add additional information (Pfefferbaum, Lim, & Rosenbloom, 1992). Jernigan, Butters, and Cermak (1992) compared the MR images of the brains of alcoholic and nonalcoholic individuals. They concluded that the alcoholic patients had increased cerebral spinal fluid in the ventricles and sulci attributable to the reduced volume of the adjacent gray matter of the diencephalon, basal ganglia, and cerebral cortex. Increased white-matter abnormalities also were noted in the alcoholic patients.

In addition to these structural changes, abnormalities in brain function have been noted. PET scan studies of alcoholic patients indicated lowered brain metabolism throughout the brain, as measured by glucose uptake (Sachs, Russell, Christman, & Cook, 1987). Electrophysiological investigations, using measures such as event-related potentials also have shown changes suggestive of increased latencies and reduced amplitudes of brain wave responses to visual and auditory stimuli (Parsons, Sinha, & Williams, 1990; Porjesz & Begleiter, 1987). These findings are similar to those found in other groups with brain dysfunction, although to a lesser degree.

It is clear that intermediate-stage alcoholics as a group manifest many abnormalities in brain structure and function compared with nonalcoholic peers. Note, however, that these results are based on comparisons of groups of participants and that there is considerable variability among alcoholic individuals in the degree to which they manifest a given abnormal finding.

NEUROPSYCHOLOGICAL FUNCTIONING IN ALCOHOLICS: ORGANIC MENTAL DISORDERS

There are only a few clinical studies of alcoholic dementia (Carlen et al., 1994). Such patients meet the usual *DSM-II-R* or *DSM-IV* criteria for dementia (chaps. 3 and 4 in this book). By contrast, there are several investigations of the amnestic syndrome. Therefore, the latter is the focus here. The classic symptom in amnestic alcoholic patients is the striking inability to form new memories (anterograde amnesia). Victor et al. (1971) reported that their 245 patients also manifested many other deficits, such as retrograde amnesia (loss of past memories), mild impairment of perceptual and conceptual functions, and diminution in initiative and spontaneity.

Talland (1965) was one of the first psychologists to intensively and extensively study the performance of patients with Korsakoff's amnesia on tests of verbal, perceptual, perceptual–motor, motor, associative learning, immediate and remote memory, concept formation, set shifting, and so on. Compared with healthy control subjects, patients with Korsakoff's amnesia differed from control subjects on most cognitive functions, especially memory, but they did not differ from control subjects on scores on the Wechsler-Bellevue Intelligence Scale. Butters and Cermak (1980) also found that patients with Korsakoff's amnesia scored in the normal range of intelligence but that their scores on the Wechsler Memory Scale (WMS) were much below the norms for their intelligence level. Interestingly, their patients could remember strings of digits or words at the normal control level, but any delay period before the recall, especially if the delay period (e.g., 9 s) was filled with another task, gave rise to severe impairment.

Does the memory impairment in patients with Korsakoff's amnesia account for their impaired concept formation and set-shifting performance? Janowsky, Shimamura, Kritchevsky, and Squire (1989) and Joyce and Robbins (1991) investigated this question, and they found that it does not. Both areas of cognitive functioning are impaired in patients with Korsakoff's amnesia, but the deficits are not causally related.

In recent studies, mainly from Butters's laboratory, a series of systematic comparisons of patients with Korsakoff's amnesia and patients with Alzheimer's, Huntington's, and Parkinson's diseases have been conducted (Heindel, Salmon, & Butters, 1993). Patients with Korsakoff's amnesia performed more similarly to patients with Alzheimer's disease than they did to patients with Huntington's disease on tests of verbal and figural memory, verbal list learning, letter fluency (perseverative errors), and pursuit-rotor learning. Unlike patients with Alzheimer's disease, patients with Korsakoff's amnesia manifested intact implicit memory during a lexical priming task and several similar tasks. (The term *implicit memory* refers to performance benefits resulting from previous experience on a given task, despite the patient's inability to explicitly recall the experience.)

In summary, patients with Korsakoff's amnesia are typically placed in the amnestic disorder diagnostic category because of their profound and explicit (verbalizable recall) memory problems. However, they manifest many of the cognitive deficits found in the dementias, such as the Alzheimer's type.

NEUROPSYCHOLOGICAL FUNCTIONING IN INTERMEDIATE-STAGE ALCOHOLIC INDIVIDUALS

Over the past several decades, there have been numerous reviews of neuropsychological functioning in detoxified intermediate-stage alcoholic patients (Parsons, 1987; Parsons & Nixon, 1993). Typically, these studies have been conducted on detoxified alcoholic patients, sober for 2–4 weeks, who are in treatment programs and who do not have other medical disorders that could affect brain functioning. Their performance on neuropsychological tests is then compared with age- and education-equated groups of nonalcoholic control peers. The consensus of such reviews is that sober alcoholic patients manifest a mild-to-moderate impairment on tests measuring memory and learning, abstracting and problem solving, perceptual–spatial abilities, perceptual–motor speed, and information-processing speed. Verbal abilities, such as those measured by the Wechsler Adult Intelligence Scale–Revised (WAIS-R; Wechsler, 1981), usually fall within normal limits. However, if tests of verbal problem solving or more demanding tests of verbal abstracting abilities are given, alcoholic patients perform significantly more poorly than do nonalcoholic control peers (Yohman & Parsons, 1987).

Given these conclusions, several questions arise that are of interest to practitioners. How was the conclusion that alcoholic patients manifest a "mild-to-moderate impairment" determined? Is there a typical pattern of test results? Do the neuropsychological test results suggest a specific model of brain dysfunction? What is the course of recovery of neuropsychological functions (i.e., how long the impairment persists)? Do the neuropsychological test results obtained during the treatment program predict resumption of drinking?

DETERMINATION OF THE DEGREE OF IMPAIRMENT

There are four studies that have helped to establish the degree of impairment in alcoholic individuals. Each of these studies compared groups of sober alcoholic individuals, age- and education-matched medically diagnosed patients with brain damage, and nonalcoholic control peers. All of the researchers used the Halstead–Reitan Neuropsychological Test Battery (HRNTB), which is widely recognized as a highly reliable and valid battery of neuropsychological tests (Reitan & Wolfson, 1993), and all had samples of 30 or more participants in each group. The groups with brain damage had mild-to-severe impairment.

Fitzhugh, Fitzhugh, and Reitan (1965) found that their alcoholic respondents performed significantly more poorly than did the control group and more similarly to the group with brain damage. Jones and Parsons (1971) found that their alcoholic patients and their patients with mild-to-moderate brain damage had similar levels of performance on the Halstead Category test, one of the more brain-sensitive tests from the HRNTB, and that both groups of patients scored more poorly than did the control group. Using 18 measures derived from the HRNTB, Miller and Orr (1980) reported that alcoholic patients and those with brain damage did not differ in performance levels on 17 of the 18 measures but that both patient groups differed on the 18 measures from the control group. Goldstein and Shelly (1982) compared patients with diffuse brain damage with alcoholic patients on the HRNTB as well as other tests; the two groups performed similarly, and the HRNTB overall impairment index fell in the moderate-to-severely impaired range. Considering all of these results, the conclusion is clear: Sober alcoholic individuals who are tested after withdrawal symptoms have subsided manifest impairment on neuropsychological tests equivalent to that of patients with mild-to-moderate impairment and, in some cases, to those with severe brain damage.

NEUROPSYCHOLOGICAL AND COGNITIVE MODELS OF THE DEFICITS

In one of the first papers from our laboratories, Jones and Parsons (1971) suggested that the pattern of neuropsychological impairment obtained in studies comparing alcoholic and nonalcoholic participants could be consistent with any one of three hypotheses. According to the first hypothesis, the functions subserved by the right hemisphere are more vulnerable to the toxic effect of alcohol than are those of the left hemisphere. This hypothesis was based on the consistent findings of greater impairment on perceptual–spatial tasks than on verbal tasks, such as found on the Wechsler Verbal scales (Parsons & Farr, 1981). According to the second hypothesis, the frontal lobes are more susceptible to alcohol's effects than are other brain regions. This hypothesis was developed because of the difficulties alcoholic patients had on problem-solving and abstracting tasks, such as on the Wisconsin Card Sorting Task (WCST; Tarter & Parsons, 1971), and the clinical observations that many alcoholic patients fail to benefit from their experiences in a manner similar to that of patients with frontal lobe damage.

In the third hypothesis, the deficits are due to a mild generalized dysfunction of the brain. This hypothesis was based on the possibility that the apparent resiliency of the verbal functions to alcohol's toxic effects might be a function of the type of tasks used (e.g., the Wechsler Verbal subtests). The latter might be tapping overlearned verbal skills within a language system and thus would be less vulnerable than the more novel perceptual–spatial tasks mediated by the right hemisphere or the abstracting and executive skills mediated by the frontal lobes.

These hypotheses have been tested in several different experiments and by many different investigators. In light of the evidence, especially that of alcoholic patients' impairment on verbal problem-solving tests (Yohman & Parsons, 1987), it has been concluded (Parsons & Nixon, 1993; USDHHS, 1974) that the mild generalized brain dysfunction hypothesis, with some qualifications, best fits the data. This hypothesis suggests that alcoholism results in a mild-to-moderate generalized dysfunction characterized by a variable pattern of impairment. The latter depends on the characteristics of the tasks used and individual differences in cognitive–perceptual functions.

Two cognitive models of alcoholic patients' neuropsychological deficits have been proposed. Barron and Russell (1992), using Cattell's (1963) model of fluid versus crystallized abilities, pointed out that alcoholic patients' deficits are most clearly found on tests that involve the fluid abilities of abstracting, problem solving, and so on, as opposed to the crystallized overlearned functions such as vocabulary, and so on. However, this model does not account for alcoholic patients' impaired perceptual–motor performance and the recent evidence that they take significantly longer to perform all types of tasks (both fluid and crystallized) than do nonalcoholic individuals (Glenn & Parsons, 1992).

A second, more limited cognitive model has been proposed by Nixon and Parsons (1991). Recognizing that abstracting and problem-solving functions are typically impaired in sober alcoholic patients, Nixon and Parsons assumed that these functions are performed in knowledge memory as defined by Tariot and Weingartner (1986). Knowledge memory comprises the processes of access, availability, and efficiency. The term *access* refers to a person's ability to extract information from memory. *Availability* is defined as the persistence of information over time. *Efficiency*, in this model, is the effective use of accurate information while ignoring irrelevant, inaccurate, or interfering information. An initial test of the model provided support for the prediction that alcoholic patients are less efficient than nonalcoholic individuals in solving an ecologically valid task (Nixon & Parsons, 1991). Further tests of this model are necessary before its explanatory power can be assessed.

RECOVERY OF NEUROPSYCHOLOGICAL FUNCTIONS IN ALCOHOLIC PATIENTS

Before discussing recovery of neuropsychological functioning in alcoholic patients, I thought it important to recognize that alcoholic patients manifest significant psychological disturbance both during treatment and for some time after discharge and that this can be related to outcome. For example, the presence of a dual diagnosis (alcohol dependence plus another psychiatric diagnosis) can significantly increase recidivism (Moos, Mertens, & Brennan, 1994).

DeSoto and his colleagues (DeSoto, O'Donnell, Allred, & Lopes, 1985; DeSoto, O'Donnell, & DeSoto, 1989) conducted a cross-sectional and then a longitudinal study of the posttreatment psychological adjustment of members of Alcoholics Anonymous using the Brief Symptom Inventory (BSI; Derogatis & Spencer, 1982). The BSI is a refinement of the Symptom Check List (Derogatis, 1977), a widely used inventory of established reliability and validity, and measures nine primary psychiatric symptom groupings (e.g., anxiety, depression, hostility, somatization, etc.). The BSI also contains an overall measure of the severity of symptoms or pathology: the Global Severity Index (GSI). The results from both studies indicated that in the first several months after treatment, GSI scores were the highest and in the range of psychiatric inpatients. Scores dropped sharply at around 3 years but remained significantly higher than those of control patients; scores then dropped more gradually at about 7 years but were still mildly elevated but within the range of control patients. The obvious conclusion is that it can take years for the psychological disturbance in alcoholic patients to resolve.

What is found in the neuropsychological studies? Both cross-sectional and longitudinal studies of the neuropsychological functioning in alcoholic patients have been done. The results of the two largest cross-sectional studies suggest that there is improvement in functioning over a 4- to 5-year period. Brandt, Butters, Ryan, and Bayog (1983) found that a group of recovering alcoholic patients who had been sober for 5 or more years (long-term group) had significantly better scores than did 1- to 2-month-abstinent alcoholic patients (short-term group) on measures of short-term memory, delayed visual–spatial memory, and psychomotor speed. However, on a symbol–digit paired-associates learning task and an embedded figures perceptual task, both the long- and short-term recovery groups had impaired performance. The performance of alcoholic patients who had been abstinent for 1–3 years fell in between that of the long- and short-term recovery groups on all tests.

Fabian and Parsons (1983) compared 4-year-abstinent with 1-month-abstinent alcoholic women and nonalcoholic control peers. The 1-month-abstinent group was significantly impaired compared with control peers; the 4-year-sober group performed significantly better than did the 1-month-sober group and scored at or nearly at the level of the control group on individual tests, including many tests from the HRNTB. However, on an overall average measure of performance, the 4-year-sober group performed significantly lower than did the control group but significantly higher than did the 1-month-sober group. Thus, the results of cross-sectional studies suggest that improvement does occur with continued abstinence but that the process may be a slow one, extending over 4–5 years (or longer).

Longitudinal studies of the same patients, tested and retested, would provide a more definitive test, provided that a comparison nonalcoholic control group were also followed. In a review of studies meeting this criterion, Parsons and Leber (USDHHS, 1974) found seven that followed patients for 1–4 years. In five of the seven studies, there was evidence for improved neuropsychological functioning, although some deficits remained. Since that time, I and my colleagues have conducted three studies in which both alcoholic and control groups were tested with a large battery of neuropsychological tests during or at the end of treatment and then 12–18 months later (Fabian & Parsons, 1983; Parsons, Schaeffer, & Glenn, 1990; Yohman, Parsons, & Leber, 1985). The same basic findings emerged in each study. Alcoholic patients performed more poorly than did the control patients at initial testing. Both groups improved significantly, but the alcoholic patients still differed significantly from the control patients at retesting. Finally, the most recent longitudinal study indicated that alcoholic patients who had been sober for 1.8 years still manifested impairments on attention and learning but that those who had been sober for 6.7 years manifested no impairments on the neuropsychological tests (Rourke & Grant, 1995).

Comparing these results with those of the cross-sectional studies and the time course of symptom remission in the studies of DeSoto et al. (1985, 1989), it would appear that gradual improvement in neuropsychological functions can be expected, paralleling the improved psychiatric status, but that the process may be slow. The implications for the practitioner are twofold. First, it is important to obtain a good history of alcohol use or abuse, as well as other drug use, from every patient referred for a neuropsychological assessment. Second, recovering alcoholic patients and their families should be informed that recovery of impaired functions will be gradual and may take several years.

Other observations of relevance to recovery can be made. Alcoholic patients without cognitive changes should be advised that resumption of drinking might well lead to the onset of such changes. Alcoholic patients with cognitive changes should be made aware that resumption of drinking could result in increased cognitive deficits or retard recovery to normal cognitive functioning.

For patients who have cognitive changes, depending on the type of cognitive deficits shown, recommendations about everyday measures to improve functioning can be offered. For example, if, as so frequently happens, alcoholic patients complain of memory problems, the patients can be advised to carry and use a small notebook for recording things to be remembered (e.g., shopping lists, appointments, other events), use mental rehearsal and visual imagery for important things to remember, and practice focusing attention in social situations in which recall may be important (e.g., names of people whom patients have just met). (For a discussion of such techniques, see Wilson, 1987.)

Discussions of broader issues in the recovery and treatment of alcoholic patients can be found in current issues of the leading journals in the field: *Addictive Behaviors, Alcoholism: Clinical and Experimental Research, Archives of General Psychiatry, British Journal of Addiction, International Journal of Addictions, Journal of Studies on Alcohol,* and the *Psychology of Addictive Behaviors.*

PREDICTION OF RESUMPTION OF DRINKING

One question of potential importance for practitioners is whether neuropsychological tests given during or at the end of treatment predict posttreatment drinking status. Studies investigating this question have shown mixed results. The results of four studies showed that alcoholic patients tested during treatment who later resumed drinking performed more poorly than did comparable alcoholic patients who did not resume drinking (Abbott & Gregson, 1981; Fabian & Parsons, 1983; Gregson & Taylor, 1977; Yohman et al., 1985). By contrast, other researchers have found either no relationship between neuropsychological test performance and the resumption of drinking (Donovan, Walker, & Kivlahan, 1987) or an inconsistent one (Eckardt et al., 1988).

In considering these results, Parsons, Schaeffer, and Glenn (1990) suggested that sampling differences with respect to uncontrolled variables known to affect neuropsychological functioning (e.g., depression, anxiety, childhood history of attention deficit and conduct disorders, family history of alcoholism) might contribute to the discordant results. To investigate this possibility, male and female middle-aged alcoholic patients (n = 103) were tested at the end of inpatient treatment and then again an average of 14 months later on the same neuropsychological battery. Seventy-two peer community nonalcoholic men and women tested and retested over the same time interval were in the comparison group. The neuropsychological battery included test clusters of verbal, learning and memory, problem-solving, and perceptual–motor functions. An overall performance measure was derived. Depressive and anxiety symptoms were measured by the Beck Depression Inventory (Beck, 1967) and the State-Trait Anxiety Inventory (Spielberger, Gorsuch, & Lushene, 1970); attention deficit and conduct disorders were assessed with the Hyperkinesis/Minimal Brain Damage Questionnaire (Tarter, McBride, Buonpane, & Schneider, 1977); and family history of alcoholism was measured with a standardized interview.

Alcoholic patients were divided into two groups: resumers, those who had resumed drinking (but only at about one third their pretreatment levels), and abstainers, those who had not. These two groups did not differ in their pretreatment alcohol intake or duration of alcoholism. Their initial and retest standard (T) scores for the overall performance score measure are given in Table 1 (the groups also

TABLE 1

Overall Performance *T* Scores, Means, and Standard Deviations for Resumers, Abstainers, and Control Participants

		Overall performance score[a]			
		Initial test		Retest	
Group	*n*	*M*	*SD*	*M*	*SD*
Resumers	41	46.1	7.04	49.2	5.35
Abstainers	62	49.5	6.75	51.9	6.70
Nonalcoholics	72	52.6	5.73	55.5	5.53

[a]A repeated measures analysis of variance resulted in a significant group effect, $F(2, 172) = 15.0$, $p < .001$, but a nonsignificant Group × Test–Retest interaction, $F(2, 172) = 1.0$, $p = .371$. Duncan's multiple-range tests for significant ($p < .05$) group differences indicated that resumers performed more poorly than abstainers, who performed more poorly than control peers at both initial testing and retesting.

differed significantly on each of the aforementioned clusters). As can be seen, at initial testing the groups who would later become resumers and abstainers differed significantly from each other and from their control nonalcoholic peers. At retesting, the same ordering of results was obtained. Although all three groups improved significantly from testing to retesting, they did so at the same rate.

To determine whether variables such as anxiety, depression, attention deficit and conduct disorders, and family history of alcoholism, in addition to the overall neuropsychological performance score, would predict resumer–abstainer status, scores for these variables were placed in a stepwise multiple regression equation. Three variables were significant predictors (in order of significance): the Beck Depression Inventory, the attention deficit disorder score, and the overall neuropsychological performance score. The combined squared multiple correlation explained 26% of the variance, with the Beck score being the best predictor.

Parsons, Schaeffer, and Glenn (1990) concluded that neuropsychological test performance at the end of treatment clearly differentiated future resumers from abstainers. However, the contributions of depressive symptoms and childhood history of attention deficit disorders to the prediction of resumption status suggest that such variables may play a contributing role. Attention to these variables in the neuropsychological assessment process is both clinically and scientifically important.

NEUROPSYCHOLOGICAL ASSESSMENT OF ALCOHOLIC PATIENTS

Indications for Neuropsychological Assessment

For patients who meet the clinical criteria for alcoholic dementia or amnestic disorder, the major contribution of a neuropsychological assessment is the identification of the neuropsychological functions that are impaired, the severity of impairment, and the implications of these findings for the patient's competency to meet the tasks of everyday living. As indicated earlier, only a small percentage of alcoholic patients fall into those diagnostic categories and, therefore, such assessments are relatively rare. The case is different for the intermediate-stage alcoholic patient.

There is ample evidence in the preceding sections that intermediate-stage alcoholic patients have both biomedical and neuropsychological changes indicative of brain dysfunction. Obviously, one indication for assessment would be whether the alcoholic patient in treatment or posttreatment complains of cognitive difficulties in attention, memory, thinking, spatial difficulties, problem solving, and so on. Alcoholic patients frequently do recognize that they are functioning less effectively in one or more of these areas (Shelton & Parsons, 1987). More commonly, referral for assessment occurs when the treatment team, family, or court suspects that such problems exist. Also, as noted earlier, neuropsychological test performance, at least with our battery, does predict resumption of drinking and may point to other areas of importance in recovery, such as employability (Donovan et al., 1987).

Given the prevalence of alcohol abusers in American society, it is inevitable that a high percentage of patients referred for psychological assessment (other than a neuropsychological one) will have had or have an alcohol problem. If the drinking problem is current or if the person had an alcohol abuse problem within the past 5 years, neuropsychological assessment should be considered. Actually, compared with several decades ago, usage patterns today indicate that such patients are likely to have a polydrug problem. In an unpublished study of alcoholic women in treatment programs who were screened for projects at our center, it was found that in addition to the alcoholism, approximately 38% of the women regularly used stimulants (primarily cocaine and amphetamines) and that 27% used depressants (primarily benzodiazepines). Marijuana was widely used by both groups.

A few researchers have reported neuropsychological deficits in detoxified long-term benzodiazepine users (Golonbok et al., 1988), cocaine abusers (Ardila, Rosselli, & Strumwasser, 1991; Hoff et al., 1991), and polydrug abusers (I. Grant & Judd, 1976). The results of these studies, in addition to the fact that there is a paucity of investigations on the possible additive or interactive effects of the different combinations of drugs and alcohol abuse, suggest that a thorough history of both drug and alcohol usage should be part of the neuropsychological examination.

Neuropsychological Assessment of Alcoholic Patients: Preliminary Considerations

There are a number of recommendations for the neuropsychological assessment of current alcoholic patients, drug abusers, or individuals referred for assessment who may have, or are suspected of having, a history of past alcohol or drug abuse or who are referred for assessment for other reasons.

Considering the latter group first, one of the first steps is to screen for possible alcohol or drug problems. There are several short screening tests for alcohol problems that have demonstrated validity. These tests are listed in Exhibit 1. The CAGE test (Ewing, 1984) is a four-item questionnaire whose acronym stands for felt need to Cut down on drinking, Annoyed by criticism of drinking, Guilty about drinking, and Eye opener (morning drinking). Two or more positive responses are indicative of problem drinking or abuse. The advantages of the CAGE are its brevity and sensitivity, but it has not been shown to be effective in certain populations such as college students, and it focuses on lifetime as opposed to current problems (Chan, Pristach, Welte, & Russell, 1993).

The more recently developed TWEAK scales (the acronym stands for questions about Tolerance, Worry about drinking, Eye opener (morning drinking), Amnesia, K/Cut-down) appears to be more suitable for clinical psychiatric outpatients and the general population (Chan et al., 1993; Russell et al., 1994). As can be seen in Exhibit 1, unlike the CAGE, the questions all were designed to elicit responses of current drinking experiences. Questions 1 and 2 (tolerance) give rise to two alternative forms of the TWEAK: T-1 and T-2. T-1 uses a Question 1 answer of three drinks or more to define tolerance; al-

EXHIBIT 1

Screening Tests for Alcohol Problems

CAGE Test

1. Have you ever felt that you ought to Cut down on your drinking?
2. Have people Annoyed you by criticizing your drinking?
3. Have you ever felt bad or Guilty about your drinking?
4. Have you ever had a drink the first thing in the morning to steady your nerves or get rid of a hangover (Eye opener)?

Score 1 for each positive answer; a score of 2 or more suggests possible alcohol problems

TWEAK Test[a]

1. How many drinks does it take before you begin to feel the first effects of alcohol? (Tolerance 1)
2. How many drinks does it take before the alcohol makes you fall asleep or pass out? Or if you never drink until you pass out, what is the largest number of drinks you have? (Tolerance 2)
3. Have your friends or relatives, worried or complained about your drinking in the past year? (Worried)
4. Do you sometimes take a drink in the morning when you first get up? (Eye opener)
5. Are there times when you drink and afterward you can't remember what you did or said? (Amnesia)
6. Do you sometimes feel the need to cut down on your drinking? (K/Cut down)

See text for scoring.

[a]*From "Use of the TWEAK Test in Screening for Heavy Drinking in Three Populations," by W. K. Chan, E. A. Pristach, J. W. Welte, & M. Russell, 1993,* Alcoholism: Clinical and Experimental Research, 17, *1188–1192. Copyright 1993 by Williams & Wilkins. Reprinted with permission.*

ternatively, the T-2 version uses a Question 2 answer of five or more drinks to define it. A positive answer to either is scored 2; a positive answer to Question 3 is also scored 2; positive answers to the remaining questions are scored 1 each. A score of 3 or more out of the total possible 7 points is considered positive for possible alcohol problems. In comparison with the CAGE and the Brief Michigan Alcoholism Screening Test (Pokorny, Miller, & Kaplan, 1972), using a *DSM-III-R* interview as the "gold standard," the TWEAK scales had higher sensitivity and specificity scores in the outpatient and general population (male and female) samples. For those with positive scores, the scales and procedures mentioned shortly can be applied.

For people suspected of having an alcohol or drug problem, obtaining a valid history may be difficult given that denial is a commonly used defense by alcohol and drug abusers. In this regard, Babor, Stephens, and Marlatt (1987) provided a number of helpful recommendations: assure patients of confidentiality; provide clear descriptions of the assessment tasks and engage patients in the process; encourage patients and provide prompts when they have difficulty recalling past drinking and associated events; and attempt to gather data from other sources, such as significant others or collaterals, to verify patients' self-reports.

In my experience, the problem of obtaining a good history differs depending on the patient's willingness to admit to being an alcoholic or drug abuser. For a patient who is willing to do so, obtaining a good history is mainly a question of whether the patient has a severe memory impairment. For the suspected substance user or abuser who does not admit to being an alcoholic or drug abuser, obtaining a valid history is more difficult; for such patients, the use of collateral sources and biomedical findings is most important.

There are a number of procedures and scales that provide good coverage of this area (see Maisto & Connors, 1990, for a review of them). Typically, these procedures provide information about the frequency of alcohol or drug intake; the amount ingested per day, week, and month; the duration of usage; the temporal gradient of usage (i.e., gradual or abrupt increases); the duration of heavy usage; the year of first usage; the number of blackouts or overdoses; the kinds of alcoholic beverages or drugs used; physiological symptoms of dependence and tolerance; severity of withdrawals; reasons for drinking, and so forth.

One comprehensive standardized interview instrument that covers much of that information is the Comprehensive Drinker Profile by Miller and Marlatt (1984). The Michigan Alcoholism Screening Test (Selzer, 1971) is the most frequently used screening instrument for alcohol problems. It is a 25-item scale with well-established validity that assesses the consequences of alcohol use on social, legal, and physical dimensions. More specialized instruments include the Alcohol Use Inventory–Revised (Horn, Wanberg, & Foster, 1987) and the Alcohol Dependence Scale (Skinner & Allen, 1982; Skinner & Horn, 1984). The Alcohol Use Inventory–Revised measures areas such as the style of drinking, concerns about drinking, the benefits of drinking, and the consequences of drinking, as well as provides a general alcoholism factor. The Alcohol Dependence Scale measures the severity of alcohol dependence (for drug screening questions, see chap. 7, Exhibit 2, in this book).

Of course, a good medical workup, including a neurological examination and neuroimaging studies, would be useful to identify whether any other disorders or conditions may be present that might also affect brain functioning (e.g., previous head trauma, seizures, kidney or liver disease, endocrine dysfunction). In the absence of such a workup, or if the results of the biomedical examination are negative, it is advisible to ask questions to elicit a history of such disorders and conditions (see chap. 7, Exhibit 3, in this book for a listing of such questions).

Another important point is the timing of the assessment with respect to last alcohol or drug usage. For inpatients, a period of at least 2 weeks after the last drink or drug use is the minimum interval before testing; preferably, 3 or 4 weeks of sobriety should elapse. For outpatients, the situation is more complicated. Because these patients may be secretly using drugs or alcohol, a blood or urine screen immediately preceding or following the neuropsychological examination is preferable; at the least, a breathalyzer reading for alcohol should be obtained. If the patient has a significant level of alcohol or drug in his or her system at the time of testing, the interpretation of the results of the assessment is compromised with respect to chronic effects.

If a biomedical screen is not obtained, the neuropsychologist should be alert to any behavioral signs at the time of testing that may suggest the presence of alcohol or drugs, particularly tremulousness, restlessness, nystagmus, dilated or pinpoint pupils, excessive sweating, increased respiration rate, and anxiety (Parsons & Adams, 1983).

Finally, some assessment of the degree of affective and personality disturbance in the alcohol or drug abuser should be made. In our laboratories, for our clinical cases we routinely use the Minnesota Multiphasic Personality Inventory–2 (MMPI-2; Butcher, Dahlstrom, Graham, Tellegen, & Kaemmer, 1989). In our research, we use the Beck Depression Inventory (Beck, 1967) and the State-Trait Anxiety Inventory (Spielberger et al., 1970). The latter two are widely recognized as reliable and valid tests of depression and anxiety, respectively. Depression in particular has been shown to be correlated with neuropsychological performance (Glenn, Errico, Parsons, King, & Nixon, 1993) and with recidivism (Parsons, Schaeffer, & Glenn, 1990).

Is There a Typical Alcoholic Neuropsychological Test Pattern?

Parsons and Farr (1981) examined the results of 15 studies in which the performance of alcoholic patients was compared with control peers on the HRNTB and made a similar examination of seven studies comparing the groups' performance on the WAIS and WAIS-R. They identified 8 out of a total of 19 subtests on which alcoholic patients consistently performed more poorly than did peers. These subtests are listed in Table 2. For the neuropsychologist who uses the HRNTB (it is still the most widely used neuropsychological test battery) and the WAIS-R, these 8 subtests are the ones most likely to reveal performance deficits in alcoholic patients, especially in comparison with the scores on the Verbal IQ subtests of the WAIS and WAIS-R. On these latter subtests, alcoholic patients may perform somewhat more poorly than control peers, but they are typically not significantly impaired. An additional advantage of using this battery is that the four measures from the HRNTB can now be adjusted for age and education according to the norms of Heaton, Grant, and Matthews (1991). These norms also can be used if the four subtests are from the WAIS. If, as is more likely, the WAIS-R subtests will be used, these subtests can be corrected for age on the basis of the national standardization sample.

TABLE 2

Tests on Which Alcoholic Patients Consistently Perform More Poorly Than Control Peers

Measure	Studies in which alcoholic patients perform worse than controls (%)
Halstead–Reitan Neuropsychological Test Battery studies (*n* = 15)	
Category test[a]	87
Tactual Performance Test–Time[a]	80
Trails B[a]	73
Tactual Performance Test–Location[a]	62
Wechsler Adult Intelligence Scale studies (*n* = 7)	
Block Design[a]	100
Object Assembly	86
Digit Symbol[a]	75
Picture Arrangement	71

[a]Tests identified by Reitan and Wolfson (1986) as the best measures of "current problem-solving ability" and the most sensitive tests to brain dysfunction and aging.

If the question for assessment is, Is this alcoholic patient impaired in his or her neuropsychological functioning? then these tests would suffice. However, if the question is, What cognitive functions are impaired? there are some notable gaps in the functions measured by these tests (e.g., tasks that may have a more direct relation to the problems of everyday living such as reaction time, learning, memory, and verbal problem solving).

In the literature since 1981, in addition to the HRNTB, a variety of different neuropsychological tests have been used in studies of alcoholic patients. Many of these studies have been done in our laboratories. In almost every study, alcoholic patients performed more poorly on all tests compared with than control patients. However, in any given study, the test that best discriminated between alcoholic pa-

EXHIBIT 2

Neuropsychological Test Battery for Prediction of Resumption of Drinking

Verbal cluster

WAIS-R Comprehension (Wechsler, 1981)
WAIS-R Information (Wechsler, 1981)
Shipley Institute of Living Scale Vocabulary subtest (Shipley, 1940)

Learning and memory cluster

Wechsler Memory Scale–Logical Memory, Immediate and Delayed (Russell, 1975)
Wechsler Memory Scale–Figural Memory, Immediate and Delayed (Russell, 1975)
Symbol-Digit Paired Associate Test (Ryan & Butters, 1980)
Face-Name Learning Test (Schaeffer & Parsons, 1987)

Problem-solving cluster

Booklet Category Test (DeFillipis, McCampbell, & Rogers, 1979)
Levine Hypothesis Test (Levine, 1966)
Conceptual Level Analogy Test (Willner, 1970)
Shipley Institute of Living Scale Abstracting subtest (Shipley, 1940)
WAIS-R Block Design (Wechsler, 1981)
Word Finding Test (Reitan, 1972)

Perceptual–motor cluster

Grooved Pegboard (Lewis & Rennick, 1979)
Trails A and B (Reitan & Wolfson, 1993)
WAIS-R Digit Symbol (Wechsler, 1981)

WAIS-R = Wechsler Adult Intelligence Scale–Revised.

tients and control patients turned out to be a poor discriminator or even failed to be significant in the next study (Parsons, 1994a). In part, this variability may be due to the reliability of the given test. However, if tests are grouped by either a logical categorization or by factor analysis and averaged by *T* scores or *z* scores, much more reliable measures are obtained (Parsons, 1994b). For example, in the study of resumers and abstainers cited earlier (Parsons, Schaeffer, & Glenn, 1990), there were four logical test clusters, each with three to six individual tests (see Exhibit 2). The test–retest (14 months) reliabilities for the neuropsychological test clusters were .80 or above ($ps < .001$). By contrast, reliabilities for individual tests were .50–.70 (Parsons, 1994b). It is obvious that multiple measures of any given neuropsychological function are preferable.

Recommended Battery of Tests

The following principles have guided the selection of tests: (a) The tests have been shown to discriminate between alcoholic patients and control peers (except verbal tests of crystallized intelligence); (b) the tests have a reasonable set of norms, preferably adjusted when needed, for age, education, and sex; (c) the tests reflect psychological processes that are noted in the clinical or experimental literature to be frequently impaired in alcoholic patients; and (d) the tests can be placed into clusters of neuropsychological functions on the basis of either face validity or factor analyses.

The recommended battery is presented in Exhibit 3. Note that it includes all of the battery in Table 2, except for the WAIS-R Object Assembly and Picture Arrangement tests. Also, I have included several tests

EXHIBIT 3

Recommended Battery for Alcohol and Drug Abusers

Tests of verbal (crystallized) intelligence

WAIS-R Comprehension
WAIS-R Information[a]
WAIS-R Vocabulary[a]
Shipley Institute of Living Scale Vocabulary subtest

Tests of perceptual–motor speed

Simple and choice reaction time
Grooved Pegboard
Trails A and B[a]
WAIS-R Digit Symbol[a]

Tests of learning and memory

California Verbal Learning Test[a]
Face-Name Learning Test
HRNTB TPT–Memory for Location
WMS-R Memory for Paragraphs, Immediate[a]
WMS-R Memory for Paragraphs, Delayed[a]
WMS-R Figural Memory, Immediate[a]
WMS-R Figural Memory, Delayed[a]

Tests of verbal problem solving

Shipley Institute of Living Scale Abstracting subtest[a]
Conceptual Level Analogy Test

Tests of perceptual–spatial problem solving

WAIS-R Block Design[a]
HRNTB Category test[a]
HRNTB TPT–Total Time[a]
Levine Hypothesis Test
Wisconsin Card Sorting Test

References for tests are given in the text. WAIS-R = Wechsler Adult Intelligence Scale–Revised; HRNTB = Halstead–Reitan Neuropsychological Test Battery; TPT = Tactual Performance Test; WMS-R = Wechsler Memory Scale–Revised.
[a]Recommended short battery.

that do not meet the criterion of adequate norms but, on the basis of our clinical research, may contribute significantly to the assessment process. Finally, the battery is not set in stone. Tests should be omitted or added depending on the patient's unique assessment needs, as decided by the neuropsychologist.

In the tests of crystallized intelligence, I have included two measures of vocabulary: the WAIS-R Vocabulary test, the best single indicator of premorbid intelligence on the WAIS-R, and the Shipley Institute of Living Scale Vocabulary subtest (Shipley, 1940). The latter is a well-standardized, 20-item test with a 10-min time limit. Both tests usually show a lack of impairment in alcoholic patients. The WAIS-R Information and Comprehension subtests provide measures of long-term memory and practical verbal problem-solving ability. They provide useful comparisons for the episodic memory tests (memory for specific events) and the nonverbal problem-solving tests in subsequent clusters. All WAIS-R subtests are, of course, well-standardized and their scores can be adjusted for age.

Alcoholic patients have been found to perform all cognitive neuropsychological tests more slowly than control peers (Glenn & Parsons, 1992). Measures of the speed of information processing are recommended in the second cluster in Exhibit 3, tests of perceptual–motor speed. The first test recommended is that of simple and choice reaction time. Slowed reaction times under either condition clearly have implications for driving or working with machines in industry. Unfortunately, although reaction time paradigms are often used in research on organic brain conditions, there is no widely accepted reaction time technique with norms that adjust for age and sex. Until such a technique becomes available, and there are some indications that there may soon be such tests, the reaction time paradigm recommended to AIDs researchers by Butters et al. (1990) should be considered. The remaining perceptual–motor tests—WAIS-R Digit Symbol, Trails A and B, and the

Grooved Pegboard (Lewis & Rennick, 1979)—are all commonly used neuropsychological tests in which the speed of perceptual–motor performance plays a major role. Heaton et al. (1991) provided age- and education-corrected norms for these tests.

Sober alcoholic patients frequently complain of memory and learning problems, and, given the results of many experimental studies, their complaints are justified. In the third cluster, tests of learning and memory, the HRNTB Tactual Performance test (TPT)–Memory for Location, provides a measure of incidental memory for tactually perceived forms placed in a formboard by the blindfolded patient. (The patient is not told that he or she will be asked to draw the location of the forms after completing the test.) Age- and education-adjusted norms are available for this frequently used neuropsychological test (Heaton et al., 1991).

The revised WMS (WMS-R; Wechsler, 1987) logical memory (memory for a paragraph story) and figural memory and immediate and delayed conditions are frequently used tests in assessment. Alcoholic patients perform more poorly on both immediate and delayed conditions on logical and figural memory (Nixon, Kujawski, Parsons, & Yohman, 1987; Wechsler, 1987). Alternatively, the Russell modification of these subtests (Russell, 1975, 1988) can be used. The 1988 modification provides norms adjusted for age and education and may be more useful clinically than the WMS-R until the latter has a larger research base.

The California Verbal Learning Test (Delis, Kramer, Kaplan, & Ober, 1987) is a list-learning task in which the patient has to learn a shopping list of 16 common items over five trials. After an interference trial, recall of the original list is tested. Delayed free recall, cued recall, and recognition trials are given. Measures of learning, interference, learning strategy (clustering semantically related items), immediate and delayed recall, and recognition are obtained. Alcoholic patients are impaired in learning the lists. Norms for age by decade and sex are provided.

The Face-Name Learning Test has been shown in several studies to distinguish between alcoholic and control groups (Becker, Butters, Hermann, & D'Angelo, 1983; Schaeffer & Parsons, 1987). In our studies, we present 12 faces, 6 males and 6 females of middle age, and verbally name each. Alcoholic patients perform more poorly than do control peers in learning the names; alcoholic patients' scores are significantly correlated with their drinking history, in that the more they drink both in quantity and frequency, the poorer their learning scores. Also, alcoholic patients' learning scores are correlated with their therapist's ratings of them in terms of the ability to learn, remember, and plan. Given its ecological validity, it is unfortunate that there are no norms for this test other than those for control groups in each of these studies.

In the tests of verbal problem-solving cluster, two tests are recommended. The Shipley Institute of Living Scale (Shipley, 1940) Abstracting subtest distinguishes alcoholic patients from nonalcoholic control peers (Nixon, Parsons, & Schaeffer, 1988). It is a self-administered scale of 20 items to be completed in 10 min. It then can be combined with the Shipley Vocabulary subtest to get a conceptual quotient. In other words, a fluid reasoning test (abstracting) is compared with a measure of crystallized intelligence (vocabulary). The Conceptual Level Analogy Test, devised by Willner (1970), is constructed to eliminate the solution of the analogy by word association, a problem with most analogy tests. It requires only a fourth-grade level of vocabulary and has been well standardized. It measures analogical reasoning over six levels of difficulty ranging from easy to very hard. It has been shown to be sensitive to central nervous system impairment (Willner & Struve, 1970) and to be impaired in alcoholic patients (Yohman & Parsons, 1987).

In the last cluster in Exhibit 3, tests of perceptual–spatial problem solving, I have listed a number of well-known tests that consistently distinguish between alcoholic patients and nonalcoholic individuals and are commonly used in clinical neuropsychological assessment of patients with brain dysfunction. The HRNTB Category test and TPT–Total Time scores and the WCST Perseveration scores can be adjusted for age and education by using the Heaton et al. (1991) norms. For other WCST-derived measures (e.g., categories completed, number of trials to criterion), Heaton (1981) should be consulted. I have included both the Category test and the WCST because there is only a low correlation, if any, between the two tests. For example, in a factor analysis that was performed on 80 alcoholic patients and 40 control peers, the two tests loaded on different factors (Fabian, Parsons, & Silberstein, 1981). Furthermore, the WCST Response Perseveration score has been useful in identifying frontal lobe as well as generalized, diffuse dysfunction (Heaton, 1981). Perrine (1993) found that WCST scores were associated with attribute identification (i.e., discrimination of relevant features), whereas the Category test was associated more with rule learning (i.e., deduction of classification rules). The two tests clearly measure different aspects of problem solving.

The WAIS-R Block Design subtest, as noted earlier, is one of the more sensitive tests to impairment in alcoholic patients. It also can be corrected for age and education using the norms of Heaton et al. (1991). In our studies it typically loads on the same factor as the Category test and the TPT. The Levine Hypothesis Testing procedure (Levine, 1966) is an ingenious concept identification test in which the patient has to identify the relevant attribute of visually presented stimuli. By reinforcing only occasional trials, the strategy of the patient can be detected (e.g., win–stay and lose–shift) in addition to trials to completion, errors, and so forth. Whether the poor performance is attributable to impaired memory or impaired problem solving independent of memory can be determined. Alcoholic patients and patients with Korsakoff's amnesia perform poorly on this task (Klisz & Parsons, 1977; Oscar-Berman, 1973).

Under certain conditions, other tests might be added to or dropped from this battery, as noted earlier. For example, for alcoholic patients who have a history of head injury severe enough to be hospitalized, the HRNTB Finger Tapping and Sensory Perceptual test may be useful in lateralization (Reitan & Wolfson, 1993) of the effects of that injury. Also, as new tests are developed that clearly measure specific relevant cognitive functions and have adequate norms, they can replace tests in the battery that are less able to meet these criteria. Finally, it is frequently useful to estimate premorbid intelligence on the basis of demographic factors such as education, type of occupation, and so on. Formulas for such estimations are discussed in chapter 2 of this book.

The minimum time for administering the battery in Exhibit 3 is about 4 hr; the maximum time is around 6 hr for a slow-performing patient. The average is about 5 hr. If time is a consideration, the WAIS-R Information and Vocabulary subtests, Shipley Abstracting, WAIS-R Digit Symbol, Trails A and B, California Verbal Learning Test, WMS-R Immediate and Delayed Memory tests, Category test, TPT, and WAIS-R Block Design could be given. This would be approximately a $2^1/_2$- to $3^1/_2$-hr assessment, with at least one test from each of the categories in Exhibit 3, except reaction time, being sampled. This battery would contain six of the eight tests previously found by Parsons and Farr (1981) to be the most consistently differentiating tests between alcoholic patients and control peers.

CASE EXAMPLES

I present three case summaries to illustrate several different aspects of neuropsychological assessment.

Case 1: Mr. A

This case was selected to (a) provide a concrete example of the use of the norms of Heaton et al. (1991); (b) demonstrate the discriminating ability of the HRNTB tests identified by Reitan and Wolfson (1986) as those most sensitive to brain dysfunction; and (c) consider the combined effects of head trauma and alcoholism (in this case, the alcoholism preceded the head trauma).

Mr. A was referred for a neuropsychological examination because of a history of alcoholism and head trauma and periods of disorganization sufficient for hospitalization and inability to carry out his job duties as an accountant. Mr. A was a 58-year-old married White man who had a bachelor's degree in accounting. He had been a heavy beer drinker for about 10 years. Approximately 6 years after starting heavy drinking, he was hospitalized for a blow to the head in the left temporal–parietal region. According to the wife, the neurosurgeon removed bone fragments but told her that there was no damage to the brain. He retired because of physical disability the year thereafter. He resumed drinking and, 4 years later, fell while drunk, hitting his head. According to his wife, there was a crack in his skull from the base to the right eardrum. After several weeks, his behavior became disorganized and he was hospitalized in a psychiatric ward. After he had improved, he was referred to us. The neurological examination results were within normal limits at this time, except for some mild memory problems. The referral question requested information on the patient's strengths and weaknesses regarding possible rehabilitation.

The patient was cooperative and appeared to be trying to do as well as he could. There were no signs of disorganized behavior during the testing session. He was given the tests listed in Table 3.

In the second column, the raw scores on each test are listed; in the third column, the standard scores ($M = 50$, $SD = 10$) based on the Heaton et al. (1991) norms are given. For example, for the second test, TPT–Total Time, there was a raw score of 30 min which gave rise to a standard score of 15. In other words, the patient scored 3.5 standard deviations below the mean for normal performance. Note that the Halstead Impairment Index of 1.0 gave rise to a standard score of 8, or 4.2 standard deviations away from the mean for normal individuals. Of course, using either measure, there is no question that the patient's higher cortical functions were severely impaired. There is, however, obvious variability in the severity of impairment over the various tests, with some test scores falling in the normal range.

One way of assessing this variability is to compare the mean of the six tests that Reitan and Wolfson (1986) identified as the most sensitive to brain dysfunction ($M = 30.3$, mild-to-moderate impairment) with those of the rest of the battery (down to the dotted line); the mean for the latter is 41.1 (below average). There is little doubt that the six tests are much more discriminating. It is also clear that motor, sensory–perceptual, and language functions, as measured respectively by the Finger Tapping test, the Sensory Perceptual test, and Aphasia Screening test, are at the average level. These findings are fairly important because they show that basic sensory and motor functions appear to be intact.

Considering the tests under the dotted line, the Wechsler IQ scores, although in the normal range, are certainly much lower than expected for a person of Mr. A's age and educational level. Applying the Heaton et al. (1991) norms, the Full-Scale IQ resulted in a standard score of 27, 2.3 standard deviations away from the mean and in the moderately impaired range. These analyses confirm the utility of having a resource such as age- and education-corrected norms. Unfortunately, there are no such norms for the original WMS, but the memory quotient of 89 indicated a moderate impairment in view of his educational level. Furthermore, in a within-test analysis (data are not presented in Table 3), he learned only one hard associate out of 12 tries on the WMS Paired Associate test, a grossly impaired performance. Finally, this patient also was given the MMPI; the profile was within normal limits.

TABLE 3

Mr. A's Raw Scores and Standard Scores on the Neuropsychological Battery

Measure	Raw score	Standard score
Halstead–Reitan Neuropsychological Test Battery		
Category test[a]	104	33
TPT–Total Time[a]	30 min	15
TPT–Memory	4	31
TPT–Location[a]	0	34
Seashore Rhythm	23	40
Speech Sounds Perception	11	37
Finger Tapping	48	48
Trails B[a]	170 s	32
WAIS Digit Symbol[a]	6[b]	36
WAIS Block Design[a]	6[b]	32
Aphasia Screening	3	51
Spatial Relations	4	32
Sensory Perceptual Test	6	49
Halstead Impairment Index	1.0	8
Wechsler test		
WAIS Verbal IQ	101	30
WAIS Performance IQ	96	31
WAIS Full-Scale IQ	99	27
Wechsler Memory Scale MQ	89	NA

Note: TPT = Tactual Performance Test; WAIS = Wechsler Adult Intelligence Scale; MQ = memory quotient; NA = not applicable.
[a]Tests most sensitive to brain dysfunction (Reitan & Wolfson, 1986).
[b]Scaled scores.

In summary, although the patient achieved WAIS IQ scores in the normal or average range, the actual scores were decidedly below the norms for a person of his age and educational level. Overall, the neuropsychological tests indicated moderate-to-severe impairment of higher cortical functions, impairment that could not be accounted for by problems in sensory or motor functions. Impairment was greatest in nonverbal problem solving, abstracting, perceptual–motor speed, learning, and memory. This impairment is characteristic of a static, diffuse brain dysfunctional condition and appears to be a product of head trauma and alcoholism. The recommendations were for complete abstinence from all alcohol; a structured work (other than auditing) or hobby experience; counseling for at least 6 months; and, if these recommendations were followed, retesting at 1 year to determine progress.

Case 2: Mr. B

This case illustrates the value of expanding the test battery to include tests such as the California Verbal Learning Test, the Continuous Visual Memory Test, WMS-R, and the Shipley Institute of Living Scale. In contrast to Mr. A, Mr. B's head trauma preceded his alcoholism. Mr. B was a White married veteran with 12 years of education who was seen at the Oklahoma City Veterans Administration (VA) Medical Center on two occasions: when he was 39 and 44 years of age. While in the military, Mr. B was in an automobile accident that resulted in a penetrating injury to the left frontal lobe, a period of unconsciousness for 2 weeks, and a year of hospitalization. He began to suffer from grand mal-type seizures, which occurred once a month despite attempts to control them with medication. Over the years, he gradually increased his drinking to the alcoholic level. Approximately 17 years after the onset of seizures, he came to the VA hospital for treatment on the alcohol ward. He was given a neuropsychological test battery (by William Leber, to whom I am indebted for permission to use these results). The patient was noted to be cooperative and hardworking. The tests administered at the first admission are listed in Table 4.

In the absence of the complete WAIS-R, the Shipley Institute of Living Scale was used to estimate intelligence. As can be seen in Table 4, the estimated Full-Scale IQ was 102. Verbal abstracting ability was relatively preserved (109) compared with vocabulary (91). The Halstead Impairment Index of 0.7 and its corresponding standard score of 27 placed him at a moderate level of impairment. Again, there was considerable variability in the scores. The mean standard score for the six brain-sensitive tests was 33.8 (mild-to-moderate impairment) compared with 41 (below average) for the other three tests that have standard scores. The WMS, as modified by Russell (1975), gave rise to nonimpaired scores for immediate and delayed figural memory, but severe impairment for both immediate and delayed logical memory. Leber noted that the patient's perseverative tendencies caused him to obtain lower scores on timed tests.

Overall, he performed poorly on the tests of nonverbal abstracting and problem-solving abilities. When coupled with his moderate impairment in logical memory, relatively low vocabulary, and perseverative tendencies, the results were considered consistent with the history of left frontal lobe injury. Alcoholism was considered to be a secondary factor.

Five years later, Mr. B was seen for a second time. During the interim period, his seizures were better controlled; he stated he had not had one for a year. He had several jobs during this period, but he usually quit them after arguing with his boss. His wife stated that when he drank, he became verbally and physically aggressive. She also reported that he had severe memory problems and difficulty in finding his way around. He had, however, done small-engine repair, which he liked, coached soccer, and taken his children for hikes in the woods and fishing.

Mr. B had two hospitalizations for alcoholism in his recent past, with the last one being at the VA medical center. At that time, he was again given a neuropsychological examination that included a number of different tests. The results are listed in Table 5.

On the four tests that were administered at both sessions, Mr. B improved on two (Trails B and Digit Symbol), stayed the same on Block Design, and performed significantly lower on Finger Tapping. In this testing, the full WAIS-R was given. The Verbal and

TABLE 4

Mr. B's First Testing: Raw Scores and Standard Scores on the Neuropsychological Battery

Measure	Raw score	Standard score	Russell norm
Halstead–Reitan Neuropsychological Test Battery			
Category test[a]	80	32	
TPT—Total Time[a]	24.3 min	17	
TPT—Memory	6	34	
TPT—Location[a]	2	39	
Seashore Rhythm	21	35	
Speech Sounds Perception	10	35	
Finger Tapping	55	53	
Trails B[a]	129 s	33	
Halstead Impairment Index	.7	27	
WAIS-R Block Design[a]	10[b]	44 (estimate)	
WAIS-R Digit Symbol[a]	6[b]	34	
Wechsler Memory Scale[c]			
Logical Memory–Immediate	12		4
Logical Memory–Delayed	7		4
Figural Memory–Immediate	11		1
Figural Memory–Delayed	9		1
Shipley Institute of Living Scale			
Vocabulary estimated IQ	91		
Abstracting estimated IQ	109		
Estimated IQ	102		

Note: TPT = Tactual Performance Test; WAIS-R = Wechsler Adult Intelligence Scale–Revised.
[a]Tests most sensitive to brain dysfunction (Reitan & Wolfson, 1986).
[b]Scaled scores.
[c]Norms for Russell's (1975) modification of the Wechsler Memory Scale range from 0 (*not impaired*) to 5 (*severely impaired*).

Full-Scale IQs of 87 and 94, respectively, were similar to the Shipley estimates of 91 and 102 of the previous testing when the fact that the WAIS estimates IQs 4–7 points higher than the WAIS-R. Mr. B also improved his performance on the WMS in that on the revised version, his immediate logical memory was in the normal range and his delayed memory was not as impaired as on first testing. On the other hand, his performance on figural memory was poorer, especially on delayed memory.

The California Verbal Learning Test, however, gave rise to the most severe impairment scores. His learning score over five trials was 3.3 standard deviations below the mean for normal individuals. Similarly, both short and long delay and free and cued recall scores were 3–5 standard deviations below the mean, averaging in the severely impaired range. On the Continuous Visual Memory Test, a memory recognition test, he consistently scored in the lowest fifth percentile and had a very high false-alarm score.

On his other tests, surprisingly, his WCST Perseveration score was only 0.7 standard deviations below average. Individuals with left frontal lobe damage typically score lower on this measure. The Sensory Perceptual score was in the impaired range. There were twice as many errors on the right side than on the left (data are not presented in Table 5),

TABLE 5

Mr. B's Retesting Results

Measure	Raw score	Standard score	z score or percentile[a]
Halstead–Reitan Neuropsychological Test Battery			
Finger Tapping	46	38	
Trails B	91 s	44	
Sensory Perceptual	21	30	
Aphasia Screening	13	33	
WAIS-R[b]			
Verbal IQ	87	—	
Performance IQ	93	—	
Full-Scale IQ	94	—	
Block Design	10	46[c]	
Digit Symbol	7	40	
Wisconsin Card Sorting Test			
Perseveration Responses	22	43	
California Verbal Learning Test			
List A Trails 1–5	33		−3.3
List A Trail 1	5		−2.0
List A Trail 5	6		−5.0
List B	7		0.0
List A Short Delay Recall	4		−4.0
List A Short Delay Cued Recall	4		−4.0
List A Long Delay Recall	4		−3.0
List A Long Delay Cued Recall	3		−5.0
Continuous Visual Memory Test			
Hits	34		5%
False-alarms	28		99%
A Prime	83		<2%
Total	60		<1%
Delay Recognition	2		4%
Wechsler Memory Scale–Revised			
Logical Memory–Immediate	28		59%
Logical Memory–Delayed	16		27%
Figural Memory–Immediate	32		40%
Figural Memory–Delayed	20		13%

Note: TPT = Tactual Performance Test; WAIS-R = Wechsler Adult Intelligence Scale–Revised.
[a]In the California Verbal Learning Test, *z* scores are standard deviations away from the mean; percentile scores are used in the Continuous Visual Memory Test.
[b]Heaton, Grant, and Matthews's (1991) norms are based on the WAIS. However, the Digit Symbol test was not changed on the WAIS-R; therefore, the WAIS score could be used for the standard score. The Block Design test was changed; therefore, the standard score was estimated.
[c]Estimate.

suggesting left-hemisphere sensory–perceptual dysfunction. Consistent with this interpretation was the impaired Aphasia Screening score.

Finally, Mr. B's MMPI results showed significant distress and anxiety, with elevated depression, low ego strength, mild-to-moderate social isolation, and emotional isolation.

In summary, in this retesting, which used a greatly expanded battery, Mr. B was found to have improved in some areas of his functioning and to have maintained his overall level of general intelligence. However, the new tests that were administered clearly indicated that severe problems remained in verbal learning and memory as well as visual memory, especially in delayed recall. Mild aphasic problems and impaired sensory–perceptual performance suggested left-hemisphere dysfunction. Significant depression was present. The role of the latter in the learning and memory problems Mr. B exhibited is difficult to specify but should be considered.

In this case, the alcoholism was subsequent to a left frontal lobe injury and undoubtedly played a role in his overall pattern of neuropsychological functioning. It was difficult to attribute all of the widespread indications of neuropsychological impairment to a circumscribed lesion in the left frontal lobe. Recommendations for the patient were that he should stop drinking alcohol completely (the patient said that drinking alcohol helped prevent seizures). Marital or family therapy directed at educating all members about the organic etiology of much of his problematic behavior should be undertaken. He also was advised to maintain high levels of activity in current and previous behaviors, such as coaching soccer, small-engine repair, and recreational pursuits.

Case 3: Mr. C

This patient's case illustrates the problems in interpreting the results of neuropsychological examination of minority patients, especially when complicated by the presence of depression. Mr. C was a 59-year-old married Black man who was left-handed and had 8 years of education in a segregated school. He had worked as a concrete finisher for most of his life. He had a history of alcohol use since the age of 16. Prior to admission to the VA medical center, he had been drinking about a pint of whiskey a day for years. He had been arrested and charged with driving under the influence of alcohol and sought treatment as a result. He was referred for a neuropsychological examination by the alcohol and drug treatment team to assess his present level of functioning and determine whether there was alcohol-related cognitive impairment.

The patient was dressed neatly, cooperative, alert, oriented, but moderately depressed. The neuropsychological test results are listed in Table 6. (Again, I am indebted to William Leber for permission to use these results.)

Mr. C's WAIS-R scores were at the borderline level of intellectual functioning. Adjusting for his age and educational level, this gave him standard scores in the moderate-to-severe impairment range. However, these scores were probably an underestimate of his abilities, given the poorer educational programs in the segregated school of his day.

The mean standard score on the motor and perceptual–motor tests (Trails B, Finger Tapping, Grooved Pegboard, and Digit Symbol) was 27, a score that indicates moderate impairment. On the other hand, the WCST Perseveration Response score was within normal limits, as were his short- and long-term delayed recall and cued recall on the California Verbal Learning Test. Nevertheless, significant learning and memory problems were present, as indicated by the California Verbal Learning Test Total Correct score and the Recognition score, both of which are in the moderate-to-severe range of impairment. Similarly, on the WMS he scored in the moderately impaired range for immediate and delayed logical and figural recall.

Mr. C's MMPI-2 scores indicated that it was taken validly. His profile showed significant elevations on Scales 1, 2, 3, 7, and 8 and a significant lowering of Scale 9. The profile indicated an acute depressive state with considerable tension and anxiety, low self-esteem, and the biological concomitants of low energy level, sleep disturbance, reduced appetite, and depressive rumination. The depressive symptomatology was severe enough that it certainly could have accounted for a significant degree of the impairment in Mr. C's performance, especially in motor speed and memory.

In summary, although Mr. C performed at a moderate-to-moderately severe level on many of the test measures, there were two major complicating factors in interpreting these results. The first was that he was a member of a minority group who, when he was attending school, was segregated and provided with a poorer education. Second, he was in an acute depressive state, one that could have affected his performance on many neuropsychological tests, especially those involving motor, perceptual–motor speed, or memory. The recom-

TABLE 6

Mr. C's Raw Scores and Standard Scores on the Neuropsychological Test Battery

Measure	Raw score	Standard score	z score
Halstead–Reitan Neuropsychological Test Battery			
Trails B[a]	247 s	35	−1.5
Finger Tapping	16	13	−2.7
Aphasia Screening	15	40	−1.0
WAIS-R			
Digit Symbol[a]	2[b]	39	−1.1
Block Design[a]	4[b]	30	−2.0
Verbal IQ	78	28	−2.2
Performance IQ	70	23	−2.7
Full-Scale IQ	74	24	−2.6
Grooved Pegboard	200 s	21	−2.9
Wisconsin Card Sorting Test			
Perseverative Response	21	58	0.8
California Verbal Learning			
List A, 1–5 Total	35		−3.2
List A, 1	6		0.0
List A, 5	8		−2.0
List B	1		−3.0
List A, Short Delay Free Recall	7		−1.0
List A, Short Delay Cued Recall	9		−1.0
List A, Long Delay Free Recall	8		−1.0
List A, Long Delay Cued Recall	8		−1.0
Recognition hits	10		−3.0
Wechsler Memory Scale[c]			
Logical Memory–Immediate Recall	12		3.75
Logical Memory–Delayed Recall	11		2.75
Figural Memory–Immediate Recall	4		3.5
Figural Memory–Delayed Recall	3		3.5

Note: WAIS-R = Wechsler Adult Intelligence Scale–Revised.
[a]Tests most sensitive to brain dysfunction (Reitan & Wolfson, 1986).
[b]Scaled scores.
[c]The score for the Wechsler Memory Scale variables are from Russell's (1988) revised norms; scores range from 0 (*not impaired*) to 6 (*severely impaired*).

mendation was for immediate treatment of the depression and alcoholism. Follow-up in 6 months was advised. If the depression treatment regime were to be successful, a better estimate of any residual deficits in neuropsychological functioning should be obtained.

SUMMARY

Alcohol and drug abuse continue to be major problems in Western society. The neuropsychological deficits associated with alcohol abuse, the most commonly abused drug, have been thoroughly studied over the past 3 decades and provide a useful context for discussing the research findings and problems in assessing patients with alcohol and drug problems. The etiology of alcoholism is multiply determined with biopsychosocial factors, including genetics, all of which play a role. About 10% of alcoholic patients eventually meet the criteria for organic mental disorder, such as dementia or amnestic syndrome, and have well-documented brain changes. The remaining 90% have brain changes of a less severe but significant nature. Alcoholic patients perform more poorly than nonalcoholic peers on neuropsychological tests measuring memory and learning, abstracting and problem solving, perceptual–spatial abilities, perceptual–motor speed, and information-processing speed. The level of performance is similar to that of patients with mild-to-moderate brain damage and is of a generalized or diffuse nature.

Recovery of cognitive functions in alcoholic patients who remain sober appears to be one of slow improvement over a period of several years. Neuropsychological performance measured at the end of treatment in our studies has predicted resumption of drinking months later (i.e., resumers have poorer neuropsychological performance than abstainers).

Neuropsychological assessment should include a thorough interview about the history of alcohol and drug usage, with particular attention given to any other medical condition that could affect brain function (e.g., head trauma, possible HIV infection, etc.). Blood screens for drugs before testing, particularly in outpatients, should be used. Some assessment of the patient's affective state should be made.

Neuropsychological tests that, over several decades, have consistently distinguished between alcoholic and control patients are the Category test, TPT–Total Time and TPT–Memory for Location, Trails B, and Block Design and Digit Symbol. However, for a more comprehensive assessment, clusters of a number of additional tests are recommended. These clusters measure verbal (crystallized) abilities, learning and memory performance, perceptual–motor speed, verbal problem solving, and perceptual–spatial problem-solving functions. Case examples indicate how the recently developed norms for various tests can be used to gain a better appreciation for the nature and severity of the neuropsychological changes in alcoholic patients.

References

Abbott, M. W., & Gregson, R. A. M. (1981). Cognitive dysfunction in the prediction of relapse in alcoholism. *Journal of Studies on Alcohol, 43*, 230–243.

American Psychiatric Association. (1987). *Diagnostic and statistical manual of mental disorders* (3rd ed., revised). Washington, DC: Author.

American Psychiatric Association. (1994). *Diagnostic and statistical manual of mental disorders* (4th ed.). Washington, DC: Author.

Ardila, A., Rosselli, M., & Strumwasser, S. (1991). Neuropsychological deficits in chronic cocaine abusers. *International Journal of Neuroscience, 57*, 73–79.

Babor, T. F., Stephens, R. S., & Marlatt, G. A. (1987). Verbal report methods in clinical research on alcoholism: Response bias and its minimization. *Journal of Studies in Alcohol, 48*, 410–424.

Barron, J. H., & Russell, E. W. (1992). Fluidity theory and neuropsychological impairment in alcoholism. *Archives of Clinical Neuropsychology, 7*, 175–188.

Beck, A. T. (1967). *Depression: Clinical, experimental and theoretical aspects.* New York: Harper & Row.

Becker, J. R., Butters, N., Hermann, A., & D'Angelo, N. (1983). Learning to associate names and faces: Impaired acquisition on an ecologically-relevant memory task by male alcoholics. *Journal of Nervous and Mental Disease, 171*, 617–623.

Begleiter, H., & Porjesz, B. (1979). Persistence of a "subacute withdrawal syndrome" following chronic ethanol intake. *Drug and Alcohol Dependence, 4*, 353–357.

Bennett, A. E., Mowery, G. L., & Fort, J. T. (1960). Brain damage from chronic alcoholism: The diagnosis of intermediate stage of alcoholic brain disease. *American Journal of Psychiatry, 116*, 705–711.

Bergman, H. (1987). Brain dysfunction related to alcoholism: Some results from the KARTAD project. In O. A. Parsons, N. Butters, & P. E. Nathan (Eds.), *Neuropsychology of alcoholism: Implications for diagnosis and treatment* (pp. 21–44). New York: Guilford Press.

Blum, K., Noble, E. P., Sheridan, P. J., Montgomery, A., Ritchie, T., & Cohn, J. B. (1990). Allelic association of human dopamine D_2 receptor gene in alcoholism. *Journal of the American Medical Association, 263*, 2055–2060.

Brandt, J., Butters, N., Ryan, C., & Bayog, R. (1983). Cognitive loss and recovery in long-term alcohol abusers. *Archives of General Psychiatry, 40*, 435–442.

Butcher, J. N., Dahlstrom, W. G., Graham, J. R., Tellegen, A., & Kaemmer, B. (1989). *Minnesota Multiphasic Personality Inventory (MMPI-2) manual for administration and scoring.* Minneapolis: University of Minnesota Press.

Butters, N., & Cermak, L. S. (1980). *Alcoholic Korsakoff's syndrome.* San Diego, CA: Academic Press.

Butters, N., Grant, I., Haxby, J., Judd, L. L., Martin, A., McClelland, J., Pequegnat, W., Schacter, D., & Stover, E. (1990). Assessment of AIDS-related cognitive changes: Recommendations of the NIMH Workshop on Neuropsychological Approaches.

Journal of Clinical and Experimental Neuropsychology, 12, 963–978.

Butters, N., & Salmon, D. P. (1986). Etiology and neuropathology of alcoholic Korsakoff's syndrome: New findings and speculations. In I. Grant (Ed.), *Neuropsychological correlates of alcoholism* (pp. 61–108). Washington, DC: American Psychiatric Press.

Cadoret, R. J. (1990). Genetics of alcoholism. In R. L. Collins, K. E. Leonard, & J. S. Searles (Eds.), *Alcohol and the family* (pp. 39–78). New York: Guilford Press.

Carlen, P. L., McAndrews, M. P., Weiss, R. T., Dongier, M., Hill, J.-M., Menzano, E., Forcnik, K., Abarbanel, J., & Eastwood, M. R. (1994). Alcohol-related dementia in the institutionalized elderly. *Alcoholism: Clinical and Experimental Research, 18*, 1130–1134.

Cattell, R. B. (1963). Theory of fluid and crystallized intelligence. *Journal of Educational Psychology, 54*, 1–22.

Chan, W. K., Pristach, E. A., Welte, J. W., & Russell, M. (1993). Use of the TWEAK Test in screening for heavy drinking in three populations. *Alcoholism: Clinical and Experimental Research, 17*, 1188–1192.

Cloninger, C. R. (1987). Neurogenetic adaptive mechanisms in alcoholism. *Science, 236*, 410–436.

DeFillipis, N. A., McCampbell, E., & Rogers, P. (1979). Development of a booklet form of the Category test: Normative and validity data. *Journal of Clinical Neuropsychology, 1*, 339–342.

Delis, D. C., Kramer, J. H., Kaplan, E., & Ober, B. A. (1987). *The California Verbal Learning Test.* New York: Psychological Corporation.

Derogatis, L. R. (1977). *SCL 90: Administration, scoring and procedures manual.* Baltimore: Johns Hopkins University School of Medicine, Clinical Psychometrics Research Unit.

Derogatis, L. R., & Spencer, P. M. (1982). *The Brief Symptom Inventory (BSI): Administration, scoring and procedures manual I.* Baltimore: Johns Hopkins University School of Medicine, Clinical Psychometrics Research Unit.

DeSoto, C. B., O'Donnell, W. E., Allred, L. J., & Lopes, C. E. (1985). Symptomatology in alcoholics at various stages of abstinence. *Alcoholism: Clinical and Experimental Research, 9*, 505–512.

DeSoto, C. B., O'Donnell, W. E., & DeSoto, J. L. (1989). Long-term recovery in alcoholics. *Alcoholism: Clinical and Experimental Research, 13*, 693–697.

Donovan, D. M., Walker, R. D., & Kivlahan, D. R. (1987). Recovery and remediation of neuropsychological functions: Implications for alcoholism rehabilitation process and outcome. In O. A. Parsons, N. Butters, & P. E. Nathan (Eds.), *Neuropsychology of alcoholism: Implications for diagnosis and treatment* (pp. 339–360). New York: Guilford Press.

Eckardt, M. J., Rawlings, R. R., Graubard, B. I., Faden, V., Martin, P. R., & Gottschalk, L. A. (1988). Neuropsychological performance and treatment outcome in male alcoholics. *Alcoholism: Clinical and Experimental Research, 12*, 88–93.

Ewing, J. A. (1984). Detecting alcoholism: The CAGE questionnaire. *Journal of the American Medical Association, 252*, 1905–1907.

Fabian, M. S., & Parsons, O. A. (1983). Differential improvement of cognitive functions in recovering alcoholics. *Journal of Abnormal Psychology, 92*, 87–95.

Fabian, M. S., Parsons, O. A., & Silberstein, J. A. (1981). Impaired perceptual-cognitive functioning in alcoholic women: Cross-validated findings. *Journal of Studies on Alcohol, 4*, 217–229.

Fitzhugh, L. C., Fitzhugh, K. B., & Reitan, R. M. (1965). Adaptive abilities and intellectual functioning of hospitalized alcoholics: Further considerations. *Quarterly Journal of Studies on Alcoholism, 26*, 402–411.

Glenn, S. W., Errico, A. L., Parsons, O. A., King, A. C., & Nixon, S. J. (1993). The role of antisocial, affective, and childhood behavioral characteristics in alcoholics' neuropsychological performance. *Alcoholism: Clinical and Experimental Research, 17*, 162–169.

Glenn, S. W., & Parsons, O. A. (1992). Neuropsychological efficiency measures in male and female alcoholics. *Journal of Studies on Alcohol, 53*, 546–552.

Goldstein, G., & Shelly, C. (1982). A multivariate approach to brain lesion localization in alcoholism. *Addictive Behaviors, 7*, 165–175.

Golonbok, S., Moodley, P., & Lader, M. (1988). Cognitive impairment in long-term benzodiazepine users. *Psychological Medicine, 18*, 365–374.

Grant, B. F., Harford, T. C., Hasin, D. S., Chou, P., & Pickering, R. (1992). *DSM-III-R* and the proposed *DSM-IV* alcohol use disorders, United States 1988: A nosological comparison. *Alcoholism: Clinical and Experimental Research, 16*, 215–221.

Grant, I., Adams, K. M., & Reed, R. (1987). Intermediate-duration (subacute) organic mental disorder of alcoholism. In I. Grant (Ed.), *Neuropsychological correlates of alcoholism* (pp. 37–60). Washington, DC: American Psychiatric Press.

Grant, I., & Judd, L. L. (1976). Neuropsychological and EEG disturbances in polydrug users. *American Journal of Psychiatry, 133*, 1039–1042.

Gregson, R. A. M., & Taylor, G. M. (1977). Prediction of relapse in men alcoholics. *Journal of Studies on Alcohol, 38*, 1749–1759.

Harper, C. G., & Kril, J. J. (1993). Neuropathological changes in alcoholics. In W. A. Hunt & S. J. Nixon (Eds.), *Alcohol-induced brain damage* (Monograph No.

22, pp. 39–70). Rockville, MD: National Institute on Alcohol Abuse and Alcoholism.

Hasin, D., & Grant, B. (1994). 1994 draft *DSM-IV* criteria for alcohol use disorders: Comparison to *DSM-III-R* and implications. *Alcoholism: Clinical and Experimental Research, 18*, 1348–1353.

Heaton, R. K. (1981). *Wisconsin Card Sorting Test manual.* Odessa, FL: Psychological Assessment Resources.

Heaton, R. K., Grant, I., & Matthews, C. G. (1991). *Comprehensive norms for an expanded Halstead-Reitan Battery.* Odessa, FL: Psychological Assessment Resources.

Heindel, W. C., Salmon, D. P., & Butters, N. (1993). Cognitive approaches to the memory disorders of demented patients. In P. B. Sutker & H. E. Adams (Eds.), *Comprehensive handbook of psychopathology* (2nd ed., pp. 735–764). New York: Plenum.

Hoff, A. L., Riordan, H., Alpert, R., & Volkow, N. (1991, February). *Cognitive function in chronic cocaine abusers.* Paper presented at the annual meeting of the International Neuropsychological Society, San Antonio, TX.

Horn, J., Wanberg, K., & Foster, F. (1987). *Guide to the Alcohol Use Inventory.* Minneapolis, MN: National Computer Systems.

Horvath, T. B. (1975). Clinical spectrum and epidemiological features of alcoholic dementia. In G. Rankin (Ed.), *Alcohol, drugs, and brain damage* (pp. 1–16). Toronto: Addiction Research Foundation.

Institute of Medicine. (1987). *Causes and consequences of alcohol problems.* Washington, DC: National Academy Press.

Janowsky, J. S., Shimamura, A. P., Kritchevsky, M., & Squire, L. (1989). Cognitive impairment following frontal lobe damage and its relevance to human amnesia. *Behavioral Neuroscience, 103*, 548–560.

Jernigan, T., Butters, N., & Cermak, L. S. (1992). Studies of brain structure in chronic alcoholism using magnetic resonance imaging. In S. Zakhari & E. Witt (Eds.), *Imaging in alcohol research* (pp. 121–134). Rockville, MD: National Institute on Alcohol Abuse and Alcoholism.

Jones, B., & Parsons, O. A. (1971). Impairment of abstract ability in chronic alcoholics. *Archives of General Psychiatry, 24*, 71–75.

Joyce, E. M., & Robbins, T. W. (1991). Frontal lobe function in Korsakoff and non-Korsakoff alcoholics: Planning and spatial working memory. *Neuropsychologia, 29*, 709–723.

Kendler, K. S., Heath, A. C., Neale, M. C., Kessler, R. C., & Eaves, L. J. (1992). A population-based twin study of alcoholism in women. *Journal of the American Medical Association, 268*, 1877–1882.

Klisz, D. K., & Parsons, O. A. (1977). Hypothesis testing in younger and older alcoholics. *Journal of Studies on Alcohol, 38*, 1718–1729.

Levine, M. (1966). Hypothesis behavior by humans during discrimination learning. *Journal of Experimental Psychology, 71*, 331–338.

Lewis, R. F., & Rennick, P. M. (1979). *Manual for the Repeatable Cognitive-Perceptual-Motor Battery.* Grosse Pointe Park, MI: Axon Publishing.

Maisto, S. A., & Connors, G. J. (1990). Clinical diagnostic techniques and assessment tools in alcohol research. *Alcohol Health & Research World, 14*, 232–238.

McGue, M., Pickens, R. W., & Svikis, D. S. (1992). Sex and age effects on the inheritance of alcohol problems: A twin study. *Journal of Abnormal Psychology, 101*, 3–17.

Miller, W. R., & Marlatt, G. A. (1984). *Manual for the Comprehensive Drinker Profile.* Odessa, FL: Psychological Assessment Resources.

Miller, W. R., & Orr, J. (1980). Nature and sequence of neuropsychological deficits in alcoholics. *Journal of Studies in Alcohol, 41*, 325–337.

Moos, R. H., Mertens, J. R., & Brennan, P. L. (1994). Rates and predictors of four-year readmission among late-middle-aged and older substance abuse patients. *Journal of Studies on Alcohol, 55*, 561–570.

Narrow, W. E., Regier, D. A., Rae, D. S., Manderscheid, R. W., & Locke, B. Z. (1993). Use of services by persons with mental and addictive disorders. *Archives of General Psychiatry, 50*, 95–107.

Nixon, S. J., Kujawski, A., Parsons, O. A., & Yohman, J. R. (1987). Semantic and figural memory impairment in alcoholics. *Journal of Clinical and Experimental Neuropsychology, 9*, 311–322.

Nixon, S. J., & Parsons, O. A. (1991). Alcohol-related efficiency deficits using an ecologically valid test. *Alcoholism: Clinical and Experimental Research, 15*, 601–606.

Nixon, S. J., Parsons, O. A., & Schaeffer, K. W. (1988). Subject selection biases in alcoholic samples: Effects on cognitive performance. *Journal of Clinical Psychology, 44*, 831–836.

Oscar-Berman, M. (1973). Hypothesis testing and focusing behavior during concept formation by amnesic Korsakoff patients. *Neuropsychologica, 11,* 191–198.

Parsons, O. A. (1986). Cognitive functioning in sober social drinkers: A review and critique. *Journal of Studies on Alcohol, 47*, 387–404.

Parsons, O. A. (1987). Neuropsychological aspects of alcohol abuse: Many questions—Some answers. In O. A. Parsons, N. Butters, & P. E. Nathan (Eds.), *Neuropsychology of alcoholism: Implications for diagnosis and treatment* (pp. 153–175). New York: Guilford Press.

Parsons, O. A. (1994a). Determinants of cognitive deficits in alcoholics: The search continues. *The Clinical Neuropsychologist, 8*, 39–58.

Parsons, O. A. (1994b). Neuropsychological measures and event-related potentials in alcoholics: Interrelationships, long-term reliabilities and prediction of resumption of drinking. *Journal of Clinical Psychology, 50*, 37–46.

Parsons, O. A., & Adams, R. L. (1983). Neuropsychological examination of alcohol and drug abuse patients. In C. J. Golden & P. Vincente (Eds.), *Foundations of clinical neuropsychology* (pp. 215–248). New York: Plenum.

Parsons, O. A., & Farr, S. P. (1981). Neuropsychology of alcohol and drug use. In S. Filskov & T. Boll (Eds.), *Handbook of clinical neuropsychology* (pp. 320–365). New York: Wiley Interscience.

Parsons, O. A., & Nixon, S. J. (1993). Neurobehavioral sequelae of alcoholism. *Neurologic Clinic, 11*, 205–218.

Parsons, O. A., Schaeffer, K. W., & Glenn, S. W. (1990). Does neuropsychological test performance predict resumption of drinking in posttreatment alcoholics? *Addictive Behaviors, 15*, 297–307.

Parsons, O. A., Sinha, R., & Williams, H. L. (1990). Relationships between neuropsychological test performance and event-related potentials in alcoholic and nonalcoholic samples. *Alcoholism: Clinical and Experimental Research, 14*, 746–755.

Perrine, K. (1993). Differential aspects of conceptual processing in the Category test and the Wisconsin Card Sorting Test. *Journal of Clinical and Experimental Neuropsychology, 15*, 461–473.

Pfefferbaum, A., Lim, K. O., & Rosenbloom, M. (1992). Structural imaging of the brain in chronic alcoholism. In S. Zakhari & E. Witt (Eds.), *Imaging in alcohol research* (pp. 99–120). Rockville, MD: National Institute on Alcohol Abuse and Alcoholism.

Pokorny, A. D., Miller, B. A., & Kaplan, H. B. (1972). The brief MAST: A shortened version of the Michigan Alcoholism Screening Test. *American Journal of Psychiatry, 129*, 118–120.

Porjesz, B., & Begleiter, H. (1987). Evoked brain potentials and alcoholism. In O. A. Parsons, N. Butters, & P. E. Nathan (Eds.), *Neuropsychology of alcoholism: Implications for diagnosis and treatment* (pp. 45–63). New York: Guilford Press.

Reitan, R. M. (1972). Verbal problem-solving as it relates to cerebral damage. *Perceptual and Motor Skills, 34*, 515–524.

Reitan, R. M., & Wolfson, D. (1986). The Halstead–Reitan Neuropsychological Test Battery and aging. *Clinical Gerontologist, 5*, 39–61.

Reitan, R. M., & Wolfson, D. (1993). *The Halstead–Reitan Neuropsychological Test Battery* (2nd ed.). Tucson, AZ: Neuropsychology Press.

Ross, H. E., Glaser, F. B., & Germanson, T. (1989). The prevalence of psychiatric disorders in patients with alcohol and other drug problems. *Archives of General Psychiatry, 45*, 1023–1031.

Rourke, S. B., & Grant, I. (1995). A regression approach to measuring patterns of neuropsychological recovery in alcoholics with increasing abstinence. *Journal of the International Neuropsychological Society, 1*, 165.

Russell, E. W. (1975). A multiple scoring method for assessment of complex memory functions. *Journal of Consulting and Clinical Psychology, 43*, 800–809.

Russell, E. W. (1988). Renorming Russell's version of the Wechsler Memory Scale. *Journal of Clinical and Experimental Neuropsychology, 10*, 235–249.

Russell, M., Martier, S. S., Sokol, R. J., Mudar, P., Bottoms, S., Jacobson, S., & Jacobson, J. (1994). Screening for pregnancy risk-drinking. *Alcoholism: Clinical and Experimental Research, 18*, 1156–1161.

Ryan, C., & Butters, N. (1980). Learning and memory impairments in young and old alcoholics: Evidence for the premature aging hypothesis. *Alcoholism: Clinical and Experimental Research, 4*, 288–303.

Sachs, H., Russell, J. A. G., Christman, D. R., & Cook, B. (1987). Alteration of regional cerebral glucose metabolic rate in non-Korsakoff chronic alcoholism. *Archives of Neurology, 44*, 1242–1251.

Schaeffer, K. W., & Parsons, O. A. (1987). Learning impairment in alcoholics using an ecologically-relevant test. *Journal of Nervous and Mental Disease, 175*, 213–218.

Schuckit, M. A., Klein, J. L., Twitchell, G. R., & Springer, L. M. (1994). Increases in alcohol-related problems for men on a college campus between 1980 and 1992. *Journal of Studies on Alcohol, 55*, 739–742.

Searles, J. S. (1990). The contribution of genetic factors to the development of alcoholism: A critical review. In R. L. Collins, K. E. Leonard, & S. Searles (Eds.), *Alcohol and the family* (pp. 3–38). New York: Guilford Press.

Selzer, M. L. (1971). The Michigan Alcoholism Screening Test: The quest for a new diagnostic instrument. *American Journal of Psychiatry, 127*, 1653–1658.

Shelton, M. D., & Parsons, O. A. (1987). Alcoholics' self-assessment of their neuropsychological functioning in everyday life. *Journal of Clinical Psychology, 43*, 395–403.

Shipley, W. C. (1940). A self-administering scale for measuring intellectual impairment and deterioration. *Journal of Psychology, 9*, 371–377.

Skinner, H. A., & Allen, B. A. (1982). Alcohol dependence syndrome: Measurement and validation. *Journal of Abnormal Psychology, 91*, 199–209.

Skinner, H. A., & Horn, J. (1984). *Alcohol Dependence Scale (ADS) user's guide.* Toronto: Addiction Research Foundation.

Spielberger, C. D., Gorsuch, R. L., & Lushene, R. E. (1970). *Test manual for the State-Trait Anxiety Inventory.* Palo Alto, CA: Consulting Psychologists Press.

Talland, G. (1965). *Deranged memory.* San Diego, CA: Academic Press.

Tariot, P. N., & Weingartner, H. (1986). A psychobiologic analysis of cognitive failures. *Archives of General Psychiatry, 43*, 1183–1188.

Tarter, R. E., McBride, H., Buonpane, N., & Schneider, D. U. (1977). Differentiation of alcoholics. *Archives of General Psychiatry, 34*, 761–768.

Tarter, R. E., & Parsons, O. A. (1971). Conceptual shifting in chronic alcoholics. *Journal of Abnormal Psychology, 77*, 71–75.

U.S. Department of Health and Human Services. (1974). *Second special report to the U.S. Congress on alcohol and health* (DHHS Publication No. ADM 92-1191). Washington, DC: U.S. Government Printing Office.

U.S. Department of Health and Human Services. (1990). *Seventh special report to the U.S. Congress on alcohol and health* (DHHS Publication No. ADM 90-1656). Washington, DC: U.S. Government Printing Office.

U.S. Department of Health and Human Services. (1993). *Eighth special report to the U.S. Congress on alcohol and health* (DHHS Publication No. ADM 94-3699). Washington, DC: U.S. Government Printing Office.

Victor, M., Adams, R. D., & Collins, G. H. (1971). *The Wernicke-Korsakoff syndrome.* Philadelphia: F. A. Davis.

Wechsler, D. (1981). *WAIS-R manual: Wechsler Adult Intelligence Scale-Revised.* New York: Harcourt, Brace & Jovanovich.

Wechsler, D. (1987). *WMS-R: Wechsler Memory Scale-Revised Manual.* New York: Psychological Corporation.

Wilkinson, D. A. (1987). CT scan and neuropsychological assessment of alcoholism. In O. A. Parsons, N. Butters, & P. E. Nathan (Eds.), *Neuropsychology of alcoholism: Implications for diagnosis and treatment* (pp. 76–102). New York: Guilford Press.

Willner, A. E. (1970). Toward the development of a more sensitive clinical test of abstraction: The Analogy Test. *Proceedings of the 78th Annual Convention of the American Psychological Association, 5*, 553–554.

Willner, A. E., & Struve, F. A. (1970). An analogy test that predicts EEG abnormality in hospitalized psychiatric patients. *Archives of General Psychiatry, 23*, 428–437.

Wilson, B. (1987). Identification and remediation of everyday problems in memory impaired patients. In O. A. Parsons, N. Butters, & P. E. Nathan (Eds.), *Neuropsychology of alcoholism: Implications for diagnosis and treatment* (pp. 322–338). New York: Guilford Press.

Winger, G., Hofman, F. G., & Woods, J. H. (1992). *A handbook on drug and alcohol abuse* (3rd ed.). New York: Oxford University Press.

Worton, R. G. (1991). Molecular genetic approaches to the study of individual risk in alcoholism. In H. Kalant, J. M. Khanna, & Y. Israel (Eds.), *Advances in biomedical alcohol research* (pp. 19–26). Elmsford, NY: Pergamon Press.

Yohman, J. R., & Parsons, O. A. (1987). Verbal reasoning deficits in alcoholics. *Journal of Nervous and Mental Disease, 175*, 219–223.

Yohman, J. R., Parsons, O. A., & Leber, W. R. (1985). Lack of recovery in male alcoholics' neuropsychological performance one year after treatment. *Alcoholism: Clinical and Experimental Research, 9*, 114–117.

Zakhari, S., & Witt, E. (1992). *Imaging in alcohol research* (Research Monograph No. 21, DHHS Publication No. ADM 92-1890). Rockville, MD: National Institute on Alcohol Abuse and Alcoholism.

CHAPTER 7

HUMAN IMMUNODEFICIENCY VIRUS (HIV-1)

Oscar A. Parsons

In 1981, five gay men in the United States were diagnosed as suffering from pneumocystis carinii pneumonia and other symptoms, a condition that rapidly became known as *acquired human immunodeficiency syndrome* (AIDS; Chesney, 1993). Few people at that time realized that "a microbiological time bomb" had been planted (Osborn, 1990) and that within a decade, AIDS would become a worldwide epidemic. Early on, it was clear from clinical examinations that a large number of patients with AIDS had neurological symptoms, including a dementia that became known as the *AIDS dementia complex* (ADC; Navia, Cho, Petito, & Price, 1986). This dementia has been reported in 40–90% of patients with AIDS, depending on the samples studied (Brew, 1993). Neuropsychological research on patients with AIDS has confirmed the presence of dementia in a high percentage of the samples tested. Less clear is the degree to which HIV-1 seropositive individuals, who do not yet have full-blown AIDS, manifest cognitive neuropsychological deficits and which neuropsychological tests may hold the most promise for identifying such deficits. These latter topics, including several illustrative cases and a brief discussion of treatment and prevention, are the focus of this chapter. First, however, I discuss the epidemiology, genetics, clinical symptomatology, and biological aspects of the HIV-1 disorder.

EPIDEMIOLOGY

The rate of infection with HIV-1 is out of control (Coates, 1993). As of late 1992, more than 600,000 cases worldwide of AIDS had been reported to the World Health Organization (WHO), but the true number was thought to be closer to 2.5 million. By 1995, however, the estimate of the number of HIV-positive people throughout the world was 19.5 million, with 6,000 people becoming infected each day, or 2,190,000 new cases each year (Centers for Disease Control and Prevention [CDC], 1994; 1995b). One of the most alarming developments is the rapid spread of infection in the great population centers of South and Southeast Asia.

In the United States, estimates of infected individuals range from 1 to 1.5 million; in Northern Europe the estimate is 500,000 (Chesney, 1993; Touchette, 1993). In the United States, as of October 1995, cumulative statistics indicated that 493,493 adults and adolescents and 7,817 children had been identified as having AIDS; 62% of those patients have died.

In the United States during 1991, there were 29,850 residents who died of HIV disease. Tragically, 75% of these deaths occurred among individuals aged 25–44 years, the years during which many people are the most productive in society. HIV infection was the ninth leading cause of death overall, but it was the third leading cause of death among 25- to 44-year-olds; the death rate for men was seven times that for women. By 1995, HIV infection was the leading cause of death in men and women aged 25–44 years and the seventh cause of death over all ages (CDC, 1995a, 1995b). The proportionate increases in the death rate for women have been greater than for men since 1985 (CDC, 1995a). The death rates from HIV infection are higher in minority groups. In 1990, the percentages of total deaths among men in the following groups were as follows: Hispanic, 22%; Black, 19%; White, 15%; and Asian and Native American, 10% (CDC, 1993b).

The magnitude of the health problem also can be seen in the fact that in 1990, 225,000 HIV-infected patients were cared for in acute-care hospitals in the United States. Interestingly, 63%–65% of these HIV-positive patients were unaware of their HIV infection before entering the hospital (CDC, 1993a).

Considering the epidemiological data and the evidence of cognitive deficits in patients with AIDS, it is apparent that unless prevention and treatment procedures are developed that can contain the rapid spread of HIV-1 infection, these patients will make up a substantial percentage of the referrals for neuropsychological assessment in the next decade.

GENETICS

There is little information on the genetic contributions to the susceptibility of HIV-1 infection. There are, however, wide differences in the rapidity of progression of the disease. Some individuals progress to AIDS within 1 year of seroconversion; at the other extreme, some remain asymptomatic for 10 or more years (Ezzell, 1993; Tersmette & Schuitemaker, 1993). Although the number of patients in the latter category is small, they are being intensively studied and a number of possible genetic contributions are being investigated. For example, variations in the envelope gene that encodes the HIV-1 envelope proteins could possibly lead to a greater number of mutations influencing the course of the disease (Ezzell, 1993).

A second example is the interesting model of HIV population dynamics offered by Coffin (1995). Coffin pointed out that the supposed latent phase of the HIV infection is actually a highly active phase in which cells are being infected and dying at a high rate and in large numbers but equally large cell replacements are occurring. This turnover drives the mutation rate and the development of specific genetic variations that resist the pharmacological therapeutic agents and hasten the pathogenic process. Given the preliminary stage of these investigations, it is likely that any definitive identification of genetic factors in HIV-1 infections is still some years away.

CLINICAL SYMPTOMATOLOGY AND CLASSIFICATION

A landmark article on the clinical features of ADC was published 5 years after AIDS was identified (Navia, Jordan, & Price, 1986). Using 46 autopsy-verified patients whose mental changes could not be ascribed to opportunistic infections or other disorders likely to affect the brain, Navia, Jordan, and Price retrospectively described the course of symptom development. Early in the syndrome, 29 of 44 patients reported minor cognitive changes such as forgetfulness, loss of concentration and attention, confusion, and slowness of thought. Twenty patients reported motor symptoms such as loss of balance, leg weakness, and a deterioration in handwriting. Behavioral changes were reported by 17 patients. These changes included apathy, social withdrawal, and dysphoric mood. Results of routine bedside mental status examination indicated that 12 fell in the normal range; the remaining patients had either motor–verbal slowness or impaired cognition (e.g., performing serial sevens). Neurological findings were abnormal in 18 of the patients, with ataxia, pyramidal signs, and leg weakness predominating.

Thirty-four of 45 patients who had progressed to the late stage of the illness were classified as having severe dementia; 11 fell in the moderate dementia category. Many of the patients with severe dementia had psychomotor retardation and only rudimentary intellectual and social functions. The neurological signs were exaggerated and extensive. Peripheral neuropathy was present in 22 patients in the demented group. Navia, Jordan, and Price (1986) concluded that ADC was sufficiently distinct in its presentation to permit accurate clinical diagnosis in most patients and differentiation from the other neurological complications of AIDS.

Subsequent publications in this area, including a prospective study by McArthur (1987), have confirmed most of the observations noted earlier. Given the consistency of the findings, the American Academy of Neurology AIDS Task Force (1991) proposed a nomenclature for the diagnosis of HIV-positive individuals. The HIV-1-associated cognitive–motor complex is divided into severe manifestations and mild manifestations. The former has two subdivisions: HVI-1 associated dementia complex and HIV-1 associated myelopathy. The mild category has one: HVI-1 associated minor cognitive–motor disorder. Provisions are made for "probable" and "possible" as well as definite diagnoses. Criteria for classification are discussed in the article. The utility of the minor cognitive–motor disorder category was demonstrated in a recent study by Diehr et al. (1995). One hundred HIV-positive men were given a battery of neuropsychological tests. The results for eight cognitive ability areas were then rated by experienced clinicians as to either normal or meeting the criteria for minor cognitive–motor disorder. Twenty-two percent (n = 42) of the 190 patients met the criteria.

Several other classification systems have been used, the most common of which is that of the CDC. The latest revised system (CDC, 1992) is presented in Table 1. Note that it combines the cell count of CD4+ T lymphocytes with clinical symptomatology. The patient is first classified as falling into one of the three groups: A, B, or C. They are then subclassified on the basis of their CD4+ T cell count. For example, an HIV-1 seropositive, symptomatic patient would be placed in Class B. If the patient's CD4+ T cell count was 300 μl, the patient would be classified as B2. For surveillance purposes, the new system identifies all HIV-1-infected individuals with CD4+ T cell counts less than 200 μl as having AIDS regardless of the specific illness diagnosed. The CDC predicted that reports of AIDS incidence will increase by approximately 75% above previously projected levels in 1993 and by 10%–20% in 1994, providing that state health departments implement the new surveillance procedures successfully (Buehler, Ward, & Berkelman, 1993). Another classification system occasionally used in research reports is the Walter Reed Stage classification (Redfield, Wright, & Tramont, 1986). This system consists of seven stages that are based on the documented presence of the HIV-1 virus, CD4+ T cells, and clinical symptoms.

Finally, occasional reports have used the classification of AIDS-related complex (ARC) to distinguish infected individuals who do not meet the criteria for AIDS but who have other medical HIV-related symptoms such as generalized lymphadenopathy. These patients are usually compared with HIV-1 seronegative control peers, HIV-1 seropositive individuals with no or transient symptoms, and patients with AIDS, resulting in a four-group comparison (Grant et al., 1987; Ollo, Johnson, & Grafman, 1991).

TABLE 1

Centers for Disease Control and Prevention 1993 Revised Classification System for HIV Infection and Expanded Surveillance Case Definition

	A	B[a]	C[b]
CD4+ T Cell categories	Asymptomatic or acute HIV infection or persistent generalized lymphadenopathy	Symptomatic but not conditions A or C	AIDS-indicator conditions
≥ 500/μl	A1	B1	C1
200–499/μl	A2	B2	C2
< 200/μl[c]	A3	B3	C3

Note: For surveillance purposes, all HIV-infected individuals with CD4+ counts less than 200/μl are identified as having AIDS. In the public domain.
[a]Constitutional symptoms such as fever or diarrhea lasting longer than 1 month.
[b]Opportunistic infections, preliminary TB, recurrent pneumonia, wasting syndrome.

BIOLOGICAL ASPECTS

In the second part of their landmark study, Navia, Cho, et al. (1986) reported on their neuropathological examination of the brains of 70 autopsied adult patients with AIDS, 46 of whom had exhibited clinically defined dementia during the course of their disease. Overall, less than 10% of the brains were histologically normal. Abnormalities were found predominantly in the white matter and subcortical structures. There was relative sparing of the cortex. As might be expected, the frequency and severity of the abnormalities were greater in the dementia subgroup. Pallor of the white matter was noted in 64 of 70 brains and was most prominent in the centrum semiovale. Inflammation of the brain, often associated with reactive astrocytosis, occurred in 75% of the patients. Reactive vacuolation of the white matter was present in more than 50% of the patients, chiefly in the centrum semiovale and less commonly in the internal capsule, brain stem, and cerebellum. Multinucleated giant cells were found in a subgroup ($n = 18$) of the patients with dementia. In this group macrophages, lymphocytes, and reactive astrocytosis were found in the subcortical gray matter (i.e., the basal ganglia), most commonly involving the putamen, caudate, and claustrum, and in the pons. Computed tomography scans of 38 patients showed variable degrees of cortical atrophy in 32. Magnetic resonance imaging was performed on several patients, which indicated diffuse cortical atrophy as well as focal areas of increased signal in white matter. The authors presciently commented that the magnetic resonance imaging would be a more sensitive method for detecting HIV-related brain changes.

Considering all the results, the most frequent and prominent findings were present in the white matter and subcortical structures, whereas the cortex was relatively spared. Navia, Cho, et al. (1986) concluded that the progressive cognitive decline accompanied by motor and behavioral disturbances in their patients resembled other subcortical dementias. Finally, they suggested that the dementia complex may result from the direct brain infection by the HIV.

The conclusion that many patients with AIDS suffer from a subcortical dementia is not uncontroversial. Kaemingk and Kaszniak (1989) reviewed the evidence and suggested that although the existence of "subcortical" dementia as an entity has not been firmly established, it serves as a useful framework for looking at HIV dementia. Aside from the neuropathological evidence (such as that cited earlier), a study by Rottenberg et al. (1987) provides some confirmatory evidence. Those investigators compared 12 patients with ADC and 18 healthy individuals on regional cerebral metabolic rates for glucose, as measured by positron emission tomography. Relatively high metabolic activity was found in the thalamus and basal ganglia in early ADC, but as the disease progressed cortical and subcortical hypometabolism were found. Interestingly, subcortical metabolism was significantly related to performance on the Grooved Pegboard test, but cortical metabolism was related to Verbal Fluency and Trails B results. These findings were confirmed by Van Gorp et al. (1992), who also used positron emission tomography scans to measure regional brain metabolic rates for glucose. Seventeen patients with AIDS were compared with 14 HIV-negative control peers. The patients with AIDS had relative regional hypermetabolism in the basal ganglia and thalamus and a relative hypometabolism in the temporal lobe region. The temporal lobe metabolism and severity of dementia were inversely related. As ADC progresses, it appears that cortical areas become more involved.

In a recent article, Brew (1993) concurred that the major characteristic of the ADC is a subcortical dementia with dominant slowing of intellectual processing and poor attention coupled with scattered motor symptoms. Brew also addressed the question of whether the dementia is a direct effect of viral infection of the brain and concluded that it could not account for all of the results. He suggested that host-mediated responses or certain viral products might be involved. For the former, he suggested quinolinic acid (found at heightened levels in the cerebrospinal fluid of patients with AIDS) and for the latter, the neurotoxic glycoprotein gp 120 of the envelope of HIV-1. The importance of quinolinic acid is supported by a recent report in which levels of cerebrospinal fluid quinolinic acid in 95 HIV-positive men were found to be significantly inversely correlated with the quality of performance on executive, memory, reasoning, and verbal and visual memory tasks (Kaderman, Levin, & Berger, 1995).

Another autopsy study (Masliah et al., 1992) of the brains of patients with AIDS showed a strong correlation between neocortical dendritic and presynaptic damage and the presence of another HIV envelope protein, gp 41, in the neocortical gray and deep white matter. Masliah et al. concluded that the presence of HIV-1 in the neocortex may be responsible by direct or indirect mechanisms for the up to 40% loss of neocortical dendritic area and 20% loss of synapses in the areas examined.

Finally, Epstein and Gendelman (1993), on the basis of their laboratory experiments, suggested that HIV-1-infected macrophages can initiate neurotoxicity, which is then amplified through cell-to-cell interactions with astrocytes, resulting in astroglial proliferation and neuronal injury. Obviously, the mechanisms by which the HIV-1 infection in the brain results in brain injury and dysfunction remain to be definitively established, but it is also clear that much progress in that area has been made.

Several studies have shown electroencephalographic abnormalities in patients who are HIV-1 seropositive or have ARC or AIDS (Kaemingk & Kaszniak, 1989). An event-related potential study of patients with ARC or AIDS compared with asymptomatic HIV-positive patients (Ollo et al., 1991) showed reduced P-300 amplitudes and increased P-300 latencies to visual and auditory stimuli in the patients with ARC or AIDS; in the asymptomatic HIV-positive group, these results held only for the visual modality.

In summary, there is biomedical evidence for a continuum of increasing brain abnormalities from HIV-positive individuals without symptoms to HIV-positive patients with symptoms (ARC) to nondemented patients with AIDS, to patients with AIDS and ADC. The progression seems to be from primarily a subcortical brain dysfunction in the early-to-middle stages to an increased involvement of the cortex in the later stages of AIDS dementia.

NEUROPSYCHOLOGICAL RESEARCH ON HIV-POSITIVE INDIVIDUALS

Since the time of the first description of the ADC (Navia, Jordan, & Price, 1986), the clinical symptoms of dementia in patients with AIDS, especially toward the latter stages of the disease, have been noted repeatedly. Neuropsychological assessment of such patients is typically used to help define the extent and severity of the dementia. The neuropsychological tests used in assessing these patients are those commonly used for assessing dementia associated with other neurological disorders.

More recent studies have been concerned with the question of the extent to which neuropsychological deficits are found in people who are HIV-positive, both asymptomatic and symptomatic (but not full-blown AIDS). In the most comprehensive of these studies, four groups of patients were compared: HIV-1 seronegative (but drawn from the same demographic sample as the HIV-1 seropositive patients); HIV-1 seropositive and asymptomatic; HIV-1 seropositive and symptomatic; and patients with AIDS (Ayers, Abrams, Newell, & Friedrich, 1987; Bornstein, Nasrallah, et al., 1993; Grant et al., 1987).

TABLE 2

Percentages of HIV− (Seronegative) and HIV+ (Seropositive) Patients Who Were Impaired on 6 or More Tests Out of 15 Administered

Deviations	% impaired			
from mean	HIV−	HIV+	ARC	AIDS
1 *SD* below mean of HIV−	14.3	22.1	41	51.3
1.5 *SD*s below mean of HIV−	5.2	10.1	18	20.5

Note: ARC = AIDS-related complex. Data are from Bornstein, Nasrallah, et al. (1993).

Of these studies, the one by Bornstein, Nasrallah, et al. (1993) was the largest and best controlled. Those investigators compared four groups of homosexual and bisexual men ($N = 310$) on a battery of 15 neuropsychological measures derived from the Wisconsin Card Sorting Test (Berg, 1948), Trail Making test (Reitan, 1958), Visual Span (Wechsler, 1987), Grooved Pegboard (Kløve, 1963), Verbal Fluency (Benton & Hamsher, 1977), Figural Fluency (Jones-Gotman & Milner, 1977), Verbal Concept Attainment Test (Bornstein, 1994), Paced Auditory Serial Addition Test (Gronwall, 1977), and the Selective Reminding Test (Buschke & Fuld, 1974). Using the criteria of 1 and 1.5 standard deviations below the mean of the HIV-negative group on 6 or more (40%) of the 15 measures, they found a systematic progression of the percentage of patients in the group meeting these criteria from the HIV-negative group to the group with AIDS (see Table 2). Using the more lenient criterion of 1 standard deviation, the range was 14.3% in the HIV-negative to 51.3% in the group with AIDS. Using the more stringent criterion of 1.5 standard deviations, the comparable range was 5.2%–20.5%. These data strongly suggest that there is a relationship between the stage of the disorder and neuropsychological impairment.

Other researchers have compared three groups. Skoraszewski, Ball, and Mikulka (1991) performed a meta-analysis of eight such studies in which nine neuropsychological dimensions (e.g., verbal processing, spatial processing, problem solving, semantic memory, motor speed, etc.) were measured. The overall effect sizes ranged from 0.29 (mild impairment) in HIV-negative groups, to 0.56 (moderate impairment) for HIV-symptomatic groups, to 1.12 (severe impairment) for groups with AIDS. Skoraszewski et al. then conducted their own study of the performance of 30 HIV-negative patients, 27 HIV-positive (both symptomatic and asymptomatic) patients, and 26 patients with AIDS on the Shipley Institute of Living Scale (Shipley, 1946), Wechsler Memory Scale (Russell, 1975), Finger Tapping test (Halstead, 1947; Reitan & Wolfson, 1993), Controlled Oral Word Association (Benton & Hamsher, 1977), Trail Making test (Reitan, 1958; Reitan & Wolfson, 1993), and Digit Span and Digit Symbol tests (Wechsler, 1981). Patients with AIDS performed more poorly than did the HIV-negative group on all tests; the HIV-positive group had poorer performance than did the HIV-positive group on 3 of 14 measures and performed significantly better than did the patients with AIDS on 9 of 14 measures. The authors concluded that their results indicated a milder degree of impairment (although significant) in the patients who were HIV-1 seropositive and had AIDS than was found in their meta-analysis.

In a recent three-group study, Peavy et al. (1994) reported that HIV-positive symptomatic patients performed more poorly than did HIV-negative control peers on measures of acquisition and retention on the California Verbal Learning Test. The performance of asymptomatic HIV-positive patients fell between the other two groups on almost every measure. Most interesting, however, was a comparison of the pattern of the three groups' performances with performances by patients with Huntington's disease (primarily subcortical) and a group of patients with Alzheimer's dementia (primarily cortical) on the same test. The performance of the HIV-1 symptomatic group was most similar to the patients with Huntington's disease, thus providing additional support for the subcortical hypothesis of HIV-1 effects on the brain.

Finally, Heaton (1993) reported that out of 50 studies in which HIV-1 seropositive patients were compared with HIV-1 seronegative patients, 21 studies indicated that HIV-1 seropositive patients performed more poorly than did HIV-1 seronegative patients. Studies in which larger batteries were used were more likely to demonstrate differences; in such studies, 34% of the patients were impaired in the HIV-positive groups compared with 16% in the HIV-negative groups.

There are, however, several large-scale studies that have not shown differences between HIV-positive and HIV-negative patients. For example, McAllister et al. (1992) tested 95 HIV-positive and 32 HIV-negative gay men on a battery of neuropsychological tests, some 15 different measures, and found significant differences only in the symptomatic HIV-positive men (n = 15). No differences were found for event-related potentials (P-300), somatosensory potentials in the legs, or magnetic resonance imaging abnormalities of the brain. Obviously, this type of variability in results across studies suggests caution in generalizing results from any one study.

Considering all the evidence, aside from the patients with AIDS, approximately one third of the HIV-positive patients, especially the symptomatic patients, may manifest a mild impairment on neuropsychological test batteries, providing that the battery measures several different cognitive functions. Also, the pattern of cognitive deficits is highly variable across studies.

RECOMMENDED NEUROPSYCHOLOGICAL TESTS FOR PATIENTS WITH HIV-1

A recommended battery of neuropsychological tests for HVI-1-infected patients has been published (Butters et al., 1990), a result of a workshop sponsored by the National Institute of Mental Health. Because of the evidence from the neuropathological and neuroradiological studies of subcortical changes in some HIV-infected individuals, the report suggested that tests measuring attentional and speed-of-processing functions should receive special emphasis in the assessment process. A second recommendation was that HIV-positive patients who do not yet have AIDS are likely to have subtle indications of impairment; therefore, clinical ratings of the testing results for a patient should be made. The third recommendation was that measures of depression and anxiety be included as part of the neuropsychological battery, given the evidence that disturbances in these affects have been shown to adversely affect cognitive performance.

The recommended battery, consisting of 26 tests covering 10 domains of functioning, is presented in Exhibit 1. As can be seen, the domains cover most of the areas considered to be important in neuropsychological assessment and, except for a few tests (e.g., Sternberg Search Task, Working Memory Test), are tests of known reliability and validity in neuropsychological research and assessment. The battery takes 7–9 hr to complete. For detailed information on all 26 tests, see Butters et al. (1990).

Recognizing that assessment time is frequently much more limited, the authors recommended a short battery of 6 of the 26 tests that takes 1–2 hr to administer. This battery consists of the Wechsler Adult Intelligence Scale–Revised (WAIS-R) Vocabulary subtest (Wechsler, 1981), the Wechsler Memory Scale–Revised (WMS-R) Visual Span subtest (Wechsler, 1987), the Paced Auditory Serial Addition Test (Gronwall, 1977), the California Verbal Learning Test (Delis, Kramer, Kaplan, & Ober, 1987), the Hamilton Rating Scale for Depression (Williams, 1988), and the State-Trait Anxiety Inventory (Spielberger, Gorsuch, & Lushene, 1970).

Bornstein (1994) pointed out that current conceptualizations about the nature of the HIV-related neurobehavioral dysfunction have not generated a clear consensus about which functions are impaired. He suggested that a broad neuropsychological battery be used, one that includes measures of functioning that are expected to be abnormal (e.g., the Butters et al., 1990, divided attention, speed of information processing, and speed of processing and retrieval from working and long-term memory) but that also includes measures of a range of functions not yet implicated in HIV-positive individuals. In other words, the typical full neuropsychological battery used by most clinicians will provide relevant information for the examination of HIV-1-infected patients.

There is one recommended test by Butters et al. (1990) that is not typically used in neuropsychological examinations (i.e., simple and choice reaction time [RT]). The possible value of including such measures is illustrated by Martin et al. (1992). They reported that their sample of HIV-positive patients ($n = 52$), symptomatic (29%) and asymptomatic (71%), had a highly significant slowing of RT under both simple and choice conditions compared with 33 HIV-negative peers. Martin et al. also found that a group of 17 HIV-positive patients, retested after 6 months, had significantly higher levels of quinolinic acid (an endogenous neurotoxin) than did control peers both at initial testing and at retesting. There was a significant correlation between the increases in quinolinic acid and slowing of simple RT from testing to retesting, $r(14) = .68$, $p < .01$. Other, more recent studies also have shown HIV-1 deficits in RT (Mapou et al., 1995; Stroup, Hunter, & Bornstein, 1995). Considering these findings, it would seem that the addition of a well-designed RT test would be useful in studying individuals who are HIV-positive.

For practitioners today, the examination of individuals with AIDS who have clinically diagnosed dementia consists of the neuropsychological tests customarily used in evaluating any patient with dementia. For patients with AIDS who do not have clinically diagnosed dementia, HIV-positive, and HIV-positive symptomatic groups, as Butters et al. (1990) and Bornstein (1994) have recommended, a battery of neuropsychological tests covering diverse cognitive functions should be used. Given the neuropathological evidence, this battery should certainly include measures of information-processing speed, motor speed (as in pegboards and finger tapping), attention and concentration, and immediate and delayed verbal and visual memory.

SUBJECTIVE SYMPTOMS AND NEUROPSYCHOLOGICAL IMPAIRMENT

The relation between subjective physical and mental symptoms in HIV-1-infected patients and performance on neuropsychological tests has been investigated by several researchers. Initial studies gave rise to null or inconsistent results (Van Gorp, Satz, & Hinkin, 1991; Wilkins et al., 1991), although sub-

EXHIBIT 1

Recommended NIMH Core Neuropsychological Battery for Assessment of HIV-1 Patients

A. Indication of premorbid intelligence
   1. Vocabulary (WAIS-R; Wechsler, 1981)[a]
   2. National Adult Reading Test (Grober, Sliwinski, & Buschke, 1990).

B. Attention
   1. Digit Span (WMS-R; Wechsler, 1987)
   2. Visual Span (WMS-R; Wechsler, 1987)[a]
   3. Visual Search Test (Rennick, 1979)

C. Speed of processing
   1. Sternberg Search Task (Sternberg, 1966)
   2. Simple and choice reaction time tests (Martin, Robertson, & Edelstein, 1989)
   3. Paced Auditory Serial Addition Test (Gronwall, 1977)[a]

D. Memory
   1. California Verbal Learning Test (Delis, Kramer, Kaplan, & Ober, 1987)[a]
   2. Working Memory Test (Baddeley, Logie, Bressi, Della Sala, & Spinnler, 1986)
   3. Modified Visual Reproduction test (WMS) (Russell, 1975)

E. Abstraction
   1. Category test (Reitan & Wolfson, 1993)
   2. Trail Making test, Parts A and B (Reitan & Wolfson, 1993)

F. Language
   1. Boston Naming Test (Kaplan, Goodglass, & Weintraub, 1983)
   2. Letter and Category Fluency Test (Butters, Granholm, Salmon, Grant, & Wolfe, 1987)

G. Visuospatial
   1. Embedded Figures Test (Witkin, Ohman, Raskin, & Karp, 1971)
   2. Money's Standardized Road-Map Test of Direction Sense (Money, 1976)
   3. Digit Symbol Substitution (Wechsler, 1981)

H. Construction abilities
   1. Block Design test (Wechsler, 1981)
   2. Tactual Performance test (Reitan & Wolfson, 1993)

I. Motor abilities
   1. Grooved Pegboard (Kløve, 1963)
   2. Finger Tapping (Reitan & Wolfson, 1993)
   3. Grip Strength (Reitan & Wolfson, 1993)

J. Psychiatric assessment
   1. Diagnostic Interview Schedule (Robins, Helzer, Croughan, & Ratcliff, 1981)
   2. Hamilton Rating Scale for Depression (Hamilton, 1960; Williams, 1988)[a]
   3. State-Trait Anxiety Inventory (Spielberger, Gorsuch, & Lushene, 1970)[a]
   4. Mini-Mental State Exam (Folstein, Folstein, & McHugh, 1975)

NIMH = National Institute of Mental Health; WAIS-R = Wechsler Adult Intelligence Scale–Revised; WMS-R = Wechsler Memory Scale–Revised. From "Assessment of AIDS-Related Cognitive Changes: Recommendations of the NIMH Workshop on Neuropsychological Assessment Approaches," by N. Butters, I. Grant, et al., 1990, Journal of Clinical and Experimental Neuropsychology, 12, *pp. 963–978. Copyright 1990 by Swets & Zeitlinger. Adapted with permission.*
[a]*Abbreviated battery.*

jective cognitive complaints were related to depression. Subsequent investigators using a broader range of HIV-1-infected individuals have more consistently found relationships. Stern et al. (1991) correlated complaints of cognitive difficulties in everyday life (reading, watching TV, speed of thought, and memory) with cognitive test performance in areas assessing similar functions in 124 HIV-negative and 84 HIV-positive gay men. Significant positive correlations were found in the HIV-positive but not the HIV-negative men.

More recently, Mapou et al. (1993) compared 79 HIV-positive (23 reporting constitutional symptoms) and 27 HIV-negative men in the military on a wide variety of subjective complaints and results of an extensive neuropsychological battery. The percentage of men claiming subjective symptoms was higher in every category (e.g., sleep disturbances, sensory, motor, memory problems, etc.) in the HIV-positive group than the HIV-negative group. The HIV-positive group was divided into those who had subjective complaints for a given area (e.g., motor, sensory, memory) and those without complaints in that area. The percentage of men falling 1.5 standard deviations below the mean of the control group was calculated for each complaint group. On 14 different neuropsychological tests covering similar domains of functioning, the complaint group differed significantly from the group without complaints for the given area of functioning. These results held across both the HIV-positive asymptomatic and symptomatic groups. Finally, although depression and anxiety measures were significantly higher in the complaint groups, neither was significantly related to neuropsychological test performance.

A similar pattern of results was found by Beason-Hazen and Bornstein (1994) in a study of HIV-positive but asymptomatic sample of gay and bisexual men ($N = 133$). The prevalence and duration of self-reported symptoms were related to neuropsychological test performance on the battery described earlier (Bornstein, Nasrallah, et al., 1993), especially to measures of information processing and RT. The relationships remained significant when the effect of depression was removed. Beason-Hazen and Bornstein concluded that the early appearance of physical symptoms may represent a risk factor for the subsequent development of neuropsychological impairment.

The two studies just cited illustrate an important point: the possible role of depression and anxiety in the neuropsychological impairment found in HIV-1-infected individuals. In both studies, it was shown that the relationships between subjective symptoms and neuropsychological impairment could not be accounted for by anxiety or depression and that these affective variables were not predictors of the neuropsychological impairment. This lack of relationship also was reported by Hinkin et al. (1992), who compared groups of HIV-positive men ($n = 18$) who had low scores on the Beck Depression Inventory with a peer seropositive group ($n = 19$) who had high scores (> 20). Of a number of neuropsychological measures, the high-depression group performed significantly worse only on the Grooved Pegboard test. In another recent report, Grant et al. (1993) found no systematic relationship between depression and performance on a battery of neuropsychological tests in a wide range of HIV-1-infected patients, although the HIV-positive symptomatic patients had higher levels of depression and neuropsychological impairment. Grant et al. concluded that depressed mood and cognitive disturbance each seem to have unique associations with HIV illness status.

In summary, subjective complaints in HIV-positive individuals may indicate the likelihood of mild or incipient neuropsychological inefficiencies. Although depression and anxiety may contribute to their subjective complaints, they are not systematically related to neuropsychological performance in these patients. Nevertheless, neuropsychologists would be well advised to include measures of affective distress in their examinations of HIV-1-infected individuals. For any given individual, moderate-to-high levels of depression or anxiety might result in greater cognitive inefficiency (Cassens, Wolfe, & Zola, 1990).

CLINICAL NEUROPSYCHOLOGICAL EXAMINATION OF HIV-1-INFECTED INDIVIDUALS

Referrals of HIV-1-infected individuals for a neuropsychological examination are made by a variety of health professionals (e.g., neurologists, psychiatrists, internal medicine specialists, pediatricians, family medicine physicians, vocational rehabilitation workers, etc.). The referrals are made for a number of reasons. Most of them are concerned with questions of the presence and severity of any cognitive impairment; the possible role of affective factors in any impairment; and the implication of these findings for the adjustment, capacity for work, or rehabilitation of the patient. The patients range from asymptomatic HIV-1-infected individuals to patients with ADC.

In the clinical examination of suspected or identified HIV-positive patients, it is important to recognize that the primary mode of transmission of the virus is by sexual intercourse, transfusion of infected blood, or contaminated needles. Casual exposure such as a handshake, sneezing, or being in close physical proximity to an infected person does not result in transmission. Obviously, contact with any open wound or bleeding by the patient should be avoided, and any examination should not proceed without adequate treatment of those conditions by people wearing protective gloves.

Earlier I made recommendations for using a battery of neuropsychological tests and measuring the affective status of the patients. I must reemphasize that the current research evidence does not identify any specific neuropsychological test as being uniquely sensitive to HIV-1 infection, although measures of speed of information processing, perceptual–motor speed, RT, and memory frequently (but not always) are found to be mildly impaired. Of course, the patient's performance on the neuropsychological tests should be compared with the best norms available. The patient's subjective complaints should be registered.

Furthermore, as in examining any patient with suspected neuropsychological deficits, a comprehensive interview should be done to eliminate the possibility that any deficits found are the result of factors other than HIV-1 infection. The measurement of depression and anxiety has already been mentioned. Other psychiatric symptoms or disorders can be identified through the use of instruments such as the Minnesota Multiphasic Personality Inventory (MMPI) or standardized psychiatric interview procedures. The patient's current and past alcohol and drug use histories should be obtained. Moderate-to-severe alcohol abuse, in particular, could result in mild-to-moderate cognitive deficits, despite the findings by Bornstein, Fama, et al. (1993). Systematic interviews and questionnaires have been developed to measure alcohol and drug use (see chap. 5 in this book). A substantial number of HIV-positive individuals have been infected by sharing drug injection needles. Given the possible residual effects of taking drugs on neuropsychological functioning, the patient's drug history should be explored carefully. Questions to elicit such information are provided in Exhibit 2.

A patient's history of any other disorder or experience that could result in central nervous system dysfunction should be obtained. Questions to elicit this information are provided in Exhibit 3. The possibility of previous learning disorders should be investigated by inquiring about any repeating of grades in school or placement in special classes. All medications currently being taken by the patient should be recorded. Any sensory problems (poor visual, auditory, or tactual abilities) or motor problems also should be noted. Premorbid special cognitive competencies as indicated by vocations (e.g., accounting, engineer or carpenter, lawyer, etc.) should be registered.

Recommendations for work capacity should be based on a comprehensive medical and clinical psychological examination as well as on a neuropsychological examination. Obviously, at advanced stages of AIDs, the patient's physical condition and mental condition may preclude any sustained work effort. At the symptomatic HIV-positive stage, the patient's symptoms, psychiatric status, and cognitive functioning status are important. In a sample of 289 HIV-positive men without dementia, a significantly higher unemployment rate ($p < .001$) was found in those who had neuropsychological impairment than in their nonimpaired peers. In addition, for those HIV-positive men who remained employed, there was a strong association between neuropsychological impairment and subjective decreases in job-related abilities. Neither depression nor medical symptoms could account for this relationship (Heaton et al., 1994).

Another factor that could affect work productivity in HIV-infected individuals is that, if their condition

EXHIBIT 2

Drug-Screening Questions

Interviewer: I am going to ask you about drugs that you have taken at any time for treatment of medical problems or on your own.

1. Have you ever used drugs for anxiety such as Librium, Valium, Xanex, Serax, Miltown, or Equinal? (Note to interviewer: For each drug taken in this class and the subsequent classes of drugs, record the following information:
   a. Length of time used (years or months)
   b. Average daily dose
   c. Date of most recent use
   d. Route of administration
2. Have you ever used drugs for psychotic illnesses such as Lithium, Thorazine, Mellaril, Haldol, Navane, Prolixin, and so on?
3. Have you ever used drugs for depression such as Zoloft, Prozac, Welbutrin, Elavil, Triavil, Sinequan, Vivacticl, Nardil, Parnate, Marplan, and so on?
4. Have you ever used barbiturates such as phenobarbital, nembutal, chloral hydrate, paraldehyde, red devils, downers, and so on?
5. Have you ever used cocaine or crack?
6. Have you ever used other stimulants (amphetamines) such as speed, crystal, crank, white crosses, methamphetamine, methylphenidate, and so on?
7. Have you ever used opiates such as heroin, opium, morphine, methadone, and so on? (record codeine under pain killers below)
8. Have you ever used hallucinogens such as LSD ("acid"), PCP, mushrooms, peyote, and so on?
9. Have you ever used other street drugs such as marijuana, ecstasy, designer drugs, quaaludes, and so on?
10. Have you ever used pain killers such as Darvon, Demerol, Percocet, Percodan, Codeine, Fiorinal, Darvocet, Tylenol III, and so on?
11. Have you ever inhaled substances such as glue, paint thinner, freon, White-Out, paint, gasoline, hair spray, or nitrous oxide?
12. Have you ever used Antabuse?
13. Have you ever used any other drugs that we haven't already discussed? (include current medications)
14. Have you ever drunk alcohol at the same time that you were taking any of these drugs?
15. Have you ever tried to stop taking a drug but were unsuccessful? (If the answer is yes, ask which drugs)
16. Have you ever had to increase the amount of the drug you were taking in order to get the same effect as when you first started?
17. Have you ever taken a drug in a larger amount or for a longer period than you intended?
18. Has taking any drug or drugs led to difficulties with the law, your spouse or significant other, your family, your health, your work, your finances, your friends? (Have the patient explain each positive response)
19. Have you ever shared drug injection needles with someone else?
20. Have you ever been in treatment for drug abuse or attended Narcotics Anonymous or Alcoholics Anonymous? (If yes, have patient explain)

If a positive response is given to 3 of Questions 15–18, the possibility of a past or current diagnosis of psychoactive substance dependence (revised third edition of the Diagnostic and Statistical Manual of Mental Disorders*) should be considered.*

EXHIBIT 3

Questions for Possible Brain Dysfunction Conditions

1. Were there any complications at the time of the patient's birth such as low birth weight, oxygen deprivation, prematurity, or deformity?
2. What childhood or adolescent diseases, trauma, or surgery did the patient have? Inquire about any loss of consciousness, concussions, convulsions, encephalitis, meningitis, high fevers about 104°, seizures, oxygen deprivation or near drowning, diabetes, poisoning, and head trauma.
3. What adult diseases, trauma, or surgery did the patient have? Inquire about high blood pressure, operations, auto accidents, electrical shock treatments or accidents, any diagnosis of central nervous system disorder such as multiple sclerosis, minor strokes, being dazed or losing consciousness from sports trauma, epilepsy or fits, fainting, sunstroke, recreational and prescription drug usage, alcohol use and abuse, and any partial paralysis or sensory loss.
4. What is the patient's educational history? Is there evidence of learning disabilities? If so, in reading, spelling, mathematics, or other? Did the patient fail any grade? Did the patient attend special classes? If so, for how long and in what subjects?

is known by coworkers, interpersonal isolation and rejection might occur and adversely affect work effectiveness. In this regard, all HIV-positive individuals should be encouraged to join one of the many HIV-1 support groups that have been formed throughout the country.

The same general considerations hold for recommendations for treatment. Aside from HIV-1 patients with ADC, the cognitive changes in HIV-1 patients are probably less important than the psychological and psychiatric reactions to their illness. The usual clinical psychological assessment of the patient's personality and affective difficulties and resources, as well as overall intelligence level, will provide information on treatment. Again, at a minimum, the patient should be advised to join an HIV-1 support group.

CASE EXAMPLES

The cases of 4 HIV-1-infected patients are presented. They illustrate some of the typical problems encountered in the clinical neuropsychological examination of such patients. Selected data from the neuropsychological examination are presented first, followed by individual summaries of case histories and interpretation of the results of the neuropsychological findings.

Summary of Selected Neuropsychological Findings

Data for the 4 HIV-1-infected individuals are presented in Tables 3 and 4. Note that in Table 3, all patients are in their 30s and have Full-Scale WAIS-R IQs in the average range. Two of the four, Patients A and B, have significantly lower Performance IQs than Verbal IQs, but the other two patients do not.

In the next grouping of tests, the results are presented for selected tests from the Halstead–Reitan Neuropsychological Test Battery (Reitan & Wolfson, 1993), which, according to Reitan and Wolfson (1986), are the most sensitive to brain dysfunction. In our laboratory, these tests provide good discrimination between alcoholic and nonalcoholic patients (Hochla, Fabian, & Parsons, 1982). The tests also are among the 26 recommended by Butters et al. (1990). The *T* scores ($M = 50$, $SD = 10$) are based on the most comprehensive set of norms currently available for the extended Halstead–Reitan Battery. These norms (Heaton, Grant, & Matthews, 1991) are adjusted for age and education. As can be seen, the Category test results all were in the average (nonimpaired) range. By contrast, for the Tactual Performance test (TPT)–Total Time, the scores of Patients A and B fell in the impaired range, whereas Patient C's was above average on this test. Patient D was not given the

TPT. For TPT–Location, Patients A and C scored in the mildly impaired range and Patient B in the average range. For Trail Making (Trails) B, Patients A and B scored below average; Patients C and D scored in the mildly impaired range. On the WAIS-R Block Design subtest, Patients A and B scored in the mildly impaired range and Patients C and D in the above-average and average ranges, respectively. For the WAIS-R Digit Symbol test, all 4 patients scored in the impaired range. Averaging *T* scores over the six tests (see the lower section of Table 3) placed Patients A and B in the mildly impaired, Patient D in the below-average, and Patient C in the average ranges. By contrast, the average *T* scores for the three clearest tests of perceptual–motor speed (i.e., Digit Symbol, Finger Tapping, and Trails B) placed 3 of the 4 patients, B,

TABLE 3

Patients' Ages, Years of Education, and Scores on the WAIS-R and Selected Tests From the Extended HRNTB

	Patient			
Variable	**A**	**B**	**C**	**D**
Age	38	39	35	32
Education (years)	15	14	GED	11
Intelligence				
WAIS-R Full-Scale IQ	108	100	107	90
Verbal IQ	125	110	110	93
Performance IQ	88	90	104	88

	Scores							
	Raw	***T*[b]**	**Raw**	***T*[b]**	**Raw**	***T*[b]**	**Raw**	***T*[b]**
HRNTB tests								
Category test[a]	30	47	35	47	20	55	38	47
TPT–Total Time[a]	17.1 min	40	24 min	32	7.7 min	63	—	—
TPT–Dominant Hand	4.6 min	52	10 min	33	4.0 min	56	—	—
TPT–Nondominant Hand	8.2 min	34	9.8 min	30	2.4 min	58	—	—
TPT–Both Hands	4.3 min	36	4.2 min	36	1.3 min	65	—	—
TPT–Memory	6	37	8	49	9	57	—	—
TPT–Location[a]	2	38	4	46	2	38	—	—
Block Design (scaled score)[a]	8	34	6	34	12	61	10	54
Trails B[a]	69 s	44	70 s	44	96 s	38	110 s	38
Digit Symbol (scaled score)[a]	7	35	6	31	5	29	6	37
Finger Tapping	52	48	—	—	45	37	46.6	41
Reitan's six best discriminating tests (mean *T* scores)	39.7		39.0		47.3		44.0	
Tests of motor and perceptual–motor speed (Digit Symbol, Trails B, and Finger Tapping)	42.3		37.5		34.7		38.7	

Note: WAIS-R = Wechsler Adult Intelligence Scale–Revised; TPT = Tactual Performance Test; GED = general equivalency diploma; HRNTB = Halstead–Reitan Neuropsychological Test Battery. Dashes indicate that these tests were not given.

[a]Reitan and Wolfson's (1986) six tests that best discriminate patients with brain damage.

[b]Heaton, Grant, and Matthews's (1991) age- and education-adjusted *T* scores ($M = 50$, $SD = 10$). *T* score classification: 25–29 = moderate impairment, 30–34 = mild-to-moderate impairment, 35–39 = mild impairment, 40–44 = below average, 44–54 = average, and 55+ = above average.

TABLE 4

Patients' Scores on Tests of Learning and Memory

Measure	A	B	C	D	*M*
Wechsler Memory Scale					
Stories: Immediate	16.8 (0)	13.0 (1)	12.5 (1)	10.0 (2)	(1)
Stories: Delayed	13.0 (0)	10.3 (1)	11.5 (1)	8.5 (2)	(1)
Figural Memory: Immediate	7 (3)	10 (1)	11 (1)	4 (4)	(2.25)
Figural Memory: Delayed	7 (3)	7 (2)	10 (1)	4 (3)	(2.25)
Luria Words Test					
Trial	4 (0)	9 (2)	10 (3)	10 (3)	(2)
Words learned	10 (0)	10 (0)	9 (2)	9 (2)	(1)
5-min Recall words recalled	10 (0)	7 (3)	9 (1)	7 (3)	(1.75)
10-min Recall words recalled	10 (0)	6 (4)	8 (1)	4 (4)	(2.25)

Note: Scores for the Wechsler Memory Scale are represented in terms of Russell's (1975) impairment scores: 0–1 = not impaired, 2 = mild impairment, 3–4 = moderate-to-severe impairment. Scores in parentheses are the equivalent of Russell's impairment index but are based on data from our laboratory. On the Luria Words Test, numbers represent the trial at which the best performance was reached.

C, and D, in the mildly to moderately impaired range and Patient A as below average.

In Table 4, the results of the administration of tests of memory for stories and figures and for list learning and memory are presented. Russell's (1975) method of scoring the WMS stories and figures both immediate and delayed (20 s) was used. The scores presented are ratings of impairment (0–1 = nonimpaired, 2 = mildly impaired, 3–4 = moderately to severely impaired, and 5 = severely impaired). Memory for stories was impaired only for Patient D, whose immediate and delayed scores were in the mildly impaired range. However, scores for figural memory were impaired in 3 of the 4 patients, especially delayed memory. Patient D was impaired on the stories and the figures for both the immediate and delayed trials.

The Luria Words Test (Sherer, Nixon, Parsons, & Adams, 1992) consists of learning 10 common nouns (e.g., *house, night, bridge, pie,* etc.) to a criterion of four successive correct recall of all 10 words (in any order) or 10 trials, whichever comes first. The average control subject learns the list in four or five trials. The data presented are for the trial of highest performance, (i.e., how rapidly the patient achieved his peak performance) and both 5- and 20-min recall. On the basis of our laboratory's norms, Patient A was clearly nonimpaired, Patient B was mildly impaired in acquisition and moderately to severely impaired in delayed recall, Patient C was moderately impaired in acquisition but not impaired in recall, and Patient D was moderately impaired in acquisition, moderately impaired at 5-min recall, and moderately to severely impaired at 20-min recall. In summary, 3 of the 4 patients were mildly to moderately impaired in acquisition and 2 of the 4 were impaired in delayed recall.

Case History Summaries and Integration of Findings

Case A. This patient was a 38-year-old single gay White man with 15 years of education who was referred by his physician from the infectious disease unit for testing of his cognitive abilities. According to his physician, the patient reported fears of becoming demented because of the progression of the HIV for which he had tested positive 2 years earlier. He complained of memory problems, believed his cognitive functions were slipping, and was experiencing depression. However, before testing could be accomplished, consultation with a vocational rehabilitation counselor indicated that he was eligible to receive support for completing his college degree in a health-related field. This information appeared to alleviate his depression and subjectively improve his cognitive functions.

Patient A had been an equity actor and then became a medical laboratory technician. He had made two serious suicide attempts by drug overdose: one 12 years previously when he lost his acting job and one a year ago when he lost his current job. He was hospitalized both times. He had a 10-year history of heavy alcohol consumption before his last hospitalization. Since then, he has been sober but unemployed. During his last hospitalization, he suffered injuries to his left arm and shoulder caused by tight restraints and complained of pain associated with left arm movements. No history of head trauma or other disorders that could compromise the central nervous system were reported. During testing, he was alert, responsive to questioning, and consistently put forth good effort. Mood and speech were considered normal, there was no evidence of any thought disorder, and affect was considered appropriate.

Of relevance to the interpretation of neuropsychological findings are the following: (a) The 10-year history of heavy alcohol intake could result in some neuropsychological decrements in performance; (b) the history of depression and suicide attempts suggested that an underlying depression may be present despite the patient's claims of feeling normal; and (c) the patient's injury to his left arm might compromise his motor performance with that extremity.

Tables 3 and 4 show a wide discrepancy between this patient's Verbal IQ (125) and Performance IQ (88). He also was impaired in visual figural memory on both immediate and delayed trials and on TPT–Location. These findings suggest the presence of right-hemisphere dysfunction. Consistent with this interpretation, his left-hand performance on the TPT–Total Time was impaired and his grip strength and finger tapping with the left hand were significantly lower than the right-hand performance (the latter data are not given in Tables 3 and 4). These impaired motor performances, however, were probably due in large part to the painful injury to his left arm. On the other hand, this patient had a Verbal IQ in the superior range, a nonimpaired Category test score, an excellent memory for stories both immediate and delayed, and excellent list learning with perfect delayed recall. Interpretation of the data was that his poor performance on tests associated with right-hemisphere functions could be attributable to a premorbid difference in cognitive abilities, plus a residual deficit from alcohol abuse. Whether the HIV-1 infection would selectively affect such functions seemed unlikely but remained a possibility. The one test consistent with that hypothesis was his relatively poor performance on the Digit Symbol test. Finally, Patient A's MMPI profile indicated characterological problems, but it was within normal limits for the presence of affective or thought disturbances. It was concluded that this patient had the cognitive resources to benefit from further college education and that the deficits in visual memory and perceptual organization and performance could gradually but partially resolve over time.

Case B. This patient was referred by a psychiatrist who wanted baseline cognitive functioning in anticipation of follow-up studies at a later time. Patient B had suffered from hemophilia since childhood. He was 39 years of age, had 14 years of education, and was married with two children. He worked as printer and publisher of a weekly newspaper, but several years ago he became so disabled that he took himself off of the payroll and his wife assumed most of the duties. As a result of his hemophilia, he suffered repeated hemorrhages that caused painful damage to his joints. Nine years ago, he had bilateral hip replacements; the right replacement is now deteriorating and causing considerable pain. He was confined to a wheelchair. He had been taking codeine for the past 15 years for the pain. Three years ago he was diagnosed as being HIV-positive, the result of contaminated blood transfusions some years previously. He is currently being successfully treated with methadone to break the addiction to codeine and this is going well. Other medications included AZT (azidothymidine), Septra (clorazepate depotassium), and Tranxene (trimethoprin and sulfamethoxazole). About 3.5 years ago, he suffered a subdural hematoma. Medical records were not available, but the patient indicated that the bleed began in the right posterior portion of the head and spread to the right frontal region. He denied any cognitive or physical sequelae of the bleed. Patient B reported that he had been depressed for the past 2 years and that the symptoms had worsened in the past 3–4 months. Also, he experienced symptoms of anxiety and panic and complained of poor short-term memory. He was pleasant and cooperative throughout the testing. Affect was flat and he appeared dysphoric, but he gave good effort on all the tasks.

Of relevance to the interpretation of the neuropsychological findings is the following: (a) the history of a right frontal bleed and subdural, (b) the subjective complaints of depression and anxiety, (c) subjective complaints of short-term memory problems, and (d) joint pains that might compromise motor speed.

As can be seen in Tables 3 and 4, there was a 20-point discrepancy between Patient B's Verbal IQ of 110 and his Performance IQ of 90, suggesting the presence of mild right-hemisphere dysfunction. His impaired scores on TPT–Total Time, Block Design, and Digit Symbol were consistent with this interpretation. His overall score on the tests most sensitive to brain dysfunction placed him 1.1 standard deviations lower than the mean of control peers (mildly impaired range). Perceptual–motor speed was mildly impaired (Trails B and Digit Symbol). Memory for stories both immediate and delayed was intact; figural memory was mildly impaired on the delayed recall. The acquisition of the Luria Words Test was mildly impaired, but his delayed recall was moderately to severely impaired. Areas of cognitive strengths were his verbal abilities and nonverbal abstracting as measured by the Category test. Finally, his MMPI profile suggested the presence of a severe depression and anxiety state, including feelings of worthlessness, hopelessness, low energy level, social withdrawal, tension, and agitation.

Interpretation of these data (and the rest of the testing, which was not reported) was that this patient was showing mild residual effects of the right frontal bleed and hematoma in his poorer performance on the tests involving visual–spatial organization and perceptual–motor skills. His interview complaints about severe depression and anxiety were corroborated by his MMPI profile and might well account for the short-term memory problems he noted. Some of the difficulties in motor speed and strength could be accounted for by the effects of hemorrhages in his joints. Although it was possible that some of the impaired performances could be accounted for by HIV-1 infection, a more parsimonious explanation was offered earlier. It was strongly advised that he receive treatment for the affective disturbances.

Case C. This patient was referred by his physician to assess the degree of cognitive decline associated wit his HIV-1 symptomatic infection. Patient C was 35-year-old gay male with a high school equivalency who was diagnosed as HIV-positive about 3.5 years previously. One year before testing, he was troubled by body aches, nausea, and a sudden onset of visual change and left face and arm numbness, which lasted for several hours. Several months later he started treatment with AZT. Two months ago he complained of reading and memory problems and felt that he was "going crazy." At that time, a computed tomography scan of the brain was within normal limits. The patient had been a professional ice skater for 15 years. On diagnosis of his HIV-positive status, he quit skating and became a barber. After working several years, he stopped working because of fatigue, nausea, and memory problems.

The patient stated that he currently had difficulty in organizing his thoughts and continued to have memory problems. He also indicated that his memory problems varied from day to day and admitted to a significant degree of depression. He lived in a stable relationship with his lover, who had AIDS. His past medical history was positive for three mild head injuries, one of which resulted in unconsciousness for 2 or 3 min. He admitted to heavy use of alcohol in the past and experimentation with other drugs. The patient was cooperative, alert, and fully oriented. There were no indications of thought disturbance, but he did appear to be distressed and tearful several times during the testing session. Nonetheless, he appeared to give consistent effort on all of the tests.

Of relevance for the interpretation of the neuropsychological test findings are (a) the subjective complaints of depression, (b) the possible effect of three apparently minor head injuries, and (c) the history of heavy use of alcohol.

Considering the results in Tables 3 and 4, Patient C was functioning at the average level of intelligence with no significant difference between his Verbal IQ and Performance IQ. His performance on the tests most sensitive to brain dysfunction (see Table 3) placed him in the average range. This is somewhat misleading in that his performance on the Category test, TPT–Total Time, and Block Design was above average, but his performance on the TPT–Location, Trails B, and especially Digit Symbol was impaired. Indeed, the three measures of perceptual–motor speed indicated a mild-to-moderate impairment. His memory for stories and figures, both immediate and delayed, was intact. Learning of the Luria Words List was mildly impaired, but delayed recall was within normal limits. His MMPI indicated moderate depression.

It was concluded that Patient C performed in the unimpaired range for most of the neuropsychological tests administered (including others not reported here) and that his speed-of-performance deficits could be the result of his moderate level of depression or his HIV-1 infection. Treatment for the depression was advised. Retesting after successful treatment could help in arriving at a more definitive identification of the possible cause of the impairment in speed of performance.

Case D. This patient was a 32-year-old gay man with 11 years of education. He was unemployed and had worked as a shipping-and-receiving clerk for about 10 years previously. He had to terminate work because of physical problems. He lived with his lover in a stable relationship. He was referred by his physician in the infectious disease unit because of his complaints about memory impairment. The patient was diagnosed as HIV-positive about 3 years ago and within 6 months was diagnosed as having ARC. Two years ago, he had complaints of pain and parathesias in his lower extremities. Magnetic resonance imaging of the head was done and found to be normal, although there was significant artifact in the region of the brain stem, particularly the right pons. Approximately 1 year ago, he was diagnosed as having AIDS and placed on AZT. Shortly after that, he attempted suicide by overdose of AZT and was referred to a mental health clinic, but he never contacted them.

During the interview he stated that his memory was worsening and that he had anxiety attacks. His memory was such that he had to write things down in order to be sure to do them; his anxiety attacks were characterized by difficulty catching his breath and having a rapid heart beat. His medications included Dilantin, which helped with fasiculations in his legs, Pentanomine for his pneumocystitis, AZT, and other medicine for periodic bouts of thrush. He reported past heavy alcohol use and intravenous drug use, but he was currently not using. He reported having been knocked unconscious by an automobile at about age 10, but he did not think that there had been any long-term sequelae from this injury. During the examination, Patient D displayed good motivation and cooperation. No signs of thought disturbance were present, and generally he displayed a normal range of affect. However, several times when difficult topics were discussed in the interview, he became abruptly tearful and distressed but just as quickly resumed normal affective status.

Of relevance to the neuropsychological evaluation were (a) subjective complaints of memory problems, (b) subjective complaints of anxiety attacks, and (c) a possible underlying depression.

Tables 3 and 4 indicate that Patient D was functioning at the average level of intelligence (Full-Scale IQ of 90), with Verbal IQ in the average range and Performance IQ in the below-average range, but this difference was not significant. On the tests most sensitive to brain damage (only four of the six given), he scored in the below-average range (see Table 3), although on the Category test his performance was in the average range. On the tests of perceptual–motor speed (see Table 3), his scores were in the mildly impaired range, with Digit Symbol being the most impaired. His memory for stories both immediate and delayed was mildly impaired; figural memory scores fell in the moderately to severely impaired range (see Table 4). On the Luria Words Test, he had a moderate impairment in acquisition and a moderate-to-severe impairment in delayed recall. His MMPI was grossly elevated, with a profile indicating a moderate-to-severe depression and anxiety syndrome.

It was concluded from these results (and other test results not presented) that this patient manifested a mild-to-moderate overall impairment with mild-to-moderate impairments in perceptual–motor speed, acquisition (word-list learning), and immediate and delayed memory. His level of depression and anxiety could contribute to these deficits and to the course of his AIDS condition. He was considered a suicide risk, and supportive counseling was recommended.

In summary, these abbreviated case histories and reported results illustrate a number of important points for the clinical neuropsychologist and other practitioners.

1. The data suggest that patients referred for clinical neuropsychological examinations often manifest a variety of medically relevant current and past problems that should be considered in interpreting the results.
2. Despite the research findings cited earlier that indicated that depressive symptoms could not account for the cognitive impairment occasionally found in HIV-1-infected individuals, it is my clinical impression that the role of the affective distress (depression and anxiety) that frequently accompanies the HIV-positive status must be considered. This is especially true when speed-of-performance and memory problems, two of the more common findings among HIV-positive patients, are present.
3. The Category test, one of the most sensitive tests in the neuropsychological battery for other types of brain damage, was consistently in the nonimpaired range for the 4 patients, suggesting relative intactness of cortical functioning. The TPT (which involves perceptual–motor as well as problem-solving abilities), on the other hand, was impaired in 2 of the 3 patients to whom it was given.
4. Performance on the three tests of perceptual–motor speed was below average to moderately impaired in the 4 patients. This finding is consistent with the subcortical neuropathological changes previously described for HIV-1-infected individuals. Three of the 4 patients had impairments in learning and memory, especially delayed recall. This finding is consistent with the patients' subjective complaints.
5. Considering the presence of a variety of other problems such as alcohol abuse, drug use, feelings of low energy and fatigue, minor head trauma, and HIV-1 infections, the 4 patients were reasonably intact in their cognitive functioning. This finding parallels those obtained in the research studies referred to in the earlier part of this chapter.

TREATMENT AND PREVENTION

There is still no known cure for HIV-1 immunodeficiency infections. Drugs such as AZT, ddI (2′,3′-dideoxyinosine), or ddC (2′,3′-dideoxycytidine), used individually or in combination, may alleviate some of the symptoms and prolong life, although the use of ddC has been questioned by some researchers (Coates, 1993). Given these facts, primary and secondary prevention strategies become extremely important. As pointed out by the National Commission on AIDS (1993), the social behavioral approaches to AIDS prevention have been chronically underfunded by the National Institutes of Health. According to the commission, "it is critically important to immediately make effective use of behavioral and social science knowledge in the national response to the HIV/AIDS epidemic" (National Commission on AIDS, 1993, p. 9).

The commission's recommendation was based, in part, on the success of the few large-scale HIV-1 infection prevention studies that have been undertaken. The San Francisco Men's Health Study, in collaboration with the San Francisco AIDS Foundation and other community-based organizations, carried out a multifaceted, community-level HIV-1 risk reduction program. Rates of new infection fell to less than 1% per year over a 6-year period in the target populations of gay and bisexual men. In Zaire, a condom usage promotion, which included mass media, interviews, theaters, bars, and village seminars, resulted in sales of condoms in 1988 of 800,000 and 18,000,000 in 1990 (Coates, 1993).

The role of psychologists in treatment and prevention has been examined by a number of writers. Chesney (1993) pointed out the challenges to health psychologists posed by the AIDS epidemic, such as the rising expectations for successful behavior change programs, providing services to the growing number of people who are coping with chronic disease, and an increasing shift to community and public health perspectives in dealing with the epidemic.

Priorities for the roles of psychologists in the "second decade" of the AIDS epidemic were formulated by Kelly, Murphy, Sikkema, and Kalichman (1993):

> *Behavior change efforts must now rapidly move to second generation approaches that incorporate methods to change social and peer norms concerning risk behavior avoidance, facilitate acquisition of cognitive and behavioral skill competencies needed to implement and sustain change, foster accurate appraisals of risk vulnerability, strengthen behavior change motivation, and target situational factors—such as recreational drug use—that interfere with change implementation. (p. 1024)*

To the extent that neuropsychologists have interests and competencies in these areas, their contributions, together with other clinical, social, and health psychologists, are sorely needed.

SUMMARY

In the United States, AIDS is already the seventh leading cause of death overall and the leading cause among 25- to 44-year-olds. There are no indications that the disease is abating. There is biomedical evidence for a continuum of increasing brain abnormalities ranging from HIV-positive individuals who do not have any symptoms (and a low incidence of brain abnormalities), to HIV-positive patients who do have symptoms (ARC), to patients with AIDS who are not demented, to AIDS patients with ADC. Up to 90% of the latter group exhibit brain abnormalities. From 40% to 90% of patients with AIDS (depending on the sample studied) exhibit ADC. The progression of brain dysfunction seems to be from primarily a subcortical locus in the early and middle stages to an increased involvement of the cortex in patients with ADC. There is no known cure for HIV-1 infection, although drugs such as AZT may alleviate some symptoms. Primary prevention is the current preferred method of containing the disorder.

Recent neuropsychological research on HIV-1-infected individuals has focused on the progression in the development of neuropsychological impairment in peers who are HIV-negative, HIV-positive but asymptomatic, HIV-positive and symptomatic, and in patients with AIDS. Considering all the evidence, aside from patients with AIDS, approximately one third of the HIV-positive patients manifest mild impairments on neuropsychological test batteries. These impairments are more prominent in patients who are HIV-positive and symptomatic. Although there is no consistency across studies as to which cognitive functions are impaired, deficits in speed of information processing, perceptual–motor performance, attention, concentration, and memory have been reported most frequently. These areas of cognitive deficits match the subjective complaints of the HIV-1-infected patients. Affective distress cannot account for the neuropsychological impairment in these patients.

The clinical neuropsychological examination of individual patients with ADC should consist of tests that are commonly used to assess functioning in cases of dementia. For the other HIV-1-infected individuals, a battery of neuropsychological tests including measures of RT, speed of information processing, perceptual–motor speed, attention and memory, especially delayed memory, and selected tests of higher cognitive functions should be used. These patients should be given a comprehensive interview to eliminate the possibility that any deficits found are not attributable to premorbid or current confounding factors. Any sensory or motor impairments that could affect performance should be noted. All medications currently taken should be recorded. The importance of such factors in interpreting the results of the clinical neuropsychological examination was illustrated in each of four case examples.

References

American Academy of Neurology AIDS Task Force. (1991). Nomenclature and research case definitions for neurologic manifestations of human immunodeficiency virus type (HIV-1) infection. *Neurology, 41,* 778–785.

Ayers, M. R., Abrams, D. L., Newell, T. G., & Friedrich, F. (1987). Performance of individuals with AIDS on the Luria–Nebraska Neuropsychological Battery. *International Journal of Clinical Neuropsychology, 9,* 101–105.

Baddeley, A., Logie, R., Bressi, S., Della Sala, S., & Spinnler, H. (1986). Dementia and working memory.

Quarterly Journal of Experimental Psychology, 38A, 603–618.

Beason-Hazen, S., & Bornstein, R. A. (1994). Self-report of symptoms and neuropsychological performance in HIV+ asymptomatic individuals. *Journal of Neuropsychiatry and Clinical Neurosciences, 6,* 43–49.

Benton, A., & Hamsher, K. (1977). *Multilingual Aphasia Examination manual.* Iowa City: University of Iowa.

Berg, E. A. (1948). A simple objective test for measuring flexibility in thinking. *Journal of General Psychology, 39,* 15–22.

Borkowski, J. G., Benton, A. L., & Spreen, O. (1967). Word fluency and brain damage. *Neuropsychologia, 5,* 135–140.

Bornstein, R. A. (1994). Methodological and conceptual issues in the study of cognitive change in HIV infection. In I. Grant (Ed.), *Neuropsychology of HIV infections* (pp. 146–160). New York: Oxford University Press.

Bornstein, R. A., Fama, R., Rosenberger, P., Whitacre, C. C., Para, M. F., Nasrallah, H. A., & Foss, R. J. (1993). Drug and alcohol use and neuropsychological performance in asymptomatic HIV infection. *Journal of Neuropsychiatry and Clinical Neurosciences, 5,* 254–259.

Bornstein, R. A., Nasrallah, H. A., Para, M. F., Whitacre, C. C., Rosenberger, P., & Foss, R. J. (1993). Neuropsychological performance in symptomatic and asymptomatic HIV infection. *AIDS, 7,* 519–524.

Brew, B. J. (1993). HIV-1-related neurological disease. *Journal of Acquired Human Immunodeficiency Syndromes, 6*(Suppl. 1), 510–515.

Buehler, J. W., Ward, J. W., & Berkelman, R. L. (1993). The surveillance definition for AIDS in the U.S. *AIDS, 7,* 585–587.

Buschke, H., & Fuld, P. A. (1974). Evaluating storage, retention and retrieval in disordered memory and learning. *Neurology, 24,* 1019–1025.

Butters, N., Granholm, E., Salmon, D. P., Grant, I., & Wolfe, J. (1987). Episodic and semantic memory: A comparison of amnesic and demented patients. *Journal of Clinical and Experimental Neuropsychology, 9,* 479–497.

Butters, N., Grant, I., Haxby, J., Judd, L. L., Martin, A., McClelland, J., Pequegnat, W., Schacter, D., & Stover, E. (1990). Assessment of AIDS-related cognitive changes: Recommendations of the NIMH workshop on neuropsychological assessment approaches. *Journal of Clinical and Experimental Neuropsychology, 12,* 963–978.

Cassens, G., Wolfe, L., & Zola, M. (1990). The neuropsychology of depressions. *Journal of Neuropsychiatry and Clinical Neurosciences, 2,* 202–213.

Centers for Disease Control and Prevention. (1992). 1993 revised classification system for HIV infection and expanded surveillance case definition for AIDS among adolescents and adults. *Morbidity and Mortality Weekly Report, 41,* 1–19.

Centers for Disease Control and Prevention. (1993a). Update: Mortality attributable to HIV infection/AIDS among persons aged 24–44 years—United States, 1990 and 1991. *Morbidity and Mortality Weekly Report, 42,* 481–485.

Centers for Disease Control and Prevention. (1993b). Recommendations for HIV testing services for inpatients and outpatients in acute-care hospital settings. *Morbidity and Mortality Weekly Report, 42,* 1–6.

Centers for Disease Control and Prevention. (1994). *Morbidity and Mortality Weekly Report, 43,* 825–843.

Centers for Disease Control and Prevention. (1995a). *Morbidity and Mortality Weekly Report, 44,* 87–100.

Centers for Disease Control and Prevention. (1995b). *Morbidity and Mortality Weekly Report, 44,* 849–853.

Chesney, M. A. (1993). Health psychology in the 21st century: Acquired immunodeficiency syndrome as a harbinger of things to come. *Health Psychology, 12,* 259–268.

Coates, T. J. (1993). Prevention of HIV-1 infection: Accomplishments and priorities. *Journal of NIH Research, 5,* 73–76.

Coffin, J. M. (1995). HIV population dynamics in vivo: Implications for genetic variation, pathogenesis and therapy. *Science, 267,* 483–489.

Diehr, M. C., White, D. A., Heaton, R. K., McCutchan, J. A., Wallace, M. R., Grant, I., Atkinson, H., & the HNRC Group. (1995). Neuropsychological profile of HIV-1 associated minor cognitive motor disorder. *Journal of the International Neuropsychological Society, 1,* 138.

Delis, D. C., Kramer, J. H., Kaplan, E., & Ober, B. A. (1987). *The California Verbal Learning Test.* New York: Psychological Corporation.

Epstein, L. G., & Gendelman, H. E. (1993). Human immunodeficiency virus type 1 infection of the nervous system. *Annals of Neurology, 33,* 429–435.

Ezzell, C. (1993). On borrowed time: Long-term survivors of HIV-1 infection. *Journal of NIH Research, 5,* 77–82.

Folstein, M. F., Folstein, S. E., & McHugh, P. R. (1975). Mini-Mental State: A practical method for grading the cognitive state of patients for the clinician. *Journal of Psychiatric Research, 12,* 189–198.

Grant, I., Atkinson, J. H., Hesselink, J. R., Kennedy, C. J., Richman, D. D., Spector, S. A., & McCutchan, J. A. (1987). Evidence for early central nervous system involvement in the acquired immunodeficiency syndrome (AIDS) and other human immunodeficiency virus (HIV) infections. *Annals of Internal Medicine, 107,* 828–836.

Grant, I., Olshen, R. A., Atkinson, J. H., Heaton, R. K., Nelson, J., McCutchan, J. A., & Weinrich, J. D. (1993). Depressed mood does not explain neuropsychological deficits in HIV-infected persons. *Neuropsychology, 7,* 53–61.

Grober, E., Sliwinski, M., & Buschke, H. (1990). Premorbid intelligence in the elderly. *Journal of Clinical and Experimental Neuropsychology, 12,* 30.

Gronwall, D. M. A. (1977). Paced auditory serial-addition task: A measure of recovery from concussion. *Perceptual and Motor Skills, 44,* 367–373.

Halstead, W. C. (1947). *Brain & intelligence: A quantitative study of the frontal lobes*. Chicago: University of Chicago Press.

Hamilton, M. A. (1960). A rating scale for depression. *Journal of Neurology, Neurosurgery and Psychiatry, 23,* 56–62.

Heaton, R. K. (1993, August). Neuropsychological impairment and vocational difficulties in HIV-1 infected persons. Symposium conducted at the 101st Annual Convention of the American Psychological Association, Toronto.

Heaton, R. K., Grant, I., & Matthews, C. G. (1991). *Comprehensive norms for an Extended Halstead-Reitan Battery*. Odessa, FL: Psychological Assessment Resources.

Heaton, R. K., Velin, R. A., McCutchan, J. A., Gulevich, S. J., Atkinson, J. H., Wallace, M. R., Hamish, H. P. D., Kirson, D. A., Grant, I., & the HNRC Group. (1994). Neuropsychological impairment in human immunodeficiency virus infection: Implications for employment. *Psychosomatic Medicine, 56,* 8–17.

Hinkin, C. H., Van Gorp, W. G., Satz, P., Weisman, J. D., Thommes, J., & Buckingham, S. (1992). Depressed mood and its relationship to neuropsychological test performance in HIV-1 seropositive individuals. *Journal of Clinical and Experimental Neuropsychology, 14,* 289–297.

Hochla, N. A. N., Fabian, M. S., & Parsons, O. A. (1982). Brain-age quotients in recently detoxified alcoholic, recovered alcoholic and nonalcoholic women. *Journal of Clinical Psychology, 38,* 207–212.

Jones-Gotman, N., & Milner, B. (1977). Design fluency: The invention of nonsense drawings after focal cortical lesions. *Neuropsychologia, 15,* 653–674.

Kaderman, R., Levin, B., & Berger, J. (1995). Relationship between cerebrospinal fluid grunolinic acid and cognitive functioning in HIV-1. *Journal of the International Neuropsychological Society, 1,* 161.

Kaemingk, K. L., & Kaszniak, A. W. (1989). Neuropsychological aspects of human immunodeficiency virus infection. *The Clinical Neuropsychologist, 4,* 309–326.

Kaplan, E., Goodglass, H., & Weintraub, S. (1983). *Boston Naming Test*. Philadelphia: Lea & Febiger.

Kelly, J. A., Murphy, D. A., Sikkema, K. J., & Kalichman, S. C. (1993). Psychological interventions to prevent HIV infection are urgently needed. *American Psychologist, 48,* 1023–1034.

Kløve, H. (1963). Clinical neuropsychology. *Medical Clinics of North America, 47,* 1647–1658.

Mapou, R. L., Law, W. A., Kay, G. G., Clasby, S., Roller, T. L., & Temoshok, L. R. (1995). Performance on conventional and computerized reaction time measures in HIV-1-infected individuals. *Journal of the International Neuropsychological Society, 1,* 162.

Mapou, R. L., Law, W. A., Martin, A., Kampen, D., Salazar, A. M., & Rundell, J. R. (1993). Neuropsychological performance, mood and complaints of cognitive and motor difficulties in individuals infected with the human immunodeficiency virus. *Journal of Neuropsychiatry and Clinical Neurosciences, 5,* 86–93.

Martin, A., Heyes, M. P., Salazar, A. M., Kampen, D. L., Williams, J., Law, W. A., Coats, M. E., & Markey, S. P. (1992). Progressive slowing of reaction time and increasing cerebrospinal concentrations of quinolinic acid. *Journal of Neuropsychiatry and Clinical Neurosciences, 4,* 270–279.

Martin, E. M., Robertson, L. C., & Edelstein, H. E. (1989). Decision-making speed is impaired in early-stage HIV infection. *Journal of Clinical and Experimental Neuropsychology, 11,* 78.

Masliah, E., Achim, C. L., Nianfeng, G. C., DeTeresa, R., Terry, R. D., & Widey, C. A. (1992). Spectrum of human immunodeficiency virus-associated neocortical damage. *Annals of Neurology, 32,* 321–329.

McAllister, R. H., Herns, M. V., Harrison, M. J. G., Newman, S. P., Connolly, S., Fowler, C. J., Fell, M., Durrance, P., Maryi, H., Kendall, B. E., Valentine, A. R., Weller, I. V. D., & Adler, M. (1992). Neurological and neuropsychological performance in HIV seropositive men without symptoms. *Journal of Neurology, Neurosurgery and Psychiatry, 55,* 143–148.

McArthur, J. C. (1987). Neurologic manifestations of AIDS. *Medicine, 66,* 407–437.

Money, J. (1976). *A standardized road-map test of directional sense*. San Rafael, CA: Academic Therapy Publications.

National Commission on AIDS. (1993). *Behavioral and social sciences and the HIV/AIDS epidemic*. Washington, DC: CDC National AIDS Clearinghouse.

Navia, B. A., Cho, E. S., Petito, C. K., & Price, R. W. (1986). The AIDS dementia complex: II. Neuropathology. *Annals of Neurology, 19,* 525–535.

Navia, B. A., Jordan, B. D., & Price, R. W. (1986). The AIDS dementia complex: I. Clinical feature. *Annals of Neurology, 19,* 517–524.

Ollo, C., Johnson, R., Jr., & Grafman, J. (1991). Signs of cognitive change in HIV disease: An event-related brain potential study. *Neurology, 41,* 209–215.

Osborn, J. E. (1990). AIDS: Politics and science. *Preventive Medicine, 19,* 744–751.

Peavy, G., Jacobs, D., Salmon, D., Butters, N., Delis, D. C., Taylor, M., Massman, P., Stout, J. C., Heindel, W. C., Kirson, D., Atkinson, J. H., Chandler, J. L., Grant, I., & the HNRC Group. (1994). Verbal memory performance of patients with human immunodeficiency virus infection: Evidence of subcortical dysfunction. *Journal of Experimental and Clinical Neuropsychology, 16,* 508–523.

Redfield, R. R., Wright, D. C., & Tramont, E. C. (1986). The Walter Reed staging classification for HTLV III/LAV infection. *New England Journal of Medicine, 314,* 131–132.

Reitan, R. M. (1958). Validity of the Trail Making Test as an indicator of organic brain damage. *Perceptual and Motor Skills, 8,* 271–276.

Reitan, R. M., & Wolfson, D. (1986). The Halstead–Reitan Neuropsychological Test Battery and aging. *Clinical Gerontologist, 5,* 39–61.

Reitan, R. M., & Wolfson, D. (1993). *The Halstead–Reitan Neuropsychological Battery* (2nd ed.). Tucson, AZ: Neuropsychology Press.

Rennick, P. M. (1979). *Color-naming and visual search tests for Repeatable Cognitive-Perceptual Motor Battery.* Grosse Point Park, MI: Axon Publishing.

Robins, L. N., Helzer, J. E., Croughan, J., & Ratcliff, K. S. (1981). National Institute of Mental Health Diagnostic Interview Schedule: Its history, characteristics and validity. *Archives of General Psychiatry, 38,* 381–389.

Rottenberg, D. A., Moeller, J. R., Strother, S. C., Sidtis, J. J., Navia, B. A., Dhaivan, V., Genos, J. Z., & Price, R. W. (1987). The metabolic pathology of the AIDS dementia complex. *Annals of Neurology, 22,* 700–706.

Russell, E. W. (1975). A multiple scoring method for the assessment of complex memory functions. *Journal of Consulting and Clinical Psychology, 43,* 800–809.

Sherer, M., Nixon, S. J., Parsons, O. A., & Adams, R. L. (1992). Performance of alcoholic and brain-damaged subjects on the Luria Memory Words Test. *Archives of Clinical Neuropsychology, 7,* 499–504.

Shipley, W. C. (1946). *A self-administering scale of measuring intellectual impairment: Manual of directions and scoring key.* Los Angeles: Western Psychological Services.

Skoraszewski, M. J., Ball, J. D., & Mikulka, P. (1991). Neuropsychology functioning of HIV-infected males. *Journal of Clinical and Experimental Neuropsychology, 13,* 278–290.

Spielberger, C. D., Gorsuch, R. C., & Lushene, R. E. (1970). *Manual for the State-Trait Inventory.* Palo Alto, CA: Consulting Psychologists Press.

Stern, Y., Marder, K., Bell, K., Chen, J., Dooneref, G., Goldstein, S., Mindry, R. D., Richards, M., Sano, M., Wellcones, J., Gorman, J., Ehrhardt, A., & Wayeux, R. (1991). Multidisciplinary baseline assessment of homosexual men with and without human immunodeficiency virus infection: III. Neurologic and neuropsychological findings. *Archives of General Psychiatry, 48,* 131–138.

Sternberg, S. (1966). High-speed scanning in human memory. *Science, 153,* 652–654.

Stroup, E. S., Hunter, M., & Bornstein, R. A. (1995). Subtle cognitive deficit and psychological distress in asymptomatic HIV infection. *Journal of the International Neuropsychological Society, 1,* 138.

Tersmette, M., & Schuitemaker, H. (1993). Virulent HIV strains? *AIDS, 7,* 1123–1125.

Touchette, N. (1993). Asia now second only to Africa in total HIV infections. *Journal of NIH Research, 5,* 47–48.

Van Gorp, W. G., Mandelbaum, M. A., Gee, M., Hinkin, C. H., Stern, C. E., Paz, D. K., Dixon, W., Evans, G., Flynn, F., Frederick, C. J., Ropchau, J. R., & Blahd, W. H. (1992). Cerebral metabolic dysfunction in AIDS: Findings with and without dementia. *Journal of Neuropsychiatry and Clinical Neurosciences, 4,* 281–287.

Van Gorp, W. G., Satz, P., & Hinkin, C. H. (1991). Metacognition in HIV-1 seropositive asymptomatic individuals: Self ratings vs. objective neuropsychological performance. *Journal of Experimental and Clinical Neuropsychology, 13,* 812–817.

Wechsler, D. (1981). *Wechsler Adult Intelligence Scale-Revised manual.* New York: Psychological Corporation.

Wechsler, D. (1987). *Wechsler Memory Scale-Revised.* New York: Psychological Corporation.

Wilkins, J. W., Robertson, K. R., Snyder, C. R., Robertson, W. K., van der Horst, C., & Hall, C. D. (1991). Implications of self-reported cognitive and motor dysfunction in HIV-positive patients. *American Journal of Psychiatry, 148,* 641–643.

Williams, J. B. W. (1988). A structured interview guide for the Hamilton Depression Rating Scale. *Archives of General Psychiatry, 45,* 742–746.

Witkin, H., Ohman, P., Raskin, E., & Karp, S. (1971). *Embedded Figures Test.* Palo Alto, CA: Consulting Psychologists Press.

CHAPTER 8

MULTIPLE SCLEROSIS

William W. Beatty

In this chapter, I hope to acquaint readers with the cognitive features of multiple sclerosis (MS). After a brief consideration of the purely medical aspects of the disease, I summarize the current state of knowledge about the major cognitive changes associated with MS, which is based primarily on studies of groups of patients who have MS. This approach has significant limitations, as I attempt to demonstrate with four single-case studies. Finally, I discuss what I believe the roles of clinical neuropsychologists should be in the evaluation and treatment of patients with MS. I come by my opinions on the basis of 10 years of experimental research on cognition in MS and as the spouse of a woman who became wheelchair bound 5 years after being diagnosed with this disease.

NEUROLOGY AND NEUROPATHOLOGY

MS is characterized by inflammatory demyelination, which can occur anywhere in the central nervous system. Although cognitive symptoms may predominate initially, more typically the first symptoms are associated with involvement of the white-matter tracts of the spinal cord, optic nerves, brain stem, cerebellum, and the periventricular regions throughout the brain. Common initial symptoms are blurred or double vision, numbness or tingling in the limbs, and gait or balance problems. The numerous possible locations of the lesions guarantees, as Ebers (1986) has stated, that "the symptoms of the disease are protean" (p. 1268).

After the appearance of the initial symptoms (whatever they may be), the typical outcome is that the symptoms spontaneously remit. Then—weeks, months, or years later—the same or different symptoms reappear, only to wane or disappear completely, as if by magic. Some patients have several relapses a year, whereas others may have none. Patients who have frequent relapses for several years may subsequently enter a period in which no relapses occur for many years.

There is little wonder that this confusing and disorderly state of affairs has often led physicians to conclude that their patients' problems were psychiatric rather than neurologic. The clinical histories of many MS patients record years of treatment for "hysteria" or "conversion disorder." (Conversely, one wonders if any of Freud's patients may actually have had MS.)

Fortunately, the introduction of new technologies—such as magnetic resonance imaging and evoked potentials—has improved diagnosis by permitting earlier demonstration of "real" changes in biological variables. It is important to note, however, that none of these procedures can yield a sign that is specific for MS. Various diagnostic criteria for MS

The research reported in this chapter was supported by Grant HR3-005 from the Oklahoma Center for the Advancement of Science and Technology and by funds provided by the Neuropsychiatric Research Institute, Fargo, ND. Special thanks are due to Nancy Monson, Karen Hames, Susan Wilbanks, Carlos Blanco, and Robert Paul—all of whom provided skilled technical assistance—and to all of the patients and control participants from North Dakota, Minnesota, and Oklahoma who generously donated their time to provide data for the studies described herein.

have been used, but all require the demonstration of white-matter lesions that are disseminated in time and space. In effect, this means that there must be at least two episodes and that the patient's symptoms cannot be explained by a single lesion anywhere in the central nervous system. Other neurological disorders can fulfill these criteria, so the actual diagnosis of MS ultimately rests on clinical judgment.

After the appearance of the first symptoms, the clinical course of the disease is extremely variable and, for the individual patient, completely unpredictable. In the older literature, relapsing–remitting and chronically progressive disease courses were recognized. In the former type, patients were said to exhibit bouts of worsening (relapses) separated by periods of recovery to relatively normal functioning (remitting). In the latter type, patients supposedly showed a steadily (chronically) downward course, with severe disability likely within 2 years. In an important study, Goodkin, Hertsgaard, and Rudick (1989) demonstrated that this chronically progressive scheme has almost no predictive validity in forecasting disability 2 years after diagnosis, even when the initial diagnostic categories are defined by rigorous operational definitions.

A more recent taxonomic scheme recognizes five disease courses: (a) benign sensory (1–2 attacks of mainly sensory symptoms in a lifetime); (b) benign relapsing–remitting (periodic relapses, with nearly complete recovery after each); (c) progressive relapsing–remitting (periodic relapses with partial but incomplete recovery after each relapse); (d) chronic progressive (steady but slow worsening without significant recovery); and (e) acute progressive (rapid deterioration, often leading to death). Because this nosology is new, its prospective utility is unknown.

Measurement of disability for MS patients in neurological terms is most often accomplished with Kurtzke's (1983) Expanded Disability Status Scale (EDSS). On the basis of a detailed neurological examination, ratings are made of the status of several functional systems (e.g., cerebral or cerebellar). These scores are then combined into an overall summary score, with values ranging from 0 (*unaffected*) to 10 (*death due to MS*) in 0.5-point steps (see Exhibit 1). Unfortunately, this scale is rarely used by clinical neurologists unless they are also researchers. Indeed, in my experience, most clinical neurologists do not systematically examine their MS patients at all, except during relapses and at diagnosis.

A crude, but effective method for quantifying disability that does not require a neurological examination is the Ambulation Index (Hauser et al., 1983), which is also shown in Exhibit 1. This measure of walking ability requires only a hallway, a stopwatch, simple observation, and a few straightforward questions. Scores range from 0 (*unaffected*) to 9 (*wheelchair bound and unable to transfer without assistance*) and are highly and positively correlated ($r = .96$; Beatty, Goodkin, Hertsgaard, & Monson, 1990) with the EDSS summary score. The major limitations of the Ambulation Index are that it does not measure visual and upper-limb functions, but there are many simple and effective ways of measuring these capacities, such as using a standard eye chart or the Purdue Pegboard Test (Purdue Research Foundation, 1948).

The neuropathological signature of MS is the plaque that indicates a lesion in the myelin surrounding the nerve axon. (Note, however, that the MS plaque is altogether different from the senile plaques characteristic of Alzheimer's disease, which are composed of degenerating neurites.) Within the MS plaques, there is myelin loss, gliosis, and relative sparing of axons, although damage is sometimes severe enough to disrupt or destroy axons (Raine, 1990). Immunological techniques have suggested that invasion of CD4 helper cells from the thymus herald lesion progression, whereas increased macrophage activity leads to active breakdown of myelin. The processes associated with active lesions produce edema (swelling) that is not present in old lesions, which in autopsy specimens appear sclerotic (scarred).

The exact sequence of events that culminates in the active formation of plaques is not known with certainty. The best current guess is as follows: (a) The blood–brain barrier, which ordinarily separates the myelin from the body's immune system, is somehow breached; (b) this exposes the proteins of the myelin, which are potent antigens, to detection by the immune system; and (c) the immune system launches an attack on the myelin, led by the CD4 cells. The control systems are actually considerably

EXHIBIT 1

The Expanded Disability Status Scale and the Ambulation Index

Expanded Disability Status Scale[a]

0 Normal neurologic exam.

1 No disability, minimal signs in one functional system.

2 Minimal disability in one functional system.

3 Moderate disability in one functional system or mild disability in three or four functional systems.

4 Fully ambulatory without aid despite relatively severe disability in one functional system; able to walk 500 m without aid or rest.

5 Able to walk 200 m without aid or rest, but cannot complete a normal day's activities without special provisions.

6 Able to walk 100 m without rest with unilateral support.

7 Restricted to wheelchair, but can wheel and transfer self.

8 Restricted to bed or motorized wheelchair.

9 Helpless bed patient, can communicate and eat.

10 Death due to MS.

Ambulation Index[b]

0 Asymptomatic; fully active.

1 Walks normally, but reports fatigue that interferes with athletic or other demanding activities.

2 Abnormal gait or episodic imbalance; gait disorder is noticed by family and friends; able to walk 25 ft (8 m) in 10 s or less.

3 Walks independently; able to walk 25 ft in 20 s or less.

4 Requires unilateral support (cane or single crutch) to walk; walks 25 ft in 20 s or less.

5 Requires bilateral support (canes, crutches or walker) and walks 25 ft in 20 s or less; or requires unilateral support but needs more than 20 s to walk 25 ft.

6 Requires bilateral support and more than 20 s to walk 25 ft; may use wheelchair on occasion.

7 Walking limited to several steps with bilateral support; unable to walk 25 ft; may use wheelchair for most activities.

8 Restricted to wheelchair; able to transfer self independently.

9 Restricted to wheelchair; unable to transfer self independently.

[a]*The actual scale has 0.5-point intervals (see Kurtzke, 1983). From "Rating Neurological Impairment in Multiple Sclerosis: An Expanded Disability Status Scale (EDSS)," by J. Kurtzke, 1983,* Neurology, 33, *pp. 1451–1452. Copyright 1983 by* Neurology. *Reprinted with permission.*

[b]*From "Intensive Immunosuppression in Progressive Multiple Sclerosis," by S. L. Hauser, D. M. Dawson, J. R. Lehrich, M. F. Beal, S. V. Kevy, R. D. Propper, J. A. Mills, and H. L. Weiner, 1983,* New England Journal of Medicine, 308, *p. 180. Copyright 1983 by the* New England Journal of Medicine. *Adapted with permission.*

more complicated, but for present purposes, this simplified model is sufficient. The central point is that MS is clearly an autoimmune disease, in which the body attacks itself (Ebers, 1986).

Because of the involvement of the immune system, drug treatments intended for MS act on that system. Adrenocorticotropic hormone (ACTH) and various corticosteroids (e.g., prednisone) are anti-inflammatory and immunosuppressant, but they do not affect the course of the disease and have many undesirable side effects if given chronically. These agents are, however, useful in ameliorating relapses. Powerful immunosuppressants (e.g., imuran or cytoxin) have modest benefits if taken chronically, but the side effects can be extremely noxious. Only a few patients who can tolerate the side effects continue to use these drugs. In June 1993, the Federal Drug Administration approved interferon-beta-1b (Betaseron) for use by ambulatory patients with relapsing–remitting MS. The drug reduces the frequency and severity of relapses and the number of plaques detected on magnetic resonance imaging (IFNB Multiple Sclerosis Study Group, 1993; Paty et al., 1993), but there has been no proof of its effect on the course of the disease.

Because there is no really effective therapy for MS, folk medicine cures and treatments frequently appear, supported by predictable testimonial claims. The highly unpredictable course of the disease, which makes it very difficult to demonstrate that a treatment has a genuine benefit, makes it equally hard to expose quackery. Recently touted treatments range from the slightly wacky (e.g., eating colostrum, the bloody first milking after the birth of a calf) to the potentially dangerous (e.g., being stung by live bees). In their desperation, highly intelligent patients—even people with scientific training—will try these treatments. Some patients have tried nearly every treatment that was ever made available.

EPIDEMIOLOGY AND GENETICS

There are between 250,000 and 350,000 persons with MS living in the United States (Anderson et al., 1992). Within the United States, prevalence of the disease is not uniform, however. Residents of the northern states (north of about 40° N latitude) are about 3 times as likely to have MS as are residents of southern states. In North America, the region of high risk for MS extends into the more populated regions of southern Canada, which have prevalence rates as high as or higher than those in the northern United States. Within the United States, the prevalence of MS is much higher among Whites than among people of other racial groups (Ebers, 1986).

In Europe, the prevalence of MS is also high, and, again, residents of more northerly areas (parts of the British Isles, The Netherlands, northern Germany, and Scandinavia) are at greater risk than residents of southern Europe. The highest known prevalence of MS in the world is about 300 persons per a population of 100,000, in the Orkney Islands, an old Viking colony off the north coast of Scotland.

In the southern hemisphere, MS is common in Australia and New Zealand. By contrast, MS is rare in Asia (prevalence rates of less than 5 per 100,000) and unknown among native African peoples (Sadovnick & Ebers, 1993).

Worldwide, MS affects about twice as many women as men. A predominance of women is usual in autoimmune diseases. For example, in lupus (systemic lupus erythematosus), 10 times as many women as men are affected.

The interesting relationship between geographic latitude and prevalence, together with an early failure (Mackay & Myrianthopoulos, 1966) to find a difference in concordance rates for MS between pairs of identical and fraternal twins, inspired searches for purely environmental causes of the disease. More recent data, however, indicate a concordance rate for MS of 26% for identical twins in comparison with 2.3% for fraternal twins and 1.9% for siblings (Ebers et al., 1986). These findings are in agreement with the roughly 20-fold increase in the risk of MS for first-degree relatives. Further support for a genetic influence comes from the strong association of MS with certain histocompatibility antigens. Knowledge of the genetic control of these factors is advancing rapidly.

A genetic explanation for MS can account for the marked variation in prevalence among people of different racial groups. It can also explain the marked similarity in the north versus south prevalence gradients in Europe and North America, because most of the immigrants to the northern United States and Canada formerly resided in northern Europe (Page, Kurtzke, Murphy, & Norman, 1993). A similar line of reasoning explains the relatively high prevalence of MS among Whites in Australia.

However, an entirely genetic model cannot explain changes in risk for MS that seem to occur when a person moves from one geographic region to another early in life. For example, people who were born in northern Europe (a region of high risk) and moved to Israel (a region of low risk) before about age 15 have been shown to have acquired the low risk for MS typical of people born and raised in Israel. Migrants to Israel from northern Europe who moved after age 15 retained the high risk of their birth region (Alter, Kahana, & Loewenson, 1978). This observation, which has been replicated, can best be explained as follows: MS develops in people who have a genetic susceptibility and who are also exposed to some unknown environmental "trigger" some time before 15 years of age. Presumably, the likelihood of exposure to the trigger early in life is greater in northern than in southern regions.

MS is a disease of young and middle-aged adults. The median age at first symptom is about 25 years; roughly 85% of patients who have MS experience their first symptoms between the ages of 20 and 50 years. The median age at diagnosis is about 30 years (Ebers, 1986). The interval between first symptoms and diagnosis is due partially to the wide range in interrelapse intervals and partially to the difficulties of making a reasonably certain diagnosis, which were described earlier.

COGNITIVE ASSESSMENT AND MS: A BRIEF HISTORY

An early account of mental function in MS was provided by Charcot (1877), who noted that "at a certain stage of the disease," patients with MS may show "marked enfeeblement of the memory; conceptions are formed slowly; the intellectual and emotional faculties are blunted in their entirety" (p. 194). Despite what has proved to be quite an accurate characterization of the cognitive disturbances most often exhibited by MS patients, until recently, most physicians and psychologists continued to hold that cognitive impairments were uncommon in MS and were observed only in patients with long-standing disease and severe physical disability (McKhann, 1982). This position was defensible because estimates of the prevalence of organic mental impairment in MS based on clinical examination had suggested rates of 5% or less (Kahana, Leibowitz, & Alter, 1971; Kurtzke et al., 1972). It was not until the publication of Rao's (1986) review that neuropsychologists began to appreciate the extent and nature of cognitive impairment in MS.

Why did it take more than 100 years for the accuracy of Charcot's (1877) description to be recognized? Mahler and Benson (1990) suggested that neurologists and other physicians tended to equate organic mental impairment with the severe, global, and relentlessly progressive dementia associated with Alzheimer's disease, which is, of course, readily detectable on clinical examination in its more advanced stages. With this inappropriate model, it is easy to see how the incorrect idea that cognitive impairment in MS was rare and strongly correlated with disease duration and severity of physical disability became entrenched.

I believe that changes in the organization of society have also contributed to the recent recognition that cognitive deficits are more common in MS than was once supposed and that these impairments can have implications for patients' ability to function at home and at work that are just as significant as the physical symptoms of the disease described above. In the 1920s, when neurology and psychiatry evolved as separate medical subspecialties, men held jobs outside the home, whereas most women were homemakers. For most people of both sexes, the cognitive demands of work were limited to the performance of highly overlearned responses, but success on the job placed a premium on strength, speed, stamina, and manual dexterity. Under these conditions, it is easy to see why clinicians paid so little attention to the cognitive abilities of their MS patients. In the past 25 years, women, who constitute roughly two thirds of MS patients, have entered the workforce in increasing numbers. Moreover, in developed nations, the cognitive demands of work for both sexes have changed. More jobs require the ability to process information quickly, to learn and remember, and to make decisions, whereas fewer jobs emphasize primarily physical abilities.

Two recent studies have demonstrated that cognitive impairment has a meaningful impact on functioning in everyday life by patients who have MS. Rao, Leo, Ellington, et al. (1991) recruited 100 patients from a local MS society register. On the basis of their performance on an extensive battery of neuropsychological tests, 52 were considered cognitively intact, and 48 were judged to be cognitively impaired. The two groups did not differ in age, gender distribution, education, occupational status, overall severity of physical disability on the EDSS, duration of disease, disease course, and self-ratings of depression. Despite the many similarities, the cognitively impaired patients were more likely to be unemployed, engaged in fewer social activities, and required more assistance in performing activities of daily living. Ratings by friends and relatives indicated that the cognitively impaired patients were more often confused and were less emotionally stable than the cognitively intact patients.

Wild, Lezak, Whitham, and Bourdette (1991) compared groups of patients whose lesions were primarily cerebral or predominantly spinal in locus. Patients with spinal lesions were substantially more severely disabled than patients with cerebral lesions (on the EDSS, $Ms = 6.2$ vs. 2.3, respectively). Nevertheless, the patients in the spinal group were more likely to be employed and to be currently married and were less likely to have been divorced or to have received psychiatric care.

These findings make it clear that the cognitive impairments that may accompany MS can be as disabling as the physical limitations, and sometimes more so. Identifying MS patients' cognitive strengths and weaknesses, and helping them to accept and compensate for their impairments is a role that clinical neuropsychologists should be filling. Unfortunately, in most areas of the United States, few patients with MS ever see a neuropsychologist. For example, of the approximately 100 MS patients who have volunteered for ongoing studies of cognition I have conducted at the University of Oklahoma Health Sciences Center, only about 10% have received a previous neuropsychological evaluation.

MS AS SUBCORTICAL DEMENTIA: A CONTEMPORARY VIEW

Rao (1986) argued that the profile of behavioral changes evident in MS fit the prototype of subcortical dementia. Cummings and Benson (1984) indicated that subcortical dementia is characterized by slowed information processing, impaired visuospatial skills, poor problem solving and abstraction, memory difficulties that are partially alleviated by cueing, and personality and mood disturbances. In contrast to the cortical dementias (typified by Alzheimer's disease), aphasia, agnosia, acalculia, and true amnesia are rarely observed in MS or the other subcortical dementias (e.g., Huntington's disease or Parkinson's disease). Several subsequent studies using large samples (e.g., Beatty, Goodkin, Monson, & Beatty, 1989; Rao, Leo, Bernardin, & Unverzagt, 1991) have shown that the average performance of patients who have MS does, indeed, conform to the profile of subcortical dementia. Below, I summarize the major findings according to cognitive domain.

Intelligence

Cross-sectional studies (see Rao, 1986) using standardized tests (e.g., Wechsler Adult Intelligence Scale, original [WAIS] or revised [WAIS-R]) have generally shown modest differences in Verbal IQ between MS patients and demographically comparable controls. These differences (rarely larger than 7 points) have only reached statistical significance when fairly large samples were used. Differences in Performance IQ between patients and controls are larger in magnitude because, for patients, Performance IQ scores average 7–14 points lower than Verbal IQ. Because response speed and the integrity of sensory and motor functions contribute more to the Performance IQ than to the Verbal IQ, it is not possible to determine whether visuospatial functions are more vulnerable to loss than are verbal abilities.

Language

Problems in speech production, such as hypophonia and dysarthria, are common in MS, but aphasia, alexia, and agraphia are rare (Mahler & Benson, 1990). Unfortunately, some neurologists and neuropsychologists, perhaps because of their experiences with other patient populations, continue to believe that slurred speech is a reliable predictor of broad cognitive impairment in MS. In my experience, this is simply not true.

Deficits in confrontation naming, although rather uncommon in MS, are correlated with more global cognitive deficits (Beatty & Goodkin, 1990). Interestingly, MS patients who performed poorly on the Boston Naming Test (Kaplan, Goodglass, & Weintraub, 1983) did not exhibit the obvious word-finding difficulties in ordinary conversation of the sort shown by patients with Alzheimer's who had comparably low scores on naming tests.

Although aphasia and anomia are not common in MS, impairments on verbal fluency tests have repeatedly been demonstrated (e.g., Beatty, Goodkin, Monson, et al., 1989; Rao, Leo, Bernardin, et al., 1991). Occasionally, such deficits are evident in the absence of any other cognitive impairment. Except in cases with severe and obvious dysarthria, the most reasonable interpretation of these results is that the commonly observed deficits on verbal fluency tests—as well as the less common difficulties on confrontation naming tests—represent different degrees of impairment in access to established knowledge (Rao, 1990). From this perspective, it is not surprising that patients with naming difficulties are likely to exhibit impairments on a broad range of other cognitive tasks (Beatty & Goodkin, 1990).

Attention and Information-Processing Speed

Because MS affects the myelin sheath, it is not entirely expected that the ability to process information quickly is often compromised. Many MS patients are at least vaguely aware of this problem, although they usually cannot describe their difficulty very precisely. Measurement of speed of information processing is best accomplished by using the oral version of the Symbol Digit Modalities Test (SDMT; Smith, 1982) or the Paced Auditory Serial Addition Test (PASAT; Gronwall, 1977). Both tests avoid the interpretative problems posed by other tests that require written responses, but each test is susceptible to other potential confounds (e.g., problems with visual or auditory perception, visual tracking, short-term memory, or arithmetic). Provided that appropriate assessments of these functions are performed however, either the SDMT or the PASAT can provide a satisfactory measure of information-processing speed. The SDMT takes much less time to administer, however.

Slowed information processing, as revealed by the SDMT or the PASAT, could reflect central influences, peripheral influences, or both. Studies of MS patients in which the Sternberg Memory Scanning Test was used (Rao, 1990) demonstrated that central processing is slowed: Patients required 20–30 ms longer than controls to process each additional bit of information, an increase of about 25%.

Attention and concentration have most often been studied by using the Digit Span test from the WAIS (Wechsler, 1981), which is also a measure of immediate memory. The available data are in conflict. Mild deficits on the Digit Span test have been reported in some studies (e.g., Rao, Leo, Bernardin, et al., 1991), but not in others (e.g., Heaton, Nelson, Thompson, Burks, & Franklin, 1985). The contradictory findings cannot be explained by illness variables, because impairment has been reported in mildly disabled patients (Lyon-Caen et al., 1986), whereas intact performance has been found in more severely disabled patients (Rao, Hammeke, McQuillen, Khatri, & Lloyd, 1984). Some evidence (Rao, Leo, Bernardin, et al., 1991) has indicated that deficits may occur on Digits Backward, but not on Digits Forward, which could suggest that MS patients' major difficulties involve manipulating information in their immediate memory. Because most studies do not report data separately for the two components of the Digit Span test, the generality of this finding cannot be presently determined.

Memory

Complaints about memory problems are commonly made by patients who have MS, and various aspects of patients' anterograde memory have been extensively studied. The decay of information from short-term memory has been studied by using the Brown–Peterson technique. In three of four studies

(Beatty, Goodkin, Monson, et al., 1989; Litvan et al., 1988; Rao, Leo, & St. Aubin-Faubert, 1989) with mildly to moderately disabled patients (most with a relapsing–remitting disease course), no deficits were noted. In the fourth study (Grant et al., 1984), mildly disabled patients showed significant impairments, but about two thirds of the patients were tested while hospitalized (presumably for a relapse). In the only study of chronic progressive patients, deficits in short-term memory were observed (Beatty, Goodkin, Monson, Beatty, & Hertsgaard, 1988). Taken together, these findings indicate that the registration and storage of information in short-term memory is reasonably intact in patients with MS, as long as patients are tested when they are in reasonably good health.

Impairments in anterograde long-term memory have been widely documented with MS. Comparably severe deficits have been observed with a variety of verbal and nonverbal materials (Beatty et al., 1988; Beatty, Goodkin, Monson, et al., 1989; Rao et al., 1989; Rao, Leo, Bernardin, et al., 1991). When tested on multitrial learning tasks, most MS patients were impaired on the first trial, showed normal acquisition over subsequent trials, and showed nearly normal rates of forgetting over a delay of 30–60 min. A subgroup of patients exhibited very slow learning and accelerated forgetting (Rao et al., 1984).

The above deficits can be easily demonstrated when recall methods are used to test patients' memory. With recognition procedures, impairments are generally less severe (Rao, 1986) and may not be evident at all, except among patients with global cognitive impairment (Beatty et al., 1988; Rao et al., 1989).

In contrast to the consistent pattern of deficits seen when memory is tested by methods that require explicit recollection, implicit memory seems fully preserved in patients who have MS. Entirely normal performance has been found on pursuit rotor learning (Beatty, Goodkin, Monson, & Beatty, 1990), several measures of priming (Rao et al., 1993), and frequency coding (Grafman, Rao, Bernardin, & Leo, 1991).

Remote memory has not been studied extensively in MS, and the available data have been somewhat contradictory. On brief tests such as the Presidents test (Rao, Leo, Bernardin, et al., 1991) or the Information test from the WAIS, performance has typically been normal. On more extensive batteries (e.g., Famous Faces or Public Events), significant impairments have been noted (Beatty et al., 1988; Beatty, Goodkin, Monson, et al., 1989). As with anterograde memory, deficits are greater on recall than on recognition.

Problem Solving and Abstraction

On nonverbal tests of conceptual function, such as Raven's Matrices, the Category Test, Levine's Hypothesis Testing Task, and the Wisconsin Card Sorting Test (WCST; Heaton, 1981), impairments in performance by MS patients have been reported consistently (Beatty, Goodkin, Monson, et al., 1989; Heaton et al., 1985; Rao, Leo, Bernardin, et al., 1991). Analyses of patterns of impairment on these tasks have emphasized the importance of perseverative responding as the main source of the MS patients' deficits. However, on the California Card Sorting Test, patients exhibited deficits in generating and identifying concepts, but they executed concepts normally and showed no increase in perseverative errors (Beatty & Monson, in press).

On the most commonly used measure of verbal abstraction—the Similarities test of the WAIS—the data are equivocal. In some studies, patients with MS have performed as well as controls, whereas in other studies, they have been impaired, but the degree of impairment on the Similarities test has been no greater than on the Vocabulary test (Rao, 1986; Ryan, 1993).

In a recent study, Beatty, Hames, Blanco, Paul, and Wilbanks (1995) examined performance by MS patients and control participants on the Shipley Institute of Living Scale (Zachary, 1986). Relative to controls, patients with MS have shown impairment on both the Vocabulary and Abstraction tests, but the relative impairment in abstraction has been greater in magnitude.

Overall, the implication of these last findings is that MS patients exhibit a primary deficit in concept formation; perseverative tendencies are secondary features and may be limited to certain testing situations or may be artifacts of particular scoring systems. In other words, Charcot (1877) had it right all along.

Visuoperceptual Processing

Patients who have MS often exhibit deficits on such measures as the Line Orientation Test (Rao, Leo, Bernardin, et al., 1991) and the Facial Recognition Test, as well as deficits in judging emotions conveyed by facial expressions (Beatty, Goodkin, Weir, et al., 1989). It is very difficult to determine whether these impairments arise from simple defects in visual perception or from higher level disturbances in visuoperceptual and visuospatial processes.

NEUROPSYCHOLOGICAL TEST BATTERIES FOR MS

Although many MS patients have been tested with the familiar Halstead–Reitan Battery (HRB), I cannot recommend this battery, for several reasons. First, patients with MS are especially susceptible to fatigue, and the long administration time of the HRB complicates interpretation. Second, many of the HRB tests, such as the Tactual Performance Test, have complicated sensory and motor demands that make isolating the source of deficits nearly impossible. Third, much of the information from the sensory–perceptual examination of the HRB is redundant with the information one should be able to get from the patient's neurologist. If the patient has not had a recent comprehensive neurological examination, then he or she should probably have one to ensure the accuracy of the diagnosis, to make certain that no other significant medical conditions exist, and to describe the functional status of various neurological systems.

Peyser, Rao, LaRocca, and Kaplan (1990) have proposed a test battery for the assessment of MS patients. Although the battery was selected for the purpose of providing a common set of measures to be collected on all patients seen by neuropsychologists at MS research centers, it serves equally well as a core battery for clinical purposes. The following tests make up this battery:

1. The Mini-Mental State Exam (MMSE; Folstein, Folstein, & McHugh, 1975), as a dementia screen;
2. The SDMT, the Auditory *A*s (an auditory test of vigilance), the PASAT, and a modified Stroop test, as measures of attention and concentration;
3. The Logical Memory test of the Wechsler Memory Scale–Revised, the California Verbal Learning Test (Delis, Kramer, Kaplan, & Ober, 1987), and the 7/24 Spatial Recall Test (Barbizet & Cany, 1968), as measures of memory;
4. An abbreviated Boston Naming Test, the Controlled Oral Word Association Test (COWAT; a verbal fluency test; Benton, 1968), and an abbreviated Token Test (Lezak, 1983), as measures of language;
5. An abbreviated Hooper Visual Organization Test (Hooper, 1958) and a modified version of the WAIS-R Block Design test, as measures of visuospatial functions;
6. The WAIS-R Information test, to assess general knowledge; and
7. The WCST, the Raven Matrices (Raven, 1960), and the WAIS-R Comprehension test, as measures of abstraction and reasoning.

Administration of this battery is short enough (2–3 hr) that the confounding effects of fatigue can usually be avoided, especially if rest periods are given as needed. Reasonably adequate norms for control patients are available for most of the component tests (norms for Auditory *A*s, the modified Stroop test, and the 7/24 test are less satisfactory), and the cognitive domains sampled are those in which MS patients will often show deficits. Finally, the tests chosen and the scoring procedures used are intended to minimize the impact of manual dexterity and speed on performance.

Administering the MMSE is probably a waste of time with patients who have MS. In three independent studies (Beatty & Goodkin, 1990; Franklin, Heaton, Nelson, Filley, & Seibert, 1988; Rao, Leo, Bernardin, et al., 1991), the sensitivity of the MMSE for detecting cognitively impaired MS patients ranged from 20% to 25% when the lower limit of control performance (28) was used as a cutoff. Had the more conventional score (< 24) been used to define suspected impairment, the sensitivity of the MMSE would have been much lower.

In some situations, it may be desirable to administer a screening examination to ascertain whether more extensive testing is warranted. Although there is no entirely satisfactory instrument, at present the best available choice for this is the Brief Cognitive Battery (Rao, Leo, Bernardin, et al., 1991). This consists of the COWAT, the PASAT, the 7/24 test, and the Buschke Selective Reminding Test (SRT; Buschke, 1973) and requires about 20 min to administer. In a study of 100 MS patients, about one half of which had cognitive impairment, the Brief Cognitive Battery had a sensitivity of 72% and a specificity of 90%.

As a final suggestion, I advise conducting some sort of assessment of mood and anxiety. Standard measures, such as the Beck Depression Inventory (BDI; Beck, Ward, Mendelson, Mock, & Erbaugh, 1961) and the State–Trait Anxiety Inventory (Spielberger, Gorsach, & Lushene, 1970), must be used cautiously because the somatic signs of depression and anxiety are also common symptoms of MS.

THE DANGERS OF AVERAGING: FOUR CASES

As a graduate student in experimental psychology, I was taught to revere the virtues of the analysis of variance design and to regard high within-group variability as a curse that had to be avoided or, at least, beaten down in my quest to reach the cherished goal of $p < .05$. When I began to study cognition in MS, I naturally used the same strategy that had served me well in my 15 postdoctoral years of conducting research in biopsychology with animals. The initial studies I was involved in were aimed at testing the idea that MS causes a form of subcortical dementia. When groups of MS patients and control participants were compared on a battery of tests, the results were unambiguous. Patients with MS performed normally on all of the measures chosen for sensitivity to cortical dementia and were impaired on all of the measures purported to be sensitive to subcortical dementia (Beatty, Goodkin, Monson, et al., 1989).

At first I was elated by the apparent clarity of the findings. Then I decided to take a closer look at the performance of individual patients. Quite a different picture emerged. First, only 10%–15% of patients with MS actually exhibited all of the deficits associated with subcortical dementia. Some of the other patients showed relatively focal cognitive impairments in memory, speed of information processing, or problem solving. The remaining patients (30%–50%) performed within normal limits on all of the tests. The concept of MS as a form of subcortical dementia, which was so beautifully supported by the group data, proved to be a piece of abstract fiction when applied to individual cases.

To illustrate this point, I have selected four case studies from the first 66 patients who volunteered for a research project on cognition in MS that is still in progress. To maximize participants' performance, the relatively short battery (2.5–3 hr, including one rest break) is administered in the patients' own homes at least 1 month after recovery from a relapse. To facilitate exposition, I have chosen four relatively young women who were only mildly disabled at the time of testing as judged by the Ambulation Index. Visual acuity varied between patients, but all could read a newspaper with glasses or contact lenses. Data from a healthy control participant of about the same age as the patients (Case 1A) are also given. In the evaluations described below, the term *clear impairment* refers to performance below the 5th percentile for control participants.

Case 1

Case 1 is a young women who had worked as an independent consultant to oil-and-gas firms. Her duties consisted of establishing the legal status of oil, gas, and other mineral rights for parcels of land that were under consideration as potential drilling sites. The work required frequent travel and on-site inspection of properties. About 1 year before testing, the physical demands of the work had become too much for her, and she retired on Social Security.

Case 1 illustrates a pattern of performance that is commonly exhibited by MS patients (see Table 1). She showed mild slowing (on the SDMT and on the FAS, a version of the COWAT) and clearly impaired verbal and nonverbal learning and memory (on the New Map Test, a visuospatial memory test [Beatty et al., 1988] and on the SRT). Detailed examination of her SRT performance suggested that retrieval failure is the principal cause of her memory difficulties. Case 1 performed normally on measures of attention (Digit Span test), visuospatial perception (Benton Line Orientation Test; Benton, Hamsher, Varney, & Spreen, 1983), naming (Boston Naming Test) and

TABLE 1

Selected Neuropsychological Test Data for Four Women With Multiple Sclerosis and One Healthy Control Participant (Case 1A)

	Case				
Type of data	**1**	**1A**	**2**	**3**	**4**
Age (years)					
at testing	39	37	39	35	38
at diagnosis	33	NA	35	30	29
at first symptoms	27	NA	32	30	25
Education (years completed)	16	14	18	10	13
Ambulation Index	3	NA	3	1	1
Beck Depression Inventory	1	7	9	36	2
SDMT (no. correct)	48	62	27	27	50
Digit Span test, from WAIS-R (scaled score)	9	12	7	6	11
Benton Line Orientation Test (no. correct)	28	21	14	14	25
WCST, categories	6	6	6	0	6
Perseverative Responses	17	4	13	124	7
NMT–Delayed Recall	4	8	4	0	11
Selective Reminding Test[a]					
Total Recall	89	130	101	44	126
Long-Term Recall	52	125	82	5	117
Consistent	28	122	25	0	106
Random	34	3	57	5	11
Short-Term Recall	37	5	19	39	9
Long-Term Storage	62	125	95	8	122
Delayed Recall	5	12	12	0	9
Recognition (% correct)	100	100	96	54	100
Boston Naming Test, no cues[b]	15	13	15	8	15
FAS (no. correct)	33	37	18	6	38

Note: NA = not applicable. SDMT = Symbol Digit Modalities Test (oral); WAIS-R = Wechsler Adult Intelligence Scale–Revised; WCST = Wisconsin Card Sorting Test; NMT = New Map Test of Spatial Memory; FAS = a version of the Controlled Oral Word Association Test.
[a]Low scores on random Long-Term Recall and Short-Term Recall in relation to the score for consistent Long-Term Recall are associated with better performance on this test.
[b]15-item version.

problem solving (WCST). Comparison of the performance of Case 1 with that of her healthy sister (Case 1A) emphasizes the patient's cognitive strengths and weaknesses.

Because I needed someone to test patients from the Tulsa area (about 100 miles from Oklahoma City) and I was impressed with Case 1's positive attitude toward herself and her disease, I recruited her to become a part-time neuropsychology technician. Although she protested that she had no training in science, I was able to convince her that neuropsychological testing is not "rocket science." She learned to administer the tests quickly and accurately. By using a tape recorder, she has compensated completely for her cognitive limitations (of which she was well aware before she was tested). Her performance has been so consistently excellent that I consider hiring her to be the smartest personnel decision I've made in my 25-year-long professional career.

Case 2

Case 2 exhibits more severe cognitive deficits. She processes information very slowly (measured with the SDMT and FAS), shows clear impairments in spatial memory (New Map test) and visuospatial perception (Line Orientation test), and has difficulty in attention (Digit Span). Naming (Boston Naming Test) and problem solving (WCST) are intact. Verbal memory (SRT) is somewhat below average but clearly better than nonverbal memory. Her excellent performance on delayed recall (12 out of 12) suggests an acquisition deficit rather than a memory disorder. If one were to follow the recommendations of Cummings and Benson (1984) for defining dementia as the presence of clear impairments in three different cognitive domains, then Case 2 would be considered to have dementia. Yet she remains gainfully employed as a computer programmer. She and her employer are fully aware of her cognitive and physical limitations (mainly fatigue), and she no longer works in settings where she would have to process information quickly and remember several things at the same time. Instead, she is given programming assignments with adequate time so that she can complete them, either in the office or at home. With this accommodation, she has maintained satisfactory performance at work despite her cognitive deficits.

Case 3

Case 3 is a patient with severe dementia who performed poorly on all of the tests administered. Her verbal memory impairment undoubtedly reflects retrieval difficulties, but there is little doubt that acquisition and storage processes are seriously compromised as well. Although Case 3 appears depressed on the basis of her BDI score, it is unlikely that depression is a major factor in her cognitive disturbance (see the discussion of noncognitive factors below). Case 3 continues to live at home, under the care of her husband. The mildness of her physical symptoms is, in a sense, a burden, because she is quite capable of wandering off and getting lost, which she has done on several occasions. Fortunately, MS patients such as Case 3, who exhibit features of both cortical and subcortical dementia, are rare.

Case 4

Case 4 is a patient with no meaningful cognitive deficits at all, except perhaps for very slight slowing of information processing (measured on the SDMT and FAS) and slightly below-average delayed recall on the SRT. She is employed full-time as a data clerk.

Summary

These four cases illustrate the enormous range in cognitive function in a group of MS patients who are relatively similar in age, disease duration, and level of physical disability. When the data are examined in this way, it is clear that there is no "MS pattern of cognitive deficit." Yet, if you average their results, you will come very close to the pattern of "subcortical dementia" reported for group studies by Rao and myself (e.g., Beatty, Goodkin, Monson, et al., 1989; Rao, 1990).

PREDICTORS OF COGNITIVE IMPAIRMENT IN MS: INFLUENCES OF NONCOGNITIVE FACTORS

As mentioned earlier, the idea that cognitive impairment only occurs in severely disabled MS patients with long-standing disease has endured in neurology for about a century. Although the cases described above should raise doubts about that view, I am aware that most psychologists have a healthy distrust of single-case studies. Table 1 summarizes demographic and clinical data for the first 66 patient volunteers in an ongoing study of cognition in MS. Because the patients volunteered for the research study, the sample may have been biased in unknown ways. For example, the average level of education for the sample (14.7 years) is probably higher than for the overall MS population in Oklahoma, but because there are no epidemiological data on this point, I cannot be certain.

In Table 2, patients have been classified as either having or not having dementia on the basis of their performance on tests sampling seven different cognitive domains. Impairment was defined as a score below the 5th percentile for control participants, and patients were considered to have dementia if they were impaired in at least three cognitive domains. This definition was suggested by Cummings (1990) and is not necessarily identical to the definition of dementia given in the *Diagnostic and Statistical Manual of Mental Disorders* (4th ed., revised; American Psychiatric Association, 1994). Patients who did not show dementia included those with focal cognitive deficits (e.g., Case 1) as well as those with no cognitive deficits (e.g., Case 4). Inspection of Table 2 reveals the striking absence of any rela-

TABLE 2

Demographic and Clinical Characteristics of Multiple Sclerosis Patients Without Dementia and With Dementia

	Without dementia (n = 50; 19 M, 31 F)		With dementia (n = 16; 6 M, 10 F)	
Characteristic	***M***	**Range**	***M***	**Range**
Age (years)	46.0	32–72	46.1	31–71
Education (years)	15.4	11–20	12.4	9–18
Ambulation Index	3.6	0–9	4.4	0–9
Disease duration (years since diagnosis)	10.6	1–29	8.4	1–23
Beck Depression Inventory	11.9	1–30	14.5	1–36

Note: M = male; F = female.

tionship between dementia status and gender, age, disability status, or disease duration. Patients with and without dementia occur at every age, disability level, and duration of disease. Although BDI scores are somewhat higher among the patients with dementia, it is clear that depression is not a useful predictor of dementia status. Of the measures considered, only education is a potentially valid predictor. It should be noted, however, that 3 of the 16 patients with dementia had college degrees.

Although these findings may seem surprising, they are in accordance with most of the literature on cognition in MS. Attempts to demonstrate a significant correlation between disease duration and cognitive performance have consistently failed (see Beatty, Goodkin, Hertsgaard, et al., 1990). Although patients who are severely disabled perform, on average, somewhat more poorly on cognitive tests than those who are less severely disabled, the relationship is much too weak to be of any predictive value (Beatty et al., 1990). Likewise, although there is generally a negative correlation between BDI scores and test performance by patients with MS, depression contributes very little to the variance in their performance on neuropsychological measures (Beatty, Goodkin, Hertsgaard, et al., 1990; Rao, Leo, Bernardin, et al., 1991). Finally, the apparent "buffering" influence of education has been reported repeatedly in the literature on Alzheimer's disease (Berkman, 1986; Mortimer & Graves, 1993). Whether or not the brains of highly educated people have greater "reserve capacity" than those of people who are less well educated (Stern, Alexander, Prohovnik, & Mayeux, 1992) is a fascinating but unproven concept.

Several years ago, Heaton et al. (1985) claimed that both the pattern and severity of impairment on neuropsychological tests were different for patients with chronically progressive as opposed to relapsing–remitting disease courses. Although it is not difficult to demonstrate statistically significant differences on neuropsychological tests in the mean performance of relatively large groups of chronically progressive and relapsing–remitting patients, disease course is not useful in predicting the performance of individual patients (Beatty, Goodkin, Hertsgaard, et al., 1990).

The final potential influence on test performance by patients with MS—their medication status—is poorly understood. At present, there is no evidence that any of the drugs prescribed to alleviate spasticity, to aid in bladder control, or to reduce fatigue have any effect on neuropsychological test performance; because patients with MS usually take many medications, it is not possible to isolate effects of specific drugs, so these conclusions are tentative. Likewise, the effects on cognition, if any, of interferon-beta-1b (Betaseron), which was recently approved for the treatment of relapsing–remitting MS, are unknown. Benzodiazepines (such as Valium) are frequently prescribed as antispastics, and some physicians still prescribe strongly anticholinergic antidepressants, such as amitriptyline (Elavil). The adverse effects of these agents on attention and anterograde memory, even in therapeutic doses, have been well documented (Branconnier, DeVitt, Cole, & Spera, 1982; Preston et al., 1988). At the very least, the use of any of these drugs should be noted; a discreet suggestion to the patient's physician to consider alternative medications might be in order.

Finally, there is the matter of steroids. ACTH and various adrenocortical steroids can alleviate and shorten relapses, and these drugs have a perfectly legitimate use for this purpose. There are no demonstrated benefits of maintenance steroid treatment in MS; chronic steroid treatment increases the risk of fractures as well as induces manic reactions in some patients and dysphoric reactions in others. My advise is, first, to avoid assessing the patient during relapse and, second, to try to improve the patient's energy level and mood without using steroids.

THE CLINICAL NEUROPSYCHOLOGIST AND THE MS PATIENT

As noted earlier, the cognitive status of most MS patients is never assessed except by clinical examination. Most referrals of MS patients to psychologists are likely to be for "psychological" problems—most often, for suspected mood disturbances. Another common concern is sexual dysfunction, particularly in men, who often experience impotence.

Although mood disturbance, particularly depression, may be the referral question, it is important for the neuropsychologist to determine (if possible) the factors leading to the depression. Does the depression pre-date the onset of MS? Has it been recurrent? Is the patient depressed about his or her current physical disability, about fear of future disability, or about problems at work? Depending on the patient's occupation and level of physical disability, concerns about work performance might raise issues of cognitive impairment, even if the patient does not mention these issues.

Any evaluation of an MS patient should include an interview with a spouse, partner, or other close relative, if possible (see Nixon, chap. 3, this book). Although many MS patients can appraise their cognitive assets and limitations quite accurately, some cannot. Because partners and relatives will, by necessity, be an important part of any plan to help the patient cope with his or her disease, early involvement of these individuals is important.

In an ideal world, every MS patient would receive at least a brief cognitive screening examination soon after diagnosis of the disease was reasonably certain. There is now good evidence that small but meaningful cognitive declines are likely to occur even in this early stage (Canter, 1951; Ron, Callanan, & Warrington, 1991). Although the deficits are subtle and unlikely to be incapacitating in their own right, coupled with fear engendered by the physical losses associated with a relapse and being diagnosed with a potentially crippling disease, the vague sense of cognitive loss may add to the patient's already considerable psychological distress. Worse yet, lapses of attention and memory may be misinterpreted by family, friends, and employers as intentional acts of malingering to gain sympathy and escape responsibility. This is especially likely to occur if the patient seems fully recovered from the physical symptoms of the relapse.

Educating families, as well as patients, about MS and its varied possible outcomes is an important task that is often overlooked. In my experience, only a few physicians do a good job of educating their MS patients. Helping patients and their families adapt to a disease that is as capricious as MS is a largely unmet need, which clinical psychologists could potentially fill in a number of ways. Providing education is one way of doing this, and, fortunately, good information sources are readily available.

The National Multiple Sclerosis Society disseminates nontechnical abstracts to local chapters for publication in their newsletters. This information is timely and readable. If you plan to work with MS patients, I advise you to subscribe to the local chapter newsletter. Many of your patients will have read the latest issue and may ask your opinion of the most recent research.

Finally, nearly every community of any size has one or more MS support groups, which are organized by patients and their spouses or partners. The better groups provide useful information about coping with MS as well as social support. Knowing the support group leaders in your area can greatly enhance your effectiveness.

Curiously, some physicians discourage their MS patients from attending support groups or becoming involved in their local MS Society chapters. The supposed reason is that they are afraid that their mildly disabled patients will see other patients in wheelchairs and "fall apart." There is some validity to this position, and so, these days in most larger cities, there are support groups specifically for newly diagnosed and mildly disabled patients. More generally, providing accurate information about the disease and its many courses, together with the assurance that most physical and mental consequences can be dealt with by using various compensatory devices and behavioral strategies, would seem to be a wiser course than attempting to isolate people newly diagnosed with MS from all other people who have MS.

If the initial neuropsychological evaluation reveals some cognitive impairments, the patient is likely to ask, "Will it get worse?" On the basis of the results of longitudinal studies with 1.5- to 3-year test–retest intervals (Bernardin, 1992; Filley, Heaton, Thompson, Nelson, & Franklin, 1990; Ivnik, 1978), this is the best current answer: Not very much and not very fast. This is an extremely important finding, because it gives the clinician—working together with the patient, family members, and patient's employer—adequate time to try out strategies that can allow the patient to best compensate for his or her cognitive and physical limitations. In the only published study of cognitive rehabilitation in MS, Jonsson, Korfitzen, Heltberg, Ravnborg, and Byskov-Ottosen (1993) found that a formal cognitive rehabilitation program of the sort used with head-injured patients was slightly more effective than an active diffuse-stimulation control program, but both interventions led to substantial improvement that was sustained for a few months. These results are encouraging, but, as Cases 1 and 2 demonstrate, elaborate and costly cognitive rehabilitation is often unnecessary. Simple and cheap strategies (e.g., note taking, list making, and tape recording) that many MS patients adopt spontaneously can solve most memory problems. What is essential is that all of the important players (the patient, the family, and the employer) understand the patient's physical and cognitive limitations, as well as his or her strengths. Only with this knowledge can a reasonable plan for determining employability be formulated. Although Case 2 and her employer worked out the necessary accommodations without professional assistance, that situation is probably not typical. Clearly, the clinical neuropsychologist is the only professional qualified to conduct the essential analysis of the patient's strengths and weaknesses and to serve as a liaison (and, if necessary, an advocate) to the patient's employer. Although it is not widely known, the 1990 Americans With Disabilities Act requires that employers make reasonable accommodations for their employees' disabilities.

Despite everyone's best efforts, it is likely that individuals who have MS will eventually have to stop working and seek Social Security disability. In addition to helping document the patient's claim, clinical neuropsychologists can provide an important service by vigilantly monitoring their patient's emotional status at this time. Although MS patients are vulnerable to depression throughout the course of their disease (Devins & Seland, 1987), on the basis of my personal experience, I can attest that the time of forced and premature retirement can be especially distressing. In addition to possible financial problems associated with loss of income, patients may experience a profound loss of self-esteem and self-worth. The difficulties of dealing with the seemingly arbitrary and inconsistent policies of the Social Security system only make matters worse.

I indicated earlier that depression poses little threat to the validity of neuropsychological test data of patients with MS. However, neuropsychologists should be concerned about depression in their MS patients for the same reasons they would be concerned about depression in anyone else, only more so. Depression saps motivation, increases the risk of suicide, and can poison personal relationships.

Some MS patients never recover their spirit after forced retirement, whereas others adapt successfully and go on to lead productive lives in different ways. Virtually nothing is known about the variables that determine successful coping with MS. Clinical neuropsychologists who work with MS patients could make a significant contribution by helping to fill this void.

References

Alter, M., Kahana, E., & Loewenson, R. (1978). Migration and risk of multiple sclerosis. *Neurology, 28,* 1089–1093.

American Psychiatric Association. (1994). *Diagnostic and statistical manual of mental disorders* (4th ed., revised). Washington, DC: Author.

Anderson, D. W., Ellenberg, J. H., Leventhal, C. M., Reingold, S. C., Rodriguez, M., & Silberberg, D. H. (1992). Revised estimate of the prevalence of multiple sclerosis in the United States (1992). *Annals of Neurology, 31,* 333–336.

Barbizet, J., & Cany, E. (1968). Clinical and psychometrical study of a patient with memory disturbances. *International Journal of Neurology, 7,* 44–54.

Beatty, W. W., & Goodkin, D. E. (1990). Screening for cognitive impairment in multiple sclerosis: An evaluation of the Mini-Mental State Exam. *Archives of Neurology, 47,* 297–301.

Beatty, W. W., Goodkin, D. E., Hertsgaard, D., & Monson, N. (1990). Clinical and demographic predictors of cognitive performance in multiple sclerosis: Do diagnostic type, disease duration and disability matter? *Archives of Neurology, 47,* 305–309.

Beatty, W. W., Goodkin, D. E., Monson, N., & Beatty, P. A. (1989). Cognitive disturbances in patients with relapsing remitting multiple sclerosis. *Archives of Neurology, 46,* 1113–1119.

Beatty, W. W., Goodkin, D. E., Monson, N., & Beatty, P. A. (1990). Implicit learning in patients with chronic progressive multiple sclerosis. *International Journal of Clinical Neuropsychology, 12,* 166–172.

Beatty, W. W., Goodkin, D. E., Monson, N., Beatty, P. A., & Hertsgaard, D. (1988). Anterograde and retrograde amnesia in patients with chronic progressive multiple sclerosis. *Archives of Neurology, 45,* 611–619.

Beatty, W. W., Goodkin, D. E., Weir, W. S., Staton, R. D., Monson, N., & Beatty, P. A. (1989). Affective judgments by patients with Parkinson's disease or chronic progressive multiple sclerosis. *Bulletin of the Psychonomic Society, 27,* 361–364.

Beatty, W. W., Hames, K. A., Blanco, C. R., Paul, R. H., & Wilbanks, S. L. (1995). Verbal abstraction deficit in multiple sclerosis. *Neuropsychology, 9,* 198–205.

Beatty, W. W., & Monson, N. (in press). Problem solving in multiple sclerosis: Comparison of the Wisconsin and California Card Sorting Tests. *Journal of the International Neuropsychological Society.*

Beck, A. T., Ward, C. H., Mendelson, M., Mock, J., & Erbaugh, J. K. (1961). An inventory for measuring depression. *Archives of General Psychiatry, 4,* 561–571.

Benton, A. L. (1968). Differential behavioral effects in frontal lobe disease. *Neuropsychologia, 6,* 53–60.

Benton, A. L., Hamsher, K. S., Varney, N. R., & Spreen, O. (1983). *Contributions to neuropsychological assessment.* New York: Oxford University Press.

Berkman, L. F. (1986). The association between educational attainment and mental status examinations: Of etiologic significance for senile dementia or not? *Journal of Chronic Diseases, 39,* 171–174.

Bernardin, L. (1992, June). *A prospective long-term study of cognitive dysfunction in MS.* Paper presented at the Workshop on Neurobehavioral Disorders in MS: Diagnosis, underlying pathology, natural history, and therapeutic intervention, Bergamo, Italy.

Branconnier, R. J., DeVitt, D. R., Cole, J. O., & Spera, K. F. (1982). Amitriptyline selectively disrupts verbal recall from secondary memory of normal aged. *Neurobiology of Aging, 3,* 55–59.

Buschke, H. (1973). Selective reminding for analysis of memory and learning. *Journal of Verbal Learning and Verbal Behavior, 12,* 543–550.

Canter, A. H. (1951). Direct and indirect measures of psychological deficit in multiple sclerosis. *Journal of General Psychology, 44,* 3–50.

Charcot, J.-M. (1877). *Lectures on the diseases of the nervous system.* London: New Sydenham Society.

Cummings, J. L. (1990). Introduction. In J. L. Cummings (Ed.), *Subcortical dementia* (pp. 3–16). New York: Oxford University Press.

Cummings, J. L., & Benson, D. F. (1984). Subcortical dementia: Review of an emerging concept. *Archives of Neurology, 41,* 874–879.

Delis, D. C., Kramer, J., Kaplan, E., & Ober, B. A. (1987). *California Verbal Learning Test manual.* San Antonio, TX: Psychological Corporation.

Devins, G. M., & Seland, T. P. (1987). Emotional impact of multiple sclerosis: Recent findings and suggestions for future research. *Psychological Bulletin, 101,* 363–375.

Ebers, G. C. (1986). Multiple sclerosis and other demyelinating diseases. In A. K. Asbury, G. M. McKhann, & W. I. McDonald (Eds.), *Diseases of the nervous system: Clinical neurobiology. II* (pp. 1268–1281). Philadelphia: W. B. Saunders.

Ebers, G. C., Bulman, D. E., Sadovnick, A. D., Paty, D. W., Warren, S., Hader, W., Murray, T. J., Seland, P., Duquette, P., Grey, T., Nelson, R., Nicolle, M., & Brunet, D. (1986). A population-based study of multiple sclerosis in twins. *New England Journal of Medicine, 315,* 1638–1642.

Filley, C. M., Heaton, R. K., Thompson, L. T., Nelson, L. M., & Franklin, G. M. (1990). Effects of disease course on neuropsychological functioning. In S. M. Rao (Ed.), *Neurobehavioral aspects of multiple sclerosis* (pp. 136–148). New York: Oxford University Press.

Folstein, M. F., Folstein, S. E., & McHugh, P. R. (1975). "Mini-Mental State": A practical method for grading the cognitive state of patients for the clinician. *Journal of Psychiatric Research, 12*, 189–198.

Franklin, G. M., Heaton, R. K., Nelson, L. M., Filley, C. M., & Seibert, C. (1988). Correlation of neuropsychological and MRI findings in chronic progressive multiple sclerosis. *Neurology, 38*, 1826–1829.

Goodkin, D. E., Hertsgaard, D., & Rudick, R. (1989). Exacerbation rates and adherence to disease type in a prospectively followed-up population with multiple sclerosis: Implications for clinical trials. *Archives of Neurology, 46*, 1107–1112.

Grafman, J., Rao, S. M., Bernardin, L., & Leo, G. J. (1991). Automatic memory processes in patients with multiple sclerosis. *Archives of Neurology, 48*, 1072–1075.

Grant, I., McDonald, W. I., Trimble, M. R., Smith, E., & Reed, R. (1984). Deficient learning and memory in early and middle phases of multiple sclerosis. *Journal of Neurology, Neurosurgery, and Psychiatry, 47*, 250–255.

Gronwall, D. M. A. (1977). Paced auditory serial-addition task: A measure of recovery from concussion. *Perceptual and Motor Skills, 44*, 367–373.

Hauser, S. L., Dawson, D. M., Lehrich, J. R., Beal, M. F., Kevy, S. V., Propper, R. D., Mills, J. A., & Weiner, H. L. (1983). Intensive immunosuppression in progressive multiple sclerosis. *New England Journal of Medicine, 308*, 173–180.

Heaton, R. K. (1981). *Wisconsin Card Sorting Test manual.* Odessa, FL: Psychological Adjustment Resources.

Heaton, R. K., Nelson, L. M., Thompson, D. S., Burks, J., & Franklin, G. M. (1985). Neuropsychological findings in relapsing–remitting and chronic progressive multiple sclerosis. *Journal of Consulting and Clinical Psychology, 53*, 103–110.

Hooper, H. E. (1958). *The Hooper Visual Organization Test manual.* Los Angeles: Western Psychological Services.

IFNB Multiple Sclerosis Study Group. (1993). Interferon beta-1b is effective in relapsing–remitting multiple sclerosis, I. Clinical results of a multicenter, randomized, double-blind, placebo-controlled trial. *Neurology, 43*, 655–661.

Ivnik, R. J. (1978). Neuropsychological stability in multiple sclerosis. *Journal of Consulting and Clinical Psychology, 46*, 913–923.

Jonsson, A., Korfitzen, E. M., Heltberg, A., Ravnborg, M. H., & Byskov-Ottosen, E. (1993). Effects of neuropsychological treatment on patients with multiple sclerosis. *Acta Neurologica Scandinavica, 88*, 394–400.

Kahana, E., Leibowitz, V., & Alter, M. (1971). Cerebral multiple sclerosis. *Neurology, 21*, 1179–1185.

Kaplan, E., Goodglass, H., & Weintraub, S. (1983). *Boston Naming Test.* Philadelphia: Lea & Febiger.

Kurtzke, J. (1983). Rating neurological impairment in multiple sclerosis: An Expanded Disability Status Scale (EDSS). *Neurology, 33*, 1444–1452.

Kurtzke, J. F., Beebe, G. W., Nagler, B., Auth, T. L., Kurland, L. T., & Nefzger, M. D. (1972). Studies on the natural history of multiple sclerosis, 6. Clinical and laboratory findings at first diagnosis. *Acta Neurologica Scandinavica, 48*, 19–46.

Lezak, M. D. (1983). *Neuropsychological assessment* (2nd ed.). New York: Oxford University Press.

Litvan, I., Grafman, J., Vendrell, P., Martinez, J. M., Junque, C., Vendrell, J. M., & Barraquer-Bordas, J. L. (1988). Multiple memory deficits in patients with multiple sclerosis: Exploring the working memory system. *Archives of Neurology, 45*, 607–610.

Lyon-Caen, O., Jouvent, R., Hauser, S., Chaunu, M.-P., Benoit, N., Widlocher, D., & Lhermitte, F. (1986). Cognitive function in recent-onset demyelinating disease. *Archives of Neurology, 43*, 1138–1141.

Mackay, R., & Myrianthopoulos, X. (1966). Multiple sclerosis in twins and their relatives: Final report. *Archives of Neurology, 15*, 449–462.

Mahler, M. E., & Benson, D. F. (1990). Cognitive dysfunction in multiple sclerosis: A subcortical dementia? In S. M. Rao (Ed.), *Neurobehavioral aspects of multiple sclerosis* (pp. 88–101). New York: Oxford University Press.

McKhann, G. M. (1982). Multiple sclerosis. *Annual Review of Neuroscience, 5*, 219–239.

Mortimer, J. A., & Graves, A. B. (1993). Education and other socioeconomic determinants of dementia and Alzheimer's disease. *Neurology, 43*, S39–S44.

Page, W. F., Kurtzke, J. F., Murphy, F. M., & Norman, J. E. (1993). Epidemiology of multiple sclerosis in U.S. veterans, V. Ancestry and the risk of multiple sclerosis. *Annals of Neurology, 33*, 632–639.

Paty, D. W., Li, D. K. B., UBC MS/MRI Study Group, IFNB MS Study Group. (1993). Interferon beta-1b is effective in relapsing–remitting multiple sclerosis, II. MRI analysis of results of a multicenter, randomized, double-blind, placebo-controlled trial. *Neurology, 43*, 662–667.

Peyser, J. M., Rao, S. M., LaRocca, N. G., & Kaplan, E. (1990). Guidelines for neuropsychological research in multiple sclerosis. *Archives of Neurology, 47*, 94–97.

Preston, G. C., Broks, P., Traub, M., Ward, C., Poppleton, P., & Stahl, S. M. (1988). Effects of lorazepam on memory, attention and sedation in man. *Psychopharmacology, 95*, 208–215.

Purdue Research Foundation. (1948). *Examiner's manual for the Purdue Pegboard*. Chicago: Science Research Associates.

Raine, C. S. (1990). Neuropathology. In S. M. Rao (Ed.), *Neurobehavioral aspects of multiple sclerosis* (pp. 15–36). New York: Oxford University Press.

Rao, S. M. (1986). Neuropsychology of multiple sclerosis: A critical review. *Journal of Clinical and Experimental Neuropsychology, 8*, 501–542.

Rao, S. M. (1990). Multiple sclerosis. In J. L. Cummings (Ed.), *Subcortical dementia* (pp. 164–180). New York: Oxford University Press.

Rao, S. M., Grafman, J., DiGiulio, D., Mittenberg, W., Bernardin, L., Leo, G. J., Luchetta, T., & Unverzagt, F. (1993). Memory dysfunction in multiple sclerosis: Its relation to working memory, semantic encoding, and implicit learning. *Neuropsychology, 7*, 364–374.

Rao, S. M., Hammeke, T. A., McQuillen, M. P., Khatri, B. O., & Lloyd, D. (1984). Memory disturbance in chronic progressive multiple sclerosis. *Archives of Neurology, 41*, 625–631.

Rao, S. M., Leo, G. J., Bernardin, L., & Unverzagt, F. (1991). Cognitive dysfunction in multiple sclerosis, I. Frequency patterns and predictions. *Neurology, 41*, 685–691.

Rao, S. M., Leo, G. J., Ellington, L., Nauertz, T., Bernardin, L., & Unverzagt, F. (1991). Cognitive dysfunction in multiple sclerosis, II. Impact on employment and social functioning. *Neurology, 41*, 692–696.

Rao, S. M., Leo, G. J., & St. Aubin-Faubert, P. (1989). On the nature of memory disturbance in multiple sclerosis. *Journal of Clinical and Experimental Neuropsychology, 11*, 699–712.

Raven, J. C. (1960). *Guide to the Standard Progressive Matrices*. London: H. K. Lewis.

Ron, M. A., Callanan, M. M., & Warrington, E. K. (1991). Cognitive abnormalities in multiple sclerosis: A psychometric and MRI study. *Psychological Medicine, 21*, 59–68.

Ryan, L. (1993). *Patterns of cognitive impairment in multiple sclerosis and their relationship to neuropathology on magnetic resonance imaging*. Unpublished doctoral dissertation, University of British Columbia, Vancouver.

Sadovnick, A. D., & Ebers, G. C. (1993). Epidemiology of multiple sclerosis: A critical overview. *Canadian Journal of Neurological Sciences, 20*, 17–29.

Smith, A. A. (1982). *Symbol Digit Modalities Test manual*. Los Angeles: Western Psychological Services.

Spielberger, C. D., Gorsach, R. L., & Lushene, R. E. (1970). *Manual for the State–Trait Anxiety Inventory*. Palo Alto, CA: Consulting Psychologists Press.

Stern, Y., Alexander, G. E., Prohovnik, I., & Mayeux, R. (1992). Inverse relationships between education and parietotemporal perfusion deficit in Alzheimer's disease. *Annals of Neurology, 32*, 371–375.

Wechsler, D. (1981). *Wechsler Adult Intelligence Scale–Revised*. New York: Psychological Corporation.

Wild, K. V., Lezak, M. D., Whitham, R. H., & Bourdette, D. N. (1991). Psychosocial impact of cognitive impairment in the multiple sclerosis patient. *Journal of Clinical and Experimental Neuropsychology, 13*, 74.

Zachary, R. A. (1986). *Shipley Institute of Living Scale, revised manual*. Los Angeles: Western Psychological Services.

CHAPTER 9

PARKINSON'S DISEASE

Vicki M. Soukup and Russell L. Adams

Parkinson's disease (PD), or primary parkinsonism, is an idiopathic, progressive neurological disorder that is manifested clinically by bradykinesia (or slowness in the initiation of voluntary movement), resting tremor, cogwheel rigidity, and postural reflex impairment. The disorder has specific histological features that involve the loss of pigmented neurons in the substantia nigra and the presence of characteristic eosinophilic cytoplasmic inclusions (or Lewy bodies). The prototypic form described in this chapter is distinguished from other parkinsonism disorders on the basis of unknown etiology and onset after age 40.

James Parkinson (1817) is credited with providing the first description of the disorder, in a classic monograph titled *An Essay on the Shaking Palsy*. From his observation of 6 patients, only 3 of whom had been examined in detail, he presented a strikingly accurate portrayal of the malady. The disorder was characterized as a chronic progressive illness that appears insidiously in middle age. The initial symptom involves a mild tremor and weakness of one hand. The affliction progresses to involve the other limbs, posture becomes less erect, and general slowness develops. The patient has difficulty initiating voluntary movement. As the disease advances, the patient exhibits "a propensity to bend the trunk forward, and to pass from a walking to a running pace" (p. 1). Parkinson noted that the motor abnormalities eventually result in significant disability and invalidism, but mental faculties are preserved until the terminal stages of the disease. Subsequent research has challenged this final point; but more important, PD has emerged as a significant prototype for the study of degenerative neurological diseases.

The preponderance of the research in this area has been conducted from a biomedical perspective. This chapter introduces the practitioner to the complexity in diagnosis and symptomatic manifestations of the disease. Within this framework, we provide a summary of the epidemiology, proposed etiology, pathophysiology, and prognosis of the disorder. After describing the essential clinical features, we turn to a review of the prominent neuropsychological deficits, concomitant psychiatric concerns, and associated psychosocial issues experienced by individuals with PD. In this section, we address essential referral concerns and assessment tools developed for this population. A suggested neuropsychological test battery and sample case are presented. Finally, we conclude with a brief note regarding the status of various pharmacological and surgical treatment options.

CLINICAL DIAGNOSIS

As yet, there is no definitive biological marker to confirm a diagnosis of PD. Diagnosis is made on the basis of clinical findings, medical history, and physical examination. Considering the heterogeneous clinical presentation of PD and the overlap with other parkinsonism disorders, there are significant problems in diagnostic accuracy. Indeed, varying definitions of diagnostic criteria have made comparisons between studies difficult and have contributed to the array of disparate, often contradictory, findings in PD research. In an effort to minimize diagnostic inaccuracies, the United Kingdom Parkinson's Disease

EXHIBIT 1

Clinical Diagnostic Criteria Proposed by United Kingdom Parkinson's Disease Society Brain Bank

Step 1: Diagnosis of Parkinsonian syndrome

- Bradykinesia (slowness of initiation of voluntary movement with progressive reduction in speed and amplitude of repetitive actions)
- And at least one of the following:
  - Muscular rigidity
  - 4–6 Hz rest tremor
  - Postural instability not caused by a primary visual, vestibular, cerebellar, or proprioceptive dysfunction

Step 2: Exclusion criteria for Parkinson's disease (PD)

- History of repeated strokes with stepwise progression of parkinsonian features
- History of encephalitis or repeated head injury
- Oculogyric crises
- Neuroleptic treatment at onset of symptoms
- More than one affected relative
- Sustained remission
- Strictly unilateral features after 3 years
- Supranuclear gaze palsy
- Cerebellar signs
- Early severe autonomic involvement
- Early severe dementia with disturbances of memory, language, and praxis
- Babinski sign
- Presence of cerebral tumor or communicating hydrocephalus on computed tomography scan
- Negative response to large doses of levodopa (if malabsorption is excluded)
- MPTP (1-methyl-4-phenyl-1,2,3,6-tetrahydropyridine) exposure

Step 3: Supportive prospective positive criteria for PD[a]

- Unilateral onset
- Rest tremor present
- Progressive disorder
- Persistent asymmetry affecting side of onset most
- Excellent response (70%–100%) to levodopa
- Severe levodopa-induced chorea
- Levodopa response for 5 years or more
- Clinical course of 10 years or more

From "The Relevance of the Lewy Body to the Pathogenesis of Idiopathic Parkinson's Disease," by W. R. Gibb and A. J. Lees, 1988, Journal of Neurology, Neurosurgery, and Psychiatry, 51, *p. 746. Copyright 1988 by BMJ Publishing. Adapted with permission.*

[a]*Three or more are required for diagnosis of definite PD.*

Society Brain Bank (Gibb & Lees, 1988) has proposed guidelines for diagnosis (shown in Exhibit 1).

Investigators using autopsy confirmation to assess the accuracy of clinical diagnosis have estimated that misdiagnosis occurs in approximately 20% of cases. A recent analysis of donor tissue from 100 consecutive cases at London's Parkinson's Disease Society Brain Bank (PDSBB) indicated that 76% of individuals with a diagnosis of idiopathic PD (IPD) satisfied the established neuropathological criteria for IPD (Hughes,

Daniel, Kilford, & Lees, 1992). Diagnostic accuracy was improved to 82% through the use of the recommended PDSBB diagnostic criteria shown in Exhibit 1. Misdiagnoses consist of such disorders as multiple system atrophy, progressive supranuclear palsy, Alzheimer's disease, and basal ganglia vascular disease.

Parkinsonism, defined as the clinical expression of dysfunction in the dopaminergic nigra-neostriatal system, is seen in a variety of disorders. Exhibit 2 provides a summary of the various conditions and disease processes that give rise to parkinsonism. Despite this impressive array, sample estimates provided by Stacy and Jankovic (1992) indicate that the vast majority of patients (78%) referred to specialized movement disorder clinics are presumed to have PD.

In the remaining portion of this section, we provide a brief description of the major parkinsonism

EXHIBIT 2

Classification of Parkinsonism

Primary (idiopathic) parkinsonism
- Parkinson's disease
- Juvenile parkinsonism

Secondary (acquired, symptomatic) parkinsonism
- Infectious: postencephalitic, slow virus
- Drugs: dopamine-receptor blocking drugs (antipsychotic, antiemetic drugs), reserpine, tetrabenazine, alpha-methyl-dopa, lithium, flunarizine, cinnarizine
- Toxins: MPTP, CO, Mn, Hg, Cs2, methanol, ethanol
- Vascular: multi-infarct
- Trauma: pugilistic encephalopathy
- Other: Parathyroid abnormalities, hypothyroidism, hepatocerebral degeneration, brain tumor, normal pressure hydrocephalus, syringomesencephalia

Heredodegenerative parkinsonism
- Huntington's disease
- Wilson's disease
- Hallervorden–Spatz disease
- Olivopontocerebellar and spinocerebellar degenerations
- Familial basal ganglia calcification
- Familial parkinsonism with peripheral neuropathy
- Neuroacanthocytosis

Multiple systems degenerations (parkinsonism plus)
- Progressive supranuclear palsy
- Shy–Drager syndrome
- Striatonigral degeneration
- Parkinsonism-dementia-ALS complex
- Corticobasal ganglionic degeneration
- Autosomal dominant Lewy body disease
- Alzheimer's disease

From "Differential Diagnosis of Parkinson's Disease and the Parkinsonism Plus Syndromes," by M. Stacy and J. Jankovic, 1992, Neurologic Clinics (Parkinson's Disease), 10, *p. 343. Copyright 1992 by W. B. Saunders. Reprinted with permission. ALS = amyotrophic lateral sclerosis.*

disorders. The intent is not to provide a comprehensive treatise but, rather, to illustrate the differential features associated with dopaminergic nigrostriatal dysfunction.

Juvenile parkinsonism is a heterogeneous group of clinicopathologic entities with onset before age 21 years. Youth-onset PD (YOPD) is arbitrarily defined as parkinsonism that produces initial symptoms between the ages of 21 years and 39 years, inclusive. In contrast to PD, a frequent early feature of YOPD is focal dystonia, or stiff muscles. The disorder tends to have a more gradual progression of signs and symptoms as well as an earlier appearance of levodopa-related dyskinesias and dose-related motor fluctuations. YOPD warrants recognition as a separate group because differential diagnosis entails consideration of other neurological conditions that are not generally seen in older patients (Golbe, 1991). Specifically, three other diseases (i.e., Wilson's disease, or hepatolenticular degeneration; Hallervorden–Spatz disease; and Huntington's chorea) may initially have parkinsonism features for individuals in this age group.

The second largest group of parkinsonism disorders is classified clinically as *parkinsonism plus syndromes* and neuropathologically as *multiple systems degeneration*. This group of patients represents approximately 12% of all parkinsonian referrals (Stacy & Jankovic, 1992). These individuals typically display additional neurologic abnormalities, such as supranuclear ophthalmoparesis or paralysis of downward gaze (progressive supranuclear palsy), dysautonomia (Shy–Drager syndrome), dementia (Alzheimer's disease with parkinsonism), and dementia coupled with motor neuron disease (parkinsonism-dementia-amyotrophic lateral sclerosis complex of Guam). Other features useful in differentiating these disorders from PD include the absence or paucity of tremor, early gait abnormalities (such as freezing), postural instability, and pyramidal findings. In contrast to a relative preservation of postsynaptic dopamine receptors in PD, the other parkinsonian disorders reveal reduced postsynaptic receptors, resulting in the poor response to levodopa.

Secondary (or acquired) parkinsonism is thought to represent approximately 8% of all parkinsonism patients (Stacy & Jankovic, 1992). Patients in this group exhibit symptomatic manifestations as a result of an identifiable etiologic agent, such as toxic exposure, trauma, metabolic derangement, infection, stroke, or tumor. For example, postencephalitic parkinsonism appeared as the sequela of an epidemic of encephalitis lethargica in 1917–1928. Although the population affected by this virus has largely disappeared, sporadic cases still occur from the effects of Eastern Equine viral encephalitis or Japanese B virus infections. Patients with this form of parkinsonism show other neurological findings such as oculogyric crises, dystonic spasms, nystagmus, and cranial nerve palsies. Changes in mentation, including hallucinations, psychosis, and dementia are observed.

Another subtype of secondary parkinsonism is seen in the patient with a history of repeated transient ischemic attacks and findings suggestive of one or more episodes of infarction, in addition to the classic PD symptoms. The disorder is due to infarct damage in the brain stem and basal ganglia, which produces a disruption of the dopaminergic systems in the brain.

The effects of medications that prompt a drug-induced parkinsonism are included in the category of secondary parkinsonism and account for approximately 4% of all patient referrals (Stacy & Jankovic, 1992). Specifically, dopamine receptor blocking drugs, such as antipsychotics and antiemetics, as well as dopamine-depleting drugs, such as reserpine, tetrabenazine, and alpha-methyldopa are responsible for symptoms of rigidity, masklike facies, bradykinesis, and tremor. In most instances, the symptoms are reversible when the causative drug is withdrawn or reduced.

Rare causes of parkinsonism include heredodegenerative diseases, such as Huntington's disease, Wilson's disease, Hallervorden–Spatz disease, and familial basal ganglia calcification. Patients with diagnoses in this category account for less than 1% of patient referrals seen in specialized PD clinics (Stacy & Jankovic, 1992).

EPIDEMIOLOGY AND ETIOLOGIC CONCERNS

PD is one of the more frequently occurring degenerative diseases of the nervous system in middle and later life, affecting about 1% of the population over 50 years of age. The mean age of onset is in the mid-50s, with approximately 40% of patients developing the disease between ages 50 and 60. Increased incidence is associated with increased age. Most studies report no significant gender differences in the prevalence of PD; except in China, where PD is 3 times more common in men than in women (Li et al., 1985).

Although PD is observed in all countries and in all ethnic groups, it is less common among non-White populations. Two U.S. hospital surveys have revealed an estimated prevalence of 128 and 121 per 100,000 for White men and women, respectively, but only 30 and 7 per 100,000 for Black men and women, respectively (Kessler, 1972; Paddison & Griffith, 1974; Stern et al., 1991). Community-based surveys indicate that for unknown reasons, the prevalence of PD is lower in China, Japan, and Africa as compared with Europe and North America (Tanner, 1989).

Etiologic concerns about exogenous agents related to agricultural activities as the causative factor are undergoing careful review. Studies conducted in the United States to examine risk factors have found that rural living and drinking well water are associated with increased risk of PD (Koller et al., 1990). This was observed regardless of age at disease onset. A cross-sectional survey in Hong Kong found that rural living, engagement in farming, previous use of herbicides or pesticides, and habitual consumption of raw vegetables were associated with significantly increased risk of PD (Ho, Woo, & Lee, 1989). Other studies performed in Spain, Canada, and China have reported increased risk for PD in association between pesticide and herbicide exposure, metal industries, and well-water drinking, but results have been contradictory and inconclusive (Semchuk, Love, & Lee, 1992; Tanner et al., 1989).

The discovery of the biological effects associated with the repeated intravenous use of MPTP (1-methyl-4-phenyl-1, 2, 3, 6-tetrahydropyridine) has contributed to an increased interest in the environmental toxin hypothesis. In 1983, MPTP was identified as a human neurotoxin that could selectively destroy the substantia nigra, resulting in neuropathological and neurochemical changes similar to those in PD. The clinical presentation of these individuals is virtually indistinguishable from PD, with the primary difference being in the onset of symptoms. Unlike the slow progressive course of PD, the onset of symptoms in MPTP-induced parkinsonism is abrupt, typically within 2–4 days after stopping the drug, and it evolves over 4–14 days (Tanner & Langston, 1990). Given these clinical and anatomical similarities, this agent has served as a laboratory model by which to understand the process of selective neuronal degeneration.

Other intriguing lifestyle considerations have been linked to the development of PD. An inverse relationship between PD and cigarette smoking has been reported, with a tendency of PD patients to be nonsmokers (Tanner, 1989). Lower alcohol consumption has also been reported in this patient group. Other potentially protective factors, such as the taking of antioxidant vitamins, are presently undergoing careful review, because several small studies have suggested that consumption of foods rich in tocopherol and the use of supplemental vitamins, Vitamin E, or cod liver oil may be associated with decreased risk of developing PD. These hypotheses remain under investigation because the evidence to date is inconclusive.

GENETICS

Early reports have shown that 10%–15% of individuals with PD have relatives similarly affected (Duvoisin, 1986). Yet, findings of a low concordance rate among monozygotic twins suggest that simple Mendelian genetic factors play a limited role in the development of the disease (Marsden, 1987; Marttila, Kaprio, Koskenvuo, & Rinne, 1988). In a recent review, Johnson, Hodge, and Duvoisin (1990) concluded that an autosomal dominant mode of inheritance with low penetrance could not be ruled out. The strongest evidence for a significant genetic component has been provided by Golbe, Di Iorio, Bonavita, Miller, and Duvoisin's (1990) recent description of a large kindred with nearly fully penetrant PD.

The general conclusion derived from these studies is that although there may be a role for inheritance in some cases of PD, heredity alone cannot be responsible for the illness. It has been suggested, however, that there may be a genetic susceptibility to develop PD based on a reduced ability to metabolize toxins from the environment or to inactivate toxic radicals that are formed within the body (Johnson, 1991). The defective antioxidant theory proposes that a failure in the detoxification system leads to an increased proliferation of free oxygen radicals, which are toxic and result in nigral cell death. Comparisons between early and late-stage PD patients have revealed lower antioxidant activity among late-stage PD patients. These results support the notion of a general defect in the free-radical-protecting enzymes, but the defect may be a secondary consequence of the illness, rather than a primary etiologic agent. Findings of enzymatic dysfunction in PD (Bindoff, Birch-Machin, Cartlidge, Parker, & Turnbull, 1989), reports of defective sulfur metabolism (Steventon, Heafield, Waring, & Williams, 1989), and evidence of Mitochondrial Complex I deficiency in PD patients (Schapira et al., 1990) strengthen the possibility that the development of PD is associated with susceptibility to toxic metabolites.

PATHOPHYSIOLOGY

All individuals with PD show a moderately severe, highly focal nerve-cell loss (of at least 60%) in the pars compacta of the substantia nigra (Gibb, 1992). The neuronal loss shows a characteristic pattern involving the preferential degeneration of the ventral tier cells of the pars compacta and a relative preservation of dorsal tier cells. The anatomic and functional significance of this division of the pars compacta is unknown.

A proportion of the remaining cells contain Lewy bodies, which signify neuronal degeneration. Lewy bodies are not specific to PD; their greatest power in diagnosis is to exclude PD if they are absent. Lewy bodies appear at an early stage of the degenerative process, and because of their distinctive appearance, they can be readily found before significant cell loss is apparent. Their distribution in the nervous system provides a map of the territories involved in the degeneration. Lewy bodies have been found not only in the substantia nigra, but also in the locus coeruleus, ventral tegmental area, nucleus basalis of Meynert, raphe nuclei, thalamus, cerebral cortex, and entire autonomic nervous system (Gibb, 1992).

Gibb's (1992) report indicates that the extent of spread into the cerebral cortex is variable. All patients show at least a couple of Lewy bodies in the cingulate cortex but not in the hippocampus. In some individuals, there is further spread of Lewy bodies into the temporal and frontal cortices and, less commonly, into parietal and occipital regions.

The dopamine depletion that occurs as a result of the nerve-cell degeneration in PD reduces the concentration of this neurotransmitter along the nigrostriatal pathway, resulting in an imbalance in the activity of alpha and gamma motor systems. Increased inhibition of gamma motor neurons produces the tremor, and increased alpha motor neuron activity results in rigidity. Bradykinesia is the end result of the imbalance.

An 80% depletion of striatal dopamine must occur before clinical symptoms are noted. Symptoms are not seen initially because the striatal system seemingly compensates for cell loss or denervation by presynaptic hyperactivity and postsynaptic dopamine-receptor hypersensitivity (Agid et al., 1989; Riederer & Wuketich, 1976).

Consistent evidence of a decline in nigral cell numbers associated with aging, along with reports of increased incidence of PD with age, has prompted concerns that PD may be related to an acceleration of the normal aging process. However, studies that have examined the pattern of cell loss that occurs in the substantia nigra as a function of normal aging have not provided support for this model. Patients with PD show marked pathology in the ventrolateral regions of the substantia nigra, whereas with age, the dorsal tier is more affected by neuronal cell loss (Gibb, 1992).

IMAGING TECHNIQUES

In general, electroencephalographic findings show progressive, generalized slowing as the disease progresses, and in advanced cases, computed tomography scanning will reveal diffuse cortical atrophy with widening of the sulci and hydrocephalus ex vacuo.

Electrophysiological studies, designed to evaluate speed of processing as measured by positive event-related potential (P3) latency, have observed that, prior to treatment, newly diagnosed PD patients exhibit normal P3 and task performance, with prolonged reaction time. After treatment, P3 latency is significantly prolonged, with reduced reaction time.

These findings suggest a dopamine-induced dissociation between cognitive and motor processing (Prasher & Findley, 1991).

Positron emission tomography (PET) scanning has been used to assess changes in the nigrostriatal dopamine system. Among affected PD patients, Leenders et al. (1986) reported a 60% reduction of L-6 18F Fluoro-Dopa (F-Dopa) uptake into striatal tissue. In comparison with age-matched controls, PD patients showed reduced uptake of F-Dopa in the putamen and, to a lesser degree, in the caudate nucleus (Leenders et al., 1990).

Comparison PET studies have also indicated subtle differences between PD and atypical PD cases. Brooks et al. (1990) reported that among PD patients, uptake is relatively preserved in the caudate and anterior putamen, with severe involvement of the posterior putamen. In contrast, uptake in the caudate and putamen is globally impaired in patients with progressive supranuclear palsy. Similarly, Otsuka et al. (1991) observed decreased uptake in the putamen (with a relative sparing of the caudate) among IPD patients, whereas equally decreased up take in the caudate and putamen was found among patients with atypical parkinsonism. Atypical PD patients have also shown decreased blood flow and glucose metabolism of the caudate and putamen as well as global cerebral decrease; in contrast, early stage, PD patients without dementia have shown normal blood flow and glucose metabolism.

PET imaging has contributed to elucidating the pathophysiology of parkinsonism and holds promise in the preclinical screening of individuals at risk for PD (Eidelberg, 1992). The technique also has great potential in objectively measuring rates of disease progression in normal and treated populations. However, clinical application of the procedure is currently restricted, because of the limited availability in only a few research centers.

Magnetic resonance (MR) imaging has proved to be of great value in excluding secondary causes of parkinsonism, such as basal ganglia infarction, hemorrhage, calcification, and hydrocephalus. However, the more important role of MR imaging relates to its capacity to image iron and detect pathologic accumulations in the putamen and substantia nigra. Specifically, signal hypodensity (or attenuation) within the putamen of patients with parkinsonian features is a marker for atypical parkinsonism.

In the initial studies reported by Olanow (1992) on parkinsonian patients, two patterns were observed that were different from those found in normal controls: (a) nigral changes, involving smudging or narrowing of the area of high signal separating the red nucleus and the substantia nigra and (b) striatal changes, involving signal attenuation in the putamen that equals or exceeds that found in the globus pallidus. Subsequent analyses have indicated that patients with nigral parkinsonism do not show signal attenuation in the putamen exceeding that found in age-matched controls. Among patients considered to have IPD, degeneration is confined to the nigra, with relative preservation of striatal neurons and dopamine receptors. This finding presumably accounts for the capacity of these patients to respond to levodopa therapy. In contrast, patients with striatal patterns likely have atypical parkinsonism involving degeneration of striatal neurons and their dopamine receptors. The loss of dopamine receptors accounts for the lack of response to levodopa therapy in patients with atypical parkinsonism. These studies suggest that the MR imaging is the first laboratory marker that has the capacity to differentiate PD from atypical parkinsonism (Olanow, 1992).

SYMPTOM PRESENTATION

The most common presenting symptom is a unilateral resting tremor of 3–5 cycles per s. It is first seen in the fingers and thumb, producing a characteristic pill-rolling action. The tremor is temporarily inhibited with voluntary movement, but becomes more prominent as the action continues. The tremor is markedly increased by tension or exertion and disappears during sleep. Many patients report vague, prodromal symptoms that antedate the appearance of obvious tremor by several years. These include paresthesias, aching or cramping muscles, a sensation of pulling or tenseness in the muscles, focal dystonia, generalized fatigue, depression, anxiety and restlessness, loss of dexterity, deterioration of handwriting, and changes in posture and balance (Hoehn, 1992). Given the elusive, ill-defined nature of these complaints, these symptoms are frequently ignored by the patient or dismissed as being insignificant and attributed to advancing age. In most cases, the diagnosis of PD follows the onset of symptoms by 1 to 2 years.

Observation of the patient may reveal diminished swing of the involved upper limb while walking, a slight lateral tilt of the trunk away from the affected side, and decreased facial expression, typically referred to as a masklike facies. Seborrhea of the forehead is occasionally present. Conversational speech reveals reduced amplitude and a slow, monotonic cadence. When the dominant hand is involved, handwriting will show characteristic changes, including micrographia, tremulousness, and poorly formed loops.

Tests of rapid alternating movements and finger dexterity may reveal slow, poorly coordinated movements, with rapidly deteriorating performance over time (Duvoisin, 1976). An exaggerated blink reflex (glabellar reflex) can be obtained by rhythmical tapping of the forehead. In the normal patient, blinking accompanies the initial taps, but rapidly subsides; in contrast, the PD patient continues to blink in response to each tap. Muscle tone is increased, giving rise to a plastic quality when muscle groups are passively stretched. This phenomenon, referred to as *cogwheeling*, is apparent during passive stretching, in which there is free movement between 5° and 10° accompanied by a tonic contraction of the stretched muscle.

As the clinical manifestations progress to bilateral involvement of limbs, the patient tends to assume a stooped posture when standing and walking (Duvoisin, 1976). Gradually, a mild, generalized slowness of all body movement develops that may be perceived by the patient as fatigue, weakness, or lethargy. There is a general poverty of spontaneous activity in hand gestures, eye blinking, facial expressions, and postural adjustments, and the patient appears to be relatively immobile. Even though physical disability is still minimal, many patients withdraw from social activities at this stage and exhibit depressive symptomatology.

The onset of gait disturbance signals the beginning of moderate generalized disability. Episodes of retropulsion and propulsion reflect increasing impairment of righting reflexes. Propulsion is manifested as a festinating gait or an inability to catch up with the center of gravity, with a quickening of pace as if propelled forward. Gait is slow and shuffling and fine motor activities are difficult. Assistance is frequently required in completing ordinary activities of daily living as a result of increased movement difficulties.

The clinical characteristics described above represent a broad generalization in terms of the expression and progression of PD. Recent evidence has demonstrated that within the realm of PD there are different subgroups with relatively specific clinical patterns. For example, patients with tremor as the dominant symptom generally have less bradykinesia and slower progression of the disease than those with postural instability and gait difficulty as dominant features (Jankovic et al., 1990). The latter group generally is older, is more likely to be cognitively impaired, and experiences a more rapidly progressive course than the tremor group. Whether these different subgroups represent variations of the same disease or etiologically distinct entities remains in question. However, further validation of these subtypes has implications for predicting the relative progression, complications, and prognosis of the disorder.

PROGNOSIS

The clinical symptoms of PD progressively worsen over a period of 10–20 years before culminating in severe invalidism. However, the rate of progression is highly variable between individuals, particularly with the introduction of neuroprotective agents (Langston, 1990a, 1990b). Only 25% of patients who have the disease less than 5 years are severely disabled. Two thirds of PD patients are markedly incapacitated in 5–9 years, whereas 80% of patients show significant disability in 10–14 years. There is a small group of atypical patients who show an unusually slow evolution of the disease and tend to remain in the early stages of the illness for 10 years or longer. Individuals in this group, comprising 10%–20% of PD patients, maintain righting reflexes and balance for more than 10 years and do not become severely disabled for 20 years or more.

There is evidence that when the initial symptom is tremor, the rate of progression through the stages is less rapid. However, recent reports by Hershey and associates (Hershey, Feldman, Kim, Commichau, &

Lichter, 1991) have indicated that tremor predominance after 5–7 years appears to be a better predictor of a benign clinical course and good cognitive outcome than tremor at onset. Tremor predominance refers to those patients who experience tremor as the initial symptom and continue to manifest tremor as the prominent feature, rather than disabling rigidity, bradykinesia, or gait disorder. This group of patients may represent a different subtype of PD as compared with those for whom the onset is characterized by rigidity, bradykinesia, or gait disturbance.

NEUROPSYCHOLOGICAL STUDIES

Early studies of the neuropsychological deficits in PD have been marked by methodological imprecision. Heterogeneous samples with varying levels of disability have yielded inconsistent results. Comparisons between studies have been hindered by the failure to control for depression, dementia, or duration of illness. Each of these factors has been shown to exert a dramatic influence on cognitive performance. Therefore, it is not surprising that a range of specific cognitive deficits have been associated with the disease and no consistent neuropsychological profile has emerged.

General intellectual evaluations have indicated that even though the mean IQ of PD patients is 5 to 10 points lower than that of age- and education-matched individuals in a control group, it is still within the normal range (Lees & Smith, 1983; Reitan & Boll, 1971; Talland, 1962). Loranger's data (Loranger, Goodell, McDowell, Lee, & Sweet, 1972) indicated that 85% of PD patients show Wechsler Adult Intelligence Scale (WAIS) Verbal IQ–Performance IQ discrepancies of greater than 10 points as compared with 15% of the normal population. According to estimates by Mayeux and Stern (1983), between 20% and 30% of PD patients have cognitive impairments sufficient to cause pronounced difficulties in their lives. Dakof and Mendelsohn's (1986) review noted that the most commonly reported impairment is a slowing down of thinking processes (bradyphrenia). In addition to the obvious motor difficulties that arise from the disorder, various focal deficits have been found on measures of visuospatial ability, memory, concept formation, and cognitive flexibility.

Visuospatial dysfunction, as one of the most frequently reported cognitive deficits in PD, reveals an interesting gradient of functional decline. A series of studies by Levin and colleagues (Levin et al., 1991; Levin, Llabre, & Weiner, 1989) suggested that facial recognition is one of the initial visuospatial skills to show decline in patients both with and without dementia. By middle-stage PD, patients with dementia experience difficulties mentally assembling puzzles, formulating angular judgments, and identifying embedded objects and geometric figures. In contrast, PD patients without dementia retain the ability to formulate angular judgments and to identify verbal and geometric embedded figures. Tasks involving mental object assembly (e.g., Hooper Visual Organization Test; Hooper, 1958) and manual visuoconstruction show a decline as a function of disease duration and are independent of dementia. In the advanced stages of PD, patients with dementia show pervasive impairment in all areas of visuospatial functioning.

Memory deficits among PD patients have been observed on a variety of measures, including paired-associate tasks, immediate recall of verbal narrative material, and verbal learning tasks. The fact that patients perform normally on delayed recall of the Logical Memory task suggests that encoding, consolidation, and retrieval processes are intact (Karayanidis, 1989). This differential recall at immediate and delayed stages has prompted speculations that the rate of stimulus presentation exceeds the patient's rate of processing, particularly because PD patients appear to benefit from recall cues more than age-matched controls (Scholz & Sastry, 1985). There are relatively consistent data indicating that PD patients have intact immediate auditory memory (Digit Span test) as well as adequate recognition memory.

Overall, a definite deficit in verbal memory has been documented only in tasks that involve free recall of novel items from short-term memory and trial-by-trial learning. The verbal memory deficit is independent of disease duration and levodopa treatment, with symptom severity contributing only moderately to performance decline.

Defective concept formation and cognitive inflexibility is perhaps the most consistently obtained finding in the cognitive assessment of PD patients.

Specifically, patients with PD who do not have dementia reveal cognitive deficits that are similar to those observed in patients with frontal lobe lesions (Caltagirone, Carlesimo, Nocentini, & Vicari, 1989). Impaired performance is observed in tasks of concept formation, sequence planning, shifting and maintaining sets, and temporal ordering. These deficits have been observed on a variety of measures, including the Wisconsin Card Sorting Test (Berg, 1948; Heaton, 1981), the Stroop test (Stroop, 1935), and the Trail Making Test (Reitan & Wolfson, 1985; U.S. War Department, 1944).

Verbal fluency measures have revealed a selective deficit associated with category naming. Specifically, PD patients without dementia show significant impairment in category naming for a semantic target, such as *fruit*, but perform normally on tests of letter fluency (Auriacombe et al., 1993; Lees & Smith, 1983; Raskin, Sliwinski, & Borod, 1992; Weingartner, Burns, Diebel, & LeWitt, 1984). Although several explanations have been proposed to account for this selective fluency deficit, preliminary reports by Auriacombe et al. have suggested that impaired category naming is related to the lexical retrieval impairment that has been observed in PD (Matison, Mayeux, Rosen, & Fahn, 1982).

Reports of linguistic functions among PD patients indicate a relative preservation of verbal abilities (Levin, Llabre, & Weiner, 1989). However, a proportion of PD patients suffer from speech problems, most commonly referred to as *hypokinetic dysarthria*. This disorder is characterized by monotony of pitch and loudness, reduced stress, short phrases, imprecise consonants, and segmented rushes of speech. These speech impairments, coupled with the mask-like facies and reduced gestural movements, compromise communication skills.

Nevertheless, although a variety of specific cognitive deficits have been observed in PD, the most salient feature that emerges from these studies is the extensive individual variation in the patterning of the motoric, affective, and cognitive symptomatology of the disease. The failure to identify a specific profile of deficits characteristic of PD has prompted some researchers to propose subtypes of PD, differentiable by the extent or patterning of cognitive deficits. For example, Mortimer and colleagues (Mortimer, Jun, Kuskowski, & Webster, 1987) identified three clusters of patients on the basis of their neuropsychological performance: Those with both verbal memory and visuospatial reasoning disorders, those with memory impairment alone, and those with normal intellectual function.

Another typology, proposed by Lieberman et al. (1979), was derived from the finding that PD patients with dementia were significantly older at the time of disease onset than PD patients who did not have dementia. Their findings were interpreted as suggesting two types of PD: one an exclusively motor disorder found in younger patients and the other a motor and cognitive disorder found in older patients.

A significant relationship between cognitive disability and disturbed affect has been observed in several studies, prompting researchers to speculate the existence of two subtypes of PD, according to the presence or absence of major depression. A longitudinal study of depression and intellectual decline among 92 PD patients indicated that patients with major depression exhibit a significantly greater cognitive decline, greater deterioration in activities of daily living, and faster progression through the Hoehn and Yahr (1967) stages than patients with either minor depression or no depression (Starkstein, Mayberg, Leiguarda, Preziosi, & Robinson, 1992). Further evidence for a biological difference between depressed and nondepressed PD patients has been provided by studies by Mayeux and associates (Mayeux et al., 1986, Mayeux, Stern, Sano, Williams, & Cote, 1988). Lower concentrations of 5-hydroxy-indoleacetic acid (5-HIAA) were found in the cerebrospinal fluid of depressed PD patients as compared with nondepressed PD patients. The lowest 5-HIAA concentrations were observed among patients who had both depression and dementia, suggesting that the association of dementia and depression in PD may represent a unique clinical entity (Sano et al., 1989).

Currently, these typologies are post hoc formulations that lack consistent cross-validation evidence. Further systematic study in large samples is needed to confirm the validity of these initial findings.

DEMENTIA

Approximately 15.9% of patients with PD show symptoms of dementia. This incidence rate is 6.65

times the rate that would be expected when compared with a cohort of individuals over age 60 (Marder et al., 1991). Even when age and disease duration are controlled, PD patients with dementia have significantly reduced survival rates in comparison with PD patients who do not have dementia. Questions remain as to whether the dementia is part of the natural history of PD or whether it is due to coincident Alzheimer's disease.

NEUROPSYCHOLOGICAL ASSESSMENT

In the initial stages of PD, cognitive impairments are subtle, if present at all, and dementia is rarely encountered. At the other end of the PD spectrum, some elderly patients with advanced PD may show obvious dementia, with cognitive impairments characteristic of Alzheimer's disease. The primary diagnostic concerns arise in the large group of patients with PD of mild-to-moderate severity who report complaints of forgetfulness or mild cognitive impairments. Most typically, the referral question is related to one of the following issues:

1. Concerns about dementia, depression, or both
2. Ability to operate a motor vehicle and driving restrictions
3. Management of financial affairs
4. Medication compliance and related memory concerns.

In all cases, psychometric data must be integrated with the patient's current and premorbid functional abilities. For this reason, an extensive history and assessment of current functional status must be obtained.

Rating Scales for Assessing Level of Disability

Given that neuropsychological test performance is strongly related to the patient's stage of illness, the evaluation should include an assessment of the patient's functional status and current level of disability. Although a variety of general functional status measures are available, there are instruments that have been specifically developed for and used extensively in the evaluation of the PD patient. These measures have the advantage of an extensive database with this population and they also target the unique features and consequences of the disorder.

The Hoehn and Yahr Scale. This scale is one of the measures used most widely in PD research to assess stages of severity. The scale is simply a grading of severity from 1 to 5, developed to reflect the progressive level of disability manifested in the course of PD. The scale was devised in the late 1960s and reported in 1967. According to Hoehn's description (1992), the scale is a "potpourri" of clinical signs and functional ability. The advantage seems to be that the stages of severity are easily defined by both patient and clinician and also provide a method of determining rate of progression in PD. This scale is reproduced in Exhibit 3.

The Northwestern University Disability Scales. This measure, developed by Canter, LaTorre, and Mier (1961), was designed to evaluate the extent to which a patient has lost premorbid efficiency in daily living. It evaluates five areas of patient functioning affected by the disorder: walking, dressing, hygiene, eating and feeding, and speech (see individual scales in Exhibit 4). The numerical value for each scale is multiplied by 2 to yield a maximum of 20 points per scale, with the possible total of 100 points. Complete failure to walk, for example, is rated 0. The walking scale defines 10 more points of increasing independence and efficiency in locomotion, ending in normal walking, which is given a value of 20. Although the scores represent an ordinal level of measurement, the degree of disability can be expressed as a percentage and serve as a baseline against which changes can be compared.

The Unified Parkinson's Disease Rating Scale. This measure, developed by Fahn et al. (1987), has become a standard scale in clinical studies of PD. The instrument is a composite of several assessments, with subcategories focusing on various aspects of parkinsonism. Signs and symptoms are graded on a well-defined scale ranging from 0 (*normal*) to 4 (*most severe*). It was initially devised in the late 1980s and has undergone revision to include the Schwab and England Activities of Daily Living Scale and the Hoehn and Yahr Clinical Rating of Severity Scale.

EXHIBIT 3

Hoehn and Yahr's Rating Scale: Level of Clinical Disability in Patients With Parkinson's Disease

Stage I	Unilateral involvement with minimal or no functional impairment.
Stage II	Bilateral or midline involvement, without impairment of balance; early postural changes are revealed.
Stage III	Impaired righting reflexes (mild disability); patient reveals unsteadiness when turning or when pushed from a standing position with eyes closed and feet together. (The onset of disturbance of balance heralds the beginnings of significant disability.)
Stage IV	Fully developed symptomatology (moderate); patient is able to ambulate and stand unassisted, but is markedly incapacitated; presence of disabling rigidity and bradykinesia.
Stage V	Confinement to bed or wheelchair unless aided (severe).

From "Parkinsonism: Onset, Progression, and Mortality," by M. M. Hoehn and M. D. Yahr, 1967, Neurology, 17, *p. 433.*

Depression as the Primary Psychological Feature

The assessment of cognitive dysfunction in PD is complicated by the presence of depression. Depression is the most frequent psychological dysfunction associated with PD (Mayeux, Stern, Rosen, & Leventhal, 1981), observed in approximately 40% of neurology clinic cases (Starkstein, Preziosi, Bolduc, & Robinson, 1990). The frequency and severity of depression is reported to be higher in both early and late stages of the disease, in comparison with the middle stages. Debate continues about whether the high frequency of depression occurs as a consequence of progressive physical impairment or whether the depression is a manifestation of the neurochemical changes in specific brain areas.

A recent survey of 339 PD patients, conducted by Dooneief and associates (1992), revealed a 47% prevalence of depression. Their report predicts that PD patients have about an 8%–9% chance of developing depression over a 5-year period, with an estimated incidence of 14.5% per year. Given that the prevalence of depression is 3%–4% among healthy elderly people (Boyd & Weissman, 1981), these findings are consistent with clinical observations that depression is more prevalent in individuals with PD.

In numerous studies, the severity of depression has been found to be a critical factor in evaluating the severity of cognitive impairment (Starkstein et al., 1989, 1990, 1992). Even when age, education, and illness variables are controlled, PD patients with major depression reveal impaired performance in a number of cognitive domains, with the most severe impairments in frontal lobe-related functions. In contrast, PD patients with minor depression do not reveal significant evidence of cognitive impairment in comparison with nondepressed PD patients. Although further replication of these findings is required, these preliminary findings have significant implications for the neuropsychological assessment of PD patients.

Additional Social–Psychological Issues

In addition to neurological symptoms, PD patients experience what have been referred to as secondary disease symptoms across a range of psychological and behavioral domains. Furthermore, data from Ellgring and associates (1990) have indicated that the stress experienced by these patients is considerably greater than that found in elderly people without the disease. Yet, with few exceptions, there has been little attention directed toward the broader question of psychosocial adaptation to PD.

Early work by Singer (1973, 1974a, 1974b, 1976) examined the effects of levodopa-treated PD patients in terms of activity level, social participation,

EXHIBIT 4

Northwestern University Disability Scales

Scale A: Walking

Never walks alone

0 Cannot walk at all, even with maximum assistance.
1 Needs considerable help, even with short distances; cannot walk outdoors with help.
2 Requires moderate help indoors; walks outdoors with help.
3 Requires potential help indoors and active help outdoors.

Sometimes walks alone

4 Walks from room to room without assistance, but moves slowly and uses external support; never walks alone outdoors.
5 Walks from room to room with moderate difficulty; may occasionally walk outdoors without assistance.
6 Walks short distances with ease; walking outdoors is difficult but often accomplished without help; rarely walks long distances alone.

Always walks alone

7 gait is extremely abnormal; very slow and shuffling; posture grossly affected; there may be propulsion.
8 Quality of gait is poor, slow rate; posture moderately affected; mild propulsion; turning is difficult.
9 Gait only slightly deviant from normal in quality and speed; turning is the most difficult task; normal posture.
10 Normal.

Scale B: Dressing

Requires complete assistance

0 Patient is a hindrance rather than a help to assistant.
1 Movements of patient neither help nor hinder assistant.
2 Can give some help through bodily movements.
3 Gives considerable help through bodily movements.

Requires partial assistance

4 Performs only gross dressing activities alone (hat, coat).
5 Performs about half of dressing activities independently.
6 Performs more than half of dressing activities alone, with considerable effort and slowness.
7 Handles all dressing alone with the exception of fine activities (tie, buttons).

Complete self-help

8 Dresses self completely with slowness and great effort.
9 Dresses self completely with only slightly more time and effort than normal.
10 Normal.

(continues)

EXHIBIT 4 (*Continued*)

Scale C: Hygiene

Requires complete assistance

0 Unable to maintain proper hygiene even with maximum help.
1 Reasonably good hygiene with assistance, but does not provide assistant with significant help.
2 Hygiene maintained well; gives aid to assistant.

Requires partial assistance

3 Performs a few tasks alone with assistant nearby.
4 Requires assistance for half of toilet needs.
5 Requires assistance for some tasks not difficult in terms of coordination.
6 Manages most of personal needs alone; has substituted methods for accomplishing difficult tasks (e.g., electric razor).

Complete self-help

7 Hygiene maintained independently, but with effort and slowness; accidents are not infrequent; may use substitute methods.
8 Hygiene activities are moderately time-consuming; no substitute methods and few accidents.
9 Hygiene maintained normally, with slight slowness.
10 Normal.

Scale D: Eating and feeding[a]

Eating

0 Eating is so impaired that a hospital setting is required to get adequate nutrition.
1 Eats only liquid and soft food; these are consumed slowly.
2 Liquids and soft foods handled with ease; hard foods are occasionally eaten, but require great effort and much time.
3 Eats some hard foods routinely, but these require time and effort.
4 Follows a normal diet, but chewing and swallowing are labored.
5 Normal.

Feeding

0 Requires complete assistance.
1 Performs only a few feeding tasks independently.
2 Performs most feeding tasks alone, slowly and with effort; requires help with some tasks (e.g., cutting meat or filling cup).
3 Handles all feeding alone with moderate slowness; still may get assistance in specific situations (e.g., cutting meat in restaurant); accidents not infrequent.
4 Fully feeds self with rare accidents; slower than normal.
5 Normal.

EXHIBIT 4 (*Continued*)

Scale E: Speech

0 Does not vocalize at all.
1 Vocalizes, but rarely for communicative purposes.
2 Vocalizes to call attention to self.
3 Attempts to use speech for communication, but has difficulty in initiating vocalization; may stop speaking in middle of phrase and be unable to continue.
4 Uses speech for most communication, but articulation is highly unintelligible; may have occasional difficulty in initiating speech; usually speaks in single words or short phrases.
5 Speech always used for communication, but articulation is still very poor; usually uses complete sentences.
6 Speech can always be understood if listener pays close attention; both articulation and voice may be defective.
7 Communication accomplished with ease, although speech impairment detracts from content.
8 Speech easily understood, but voice or speech rhythm may be disturbed.
9 Speech entirely adequate; minor voice disturbances present.
10 Normal.

From "A Method for Evaluating Disability in Patients With Parkinson's Disease," by G. J. Canter, R. LaTorre, and M. Mier, 1961, Journal of Nervous and Mental Disease, 133, *pp. 144–145. Copyright 1961 by Williams & Wilkins. Reprinted with permission.*
[a]Eating and feeding are figured separately, and the two scores are added.

depression, and enjoyment of life. Subsequent studies by Dakof and Mendelsohn (1986, 1989) identified four distinct adaptational patterns exhibited by PD patients. Cluster I patients, described as sanguine and engaged, exhibited characteristic cognitive styles that involved (a) deliberately putting negative thoughts out of mind and remaining optimistic, (b) believing that there were worse fates than having PD, and (c) maintaining a sense that certain aspects of their disease status were within their control and that actions and attitudes could affect the course of the illness. In contrast, Cluster II PD patients struggled with feelings of anxiety, frustration, and depression. These patients felt stigmatized, embarrassed, and resentful of their limitations, with prominent fears of the future. Cluster III patients were similar to those in Cluster II in terms of depression and preoccupation with their disease, but the distress experienced by Cluster III patients centered on past roles; specifically, the loss of participation in family and work roles was associated with feelings of powerlessness, loss of dignity, and loss of self-esteem. These individuals were characteristically more socially isolated, preferring the company of other PD patients as the only people who could understand them. Cluster IV patients were distinguished by their passivity and resignation to their fate, with little emotion expressed over the loss of personal power and influence. The two key factors that emerged to distinguish various patient adaptations were disease severity and attitudinal stance. Although the case-centered methodology used in Dakof and Mendelsohn's (1989) report has inherent limitations, their work has provided a empirical foundation from which other research has emerged.

One of the largest studies to date in the area of psychosocial issues in PD was recently conducted in Germany by Ellgring et al. (1993). From a survey of 325 PD patients, these researchers identified four primary areas of psychosocial dysfunction: (a) stress from bodily symptoms, (b) lack of efficiency, (c) anxiety, and (d) interpersonal discomfort (Ellgring et al., 1993). Specifically, 97% of the sample experienced distress associated with reduced manual skills; 90% of the sample noted that bradyphrenia and an increase of symptoms under stress were problematic concerns. A stress-induced increase of motor symptoms is a common phenomenon in PD. Even minor stressors, particularly social in nature, have extreme effects and may elicit or increase tremor. Some patients report freezing, particularly in circumstances that promote a sense of being pushed or rushed. In interpersonal settings, over 80% of the sample described having fewer activities, increased anxiety or insecurity in social interactions, and inability to cope with many people. The social anxiety is thought to evolve as an indirect consequence of the motor symptoms. These patients fear negative evaluation in public and, as a result, social withdrawal increases.

Cognitive–behavioral interventions involving group training in stress management and individual counseling to enhance coping skills have been adapted for the specific concerns of the PD patient (described in Ellgring et al., 1993). Group seminars address such topics as (a) coping with difficult social situations; (b) psychoeducation about stress and disease; (c) methods for increasing activity, initiative, and independence; and (d) ways to change attitudes about disease. Individual counseling uses stress inoculation, cognitive restructuring, social skills training, modeling or role-playing, relaxation training, and transfer of contents to daily activities. The maintenance of motivation remains a critical problem in working with the PD patient. These initial studies provide an empirical framework for developing a specific treatment plan or program designed to manage the psychological components of the illness.

Education and support services are an essential component in the management of PD. Special attention should be given to the psychological condition of relatives and the primary caretaker, because patients themselves can receive adequate support only when the health of their relatives is maintained. The family and patient should be made aware of the more common psychological features, medication side effects, and less frequent psychotic disturbances that may arise during treatment. Many patients benefit from local support networks that provide physical therapy services, caregiver support groups, and educational conferences. Several national organizations publish newsletters that provide practical, educational, and referral information regarding PD. Information can be obtained by contacting these sources:

The American Parkinson Disease Association, Inc.
60 Bay Street, Suite 401, Staten Island, NY 10301; (800) 223-2732

National Parkinson Foundation, Inc.
1501 Northwest 9th Avenue, Miami, FL 33136-1494; (800) 433-7022

Parkinson's Disease Foundation
650 West 168th Street, New York, NY 10032; (212) 923-4700, (800) 457-6676

United Parkinson's Foundation
833 West Washington Boulevard, Chicago, IL 60607; (312) 733-1893

Recommended Neuropsychological Test Battery for PD Patients

On the basis of an extensive literature review of the cognitive deficits associated with this disorder, Raskin, Borod, and Tweedy (1990) formulated a comprehensive neuropsychological battery tailored to the patient with PD. As shown in Exhibit 5, the battery begins with a screening for dementia, because of the frequent occurrence of dementia in PD and to eliminate the need for further testing if a patient is initially found to have dementia. The battery includes measures of immediate and delayed memory, verbal fluency, set shifting, spatial orientation, and depression, because these are areas where deficits have commonly been reported in PD patients. In addition, a writing sample is obtained to assess micrographia. Tests of semantic memory, abstract reasoning, and basic visual discrimination, generally found to be intact in PD patients, are included to determine the specificity of any observed deficits. For each of these cognitive areas (except writing), tasks were selected that minimize motor output. Administration time is estimated at approximately 3 hr, and the battery can be administered on successive days to reduce fatigue.

EXHIBIT 5

Neuropsychological Test Battery for Parkinson's Disease

Dementia
- Dementia Rating Scale (Mattis, 1976)

General cognitive functioning
- Fund of information
  - WAIS-R Information subtest (Wechsler, 1981)
- Abstract reasoning
  - WAIS-R Similarities subtest (Wechsler, 1981)

Basic visual discrimination
- Benton Visual Discrimination Test (Benton, Hamsher, Varney, & Spreen, 1983)

Spatial orientation
- Benton Line Orientation (Benton et al., 1983)
- Money Map Test (Money, 1976)
- Benton Right–Left Orientation (Benton et al., 1983)

Set shifting
- Stroop Color and Word Interference Test (Stroop, 1935)
- Competing Programs (Luria, 1966)
- Trail-Making Test (Army Individual Test Battery, 1944)

Memory and attention
- Immediate recall
  - Wechsler Memory Scale–Revised (WMS-R) Digit Span (Wechsler, 1987)
  - WMS-R Logical Memory
  - California Verbal Learning Test (Delis, Kramer, Kaplan, & Ober, 1987)
  - Benton Visual Retention, 10-sec exposure (Benton, 1974)
- Delayed recall
  - WMS-R Logical Memory
  - California Verbal Learning Test delay trial
- Recognition
  - California Verbal Learning Test recognition trial
  - Randt picture recognition

Verbal fluency
- Controlled Word Association Test (FAS) (Benton, 1968)
- Animal Naming (Goodglass & Kaplan, 1972)

Naming
- Boston Naming Test (Kaplan, Goodglass, & Weintraub, 1983)

Depression
- Zung Depression Index (Zung, 1965)

Motoric functioning
- Finger Tapping Test (Halstead, 1947)

Writing
- Sentence Writing from the Boston Diagnostic Aphasia Exam (Goodglass & Kaplan, 1983)

WAIS-R = Wechsler Adult Intelligence Scale–Revised. From "Neuropsychological Aspects of Parkinson's Disease," by S. A. Raskin, J. C. Borod, and J. Tweedy, 1990, Neuropsychology Review, 1, *p. 213. Copyright 1990 by Plenum. Reprinted with permission.*

Illustrative Case Using the Halstead–Reitan Neuropsychological Test Battery

Neuropsychological assessment with the Halstead–Reitan battery has been used in the evaluation of PD. The case described here illustrates the use of this battery, along with supplemental measures, in evaluating this population. A summary of the test results is provided in Table 1.

Mr. A . is a 70-year-old college-educated, White man recently diagnosed with PD and referred for evaluation by his neurologist. His chief complaint was expressed as "I feel depressed." Further questioning indicated concerns about slowed thinking, lack of initiative, driving difficulties, and problems with recent memory. Interviews with family members revealed that although the patient had remained employed in his own consulting business, he had be-

TABLE 1

Mr. A.'s Test Results on the Neuropsychological Test Battery

Measure	Raw score	T score	Percentile
Halstead–Reitan Neuropsychological Test Battery			
Category test	93	43	
TPT–Memory	4	36[b]	
TPT–Location	0	36[b]	
Speech-Sounds Perception Test	7	43	
Finger Tapping Dominant	50	51	
Trails A	35 s	51	
Trails B	195 s	33[b]	
Halstead Impairment Index	.6	48	
WAIS-R Verbal IQ	104		61
WAIS-R Performance IQ	99		47
WAIS-R Full Scale IQ	102		55
WAIS-R Block Design[a]	10		50
WAIS-R Digit Symbol[a]	9		37
Luria Memory Words (Maximum = 10)			
2-min recall	8		89
20-min recall	8		89

Note: TPT = Tactual Performance Test; WAIS-R = Wechsler Adult Intelligence Scale—Revised.
[a]WAIS-R raw score values are age-corrected scale scores.
[b]Mild-to-moderate impairment.

come increasingly wary of tackling new business-related projects, more withdrawn in social settings, and reluctant to participate in outside activities.

The history of the complaint indicated that Mr. A. had consulted his family physician approximately 1 year before with complaints of depression. An extended trial of antidepressants was prescribed, but the patient did not experience significant change in his status and was subsequently referred to the neurologist. The initial neurological exam revealed marked facial immobility, decreased arm swing, and a hint of cogwheel rigidity, insufficient to warrant a diagnosis of PD at the time. The computed tomography scan was unremarkable, except for mildly prominent, dilated sulci, consistent with age-related cerebral atrophy. His medical and psychiatric history was unremarkable. At a 6-month follow-up, the patient had a mild tremor of the left hand. At that time, he was diagnosed with PD and prescribed a trial of Symmetrel.

The patient's social and family background revealed a relatively stable individual who had been married 35 years and self-employed in a consulting capacity for approximately 15 years. He characterized himself before being diagnosed as active and involved in church and social activities.

The following neuropsychological instruments were administered: the revised WAIS (WAIS-R; Wechsler, 1981), the Halstead–Reitan Neuropsychological Test Battery (Reitan & Wolfson, 1993), the Controlled Word Association Test (Benton, 1968), the Wechsler Memory Scale–Revised (Wechsler, 1987), the Luria Memory Words (Sherer, Nixon, Parsons, & Adams, 1992), the Bender Gestalt Visual Motor Test (Bender, 1938), the Beck Depression Inventory (Beck, 1967), and the Minnesota Multiphasic Personality Inventory (Butcher, Dahlstrom, Graham, Tellegen, & Kaemmer, 1989).

Neuropsychological test results indicated current intellectual functioning in the average range (WAIS-R Verbal IQ = 104, Performance IQ = 99, Full-Scale IQ = 102). These findings were lower than would be expected (given the patient's educational history and occupational status) and suggested the presence of a decline in cognitive capacity relative to premorbid abilities. Specific deficits were observed in areas requiring sequencing of social situations, calculation ability, and psychomotor speed. Relative strengths were displayed in verbal tasks, with some reduced efficiency associated with abstract reasoning and judgment.

Fine motor skills and motor strength ability revealed a mild unilateral decline associated with the left upper extremity, consistent with the left-handed tremor.

On measures of learning and verbal memory functions, the patient displayed adequate retention and recall of verbal material. Immediate recall for auditory material was above average (Digit Span = 14, age-corrected scale score) and delayed recall of word lists showed no significant decay of information (89%). However, the patient's ability to learn new information was slower than would be expected (9 words in 8 trials), in view of his premorbid abilities.

Performance on visuospatial tasks was marked by considerable disparity. Visual tracking skills (Trails A = 35 s, no errors), visual attention to detail (Picture Completion = 11, age-corrected scale score) and constructional assembly abilities (Block Design = 10; Object Assembly = 13, age-corrected scale scores) were average to above average. However, constructional graphomotor abilities were below average and suggestive of mild dyspraxia. Specifically, performance on the Bender Gestalt Test revealed overlapping figures, angulation difficulties, and loss of gestalt. Memory for geometric shapes and spatial position was severely impaired (Tactual Performance Test–Memory = 4; Tactual Performance Test–Location = 0).

Similarly, complex problem solving (requiring visuospatial analysis) and tasks requiring visuospatial scanning, motor skills, and conceptual set shifting were markedly deficient (Category test = 93, Tactual Performance Test–Total = 29 s, Trails B = 195 s with 4 errors). Verbal fluency skills were at the 11th percentile.

The patient's psychological profile revealed a mildly depressed and anxious individual who was experiencing significant concern about his present health problems. His depression was primarily manifested as ruminative and agitated, with a tendency toward introversion when under stress. His emotional status revealed no evidence of significant psychopathology.

In summary, the results of the neuropsychological evaluation showed a decline in general cognitive functioning, although functionally within normal limits. The patient displayed specific deficits in visuospatial skills, visual memory, and complex problem solving. His ability to learn new material was compromised to some extent, and he displayed reduced processing speed. Immediate auditory attention and verbal memory skills were intact. A mild lateralized decline in motor skills was present in the left extremity. His psychological status was suggestive of mild depression, but indicated no significant psychopathology.

The patient was given his test results and advised that he should no longer drive a motor vehicle, given the observed visuospatial deficits and decreased cognitive processing speed. He was provided with compensatory techniques to assist him with his visual memory deficits. The patient disclosed that he had experienced intermittent worry that he was "going crazy" and expressed considerable relief that his symptoms had been validated to some extent by the testing and were not suggestive of psychiatric decompensation. In view of his concerns about the progression of his illness, the patient was advised to return for a follow-up visit in 1 year to reevaluate his status and render impressions regarding the relative progression of his deficits.

TREATMENT

The lack of definitive data on how to best treat PD has prompted some experts in the field to formulate general management guidelines (described in Koller, Silver, & Lieberman, 1994). Their efforts have led to the construction of an algorithm to address the pharmacological as well as nonpharmacological factors in the treatment of PD. The information provided in the supplement represents perhaps the most current, comprehensive problem-solving procedure available for addressing the many problems afflicting the patient with PD.

A key component to early PD management involves education and group support for patients and their families. The value of exercise and adequate nutrition is frequently overlooked as a contributing factor in overall well-being.

Decisions associated with the pharmacological management of early stage PD are mediated in part by age considerations, presence of cognitive disability, and degree of functional impairment. Patients without significant cognitive decline may be candidates for Selegiline, a selective monoamine oxidase inhibitor (MAOI) hailed as a neuroprotective agent that purportedly delays the progression of PD symptoms. Amantadine (Symmetrel) provides transient benefits as short-term monotherapy for a period as long as 6 to 12 months in patients with mild-to-moderate parkinsonism. Anticholinergic drugs, such as trihexyphenidyl and benztropine, are reported to be effective in reducing tremor; however, the high incidence of delirium, confusion, and other side effects—particularly among elderly patients or those with cognitive impairment—limit widespread use of these drugs.

Levodopa therapy is the most effective drug available for the treatment of PD. Peak plasma concentrations occur within the first hour after oral ingestion. Long-acting levodopa-carbidopa preparations, such as Sinemet CR, have been increasingly advocated to avoid response fluctuations, although their ability to produce smooth plasma levodopa levels and prevent motor fluctuations has not been proven. Most patients report a dramatic response in terms of regaining normal physical abilities during the initial phases of this treatment. However, after 5–6 years of treatment, approximately one third of patients either fail to maintain benefit or develop intolerable side effects, necessitating a change in regimen (J. R. Calverley, personal communication, January 23, 1995). Clinical experts have noted that most of these patients respond to an added second agent. The dopamine agonists (such as bromocriptine and pergolide) may be used to supplement the levodopa regimen as response fluctuations and dyskinesias develop. Psychotic complications with levodopa therapy are seen in about 22% of PD patients (Friedman & Sienkiewicz, 1991). This percentage is considerably lower among patients seen at specialized PD clinics, with estimates at 10% or less (J. R. Calverley, personal communication, January 23, 1995). Psychotic complications are dose related, and these patients generally tend to be older (mean age 72 years), with later onset of the disease.

The limitations of symptomatic treatment have led researchers to investigate pharmacologic agents that may have a potential to delay the progression of PD. The initial clinical trials evaluating the efficacy of Selegiline showed that the rate of symptom development and need for levodopa was delayed by 40%–83% per year among treated patients as compared with placebo controls (Tetrud & Langston, 1989). The results of a large, multi-institutional study ($N = 800$), DATATOP (Parkinson Study Group, 1989), indicated that the average time before levodopa was initiated in the placebo group was 312 days as compared with 549 days for patients in the Selegiline group. Although there is continued controversy as to whether the delay in the need for levodopa results from a symptomatic or a neuroprotective effect, the weight of the evidence and paucity of adverse effects argue for treating all newly diagnosed PD patients with Selegiline (Lieberman, 1993). Selegiline became available for prescription use in the fall of 1989. Unlike other MAOIs, the drug selectively inhibits MAO-B, precluding the dietary restrictions associated with general MAOIs. However, the medication is expensive: $2.60 per tablet, for an average cost of $156.00 per month. Some experts in the field contend that the beneficial effects rarely last more than 1 year (J. R. Calverley, personal communication, January 23, 1995).

Neurosurgical treatments for PD have consisted of strategies aimed either at alleviating the underlying dopamine deficiency or at correcting abnormal compensatory effects in neural circuits within the basal ganglia. Four different neurosurgical approaches have been reviewed: intracerebral transplantation of fetal dopamine neurons, implantation of autologous adrenal medulla tissue, tremor-reducing surgical lesions in the ventrolateral thalamus, and ventroposterior pallidotomy aimed at reducing akinesia and rigidity (Widner & Rehncrona, 1993).

For fetal neural tissue transplants, the findings to date indicate that further refinement of the technique is needed to enhance graft survival. In contrast, adrenal implants have been suspended as a result of unacceptable complication rates. A follow-up report by the United Parkinson's Foundation Registry on adrenal medullary transplants (Goetz et al., 1991) indicated that only 19% of the patients demonstrated improvement 2 years after surgery. Twenty-two percent of survivors had persistent psychiatric morbidity that was not present prior to surgery. Evidence from PET scanning in life and postmortem studies has shown poor graft survival. Reports of high postoperative mortality and surgical complications in 10%–20% of cases have tempered the initial enthusiasm, particularly because patients continue to require levodopa therapy. Stereotactic ventrolateral thalamotomy for medically resistant tremor has been shown to provide several tremor-free years among carefully selected patients, along with a reduction in medication and few permanent complications (Widner & Rehncrona, 1993). Pallidotomy remains under investigation, particularly with regard to long-term effects and complication rates.

SUMMARY

PD has been thus far the only neurodegenerative disease to respond to the principle of neurotransmitter replacement therapy. From the discovery of levodopa treatment in the late 1960s, the field has advanced toward the identification of a substance (MPTP) that produces a laboratory model of selective neuronal degeneration in the substantia nigra. These animal models allow the identification of potential neuroprotective agents or surgical implantation mechanisms for treatment. In this chapter, we have presented a summary of the diagnostic concerns, clinical features, and associated neuropsychological deficits presented by patients who have PD. The clinical management of these individuals requires a multidisciplinary approach, involving neurological, geropsychiatric, and neuropsychological expertise.

Behavioral changes are a common cause of disability among PD patients, with depression noted as the most frequent psychological disturbance. Assessment can be problematic because of the overlap between somatic symptoms related to PD and those related to depression. Less common, but possibly the most serious psychiatric side effects associated with all the antiparkinsonian medications, are delirium and psychosis. These episodes are generally reversible, with initial management aimed at dosage reduction. In addition, some degree of intellectual impairment can be expected in the vast majority of patients, but the range of severity among patients is extensive. Characteristic cognitive prototypes have been identified and may provide conceptual templates for continued research efforts, but current clinical approaches acknowledge the extensive variation among these patients via a multifactorial assessment. This approach entails the evaluation of functional disability and assessment of specific psychiatric features, in addition to the delineation of neuropsychological deficits.

References

Agid, Y., Cervera, P., Hirsch, E., Javoy-Agid, F., Lehericy, S., Raisman, R., & Ruberg, M. (1989). Biochemistry of Parkinson's disease 28 years later: A critical review. *Movement Disorders*, *4*(Suppl. 1), S126–S144.

Army Individual Test Battery. (1944). *Manual of directions and scoring*. Washington, DC: War Department, Adjutant General's Office.

Auriacombe, S., Grossman, M., Carvell, S., Gollomp, S., Stern, M., & Hurtig, H. (1993). Verbal fluency deficits in Parkinson's disease. *Neuropsychology*, *7*, 182–192.

Beck, A. (1967). *Depression: Clinical, experimental and theoretical aspects*. New York: Harper & Row.

Bender, L. (1938). *A visual motor gestalt test and its clinical use*. (American Orthopsychiatric Association Research Monographs No. 3).

Benton, A. (1968). Differential behavioral effects in frontal lobe disease. *Neuropsychologia*, *6*, 53–60.

Benton, A. (1974). *The revised visual retention test*. New York: Psychological Corporation.

Benton, A., Hamsher, K., Varney, N., & Spreen, O. (1983). *Contributions to neuropsychological assessment*. New York: Oxford University Press.

Berg, E. A. (1948). A simple objective technique for measuring flexibility of thinking. *Journal of General Psychology*, *39*, 15–22.

Bindoff, L. A., Birch-Machin, M., Cartlidge, N. E., Parker, W. D., Jr., & Turnbull, D. M. (1989). Mitochondrial function in Parkinson's disease. *Lancet*, *2*, 49.

Boyd, J. H., & Weissman, M. M. (1981). Epidemiology of affective disorders: A reexamination and future directions. *Archives of General Psychiatry*, *38*, 1039–1046.

Brooks, D. J., Ibanez, V., Sawle, G. V., Quinn, N., Lees, A. J., Mathias, C. J., Bannister, R., Marsden, C. D., & Frackowiak, R. S. (1990). Differing patterns of striatal F18–dopa uptake in Parkinson's disease, multiple system atrophy, and progressive supranuclear palsy. *Annals of Neurology*, *28*, 547–555.

Butcher, J., Dahlstrom, W., Graham, J., Tellegen, A., & Kaemmer, B. (1989). *Minnesota Multiphasic Personality Inventory (MMPI-2) manual for administration and scoring*. Minneapolis: University of Minnesota Press.

Caltagirone, C., Carlesimo, A., Nocentini, U., & Vicari, S. (1989). Defective concept formation in parkinsonians is independent from mental deterioration. *Journal of Neurology, Neurosurgery, and Psychiatry*, *52*, 334–337.

Canter, G. J., LaTorre, R., & Mier, M. (1961). A method for evaluating disability in patients with Parkinson's Disease. *Journal of Nervous and Mental Disease*, *133*, 143–147.

Dakof, G., & Mendelsohn, G. (1986). Parkinson's disease: The psychological aspects of a chronic illness. *Psychological Bulletin*, *99*, 375–387.

Dakof, G., & Mendelsohn, G. (1989). Pattern of adaptation to Parkinson's disease. *Health Psychology*, *8*, 355–372.

Delis, D., Kramer, J., Kaplan, E., & Ober, B. (1987). *California Verbal Learning Test manual*. New York: Psychological Corporation.

Dooneief, G., Mirabello, E., Bell, K., Marder, K., Stern, Y., & Mayeux, R. (1992). An estimate of the incidence of depression in idiopathic Parkinson's disease. *Archives of Neurology*, *49*, 305–307.

Duvoisin, R. C. (1976). Parkinsonism. *Clinical Symposia*, *28*, 2–29.

Duvoisin, R. C. (1986). Genetics of Parkinson's disease. *Advances of Neurology*, *45*, 307–312. New York: Raven Press.

Eidelberg, D. (1992). Positron emission tomography studies in parkinsonism. *Neurologic Clinics*, *10*, 421–433.

Ellgring, H., Seiler, S., Nagel, U., Perleth, B., Gasser, T., & Oertel, W. (1990). Psychosocial problems of Parkinson's patients: Approaches to assessment and treatment. *Advances in Neurology*, *53*, 349–353.

Ellgring, H., Seiler, S., Perleth, B., Frings, W., Gasser, T., & Oertel, W. (1993). Psychosocial aspects of Parkinson's disease. *Neurology*, *43*(Suppl. 6), S41–S44.

Fahn, S., Elton, R., & Members of the UPDRS Development Corporation. (1987). Unified Parkinson's disease rating scale. In S. Fahn, C. Marsden, D. Calne, & M. Goldstein (Eds.), *Recent developments in Parkinson's disease* (Vol. 2, pp. 153–164). Florahm Park, NJ: MacMillan Healthcare Information.

Friedman, A., & Sienkiewicz, J. (1991). Psychotic complications of long-term levodopa treatment of Parkinson's disease. *Acta Neurologia Scandinavia*, *84*, 111–113.

Gibb, W. R. (1992). Neuropathology of Parkinson's disease and related syndromes. In J. M. Cedarbaum & S. T. Gancher (Eds.), *Parkinson's disease* (pp. 361–376). Philadelphia: W. B. Saunders.

Gibb, W. R., & Lees, A. J. (1988). The relevance of the Lewy body to the pathogenesis of idiopathic Parkinson's disease. *Journal of Neurology, Neurosurgery, and Psychiatry*, *51*, 745–752.

Goetz, C. G., Stebbins, G. T., Klawans, H. L., Koller, W. C., Grossman, R. G., Bakay, R. A., Penn, R. D., & the United Parkinson Foundation Neural Transplantation Registry. (1991). United Parkinson Foundation Neurotransplantation Registry on adrenal medullary transplants: Presurgical, and one and two year follow-up. *Neurology*, *41*, 1719–1722.

Golbe, L. I. (1991). Young-onset Parkinson's disease: A clinical review. *Neurology*, *41*, 168–173.

Golbe, L. I., Di Iorio, G., Bonavita, V., Miller, D. C., & Duvoisin, R. C. (1990). A large kindred with autosomal dominant Parkinson's disease. *Annals of Neurology*, *27*, 276–282.

Goodglass, H., & Kaplan, E. (1972). *Assessment of aphasia and related disorders*. Philadelphia: Lea & Febiger.

Goodglass, H., & Kaplan, E. (1983). *Assessment of aphasia and related disorders* (2nd ed.). Philadelphia: Lea & Febiger.

Halstead, W. (1947). *Brain and intelligence*. Chicago: University of Chicago Press.

Heaton, R. K. (1981). *Wisconsin Card Sorting Test: Manual*. Odessa, FL: Psychological Assessment Resources.

Hershey, L. A., Feldman, B. J., Kim, K. Y., Commichau, C., & Lichter, D. G. (1991). Tremor at onset: Predictor of cognitive and motor outcome in Parkinson's disease? *Archives of Neurology*, *48*, 1049–1051.

Ho, S. C., Woo, J., & Lee, C. M. (1989). Epidemiologic study of Parkinson's disease in Hong Kong. *Neurology*, *39*, 1314–1318.

Hoehn, M. M. (1992). The natural history of Parkinson's disease in the pre-levodopa and post-levodopa eras. *Neurologic Clinics*, *10*, 331–339.

Hoehn, M. M., & Yahr, M. D. (1967). Parkinsonism: Onset, progression and mortality. *Neurology*, *17*, 427–442.

Hooper, H. E. (1958). *The Hooper visual organization test*. Los Angeles: Western Psychological Services.

Hughes, A. J., Daniel, S. E., Kilford, L., & Lees, A. J. (1992). Accuracy of clinical diagnosis of idiopathic Parkinson's disease: A clinico-pathological study of 100 cases. *Journal of Neurology, Neurosurgery, and Psychiatry*, *55*, 181–184.

Jankovic, J., McDermott, M., Carter, J., Gauthier, S., Goetz, C., Golbe, L., Huber, S., Koller, W., Olanow,

C., Shoulson, I., Stern, M., Tanner, C., Weiner, W., & the Parkinson's Study Group. (1990). Variable expression of Parkinson's disease: A base-line analysis of the DATATOP cohort. *Neurology, 40,* 1529–1534.

Johnson, W. G. (1991). Genetic susceptibility to Parkinson's disease. *Neurology, 41,* 82–87.

Johnson, W. G., Hodge, S. E., & Duvoisin, R. C. (1990). Twin studies and the genetics of Parkinson's disease—A reappraisal. *Movement Disorders, 5,* 187–194.

Kaplan, E., Goodglass, H., & Weintraub, S. (1983). *The Boston Naming Test.* Philadelphia: Lea & Febiger.

Karayanidis, F. (1989). Parkinson's disease: A conceptualization of neuropsychological deficits within an information-processing framework. *Biological Psychology, 29,* 149–179.

Kessler, I. I. (1972). Epidemiologic studies of Parkinson's disease: III. A community-based survey. *American Journal of Epidemiology, 96,* 242–254.

Koller, W., Silver, D., & Lieberman, A. (1994). An algorithm for the management of Parkinson's Disease. *Neurology, 44*(Suppl. 10), S1–S52.

Koller, W., Vetere-Overfield, B., Gray, C., Alexander, C., Chin, T., Dolezal, J., Hassanein, R., & Tanner, C. (1990). Environmental risk factors in Parkinson's disease. *Neurology, 40,* 1218–1221.

Langston, J. W. (1990a). Predicting Parkinson's disease. *Neurology, 40*(Suppl. 3), 70–74.

Langston, J. W. (1990b). Selegiline as neuroprotective therapy in Parkinson's disease: concepts and controversies. *Neurology, 40*(Suppl. 3), 61–66.

Leenders, K. L., Palmer, A. J., Quinn, N., Clark, J. C., Firnau, G., Garnett, E. S., Nahmias, C., Jones, T., & Marsden, C. D. (1986). Brain dopamine metabolism in patients with Parkinson's disease measured with positron emission tomography. *Journal of Neurology, Neurosurgery, and Psychiatry, 49,* 853–860.

Leenders, K. L., Salmon, E. P., Tyrrell, P., Perani, D., Brooks, D. J., Sager, H., Jones, T., Marsden, C. D., & Frackowiak, R. (1990). The nigrostriatal dopaminergic system assessed in vivo by positron emission tomography in healthy volunteer subjects and patients with Parkinson's disease. *Archives of Neurology, 47,* 1290–1298.

Lees, A. J., & Smith, E. (1983). Cognitive deficits in the early stages of Parkinson's disease. *Brain, 106,* 257–270.

Levin, B. E., Llabre, M. M., Reisman, S., Weiner, W. J., Sanchez-Ramos, J., Singer, C., & Brown, M. C. (1991). Visuospatial impairment in Parkinson's disease. *Neurology, 41,* 365–369.

Levin, B. E., Llabre, M. M., & Weiner, W. J. (1989). Cognitive impairments associated with early Parkinson's disease. *Neurology, 39,* 557–561.

Li, S. C., Schoenberg, B. S., Wang, C. C., Cheng, X. M., Rui, D. Y., Bolis, C. L., & Schoenberg, D. G. (1985). A prevalence survey of Parkinson's disease and other movement disorders in the People's Republic of China. *Archives of Neurology, 42,* 655–657.

Lieberman, A. (1993). Treatment of Parkinson's disease. *Current Opinion in Neurology and Neurosurgery, 6,* 339–343.

Lieberman, A., Dziatolowski, M., Kupersmith, M., Serby, M., Goodgold, A., Korein, J., & Goldstein, M. (1979). Dementia in Parkinson's disease. *Annals of Neurology, 6,* 355–357.

Loranger, A. W., Goodell, H., McDowell, F. H., Lee, J. E., & Sweet, R. D. (1972). Intellectual impairment in Parkinson's disease. *Brain, 95,* 405–412.

Luria, A. (1966). *Higher cortical functions in man.* New York: Basic Books.

Marder, K., Leung, D., Tang, M., Bell, K., Dooneief, G., Cote, L., Stern, Y., & Mayeux, R. (1991). Are demented patients with Parkinson's disease accurately reflected in prevalence surveys? A survival analysis. *Neurology, 41,* 1240–1243.

Marsden, C. D. (1987). Parkinson's disease in twins. *Journal of Neurology, Neurosurgery, and Psychiatry, 50,* 105–106.

Marttila, R. J., Kaprio, J., Koskenvuo, M., & Rinne, U. K. (1988). Parkinson's disease in a nationwide twin cohort. *Neurology, 38,* 1217–1219.

Matison, R., Mayeux, R., Rosen, J., & Fahn, S. (1982). "Tip-of-the-tongue" phenomenon in Parkinson's disease. *Neurology, 32,* 567–570.

Mattis, S. (1976). Mental status examination for organic mental syndrome in the elderly patient. In R. Bellack & B. Karasu (Eds.), *Geriatric psychiatry* (pp. 77–121). New York: Grune and Stratton.

Mayeux, R., & Stern, Y. (1983). Intellectual dysfunction and dementia in Parkinson's disease. In R. Mayeux & W. G. Rosen (Eds.), *The dementias* (pp. 211–227). New York: Raven Press.

Mayeux, R., Stern, Y., Rosen, J., & Leventhal, J. (1981). Depression, intellectual impairment, and Parkinson disease. *Neurology, 31,* 645–650.

Mayeux, R., Stern, Y., Sano, M., Williams, J. B., & Cote, L. J. (1988). The relationship of serotonin to depression in Parkinson's disease. *Movement Disorders, 3,* 237–244.

Mayeux, R., Stern, Y., Williams, J. B., Cote, L., Frantz, A., & Dyrenfurth, I. (1986). Clinical and biochemical features of depression in Parkinson's disease. *American Journal of Psychiatry, 143,* 756–759.

Money, J. (1976). *A standardized road map test of direction sense*. San Rafael, CA: Academic Therapy Publications.

Mortimer, J. A., Jun, S. P., Kuskowski, M. A., & Webster, D. D. (1987). Subtypes of Parkinson's disease defined by intellectual impairment. *Journal of Neural Transmission, 24*(Suppl.) 101–104.

Olanow, C. W. (1992). Magnetic resonance imaging in Parkinson's disease. *Neurologic Clinics, 10*, 405–420.

Otsuka, M., Ichiya, Y., Hosokawa, S., Kuwabara, Y., Tahara, T., Fukumura, T., Kato, M., Masuda, K., & Goto, I. (1991). Striatal blood flow, glucose metabolism and 18 F-Dopa uptake: Difference in Parkinson's disease and atypical parkinsonism. *Journal of Neurology, Neurosurgery, and Psychiatry, 54*, 898–904.

Paddison, R. M., & Griffith, R. P. (1974). Occurrence of Parkinson's disease in Black patients at Charity Hospital in New Orleans. *Neurology, 24*, 688–690.

Parkinson, J. (1817). *An essay on the shaking palsy*. London: Sherwood, Neely, & Jones.

Parkinson Study Group. (1989). DATATOP: A multicenter controlled clinical trial in early Parkinson's disease. *Archives of Neurology, 46*, 1052–1060.

Prasher, D., & Findley, L. (1991). Dopaminergic induced changes in cognitive and motor processing in Parkinson's disease: An electrophysiological investigation. *Journal of Neurology, Neurosurgery, and Psychiatry, 54*, 603–609.

Raskin, S., Borod, J., & Tweedy, J. (1990). Neuropsychological aspects of Parkinson's disease. *Neuropsychology Review, 1*, 185–221.

Raskin, S., Sliwinski, M., & Borod, J. (1992). Clustering strategies on tasks of verbal fluency in Parkinson's disease. *Neuropsychologia, 30*, 95–99.

Reitan, R. M., & Boll, T. J. (1971). Intellectual and cognitive functions in Parkinson's disease. *Journal of Consulting and Clinical Psychology, 37*, 364–369.

Reitan, R. M., & Wolfson, D. (1985). *The Halstead–Reitan Neuropsychological Test Battery*. Tucson, AZ: Neuropsychology Press.

Reitan, R. M., & Wolfson, D. (1993). *The Halstead–Reitan Neuropsychological Test Battery* (2nd ed.). Tucson, AZ: Neuropsychology Press.

Riederer, P., & Wuketich, S. (1976). Time course of nigrostriatal degeneration in Parkinson's disease. *Journal of Neural Transmission, 38*, 277–301.

Sano, M., Stern, Y., Williams, J., Cote, L., Rosenstein, R., & Mayeux, R. (1989). Coexisting dementia and depression in Perkinson's disease. *Archives of Neurology, 46*, 1284–1286.

Schapira, A. H., Cooper, J. M., Dexter, D., Clark, J. B., Jenner, P., & Marsden, C. D. (1990). Mitochondrial complex I deficiency in Parkinson's disease. *Journal of Neurochemistry, 54*, 823–827.

Scholz, O. B., & Sastry, M. (1985). Memory characteristics in Parkinson's disease. *International Journal of Neuroscience, 27*, 229–234.

Semchuk, K. M., Love, E. J., & Lee, R. G. (1992). Parkinson's disease and exposure to agricultural work and pesticide chemicals. *Neurology, 42*, 1328–1335.

Sherer, M., Nixon, S., Parsons, O., & Adams, R. (1992). Performance of alcoholic and brain damaged subjects on the Luria Memory Words Test. *Archives of Clinical Neuropsychology, 7*, 499–504.

Singer, E. (1973). Social costs of Parkinson's disease. *Journal of Chronic Disease, 26*, 243–254.

Singer, E. (1974a). The effect of treatment with levodopa on Parkinson patients' social functioning and outlook on life. *Journal of Chronic Disease, 27*, 581–594.

Singer, E. (1974b). Premature social aging: The social psychological consequences of a chronic illness. *Social Science and Medicine, 8*, 143–151.

Singer, E. (1976). Sociopsychological factors influencing response to levodopa therapy for Parkinson's disease. *Archives of Physical Medicine & Rehabilitation, 57*, 328–334.

Stacy, M., & Jankovic, J. (1992). Differential diagnosis of Parkinson's disease and the parkinsonism plus syndromes. *Neurologic Clinics, 10*, 341–359.

Starkstein, S. E., Mayberg, H. S., Leiguarda, R., Preziosi, T. J., & Robinson, R. G. (1992). A prospective longitudinal study of depression, cognitive decline, and physical impairments in patients with Parkinson's disease. *Journal of Neurology, Neurosurgery, and Psychiatry, 55*, 377–382.

Starkstein, S. E., Preziosi, T. J., Berthier, M. L., Bolduc, P. L., Mayberg, H. S., & Robinson, R. G. (1989). Depression and cognitive impairment in Parkinson's disease. *Brain, 112*, 1141–1153.

Starkstein, S. E., Preziosi, T. J., Bolduc, P. L., & Robinson, R. G. (1990). Depression in Parkinson's disease. *Journal of Nervous and Mental Disease, 178*, 27–31.

Stern, M., Dulaney, E., Gruber, S. B., Golbe, L., Bergen, M., Hurtig, H., Gollomp, S., & Stolley, P. (1991). The epidemiology of Parkinson's disease: A case-control study of young-onset and old-onset patients. *Archives of Neurology, 48*, 903–907.

Steventon, G. B., Heafield, M. T., Waring, R. H., & Williams, A. C. (1989). Xenobiotic metabolism in Parkinson's disease. *Neurology, 39*, 883–887.

Stroop, J. (1935). Studies of interference in serial verbal reactions. *Journal of Experimental Psychology, 18*, 643–662.

Talland, G. A. (1962). Cognitive function in Parkinson's disease. *Journal of Nervous and Mental Disease, 135,* 196–205.

Tanner, C. M. (1989). The role of environmental toxins in the etiology of Parkinson's disease. *Trends in Neuroscience, 12,* 49–54.

Tanner, C. M., Chen, B., Wang, W., Peng, M., Liu, Z., Liang, X., Kao, L. C., Gilley, D. W., Goetz, C. G., & Schoenberg, B. S. (1989). Environmental factors and Parkinson's disease: A case-control study in China. *Neurology, 39,* 660–664.

Tanner, C. M., & Langston, J. W. (1990). Do environmental toxins cause Parkinson's disease? A critical review. *Neurology, 40*(Suppl. 3), 17–30.

Tetrud, J. W., & Langston, J. W. (1989). The effect of deprenyl (Selegiline) on the natural history of Parkinson's disease. *Science, 245,* 519–522.

U.S. War Department, Adjutant General Office, Classification and Replacement Branch, Staff, Personnel Research Section. (1944). The new army individual test of general mental ability. *Psychological Bulletin, 41,* 532–538.

Wechsler, D. (1981). *Wechsler Adult Intelligence Scale—Revised manual.* New York: Psychological Corporation.

Wechsler, D. (1987). *Wechsler Memory Scale—Revised manual.* New York: Psychological Corporation.

Weingartner, H., Burns, S., Diebel, R., & LeWitt, P. (1984). Cognitive impairments in Parkinson's disease: Distinguishing between effort-demanding and automatic cognitive processes. *Psychiatry Research, 11,* 223–235.

Widner, H., & Rehncrona, S. (1993). Transplantation and surgical treatment of parkinsonian syndromes. *Current Opinion in Neurology and Neurosurgery, 6,* 344–349.

Zung, W. (1965). A self-rating scale of depression. *Archives of General Psychiatry, 12,* 63–70.

Section II

CHILD AND LIFE-SPAN DEVELOPMENTAL NEUROPSYCHOLOGY

Chapter 10

ATTENTION DEFICIT HYPERACTIVITY DISORDER

Jan L. Culbertson and Kevin R. Krull

Attention deficit hyperactivity disorder (ADHD) is one of the most studied disorders in existence and is one of the most frequent reasons for referral to child mental health clinics today. Practitioners are often asked to assist in the diagnosis of ADHD, make recommendations about pharmacotherapy and psychotherapy, educate parents about the ramifications of ADHD for the family, and provide suggestions to teachers about managing the behavior of children with ADHD in the classroom. As ADHD becomes better recognized as a problem for adolescents and adults as well as children, there will be increasing demands for information about treatment and the implications of ADHD in the college classroom and workplace. The past decade has witnessed an explosion in research about the etiology, diagnosis, and treatment of ADHD. The field of neuropsychology has contributed to many aspects of this research, particularly in providing information about the pathophysiology of ADHD. Neuropsychology can provide useful means of conceptualizing ADHD and a framework for planning evaluation and treatment.

In this chapter we provide a neuropsychological approach to understanding and evaluating ADHD in children, adolescents, and adults. We focus on definition and classification of the disorder using contemporary nosology, prevalence and epidemiological data, and detailed descriptions of the core symptoms. With this information as foundation, current conceptualizations of ADHD are described from the perspectives of Barkley, Mirsky, Denckla, and others. The empirical evidence and current theories regarding etiology, comorbidity, and prognosis of ADHD are presented, along with a detailed discussion of the contributions of pathophysiological research to our understanding of the disorder. Next, we present a two-stage model for approaching evaluation of ADHD in children, adolescents, and adults, along with a discussion of suggested tests and measures. The chapter concludes with a discussion of treatment issues and the need for longitudinal research.

HISTORY AND DESCRIPTION

Historical Overview

The history of ADHD has evolved primarily in the twentieth century, although early descriptions of behavioral disorders occurring after an insult to the brain date back to the late nineteenth century (Shaywitz & Shaywitz, 1988). In the early twentieth century, descriptions of hyperactivity, inattention, and poor impulse control appeared in the medical literature as sequelae of head injuries (Goldstein, 1936; Meyer, 1904), encephalitis (Hohman, 1922), or various central nervous system infections (Bender, 1942). Researcher G. F. Still (1902) referred to children who were aggressive and defiant, displayed "lawlessness" (p. 1009), had little "inhibitory volition" (p. 1008), and had a major "defect in moral control" (p. 1009). Still reported that these conditions occurred most often secondary to acute brain disease and could remit upon recovery or follow a chronic course (Barkley, 1990). This early literature accounted for the link between brain damage and the symptoms we currently consider representative of ADHD.

In the 1940s, Strauss and his colleagues were influential in conceptualizing the "brain damage syndrome" characterized by numerous learning and behavioral impairments, including symptoms of hyperactivity, distractibility, and impulsivity (Barkley, 1990; Shaywitz & Shaywitz, 1988; Strauss & Lehtinen, 1947; Werner & Strauss, 1941). Children thought to have brain damage syndrome often did not have documented evidence of brain damage, other than learning and behavioral problems, but Strauss promulgated the notion that all brain lesions are followed by similar kinds of disordered behavior (Strauss & Lehtinen, 1947). In the 1950s and 1960s, critical reviews began to appear challenging Strauss's ideas about a unitary syndrome of brain damage in children (Birch, 1964; Herbert, 1964; Rapin, 1987). A new term, *minimal brain dysfunction*, came into vogue, in part as a result of the work of Clements and Peters (1962), who argued that neurologic soft signs might be considered evidence of organic brain damage, without other corroborating evidence of damage. Unfortunately, the symptoms of minimal brain dysfunction were vaguely defined and included disorders that would now be considered as ADHD, learning disabilities, developmental language disorders, and dyslexia. Use of the term *minimal brain dysfunction* led to confusion in diagnosis and was gradually dropped from use due to its lack of specificity, poor prescriptive value, and lack of neurologic evidence (Barkley, 1990; Kirk, 1963; Rie & Rie, 1980).

Other terms emerged in the literature during the 1950s and 1960s as dissatisfaction with minimal brain dysfunction continued. The term *hyperactive child syndrome* (Chess, 1960; Laufer & Denhoff, 1957) reflected the growing emphasis on excessive activity as the defining symptom of the disorder, and led to the term *Hyperkinetic Reaction of Childhood* that appeared in the second edition of the *Diagnostic and Statistical Manual of Mental Disorders* (*DSM-II*; American Psychiatric Association, 1968). It was not until the 1970s that problems with sustained attention and impulse control began receiving notice from researchers (Barkley, 1990; Douglas, 1972; Werry & Sprague, 1970). Douglas developed a theory of ADHD in which four major deficits could account for the symptoms: (a) deficits in investment, organization, and maintenance of attention and effort; (b) poor ability to inhibit impulsive responses; (c) poor ability to modulate arousal levels to meet situational demands; and (d) a strong inclination to seek immediate reinforcement (Barkley, 1990; Douglas, 1980a, 1980b, 1983; Douglas & Peters, 1979). This theory guided research for the next 15 years and led to adoption of the term *attention deficit disorder* (ADD) for use in the *DSM-III* (American Psychiatric Association, 1980). According to Barkley (1990), Douglas's theory was seminal in leading researchers to acknowledge that hyperactivity was a multidimensional construct and that the symptoms of hyperactivity were quite situational in nature. Furthermore, it was accepted that some children could exhibit symptoms of inattention in the absence of hyperactivity. There was for the first time a clear subtyping of ADD on the basis of the presence or absence of hyperactivity (Barkley, 1990).

Just as the construct of hyperactivity was criticized in the early 1980s due to its multidimensional features, the construct of attention also received similar criticism by the end of the 1980s. There was the realization that the subtyping of ADD had been done with little empirical research to support its validity. The 1980s witnessed a continuation of the explosion in research that had begun in the 1970s and a movement toward empirical validation of the subtypes of ADD across such dimensions as presence of aggression, pervasiveness across situations, stimulant drug response, and so forth (Barkley, 1990). Much of the research of that era was directed toward distinguishing hyperactivity from other types of disorders such as aggression or conduct problems (Loney, Langhorne, & Paternite, 1978; Loney & Milich, 1982) and learning disabilities (Ackerman, Dykman, & Oglesby, 1983; Dykman, Ackerman, & Holcomb, 1985). Most of this research came too late to be considered for the revision of the *DSM-III* in 1987 (*DSM-III-R*, American Psychiatric Association, 1987). In the *DSM-III-R*, the subtype of ADD without hyperactivity was no longer recognized but was relegated to a vague and largely undefined category of *undifferentiated ADD*. The term *ADHD* was adopted, reflecting a single disorder rather than the dichotomous diagnostic system used in *DSM-III*. The *DSM-III-R* conceptualization of ADHD contained a single list of empirically derived behavioral dimensions and a single cutoff score. These criteria had undergone an extensive field trial to determine their sensitivity, power, and specificity to distinguish children with ADHD from those with other psychiatric conditions (Barkley, 1990). The conceptualization of *DSM-III-R* reflected the continuing attempts to explore the unique features of ADHD, but it also reflected continuing problems with specificity of the syndrome.

Current Definition and Classification of ADHD

The nosology used in *DSM-III-R* was hampered by the preliminary nature of empirical research to substantiate that two distinct disorders existed. Research throughout the latter 1980s and early 1990s has led to the current conceptualization, as reflected in the recently published *DSM-IV* (American Psychiatric Association, 1994). The *DSM-IV* conceptualization of ADHD has resulted in three primary subtypes: *predominantly inattentive type, predominantly hyperactive–impulsive type*, and *combined type*. The term *ADHD* is retained, but the subtypes are specified according to the criteria listed in Exhibit 1 (American Psychiatric Association, 1994).

The diagnosis of ADHD, predominantly inattentive type, is made if Criterion A1 is met but not Criterion A2 for the past 6 months. The diagnosis of ADHD, predominantly hyperactive–impulsive type, is made if Criterion A2 is met but not Criterion A1 for the past 6 months. The diagnosis of ADHD, combined type is made if both Criteria A1 and A2 are met for the past 6 months. There also is a category for ADHD *not otherwise specified*, which is appropriate for disorders with prominent symptoms of attention deficit or hyperactivity–impulsivity that do not meet criteria for ADHD. The nosology in the *DSM-IV* is used for the remainder of this chapter, as it reflects the growing awareness of the distinction between primarily inattentive versus primarily hyperactive–impulsive symptomatology, the pervasiveness of the disorder, and the clinically significant adjustment problems often associated with the disorder.

Barkley (1982, 1990) proposed a list of criteria to be used in association with those in *DSM-III-R*. Because only one of these proposed criteria has been incorporated into *DSM-IV*, they continue to be worthy of consideration along with the criteria listed for *DSM-IV*:

1. Use standardized parent or teacher child behavior rating scales or both with age-appropriate norms to determine if a particular child's behavior deviates at greater than the 97th percentile (2 standard deviations above the mean) for his or her age.
2. Document that the duration of symptoms is at least 12 months rather than 6 months.
3. Onset should occur by 6 years rather than 7 years.
4. Symptoms must be pervasive across settings.
5. If child's intelligence quotient is less than 78–80, make behavioral comparisons with children of a similar mental or developmental age rather than chronological age.

Of the five recommended criteria, only the fourth was incorporated into the criteria for *DSM-IV*. Barkley recommended the first of these criteria as a means of increasing the reliability and validity of diagnosis by using clear behavioral descriptions of the symptoms and by using age-normed comparisons for each child. Setting the criteria for clinical significance at greater than the 97th percentile on behavior rating scales also increases the diagnostic rigor. The criterion related to duration of symptoms was designated in part due to the variability in presence of symptoms across the age span, and the difficulty in making a valid diagnosis with younger children. The *DSM-III-R* criteria required that 8 of 14 symptoms be present before making the diagnosis. This approach is generally appropriate for early elementary age children (approximately 6 to 12 years). However, Barkley (1990) suggested that clinical significance for the preschool child would require 10 of 14 symptoms, whereas only 6 of 14 symptoms is significant in adolescents. Establishing the criterion of 12 months duration of symptoms means there is less chance of error in the younger age range. As many as 45% of preschool children have concerns raised about their attention or activity level, but only 5%–10% will have persistent concerns beyond 12 months (Barkley, 1990). The criterion related to age of onset of symptoms was developed due to concern

EXHIBIT 1

DSM-IV Diagnostic Criteria for Attention Deficit Hyperactivity Disorder

Attention Deficit Hyperactivity Disorder

A. Either 1 or 2:

1. Inattention: At least six of the following symptoms of inattention have persisted for at least six months to a degree that is maladaptive and inconsistent with developmental level:

Inattention

a. often fails to give close attention to details or makes careless mistakes in schoolwork, work, or other activities
b. often has difficulty sustaining attention in tasks or play activities
c. often does not seem to listen when spoken to directly
d. often does not follow through on instructions and fails to finish schoolwork, chores, or duties in the workplace (not due to oppositional behavior or failure to understand instructions)
e. often has difficulty organizing tasks and activities
f. often avoids, dislikes, or is reluctant to engage in tasks that require sustained mental effort (such as schoolwork or homework)
g. often loses things necessary for tasks or activities (e.g., toys, school assignments, pencils, books, or tools)
h. is often easily distracted by extraneous stimuli
i. is often forgetful in daily activities

2. Hyperactivity–Impulsivity: At least four of the following symptoms of hyperactivity–impulsivity have persisted for at least six months to a degree that is maladaptive and inconsistent with developmental level:

Hyperactivity

a. often fidgets with hands or feet or squirms in seat
b. often leaves seat in classroom or in other situations in which remaining seated is expected
c. often runs about or climbs excessively in situations in which it is inappropriate (in adolescents or adults, may be limited to subjective feelings of restlessness)
d. often has difficulty playing or engaging in leisure activities quietly
e. is often "on the go" or often acts as if "driven by a motor"
f. often talks excessively

Impulsivity

h. often blurts out answers before questions have been completed
i. often has difficulty awaiting turn
j. often interrupts or intrudes on others (e.g., butts into conversations or games)

B. Some hyperactive–impulsive or inattentive symptoms that caused impairment were present before age 7 years.

C. Some impairment from the symptoms is present in two or more settings (e.g., at school [or work] and at home).

D. There must be clear evidence of clinically significant impairment in social, academic, or occupational functioning.

EXHIBIT 1 (*Continued*)

E. The symptoms do not occur exclusively during the course of a Pervasive Developmental Disorder, Schizophrenia or other Psychotic Disorder, and are not better accounted for by another mental disorder (e.g., Mood Disorder, Anxiety Disorder, Dissociative Disorder, or a Personality Disorder).

From Diagnostic and Statistical Manual of Mental Disorders (DSM-IV; *4th ed., pp. 83–85), by the American Psychiatric Association, 1994, Washington, DC: Author. Copyright 1994 by the American Psychiatric Association. Adapted with permission.*

that at 7 years of age, learning disabilities may be present or may be first detected, and the frustration associated with these disabilities may lead to secondary expressions of agitation, hyperactivity, and behavioral problems. Barkley's reasoning was that if the onset of ADHD is documented by 6 years of age, it would be easier to discriminate those youngsters who have the more chronic developmental symptoms associated with ADHD, rather than secondary symptomatology associated with learning disabilities. Finally, using mental age comparisons for children with intelligence quotients below 78–80 helps the examiner distinguish whether the current symptoms are developmentally appropriate for the child's functioning level rather than relying solely on chronological age. As Barkley (1982) noted, the additional criteria help to refine the diagnostic process and decrease the possibility of error.

The many changes in diagnostic criteria for ADHD over the past decades reflect the growing understanding and increased sophistication of research on this important disorder. The changes have also led to much confusion about interpretation of past research studies, where the definition of the disorder has varied widely. Thus, we are entering a new era of research sophistication that should lead to better understanding of the characteristics of ADHD and the neuropathological basis of the disorder.

Epidemiology of ADHD

On the basis of *DSM-III-R* criteria, the occurrence of ADHD in the general population is generally thought to be 3% to 5% (American Psychiatric Association, 1987). Other estimates have ranged from 1% to 20%, depending on the definition used for ADHD, the population studied (whether community or clinic samples), the geographic locale of the survey, and the degree of agreement required among parents, teachers, and professionals (Barkley, 1990; DuPaul, 1990; Lambert, Sandoval, & Sassone, 1978; Ross & Ross, 1982; Szatmari, Offord, & Boyle, 1989b). The use of age-normed rating scales has raised the question of the appropriate cutoff level for clinical significance of symptoms. Trites, Dugas, Lynch, and Ferguson (1979) surveyed symptoms of over 14,000 school children using a cutoff of 1.5 standard deviations above the mean on parent and teacher rating scales: This survey showed that an average of 14% of that population was hyperactive. In contrast, DuPaul (1990) used a cutoff of 2 standard deviations (97th percentile) from the mean in a separate study, and found a prevalence rate of 2% to 9%. It is apparent that the more stringent criterion of the 97th percentile appears to identify a group of children whose ADHD symptoms are more seriously deviant, are stable over as long as 8 to 10 years, and are predictive of later adjustment (Barkley, 1990; Barkley, Fischer, Edelbrock, & Smallish, 1990).

The prevalence of ADHD among boys has been consistently higher than among girls, although the proportion has varied dramatically across studies from 2:1 to 10:1 (American Psychiatric Association, 1980; Ross & Ross, 1982). There is an average 6:1 male to female ratio most often cited for clinic-referred children (Barkley, 1990). However, epidemiological studies find the proportion to be approximately a 3:1 male to female ratio among community samples of nonreferred children (Szatmari et al., 1989b; Trites et al., 1979). Barkley (1990) hypothesized that the considerably higher rate of boys among clinic samples may be due to referral bias, in that boys are more likely than girls to be aggressive and antisocial. Therefore, more boys than girls are likely to be referred to mental health centers. However, boys are more likely to manifest ADHD symptoms than girls even in community-based samples, suggesting a possible sex-linked mechanism in the expression of the disorder (Barkley, 1990).

Recent studies of clinic-referred children with ADHD have found no differences between boys and girls on measures of intelligence, academic achievement, peer relations, emotional problems, or behavioral disorders (Breen, 1989; Horn, Wagner, & Ialongo, 1989; McGee, Williams, & Silva, 1987). However, ADHD girls within community samples may have fewer conduct problems than boys. In clinic samples the girls who get referred to psychiatric clinics may be as aggressive or conduct disordered as boys (Barkley, 1990).

Conceptualization and Etiologic Considerations in ADHD

Various hypotheses have been proposed regarding the constructs underlying the symptoms of ADHD. Zentall (1985) hypothesized that children with ADHD have higher than normal thresholds for arousal by stimulation, so that when environmental stimulation decreases, hyperactivity and inattention increase as a means of compensating for this reduction. This would serve to maintain an optimal level of central nervous system arousal (Barkley, 1990; Zentall, 1985). Haenlein and Caul (1987) proposed that thresholds for reinforcement within the brain may be set too high; therefore, rewards may be less reinforcing or weaker for children with ADHD, leading to decreased persistence and responding to tasks (Barkley, 1990). Finally, Quay (1988) proposed that the symptoms of ADHD may relate to decreased activity in the brain's behavioral inhibition system, so that punishment fails to inhibit or regulate behavior as well as it would in children who do not have ADHD (Barkley, 1990). Other conceptualizations related to neuropathology will be presented in the next section of this chapter. This section will elaborate three conceptualizations that are receiving attention currently in the research literature.

Deficiency in regulation and maintenance of behavior. Barkley (1990) has proposed that ADHD may be explained by a deficit involving diminished regulation of behavior by rules. One can examine several components to rule-governed behavior, including the child's ability to change his or her behavior immediately following the statement of a rule versus the child's ability to remember a rule over time and bring his or her behavior into correspondence with the rule even without repetition. The latter skill is referred to as "self-control." Children with ADHD typically have problems with self-control and problem solving, particularly when they must remember rules over a period of time and bring their behavior into correspondence with these rules. Barkley (1990) therefore suggested that the primary symptoms of ADHD may be better conceptualized as "deficits in the functional relationships between child behavior and environmental events than as cognitive constructs or capacities" (p. 71). He further suggested that the deficit in behavioral regulation may stem from one or more of the following impairments:

1. Diminished sensitivity to behavioral consequences
2. Diminished control of behavior by partial schedules of consequences
3. Poor rule-governed behavior.

Barkley went on to suggest a redefinition of ADHD as follows:

> *ADHD consists of developmental deficiencies in the regulation and maintenance of behavior by rules and consequences. These deficiencies give rise to problems with inhibiting, initiating, or sustaining responses to tasks or stimuli, and adhering to rules or instructions, particularly in situations where consequences for such behavior are delayed, weak, or nonexistent. The deficiencies are evident in early childhood and are probably chronic in nature. Although they may improve with neurologic maturation, the deficits persist in comparison to same-age normal children, whose performance in these areas also improves with development. (p. 71)*

Barkley (1990) presumes that the deficiencies in regulation and maintenance of behavior are biologically based and have implications for social interactions and social development of the child with ADHD. The presumed biological basis of the disorder implies that the disorder has a lifelong course, but it also serves to remove blame from these children, who often find themselves labeled as noncompliant, nonconformist, or lazy (Barkley, 1990). Barkley's view of the conceptualization of ADHD also specifies the types of environments and tasks in which children with ADHD may perform better, and those in which their disorder will be more problematic. Barkley argued that the biologically based deficiencies in the regulation of behavior by rules and consequences becomes the core problem in ADHD, as opposed to an attentional deficit.

Attention as the core deficit. In contrast to Barkley, Mirsky (1987, 1989) argued that disordered attention may provide a reasonable explanation for the symptoms associated with ADHD. Mirsky approached the conceptualization of ADHD from the perspective of cognitive psychophysiological research applied to attention or information processing. On the basis of research and analyses by several cognitive psychologists (Kahneman, 1973; Nuechterlein & Dawson, 1984; Posner, 1978; Shiffrin & Schneider, 1977; Zubin, 1975), Mirsky proposed that attention may be subdivided into a number of different elements, including the capacity to focus on or select some aspect of the environment, the ability to sustain or maintain focus for a period of time, the ability to encode or manipulate information held in memory, and the ability to shift adaptively from one aspect of the environment to another (Mirsky, 1987). These four elements of attention (focus–execute, sustain, encode, and shift), can be measured through a variety of neuropsychological tests of attention. A recent study through the Laboratory of Psychology and Psychopathology of the National Institute of Mental Health used a factor analysis of a battery of neuropsychological tests thought to be sensitive to various aspects of attention; the factor analysis yielded four main factors, as illustrated in Table 1. The factors associated with the "focus–execute" component of attention related to perceptual motor speed, and involved such tests as Trail Making (Reitan, 1979), a letter cancellation procedure, a measure similar to Coding from the Wechsler scales (Wechsler, 1981, 1989, 1990), and the Stroop test (C. J. Golden, 1978). The factor best able to measure the "sustain" element of attention was vigilance, and was reflected in omission and commission errors and reaction time on a Continuous Performance Test (Rosvold, Mirsky, Sarason, Bransome, & Beck, 1956). The "encode" element of attention was best captured by a factor involving numerical or mnemonic tasks, as reflected in Digit Span and Arithmetic from the Wechsler scales. Finally, the "shift" element of attention was best measured by a factor involving flexibility, as reflected in scores from the Wisconsin Card Sorting Test

TABLE 1

The Relation Among Elements of Attention, Neuroanatomic Localization, and Neuropsychological Evaluation

Component of attention	Brain regions involved in attention	Neuropsychologic function	Neuropsychologic measures of attention
Focus–execute	Superior temporal cortex Inferior parietal cortex Corpus striatum structures (including caudate, putamen, globus pallidus)	Perceptual–motor speed	Trail-Making Test Talland Letter Cancellation Stroop Color and Word Test Digit-Symbol substitution
Sustain	Rostral midbrain structures (including tectum, mesopontine, reticular formation, and midline and reticular thalamic nuclei)	Vigilance	Continuous Performance Test: commission errors, omission errors, response time
Encode	Hippocampus	Numerical–mnemonic	Digit Span Arithmetic
Shift	Prefrontal cortex	Flexibility	Wisconsin Card Sorting Test

(WCST; Heaton, 1981). Mirsky proceeded to integrate the neuropsychological testing with descriptions of the neuroanatomic localization of the elements of attention (Mirsky, 1987). As noted in Figure 1, there are numerous brain regions implicated through research as being involved in attention. At the most rostral level, the tectum and the mesopontine regions of the reticular formation have been established as relating to consciousness and attention (Lindsley, Bowden, & Magoun, 1949; Moruzzi & Magoun, 1949). The mesial view of the right hemisphere depicts the midline thalamic region, including the reticular nuclei, whose role in attention is supported by the work of Ajmone Marsan (1965) and Jasper (1958). Other areas depicted in Figure 1 include the corpus striatum, the hippocampus, and the anterior cingulate gyrus. The corpus striatum has been implicated in the neglect phenomenon (Healton, Navarro, Bressman, & Brust, 1982; Heilman, Watson, Valenstein, & Damasio, 1983). The top two views in Figure 1 illustrate cortical areas implicated in attention, including the prefrontal cortex (Milner, 1963) and the inferior parietal lobule, which also has been implicated in the neglect phenomenon. Because lesions of the right hemisphere are more likely to result in neglect, the inferior parietal lobule is depicted of greater size in the right hemisphere (Heilman et al., 1983). Finally, the superior temporal cortex is felt to be a multimodal sensory convergence area with an important role in attention (Pandya & Yeterian, 1985). The brain structures depicted in Figure 1 are thought to represent a system, with well-defined anatomical connections among the various areas (Jones & Peters, 1986; Mirsky, 1987). The schematic representation of these brain centers and the interconnections among the re-

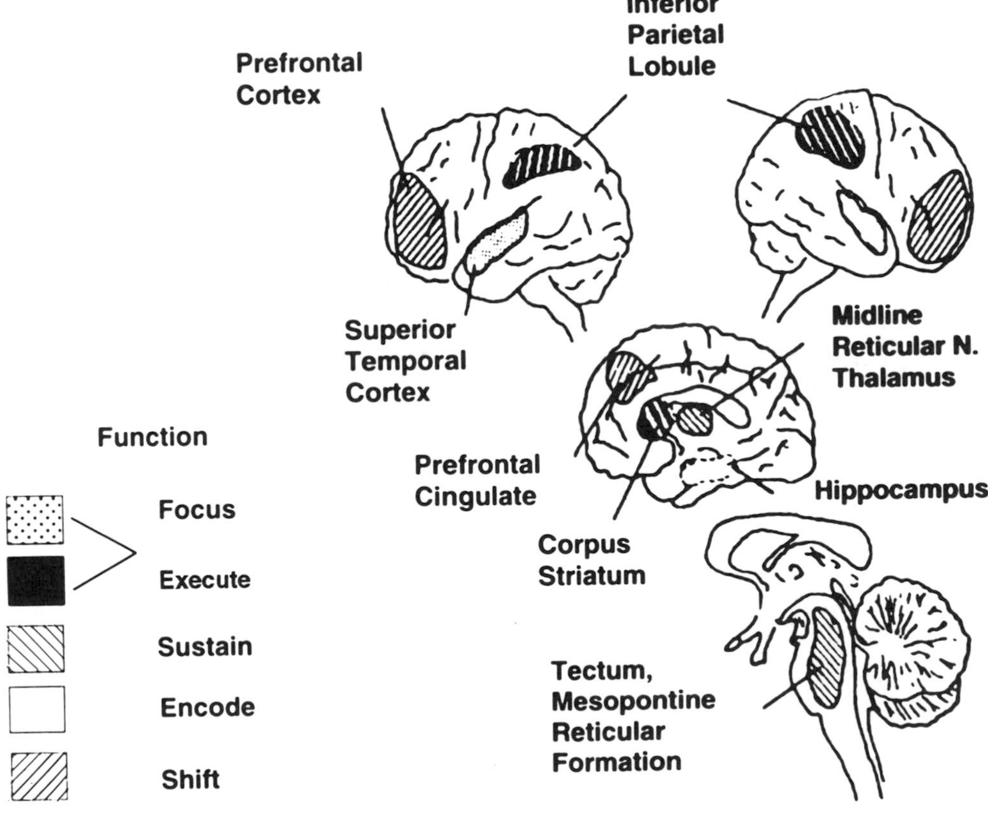

FIGURE 1. Semischematic representation of brain regions involved in attention, with tentative assignment of functional specializations to the regions. From "Behavioral and Psychophysiological Markers of Disordered Attention," by A. F. Mirsky, 1987, *Environmental Health Perspectives*, *74*, p. 196. In the public domain.

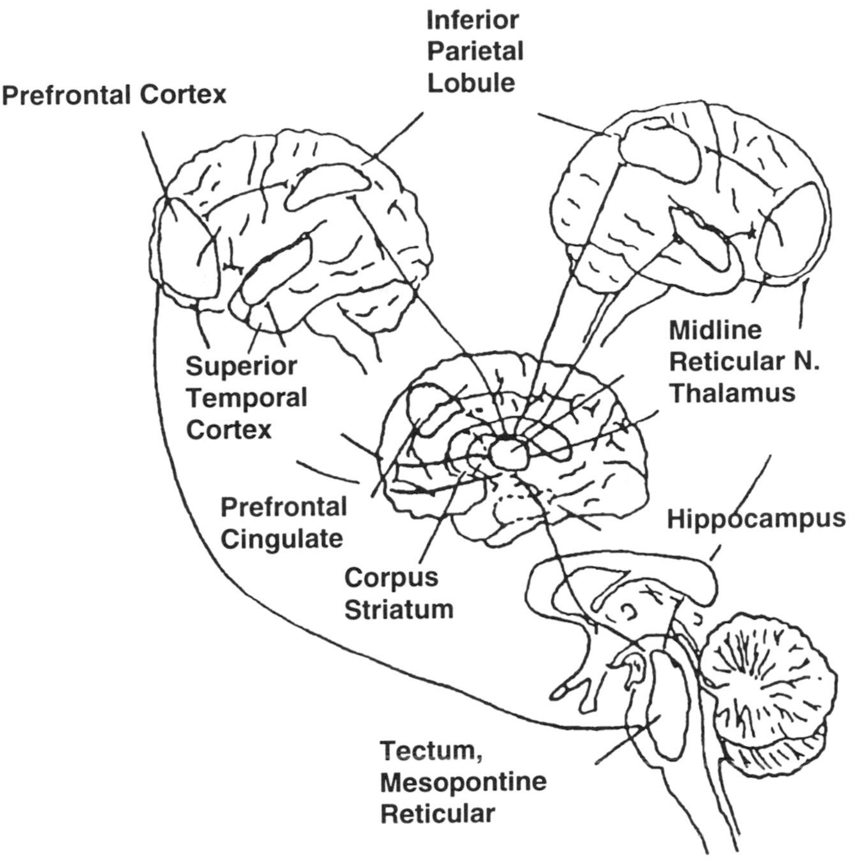

FIGURE 2. Semischematic representation of brain regions involved in attention; some interconnections among the regions are shown; the connections are conceivably sufficient to support the concept of an attention system. From "Behavioral and Psychophysiological Markers of Disordered Attention," by A. F. Mirsky, 1987, *Environmental Health Perspectives*, 74, p. 197. In the public domain.

gions are depicted in Figure 2. According to Mirsky (1987), the connections depicted are conceivably sufficient to support the concept of an attentional system.

In summary, Mirsky (1987, 1989) has subdivided attention into a number of separate functions, which are thought to be supported by different brain regions that have become specialized for this purpose, but that are organized into a system. The attentional system within the brain is thought to be widespread and, therefore, quite vulnerable so that damage or dysfunction in any one of the brain regions can lead to specific deficits in attentional function. As illustrated in Table 1, the four elements of attention can be assigned in a preliminary fashion to differing brain regions, although it must be understood that ongoing research will most likely provide greater specificity. However, at the current state of our knowledge, the following functional specialization is suggested by Mirsky (1987, 1989): The focus–execute function is likely shared by superior temporal and inferior parietal cortices, as well as by structures that make up the corpus striatum (including the caudate, putamen, and globus pallidus). The motor execute function is felt to be mediated by the inferior parietal and corpus striatal regions of the brain. The sustained function of attention is felt to be mediated by rostral structures, including the tectum, mesopontine reticular formation, and reticular and midline thalamic nuclei. The encoding function is thought to be accomplished by the hippocampus, which provides an essential mnemonic function required for some aspects of attention. Finally, the ability to shift attention from one aspect of the environment to the other is supported by the prefrontal cortex. Although preliminary, these initial attempts to examine functional specialization of components of attention to different brain regions promise to have a strong heuristic effect on our understanding of the core deficits in ADHD.

Executive dysfunction. Denckla (1989, 1991) proposed that the neuropsychological domain of executive function would encompass many of the attentional and impulse control characteristics seen in adults who have residual type ADHD (ADHD-RT). Executive function refers to the capacity to attend to more than one component of a situation at a time while filtering outside interference or distractions; inhibiting responses that would be off task or inappropriate; and planning, sequencing, and maintaining appropriate responses for a sufficient period of time (Denckla, 1991). The subcortical structures including basal ganglia and limbic system, along with interconnections to the frontal lobes, and structures of the frontal lobes themselves, are felt to be responsible for the functional elements of attention (Denckla, 1989). Citing constructs similar to those proposed by Mirsky (1987, 1989), Denckla delineates the attentional constructs *initiate* (e.g., to focus, select, engage), *sustain* (e.g., to concentrate), *inhibit* (e.g., self-control), and *shift* (e.g., to reengage). Denckla and colleagues proposed a brief battery of neuropsychological tests that would tap the four constructs included in executive functioning and thus would operationalize the definition of executive functioning through each one of these aspects of rule-governed mental performance. The construct *initiate*, involving planning and organization, was felt to be tapped by the WCST (Grant & Berg, 1948; Heaton, 1981), a verbal fluency measure derived from the Multilingual Aphasia Exam (Benton & Hamsher, 1983), scores derived from verbal memory on the California Verbal Learning Test (Delis, Kramer, Kaplan, & Ober, 1986), and scores derived from the Rey–Osterreith Complex Figure (Rey-O; Waber & Holmes, 1985). The *sustain* construct, involving concentration and vigilance, was tapped by the Continuous Performance Test (Klee & Garfinkel, 1983), Trails A and B from the Halstead–Reitan Neuropsychological Test Battery (Reitan, 1979), the Stroop Color and Word Test (C. J. Golden, 1978), and the verbal fluency measure. The *inhibit* construct, involving self-control and self-monitoring, was tapped by the Stroop, the Matching Familiar Figures Test (Cairns & Cammock, 1978), the verbal fluency measure, and scores derived from verbal memory on the California Verbal Learning Test. Finally, the *shift* construct, tapping cognitive flexibility, was measured by the WCST, the Stroop, the verbal fluency measure, and the verbal learning measure from the California test. According to Denckla, these measures of executive function allow one to examine an individual's capacity to deal with the demands inherent in a task, as well as the content (verbal vs. nonverbal, simultaneous vs. sequential processing, visual vs. auditory modality, etc.) in assessing different information processing abilities. Thus, use of the concept of executive function is productive in assessment of ADHD-RT in adults, and allows one to develop different aspects of this heterogeneous disorder. This approach may improve on the typical self-report measures used with adult patients regarding their current and historical symptoms.

Pathophysiology of ADHD

Attempts to identify pathophysiological substrates of ADHD have produced many theories of neurophysiological dysfunction. Dysfunction has been inferred from imaging studies, including magnetic resonance (MR) imaging, positron emission tomography (PET), single photon emission computerized tomography (SPECT), electrophysiological responses such as event-related potentials (ERPs), and neurochemical assays. MR images provide an image of brain structure, but they indicate nothing about function. PET and SPECT functional imaging depends on the uptake of tracers, thus giving an indication of metabolism in active areas of the brain. ERPs on the other hand are a noninvasive technique for examining electrochemical activity in general brain areas. Although data from these functional imaging studies do not demonstrate neuroanatomical abnormalities, brain areas of reduced activity can be determined in general cortical or subcortical areas and associated with specific cognitive processes.

Brain dymorphology. Hynd and colleagues have reported structural differences in the brain between individuals with and without ADHD. Through morphometric analysis, individuals who have ADHD or dyslexia have been found to have smaller right anterior width regions when compared with controls (Hynd, Semrud-Clikeman, Lorys, Novey, & Eliopulos, 1990). Children with ADHD also have been found to have a smaller corpus callosum, particularly in the area of the genu and splenium (Hynd et al., 1991). More recently, these children have been found to have a pattern of asymmetry of the head of the caudate nucleus (Hynd et al., 1993). In this study, 72.7% of normal children were found to have a larger left caudate, whereas 63.6% of the children with ADHD were found to have a larger right caudate. This reversal of the typical asymmetry was attributed to a significantly smaller left caudate in the children with ADHD, which was interpreted as contributing to behavioral disinhibition of the dominant hemisphere. An important point to keep in mind is that in all of these studies, the MR images from the children with ADHD were interpreted as being clinically normal, though significant group differences were found.

Electrophysiologic processes. Because PET and SPECT analyses involve the use of radioactive tracers and thus are invasive in nature, studies of childhood ADHD obviously are not abundant. Recent research with adults, however, suggests global and regional impairment in brain functioning. Zametkin et al. (1990) reported global reduction of brain activity during performance on a continuous performance task in adults diagnosed with ADHD. Regional reduction in premotor and superior prefrontal activity also was evident in comparison with a control group.

Electrophysiological processes in children with ADHD have received much more attention. Some investigators have examined sensory and perceptual processes involved in this disorder, whereas others have focused more on cognitive processes. A common component of analysis is the P3 waveform, which is associated with target identification and resource allocation processes in a vigilance task. Holcomb and colleagues reported decreased visual and auditory P3 amplitudes in children with ADHD compared with controls (Holcomb, Ackerman, & Dykman, 1985, 1986). Harter and colleagues have reported differences between children with ADHD and children with specific learning disabilities (Harter, Anllo-Vento, & Wood, 1989; Harter, Anllo-Vento, Wood, & Schroeder, 1988; Harter, Diering, & Wood, 1988). Furthermore, children with inattention were described as having increased amplitudes of an orienting response (O-Wave) found primarily over the frontal cortical areas. This O-Wave has a developmental trend, reducing in amplitude with maturation of cortical areas (J. Rorbaugh, personal communication, February, 1992) and thus may suggest delays in cortical development of children with ADHD. Satterfield and colleagues reported ERP abnormalities to selective attention tasks in children with ADHD (Satterfield, Schell, Nicholas, & Backs, 1988; Satterfield, Schell, Nicholas, Satterfield, & Freese, 1990). The major differences found between children with and without ADHD were in the P3 component and in an index of selective attention recorded over the frontal cortex. In a longitudinal study, it was further reported that the degree of abnormality found in the children with ADHD increased with age (Satterfield et al., 1990). More recent studies suggest that these abnormal processes found in children with ADHD improve following treatment with stimulant medication (Klorman, 1991; Klorman et al., 1990). These studies suggest that processing deficits seen in children with ADHD involve impairment in sustained as well as selective attention processes and that these processes can be identified with ERP techniques. Furthermore, for selective attention processes, these differences are primarily detected over frontal scalp areas, which is consistent with findings reported from PET imaging in adults.

Frontal lobe dysfunction. The theory of frontal lobe dysfunction in children with ADHD, as evidenced from the aforementioned discussion of pathophysiological studies, has also been investigated through neuropsychological procedures. Chelune, Ferguson, Koon, and Dickey (1986) conducted one of the first studies to report deficits on frontal lobe tests in children with ADHD. These investigators reported a greater degree of perseverative errors and fewer categories on the WCST, a measure of nonverbal abstract reasoning and problem solving. This impairment on the WCST also has been reported in several subsequent studies (Boucugnani & Jones, 1989; Gorenstein, Mammato, & Sandy, 1989; Shue & Douglas, 1992), though others have reported no significant differences on this test in individuals with ADHD (Loge, Staton, & Beatty, 1990).

Other frontal lobe tasks that have been used in the analysis of cognitive abilities of children with ADHD include measures of vigilance, selective attention, and impulsivity. Loge and colleagues (1990) reported a larger number of errors of commission and omission on the Vigilance and Distractibility Tasks from the Gordon Diagnostic System (GDS) in children with ADHD. Errors of commission, or false alarms, often are taken as an indication of impulsive responding. This type of behavior also has been studied using a go/no–go task. In this procedure an individual is required to produce a specific response following a signal given by the examiner and inhibit a response following a slightly different stimulus. Using this procedure, Trommer, Hoeppner, Rosenberg, Armstrong, and Rothstein (1988) found a larger number of errors of omission in children with ADHD compared with children with primarily inattentive type of ADHD and normal controls. The performance of children with ADHD was demonstrated to improve following stimulant medication (Trommer, Hoeppner, & Zecker, 1991). In view of these findings, Barkley, Grodzinsky, and DuPaul (1992) concluded that some measures of frontal lobe dysfunction are not reliably sensitive to ADHD pathology. Those measures that tend to be more reliable include response inhibition (as in errors of commission and performance on the go/no–go tasks), and performance on tests of sustained attention or vigilance (i.e., GDS or the Conners Continuous Performance Test).

Influences on corticogenesis. Attention is a process that is extremely sensitive to external and internal factors that may affect normal homeostasis of the individual. Insults or injuries to the developing brain may alter corticogenesis, thereby producing permanent changes in the organism's ability to be attentive and to regulate behavior. These insults or injuries may be produced by identified or unidentified toxins introduced during fetal development (i.e., alcohol, nicotine, food additives), minor physical injuries to the developing fetus, or anoxic or hypoxic events during delivery. Data from longitudinal studies have indicated a significant association between maternal cigarette smoking and hyperactivity in the offspring (Nichols & Chen, 1981; Streissguth et al., 1984). The amount of maternal alcohol consumption prenatally also appears to be related directly to the degree of inattention in the offspring at age 4 years (Streissguth et al., 1984). A pattern of binge drinking (five or more drinks per occasion) may result in more significant sequelae than moderate levels of drinking (0.1 to 0.9 ounces per day) for a more prolonged period of time. However, even moderate amounts of maternal alcohol consumption during pregnancy are associated with inattention and fidgety and restless behavior (Landesman-Dwyer, Ragozin, & Little, 1981; Streissguth et al., 1984). Although correlation does not imply causation, the research to date suggests it is likely that alcohol has teratogenic effects on the developing fetus. Interpretation of the correlation between cigarette smoking or alcohol consumption and ADHD is complicated by the association of these factors with other confounding factors that may lead to perinatal adversity.

Other environmental toxins have been explored as possible correlates with ADHD. There is a mild correlation between elevated blood lead levels in children and symptoms of hyperactivity and inattention (Thomson et al., 1989), but the association is attenuated when other possible confounding factors are taken into account (Fergusson, Fergusson, Horwood, & Kinzett, 1988; Milar, Schroeder, Mushak, & Boone, 1981; Silva, Hughes, Williams, & Faed, 1988). Food additives, particularly salicylates, preservatives, and food dyes, received popular attention as a potential cause of ADHD in the 1970s and 1980s, primarily on the basis of the work of Feingold (1975). This view was not substantiated in subsequent research (Conners, 1980; J. F. Taylor, 1980). Sugar also received attention in the scientific and lay literature, but has been refuted as a cause of ADHD through carefully controlled studies (Gross, 1984; Wolraich, Milich, Stumbo, & Schultz, 1985). Although some youngsters may have sensitivity to particular foods or additives, in general controlled scientific studies have failed to prove a link between food additives or sugar and ADHD.

Finally, it has been suggested that ADHD symptoms may occur as a result of brain infections, trauma, or perinatal complications that may result in hypoxic or anoxic insults (Cruikshank, Eliason, & Merrifield, 1988; O'Dougherty, Nuechterlein, & Drew, 1984). Other studies have not found a greater incidence of perinatal complications in children with ADHD compared with normal children (Barkley, DuPaul, & McMurray, 1990). Large scale epidemiological studies generally have not found a strong association between perinatal complications and symptoms of ADHD, once other confounding factors are taken into account, such as maternal smoking and alcohol use or socioeconomic disadvantage (Goodman & Stevenson, 1989; Nichols & Chen, 1981).

Genetic predispositions. Genetic predispositions for ADHD also have been suggested. Biederman et al. (1992) conducted a large family study of 140 children with ADHD, 120 matched controls, and 840 primary relatives to examine this relationship. These investigators found that when compared with the relatives of the control group, relatives of the children with ADHD had higher risks for ADHD, antisocial personality disorder, substance abuse, depression, and anxiety. However, this study did not rule out environmental causes. Cadoret and Stewart (1991) examined patterns of attention deficits and hyperactivity in 283 male adoptees. In this study, having a biological parent with a history of delinquent or criminal behavior significantly increased the likelihood of ADHD in sons who had been given up for adoption. However, socioeconomic status and psychiatric problems in the adoptive family members also correlated with outcomes of aggressive behavior and ADHD.

In a more definitive study of 91 identical and 105 same-sex fraternal twins, Stevenson (1992) reported a heritability factor of .75 for rating of activity levels and .76 for measures of attention deficits. The results of these studies appear to indicate that ADHD is associated with both genetic predispositions and environmental factors.

Neurochemical theories. Whether ADHD is caused by internal or external factors is not clear at this time. Still, the notion of chemical imbalances in the brains of these individuals, which also could be genetically or environmentally determined, has good support. One of the current neurochemical theories on the etiology of ADHD involves the notion of neurotransmitter imbalances. The class of neurotransmitter believed to be involved is the catecholamines, particularly dopamine and noradrenaline (Clark, Geffen, & Geffen, 1987; Oades, 1987; Rogeness et al., 1989). Catecholamines have been known to be associated with mechanisms of attention for quite some time. Furthermore, medications commonly used to treat ADHD influence levels of the catecholamines. Methylphenidate (Ritalin), which has been demonstrated to increase attentional capacity in normal individuals and individuals with ADHD, increases catecholamine levels in the brain (Clark et al., 1987). Cylert is a dopamine agonist, whereas the MAO inhibitors such as desipramine influence noradrenergic levels (Zametkin, 1989). This influence on catecholamine activity, combined with no effect on serotonergic activity, suggests that the drugs shown to be effective in treating ADHD address dopaminergic and noradrenergic dysfunction.

Rogeness and colleagues (1989) collected samples of urinary and plasma catecholamine levels in children diagnosed by *DSM-III* criteria as having ADD. They found that low plasma dopamine-B-hydroxylase activity, which converts dopamine to norepinephrine, correlated with ADD symptomatology. Further neurochemical imbalances have been attributed to dysfunction of the hypothalamic-pituitary-adrenal axis. This axis is responsible for determining adrenal activity, with plasma or salivary cortisol often used as an indirect measure of this activity. Recent evidence suggests that functioning of this feedback system is associated with symptoms of ADHD. Kaneko, Hoshino, Hashimoto, Okano, and Kumashiro (1993) reported abnormal hypothalamic-pituitary-adrenal functioning in a group of children with ADHD. Furthermore, abnormal diurnal rhythms were more common as degree of hyperactivity increased in severity.

Primary Symptoms of ADHD

Inattention. Children with ADHD often display marked inattention compared with other children of their age. Inattention includes many different aspects such as alertness, arousal, selectivity, sustained attention, distractibility, or span of attention (Hale & Lewis, 1979). Behavioral descriptors provided by parents and teachers include "can't concentrate," "easily distracted," "shifts from one uncompleted activity to another," "doesn't seem to listen to what is being said," "fails to finish tasks required for schoolwork or play," "daydreams," "often loses things," or "confused and seems to be in a fog" (Barkley, DuPaul, & McMurray, 1990; Stewart, Pitts, Craig, & Dieruf, 1966). Although these behaviors are sometimes seen in play situations, they are seen most often in situations requiring the child to sustain attention to tasks that are less interesting, such as independent schoolwork or doing chores at home (Barkley, 1990). Although these children are described as distractible, some research has shown children with ADHD to be no more distractible than other children (Campbell, Douglas, & Morganstern, 1971; Cohen, Weiss, & Minde, 1972; Rosenthal & Allen, 1980; Steinkamp, 1980). However, the problem appears more consistently to be one of poor persistence or effort in responding to tasks that have little appeal or have few immediate consequences for completion (Barkley, 1990). In those situations in which a child appears distractible, it is important to examine whether other competing activities might offer stronger reinforcement or gratification compared with the assigned task. It is not clear whether the off-task behavior represents distractibility or behavioral disinhibition, as described in the following section.

Behavioral disinhibition. Children with ADHD often are described as taking unnecessary risks or engaging in dangerous activities without considering the consequences. In general, they are described as acting before they think, or having difficulty delaying gratification and working for longer term goals. They may respond to questions before the questions have been completed, resulting in careless errors in school work. They also may be seen as intrusive and rude, in that they may often interrupt or intrude on activities of others.

The symptom of impulsivity has been difficult to separate from the hyperactivity dimension, and Barkley (1990) hypothesized that the more global problem of behavioral disinhibition may unite these two symptoms. Behavioral disinhibition refers to poor regulation and inhibition of behavior, as when a child fails to follow rules or instructions in the face of competing and highly rewarding activities. Several lines of research have indicated that symptoms of behavioral disinhibition can better discriminate ADHD children from non-ADHD children, compared with the symptom of inattention (Barkley, DuPaul, & McMurray, 1990; Grodzinsky, 1990; Spitzer, Davies, & Barkley, 1990). Barkley (1990) suggested that behavioral disinhibition, or poor regulation and inhibition of behavior, may be the hallmark of ADHD.

Hyperactivity. Children with ADHD often are described as "motor driven," "talking excessively," "squirmy and fidgety," "unable to sit still when required to do so," and "often humming and making odd noise." They are characterized by generally excessive and developmentally inappropriate levels of activity, whether motor or vocal (Barkley, 1990). They engage in generally excessive and unnecessary gross bodily movements, which, at times, seem irrelevant to the task or situation, or seem purposeless (Barkley, 1990; Stewart et al., 1966). Scientific studies, such as those of Barkley and Cunningham (1979), reveal that measures of ankle movement and locomotion seem to differentiate children with ADHD from normal children more reliably than other measures. There is growing evidence that the impairment may lie not so much in level of activity as in the failure of the child to regulate his or her activity level to the setting or to task demands (Routh, 1978). Also, the pervasiveness of hyperactivity across both home and school settings may help to separate ADHD from other diagnostic categories in clinic-referred children (E. A. Taylor, 1986).

Deficient rule-governed behavior. Although not as widely accepted as the core symptoms of ADHD described earlier, deficient rule-governed behavior has been suggested by Barkley and others as one of the primary deficits of ADHD (Barkley, 1981, 1982, 1990; Kendall & Braswell, 1984). Children with deficits in rule-governed behavior may be unable to follow rules immediately after they are stated (compliance) or rules that have been stated previously (tracking). Barkley (1990) cautioned that deficiencies in rule-governed behavior should be distinguished from oppositional defiant behavior, in which there is an active refusal to obey rules. In contrast, children with problems in rule-governed behavior may not respond to the stimulus control of previously stated rules in a given situation, so that their behavior is not in correspondence with situational demands. These children commonly may be described as not listening, failing to comply to instructions, unable to maintain compliance to an instruction over time, and having problems adhering to directions associated with a particular task (Barkley, 1990).

Variability in task performance. It is often the rule that children with ADHD are quite variable in the quality and quantity of their task performance. For instance, teachers frequently complain that children can perform academic tasks on one occasion but not on another. This leads to judgments that children with ADHD are capable of performing but are merely lazy. Parents also note variability in completion of household chores or adherence to family routines. This description occurs so frequently in children with ADHD that Barkley (1990) suggested that it may be one of the primary diagnostic criteria of the disorder.

Several factors have been noted to affect the situational and temporal variation in the symptoms of children with ADHD. For instance, the degree of environmental demands for inhibition can affect behavior in ADHD children. Children with ADHD appear less distinguishable from normal children in free-play or low-demand settings than in highly restrictive settings (Barkley, 1985; Routh & Schroeder, 1976). The more complicated the task, with greater demands for planning, organization, and executive functions, the greater the likelihood that children with ADHD will perform more poorly than children who do not have the disorder (Douglas, 1983). Children with ADHD have also been found to be more compliant and less disruptive with their fathers than with their mothers (Tallmadge & Barkley, 1983; Tarver-Behring, Barkley, & Karlsson, 1985). Children with ADHD also perform better on tasks where instructions are repeated frequently (Douglas, 1983) and on tasks that are novel or are in unfamiliar surroundings (Zentall, 1985). Children with ADHD may perform better at the beginning of an academic year when there is more novelty inherent in the situation than as the academic year progresses. Similarly, children with ADHD may be able to inhibit the primary symptoms of their disorder during brief diagnostic office visits to physicians, for instance, but may not be able to inhibit over time during more detailed evaluations. Children with ADHD may perform better on tasks that involve a high rate of immediate reinforcement for compliance, or punishment for noncompliance (Barkley, 1990; Douglas, 1983). Parents often report that their child has no attentional deficit when playing popular video games, such as Nintendo. It has been suggested that ADHD may be a problem in the manner in which behavior is regulated by its consequences (Barkley, 1990). Finally, fatigue may affect the degree to which ADHD symptoms are exhibited so that performance later in the school day may be diminished compared with earlier in the school day (Zagar & Bowers, 1983). These observations of variability in symptom presentation for the child with ADHD also lend themselves to constructive suggestions for management that are discussed in a later section of this chapter.

Developmental Considerations in ADHD

Presentation during preschool years. Inattention and high activity level are very common in preschool-age children and are particularly recognized when children attend structured preschool or Head Start programs. Palfrey, Levine, Walker, and Sullivan (1985) found that approximately 40% of children up to the age of 4 years are considered to have significant problems with inattention, yet only a small proportion of these children go on to have ADHD. Campbell (1990) cautioned practitioners to consider developmental factors when making diagnoses such as ADHD during the preschool years, considering that inattention and overactivity may be normal developmental characteristics of the preschool-age child. Campbell and colleagues (Campbell, 1990; Campbell & Ewing, 1990) have shown that, in preschoolers who have significant inattention and overactivity, the symptoms typically disappear within 3 to 6 months. Only a small majority have symptoms that persist 12 months and beyond, and those children are the ones who are at risk of behavioral problems, poor academic performance, or ADHD. Particularly in those children whose high activity level and behavioral problems begin at age 3 years and then persist to age 4 years, there is a risk for significant problems with hyperactivity and behavior at later ages.

To distinguish normal developmental patterns of overactivity and inattention from clinically significant symptoms of ADHD, we suggest that practitioners consider both duration and severity of symptoms to assist in diagnosis. Making a formal diagnosis of ADHD during the preschool years often does not result in drastic changes in management, because drug therapy is rarely prescribed during that age range. Management in the preschool classroom setting can be addressed with or without a formal diagnosis, by consulting with teachers and providing anticipatory guidance to parents regarding effective behavior management strategies. In the majority of cases, awareness of the symptoms so that they can be monitored for persistence and severity and implementation of behavior management strategies will be effective prior to school age.

In the small minority of preschoolers whose symptoms are extreme, there are several risk factors that need to be monitored. First, these children are at risk for accidents and injuries due to their impulsive, risk-taking behavior in the home and school environments. Child proofing the environment and providing close supervision may be necessary to prevent accidental injury. Second, these children are at risk for frequent discipline, punishment, or even expulsion from preschool programs that find their behavior excessively disruptive and difficult to manage. For those children whose symptoms of hyperactivity and inattention are accompanied by oppositionality and aggression, there is greater risk for a poor outcome in school programs. Such children may have frequent temper tantrums, low frustration tolerance, demanding and intrusive interactions with peers and adults, and excessive moodiness. Parents often report that they give more negative feedback or criticism to these children than to their other children, and that the typical behavior management strategies are ineffective (Barkley, 1988b; Battle & Lacey, 1972; Campbell, 1990; Cohen, Sullivan, Minde, Novak, & Helwig, 1981). Parents of preschool children with ADHD report that their lives are much more stressful related to their parental role than mothers of other preschoolers, or even mothers of older ADHD children (Mash & Johnston, 1982, 1983). Intervention with families of preschool children who have severe symptoms that persist over time may prevent or lessen adjustment problems that can emerge secondary to the symptoms. In the more severe cases in which the symptoms of ADHD are disruptive to the home or school adjustment of the child to a significant degree, referral for behavior management counseling, particularly oriented toward parent–child interaction (Eyberg & Boggs, 1989; Eyberg & Robinson, 1982; Forehand & McMahon, 1981) is recommended.

Presentation during the early to middle school-age years. School-age children with ADHD are at risk for many adjustment problems related to academic, social, behavioral, and emotional functioning. When one considers that a core deficit in ADHD involves a deficiency in rule-governed behavior, it is not surprising that adjustment problems will occur in school settings, where many rules apply. Children with ADHD often find themselves at odds with the social ecology of the classroom, where there are rules for speaking, being out of one's seat, talking with peers, and completing independent classwork. On the playground, the often unspoken social rules of peer interaction create a different ecology, but one that is equally difficult for the child with ADHD. The tendency for the child with ADHD to be intrusive, overly excited, emotionally labile, excessively active, and distractible may lead peers to consider the child to be irritating or a pest. The child with ADHD may be hampered in playing sports activities or group games by distractibility, inability to remember rules, difficulty following the rules of the game, and impulsivity (which can lead to careless errors). Thus, the school setting may represent a negative environment in which the child with ADHD feels out of sync and ostracized.

Academically, the child with ADHD is at risk for poor performance due to difficulty completing work, staying on task during assignments or tests, and because of the high co-occurrence of learning disorders among this population. Children with ADHD are at risk for being labeled immature at younger ages and being retained in school more often than children who do not have ADHD. Often the retention does little to change the pattern of classroom behavior and only serves to hold back an otherwise bright child who is capable of learning along with age mates. Homework assignments may lead to battlegrounds in the home environment, as fatigue sets in late in the day and children struggle to stay on task doing work that is typically unrewarding. The potential for frustration to mount in both children and parents is high. Academic risk also relates to the variability in performance among children with ADHD, which places them at risk for being labeled lazy. Many teachers do not realize that the variability is characteristic of ADHD and that the child may have little control over it. Finally, problems with organization can lead to conflicts with parents and teachers due to lost assignments, lost materials (e.g., pencils, notebooks, textbooks), messy desks, and inability to remember schedules. It is often necessary for parents and teachers to help provide structure and organization that the child is unable to provide for himself or herself.

Despite the many potential risk factors and adjustment problems faced by school-age children with ADHD, a positive outcome is possible with the support of family and school personnel. The situation is complicated when there is family psychopathology, and parents may not have the resources to provide assistance for their child. Likewise, parents may be suffering from many of the same symptoms of ADHD as their children and may find it hard to provide a structured and organized environment for their child.

Presentation during adolescence. The presentation of behavioral symptoms associated with ADHD is slightly different in adolescence compared with that typically seen in younger children. Hyperactivity tends to decrease in severity with age, though adolescents continue to display impaired attention and impulsivity (Brown & Borden, 1986). Academic failure and emotional immaturity also are frequently reported.

The academic failure may result from two processes affecting the adolescent with ADHD. First, the increased scholastic demands for completion of lengthy assignments and for independent functioning in the classroom are countered by the adolescent's continuing difficulty with inattention and impulsivity. The adolescent may continue to need a highly structured environment with frequent teacher feedback, but teachers often are unwilling to provide this help because of the developmental expectation that adolescents should be able to work more independently. The second process affecting scholastic achievement in adolescents with ADHD is reflected in the declining IQ pattern as these youngsters get older. The decline in IQ likely reflects the failure of adolescents with ADHD to acquire information and skills at a rate commensurate with their age mates, most likely due to interference from the primary symptoms of ADHD that take their toll over the years. The result is a lag in academic achievement that is cumulative and that may cause adolescents with ADHD to struggle during the high school years. Studies examining the educational outcome of adolescents (at 17 and 18 years) with ADHD have reported a poorer outcome compared with non-ADHD peers (Lambert, 1988).

Specific cognitive deficits reported in adolescents with ADHD appear restricted to disorders of attention. In an 8-year follow-up study of hyperactive children, Fischer, Barkley, Edelbrock, and Smallish (1990) reported continued academic problems combined with inattentiveness and behavioral disinhibition, though no deficits on neuropsychological measures of frontal lobe functions were found; verbal memory, fluency, and nonverbal abstract reasoning skills were not significantly different from controls.

Emotional immaturity is another frequently reported characteristic of the adolescent with ADHD. The adolescent may continue to be interested in activities that are more typical of younger children, activities that often require less diligence or sustained attention to complete. Because of this, the adolescent with ADHD may choose to associate with younger peers in order to compete on an equal par in games and activities, while developmentally feeling the need to associate with same-age peers to avoid ostracism. Thus, identity issues may be more conflictual for the adolescent with ADHD, as the symptoms of their developmental disability may interfere with normal peer interactions, age appropriate activities, and their sense of mastery. The most common complaints associated with adolescents who have ADHD center around social interactions and conduct problems. Conduct problems, including aggressive behavior and conflicts with authority, are quite common (Hechtman, 1991; Lambert, 1988). Adolescents at greatest risk are those who have had a history of oppositional–defiant problems in the past, with those problems escalating as the adolescent gets older. The risks involved in comorbid ADHD and conduct disorders are discussed in the next section. However, the adolescent with these comorbid disorders is at greater risk for poor outcome, including the possibility of antisocial personality disorder, delinquency, and poor vocational adjustment.

Finally, the period of adolescence is an important time for vocational planning and preparation. However, the options for future schooling and employment for the adolescent with ADHD may be limited due to the primary symptoms of ADHD that persist into adulthood. The adolescent is at high risk for school failure and school dropout during this age range and may feel discouraged or incompetent compared with peers in vocational preparation. School vocational counseling and support from guidance counselors can make a significant difference to adolescents with ADHD who must select a vocational path that takes into account their strengths while working around the deficits associated with their disability.

Presentation in adulthood. The presentation of ADHD in adults is similar to that seen in adolescence, with the addition of vocational difficulties and occasionally substance abuse. In prospective follow-up studies of children identified as having ADHD, outcome typically includes poorer academic achievement and impulsive behavioral problems compared with individuals without ADHD (Fischer et al., 1990; Gittelman, Mannuzza, Shenker, & Bonagura, 1985; Hechtman, 1991; Satterfield, Hoppe, & Schell, 1986; Shekim, Asarnow, Hess, Zaucha, & Wheeler, 1990; Weiss & Hechtman, 1986; Weiss, Hechtman, Perlman, Hopkins, & Wener, 1979). In their longitudinal analysis of outcome of ADHD, Weiss and Hechtman (1986), Weiss et al. (1979), and Hechtman (1991) described increased delinquency in adolescence and higher rates of antisocial personality disorder in adulthood. In fact, at a 15-year follow-up, 23% of the children with ADHD were diagnosed with an antisocial personality disorder as adults. Mannuzza, Klein, Bessler, Malloy, and LaPadula (1993) reported lower occupational status in a group of adults with ADHD compared with matched controls, both of which were followed over a 16-year period. The adult ADHD group was also 10 times more likely to have an antisocial personality disorder and five times more likely to have an ongoing drug abuse problem.

Adults who have been or are identified as having ADHD appear to be at risk for other psychiatric disorders as well. Shekim et al. (1990) found that over 25% of adults with ADHD could also be diagnosed with an affective disorder, 34% displayed alcohol dependence, 30% displayed drug abuse\dependence, and 53% displayed a generalized anxiety disorder. In fact, it is common for these individuals to be misdiagnosed numerous times prior to having the ADHD recognized, particularly if they do not present a clear developmental history of learning disability or delay.

Loney, Kramer, and Milich (1981) were instructive in separating the trait of aggressiveness from the other primary symptoms of ADHD when interpreting longitudinal outcome studies of children diagnosed as having ADHD. The high prevalence of poor outcome in the areas of antisocial personality and delinquency often is associated with comorbid aggression rather than with the ADHD symptoms. On the positive side, Weiss and Hechtman (1986), in their longitudinal follow-up of over 100 adults who had been diagnosed with ADHD as children, found that most were employed, were not shorter or in other ways physiologically different from non-ADHD controls, were not more abusive of drugs or alcohol than controls, and were not psychotic or in prison (Denckla, 1991). However, they were reported to have more frequent job changes and more frequent changes of important intimate relationships, which suggests generally less stability in their adult lives (Weiss & Hechtman, 1986).

The diagnosis of ADHD-RT in adults often is complicated by reliance on retrospective historical information and primarily self-report data from the individual being diagnosed. Wender, Reimherr, and Wood (1981) suggested that a diagnosis of ADHD-RT must include documentation that an individual had a history of the disorder during childhood, and must currently have both hyperactivity and attentional deficits as an adult. In addition, the individual must have two of the characteristics encompassing poor attention, poor concentration or task persistence, and impulsivity (Denckla, 1991; Wender et al., 1981). There continues to be some controversy in the literature regarding the integrity of the construct of ADHD-RT (Gualtieri, Ondrusek, & Finlay, 1985), and there certainly continues to be discussion regarding appropriate diagnostic criteria. Further research will be needed to further define the core characteristics of ADHD in adulthood, and only then can one better understand the implications for vocational and social–emotional functioning for these individuals.

Conditions Comorbid With ADHD

Conduct problems. There is abundant research literature to support the co-occurrence of aggression, oppositional, defiant, and even antisocial characteristics in children with ADHD. Over 65% of clinic-referred children with ADHD meet criteria for an oppositional defiant disorder (ODD; per the *DSM-III-R*, American Psychiatric Association, 1987), characterized by a disturbance of mood (hostile or angry and negative temperament) and defiant, resistant, oppositional behavior (Loney & Milich, 1982; Stewart et al., 1966). Oppositional defiant disorder (ODD) in its most severe presentation may be detected even during the preschool years but more often is diagnosed during middle childhood. Studies by Barkley, DuPaul, and McMurray (1990) and Barkley, Fischer, et al. (1990) have indicated that 40% of children with ADHD and 65% of adolescents with ADHD will meet full diagnostic criteria for ODD.

The more serious problem of conduct disorder, as defined by *DSM-III-R* guidelines (American Psychiatric Association, 1987), also is comorbid with a large percentage of children who have ADHD. This disorder is characterized by a higher rate of physical aggression and antisocial behaviors, including lying, stealing, destruction of property, and truancy. Studies have indicated that as many as 21%–45% of children with ADHD and 44%–50% of adolescents with ADHD will meet diagnostic criteria for conduct disorder. The risk for developing conduct disorder increases in those children whose parents have psychopathology and come from lower socioeconomic backgrounds (McGee, Williams, & Silva, 1984; Reeves, Werry, Elkind, & Zametkin, 1987; Szatmari et al., 1989b).

Academic performance problems. Children with ADHD are likely to be delayed in both intellectual and academic development compared with siblings and non-ADHD peers. Intellectual ability on standardized tests averages 7 to 15 points below both control groups (Fischer et al., 1990; McGee, Williams, Moffitt, & Anderson, 1989; Prior, Leonard, & Wood, 1983; Tarver-Behring et al., 1985). According to Barkley (1990), it is unclear whether the lower intellectual performance is related to cognitive ability or whether these children do poorly on standardized tests because of their inattention and problems with test-taking behavior. The lower scores on intellectual tests also may relate to comorbid learning disability in many children who have ADHD. Learning disabilities have been reported in 20% to 50% of children with ADHD, with the variation accounted for largely by the definition used for learning disability. Using a discrepancy formula in which comparisons are made between intellectual and academic achievement, a 15-point discrepancy (1 standard deviation) results in the higher percentage of children diagnosed with learning disabilities, whereas a 1.5 or 2 standard deviation discrepancy (21 to 30 standard score points) would provide a lower and more conservative rate of co-occurring learning disability among children with ADHD.

Academic performance problems occur even in children who do not have learning disabilities because of the problems with impersistence and variability in performance, and inattentive, impulsive, and restless behavior in the classroom. In children who do have comorbid learning disabilities, several studies have indicated significant improvement in academic productivity following initiation of stimulant medication (Barkley, 1977a; Pelham, Bender, Caddell, Booth, & Moorer, 1985; Rapport, DuPaul, Stoner, & Jones, 1986). Barkley (1990) reported that approximately 40% of children with ADHD may be placed in formal special educational programs for learning disabilities or behavior disorders for some period of time during their education, and that 23% to 35% will be retained in at least one grade before reaching high school.

Social skills problems. Significant problems in social relationships with other children are found in approximately 50% of children with ADHD (Pelham & Bender, 1982). Children with ADHD often are rejected by their peers and are viewed as overly intrusive, bossy, domineering, aggressive, and noisy, compared with children who do not have ADHD (Milich & Landau, 1982; Pelham & Bender, 1982). They often are viewed as emotionally immature and as having little regard for social consequences. They may talk excessively but they are less likely to respond to verbal interactions of their peers. The decreased reciprocity in social exchanges leads to social interaction problems (Cunningham & Siegel, 1987; Landau & Milich, 1988). Some studies indicate that children with ADHD may misinterpret the intentions or actions of others toward them, which suggests the possibility of social perception problems (Milich & Dodge, 1984). These problems in social interaction may result in peers withdrawing from children who have ADHD, and consequently, painful isolation for these youngsters. It has been hypothesized that the roots of later antisocial personality problems may be found in the earlier social interaction experiences of children with ADHD.

Emotional disturbances. Szatmari et al. (1989b), in their large epidemiological survey, found that emotional disorders frequently are comorbid with ADHD. Up to 44% of children with ADHD have at least one other psychiatric disorder, 32% have two disorders, and 11% have at least three other disorders. Several studies have reported that children with ADHD have more symptoms of anxiety, depression, and low self-esteem than learning disabled children without ADHD and normal children (Breen & Barkley, 1983, 1984; Margalit & Arieli, 1984).

Apart from diagnosable emotional disorders, children with ADHD generally have been noted to have emotional immaturity, characterized by exaggerated responses to situations, low frustration tolerance, and poor self-esteem. They also have been noted to have a greater number of somatic complaints compared with normal children (Barkley, DuPaul, & McMurray, 1990). Szatmari et al. (1989b) found that a large percentage of children with ADHD (24% of boys and 35% of girls) between 12 and 16 years met criteria for somatization disorder.

Developmental and medical problems. A variety of other developmental and medical anomalies have been reported with a higher rate of frequency in children with ADHD compared with normal children. Developmental problems include a higher frequency of speech delay (Barkley, DuPaul, et al., 1990) and more dysfluency in language production (Hamlett, Pellegrini, & Conners, 1987; Zentall, 1985). Language problems are more apparent when children with ADHD must organize and generate their speech in response to specific task demands (Barkley, 1990). Motor coordination problems have been reported in as many as 52% of children with ADHD, compared with 35% of normal children (Barkley, DuPaul, & McMurray, 1990; Szatmari et al., 1989b). Motor coordination problems are especially noted on fine motor tasks, such as peg boards or mazes (McMahon & Greenberg, 1977; Shaywitz & Shaywitz, 1988). Children with ADHD may have more neurologic soft signs and motor overflow movements during a medical screening compared with normal and purely learning disabled children (Denckla & Rudel, 1978; Denckla, Rudel, Chapman, & Krieger, 1985).

Sensory deficits in visual and auditory acuity are not especially common in children with ADHD, although there is a higher incidence of otitis media or middle ear infections compared with normal children (Mitchell, Aman, Turbott, & Manku, 1987).

Children with ADHD also have been shown to have more minor physical anomalies (e.g., single transverse palmar crease, greater than normal head circumference, low set ears, electric or fine hair, eyes placed slightly farther apart than normal) compared with other children (Firestone, Lewy, & Douglas, 1976; Lerer, 1977; Quinn & Rapoport, 1974). Although these minor anomalies occur more frequently in children with ADHD, the literature is mixed regarding whether there is a relationship between these anomalies and hyperactive behavior (Firestone et al., 1976). Other studies have found a more frequent occurrence of certain health problems in children with ADHD, including recurrent upper respiratory infections, allergies, and asthma (Hartsough & Lambert, 1985; Szatmari, Offord, & Boyle, 1989a).

Children with ADHD have been reported to be more prone to accidents, such as broken bones, head injuries, bruises, lacerations, or accidental poisonings (Hartsough & Lambert, 1985; Stewart et al., 1966). However, children with ADHD have not been found to have more hospitalizations or surgeries than non-ADHD children (Barkley, DuPaul, & McMurray, 1990; Hartsough & Lambert, 1985; Stewart et al., 1966).

The literature has been inconsistent regarding the incidence of enuresis and encopresis in children with ADHD. Some studies have reported a high incidence of enuresis (43%) in children with ADHD compared with non-ADHD children (28%; Stewart et al., 1966), although those figures have not been replicated recently (Barkley, DuPaul, & McMurray, 1990). However, several studies have found children with ADHD to have a higher number of sleep problems than non-ADHD children, including difficulty falling asleep (56% of children with ADHD, compared with 23% of controls), and problems with waking in the middle of the night (39% of ADHD children). This higher incidence of sleep problems may appear in infancy or early childhood and persist over the years (Kaplan, McNichol, Conte, & Moghadam, 1987; Stewart et al., 1966; Trommer et al., 1988).

ASSESSMENT OF CHILDREN, ADOLESCENTS, AND ADULTS WITH ADHD

Despite the considerable research on ADHD, there is no one test or set of test procedures that can be used to provide a definitive diagnosis of the disorder. ADHD remains a diagnosis made primarily by history and observation. The diagnostic process becomes more complex and time consuming when other comorbid features are present along with symptoms of ADHD, and the practitioner must rule in or rule out these disorders in order to develop an effective treatment plan. The purpose of this section of the chapter is to describe a two-tier model for assessment, with the first tier involving brief screening procedures, and the second tier a more comprehensive evaluation process that can be used as the basis for a treatment program. This section describes assessment procedures appropriate for preschool, school age, adolescent, and adult populations who are suspected of having ADHD, with particular attention to developmental issues within each age group.

A Screening Model for ADHD

The first step in evaluating a child, adolescent, or adult for ADHD involves screening for the presence of the primary ADHD symptoms, the pervasiveness of the symptoms, and the presence of comorbid disorders. The screening should help the practitioner determine whether an evaluation focused specifically on ADHD symptoms will suffice for treatment planning, or whether a more comprehensive evaluation process will be needed. In the latter case, there may be concerns about comorbid learning disability, behavior disorder, or emotional disorder that will require further evaluation in order to make a differential diagnosis and plan the most appropriate treatment strategy.

Screening of primary symptoms to determine whether they fit the diagnostic criteria for ADHD can be accomplished in two ways. A semistructured interview with parents, teachers, or both using a rating scale based on *DSM-IV* criteria can provide information regarding the presence and intensity of the symptoms. In our clinic, parents are asked to rate on a 4-point scale (*rarely, occasionally, pretty often, very often*) to what degree the primary symptoms have been present in their child for the past 6 months, as illustrated in Exhibit 2. For preschool-aged children, parents are asked to rate those symptoms that have persisted for the past 12 months in order to assess the child for more pervasive symptomatology. The second procedure involves asking parents and teachers to complete age-normed behavioral checklists designed to determine whether the child's behaviors are deviant from those to be expected for their age and gender. This is particularly important for preschoolers and young elementary school children, in whom it may be more difficult to separate symp-

EXHIBIT 2

DSM-IV Checklist of Primary Symptoms of Attention Deficit Hyperactivity Disorder (ADHD)

I. ADHD, Predominantly Inattentive Type (314.00)
A. Have the symptoms been present at least 6 months? ______
At least 12 months for preschoolers? ______
B. Compared to other children the same age, are at least 6 of the following symptoms present? ______
(either "3" or "4" must be circled)

Inattention

1 2 3 4 1. often fails to give close attention to details or makes careless mistakes in schoolwork, work, or other activities
1 2 3 4 2. often has difficulty sustaining attention in tasks or play activities
1 2 3 4 3. often does not seem to listen when spoken to directly
1 2 3 4 4. often does not follow through on instructions and fails to finish schoolwork, chores, or duties in the workplace (not due to oppositional behavior or failure to understand instructions)
1 2 3 4 5. often has difficulty organizing tasks and activities
1 2 3 4 6. often avoids, dislikes, or is reluctant to engage in tasks that require sustained mental effort (such as schoolwork or homework)
1 2 3 4 7. often loses things necessary for tasks or activities (e.g., toys, school assignments, pencils, books, or tools)
1 2 3 4 8. is often easily distracted by extraneous stimuli
1 2 3 4 9. is often forgetful in daily activities

II. ADHD, Predominantly Hyperactive–Impulsive Type (314.01)
A. Have the symptoms been present at least 6 months? ______
At least 12 months for preschoolers? ______
B. Compared to other children the same age, are at least 4 of the following symptoms present? ______
("3" or "4" must be circled)

Hyperactivity

1 2 3 4 1. often fidgets with hands or feet or squirms in seat
1 2 3 4 2. often leaves seat in classroom or in other situations in which remaining seated is expected
1 2 3 4 3. often runs about or climbs excessively in situations in which it is inappropriate (in adolescents or adults, may be limited to subjective feelings of restlessness)
1 2 3 4 4. often has difficulty playing or engaging in leisure activities quietly
1 2 3 4 5. is often "on the go" or often acts as if "driven by a motor"
1 2 3 4 6. often talks excessively

Impulsivity

1 2 3 4 7. often blurts out answers before questions have been completed
1 2 3 4 8. often has difficulty awaiting turn
1 2 3 4 9. often interrupts or intrudes on others (e.g., butts into conversations or games)

EXHIBIT 2 (*Continued*)

III. ADHD, Combined Type (314.01)
Code if criteria for both I and II are met for the past 6 months (12 months for preschoolers)

Check the appropriate level of severity (make this rating at the conclusion of the intake)

______ Mild Few, if any, symptoms in excess of those required to make the diagnosis, and only minimal or no impairment in school and social functioning.

______ Moderate Symptoms of functional impairment intermediate between mild and severe.

______ Severe Many symptoms in excess of those required to make the diagnosis and significant and pervasive impairment in functioning at home and in school and with other adults and peers.

1 = rarely; *2* = occasionally; *3* = pretty often; *4* = very often. *From* Diagnostic and Statistical Manual of Mental Disorders (DSM-IV; *4th ed., pp. 83–84), by the American Psychiatric Association, 1994, Washington, DC: Author. Copyright 1994 by the American Psychiatric Association. Adapted with permission.*

toms of ADHD from behavior problems or age-appropriate exploratory activity. Exhibit 3 provides examples of general broad-band inventories and narrow-band rating scales specific to ADHD for use in the screening. It is recommended that at least one broad-band and one narrow-band behavioral rating scale be administered to both parents and teachers as part of the initial screening of children and youth. Several goals can be accomplished through review of parent and teacher responses to these scales. In addition to screening for the presence or absence of ADHD symptoms compared with age norms, one can also screen for other potential comorbid behavioral and emotional problems, learning problems, and social interaction problems. The narrow-band rating scales specific to ADHD can help with the initial processes of subtyping according to the presence or absence of hyperactivity–impulsivity, primarily inattentive symptoms, or the combined symptoms. With adults, behavioral ratings such as the Wender Utah Rating Scale (Ward, Wender, & Reimherr, 1993) help with the differential diagnosis between ADHD and other types of adult psychopathology. The Wender Utah Rating Scale includes an adult self-report scale and also a parent rating scale in which retrospective information is provided about symptoms during childhood.

Another essential part of the initial screening with children is review of the child's developmental history with the parents, based on either a written history form or an interview. This history should include details of medical, school, and family history, along with developmental, behavioral, and social–emotional progress in the child. The history may be broadened to help the practitioner determine whether the symptoms of ADHD relate to other significant family events (e.g., the recent birth of a new sibling), which would suggest that the symptoms may be transient in nature rather than representing true symptoms of ADHD. The interview might also provide information that the child has just been diagnosed with a learning disability, and the symptoms of ADHD are of recent onset, coinciding with the learning problems in the classroom. Again, in this case the symptoms of ADHD may be secondary to the primary disability in the area of learning. In other cases, the history may provide clear evidence of chronic excessive activity, distractibility, and impulsivity over the age span from the toddler years through the early school years, and across multiple settings. This type of history would more strongly suggest the presence of ADHD.

A Model for Comprehensive Evaluation of ADHD

Once screening has been completed, the practitioner will have information regarding the primary symptoms of ADHD, and hypotheses about subtypes of ADHD and the presence or absence of comorbid symptomatology. This information guides the plan-

EXHIBIT 3

Examples of Behavioral Rating Scales Useful in Screening for Symptoms of Attention Deficit Hyperactivity Disorder (ADHD), Learning Problems, and Behavioral and Emotional Problems

General Broad-Band Inventories

Burks' Behavior Rating Scales: Child and Adolescent Version and Preschool and Kindergarten Edition (Burks, 1977)

The child and adolescent version (Grades 1–9) is a 110-item paper-and-pencil inventory used by parents and teachers to rate a child's observed behavior over 19 subscales. The preschool and kindergarten version (ages 3 to 6 years) is a 105-item paper-and-pencil inventory used by parents and teachers to identify patterns of behavior problems in the young child. *Publisher*: Western Psychological Services.

Child Behavior Checklist (CBCL), Revised Child Behavior Profile, and Child Behavior Checklist–Teacher Report Form (CBCL-TRF; Achenbach & Edelbrock, 1983)

Assesses behavioral problems and social competencies of children from ages 4 to 16 years. Separate forms are available for boys and girls. Both internalizing and externalizing behaviors are screened. The CBCL assesses behaviors from the parents' point of view, whereas the CBCL-TRF assesses the child's classroom behavior. *Publisher*: University of Vermont.

Personality Inventory for Children—Revised Format (Wirt, Lachar, Klinedinst, Seat, & Broen, 1984)

Evaluates the personality attributes of children and adolescents on a 280-item paper-and-pencil true–false inventory completed by parents. The 16 scales include Intellectual Screening, Family Relations, Hyperactivity, Somatic Concern, Social Skills, Achievement, Development, Depression, Delinquency, Withdrawal, Psychosis, Anxiety, Lie, Frequency, Defensiveness, and Adjustment. Used to identify psychopathology, developmental problems, and social disabilities. *Publisher*: Western Psychological Services.

Revised Behavior Problem Checklist (RBPC; Quay & Peterson, 1983)

Assesses the nature of behavior problems in educational, mental health, pediatric, and correctional settings. The RBPC is an 85-item observational inventory that includes statements about problem behaviors commonly seen in children and adolescents. Behavior can be rated by parent, teacher, child care worker, or other knowledgeable observers. *Publisher*: Herbert C. Quay.

Narrow-Band Scales Specific to ADHD

ADD-H Comprehensive Teacher Rating Scale (ACTeRS; Ullmann, Sleator, & Sprague, 1984)

Aids in diagnosing attention deficit disorder with or without hyperactivity in children ages 5 to 12 years. Also provides teacher ratings of social skills and oppositional behavior. Used as a screening device to discriminate children with ADHD from those who may be learning disabled. *Publisher*: PRO-ED.

EXHIBIT 3 (*Continued*)

Attention Deficit Disorders Evaluation Scale (McCarney, 1989)
Measures inattention, impulsivity, and hyperactivity in children and youth ages 4 to 18 years. Parent version contains 46 items and teacher version contains 60 items. Has excellent national normative sample that is larger than the normative sample of any other published rating scale for youths with ADHD. Scale development did not include factor or cluster analysis, so that the three behavioral dimensions may not hold up under research scrutiny. Needs further research to determine sensitivity to treatment effects. *Publisher*: Hawthorne Educational Services.

Conners Parent Rating Scale–Revised, and Conners Teacher Rating Scale–Revised (Conners, 1989)
Measures hyperactivity and other patterns of child behavior. Two parent versions (48- or 93-item) available, measuring conduct, psychosomatic, and learning problems; impulsivity–hyperactivity; anxiety–passivity; and antisocial behaviors among others. Two teacher versions (28- or 39-item) available, measuring hyperactivity, conduct problems, anxiety–passivity, emotional–overindulgent behavior, and daydreaming. *Publisher*: Multi-Health Systems.

Iowa Conners Teacher Rating Scale (Milich, Loney, & Landau, 1982)
Discriminates aggression and inattention–overactivity. A 10-item teacher report measure with items from original Teacher Rating Scale (CTRS) for Grades 1–5. Developed to distinguish purely aggressive from purely hyperactive children. *Publisher*: Jan Loney.

Self-Control Rating Scale (Kendall & Wilcox 1979)
Assesses deficits in self-control in children ages 8 to 11 years. Completed by teachers, parents, or other caregivers. Has restricted sample size and age range. Developed to assess a narrow constellation of behaviors associated with self-control and to evaluate changes in this behavior associated with cognitive–behavioral intervention. *Publisher*: Philip C. Kendall.

Swanson, Nolan, and Pelham Rating Scales (Swanson & Pelham, 1988)
Provides teacher ratings on inattention, hyperactivity, impulsivity, and peer problems for children ages 6 to 11 years. Based on *DSM-III* criteria for ADD, so it may have limited utility with the advent of DSM-IV. *Publisher*: William Pelham.

Wender Utah Rating Scale (Ward, Wender, & Reimherr, 1993)
Assesses symptoms of ADHD and other forms of psychopathology in adult life. Requires adults to rate on a 5-point scale 61 items that provide retrospective information about symptoms during childhood. Also includes a 10-item parent rating scale in which parent rates the presence and severity of symptoms when the child was 6 to 10 years old. *Publisher*: Paul Wender.

Werry-Weiss-Peters Activity Rating Scale (Routh, Schroeder, & O'Tuama, 1974)
Discriminates effectively between hyperactive and normal children and is sensitive to drug treatment or parent training programs. Norms available for ages 3–9 years, based on parent ratings. *Publisher*: John Werry.

DSM = Diagnostic and Statistical Manual of Mental Disorders.

ning for the remainder of the evaluation. The decision-making process about the evaluation is facilitated by the following guidelines:

1. If screening and initial intake history reveal no concerns about development, intelligence, pre-academic or academic achievement, or behavioral–social–emotional problems, proceed with evaluation of the symptoms of ADHD, intended to describe both qualitatively and quantitatively the nature and severity of the disorder. Both direct observational procedures (for children and youth) and measures of attention and impulsivity are useful in completing this evaluation. See Exhibits 4 and 5 for examples of measures that are discussed further in later sections of this chapter.
2. If screening and initial intake history reveal decreased academic performance along with symptoms of ADHD, but no behavioral–social–emotional problems, add to Number 1 an evaluation of intellectual, academic, and information-processing abilities to rule out a learning disability or other causes of achievement problems (such as low IQ, perceptual deficits, etc.).
3. If academic performance is average and there are no concerns about learning, but social–behavioral–emotional problems exist, then proceed with measures in Number 1 and add other measures sensitive to emotional and behavioral functioning. These measures might include projective story telling or projective drawing procedures, sentence completion tasks, and interview of the child directly.

EXHIBIT 4

Direct Observational Procedures Useful in Evaluating Children and Youth With Symptoms of Attention Deficit Hyperactivity Disorder (ADHD)

Child Behavior Checklist—Direct Observation Form (Achenbach, 1986)

Direct observations made in group or classroom settings provide scores for mean time on task, total problems, and total internalizing and externalizing symptoms. Normed scale of 96 items provides six factors: Withdrawn–Inattentive, Nervous–Obsessive, Depressed, Hyperactive, Attention-Demanding, and Aggressive.

Classroom Behavioral Observations (Abikoff, Gittelman-Klein, & Klein, 1977)

Observers classify behaviors in the classroom setting on dimensions such as activity, off-task behavior, disruptiveness, verbal or physical aggression, excessive verbalization, and daydreaming. Uses interval sampling procedures, and results discriminate children with ADHD from normal classmates. Results also correlate highly with teacher ratings on the Conners Teacher Rating Scale.

Dyadic Parent–Child Interaction Coding System–II (Eyberg, Bessmer, Newcomb, Edwards, & Robinson, 1993)

Assesses child and parent behavior and parent–child interaction in an informal playroom environment. The observation includes three segments: child-directed interaction (in which child has free play without direction from parent), parent-directed interaction (in which parent must get the child to play according to the parent's rules), and clean up (in which parent must direct the child in cleaning up the playroom). Each 5-min segment allows coding of child compliance and negative behaviors, along with parent commands, praises, and negative behavior.

Hyperactive Behavior Code (Jacob, O'Leary, & Rosenblad, 1978)

Observers classify behaviors in the classroom setting on the dimensions of daydreaming, aggression, and so forth. Uses interval sampling procedures, and the results discriminate children with ADHD

EXHIBIT 4 (*Continued*)

from normal classmates. Results also correlate highly with teacher ratings on the Conners Teacher Rating Scale.

Parent–Adolescent Interaction Coding System (Robin & Foster, 1989)
Provides observations of parents and adolescents during problem-centered discussion involving three topics: a neutral discussion, a current list of disagreements, and then a positive discussion. The verbal behavior of the parent–adolescent dyad is coded using 6 mutually exclusive categories: *puts down/commands*, *defends/complains*, *facilitates*, *problem-solves*, *defines/evaluates*, and *talks*. Discriminates between adolescents with ADHD and normal adolescents.

Playroom Observations of Mother–Child Interactions (Barkley, 1987)
Modified from the Forehand and McMahon (1981) parent–child coding system, this observational system assesses oppositional and defiant behavior in children during task performance with their mothers, and records parental behaviors during these interactions. The setting is an informal playroom during which the child is given 5 min of free play, and then asked to complete seven tasks involving cleaning, interaction with the mother, or completing tasks directed by the mother. The observer uses an interval coding method to code child compliance; child negative behavior; and parental commands, praises, and negative behavior.

Restricted Academic Playroom Situation (Barkley, 1988a)
This modified version of the Roberts (1979) coding system provides a situation designed for observing and recording symptoms of ADHD during individual academic work. The child or adolescent is observed during performance of independent math problems in a clinic playroom with toys or age-appropriate materials present. The child is told to complete as many math problems as possible, not to leave the chair at the table, and not to touch the toys/materials. Interval ratings are made in 5 behavior categories: *off task*, *fidgets*, *out of seat*, *vocalizes*, and *plays with objects*.

The guidelines listed earlier are helpful when the symptom presentation is clear and provides the practitioner a clear direction about functional impairment. However, it is often the case that symptoms are presented much less clearly, and it would benefit the child or youth to conduct a more comprehensive evaluation, given the high risk of comorbid learning and behavioral–emotional problems with ADHD. Clinical judgment following the initial screening and intake interview will assist in decision making about the nature of the evaluation. Table 2 provides a conceptualization of a neuropsychological approach to evaluation of the child, adolescent, and adult suspected of having ADHD. This model is based on current empirical literature that suggests certain functional areas that need to be tapped during an evaluation and suggests the measures that are likely to be most sensitive to symptoms of ADHD. The following sections elaborate on this model from a developmental perspective, with discussions of assessment during the preschool, school-age, adolescent, and adult years.

Assessment of the preschool-age child. As noted in an earlier section, symptoms of decreased attention and increased activity level are common during the preschool years. They are of concern clinically only when they persist for at least 12 months and are of sufficient severity to disrupt the child's functioning in a structured preschool environment or the home.

In the preschool-age range, parental interview should provide information for a differential diagnosis between symptoms of ADHD and other childhood disorders, particularly those that may appear superficially as ADHD. These may include pervasive

EXHIBIT 5

Laboratory Tests and Measures for Assessment of Vigilance, Sustained Attention, and Impulsivity

Cancellation Tasks

Several paper-and-pencil versions of Cancellation Tasks have been used to assess attention. The Wechsler Intelligence Scale for Children, third edition, Symbol Search subtest (Wechsler, 1990) involves cancellation of geometric symbols within a 2-min time limit. The Children's Checking Task (Keogh & Margolis, 1976; Margolis, 1972) involves drawing a line through numbers that are read on a tape and ability to recognize discrepancies between the tape and printed pages of numbers. This test is scored for errors of omission (missed discrepancies) and errors of commission (numbers circled that were not discrepancies).

Gordon Diagnostic System (Gordon, 1983)

Measures of sustained attention and vigilance are obtained from the Vigilance task and Distractibility task, with scores derived from the number of correct responses, number of target stimuli missed (omission errors), and number of responses following nontarget or incorrect stimuli (commission errors). Commission errors are presumed to tap sustained attention and impulse control, while number of correct responses and omission errors tap sustained attention only. The Delay task measures impulse control using a differential reinforcement of low rates paradigm, in which the child sits before the computerized device and is told to wait before pressing a large blue button on the front panel of the device. The child is told that he or she will earn points by waiting long enough before pushing the button. The child is not informed of the actual delay required to earn a point.

Matching Familiar Figures Test (MFFT; Kagan, 1966; Cairns & Cammock, 1978)

Requires the child to match a picture of a recognizable object to an identical picture among an array of six similar images. Scores include latency (average time to initial response) and total errors (incorrectly identified pictures). The Cairns and Cammock (1978) version of the MFFT is longer (20 stimulus trials) and purported to have greater reliability among older children and adolescents. However, the MFFT does not reliably discriminate among children with and without ADHD.

Stroop Color and Word Test (Golden, 1978)

Brief screening measure for Grades 2 and higher. Consists of a Word Page in which color words are printed in black ink, a Color Page with *X*s printed in color, and a Word-Color Page with words from the first page printed in colors from the second. The individual must read the list of color names in which no name is printed in its matching color; the Word-Color Page requires naming the color of ink in which the color names are printed. Measures sustained attention, impulsivity, and mental flexibility. The impulsivity components of this test are felt to discriminate children with ADHD from those without.

Wisconsin Card Sorting Test (Grant & Berg, 1948; Heaton, 1981)

Involves cards with various colored geometric shapes and numbers of shapes on them. Requires sorting these cards based on a categorizing rule known only to the examiner (color, number, shape). Feedback is given regarding correct or incorrect responses, and this feedback can be used to deduce the categorizing rule as quickly as possible in order to limit the number of sorting errors. The evidence for this task discriminating children with and without ADHD is limited.

TABLE 2

Conceptualization of a Neuropsychologic Battery for Children, Adolescents, and Adults With Attention Deficit Hyperactivity Disorder (ADHD)

	Measure		
Function	**Child**	**Adolescent**	**Adult**
Cognitive	WPPSI-R[a] WISC-III	WISC-III[b] WAIS-R	WAIS-R[c]
Achievement	WJ-R[d] WIAT[e]	WJ-R WIAT	WJ-R WRAT-3[f]
Attention:			
Focus–execute Initiate	WISC-III: Coding Symbol Search Fluency[g]	WISC-III: Coding Symbol Search Fluency Stroop[h]	WAIS-R: Digit Symbol Fluency Stroop Letter Cancellation
Sustain	GDS:[i] Vigilance task (errors of omission)	GDS: Vigilance task (errors of omission)	GDS: Vigilance task (errors of omission)
Encode	WISC-III: Digit Span Arithmetic	WISC-III/WAIS-R: Digit Span Arithmetic	WAIS-R: Digit Span Arithmetic
Inhibit	Stroop MFFT[j] GDS: Vigilance task (errors of commission)	Stroop MFFT GDS: Vigilance task (errors of commission)	Stroop MFFT GDS: Vigilance task (errors of commission)
Shift–mental flexibility	WCST[k] Trails B[l]	WCST Trails B	WCST Trails B
Memory	WRAML[m] TOMAL[o] CAVLT[q]	WRAML TOMAL CAVLT Rey-O[r]	WMS-R[n] RAVLT[p] Rey-O
Emotional–personality	CBCL[s] Reynolds[v] Roberts[x] RCMAS[z]	MMPI-A[t] Reynolds STAI[y]	MMPI-2[u] BDI[w] STAI

[a]Wechsler Preschool and Primary Scale of Intelligence–Revised.
[b]Wechsler Intelligence Scale for Children–Third Edition.
[c]Wechsler Adult Intelligence Scale–Revised.
[d]Woodcock–Johnson Psychoeducational Battery–Revised Edition.
[e]Wechsler Individual Achievement Test.
[f]Wide Range Achievement Test–Third Edition.
[g]FAS Fluency Task.
[h]Stroop Color and Word Test.
[i]Gordon Diagnostic System.
[j]Matching Familiar Figures Test.
[k]Wisconsin Card Sorting Test.
[l]Trail-Making Test B (from Halstead–Reitan Neuropsychological Battery).
[m]Wide Range Assessment of Memory and Learning.
[n]Wechsler Memory Scale–Revised.
[o]Test of Memory and Learning.
[p]Rey Auditory Verbal Learning Test.
[q]Children's Auditory Verbal Learning Test.
[r]Rey–Osterreith Complex Figure.
[s]Child Behavior Checklist.
[t]Minnesota Multiphasic Personality Inventory–Adolescent.
[u]Minnesota Multiphasic Personality Inventory–Second Edition.
[v]Reynolds Child Depression Scale.
[w]Beck Depression Inventory.
[x]Roberts Apperception Test.
[y]State–Trait Anxiety Inventory.
[z]Revised Children's Manifest Anxiety Scale.

developmental disorder or ODD. Children with pervasive developmental disorder often present with overactivity and inattention as primary symptoms, but they also exhibit inappropriate thinking and affect, a restricted repertoire of activities and interests, and poor social interaction skills. Children with ODD often have increased activity and agitation, along with frequent temper outbursts, argumentative behavior, and increased aggression. However, deliberate defiance or aggression rather than motor overactivity are the predominant symptoms in children with ODD.

Interview with the parents can provide useful information on the nature of the parent–child interaction, the child's compliance to parental directions, and the child's ability to demonstrate age appropriate self-control. The Home Situations Questionnaire (Barkley, 1981) generates a parental report about *where* children display behavioral problems as opposed to the type of problems they have. The questionnaire requires a parent to answer yes or no as to whether the child has difficulty in any of 16 situations typically found in the home or public, such as when asked to do homework, when visiting others, at bedtime, and so forth. Normative data are available for children ages 4 to 12 years (Barkley & Edelbrock, 1987), and the scale can differentiate children with and without ADHD.

Direct observations of the child's behavior and of parent–child interaction can provide useful information in the evaluation of a preschool child. Several models have been developed for direct observation, as described in Exhibit 4. Roberts (1979) developed a widely used code for observation in a clinic playroom setting. Using a large grid drawn on the floor, observers continually record grid crossings, out-of-seat behavior, fidgeting, vocalization, attention shifts, and on-task behavior in a free-play situation. For older children, an academic situation can be used in which the child is asked to complete worksheets similar to the Wechsler Intelligence Scale for Children–Third Edition (WISC-III) Coding subtest and asked not to play with any of the toys in the room. For the younger child the play situation provides a more appropriate condition. This model for child observation allows the examiner to record ADHD behaviors objectively, to discriminate between those children with and without ADHD, and to detect additional problems such as aggression (Milich, 1984; Milich, Loney, & Landau, 1982; Roberts, 1979). Barkley (1988a) and Barkley, Fischer, Newby, and Breen (1988) modified the Milich–Roberts procedure to allow the child's mother to sit in the playroom during the observation while the examiner records behavior from behind a one-way observation mirror. This procedure prevents separation anxiety for the young preschool child and may reduce the occurrence of oppositional behavior.

Parent–child interactions allow for observations of the child's compliance in completing assigned tasks, and the occurrence of oppositional or deviant behaviors. A model for parent–child interaction developed by Robinson and Eyberg (1981) and recently revised (Eyberg, Bessmer, Newcomb, Edwards, & Robinson, 1993) uses a systematic coding system for dyadic interactions over a 15-min period divided into three situations. The first 5-min segment is a free-play condition during which the child and parent are together in a playroom setting with a variety of age-appropriate toys, and the child is told that he or she can play freely with the available toys. The parent participates in the play, but does not direct the play. In the second 5-min segment, the parent is told to choose the activity and get the child to play along with the parent. In the third 5-min segment, the parent is told to have the child clean up all the toys. The parent is directed not to help. Ratings are made on child compliance and noncompliance to the parent's directions as well as oppositional behaviors (e.g., whining, sassing, yelling, physical aggression, destructive behavior). Observations of the parent's style of giving commands and praise are made also. This direct observation format is helpful in discriminating symptoms of ADHD from those of ODD.

Where possible, observation of the child within a preschool environment such as a structured preschool or Head Start classroom can provide useful information about the child's ability to adjust to the structure and rules of the group setting, interact with peers, and respond to directions from teachers. Observations in the natural school environment may elicit more typical behavior than may be seen in the clinic environment, where children often can inhibit their impulsive and hyperactive behaviors for brief periods of time. This suggests several potential limitations of behavioral observations that should be considered. First, care must be taken to provide a clinic observation situation that is similar to situations in which the deviant behavior is likely to occur. For older children, presentation of worksheets or academic assignments during the observation provides an opportunity for observation of on-task and off-task behavior. Observing the child without a parent present often leads to better observations of ADHD symptoms, whereas observing with the parent present may provide opportunity for observing oppositional defiant behaviors. Finally, the observer must take care to define carefully the behaviors being observed, and practice until reliability is achieved (Barkley, 1990). The child with ADHD may inhibit hyperactive and impulsive behaviors during the initial stages of the clinic visit, and it is important for observations to be delayed for 1 to 2 hours so that there is a greater likelihood of seeing typical behavior from the youngster.

Other aspects of the evaluation of preschoolers are determined by the presenting symptoms and situational demands. For the older preschooler who is about to enter kindergarten, or who is already showing signs of developmental delay, it is important to include assessment of cognitive, preacademic, and other developmental skills as part of the comprehensive evaluation. Portions of the model described in Table 2 can be adapted for the preschool-age child. The cognitive measure would be chosen depending on the age and functioning level of the child, but generally should include a broad range of measures tapping verbal, perceptual performance, and memory functions. Screening of preacademic readiness skills (e.g., knowledge of colors and shapes, ability to recite the alphabet and count by rote) is important. Children who show delays in cognitive or preacademic learning, or in other areas of development such as speech–language or motor skills, are candidates for placement in structured preschool or Head Start programs that can facilitate preparation for formal schooling. Special education services may be provided through the public school, depending on the severity of the child's disability or risk for disability. Assessment of other areas of development as part of the workup for possible ADHD would be dependent on presenting symptoms and parental or teacher concerns.

Laboratory measures of vigilance may be used during the preschool years, but are rather demanding on the young child's attention and cooperation due to their length. The GDS (Gordon, 1983) has norms for 4- and 5-year olds, but some other measures listed in Exhibit 5 do not have preschool versions available (e.g., Stroop Color and Word Test, WCST). In most instances, other evaluation procedures described in this section would be appropriate for use with preschoolers, and would suffice for making a diagnosis without the use of laboratory measures of vigilance and sustained attention.

Finally, evaluation of the child's behavioral and emotional functioning would need to be conducted if symptoms suggestive of a disorder in this area are presented. Behavioral evaluation through rating scales, observations, and interview has been discussed previously. Evaluation of emotional functioning can include structured and unstructured play observation, or use of projective drawings or storytelling techniques. It is possible for children even in the preschool range to have lowered self-esteem and to develop a self-concept of a troublemaker or pest. Particularly if symptoms of ADHD have been present since the toddler years, the preschool child most likely has received much negative feedback for his or her behavior related to symptoms of overactivity, distractibility, and poor attention. Even if primary emotional or behavioral problems are not present during the preschool years, the risk of secondary emotional adjustment problems should be considered.

Case example. Michael is a 4-year, 11-month-old boy of average height and weight, who was brought to the clinic by his mother (H.) for screening. The screening exam included intake interview with the mother, semistructured parental interview regarding *DSM-IV* criteria for disruptive behavior disorders, and review of behavioral checklists completed by the mother and a recent preschool teacher.

Initial contact with the mother began with her statement that she is a single (divorced) mother, and that Michael was "driving (her) crazy." The mother wept frequently during the initial interview as she described the stress in her current family situation due to Michael's behavior. She reported that she was divorced from Michael's father when Michael was 2 years old, and does not know the whereabouts of the father. He provides no financial support and has not been in contact with the family since the divorce. H. has a 2-year-old son who is the biological sibling of Michael. She currently works 9-hr shifts as a waitress 6 days a week but is threatened with losing her job due to frequent absences to take care of Michael. She has lost numerous babysitters, who have refused to continue caring for Michael due to his noncompliant, risk-taking, and hyperactive behavior. Michael has attended three daycare and preschool programs but has been expelled from each after brief periods of time because of his disruptiveness and aggression. He is in perpetual movement, talks excessively, and often intrudes into the activities of other children. The mother described how Michael will not follow her directions, is openly defiant with her, and seems to be controlling the household. She said that she gives in to Michael rather than endure his tantrums and demanding behavior. Although she acknowledged that this may make his behavior worse, she reported that she is "too tired" to fight the battles with Michael any longer. Now, her 2-year-old son is beginning to show similar symptoms, and she is concerned that he will be equally difficult to manage as he gets older.

Prior medical history was unremarkable with regard to the pregnancy, labor, and delivery. Michael has had occasional ear infections, but no serious illnesses or injuries that would be expected to affect his development. The mother reported that she did not use alcohol or drugs during pregnancy or since pregnancy but reported that her former husband had abused alcohol during their marriage. He was not physically abusive to the mother or to Michael. Michael's developmental milestones were met at the expected times, and his development appeared to be normal intellectually, motorically, and linguistically. However, he has not developed age-appropriate social skills with peers, and in fact is rejected by most peers because of his aggressive and intrusive behavior. The mother lives alone in a small apartment with Michael and her other son and has extended family support from the maternal grandparents, who live nearby.

Assessment of behavioral functions included the interview with the mother, phone interview with the most recent preschool teacher, behavioral rating scales completed by the mother and the most recent preschool teacher, direct observations of Michael's behavior, and direct observations of parent–child interaction. Interview with the mother regarding primary symptoms revealed that Michael met *DSM-IV* criteria for both ADHD-combined type (severe) and ODD. However, due to the intensity of the mother's distress and self-described depression, it was felt to be necessary to obtain corroborative information from direct observations in the clinic and from other informants. Michael's most recent preschool teacher, who had worked with him for a period of 6 months prior to the current evaluation, was willing to complete the Conners Questionnaire (Conners, 1989) and Achenbach Child Behavior Checklist (CBCL; Achenbach & Edelbrock, 1983), as well as engage in a phone interview regarding primary symptoms. She described Michael as being extremely active and disruptive in the classroom, but she did not observe him to be aggressive or noncompliant within the structured classroom environment. However, in an unstructured setting such as the playground, he played roughly with the other children, often pushing them or demanding his way. He often seemed to come to school angry, and he carried these feelings through the day. He was ultimately expelled from the preschool due to complaints of other parents about his rough behavior during free-play time. The teacher described Michael as an endearing youngster who seemed very needy for attention, and who had learned many negative attention-seeking behaviors. The teacher's responses to the Conners Questionnaire revealed clinically significant elevations on the Conduct Problems factor (*T* score = 77), the Hyperactivity factor (*T* score = 75), and the Hyperactivity Index (*T* score = 73). The mother's responses to the Conners Questionnaire revealed elevations in all the factors at greater than the 90th percentile, indicating that the mother perceived a clinically significant level of problems in conduct, learning, psychosomatic complaints, impulsive–

hyperactive behavior, and anxiety. Likewise, on the CBCL, the mother's responses were elevated in the internalizing areas of social withdrawal, depression, immaturity, and somatic complaints as well as the externalizing areas of aggression and delinquency. Based on the data obtained to this point, the differential diagnosis could include ADHD, ODD, or both. Significant learning problems have been ruled out, with the exception of motor skills problems that might interfere with beginning schoolwork. The possibility of more severe emotional problems remains as well, though this seems unlikely given the information thus far. On the basis of the screening it was decided that a more comprehensive evaluation was needed to provide additional information to assist with the differential diagnosis.

For the comprehensive evaluation, Michael came to the clinic as an attractive, gregarious, smiling young boy who eagerly asked to come with the examiner and explore the building. He showed no signs of anxiety or oppositional behavior at the outset of testing. He cooperated in completing the Wechsler Preschool and Primary Scale of Intelligence–Revised (Wechsler, 1989) but was noted to be highly distractible and extremely talkative throughout the testing period. He achieved a Verbal IQ score of 126, a Performance IQ score of 116, and a Full-Scale IQ score of 125. He proudly counted from 1 to 100, recited all the alphabet correctly, and spelled his first name for the examiner. He stated that he was ready to begin school with the "big kids" so he could ride the school bus each day. Measures of language, motor, and perceptual functioning were somewhat variable. Michael's performance on the Preschool Language Scale–3 (Zimmerman, Steiner, & Pond, 1992) was congruent with his intellectual functioning, with an Auditory Comprehension score of 125, Expressive Communication score of 127, and a Total Language score of 129. Michael's performance on motor tasks was in the low-average-to-borderline range, however. On the Beery Test of Visual–Motor Integration (Beery, 1982), he copied only three designs correctly and achieved a standard score of 79 with a corresponding age equivalent of 3 years, 6 months. On the McCarthy Scales of Children's Abilities (McCarthy, 1972), his performance on the Motor scale fell between 1 and 1.5 standard deviations below the mean for his age. He had difficulty with gross motor tasks involving balance, skipping, catching a bean bag, and throwing toward a target. He had difficulty with fine motor and graphomotor tasks involving copying geometric shapes and drawing a person. Michael's visual perception abilities were excellent when the motor component was removed from the task. His performance on the Motor Free Visual Perception Test (Colarusso & Hammill, 1972) resulted in a Perceptual Quotient of 118. Finally, evaluation of adaptive functioning using the Vineland Adaptive Behavior Scales (Sparrow, Balla, & Cicchetti, 1984) revealed extreme variability in scores based on the mother's perception. A relative strength was noted on the Communication Domain, with a score of 120, compared with low average scores in the Daily Living Skills Domain (standard score 83) and Motor Skills Domain (standard score 85). The lowest rating was on the Socialization Domain with a score of 71. Based on evaluation of current intellectual, preacademic, language, perceptual, and motor functions, Michael appeared to have focal deficits in the area of fine motor, gross motor, and visuomotor integration skills but to be functioning at an average to bright–average level in all other areas. However, the variable ratings on the adaptive measure suggested that behavioral or ADHD factors may have been interfering with his daily functioning to a significant degree.

Because of concerns about the parent–child relationship, Michael and his mother were observed in a playroom setting using the Eyberg et al. (1993) Parent–Child Interaction Dyadic Coding System–II. The 15-min observation revealed that Michael complied with his mother's commands only 21% of the time (compared with an expected 64% compliance rate for his age). Michael also had more than the expected number (i.e., 3 to 6) of deviant behaviors within a 15-min period, including whining, yelling at his mother, sassing, destructive play, and striking at his mother on two occasions following her insistence that he pick up a toy. On the other hand, it was noted that the mother used frequent critical statements, responded to Michael each time he exhibited an inappropriate or deviant behavior (which provided attention and reinforcement for his negative behaviors), and tended to engage in verbal battles with Michael, which he prolonged. The mother's commands tended to be nondirect, saying, "let's pick up the toys," or asking, "would you pick up the toys now?" rather than stating directly that she wanted him to pick up the toys. The mother often gave several commands in succession without allowing Michael the opportunity to comply, and he often responded by ignoring her. Thus, the parent–child interaction revealed numerous problems related to Michael's oppositional–defiant behavior. The 15-min observation also revealed periods of several minutes during which Michael sat at a small table playing appropriately with toys of his choosing. He eagerly showed his mother his block-building skills and asked for her approval. Her response often was to nod or provide an unenthusiastic approval, rather than expressing strong interest in his achievements. A later interview with the mother revealed several clinical signs of depression, including recent decreased appetite and weight loss of approximately 10 pounds, difficulty sleeping, prolonged bouts of crying, and difficulty keeping her mind on her job. She reported that she dreaded returning home in the evening because of Michael's demands for attention and his anger when she was not forthcoming. She reported that her symptoms of depression had been present to a mild degree for the past 2 years, but had become worse in the last month. She had not sought medical or psychological treatment but was willing to accept a referral at this time.

The evaluation of the presenting question with regard to ADHD and ODD was less clear given the familial situation, particularly with regard to the mother's depressive symptoms and problems in parent–child interaction. Following the initial evaluation of Michael, a diagnosis was deferred pending involvement of the mother and Michael in a treatment program to allow for more prolonged observation of the parent–child interaction, direct observations of Michael's behavior, and Michael's response to behavioral interventions. A subsequent interview with the maternal grandparents revealed their willingness to provide caretaking for Michael and his brother and a respite for the mother for a brief period during which she could receive treatment and rest for her own symptoms. The mother subsequently was evaluated for depression and was prescribed medication for symptoms of a major depressive disorder. Within approximately 3 weeks, she reported a significant reduction in her symptoms and a willingness to become involved in a parent–child behavioral treatment program with Michael. The model of parent training called Parent–Child Interaction Therapy, described by Eyberg and Boggs (1989), was used. This program is a two-stage parent training model for noncompliant children that involves direct coaching of the parent during parent–child play interactions and sequential training in differential social attention and time-out. The intervention involved the mother and Michael attending weekly sessions for approximately 14 weeks, until behavioral assessment revealed that improvement in oppositional–defiant symptomatology had occurred. In the case of Michael and his mother, the first stage of training involved working with the mother to help her attend to Michael's positive attention-seeking behaviors, praise appropriate behavior, and use withdrawal of her attention rather than criticism for negative attention-seeking behaviors. Michael's response to the change in his mother's behavior was immediate, and over the first several weeks of intervention he exhibited calmer behavior, more prolonged periods of quiet play and conversation with his mother, a decrease in negative behaviors (whining, yelling, and physically destructive behavior), and reduced activity and agitation. The second stage of the program involved teaching the mother to use direct commands rather than indirect and to follow a system of providing a command, one warning, and then consequences involving use of a time-out chair for noncompliant behavior. Michael quickly learned to listen to the mother's direct commands and he usually complied after a warning had been given. As time progressed, the warnings were unnecessary and Michael successfully avoided the consequence of the time-out chair in clinic. Generalization to the home environment worked equally well, as H. successfully carried out the carefully rehearsed procedures in the home environment. About midway through the program, Michael reentered a preschool program. No direct intervention was provided in the preschool, but subsequent teacher reports indicated no problems with overactive, destructive, aggressive, or noncompliant behavior either in the structured classroom setting or on the playground during free play. Assessment of Michael's behavioral functioning using the Conners and CBCL at the end of treatment revealed that there were no clinically significant elevations by either parent or teacher report. Review of primary symptoms of ADHD and ODD with both parent and teacher revealed that Michael did not meet criteria for either disorder by the end of the treatment period. At both 3-month and 6-month follow-up sessions, Michael continued to maintain the positive changes in his behavior, and H. maintained her adherence to the routines learned in the behavioral intervention program. The mother continued to receive psychotherapy and she reported that her symptoms of depression were reduced.

This case illustrates the necessity of considering familial factors as they may influence a child's level of agitation and activity. It also illustrates that severe oppositional–defiant behavior may sometimes present in the form of ADHD, whereas treatment of the oppositional–defiant symptoms may reduce both the overactivity and the oppositional–defiant behaviors. In our clinic, preschoolers who present with significant oppositional behavior often undergo Parent–Child Interaction Therapy prior to our making a differential diagnosis of ADHD versus ODD in order to sort out more carefully the nature and the etiology of the presenting symptoms.

Assessment of children during the early to middle school-age years. Assessment for ADHD during the school-age years often involves making a differential diagnosis among ADHD-predominantly inattentive type, ADHD-predominantly hyperactive–impulsive type, or ADHD-combined type; learning disabilities; anxiety or other internalizing disorders; and a variety of disruptive behavioral disorders. The screening evaluation described earlier is a helpful starting point for surveying the symptomatology related to the differential diagnosis. However, given the risk for comorbid learning and behavioral problems among school-age children, it is often necessary to conduct a more comprehensive evaluation to provide appropriate intervention. The neuropsychological conceptualization for evaluation of school-age children with ADHD described in Table 2 provides a useful model.

Prior to beginning formalized evaluation, one should undertake a structured interview with a parent (and teacher, if available) to elicit additional information regarding primary symptoms and concerns. Furthermore, a developmental history obtained from the parent will provide information about the chronicity of the symptoms as well as associated health, developmental, school, and family factors that need to be considered.

Direct observation of the child's behavior should be included in the formal evaluation of a school-age child with ADHD. The Restricted Academic Situation Observation, described by Barkley (1990) and discussed in the section on evaluation of preschool-age children, provides a useful observational paradigm for school-age children. Typically, children in this age range are asked to complete a packet of math problems independently while alone in a clinic play room, with observers coding behavior from behind a one-way mirror. The child's behavior is scored according to the amount of time he or she is off task, fidgeting, out of seat, vocalizing, or playing with objects. If classroom observations are possible, then the CBCL–Direct Observation Form (Achenbach, 1986) is a useful measure. It is comparable to the parent and teacher report forms of the CBCL, with scores provided for mean time on tasks, total problems, and total internalizing and externalizing symptoms. It is recommended that each child be observed on three or more occasions for at least 10 min each, so that the observer can take the average of the observations for that particular setting (Achenbach, 1986; Barkley, 1990). This is the only observational system with normative data for elementary-age children during classroom observation. Its scales were empirically developed and have been shown to discriminate among various types of child psychopathology and their behavioral profiles (McConaughy & Achenbach, 1988; McConaughy, Achenbach, & Gent, 1988). Also, direct observation of child behavior can occur during administration of tests of vigilance, such as the GDS (Gordon, 1983). Research has indicated that such observations may be sensitive in discriminating children with ADHD from other diagnostic groups (Barkley, DuPaul, & McMurray, 1990). Other direct observation methods are listed in Exhibit 4.

Observation of parent–child interactions also may be useful if there are concerns or questions about the child's compliance and the occurrence of oppositional or defiant behaviors. Procedures outlined in the section on evaluating preschool children may be applied for young school-age children as well. The parent–child interaction models described by Eyberg and colleagues (Eyberg et al., 1993) or Forehand and colleagues (Forehand & McMahon, 1981) are typically useful up to the age of 7 years, and less appropriate for older youngsters. Barkley's coding system for Playroom Observations of Mother–Child Interactions is useful for children under and over the age of 7 years. This system is fully described and accompanied by sample coding sheets in Barkley's texts (Barkley, 1981, 1987).

Formal evaluation of the school-age child begins with assessment of cognitive and academic functioning to rule in or rule out a learning disability or other problems with academic achievement. This portion of the evaluation is particularly helpful when children present with school failure, and the etiology is unclear. The school failure may result from interference related to symptoms of ADHD, or may be due to lowered cognitive functioning or a learning disability. This differential diagnosis needs to be explored. The Wechsler or other age-appropriate intelligence scales may be selected. Academic achievement measures that sample a broad range of academic functioning and include writing samples as a measure of written language are useful (see Table 2).

Measurement of attention in the school-age child follows guidelines set forth in the literature discussed earlier. The various aspects of attention (focus–execute, sustain, encode, inhibit, shift) are measured systematically to survey the range and severity of problems. The attention function of focusexecute or initiate may be tapped through the WISC-III Coding and Symbol Search subscales (Wechsler, 1990), which require vigilance and rapid performance of visuomotor tasks within a specific time limit. The FAS fluency task (Benton & Hamsher, 1983) also taps this functional area by requiring the child to recite as many words as possible beginning with the letters *f*, *a*, and *s* within a specific time frame. The functional area of sustained attention can be tapped through continuous performance tests such as the GDS Vigilance Task (Gordon, 1983), particularly attending to the errors of omission. The Vigilance task requires the child to press a button each time a specific numerical sequence (e.g., a 1 followed by a 9) appears on a screen. Research indicates that this task discriminates children with ADHD from children without ADHD (Barkley, DuPaul, & McMurray, 1990; Gordon & Mettelman, 1988). Its advantages include standardized administration procedures, reliable results, and normative data. However, the GDS Vigilance task also has been reported to have a high number of false negatives (i.e., underidentifying children who actually meet criteria for ADHD by other established standards). This factor should be kept in mind by the practitioner when deciding how much weight to give GDS scores in the overall diagnostic decision-making process (DuPaul, Anastopoulos, Shelton, Guevremont, & Metevia, 1992; Gordon, DiNiro, & Mettelman, 1988). The encode aspect of attention taps numerical–mnemonic functions, as measured by the WISC-III Digit Span and Arithmetic subtests. The inhibit aspect of attention taps mental control and impulsivity and is measured by tests such as the Stroop Color and Word Test (C. J. Golden, 1978), the Matching Familiar Figures Test (Cairns & Cammock, 1978; Kagan, 1966), and the GDS Vigilance task (errors of commission). The Stroop Color and Word Test is a brief screening measure appropriate for Grades 2 and up that requires a child to read a list of color names in which no name is printed in its matching color. The Matching Familiar Figures Test is a match-to-sample test in which the child must match a picture with an identical picture from among an array of six similar images. The longer version of the Matching test has 20 stimulus trials and is reported to have greater reliability among older children and adolescents (Cairns & Cammock, 1978; Messer & Brodzinski, 1981), but has not always been shown to discriminate between children with and without ADHD (Barkley, DuPaul, & McMurray, 1990; Fischer et al., 1990). Finally, the GDS Vigilance task provides an indicator of impulsivity through measurement of errors of commission, in which the child responds to an incorrect stimulus sequence. The final functional area of attention relates to mental flexibility or the shift dimension. The WCST (Heaton, 1981) assesses the ability to form abstract concepts and to shift and maintain the set. The Trails B test from the Halstead–Reitan Neuropsychological Test Battery (Reitan, 1979) assesses speed of visual search, mental flexibility, attention, and motor function. The intermediate form of Trails B for children ages 9 through 14 has normative data for each year, and the adult form is used for adolescents aged 15 and older.

Memory functions in the school-age child may be tapped by a number of recently developed measures. The assessment of memory problems in children with ADHD is complicated because of interference from variable attention or poorly sustained attention on tasks. The practitioner must watch for behavioral indications of variable attention during the memory task, but even this is not always sufficient for discriminating between the effects of poor memory versus poor attention. By varying the dimensions of memory assessed (e.g., according to sensory modality, recall versus recognition, immediate versus delay, and motor output versus verbal output), one can better understand the relative influence of attention versus memory functions on task performance. The Wide Range Assessment of Memory and Learning (Sheslow & Adams, 1990) includes three tests of verbal memory, three tests of visual memory, and three tests assessing the child's ability to learn novel information across repeated trials. Several of the subtests have immediate and delayed trials. This test is appropriate for children and adolescents ages 5 to 17 years. The Test of Memory and Learning (C. R. Reynolds & Bigler, 1994) is a new memory assessment tool that measures verbal memory, nonverbal memory, and delayed recall, with supplementary composite scores that include a Learning Index, Attention and Concentration Index, Sequential Recall Index, Free Recall Index, and an Association Recall Index. The test is appropriate for children and adolescents ages 5 through 19 years. The Children's Auditory Verbal Learning Test–2 (Talley, 1993) yields measures of immediate memory span, level of learning, immediate recall, delayed recall, recognition accuracy, and total intrusions. The test is composed of one recognition and two free-recall memory word lists designed specially for children and adolescents from ages 6 years, 6 months to 17 years, 11 months. The first free-recall word list is presented for five trials, and the second free-recall word list is presented as an interference test, after which the individual is asked to recall words from the first list. Following a brief delay, the individual is asked to recall the initial word list for a second time. Finally, a new recognition list is presented and the individual must decide whether each word was included in the original free-recall word list. Normative data are provided for this measure. These recently developed tests of memory and learning are a superb addition to the literature in clinical assessment of children's memory and provide the practitioner a broad range of options.

Finally, assessment of the school-age child must include attention to emotional and personality functioning to determine whether primary or secondary emotional factors accompany the symptoms of ADHD. As a group, children with ADHD are reported to have more symptoms of anxiety, depression, and low self-esteem than children without ADHD (Breen & Barkley, 1983, 1984; Margalit & Arieli, 1984). Szatmari et al. (1989b) also reported that co-occurrence of behavioral and emotional disorders with ADHD is quite common. In their survey, up to 44% of individuals with ADHD had at least one other psychiatric disorder, and 32% had two other disorders. Therefore, evaluation for co-occurrence of emotional psychopathology is an important part of the comprehensive assessment of children with ADHD. The range of possible measures is very high, but a representative battery might include the CBCL (previously discussed), Roberts Apperception Test for Children (McArthur & Roberts, 1982), the Reynolds Child Depression Scale (W. M. Reynolds, 1989), The State–Trait Anxiety Inventory for Children (Spielberger, 1973), and the Revised Children's Manifest Anxiety Scale (C. R. Reynolds & Richmond, 1985). Certainly other projective measures, clinical interview, and behavioral rating scales might be used in addition to those mentioned, but the current battery is suggested because it includes measures sensitive to symptoms of depression, anxiety, and externalizing behavioral problems.

Case example. Jamie is an attractive 11-year, 5-month-old boy currently placed in fifth grade. He was referred for evaluation by his pediatrician, who cited a long history of academic and school performance problems, distractibility, and noncompliant behavior at home. Jamie has never been referred for psychological evaluation in the past, and referral questions involve ruling out ADHD, a learning disability, and a possible ODD.

The initial interview with Jamie's mother revealed that she had made repeated attempts to convince the school psychometrist to evaluate Jamie but had been told by teachers that Jamie is merely unmotivated and disorganized, but capable of grade-appropriate work if he only tries. Jamie frequently does not remember to write down assignments, does not turn in assignments that are completed, loses books and materials necessary for academic work, and is particularly resistive to homework or classwork that involves writing. An interview with the teacher revealed that Jamie is well liked. He was described as warm, sensitive, gregarious, polite, and helpful to the teachers, yet at the same time he exhibits impulsive, distractible, overactive, disorganized, and unmotivated behavior. Jamie's school performance has been variable, with grades ranging from *A*s to *F*s over the course of the previous school year. He had been retained 1 year (first grade) because of supposed immaturity, but had never received special education services.

Early medical history revealed perinatal risk factors associated with postterm (44-week) gestation, moderate maternal alcohol use and heavy smoking during pregnancy, and a 46-hr labor complicated by maternal pre-eclampsia. Jamie was initially hypoxic and cyanotic at birth, with Apgar scores of 5 at 1 min and 9 at 5 min. He required treatment in the neonatal intensive care unit due to metabolic acidosis, meconium aspiration, and hyperbilirubinemia requiring phototherapy for 4–5 days. He was discharged home at 6 days, and subsequently did well until he contracted Rocky Mountain Spotted Fever at age 10 years. Elevated temperature to 105° persisted for 1 week, accompanied by hallucinations. However, he recovered from this disease without residual liver, spleen, or kidney damage and without noticeable changes in behavior, learning ability, or activity and attentional level. Otherwise, Jamie had been healthy.

Developmental milestones were attained at the expected ages, although Jamie was described by his mother as being "extremely clumsy" and poor at athletics. Jamie's father reported that he was exceptionally well-coordinated and excelled at sports. Discrepancies in parental history were apparent in a number of areas, as will be illustrated.

Family history was remarkable for parental divorce when Jamie was 5 years old following 3 to 4 years of marital conflict. Divorce was followed by a prolonged custody battle, during which the mother and Jamie lived briefly with a boyfriend who physically abused both of them. The mother remarried when Jamie was 8 years old, and Jamie was placed in her custody. He had a stepbrother 7 months younger, who was described as "extremely compliant." Jamie's mother and father provided highly conflicting histories that reflected their different perceptions of Jamie's behavior, school performance, and general functioning. Jamie's mother is an extremely organized person who described Jamie as impulsive, irresponsible, disorganized, forgetful, and unable to control himself. The father, who is relaxed and easygoing, described Jamie as having no behavioral or adjustment problems. The teachers reported that Jamie can be very disruptive in class, talks excessively, and has difficulty keeping his hands to himself and staying in his seat. He has low tolerance for frustration or failure and does not work up to his full potential.

Given the broad range of presenting concerns, the neuropsychologist conducted a comprehensive evaluation. Measurement of cognitive functioning on the WISC-III revealed a Verbal IQ score of 115, Performance IQ score of 110, and Full-Scale IQ score of 113—all of which are in the high average range. However, variability was noted among the four factor scores derived from the WISC-III, with relative strengths noted on the Verbal Comprehension Index (standard score [SS] = 118) and Perceptual Organization Index (SS = 111) compared with the Processing Speed Index (SS = 91) and the Freedom From Distractibility Index (SS = 87). Scaled scores on the WISC-III ranged from 5 to 15, with relative weaknesses on the Digit Span (SS = 5), Symbol Search (SS = 6), and Picture Completion (SS = 7) subtests. This performance suggests difficulty with short-term auditory memory or attention, speed of information processing, and attention to visual detail.

Assessment of academic achievement was based on comparisons to an expected standard score of 108, derived from a regression formula applied to Jamie's WISC-III Full-Scale IQ of 113. Given this comparison, Jamie's performance was in the expected range on the Woodcock–Johnson Psychoeducational Battery–Revised Tests of Achievement on all measures of reading (including word identification, comprehension, and phonetic analysis skills) and mathematics reasoning. However, Jamie's performance was significantly discrepant from the expected level in the area of math calculation (SS = 87) and several areas of written language (grammatic usage, punctuation and capitalization, spelling, and proofing). Further evaluation of written language was obtained from the Test of Written Language–2 (Hammill & Larsen, 1988), which revealed a Spontaneous Writing Quotient of 68. On this task requiring Jamie to create a written story related to a picture, his performance was deficient in thematic maturity, contextual spelling, and contextual style. Qualitative analysis of his writing revealed extremely poor production of letters, inappropriate use of punctuation, and extremely poor spelling, which resulted in writing samples that were poorly legible and incoherent. In contrast, Jamie's ability to produce stories orally was excellent, revealing a rich and sophisticated vocabulary, creative ideas, and good use of grammar and syntax. Jamie's performance on these tests of academic achievement suggest that he has a specific learning disability in two areas: mathematics calculation and written expression.

Assessment of attention was subdivided into several components. The focus–execute function was assessed through the Coding and Symbol Search subtests of the WISC-III. Jamie's average scaled score on the WISC-III was 11.3, but the Coding scaled score was 9 and the Symbol Search scaled score was 6. Jamie not only worked more slowly than would be expected for his age on these tasks but made errors of commission as well. His performance suggested difficulty with the focus–execute dimension of attention. Measurement of sustained attention involved use of the GDS Vigilance task and Distractibility task. On both tasks, Jamie's errors of omission were in the abnormal range for his chronologic age, suggesting significant difficulty with sustained attention. Observations of his behavior during the task revealed that he talked about extraneous matters as the task was going on, moved from his seat to the window on one occasion during the Vigilance task, and complained that he lost his place on several occasions. He appeared frustrated by the Distractibility task and asked if it could be ended early. The encode aspect of attention was measured with the WISC-III Digit Span and Arithmetic subtests. Jamie's arithmetic functioning was at the average level with a scaled score of 10. He appeared to use compensation strategies of rehearsal and counting on his fingers to facilitate his performance. However, he achieved only a scaled score of 5 on Digit Span. He appeared to lose focus. Jamie's ability to inhibit or control impulsive behavior was measured from the GDS Vigilance task by assessing errors of commission. Again, Jamie's responses were in the abnormal range for chronologic age, and behavioral observations corroborated impulsive behavior on the GDS and also throughout the remainder of the evaluation.

Assessment of memory functions was obtained from the Wide Range Assessment of Memory and Learning. Jamie had superior performance on the Verbal Memory scale, with a standard score of 121. His score reflected superior performance on recall of the main ideas of a story (SS = 16) and verbatim recall of sentences (SS = 15). However, recall of number or letter sequences was average (SS = 9). In contrast, Jamie's Visual Memory Index was only 89, which is in the low average range. His performance was consistent across the three subtests tapping picture memory (SS = 8), reproduction of geometric designs (SS = 9), and reproduction of finger movement patterns (SS = 8). Jamie's Learning Index was average at a standard score of 98, but his performance was variable depending on the modality of the learning task. His performance on a verbal learning (serial word list) measure was a relative strength, with a standard score of 12. In contrast, his visual learning score was borderline at a standard score of 7, and his performance on a sound–symbol association measure was average at a standard score of 10. Jamie's performance on the Wide Range test provides clues about his information processing strengths and the weaknesses that most likely underlie his learning disability.

Assessment of social and behavioral functioning was accomplished through interviews with the mother and father, interview with Jamie, and review of behavioral checklists completed by the parents and teacher. The interview with the father revealed no concerns about attention, hyperactivity, learning, or behavioral problems. The structured interview with the mother using the *DSM-IV* Checklist of Primary Symptoms of ADHD revealed that Jamie meets criteria for ADHD-predominantly inattentive type by meeting 8 of the 9 symptoms at a level that is considered to cause significant distress in his daily functioning. The particular symptoms involve failing to give close attention to details, making careless errors in schoolwork, having difficulty sustaining his attention on tasks, not listening to what is being said to him, not following through on instructions or completing homework, often losing things necessary for tasks or activities, and being easily distracted and forgetful. The mother's responses to the Conners Questionnaire revealed ratings in the clinically significant range on the factors of learning problems, impulsivity, and the hyperactivity index. The father's responses to the Conners revealed no clinically significant concerns. However, the teacher's responses to the Conners were congruent with the mother's, revealing ratings in the clinically significant range for inattention–passivity, hyperactivity, and the hyperactivity index. The mother expressed concerns about Jamie's compliance and ability to follow rules, but neither the teacher nor the father had concerns in this area. Interview with the mother indicated that her concerns about Jamie's behavior could be explained by his symptoms of ADHD, in that he was forgetful about chores, disorganized, sloppy, and failed to follow through on directions without distraction. She admitted that her personality style and Jamie's personality style were quite different, and that the ADHD symptoms were particularly bothersome to her. She did not endorse symptoms that suggested an ODD, as Jamie was not deliberately defiant, aggressive, or argumentative with the mother. Interview with Jamie revealed a perception that things were much more relaxed and pleasant for him at his dad's home, and he felt less pressure when he was staying with his father. He admitted that his mother was often angry at him, and seemed to nag a lot.

Projective evaluation with Jamie revealed that his primary concerns related to the conflict between his parents and reflected his sadness and anxiety about being caught in the middle of the parental battleground. He expressed a desire to live with his father rather than his mother, although acknowledging his affection for his mother and his desire for her approval. Other than the distress related to his parents' conflict, there were no indications of significant emotional pathology.

This case illustrates the comorbidity of a learning disability and ADHD-predominantly inattentive type in a child with good social skills and the ability to win the teachers' approval and affection. His social prowess most likely contributed to the teachers minimizing his academic and attentional difficulty in the classroom. He was misperceived as unmotivated and lazy, but was well liked and often forgiven for his infractions. The evaluation revealed two areas of disability that resulted in Jamie's becoming eligible for special education services within the schools: learning disability and ADHD. A meeting with school officials resulted in Jamie's receiving itinerant services from the special education teacher certified in learning disabilities, who consulted with Jamie's regular classroom teachers about curriculum modifications to address his learning disability and ADHD. Specific recommendations with regard to his learning disability involved reduction in the quantity of writing assignments, teaching Jamie keyboard skills so that he could use a typewriter or a word processor for completing assignments, allowing Jamie the opportunity to take tests and present book reports orally at times, and monitoring his need for assistance in mathematics calculation. School interventions related to Jamie's ADHD included assistance with organization by assuring that all assignments were written down, that the correct study materials were taken home each evening, and that completed homework assignments were turned in daily. Special instruction was provided with regard to study habits, including organization of study materials and notebooks for keeping assignments; breaking assignments into small steps with frequent feedback as to progress or completion of tasks; and reducing distraction in the classroom environment to the extent possible, or allowing Jamie the opportunity for small group work away from the larger classroom environment. Recommendations to the parents included monitoring of completion of homework assignments; maintaining a structured and organized time and place for study; reminders and positive reinforcement for Jamie's remembering to turn in assignments daily; using tangible reminders for daily chores, such as lists, tape-recorded messages, and so forth; and helping Jamie to identify compensation strategies for the potential school problems caused by his ADHD. The recommendation for both biological parents to be involved in therapy with Jamie was vehemently rejected by both parents.

Assessment of adolescents. The first stage of the assessment process with adolescents is similar to that used with younger children. Much of the initial data is provided by parents and teachers. For adolescents up to 18 years of age, the same behavioral rating scales can be used (see Exhibit 3). Teachers are asked to complete the CBCL, the Conners Teacher Rating Scale, the Attention Deficit Disorder Evaluation Scale (McCarney, 1989), and the ADD-Hyperactive Comprehensive Teacher Rating Scale (Ullman, Sleator, & Sprague, 1984). Parents are asked to complete the parent versions of the CBCL, the Attention Deficit Disorder Evaluation Scale, and the Conners Parent Rating Scale. Separate clinical interviews are conducted with the adolescent and the parents in order to identify problem areas. Adolescents often can provide information about their cognitive functioning, particularly their ability to complete tasks and focus on activities, though parents frequently may have different opinions. Furthermore, adolescents may be more willing to discuss certain emotional or behavioral problems without a parent present.

In addition to rating scales and interviews, observation of the adolescent's behavior is recommended. The adolescent should be observed in the classroom environment as well as the clinic setting. With observations in the clinic setting, structured cognitive tasks (e.g., solving mathematical problems) should be used while on- and off-task behavior is coded. The Restricted Academic Playroom Situation (Barkley, 1988a) requires the adolescent to complete mathematics problems in a clinic room that contains distracting objects. Behavior typically is coded in five behavioral categories (*off-task, fidgets, out of seat, vocalizes*, and *plays with objects*) during 10- or 15-s intervals. A similar, though less structured, procedure can be employed in the classroom setting. Observations of parent–adolescent interaction and communication, using the paradigm and coding system developed by Robin and Foster (1989), often is informative. Refer to Exhibit 4 for examples of direct observational methods.

The second stage of testing involves assessment of cognitive functions. Intellectual ability and achievement is assessed by one of the standard batteries. The Wechsler series of IQ tests are the most commonly used for measurement of ability. The WISC-III (Wechsler, 1990) is used for younger adolescents, and the Wechsler Adult Intelligence Scale–Revised (WAIS-R; Wechsler, 1981) is used for older adolescents. The Woodcock–Johnson Psychoeducational Battery–Revised Tests of Achievement (Woodcock & Johnson, 1989) and the Wechsler Individual Achievement Test (1992) are recommended for assessment of achievement levels. The latter is useful when IQ is measured with the WISC-III, because the tests share the same normative sample.

Attention and concentration is typically assessed with cancellation or other perceptual-motor tasks in combination with a continuous performance measure, such as the GDS (Gordon, 1983). See Exhibit 5 for further examples. Cancellation and perceptual motor tests include tasks involving sequential processing (Coding, Digit Symbol, Trails A, etc.) or mental flexibility (Trails B). The Stroop Color and Word Test (C. J. Golden, 1978) and the Paced Auditory Serial Addition Test (Gronwall, 1977) are useful in the assessment of mental control, and to a certain extent selective attention. The Stroop requires a selective attention process involving response inhibition, whereas the Paced test involves mental arithmetic and short-term memory. The focus–execute or initiate function can be assessed with the perceptual-motor tasks. Sustained attention can be assessed with the GDS or another Continuous Performance Test procedure. The WCST and Trails B are often used as measures of set-shifting or mental flexibility.

Memory and learning can be assessed either with a complete battery or by piecing together individual subtests. For younger adolescents, the Wide Range Assessment of Memory and Learning (Sheslow & Adams, 1990) or the newer Test of Memory and Learning (C. R. Reynolds & Bigler, 1994) can be used to obtain measures of verbal and visual immediate and delayed recall. Both of these batteries have subtests that present lists of information over respective trials to examine learning potential. Individual tests that are frequently employed, though are not as comprehensive as the batteries listed earlier, include the Rey Auditory Verbal Learning Test (Lezak, 1983) and the Rey-O (Spreen & Strauss, 1991). The former is a verbal list learning procedure that employs the use of a distracter. The Rey-O is a visuospatial memory test that also can be used as a measure of planning and organization because of the complexity of the design. The memory tests, along with Digit Span and the Paced test, are good measures of the encode function discussed previously.

Finally, assessment of emotional–personality functioning is suggested to aid in ruling out a primary depressive disorder or psychotic disorder. The Reynolds Child Depression Scale (W. M. Reynolds, 1989) or Reynolds Adolescent Depression Scale (W. M. Reynolds, 1987) and the State–Trait Anxiety Inventory–Children's Version, can be used as a guide to assessment of depression and anxiety. The Minnesota Multiphasic Personality Inventory–Adolescent Version (MMPI-A; Butcher, Graham, Williams, & Kaemmer, 1992) can be used up to 18 years of age to obtain a more detailed assessment of personality and emotional functioning.

Case example. Daniel is a 14-year, 4-month-old White male adolescent referred for neuropsychological evaluation to address poor performance in school. His parents were concerned primarily that he might have ADHD. Because Daniel was raised in a rural area of the state and attended a small school system, assessments for ADHD were not conducted when Daniel was younger. Although in mainstream classes, Daniel has a long history of academic failure; he has received special education services in a learning disability resource lab for mathematics since the second grade and for reading since the third grade. Daniel apparently repeated the second grade due to academic failure. Current school grades were reportedly *D*s and *F*s. Problems in social and behavioral interaction were also reported by his parents. Daniel's parents reported that Daniel has very few friends at school, though because they lived on a farm in an isolated area, interactions with peers were not readily available. Daniel frequently fought with his sisters as well as other children within the school system. Daniel was viewed by his parents as having a short fuse and was somewhat oppositional in terms of compliance with commands and chores. He was viewed as becoming easily frustrated, and he often reacted to this frustration with anger outbursts. Symptoms of depression or anxiety were denied by his parents. No major medical illnesses were reported and Daniel was described as reaching developmental milestones within the average range. Head injuries and loss of consciousness were also reported absent.

On the initial screening, observations of Daniel's behavior were recorded and rating scales were collected from the parents as well as two of his teachers. On the Conners Parent Rating Scale the parents independently reported that Daniel displayed a significant degree of hyperactive behavior, combined with learning problems and conduct problems. The *T* score on the Impulsive–Hyperactive Index was 76 for the mother and 81 for the father. The overall Hyperactivity Index was 90 for the mother and 92 for the father. The Psychosomatic and Anxiety indexes were within the normal range. Both parents also reported significant elevations on the Attention, Aggression, and Hyperactive indexes on the parents' version of the CBCL. The Conners Teacher Rating Scale and the ACTeRS were completed by two of Daniel's teachers. On the Conners for Teacher 1, the only significant elevation was on the Attention subscale, which fell at a *T* score of 75. This teacher also rated Daniel below the 10th percentile on the Attention scale from the ACTeRS. The Conners completed by the second teacher was significant for inattentive and hyperactive behavior, with *T* scores at 78 and 80, respectively. This teacher also placed Daniel below the 10th percentile on the Attention subscale from the ACTeRS, as well as at the 15th percentile for the Hyperactivity subscale. Observations of Daniel's behavior during current evaluation revealed inattentive and overactive behaviors. Daniel was observed to be in continual movement, though he was able to remain seated throughout the observation period. The overactive behavior was restricted to frequent limb movements.

The neuropsychological evaluation revealed several problem areas. On the WISC-III Daniel achieved a Verbal IQ of 89, a Performance IQ of 79, and a Full-Scale IQ of 83. Digit Span fell at a scaled score of 6, whereas Coding and Symbol Search fell at scaled scores of 4 and 5, respectively. Administration of the Woodcock–Johnson–Revised revealed a Broad Reading score of 99, a Broad Mathematics score of 76, and a Broad Written Language score of 76. Daniel was also administered the Wide Range Assessment of Memory and Learning, which revealed a General Memory Index of 85. The Verbal Memory Index score was 85, with scaled scores of 12, 7, and 4, for stories, sentences, and number–letter recall, respectively. The Visual Memory Index score was 81, with scaled scores of 10, 9, and 3, on picture memory, designs, and finger windows, respectively. Daniel was thus impaired on measures of encoding, as evidenced by his digit span and finger window performances. The GDS revealed abnormal scores for the Vigilance and Distractibility Tasks, with borderline performance on measures of impulsivity (errors of commission) during the distractibility portion, indicating deficits in sustaining attention. Poor planning and organization (initiation) of visuospatial construction was revealed by his standard score of 67 on the Rey-O. Reproduction of simple designs was in the normal range with a standard score of 97 on the Beery Visual Motor Integration Test. The Stroop Color and Word Test revealed delayed processing speed with *T* scores of 32 on word naming, 20 on color naming, and 27 on color-word naming. Mental flexibility or set shifting was also impaired as measured by the WCST, with standard scores of 61 for number of categories achieved, 69 for percentage of perseverative errors, and 58 for percentage of conceptual level. The Sensory Perceptual Examination was within normal limits with no tactile, auditory, or visual suppressions noted.

The results of this evaluation led to a diagnosis of an ADHD-combined type, because the primary cluster of symptoms appeared to be inattention combined with hyperactivity. Recommendations for treatment included a combined pharmacological therapy and behavioral management approach. This combined treatment approach led to significant improvements in compliance and reductions of oppositional behavior in the school and home envi- ronments. Over the next semester Daniel showed increases in his grades so that he was now receiving *B*s and *C*s. The behavioral management program also appeared to alleviate some of the aggressive tendencies that Daniel was displaying and improved interactions with his family.

Assessment of adults. The diagnosis of ADHD in adults often is more difficult than with children or adolescents. In the rare event that clear developmental and early educational data are available, the diagnostic process can move along with relative ease. However, frequently this information is not available, or when available it often is not clear. The validity of diagnosis of ADHD-RT in adults has been criticized because of its reliance on retrospective data and self-report from the patient (Denckla, 1991; Gualtieri et al., 1985). The Utah criteria for adult ADHD-RT are recommended to survey past and present symptoms (Wender et al., 1981). These criteria require the presence of ADHD symptomatology as a child, as well as current symptoms of hyperactivity and attentional deficits as an adult. The patient must have two of the characteristics encompassing poor attention, poor concentration or task persistence, and impulsivity (Denckla, 1991; Wender et al., 1981). Retrospective rating scales are useful in determining the history of ADHD symptoms during childhood. The Wender Utah Rating Scale (Ward et al., 1993) has been revised recently to aid in this process. This scale includes self-rating and parental rating sections. For each section the rater is instructed to rate items based on the patient's behavior between the ages of 6 and 10 years. The Hyperkinesis/Minimal Brain

Dysfunction Scale also has been used extensively to examine retrospective ratings of behavior in alcoholic and control populations (Tarter, McBride, Boupane, & Schneider, 1977). The items on this scale load on four factors: Hypomania/Impulsiveness, Attention/Social Problems, Antisocial Behavior, and Visuospatial Deficits (Alterman, Tarter, Baughman, Bober, & Fabian, 1985).

In addition to behavioral rating scales, the practitioner should conduct a thorough interview with the patient and obtain as much data on early education and development as possible. Obtaining information about current vocational functioning aids in assessing the impact of ADHD on current functioning.

As with adolescents, the second stage of testing involves assessment of cognitive functioning. In adults, intellectual ability is assessed with the WAIS-R (Wechsler, 1981). A brief academic screening of word recognition, spelling, and mathematics calculation can be accomplished with the Wide Range Achievement Test–Third Edition (Wilkinson, 1993). This test is usually sufficient, but it can be supplemented by the Woodcock–Johnson Psychoeducational Battery–Revised Tests of Achievement (Woodcock & Johnson, 1989) if performance is deficient.

Attention and concentration is assessed in a similar manner to that used with adolescents, as is memory and learning. Table 2 presents examples of the different tests that can be used in the evaluation.

Emotional–personality functioning is assessed with the MMPI-2 (Hathaway & McKinley, 1989), as well as the Beck Depression Inventory (Beck, 1987) and the State–Trait Anxiety Inventory (Spielberger, 1983). Of particular concern for comorbidity are the diagnoses of antisocial personality disorder, generalized anxiety disorder or other affective disorders, and substance abuse or dependence.

In addition to assessment of the standard cognitive processes, it is advised that tests to determine the likelihood of malingering also be included. Given that a diagnosis of ADHD in adults may lead to a prescription for stimulant medications (a highly addictive class of drugs), the practitioner is likely to be faced with individuals who are drug seeking. Forced choice memory tests are useful in identifying those individuals who are malingering. Performance that is significantly less than chance on a two-choice test indicates that the individual must have identified the correct answer in order to consistently give the incorrect answer.

Case example. C. is a 40-year-old man, employed as a manager in a machine shop. He reported a long history of problems with attention, concentration, overactivity, and impulsiveness. He stated that at times he feels as if his mind is in a fog. This fog was described as a feeling of being drained though not necessarily sleepy. He described interference from his attention and concentration problems in a variety of situations. He indicated that he has a difficult time finishing tasks that he begins. For example, in his carpentry business, which he reportedly enjoys immensely, he tends to start many projects without completing any of them. He often will begin one project, only to become distracted and switch to another project, only to move to yet a third project. Examples of impulsive behavior included saying things before thinking through the consequences. C. described feeling uneasy in group interactions because of his difficult time thinking and his tendency to become easily distracted. He described having trouble organizing his thoughts and planning events, and is reportedly late everywhere he goes. C. apparently has had these symptoms since childhood, when he was described as an impulsive and distractible child. During his late adolescent and early adult years, he reported a tendency toward substance abuse, though as an older adult he restricts his drinking to one to two beers per occasion. He will frequently drink 10–12 cups of coffee per day, and described his reaction to the coffee as being relaxing.

Observations from the initial screening revealed significant motor overactivity and distractibility. C. would frequently jump from one topic to another and frequently interrupt the examiner's conversation. Motor activity was restricted to limb movements. C. frequently tapped his foot or moved his hands about his chair. He had no problem remaining in his seat, though he would frequently shift around during the conversation. Rating scales completed at this time included the Wender Utah Rating Scale, with the addition of the parents' rating scale, and the Hyperkinesis/Minimal Brain Dysfunction Rating Scale.

Significant hyperactive behavior was reported on both of these scales; C. rated himself as being above the 99th percentile. On the parents' rating scale, which was completed by his mother, his performance was again above the 95th percentile. This scale required the mother to rate C.'s behavior when he was between the ages of 6 and 10 years.

The neuropsychological evaluation of C. included the WAIS-R, the Selective Reminding Test (Bushchke, 1973; Bushchke & Fuld, 1974), selected tests from the Wechsler Memory Scale–Revised (Wechsler, 1987), the Rey-O (Osterreith, 1944; Rey, 1941), the GDS, Trail-Making A and B from the Halstead battery (Reitan, 1979), the Stroop Color and Word Test, the WCST, and sensory and motor examinations. Emotional and personality functioning was also evaluated by the MMPI-2, the Beck Depression Inventory, and the State–Trait Anxiety Inventory.

On the WAIS-R, C. achieved a Verbal IQ of 106, a Performance IQ of 115, and a Full-Scale IQ of 110. The Digit Span scaled score was 8, whereas the Digit Symbol scaled score was 7. These were the two lowest scaled scores on the intellectual assessment. On the GDS, C. achieved normal performance on the Vigilance task, though he had borderline performance on the Distractibility task. A normal degree of errors of commission were present on both of these subtests. Additional assessment of attention and concentration revealed a score below the 10th percentile on Trail-Making A, as well as *T* scores of 40 for the word portion of the Stroop, 30 for the color naming, and 28 for the color-word naming. Thus, the focus–execute function appeared mildly to moderately impaired.

Memory assessment revealed significant problems in recall of verbal information. On story memory from the Wechsler Memory Scale–Revised, his performance was at the 14th percentile for immediate recall and at the 6th percentile for 30-min delay. Figure memory was at the 98th percentile for immediate recall and 94th percentile at delay. A measure of word learning and delayed recall (Selective Reminding Test) revealed a long-term storage standard score of 58, a consistent long-term retrieval standard score of 65, and a 30-min delayed recall standard score of 47. Encoding of verbal material was therefore judged to be significantly impaired. Average performance was present on the WCST. Average performance also was present on the Rey-O. Sensory examination revealed no suppressions in the tactile, auditory, or visual modalities. Assessment of emotional and personality functioning revealed a Beck Depression Inventory score of 8 and standard scores on the State–Trait Anxiety Inventory of 76 for State and 62 for Trait. The MMPI-2 was valid and indicated a mild degree of anxiety, with a *T* score of 67 on scale 7.

The results of this evaluation led to a conclusion that C. did indeed have ADHD. He was subsequently placed on a low dose of Ritalin, which was gradually increased to 20 mg twice a day. At this dose, C. reported significant improvement in his behavior. He subsequently was able to complete tasks that he has begun and displayed significant modification of his work habits. C. also participated for a brief period in a group therapy program. This program addressed issues of education concerning medication, as well as the etiology of ADHD. Problem-solving strategies also were discussed and appeared quite helpful to C.

Medical consultation. Medical consultation may be obtained either during the initial workup with the child for suspected ADHD or after the diagnosis is made. In our clinic, the physician often prefers to wait until psychological tests have been completed before being called for consultation. At that point, additional information is available regarding the nature and severity of ADHD symptoms so that a clearer recommendation can be made regarding a trial of stimulant medication. If the clinician is considering stimulant medication, the medical consultation can serve several purposes. First, the patient (or his or her parents) needs to be educated about the potential benefits and side effects of stimulant medication. The parents and often the teachers of children and adolescents with ADHD will be enlisted to monitor the child's response to medication if a trial of stimulants is begun. Second, the medical consultation can provide a baseline physical evaluation of the child's growth parameters so that the risks of appetite suppression and possible weight loss can be weighed in the context of current parameters. The medical exam can rule out thyroid dysfunction and assess for adrenal overactivity. Persons with thyroid dysfunction may have symptoms of overactivity that simulate ADHD, but they also will have other physical symptoms that make differential diagnosis clear. The medical exam also assesses for associated soft neurologic signs, motor uncoordination, enuresis or encopresis, sleep problems, otitis media, and allergies, all of which may be found at a higher rate in children with ADHD. Finally, the medical exam provides an opportunity for a thorough past medical history and family medical history to determine the presence of tics or Tourette's disorder, seizures, or other medical problems that might contraindicate the use of stimulant medications. The physician plays an important role in monitoring the dosage level and effectiveness of stimulant medication; this is discussed further in the next section of the chapter, along with other treatment approaches for ADHD.

TREATMENT OF CHILDREN, ADOLESCENTS, AND ADULTS WITH ADHD

Treatment of children and youth with ADHD typically involves multiple types of intervention over the course of the child's life, ranging from special education, tutoring, or other academic interventions in the school setting; parent training to assist with behavioral management; psychostimulant medication to address the primary symptoms of overactivity and reduced attention span; and individual treatment programs for the child or youth with ADHD, focused on such areas as social skills development, peer relations, anger management, or behavioral self-control. Although psychostimulant medication is by far the most common treatment for children and youth with ADHD, the most successful outcome occurs when medication is used in conjunction with other types of intervention that emphasize behavioral change. Usually intervention strategies will be chosen on the basis of the most significant concerns to the parents or teachers, the areas interfering most with the child's current functioning, the most salient or severe symptoms, or those symptoms having the greatest impact on later adjustment (Shelton & Barkley, 1993). Many interventions have been used with ADHD children, but not all have been effective. Currently, interventions that are unproven or that have been discredited include removal of sugar or food additives from the child's diet, megavitamin therapy, caffeine, removal of fluorescent lights, sensory motor integration therapy, biofeedback training, and treatment for inner ear disturbances. The treatments that have some proven efficacy are discussed in the following sections.

Educational and School Interventions

Classroom management of ADHD often is a challenge to school professionals, depending on the nature and severity of the symptoms. Even if no comorbid behavioral or learning problems are associated with ADHD, the primary symptoms can create disruptions for the child's individual learning as well as disruptions for peers in the classroom setting. Most children with ADHD will be educated in mainstream classes rather than more restrictive environments such as resource labs or self-contained special classes. The most common intervention involves the regular classroom teacher modifying the curriculum or structuring the classroom environment in such a way that it is more conducive for learning for the child with ADHD. However, some children with ADHD have symptoms so severe that learning is impaired in a regular classroom environment that has numerous distractions and activities. These children may need some periods of time throughout the day for work in small group settings with fewer distractions and with a smaller teacher–pupil ratio.

Only recently have children with ADHD been recognized under the Education for the Handicapped Act (Public Law 94-142), now known as the Individuals with Disabilities Education Act. These laws provide for a free and appropriate public education to all children who by reason of their disability require special education and related services. Children with ADHD most often receive services under the category "Other Health Impaired," though many are eligible for services under other categories as well, including "Learning Disability" and "Severely Emotionally Disturbed." Prior to 1991 or 1992, few children with ADHD were identified by school personnel as having a disability. This likely is related to the methods of assessment used in most schools that emphasize discrepancy formulas solely on the basis of numeric measures to determine disability and therefore eligibility for services (Learning Disabilities Association, 1991). Currently, schools nationwide are doing a better job of recognizing that ADHD is a disability that can interfere with school functioning, and they are working to assure that appropriate evaluations are being done. Children and youth whose symptoms of ADHD can be shown to interfere with academic achievement may receive special education services and an Individualized Education Plan.

Special education services vary in the degree of restrictiveness, with the least restrictive services involving monitoring of the child's progress in the regular classroom, consultation with the regular education teacher, or both. The special education teacher can provide consultation on behavioral management techniques or ways to structure the classroom environment, to create a setting that is more conducive to learning for the child with ADHD. Suggestions often used in the classroom include preferential seating (so that the child with ADHD may be close to the teacher's desk or away from distracting stimuli in the classroom, such as air conditioners, windows, high traffic areas, etc.); increasing the structure and organization in the classroom so that a consistent routine is followed; and surrounding the child with good peer role models, to encourage peer tutoring and collaborative learning. Often an area of the classroom may be developed that has reduced distractions, so the child with ADHD can work in that setting at times. However, it is important to let all students have access to the area so the child with ADHD will not feel different.

Teachers may need to implement more formalized behavior management strategies with the child who has ADHD. These may include token reinforcement systems, increased attention to the child's compliance to classroom rules and assignments, use of time-out procedures in the classroom, and behavioral contracts. Use of the "drag sheet" between parents and teachers often assures that teachers monitor the child on writing down assignments and taking home the necessary study materials, and parents monitor the child in completing homework and returning the homework to the teacher the following day. Having the parent and teacher sign off on the drag sheet assures close monitoring of child compliance (Shelton & Barkley, 1993).

Finally, teaching strategies designed to increase the child's optimal performance may be useful. These include giving only one task at a time with frequent feedback as to progress and completion of tasks; allowing the child to work in short bursts, with an opportunity to move about the room quietly or take a break after completion of brief assignments; and allowing extra time for certain tasks, if the child tends to become distracted and to work more slowly than classmates. Test taking is often a difficult time for the child with ADHD, and the teacher must be aware of the performance demands being placed on the child for a given test. The child who has poor attention and slow writing may be hampered on a written test, but may perform quite well on an oral test. It is important to ensure that the child's knowledge is being tested rather than the child's attention span. The child with ADHD often has difficulty with behavioral control and is easily frustrated. Increased frustration and fatigue can break down the child's self-control and lead to misbehavior. The teacher who understands the nature of the child's frustration and the reasons for the misbehavior will likely respond by reducing the stressors in the environment rather than merely punishing the misbehavior. These and other recommendations for teaching children with ADHD have been described by the Education Committee of the Children With Attention Deficit Disorders (CHADD) organization (Children With Attention Deficit Disorders, 1988).

Parent Training and Parent Support Programs

One of the first steps in working with parents of a child diagnosed with ADHD is to provide education. Often a few brief sessions focused on providing an overview of ADHD, its course and outcome, and useful treatments will be reassuring. Referral of parents to local chapters of CHADD or other community support groups may also be helpful.

When behavioral problems accompany the symptoms of ADHD, more formalized parent training programs may be needed to teach parents behavioral management strategies. Several models exist and have already been discussed in this chapter, including those by Eyberg and colleagues (Eyberg & Boggs, 1989), Forehand and McMahon (1981), and Barkley (1987). These programs use various methods to educate the parent about the causes of child misbehavior, to enhance parental attending skills, and to teach parents how to attend to child compliance, use time-out procedures for noncompliance, manage the child's behavior in public places, and cope with future behavioral problems. If behavioral problems can be brought under better control through treatment, and management problems decrease in the home and school environments, the child may be able to function adequately without medical treatment. However, if medication is needed in the more severe cases, often parent training programs are a useful adjunct to the medical treatment.

Stimulant Medications

By far the most common treatment for ADHD involves psychostimulant medications. According to Barkley (1990), more children receive medication to manage ADHD than any other childhood disorder. Current estimates suggest that between 1% and 2% of the school-age population is currently on psychostimulant medication (Safer & Krager, 1983). The key to successful use of psychostimulant medication involves proper dosages and adequate monitoring to determine the efficacy of treatment. The most common stimulants are Ritalin (methylphenidate), Cylert (pemoline), and Dexedrine (dextroamphetamine). There are many scientific reviews of the clinical effects of these medications that attest to their usefulness. Barkley (1977b) reported in his review that stimulant medications as a group led to an average improvement rate of between 73% and 77% among patients treated. In addition, several studies reported improvement rates in the range of 39% for placebo effects (Barkley, 1977b). The available research suggests that approximately 25% of children will have no change as a result of stimulant medication, so it should not be assumed that all children will benefit.

Ritalin (methylphenidate) is the most commonly used stimulant medication because of its quick onset of action, minimal side effects, and generally good results (Rostain, 1991). The usual effective dose ranges from 0.3 to 0.7 mg/kg. For children less than 8 years of age (or under 25 kg), the typical starting dose is 5 mg. For older or heavier children, the typical starting dose is 10 mg. Typically, it is recommended to begin with a single morning dose given at a time when parents can observe the child's behavior and note any adverse side effects. If the dose appears to be effective, the child may be given the medication before leaving for school for 1 week. If teachers report an improvement in morning classroom performance, the child may be maintained on the initial dose. If not, the dose may be increased on a weekly basis in increments of 2.5 or 5.0 mg, depending on the child's weight (Rostain, 1991). Once an effective dose is determined, the medication typically is given in 2 or 3 daily doses at intervals of 3 to 4 hr. Careful monitoring through age-normed behavioral checklists completed by teachers and parents will assist the physician in determining if the dosage is correct. After several weeks on a steady dosage schedule, it may be necessary to increase the dosage slightly, with careful measurement of growth parameters and blood pressure and a brief physical exam conducted approximately every 2 months if there are no adverse side effects (Rostain, 1991).

With Dexedrine, the usual starting dose is 2.5 to 5.0 mg in the morning; this medication is typically taken only once a day. The protocol for initiating and increasing the dose is similar to that suggested for methylphenidate. According to Rostain (1991), greater appetite suppression and sleep disturbances are seen with this medication. Cylert (pemoline) has the longest duration of action (half life of 12 hr) among the psychostimulant medications. It is administered in a single dose in the morning, with the initial dosage typically 37.5 mg. After 1 to 2 weeks, the dosage may be increased by increments of 18.75 mg (Rostain, 1991).

Concerns about side effects associated with psychostimulant medication have filled the scientific and lay literature. The most frequently reported side effects in the literature are insomnia and decreased appetite, found in 90% and 79%, respectively, of the studies reviewed by Barkley (1977b). Irritability and weight loss were the next most frequently reported, although they were noted in fewer than half of the studies. Other studies have indicated a high percentage of behavioral changes. Barkley, McMurray, Edelbrock, and Robbins (1990) found that over half of their sample of ADHD children exhibited decreased appetite, insomnia, anxiety, irritability, and proneness to crying with both a low dose (0.3 mg/kg) and medium dose (0.5 mg/kg) of methylphenidate. Another potential side effect, though present in only a small percentage of cases, involves an increase in nervous tics. There are reports of irreversible Tourette's syndrome presumed to be secondary to stimulant medication treatment (G. S. Golden, 1988). Barkley has estimated that fewer than 1% of children with ADHD who are treated with stimulants will develop a tic disorder, but preexisting tics may be exacerbated in as many as 13% of the children (Denckla, Bemporad, & MacKay, 1976). Therefore, it is important to screen children carefully for a personal or family history of tics or Tourette's disorder and to monitor carefully those children who have positive histories. If a child on psychostimulant medication should develop motor or vocal tics, the medication should be discontinued immediately.

Finally, the behavioral rebound phenomenon has been described frequently as a side effect of psychostimulant medication. The rebound effect involves an exacerbation of ADHD symptoms, typically exceeding those that were evidenced at baseline. These effects typically occur in late afternoon or evening following daytime administrations of medication. The type and severity of symptoms are variable, but may include an increase in activity, insomnia, and increased irritability. The rebound effects often can be managed by changing the time of administration or the dosage level of medications.

Finally, certain medications can lead to possible medical side effects that need to be monitored. Pemoline has been reported to cause impaired liver functioning in approximately 3% of children, and these effects may not be reversible. Children on this medication are monitored carefully by their physician for liver functioning. The long-term side effects of psychostimulant medications have not been well studied to date. However, Barkley (1990) reported that there is no evidence to suggest addictive effects from the medications.

Indicators for use of stimulant medication are based on the baseline medical exam of the child (ruling out high risk medical factors that would contraindicate use of medication), the severity of the current symptoms, the level of disruptiveness to the child's school or family functioning, the parents' attitude toward pharmacotherapy, and the absence of internalizing symptoms (such as anxiety, fearfulness, and psychosomatic disturbances) in the child. Such symptoms have been noted in children who are less likely to respond positively to stimulant medications and who may exhibit a better response to antidepressant medications (Barkley, 1990). Contraindications for psychostimulant medication include those children who are less than 4 years of age; those with a personal or family history of tics, psychosis, or thought disorder; children with comorbid severe behavioral problems; and children with internalizing symptoms (Barkley, 1990).

In summary, between 70% and 80% of children with ADHD have been reported to show a positive response to psychostimulant medication, with improvement in attention span and a reduction of disruptive, hyperactive, and impulsive behaviors (Barkley, 1990). Although the medications are not designed to treat behavioral disorders, parents often report an increase in behavioral compliance and a decrease in behavioral management problems once their child receives medication. The side effects of psychostimulant medication are mild in most cases and diminish with the reduction or discontinuance of medication. However, certain children who have a family history of tics or Tourette's disorder probably should not receive the medications, as these conditions may be exacerbated and possibly become irreversible (Barkley, 1990). Barkley pointed out that stimulant medications are not a panacea for ADHD and should not be the sole treatment used in most cases. Continued use of educational interventions and parent interventions to supplement medical management of ADHD is important.

Direct Interventions With Children and Adolescents Who Have ADHD

A number of psychotherapeutic interventions have been used with children and adolescents who have ADHD, including social skills and peer relationship training, cognitive–behavioral approaches designed to assist with anger management and self-control, traditional behavioral therapy in the form of token economies or behavioral contracts, as well as traditional play therapy and other approaches.

Often group therapy approaches are useful for providing training in social skills and peer relationships. Social skills training sessions may provide a rationale for discussion of social skills, verbal instructions on the performance of the skills, modeling by therapists, role-playing between the therapist and among children, coaching and feedback as children develop skills, and videotaping interactions between children for the purpose of review and modification (Guevremont, 1990). There are a variety of models for social skills training, but most have the following steps in common: problem identification (accurately identifying a problem and planning a goal); alternative thinking (the ability to generate many possible solutions to a particular interpersonal conflict); consequential thinking (the ability to anticipate immediate and longer term consequences of one's actions); and means–ends thinking (the ability to plan one's actions to attain a goal while recognizing potential obstacles). The main goal of these types of training programs is to encourage a reflective style of thinking with a goal of increasing social behavior likely to result in more positive consequences for the child or adolescent (Guevremont, 1990).

Interventions involving cognitive–behavioral strategies for anger management and behavioral control have been successful with children and youth who have ADHD. Hinshaw, Henker, and Whalen (1984) developed an anger-control program for boys with ADHD, using principles and procedures derived from cognitive–behavioral therapy and stress inoculation procedures. These procedures involve such steps as (a) learning to identify external events (e.g., being teased) and internal events (e.g., thoughts, muscle tension) associated with emotional arousal; (b) learning a variety of coping skills to use when the stressful event is present; and (c) actively practicing use of the coping skills while being exposed to different degrees of stress (Guevremont, 1990). The intervention model espoused by Guevremont (1990) incorporates anger control training with emphasis on stopping and thinking before acting, and the use of a reflective sequence for approaching conflicts. In general, empirical investigations of cognitive–behavioral approaches to achieve increased behavioral control have produced positive results.

For older children and adolescents, the recommended interventions include behavior management techniques such as token economies to improve compliance with commands as well as to reward the child for on-task behavior. Because adolescents often display problems in social interactions, a group therapy program may be used to address educational aspects of the medication therapy and etiology of the disorder as well as give the adolescent experience and feedback in interacting with peers. Interventions discussed in previous paragraphs are appropriate for social skills training and so on in adolescence.

Intervention with adults is slightly different than that with adolescents and includes medication management as well as a group therapy program. Medication for adults is started at a very low dose and increased slightly to a level that leads to improvement in the desired behaviors. The group therapy program used with adults serves mainly as an educational and problem-solving format. Adults typically are concerned with the etiology and future consequences of the disorder. In addition, many adults have found compensatory techniques that prove useful for them in overcoming the problems associated with their disorder. As a result, they can be a good source of information for other patients.

CONCLUSION

ADHD is one of the most common, and perhaps one of the most misunderstood, disorders in the mental health field. The changing definitions and conceptualizations of the disorder over the years have been confusing to professionals but have moved the field toward more rigorous empirical research to define the diagnostic criteria and the subtypes of ADHD. With the publication of *DSM-IV*, practitioners and researchers have an opportunity to move toward even greater understanding of the ramifications of ADHD. This chapter has reviewed current conceptualizations and definition of ADHD, along with discussion of electrophysiologic and pathophysiologic processes presumed to underlie this disorder. A developmental focus has been maintained so that the practitioner can better understand the differing presentations of ADHD across the age span, with resultant implications for assessment and treatment. A two-tier model for assessment, including screening and comprehensive evaluation, has been presented, with recommendations based on the empirical literature to date. As more children and individuals in late adolescence or adulthood become aware of ADHD and seek professional assistance for their symptoms, the information presented in this chapter should assist in planning an optimal assessment and intervention program.

References

Abikoff, H., Gittelman-Klein, R., & Klein, D. (1977). Validation of a classroom observation code for hyperactive children. *Journal of Consulting and Clinical Psychology, 45,* 772–783.

Achenbach, T. M. (1986). *Manual for the Child Behavior Checklist–Direct Observation Form.* Burlington: University of Vermont, Department of Psychiatry.

Achenbach, T. M., & Edelbrock, C. (1983). *Manual for the Child Behavior Checklist and Revised Child Behavior Profiles.* Burlington: University of Vermont, Department of Psychiatry.

Ackerman, P. T., Dykman, R. A., & Oglesby, D. M. (1983). Sex and group differences in reading and attention disordered children with and without hyperkinesis. *Journal of Learning Disabilities, 16,* 407–415.

Ajmone Marsan, C. (1965). The thalamus. Data on its functional anatomy and on some aspects of thalamocortical integration. *Archives of Italian Biology, 103,* 847–882.

Alterman, A., Tarter, R., Baughman, T., Bober, B., & Fabian, S. (1985). Differentiation of alcoholics high and low in childhood hyperactivity. *Drug and Alcohol Dependence, 15,* 111–121.

American Psychiatric Association. (1968). *Diagnostic and statistical manual of mental disorders* (2nd ed.). Washington, DC: Author.

American Psychiatric Association. (1980). *Diagnostic and statistical manual of mental disorders* (3rd ed.). Washington, DC: Author.

American Psychiatric Association. (1987). *Diagnostic and statistical manual of mental disorders* (3rd ed., revised). Washington, DC: Author.

American Psychiatric Association. (1994). *Diagnostic and statistical manual of mental disorders* (4th ed.). Washington, DC: Author.

Barkley, R. A. (1977a). The effects of methylphenidate on various measures of activity level and attention in hyperkinetic children. *Journal of Abnormal Child Psychology, 5,* 351–369.

Barkley, R. A. (1977b). A review of stimulant drug research with hyperactive children. *Journal of Child Psychology and Psychiatry, 18,* 137–165.

Barkley, R. A. (1981). *Hyperactive children: A handbook for diagnosis and treatment.* New York: Guilford Press.

Barkley, R. A. (1982). Specific guidelines for defining hyperactivity in children (attention deficit disorder with hyperactivity). In B. Lahey & A. Kazdin (Eds.), *Advances in clinical child psychology* (Vol. 5, pp. 137–180). New York: Plenum.

Barkley, R. A. (1985). The social interactions of hyperactive children: Developmental changes, drug effects, and situational variation. In R. McMahon & R. Peters (Eds.), *Childhood disorders: Behavioral-developmental approaches* (pp. 218–243). New York: Brunner/Mazel.

Barkley, R. A. (1987). *Defiant children: A clinician's manual for parent training* (pp. 33–37). New York: Guilford Press.

Barkley, R. A. (1988a). *Attention deficit–hyperactivity disorder.* In E. Mash & L. Terdal (Eds.), *Behavioral assessment of childhood disorders* (2nd ed., pp. 69–104). New York: Guilford Press.

Barkley, R. A. (1988b). The effects of methylphenidate on the interactions of preschool ADHD children and their mothers. *Journal of the American Academy of Child and Adolescent Psychiatry, 27,* 336–341.

Barkley, R. A. (1990). *Attention deficit hyperactivity disorder: A handbook for diagnosis and treatment.* New York: Guilford Press.

Barkley, R. A., & Cunningham, C. E. (1979). Stimulant drugs and activity level in hyperactive children. *American Journal of Orthopsychiatry, 49,* 491–499.

Barkley, R. A., DuPaul, G. J., & McMurray, M. B. (1990). Comprehensive evaluation of attention deficit disorder with or without hyperactivity as defined by research criteria. *Journal of Consulting and Clinical Psychology, 58,* 775–789.

Barkley, R. A., & Edelbrock, C. (1987). Assessing situational variation in children's problem behaviors: The Home and School Situations Questionnaire. In R. J. Prinz (Ed.), *Advances in behavioral assessment of children and families* (Vol. 3, pp. 157–176). Greenwich, CT: JAI Press.

Barkley, R. A., Fischer, M., Edelbrock, C. S., & Smallish, L. (1990). The adolescent outcome of hyperactive children diagnosed by research criteria: I. An 8 year prospective follow-up study. *Journal of the American Academy of Child and Adolescent Psychiatry, 29,* 546–557.

Barkley, R. A., Fischer, M., Newby, R., & Breen, M. (1988). Development of a multi-method clinical protocol for assessing stimulant drug responses in ADHD children. *Journal of Clinical Child Psychology, 17,* 14–24.

Barkley, R. A., Grodzinsky, G., & DuPaul, G. J. (1992). Frontal lobe functions in attention deficit disorder with and without hyperactivity: A review and research report. *Journal of Abnormal Child Psychology*, *20*, 163–188.

Barkley, R. A., McMurray, M. B., Edelbrock, C. S., & Robbins, K. (1990). Side effects of methylphenidate in children with attention deficit hyperactivity disorder: A systemic placebo-controlled evaluation. *Pediatrics*, *86*(2), 184–192.

Battle, E. S., & Lacey, B. (1972). A context for hyperactivity in children over time. *Child Development*, *43*, 757–773.

Beck, A. T. (1987). *Beck Depression Inventory manual*: New York: Psychological Corporation.

Beery, K. E. (1982). *Revised administration, scoring, and teaching manual for the Developmental Test of Visual–Motor Integration*. Cleveland, OH: Modern Curriculum Press.

Bender, L. (1942). Postencephalitic behavior disorders in childhood. In J. B. Neal (Ed.), *Encephalitis: A clinical study* (pp. 361–384). New York: Grune & Stratton.

Benton, A. L., & Hamsher, K. (1983). *Multilingual aphasia examination*. Iowa City, IA: AJA Associates.

Biederman, J., Faraone, S. V., Keenan, K., Benjamin, J., Krifcher, B., Moore, C., Sprich-Buckminster, S., Ugaglia, K., Jellinek, M. S., & Steingard, R. (1992). Further evidence for family-genetic risk factors in attention deficit hyperactivity disorder. Patterns of comorbidity in probands and relatives of psychiatrically and pediatrically referred samples. *Archives of General Psychiatry*, *49*, 728–738.

Birch, H. G. (1964). *Brain damage in children: The biological and social aspects*. Baltimore: Williams & Wilkins.

Boucugnani, L. L., & Jones, R. W. (1989). Behaviors analogous to frontal lobe dysfunction in children with attention deficit hyperactivity disorder. *Archives of Clinical Neuropsychology*, *4*, 161–173.

Breen, M. J. (1989). ADHD girls and boys: An analysis of attentional, emotional, cognitive, and family variables. *Journal of Child Psychology and Psychiatry*, *30*, 711–716.

Breen, M., & Barkley, R. A. (1983). The Personality Inventory for Children (PIC): Its clinical utility with hyperactive children. *Journal of Pediatric Psychology*, *8*, 359–366.

Breen, M. J., & Barkley, R. A. (1984). Psychological adjustment of learning disabled, hyperactive, and hyperactive-learning disabled children as measured by the Personality Inventory for Children. *Journal of Clinical Child Psychology*, *13*, 232–236.

Brown, R. T., & Borden, K. A. (1986). Hyperactivity at adolescence: Some misconceptions and new directions. *Journal of Clinical Child Psychology*, *15*, 194–209.

Burks, H. F. (1977). *Burks Behavior Rating Scales*. Los Angeles, CA: Western Psychological Services.

Buschke, H. (1973). Selective reminding for analysis of memory and learning. *Journal of Verbal Learning and Verbal Behavior*, *12*, 543–550.

Buschke, H., & Fuld, P. A. (1974). Evaluating storage, retention, and retrieval in disordered memory and learning. *Neurology*, *24*, 1019–1025.

Butcher, J. N., Graham, J. R., Williams, C. L., & Kaemmer, B. (1992). *Minnesota Multiphasic Personality Inventory–Adolescent*. Minneapolis: University of Minnesota Press.

Cadoret, R. J., & Stewart, M. A. (1991). An adoption study of attention deficit/hyperactivity/aggression and their relationship to adult antisocial personality. *Comprehensive Psychiatry*, *32*, 73–82.

Cairns, E., & Cammock, T. (1978). Development of a more reliable version of the "Matching Familiar Figures Test." *Developmental Psychology*, *14*, 555–560.

Campbell, S. B. (1990). *Behavior problems in preschoolers: Clinical and developmental issues*. New York: Guilford Press.

Campbell, S. B., Douglas, V. I., & Morganstern, G. (1971). Cognitive styles in hyperactive children and the effect of methylphenidate. *Journal of Child Psychology and Psychiatry*, *12*, 55–67.

Campbell, S. B., & Ewing, L. J. (1990). Follow-up of hard-to-manage preschoolers: Adjustment at age 9 years and predictors of continuing symptoms. *Journal of Child Psychology and Psychiatry and Allied Disciplines*, *36*, 870–889.

Chelune, G. J., Ferguson, W., Koon, R., & Dickey, T. O. (1986). Frontal lobe disinhibition in attention deficit disorder. *Child Psychiatry and Human Development*, *16*, 211–234.

Chess, S. (1960). Diagnosis and treatment of the hyperactive child. *New York State Journal of Medicine*, *60*, 2379–2385.

Children With Attention Deficit Disorders. (1988). *Attention deficit disorders: A guide for teachers*. Plantation, FL: Author.

Clark, C. R., Geffen, G. M., & Geffen, L. B. (1987). Catecholamines and attention: II. Pharmacological studies in normal humans. *Neuroscience and Biobehavioral Review*, *11*, 353–364.

Clements, S. D., & Peters, J. E. (1962). Minimal brain dysfunctions in the school-aged child. *Archives of General Psychiatry*, *6*, 185–187.

Cohen, N. J., Sullivan, J., Minde, K., Novak, C., & Helwig, C. (1981). Evaluation of the relative effectiveness of methylphenidate and cognitive behavior modification in the treatment of kindergarten-aged hyperactive children. *Journal of Abnormal Child Psychology*, 9, 43–54.

Cohen, N. J., Weiss, G., & Minde, K. (1972). Cognitive styles in adolescents previously diagnosed as hyperactive. *Journal of Child Psychology and Psychiatry*, *13*, 203–209.

Colarusso, R. P., & Hammill, D. D. (1972). *Motor-Free Visual Perception Test*. Novato, CA: Academic Therapy Publications.

Conners, C. K. (1980). *Food additives and hyperactive children*. New York: Plenum.

Conners, C. K. (1989). *Manual for Conners' Rating Scales (Conners' Teacher Rating Scales, Conners' Parent Rating Scales)*. North Tonawanda, NY: Multi-Health Systems.

Cruikshank, B. M., Eliason, M., & Merrifield, B. (1988). Long-term sequelae of cold water near-drowning. *Journal of Pediatric Psychology*, *13*, 379–388.

Cunningham, C. E., & Siegel, L. S. (1987). Peer interactions of normal and attention-deficit disordered boys during free play, cooperative tasks, and simulated classroom situations. *Journal of Abnormal Child Psychology*, *15*, 247–268.

Delis, D. C., Kramer, J. H., Kaplan, E., & Ober, B. A. (1986). *The California Verbal Learning Test*. New York: Psychological Corporation.

Denckla, M. B. (1989). Executive dysfunction. *International Pediatrics*, *4*, 155–160.

Denckla, M. B. (1991). Attention deficit hyperactivity disorder: Residual type. *Journal of Child Neurology*, 6(Suppl.), S44–S50.

Denckla, M. B., Bemporad, J. R., & MacKay, M. C. (1976). Tics following methylphenidate administration. *Journal of the American Medical Association*, *235*, 1349–1351.

Denckla, M. B., & Rudel, R. G. (1978). Anomalies of motor development in hyperactive boys. *Annals of Neurology*, *3*, 231–233.

Denckla, M. B., Rudel, R. G., Chapman, C., & Krieger, J. (1985). Motor proficiency in dyslexic children with and without attentional disorders. *Archives of Neurology*, *42*, 228–231.

Douglas, V. I. (1972). Stop, look, and listen: The problem of sustained attention and impulse control in hyperactive and normal children. *Canadian Journal of Behavioral Science*, *4*, 259–282.

Douglas, V. I. (1980a). Higher mental processes in hyperactive children: Implications for training. In R. Knights & D. Bakker (Eds.), *Treatment of hyperactive and learning disordered children* (pp. 65–92). Baltimore: University Park Press.

Douglas, V. I. (1980b). Treatment and training approaches to hyperactivity: Establishing internal or external control. In C. Whalen & B. Henker (Eds.), *Hyperactive children: The social ecology of identification and treatment* (pp. 283–318). San Diego, CA: Academic Press.

Douglas, V. I. (1983). Attention and cognitive problems. In M. Rutter (Ed.), *Developmental neuropsychiatry* (pp. 280–329). New York: Guilford Press.

Douglas, V. I., & Peters, K. G. (1979). Toward a clearer definition of the attentional deficit of hyperactive children. In G. A. Hale & M. Lewis (Eds.), *Attention and the development of cognitive skills* (pp. 173–248). New York: Plenum.

DuPaul, G. J. (1990). *The ADHD Rating Scale: Normative data, reliability, and validity*. Unpublished manuscript, University of Massachusetts Medical Center, Worcester.

DuPaul, G. J., Anastopoulos, A. D., Shelton, T. L., Guevremont, D. C., & Metevia, L. (1992). Multimethod assessment of attention deficit hyperactivity disorder: The diagnostic utility of clinic-based tests. *Journal of Clinical Child Psychology*, *21*, 394–402.

Dykman, R. A., Ackerman, P. T., & Holcomb, P. J. (1985). Reading disabled and ADD children: Similarities and differences. In D. B. Gray & J. F. Kavanagh (Eds.), *Biobehavioral measures of dyslexia* (pp. 47–62). Parkton, MD: York Press.

Eyberg, S. M., Bessmer, J., Newcomb, K., Edwards, D., & Robinson, E. (1993). *Dyadic parent–child interaction coding system, II: A manual*. Unpublished manuscript, University of Florida.

Eyberg, S. M., & Boggs, S. R. (1989). Parent training for oppositional-defiant preschoolers. In C. E. Schaefer & J. M. Briesmeister (Eds.), *Handbook of parent training: Parents as cotherapists for children with behavior problems* (pp. 105–132). New York: Wiley.

Eyberg, S. M., & Robinson, E. A. (1982). Parent–child interaction training: Effects on family functioning. *Journal of Clinical Child Psychology*, *11*, 130–137.

Feingold, B. (1975). *Why your child is hyperactive*. New York: Random House.

Fergusson, D. M., Fergusson, J. E., Horwood, L. J., & Kinzett, N. G. (1988). A longitudinal study of dentine lead levels, intelligence, school performance, and behaviour. *Journal of Child Psychology and Psychiatry and Allied Disciplines*, *29*, 811–824.

Firestone, P., Lewy, F., & Douglas, B. I. (1976). Hyperactivity and physical anomalies. *Canadian Psychiatric Association Journal*, *21*, 23–26.

Fischer, M., Barkley, R. A., Edelbrock, C. S., & Smallish, L. (1990). The adolescent outcome of hyperactive children diagnosed by research criteria: II. Academic, attentional, and neuropsychological status. *Journal of Consulting and Clinical Psychology, 58,* 580–588.

Forehand, R., & McMahon, R. (1981). *Helping the noncompliant child: A clinician's guide to parent training.* New York: Guilford Press.

Gittelman, R., Mannuzza, S., Shenker, R., & Bonagura, N. (1985). Hyperactive boys almost grown up: I. Psychiatric status. *Archives of General Psychiatry, 42,* 937–947.

Golden, C. J. (1978). *Stroop Color and Word Test: A manual for clinical and experimental users.* Chicago: Stoelting.

Golden, G. S. (1988). The use of stimulants in the treatment of Tourette's syndrome. In D. J. Cohen, R. D. Bruun, & J. F. Lechman (Eds.), *Tourette's syndrome and tic disorders: Clinical understanding and treatment* (pp. 317–327). New York: Wiley.

Goldstein, K. (1936). Modification of behavior consequent to cerebral lesion. *Psychiatric Quarterly, 10,* 539–610.

Goodman, R., & Stevenson, J. (1989). A twin study of hyperactivity: II: The aetiological role of genes, family relationships, and perinatal adversity. *Journal of Child Psychology and Psychiatry, 30,* 691–709.

Gordon, M. (1983). *The Gordon Diagnostic System.* Boulder, CO: Clinical Diagnostic Systems.

Gordon, M., DiNiro, D., & Mettelman, B. B. (1988). Effect upon outcome of nuances in selection criteria for ADHD/Hyperactivity. *Psychological Reports, 62,* 539–544.

Gordon, M., & Mettelman, B. B. (1988). The assessment of attention: I. Standardization and reliability of a behavior-based measure. *Journal of Clinical Psychology, 44,* 682–690.

Gorenstein, E. E., Mammato, C. A., & Sandy, J. M. (1989). Performance of inattentive–overactive children on selected measures of prefrontal-type function. *Journal of Clinical Psychology, 45,* 619–632.

Grant, D. A., & Berg, E. A. (1948). A behavioral analysis of degree of reinforcement and ease of shifting of new responses in a Weigl-type card-sorting problem. *Journal of Experimental Psychology, 38,* 404–411.

Grodzinsky, G. (1990). *Assessing frontal lobe functioning in 6 to 11 year old boys with attention deficit hyperactivity disorder.* Unpublished doctoral dissertation, Boston College.

Gronwall, D. (1977). Paced auditory serial-addition task: A measure of recovery from concussion. *Perceptual and Motor Skills, 44,* 367–373.

Gross, M. D. (1984). Effects of sucrose on hyperkinetic children. *Pediatrics, 74,* 876–878.

Gualtieri, C. T., Ondrusek, M. G., & Finlay, C. (1985). Attention deficit disorders in adults. *Clinical Neuropharmacology, 8,* 343–356.

Guevremont, D. (1990). Social skills and peer relationship training. In R. A. Barkley (Ed.), *Attention deficit hyperactivity disorder* (pp. 540–572). New York: Guilford Press.

Haenlein, M., & Caul, W. F. (1987). Attention deficit disorder with hyperactivity: A specific hypothesis of reward dysfunction. *Journal of the American Academy of Child and Adolescent Psychiatry, 26,* 356–362.

Hale, G. A., & Lewis, M. (1979). *Attention and cognitive development.* New York: Plenum.

Hamlett, K. W., Pellegrini, D. S., & Conners, C. K. (1987). An investigation of executive processes and the problem solving of attention deficit disorder–hyperactive children. *Journal of Pediatric Psychology, 12,* 227–240.

Hammill, D. D., & Larsen, S. C. (1988). *Test of Written Language–2nd edition examiner's manual.* Austin, TX: PRO-ED.

Harter, M. R., Anllo-Vento, L., & Wood, F. B. (1989). Event-related potentials, spatial orienting, and reading disabilities. *Psychophysiology, 26,* 404–421.

Harter, M. R., Anllo-Vento, L., Wood, F. B., & Schroeder, M. M. (1988). Separate brain potential characteristics in children with reading and attention deficit disorder: Color and letter relevance effects. *Brain and Cognition, 7,* 115–140.

Harter, M. R., Diering, S., & Wood, F. B. (1988). Separate brain potential characteristics in children with reading and attention deficit disorder: Relevance-independent effects. *Brain and Cognition, 7,* 54–86.

Hartsough, C. S., & Lambert, N. M. (1985). Medical factors in hyperactive and normal children: Prenatal, developmental, and health history findings. *American Journal of Orthopsychiatry, 55,* 190–210.

Hathaway, S. R., & McKinley, J. C. (1989). *Minnesota Multiphasic Personality Inventory–2.* Minneapolis: University of Minnesota Press.

Healton, E. B., Navarro, C., Bressman, S., & Brust, J. C. M. (1982). Subcortical neglect. *Neurology, 32,* 776–778.

Heaton, R. K. (1981). *A manual for the Wisconsin Card Sorting Test.* Odessa, FL: Psychological Assessment Resources.

Hechtman, L. (1991). Resilience and vulnerability in long term outcome of attention deficit hyperactivity disorder. *Canadian Journal of Psychiatry, 36,* 415–421.

Heilman, K. M., Watson, R. T., Valenstein, E., & Damasio, A. R. (1983). Localization of lesions in neglect. In A. Kertesz (Ed.), *Localization in neuropsychology* (pp. 471–492). San Diego, CA: Academic Press.

Herbert, M. (1964). The concept and testing of brain damage in children: A review. *Journal of Child Psychology and Psychiatry, 5,* 197–217.

Hinshaw, S. P., Henker, B., & Whalen, C. K. (1984). Self-control in hyperactive boys in anger inducing situations: Effects of cognitive–behavioral training and of methylphenidate. *Journal of Abnormal Child Psychology, 12*, 55–77.

Hohman, L. B. (1922). Post-encephalitic behavior disorders in children. *Johns Hopkins Hospital Bulletin, 33*, 372–375.

Holcomb, P. J., Ackerman, P. T., & Dykman, R. A. (1985). Cognitive event-related brain potentials in children with attention and reading deficits. *Psychophysiology, 22*, 656–667.

Holcomb, P. J., Ackerman, P. T., & Dykman, R. A. (1986). Auditory event-related potentials in attention and reading disabled boys. *International Journal of Psychophysiology, 3*, 263–273.

Horn, W. F., Wagner, A. E., & Ialongo, N. (1989). Sex differences in school-age children with pervasive attention deficit hyperactivity disorder. *Journal of Abnormal Child Psychology, 17*, 109–125.

Hynd, G. W., Hern, K. L., Novey, E. S., Eliopulos, D., Marshall, R., Gonzalez, J. J., & Voeller, K. K. (1993). Attention deficit–hyperactivity disorder and asymmetry of the caudate nucleus. *Journal of Child Neurology, 8*, 339–347.

Hynd, G. W., Semrud-Clikeman, M., Lorys, A. R., Novey, E. S., & Eliopulos, D. (1990). Brain morphology in developmental dyslexia and attention deficit disorder/hyperactivity. *Archives of Neurology, 47*, 919–926.

Hynd, G. W., Semrud-Clikeman, M., Lorys, A. R., Novey, E. S., Eliopulos, D., & Lyytinen, H. (1991). Corpus callosum morphology in attention deficit-hyperactivity disorder: Morphometric analysis of MRI. *Journal of Learning Disabilities, 24*, 141–146.

Jacob, R. G., O'Leary, K. D., & Rosenblad, C. (1978). Formal and informal classroom settings: Effects on hyperactivity. *Journal of Abnormal Child Psychology, 6*, 47–59.

Jasper, H. H. (1958). Recent advances in our understanding of ascending activities of the reticular system. In H. H. Jasper (Ed.), *Reticular formation of the brain* (pp. 319–331). Boston: Brown.

Jones, E. G., & Peters, A. (Eds.). (1986). *Cerebral cortex: Sensory-motor areas and aspects of cortical connectivity* (Vol. 5). New York: Plenum.

Kagan, J. (1966). Reflection–impulsivity: The generality and dynamics of conceptual tempo. *Journal of Abnormal Psychology, 71*, 17–24.

Kahneman, D. (1973). *Attention and effort*. Englewood Cliffs, NJ: Prentice Hall.

Kaneko, M., Hoshino, Y., Hashimoto, S., Okano, T., & Kumashiro, H. (1993). Hypothalamic-pituitary-adrenal axis function in children with attention deficit–hyperactivity disorder. *Journal of Autism and Developmental Disorders, 23*, 59–65.

Kaplan, B. J., McNichol, J., Conte, R. A., & Moghadam, H. K. (1987). Sleep disturbance in preschool age hyperactive and non-hyperactive children. *Pediatrics, 80*, 839–844.

Kendall, P. C., & Braswell, L. (1984). *Cognitive–behavioral therapy for impulsive children*. New York: Guilford Press.

Kendall, P. C., & Wilcox, L. E. (1979). Self-control in children: Development of a rating scale. *Journal of Consulting and Clinical Psychology, 47*, 1020–1029.

Keogh, B. K., & Margolis, J. S. (1976). A component analysis of attentional problems of educationally handicapped boys. *Journal of Abnormal Child Psychology, 4*, 349–359.

Kirk, S. A. (1963). Behavioral diagnoses and remediation of learning disabilities. In *Proceedings of the annual meeting: Conference on exploration into the problems of the perceptually handicapped child* (Vol. 1, pp. 1–7). Evanston, IL: Perceptually Handicapped Children.

Klee, S. H., & Garfinkel, B. D. (1983). The computerized CPT: A new measure of inattention. *Journal of Abnormal Child Psychology, 11*, 487–496.

Klorman, R. (1991). Cognitive event-related potentials in attention deficit disorder. *Journal of Learning Disabilities, 24*, 130–140.

Klorman, R., Brumaghim, J. T., Salzman, L. F., Strauss, J., Borgtedt, A. D., McBride, M. C., & Loeb, S. (1990). Effects of methylphenidate on processing negativities in patients with attention deficit hyperactivity disorder. *Psychophysiology, 27*, 328–337.

Lambert, N. M. (1988). Adolescent outcomes for hyperactive children: Perspectives on general and specific patterns of childhood risk for adolescent educational, social, and mental health problems. *American Psychologist, 43*, 786–799.

Lambert, N. M., Sandoval, J., & Sassone, D. (1978). Prevalence of hyperactivity in elementary school children as a function of social system definers. *American Journal of Orthopsychiatry, 48*, 446–463.

Landau, S., & Milich, R. (1988). Social communication patterns of attention deficit-disordered boys. *Journal of Abnormal Child Psychology, 16*, 69–81.

Landesman-Dwyer, S., Ragozin, A. S., & Little, R. E. (1981). Behavioral correlates of prenatal alcohol exposure: A four-year follow-up study. *Neurobehavioral Toxicology and Teratology, 3*, 187–193.

Laufer, M., & Denhoff, E. (1957). Hyperkinetic behavior syndrome in children. *Journal of Pediatrics, 50*, 463–474.

Learning Disabilities Association. (1991, March–April). Response to notice of inquiry regarding Attention Deficit Disorder. *LDA Newsbriefs, 26(2)*, 1–6.

Lerer, R. J. (1977). Do hyperactive children tend to have abnormal palmar creases? Report of a suggestive association. *Clinical Pediatrics, 16*, 645–647.

Lezak, M. D. (1983). *Neuropsychological assessment* (2nd ed.). New York: Oxford University Press.

Lindsley, D. B., Bowden, J. W., & Magoun, H. W. (1949). Effect upon EEG of acute injury to the brain stem activating system. *Journal of Electroencephalography and Clinical Neurophysiology, 1*, 547–558.

Loge, D. V., Staton, R. D., & Beatty, W. W. (1990). Performance of children with ADHD on tests sensitive to frontal lobe dysfunction. *Journal of the American Academy of Child and Adolescent Psychiatry, 29*, 540–545.

Loney, J., Kramer, J., & Milich, R. (1981). The hyperkinetic child grows up: Predictors of symptoms, delinquency and achievement at follow-up. In K. Gadow & J. Loney (Eds.), *Psychosocial aspects of drug treatment for hyperactivity* (pp. 381–415). Boulder, CO: Westview Press.

Loney, J., Langhorne, J., & Paternite, C. (1978). Empirical basis for subgrouping the hyperkinetic/minimal brain dysfunction syndrome. *Journal of Abnormal Psychology, 87*, 431–441.

Loney, J., & Milich, R. (1982). Hyperactivity, inattention, and aggression in clinical practice. In D. Routh & M. Wolraich (Eds.), *Advances in developmental and behavioral pediatrics* (Vol. 3, pp. 113–147). Greenwich CT: JAI Press.

Mannuzza, S., Klein, R. G., Bessler, A., Malloy, P., & LaPadula, M. (1993). Adult outcome of hyperactive boys: Educational achievement, occupational rank, and psychiatric status. *Archives of General Psychiatry, 50*, 565–576.

Margalit, M., & Arieli, N. (1984). Emotional and behavioral aspects of hyperactivity. *Journal of Learning Disabilities, 17*, 374–376.

Margolis, J. S. (1972). *Academic correlates of sustained attention*. Unpublished doctoral dissertation, University of California—Los Angeles.

Mash, E. J., & Johnston, C. (1982). A comparison of the mother–child interactions of younger and older hyperactive and normal children. *Child Development, 53*, 1371–1381.

Mash, E. J., & Johnston, C. (1983). Parental perceptions of child behavior problems, parenting self-esteem, and mothers' reported stress in younger and older hyperactive and normal children. *Journal of Consulting and Clinical Psychology, 51*, 68–99.

McArthur, D. S., & Roberts, G. E. (1982). *Roberts Apperception Test for Children manual* (9th ed.). Los Angeles: Western Psychological Services.

McCarney, S. B. (1989). *Attention Deficit Disorder Evaluation Scale (ADDES)*. Columbia, MO: Hawthorne Educational Services.

McCarthy, D. (1972). *McCarthy Scales of Children's Abilities*. New York: Psychological Corporation.

McConaughy, S. H., & Achenbach, T. M. (1988). *Practical guide for the Child Behavior Checklist and related materials*. Burlington: University of Vermont, Department of Psychiatry.

McConaughy, S. H., Achenbach, T. M., & Gent, C. L. (1988). Multiaxial empirically-based assessment: Parent, teacher, observational, cognitive, and personality correlates of Child Behavior Profile types for 6- to 11-year-old boys. *Journal of Abnormal Child Psychology, 16*, 485–509.

McGee, R., Williams, S., Moffitt, T., & Anderson, J. (1989). A comparison of 13-year-old boys with attention deficit and/or reading disorder on neuropsychological measures. *Journal of Abnormal Child Psychology, 17*, 37–53.

McGee, R., Williams, S., & Silva, P. A. (1984). Background characteristics of aggressive, hyperactive, and aggressive–hyperactive boys. *Journal of the American Academy of Child and Adolescent Psychiatry, 23*, 280–284.

McGee, R., Williams, S., & Silva, P. (1987). A comparison of girls and boys with teacher-identified problems of attention. *Journal of the American Academy of Child and Adolescent Psychiatry, 26*, 711–717.

McMahon, S. A., & Greenberg, L. M. (1977). Serial neurologic examination of hyperactive children. *Pediatrics, 59*, 584–587.

Messer, S., & Brodzinsky, D. M. (1981). Three-year stability of reflection–impulsivity in young adolescents. *Developmental Psychology, 17*, 848–850.

Meyer, A. (1904). The anatomical facts and clinical varieties of traumatic insanity. *American Journal of Insanity, 60*, 373–441.

Milar, C. R., Schroeder, S. R., Mushak, P., & Boone, L. (1981). Failure to find hyperactivity in preschool children with moderately elevated lead burden. *Journal of Pediatric Psychology, 6*, 85–95.

Milich, R. (1984). Cross-sectional and longitudinal observations of activity level and sustained attention in a normative sample. *Journal of Abnormal Child Psychology, 12*, 261–276.

Milich, R., & Dodge, K. A. (1984). Social information processing in child psychiatric populations. *Journal of Abnormal Child Psychology, 12*, 471–490.

Milich, R., & Landau, S. (1982). Socialization and peer relations in hyperactive children. In K. Gadow & I. Bialer (Eds.), *Advances in learning and behavioral disabilities* (Vol. 1, pp. 283–339). Greenwich, CT: JAI Press.

Milich, R., Loney, J., & Landau, S. (1982). Independent dimensions of hyperactivity and aggression: A validation of playroom observation data. *Journal of Abnormal Psychology*, *91*, 183–198.

Milner, B. (1963). Effects of different brain lesions on card sorting. *Archives of Neurology*, *9*, 90–100.

Mirsky, A. F. (1987). Behavioral and psychophysiological markers of disordered attention. *Environmental Health Perspectives*, *74*, 191–199.

Mirsky, A. F. (1989). The neuropsychology of attention: Elements of a complex behavior. In E. Perecman (Ed.), *Integrating theory and practice in clinical neuropsychology* (pp. 75–91). Hillsdale, NJ: Erlbaum.

Mitchell, E. A., Aman, M. G., Turbott, S. H., & Manku, M. (1987). Clinical characteristics and serum essential fatty acid levels in hyperactive children. *Clinical Pediatrics*, *26*, 406–411.

Moruzzi, G., & Magoun, H. W. (1949). Brain stem reticular formation and activation of the EEG. *Journal of Electroencephalography and Clinical Neurophysiology*, *1*, 455–473.

Nichols, P. L., & Chen, T. C. (1981). *Minimal brain dysfunction: A prospective study*. Hillsdale, NJ: Erlbaum.

Nuechterlein, K. H., & Dawson, M. E. (1984). Information processing and attentional functioning in the developmental course of schizophrenic disorders. *Schizophrenia Bulletin*, *10*, 160–203.

Oades, R. D. (1987). Attention deficit disorder with hyperactivity (ADDH): The contribution of catecholamine activity. *Progress in Neurobiology*, *29*, 365–391.

O'Dougherty, M., Nuechterlein, K. H., & Drew, B. (1984). Hyperactive and hypoxic children: Signal detection, sustained attention, and behavior. *Journal of Abnormal Psychology*, *93*, 178–191.

Osterreith, P. A. (1944). Le test de copie d'une figure complex: Contribution a l'étude de la perception et de la memoire [A test of copying a complex figure: Contributions to the study of perception and memory]. *Archives de Psychologie*, *30*, 286–356.

Palfrey, J. S., Levine, M. D., Walker, D. K., & Sullivan, M. (1985). The emergence of attention deficits in early childhood: A prospective study. *Developmental and Behavioral Pediatrics*, *6*, 339–348.

Pandya, D. N., & Yeterian, E. H. (1985). Architecture and connections of cortical association areas. In A. Peters & E. G. Jones (Eds.), *Cerebral cortex: Association and auditory cortices* (Vol. 4, pp. 3–61). New York: Plenum.

Pelham, W. E., & Bender, M. E. (1982). Peer relationships in hyperactive children: Description and treatment. In K. Gadow & I. Bialer (Eds.), *Advances in learning and behavioral disabilities* (Vol. 1, pp. 365–436). Greenwich, CT: JAI Press.

Pelham, W. E., Bender, M. E., Caddell, J., Booth, S., & Moorer, S. H. (1985). Methylphenidate and children with attention deficit disorder. Dose effects on classroom academic and social behavior. *Archives of General Psychiatry*, *42*, 948–952.

Posner, M. I. (1978). *Chronometric explorations of mind*. Hillsdale, NJ: Erlbaum.

Prior, M., Leonard, A., & Wood, G. (1983). A comparison study of preschool children diagnosed as hyperactive. *Journal of Pediatric Psychology*, *8*, 191–207.

Quay, H. C. (1988). Attention deficit disorder and the behavioral inhibition system: The relevance of the neuropsychological theory of Jeffrey A. Gray. In L. Bloomingdale & J. Sergeant (Eds.), *Attention deficit disorder: Criteria, cognition, and intervention* (pp. 117–126). Elmsford, NY: Pergamon Press.

Quay, H. C., & Peterson, D. R. (1983). *Interim manual for the Revised Behavior Problem Checklist*. Unpublished Manuscript, University of Miami.

Quinn, P. O., & Rapoport, J. L. (1974). Minor physical anomalies and neurological status in hyperactive boys. *Pediatrics*, *53*, 742–747.

Rapin, I. (1987). Brain damage in children. In V. C. Kelley (Ed.), *Practice of pediatrics* (Vol. 9, revised ed., pp. 1–95). New York: Harper & Row.

Rapport, M. D., DuPaul, G. J., Stoner, G., & Jones, J. T. (1986). Comparing classroom and clinic measures of attention deficit disorder: Differential, idiosyncratic, and dose-response effects of methylphenidate. *Journal of Consulting and Clinical Psychology*, *54*, 334–341.

Reeves, J. C., Werry, J., Elkind, G. S., & Zametkin, A. (1987). Attention deficit, conduct, oppositional, and anxiety disorders in children: II. Clinical characteristics. *Journal of the American Academy of Child and Adolescent Psychiatry*, *26*, 144–155.

Reitan, R. M. (1979). *Manual for administration of neuropsychological test batteries for adults and children*. Tucson, AZ: Neuropsychological Laboratory.

Rey, A. (1941). L'examen psychologique dans les cas d'encephalopathie traumatique [Psychological examination of cases with traumatic encephalopathy]. *Archives de Psychologie*, *28*, 286–340.

Reynolds, C. R., & Bigler, E. D. (1994). *Test of memory and learning*. Austin, TX: PRO-ED.

Reynolds, C. R., & Richmond, B. O. (1985). *Revised Children's Manifest Anxiety Scale*. Los Angeles: Western Psychological Services.

Reynolds, W. M. (1987). *Reynolds Adolescent Depression Scale*. Odessa, FL: Psychological Assessment Resources.

Reynolds, W. M. (1989). *Reynolds Child Depression Scale*. Odessa, FL: Psychological Assessment Resources.

Rie, H. E., & Rie, E. D. (Eds.). (1980). *Handbook of minimal brain dysfunction: A critical review*. New York: Wiley.

Roberts, M. (1979). *A manual for the Restricted Academic Playroom Situation*. Iowa City, IA: Author.

Robin, A. L., & Foster, S. L. (1989). *Negotiating parent–adolescent conflict: A behavioral family systems approach*. New York: Guilford Press.

Robinson, E. A., & Eyberg, S. N. (1981). The Dyadic Parent–Child Interaction Coding System: Standardization and validation. *Journal of Consulting and Clinical Psychology, 49*, 245–250.

Rogeness, G. A., Maas, J. W., Javors, M. A., Macedo, C. A., Fischer, C., & Harris, W. R. (1989). Attention deficit disorder symptoms and urine catecholamines. *Psychiatry Research, 27*, 241–251.

Rosenthal, R. H., & Allen, T. W. (1980). Intratask distractibility in hyperkinetic and non-hyperkinetic children. *Journal of Abnormal Child Psychology, 8*, 175–187.

Ross, D. M., & Ross, S. A. (1982). *Hyperactivity: Current issues, research, and theory* (2nd ed.). New York: Wiley.

Rostain, A. L. (1991). Attention deficit disorders in children and adolescents. *Pediatric Clinics of North America, 38*, 607–635.

Rosvold, H. E., Mirsky, A. F., Sarason, I., Bransome, E. D., & Beck, L. H. (1956). A continuous performance test of brain damage. *Journal of Consulting Psychology, 20*, 343–350.

Routh, D. K. (1978). Hyperactivity. In P. Magrab (Ed.), *Psychological management of pediatric problems* (pp. 3–48). Baltimore: University Park Press.

Routh, D. K., & Schroeder, C. S. (1976). Standardized playroom measures as indices of hyperactivity. *Journal of Abnormal Child Psychology, 4*, 199–207.

Routh, D. K., Schroeder, C. S., & O'Tuama, L. (1974). The development of activity level in children. *Developmental Psychology, 10*, 163–168.

Safer, D. J., & Krager, J. M. (1983). Trends in medication treatment of hyperactive school children. *Clinical Pediatrics, 22*, 500–504.

Satterfield, J. H., Hoppe, C., & Schell, A. M. (1986). Prospective study of delinquency in 110 adolescent boys with attention deficit disorder and 88 normal adolescent boys. *American Journal of Psychiatry, 139*, 797–798.

Satterfield, J. H., Schell, A. M., Nicholas, T., & Backs, R. W. (1988). Topographic study of auditory event-related potentials in normal boys and boys with attention deficit disorder with hyperactivity. *Psychophysiology, 25*, 591–606.

Satterfield, J. H., Schell, A. M., Nicholas, T. W., Satterfield, B. T., & Freese, T. E. (1990). Ontogeny of selective attention effects on event-related potentials in attention-deficit hyperactivity disorder and normal boys. *Biological Psychiatry, 28*, 879–903.

Shaywitz, S. E., & Shaywitz, B. A. (1988). Attention deficit disorder: Current perspectives. In J. F. Kavanagh & T. J. Truss, Jr. (Eds.), *Learning disabilities: Proceedings of the national conference* (pp. 369–523). Parkton, MD: York Press.

Shekim, W. O., Asarnow, R. F., Hess, E., Zaucha, K., & Wheeler, N. (1990). A clinical and demographic profile of a sample of adults with attention deficit hyperactivity disorder, residual state. *Comprehensive Psychiatry, 31*, 416–425.

Shelton, T. L., & Barkley, R. A. (1993). Assessment of attention deficit hyperactivity disorder in young children. In J. L. Culbertson & D. J. Willis (Eds.), *Testing young children: A reference guide for developmental, psychoeducational, and psychosocial assessments* (pp. 290–318). Austin, TX: PRO-ED.

Sheslow, D., & Adams, W. (1990). *Wide Range Assessment of Memory and Learning administration manual*. Wilmington, DE: Jastak Associates.

Shiffrin, R. M., & Schneider, W. (1977). Controlled and automatic human information processing: II. Perceptual learning, automatic attending, and a general theory. *Psychological Review, 84*, 127–190.

Shue, K. L., & Douglas, V. I. (1992). Attention deficit hyperactivity disorder and the frontal lobe syndrome. *Brain and Cognition, 20*, 104–124.

Silva, P. A., Hughes, P., Williams, S., & Faed, J. M. (1988). Blood lead, intelligence, reading attainment, and behaviour in eleven-year-old children in Dunedin, New Zealand. *Journal of Child Psychology and Psychiatry, 29*, 43–52.

Sparrow, S. S., Balla, D. A., & Cicchetti, D. V. (1984). *Vineland Adaptive Behavior Scales*. Circle Pines, MN: American Guidance Service.

Spielberger, C. D. (1973). *State–Trait Anxiety Inventory for Children*. Palo Alto, CA: Consulting Psychologists Press.

Spielberger, C. D. (1983). *State–Trait Anxiety Inventory (Form Y)*. Palo Alto, CA: Consulting Psychologists Press.

Spitzer, R. L., Davies, M., & Barkley, R. A. (1990). The *DSM-III-R* field trial of disruptive behavior disorders. *Journal of the American Academy of Child and Adolescent Psychiatry, 29*, 690–697.

Spreen, O., & Strauss, E. (1991). *A compendium of neuropsychological tests*. New York: Oxford University Press.

Steinkamp, M. W. (1980). Relationships between environmental distractions and task performance of hyperactive and normal children. *Journal of Learning Disabilities, 13*, 40–45.

Stevenson, J. (1992). Evidence for a genetic etiology in hyperactivity in children. *Behavior Genetics, 22*, 337–344.

Stewart, M. A., Pitts, F. N., Craig, A. G., & Dieruf, W. (1966). The hyperactive child syndrome. *American Journal of Orthopsychiatry, 36*, 861–867.

Still, G. F. (1902). The Coulstonian Lectures on some abnormal physical conditions in children. *Lancet, 1*, 1008–1012, 1077–1082, 1163–1068.

Strauss, A. A., & Lehtinen, L. E. (1947). *Psychopathology and education of the brain-injured child*. New York: Grune & Stratton.

Streissguth, A. P., Martin, D. C., Barr, H. M., Sandman, B. M., Kirchner, G. L., & Darby, B. L. (1984). Intrauterine alcohol and nicotine exposure: Attention and reaction time in four-year-old children. *Developmental Psychology, 20*, 533–541.

Swanson, J., & Pelham, W. (1988). *A rating scale for the diagnosis of attention deficit disorder: Teacher norms and reliability*. Unpublished manuscript, University of Pittsburgh, Western Psychiatric Institute.

Szatmari, P., Offord, D. R., & Boyle, M. H. (1989a). Correlates, associated impairments, and patterns of service utilization of children with attention deficit disorders: Findings from the Ontario child health study. *Journal of Child Psychology and Psychiatry, 30*, 205–217.

Szatmari, P., Offord, D. R., & Boyle, M. H. (1989b). Ontario child health study: Prevalence of attention deficit disorder with hyperactivity. *Journal of Child Psychology and Psychiatry, 30*, 219–230.

Talley, J. L. (1993). *Children's Auditory Verbal Learning Test–2*. Odessa, FL: Psychological Assessment Resources.

Tallmadge, J., & Barkley, R. A. (1983). The interactions of hyperactive and normal boys with their mothers and fathers. *Journal of Abnormal Child Psychology, 11*, 565–579.

Tarter, R., McBride, H., Boupane, N., & Schneider, D. (1977). Differentiation of alcoholics: Childhood history of minimal brain dysfunction, family history, and drinking pattern. *Archives of General Psychology, 34*, 761–768.

Tarver-Behring, S., Barkley, R., & Karlsson, J. (1985). The mother–child interactions of hyperactive boys and their normal siblings. *American Journal of Orthopsychiatry, 55*, 202–209.

Taylor, E. A. (1986). Childhood hyperactivity. *British Journal of Psychiatry, 149*, 562–573.

Taylor, J. F. (1980). *The hyperactive child and the family*. New York: Random House.

Thomson, G. O. B., Raab, G. M., Hepburn, W. S., Hunter, R., Fulton, M., Laxen, D. P. H. (1989). Blood-lead levels and children's behaviour: Results from the Edinburgh lead study. *Journal of Child Psychology and Psychiatry, 30*, 515–528.

Trites, R. L., Dugas, F., Lynch, G., & Ferguson, B. (1979). Incidence of hyperactivity. *Journal of Pediatric Psychology, 4*, 179–188.

Trommer, B. L., Hoeppner, J. B., Rosenberg, R. S., Armstrong, K. J., & Rothstein, J. A. (1988). Sleep disturbances in children with attention deficit disorder. *Annals of Neurology, 24*, 325.

Trommer, B. L., Hoeppner, J. B., & Zecker, S. G. (1991). The go–no-go test in attention deficit disorder is sensitive to methylphenidate. *Journal of Child Neurology, 6*(Suppl.), S128–S131.

Ullmann, R. K., Sleator, E. K., & Sprague, R. L. (1984). A new rating scale for diagnosis and monitoring of ADD Children. *Psychopharmacology Bulletin, 20*, 160–164.

Waber, D. P., & Holmes, J. M. (1985). Assessing children's copy productions of the Rey–Osterreith Complex Figure. *Journal of Clinical and Experimental Neuropsychology, 7*, 264–280.

Ward, M. F., Wender, P. H., & Reimherr, F. W. (1993). The Wender-Utah Rating Scale: An aid in the retrospective diagnosis of childhood attention deficit hyperactivity disorder. *American Journal of Psychiatry, 150*, 885–890.

Wechsler, D. (1981). *Wechsler Adult Intelligence Scale–Revised manual*. New York: Psychological Corporation.

Wechsler, D. (1987). *Wechsler Memory Scale–Revised manual*. New York: Psychological Corporation.

Wechsler, D. (1989). *Manual for the Wechsler Preschool and Primary Scales of Intelligence–Revised*. New York: Psychological Corporation.

Wechsler, D. (1990). *Wechsler Intelligence Scale for Children–Third edition manual*. New York: Psychological Corporation.

Wechsler Individual Achievement Test. (1992). *Manual*. New York: Psychological Corporation.

Weiss, G., & Hechtman, L. T. (1986). *Hyperactive children grown up*. New York: Guilford Press.

Weiss, G., Hechtman, L., Perlman, T., Hopkins, J., & Wener, A. (1979). Hyperactives as young adults: A controlled prospective ten-year follow-up of 75 children. *Archives of General Psychiatry*, *36*, 675–681.

Wender, P. H., Reimherr, F. W., & Wood, D. R. (1981). Attention deficit disorder (minimal brain dysfunction in adults). *Archives of General Psychiatry*, *38*, 449–456.

Werner, H., & Strauss, A. A. (1941). Pathology of figure–background relation in the child. *Journal of Abnormal and Social Psychology*, *36*, 236–248.

Werry, J. S., & Sprague, R. L. (1970). Hyperactivity. In C. G. Costello (Ed.), *Symptoms of psychopathology* (pp. 397–417). New York: Wiley.

Wilkinson, G. S. (1993). *Wide Range Achievement Test–Third edition administration manual*. Wilmington, DE: Jastak Associates.

Wirt, R. D., Lachar, D., Klinedinst, J. K., Seat, P. D., & Broen, W. E. (1984). *Multidimensional description of child personality: A manual for the Personality Inventory for Children, revised 1984*. Los Angeles: Western Psychological Services.

Wolraich, M., Milich, R., Stumbo, P., & Schultz, F. (1985). The effects of sucrose ingestion on the behavior of hyperactive boys. *Pediatrics*, *106*, 675–682.

Woodcock, R. W., & Johnson, M. B. (1989). *Woodcock–Johnson Psycho-Educational Battery–Revised tests of achievement*. Allen, TX: DLM Teaching Resources.

Zagar, R., & Bowers, N. D. (1983). The effect of time of day on problem-solving and classroom behavior. *Psychology in the Schools*, *20*, 337–345.

Zametkin, A. J. (1989). The neurobiology of ADHD: A synopsis. *Psychiatric Annals*, *19*, 584–586.

Zametkin, A. J., Nordahl, T. E., Gross, M., King, A. C., Semple, W. E., Rumsey, J., Hamburger, S., & Cohen, R. M. (1990). Cerebral glucose metabolism in adults with hyperactivity of childhood onset. *New England Journal of Medicine*, *323*, 1361–1366.

Zentall, S. S. (1985). A context for hyperactivity. In K. D. Gadow & I. Bialer (Eds.), *Advances in learning and behavioral disabilities* (Vol. 4, pp. 273–343). Greenwich, CT: JAI Press.

Zimmerman, I. L., Steiner, V. G., & Pond, R. E. (1992). *Preschool Language Scale–3*. New York: Psychological Corporation.

Zubin, J. (1975). Problem of attention in schizophrenia. In M. L. Kietzman, S. Sutton, & J. Zubin (Eds.), *Experimental approaches to psychopathology* (pp. 139–166). San Diego, CA: Academic Press.

CHAPTER 11

LEARNING DISABILITIES

Jan L. Culbertson and Jane E. Edmonds

Children with learning disabilities constitute one of the largest referral populations to child neuropsychology clinics. In recent years, adolescents and adults with learning disabilities increasingly have sought evaluation and treatment in neuropsychological clinics as awareness of the lifelong impact of this disorder has increased. Given the presumed neurologic basis of learning disability, there is an evolving theoretical and empirical foundation within the field of neuropsychology for the study of learning disabilities. Since the late 1960s and early 1970s, multiple disciplines have contributed to understanding the etiology, diagnosis, and remediation of learning disabilities. The neuropsychological approach to evaluation is particularly valuable, in that it provides for integration of the neurologic, cognitive, academic, and social–emotional components of this disorder. This chapter provides a theoretically based model for neuropsychological assessment of children, adolescents, and adults with learning disabilities. The chapter is divided into sections dealing with the definitions and symptoms of learning disabilities, conceptual issues in the diagnosis of learning disability, the epidemiology and pathophysiology of learning disabilities, an overview of subtyping research and selected neuropsychological research on learning disabilities, and finally a neuropsychological approach to clinical assessment of children, adolescents, and adults with learning disabilities. Case examples are provided as well.

LEARNING DISABILITIES: AN OVERVIEW

Terminology

Kirk (1963) is credited with originally coining the term *learning disability*. However, the conceptualization of childhood learning disabilities spans 100 years, with case reports of patients who had adequate visual acuity but inability to read words (Hinshelwood, 1895; Kussmaul, 1877; Morgan, 1896). Such terms as *congenital word blindness*, *developmental alexia*, *minimal brain dysfunction*, *perceptual handicaps*, *developmental aphasia*, *dysgraphia*, *dyslexia*, and *dyscalculia* have been used in the intervening time. In fact, Cruickshank (1972) published a list of 40 different terms used to describe the disorder. The various disciplines (e.g., medicine, psychology, education, speech–language pathology) contributing to research on learning disability have lead to diverse terminology and consequently, much confusion.

Historical Overview

By the early 1900s, a knowledge base began to be established regarding learning disabilities (i.e., mainly reading disorders). The cumulative data by that time suggested that learning disability was present in children, adolescents, and adults with relatively normal cognitive abilities; occurred more frequently among men than women; was heterogeneous in terms of symptom presentation; was generally unresponsive to traditional teaching approaches; and appeared to have a familial or genetic component (Hooper & Willis, 1989). There followed a period of many years during which researchers attempted to identify a single deficient process that would explain learning disabilities. Most of this research stemmed from the work of Orton (1928, 1937), who advanced the theory that learning disabilities could be attributed to a neurodevelopmental failure in establishing cerebral dominance. Other theories of the etiology of learning disability included visual–perceptual deficits (Frostig, 1964; Kephart, 1971; Lyle & Goyen, 1968, 1975); auditory–perceptual deficits and associated language deficiencies (de Hirsch, Jansky, & Langford, 1966); deficits in intersensory integration (Birch & Belmont, 1964, 1965; Senf, 1969); and attention–memory deficits (Lyle & Goyen, 1968, 1975; Thomson & Wilsher, 1978). Although the single-factor conceptualizations were popular for many decades, more complex conceptualizations of learning problems have now emerged from sophisticated neuropsychological studies, such as cerebral hemisphere studies using dichotic listening and visual-field paradigms (McKeever & Van Deventer, 1975; Witelson & Rabinovitch, 1972; Yeni-Komshian, Isenberg, & Goldstein, 1975). It is now accepted that single-factor conceptualizations are not broad enough to account for all of the psychoeducational problems manifested by individuals with learning disabilities. Therefore, more recent research has relied on neurolinguistic, neuroanatomical, and neuropsychological data to suggest a variety of learning disability subtypes and related etiologies. Examples of these models for subtype analysis are discussed at a later point in this chapter.

In summary, the more than 100-year history of research in the field of learning disabilities has produced numerous terms and conceptualizations of the disorder, all of which have led to present-day definitions and research protocols based on the research data. For the purposes of this chapter, the term *learning disabilities* is used as a generic term inclusive of disorders involving reading, writing, spelling, arithmetic, listening, thinking, talking, and social perception. Subtypes of learning disabilities will be specified when referring to learning disabilities in reading (i.e., dyslexia); mathematics (i.e., dyscalculia); written expression (i.e., dysgraphia); and social–emotional functioning (i.e., social–emotional learning disabilities). *Dyslexia* is functionally defined as a disorder in one or more of the basic skills involved in reading, including decoding (i.e., letter–word recognition, phonetic analysis) and comprehension. *Dyscalculia* is functionally defined as a disorder in one or more of the basic skills involved in mathematics, including mechanical (computational) arithmetic and mathematics reasoning abilities. *Dysgraphia* is functionally defined as a disorder in written expression that involves deficits in one or more of the following: (a) the motor production of writing, including letter formation, speed of writing production, and spatial organization of writing; (b) knowledge of rules for spelling, punctuation and capitalization, and grammatical usage; (c) semantic abilities related to clear expression of information in written form; and (d) organizational ability, related to the thematic construction and organization of written discourse. *Social–emotional learning disability* is functionally defined as a form of socioemotional disturbance caused by specific patterns of central processing abilities and deficits (Rourke, 1989), as opposed to socioemotional reactions that often develop secondary to the frustration inherent in dealing with the consequences of learning disabilities. The former definition presumes a primary neuropsychological basis to the social–emotional problems, similar to the neuropsychological basis of other subtypes of learning disabilities. The functional social–emotional deficits lie in the areas of adaptation to novel situations, social competence (e.g., judgment, social interaction, social perception), poor pragmatic communication ability, risk for secondary emotional disturbance (both internalized and externalized forms of psychopathology) over time, and abnormal activity level, which often presents as hyperactive at younger ages and then progresses to normoactive and eventually hypoactive (Rourke, 1989).

Definitions of Learning Disabilities

Adding to the confusion in learning disability terminology is controversy regarding the definition of learning disabilities. Over 20 years ago, Vaughan and Hodges (1973) compiled a list of 38 different definitions. However, only five definitions have been adopted officially by the U.S. government or major professional organizations concerned with the study of learning disabilities. Four of these definitions, representing variations in the conceptualization of learning disabilities over the years, are printed in Exhibit 1.

One of the first formal definitions was developed by the National Advisory Committee on the Handicapped, and it was eventually adopted into the federal definition of learning disability (with only slight modifications) in the Rules and Regulations Implementing Education for All Handicapped Children Act of 1975 (PL 94–142). The modified version of this definition is printed in Exhibit 1. This definition, and later the federal definition included in PL 94–142, have been criticized for being too general, lacking operational criteria, and treating learning disability as a single disorder rather than a heterogeneous disorder (Hooper & Willis, 1989). Despite the adoption of PL 94–142 by nearly all state governments, there has never been unanimous agreement among professionals about this definition.

In 1981, the National Joint Committee for Learning Disabilities developed a new definition that was felt to represent an improvement over its predecessors (Hammill, Leigh, McNutt, & Larsen, 1981). The committee was formed by representatives of six groups (The Association for Children and Adults With Learning Disabilities, the American Speech–Language–Hearing Association, The Council for Learning Disabilities, the Division for Children With Communication Disorders, the International Reading Association, and the Orton Dyslexia Society) to generate a more acceptable definition of learning disability. The committee definition was felt to improve on prior definitions specifically by recognizing the heterogeneous nature of learning disability (and thus providing a conceptual foundation for subtyping), acknowledging the neurobiological basis presumed to underlie disorders of learning, and allowing for learning disabilities to exist concurrently with other handicapping conditions (Hooper & Willis, 1989). This definition has been adopted by Congress and has led to an evolution in the field of learning disability regarding the causal status of neurologic factors (Heath & Kush, 1991).

The Association for Children and Adults With Learning Disabilities, now renamed the Learning Disabilities Association, published a definition in 1985 that introduced the idea of the chronic nature of learning disability. Written from the perspective of those who experience the disorder, this definition was the first to acknowledge that not all cases of learning disability can be remediated through treatment, and it refers to the pervasive impact that learning disabilities can have on an individual's academic and nonacademic functioning (Hooper & Willis, 1989).

One of the most recent and most controversial definitions to date was developed in 1987 by the Interagency Committee on Learning Disabilities, a multidisciplinary group of professionals. This definition, like the Association for Children and Adults with Learning Disabilities definition, acknowledges that the disorder is presumed to be due to central nervous system dysfunction. However, controversy over this definition relates to its inclusion of deficiencies in social skills within the parameters of learning disabilities, and its acknowledgment that learning disabilities may co-occur with other handicapping conditions such as attention deficit disorder, socioenvironmental influences, and other handicapping conditions (including sensory impairment, mental retardation, and emotional disturbance). This definition is controversial because of the increased diagnostic dilemmas caused by including social skills and attention deficit disorders as part of the definition (Hooper & Willis, 1989). To date, the United States Department of Education has not endorsed this definition.

The four definitions are informative about changes in the conceptualization of learning disabilities, but most school systems continue to use the definition in PL 94–142 published in 1977. Practitioners will find it most useful to contact their state department of education or the special education offices in their local school district to ascertain the definition of learning disabilities being used locally.

Despite the evolution in diagnoses of learning disabilities, there remain many questions about the operational criteria for diagnosis and, consequently, the validity of the diagnosis. An overview of concep-

EXHIBIT 1

Four Official Definitions of Learning Disabilities

Education for All Handicapped Children Act of 1975

Specific learning disability means a disorder in one or more of the basic psychological processes involved in understanding or using language, spoken or written, in which the disorder may manifest itself in an imperfect ability to listen, think, speak, read, write, spell, or to do mathematical calculations. The term includes such conditions as perceptual handicaps, brain injury, minimal brain dysfunction, dyslexia, and developmental aphasia. The term does not include children who have learning problems which are primarily the result of visual, hearing, or motor handicaps, or mental retardation, or emotional disturbance, or of environmental, cultural, or economic disadvantage. (U.S. Office of Education, 1977, p. 65083)

National Joint Committee for Learning Disabilities (NJCLD)

Learning Disabilities is a generic term that refers to a heterogeneous group of disorders manifested by significant difficulties in the acquisition and use of listening, speaking, reading, writing, reasoning, or mathematical abilities. These disorders are intrinsic to the individual and presumed to be due to central nervous system dysfunction. Even though a learning disability may occur concomitantly with other handicapping conditions (e.g., sensory impairment, mental retardation, social and emotional disturbance) or environmental influences (e.g., cultural differences, insufficient/inappropriate instruction, psychogenic factors), it is not the direct result of those conditions or influences. (Hammill, Leigh, McNutt, & Larsen, 1981, p. 336)

Association for Children and Adults With Learning Disabilities (ACLD)

Specific Learning Disabilities is a chronic condition of presumed neurological origin which selectively interferes with the development, integration, and/or demonstration of verbal and/or non-verbal abilities. Specific Learning Disabilities exists as a distinct handicapping condition in the presence of average to superior intelligence, adequate sensory motor systems, and adequate learning opportunities. The condition varies in its manifestations and in degree of severity. Throughout life the condition can affect self-esteem, education, vocation, socialization, and/or daily living activities. (ACLD, 1985, pp. 1, 19)

Interagency Committee on Learning Disabilities (ICLD)

Learning disabilities is a generic term that refers to a heterogeneous group of disorders manifested by significant difficulties in the acquisition and use of listening, speaking, reading, writing, reasoning, or mathematical abilities, or of social skills. These disorders are intrinsic to the individual and presumed to be due to central nervous system dysfunction. Even though a learning disability may occur concomitantly with other handicapping conditions (e.g., sensory impairment, mental retardation, social and emotional disturbance), with socioenvironmental influences (e.g., cultural differences, insufficient or inappropriate instruction, psychogenic factors), and especially with attention deficit disorder, all of which may cause learning problems, a learning disability is not the direct result of those conditions or influences. (ICLD, 1987, p. 222)

From Learning Disability Subtyping *(p. 14), by S. R. Hooper and W. G. Willis, 1989, New York: Springer-Verlag. Copyright 1989 by Springer Verlag. Adapted with permission.*

tual issues in the diagnosis of learning disability is presented in the following section.

Conceptual Issues in the Diagnosis of Learning Disabilities

Although some researchers have argued that learning disability should be considered a heterogeneous disorder characterized by a variety of subtypes (Rourke, 1975, 1978, 1983), other researchers (Algozzine & Ysseldyke, 1986) question whether learning disability constitutes a unique behavioral syndrome and whether it should be considered as a type of disability (Heath & Kush, 1991). Arguments of this type are concerned primarily with the validity of diagnostic procedures for learning disability. The original rules and regulations implementing PL 94–142 (the Rules and Regulations Implementing Education for All Handicapped Children Act of 1975, 1977) provided a definition of learning disability for use by all states receiving federal funds for special education programs (Reynolds, 1990). According to this law, the diagnosis of learning disability

> *is made based on (1) whether a child does not achieve commensurate with his or her age and ability when provided with appropriate educational experience and (2) whether the child has a severe discrepancy between achievement and intellectual ability in one or more of seven areas relating to communication skills and mathematical abilities.*
>
> *These concepts are to be interpreted in a case by case basis by the qualified evaluation team members. The team must decide that the discrepancy is not primarily the result of (1) visual, hearing, or motor handicaps; (2) mental retardation; (3) emotional disturbance; or (4) environmental, cultural, or economic disadvantage. (Rules and Regulations Implementing Education for All Handicapped Children Act of 1975, 1977, p. 65083)*

Although this definition gives some guidance, operationalization of the federal guidelines has largely been left up to individual states, and the criteria vary widely (Reynolds, 1990). Chalfant's (1984) review of state education agency definitions of learning disability across the United States revealed five components that were generally consistent across states:

1. *Failure to achieve* refers to a lack of academic achievement in one of the principle areas of academic learning. This lack of achievement is sometimes compared to grade placement and at other times compared to intellectual functioning.
2. *Psychological process disorders* refer to those basic psychological processes believed to underlie academic learning, including attention and concentration, understanding and using oral and written language, conceptualization, and various types of information processing.
3. *Exclusionary criteria* require that the observed symptoms not be due to such factors as sensory problems; mental retardation; educational, economic, or cultural disadvantage; or emotional disturbance.
4. *Etiology* generally reflects a student's medical and developmental histories, which are reviewed in an attempt to determine factors important in the eti ology of learning disability (e.g., neurological problems, brain injury, delayed speech and language development, perinatal difficulties).
5. *Severe discrepancy* between achievement and intellectual ability in one of the seven areas listed in the federal regulations is required. Some states define the discrepancy by comparing a child's actual achievement with the mean achievement level of all children of the same age, rather than using the child's intellectual ability as the basis for a discrepancy.

Despite the commonalities across states in the components of the learning disability diagnosis, there remains a problem with subjectivity. For instance, when setting a specific operational criterion for a "severe" discrepancy between aptitude and achievement, how is the discrepancy defined? There are many variations across states in the models for determining a severe discrepancy. These range from use of constant grade-equivalent discrepancies (e.g., performing 2 years below grade level for age), to standard score difference methods, to requiring both an achievement deficit and a processing strength (i.e., a processing ability that exceeds intellectual ability), to use of various regression models of aptitude–achievement discrepancies (Reynolds, 1990).

Grade level discrepancy models use arbitrary grade cutoffs (e.g., performance two grade levels below actual placement) to determine discrepancies. They are problematic in that they overidentify children who fall in the slow learner range of intellectual ability, with IQs between 70 and 90. Although these children have academic delays, their performance often is commensurate with their intellectual ability, and there is no severe discrepancy between aptitude and achievement (Reynolds, 1990). For that reason, grade-level discrepancy models are no longer widely used to identify children with learning disability.

Likewise, standard score comparison models require that a child's academic scores fall below their intellectual scores by some predetermined amount. However, these models fail to take into consideration the regression toward the mean that occurs in achievement scores compared with intellectual scores. The concept *regression* indicates that when a dependent variable (academic achievement) is predicted from a correlated measure (IQ), the predicted value of the dependent variable will regress toward the mean over time (Heath & Kush, 1991). The correlation between most IQ and achievement measures ranges between .50 and .65. Because of the effects of regression toward the mean, a child with an IQ of 130 would be expected to achieve around the level of 118–122. Conversely, a child with an IQ of 85 would be expected to achieve at a level of approximately 88–91 (Heath & Kush, 1991). Using straight standard score comparisons without consideration of regression toward the mean results in overidentification of underachieving children in the upper IQ range, and underidentification of children in the lower IQ range (Reynolds, 1990).

Another problem with standard score comparisons is the failure to consider measurement error across different tests, which occurs because IQ and achievement tests are not perfectly correlated. Difference-score reliabilities are less reliable than the reliabilities of the two test scores used to create the difference score. This occurs because the difference-score reliability is determined not only by the reliability of the different tests used, but also by the correlation between the two measures (Heath & Kush, 1991). Thus, it is important to use IQ and achievement tests that have high reliability (greater than .80) and that are highly correlated with each other. Examples include the Kaufman Assessment Battery for Children (Kaufman & Kaufman, 1983) and the Kaufman Test of Educational Achievement (Kaufman & Kaufman, 1985); the Woodcock–Johnson Psychoeducational Battery–Revised Tests of Cognitive Ability and Tests of Achievement (Woodcock & Johnson, 1989); and the Wechsler Intelligence Scale for Children–Third Edition (WISC-III; Wechsler, 1990) and the Wechsler Individual Achievement Test (Psychological Corporation, 1992). In the manual to the last test, for example, a table provides expected or "predicted" achievement levels based on the WISC-III IQ scores, and this makes comparisons easier for the practitioner.

A regression approach to quantify IQ–achievement discrepancies is thought to be the most psychometrically defensible method (Heath & Kush, 1991; Reynolds, 1984; Shepard, 1980; Thorndike, 1963; Wilson & Cone, 1984). This method uses a prediction equation based on the correlation between IQ and achievement scores. For a given individual, his or her IQ score is used to determine an expected or predicted achievement score that is then compared with the actual level of achievement. Only those individuals whose actual level of achievement falls significantly below the expected level would meet the criterion of having a severe discrepancy. According to Heath and Kush (1991), the regression model most appropriate for establishing an IQ–achievement discrepancy indicates that a severe discrepancy exists when the difference between the student's predicted achievement score and the student's actual achievement score exceeds a certain z value.

The choice of a z value is determined by the number of IQ–achievement comparisons being made, because multiple comparisons will lead to an inflated alpha level (resulting in a potentially large number of chance significant discrepancies and overidentification of learning disability). For only one IQ–achievement comparison, a 90% confidence level is appropriate, whereas with two or three comparisons a 95% level is suggested. For more than three comparisons, a 99% confidence level is needed

(Heath & Kush, 1991). For ease of computation and to avoid the possibility of mathematical error, several computer programs are available that calculate significant IQ–achievement discrepancies using a regression approach for IBM-compatible (McDermott & Watkins, 1987) and Apple (McDermott & Watkins, 1985; Reynolds & Snow, 1985; Watkins & Kush, 1988) microcomputers. This rather conservative approach to setting a z level is based on the assumption that for a discrepancy to be considered severe, it should occur relatively infrequently in the normal population of individuals under consideration (Kamphaus & Reynolds, 1987; Reynolds, 1984; Reynolds, 1990).

The preceding discussion illustrates several advantages to the regression approach for determining a severe discrepancy between aptitude and achievement. By taking into account the correlation between IQ and achievement tests, it is possible to assess children across all IQ levels and clearly distinguish between those who have learning disabilities and those who are slow learners (Heath & Kush, 1991). There are some data to support that regression methods produce more proportionate racial representation in learning disability classes than do fixed standard-score definitions (Braden, 1987). Finally, IQ remains the best single predictor of academic achievement, and that prediction can be thought of as an expected level of achievement (Heath & Kush, 1991; Thorndike & Hagen, 1977). Despite the advantages of the regression method, it should be considered a necessary but not sufficient condition for the diagnosis of learning disability (Reynolds, 1984). The other components of the learning disability definition described earlier in this section are also important considerations for diagnosis, but additional research is needed to better operationalize these components. Until then, it is important for practitioners to adopt a theoretical model and to strive to achieve internal consistency in their own diagnostic work with learning disability (Reynolds, 1984). The sections in this chapter reviewing subtyping research and other neuropsychological research on learning disability provide a variety of theoretical perspectives for review as well as a suggested model for learning disability evaluation.

EPIDEMIOLOGY OF LEARNING DISABILITIES

Learning disability is the most frequently diagnosed type of disability among American school-age children. According to Reynolds (1984), the number of school age children diagnosed with learning disability in the United States tripled from 1976 to 1982, with more than 40% of the special education population diagnosed as having learning disabilities. This represents 4% of all school-age children (Chalfant, 1989). As discussed in the section on conceptual issues related to diagnosis of learning disability, the high prevalence rate has led to diagnostic criteria that vary considerably across states. The economic implications of the high prevalence rate (e.g., the additional personnel, space, materials, costs associated with special education services) generally have led states to adopt more stringent criteria for diagnosis. Thus the epidemiology data are confounded by the conceptual problems inherent in the definitional and diagnostic debate related to learning disability among school-age children.

The information on epidemiology of learning disability among the adult population is even more difficult to ascertain. At the postsecondary level, adults with learning disabilities are the fastest growing group of students with disabilities receiving services (Brill, 1987; Gajar, 1992; Gajar, Murphy, & Hunt, 1982; King, 1987). Hirschorn (1988) reported that approximately 1% of the total college freshman population were self-identified as learning disabled. Other studies have reported that over half of the 50,000 high school graduates identified as learning disabled will go on to some form of postsecondary education (Mithaug, Horiuchi, & Fanning, 1985; Shaw & Shaw, 1989; White et al., 1982). These statistics suggest that the over 10-fold increase in college freshmen with learning disabilities through the 1980s will continue through the 1990s and beyond (Shaw & Shaw, 1989). Unfortunately, there is a paucity of information about adults with learning disabilities in community or vocational settings. Obviously much information is needed about the incidence of learning disabilities across a variety of adult populations.

In the following sections, we present the literature with regard to epidemiology across three major types of learning disabilities: dyslexia, dyscalculia, and dysgraphia. This literature by and large pertains to school-age children and adolescents.

Dyslexia

Recognizing the possible effects of varied diagnostic and definitional criteria, conservative estimates suggest that the incidence of dyslexia is about 3:100 to 6:100 (Hynd & Cohen, 1983; Stanovich, 1986). Among the population of school age children, estimates range from 3% to 15%, with boys outnumbering girls by a ratio of approximately 3:2 (Nass, 1992). However, controversy has arisen over the gender issue when sample selection is considered. One group of researchers (Shaywitz, Shaywitz, Fletcher, & Escobar, 1990) investigated results from the Connecticut Longitudinal Study and found gender differences in the prevalence of dyslexia among research-identified and school-identified groups. Among second and third graders, no significant gender differences emerged in the prevalence of dyslexia when research-identified girls were compared with the research-identified boys. However, the school-identified sample classified significantly more boys than girls, and this corresponds to other prevalence statistics on dyslexia (Nass, 1992). Shaywitz et al. (1990) contend that school based referrals may be biased by teachers who are confounding behavior with achievement. Nevertheless, the current *Diagnostic and Statistical Manual of Mental Disorders* (*DSM-IV*, American Psychiatric Association, 1994) supports gender differences, indicating that more men than women have dyslexia.

Dyscalculia

The incidence of dyscalculia has been estimated at 6% of the school population, suggesting that the disorder is not uncommon (Badian, 1983; Gordon, 1992). Norman and Zigmond (1980), reporting on the characteristics of learning disabled students served by Child Service Demonstration Centers, found that 8.1% of their sample had learning disabilities in math, whereas 13.1% had disabilities in both reading and math. A survey of elementary and secondary school learning disability teachers indicated that the typical student with learning disabilities spends a third of his or her time in the resource room for math instruction (Carpenter, 1985). Approximately 26.2% of the learning disabled students from another survey received primary services for math, and an additional 40.3% were served when math was a concern along with another type of learning disability (McLeod & Armstrong, 1982).

Although the estimates of dyscalculia are considerable, the actual incidence of primary mathematics disorders is largely unknown (Semrud-Clikeman & Hynd, 1992). This may be attributed in part to a societal tendency to be more accepting of deficient mathematics abilities, which apparently have a less significant effect on the content areas of academics than do reading or writing disabilities (Gordon, 1992).

Dysgraphia

The existence of dysgraphia, especially in the absence of dyslexia, is thought to be minimal in comparison with other learning disabilities. However, because definitions vary widely, and because schools generally have not attended to this type of learning disability as much as other types, the prevalence is difficult to establish. Rather dated estimates from a review on dysgraphia by Benton (1975) reported a 3% to 4% incidence among children. Similar to dyslexia, dysgraphia is reported to be more prevalent among boys (O'Hare & Brown, 1989b). The paucity of information on dysgraphia reflects the rather meager attention given to this type of learning disability by educators, researchers, and practitioners to date.

PATHOPHYSIOLOGY OF LEARNING DISABILITIES

Neurologic dysfunction among populations who are learning disabled has been inferred for almost a century. Evidence revealing deviations in brain morphology among adults has accumulated and has led to many correlative studies in children. Recent technology (computed tomography, magnetic resonance [MR] imaging, and brain electrical activity mapping [BEAM] studies) has begun to replace correlative data with direct documentation of neurologic involvement. This section of the chapter reviews current thinking surrounding the neuropathogenesis of dyslexia, dyscalculia, and dysgraphia. The majority of research has focused on dyslexia, and this overrepresentation is reflected here.

Dyslexia

Brain morphology studies. From the beginning of the 20th century, early investigators (Fisher, 1905; Hinshelwood, 1895, 1900) recognized similarities between children with reading problems and adults with known brain damage, and they hypothesized that developmental dyslexia was associated with some form of neuropathogenesis. It has been only within the last 2 decades that direct neurologic evidence has been correlated with the pathological neurodevelopmental processes characterized by dyslexia. The preponderance of data has focused on the left central language cortex otherwise known as the planum temporale (See Figure 1). Based on the observations of early investigators like Hinshelwood (1895, 1990) and Fisher (1905), Geschwind and Levitsky (1968) elected to study the morphology of the planum temporale in 100 normal adult brains. They found a reliable pattern of asymmetry in which the left planum appeared to be significantly larger and one third longer than the right in 65% of the normal brains. This pattern of asymmetry has been established as early as the 20th week of gestation (Weinberger, Luchins, Morihisa, & Wyatt, 1982). In the brain of individuals with dyslexia, however, this asymmetrical pattern of the planum has not been found (See Figure 1). Two recent studies (Galaburda, Sherman, Rosen, Aboitiz, & Geschwind, 1985; Humphreys, Kaufman, & Galaburda, 1990) not only have documented alterations in the pattern of brain asymmetry of language areas but also have revealed the presence of minor cortical malformations in the brains of four male and three female individuals with dyslexia. These authors discovered abnormal symmetrical planum temporale and glial scarring among ectopic neurons in the molecular layer of the perisylvian cortex (predominately frontal and involving the vascular watershed of the anterior and middle cerebral arteries). Humphreys et al. (1990) contended that the same insult responsible for the scarring is also responsible for the minor cortical malformations and that a manifestation of dyslexia is dependent on both symmetric plana and microscopic pathology.

Other lines of research have documented deviations from normal asymmetries favoring the left side in the anterior speech region (pars opercularis and pars triangularis of the third frontal convolution; Falzi, Perrone, & Vignolo, 1982), the auditory cortex (Galaburda & Sanides, 1980), the inferior parietal lobe and the posterior thalamus (Eidelberg & Galaburda, 1982). Further investigation of the thalamus (Galaburda & Livingstone, 1993) has revealed a magnocellular defect within the lateral geniculate nuclei in which the average magnocellular areas were 27% smaller in the brains of individuals with dyslexia when compared with nondyslexic brains. Histological sections of the lateral geniculate nuclei evinced more disorganization among the magnocellular layers of the dyslexic brains and more variation in the size and shape of the cell bodies. Additional examination of the medial geniculate nuclei among the same sample failed to reveal any significant differences between the dyslexic and control brains but demonstrated a reverse asymmetry in the proportion of large cells in favor of the right medial geniculate nuclei in the dyslexic group ($n = 5$). Neuroanatomical research implicating both the linguistic nature of dyslexia (Humphreys et al., 1990) and perceptual processing factors (Galaburda & Livingstone, 1993) seems to be pertinent to understanding the etiology.

FIGURE 1. Coronal section of the brain illustrating the normal asymmetry of the planum temporale, with the left-hemisphere planum larger than the right.

Immune disturbances. Although animal studies (Humphreys, Rosen, Press, Sherman, & Galaburda, 1991; Sherman, Galaburda, & Geschwind, 1985) have intimated that autoimmune damage of vessel walls produces ischemic insult to the developing cortex, leading to cortical injury, scars, and malformations, the possible role of immune disturbances as the etiologic basis of dyslexia among humans remains unknown (Galaburda, 1993). One hypothesis that continues to precipitate etiologic investigations is that of Geschwind (Geschwind & Behan, 1982), which proposes a positive correlation between left-handedness, immune disturbances (allergic and autoimmune), and learning disabilities (mainly dyslexia). The hypothesis contends that normal development of left-hemisphere dominance is suppressed by testosterone in utero, consequently resulting in an increased incidence of left-handedness, developmental language disorders, and autoimmune or atopic diseases.

Hugdahl, Synnevag, and Satz (1990) found significant increases in allergic and autoimmune illness among 105 children with dyslexia when compared with an equivalent control group. However, no significant handedness differences were revealed between the groups. Galaburda (1993) suggested that before this issue is successfully resolved, research with large populations using standard measures of handedness and diagnostic criteria for learning and immunological dysfunctions will need to be conducted. Presently, the learning–immunological association seems to be more viable than the learning disorders–left-handedness relationship.

Neuroimaging studies. Neuroimaging studies of dyslexics have supported and supplemented Galaburda's neuroanatomical studies. Two MR imaging studies conducted recently (Hynd, Semrud-Clikeman, Lorys, Novey, & Eliopulos, 1990; Larsen, Høien, Lundberg, & Ødegaard, 1990) revealed that children with dyslexia demonstrated either equal symmetry or reversed asymmetry of the planum (See Figure 1). Hynd et al. (1990) also found that children with dyslexia had smaller insular regions bilaterally and significantly reduced size of the left planum temporale when compared with controls and children with attention deficit hyperactivity disorder (ADHD). Larsen et al. (1990) distinguished subtypes among the dyslexics in their sample and found that all of the phonological dyslexics were found to have symmetry of the planum. Because this consistency was not demonstrated within other subtypes, the authors suggested that normal phonological awareness was dependent on asymmetry of the planum.

Morphology studies utilizing MR imaging have also investigated the corpus callosum in children with dyslexia. Because frontal lobe involvement has been implicated among dyslexics, researchers in one study (Hynd et al., 1993) hypothesized that the genu of the corpus callosum would be morphologically different than that found in normal brains. Indeed, children with developmental dyslexia were found to have significantly smaller genu regions of the corpus callosum than controls, implying differences in interhemispheric connections that may affect reading. Positron emission tomography has also been used among dyslexic populations. This method has allowed researchers to observe true brain–behavior relationships as they occur during various functions. In two recent studies (Gross-Glenn et al., 1991; Rumsey et al., 1992), adults with dyslexia read or performed a related task while brain activation was observed simultaneously. As expected, activation was absent in the left occipital, temporoparietal, and midtemporal regions. These results appear to support the data that suggest left temporoparietal impairment in children and adults with dyslexia.

Although children with dyslexia reportedly have demonstrated altered brain potentials, electroencephalographic abnormalities are not uncommon in the normal child, with paroxysmal abnormalities in about 1%, and other minor abnormalities found in up to 5%, of the normal population (Nass, 1992). Nevertheless, many studies investigating the electroencephalogram (EEG) spectra revealed differences between dyslexics and normals. In a recent study (Ortiz, Exposito, Miguel, Martin-Loeches, & Rubia, 1992), carefully screened samples of 9- to 12-year-old dysphonemic-sequencing dyslexic children and normal controls were compared via topographic mapping of EEG bands and alpha asymmetry. During resting conditions, no significant differences were revealed. However, while participants were engaged in an auditory phonemic discrimination task, the dyslexic group demonstrated a left-hemisphere alpha responsiveness and a beta 2 decrease in the left posterior quadrant. The authors concluded that this atypical pattern may be indicative of disorganized neural processors, such as poor attention to external stimuli or dysfunctional cognitive processing, that are directly related to the task demands of an auditory phonemic discrimination problem.

Event-related potentials are perhaps of more relevance than EEGs or evoked potentials to the neuropsychologist, who may be interested in clinical disorders that manifest as cognitive or behavioral problems. Various types of computerized systems exist, so that the event-related potentials can be mapped or imaged as they evolve throughout the cortex. Hynd and Willis (1988) illustrated differences between the topographical maps of an individual with dysphonetic dyslexia and an age-matched control. The distribution of the P3 component of event-related potentials in the nondyslexic individual was symmetrical, but there was a marked left-sided asymmetry in the P3 response of the individual with dysphonetic dyslexia (Hynd & Willis, 1988).

Genetic studies. Increased genetic research over the last decade has provided evidence for familial dyslexia. Genetic research since the study by Hallgren (1950) has strongly suggested an autosomal dominant mode of inheritance for many cases of developmental dyslexia. The study by S. D. Smith, Kimberling, Pennington, and Lubs (1983) indicated a link to the 15th chromosome, and this became the fulcrum for future studies on this topic. However, interpretation of many genetic studies of dyslexia has been compromised because they have used criteria for subject selection (i.e., patients with normal IQ, evidence of a relatively pure reading disability, and absence of other etiologic factors) that resulted in a probable mixture of genetic transmission modes, including generation-to-generation transmission (autosomal dominant inheritance), affected siblings with normal parents (autosomal recessive inheritance), and sporadic cases that are often multifactorial (DeFries & Decker, 1982; Finucci, Guthrie, Childs, Abbey, & Childs, 1976; Lubs et al., 1991). According to DeFries and Decker (1982), the statistical techniques necessary to justify different genetic mechanisms in the presence of phenotypic similarities are inadequate, although they may show a significant genetic component and may be consistent with a major gene defect (Lubs et al., 1991). For instance Pennington et al. (1991), in a recent article, reported that a significant proportion of the 204 families studied demonstrated a sex-influenced, additive, and major gene transmission. However, the authors warn that the etiology of dyslexia remains heterogeneous even in the presence of dominant transmission. Conclusions about the specific transmission of dyslexia will vary widely depending on the proportion of families with each type of inheritance that were included in a particular study (Lubs et al., 1991).

Dyscalculia

Neuroanatomical studies. Several hypotheses regarding the neuroanatomical basis for dyscalculia have emerged, including the right-hemisphere dysfunction hypothesis, the shared-hemisphere hypothesis, and the subcortical dysfunction hypothesis. Because mathematics clearly has spatial components, the link to right cerebral hemisphere function is perhaps the most strongly supported of the hypotheses. Researchers (Ozols & Rourke, 1985; Rourke & Strang, 1983) have demonstrated the spatial–right-hemisphere association by investigating different dyscalculia subtypes among children. The results indicated that those children who demonstrate a mathematics disorder exclusively perform more poorly on visual-perceptual and visuospatial measures than those children with multiple academic disorders. This finding corroborates right cerebral hemisphere dysfunction for some advanced mathematics skills.

Compromised bilateral hemisphere dysfunction has been suggested as an etiologic factor in dyscalulia by a number of researchers (Giannitrapani, 1982; Katz, 1980), acknowledging the many processes involved in mathematical tasks. Boller and Grafman (1985) reported that 84% of patients with left temporo-occipital lesions presented with alexia or agraphia for numbers, whereas 89% of patients with right-sided lesions exhibited spatial acalculia. Math problems that are spatial in nature often require both reading and writing the numbers, thereby supporting the hypothesis that implicates bilateral hemispheric mediation (Grafman, Passaflume, Faglioni, & Boller, 1982). Children who have math deficits in conjunction with reading and spelling deficiencies (left-hemisphere mediated tasks) may be the best examples of shared hemisphere dysfunction (Semrud-Clikeman & Hynd, 1992).

A third hypothesis regarding the etiology of dyscalculia involves subcortical dysfunction. An early study by Ojemann (1974), involving the electrical stimulation of the thalamus, suggested that subcortical processes may be significantly involved in mathematical skills. An orienting response and an acceleration of mental arithmetic abilities were produced by stimulation of the left thalamic region, whereas right-side stimulation resulted in more calculation errors and a decrease in the speed of counting and number identification. Therefore, sensory input may be oriented within the thalamic region and integrated with other subprocesses necessary for successful mathematics performance (Semrud-Clikeman & Hynd, 1990).

An awareness of the many neuropsychological processes (i.e., perceptual, linguistic, cognitive, and functional) involved in dyscalculia has contributed to hypotheses about possible dysfunctional brain–behavior connections that may underlie dyscalculia (Spiers, 1987). The cortical regions that have been associated with specific mathematical proficiencies are listed in Table 1.

According to Keller and Sutton (1991), the perceptual skills of visuospatial organization (needed for comprehension and production of written math) are mediated by the right hemisphere, whereas the hemisphere that is dominant for language mediates the linguistic skills necessary for math performance (Novick & Arnold, 1988). The higher association areas of the dominant hemisphere are critical in reading and comprehending word problems, as well as understanding math concepts and procedures (Novick & Arnold, 1988). The frontal lobes are important in the processes of quick mental calculations and abstract conceptualization (Gaddes, 1985), as well as for problem-solving skills and for written and oral performance (Novick & Arnold, 1988). The parietal lobes mediate motoric functions and tactile sensory discriminations, both of which can be involved in math performance (Gaddes, 1985; Keller & Sutton, 1991). The left parietal lobe is particularly important in sequencing abilities (Novick & Arnold, 1988), and the parietal lobes in general play an im-

TABLE 1

Cortical Regions and Abilities Associated With Mathematical Proficiency

Cortical region	Ability
Right hemisphere	Visuospatial organization
Language-dominant hemisphere	Linguistic skills
Higher association areas of the dominant hemisphere	Reading and understanding word problems and mathematical concepts and procedures
Frontal lobes	Quick mental calculations, abstract conceptualizing, problem-solving skills, and oral and written performance
Parietal lobes	Motoric functions, use of tactile sensations
Left parietal lobes	Sequencing abilities
Occipital lobes	Visual discrimination of written mathematical symbols
Temporal lobes	Auditory perception, long-term verbal memory
Dominant temporal lobe	Memory of series, basic math facts, and subvocalization during problem solving

Note: From "Specific Mathematics Disorders," by C. E. Keller and J. P. Sutton. In *Neuropsychological Foundations of Learning Disabilities* (p. 555), edited by J. E. Obrzut and G. W. Hynd, 1991, San Diego, CA: Academic Press. Copyright 1991 by Academic Press. Adapted with permission.

portant integrative role in the cortical organization of the senses (Keller & Sutton, 1991). The occipital lobes mediate the process of visual discrimination of written mathematical symbols (Novick & Arnold, 1988), and are important in routine calculations and geometry (Gaddes, 1985). The temporal lobes are necessary for mathematical skills involving auditory perception and long-term verbal memory (Gaddes, 1985), whereas the dominant temporal lobe is responsible for memory of basic math facts, memory of series, and subvocalization during problem solving (Novick & Arnold, 1988).

Given the complexity of the processes involved in mathematical performance and the likely interaction or interplay of these various processes it is difficult to discern specific neuroanatomic dysfunctions associated with specific neuropsychological deficits (Grunau & Low, 1987; Novick & Arnold, 1988). Research designs that consider the relationship among the component processes in mathematics performance will likely add to our understanding of the heterogeneity of dyscalculia and extend our knowledge of pathogenesis beyond its current rudimentary state (Keller & Sutton, 1991).

Neuroimaging studies. At present there is little research investigating the neurologic basis of dyscalculia using noninvasive techniques, such as evoked potentials, CT scans, and MR imaging (Semrud-Clikeman & Hynd, 1992). Because these techniques typically have been reserved for the more common reading disorders, potential deviations in the brains of children with dyscalculia have not been well documented. However, a few EEG studies have revealed that when normal individuals are compared with patients with documented right-hemispheric brain damage and arithmetic deficits, significant psychophysiological differences are found. One such study (Mattson, Sheer, & Fletcher, 1991) found that during a nonverbal task, children with arithmetic learning disorders generated proportionally less right-hemisphere 40-Hz EEG activity than did either the reading disabled children or controls.

Despite these results suggesting right-hemispheric dysfunction, there is also electrophysiological evidence (Grunau & Low, 1987) implicating a relationship between bilateral posterior association regions and mathematics difficulties. This finding corresponds to Luria's (1980) original hypothesis implying the bilateral involvement of the parieto-temporo-occipital areas in dyscalculia.

Dysgraphia

As with most childhood disorders, the neurophysiological basis of developmental dysgraphia has been gradually understood by observing similar behaviors exhibited by adults with acquired brain dysfunction. Clinical markers that might distinguish the written output of persons with developmental dysgraphia compared with persons with acquired dysgraphia resulting from postnatal brain injury do not exist (O'Hare & Brown, 1989a). Writing has been shown to be compromised in adults with lesions found in left-hemispheric language areas, the bilateral posterior cerebral areas (occipito-temporal-parietal), and the sensorimotor strips localized to the left (Luria, 1966). One might expect that by virtue of its complexity, written language is dependent on many, if not most, regions of the cerebrum. Developmentally speaking, normal written language skills emerge only when the brain mechanisms responsible for earlier developing language functions (speaking and reading) have matured properly (Myklebust, 1973). Unfortunately, neurophysiological studies investigating dysgraphia have been overshadowed by those pursuing dyslexia. The paucity of research, especially that investigating developmental dysgraphia, may be somewhat attributed to the multifarious nature of the disorder. Children who exhibit writing disorders may manifest difficulties at early ages with the graphomotor aspects of writing (legibility, rate of production, spatial presentation, punctuation, and capitalization), with the phonological–linguistic features (grammar, sentence formulation, and spelling), or with both, and may evidence semantic or compositional problems at later ages. This final genre of written language is sometimes neglected, particularly in the school setting. Johnson and Myklebust (1967) first addressed the formation of abstract–imaginative writing (e.g., character and plot development, moral themes, etc.) and deemed it, ontogenically, the highest stage of written language development. More recently, research suggesting an association to frontal brain maturation has evolved (Dennis, 1991) and has delineated additional characteristics typically found in this highest stage (e.g., comprehension of words and events, use of metaphors and analogies). Children exhibiting a semantic dysgraphia may in fact have compromised frontal lobes (resulting from prenatal or genetic circumstances) that would generate relatively few difficulties in the primary levels of school but would keep them from developing to their full potential during their later educational career. The Kennard Principle (Kolb & Whishaw, 1985), which explains how an early neurologic insult may not have an effect on a child's behavior until the neurologic site responsible for that behavior is fully developed, would support this hypothesis.

Although Luria's adult clinical studies of dysgraphia have provided information regarding localization of brain dysfunction across the various components of written language, O'Hare and Brown (1989a) have devised a concise review of childhood dysgraphia via the medical model (see Table 2). The heterogeneous nature of dysgraphia dictates that the practitioner be familiar with specific categories before hypothesizing neuroanatomical substrates.

Genetic research on dysgraphia has not advanced to the level of designating an actual chromosome responsible for this disorder. However, children with the XXY presentation have been shown to demonstrate congenital markers similar to children with acquired dysgraphia (Ratcliffe, 1982).

Genetic activation that may dictate brain maturation among individuals has also been hypothesized from cases of spelling dysgraphia, which is occasionally inherited in the absence of delayed or abnormal speech development (O'Hare & Brown, 1989a). This presentation is perhaps an exception to Myklebust's hierarchical conceptualization of acquisition of written language skills (Myklebust, 1965b; see Exhibit 2).

Finally, linguistic dysgraphics may follow a course of brain maturation similar to that suggested for dyslexics by Geschwind and Galaburda (1985). Delays in reading decoding and comprehension in

TABLE 2

Clinical Classification of Dysgraphia Related to Underlying Brain Mechanisms

Category	Clinical expression	Underlying brain mechanism
Motor dysgraphia		
Visual–spatial	Recognition of faces, shapes, objects, places, and directions	Occipital and parietal lobes on nondominant side; angular gyrus
Executive–coordination	Speed of movement Grip strength Execution of a movement	Extrapyramidal and cerebellar systems Pyramidal tract
Dyspraxia	Motor planning Motor sequence Automaticity	Precentral motor cortex Cerebellum Parietal lobes
Spelling–syntactical	Spelling Punctuation Sentence structure	Motor association areas Broca's region Related subcortical structures Early neuronal migration and assembly in cortex
Semantic composition	Conceptualization Understanding of metaphors and analogies	Left frontal cortex Left temporal cortex

Note: From "Childhood Dysgraphia: Part 1. An Illustrated Clinical Classification," by A. E. O'Hare and J. K. Brown, 1989, *Child: Care, Health, and Development*, *15*, pp. 79–104. Copyright 1989 by Blackwell Science. Adapted with permission.

EXHIBIT 2

Hierarchy for Acquisition of Verbal Language Skills

Writing
(Visual expressive language)

Reading
(Visual receptive language)

Speaking
(Auditory expressive language)

Comprehension of Spoken Word
(Auditory receptive language)

Inner Language
(Auditory symbol and experience)

Experience

This hierarchy illustrates the progression of the development of human language from the most basic level (experience) to the highest level (writing). From The Psychology of Deafness *(2nd ed., p. 232), by H. Myklebust, 1965, New York: Grune & Stratton. Copyright 1965 by Grune & Stratton. Adapted with permission.*

addition to dysphonetic spelling errors are typically seen in children with a linguistic writing disorder (Sandler et al., 1992). The difficulty in making a differential diagnosis between dysgraphia and dyslexia provides further support for a common neurologic etiology. O'Hare and Brown (1989a) suggest that children may be incorrectly diagnosed as dyslexic, only later to make improvements in reading and continue to exhibit dysgraphia as their primary disability. Because such similarities exist, readers are referred to the pathophysiological section concerning dyslexia, which explains theories of neuronal migration, cortex assembly, and subcortical connections.

Gregg (1992) contends that although the neurophysiological aspects of dysgraphia have been somewhat neglected in the past, recent interest may provide evidence for the neural integration of the many skills (visual, motor, linguistic, etc.) required for written output.

SUBTYPING OF LEARNING DISABILITIES

The present-day conceptualization of learning disabilities suggests that it is a heterogeneous disorder with different subtypes based on either the presumed underlying pathology or the clinical presentation. Since 1963, over 100 learning disabilities classification studies have appeared in the literature, about half of which are clinical–inferential models and the rest empirical classification models (Hooper & Willis, 1989). Clinical–inferential models attempt to group individuals into homogeneous clusters through post hoc analyses based on patterns of test performance. The variables used to derive subtypes include achievement, neurocognitive (intellectual and neuropsychological), and neurolinguistic measures, as well as combinations of these measures. Although clinical–inferential models have provided a foundation for the multidimensional nature of learning disabilities, they have given way to empirical classification models during the 1980s—paralleling advances in computer technology (Hooper & Willis, 1989). Despite their intuitive appeal, the clinical–inferential approaches have been criticized methodologically due to limited data reduction strategies and questionable validity (Hooper & Willis, 1989). In contrast, empirical classification approaches are designed to group individuals on the basis of test performance profile similarities using advanced statistical procedures such as Q factor analysis and cluster analysis. These empirical classification schemes are limited by the quality of the data input, however, and require sound clinical judgment on the part of the investigator for interpretation. It is beyond the scope of this chapter to provide a detailed review of the various classification schemas developed to date; the interested reader is referred to Hooper and Willis (1989) for a detailed overview of subtyping models developed through the late 1980s.

Even a cursory overview of the subtyping approaches in the literature leaves one wondering about their clinical applicability. Given the number of syndromes described and the need for further validation research, it is difficult to select a subtyping model for use in clinical practice. It is clear that subtyping research can lead to increased understanding of possible neuroanatomic correlates with clinical syndromes and eventually can lead to more precise information about the effectiveness of different intervention approaches. The evolution of the subtyping research from clinical–inferential to empirical approaches has paved the way to explore the complexities associated with degree of severity and specificity of impairment across, as well as within, a wide array of functional domains (Hooper & Willis, 1989). However, many of the empirical studies have been criticized for their tendency to use tests without a specific theoretical rationale for their selection, leading to subtypes that have little clinical utility and little significance in helping us understand why children cannot learn normally (Hynd, Connor, & Nieves, 1988). Hynd et al. (1988), Satz and Morris (1981), and Taylor, Fletcher, and Satz (1982) have argued that subtypes should be defined in terms of actual patterns of deficient learning behaviors and then studied neuropsychologically. According to Hynd et al. (1988), this approach allows for careful analysis of patterns of errors in reading, math, and so forth that may eventually reveal potential subprocesses directly involved in learning within a specific domain. By assessing actual processes involved in fluent reading, the assessment achieves greater ecological validity, and the derived subtypes may actually be observed in the clinical setting. Finally, if the actual neurocognitive behaviors that characterize learning disability subtypes can be delineated, direct treatment implications may result (Hynd et al., 1988).

At the present stage of our knowledge, it is probably best for the practitioner to use the subtyping literature as a guide for examining the various cognitive, perceptual, linguistic, and neuropsychological processes that may underlie disorders of learning, and to subtype on an individual basis for each client. Subsequent sections will provide a conceptual model for a neuropsychological approach to assessment of learning disabilities.

NEUROPSYCHOLOGICAL RESEARCH ON LEARNING DISABILITIES

Neuropsychological studies continue to provide at least indirect evidence reflecting the neuropathogenesis of learning disabilities. Although neuropathological research has been accepted with regard to the adult population with acquired learning deficits, some researchers (Fletcher & Taylor, 1984) argued that to infer central nervous system abnormalities on the basis of a child's performance on certain neuropsychological tests perpetuates faulty logic and inadequate research. This contention was predicated both on the lack of specific brain–behavior relationships confirming a central nervous system etiology of learning disabilities in children a decade ago, and the process of change that separates children from adults (i.e., the developing brain of children compared with the fully mature brain of adults). However, the relevance of neuropsychological testing among children with learning disabilities has been justified in recent years by its discriminant power (distinguishing disabled from nondisabled learners), its appraisal of the processes that preclude learning, its predictive capabilities, and its value in the development of treatment interventions (Taylor, 1988).

This section focuses on the contributions made by neuropsychological studies of learning disabilities and the salient features that best characterize learning disabilities from onset to adulthood. It is beyond the scope of this chapter to provide a detailed review of this extensive body of research; rather, the important neuropsychological findings and trends in neuropsychological research are summarized. Reflective of the current literature, most studies reviewed focus on children and adolescents. There is little neuropsychological research regarding learning disabilities in adults, but the available research is discussed.

Dyslexia

Neuropsychological research on developmental dyslexia has explored several conceptualizations. Early investigators attributed dyslexia to a variety of single-factor conceptualizations, as discussed earlier, whereas later investigators (Mattis, Erenberg, & French, 1978; Mattis, French, & Rapin, 1975; Rourke, Young, & Flewelling, 1971) proposed a dual conceptualization model involving generally auditory–linguistic versus visuospatial deficits. The various single and dual conceptualization models have been investigated and have for the most part been set aside in favor of a multidimensional conceptualization that better incorporates the complexities of processes involved in dyslexia.

The Mattis et al. studies (1975, 1978) represent the emergence of subtyping research that has been so popular in recent years and has guided most of the neuropsychological research in this field. However, subtyping research has not been without controversy. Satz and colleagues took issue with studies that used neuropsychological measures for subtyping without a specific rationale for their selection and without first delineating the patterns of deficient reading behaviors (Satz & Morris, 1981; Taylor et al., 1982). Currently, researchers have begun to group children based on the type of errors they make in an effort to discover which processes are deficient or adequate in the learning of new material. Most of the current studies have focused on the underlying linguistic deficits in dyslexia. This has occurred as a result of the neuroanatomical and neurophysiological studies that implicate language centers of the brain (Galaburda et al., 1985; Hynd et al., 1990; Larsen et al., 1990).

Dyslexia investigators (Deloche, Andreewsky, & Desi, 1982) who have followed this line of research have expanded our knowledge of the linguistic processes underlying reading. These authors, in particular, have discovered by error analysis that dyslexic readers can be categorized into two types: *surface* dyslexics or *deep* dyslexics. Surface dyslexics were found to overrely on phonological rules, struggle with visual features of unfamiliar words, and exhibit impaired comprehension. Deep dyslexics present with semantic paralexias during oral reading and have poor visual–semantic associations. Deep dyslexics may see the word *airplane* and read *jet*. Both types appear to have visual memory problems.

Fletcher (1985) investigated specific aspects of memory, including both storage and retrieval mechanisms via a selective reminding task. He found that children who had a reading or spelling disability actually performed worse on a verbal memory task than on a nonverbal visual memory task.

After reviewing the research on dyslexia, Ellis (1987) contended that dyslexia research needed to focus on early cognitive systems (i.e., attention, memory, perception, etc.) that use visual, semantic, and phonological processes that are subsequently used by later reading systems. One longitudinal study (Wolf & Obregon, 1992) investigated early naming deficits in an effort to incorporate visual, semantic, phonological, and other processes associated with reading development. Retrieving words from lexical storage has been shown to encompass many of the cognitive systems (attention, memory, and perception) via phonological, semantic, and motoric procedures (Goodglass, 1980). Moreover, "subtle dysnomia" (Rudel, 1985) has been noted most often as a salient feature of children with dyslexia. *Subtle dysnomia* refers to either the slow naming access speed individuals use on rapid naming tasks or to inadequate naming. Murphy, Pollatsek, and Well (1988) found that these naming problems translated to other natural speech situations such as retelling stories. Wolf and Obregon (1992) found that children with dyslexia (kindergarten through fourth grade) had considerable difficulty retrieving words when compared with nondyslexic children, and this discrepancy increased over time. These early and middle stages of reading development appear to be marked by a significant subtle dysnomia (Denckla & Rudel, 1976) during confrontational naming tasks. Moreover, other studies (Spring & Davis, 1988; Swanson, 1989) have demonstrated pervasive latency problems with word-retrieval throughout adolescence and into adulthood among individuals with dyslexia.

Cornwall (1992) illustrated the numerous cognitive and linguistic processes that seem to be impaired among children with severe reading disabilities. Following Fletcher's (1985) findings that implicated verbal memory, Cornwall further investigated verbal memory, phonological awareness, and naming speed and their association to five tasks readily assessed in dyslexia evaluations (e.g., word attack, word identification, reading comprehension, spelling). This carefully constructed study controlled for socioeconomic status, age, IQ, and behavior problems. Results revealed that verbal memory was a good predictor of word recognition skills; that phonological awareness was a good predictor of word attack, spelling, and reading comprehension skills; and that rapid naming was a good predictor of word identification, prose passage speed, and accuracy scores. These findings support the notion that it is the interaction of many exclusive processes that provides information concerning the existence and severity of dyslexia.

Along the lines of exploring the processes that contribute to reading failure emerges research that has investigated the organizational or executive function deficits in dyslexic children (Levin, 1990). In her study, Levin revealed that several frontal lobe functions, including verbal fluency, verbal learning, and conceptual problem solving, were compromised in children with dyslexia when compared with nondyslexic children. Specifically, strategies for solving problems were poorly generated and executed by the dyslexic group.

Levin's (1990) study appears not only to corroborate the neuroanatomical investigations of dyslexia, but also to provide a good representation of the direction in which neuropsychological research of dyslexia is heading. Research is beginning to depart from the multivariate studies that cluster variables (only vaguely related to reading) into subtypes that offer little information about how dyslexics process information.

Dyscalculia

Many of the early neuropsychological studies were guided by the premise that dyscalculia was most often associated with visuospatial deficits (Johnson & Myklebust, 1967; Kaliski, 1962; Strauss, 1951; Strauss & Lehtinen, 1947). Although Rourke and Finlayson (1978) reported that children with developmental dyscalculia could be discriminated reliably from those with other academic disorders by their poor visuospatial skills, other researchers (McLeod & Crump, 1978) were beginning to acknowledge the verbal aspects involved in mathematics performance. McLeod and Crump (1978) conducted a correlational analysis of several variables presumed related to dyscalculia and found that two verbal variables ranked slightly higher than the visuospatial variables when predicting mathematical performance. Despite the statistical limitations of this study (i.e., low subject representation), these authors provided some support for the importance of linguistic mechanisms underlying dyscalculia.

Other researchers have validated a subtype format by investigating conceptually derived subtypes of learning-disabled students with mathematic disorders (Rourke & Finlayson, 1978; Strang & Rourke, 1983; 1985). Briefly, these researchers found that, based on the Wide Range Achievement Test reading, spelling, and arithmetic subtests, one group (Group 1) emerged with difficulties in all academic areas, the second group (Group 2) demonstrated higher math than reading and spelling scores although all areas were depressed, and the final group (Group 3) had average reading and spelling skills with deficient arithmetic ability. Further neuropsychological tests revealed that Group 2 (i.e., deficient reading and spelling) exhibited poor auditory perceptual skills, whereas Group 3 (i.e., deficient arithmetic) had impairment in tactile perceptual tasks bilaterally, delayed psychomotor abilities, and difficulties with spatial organizational and analysis skills. When an error analysis was conducted between children in Group 3 and other children who had less significant mathematic difficulties, Group 3 demonstrated more mechanical arithmetic errors overall but apparently had little difficulty with tasks involving judgment and reasoning. Characteristics of these errors include

- Spatial organization problems
- Inadequate attention to visual detail
- Sequential difficulties in process
- Mental flexibility problems (shifting set)
- Poor graphomotor technique
- Compromised storage and retrieval of number facts
- Poor number logic.

Strang and Rourke (1983) suggested that disturbed development in sensorimotor processes impaired the ability of Group 3 children to acquire the primary fundamentals necessary for higher mathematics development. Possibly, precursors to these fundamental deficits may be apparent within a child's developmental history regarding the acquisition of motor milestones.

The subtyping approach introduced by Rourke and his associates to identify the neuropsychological patterns of developmental dyscalculia may be clinically valuable. Nevertheless, the cognitive processes responsible for mathematical performance (both visual and aural) cannot be overlooked. Similar to the evolution of dyslexia research, research on dyscalculia has evolved from single conceptualization models, to subtyping, to an examination of the cognitive processes underlying the disorder. An example of the latter approach is provided by Batchelor, Gray, and Dean (1990), who applied a multivariate procedure to examine the association between aural (revised WISC [WISC-R; Wechsler, 1974], Arithmetic subtest) and visual (revised Wide Range Achievement Test, Math subtest) math performance compared with several neuropsychological tasks. Their analysis revealed that mental flexibility (Trails B from the Halstead–Reitan Neuropsychological Test Battery), verbal–auditory discrimination (Speech Sounds Perception test from the Halstead–Reitan), long-term memory for general information (WISC-R, Information subtest), and visuospatial processing (WISC-R, Block Design) were all related to increased scores on both the arithmetic subtests of the WISC-R and the revised Wide Range Achievement Test. This study demonstrated that both verbal and nonverbal neuropsychological functions, as well as visual and aural memory processing, are necessary in mathematical problem solving.

As a further analysis, Batchelor et al. (1990) empirically tested a cognitive model to account for the neuropsychological functioning underlying mathematical problem solving. The cognitive model investigated was developed by Dinnel, Glover, and Ronning (1984) and Dinnel, Glover, and Halpain (in press). This model relies on the visual stimuli surrounding the task to be solved as an operational extension of the working memory. Batchelor et al. (1990) were interested in investigating the proportion of children's math performance that was reliant on continuous visual stimuli. Results revealed that verbal facility, nonverbal intermediate memory, and verbal abstract reasoning accounted for approximately 12% of the variance associated with the continuous visual stimulus. This suggests that the neuropsychological underpinnings of dyscalculia may be much more complex than originally hypothesized. Keller and Sutton (1991) have suggested that future studies, similar to the last one discussed, that combine a cognitive with a neuropsychological perspective may be most informative in explaining how compromised neuropsychological processes and skills contribute to dyscalculia. One neuropsychological process important to mathematical performance that has not been discussed thus far is attention. Rosenberger (1989) investigated both the perceptual-motor and attentional correlates of developmental dyscalculia in comparison with children with reading deficits. Children with dyscalculia displayed significantly lower performance on the Bender–Gestalt Test for Young Children (Koppitz, 1975) and the Arithmetic subtest of the WISC-R, along with more symptoms of impaired attention (based on *Diagnostic and Statistical Manual of Mental Disorders*, third edition criteria for attention deficit disorder without hyperactivity; American Psychiatric Association, 1980). This author contended that attentional deficits may preclude children from developing an aptitude for math, as automatization of number facts is difficult when attention and concentration are compromised.

Rosenberger (1989) and the researchers discussed earlier have contributed greatly to the understanding of dyscalculia and have prompted other investigators to consider neuropsychological potentiators of dyscalculia. Future researcher will need to consider the conceptual, linguistic, and attentional components of mathematics in addition to the well researched visuospatial deficits.

Dysgraphia

In comparison with dyslexia and dyscalculia, the neuropsychological research on developmental dysgraphia is extremely limited. Perhaps this lack of research reflects both dysgraphia's subordinate position in many school environments (compared with reading and mathematics) and the limited use of written expression measures in the course of a psychoeducational assessment. In addition, there seems to be a tendency to link dysgraphia with dyslexia (Hanley, Hastie, & Kay, 1992) because of the many similarities in phonological processing deficits underlying the two disorders. However, early researchers suggested that phonological deficits assist a diagnostician in differentiating dyslexia and dysgraphia. Nelson and Warrington (1974) discovered that dyslexic children who could not spell exhibited disphonetic errors, whereas dysgraphic children who read well made fewer disphonetic errors and approximately the same amount of sequential errors. One other notable difference found in this study of 121 children concerned intelligence. A pattern of lower verbal IQ on the WISC was demonstrated by the children with both dyslexia and dysgraphia. The children who exhibited only spelling problems had no significant discrepancy between verbal and performance IQs. Frith (1983) likewise acknowledged dysgraphic children who are able to read well. She found that these children use only partial cues within the lexical visual route. This route refers to a neural pathway used by normal individuals when reading a word (e.g., occipital to temporal to frontal). Because only partial cues are used when viewing words, dysgraphic children neglect some letters, and this is unproductive for letter-by-letter spelling precision.

It seems that although dysgraphia has been discussed as a heterogeneous disorder like dyslexia and dyscalculia (Myklebust, 1965a), most of the early research has focused on the spelling deficits alone. However, one recent study (Sandler et al., 1992) exemplified the diverse nature of dysgraphia by taking both a neuropsychological and developmental approach to investigate empirically derived clusters of writing disorders. These authors evaluated children ages 9 to 14 years old and revealed four dysgraphic clusters, each with a distinct pattern of writing characteristics. The subtypes were discriminated from one another by teacher observations of writing samples and 12 selected neurodevelopmental subtests in a discriminant function analysis. Neurodevelopmental subtests requiring retrieval memory such as rapid naming tasks, oral sentence formation, digit span, and visual retrieval were the most distinguishing, thus providing support for the subtyping of writing disorders. However, Sandler et al. (1992) were quick to explain that neurodevelopmental testing only provides evidence of relative strengths and weaknesses rather than disorders or abnormalities.

The first cluster from this study (Sandler et al., 1992) revealed a writing disorder with fine motor and linguistic deficits. Typical manifestations included delays in both reading decoding and comprehension, and writing was characterized by dysphonetic spelling errors. This group additionally demonstrated fine motor weaknesses (i.e., finger agnosia, reduced eye–hand coordination, and dyspraxia), which may have contributed to the development of the writing disorder.

The next most frequently occurring cluster was identified as writing disorder with visuospatial deficits. Reading and spelling among this group were virtually normal, but legibility of writing was poor. Their disorganized style of writing involved spatial planning problems and inconsistent letter formation. The authors concluded that these weaknesses in visuospatial processing possibly imply localization to the right hemisphere.

The third cluster, writing disorder with attention and memory deficits, revealed a group with relative weaknesses in reading decoding and spelling. This group differed from the first group by evidencing phonetic approximations within the spelling errors; legibility, mechanics, and rate of writing generally were not concerns for this group. Neurodevelopmentally, this group displayed considerable weaknesses in both visual retrieval memory as well as auditory short-term memory as measured by WISC-R, Digit Span performance.

The final cluster, titled writing disorder with sequencing deficits, revealed a group of children similar to those with Developmental Gerstmann Syndrome. This syndrome presents with a constellation of symptoms that include dyscalculia, finger agnosia, right–left confusion, and dysgraphia. The final cluster obtained in this study demonstrated strong reading and writing composition skills but struggled dramatically in math computation. Mechanical writing skills were characterized by poor legibility and spelling errors, and the errors were sequential in nature (omissions, insertions, and transpositions of letters and syllables). Neurodevelopmental testing showed signs of finger agnosia in addition to poor fine motor and visual sequencing skills. Moreover, this group tended to exhibit a discrepant WISC-R profile with the Verbal IQ higher than the Performance IQ.

Future research investigating not only the neuropsychological deficits but also the processes underlying dysgraphia is needed. As standardized tests for writing disorders are developed and improved, more sophisticated research on the neuropsychological basis of dysgraphia should follow.

Adults With Learning Disabilities

Just as the neuropsychological research on learning disabilities in children has primarily investigated dyslexia, studies on adults with residual developmental learning problems also have this focus. In a review of dyslexia research with adults, Bigler (1992) documented results of several studies that focused on reading, spelling, and handwriting and found that the neuropsychological deficits that surface in childhood fail to remit in adulthood. Consequently, adults with dyslexia have been found to exhibit lower verbal than performance IQs on the Wechsler Adult Intelligence Scale (WAIS; Lawson & Inglis, 1989), poor verbal fluency (Kinsbourne, Rufo, Gamzu, Palmer, & Berliner, 1991), and compromised auditory discrimination and other linguistic functions (DeRenzi & Lucchelli, 1990).

Bigler (1992) concurrently described the neuropsychological test results of three adults with residual developmental reading and spelling problems. A pattern of subtle motor deficits emerged, with all three participants not displaying the normal dominant hand advantage on finger oscillation and grip strength measures. Similarly, the participants demonstrated slightly more dominant hand errors on the sensory–perceptual tasks (i.e., tactile discrimination via finger number writing), again suggesting inadequate language lateralization. Expressive language testing (e.g., articulation) was unremarkable, but significant difficulties were demonstrated on memory tests that tap sequential auditory processing. Reading and spelling test results were significantly compromised and related to graphomotor deficits in specific instances. Neuropsychological functions that appeared to be intact included rote verbal memory, visual memory, and visuospatial processing.

A number of recent studies on adults diagnosed with learning disability have supported the pervasive nature of this disorder. Some researchers have restricted their adult studies to specific symptoms manifested by children with learning disabilities, but others have taken a broader approach and attempted to validate some of the subtyping formats among adults that were derived from children. In effect, some of the literature suggests that phonological processing deficits (i.e., auditory discrimination, attention, perception, decoding, etc.) are persistent over time. Bowen and Hynd (1988) revealed that adults demonstrate the selective auditory attention deficits typically seen in children with learning disabilities, whereas Bruck (1990) suggested that an arrest rather than delay in word recognition and decoding of real and nonsense words may be present among adults who were diagnosed with learning disabilities as children. Academically, adults on follow-up also have been shown to exhibit low patterns of achievement typically seen in children (Spreen, 1988). One study (Shafrir & Siegel, 1994) revealed that subtypes that appear to be clinically useful among childhood populations (Rourke & Finlayson, 1978; Siegel & Heaven, 1986) are also justified with adolescents and adults with learning disabilities. Shafrir and Siegel (1994) compared groups of adolescents and adults with arithmetic disabilities, reading disabilities, and reading and arithmetic disabilities, with normal achieving adolescents and adults across several cognitive and academic measures. Phonological processing deficits in reading and spelling, as well as short-term memory problems, were demonstrated by both groups with reading disabilities. Moreover, multivariate procedures correlated a phonological deficit with decoding problems observed among the adolescents and adults with a reading disability. The reading and arithmetic group had difficulty with visual recognition of a correct word. The arithmetic group achieved lower scores on vocabulary and word identification measures than the normal group but not to a significant degree, thus negating the presence of a phonological processing problem among this group. Visuospatial difficulties were demonstrated by both the arithmetic and the reading and arithmetic groups, but not among the reading group. This finding suggests that within the context of this study, visuospatial abilities among adolescents and adults with reading disabilities alone appear to be intact. Although this study added an educational component (postsecondary vs. nonpostsecondary) to the subtyping model, subtypes remained consistently similar to those seen in children.

Although the literature reviewing the neuropsychological characteristics of learning disability in adults is in the early stages, it appears to validate the persistence of the disorder over the lifespan. Conclusively, it would appear that research in the area of learning disability has come full circle. Much of the early neuropsychological research demonstrates a downward comparison of adult acquired-brain-injury studies to children with learning disabilities. This trend was followed by a focus on the important developmental aspects of learning disabilities, which in turn has brought investigators back to the study of adults.

CLINICAL SYMPTOMS OF LEARNING DISABILITIES

Because of the heterogeneous nature of learning disabilities, the presenting symptoms can vary tremendously, ranging from verbal to motor, academic, social, or behavioral. The presentation of learning disability symptoms will vary depending on the age and developmental level of the child.

Preschool Years

Symptoms representing precursors to learning disability may be apparent even in the preschool-age range. Although a diagnosis of learning disability typically is not made during the preschool years, factors that place a child at risk for development of learning disability can and should be identified. The Myklebust Hierarchy for Acquisition of Verbal Language Skills (Myklebust, 1965b) provides an important conceptual framework for the developmental sequence of abilities underlying later academic learning. As displayed in Exhibit 2, this hierarchy illustrates the importance of early language abilities as a foundation to the development of higher order symbolic skills needed for reading and writing. This conceptual hierarchy has been validated empirically by neuropsychological research indicating that deficient verbal and phonologic processes underlie many of the dyslexia, dysgraphia, and dyscalculia subtypes of learning disability. Children with developmental lag or disorders of speech and language often experience difficulty with symbol-associative learning required in the early stages of formal education. Symbol-associative learning involves associating meaning to the symbols of written language or numerical system (i.e., letters of the alphabet, numerals). This type of learning is a major hurdle faced by youngsters who are acquiring the ability to read, write, or spell. However, it is difficult for most children to make sense of a symbolic language system without first having a foundation based on their early oral language development. Thus, delayed or disordered speech–language abilities during the preschool years represent a risk factor for learning disability. Children noted to have such delays should be monitored carefully and referred for evaluation if their early language delays persist.

Likewise, perceptual abilities also provide an important foundation to academic achievement. The ability to perceive and to process information accurately through a variety of sensory modalities provides the basis for the more complex multimodality integration of information required for most academic skills. Preschool-age children may be noted to have difficulty with perceptual processing within individual modalities, such as auditory or visual. Symptoms might include difficulty discriminating between similar-sounding words (auditory discrimination) or problems in memory for simple verbal instructions (auditory–verbal memory). In the visual modality, youngsters may have difficulty visually matching similar shapes or completing puzzles.

Delays or disorders of the fine and gross motor system may also be detected during the preschool years. On a gross motor level, one might note that a child has difficulty with directional (left–right) skills, or motor planning skills needed for moving through space in a coordinated fashion. On a fine motor level, there may be difficulty manipulating crayons, using scissors to cut out shapes, working puzzles, or building with blocks. Indeed, one of the red flags of motor or visuospatial problems during the preschool years is a history of a child avoiding many of the developmental activities or tasks that would be expected during those years. For instance, a 4–year-old child with visuospatial and visuomotor deficits may simply avoid coloring or working puzzles. Exhibit 3 lists a sample of frequently presenting symptoms during the preschool years (i.e., symptoms that may place a child at high risk for learning disability) as well as symptoms that present during the school-age years. Social and behavioral symptoms are discussed in detail in the section on social–emotional learning disability.

EXHIBIT 3

Examples of Frequent Presenting Symptoms of Learning Disabilities

Early Emerging Symptoms

Language
- Hesitates when speaking (e.g., searching for the correct word)
- Delay/disorder in development of articulation
- Poor verbal expression (e.g., immature vocabulary, sentence structure, and grammatic usage)
- Misunderstands, forgets oral directions

Perceptual
- Confuses similar-sounding words
- Has trouble remembering simple directions
- Difficulty matching and discriminating colors or shapes
- Decreased attention to detail in pictures
- Poor construction ability (i.e., building objects or designs from blocks)

Motor
- Avoids puzzle, drawing, coloring, block-building tasks
- Difficulty using scissors, manipulating buttons, tying shoes
- Poor motor planning ability
- Confuses left-right on self
- Poor ability to grasp or manipulate a pencil or crayons for tracing or drawing

Social–behavioral
- May talk excessively, along with poor pragmatic communication skills
- May be either clingy and overly intrusive or withdrawn and in his or her own world
- Avoids or gets upset when confronted with novel situations
- Prolonged periods of isolated or parallel play in lieu of symbolic and integrative play

Later Emerging Symptoms

Academic
- Spelling characteristics
  - Uses incorrect letter order (i.e., sequencing errors)
  - Has difficulty associating the correct sound to letter
  - Reverses letter or entire word (*b–d*, *saw–was*)
- Writing characteristics
  - Cannot write on the line
  - Very slow in writing production
  - Errors in copying written material (especially from board)
  - Mixes upper- and lowercase letters within a word
  - Poor letter formation
  - Use of simpler vocabulary, shorter sentences, fewer ideas when required to write versus speak
- Reading characteristics
  - Loses place
  - Repeats, omits, or adds words
  - Does not read fluently

(*continues*)

EXHIBIT 3 (*Continued*)

Confuses similar words or letters as to their visual configuration (e.g., *b–d*, *was–saw*)
Has to use fingers to follow a line of print
Does not like reading
Math characteristics
Has difficulty associating number name with written symbol
Cannot recall math facts instantly (i.e., automatic, rote memory problems)
Confuses columns and spacing (i.e., spatial orientation problems)
Has difficulty with story problems
Fails to comprehend math concepts
Social–behavioral
Forgets easily
Makes inappropriate "out of context" statements, fails to see humor
Easily led by peers
Overly rigid and bossy
Is disorganized, messy, loses materials, looks disheveled
Has difficulty beginning or completing a task
Moves constantly
Is easily distracted
Poor peer relationships, especially in a group
Poor sense of time, needs many reminders, often late
Could be extremely quiet and withdrawn or impulsive and explosive
Displays inconsistencies in behavior—can do tasks sometimes but not at other times
Is clumsy, bumps into things, spills things
Child described by teacher or parents as "immature."

Referral decisions during the preschool-age range often are complicated by the question of whether the observed deficit represents merely a maturational lag in development that will resolve on its own over time, or whether it represents a more permanent neuropsychological deficit that will persist and might benefit from early intervention and remediation. An evaluation can clearly document the nature and severity of the deficits but can rarely distinguish between those caused by maturational lag and a permanent neuropsychological problem. The decision about when to refer should be guided by the severity and persistence of the delay in language, perceptual, and motor development as the child nears kindergarten age.

Early to Middle School-Age Years

The most easily detected symptoms of learning disability during the school-age years involve failure to acquire academic skills at the expected rate in one or more areas. Both teachers and parents may detect symptoms in reading, spelling, or mathematics during the early elementary years, as illustrated in Exhibit 3. Typically, learning disability symptoms in reading are detected earliest, and those involving math and written language are apparent at later ages. Written language disabilities may not be apparent until third or fourth grade, when the writing demands increase dramatically in most school curricula. Occasionally, children with clear symptoms of learning disability in the early elementary years are not referred for evaluation by teachers. Rather, many teachers will simply label the child immature and advise waiting to see if he or she catches up. Although some youngsters do have maturational lags and eventually catch up to their peers without special intervention, many children with learning disabilities are mislabeled as immature and therefore do not receive appropriate special education services in the early elementary years due to delay in identification of their disability. These children may be retained for 1 or more years, receiving the same curriculum repeatedly rather than an individualized curriculum designed to address their learning deficits. It is important to refer these youngsters for evaluation before they are retained multiple times, because their educational needs will be met more appropriately in a special education curriculum.

During the school age years, motor, verbal, and behavioral symptoms may persist. The behavioral symptoms particularly may be easily confused with other types of disorders, such as oppositional defiant disorder, conduct disorder, ADHD, or simply being lazy or unmotivated. Several researchers have suggested that children with learning disabilities are at greater risk for social adjustment problems than their normal achieving peers (Bryan & Bryan, 1986) and are at greater risk for developing secondary emotional problems and dropping out of school (Rutter, Tizard, Yule, Graham, & Whitmore, 1976; Spreen, 1978). Children with learning disabilities have been shown to have a higher incidence of delinquency and psychopathology, although the evidence for this relationship is correlational (Schonhaut & Satz, 1983). The primary differential diagnostic question involves whether the child has a primary emotional or behavioral disorder, or whether the symptoms may be reflective of a secondary emotional or behavioral response to the frustration of having learning disabilities. Larry Silver (1979) discussed several types of secondary emotional–behavioral responses that may be found in children with learning problems (see Exhibit 4). When these characteristics are observed, it is important to rule out a primary disorder in learning disability that may be causing frustration and the need to develop defenses in the form of behavioral symptoms.

Symptoms and Clinical Issues During Adolescence and Young Adulthood

Although many of the academic symptoms of learning disability already described persist into the adolescent and young adult years, they may be more difficult to detect for several reasons. Adolescents and young adults who have struggled for many years with learning disability often develop excellent compensation strategies for recognizing the types of errors they are likely to make (e.g., spelling errors, failure to pay attention to the operational sign in mathematics problems, visual confusion of similar letters such as *b* and *d*), and correcting their errors. Thus, classwork or homework may be turned in to the teacher or college professor with few errors, but this masks the additional time and effort needed to prevent or to correct the mistakes. One of the clinical red flags of learning disability in adolescents and young adults is the struggle behavior often noted in their information-processing abilities and academic performance. They may be hesitant or dysfluent in reading, laborious in producing writing samples, or unsure of the steps to performing a mathematics problem, or they may need more time than typical to process information before responding to a test item. When completing long writing assignments, inordinant time may be spent with a dictionary or spell check on a computer to correct spelling errors. Although their final response or written product may be correct, the struggle indicates that the process of obtaining the response is not yet automatic; the cost in terms of time and additional effort needed to complete the tasks is one of the most profound sequelae of learning disability.

Another clinical problem noted with adolescents and young adults who are learning disabled relates to the cumulative effect of their academic underachievement over many years. As the learning disability symptoms take their toll on the student's achievement, it is common for the student to fall behind his or her peer group in the areas affected by the learning disability, even with remedial efforts. Subsequent IQ testing may reflect a declining IQ pattern compared with earlier performances, and this also is related to the chronic underachievement. Many IQ tests include items reflective of school learning, and the student with learning disability is at a disadvantage when he or she falls behind the peer group on these measures. The impact of this clinical problem is that the student with learning disability may begin to appear more as a slow learner than a student with average IQ to school personnel and others. It becomes more difficult to demonstrate an average level of cognitive functioning, due to the confounding effects of the chronic academic under-

EXHIBIT 4

Secondary Emotional–Behavioral Responses of Children With Learning Problems

Withdrawal reaction: The child avoids situations that are frustrating and becomes "unavailable for learning."

Regression: The child reverts to an immature style of behavior with peers or adults, such as using baby talk or becoming enuretic.

Fear reactions: The child may develop a fear of a specific situation or person rather than display generalized anxiety or depression. This specific fear may be a way of displacing anxiety about school failure.

Somatic complaints: The child may develop stomachaches, headaches, or other physical symptoms, which are present only on school days and not at other times. Although the discomfort may be real, the pain often disappears when the child is allowed to stay home.

Paranoia: The child may attempt to avoid stress by projecting his or her feelings and thoughts to others, blaming them for problems. The child may feel that teachers, classmates, or others are trying to get him or her into trouble or show him or her up.

Diagnosis as the excuse: A child who has been tested and examined by various professionals may come to use the various labels and descriptions as an excuse. For instance, a child who had been labeled as dyslexic said, "I can't read because my eyes don't work right."

Depression: A child with repeated school failures, poor interaction with peers and adults, and feelings of inadequacy may feel angry and useless. Children of preschool age may express their depression by aggressive or irritable behavior. These children may internalize their anger and often develop a poor self-image so that they feel they are worthless. Even when they are given praise, they often are unable or unwilling to accept it.

Passive–aggressive reaction: A child may choose to deal with his or her anger indirectly, in such a way that people become angry with him or her even when the behavior itself is not aggressive. For example, a child who dawdles may infuriate parents, even though the child is not behaving aggressively.

Passive–dependent reaction: A child may choose to deal with his or her anger by simply avoiding situations that might result in failure or unpleasant feelings. The child's helplessness and dependency may create feelings of anger in others.

Clowning: The child who becomes the class clown may be doing so to cover feelings of inadequacy and depression, or to avoid situations that create stress, such as being called upon to recite in the classroom. By disrupting the classroom, the child who is clowning may divert the teacher's attention from his or her academic difficulties.

Impulse disorder: The child acts impulsively without taking time to think about the consequences of his or her actions. These children may be emotionally labile, showing explosive or aggressive reactions after only a slight provocation.

This information was compiled from Silver (1979).

achievement. The likelihood of misdiagnosis is greater at this age because of the declining IQ and the difficulty demonstrating a severe discrepancy between actual and expected achievement.

Adolescents and young adults who have learning disabilities often do not display the typical markers of perceptual deficits (e.g., phonological processing errors, visuomotor integration weaknesses) that characterize younger children. Because the adolescent and young adult have advanced neurologic maturation and cognitive development, more sophisticated thinking abilities and abstract reasoning are expected. If the adolescent or young adult has difficulty with these higher level abilities, it often is difficult to tease out the reason for this difficulty. Coupled with this problem is the fact that most tests of perceptual processing abilities are geared to the younger child and not to the level of the adolescent or adult. The compensation strategies used by older individuals also help to mask these perceptual weaknesses. Thus, the practitioner must be alert to the changing nature and symptoms of learning disability as the child grows into adolescence and adulthood. Elaboration of the clinical issues in assessing adolescents and adults is provided later in this chapter.

Some children and youth with learning disabilities display a primary disorder in social–emotional functioning that is related to their neuropsychological deficits and other types of learning disability. This form of learning disability is discussed in detail in the next section.

SOCIAL–EMOTIONAL (NONVERBAL) LEARNING DISABILITY

The concept of social perception deficits in children is not new. Johnson and Myklebust (1967) defined social perception as, "perception of oneself in relation to the behavior of others as well as to events and circumstances that involve others" (p. 295). Johnson and Myklebust (1967) were among the earliest researchers to describe children who present with nonverbal disorders of learning, who are unable to understand the relevance of time, size, space, direction, and various aspects of social perception. They described children who fail to learn the meaning of actions in others, so that they are unable to grasp the unspoken rules of a game; children who cannot pretend or anticipate; who fail to learn the implications of gestures, facial expressions, and other manifestations of attitudes. These children were thought to have a deficit in social perception—that is, an inability that precludes acquiring the significance of basic nonverbal aspects of daily living (Johnson & Myklebust, 1967). The psychoeducational profile of these children typically reveals average verbal intelligence with as much as a 20- to 30-point discrepancy between verbal and nonverbal abilities. These children were described as developing oral communication, reading and writing abilities, but not developing the ability to make social judgments. As described by Johnson and Myklebust (1967), most children learn naturally, without direct teaching, to perceive the feelings of others, the meaning conveyed by the tone of voice or overt actions, and the significance of physical contact. However, children with social perception deficits fail to learn through experience, unless they are taught by someone who verbalizes the unspoken rules for them. The primary deficit appears to be in the ability to interpret the behaviors of others from observation, including correct perception of the meaning of facial expressions, actions, and gestures. Although Johnson and Myklebust described social perception deficits eloquently, nearly 20 years lapsed before the field began to take note of this disorder and grapple with the difficult question of how to evaluate it adequately.

Subtypes

Many authors have written about similar disorders of social perception, and many different terms have been used to describe social–emotional learning disability. Table 3 provides a comparison of the types of nonverbal or social–emotional learning disability described in the literature.

Denckla (1978) described a group of children with right-hemisphere dysfunction, including deficits in arithmetic, visuospatial, and social perception skills. She classified these children as having a left hemisyndrome. These children had at least three motor system markers indicating right-hemisphere dysfunction, including disorders of reflexes, weakness, muscle tone, incoordination, gait, tremors, and dysarthria. As noted in Table 3, social skills deficits were similar to those described currently in children with social–emotional learning disability, and their neuropsychological performance revealed deficiencies in higher order language and thinking abilities, arithmetic deficits, and mild delays in speech and reading, which later developed adequately. Denckla (1983, 1989) eventually began using the term *social–emotional learning disability* to describe this dis-

TABLE 3

Comparison of Types of Nonverbal Learning Disabilities

Type	Arithmetic	Reading	Social skills	Motor development	Right–left confusion	Usual age of identification	Visuospatial skills	Language	IQ
Left hemisyndrome	Delayed significantly	Mild delay in reading comprehension; word reading is fine	Difficulty in processing gestures and vocal expressions Peer difficulties Significant hyperactivity	Delayed on three or more motor markers	Not reported	Young childhood	Delayed	Difficulty with verbal reasoning Delayed speech initially, then overly verbal and dependent on rules	Verbal > Performance
Nonverbal perceptual–organizational output disabled	Delayed significantly	Word reading fine; comprehension is delayed	Excessive routinization of performance; difficulty understanding facial expressions; automatized sterotyped ways of relating; severe peer problems; apathetic attitude	Clumsy; poor at sports	Yes	Recognized through case histories in retrospect; recognized in 4th–5th grades	Delayed	Verbal with little content; conceptually deficient in pragmatic aspects of language	Verbal > Performance
Type R_1 and Type R_2	Problems with reiterative number tasks	Slow and methodical	Misperceive social situations, hyperemotional word usage; poor understanding of gestures; inappropriate tone of speech	Not reported	Not reported	Not reported	Variable	Excellent vocabulary; prosody is poor	Not reported

Asperger's syndrome–schizoid personality	Inconsistent reports, but found to be delayed 2 or more years in several reports	Relatively intact; a voracious reader	Relates to adults better; likes routine Limited use of facial expression, gestures, and vocal intonation, and little eye contact	Delayed High number of soft neurological signs Clumsy	Not reported	Probable onset before 30 months but not obvious until 3–4 years of age	Delayed	Large vocabulary and good grammar; pedantic conversa-tion, concrete speech	Verbal > Performance
Developmental Gerstmann's syndrome	Delayed	Delayed, but strength compared with arithmetic	Inability to perceive subtle facial expressions and vocal intonation	Delayed	Yes	Not reported	Dysgraphia; finger agnosia	Overly verbal and dependent on verbal rules and regulations	Verbal > Performance
Pervasive developmental disorder	Probably delayed	Probably delayed	Severe and sustained impairment; relates to objcts, not to people	Delayed	Not reported	30 months of age to 12 years	Delayed	Abnormalities in speech; melodic or monoto-nous voice	Verbal > Performance

Note: Type R_1 and Type R_2 are two types of developmental right-parietal-lobe syndrome. From "Right Hemisphere Dysfunction in Nonverbal Learning Disabilities: Social, Academic, and Adaptive Functioning in Adults and Children," by M. Semrud-Clikeman and G. W. Hynd, 1990, *Psychological Bulletin*, *107*, p. 201. Copyright 1990 by the American Psychological Association. Adapted with permission of the author.

order. As a pediatric neurologist, Denckla was one of the first to suggest a specific relationship between this behavioral spectrum and dysfunction of the right hemisphere.

Rourke and Finlayson (1978) discussed a disorder they termed *nonverbal perceptual organization output disorder.* Children with this disorder were found to have average reading and spelling performance but deficient arithmetic skills, along with impairment in visuospatial skills. They had bilateral tactile–perceptual impairment (more pronounced on the left), bilateral psychomotor impairment (also more pronounced on the left), and deficiencies in the pragmatic aspects of communication. Their social relations were found to be routinized and stereotypical, and their speech and affect were flat and monotonous (Rourke, 1982). These children had difficulty adapting to novel situations, difficulty benefiting from past experience, and poor social judgment and reasoning. Follow-up studies of children with nonverbal perceptual organization output disorder revealed that their difficulties persisted into adulthood, with a predominant theme of social inadequacy (Del Dotto, Rourke, McFadden, & Fisk, 1987; Rourke, Young, Strang, & Russell, 1985). As adults, 50% of the individuals had been treated in an inpatient psychiatric unit for depression and the majority of others were found to be prone to depression. Although the follow-up studies were limited by the small number of participants, they do suggest the pervasive and chronic nature of social–emotional learning disability.

Weinberg and McLean (1986) identified two different types of learning disability in children with arithmetic and social–emotional problems: Type R_1 (also called *developmental right parietal lobe syndrome*) is marked by hyperprosody and overemotionality, along with misperception of social situations and overly emotional tone of speech. The highly emotional affect of Type R_1 distinguishes it from Type R_2, which is identical except for showing a flattened emotional affect. Both of these syndromes are thought to be caused by disturbed mechanisms in the right parietal lobe. However, this subtyping research has not been supported by empirical or clinical observations that support localization to the right parietal lobe. According to Semrud-Clikeman and Hynd (1990), this syndrome may be grossly oversimplified in terms of the presumed locus of the observed deficits.

Asperger's syndrome was first identified in 1944 to describe children who had difficulty with nonverbal aspects of communication; had limited facial expressions, gestures, and vocal intonation; and maintained poor eye contact. These children were viewed as rigid and had a need for sameness, displayed repetitive play, and had poor peer relations (Wing, 1981). There is dispute regarding whether Asperger's syndrome is at the mild end of the continuum of the autistic spectrum disorders or is a separate entity (Semrud-Clikeman & Hynd, 1990). This disorder has been described as similar to both a schizotypal personality disorder and pervasive developmental disorder (Nagy & Szatmari, 1986). Now that Asperger's syndrome is included in *DSM-IV* (American Psychiatric Association, 1994), it is likely that there will be greater empirical and clinical attention given to distinguishing the critical aspects of this syndrome from pervasive developmental disorder, schizotypal personality, and social–emotional learning disability.

Another related subtype is the Developmental Gerstmann syndrome, which is characterized by dyscalculia, dysgraphia, right–left confusion, and finger agnosia (Kinsbourne, 1968). Rourke and Strang (1978) have described many similarities between the Gerstmann syndrome and the nonverbal perceptual organization–output disorder. However, the Gerstmann syndrome itself is very controversial (Benton, 1977) with regard to its neuroanatomical basis. Traditionally, the underlying mechanism for Gerstmann Syndrome has been thought to be a defect in sequential processing (Kinsbourne & Warrington, 1963b) due to left parietal dysfunction. However, some researchers have suggested that the relatively stronger verbal IQ and the presence of constructional apraxia in Gerstmann syndrome suggest the possibility of right-hemisphere impairment. Thus, it is unclear whether Gerstmann syndrome reflects left or right hemispheric dysfunction, or bilateral disturbance in children, because the pattern of symptoms could implicate many different dysfunctional symptoms (Semrud-Clikeman & Hynd, 1990).

Others have suggested that a pervasive developmental disorder may fall on a continuum with social–emotional learning disability due to the similarly impaired social perception and social interaction abilities. However, abnormalities in speech and language are characteristic of the autistic form of pervasive developmental disorder, in contrast to strengths in speech and auditory processing more typically noted in the child with social–emotional learning disability. In the case of high-functioning autism, there may be some degree of overlap with social–emotional learning disability (Shea & Mesibov, 1985), but clearer distinctions await further research.

The presumed neurologic basis for social–emotional learning disability has been addressed extensively by two researchers in recent publications. Voeller (1986) hypothesized a neurologic model of *right hemisphere deficit syndrome* and Rourke (1988a, 1988b, 1989) developed a neuropsychological model for nonverbal learning disability (NLD) syndrome. The pathophysiology of social–emotional learning disability is discussed in the next section, with emphasis on the research of Voeller and Rourke.

Pathophysiology

One of the early studies exploring neurologic correlates to social–emotional learning disability was conducted by Voeller (1986). Voeller described 15 patients who had right-hemisphere lesions as determined by either CT scan or neurologic exam and either Verbal or Performance IQ of at least 90. Each of these patients had chronic social–emotional deficits. Some of these children had acquired neurologic lesions, and others had family members who displayed similar social–emotional symptoms, suggesting a familial pattern of deficits. The CT scans of many of these patients revealed minor anomalies of the right hemisphere. Of the 15 patients, 7 had abnormal obstetric histories (e.g., prematurity, postmaturity with neonatal seizures, and hypoxic insults) and 4 had a history of postnatal injury (two with right-sided skull fractures, one with an hypoxic episode during infancy, and one who developed a left hemiparesis and seizures after elevated temperature and dehydration). Seven of the 15 patients preferred their right hand before 1 year of age and 9 patients had left-sided neurologic anomalies on exam, suggestive of right-hemisphere dysfunction. All except 1 of these patients had attentional deficits.

Voeller (1990) also reviewed the evidence from experimental animal and human studies for a neurologic substrate to social–emotional learning disability. She cited numerous animal studies that provided evidence of a neuronal substrate underlying the processing of social signals in primates. She reviewed studies with adult humans that provided evidence of a link between specific brain lesions and affective behaviors in adults. There is evidence currently to suggest that recognition of affect in facial expressions, tone of voice (prosody), and interpretation of socially complex material is impaired in adults with right-hemisphere lesions. According to Voeller (1990), studies of infants and young children suggest that the neuronal circuitry for processing affective information is hardwired and is present even in blind children. She postulated that disruption of the neuronal circuits underlying social–emotional behaviors could be genetically programmed, could result from disturbance in intrauterine brain development, or could be acquired as a result of insults during early postnatal life.

In contrast to Voeller's model, Rourke (1988a, 1988b, 1989) proposed a neurobiologic model purporting that *NLD*, as he termed social–emotional learning disability, is a disorder that is secondary to underlying primary cognitive neuropsychologic problems. Rourke (1987) postulated that NLD results from white matter destruction or dysfunction and that this white matter is necessary for intermodal integration of information related to social–emotional functioning. In general, he postulated that the neurologic substrate relates to the neuronal connections (white matter) that provide access to the right hemisphere rather than dysfunction of specific structures or cells in the right hemisphere. Rourke postulated that deterioration or destruction of white matter (i.e., long myelinated fibers) is responsible for the disruption of the connections to the right hemisphere.

Although the specific pathogenesis of social–emotional learning disability awaits clarification through further research, recent literature has provided rich clinical descriptions of children who have a pattern of specific neuropsychological deficits accompanied by chronic deficits in social perception. These descriptions are discussed in the following section.

Developmental and Clinical Characteristics

Voeller (1990) described children and adults who have chronic difficulty relating to other human beings, are on the periphery of their social group, are considered weird and have few friends, and have particular difficulty understanding the nuances of social behaviors and making sense of social interactions. In her clinical experience, two general patterns of behavior emerge. One group of children can be described as remote, withdrawn, unrelated, with decreased eye contact and limited range of affective expression. Their speech is monotonous and robotlike. The other group is described by Voeller as overly and inappropriately friendly, and somewhat sticky (i.e., invading the space of others by standing too close and touching too much). These children tend to be hyperverbal, but their speech consists of cliches and automatic phrases that often are not used in an entirely appropriate fashion.

Although the pathophysiology of social–emotional learning disability continues to be debated, there is considerable agreement from the literature of the last 20 years regarding the characteristics of social–emotional learning disability. The most commonly reported characteristics of social–emotional learning disability are described in Exhibit 5. The presence of these symptoms for a given child will vary depending on the age and developmental stage of that child. Rourke (1988b) described social–emotional learning disability (or NLD) within the context of developmental stages. He postulated that primary neuropsychological assets and deficits in the young child lead to secondary neuropsychological assets and deficits, and so on, finally resulting in the symptoms or characteristics of NLD listed in Exhibit 5. Rourke postulated that the young child with NLD may have a primary neuropsychological asset of processing information delivered through the auditory modality. Although these youngsters may have an initial delay in acquisition of language, they soon begin using speech and language very well and may even be considered loquacious. The young child may perform simple motor tasks well, may be proficient at learning material by rote (especially through the

EXHIBIT 5

Common Characteristics of Social–Emotional Learning Disabilities

- Social isolation
- Peer rejection
- Impaired ability to engage in interactive play
- Failure to respond to peer norms
- Abnormal affective expression
- Difficulty interpreting emotions
- Poor eye contact
- Defective use of gesture
- Problems with interpersonal space
- Hyperverbal–poor pragmatic skills in communication
- Obsession with narrow topics and pursuits
- Poor adaptation to novel situations
- Decreased appreciation of metaphor and humor
- Left hemisyndrome (sensory–perceptual deficits implicate the right hemisphere)
- Motor incoordination

auditory–verbal modality), and may explore the environment primarily through verbal means. In contrast, the primary neuropsychological deficits are found in tactile and visual-perceptual abilities, complex psychomotor skills, and adaptation to novel situations. This means that during the sensorimotor stage of development, the young child with social–emotional learning disability may be rather sedentary and may be reluctant to explore the world through locomotion or sensorimotor activities. Rather, the child may attempt to explore the environment verbally, by asking questions about objects or events rather than using sensory or motor exploration. The young child's reluctance to explore the environment may be due also to difficulty handling novel situations and the tendency to withdraw from the new or unusual. Parents sometimes report that these children do not tolerate change well and are rather rigid and irritable when forced to adjust to change in the environment (Rourke, 1988b).

As children with NLD progress through developmental stages, developing better attention and more sophisticated exploratory behaviors, assets and deficits once again are seen as secondary neuropsychological manifestations of the disorder (Rourke, 1988b). Particular assets are noted in auditory–verbal attention and learning through the auditory modality, whereas deficits are seen in tactile or visual attention and more sophisticated exploratory behavior. At the level of tertiary neuropsychological development, memory skills and concept formation emerge. According to Rourke (1988b), the child with social–emotional learning disability will have assets in auditory–verbal memory, but deficits in tactile–visual memory, concept formation, reasoning, and problem solving. Problems in concept formation and problem solving are noted particularly when the task is novel or complex. As the young child with NLD develops language abilities, particular assets are noted in phonologic skills (i.e., phonetic abilities may be very good), receptive language, and rote verbal memory. Verbal output may be extremely high. In contrast, the child may have deficient oral-motor praxis or articulatory skills with little or no prosody in verbal expression. The result may be a monotonic quality to verbalization with little variation and inflection of tone related to emotional content (Rourke, 1988b). For instance, a sentence with sad content (e.g., "I just lost my wallet") may be said in a neutral tone rather than in a sad or angry tone. Other verbal deficits include poor pragmatics, often illustrated by cocktail party speech and reliance on speech and language as a primary means for social relating. The result may be a high degree of verbal output combined with superficial quality and content of the language, which may be viewed as irritating to the listener (Rourke, 1988b).

In the area of academic skills, assets are noted in basic word decoding skills, spelling and verbatim memory, along with writing after it has become an automatic or overlearned skill. In contrast, deficits are seen in the early stages of writing, and later in reading comprehension, mechanical arithmetic, mathematics reasoning, and science abilities (Rourke, 1988b).

Finally, at the social–emotional, adaptive level of functioning, the child with social–emotional learning disability has poor adaptation to novel situations, poor social competence, poor emotional stability, and often an increased activity level. Because of the deficit in social–emotional–adaptive abilities, these children often present to mental health professionals in psychiatry or psychology for diagnosis. They have been diagnosed variously as having pervasive developmental disorder, schizoid or schizotypal personality disorder, high functioning autism, affective disorder, ADHD, or Asperger's syndrome (Rourke, 1988b). It is possible that the range of diagnoses associated with social–emotional learning disability may relate to the orientation of the professional evaluating the child, but it is likely that children with social–emotional learning disability are at significant risk for psychiatric disorders (especially depression) secondary to the frustrations associated with their disorder. Particular problems are noted in young adults who have difficulty holding a job and problems with meaningful relationships. The prognosis may be very guarded due to the significant risk for secondary emotional or psychiatric disorders associated with the primary effects of the social–emotional learning disability (Rourke, 1988b).

Now that the definitions, terminology, research literature on pathophysiology and subtyping, and clinical symptoms of learning disability have been presented, this chapter shifts to issues of clinical assessment. The next section provides a conceptual model for understanding neurologic functions related to learning, and it provides a basis for planning an evaluation of learning disability.

CONCEPTUAL FOUNDATIONS FOR NEUROPSYCHOLOGICAL EVALUATION OF LEARNING DISABILITIES

Luria's theory of brain organization provides a helpful conceptualization for the neuropsychological approach to evaluating children, adolescents, and adults with learning disabilities (Luria, 1973). Luria postulated that there are three basic units of the brain—the arousal unit, the sensory input unit, and the output–planning unit—each with particular functions that support the simple and complex behaviors that govern learning. The developmental sequence in which these units of the brain develop can provide information to the psychologist who is assessing the learning attributes of children. The functions of the three basic units of the brain according to Luria's model are discussed here in developmental context as they apply to children's development and learning.

Stage 1: Development of the Arousal Unit

Development of this unit begins at conception and extends to roughly three months post delivery (Golden, 1981). The arousal unit is thought to be located within the reticular activating system, which extends from the pons and medulla through the thalamus to the cortex (see Figure 2, B). The arousal unit functions to (a) raise or lower cortical arousal and (b) filter sensory input (Luria, 1973). The reticular activating system is particularly sensitive to damage during the time it is being formed. Injuries or problems in development, if severe, may result in death or severe mental retardation. Less severe impairment may result in physiologic overactivity or underactivity (as in narcolepsy) or in alteration in attentional processes (Golden, 1981).

Stage 2: Primary Motor and Sensory Areas

The primary motor and sensory areas of the brain are thought to begin development at conception and develop through approximately the 3rd month postdelivery (Golden, 1981). This stage of development involves the primary motor cortex (located in the frontal lobe, anterior to the central sulcus) and three primary sensory areas: (a) the primary sensory area (located in the parietal lobe, immediately posterior to the central sulcus), (b) the primary auditory area, located in the inferior temporal lobe, and (c) the primary visual area, located in the most posterior part of the occipital lobe (see Figure 2, C and D). The primary motor and sensory areas of the brain are thought to be the most hard wired of all the areas of the cortex; that is, the functions of the primary areas are largely predetermined by genetics (Golden, 1981; Luria, 1973). These areas of the brain act as sensory receptors and receive sensory input on a point-to-point basis from the appropriate sensory organs (auditory, visual, tactile–kinesthetic). The initial integration of sensory information occurs in these areas. The functions of the primary motor cortex in young children may include crying and grasping, whereas basic sensory functions may include depth discrimination and recognition of high-pitched voices. These behaviors are felt to have basic survival functions, as suggested by Bowlby (1969, 1973, 1980). Because the primary motor and sensory areas of the brain are duplicated in both the left and right hemispheres, and because there is contralateral control of function, injury or failure to develop in a primary sensory area of one hemisphere may result in dysfunction on the opposite side of the body. For example, severe injury to the left primary motor area may result in a right hemiparesis, or dysfunction in motor control on the right side of the body (Golden, 1981).

Milder injuries of the primary sensory areas may result in partial dysfunction involving movement or speech production, awareness of visual and auditory stimuli, or detection of tactile stimulation (Golden, 1981).

Stage 3: Secondary Motor and Sensory Areas

The secondary motor and sensory areas of the brain are thought to begin developing at conception but

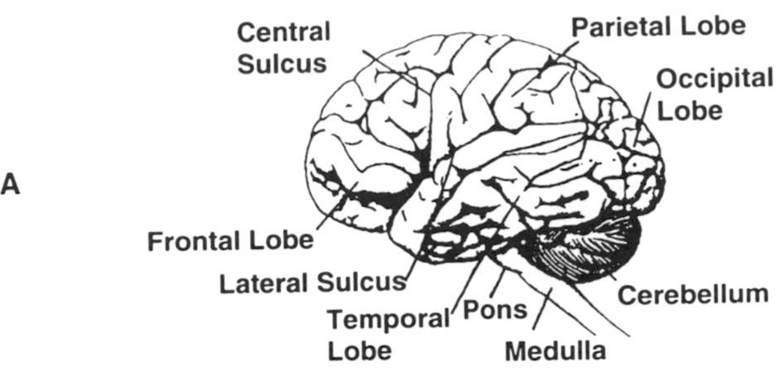

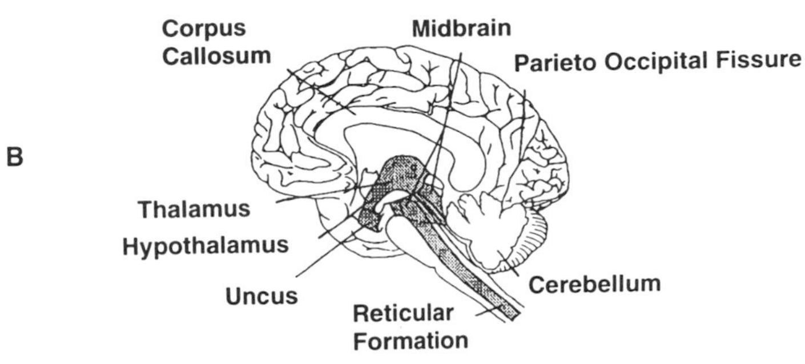

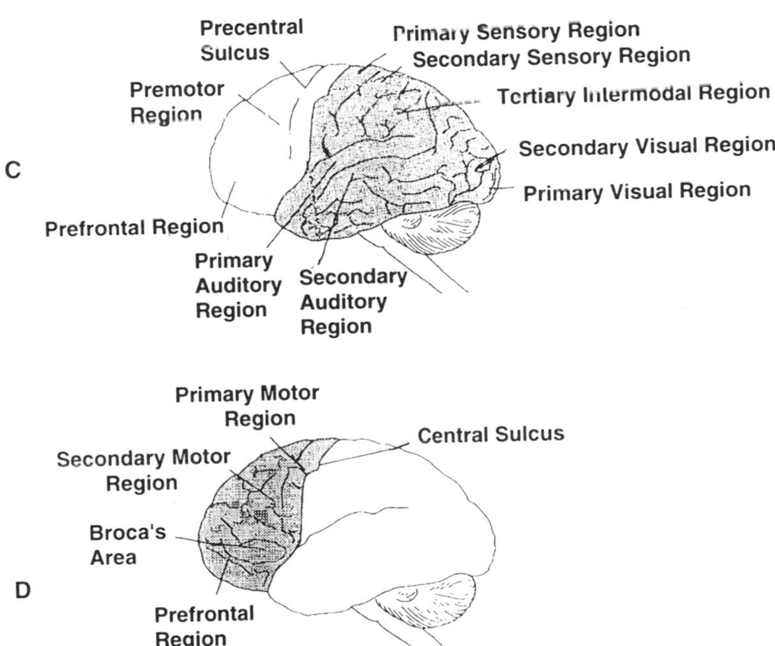

FIGURE 2. Luria's major blocks of the brain. A: Gross anatomy of the brain, left-hemisphere view. B: The first block of the brain, the brain stem, and evolutionary old cortex. C: The second block of the brain, the association area, composed of the parietal, occipital, and temporal lobes. D: The third block of the brain (shaded area), composed of the frontal areas of the brain, anterior to the central sulcus and including the motor strip of the cortex. From "The Functional Organization of the Brain," by A. R. Luria, 1970, *Scientific American*, 222, p. 67. Copyright 1970 by Scientific American. Reprinted with permission.

develop over a much longer period of time than the primary areas—to approximately 5 years of age (Golden, 1981). The secondary motor and sensory areas, referred to as association cortex, correspond to each of the primary areas and are located contiguous to the primary areas (see Figure 2, C and D). Their function is to analyze and integrate information received by the primary motor and sensory areas (Golden, 1981; Luria, 1973). For example, the secondary acoustic area of the brain functions to analyze sounds and to organize them into phonemes, pitch, tone, and rhythm. The secondary motor and sensory areas also allow information to be processed sequentially, so that the brain may be aware of stimulus changes (e.g., to detect movement) and can link events temporally (Luria, 1973). For instance, to produce speech, phonemes must be linked sequentially to form words and sentences. The secondary visual area helps one to examine more than one object, word, or letter at a time, thus providing an important foundation of the reading process. The secondary sensory area may aid in detecting two-point discrimination, or recognition of shapes or numbers traced on the skin. The secondary motor area assists in motor planning, sequencing of motor movements, and eye–hand coordination (Golden, 1981).

At the level of the secondary sensory areas, the brain is organized so that there is increased specialization of functions in the respective hemispheres. Unlike the primary cortex, where there is duplication of function in the two hemispheres, at the secondary level the left hemisphere becomes much more specialized for analyzing verbal material and for logical reasoning, and the right hemisphere is more specialized for analysis of nonverbal, visuospatial material (Luria, 1973). Most higher cortical abilities require both hemispheres, because few of the more complex learning skills are based on single-modality learning. For example, during the acquisition of reading skills, the right hemisphere is involved to a large extent through the need for visual discrimination—recognition and discrimination of letters that may be similar in shape or configuration (i.e., *b* vs. *d*, *p* vs. *q*). As reading skills become more automatic or overlearned, the letters become verbal symbols and the left hemisphere is thought to mediate reading processes more than the right (Golden, 1981). Likewise, in the acquisition of mathematics skills, the visual discrimination of numerals and the spatial aspects of math (i.e., manipulating objects and counting which stack of blocks has more blocks) involves the right hemisphere primarily. Later, as math becomes more of a verbal, logical, deductive reasoning process, the left hemisphere is thought to assume primary responsibility for mediating this ability.

Developmentally, the association cortex (secondary motor and sensory areas) discriminations begin to develop as soon as there is adequate attentional focus from Stage 1 (the arousal stage) and the capacity to relay information from the primary sensory to the secondary sensory areas via dendritic connections (Golden, 1981; Luria, 1973). Failure to develop the secondary motor or sensory areas of the brain, or injury to these areas of the brain, may result in impairment of early perceptual and motor skills that would be found typically in preschoolers. Those skills include basic discrimination, matching, and recognition abilities through the auditory, visual, tactile, and kinesthetic modalities.

Stage 4: Tertiary Area of the Sensory Input Unit

The tertiary area of the sensory input unit (Luria's second basic unit) of the brain is sometimes referred to as the *intermodal* cortex, as it is responsible for integrating and analyzing sensory information from the auditory, visual, kinesthetic, and tactile areas of the brain simultaneously (Golden, 1981; Luria, 1973). The tertiary area is located in and primarily around the parietal lobe (see Figure 2, C), and is responsible for the efficient performance of most academic functions (e.g., reading, spelling, mathematical computation). This part of the brain has a more prolonged period of development and is thought to mature during the early elementary years, roughly from 5 to 8 years. Severe injuries or aberrant development of this part of the brain may result in mental retardation, whereas milder dysfunction may provide the neurologic substrate for learning disabilities (Golden, 1981). For example, taking a spelling test requires the simultaneous analysis of information from a variety of sensory modalities. The child must process auditory information when the teacher pronounces the word aloud, then the child may visualize the word, and then the word must be translated into a sequence of kinesthetic motor movements for writing. At the same time, the child may be thinking about the sounds of each letter as the letters are written on the page. Thus, the simultaneous analysis of incoming auditory and visual and outgoing motor functions occurs. Acquired injuries or aberrant development of this part of the brain may not be apparent in young children but may become apparent in the elementary school years when the adequate functioning of this part of the brain is required for normal academic progression (Golden, 1981).

Stage 5: Tertiary Area of the Output-Planning Unit

The tertiary part of the output–planning unit (Luria's third basic unit) is commonly referred to as the prefrontal cortex and represents the highest level of development in the mammalian brain. The prefrontal lobes are located in the most anterior portion of the frontal lobes (see Figure 2, D) and are important in executive functions including planning, decision making, evaluation, temporal continuity, impulse and emotional control, focusing of attention, and cognitive flexibility (Luria, 1973). The prefrontal area of the brain receives information from the tertiary sensory input area (i.e., the intermodal area in the parietal cortex) and then analyzes this information and plans behavioral reactions (especially long-range planning). As the prefrontal lobes develop, they are thought to assume dominance over the arousal unit (reticular activating system) and thereafter regulate attentional focus. They can indirectly and consciously modulate level of arousal (Golden, 1981; Luria, 1973). The prefrontal lobes also are helpful in evaluating whether one's behavior is consistent with long-term goals and plans. The prefrontal cortex is the latest developing portion of the brain, felt to mature for the most part by mid adolescence, although maturation may continue at a slower rate up to and through the early 20s (Golden, 1981). Aberrant development or injury to this part of the brain may have severe effects on judgment, planning, and emotional control, as well as logical reasoning and problem solving abilities. Deficits in this part of the brain may not be apparent until children reach the adolescent years (Golden, 1981).

Children, adolescents, and adults with learning disabilities may have deficits at any or all levels of brain organization, from the arousal unit to the primary, secondary, and tertiary areas of the sensory input or output–planning units. The neuropsychological evaluation of learning disabilities should systematically explore the various functions as described, taking into account the developmental sequence of functional maturity. The utility of Luria's conceptual model for functional organization of the brain is that it provides a hierarchy of increasingly complex functions needed for academic achievement, and it does so within a developmental framework. Luria's conceptual model thus sets the stage for the practitioner's decisions about constructing a test battery for evaluation of learning disabilities. The next section outlines the clinical approach to neuropsychological evaluation of learning disabilities in children, adolescents, and adults.

NEUROPSYCHOLOGICAL EVALUATION OF LEARNING DISABILITIES

The neuropsychological approach to evaluation of learning disabilities presented in this chapter is guided by the conceptual model of Luria, by the vast pathophysiological and neuropsychological research to date, and also by the definitional and special educational considerations noted in the early sections of the chapter. The practitioner must first have a good understanding of learning disabilities from a theoretical and etiologic perspective, and then construct an assessment battery that taps a wide array of information-processing abilities related to academic functioning. This section of the chapter provides an overview of the neuropsychological approach to evaluation of learning disability.

Addressing Definitional and Diagnostic Criteria

One of the first steps in conducting an evaluation for learning disability is to learn about the state and local criteria in one's own locale for learning disability remedial or special educational services through either the public school system (for the child and adolescent) or through the vocational rehabilitation system (for the young adult). The definitional criteria coded in law and the typical state guidelines for diagnosis discussed in the early sections of this chapter provide a useful guideline for the general parameters of the evaluation, regardless of the age of the patient.

Specifically, it is important to demonstrate, either through history or review of school records, a "failure to achieve" in one or more of the principle areas of academic learning. Second, one must consider possible etiologic factors in development of learning disabilities, again through either the history or review of pertinent school, developmental, and medical records.

Third, the evaluation must be designed to rule out certain factors that are considered exclusionary criteria (i.e., mental retardation; sensory acuity deficits; educational, economic, or cultural disadvantage severe enough to account for the academic failure to achieve; and primary emotional disturbance that accounts for the academic failure to achieve). In other words, the academic achievement problems must be demonstrated to be related to factors other than those that involve the exclusionary criteria. Mental retardation can be ruled out as part of the cognitive evaluation for learning disabilities. Visual and auditory acuity problems can be ruled out by review of school or medical screening tests or by opthalmological, optometrical, or audiological evaluation. Ruling out educational, economic, or cultural disadvantage may be done through interview with parents, review of school records, or interview with school personnel who are acquainted with the student. However, there are many children and youth who have some form of disadvantage and also have primary processing deficits that indicate learning disabilities. Only a careful assessment of information-processing, linguistic, and motor abilities will help in the differential diagnosis with regard to the child's academic achievement problems. Finally, with regard to emotional problems, it is possible for a child with severe learning disability to develop a primary emotional problem such as depression. However, the practitioner often will be required to demonstrate that the learning disability preceded the development of the emotional disorder and that the academic problems related to learning disability are over and above those caused by the symptoms of emotional disorder. This may be a very difficult task in some cases, but often a demonstration of primary linguistic, motor, or other information-processing deficits tied to specific types of learning problems can convince schools or other agencies that learning disability is a primary diagnosis along with the emotional diagnosis.

Fourth, the neuropsychologic evaluation must address psychological process disorders believed to underlie academic learning problems, including attention and concentration, understanding and using written and oral language, conceptualization ability, and various types of information processing. The neuropsychological evaluation is well suited to this type of examination, and the practitioner has a large empirical literature to guide the neuropsychological evaluation.

Finally, determination of a severe discrepancy between achievement and ability (IQ) will be important to facilitate the acquisition of services for the learning disabled patient. Although a primary goal of the neuropsychologic evaluation is to determine the underlying processes that result in learning disabilities, the most practical goal is to provide an evaluation that can result in viable intervention. Therefore, the determination of a severe discrepancy is an important step to achieving that practical goal.

Selection of Assessment Instruments

Knowledge of a wide array of test instruments may be necessary for evaluation of the many subtypes of learning disabilities that a practitioner may encounter. Although the evaluation itself does not need to be lengthy, the process of selecting tests is determined in part by the data received throughout the evaluation, and the practitioner must be prepared to evaluate further if areas of weakness are discovered in the early stages of evaluation. In our clinic, the procedure involves starting the evaluation with broadband measures, such as cognitive and achievement batteries, that provide a profile of strengths and weaknesses across a wide range of abilities. After data from these broadband instruments are examined, then decisions are made regarding more specific perceptual, linguistic, information-processing, or motor abilities that must be examined.

Cognitive and achievement measures. Kamphaus (1993) provides a comprehensive overview of common cognitive measures for use in evaluation of learning disability. In general the Wechsler scales (Wechsler Preschool and Primary Scale of Intelligence–Revised, WISC-III, and revised WAIS [WAIS-R]), Stanford–Binet Intelligence Scale: Fourth Edition (Thorndike, Hagen, & Sattler, 1986), and the Kaufman scales (Kaufman Assessment Battery for Children [Kaufman & Kaufman, 1983]; Kaufman Adolescent and Adult Intelligence Test [Kaufman & Kaufman, 1992]) are well-respected cognitive measures that provide a profile of abilities. Exhibit 6 lists examples of achievement batteries that have either a broad focus (i.e., revised Woodcock–Johnson, Wechsler Individual Achievement Test, and Peabody Individual Achievement Test–Revised [Markwardt, 1989]) or a more circumscribed focus for evaluation of specific academic areas (e.g., Key Math–Revised, Test of Written Language–Third Edition [TOWL-3], and Woodcock Reading Mastery Tests–Revised).

Neuropsychological measures. It also is helpful to have familiarity with fixed neuropsychological test batteries, although most often the practitioner will choose to use a flexible battery approach for evaluation of learning disabilities. The flexible battery is geared to the child's symptoms and complaints at the time of referral and allows for flexibility in examining information-processing strengths and weaknesses. However, the fixed neuropsychological batteries include tasks that are unique and provide information not available in other aspects of the psychological evaluation. These tasks often embellish the battery in important and necessary ways by providing information on abstract reasoning with novel stimuli, information-processing abilities through a variety of modalities, sensory and motor functions, and memory. Examples of fixed neuropsychological batteries used for children, adolescents, and adults are found in Table 4, along with a description of their content. It should be noted that the Neuropsychological Investigation for Children–Revised is being field tested in the United States by the Psychological Corporation as this text is written. Practitioners may expect its publication for clinical use in the future.

The flexible battery approach attempts to preserve the quantitative nature of neuropsychological assessment by selecting standardized tests that measure a broad range of neuropsychological functions and combining them into a battery that assesses relevant functions and abilities (Hooper & Willis, 1989). One advantage of the flexible battery approach is that it allows flexibility in test selection, thus minimizing the time required to conduct assessment. This approach shows remarkable similarity to the factor structure of traditional, or fixed, neuropsychological test batteries (Hooper & Willis, 1989). There are several disadvantages as well, as described by Hooper and Willis (1989). The collection of tests used for the battery, although designed around broadband neuropsychological constructs, may not accurately reflect true profile differences. Also from a psychometric perspective, test data compared across different normative samples and empirical relationships among measures can only be estimated. Thus, using this approach, it is very important to look for broad patterns of intact functioning and dysfunctioning rather than overinterpreting a few minute signs of dysfunction.

Conceptual Hierarchy for Neuropsychological Assessment

A conceptual hierarchy for neuropsychological assessment was developed within the context of Luria's conceptualization of brain functioning and the developmental sequence in which certain functions develop. Exhibit 7 provides a working model for a conceptual hierarchy of skills, organized under the different sensory modalities, along with examples of tests that may be used to measure those skills. The hierarchy is organized on a continuum from basic skills to more complex abilities. Using this hierarchy, the practitioner can explore a variety of phonological, visual-perceptual, sensory, and motor abilities that may underlie learning disabilities and can determine where along the continuum of skills the student has difficulty. The conceptual hierarchy is not intended to be inclusive of all potential measures of the specific abilities but rather to provide examples of the types of measures that may be used. The practitioner may conduct a task analysis of other potential measures by asking, "What functions are being

EXHIBIT 6

Tests of Academic Functioning

Woodcock–Johnson Psychoeducational Battery–Revised (Woodcock & Johnson, 1989)

Curricular area	Standard battery	Supplemental battery
Reading	Letter–Word Identification	Word Attack
	Passage Comprehension	Reading Vocabulary
Mathematics	Calculation	Quantitative Concepts
	Applied Problems	
Written Language	Dictation	Proofing
	Writing Samples	Writing Fluency
		Punctuation and Capitalization
		Spelling
		Usage
		Handwriting
Knowledge	Science	
	Social Studies	
	Humanities	
Skills	Letter–Word Identification	
	Applied Problems	
	Dictation	

Peabody Individual Achievement Test–Revised (Markwardt, 1989)

Subtest
1. General Information
2. Reading Recognition
3. Reading Comprehension
4. Mathematics
5. Spelling
6. Written Expression

Total reading score = 2 + 3; Written language score = 5 + 6; Total test score = 1–5.

Kaufman Test of Educational Achievement (Kaufman & Kaufman, 1985)

Reading Composite:
- Reading Decoding
- Reading Comprehension

Mathematics Composite:
- Mathematics Applications
- Mathematics Computation

Spelling

Battery Composite

Key Math–Revised (Connolly, 1988)

Basic Concepts
- Numeration
- Rational Numbers
- Geometry

Operations
- Addition
- Subtraction
- Multiplication
- Division
- Mental Computation

Applications
- Measurement
- Time and Money
- Estimation
- Interpreting Data
- Problem Solving

Total Test Score

Woodcock Reading Mastery Tests–Revised (Woodcock, 1987)

Readiness Cluster:
- Visual–Auditory Learning
- Letter Identification
- (Supplemental) Letter Checklist

Basic Skills Cluster:
- Word Identification
- Word Attack

Reading Comprehension Cluster:
- Word Comprehension Subtests:
  - Antonym–Synonyms
  - Analogies
- Passage Comprehension
- Total Reading Cluster

Test of Written Language–3 (Hammill & Larsen, 1996)

Contrived Writing Cluster:
- Vocabulary
- Spelling
- Style
- Logical Sentences
- Sentence Combining

Spontaneous Writing Cluster:
- Thematic Maturity
- Contextual Vocabulary
- Syntactic Maturity
- Contextual Spelling
- Contextual Style

Overall Written Language Cluster

EXHIBIT 6 (*Continued*)

Wechsler Individual Achievement Test (Psychological Corporation, 1992)

Reading Composite:
  Basic Reading[a]
  Reading Comprehension
Mathematics Composite:
  Mathematics Reasoning[a]
  Numerical Operations
Language Comprehension:
  Listening Comprehension
  Oral Expression
Spelling[a]
Written Expression

[a]*Tests used to obtain Total Screener Score.*

measured by the test?" "How is the information being presented to the child (e.g., auditorially, visually, or through tactile or sensory avenues)?" "How is the child being asked to perform (e.g., by speaking, writing, or merely pointing to a picture)?"

From the most simple to the most complex levels of function, the neuropsychologic evaluation should

1. Examine the integrity of the arousal unit. This involves examination of a student's orientation to time, place, and setting; observations and measurement of a child's activity level; and observations and measurement of the child's ability to sustain concentration and be free from distractibility.
2. Examine the integrity of the basic sensory functions (motor, tactile, auditory, and visual reception). Neuropsychological tests such as the Halstead or Luria batteries include basic sensory and motor tasks to determine how well information is being detected through the primary sensory modalities.
3. Examine modality-specific skills (i.e., auditory or phonological, visual, sensory, motor) to assess the integrity of the secondary association areas of the brain. Tests should be selected that measure recognition, discrimination, and matching through the various sensory modalities, as well as spatial orientation and motor planning skills.
4. Examine the efficiency of sensory-integration abilities. This might include an assessment of verbal communication from both receptive and expressive perspectives; examination of age-appropriate academic functions in reading, spelling, math, and written language; and examination of multimodality integration skills (i.e., tasks that combine modalities such as visuomotor, auditory–motor, visual–auditory, etc.).
5. Examine the child's higher order cognitive abilities. These skills would include memory (i.e., long- and short-term storage, retrieval, delayed recall), concept formation, abstract thinking, problem solving through different sensory modalities, and comprehension or use of complex verbalizations such as absurdities or malaproprisms.
6. Evaluate the child's adaptive–social–emotional functioning through history, observations, interview, and direct testing of self-help and adaptive abilities, behavioral responses, and projective evaluation responses.

Once information is obtained from the neuropsychological evaluation, the next step is integration of the data. When using a flexible battery approach, it is possible to conduct a profile analysis of test results. Figure 3 illustrates a profile of a 7-year-old child who was given a battery of tests that tap cognitive, verbal comprehension, phonological processing, nonverbal reasoning, visuomotor integration, and academic skills. The child's test scores were transformed into percentiles and profiled so that they could be examined comparatively. The profile allows one to analyze the test data on the basis of a number of different dimensions: verbal versus nonverbal functioning, input versus output disorders (i.e., does the child have difficulty recognizing or decoding information versus expressing information through writing or speaking), disorders of higher order processes (e.g., memory, abstract reasoning, and problem solving), disorders of information processing through specific modalities and combinations of modalities, disorders in specific academic areas, and finally

TABLE 4

Fixed Neuropsychological Test Batteries

Test battery	Subtests or scales	Abilities assessed
Reitan–Indiana Neuropsychological Test Battery for Children (5–8 years)	Category Test	Complex concept formation, basic reasoning abilities, intelligence
	Tactual Performance Test	Right–left-sided sensory recognition, spatial memory
	Finger Oscillation Test (finger tapping)	Right–left-sided motor speed
	Sensory–perceptual Measures	Sensory localization, sensory perception, sensory recognition
	Aphasia Screening Test	Letter identification, follow directions regarding right–left hands, copy simple geometric shapes, compute simple arithmetic problems
	Grip Strength Test (dynamometer)	Right–left-sided muscle strength
	Lateral Dominance Examination	Right–left-sided preferences
	Color Form Test	Cognitive flexibility, sequential reasoning
	Progressive Figures Test	Visuospatial reasoning, cognitive flexibility, sequential reasoning
	Matching Pictures Test	Perceptual generalization, ability to categorize
	Target Test	Pattern perception, ability to attend to and copy visuospatial configurations
	Individual Performance Tests	Visual perception, visuomotor integration
	Marching Test	Visuomotor integration, coordination
Halstead–Reitan Neuropsychological Test Battery for Children (9–14 years) and Halstead–Reitan Neuropsychological Test Battery (15 years–adult)	Category Test	Complex concept formation, basic reasoning abilities, intelligence
	Tactual Performance Test	Right–left-sided sensory perception, sensory recognition, spatial memory, manual dexterity
	Seashore Rhythm Test	Sustained auditory attention, perception, and ability to match different auditory or rhythmic sequences
	Speech–Sounds Perception Test	Sustained attention, auditory perception, auditory visual integration
	Finger Oscillation (finger tapping)	Right–left-sided motor speed
	Tactile, Auditory, and Visual Imperception Test	Perception of unilateral and bilateral simultaneous sensory stimulation
	Tactile Finger-Recognition Test	Perception and localization of sensory stimulation
	Finger Number Writing Perception	Report numbers written on the fingertips
	Tactile Form Recognition Test	Sensory recognition, tactile-visual integration
	Aphasia Screening Test	Letter identification, follow directions regarding right–left hands, copy simple geometric shapes, compute simple arithmetic problems

TABLE 4 (*Continued*)

Test battery	Subtests or scales	Abilities assessed
	Grip Strength Test (dynamometer)	Right–left-sided muscle strength
	Trail-Making Test	Conceptual set shifting, memory, attention (Parts A & B)
	Lateral Dominance Examination	Right–left-sided preference
Luria–Nebraska Neuropsychological Battery–Children's Revision (8–12 years) and Luria–Nebraska Neuropsychological Battery (13 years–adult)	Motor Skills	Motor speed, coordination, ability to imitate motor movements
	Rhythm	Perceive and repeat rhythmic patterns, sing a song from memory
	Tactile	Finger localization, arm localization, two-point discrimination, movement discrimination, shape discrimination, stereognosis
	Visual	Visual recognition, visual discrimination
	Receptive Speech	Follow simple commands, comprehend visual–verbal directions, decode phonemes
	Expressive Language	Read and repeat words and simple sentences, name objects from description, use automated speech
	Writing	Analyze letter sequences, spell, write from dictation
	Reading	Letter and word recognition, sentence and paragraph reading, nonsense syllable reading
	Arithmetic	Simple arithmetical abilities, number writing, number recognition
	Memory	Verbal and nonverbal memory
	Intelligence	Vocabulary development, verbal reasoning, picture comprehension, social reasoning, deductive processes
Neuropsychological Investigation for Children–Revised Version (4–8 years)	Orientation, Attention Strategy	General orientation, strategy generation, inhibition and control, selective and sustained attention, distractibility
	Language	Auditory closure, receptive language, oral praxis (dynamic and kinesthetic), concept formation, naming, verbal fluency, reading readiness
	Motor and Sensory	Handedness, motor praxis, (dynamic and kinesthetic), tactile perception, kinesthetic feedback
	Visual and Spatial	Visual discrimination, visuospatial, left–right discrimination, neglect
	Memory	Immediate memory for numbers, words, faces, names and story; delayed recall for faces, names and story

Note: From *Pediatric Neuropsychology* (pp. 148–149), by G. W. Hynd and W. G. Willis, 1988, New York: Grune & Stratton. Copyright 1988 by Grune & Stratton. Reprinted with permission.

EXHIBIT 7

Conceptual Hierarchy for Neuropsychological Assessment

AUDITORY/VERBAL

Area to be assessed	Examples of measures
	Auditory Input/Receptive Language
Sound/word discrimination	Goldman-Fristoe-Woodcock Test of Auditory Discrimination (GFW) (Quiet, Noise) Halstead-Reitan Neuropsychological Test Battery: Seashore Rhythm Test Speech Sounds Perception Test Test of Auditory Perceptual Skills (TAPS): Auditory Discrimination Test Test of Language Development–2 (TOLD-2) Primary: Word Discrimination Wepman Auditory Discrimination Test Woodcock–Johnson Psychoeducational Test Battery–Revised (WJ-R): Sound Patterns
Auditory verbal comprehension	
Single words (receptive vocabulary)	Boehm Test of Basic Concepts–Revised Test for Auditory Comprehension of Language–Revised (TACL-R): Word Classes and Relations Peabody Picture Vocabulary Test–Revised (PPVT-R) Receptive One-Word Picture Vocabulary Test (ROWPVT) TOLD-2 Primary: Picture Vocabulary
Syntactic constructions, phrases, sentences	Illinois Test of Psycholinguistic Abilities (ITPA): Auditory Reception Northwestern Syntax Screening Test (NSST) TACL-R: Grammatical Morphemes, Elaborated Sentences TOLD-2 Intermediate: Vocabulary, Grammatic Comprehension, Malapropisms TOLD-2 Primary: Grammatic Understanding WJ-R: Oral Vocabulary (Antonyms/synonyms), Listening Comprehension
Paragraphs, stories	Durrell Analysis of Reading Difficulty: Listening Comprehension McCarthy Scales of Children's Abilities: Verbal Memory II Wechsler Individual Achievement Test (WIAT): Listening Comprehension Wechsler Memory Scale–Revised (WMS-R): Logical Memory Wide Range Assessment of Memory and Learning (WRAML): Story Memory
Comprehension of abstract verbal material	ITPA: Auditory Association Kaufman Assessment Battery for Children (K-ABC): Riddles McCarthy Scales of Children's Abilities (McCarthy): Opposite Analogies Stanford-Binet Intelligence Scale: Fourth Edition (SB-IV): Comprehension, Absurdities, Verbal Relations Test of Language Competence—Expanded Edition (TLC-E): Ambiguous Sentences, Listening Comprehension (inferences) TOLD-2 Intermediate: Generals Wechsler Intelligence Scale for Children–Third Edition (WISC-III): Similarities, Comprehension, Vocabulary Wechsler Preschool and Primary Scale of Intelligence–Revised (WPPSI-R): Similarities, Comprehension, Vocabulary
Auditory verbal memory span (recognition memory)	
Word recognition	GFW Auditory Memory Tests
Oral commissions, directions	Detroit Tests of Learning Aptitude–2 (DTLA-2): Oral Directions
Verbal sequential memory	K-ABC: Word Order

EXHIBIT 7 (*Continued*)

Area to be assessed	Examples of measures
Auditory Output/Expressive Language	
Word retrieval (naming vocabulary)	DTLA-2: Word Opposites Expressive One-Word Picture Vocabulary Test (EOWPVT) Halstead–Reitan Neurological Test Battery: Aphasia Screening K-ABC: Faces and Places WJ-R: Picture Vocabulary, Memory for Names
Short-term verbal memory	
Rote/sequential words, digits	DTLA-2: Word Sequences Luria–Nebraska Neuropsychological Battery: Luria Memory Words K-ABC: Number Recall McCarthy: Verbal Memory TAPS: Word Memory Visual Aural Digit Span (VADS) WISC-III, WPPSI-R, SB-IV: Digit Span WJ-R: Memory for Words WMS-R: Digit Span WRAML: Number–Letter Recall
Sentences	DTLA-2: Sentence Imitation McCarthy: Verbal Memory I SB-IV: Sentence Memory TAPS: Sentence Memory TOLD-2 Primary: Sentence Imitation WJ-R: Memory for Sentences WRAML: Sentence Memory
Paragraphs/stories	Durrell Analysis of Reading Difficulty: Listening Comprehension McCarthy: Verbal Memory II WMS-R: Logical Memory WRAML: Story Memory
Long-term or delayed verbal memory	Luria Memory Words: Delayed Recall Trials WISC-III, WPPSI-R, SB-IV, K-ABC: Vocabulary WISC-III, WPPSI-R, Peabody Individual Achievement Test–Revised: Information WMS-R: Delayed Recall Trials for Logical Memory, Verbal Paired Associates
Auditory analysis	GFW Sound Symbol Test Lindemood Auditory Conceptualization Test
Auditory synthesis	DTLA-2: Word Fragments GFW Sound Symbol Tests (Blending) ITPA: Auditory Closure, Sound Blending WJ-R: Word Attack, Sound Blending, Incomplete Words
Oral syntax Morphology Word Order Formulation	DTLA-2: Story Construction ITPA: Grammatic Closure Northwestern Syntax Screening Test TOLD-2 Primary: Oral Vocabulary, Grammatic Completion
Verbal/auditory learning	Luria–Nebraska: Memory Words TAPS: Auditory Processing WJ-R: Visual–Auditory Learning WMS-R: Verbal Paired Associates WRAML: Verbal Learning, Sound/Symbol

(*continues*)

EXHIBIT 7 (*Continued*)

Area to be assessed	Examples of measures
Expressive formulation of abstract information	SB-IV: Verbal Absurdities, Verbal Relations TLC-E: Oral Expression, Figurative Language TOLD-2 Intermediate: Sentence Combining, Word Ordering WJ-R: Verbal Analogies
	VISUAL
	Visual Input/Receptive
Visual discrimination/matching	Benton–Spreen Embedded Figures Test Columbia Mental Maturity Scale Hiskey–Nebraska Test of Learning Aptitude (H-N): Visual Identification Leiter International Performance Scale Motor Free Visual Perception Test (MVPT) Pictorial Test of Intelligence (PTI): Form Discrimination WJ-R: Visual Matching
Visual analysis/synthesis/spatial relations	
Visual analysis/synthesis	ITPA: Visual Closure K-ABC: Magic, Window, Triangles, Gestalt Closure Motor Free Visual Perception Test Raven Coloured Progressive Matrices SB-IV: Pattern Analysis WISC-III: Block Design, Object Assembly WJ-R: Visual Closure
Spatial relations	Primary Mental Abilities Test: Spatial Relations WJ-R: Spatial Relations
Visual recognition/recall memory	DTLA-2: Object Sequences H-N: Memory for Digits, Memory for Color, Visual Attention Span ITPA: Visual Sequential Memory K-ABC: Face Recognition, Spatial Memory Motor Free Visual Perception Test SB-IV: Bead Memory, Memory for Objects WJ-R: Picture Recognition, Spatial Relations WMS-R: Visual Paired Associates, Figural Memory WRAML: Picture Memory
Visual reproduction memory	Benton Visual Retention Test Memory for Designs Test WMS-R: Visual Reproduction WRAML: Design Memory, Finger Windows
Visual cognitive	DTLA-2: Picture Absurdities, Symbolic Relations, Conceptual Matching H-N: Picture Analogies, Visual Association Halstead–Reitan Battery: Categories Test, Trails B ITPA: Visual Association K-ABC: Matrix Analogies, Photo Series Raven Coloured Progressive Matrices SB-IV: Matrices, Paper Folding WISC-III: Picture Arrangement

EXHIBIT 7 (*Continued*)

Area to be assessed	Examples of measures
	Visual Output/Expression
Visuomotor integration	
Short-term recall	Benton Visual Retention Test
	DTLA-2: Letter Sequences
	Memory For Designs Test
	Reitan–Indiana Neuropsychological Test Battery for Children: Target Test
	Slingerland Screening Tests (Recall of geometric figures)
Drawing (long-term recall)	Goodenough Draw a Person
	House–Tree–Person Technique
	McCarthy: Draw-a-Child
Copying	Bender–Gestalt Test
	Canter Background Interference Procedure (BIP)
	DTLA-2: Design Reproduction
	Developmental Test of Visual–Motor Integration (VMI)
	Halstead–Reitan Battery: Constructional Apraxia, Aphasia Screening
	McCarthy: Figure Drawings
	Reitan–Indiana Battery: Star, Concentric Squares
	SB-IV: Copying
	WPPSI-R: Geometric Designs
Visuomotor processing speed	WJ-R: Cross Out
	WISC-III: Coding, Symbol Search
	Sensory Motor Input
Sensory recognition	Halstead Batteries: Finger agnosia bilateral simultaneous stimulation, astereognosis
Tactile-kinesthetic discrimination	Halstead–Reitan Battery: Tactile form recognition (Astereognosis), Tactual Performance Test, finger agnosia, and finger-tip number (symbol) writing
	Motor Output
Short-term recall (tactile)	Halstead–Reitan Battery: Tactual Performance Test (Memory, Localization)
Fine motor speed/coordination	Bruininks–Oseretsky Test of Motor Proficiency
	Detroit Motor Speed Test
	Halstead Batteries: Finger Tapping, Tactual Performance Test, Trails A
	Lafayette Grooved Pegboard
	Purdue Pegboard Test
	WISC-III: Coding, Mazes
Gross motor	Cerebellar Screening
	Tandem Walking
Motor speech	Diadokokinetic rates
	Tests for dysarthria
Lateral dominance—motor	Halstead Batteries: Finger Tapping, Lateral Dominance Exam, and Grip Strength (Dynamometer)

Index of Tests

Auditory–verbal

Boehm Test of Basic Concepts–Revised
Detroit Tests of Learning Aptitude–2 (DTLA-2)

(*continues*)

EXHIBIT 7 (*Continued*)

Durrell Analysis of Reading Difficulty
Expressive One-Word Picture Vocabulary Test (EOWPVT)
Goldman-Fristoe-Woodcock Test of Auditory Discrimination (GFW)
Halstead–Reitan Neuropsychological Test Battery
Illinois Test of Psycholinguistic Abilities (ITPA)
Kaufman Assessment Battery for Children (K-ABC)
Lindemood Auditory Conceptualization Test
Luria–Nebraska Neuropsychological Battery for Children
McCarthy Scales of Children's Abilities
Northwestern Syntax Screening Test (NSST)
Peabody Picture Vocabulary Test–Revised (PPVT-R)
Receptive One-Word Picture Vocabulary Test (ROWPVT)
Stanford–Binet Intelligence Scale: Fourth Edition (SB-IV)
Test for Auditory Comprehension of Language–Revised (TACL-R)
Test of Auditory Perceptual Skills (TAPS)
Test of Language Competence–Expanded Edition (TLC-E)
Test of Language Development–2 (TOLD-2): Primary
Test of Language Development–2 (TOLD-2): Intermediate
Visual Aural Digit Span (VADS)
Wechsler Individual Achievement Test (WIAT)
Wechsler Intelligence Scale for Children–Third Edition (WISC-III)
Wechsler Memory Scale–Revised (WMS-R)
Wechsler Preschool and Primary Scale of Intelligence–Revised (WPPSI-R)
Wepman Auditory Discrimination Test
Wide Range Assessment of Memory and Learning (WRAML)
Woodcock–Johnson Psychoeducational Battery–Revised (WJ-R)

Visuomotor

Bender–Gestalt Test
Benton–Spreen Embedded Figures Test
Benton Visual Retention Test
Bruininks–Oseretsky Test of Motor Proficiency
Canter Background Interference Procedure (BIP)
Columbia Mental Maturity Scale
Detroit Motor Speed Test
Developmental Test of Visual–Motor Integration (VMI)
Goodenough Draw a Person (DAP)
Halstead–Reitan Neuropsychological Test Battery
Hiskey–Nebraska Test of Learning Aptitude (H-N)
House–Tree–Person Technique
Lafayette Grooved Pegboard
Leiter International Performance Scale
Luria–Nebraska Neuropsychological Battery
Memory-for-Designs Test
Motor Free Visual Perception Test (MVPT)
Pictorial Test of Intelligence (PTI)
Primary Mental Abilities Test
Purdue Pegboard Test
Raven Coloured Progressive Matrices
Reitan–Indiana Neuropsychological Test Battery for Children
Slingerland Screening Tests

social–emotional adjustment problems. For more detailed discussion of this approach, see Culbertson (1981), Culbertson and Ferry (1982), and Culbertson, Norlan, and Ferry (1981).

The profile in Figure 3 illustrates that the child has average intellectual ability, but with a significant discrepancy between Verbal IQ and Performance IQ on the WISC-III. At a glance, it is apparent that all tests of verbal reasoning and phonologic processing are relatively lower than the child's nonverbal reasoning and visuomotor integration abilities, and that in many cases they are deficient. Specifically, the child demonstrated word-finding problems on the Expressive One-Word Picture Vocabulary Test–Revised (Gardner, 1990) and problems with fluency when asked to generate information (e.g., all the animals he could think of, or things to eat, or things to ride, etc.) within 1 min. The child's expressive speech was characterized by hesitancy and difficulty formulating his ideas into sentences. He tended to use brief, simple utterances, and simplified vocabulary in his oral discourse. Evaluation of auditory discrimination for words revealed below average performance. Verbal memory tasks from the Wide Range Assessment of Memory and Learning (WRAML; Sheslow & Adams, 1990) were variable, with low average performance on a task of memory for number or letter sequences and progressively declining performance on sentence memory and story memory tasks. As the semantic level of the verbal material increased, this child's processing ability and memory for the material decreased. The academic impact of the phonologic processing deficits were seen in depressed reading skills (including decoding, phonetic analysis of nonsense syllables, and comprehension) and written language skills (particularly spelling and grammatic usage in written passages). In contrast, this child's nonverbal reasoning and visuomotor integration abilities were average to above average. His fine motor speed and coordination were adequate to

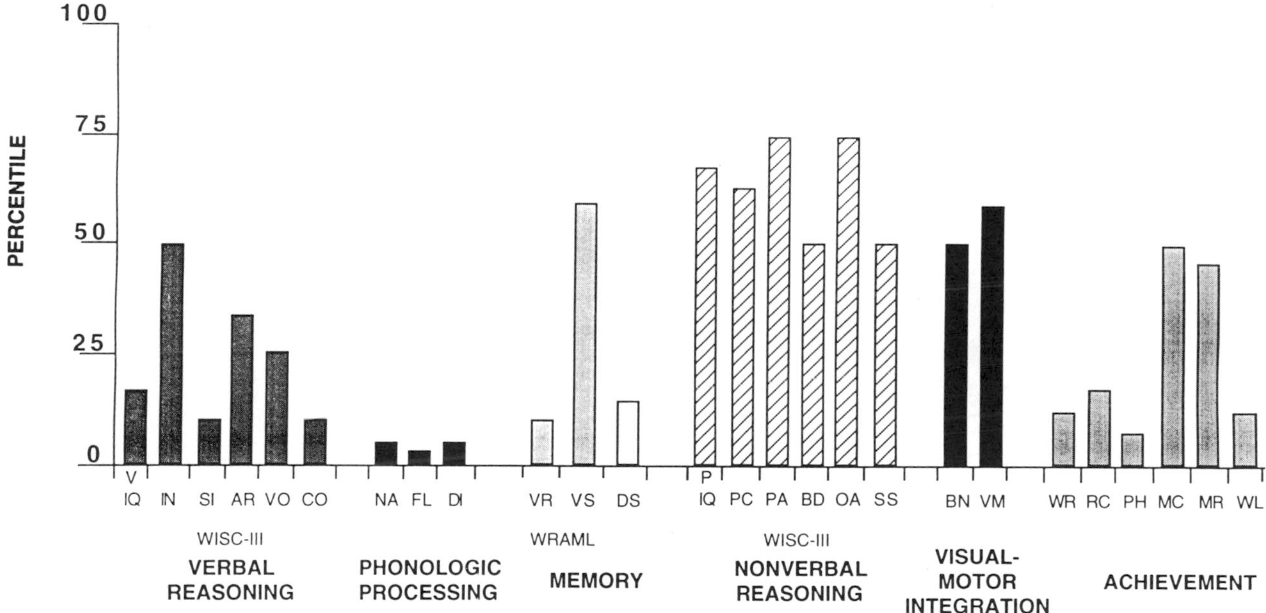

FIGURE 3. Profile of neuropsychological test results for a 7-year-old boy. WISC-III = Wechsler Intelligence Scale for Children–Third Edition; VIQ = WISC Verbal IQ; IN = WISC Information subtest; SI = WISC Similarities subtest; AR = WISC Arithmetic subtest; VO = WISC Vocabulary subtest; CO = WISC Comprehension subtest; NA = Expressive One-Word Picture Vocabulary Test; FL = FAS Fluency Test; DI = Wepman Auditory Discrimination Test; VR = Wide Range Assessment of Memory and Learning (WRAML) Verbal Memory Index; VS = WRAML Visual Memory Index; DS = WISC-III Digit Span subtest; PIQ = WISC-III Performance IQ; PC = Picture Completion subtest; PA = Picture Arrangement subtest; BD = Block Design subtest; OA = Object Assembly subtest; SS = Symbol Search subtest; BN = Bender–Gestalt Test; VM = Developmental Test of Visual–Motor Integration. WR = Woodcock–Johnson Psychoeducational Battery–Revised Letter–Word Identification subtest; RC = Passage Comprehension subtest; PH = Word Attack subtest; MC = Mathematics Calculation subtest; MR = Applied Problems subtest; WL = Written Language Cluster Score.

produce good writing and an average speed of writing production. His mathematics computation and reasoning abilities were also at the expected level. This child was diagnosed as having a learning disability in the areas of reading and written expression, with underlying deficient phonologic processing abilities.

This profile illustrates the importance of analyzing test data from various perspectives to determine the most meaningful interpretation. In this case, analysis of verbal versus nonverbal functions, modality specific (auditory, visual, motor) functions, and input versus output problems was helpful in understanding the nature of the learning disability. Following the integration and analysis of test data, the final step of the neuropsychological evaluation is providing practical recommendations for intervention (discussed later in the chapter). The process of conducting a neuropsychological evaluation of learning disability is illustrated through the following case.

Case Example

Jamie is an 11-year, 6-month-old boy referred by his pediatrician for evaluation of behavioral and attentional problems at school. Many behavioral descriptors were used by parents and teachers to characterize Jamie, including impulsive, distractible, overactive, occasionally aggressive, warm, loving, sensitive, gregarious and socially appealing, disorganized, and lazy about doing his schoolwork. By parent and teacher report as well as review of school records, it was determined that Jamie had a long-term failure to achieve at a level thought to be appropriate for his ability. However, no prior psychometric evaluations had been conducted despite the parents' concerns about his achievement. The teachers discouraged psychometric testing, suggesting that it may hurt Jamie's self-esteem; they expressed their opinion that Jamie could really do his work if he just tried.

There were several possible biologic etiologic factors to Jamie's achievement problems. The pregnancy history was remarkable for a 44 week (postterm) gestation complicated by maternal smoking, moderate alcohol use (4–5 drinks per week), and late toxemia. Labor was induced four times before it started, and it was 46 hr in length due to failure to progress. Jamie was thought to have suffered hypoxia (or decrease in oxygen) during the birth process; he was cyanotic initially after birth, had APGAR scores of 5 and 9, had meconium aspiration, metabolic acidosis, and hyperbilirubinemia requiring treatment in the neonatal intensive care unit for 4–5 days following delivery. He recovered without major developmental sequelae noted in the preschool years. Jamie developed Rocky Mountain Spotted Fever at age 6 years, accompanied by a temperature of 105° persisting for 1 week and associated with hallucinations. However, he responded to treatment and appeared to have no major residual effects. He has been healthy otherwise.

Review of history suggested that Jamie's academic problems were not due to educational, economic, or cultural disadvantage. Recent visual and audiological screenings by his pediatrician revealed normal acuity. Although his motor skills were functional, he was described by his mother as extremely clumsy and accident prone. He has had a short attention span, impulsivity, and high activity level since the preschool years. These symptoms have persisted over time, although changing in nature so that the predominant symptoms currently involve poor sustained attention, distractibility, and disorganization.

In addition to the symptoms mentioned already, the primary reason for requesting evaluation at this time relates to Jamie's problems completing written homework and classwork. The referral questions center around the reason for his poor performance and failure to complete his academic work. Parents and teachers question whether his problem is one of motivation or of interfer-

ence from a possible ADHD, an oppositional defiant disorder, or some primary learning problem.

At this stage of the evaluation, it is apparent that Jamie meets some of the definitional criteria for learning disability (i.e., documentation of academic failure, exclusionary criteria ruled out, and documentation of several possible etiologic factors that could be associated with learning disability). However, the differential diagnosis still includes a possibility of ADHD and oppositional defiant disorder as well as learning disability. Now it will be important to assess cognitive functioning, to determine whether a severe discrepancy exists between actual and expected achievement, and to evaluate possible for psychological processing deficits.

The test battery administered to Jamie is listed in Exhibit 8. The battery was selected to address the referral question about the reasons for his poor academic performance (e.g., whether he has low cognitive ability or learning disability, whether ADHD or an oppositional behavioral problem may be interfering with his school performance, and whether information-processing deficits may be present). The test data are described in Exhibit 9 and profiled in Figure 4.

Review of Jamie's test results revealed high average intellectual ability overall, with a relative strength in verbal comprehension abilities. Perceptual organization abilities involving serial order of pictures, reproduction of block designs, and puzzle assembly were relative strengths as well. However, Jamie's performance on the Picture Completion subtest suggested possible problems with visual attention to detail. The

EXHIBIT 8

Test Battery Administered to Jamie

Basic arousal, orientation, and attentional functions
- Screening for orientation to time, place, setting
- Gordon Diagnostic System (Vigilance and Distractibility tasks)
- Freedom from Distractibility Factor Score from the Wechsler Intelligence Scale for Children–Third Edition (WISC-III)

Basic sensory functions
- Halstead–Reitan Sensory Perceptual Exam
- Finger agnosia
- Finger-tip number writing
- Tactile form recognition

Modality specific perceptual functions
- Auditory
  - Expressive and Receptive One-Word Picture Vocabulary Tests
  - Wepman Auditory Discrimination Test
  - Wide Range Assessment of Memory and Learning (WRAML) Verbal Learning
- Visual
  - WISC-III Block Design, Object Assembly, Symbol Search
  - WRAML Picture Memory, Finger Windows, Visual Learning Test
- Motor
  - Halstead–Reitan Neuropsychological Test Battery: Finger Tapping
  - Purdue Pegboard Test
  - Cerebellar screening
  - Tandem walking

(*continues*)

EXHIBIT 8 (*Continued*)

Tactile-kinesthetic
- Halstead–Reitan Battery: Tactual Performance Test

Sensory-integration abilities

Visuomotor
- Developmental Test of Visual–Motor Integration
- Bender–Gestalt Test
- WRAML Design Memory

Visual–Auditory
- WRAML Sound Symbol Test

Academic
- Woodcock–Johnson Psychoeducational Battery Achievement Tests
- Test of Written Language–3
- Wide Range Achievement Test–Revised: Spelling

Psycholinguistic
- WISC-III Vocabulary
- WRAML Story Memory, Sentence Memory

Higher order cognitive abilities
- WISC-III Arithmetic, Similarities, Comprehension
- WRAML Immediate and Delayed Recall
- Category Test

Social–emotional–behavioral functioning
- Achenbach Child Behavior Checklist (CBCL)
- Conners Parent Questionnaire
- Conners Teacher Report Form
- Roberts Apperception Test
- Kinetic Family Drawing and other projective drawings
- Clinical interview with child and parent

Freedom from Distractibility Index of 87 was significantly below both the verbal comprehension and perceptual organization factors, suggesting a weakness on tasks requiring sustained attention and concentration. Also, processing speed was mildly delayed and significantly discrepant from verbal and perceptual abilities.

Jamie's expected level of academic achievement was determined by a regression formula based on his WISC-III Full-Scale IQ of 113. This resulted in a regression toward the mean, with an expected achievement level of 108. Compared with this expected level, Jamie's reading decoding, comprehension, and phonetic analysis skills were in the expected range. His knowledge of science, social studies, and humanities was above his expected achievement level, consistent with his high average IQ. Math abilities were variable, with math reasoning abilities falling above the expected range and math calculation significantly below the expected range. Jamie made numerous errors related to alignment of the numerals in computational problems, failure to attend to the operational sign, and simple errors of addition and subtraction that were not corrected. He worked very quickly on problems without checking

EXHIBIT 9

Summary of Jamie's Neuropsychological Test Results

Intellectual

Wechsler Intelligence Scale for Children–Third Edition (WISC-III): Full-Scale IQ 113 ± 7

Verbal IQ = 115 ± 7	SS	Performance IQ = 110 ± 9	SS
Information	10	Picture Completion	7
Similarities	14	Picture Arrangement	15
Arithmetic	10	Block Design	13
Vocabulary	14	Object Assembly	12
Comprehension	15	Coding	10
Digit Span	5	Symbol Search	6
		Mazes	—

Index scores:

Verbal Comprehension	118 ± 7
Perceptual Organization	111 ± 10
Freedom from Distractibility	87 ± 10
Processing Speed	91 ± 11

Academic

Woodcock–Johnson Psychoeducational Battery–Revised

Test	Grade equivalent	Actual SS	Expected SS	Discrepancy
Basic Reading	8.3	104	108	−4
Reading Comprehension	7.1	104	108	−4
Math Calculation	5.0	87	108	−21[a]
Math Reasoning	12.5	124	108	+16
Written Expression	4.2	87	108	−21[a]

Test of Written Language–3
 Spontaneous Writing Quotient: 68 (−40 discrepancy)[a]
Wide Range Achievement Test–Third Edition (WRAT-3)[a]
 Spelling: SS 84 (14th percentile)

Basic sensory functions

Halstead–Reitan Neuropsychological Test Battery: Sensory Perceptual Exam

No suppression errors on bilateral simultaneous stimulation through the visual, auditory, or tactile modalities

Tactile Finger Recognition
 Right: 0 errors
 Left: 0 errors

Finger-tip number writing:
 Right: 3 errors (36th percentile)
 Left: 5 errors (18th percentile)

Tactile Form Recognition:
 Right: 0 errors, 13 s
 Left: 0 errors, 14 s

Modality specific functions

Auditory

Expressive One-Word Picture Vocabulary Test	SS 126
Receptive One-Word Picture Vocabulary Test	SS 130

(*continues*)

EXHIBIT 9 (*Continued*)

Wepman Auditory Discrimination Test	Average
WRAML Verbal Learning Subtest	SS 13
Visual	
WISC-III	
Block Design	SS 13
Object Assembly	SS 12
Symbol Search	SS 6
WRAML	
Picture Memory	SS 5
Finger Windows	SS 6
Visual Learning	SS 10

Motor
Finger Tapping
Preferred hand: Right, M = 38 (27th percentile)
Nonpreferred hand: Left, M = 30 (9th percentile)
Purdue Pegboard
Dominant hand: 13 pegs (10th percentile)
Nondominant hand: 9 pegs (<10th percentile)
Both hands: 10 pairs (<10th percentile)
Tactile–kinesthetic
Tactual Performance Test
Dominant hand: Right, 3.2 min (35th percentile)
Nondominant hand: Left, 2.5 min (23rd percentile)
Both hands: 1.1 min (37th percentile)
Total time: 6.8 min (30th percentile)
Memory: 5 (59th percentile)
Location: 2 (5th percentile)

Sensory-integration abilities

Visuomotor
Bender–Gestalt Test
Koppitz score: 3
AE: 8 years, 6 months to 8 years, 11 months (10th–20th percentile)
Developmental Test of Visual–Motor Integration
AE: 8 years, 7 months
SS: 86 (18th percentile)

WRAML Design Memory	SS 9
Visual–auditory	
WRAML Sound Symbol	SS 10
Psycholinguistic	
WISC-III	
Vocabulary	SS 14
WRAML	
Story Memory	SS 16
Sentence Memory	SS 15

Higher order cognitive abilities

WISC-III	
Arithmetic	SS 10
Similarities	SS 14
Comprehension	SS 15
WRAML	
Verbal Memory Index	121

EXHIBIT 9 (*Continued*)

Delayed Recall for Story Memory	Average
Visual Memory Index	89
Delayed Recall for Design Memory	Average
Category Test	75th percentile
Attentional processes	
Gordon Diagnostic System	
Vigilance task	
Total correct	38 (abnormal)
Commission errors	18 (abnormal)
Distractibility task	
Total correct	10 (abnormal)
Commission errors	26 (abnormal)

SS = scaled score; AE = age equivalent.
[a]*There was a significant discrepancy between actual and expected achievement levels.*

the accuracy of his computations. Written expression was also significantly below the expected achievement level, with particular deficits on measures of spelling, rules of punctuation and capitalization, and rules for grammatical usage. Performance on the TOWL-3 spontaneous writing task was significantly below average, with specific

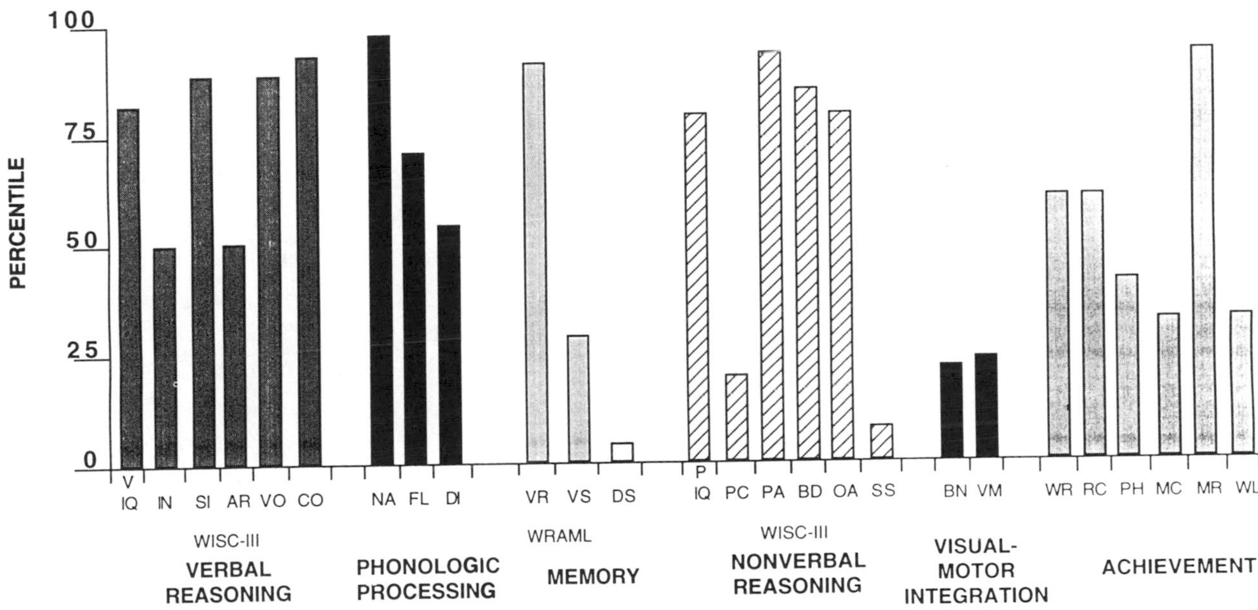

FIGURE 4. Profile of neuropsychological test results for Jamie. WISC-III = Wechsler Intelligence Scale for Children–Third Edition; VIQ = WISC Verbal IQ; IN = WISC Information subtest; SI = WISC Similarities subtest; AR = WISC Arithmetic subtest; VO = WISC Vocabulary subtest; CO = WISC Comprehension subtest; NA = Expressive One-Word Picture Vocabulary Test; FL = FAS Fluency Test; DI = Wepman Auditory Discrimination Test; VR = Wide Range Assessment of Memory and Learning (WRAML) Verbal Memory Index; VS = WRAML Visual Memory Index; DS = WISC-III Digit Span subtest; PIQ = WISC-III Performance IQ; PC = Picture Completion subtest; PA = Picture Arrangement subtest; BD = Block Design subtest; OA = Object Assembly subtest; SS = Symbol Search subtest; BN = Bender–Gestalt Test; VM = Developmental Test of Visual–Motor Integration. WR = Woodcock–Johnson Psychoeducational Battery–Revised, Letter–Word Identification subtest; RC = Passage Comprehension subtest; PH = Word Attack subtest; MC = Mathematics Calculation subtest; MR = Applied Problems subtest; WL = Written Language Cluster Score.

deficits in thematic maturity, contextual spelling, and contextual style. Writing production was generally slow and laborious, and legibility was poor. On the basis of this exam, Jamie met the learning disability criteria for a severe discrepancy in two areas: math calculation and written expression.

Jamie's performance on intellectual and academic measures has ruled out low cognitive ability as a reason for his academic difficulty but has suggested that a specific LD in math computation and written expression could account for at least a part of his poor school performance. Children with poor writing ability often present with refusal to complete written assignments at a time when writing demands increase in the school setting (e.g., generally third or fourth grade). At this point in the evaluation, it is important to evaluate possible underlying processing factors that could relate to his learning disability.

Basic sensory functions were found to be intact on the Halstead–Reitan Neuropsychological Test Battery Sensory Perceptual Exam, although there was a mild deficit in left hand sensory discrimination (finger-tip number writing). Examination of modality specific functions revealed a clear discrepancy between his generally strong auditory–verbal processing abilities and his variable, often weak visual processing abilities. Within the auditory–verbal area, he displayed excellent receptive vocabulary and naming abilities, average auditory discrimination for similar words, and good ability to learn a serial word list with repetition. Within the visual area, he had generally strong visuospatial analysis skills on block design and puzzle assembly tasks, but had difficulty on tasks requiring visual memory for pictorial details and memory for finger movement patterns. His timed visual scanning abilities were deficient on the WISC-III Symbol Search test. Fine motor speed on a finger tapping task was average for the right hand, but slow for the left. A similar pattern of performance was noted on a task of fine motor speed and dexterity with pegs (Purdue Pegboard). Tactile–kinesthetic abilities on the Tactual Performance Test were generally low average to average, with the exception of the below-average localization score. Sensory-integration abilities were delayed on tasks of visuomotor integration (Bender-Gestalt Test for Young Children [Bender-Gestalt test] and Development Test of Visual–Motor Integration [VMI]) but were average on a task of auditory–visual ability (sound–symbol association).

Jamie's psycholinguistic abilities were excellent, as were verbal measures of higher cortical abilities (e.g., abstract verbal reasoning, verbal memory). One nonverbal measure of problem-solving and abstract reasoning, the Category test, was performed at an above average level also. However, visual memory skills were impaired due to previously mentioned deficits in memory for pictorial details and movement patterns.

Evaluation of Jamie's information-processing abilities suggests several possible underlying factors related to his learning disability. First, Jamie has difficulty with attention to and memory for visual details. This processing deficit may underlie problems with spelling, punctuation, capitalization, and math computation in that these academic skills depend to some degree on visual discrimination and attention to detail. Although Jamie has some compensatory strategies (e.g., verbal mediation) for dealing with his visual processing deficits, the deficits slow his performance on some tasks and increase Jamie's frustration level. Jamie also has weaknesses in fine motor speed and coordination and in visuomotor integration, both of which could relate to his writing production problems. His writing speed is slow and his writing is poorly legible. Letter formation is poor, and he often leaves out words or critical punctuation in his writing samples. Otherwise, Jamie's test performance confirms excellent abstract reasoning, problem-solving, and verbal comprehension abilities. The testing thus far has provided the diagnosis of learning disability, and information on underlying processing deficits. However, there remain questions about the possibility of attentional and behavioral problems also interfering with Jamie's school performance.

> *Assessment of Jamie's attentional processes was accomplished through observation of his behavior during testing, administration of the Gordon Diagnostic System to examine vigilance and impulsivity, clinical interview with parents and teacher, and completion of age-normed behavioral rating scales by parents and teacher. Observation of Jamie's performance during testing revealed perseverance on tasks, but a tendency to rush through without checking his work. This resulted in some errors on easy items that probably were a result of his impulsive and inattentive work style. Excess activity level and off-task behavior were not observed. Jamie's performance on both the Vigilance and Distractibility tasks of the Gordon Diagnostic System were abnormal, indicating significantly poor vigilance abilities and increased impulsivity. These findings were confirmed by both parental and teacher ratings on the Child Behavior Checklist, with clinically elevated scores on the scale related to attention. Clinical interview with parents and teacher, reviewing* DSM-IV *criteria for ADHD, revealed that Jamie met criteria for ADHD-primarily inattentive type. Other significant oppositional behavior and conduct problems were ruled out. Projective evaluation did not reveal emotional pathology, but suggested that Jamie sometimes uses denial as a defense when confronted with difficult academic tasks and negative feedback about his performance. At other times, he uses his excellent social skills to win approval from teachers and distract them from his areas of difficulty. This may explain the teachers' discouragement of psychometric testing for many years, and their perception that Jamie was capable of doing grade-level work if he would only try harder.*

The final analysis of test data suggests that both ADHD-inattentive type and learning disability may have a negative impact on Jamie's school performance. His coping strategies for dealing with his undiagnosed problems and others' perception of him may also result in a tendency to avoid difficult tasks and try to distract others through his good social skills. In this case, the clinical issues related to Jamie's coping strategies and the response of others in the home and school environment led to an unfortunate delay in diagnosis and appropriate intervention. The resulting confusion about the cause of his academic performance problems led to a misperception of Jamie as lazy. The evaluation clarified a number of important issues related not only to his primary diagnoses of learning disability and ADHD, but also related to possible intervention strategies for addressing his learning disability and visual and visuomotor processing problems.

Special Considerations in Evaluation of Social–Emotional Learning Disability

Evaluation of children, adolescents, and adults with social–emotional learning disability should be multifaceted as outlined in Exhibit 10. The evaluation begins with a thorough review of the symptomatology as presented in the current literature. Symptoms related to the child's cognitive, academic, social, and adaptive functioning may be obtained from various caregivers including parents, teachers, and others

EXHIBIT 10

Components to Evaluation of Social–Emotional Learning Disabilities

- Review of current cognitive, academic, social, and adaptive symptoms
- History of early development with regard to social interaction, exploration, tolerance for novelty
- Formal assessment of cognitive, academic, neuropsychological, emotional, and adaptive functioning
- Direct observations of affective responsivity and expression, conversational style

who interact with the child. The history should also explore the child's early development, reviewing areas such as the child's adaptation to novel situations and the nature of early exploratory behavior. Special care must be taken to discriminate between those patients with primary emotional disorders and those who have social perception deficits that lead to disruption of their social relationships. The authors' clinical experience has revealed that children, adolescents, and adults with social–emotional learning disability often are unaware of the behaviors that disrupt their relationships with others. Because they sincerely fail to perceive social situations accurately, they often are surprised to learn that they have offended or irritated others. They may be very aware that others do not like them, they may express sadness and even anger at being rejected, but they seem to lack insight into the aspects of their behavior that create the problems. They seem to be social–emotional klutzes who inadvertently irritate and alienate others around them by their behaviors. A direct interview with the child who has social–emotional learning disability may reveal these characteristics and the lack of insight.

The formal evaluation of social–emotional learning disability includes cognitive, academic, neuropsychological, and perhaps projective assessment to make an appropriate differential diagnosis. Several cognitive and academic deficits have been associated with social–emotional learning disability and should be evaluated as part of a comprehensive workup. These include deficits in visuospatial skills, abstract reasoning and complex problem solving, decreased attention, and poor math and reading comprehension abilities. Likewise, cognitive and academic assets, including good verbal association, strong auditory–verbal memory, good reading decoding skills, and good spelling should be assessed as well. On neuropsychological evaluation, it may be possible to demonstrate a left hemisyndrome in which motor and sensory skills on the left side of the body are impaired, reflecting right-hemisphere dysfunction. Poor tactile recognition and tactile memory, particularly on the left side, may be demonstrated, as well as poor ability to adapt to novel stimuli and complex problem solving tasks (such as the Category Test or Tactual Performance Test on the Halstead-Reitan Battery).

Finally, assessment of social–emotional learning disability should include some evaluation of the child's understanding and expression of affect, direct observations of social interaction, and perhaps projective evaluation to shed insight into basic personality functioning. Assessment methods for determining the child's perception and expression of affect and emotional prosody have been developed for research purposes but are not yet clinically available. These methods are modeled after measures used with adult stroke patients and include simple tasks involving recognition of differences in facial affect as well as expression of facial affect. The examiner may instruct the patient to "show me how you would look if you were scared," or ask the patient to identify a picture displaying a certain affective facial expression. Expression of emotional prosody may be observed by asking the patient to say a neutral sentence with a sad affect or happy affect, or asking the patient to say a sentence with sad content in a neutral tone of voice. This would tap the patient's ability to express emotions. Conversely, the patient may be asked to identify the affect demonstrated by the examiner who says "I am going to the store" in a very sad voice. Other experimental measures involve asking the child to watch videotapes of social interactions in which an adult pretends to injure herself or lose an important possession. Observations are made of the child's reaction to this vignette. Although not standardized, simple screening techniques such as the ones described here may shed light on the patient's ability to understand and express affect across a variety of dimensions and may add important clinical data to the assessment.

Beyond that, more traditional projective measures such as projective storytelling, sentence completion, or drawings may be useful in understanding the patient's perception of social situations, basic personality functioning, and emotional reaction to the symptoms of their disorder. It is very common to hear patients identify the sadness and frustration they feel related to rejection from peers and family members. Psychotherapeutic intervention must not only address the need for improvement in social awareness and social perception but also provide support to the patient with regard to the secondary emotional reactions related to their primary disorder.

The following case illustrates the neuropsychological profile of a 13-year-old girl with social–emotional learning disability.

Case Example

Heather is a 13-year, 9-month-old girl referred by her pediatrician for neuropsychological evaluation because of concerns about impaired concentration and attention, poor academic progress, motor incoordination, and poor social skills. Heather is described as a teen who is extremely immature, uses baby talk, has poor perception of others' feelings and moods, talks excessively, is clingy, hugs and kisses too much, is too familiar with strangers, has poor eye contact, poor hygiene, and a very short attention span.

Pertinent medical history revealed unremarkable pregnancy, labor, and delivery of Heather as a full-term, 7 lb. 9 oz. (3,430 g) infant. The parents suspected that Heather may have had hearing loss at 17–18 months, but the loss was found to be conductive in nature and was corrected by bilateral myringotomies and tube placement. Heather's neurologic history was remarkable for report of asymmetry of motor development during infancy (e.g., strong preference for left hand and asymmetric crawling with left leg dragging). Heather's motor incoordination led to neurological examination at age 6 years, with normal EEG and CT scan. She was found to have mildly abnormal coordination on cerebellar screening, but no major motor problems.

Developmental history revealed delays in motor and speech and language development. She sat alone at 8 months, walked at 18 months, and never crawled well with alternating movements. She had no meaningful speech and language until after tubes were placed in her ears at 18 months. This was followed by rapid speech and language development.

School history revealed chronic academic delays, first noted in kindergarten. A school psychometric evaluation during kindergarten revealed a WISC-R Verbal IQ of 90, Performance IQ of 86, and Full-Scale IQ of 87. Significant motor incoordination and an attention deficit disorder were noted in contrast to well-developed verbal and auditory processing skills. Heather received special education services in a learning disability resource program for 1 period per day during first grade and continued to receive learning disability services for math since that time. She repeated first grade because of her academic problems and immaturity (e.g., short attention span and regressive behavior). Psychometric reevaluation in fourth grade revealed a WISC-R Verbal IQ of 91 and a Performance IQ of 58. Heather's current school placement is in seventh grade, with learning disability resource services for math.

Behavioral history provided by the parents revealed chronic concerns about Heather's social development. Although Heather had always seemed immature in comparison with peers, the contrast between her social behavior and that of her peers became more noticeable as she entered the teen years. Her lack of interest in personal hygiene and appearance, regressive behavior (e.g., baby talk and childish giggling), excessive need for attention and physical affection, and poor social judgment were making it embarrassing for the family to take her out in public. The parents did not consider Heather to be deliberately oppositional, but they were increasingly frustrated at her lack of improvement in social skills despite their repeated encouragement and reminders about appropriate behavior. Of more immediate concern to her parents was her boy crazy behavior; they were concerned that she is vulnerable and too gullible and that there is a high risk of pregnancy or sexually transmitted diseases. It was primarily this concern that had brought them to the clinic for neuropsychological evaluation.

EXHIBIT 11

Summary of Heather's Neuropsychological Test Results

Intellectual

Wechsler Intelligence Scale for Children–Third Edition (WISC-III): Full-Scale IQ = 62 ± 7

Verbal IQ = 81 ± 7	SS	Performance IQ = 48 ± 9	SS
Information	8	Picture Completion	1
Similarities	7	Picture Arrangement	2
Arithmetic	2	Block Design	1
Vocabulary	9	Object Assembly	1
Comprehension	7	Coding	2
Digit Span	(5)	Symbol Search	(5)
		Mazes	—

Index scores:

Verbal Comprehension	88 ± 8
Perceptual Organization	50 ± 9
Freedom From Distractibility	64 ± 10
Processing Speed	67 ± 12

Academic

Woodcock–Johnson Psychoeducational Battery–Revised

Test	Grade equivalent	Actual SS	Expected SS	Discrepancy
Basic Reading	5.1	90	89	+1
Reading Comprehension	6.2	94	89	+5
Math Calculation	2.2	47	89	−42[a]
Math Reasoning	1.6	61	89	−28[a]
Written Expression	5.6	90	89	+1

Basic sensory functions

Halstead–Reitan Neuropsychological Test Battery

Sensory Perceptual Exam

Suppression errors:

RH *0*	LH *0*
RH *4*	LF *0*
RF *1*	LH *0*
RE *1*	LE *1*
RV 2	LV *1*

Tactile Finger Recognition:
- Right: 11 errors
- Left: 7 errors

Finger-tip number writing:
- Right: 9 errors (<1st percentile)
- Left: 9 errors (<1st percentile)

Tactile Form Recognition:
- Right: 0 errors, 14 s
- Left: 0 errors, 12 s

Lateral Dominance Exam

Hand	R5	L2
Eye	R1	L1
Foot	R2	L0
Name	R19 s	L25 s

EXHIBIT 11 (*Continued*)

Modality specific functions

Auditory

Expressive One-Word Picture Vocabulary Test	SS 102
Receptive One-Word Picture Vocabulary Test	SS 98
Wepman Auditory Discrimination Test	SS average
WRAML Verbal Learning Subtest	SS 7

Visual

WISC-III	
Block Design	SS 1
Object Assembly	SS 2
Symbol Search	SS 5
WRAML	
Picture Memory	SS 6
Finger Windows	SS 2
Visual Learning	SS 2

Motor

- Finger Tapping
  - Preferred hand: Left, $M = 18$ (<1st percentile)
  - Nonpreferred hand: Right, $M = 25$ (<1st percentile)
- Purdue Pegboard
  - Dominant hand: 8 pegs (<10th percentile)
  - Nondominant hand: 8 pegs (<10th percentile)
  - Both hands: 7 pairs (<10th percentile)

Tactile–kinesthetic

- Tactual Performance Test
  - Dominant hand: Right, 10 min, 1 block (<1st percentile)
  - Nondominant hand: Left, 10 min, 1 block (<1st percentile)
  - Both hands: Discontinued
  - Total time: not applicable
  - Memory: 2 (<1st percentile)
  - Location: 0 (<1st percentile)

Sensory-integration abilities

Visuomotor

- Bender–Gestalt Test
  - Koppitz score: 10
  - AE: 5 years, 6 months to 5 years, 8 months (<5th percentile)
- Developmental Test of Visual Motor Integration
  - AE: 5 years, 10 months
  - SS: 59 (1st percentile)
- WRAML Design Memory: SS 3

Visual–auditory

- WRAML Sound Symbol: SS 3

Psycholinguistic

WISC-III	
Vocabulary	SS 9
WRAML	
Story Memory	SS 12
Sentence Memory	SS 10

Higher order cognitive abilities

WISC-III

Arithmetic	SS 2
Similarities	SS 7
Comprehension	SS 7

(*continues*)

EXHIBIT 11 (*Continued*)

WRAML
Verbal Memory Index: *98 ± 8*
Delayed Recall for Story Memory: Average
Visual Memory Index: *56 ± 10*
Delayed Recall for Design Memory: Below average
Category Test: 87 errors (<1st percentile)
Trails B: 362 s, 14 errors (<1st percentile)

[a]*There was a significant discrepancy between actual and expected achievement levels.*

The history presented thus far reveals that Heather has many symptoms suggestive of social–emotional learning disability, including immature and regressive behavior, lack of understanding or recognition of the social mores of her peer group and family, poor social judgment about her own behavior and its effect on others, and lack of regard for interpersonal space when interacting with others. Her gullibility and strong need for attention are characteristic of social–emotional learning disability. Also fitting the pattern of expected symptoms are the history of learning disability in math, the more recent psychometric profile of significantly depressed perceptual organization abilities relative to verbal abilities, and the early neurologic history reflective of left-side weakness and dyscoordination. The results of formal neuropsychological evaluation of Heather are provided in Exhibit 11 and Figure 5.

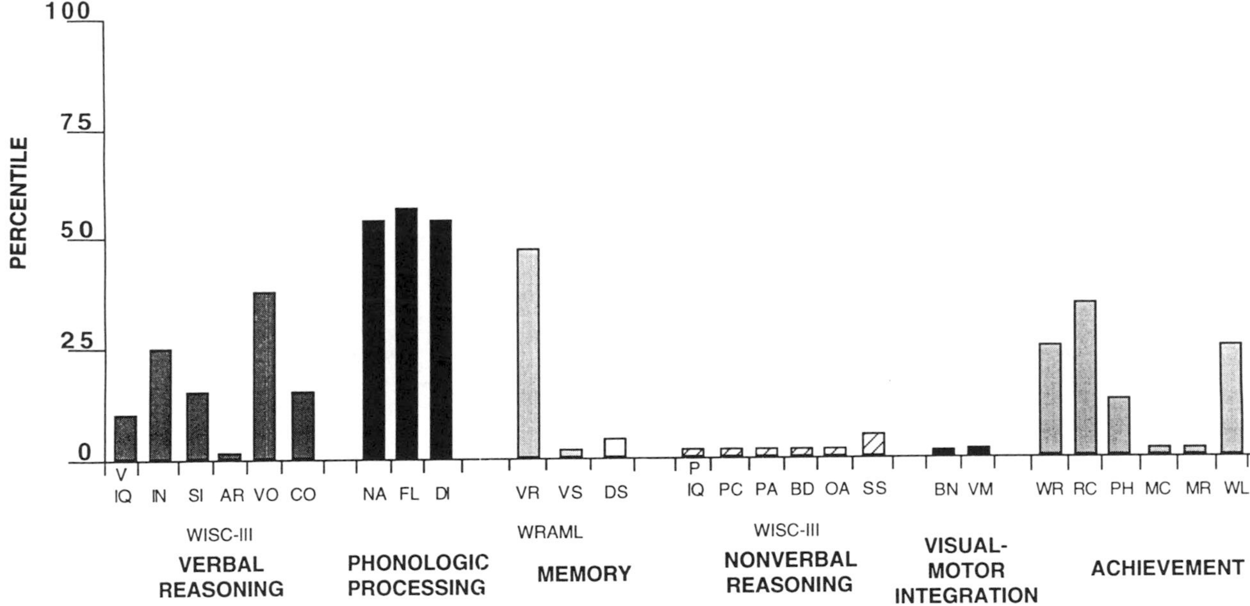

FIGURE 5. Profile of neuropsychological test results for Heather. WISC-III = Wechsler Intelligence Scale for Children–Third Edition; VIQ = WISC Verbal IQ; IN = WISC Information subtest; SI = WISC Similarities subtest; AR = WISC Arithmetic subtest; VO = WISC Vocabulary subtest; CO = WISC Comprehension subtest; NA = Expressive One-Word Picture Vocabulary Test; FL = FAS Fluency Test; DI = Wepman Auditory Discrimination Test; VR = Wide Range Assessment of Memory and Learning (WRAML) Verbal Memory Index; VS = WRAML Visual Memory Index; DS = WISC-III Digit Span subtest; PIQ = WISC-III Performance IQ; PC = Picture Completion subtest; PA = Picture Arrangement subtest; BD = Block Design subtest; OA = Object Assembly subtest; SS = Symbol Search subtest; BN = Bender–Gestalt Test; VM = Developmental Test of Visual–Motor Integration. WR = Woodcock–Johnson Psychoeducational Battery–Revised, Letter–Word Identification subtest; RC = Passage Comprehension subtest; PH = Word Attack subtest; MC = Mathematics Calculation subtest; MR = Applied Problems subtest; WL = Written Language Cluster Score.

Review of Heather's intellectual functioning revealed a more pronounced gap between verbal and performance abilities on the WISC-III than noted on previous evaluations with the WISC-R. Although Heather's Verbal IQ of 81 fell in the low-average range, her Performance IQ of 48 was in the mentally deficient range. Heather displayed extremely deficient visual attention, visuospatial reasoning, visuomotor integration, and mental arithmetic abilities, in contrast to her average to low average verbal comprehension and reasoning abilities. Of particular note was the contrast between two subtests that require some judgment and awareness of social cues. When the social information was presented nonverbally (Picture Arrangement), Heather's performance was extremely deficient, whereas her performance was in the low-average range when knowledge of social information was measured verbally (Comprehension subtest). This suggests that when social information is coded verbally, Heather can recall and discuss this information much better than when she must derive the information from nonverbal cues. Heather's attention was variable during administration of the WISC-III, suggesting a possible attention deficit. Her depressed Freedom From Distractibility factor score would seem to support this observation, but the score is somewhat deceptive because it includes the Arithmetic subtest score, and Heather had documented problems with mathematics over and above those that related to attentional factors.

Academically, a very clear profile emerged indicating a severe discrepancy between expected and actual achievement in the areas of math calculation and math reasoning. Heather's expected achievement level of 89 was determined by a regression equation based on her Verbal IQ of 81. The Verbal IQ was thought to be a better indicator of her expected achievement level than her nonverbal score because many academic subjects are language based. Also, Heather's performance on the language-based skills of reading and written expression were found to be within the expected range. Heather's current pattern of academic performance confirmed the prior diagnosis of learning disability in math calculation and math reasoning.

Heather's neuropsychological test performance revealed a pattern of assets and deficits that were characteristic of social–emotional learning disability. Her primary neuropsychological assets were noted on tasks of auditory discrimination (Wepman) and verbal learning of serial word lists. Her primary neuropsychological deficits were noted on tasks of tactile perception (finger recognition and finger-tip number writing), visual perception (visual-perceptual tasks from the WISC-III and WRAML), and more complex psychomotor tasks such as the Tactual Performance Test. Bilateral sensory and motor deficits were noted, but the severity of the deficits was greater on the left side of the body, suggesting right-hemisphere dysfunction. More complex sensory-integration abilities were strong on tests of psycholinguistic ability (from the WISC-III and WRAML) but were deficient on tests of visuomotor integration (Bender-Gestalt test and VMI). A similar pattern was noted on tests of higher order cognitive abilities, with relative strengths on verbal reasoning and comprehension tasks (WISC-III, Similarities and Comprehension tests and WRAML Verbal Memory Index) and significant deficits on nonverbal reasoning and problem-solving tasks (Halstead–Reitan Category test, Tactual Performance Test, and Trails B). Heather's style of performance on these problem-solving tasks was characterized by lack of a strategy, random responding, failure to learn from past mistakes, and inflexibility in trying new strategies. She seemed lost and quickly became frustrated on these tasks.

Heather's test profile suggests a clear pattern of deficits implicating the right hemisphere with relative sparing of left-hemisphere functions. Taking the intellectual, academic, and neuropsychological profiles together, Heather's functional assets and deficits fall into a characteristic pattern for social–emotional learning disability. One exception to this is her weaknesses in even simple motor functions (Finger Tapping, Purdue Pegboard, and writing speed); these functions often are in the average range in persons with social–emotional learning disability. The qualitative aspects of Heather's verbal abilities are not reflected in test scores, but offer important information with regard to the diagnosis of social–emotional learning disability. Heather's oral discourse was characterized by frequent topic shifts in conversation, introduction of information that was unrelated to the task at hand or current conversation, poor ability to listen and respond to comments of others, a rather flat and monotonic vocal tone, and poor eye contact while having a conversation. In addition, the parents reported that Heather was verbally intrusive with family and peers, often seeming oblivious to the feelings of others. She talks excessively, and does not detect the nonverbal cues of others that would indicate her behavior is irritating. Thus, the pragmatic aspects of communication are impaired, along with deficits in the content and prosody of her speech and language.

> *Heather has classic behavioral symptoms of social–emotional learning disability as well. Her behavior appears to others to be insensitive and rude, but when her inappropriate behavior is pointed out, Heather acts remorseful. She seems genuine in her lack of understanding of why her behavior was inappropriate. Heather is described as being socially rejected by her peer group because of her irritating behavior (e.g., talking too much, touching and hugging too much, demanding too much attention, being unable to listen to and respect the wishes of others, and being unable to take another's perspective). Her parents reported that if anyone shows some kindness to her, Heather latches on to the person and becomes possessive of their attention. Of course, Heather is soon rejected by this newfound friend and experiences yet another round of rejection and isolation.*

The information obtained from history, review of symptoms, and current test data support a diagnosis of social–emotional learning disability. However, it is important before concluding the evaluation to explore the ramifications of this diagnosis on Heather's emotional functioning. To achieve this goal, projective evaluation was added to the testing already completed.

> *The Roberts Apperception Test, a sentence-completion test, and clinical interview with Heather were completed. Results indicated that Heather had many fears and anxieties about potential loss of significant others. These fears were expressed in projective stories with regard to loss of family members to death or abandonment. Her stories also revealed her confusion about how to behave in various social situations and strongly felt rejection from others. Heather expressed wishes to be "a straight-A student," to be "beautiful," and to have "300,000 friends." Her painful desire for acceptance was compounded by her lack of understanding about why she was rejected. Heather described her mood as sad and hopeless when asked about her current life situation and the future. Although she experienced some symptoms of depression, she did not meet clinical criteria for a diagnosis of depression.*

The projective evaluation revealed the significant and pervasive impact of social–emotional learning disability on all aspects of Heather's life. Although her family expressed relief at understanding the reasons for Heather's inappropriate behavior, they admitted that they expected to still find her difficult to live with. Social–emotional learning disability is not a well-known entity to school personnel and peers, so the possibility for their understanding the nature of Heather's disability is even more remote. Finally, Heather was already showing emotional adjustment problems secondary to her primary diagnosis of social–emotional learning disability. She was at high risk for developing more serious emotional pathology, probably in the nature of internalizing disorders, as time goes on. Unfortunately, the prognosis for good adjustment and normal emotional development was poor given the circumstances of her disability.

In Heather's situation, two forms of intervention were recommended. The first involved a parent–child relational focus in which the therapist educated the family and Heather about the nature of her social perception problems. In the context of this family oriented therapy, attempts were made to code nonverbal social information (related to family interactions) into verbal cues so that Heather could use her strong verbal skills to help her process and retain this information. Siblings were included in the sessions so that role-play around typical school social situations could occur also. A very concrete, repetitive approach was used to teach Heather the rules of social interaction, such as maintaining eye contact, waiting until another person finishes speaking before starting to speak herself, maintaining the topic of conversation, remembering not to touch others too much, and so forth. Family homework assignments were developed in which Heather could practice the newly learned social skills in a variety of settings, but with supportive family members present to offer reminders and positive feedback for Heather's improving social behaviors.

The second form of intervention with Heather involved individual therapy, to provide her an opportunity to express her feelings about her life situation and to provide positive support for her. Heather had mixed feelings of dependency, support, and rejection related to family members, and it was thought that the relationship with the therapist would provide a more therapeutic means of processing the many emotions related to her disability.

These intervention approaches with Heather seemed reasonable given our knowledge about the characteristics of her social–emotional learning disability and its impact on her life. However, clinical neuropsychology research has not yet provided data about effective methods of intervention for social–emotional learning disability, and more valid recommendations for intervention await further research.

Special Considerations in Assessing Adults Who Have Learning Disabilities

Many adults who present with learning disabilities today have been previously diagnosed as children as a result of legislation passed in the 1970s and updated in the 1990s (Education of the Handicapped Act Amendments of 1990) that requires identification and remediation of these learning disorders. Lately, practitioners have found it increasingly important to familiarize themselves with the characteristics of adult learning disability and the impact this disorder has on future life experiences (e.g., work and postsecondary education). Although the chronicity of learning disability has been well established, the adult presentation of learning disability may be shrouded by the changes in the deficit over time, and any compensatory strategies that may have developed. Consequently, the evaluation of an adult with learning disabilities can be greatly enhanced by the acquisition of past test results and copies of individualized education plans. Furthermore, because diagnostic criteria are often less clear in later presentations of learning disability, records of earlier evaluations will document that the client met the specific eligibility criteria promulgated by a particular state. In addition to past evaluation results, the practitioner will want to obtain a detailed history from the client regarding his or her past, as well as present, difficulties. This collaborative participation in the evaluation is tantamount to other, more technical parts of the evaluation as it may assist the client in being actively involved in the assessment process, and it provides the examiner with clinical information (i.e., verbal presentation, prosody, time orientation, thought content, and thought process) that might not be gleaned from standardized tests.

As the practitioner considers Luria's conceptual model discussed earlier, he or she must proceed by first ruling out sensory acuity deficits and reception problems. The information on visual and auditory acuity is usually provided by medical screenings before the assessment begins. Additional information on sensory detection and perception can be obtained from the Sensory–Perceptual Exam of the Halstead–

Reitan Neuropsychological Test Battery (Reitan, 1979).

Most practitioners begin their assessment by evaluating cognitive abilities. Adults are typically administered the WAIS-R. This test can provide information regarding modality-specific skills (i.e., spatial orientation, visual recognition, visual matching, and auditory problem solving) as well as some higher order cognitive skills (i.e., abstract thinking, long-term, and short-term memory). Although various definitions have been established for learning disability, all concur that average intelligence or above is requisite to meeting the diagnostic criteria. Academic achievement tests should be administered next in an effort to establish an ability–achievement discrepancy and to gather information regarding sensory-integration efficiency. Standardized tests that cover the adult age ranges are limited. Although the third edition of the Wide Range Achievement Test covers the age span, it serves the practitioner more as a screen of academic functioning. The Woodcock–Johnson–Revised Tests of Achievement (Woodcock & Johnson, 1989) can augment the evaluation to include written expression skills (punctuation, grammar, and capitalization), mathematical reasoning, and reading comprehension. Practitioners may need to proceed further if the area of disability in question is not thoroughly covered by the Woodcock–Johnson tests. For example, the College Entrance Examination Board provides an array of tests that evaluate upper level math reasoning, written expression, and critical reasoning. These tests are referred to as the Descriptive Test of Language Skills and the Descriptive Test of Mathematical Skills (Educational Testing Service, 1989) and cover advanced sentence structure and intermediate algebra, respectively. The Nelson Denny Reading Test (Brown, Fishco, & Hanna, 1993) can be administered for upper-level (grades nine–college) reading comprehension.

Next the practitioner will need to determine processing deficits that contribute to the individual's academic difficulties. Gardner (1992) has developed an upper level of the Test of Visual–Motor Skills and the Test of Visual–Perceptual Skills for the assessment of adults. These tests provide information on visual memory, discrimination, closure, and orientation. Other useful tests include the Raven Progressive Matrices (Raven, 1977) to tap nonverbal visuospatial processing, and the Rey–Osterrieth Complex Figure (Spreen & Strauss, 1991) to assess perceptual organization. Auditory measures may include subtests from the Detroit Tests of Learning Aptitude–Adult Version (Hammill & Bryant, 1991) that tap sequencing, discrimination, and perception problems or from the Halstead–Reitan Neuropsychological Test Battery (e.g., Speech Sounds Perception and Seashore Rhythm tests).

The practitioner must then evaluate higher order cognitive abilities, such as memory, language, and abstract reasoning, to determine modality strengths and weaknesses. The Wechsler Memory Scale–Revised (Wechsler, 1987) assesses both verbal and nonverbal memory and provides a measure of delayed recall. The Rey–Osterrieth Complex Figure can also be used with a delay of 30 min to assess visual memory.

Linguistic problems are frequently present among adults with learning disabilities. The Clinical Evaluation of Language Functions–Revised (Semel, Wiig, & Secord, 1980) is occasionally used with young adults and provides assessment of syntax, semantics, and memory. Verbal fluency measures are also used to assess word retrieval skills. The Controlled Oral Word Association Test (FAS), adapted from the Multilingual Aphasia Examination (Benton & Hamsher, 1978), is a well-known verbal fluency test. The Boston Naming Test (Kaplan, Goodglass, & Weintraub, 1983) is often used as a word-retrieval measure with a visual confrontational component.

Abstract thinking, including verbal and nonverbal reasoning skills, is usually assessed among the adult population to assist with questions regarding problem-solving abilities and how these abilities relate to future vocational and educational planning. The Wisconsin Card Sorting Test (Heaton, 1981) is a nonverbal test of concept formation that reflects sources of difficulty (perseveration, inefficient learning, and failure to maintain conceptual set) attributable to critical thinking. Verbal abstract abilities can be measured by the Similarities and Comprehension subtests of the WAIS-R.

Finally, social–emotional problems are ruled out with the State–Trait Anxiety Inventory (Spielberger,

1983), the Beck Depression Inventory (Beck, 1987), and the Brief Symptom Inventory (Derogatis, 1993). If further psychopathology is indicated, then the Minnesota Multiphasic Personality Inventory, second edition (Hathaway & McKinley, 1989) is administered. Although causality cannot be implied by the empirical evidence in this area, learning disability often co-occurs with depression, ADHD, antisocial personality disorder, or conduct disorder.

INTERVENTION WITH CHILDREN, ADOLESCENTS, AND ADULTS WHO HAVE LEARNING DISABILITIES

The primary mode of intervention for learning disability has been through special education services provided by public schools. However, until recently, little attention has been given to the needs of adolescents and young adults with learning disabilities in terms of their transition from secondary schools to either vocational or college settings. Recent federal legislation has begun to address these issues while also making modifications in the special education services provided for younger children. In this section of the chapter, we discuss special education intervention for learning disabilities.

Recent Changes in Federal Legislation

Federal education legislation has ensured that students with learning disabilities are provided a free and appropriate education via Public Law 101–476, referred to as the Individuals With Disabilities Education Act (IDEA). IDEA was formerly mandated under Public Law 94–142 (Education of all Handicapped Children Act of 1975). As a result of this legislation, specialized training has been instituted at the college level for teachers who are interested in pursuing careers as learning disability specialists. These teachers, who are trained to educate children with specific learning problems, provide the bulk of intervention that is based on an individualized education plan for each student. Appropriate special education environments may range from total inclusion (full-time placement in the general education classes) to a self-contained special education placement (a full-day learning disability class for all academic subjects). Students diagnosed with learning disability most frequently access special education on a part-time basis. For example, many students are placed in learning disability resource classes for one class period per area of disability. Other supportive settings used by children with learning disabilities include Chapter 1 services (skill enhancement) and gifted programs (talent enhancement), although these programs generally are not taught by educators who are trained to work with learning disabled students.

Currently, special education programs around the country are departing from the pull-out programs (e.g., resource rooms) and moving toward the full inclusion model of education. Inclusion is to be distinguished from mainstreaming in that inclusion provides the regular classroom teacher with training, appropriate accommodations, auxiliary aids, and support from special educators (Council for Exceptional Children, 1993). Inclusion as a means of intervention is a controversial topic among parents, teachers, and administrators. Although it is a concept that is philosophically attractive because it provides students with disabilities the full opportunity to experience a realistic prototype of society, inclusion is not a strategy that national learning disability groups (e.g., the Council for Exceptional Children and the Learning Disabilities Association) subscribe to without reservation. In January 1993, the National Joint Committee for Learning Disabilities issued the following statement in response to those schools that chose to offer inclusion as the only option for serving the student with learning disabilities:

> *The Committee believes that full inclusion, when defined this way, violates the rights of parents and students with disabilities as mandated by the Individuals with Disabilities Education Act. ("Inclusion Practices Blasted," 1993)*

To date, research regarding the success of existing special education programs has been both limited and inconclusive (Council for Exceptional Children, 1993; Martin, 1994). A recent large-scale study of 8,000 high school students indicated several shortcomings of the present special education system (Wagner, 1992–1993). Approximately 65% of secondary students with learning disabilities failed at least one class during their high school career. This failure may contribute to the high drop-out rates (more than 33%) among students with learning disabilities (Wagner, 1992–1993). Although Wagner's data suggest that only 4% of students with learning disabilities enroll in 4-year college programs and even fewer obtain a degree, others (Mithaug et al., 1985; Shaw & Shaw, 1989) have indicated that approximately 50% of adolescents with learning disabilities pursue some form of postsecondary education.

One landmark change introduced by IDEA is the provision of transition services for students with learning disabilities who are 16 years or older. This legislation requires that a statement concerning each student's transition from high school to postsecondary education or a vocation appear in the individualized education plan. This mandated service is an integral part of a student's future because it addresses adult living adjustments and increases the chances of positive postschool outcomes (O'Leary, 1993).

Alternatives to transition clauses in the individualized education plan include programs provided by the Vocational Rehabilitation Agency. For example, the Job Training Partnership Act youth program is targeted to students who are between the ages of 16 and 21, are economically disadvantaged, are disabled (including learning disabled), exhibit disruptive behavior, or speak limited English as a second language. The adult program provides services to individuals who are 22 years of age or older who also exhibit the criteria discussed for their younger counterparts. Evidence of a learning disability must be provided to access vocational rehabilitation (Kyle, 1993).

Legislation mandated in the early 1970s (Rehabilitation Act of 1973) has provided adolescents and young adults diagnosed with learning disabilities legal rights that protect them from discrimination in training (i.e., college) or employment and has assisted some college students in acquiring specialized educational services (Gajar, 1992). In her review of the literature, Gajar (1992) noted that empirical studies evaluating special services at the college level are nonexistent. Others (Barsch, 1980; Geib, Guzzardi, & Genova, 1981) concur and have indicated that colleges are striving to develop appropriate programs in the absence of empirical data that would document a model program. Consequently, although legislation to provide intervention for children, adolescents, and adults is in place, the quality and availability of some of those services continues to be questionable (Mangrum & Strichart, 1988).

Trends in Special Education Services

Subsumed within the intervention of special education are many different treatment strategies. Although a full discussion of every intervention is beyond the scope of this chapter, we do highlight trends in cognitive intervention that have been empirically investigated. Because of nonexistent data with adults, as revealed earlier, this discussion is restricted to the child and adolescent populations.

Bos and Van Reusen (1991) reviewed the general trends in academic-intervention research that have focused on aspects of motivation, cognitive–metacognitive processing, and cognitive–behavioral modification. They contended that combining the neuropsychological correlates of learning disability with the difficulties these students seem to experience with complex cognitive–metacognitive strategies may increase the ecological validity of neuropsychological data within the classroom. That is, concentrating on the process that children use to comprehend a passage may be more informative than subtyping them into categories based on the difficulties they experience when trying to comprehend. In their review, Bos and Van Reusen delineated the following instructional trends: (a) the importance of self-concept and intrinsic motivation in guiding a student's endeavors and success; (b) developing and stimulating organizational frameworks for improved access of learned material and the attainment of new material; (c) the use of cognitive modeling and verbal self-instructional procedures; (d) using self-regulatory techniques; and (e) promoting the generation of strategies, competence, maintenance, and generalization.

The literature on intrinsic motivation (Perlmuter & Monty, 1977; Van Reusen, Deshler, & Schumaker, 1989) has suggested that learning disabled students who have the opportunity to voice their opinions on educational alternatives by being involved in the prioritizing of academic goals seem to be more successful. Additionally, it has been shown that teachers who monitor their own comments for messages fostering independence increase the self-concept and motivation of students with learning disabilities (Bryan, 1986; Van Reusen, Bos, Schumaker, & Deshler, 1987).

The trend of developing and activating organizational frameworks among students with learning disabilities has also proven to be productive. For example, researchers (Anderson, Reynolds, Schallert, & Goetz, 1977; Anderson, Spiro, & Anderson, 1978) have demonstrated the importance of integrating prior learning with current learning, specifically in the area of reading comprehension and content-area subjects. The interactive learning model (Bos & Anders, 1990) requires the student to consolidate old knowledge with new and has been applied in several recent studies. Substantial improvements in reading comprehension and knowledge acquisition of content areas has been demonstrated in both bilingual, upper-elementary students with learning disabilities (Bos & Reyes, 1989) and middle-school students with learning disabilities (Anders et al., 1990). These students performed at a level comparable to average achieving students and maintained this progress for 6 weeks.

The use of cognitive modeling, verbal self-instructional techniques, and self-regulation has been shown to improve reading comprehension (Graves, 1986), as well as written comprehension (Thomas, Englert, & Gregg, 1987) and mathematics (Montague & Bos, 1986). In their study of written composition, Thomas, Englert, and Gregg (1987) found that students with learning disabilities make substantially more mechanical errors and redundant comments than normal achieving students, suggesting a lack of verbal self-instruction. By utilizing self-instructional training, S. Graham and Harris (1989) were able to demonstrate improved written compositions of fifth- and sixth-grade students who have learning disabilities. This method involved generating a story from seven story-grammar questions (e.g., Who is the main character? Where does the story take place? What does the main character do? and What happens when he or she does it?). Before treatment, only 36% of the students included at least six story elements. By the completion of treatment, 86% of the students implemented this self-instructional strategy.

One study (Wood, Rosenberg, & Carran, 1993) investigated the utility of tape-recorded self-instruction cues on the mathematical performance of children with learning disabilities. The pairing of self-instruction with taped cues increased the mathematical problem-solving skills of the students. The success of the program was partly attributed to the individualized tape cues that were made by the students themselves using vocabulary at their own semantic level.

Another self-instructional approach involved the use of a mnemonic strategy to enhance and maintain reading comprehension; this strategy was shown to be significantly more effective than didactic teaching (L. Graham & Wong, 1993). The students were taught three self-questions to assist them in using the mnemonic approach: How will I answer this question? Where is the answer to this question found? and Is my answer correct? Specifically, the self-help questions focused the students' attention on the task, provided a foundation for decision making about the categories of comprehension test questions, and reminded them to check their answers (L. Graham & Wong, 1993). In addition to being successful with learning disabled students, this self-instructive technique is cost-effective and time-efficient once it is taught to the students.

The final trend of promoting strategy acquisition, competence, maintenance, and generalization focuses on the importance of considering the readiness stage of each learner. One study (E. Smith & Alley, 1981) that used a multiple-baseline design with 3 sixth-grade students looked at the efficacy of teaching strategy acquisition in the context of word problems in math. Accuracy improved with both instructional and grade-level materials. Many of the early strategies used to assist children with learning disabilities in the past have focused on traditional operant procedures. Because research (Rooney & Hallahan, 1985) has indicated a lack of generalization over tasks and settings with externally focused behavioral techniques, investigators have increasingly turned their attention to the recent success achieved with internal cognitive–behavioral approaches. Although the relationship between the neuropsychological functioning of students with learning disabilities and the cognitive treatment interventions they receive remains at a relatively primitive level (Hooper & Willis, 1989), this approach may be more productive than interventions that tend to overlook process. Further research is needed to delineate the most effective treatment strategies as a function of the specific processes that are impaired in the student with learning disabilities.

References

Algozzine, B., & Ysseldyke, J. (1986). The future of the LD field: Screening and diagnosis. *Journal of Learning Disabilities, 19*, 394–398.

American Psychiatric Association. (1980). *Diagnostic and statistical manual of mental disorders* (3rd ed.). Washington, DC: Author.

American Psychiatric Association. (1994). *Diagnostic and statistical manual of mental disorders* (4th ed.). Washington, DC: Author.

Anders, P. L., Bos, C. S., Scalon, D., Gallego, M., Duran, G. Z., & Reyes, E. (1990). [Facilitating content learning through interactive strategy instruction with middle school learning disabled students.] Unpublished raw data.

Anderson, R. C., Reynolds, R. E., Schallert, D. L., & Goetz, E. T. (1977). Frameworks for comprehending discourse. *American Educational Research Journal, 14*, 367–382.

Anderson, R. C., Spiro, R. J., & Anderson, M. C. (1978). Schemata as scaffolding for the representation of information in connected discourse. *American Educational Research Journal, 15*, 433–440.

Association for Children and Adults With Learning Disabilities. (1985). ACLD offers new definition. *Special Education Today*, 2, 1, 19.

Badian, N. A. (1983). Dyscalculia and nonverbal disorders of learning. In H. R. Mykelbust (Ed.), *Progress in learning disabilities* (Vol. 5, pp. 235–264). New York: Grune & Stratton.

Barsch, J. (1980). Community college: New opportunities for the student. *Academic Therapy, 15*, 467–470.

Batchelor, E. S., Gray, J. W., & Dean, R. S. (1990). Empirical testing of a cognitive model to account for neuropsychological functioning underlying arithmetic problem solving. *Journal of Learning Disabilities, 23*, 38–42.

Beck, A. T., (1987). *Beck Depression Inventory manual*: New York: Psychological Corporation.

Beery, K. E. (1982). *Revised administration, scoring, and teaching manual for the Developmental Test of Visual–Motor Integration*. Cleveland, OH: Modern Curriculum Press.

Benton, A. L. (1975). Developmental dyslexia: Neurological aspects. In W. J. Friedlander (Ed.), *Advances in neurology* (pp. 1–47). New York: Raven Press.

Benton, A. L. (1977). Reflections on the Gerstmann Syndrome. *Brain and Language, 4*, 45–62.

Benton, A. L., & Hamsher, K. (1978). *Multilingual Aphasia Examination*. Iowa City: University of Iowa Press.

Bigler, E. D. (1992). The neurobiology and neuropsychology of adult learning disorders. *Journal of Learning Disabilities, 25*, 488–506.

Birch, H. G., & Belmont, L. (1964). Auditory–visual integration in normal and retarded readers. *American Journal of Orthopsychiatry, 34*, 852–861.

Birch, H. G., & Belmont, L. (1965). Auditory–visual integration, intelligence, and reading ability in school children. *Perceptual and Motor Skills, 20*, 295–305.

Boller, F., & Grafman, J. (1985). Acalculia. In P. J. Vinkin, G. W. Bruyn, & H. L. Klavans (Eds.), *Handbook of clinical neurology* (pp. 315–345). Amsterdam: North Holland.

Bos, C. S., & Anders, P. L. (1990). Toward an interactive model: Teaching text-based concepts to learning disabled students. In H. L. Swanson & B. Keogh (Eds.), *Learning disabilities: Theoretical and research issues* (pp. 247–261). Hillsdale, NJ: Erlbaum.

Bos, C. S., & Reyes, E. (1989, December). *Knowledge, use, and control of an interactive cognitive strategy for learning from content area texts*. Paper presented at the annual meeting of the National Reading Conference, Austin, TX.

Bos, C. S., & Van Reusen, A. K. (1991). Academic interventions with learning-disabled students. In J. E. Obrzut & G. W. Hynd (Eds.), *Neuropsychological foundations of learning disabilities: A handbook of issues, methods, and practices* (pp. 659–683). San Diego, CA: Academic Press.

Bowen, S. M., & Hynd, G. W. (1988). Do children with learning disabilities outgrow deficits in selective auditory attention? Evidence from dichotic listening in adults with learning disabilities. *Journal of Learning Disabilities, 21*, 623–631.

Bowlby, J. (1969). *Attachment* (Vol. 1). New York: Basic Books.

Bowlby, J. (1973). *Separation: Anxiety and anger* (Vol. 2) New York: Basic Books.

Bowlby, J. (1980). *Loss: Sadness and depression* (Vol. 3) New York: Basic Books.

Braden, J. P. (1987). A comparison of regression and standard score discrepancy methods for learning disabilities identification: Effects on racial representation. *Journal of School Psychology*, *25*, 23–29.

Brill, J. (1987). *Learning disabled adults in post-secondary education*. Washington, DC: American Council on Education.

Brown, J., Fishco, V., & Hanna, G. (1993). *Nelson Denny Reading Test*. Chicago: Riverside Publishing.

Bruck, M. (1990). Word-recognition skills of adults with childhood diagnoses of dyslexia. *Developmental Psychology*, *26*, 439–454.

Bryan, T. H. (1986). Self-concept and attributions of the learning disabled. *Learning Disabilities Focus*, *1*, 82–89.

Bryan, T., & Bryan, J. (1986). *Understanding learning disabilities* (3rd ed.). Palo Alto, CA: Mayfield.

Carpenter, R. L. (1985). Mathematics instruction in resource rooms: Instruction time and teacher competence. *Learning Disability Quarterly*, *8*, 95–100.

Chalfant, J. C. (1984). *Identifying learning disabled students: Guidelines for decision-making*. Burlington, VT: Northeast Regional Resource Center.

Chalfant, J. C. (1989). Learning disabilities: Policy issues and promising approaches. *American Psychologist*, *44*, 392 398.

Connolly, A. J. (1988). *Key Math–revised: A diagnostic inventory of essential mathematics*. Circle Pines, MN: American Guidance Services.

Cornwall, A. (1992). The relationship of phonological awareness, rapid naming, and verbal memory to severe reading and spelling disability. *Journal of Learning Disabilities*, *25*, 532–538.

Council for Exceptional Children. (1993). *Inclusion: What does it mean for students with learning disabilities?* Reston, VA: Division for Learning Disabilities.

Cruickshank, W. M. (1972). Some issues facing the field of learning disability. *Journal of Learning Disabilities*, *5*, 380–388.

Culbertson, J. L. (1981). Psychological evaluation and educational planning for children with central auditory dysfunction. In R. P. Keith (Ed.), *Central auditory and language disorders in children* (pp. 13–29). Houston: College-Hill Press.

Culbertson, J. L., & Ferry, P. C. (1982). Learning disabilities. *Pediatric Clinics of North America*, *29*, 121–136.

Culbertson, J. L., Norlan, P. F., & Ferry, P. C. (1981). Communication disorders in childhood. *Journal of Pediatric Psychology*, *6*, 69–84.

DeFries, J. C., & Decker, S. N. (1982). Genetic aspects of reading disability: A family study. In R. N. Malatesha & P. G. Aaron (Eds.), *Reading disorders: Varieties and treatments* (p. 255). San Diego, CA: Academic Press.

de Hirsch, K., Jansky, J., & Langford, W. (1966). *Predicting reading failure*. New York: Harper & Row.

Del Dotto, J. E., Rourke, B. P., McFadden, G. T., & Fisk, J. L. (1987, February). *Developmental analysis of arithmetic disabled children: Impact on personality adjustment and patterns of adaptive functioning*. Paper presented at the meeting of the International Neuropsychological Society, Washington, DC.

Deloche, G., Andreewsky, E., & Desi, M. (1982). Surface dyslexia: A case report. *Brain and Language*, *15*, 12–31.

Denckla, M. B. (1978). Minimal brain dysfunction. In J. S. Chall & A. F. Mirsky (Eds.), *Education and the brain* (pp. 223–268). Chicago: University of Chicago Press.

Denckla, M. B. (1983). The neuropsychology of social–emotional learning disability. *Archives of Neurology*, *40*, 461–462.

Denckla, M. B. (1989). Social learning disabilities. *International Pediatrics*, *4*, 133–136.

Denckla, M. B., & Rudel, R. G. (1976). Naming of objects by dyslexia and other learning-disabled children. *Brain and Language*, *3*, 1–15.

Dennis, M. (1991) Frontal lobe function in childhood and adolescence: A heuristic for assessing attention regulation, executive control, and the intentional states important for social discourse. *Developmental Neuropsychology*, *7*, 327–358.

DeRenzi, E., & Lucchelli, F. (1990). Developmental dysmnesia in a poor reader. *Brain*, *13*, 1337–1345.

Derogatis, L. (1993). *Brief Symptom Inventory*. Minneapolis, MN: National Computer Systems.

Dinnel, D., Glover, J., & Halpain, D. (in press). Individual differences in mathematics achievement: A cognitive correlates approach. *Journal of Educational Psychology*.

Dinnel, D., Glover, J., & Ronning, R. (1984). A provisional mathematical problem solving model. *Bulletin of the Psychonomic Society*, *22*, 459–462.

Dunn, L. M., & Dunn, L. M. (1981). *Peabody Picture Vocabulary Test–Revised*. Circle Pines, MN: American Guidance Service.

Education of All Handicapped Children Act of 1975, Pub. L. No. 94-142.

Education of the Handicapped Act Amendments of 1990, Pub. L. No. 101-476, ß 1400–1485, 20 Stat.

Educational Testing Service. (1989). *Descriptive Test of Mathematical Skills*. Princeton, NJ: Author.

Eidelberg, D., & Galaburda, A. M. (1982). Symmetry and asymmetry in the human posterior thalamus: I. Cytoarchitectonic analysis in normal persons. *Archives of Neurology*, *39*, 325–332.

Ellis, A. W. (1987). On problems in developing culturally-transmitted cognitive modules. [Review of the book *Cognitive analysis of dyslexia*]. *Mind and Language*, *2*, 242–251.

Falzi, G., Perrone, P., & Vignolo, L. A. (1982). Right–left asymmetry in anterior speech region. *Archives of Neurology*, *39*, 239–240.

Finucci, J. M., Guthrie, J. T., Childs, A. L., Abbey, H., & Childs, B. (1976). The genetics of specific reading disability. *Annual Review of Human Genetics*, *40*, 1–23.

Fisher, J. H. (1905). Case of congenital word-blindness (inability to learn to read). *Ophthalmic Review*, *24*, 315–318.

Fletcher, J. M. (1985). Memory for verbal and nonverbal stimuli in learning disability subgroups: Analysis by selective reminding. *Journal of Experimental Child Psychology*, *40*, 244–259.

Fletcher, J. M., & Taylor, H. G. (1984). Neuropsychological approaches to children: Towards a developmental neuropsychology. *Journal of Clinical Neuropsychology*, *6*, 39–56.

Frith, U. (1983). The similarities and differences between reading and spelling problems. In M. Rutter (Ed.), *Developmental neuropsychiatry* (pp. 460–472). New York: Guilford Press.

Frostig, M. (1964). *Frostig Developmental Test of Visual Perception*. Palo Alto, CA: Consulting Psychologists Press.

Gaddes, W. H. (1985). *Learning disabilities and brain function: A neuropsychological approach* (2nd ed.). New York: Springer-Verlag.

Gajar, A. (1992). Adults with learning disabilities: Current and future research priorities. *Journal of Learning Disabilities*, *25*, 507–519.

Gajar, A. H., Murphy, J., & Hunt, F. M. (1982). A university program for learning disabled students. *Reading Improvement*, *19*, 282–288.

Galaburda, A. M. (1993). Neurology of developmental dyslexia. *Current Opinion in Neurobiology*, *3*, 237–242.

Galaburda, A., & Livingstone, M. (1993). Evidence for a magnocellular defect in developmental dyslexia. *Annals of the New York Academy of Sciences*, *682*, 70–82.

Galaburda, A. M., & Sanides, F. (1980). Cytoarchitectural organization of the human cortex. *Journal of Comparative Neurology*, *190*, 597–610.

Galaburda, A. M., Sherman, G. F., Rosen, G. D., Aboitiz, F., & Geschwind, N. (1985). Developmental dyslexia: Four consecutive patients with cortical abnormalities. *Annuals of Neurology*, *18*, 222–233.

Gardner, M. (1992). *Test of Visual Motor Skills–Upper Level*. Burlingane, CA: Psychological and Educational Publications.

Gardner, M. F. (1990). *Expressive One-Word Picture Vocabulary Test–Revised*. Novato, CA: Academic Therapy Publications.

Geib, B. B., Guzzardi, L. R., & Genova, P. M. (1981). Intervention for adults with learning disabilities. *Academic Therapy*, *16*, 317–325.

Geschwind, N., & Behan, P. (1982). Left-handedness: Association with immune disease, migraine, and developmental learning disorder. *Proceedings of the National Academy of Science*, *79*, 5097–5100.

Geschwind, N., & Galaburda, A. M. (1985). Cerebral lateralization, biological mechanisms, associations, and pathology. *Archives of Neurology*, *42*, 428–459.

Geschwind, N., & Levitsky, W. (1968). Human brain: Left–right asymmetries in temporal speech region. *Science*, *161*, 186–187.

Giannitrapani, D. (1982). Localization of language and arithmetic functions via EEG factor analysis. *Research Communications in Psychology, Psychiatry, and Behavior*, *7*, 39–55.

Golden, C. J. (1981). The Luria-Nebraska Children's Battery: Theory and formulation. In G. W. Hynd & J. E. Obrzut (Eds.), *Neuropsychological assessment and the school-age child: Issues and procedures* (pp. 277–302). New York: Grune & Stratton.

Goodglass, H. (1980). Disorders of naming following brain injury. *American Scientist*, *68*, 647–655.

Gordon, N. (1992). Children with developmental dyscalculia. *Developmental Medicine and Child Neurology*, *34*, 459–463.

Grafman, J., Passaflume, D., Faglioni, P., & Boller, F. (1982). Calculation disturbances in adults with focal hemisphere damage. *Cortex*, *18*, 37–50.

Graham, L., & Wong, B. Y. L. (1993). Comparing two modes of teaching a question-answering strategy for enhancing reading comprehension: Didactic and self-instructional training. *Journal of Learning Disabilities*, *26*(4), 270–279.

Graham, S., & Harris, K. R. (1989). Components analysis of cognitive strategy instruction: Effects on learning disabled students' compositions and self-efficacy. *Journal of Educational Psychology*, *81*, 353–361.

Graves, A. W. (1986). Effects of direct instruction and metacomprehension training on finding main ideas. *Learning Disabilities Research*, *1*, 90–100.

Gregg, N. (1992). Expressive writing disorders. In S. R. Hooper, G. W. Hynd, & R. E. Mattison (Eds.), *Developmental disorders: Diagnostic criteria and clinical assessment* (pp. 127–172). Hillsdale, NJ: Erlbaum.

Gross-Glenn, K., Duara, R., Barker, W., Loewenstein, D., Chang, J., Yoshii, F., Apicella, A. M., Pascal, S., Boothe, T., Sevush, S., Jallard, B. J., Novoa, L., & Lubs, H. (1991). Position emission tomographic studies during serial word-reading by normal dyslexia adults. *Journal of Clinical and Experimental Neuropsychology*, *13*, 531–544.

Grunau, R. V. E., & Low, M. D. (1987). Cognitive and task-related EEG correlates of arithmetic performance in adolescents. *Journal of Clinical and Experimental Neuropsychology*, *9*, 563–574.

Hallgren, B. (1950). Specific dyslexia (congenital word-blindness): A clinical and genetic study. *Acta Psychiatrica et Neurologica Scandinavica*, *65*(Suppl.), 1–287.

Hammill, D. D., & Bryant, B. R. (1991). *Detroit Tests of Learning Aptitude–Adult examiner's manual*. Austin, TX: PRO-ED.

Hammill, D. D., & Larsen, S. C. (1996). *Test of Written Language: Third edition examiner's manual*. Austin, TX: PRO-ED.

Hammill, D. D., Leigh, J. E., McNutt, G., & Larsen, S. C. (1981). A new definition of learning disabilities. *Learning Disability Quarterly*, *4*, 336–342.

Hanley, J. R., Hastie, K., & Kay, J. (1992). Developmental surface dyslexia and dysgraphia: An orthographic processing impairment. *Quarterly Journal of Experimental Psychology*, *44A*, 285–319.

Hathaway, S. R., & McKinley, J. C. (1989). *Minnesota Multiphasic Personality Inventory–2*. Minneapolis: University of Minnesota Press.

Heath, C. P., & Kush, J. C. (1991). Use of discrepancy formulas in the assessment of learning disabilities. In J. E. Obrzut & G. W. Hynd (Eds.), *Neuropsychological foundations of learning disabilities* (pp. 287–307). San Diego, CA: Academic Press.

Heaton, R. K. (1981). *Wisconsin Card Sorting Text manual*. Odessa, FL: Psychological Assessment Resources.

Hinshelwood, J. (1895). Word-blindness and visual memory. *Lancet*, *2*, 1564–1570.

Hinshelwood, J. (1900). Congenital word-blindness. *Lancet*, *2*, 1564–1570.

Hirschorn, M. W. (1988, January 20). Freshman interest in business careers hits new level and money remains a top priority, study finds. *Chronicle of Higher Education*, pp. A31, A34–A36.

Hooper, S. R., & Willis, W. G. (1989). *Learning disability subtyping: Neuropsychological foundations, conceptual models, and issues in clinical differentiation*. New York: Springer-Verlag.

Hugdahl, L., Synnevag, B., & Satz, P. (1990). Immune autoimmune disease in dyslexic children. *Neuropsychologia*, *28*, 673–679.

Humphreys, P., Kaufman, W. E., & Galaburda, A. M. (1990). Developmental dyslexia in women: Neuropathological findings in three cases. *Annuals of Neurology*, *28*, 727–738.

Humphreys, P., Rosen, G. D., Press, D. M., Sherman, G. F., & Galaburda, A. M. (1991). Freezing lesions of the developing rat brain: I. A model for cerebral cortical microgyria. *Journal of Neuropathology and Experimental Neurology*, *50*, 145–160.

Hynd, G. W., & Cohen, M. (1983). *Dyslexia: Neuropsychological theory, research, and clinical differentiation*. New York: Grune & Stratton.

Hynd, G. W., Connor, R. T., & Nieves, N. (1988). Learning disability subtypes: Perspectives and methodological issues in clinical assessment. In M. G. Tramontana & S. R. Hooper (Eds.), *Assessment issues in child neuropsychology* (pp. 281–312). New York: Plenum.

Hynd, G. W., Hall, J., Novey, E. S., Elipulos, D., Black, K., Gonzalez, J. J., Edmonds, J. E., Riccio, C., & Cohen, M. (1993). *Dyslexia and corpus callosum morphology*. Manuscript submitted for publication.

Hynd, G. W., Semrud-Clikeman, M., Lorys, A. R., Novey, E. S., & Eliopulos, D. (1990). Brain morphology in development dyslexia and attention deficit disorder/hyperactivity. *Archives of Neurology*, *47*, 919–926.

Hynd, G. W., & Willis, W. (1988). *Pediatric neuropsychology*. New York: Grune & Stratton.

"Inclusion" practices blasted by advocates. (1993, Summer). *Counterpoint*.

Interagency Committee on Learning Disabilities. (1987). *Learning disabilities: A report to the U.S. Congress*. Washington DC: Author.

Johnson, D. J., & Myklebust, H. R. (1967). Nonverbal disorders of learning. In D. J. Johnson & H. R. Myklebust (Eds.), *Learning disabilities: Educational principles and practices* (pp. 272–306). New York: Grune & Stratton.

Kaliski, L. (1962). Arithmetic and the brain-injured child. *Arithmetic Teacher*, *9*, 245–251.

Kamphaus, R. W. (1993). *Clinical assessment of children's intelligence*. Needham Heights, MA: Allyn & Bacon.

Kamphaus, R. W., & Reynolds, C. R. (1987). *Clinical and research applications of the K-ABC*. Circle Pines, MN: American Guidance Service.

Kaplan, E., Goodglass, H., & Weintraub, S. (1983). *Boston Naming Test*. Philadelphia: Lea & Febiger.

Katz, A. (1980). Cognitive arithmetic: Evidence for right hemisphere mediation in an elementary component state. *Quarterly Journal of Experimental Psychology*, *32*, 69–84.

Kaufman, A. S., & Kaufman, N. L. (1983). *Kaufman Assessment Battery for Children: Interpretive manual*. Circle Pines, MN: American Guidance Service.

Kaufman, A. S., & Kaufman, N. L. (1985). *Kaufman Test of Educational Achievement*. Circle Pines, MN: American Guidance Service.

Kaufman, A. S., & Kaufman, N. L. (1992). *Kaufman Adolescent and Adult Intelligence Test manual*. Circle Pines, MN: American Guidance Service.

Keller, C. E., & Sutton, J. P. (1991). Specific mathematics disorders. In J. E. Obrzut & G. W. Hynd (Eds.), *Neuropsychological foundations of learning disabilities* (pp. 549–571). San Diego, CA: Academic Press.

Kephart, N. C. (1971). *The slow learner in the classroom* (2nd ed.). Columbus, OH: Charles E. Merrill.

King, W. L. (1987). Students with learning disabilities and postsecondary education: National Council on the Handicapped Forum on Higher Education and Students With Disabilities. In D. Knapke & C. Lendman (Eds.), *Capitalizing on the future* (pp. 16–21). Columbus, OH: AHSSPPE.

Kinsbourne, M. (1968). Developmental Gerstmann Syndrome. *Pediatric Clinics of North America, 15,* 771–778.

Kinsbourne, M., Rufo, D. T., Gamzu, E., Palmer, R. L., & Berliner, A. K. (1991). Neuropsychological deficits in adults with dyslexia. *Developmental Medicine and Child Neurology, 33,* 763–775.

Kinsbourne, M., & Warrington, E. K. (1963). The Developmental Gerstmann Syndrome. *Archives of Neurology, 8,* 490–501.

Kirk, S. A. (1963). Behavioral diagnosis and remediation of learning disabilities. In *Proceedings of the conference on exploration into the problems of the perceptually handicapped child.* Evanston, IL: Fund for the Perceptually Handicapped Child.

Kolb, B., & Whishaw, I. Q. (1985). *Fundamentals of human neuropsychology.* New York: Freeman.

Koppitz, E. M. (1975). *The Bender Gestalt Test for Young Children.* New York: Grune & Stratton.

Kussmaul, A. (1877). Disturbance of speech. *Cyclopedia of Practical Medicine, 14,* 581.

Kyle, B. (1993). Amendments to the job training partnership act. *Learning Disabilities Association Newsletter, 28*(1), 13.

Larsen, J. P., Høien, T., Lundberg, I., & Ødegaard, H. (1990). MRI evaluation of the size and symmetry of the planum temporal in adolescents with developmental dyslexia. *Brain and Language, 39,* 289–301.

Lawson, J. S., & Inglis, J. (1989). Learning disability in adults: A comparison of two indices of differential cognitive impairment derived from the Wechsler scales. *Journal of Clinical Psychology, 45,* 106–114.

Levin, B. E. (1990). Organizational deficits in dyslexia: Possible frontal lobe dysfunction. *Developmental Neuropsychology, 6,* 95–110.

Lubs, H. A., Rabin, M., Carland-Saucier, K., Wen, X. L., Gross-Glenn, K., Duara, R., Levin, B., & Lubs, M. L. (1991). Genetic bases of developmental dyslexia: Molecular studies. In J. E. Obrzut & G. W. Hynd (Eds.), *Neuropsychological foundations of learning disabilities* (pp. 49–77). San Diego, CA: Academic Press.

Luria, A. R. (1966). *Higher cortical functions in man.* New York: Basic Books.

Luria, A. R. (1970). The functional organization of the brain. *Scientific American, 222,* 66–78.

Luria, A. R. (1973). *The working brain.* New York: Basic Books.

Luria, A. R. (1980). *Higher cortical functions in man.* New York: Basic Books.

Lyle, J. G., & Goyen, J. (1968). Visual recognition, developmental lag and strephosymbolia in reading retardation. *Journal of Abnormal Psychology, 73,* 25–29.

Lyle, J. G., & Goyen, J. (1975). Effects of speed of exposure and difficulty of discrimination on visual recognition of retarded readers. *Journal of Abnormal Psychology, 8,* 613–616.

Mangrum, C. T., & Strichart, S. S. (1988). *College and the learning disabled student.* Orlando, FL: Grune & Stratton.

Markwardt, F. C. (1989). *Peabody Individual Achievement Test–Revised manual.* Circle Pines, MN: American Guidance Service.

Martin, E. W. (1994, April). Inclusion: Rhetoric and reality. *Exceptional Parent,* pp. 39–42.

Mattis, S., Erenberg, G., & French, J. H. (1978, February). *Dyslexia syndromes: A cross validation study.* Paper presented at the sixth annual meeting of the International Neuropsychological Society, Minneapolis, MN.

Mattis, S., French, J. H., & Rapin, I. (1975). Dyslexia in children and young adults: Three independent neuropsychological syndromes. *Developmental Medicine and Child Neurology, 17,* 150–163.

Mattson, A. J., Sheer, D. E., & Fletcher, J. M. (1991). Electrophysiological evidence of lateralized disturbances in children with learning disabilities. *Journal of Clinical and Experimental Neuropsychology, 14,* 707–716.

McDermott, P. A., & Watkins, M. (1985). *McDermott Multidimensional Assessment of Children: 1985 Apple II version* [Computer program]. New York: Psychological Corporation.

McDermott, P. A., & Watkins, M. (1987). *McDermott Multidimensional Assessment of Children: 1987 IBM version* [Computer program]. New York: Psychological Corporation.

McKeever, W. F., & Van Deventer, A. D. (1975). Dyslexic adolescents: Evidence of impaired visual and auditory language processing. *Cortex, 11,* 361–378.

McLeod, T. M., & Armstrong, S. W. (1982). Learning disabilities in mathematics: Skill deficits and remedial approaches at the intermediate and secondary level. *Learning Disability Quarterly, 5,* 305–311.

McLeod, T. M., & Crump, W. D. (1978). The relationship of visuo-spatial skills and verbal ability to learning disabilities in mathematics. *Journal of Learning Disabilities, 11,* 237.

Mithaug, D., Horiuchi, C., & Fanning, P. (1985). A report on the Colorado statewide follow-up survey of special education students. *Exceptional Children, 51*, 397–404.

Montague, M., & Bos, C. S. (1986). The effects of cognitive strategy training on verbal math problem solving performance of learning disabled adolescents. *Journal of Learning Disabilities, 19*, 26–33.

Morgan, W. P. (1896). A case of congenital word-blindness. *British Medical Journal, 2*, 1978.

Murphy, L. A., Pollatsek, A., & Well, A. D. (1988). Developmental dyslexia and word-retrieval deficits. *Brain and Language, 35*, 1–23.

Myklebust, H. R. (1965a). *Development and disorders of written language* (Vol. 1). New York: Grune & Stratton.

Myklebust, H. R. (1965b). *The psychology of deafness* (2nd ed.). New York: Grune & Stratton.

Myklebust, H. R. (1973). *Development and disorders of written language* (Vol. 2). New York: Grune & Stratton.

Nagy, J., & Szatmari, P. (1986). Schizotypal personality disorders in childhood: A chart review. *Journal of Autism and Developmental Disabilities, 16*, 351–367.

Nass, R. (1992). Developmental dyslexia: An update. *Pediatrics in Review, 13*, 231–235.

Nelson, H. E., & Warrington, E. K. (1974). Developmental spelling retardation and its relation to other cognitive abilities. *British Journal of Psychology, 65*, 265–274.

Norman, C. A., & Zigmond, N. (1980). Characteristics of children labeled and served as learning disabled in school systems affiliated with Child Service Demonstration Centers. *Journal of Learning Disabilities, 13*, 542–547.

Novick, B. Z., & Arnold, M. M. (1988). *Fundamentals of clinical child neuropsychology*. New York: Grune & Stratton.

O'Hare, A. E., & Brown, J. K. (1989a). Childhood dysgraphia: Part 1. An illustrated clinical classification. *Child: Care, Health, and Development, 15*, 79–104.

O'Hare, A. E., & Brown, J. K. (1989b). Childhood dysgraphia: Part 2. A study of hand function. *Child: Care, Health and Development, 15*, 151–166.

Ojemann, G. (1974). Mental arithmetic during human malanic stimulation. *Neuropsychologia, 12*, 1–10.

O'Leary, E. (1993). Transition services and IDEA: Issues for states and local programs. *South Atlantic Regional Resource Center Newsletter, 2*, 1–11.

Ortiz, T., Exposito, F. J., Miguel, F., Martin-Loeches, M., & Rubia, F. J. (1992). Brain mapping in dysphonemic dyslexia: In resting and phonemic discrimination conditions. *Brain and Language, 42*, 270–285.

Orton, S. T. (1928). Specific reading disability—strephosymbolia. *Journal of the American Medical Association, 90*, 1095–1109.

Orton, S. T. (1937). *Reading, writing, and speech problems in children*. New York: Norton.

Ozols, E. J., & Rourke, B. P. (1985). Dimensions of social sensitivity in two types of learning-disabled children. In B. P. Rourke (Ed.), *Neuropsychology of learning disabilities: Essentials of subtype analysis* (pp. 281–301). New York: Guilford Press.

Pennington, B. F., Gilger, J. W., Pauls, D., Smith, S. A., Smith, S. D., & Defries, J. C. (1991). Evidence for major gene transmission of developmental dyslexia. *Journal of American Medical Association, 266*, 1527–1534.

Perlmuter, L. C., & Monty, R. A. (1977). The importance of perceived control: Fact or fantasy? *American Scientist, 65*, 759–765.

Psychological Corporation. (1992). *Wechsler Individual Achievement Test manual*. New York: Author.

Ratcliffe, S. G. (1982). Speech and learning disorders in children with sex chromosome abnormalities. *Developmental Medicine and Child Neurology, 13*, 3–8.

Raven, J. C. (1977). *Guide to using the Coloured Progressive Matrices*. London: HK Lewis Psychological Corporation.

Rehabilitation Act of 1973, Pub. L. No. 93-112.

Reitan, R. M. (1979). *Manual for administration of neuropsychological test batteries for adults and children*. Tucson, AZ: Neuropsychological Laboratory.

Reynolds, C. R. (1984). Critical measurement issues in learning disabilities. *Journal of Special Education, 18*, 451–476.

Reynolds, C. R. (1990). Conceptual and technical problems in learning disability diagnosis. In C. R. Reynolds & R. W. Kamphaus (Eds.), *Handbook of psychological and educational assessment of children* (pp. 571–592). New York: Guilford Press.

Reynolds, C. R., & Snow, M. (1985). *Severe discrepancy analysis* [Computer program]. College Station, TX: TRAIN.

Rooney, K., & Hallahan, D. P. (1985). Future directions for cognitive behavior modification research: The quest for cognitive change. *Remedial and Special Education, 6*, 46–51.

Rosenberger, P. B. (1989). Perceptual–motor and attentional correlates of developmental dyscalculia. *Annals of Neurology, 26*, 216–220.

Rourke, B. P. (1975). Brain–behavior relationships in children with learning disabilities: A research program. *American Psychologist, 30*, 911–920.

Rourke, B. P. (1978). Reading, spelling and arithmetic disabilities: A neuropsychologic perspective. In H. R.

Myklebust (Ed.), *Progress in learning disabilities* (Vol. 4, pp. 97–120). New York: Grune & Stratton.

Rourke, B. P. (1982). Central processing deficiencies in children: Toward a developmental neuropsychological model. *Journal of Clinical Neuropsychology*, *4*, 1–18.

Rourke, B. P. (1983). Reading and spelling disabilities: A developmental neuropsychological perspective. In U. Kirk (Ed.), *Neuropsychology of language, reading and spelling* (pp. 209–234). San Diego, CA: Academic Press.

Rourke, B. P. (1987). Syndrome of nonverbal learning disabilities: The final common pathway of white matter disease/dysfunction. *The Clinical Neuropsychologist*, *1*, 209–234.

Rourke, B. P. (1988a). Socioemotional disturbances of learning disabled children. *Journal of Consulting and Clinical Psychology*, *56*, 801–810.

Rourke, B. P. (1988b). Syndrome of nonverbal learning disabilities: Developmental manifestations in neurological disease, disorder and dysfunction. *The Clinical Neuropsychologist*, *2*, 293–330.

Rourke, B. P. (Ed.). (1989). *Nonverbal learning disabilities: The syndrome and the model*. New York: Guilford Press.

Rourke, B. P., & Finlayson, M. A. J. (1978). Neuropsychological significance of variations in patterns of academic performance: Verbal and visual–spatial abilities. *Journal of Abnormal Child Psychology*, *6*, 121–133.

Rourke, B. P., & Strang, J. D. (1978). Neuropsychological significance of variations in patterns of academic performance: Motor, psychomotor, and tactile perception abilities. *Journal of Pediatric Psychology*, *3*, 62–66.

Rourke, B. P., & Strang, J. D. (1983). Subtypes of reading and arithmetical disabilities: A neuropsychological analysis. In M. Rutter (Ed.), *Developmental neuropsychiatry* (pp. 473–488). New York: Guilford Press.

Rourke, B. P., Young, G. C., & Flewelling, R. W. (1971). The relationships between WISC verbal-performance discrepancies and selected verbal, auditory–perceptual, visual–perceptual, and problem solving abilities in children with learning disabilities. *Journal of Clinical Psychology*, *27*, 475–479.

Rourke, B. P., Young, G. C., Strang, J. D., & Russell, D. L. (1985). Adult outcomes of central processing deficiencies in childhood. In I. Grant & K. M. Adams (Eds.), *Neuropsychological assessment in neuropsychiatric disorders: Clinical methods and empirical findings* (pp. 244–257). New York: Oxford University Press.

Rudel, R. G. (1985). Definition of dyslexia: Language and motor deficits. In F. Duffy & N. Geschwind (Eds.), *Dyslexia, current status and future directions* (pp. 33–53). Boston: Little, Brown.

Rules and Regulations Implementing Education for All Handicapped Children Act of 1975, Pub. L. No. 94–142, ß 42 Fed. Reg. 42474 (1977).

Rumsey, J. M., Anderson, P., Ametkin, A. J., Aquino, T., King, A. C., Hamburger, S. D., Pikus, A., Rapoport, J. L., & Cohen, R. M. (1992). Failure to activate the left temporoparietal cortex in dyslexia. *Archives of Neurology*, *49*, 527–534.

Rutter, M., Tizard, J., Yule, W., Graham, P., & Whitmore, K. (1976). Research report: Isle of Wight studies, 1964–1974. *Psychological Medicine*, *6*, 313–332.

Sandler, A. D., Watson, T. E., Footo, M., Levine, M. D., Coleman, W. L., & Hooper, S. R. (1992). Neurodevelopmental study of writing disorders in middle childhood. *Developmental and Behavioral Pediatrics*, *13*(1), 17–23.

Satz, P., & Morris, R. (1981). Learning disabilities subtypes: A review. In F. J. Pirozzolo & M. C. Wittrock (Eds.), *Neuropsychological and cognitive processes in reading* (pp. 109–141). New York: Academic Press.

Schonhaut, S., & Satz, P. (1983). Prognosis for children with learning disabilities. A review of follow-up studies. In M. Rutter (Ed.), *Developmental neuropsychiatry* (pp. 542–563). New York: Guilford Press.

Semel, E., Wiig, E. H., & Secord, W. (1980). *Clinical Evaluation of Language Fundamentals–Revised examiner's manual*. New York: Psychological Corporation.

Semrud-Clikeman, M., & Hynd, G. (1990). Right hemisphere dysfunction in nonverbal learning disabilities: Social, academic and adaptive functioning in adults and children. *Psychological Bulletin*, *107*, 196–209.

Semrud-Clikeman, M., & Hynd, G. W. (1992). Developmental arithmetic disorder. In S. R. Hooper, G. W. Hynd, & R. E. Mattison (Eds.), *Developmental disorders: Diagnostic criteria and clinical assessment* (pp. 97–125). Hillsdale, NJ: Erlbaum.

Senf, G. M. (1969). Development of immediate memory of bisensory stimuli in normal children and children with learning disabilities. *Developmental Psychology*, *6*, 28.

Shafrir, U., & Siegel, L. S. (1994). Subtypes of learning disabilities in adolescents and adults. *Journal of Learning Disabilities*, *27*, 123–134.

Shaw, S. F., & Shaw, S. R. (1989). Learning disability college programming: A bibliography. *Journal of Postsecondary Education and Disability*, *6*, 77–85.

Shaywitz, S. E., Shaywitz, B. A., Fletcher, J. M., & Escobar, M. D. (1990). Prevalence of reading disability in boys and girls. *Journal of the American Medical Association*, *264*(8), 998–1002.

Shea, V., & Mesibov, G. B. (1985). Brief report: The relationship of learning disabilities and higher-level autism. *Journal of Autism and Developmental Disorders*, *15*, 425–435.

Shepard, L. A. (1980). An evaluation of the regression discrepancy method for identifying children with learning disabilities. *Journal of Special Education*, *14*, 79–91.

Sherman, G. F., Galaburda, A. M., & Geschwind, N. (1985). Cortical anomalies in brains of New Zealand mice: A neuropathologic model of dyslexia? *Proceedings of the National Academy of Science USA*, *82*, 8072–8074.

Sheslow, D., & Adams, W. (1990). *Wide Range Assessment of Memory and Learning administration manual*. Wilmington, DE: Jastak Associates.

Siegel, L. S., & Heaven, H. K. (1986). Categorization of learning disabilities. In S. J. Ceci (Ed.), *Handbook of cognitive, social, and neuropsychological aspects of learning disabilities* (Vol. 1, pp. 95–121). Hillsdale, NJ: Erlbaum.

Silver, L. B. (1979). The minimal brain dysfunction syndrome. In J. D. Noshpitz (Ed.), *Basic handbook of child psychiatry* (Vol. 2, pp. 416–439). New York: Basic Books.

Smith, E., & Alley, G. (1981). *The effect of teaching sixth graders with learning difficulties a strategy for solving verbal math problems* (Research Rep. No. 39). Lawrence: University of Kansas, Institute for Research in Learning Disabilities.

Smith, S. D., Kimberling, W. J., Pennington, B. F., & Lubs, H. A. (1983). Specific reading disability: Identification of an inherited form through linkage analysis. *Science*, *219*, 1345–1347.

Spielberger, C. D. (1983). *State–Trait Anxiety Inventory (Form Y)*. Palo Alto, CA: Consulting Psychologists Press.

Spiers, P. A. (1987). Acalculia revisited: Current issues. In G. Deloche & X. Seron (Eds.), *Mathematical disabilities: A cognitive neuropsychological perspective* (pp. 1–25). Hillsdale, NJ: Erlbaum.

Spreen, O. (1978). *Learning disabled children growing up* (Final report to Health and Welfare Canada, Health Programs Branch). Ottowa, Ontario, Canada: Health and Welfare Canada.

Spreen, O. (1988). *Learning disabled growing up: A follow-up into adulthood*. New York: Oxford University Press.

Spreen, O., & Strauss, E. (1991). *A compendium of neuropsychological tests*. New York: Oxford University Press.

Spring, C., & Davis, J. (1988). Relations of digit naming speed with three components of reading. *Applied Psycholinguistics*, *8*, 315–334.

Stanovich, K. E. (1986). Cognitive processes and the reading problems of learning-disabled children: Evaluating the assumption of specificity. In J. Torgeson & B. Wong (Eds.), *Psychological and educational perspectives on learning disabilities* (pp. 87–131). San Diego, CA: Academic Press.

Strang, J. D., & Rourke, B. P. (1983). Concept-formation/nonverbal reasoning abilities of children who exhibit specific academic problems with arithmetic. *Journal of Clinical Child Psychology*, *12*, 33–39.

Strang, J. D., & Rourke, B. P. (1985). Arithmetic disability subtypes: The neuropsychological significance of specific arithmetical impairment in childhood. In B. P. Rourke (Ed.), *Neuropsychology of learning disabilities: Essentials of subtype analysis* (pp. 167–183). New York: Guilford Press.

Strauss, A. (1951). The education of the brain-injured child. *American Journal of Mental Deficiency*, *56*, 712–718.

Strauss, A., & Lehtinen, L. (1947). *Psychopathology and education of the brain injured child*. New York: Grune & Stratton.

Swanson, L. B. (1989). *Analyzing naming speed–reading relationships in children*. Unpublished doctoral dissertation, University of Waterloo, Waterloo, Ontario, Canada.

Taylor, H. G. (1988). Neuropsychological testing: Relevance for assessing children's learning disabilities. *Journal of Consulting and Clinical Psychology*, *56*, 795–800.

Taylor, H. G., Fletcher, J. M., & Satz, P. (1982). Component processes in reading disabilities: Neuropsychological investigation of distinct subskill deficits. In R. N. Malatesha & P. G. Aaron (Eds.), *Reading disorders* (pp. 121–147). San Diego, CA: Academic Press.

Thomas, C. C., Englert, C. S., & Gregg, S. (1987). An analysis of errors and strategies in the expository writing of learning disabled students. *Remedial and Special Education*, *8*, 21–30, 46.

Thomson, M. E., & Wilsher, C. (1978). Some aspects of memory in dyslexics and controls. In M. M. Gruneberg, P. E. Morris, & R. N. Sykes (Eds.), *Practical aspects of memory* (pp. 545–560). San Diego, CA: Academic Press.

Thorndike, R. L. (1963). *The concepts of over- and underachievement*. New York: Columbia University, Teachers College, Bureau of Publications.

Thorndike, R. L., & Hagen, E. P. (1977). *Measurement and evaluation in psychology and education (4th ed.)*. New York: Wiley.

Thorndike, R. L., Hagen, E. P., & Sattler, J. M. (1986). *Guide for administering and scoring the Stanford–Binet Intelligence Scale* (4th ed.). Chicago: Riverside.

U.S. Office of Education. (1977). Assistance to states for education of handicapped children: Procedures for evaluating specific learning disabilities. 42 Fed. Reg. 65082–65085.

Van Reusen, A. K., Bos, C. S., Schumaker, J. B., & Deshler, D. D. (1987). *The education planning strategy*. Lawrence, KS: Edge Enterprises.

Van Reusen, A. K., Deshler, D. D., & Schumaker, J. B. (1989). Effects of a student participation strategy in facilitating the involvement of learning disabled adolescents in the IEP planning process. *Learning Disabilities: A Multidisciplinary Journal*, *1*(2), 23–34.

Vaughan, R. W., & Hodges, L. A. (1973). A statistical survey into a definition of learning disabilities. *Journal of Learning Disabilities*, *6*, 658–664.

Voeller, K. K. S. (1986). Right hemisphere deficit syndrome in children. *American Journal of Psychiatry*, *143*, 1004–1009.

Voeller, K. K. S. (1990). Right hemisphere deficit syndrome in children: A neurological perspective. *International Pediatrics*, *5*, 163–170.

Wagner, M. (1992–1993). *National longitudinal transition study of special education students*. Menlo Park, CA: SRI International.

Watkins, M., & Kush, J. (1988). *The research assistant* [Computer program]. Phoenix, AZ: SouthWest EdPsych.

Wechsler, D. (1974). *Manual for the Wechsler Intelligence Scale for Children–Revised (WISC-R)*. New York: Psychological Corporation.

Wechsler, D. (1981). *Wechsler Adult Intelligence Scale–Revised manual*. New York: Psychological Corporation.

Wechsler, D. (1987). *Wechsler Memory Scale–Revised manual*. New York: Psychological Corporation.

Wechsler, D. (1989). *Manual for the Wechsler Preschool and Primary Scales of Intelligence–Revised*. New York: Psychological Corporation.

Wechsler, D. (1990). *Wechsler Intelligence Scale for Children–Third edition manual*. New York: Psychological Corporation.

Weinberg, W. A., & McLean, A. (1986). A diagnostic approach to developmental specific learning disorders. *Journal of Child Neurology*, *1*, 158–172.

Weinberger, D. R., Luchins, D. J., Morihisa, J., & Wyatt, R. J. (1982). Asymmetrical volumes of the right and left frontal and occipital regions of the human brain. *Neurology*, *11*, 97–100.

White, W. J., Alley, G. R., Deshler, D. D., Schumaker, J. A. B., Warner, M. M., & Clark, F. L. (1982). Are there learning disabilities after high school? *Exceptional Children*, *49*, 273–274.

Wilson, L. R., & Cone, T. (1984). The regression equation method of determining academic discrepancy. *Journal of School Psychology*, *22*, 95–110.

Wing, L. (1981). Asperger's syndrome: A clinical account. *Psychological Medicine*, *11*, 115–129.

Witelson, S. F., & Rabinovitch, M. S. (1972). Hemispheric speech lateralization in children with auditory–linguistic defects. *Cortex*, *8*, 412–426.

Wolf, M., & Obregon, M. (1992). Early naming deficits, developmental dyslexia, and a specific deficit hypothesis. *Brain and Language*, *42*, 219–247.

Wood, D. A., Rosenberg, M. S., & Carran, D. T. (1993). The effects of tape-recorded self-instruction cues on the mathematics performance of students with learning disabilities. *Journal of Learning Disabilities*, *26*, 250–258, 269.

Woodcock, R. W. (1987). *Woodcock Reading Mastery Tests–Revised examiner's manual*. Circle Pines, MN: American Guidance Service.

Woodcock, R. W., & Johnson, M. B. (1989). *Woodcock–Johnson Psychoeducational Battery–Revised Manual*. Allen, TX: DLM Teaching Resources.

Yeni-Komshian, G. H., Isenberg, P., & Goldstein, H. (1975). Cerebral dominance and reading disability: Left visual-field deficit in poor readers. *Neuropsychologia*, *8*, 83–94.

CHAPTER 12

PRENATAL EXPOSURE TO ALCOHOL

Michelle R. Jenkins and Jan L. Culbertson

Concerns about the teratogenic effects of fetal alcohol exposure have been part of civilization since ancient days. Even biblical references warned of the dangers of strong drink during gestation, as in the following, "Behold, thou shalt conceive, and bear a son; and now drink no wine or strong drink" (Judges 13:7). In eighteenth-century England, a report by the College of Physicians noted a drop in birth rate and a rise in infant mortality among infants born to alcoholic mothers (Warner & Rosett, 1975). The report described the infants of alcoholic mothers as having a "starved, shriveled, and imperfect look." However, society did not begin to express widespread concern about maternal use of alcohol during gestation until the 1960s and 1970s. At this time, both French and U.S. researchers independently reported on the teratogenic effects of alcohol on the fetus as a result of maternal gestational alcoholism (Jones & Smith, 1973; Jones, Smith, Ulleland, & Streissguth, 1973; Lemoine, Harousseau, Borteyru, & Menuet, 1968). They described a specific dysmorphic condition that later was termed *fetal alcohol syndrome* (FAS). Since the 1960s, over 2,000 scientific studies have appeared about FAS alone (Streissguth et al., 1991). The effects of alcohol on the developing brain are being studied vigorously, and practitioners now have the benefit of emerging literature about the sequelae of fetal alcohol exposure. The field of neuropsychology in particular has contributed to understanding of the neuropathological impact of alcohol on the developing brain. This literature provides a basis for planning the evaluation process with children and youth and provides a foundation for this chapter.

In this chapter, we focus on the neuropsychological effects of prenatal exposure to alcohol and the implications for assessment of children and youth. We present information on the prevalence of the problem, epidemiological and genetic information on children with FAS, the neuropathological basis of the sequelae, symptom presentation, a review of neuropsychological research to date, and, finally, issues to be considered in evaluation. Case examples are used to illustrate both evaluation and treatment approaches.

FAS

Definition

FAS refers to a recognizable pattern of abnormalities found in children of alcoholic mothers (Jones & Smith, 1973). The diagnosis is made by the presence of abnormalities in each of three categories: (a) retardation of prenatal growth, postnatal growth, or both; (b) central nervous system (CNS) involvement; and (c) a characteristic set of facial features (Russell, 1991). The deleterious effects of in utero alcohol exposure are expressed on a continuum ranging from gross morphological defects at one extreme to more subtle cognitive–behavioral dysfunction at the less severe end.

Standardized criteria for clinical diagnosis were first provided in 1980 by the Fetal Alcohol Study Group of the Research Society on Alcoholism (Rosett, 1980), and modifications have since been suggested (Sokol & Clarren, 1989). Specific criteria for intrauterine growth retardation include weight or length less than the 10th percentile for gestational age and microcephaly (head circumference less than the 3rd percentile). Specific craniofacial dysmorphology includes, but is not limited to, short palpebral fissures (e.g., shortened length of the eyelids), elongated midface, a long and flattened philtrum (e.g., the vertical groove in the median portion above the upper lip), thin upper vermilion (e.g., thin upper lip), and flattened maxilla. Figure 1 shows the craniofacial dysmorphology most often noted. Damage to the CNS often is expressed as mental retardation and behavioral impairment. Use of the term *suspected fetal alcohol effects* (FAEs) has been recommended when only some of the criteria for FAS are met (Clarren & Smith, 1978). Table 1 lists the features of FAS that are found in more than 80% of the patients identified with the syndrome. Table 2 cites anomalies that are found in 25% to 80% of patients who have FAS.

Although FAS is not diagnosed in all infants whose mothers drink heavily during pregnancy, most investigators believe that all children exhibiting this pattern have mothers who have abused alcohol. The severity of the FAS features in offspring of alcoholic mothers who drink during pregnancy has been correlated positively with the amount of maternal alcohol intake (Graham, Hanson, Darby, Barr, & Streissguth, 1988) and the stage of the mother's alcoholism (Ernhart et al., 1985; Majewski, 1981).

FAS is the most common known cause of mental retardation in the United States (K. J. Smith & Eckardt, 1991). Research over the past decade has demonstrated that the teratogenic effects of alcohol on the CNS extend beyond mental retardation. Exhibit 1 provides a summary of the behavioral and developmental abnormalities associated with moderate-to-heavy drinking. The harmful effects of prenatal exposure to alcohol are now known to exist on a continuum, ranging from gross morphological defects at the more severe extreme to more subtle cognitive–behavioral dysfunctions at the other extreme.

Zuckerman and Hingson (1986) suggested that the symptoms attributed to FAS may not be specific to alcohol. They reported that the characteristic facial dysmorphology of FAS may be seen in infants born to mothers with phenylketonuria and in infants of epileptic women who take Dilantin. Lipson, Yu, and O'Halloran (1981) described 27 children of nine mothers with phenylketonuria and included pictures

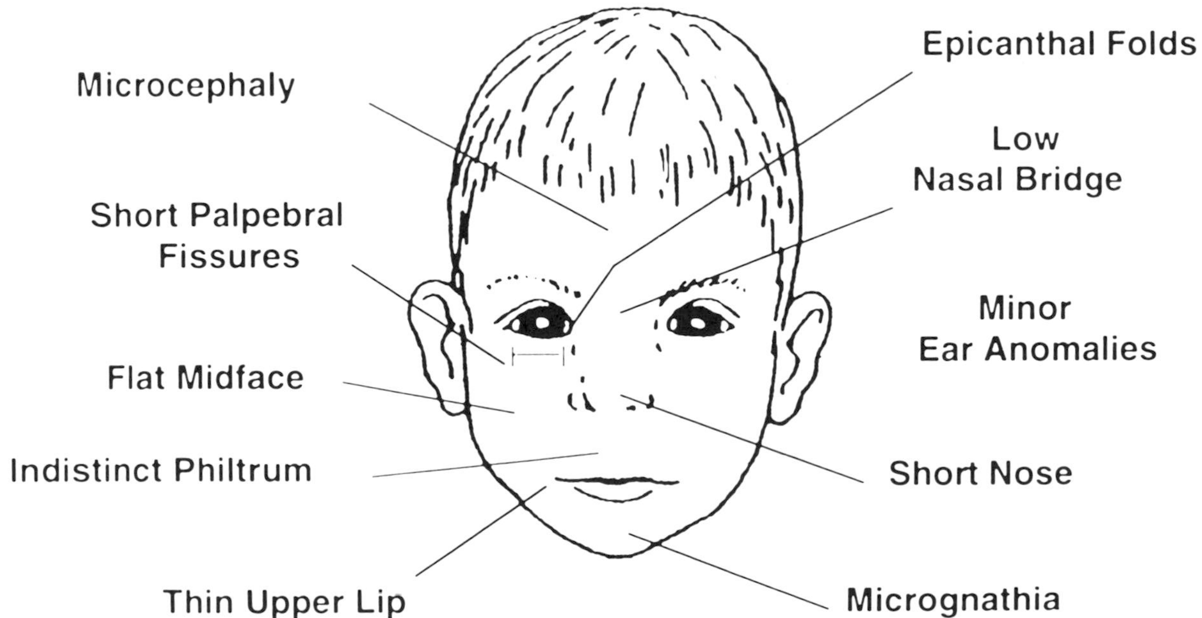

FIGURE 1. The facial features of fetal alcohol syndrome. From *Alcohol: Pregnancy and the Fetal Alcohol Syndrome* (p. 5), by R. E. Little and A. P. Streissguth, 1982, Seattle: University of Washington Health Sciences Learning Resource Center. Copyright 1982 by Project Cork Institute. Reprinted with permission.

TABLE 1

Features of Fetal Alcohol Syndrome Found in More Than 80% of Diagnosed Patients

Feature	Description
Central nervous system dysfunction	Mild to moderate mental retardation, microcephaly, irritability in infancy
Growth deficiency	Pre- and postnatal growth more than 2 standard deviations below the mean for length and weight
Facial characteristics	Short palpebral fissures, hypoplastic philtrum, thinned upper vermilion border, retrognathia in infancy

Note: From "The Fetal Alcohol Syndrome: A Review of the World Literature," by S. K. Clarren and D. W. Smith, 1978, *New England Journal of Medicine*, *298*, p. 1064. Copyright 1978 by the Massachusetts Medical Society. Adapted with permission.

of 3 of these children with facial features similar to those seen in FAS (i.e., midfacial hypoplasia, short palpebral fissures, diminished to absent philtrum, and upturned nose). These children also presented with low birth weight at term; measurements below the 3rd percentile for height and head circumference; retarded CNS development and low IQs; and an increased incidence of major and minor malformations, particularly congenital heart disease. Because lack of adequate prenatal care, poor nutrition, and metabolic problems can result in fetal abnormalities similar to those observed in FAS, practitioners should obtain a detailed description of the mother's medication and ethanol intake as well as her genetic and metabolic history before making a definitive diagnosis of FAS.

Alcohol use often is confounded with the use of other drugs, and the observed patterns may be affected, at least in part, by other teratogens (Ernhart, 1991). Stein and Kline (1983) suggested that alcohol may be a "passenger variable" that may disguise the effects of other teratogens. The teratogenic effects of such agents as ethanol and other drugs will vary according to dosage, pharmacodynamic variables of the drug, stage of fetal development during exposure, and possible genetic susceptibility to organ damage (Gallant, 1991).

Prevalence and Epidemiology of FAS and FAE

FAS is estimated to occur at a rate of 1.9 cases per 1,000 live births (Abel & Sokol, 1987). The inci-

TABLE 2

Features of Fetal Alcohol Syndrome Found in 25% to 80% of Diagnosed Patients

Feature	Description
Central nervous system dysfunction	Poor coordination, hypotonia, childhood hyperactivity
Growth	Diminished adipose tissue noted postnatally
Facial characteristics	Short, upturned nose; hypoplastic maxilla; ptosis, strabismus, and epicanthal folds; posterior rotation of ears; prominent lateral palatine ridges; micrognathia or relative prognathia in adolescence
Cardiac	Murmurs, especially atrial septal defects in early childhood
Renogenital	Labial hypoplasia
Skin	Hemangiomas, aberrant palmer creases
Skeleton	Pectus excavatum

Note: From "The Fetal Alcohol Syndrome: A Review of the World Literature," by S. K. Clarren and D. W. Smith, 1978, *New England Journal of Medicine*, *298*, p. 1064. Copyright 1978 by the Massachusetts Medical Society. Adapted with permission.

EXHIBIT 1

Behaviors and Developmental Abnormalities in Offspring Associated With Moderate-to-Heavy Drinking by Mother

Behavior

Jitteriness
Tremulousness
Unpredictable sleep–wake behavior
Decreased vigorous body activity

Developmental abnormality

Hypotonia
Poor sucking
Defects in mental development
Decreased motor performance

dence of FAE, given the less restrictive criteria, is estimated to be approximately 3 times greater than FAS, at 3–5 cases per 1,000 live births (Abel, 1984a). Among alcoholics, the incidence of FAS is considerably higher, estimated to be 25 per 1,000 whereas FAE is estimated to be 90 per 1,000 (Abel, 1984b). Based on available estimates of prevalence, the cost of providing medical, educational, psychosocial, and other auxiliary services for children with FAS-related abnormalities has been estimated at $249.7 million (Abel & Sokol, 1987). Mental retardation accounts for almost 60% of the estimated total cost.

Not all women who drink alcohol excessively during pregnancy deliver babies with FAS or FAE. Sokol, Miller, and Reed (1980) identified 204 women as alcohol abusers (out of more than 12,000 examined in a large-scale epidemiological study) and found that only 5 (2.5%) gave birth to children diagnosed with FAS. When FAE was considered, only 50% of the children born to alcohol-abusing women evidenced adverse effects attributable to prenatal alcohol exposure. Similarly, Streissguth, Barr, Martin, and Herman's (1980) study on infant neurobehavioral development revealed that only 5% to 10% of the infants born to women categorized as "heavier drinkers" during pregnancy scored abnormally low on mental and psychomotor scales at 8 months of age. Animal research also has indicated that fetuses have variable susceptibility to alcohol's adverse effects despite presumably similar levels of exposure.

A variety of factors, including genetic and maternal variables, may explain why some infants are born with FAS or FAE and others are spared. Although the full presentation of FAS has only been known to occur as a result of chronic alcoholism, individual lifestyle and constitutional, social, and environmental factors may mediate alcohol's teratogenic effects. Considerable progress has been made toward understanding the etiology of both FAS and FAE, but the knowledge is not complete. No ethnic or racial groups are immune to the teratogenic actions of alcohol; however, African Americans have been found to have increased susceptibility to the deleterious effects of prenatal alcohol exposure in epidemiological studies (Chavez, Cordero, & Beccerra, 1988; Iosub et al., 1985). Additional research aimed at identifying factors that may place the fetus at greater risk for FAS or FAE is certainly needed (Sokol & Abel, 1988). The information gained from such research will aid in the task of targeting prevention and intervention strategies more specifically to those individuals falling into high-risk categories for FAS.

Several studies have investigated the risk of FAS or FAE as a function of how much alcohol is consumed during pregnancy. Although many women spontaneously reduce their alcohol consumption during pregnancy, others continue to overindulge (Fried, Watkinson, Grant, & Knight, 1980; Weiner, Rosett, Edelin, Alpert, & Zuckerman, 1983). I. E. Smith and colleagues (I. E. Smith, Lancaster, Moss-Wells, Coles, & Falek, 1987) studied the characteristics that differentiate women who drink throughout pregnancy from those who discontinue alcohol use sometime during their pregnancy. Of the 267 pregnant women interviewed, 121 reported abstinence from alcohol during pregnancy and were classified as nondrinkers. Approximately 75% of the remaining drinkers reported continuing use of alcohol throughout pregnancy despite having received information about the harmful effects of prenatal alcohol exposure. Results revealed that women who continued to drink and those who discontinued alcohol use did not differ significantly in age, marital status, cigarette and caffeine consumption, number of previous pregnancies, amount of alcohol consumed per week, and use of other drugs. The best predictors of continued drinking throughout pregnancy were reported tolerance to alcohol, length of drinking history, a history of alcohol-related illness, and a preferred social context of drinking with other family members. These results suggest that a number of biological and behavioral factors may be useful for identifying women at greater risk for continued alcohol use throughout pregnancy.

Perhaps the most impressive epidemiological study to date is that of Streissguth and her associates (Streissguth et al., 1986; Streissguth, Barr, & Sampson, 1990; Streissguth et al., 1984; Streissguth, Martin, Martin, & Barr, 1981), who began the Seattle Longitudinal Prospective Study on Alcohol and Pregnancy in 1974 to study the effects of maternal alcohol use during pregnancy on child development. In this longitudinal study, 1,529 women were given prenatal structured interviews during the fifth month of pregnancy about their alcohol, tobacco, and other drug use, as well as about a variety of other lifestyle characteristics. These mothers were primarily White, middle-class, married, and at low risk for adverse pregnancy outcome. The average maternal age during pregnancy was 26 years, and 86% of the mothers had graduated from high school. The self-reported levels of alcohol consumption varied widely, and the group was stratified into three levels according to the amount of alcohol consumed during pregnancy and in the weeks before recognition of pregnancy. Alcohol consumption was expressed as the average daily intake of absolute alcohol, and the three levels were defined: light (less than 0.1 oz. per day), moderate (0.1 to 0.9 oz. per day), and heavy (1 oz. or more per day).

Because the Seattle Longitudinal Study relied on self-reported alcohol usage and the data are typically averaged over a period of a week or more, it is difficult to gauge clinically the impact of low-level maternal drinking on pregnancy outcome. It should be noted that these studies do not provide evidence for a threshold, or a particular level of safe social or moderate drinking during pregnancy that will not result in some degree of risk to the unborn child. However, the studies do provide evidence that even moderate drinking during pregnancy is associated with long-term deleterious effects on offspring.

Binge drinking, or relatively heavy alcohol intake, on even a few occasions appears to be more harmful than moderate intake over a more prolonged period of time (Streissguth et al., 1990; Weiner & Morse, 1988). Animal studies have indicated that high blood alcohol levels predict alcohol-related birth defects better than the total volume of alcohol consumed (Bonthius & West, 1990; Russell, 1991), and the data with humans from the Seattle Longitudinal Study are consistent with this (Sampson, Streissguth, Barr, & Bookstein, 1989; Streissguth et al., 1990). The Seattle Longitudinal Study revealed that mothers who had a binge pattern of drinking (i.e., 5 or more drinks per occasion) were more likely to have offspring who were 1 to 3 months delayed in reading and arithmetic by the end of the first grade in school, and were more likely to receive special remedial programs at school (24% of the children of binge drinkers vs. 15% of the children of nonbinge drinkers; Streissguth et al., 1990).

Although the evidence reported to date is weak, there has been a recent suggestion that heavy paternal drinking prior to conception may have an adverse affect on perinatal outcome (Hesselbrock, Bauer, Hesselbrock, & Gillen, 1991). A variety of mechanisms have been suggested for possibly producing deleterious effects, such as disrupted spermatogenesis, the presence of ethanol in the seminal fluid, or direct effects of ethanol on DNA. However, there is little empirical evidence to support any of these hypotheses (Hesselbrock et al., 1991). Detailed drinking histories of the father, particularly in the few months prior to conception, may be useful in addressing this issue in future research.

Neuropathology of FAS

Animal research. Animal research has played a major role in advancing knowledge of the numerous detrimental consequences that follow prenatal alcohol exposure. Animal studies not only provide evidence to support the CNS effects of in utero alcohol exposure but also have the advantage of allowing the control of variables that might confound clinical studies with humans (i.e., malnutrition, environmental conditions, disease, smoking, and other drug use). These studies have collectively provided strong evidence that FAEs are independent of nutrition and many other potentially confounding variables (Little, Graham, & Samson, 1982).

Chickens, mice, rats, guinea pigs, dogs, and monkeys have been used as animal models for FAS behavioral teratogenesis (Clarren, Alvord, & Sumi, 1978; DeBeukeler, Randall, & Stroud, 1977; Hanson, Streissguth, & Smith, 1978; Pfeiffer, Majewski, Fischbach, Bierich, & Volk, 1979; Tanaka, Arina, & Suzuki, 1981). Information from these studies indicates that acute as well as chronic exposure to heavy doses of ethanol can damage the fetus. Kotkoskie and Norton (1988) demonstrated that acute heavy alcohol exposure in gravid rats during Days 14 and 15—a critical period for cerebral cortex development—resulted in gross malformation of the cerebral cortex and hippocampus in the fetuses, malformations similar to those reported in human fetuses and neonates from alcoholic mothers. The specific deleterious effects of alcohol are dose related and dependent on the stage of gestation. Research has revealed that prenatal alcohol exposure alters the cytoarchitectural structure and metabolic activity of numerous brain regions and perturbs a variety of neurotransmitter systems (Norton & Kotkoskie, 1991). Several investigators using rats have reported delays in development (Abel & Dintcheff, 1978; Lee & Leichter, 1980; Martin, Martin, Sigman, & Radow, 1977; B. A. Shaywitz, Griffieth, & Warshaw, 1979) and in learning and memory performance (Abel, 1979; Riley, Lochry, & Shapiro, 1979). Reports of in utero alcohol effects on subsequent learning include impairments in shock avoidance (Abel, 1979), passive avoidance (Lochry & Riley, 1980; Riley, Lochrey, & Shapiro, 1979), operant paradigms (Martin et al., 1977), and reversal learning (Lochry & Riley, 1980).

Findings generated from animal laboratory studies suggest increased activity levels (Abel, 1982; Bond & Digiusto, 1976; Martin, Martin, Sigman, & Radow, 1978; Osborne, Caul, & Fernandez, 1980; K. J. Smith & Eckardt, 1991) and an increase in perseverative behavior (Abel 1982; Lochry & Riley, 1980; Osborne et al., 1980; Riley, Lochry, Shapiro, & Baldwin, 1979; Riley, Shapiro, Lochry, & Broide, 1980) in offspring of animals whose mothers were fed alcohol during gestation. There is disagreement about whether the increase in activity persists into adulthood (Abel, 1982; K. J. Smith & Eckardt, 1991).

In summary, results from animal studies have indicated that a short period of acute ethanol exposure early in pregnancy can result in severe developmental abnormalities of the brain. Animal research has revealed that prenatal ethanol exposure has profound effects on both structural and biochemical aspects of the brain (e.g., effects on cytoarchitectural structure, metabolic activity of numerous brain regions, and a variety of neurotransmitter systems; Clarren, 1986; Druse & Paul, 1988; Kotkoskie & Norton, 1988; Miller, 1986, 1987, 1988; Miller & Dow-Edwards, 1988; West, 1987; West & Pierce, 1986). However, additional research data suggest that decreasing or stopping ethanol intake as late as the third trimester will lessen some aspects of alcohol damaging effects on the fetus (Hanson et al., 1978).

Research evidence for CNS effects. The damaging effect of ethanol on the developing CNS was recognized early as the most characteristic feature of FAS (Norton & Kotkoskie, 1991). However, there have been relatively few studies examining CNS structure in children with FAS. Both normal (DeBeukeler et al., 1977; Tanaka et al., 1981) and abnormal (e.g., enlarged third or lateral ventricles; Clarren et al., 1978; Goldstein & Arulananthan, 1978) computed tomography scans have been reported. Severe brain malformations have been reported in approximately 33% of the 16 neuropathological cases (age 17 gestational weeks to 4.5 years) cited between 1978 and 1983 (Clarren et al., 1978; Pfeiffer et al., 1979; Wisniewski, Dambska, Sher, & Qazi, 1983). The described brain anomalies were diverse and usually consisted of small degenerative changes, such as heterotopies (e.g., displacement or misplacement of structures) and microdysplasias (e.g., minor abnormalities in cell development). Results from Wisniewski et al.'s study suggested that there was little correlation among size, weight, and maturation of the brain.

Additional evidence of the teratogenity of alcohol on the developing brain comes from studies using electroencephalograms (EEGs) and evoked potentials. Studies of sleep EEGs of neonates born to alcohol-abusing mothers have demonstrated disturbance in EEG-sleep states related to the proportion of time spent in quiet, active, or indeterminate sleep and observations of increased EEG synchrony and integrated power (Chernick, Childiaeva, & Joffe, 1983; Joffe & Chernick, 1988; Joffe, Childiaeva, & Chernick, 1984; Rosett et al., 1979). Sleep disturbances have been reported in neonates even when studies were controlled for age, sex, race, smoking history, and socioeconomic status (Chernick et al., 1983; Joffe et al., 1984; Scher, Richardson, Coble, Day, & Stoffer, 1988). Furthermore, abnormal evoked potentials in response to visual, somatosensory, and auditory stimuli have also been reported (K. J. Smith & Eckardt, 1991).

Clinical Studies of CNS Sequelae in Children With FAS or FAE

Physical sequelae. Physical signs of CNS dysfunction have been reported during the neonatal period in infants born to mothers who report consuming large quantities of alcohol during pregnancy. Several investigators report jitteriness and tremulousness, suggesting that these infants may be displaying a withdrawal reaction (Clarren & Smith, 1978; Coles, Smith, & Falek, 1987; Iosub, Fuchs, Bingol, & Gromisch, 1981; Oulette, Rosett, Rosman, & Weiner, 1977; Robe, Gromisch, & Iosub, 1981). It is not surprising that neonates of mothers who consume excessive quantities of alcohol may exhibit a full or partial withdrawal syndrome because alcohol crosses the placenta, and many mothers have been reported to have been drinking within an hour of delivery (Robe et al., 1981; K. J. Smith & Eckardt, 1991). A small number of studies have explored the possibility of a withdrawal syndrome; however, most of these studies have not been controlled and examined a small number of infants. In spite of these methodological limitations, several signs and symptoms have been reported that are consistent with withdrawal, such as seizures, irritability, low Apgar scores, autonomic instability, increased respiratory rate, hyperatusis, abnormal reflexes, increased muscle tone, hypotonia, poor habituation, low levels of arousal, less vigorous activity, increased levels of activity, low motor maturity, decreased sucking pressure, and disturbances in sleep patterns (Coles, Smith, Fernhoff, & Falek, 1984; K. J. Smith & Eckardt, 1991). Although these signs and symptoms have been reported, other investigators have reported contradictory findings with the exception of tremor and jitteriness. Further investigation is required to better understand the question of a withdrawal syndrome.

Many of the reported signs and symptoms noted during the neonatal period are suggestive of an immature CNS (K. J. Smith & Eckardt, 1991). It is important to note that these findings of CNS disturbances in the newborn infant are present prior to any impact of the postnatal environment. Furthermore, evidence is accumulating that the severity of CNS dysfunction in newborns may have a predictive value in terms of later outcome (Coles, Smith, Lancaster, & Falek, 1987; Streissguth et al., 1981).

Intellectual sequelae. Abnormalities also persist beyond the neonatal period on neurologic examination of children with full or partial FAS. Microcephaly and mental retardation in children with FAS have received the most attention in the literature. Several investigators have determined that the IQs of children with FAS can range from profound mental retardation to low average (K. J. Smith & Eckardt, 1991). Typically, the more severely a child with FAS is affected in terms of dysmorphic features and growth, the greater the intellectual impairment (Iosub et al., 1981; Streissguth, Herman, & Smith, 1978a). The relationship between physical abnormalities and intellectual impairment may not be demonstrable in FAE children. N. L. Golden, Sokol, Kuhnert, and Bottoms (1982) evaluated 12 children with FAE and found no significant correlation between the number of physical abnormalities and the mental and motor development quotients on the Bayley Scales of Infant Development. However, mental development was found to be in the borderline range or above (N. L. Golden et al., 1982).

Recent studies have suggested that even relatively low amounts of intrauterine exposure to ethanol may influence prenatal development and may have consequences for the infant's later cognitive development (Hesselbrock, Bauer, Hesselbrock, & Gillen, 1991).

Several investigations have reported neurobehavioral deficits and intrauterine growth retardation in infants born to mothers who were moderate consumers of alcohol during pregnancy (Coles, Smith, Fernhoff, & Falek, 1985; Coles, Smith, Lancaster, & Falek, 1987; Little, Asker, Sampson, & Renwick, 1986). Coles and associates reported that non-FAS 6-month-old infants of mothers who drank during their pregnancy performed more poorly on the mental and motor portions of the Bayley Scales of Infant Development than infants not exposed to alcohol in utero (Coles, Platman, & Smith, 1988). Gusella and Fried (1984) studied nondisadvantaged, well-educated mothers who received prenatal care and were social drinkers (i.e., drank an average of 0.50 oz. of absolute ethanol per day in the year prior to pregnancy). The mothers reduced their alcohol consumption during the gestational period but did not stop drinking. Gusella and Fried found that maternal alcohol consumption during pregnancy was inversely related to the infant's performance on the Mental Development Index of the Bayley Scales, which measures sensory–perceptual abilities, memory, language, and problem solving. Results also suggested that maternal drinking during pregnancy was related to reduced verbal comprehension and expressive language scores in the infants.

At the 4-year follow-up of the birth cohort from the Seattle Longitudinal Study, it was found that the prenatal alcohol effects on intelligence were stronger for the Performance scale than the Verbal scale on the Wechsler Intelligence Scale for Children–Revised (WISC-R). The follow-up of the birth cohort at age 7 years indicated that the effects of even moderate maternal alcohol consumption during pregnancy (two or more drinks per day on average) persisted during the school-age years (Streissguth et al., 1990). The cognitive disturbances found earlier had remained, but with effects seen on both the Verbal and Performance scales of the WISC-R (Streissguth, Barr, Sampson, Darby, & Martin, 1989). A 7-point decrement in IQ was found to be related to moderate prenatal alcohol consumption compared with controls. The Digit Span and Arithmetic subtests were the most strongly related to prenatal alcohol exposure as the children reached school age (Sampson et al., 1989). These tests have strong memory and attention components, and arithmetic also requires abstract problem solving. Achievement testing and teacher ratings revealed that arithmetic and reading performance was lower in the children exposed to alcohol prenatally, and both teacher and parent ratings revealed increased risk for learning problems. These findings are consistent with the view that moderate prenatal alcohol exposure throughout gestation, in the range considered to be social drinking, can have negative effects on cognitive development and learning that persist over time, even in the absence of physical abnormalities characteristic of FAS.

Longitudinal studies of children with FAS have examined whether early IQ predicts intelligence at a later age or whether the environment can alter the child's IQ. Streissguth, Herman, and Smith (1978b) published a study of 17 children with FAS (aged 18 months to 22 years) who were given repeat intelligence testing 1 to 4 years after their initial evaluation. The Bayley Scales of Infant Development were used for children under the age of 2 years, the Stanford–Binet for ages 2–5 years, the WISC-R for ages 6–15 years, and the Wechsler Adult Intelligence Scale for ages 16 years and above. On reexamination, IQ scores ranged from 10 to 96, and 13 of the 17 children had a retest IQ within one standard deviation of the initial testing. In a second follow-up study of 8 children with FAS, Streissguth, Clarren, and Jones (1985) found that the degree of intellectual impairment correlated with the severity of the mother's alcoholism at the time of the child's birth rather than with factors in the postnatal environment.

Children of alcoholic mothers may have signs of CNS damage without the complete expression of FAS and without mental retardation. S. E. Shaywitz, Cohen, and Shaywitz (1980) found that 15 of 87 children referred for learning disorders possessed some of the dysmorphic features of FAS and had a history of excessive maternal alcohol use during pregnancy. These children experienced repeated school failures and demonstrated learning disabilities and problems with attention; all but one were described as hyperactive. The children obtained normal IQ scores and there was no discrepancy between Verbal and Performance IQ on the WISC-R. Higher scores were obtained on WISC-R subtests of

Similarities, Comprehension, Object Assembly, and Block Design, and lower scores were obtained on Coding, Arithmetic, Digit Span, and Information.

Aronson, Kyllerman, Sabel, Sandin, and Olegard (1985) evaluated 21 children of alcoholic mothers who were matched to normal control participants. Results revealed that the study children had IQ scores 15 to 19 points below the controls. WISC-R subtests that measured concept formation and attention span presented the most difficulty for this group. Using the Griffith's Developmental Scales, researchers found the largest differences on the subscales of hearing and speech, eye–hand coordination, and practical reasoning. On the Frostig Test of Visual Perception, a marked perceptual delay was found in 8 of 17 study children and in none of the controls. This was typically seen if the IQ was less than 100. Ten of the 21 had traits of FAS; it was in this FAS subsample that the lowest IQ and most severe perceptual delays were found.

Eight children with FAS were examined by Darby, Streissguth, and Smith (1981). Six of the children had been placed in foster homes and 4 participated in an infant enrichment program; however, all 8 children remained in the subnormal range of intellectual functioning despite early intervention. Spohr and Steinhausen (1984) reevaluated 56 of an original cohort of 71 children 3 to 4 years after they had been diagnosed with FAS. Results suggested that although physical stigmata of FAS diminished over time, intellectual functioning typically did not show improvement. In summary, K. J. Smith and Eckardt (1991) noted the potential for catch-up in some of the growth perimeters in children with FAS; however, intelligence typically does not show improvement, even with foster home placement or other early interventions. In some studies, children with mild cognitive impairment have shown a small improvement in IQ, but these findings may be confounded because the instruments used to measure IQ changed as the child matured (K. J. Smith & Eckardt, 1991).

The long-term effects of FAS beyond childhood have also been examined. Streissguth et al. (1991) studied 61 adolescents (12 to 14 years old) and adults who had been diagnosed previously as having FAS. Results indicated that these individuals tended to remain short and microcephalic, although their weight was somewhat closer to the mean than it had been at birth. After puberty, the facies of individuals with FAS or FAE were not as distinctive as before. The average IQ was 68, but the range of IQ scores varied widely, as was found at younger ages. Average academic functioning ranged from second- to fourth-grade levels, with arithmetic deficits most characteristic. Maladaptive behaviors such as distractibility, poor judgment, and difficulty perceiving social cues were common. Family environments were remarkably unstable. These findings indicate that gestational exposure to alcohol can cause a wide spectrum of disabilities that have lifelong physical, mental, and behavioral implications.

Sensory motor effects. A variety of sensorimotor deficits have been identified in children with FAS. These include visual, auditory, vestibular, and motor coordination problems. Marcus (1987) reported on 5 children with FAS who showed cerebellar signs including kinetic tremor, axial ataxia, and dysdiadokinesis. These motor problems are typically indicative of a dysfunctional cerebellum and suggest that the cerebellum may be vulnerable to in utero alcohol exposure. In reviewing 16 autopsies of humans with FAS, Clarren (1986) also reported cerebellar dysgenesis in 10 of the cases. K. J. Smith and Eckardt (1991) found a trend for children with FAE to have more difficulty than controls and learning-disabled children on tests of cerebellar function (i.e., rapid alternating movements and finger–thumb opposition). Kyllerman, Aronson, Sabel, Karlberg, and Olegard (1985) compared 21 children of alcoholic mothers (10 with FAS) with control participants. Results suggested that children with FAS demonstrate significantly lower fine and gross motor scores on the modified Oseretsky test and inferior motor coordination.

Visual effects. Visual system anomalies are very common in FAS. Aside from the facial or morphologic malformations that comprise some of the craniofacial features used for FAS diagnosis (microphthalmia, ptosis, and short palpebral fissures), disorders of ocular muscle coordination and defects of several intraocular structures have been reported as well (Jones et al., 1973). Strabismus or esotropia (crossed eyes), optic nerve hypoplasia (a reduction in the number of optic nerve axons), and abnormal vasculature in the retina have been observed most frequently (Stromland, 1987). All of these defects contribute to compromised visual acuity, typically myopia (nearsightedness).

Auditory effects. Church (1987) suggested that the incidence of auditory problems might be quite high in children with FAS. In one study, Church found that 90% of 12 children with FAS had some degree of hearing loss. It also appears that prenatal alcohol exposure can have a negative impact at various levels of the auditory system. By measuring electrical activity in the brain stem in response to high-frequency clicking sounds, Church and Holloway (1984) found evidence of sensorineural hearing loss in rats prenatally exposed to alcohol. A follow-up study (Church, 1987) showed that the processing of auditory information at the cortical level, as measured by cortical auditory-evoked potentials, was disrupted in rats prenatally exposed to alcohol in comparison with control rats. These results have important clinical implications because auditory acuity is essential for normal speech and language development in children.

Language and speech effects. Case studies have suggested that delayed language acquisition is a common symptom of FAS (Greene, Ernhart, Martier, Sokol, & Ager, 1990). Iosub and colleagues (1981) studied 63 children who had a variety of features of FAS. These children were found to have a high prevalence of speech and language impairment, as follows: 82% had retarded speech development, 77% had voice dysfunction, 84% had an articulation disorder, and 82% had fluency–rate problems. However, Greene et al. (1990) investigated the effects of fetal alcohol exposure on language and speech acquisition in a cohort of socioeconomically disadvantaged urban children and found no statistically significant relationships between the alcohol and language indices after statistical control for confounding variables. Given that only a small number of investigations have explored the association between speech and language disorders and FAS or FAE, further investigations are needed to explore possible speech or language sequelae.

Attention and hyperactivity. Children who have FAS and FAE frequently are described as hyperactive, distractible, impulsive, and having a short attention span (Aronson et al., 1985; Streissguth et al., 1984, 1985). Even moderate amounts of maternal alcohol consumption during pregnancy are associated with inattention and fidgety and restless behavior (Landesman-Dwyer, Ragozin, & Little, 1981; Streissguth et al., 1984).

Studying a cohort of 4-year-old offspring of moderate drinkers ($M = 0.45$ oz. absolute alcohol per day during pregnancy), Landesman-Dwyer et al. (1981) found that middle-class children with different levels of prenatal alcohol exposure varied on measures associated with overactivity and attention. The sex of the child, maternal parity and smoking, and variables related to home environment were controlled. The level of environmental stimulation in the home was assessed using a standardized scale and did not covary with the level of maternal alcohol use. The offspring of the moderate drinkers were less attentive, less compliant with parental demands, and more fidgety during meals compared with offspring of abstaining or occasional drinkers. Children having the greatest alcohol and nicotine exposure were characterized as having the most problems with attention, social compliance, and fidgetiness. These investigators interpreted their data to suggest that the effects, which were similar to those characterizing attention deficit hyperactivity disorder (ADHD), could not be attributed to current environmental factors, because mother's drinking levels were low, both currently and during pregnancy, and rearing environments were supportive.

In their prospective Seattle Longitudinal Study of 475 White, middle-class children, Streissguth et al. (1984, 1986) found that performance at 4 and 7 years of age on a continuous performance test (CPT) of vigilance was associated with prenatal alcohol exposure. Prenatal alcohol exposure was significantly related to reaction time, errors of commission, and vigilance errors on the CPT as well as behavioral ratings of endurance, persistence, organization, distractibility, and impulsivity, even when adjusted for other prenatal exposures, postnatal conditions, and demographics. Moderate prenatal alcohol exposure in Streissguth's studies (1985, 1986) was correlated with impaired attention but not with hyperactivity. The researchers postulated that hyperactivity might be correlated with higher levels of alcohol use. However, not all research in this area has supported these findings. Boyd, Ernhart, Greene, Sokol, and Martier (1991) reported that when other factors were controlled statistically, no evidence for prenatal alcohol effects on attention could be identified in their sample of low-income children at a 4-year, 10-month follow-up.

Brown et al. (1991) evaluated several attention and behavioral factors in 68 children (mean age = 5 years, 10 months) whose mothers reported drinking during pregnancy to evaluate the hypothesis that such exposure contributes to deficits in attention and behavior that may be associated with ADHD. The children were predominately low-income and African American. Researchers controlled for mothers' current drinking and severity of alcohol abuse. Variables studied included sustained attention, impulsivity, behavior ratings by parents and teachers, and observed behavior in free play and in mother–child interactions. The results indicated that children exposed to alcohol throughout pregnancy showed deficits in the ability to sustain attention and were more often described by teachers, although not by their mothers, as showing attentional and behavioral problems. However, when current drinking was controlled, only acting out and other externalizing behaviors remained different by group.

In general, these results support the clinical literature which suggests that maternal alcohol use during pregnancy is associated with attention and behavior deficits in offspring. However, it appears there are some important distinctions between the attentional–activity effects of alcohol and the classic ADHD syndrome. In addition, it is not clear that attentional–activity deficits are strictly teratogenic effects. Therefore, Brown et al. (1991) recommended that practitioners consider the effects of the child's current environment in interpretation of behavior and its relationship to maternal alcohol use.

DEVELOPMENTAL PRESENTATION OF SYMPTOMS IN CHILDREN WITH FAS OR FAE

Infancy

The earliest effects of fetal exposure to alcohol occur during the gestational period, when the fetus is at increased risk for miscarriage, premature labor, or stillbirth delivery. For those infants who are delivered alive, low birth weight often is one of the first indicators of problems. Streissguth, LaDue, and Randels (1988) described the infant with FAS as having a "small, scrawny appearance" (p. 10), hypotonia (weak muscle tone), a weak sucking reflex, and "failure to thrive," meaning that they continue to lose weight longer than typical after delivery. Such infants may need a longer period of hospitalization after delivery to help stabilize their weight. Low birth weight and continued problems with weight gain are complicated by early feeding difficulties, which are a concern to caregivers during the infancy period. Often, sleep patterns may be erratic, and the infant may have difficulty establishing a normal sleep–wake cycle. These problems with feeding and sleeping may contribute to fatigue and increased stress for the caregiver, who may also be struggling with continued problems with alcoholism. The infant often is tremulous, hyperirritable, and difficult to console.

The early attachment relationship between parents and their infant develops over the first weeks and months of life. This relationship is a product of many instinctual and natural inclinations of both the caregiver and the infant but can be enhanced by the infant's responsivity to the caregiver and the caregiver's responsivity to the infant's "signalling" behaviors, such as smiling, eye contact, and so forth. In contrast, this attachment relationship can be strained by factors such as the infant's irritability, difficulty being consoled, or difficulty feeding, as well as by the caregiver's lack of responsivity to the infant's cues. Past studies of parent–infant interaction have documented the importance of the reciprocal relationship between an infant's behavioral cues (e.g., crying when hungry, alertness and eye contact with the caregiver during feeding, and vocalization to indicate a desire for attention) and the parent's response to that signal soon after it is given. The temporal contiguity of the parents' response to the infant is felt to be an important indicator of the parents' attention and sensitivity to their infant's needs as well as the strength of the attachment relationship. Imagine a young parent attempting to care for a baby who is hyperirritable, difficult to console, and has difficulty with feeding and sleeping. It would be easy for the parent to interpret the infant's behavior as an indicator of his or her own inadequacy as a parent. Depending on the degree of isolation of the parent or, conversely, the amount of positive social support available to the parent, the outcome of the parent–child attachment relationship can vary dramatically. Thus, the behavioral, temperamental, and physical characteristics of the infant with FAS or FAE must be viewed within the context of the family system, and particularly the impact on parents. The risk for potential child maltreatment is present when there is a combination of parental isolation and stress, along with infant characteristics that disrupt responsivity and make caregiving more difficult. It is common for extended family members to be involved in caregiving of infants with FAS or FAE, and custody issues must always be considered when evaluating these children and their families.

Developmental presentation of symptoms during infancy often reveals more apparent delay as the infant progresses through the first months of life. The infant with FAS or FAE may be slow to master speech–language and motor milestones and may continue to have difficulty with feeding and weight gain. Infants normally go through a period of stranger anxiety at about 8 to 12 months of age, but infants with FAS or FAE may be delayed in going through this normal period of development so that they show no signs of stranger anxiety at the typical time.

Infants exposed to alcohol in utero have been reported to have atypical head orientation and hand-to-mouth activity, decreased alertness, and decreased activity level (Landesman-Dwyer, Keller, & Streissguth, 1978); increased levels of low arousal; and decreased habituation to repetitive stimulation (Streissguth, Martin, & Barr, 1977); as well as poor state regulation (Rosett et al., 1979; Sander et al., 1977). They may be described as "very good" and their irritability may decline as they become older.

Preschool Years

Streissguth et al. (1988) described the preschool child with FAS as usually short and "elflike" in manner and appearance. These children typically are alert, outgoing, excessively friendly, and very interested in people, often moving from one activity to another with decreased attention span for their age. They may be demanding of adult attention and sometimes overly friendly.

Developmentally, preschool children with FAS develop language, but delays are noted in the lack of complexity of their vocabulary, grammatical usage, and thought processes. Because these children may be hyperverbal and prone to interrupt others, their language impairment may not be noticed readily.

Physically, preschool children with FAS continue to be small in stature, as well as slow in development. Caregivers may attribute their slow development to their small size, and this may result in a delay in detection of developmental problems and initiation of early intervention. Both motor and cognitive delays may be noted during the preschool years, as well as speech–language delays. Often, pediatricians or Head Start teachers are among the first professionals to note the delays and to conduct screening prior to a child's referral to a psychologist.

Hyperactivity may be the most pronounced behavioral symptom during the preschool years, according to Streissguth et al. (1988). In fact, the parents' concern over the child's hyperactivity may be the primary reason for referral to a practitioner during the preschool years. Children with FAS often are described as extremely busy, unable to sit still to engage in age-appropriate play activities, reckless in their movements, and prone to accidents because of their impulsivity. Parents often describe these children as needing closer supervision than their siblings because they tend to get into trouble more often. Continued delays in motoric development are noted as the child becomes old enough to attempt preschool fine motor tasks, such as coloring and drawing, or such gross motor tasks as riding a tricycle or bicycle.

Familial factors continue to be important during the preschool years and should receive consideration during evaluation. The child with FAS or FAE continues to be at risk for maltreatment, both physical and sexual. Custody issues are important, with regard to whether the child continues to live with biological parents or other relatives or caregivers. Mothers who are chronic alcoholics are at risk for early death, and leaving their child orphaned. Assessing the strengths and weaknesses of the family system is important.

Early School Years

Developmentally, the child with more significant sequelae of FAS or FAE may not be ready to begin kindergarten at the typical age, and it may be suggested that the child be held back a year before beginning school. Ideally, a structured preschool environment or Head Start program would provide early intervention for the child before school age. Developmental delays in speech–language, motor, and cognitive development can be measured reliably through diagnostic evaluations, if referrals are made. However, for those children functioning at a higher level, subtle development delays may not be noticeable during the early school years. The child may function relatively well in a regular classroom environment, particularly in acquisition of reading and written language skills, over the first 2 years of school. Arithmetic usually is more of a problem for children with FAS than writing or reading, but arithmetic problems may not be apparent until second or third grade (Streissguth et al., 1988).

Problems with attention may become more manifest during the early school years, as the child enters a structured learning environment with increased demands for attention and following classroom rules. If the child has hyperactivity and poor impulse control, there may be an early referral for psychological or medical evaluation or both to determine the most appropriate intervention for these problems. If poor attention (without hyperactivity) is the primary symptom, referral may occur at a later time and may be associated with declining academic performance.

Associated with the triad of poor attention, hyperactivity, and impulsivity may also be social interaction problems involving disruptive behavior in the classroom, intrusiveness, excessive talking, and poor tolerance for frustration. Children with FAS or FAE may also develop oppositional and defiant behavioral problems, along with the symptoms of ADHD, but the manifestation of the behavior problems is more likely to occur as a function of characteristics in the family environment than characteristics related to alcohol exposure. Factors such as parental psychopathology, continued alcohol abuse, and low socioeconomic level are associated with increased incidence of behavioral problems in the child (Barkley, 1990; Streissguth et al., 1988).

Middle School Years

As the child with FAS or FAE progresses in school, it becomes more apparent that math skills are delayed relative to reading and writing. Increased difficulty with attentional skills, and the related problems of completing classroom and homework assignments and mastering new academic skills, may lead to significant academic performance problems for the child. Referral for psychological evaluation may occur because of behavioral, attention, cognitive, or academic problems, or some combination of the above. According to Streissguth et al. (1988), it is common for children with FAS or FAE to be referred for special education services or to be retained because of lack of age-appropriate academic progress.

Depending on the skill and attention with which the child's learning and behavioral problems are handled, interventions may be adaptive or problematic. The interaction of the child's problems with the characteristics of the family and home environment become increasingly important. Effective treatment of behavioral problems requires cooperation and participation in counseling from the parents as well as the child. In family situations where parents either lack the resources or the motivation to work in the best interests of their child, there is increased risk for the child to become truant or drop out of school.

The child's prognosis for independent living and employment depends both on the degree of learning and academic problems experienced by the child with FAS or FAE and on the complex support system provided by the family and community in which the child lives. If intellectual and adaptive living skills are low, the child with FAS or FAE may not be a good candidate for employment or independent living (Streissguth et al., 1988).

Adolescence

Streissguth et al. (1988) described physical and developmental characteristics of a group of adolescents and adults with FAS. The most severely affected physical characteristic of adolescents and adults with FAS was shortness of stature, with height typically being more than two standard deviations below the average. Both weight and head circumference for the adolescents with FAS were below the mean for their age, but these were not as discrepant as height. The facial characteristics that were more apparent during infancy and preschool years often were less apparent in adolescence and adulthood. The most common facial anomalies in the older age group were an abnormal philtrum, abnormalities of the teeth and lips, hirsutism (excessive hair), abnormal shape of the head, and abnormalities associated with the fingers—particularly short, stubby fingers. The characteristic short, upturned nose usually was no longer apparent, but many of the older adolescents and adults had a rather coarse appearance of the face (Streissguth et al., 1988).

Developmentally, a broad range of intelligence was found in the adolescents and adults with FAS, ranging from the level of profound mental retardation to average intelligence. In the sample studied by Streissguth et al. (1988), 58% of the adolescents had IQ scores of 70 or below, which could be considered in the mentally deficient range. Adolescents with FAE generally had a higher range of intellectual scores, but continued to be below the norm for their age. Examination of the pattern of performance on the WISC-R revealed relative strengths on performance tasks involving visuospatial and visuomotor skills, compared with verbal tasks involving vocabulary, abstract reasoning, comprehension, and general information. Adolescents with FAS tended to perform better on the more concrete tasks and worse on the tasks requiring more abstract reasoning. Thus, there is strong evidence for persistence of the early intellectual deficits into maturity. The persistence of poor verbal comprehension skills is important to acknowledge, given the typical behavioral pattern of excessive talking and verbal fluency.

Examination of academic functioning in the adolescents studied by Streissguth et al. (1988) revealed that only 7% of the 44 adolescents were able to be in regular classes without supplementary tutoring or special education. Twenty-nine percent were in full-time, self-contained special education classrooms, and another 25% received special education services at least half of the time. An increase in truancy, refusal to attend school, and school drop out tended to occur at two critical transition periods—between elementary and middle school and between middle and high school. These should be considered high-risk periods during which it is important to reevaluate the classroom placement and educational expectations of middle school and adolescent youngsters with FAS with the goal of providing an appropriate program and keeping them in the school environment. At the point of graduating from high school, adolescents with FAS may have reached the sixth to eighth grade level of functioning, and over 95% will have experienced special education during their school years (Streissguth et al., 1988). Poor math skills, relative to reading and written language, continue to be apparent.

Socially and adaptively, adolescents with FAS are reported by their parents to have poor social interaction skills, impulsivity, lack of appropriate inhibition, and unresponsiveness to subtle social cues (Streissguth et al., 1991). They may lack reciprocal friendships and may be unlikely to show initiative. In Streissguth et al.'s study, maladaptive behaviors often were noted by parents responding to the Vineland Adaptive Behavior Scale, who reported characteristics of poor concentration and attention, excessive dependency, stubbornness, sullenness, social withdrawal, emotional lability, and periods of high anxiety, along with a tendency to lie, cheat, or steal. Streissguth et al. noted that these adolescents came from remarkably unstable family environments, often with multiple caregivers and family placements, and occasional placement in temporary shelters. Of the adolescents surveyed, only 9% were still living with both biological parents, and only 3%

were still with their biological mothers. Of those adolescents for whom reliable data could be obtained, 69% of the biological mothers were known to be dead. The adolescents surveyed in the study by Streissguth and colleagues were primarily American Indian (75% of the population studied), many of whom were living on reservations in the Southwest. The degree to which these reported characteristics among adolescents relate to cultural and environmental factors, as opposed to being representative of the larger population of adolescents with FAS, is unclear. At this point, the Streissguth et al. (1988, 1991) studies do provide a preliminary picture of the symptomatology noted in the adolescent and early adult years. Further research will be important to either replicate or refute these findings with broader populations from other ethnic and cultural groups.

CLINICAL ASSESSMENT OF CHILDREN WITH FAS OR FAE

General Considerations in Assessment of the Child With FAS or FAE

Evaluation of the child with FAS or FAE is best done in a multi-disciplinary environment that includes, at a minimum, medical and psychological components. The medical evaluation might be done by a pediatrician experienced in diagnosing FAS or FAE, with consultation as needed from a geneticist or dysmorphologist. Psychologists may assess the child's developmental, academic, and social functioning from infancy through adolescence, with consultations obtained from speech–language pathologists, educators, and occupational and physical therapists as needed. Neuropsychologic evaluation can provide more refined assessment of the child's higher cortical functioning with an understanding of the neuropathology of FAS or FAE. Social workers often are involved in the evaluation to obtain detailed family history and to provide information regarding social resources to assist the family. A setting in which the various professionals can meet to discuss and integrate data from their respective evaluations can result in a more accurate and effective comprehensive evaluation of FAS. It is ideal when the child can be seen for multiple follow-up evaluations within the same setting, and intervention can be obtained there also. This type of environment facilitates continuity and greater understanding of the developmental progress of the child as well as the family's adaptation to the child's problems.

Clinical evaluation of the child with FAS may be complicated by an unstable, chaotic family situation with parents still struggling with alcoholism. This may lead to very practical problems with parents keeping scheduled appointments or following through on recommendations. Transportation and other financial resources may be lacking. For this reason, it is helpful to the family if clinic visits can involve the multidisciplinary staff present at one time in one setting, to alleviate the need for multiple office visits and professional contacts over a long period of time. For younger children with FAS, a home-based model of evaluation often can provide information not available in a clinic setting, particularly regarding the stimulation available in the home environment and other dimensions related to the health and safety of the young child. The home-based approach may facilitate more regular follow-up and monitoring of the behavior and development of the young child with FAS as well as provide opportunities for increased rapport with the caregivers. Home visits may also may provide an opportunity for a more detailed social interview of the parents to ascertain more directly the history of alcohol abuse, prenatally, postnatally, and currently.

Otherwise, special considerations for the child with FAS or FAE relate to a good understanding of testing approaches at different developmental stages. The practitioner who is experienced in working with children across the entire age span, from infancy through adolescence, would be better equipped to distinguish normal developmental variations from abnormal manifestations of development. Assessment may be more difficult with a child who has FAS, because of the tendency toward increased activity level, decreased attention, impulsivity, and behavioral disinhibition. These characteristics will require that evaluation be done in brief segments, with increased structure and encouragement from the examiner, in order to achieve valid test results.

Assessment of Physical Characteristics

The medical component of the diagnostic evaluation should address questions related to the mother's history of alcohol abuse and assess the physical parameters of the child. The maternal history should elicit information regarding the amount and timing of alcohol consumption during pregnancy. The presence of binge drinking (more than five drinks on one occasion) versus a pattern of chronic drinking on a more regular basis should be determined if possible. The approximate amount consumed per day or per week should be elicited, as well as the timing of alcohol consumption during pregnancy (e.g., primarily first trimester, second trimester, or all three trimesters). The physician must be aware that denial of drinking is frequent, and it is helpful if other family members can corroborate the maternal history of drinking.

The physician should also examine the child to determine growth parameters, evidence of CNS dysfunction, and morphologic abnormalities, including atypical facial characteristics. A pediatrician who is experienced with the differential diagnosis of FAS may complete this part of the evaluation or he or she may choose to obtain a consultation from a geneticist or dysmorphologist. The differential diagnosis must rule out other conditions that have a pattern of malformations similar to FAS, including deLange syndrome, Noonan syndrome, Dubowitz syndrome, Stickler syndrome, X-linked mental deficiency, and fetal hydantoin effects (Little & Streissguth, 1982).

The diagnosis of FAS is made only when a maternal history of alcohol abuse is present and the child has the primary characteristics of the syndrome. A diagnosis of FAE is made when some of the characteristics are present, but not enough for a confident diagnosis of FAS (Little & Streissguth, 1982).

If the child is presented for follow-up medical evaluations after a diagnosis has been made, it is important for the physician to monitor the child's continued growth and health status through the preschool and school age years. Medical evaluation for potential cardiac defects, auditory and visual abnormalities and other potentially treatable medical problems must be considered.

Developmental Assessment of the Infant and Preschool Child

The developmental assessment of the infant and preschool-aged child is often performed by a psychologist skilled in early assessment and behavioral management. Assessment of the broad range of intelligence, preacademic readiness skills, general speech–language development, fine and gross motor coordination, social–adaptive functioning, and behavioral and emotional functioning is important for the child with FAS or FAE. All developmental assessment must be done with the awareness that the child with FAS may have decreased attention, increased distractibility, and hyperactivity, making formal testing difficult. Special adaptations of the testing situation may be required to achieve valid assessment.

Intellectual or cognitive assessment can be accomplished with a variety of standardized instruments, including the Bayley Scales of Infant Development: Second Edition (Bayley II; Bayley, 1993), the Kaufman Assessment Battery for Children (K-ABC; Kaufman & Kaufman, 1983), the McCarthy Scales of Children's Abilities (McCarthy, 1972), the Stanford–Binet Intelligence Scale: Fourth Edition (Thorndike, Hagen, & Sattler, 1986), or the Wechsler Preschool and Primary Scale of Intelligence–Revised (WPPSI-R; Wechsler, 1989). Table 3 lists examples of infant and preschool assessment instruments from which the practitioner might develop a battery of intellectual, preacademic, language, motor, and social–adaptive measures. It is recommended that a broad-based scale of intelligence be selected in order to provide information on the child's relative strengths and weaknesses across a variety of skill areas, ranging from verbal to nonverbal, receptive to expressive, and with information processed through a variety of sensory modalities (auditory, visual, kinesthetic–motor). For the infant and toddler, the Bayley II (Bayley, 1993) provides an updated, broad assessment of early developmental skills with separate indices for mental and motor development, in addition to a behavioral rating. Both the McCarthy scales and the K-ABC are engaging, interesting measures that provide information on verbal and nonverbal abilities of young children. The McCarthy scales yield verbal, perceptual performance and quantitative scales, along with separate indices of memory and motor functioning. The Binet and WPPSI-R are more demanding verbally than the K-ABC and McCarthy but provide a broad assessment of a wide range of abilities. For young children with language delay or language-based learning problems, the K-ABC provides several nonverbal processing measures and a nonverbal scale, in addition to indices of sequential and simultaneous processing.

An individualized assessment of intellectual or developmental functioning rather than developmental screening is recommended because of the high risk for future learning and cognitive problems in children with FAS or FAE. Often, screening tests will detect only the most gross deficits and will not detect more subtle indices of learning problems that may suggest greater risk for school failure. The preschool years provide an optimal time for remediation and early intervention and can be helpful in preventing a more severe negative outcome in children with FAS and FAE. Therefore, a comprehensive evaluation is warranted during this age period.

Preacademic skills in preschool and early elementary age children may be assessed by screening their ability to match, identify, or write numerals and the alphabet in lowercase and uppercase letters, identify or match colors and shapes, and perform such rote activities as counting or reciting the alphabet. The Appendix provides a sample coding sheet for informal screening of preacademic skills. In addition to the informal measures, standardized batteries of preacademic skills are available. Both the Battelle Developmental Inventory (Newborg, Stock, & Wnek, 1984) and the Bracken Basic Concept Scale (Bracken, 1984) are norm-referenced tests that measure a broad range of preschool cognitive, verbal, quantitative, and readiness skills. The Battelle also includes measures of fine and gross motor skills, as well as social–behavioral development. Criterion-referenced tests, such as the Brigance Diagnostic Inventory of Early Development (Brigance, 1978) and the Developmental Profile II (Alpern, Boll, & Shearer, 1980), provide easy-to-administer checklists of a broad range of preschool readiness, cognitive, verbal, quantitative, motor, and self-help skills. Although standard scores are not provided, these tests provide useful information for educational planning because of their emphasis on specific skill development over a broad range of areas.

Speech–language development may be evaluated in the context of general intellectual measures, but detailed assessment of the child's expressive and receptive language, phonological abilities, and oral motor functioning should be left to the speech–language pathologist. Table 3 lists examples of several preschool language instruments that may be used by the psychologist for a more formal assessment of receptive and expressive language functions, as well as the social–pragmatic aspects of communication. For the young infant or severely delayed child in whom oral communication is not yet developed, the Nonspeech Test for Receptive/Expressive Communication (Huer, 1988) can provide useful information regarding the precursors to oral communication. This test taps nonspeech communicative behavior, including gestures or eye gaze, that may precede the development of oral communication. For children at a slightly higher developmental level, the Preschool Language Scale–3 (Zimmerman, Steiner, & Pond, 1992) provides assessment of both receptive and expressive abilities from birth through 6 years. This scale taps into language concepts important for early school learning, as well as a screening for articulation skills. For children who are delayed in expressive language abilities, the Peabody Picture Vocabulary Test–Revised (Dunn & Dunn, 1981) provides a measure of receptive vocabulary that can be obtained merely by requiring the child to point to pictures after hearing a spoken word. Finally, the Test of Language Development Primary: Second Edition (Newcomer & Hammill, 1988) provides information about more sophisticated expressive and receptive communication abilities in the 4- to 8-year age range, including semantics, syntax, and phonology in both receptive and expressive areas. Each of the tests cited provides norm-referenced standard scores, percentiles, or age equivalents that can be compared with cognitive and other measures. The practitioner should assure that screening for auditory acuity is completed before language testing, to rule out sensory deficits that may impede language development.

TABLE 3

Selected Preschool Assessment Instruments

Instrument	Age range (years)	Time (minutes)	Developmental areas measured								Scores provided		
			Cognition	Verbal	Quantitative	Perceptual–fine motor	Gross motor	Social behavior	Self-help	Readiness	Standard scores	Percentiles	Age equivalent
General cognitive													
Kaufman Assessment Battery for Children	$2^1/_2$ to $12^1/_2$	60–75	X	X	X	X				X	X	X	
McCarthy Scales of Children's Abilities	$2^1/_2$ to $8^1/_2$	60–75	X	X	X	X	X				X	X	X
Stanford–Binet Intelligence Scale–Fourth Edition	2 to 18+	60–90	X	X	X	X					X		
Wechsler Preschool and Primary Scale of Intelligence–Revised	3 to $7^1/_4$	45–60	X	X	X	X					X	X	X
Bayley Scales of Infant Development–Second Edition	0 to 42 months	30–60	X	X		X	X				X		X
Preacademic													
Battelle Developmental Inventory	Birth to 8	60	X	X	X	X	X	X	X	X	X	X	
Bracken Basic Concept Scale	$2^1/_2$ to $7^1/_2$	25–30	X	X	X					X	X	X	X
Brigance Diagnostic Inventory of Early Development	Birth to 7		X	X	X	X	X		X	X			X
Developmental Profile II	Birth to 8	25–30	X	X	X	X	X		X				
Language													
Carrow Elicited Language Inventory	3 to 8	45		X[a]									
Non-Speech Test				X								X	

Peabody Picture Vocabulary Test–Revised	$2^1/_2$ to 18	20		X[b]							X	X	X
Test for Auditory Comprehension of Language	3 to 7	20		X[b]								X	X
Motor													
Bruininks–Oseretsky Test of Motor Proficiency	$4^1/_2$ to $8^1/_2$	20–30				X	X						
Developmental Test of Visual–Motor Integration	3 to 18	10–15				X					X	X	X
Motor Free Visual–PerceptionTest	4 to 8	10				X					X		X
Movement Assessment of Infants	0 to 1	30–45				X	X				X	X	X
Peabody Developmental Motor Scales and Activity Cards	0 to 7	45–60				X	X						
Adaptive													
AAMD Adaptive Behavior Scale–School Edition	3 to 17	30		X	X	X	X	X	X		X	X	
Scales of Independent Behavior	Birth to adult		X	X		X	X	X	X		X	X	X
Vineland Adaptive Behavior Scales	Birth to 18	60–90	X	X		X	X	X	X		X	X	X

Note: From "Assessment of Learning and Cognitive Dysfunction in Young Children," by M. Semrud-Clikeman and G. W. Hynd, 1993. In J. L. Culbertson and D. J. Willis (Eds.), *Testing Young Children* (pp. 176–177). Austin, TX: PRO-ED. Copyright 1993 by PRO-ED. Adapted with permission.
[a]Expressive language. [b]Receptive language.

Assessment of motor function often is included in the psychological battery for infants and young preschool children. The Bayley II (Bayley, 1993) contains a separate index of motor functioning, which provides a Psychomotor Development Index in the age range from birth to 42 months. For infants up to 12 months of age, the Movement Assessment of Infants (Chandler, Andrews, & Swanson, 1980) may be used to identify motor dysfunction and provide information useful for developing an early intervention program. This scale was first developed by physical therapists to assess motor behaviors of highrisk infants from a neonatal intensive care follow-up program. The test provides a Total Risk Score, which has at least fair (interobserver and test–retest) reliability in preliminary studies. However, the predictive validity has not yet been determined, and scores from this test should be interpreted with caution. Comprehensive measures of motor functioning at the gross motor and fine motor level for young children can be obtained on the Peabody Developmental Motor Scales (Folio & Fewell, 1983) and the Bruininks–Oseretsky Test of Motor Proficiency (Bruininks, 1978). These measures provide standard scores and a normative population for comparisons of motor development across a wide age range. Specific fine motor skills may be measured through drawing or copying tests, such as the Developmental Test of Visual–Motor Integration (Beery, 1982). This test allows for developmental assessment of the acquisition of fine motor integration skills, and provides a norm-referenced comparison group for standard scores. When fine motor functioning is seriously impaired, and the examiner wishes to examine the child's perceptual abilities free of motor interference, the Motor Free–Visual Perception Test (Colarusso & Hammill, 1972) is useful. This test provides measures of visual discrimination, memory, matching, and embedded figures to which the child can respond by pointing rather than reproducing the correct response.

Social–adaptive skills may be measured in a variety of ways, including parental interview to elicit behavioral descriptions, structured parental interview using an age-normed checklist such as the Vineland Adaptive Behavior Scales, direct observations of parent–child or child–peer interactions, or interview with preschool and Head Start professionals who have opportunity to observe the child's behavior in group social situations. A combination of these procedures would provide the most sensitive data on the social interaction and adaptive functioning of the child with FAS and FAE. Formal measures of adaptive functioning for young children (birth through adult) include the Scales of Independent Behavior (Bruininks, Woodcock, Weatherman, & Hill, 1984) and the Vineland Adaptive Behavior Scales (Sparrow, Balla, & Cicchetti, 1984). These norm-referenced standard scales provide age equivalents and standard scores comparing a child's adaptive functioning with an age-normed peer group across the areas of communication, self-help and daily living skills, socialization, and motor functioning. Although less research is available on the Scales of Independent Behavior, it does assess skills and domains similar to those of the Vineland.

Measures of adaptive functioning have the advantage of tapping information from observers (e.g., parents and teachers) who have access to the child over long periods of time in a variety of settings. Thus, the information in many ways may be more accurate than that obtained in a brief clinic examination. On the other hand, adaptive behavior scales are not as precise psychometrically as standardized cognitive ability measures, due to difficulties with norming and standardization practices (Sattler, 1988). Therefore, the practitioner should use these measures as guidelines to assist in making judgments about the presence or absence of mental retardation in young children. The American Association of Mental Retardation Adaptive Behavior Scales—School: Second Edition (Lambert, Nihira, & Leland, 1993) is particularly suited to observations of the mentally retarded child and adolescent along the dimensions of independent functioning, functional academics, and maladaptive behaviors.

Neuropsychological Assessment of the School-Age Child

As children enter the early school-age years, more sophisticated neuropsychologic tests designed to measure specialized patterns of brain dysfunction can be administered. Even when intellectual functioning is in the average range, specific neuropsychological dysfunction may be detected when measures sensitive to those functions are used. The examiner is cautioned against overuse of global batteries with summary scores that mask strengths or weaknesses in specific skill areas. The neuropsychologic battery should provide both global indices of functioning and also measures of discrete functional areas shown to be sensitive to the effects of prenatal alcohol exposure.

Few studies have reported on neuropsychological sequelae in children who have FAS or FAE. However, Streissguth, Bookstein, Sampson, and Barr (1989) reported on measures of neurobehavioral functioning in 7-1/2-year-old children who were prenatally exposed to alcohol, as part of a longitudinal study conducted to examine FAS effects. A broad selection of neuropsychologic measures was used on the basis of their presumed sensitivity to markers of prenatal alcohol exposure in the school aged child. From the broad range of measures, two primary areas emerged as most strongly associated with prenatal alcohol exposure: perceptual motor problems and memory. Streissguth, Bookstein, et al. (1989) reported that children had difficulty with the qualitative aspects of copying designs, in that they made more reversals and distortions of design elements and produced designs of poor quality and poor integration. These problems also generalized to school writing problems. Poor memory was noted across several modalities, including auditory memory on the Seashore Rhythm test from the Halstead–Reitan Neuropsychological Test Battery for Children (HRB; Reitan, 1979), and the perceptual memory component of the Tactual Performance Test from the HRB. Verbal memory problems were noted as well on the Children's Memory Test (1993), as were errors in memory for designs from that test. Finally, children with alcohol exposure were noted to have greater difficulty on tests that required shifting set and maintaining a flexible problem-solving attitude, as on the Progressive Figures Test from the Reitan–Indiana Neuropsychologic Test Battery for Children (Reitan, 1979). Distractibility and impulsivity were noted on examiner behavior ratings as being very sensitive to prenatal alcohol exposure.

Deficits in attention and vigilance were reported by Streissguth, Bookstein, et al. (1989) on CPT (Rosvold, Mirsky, Sarason, Bransome, & Beck, 1956) vigilance tasks, where errors of omission, commission, and delayed reaction time for *X* and *AX* were used. Not only did children with prenatal exposure to alcohol perform more poorly, but those children whose mothers had engaged in binge drinking were significantly worse on all measures than those children whose mothers did not engage in binge drinking. Deficits in attention have been reported by other investigators as well (Brown et al., 1991; Nanson & Hiscock, 1990), using similar measures of a computerized performance test along with parent and teacher behavioral ratings. These findings suggest that including measures of attention, vigilance, and reaction time in the neuropsychologic battery would be important. The authors made the point that the qualitative analysis of performance was as sensitive an indicator of prenatal alcohol exposure as the quantitative assessment.

Thus, a neuropsychologic battery derived from the empirical literature on children with FAS or FAE would include measures of perceptual-motor functioning, memory, sustained attention and vigilance, and cognitive flexibility in addition to global measures of intellectual and academic functioning. The functional areas to be included in the neuropsychologic battery are listed in Table 4, along with suggested measures that tap the specific functions. The general cognitive batteries provide global indexes of the child's intellectual ability as well as indexes of verbal, numerical, and perceptual reasoning abilities. Broad measures of academic functioning are always included in the battery with children and adolescents as most deficits in their neuropsychological functioning will have some impact on academic performance. The measures suggested in Table 4 for both intellectual and academic assessment are examples of recently normed, well-standardized, and psychometrically sound tests.

Perceptual motor abilities may be measured through graphomotor tests of drawing or copying geometric shapes and designs, such as on the Developmental Test of Visual–Motor Integration (Beery, 1982) or the Bender–Gestalt Test (Koppitz, 1975). The Bender can be scored for errors of rotation, perseveration, integration, and distortion, whereas the Visual–Motor test provides for both

TABLE 4

Neuropsychologic Functional Areas and Suggested Measures for Children and Youth

Functional area	Measure
General cognitive	Kaufman Assessment Battery for Children (K-ABC)
	Kaufman Adolescent and Adult Intelligence Test (KAIT)
	Stanford–Binet Intelligence Scale–Fourth Edition
	Wechsler Intelligence Scale for Children–Third Edition (WISC-III)
Academic achievement	Wechsler Individual Achievement Test (WIAT)
	Woodcock–Johnson Psychoeducational Battery–Revised (WJ-R)
Perceptual–motor	Bender–Gestalt Test for Young Children
	Developmental Test of Visual–Motor Integration (VMI)
	Lafayette Grooved Pegboard
Memory	California Verbal Learning Test for Children (CVLT-C)
	Halstead Neuropsychological Test Battery for Children
	Tactual Performance Test
	Seashore Rhythm Test
	Wide Range Assessment of Memory and Learning (WRAML)
Sustained attention/vigilance	Continuous Performance Test (CPT)
	Errors of Omission
	Errors of Commission
	Reaction Time
	Gordon's Diagnostic System
Cognitive flexibility	Reitan–Indiana Neuropsychological Test Battery for Children
	Category Test
	Color Form Test
	Progressive Figures
	Halstead–Reitan Neuropsychological Test Battery for Children (HRB)
	Category Test
	Trail Making A & B
	Stroop Color and Word Test
	Wisconsin Card Sorting Test (WCST)

qualitative analysis of developmental acquisition of visuomotor integration skills as well as quantitative scoring of the accuracy of the drawings. To measure manual dexterity and coordination, the Purdue Pegboard or Lafayette Grooved Pegboard (Trites, 1977) is useful. The Grooved Pegboard requires individuals to place grooved pegs into holes as quickly as possible, with the score being based on time to completion for each hand and number of dropped pegs. Developmental norms are available for dominant and nondominant hand performance.

Memory assessment in children has improved tremendously in recent years with the development of new test batteries, including the California Verbal Learning Test for Children (Delis, Kramer, Kaplan, & Ober, 1994) and the Wide Range Assessment of Memory and Learning (WRAML; Sheslow & Adams, 1990). The California Verbal Learning test measures both short- and long-term memory decline encoding strategies and errors such as intrusions and perseverations, list recognition ability, and the degree to which stimuli may interfere with learned material. In contrast, the WRAML has separate scales for verbal and visual memory, as well as learning. The Verbal Memory scale taps recall of the main ideas of stories, and verbatim recall of sentences and numeral and letter sequences. The Visual Memory scale taps pictorial recognition memory, ability to reproduce designs from memory, and memory for finger movement patterns. The Learning scale assesses the child's ability to learn unfamiliar material over repeated trials; the material includes word lists, sound–symbol associative tasks, and recall of the location of visual patterns. The WRAML also includes delayed recall trials to assess retention over time in the context of interference from other material.

CPTs (Gordon, 1983; Rosvold et al., 1956) have been used for over 3 decades as measures of vigilance and impulsivity. They were first developed to provide a standardized approach to assessing impulse control in children suspected of having ADHD. Empirical research has demonstrated the sensitivity of the CPT in discriminating children with ADHD from normal groups, and sensitivity to medication effects in children who have ADHD (Barkley, DuPaul, & McMurray, 1991; Barkley, Fischer, Newby, & Breen, 1988; Gordon & Mettelman, 1988). Many variations of the CPT are available (e.g., visual, auditory). However, the most common type of CPT requires the child to observe a screen while individual letters or numbers are projected onto it at a rapid pace, typically one per second. The child is instructed to press a button when a certain stimulus or pair of stimuli appear in sequence. Scores from the CPT include the number of correct responses, number of omission errors (target stimuli missed), and number of commission errors (number of responses following nontarget or incorrect stimuli). The commission errors are presumed to measure both sustained attention and impulse control, and the number of correct responses and number of omission errors are presumed to assess sustained attention only (Sostek, Buchsbaum, & Rapoport, 1980). The limitations of CPT for clinical use include lack of standardized procedures, a dearth of normative data, and the expense and size of the apparatus (Barkley, 1990). Gordon (1983) developed a version of the CPT for clinical assessment purposes in a format that is portable, solid-state, and child proof. The procedures for the Gordon Diagnostic System require a child to press a button each time a specific, randomly presented numerical sequence occurs (e.g., a 2 followed by a 7). Normative data are available on children age 3 to 16 years; Gordon's version of CPTs has been found to have good test–retest reliability (Barkley, 1990; Gordon & Mettelman, 1988). The Gordon Diagnostic System has more evidence available regarding its psychometric properties than other versions of CPTs and has sufficient normative data to be useful in clinical practice (Barkley, 1990). However, Gordon cautions the user that there is roughly a 15% to 35% false-negative rate with this type of instrument (in which children who actually have ADHD score within the normal range on the test); in contrast, the false-positive rate is extremely low, with only 2% of normal children being classified as ADHD (Barkley, 1990; Gordon, Mettelman, & DiNiro, 1989; Trommer, Hoeppner, Lorber, & Armstrong, 1988).

Finally, measures of cognitive or mental flexibility have been shown to be sensitive to the effects of prenatal exposure to alcohol,and should be included in the neuropsychologic battery. For children in the 5- to 9-year age range, three measures from the Reitan–Indiana Neuropsychological Battery for Children (Reitan, 1979) may be used. These include the Category Test, the Color Form Test, and Progressive Figures. The Category Test is a modification of the version for older children and adults. It involves presentation of abstract visual stimuli to the child, requiring the child to use concept formation and to apply organizing principles in the performance of the procedure. As the principle underlying the correct response changes from one portion of the test to another, mental flexibility and the ability to use feedback is an important part of the measure. The Color Form Test involves showing the child a form with geometric shapes depicted in different colors. The child is told to draw an imaginary line connecting the shapes, first going to a figure with the same shape, and next going to a figure with the same color, and continuing this progression by alternating between shape and color. This test was designed to be analogous to the Trail Making Test, Part B, on the Halstead–Reitan Neuropsychological Test Battery for Children and Adults. The Progressive Figures Test is similar to the Color Form Test, but somewhat more difficult. The child is shown a page depicting a number of outlined geometric shapes. Within each figure is a small and different geometric shape. The task is to connect the large figures by finding a large figure that matches the small figure where the child is located. On both the Color Form and Progressive Figures tests, scores are reflected in both errors and time to completion (Selz, 1981).

Other measures of cognitive flexibility are found on the HRB for older children. The Category Test and Trail Making Test (Parts A and B) are measures of cognitive flexibility. The Category Test on the HRB is similar to that on the Reitan–Indiana Test, except that the stimuli are black and white rather than colored, and the response involves choosing a numeral from 1 to 4 rather than choosing a color. Otherwise, the concepts and principles required for completion of the task are the same. Trails A consists of 15 circles distributed over a sheet of paper and numbered from 1 to 15. The task involves connecting the circles with a pencil line as quickly as possible, in the correct sequence from 1 to 15. Part B consists of 15 circles numbered from 1 to 8 and lettered from A to G. The task involves connecting the circles and alternating between numbers and letters as the child proceeds in sequence through the task (Selz, 1981). The Stroop Color and Word Test (C. J. Golden, 1978) is a brief screening measure appropriate for Grades 2 and up. The child is presented a Word Page in which color words are printed in black ink, a Color Page with *X*s printed in color, and a Word–Color Page with words from the first page printed in colors from the second. The task requires the child to read the list of color names in which no name is printed in its matching color. In the Color–Word Task the child must name the color of ink in which the color names are printed.

Finally, the Wisconsin Card Sorting Test (Grant & Berg, 1948; Heaton, 1981) involves showing the child four cards whose figures are different in color, form, and number of elements (a red triangle, two green stars, three yellow crosses, and four blue circles). The child is handed a pack of 128 cards that vary according to color, form, and number, and is requested to sort each consecutive card from the pack and place it in front of one of the four stimulus cards where he or she thinks it belongs. After a choice is made, the child is told whether there responses are correct or incorrect and is asked to use that information to make as many correct choices as possible. The first sorting criterion is color, and any other choice is incorrect. After the child achieves 10 consecutive color choices, the sorting criterion is changed without the child being told, and color choices are then called wrong. The criterion for correct choices then changes to form, and finally, to number. The child must use cognitive flexibility in making shifts of cognitive strategy to achieve a correct response. The tests of cognitive flexibility discussed in this section are extremely complex, and more appropriate for the older elementary or adolescent youngster, with the exception of those few measures from the Reitan–Indiana battery. These measures tap an important cognitive process not typically measured in traditional intelligence tests or other psychological measures. Therefore, they remain an important part of the neuropsychological battery.

Assessment of Social–Behavioral Functioning

Given the frequency with which behavioral problems are associated with prenatal exposure to alcohol, it is important to conduct screening on all children with suspected FAS or FAE and to follow up with more detailed diagnostic assessment if necessary. Screening measures should sample a broad range of behavior and should be obtained from multiple informants (e.g., parents, teachers, and other significant caregivers). Obtaining information from multiple sources provides observations of the child's behavior across settings and can provide an indication of the pervasiveness and severity of symptomatology. Use of behavioral rating scales that are standardized and normed by age allows more direct comparisons with developmentally appropriate behavior at a given age. These scales also provide clear descriptions of behavior that are recognizable by parents and other caregivers, to minimize the risk of error. Rating scales such as the Child Behavior Checklist (Achenbach & Edelbrock, 1983), the Conners Parent/Teacher Rating Scales (Conners, 1989), and the Eyberg Child Behavior Inventory (Eyberg & Ross, 1978) are examples of standardized rating scales that may prove helpful. Each provides parent and teacher versions of the same scale so that symptoms can be surveyed across settings. Indices of either internalizing (e.g., anxiety, depressive, and social withdrawal), or externalizing (e.g., aggressive, hyperactive, and destructive) behavior in the clinically significant range for the child's age, may be an indicator for conducting a more detailed projective or behavioral evaluation in the clinic.

For a detailed discussion of these and other behavioral assessment measures, please refer to chapter 10, on assessment of children with ADHD, in this volume. It is recommended that all children with FAS or FAE at least be screened for behavioral problems at the time of the evaluation, with more detailed assessment being included in the batteries of those children who have symptoms suggestive of behavioral disorders.

The child with FAS or FAE is at risk for secondary emotional problems related to possible chaotic family environment and also the stress associated with primary disabilities in cognition, academic achievement, or activity levels or attention. The presentation of emotional symptoms can be reflective of either internalizing or externalizing problems, which must be assessed. Detecting the primary disability is the first step in understanding the child's secondary emotional responses; once detected, the intervention often can occur in the environment to reduce the stressors associated with the primary disability. For instance, if the child with FAS has significant learning problems and borderline intelligence, an evaluation that leads to special education services and an individualized educational program may reduce the stressors associated with the primary disability.

Primary emotional problems also may develop and may indicate the need for detailed projective or other evaluation of emotional status. Detailed discussion of emotional evaluation is beyond the scope of this chapter; however, consideration of emotional factors is extremely important in evaluating children with FAS or FAE.

Family Assessment

Assessment of the family environment may not be a direct goal of the assessment of a child with FAS, but attention to certain family considerations is important. Parents of children with FAS are at risk for emotional distress related to their own problems with alcoholism and the difficulties of caring for a child who is behaviorally challenging. One or both parents may display symptoms of depression and high levels of parenting stress. Use of a questionnaire survey, such as the Parenting Stress Index (Abidin, 1985) can provide information about the parents' perception of stress related to the child, the parenting role, and life stresses. A curvilinear relationship between risk and stress level has been suggested, with extremely low levels of stress and extremely high levels of stress being associated with greater risk for poor parenting outcome and possible child maltreatment. Clinical experience with parents of children who have been exposed to alcohol in utero indicates that these parents report less satisfaction with parenting and more negative perceptions of their child. These parental reports are true even when the caregiver is a foster parent or relative, rather than the biological parent. Clinical observations have also revealed that siblings are at greater risk of developing behavioral problems in a family with a child who has FAS. Obtaining information about the support network of the parent, current and past alcohol use or abuse, and the parents perceived stress in relation to the child with FAS, would facilitate interpretation of the test results on the child. Several environmental factors must be considered when interpreting the neuropsychological test results on a child exposed to cocaine or FAS. The socioeconomic status of the family, educational level of the parents, presence of environmental toxins, nutritional status of the child, custodial placement (i.e., with biological parents, extended family, or foster or adoptive parents), the quality of housing, postnatal drug exposure, and maternal mental health are all extremely important.

CASE STUDIES

Case 1

Referral question. Melissa is a 7-year-old youngster of American Indian descent who was referred for evaluation by her adoptive parents because of concerns about poor attention, hyperactivity, behavioral problems, and persistent academic difficulties involving written language, reading, and visuospatial skills. Melissa's biological mother abused alcohol throughout her pregnancy, and Melissa is thought to have both physical and neuropsychological features suggestive of FAS.

Background. Hospital records revealed that Melissa's biological mother received no prenatal care and abused alcohol throughout her pregnancy. This pregnancy was her fourth, and records indicated three older children had been removed from the parents' custody because of substance abuse by both biological parents. Melissa was carried to 32 weeks gestation, when she was born prematurely weighing 3 lb. 1 oz. She experienced respiratory arrest and required resuscitation immediately following delivery. Melissa was hospitalized in the neonatal intensive care unit for approximately 1 month following delivery and was discharged to the care of foster parents, who subsequently adopted her at age 3 years. Melissa never lived with her biological parents. Subsequent medical history revealed intermittent treatment for pneumonia, asthma, and other respiratory ailments. No other serious illnesses or injuries were reported. Visual acuity was decreased because of astigmatism and farsightedness, which was corrected with glasses. Auditory acuity was reported to be normal. Dysmorphic facial features include low-set, posteriorly rotated ears, a high arched palate, a flat mid-face and low nasal bridge, a long philtrum, a thin upper lip, a receding chin line, and micrognathia (see Figures 2–6, illustrating Melissa's physical features from infancy through 7 years of age). Figure 2 illustrates the dysmorphic feature of hirsutism (excessive hair), which was more apparent during infancy. Melissa also has remained below her expected growth rate in both height and weight. Muscle tone is altered, with hypotonia, poor fine and gross motor coordination, and decreased muscle tone in the face and oral cavity, as illustrated by open mouth posture and drooling.

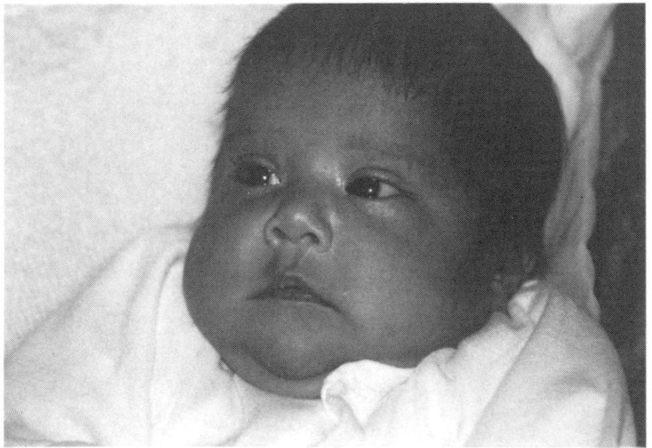

FIGURE 2. Melissa at age 2 months. Note hirsutism (excessive hair), low nasal bridge, micrognathia, and low-set, posteriorly rotated ears.

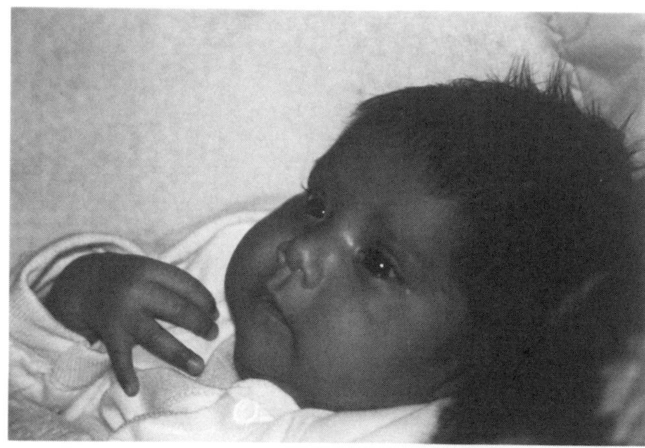

FIGURE 3. Melissa at age 2 months.

Developmental history. Developmental history revealed a consistent pattern of global developmental delays in all areas from early infancy to the present. Melissa has had repeated evaluations at the same center since 3 months of age. Early motor milestones were met at the expected age according to parent report (i.e., sitting at 6 months, crawling at 8 months, and walking at 13 months), but there has been a consistent pattern of gross motor and fine motor incoordination since that time. Melissa avoided preschool fine motor tasks such as block and puzzle construction, drawing, and coloring. She currently

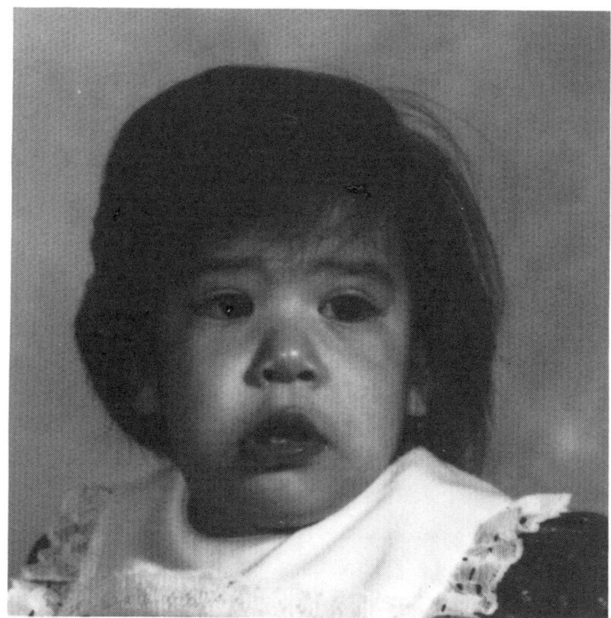

FIGURE 4. Melissa at age 2 years. Note elongated face, flat nasal bridge, elongated philtrum, thin upper lip, and micrognathia.

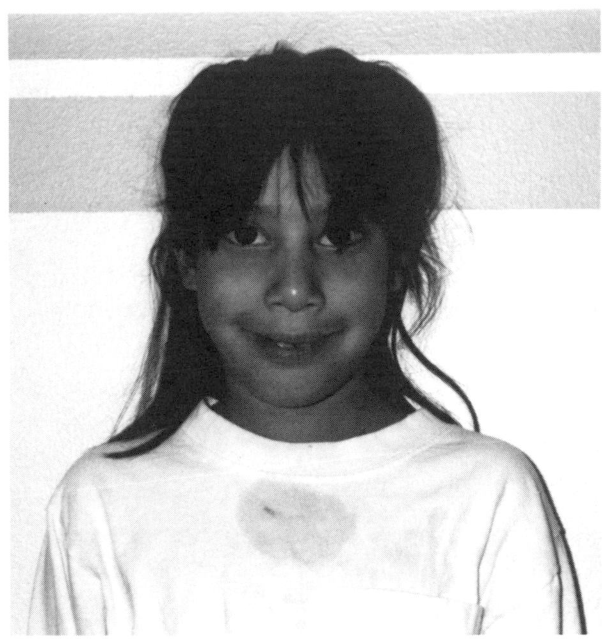

FIGURE 5. **Melissa at age 7 years. Note elongated philtrum and micrognathia.**

has an awkward pencil grasp and has difficulty with writing. She is awkward in dressing skills that involve manipulating buttons, snaps, and zippers. She continues to have decreased oral muscle tone with frequent open mouth posture and occasional drooling. Early speech–language skills were delayed, with meaningful single words being used initially at 18 months and phrases at 21–22 months. A significant receptive and expressive language delay has been noted consistently to the present, along with a moderate phonological or articulation disorder. Behavior development has been characterized by extreme hyperactivity, impulsivity, and distractibility compared with those in her peer group. In addition, there have been characteristics of low frustration tolerance, oppositional and defiant behavior, and aggressiveness. These behavioral characteristics lead to intervention with both parents and Melissa in a behavioral management program designed to increase compliance and decrease oppositional behavior.

School history. Melissa is currently placed in first grade. Melissa has not repeated a grade and has received no special education services to date; however, current school reports reveal that she is extremely below grade expectations in reading, spelling, and handwriting skills. Her mathematics skills are slightly below grade level. A major problem with school performance is related to extreme distractibility, short attention span, and hyperactivity. She is also difficult to manage behaviorally in that she disrupts the activities of the other children and is quite oppositional with teachers.

Family history. Melissa has lived with the same adoptive family since she was discharged from the hospital following her birth. She was first placed in the home with her adoptive parents as a foster child, and subsequently was adopted at age 3 years. Four biological children of the adoptive parents (ages 22, 21, 19, and 17 years) live out of the home at this time. Both parents have 14 years education and are employed. They have no history of substance abuse.

Key features. The history provides several key features that relate to current neuropsychological functioning in Melissa. The history of alcohol abuse in the biological mother during pregnancy is likely to be related to Melissa's dysmorphic physical features, developmental delays, ADHD symptoms, and oppositional–defiant behavioral symptoms. An important factor in her history is that her family since birth has been nurturing, stimulating, stable, and

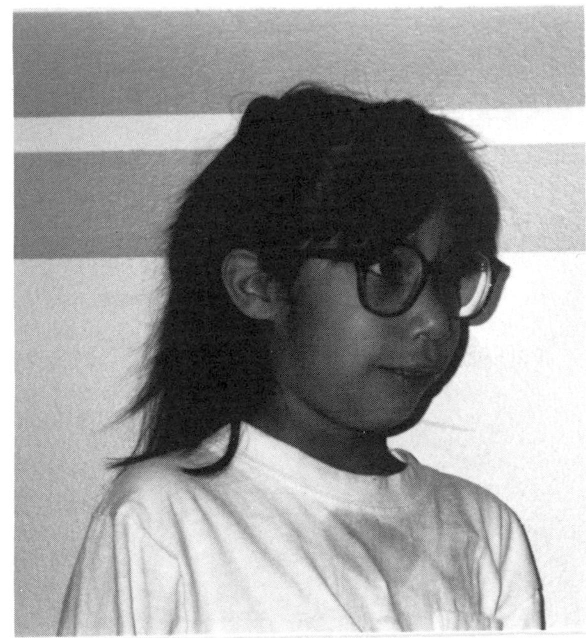

FIGURE 6. **Melissa at age 7 years, side view.**

free from major psychopathology and substance abuse. Finally, Melissa has had the advantage of early and consistent intervention through the form of infant stimulation, occupational therapy, physical therapy, speech–language therapy, and later educational tutoring to supplement the public school program.

Evaluation. Table 5 lists the assessment battery chosen for Melissa to address referral questions related to possible ADHD, academic difficulty, and behavioral problems.

Behavioral observations. Melissa presented as a small girl who wore glasses. Her behavior during evaluation was characterized by hyperactivity, impulsivity, distractibility, and extremely low frustration tolerance, which worsened as the testing session progressed. She often tested limits and required redirection to the tasks. However, her return to task was accompanied by complaints, pouting, and whining. Melissa's motor functioning was characterized by awkwardness on both a gross motor and fine motor level; her pencil grasp was inconsistent, and she had difficulty manipulating a pencil on writing tasks.

TABLE 5

Neuropsychological Test Battery for Melissa, Age 7 Years

Functional area	Measure
Cognitive	Wechsler Intelligence Scale for Children–Third Edition (WISC-III)
Academic	Woodcock–Johnson Psychoeducational Battery–Revised Tests of Achievement
Perceptual–motor	Bender–Gestalt Test for Young Children
	Motor Free Visual Perception Test
	Reitan–Indiana Neuropsychological Test Battery for Children
	Individual Performance Tests (Star; Concentric Squares; Matching Pictures, Figures, Vs)
	Tactual Performance Test
Motor–sensory	Purdue Pegboard Test
	Lateral Dominance Exam
	Sensory Perceptual Exam
	Electric Finger Tapping
Adaptive	Vineland Adaptive Behavior Scales
Cognitive flexibility	Reitan–Indiana Neuropsychological Test Battery for Children
	Category Test
	Progressive Figures
	Color Form Test
Memory	TPT: Localization and Memory
	WISC-III Digit Span
Sustained attention/vigilance	Gordon Diagnostic System
	Delay Task
	Vigilance Task
	Distractibility Task
Behavioral and emotional	Achenbach Child Behavior Checklist
	Parent Report
	Teacher Report
	Conners Questionnaire:
	Parent Rating
	Teacher Rating
	Parental Interview
	Structured Interview for *DSM-IV* Symptoms of Disruptive Behavior Disorders
	Projective Drawings

Note: DSM-IV = *Diagnostic and Statistical Manual of Mental Disorders* (4th ed.).

During the afternoon session, she became significantly more aggressive, trying to destroy test materials. She threw puzzles on the floor, hit the examiner, attempted to pull the examiner's hair, spit in the examiner's face, and kicked the examiner under the table. Time-out procedures were used with moderate success to decrease noncompliant behavior. Testing was accomplished with difficulty, although the current test results were felt to reflect Melissa's current level of functioning, given her behavioral problems and hyperactivity.

Test results. Exhibit 2 provides a summary of Melissa's evaluation results. Cognitively, Melissa's abilities fall in the borderline range, with a Full-Scale IQ from the third edition of the WISC (Wechsler, 1990) of 74 ± 7, Verbal IQ of 79 ± 8, and Performance IQ of 73 ± 9. Factor scores revealed a significantly higher Verbal Comprehension Index (87 ± 9) and Processing Speed Index (88 ± 13) than Perceptual Organization Index (70 ± 9) and Freedom From Distractibility Index (64 ± 12). Relative weaknesses were noted on tasks of mental arithmetic processing and ability to assemble parts to make a whole.

Academically, Melissa's performance was generally congruent with her expected achievement level, and there were no significant discrepancies between actual and expected achievement on any of the five areas evaluated with the Woodcock–Johnson battery (Woodcock & Johnson, 1989). Due to floor effects on the test, grade levels of functioning may be somewhat inflated. Informal academic screening revealed that Melissa still has difficulty writing some of the uppercase and lowercase alphabet, and was unable to write her last name. Because testing was conducted at the end of her first-grade year, her academic skills were felt to be delayed in comparison with her peer group.

Neuropsychological evaluation revealed evidence of impairment in several areas of neuropsychological functioning. Melissa's impulsivity, poor attention, distractibility, and hyperactivity significantly impaired her performance on age appropriate tasks. Perceptual–motor performance on the Tactual Performance Test was low average to borderline. Graphomotor and visuomotor integration task performance was impaired (Bender), although her performance on tasks requiring visual matching and discrimination was average (Matching Figures, Matching *V*s). She tended to complete graphomotor tasks quickly, but accuracy was diminished (Concentric Squares, Star). Melissa exhibited poor control of her pencil, and her drawings reflected difficulty with integration, spatial planning, and numerous distortions and rotations. Motor speed and dexterity was impaired bilaterally on a pegboard task, but more so on the left side on a finger tapping test. Sensory functions also were more impaired on the left side on tasks of finger localization and symbol discrimination. Tests of cognitive flexibility and problem solving were generally impaired as well. Memory functions were evaluated in a cursory fashion because of time constraints but they were impaired in both tactile–perceptual and auditory modalities.

Melissa was administered the Delay, Vigilance, and Distractibility tasks from the Gordon Diagnostic System. On the Delay task, she had a high number of responses, indicating high impulsivity and poor ability to suppress responding. Her number of correct responses on this task fell in the abnormal range for her age, resulting in an Efficiency Ratio of .39, which also is in the abnormal range. There was normal variability in her responses. Melissa's responses to this task indicate significant impulsivity and inability to delay responding. During the Vigilance task, Melissa complained of being bored and sometimes stared around the room rather than attending to the task. This resulted in a low number of correct responses (18) and a high number of errors of omission (27). Although motivational factors may account partially for this response pattern, there was evidence of significant difficulty sustaining and focusing her attention in a goal-directed manner. She made 28 errors of commission on the Vigilance task, which reflected her impulsivity in responding. Similar findings were noted on the Distractibility task, although her performance decreased even further. The results of this testing indicated that Melissa has significant impulsivity combined with deficits in sustained attention. She is prone to miss the salient aspects of a stimulus situation and has diminished capacity for self-control and inhibition of responding. Motivational factors also seem to interfere with per-

EXHIBIT 2

Summary of Melissa's Neuropsychological Evaluation Results

Cognitive

Wechsler Intelligence Scale for Children–Third Edition (WISC-III)

Verbal IQ	79 ± 8	Verbal Comprehension Index	87 ± 9
Performance IQ	73 ± 9	Perceptual Organization Index	70 ± 9
Full Scale IQ	74 ± 7	Freedom From Distractibility Index	64 ± 12
		Processing Speed Index	88 ± 13

Verbal	Scaled score	Performance	Scaled score
Information	7	Picture Completion	5
Similarities	8	Picture Arrangement	4
Arithmetic	1	Block Design	8
Vocabulary	8	Object Assembly	2
Comprehension	7	Coding	9
Digit Span	6	Symbol Search	6
		Mazes	7

Academic

Woodcock–Johnson Psychoeducational Battery–Revised

Test	Grade equivalent[a]	Standard score
Broad Reading	1.1	82
Broad Math	1.5	93
Broad Written Language	1.2	87
Broad Knowledge	K.4	80
Skills	1.2	82

Academic screening
- Identified all uppercase and lowercase alphabet
- Wrote 23/26 uppercase letters and 13/26 lowercase letters
- Identified numerals 1–20
- Identified 11 colors and 3 of 5 shapes

Perceptual–motor

Bender–Gestalt Test for Young Children
- Koppitz score: 18 (<5th percentile)
- Age equivalent: 4 years, 2 months to 4 years, 3 months

Motor Free Visual Perception Test
- Perceptual age: 5 years, 0 months
- Standard score: 72

Reitan–Indiana Neuropsychological Test Battery for Children
- Star
  - 16 s, Accuracy score: 2 (below average)
- Concentric Squares
  - 20 s, Accuracy score: 3 (below average)
- Matching Pictures
  - Raw score: 13 (1st percentile)
- Matching Figures
  - 27 s, 0 errors (60th percentile)
- Matching Vs
  - 38 s, 1 error (57th percentile)

EXHIBIT 2 (*Continued*)

Tactual Performance Test
Dominant hand: 6.9 min (30th percentile)
Nondominant hand: 5.2 min (30th percentile)
Both hands: 4.5 min (8th percentile)
Total time: 16.6 min (13th percentile)

Motor–sensory

Purdue Pegboard Test
Dominant hand: 7 pegs (<10th percentile)
Nondominant hand: 8 pegs (10th percentile)
Both hands: 7.5 pairs (25th percentile)
Reitan–Indiana Neuropsychological Test Battery:
Lateral Dominance Exam
Preferred right hand, eye
Mixed foot dominance
Sensory Perceptual Exam
No tactile, auditory, or visual suppressions on bilateral simultaneous stimulation
Tactile Finger Recognition
Right: 2 errors (51st percentile)
Left: 4 errors (<1st percentile)
Finger Symbol Discrimination:
Right: 6 errors (11th percentile)
Left: 8 errors (<1st percentile)
Tactile Form Recognition:
Right: 20 s, 0 errors
Left: 24 s, 0 errors
Electric Finger Tapping
Preferred hand (right): M = 36.2 (74th percentile)
Nonpreferred hand (left): M = 25.0 (7th percentile)

Cognitive flexibility

Category Test: 29 errors (17th percentile)
Progressive Figures: 36 s, 1 error (78th percentile for time)
Color Form: 15 s, 3 errors (86th percentile for time, <1st percentile for accuracy)

Memory

Tactual Performance Test
Memory: 1 (8th percentile)
Localization: 0 (<1st percentile)
WISC-III Digit Span
Standard score: 6

Sustained attention/vigilance

Gordon Diagnostic System
Delay task
Correct Responses: 32
Total Responses: 83
Efficiency Ratio: .39
Vigilance task
Total Correct: 18
Errors of Omission: 27
Errors of Commission: 28

(*continues*)

EXHIBIT 2 (*Continued*)

Distractibility task
Total Correct: 10
Errors of Omission: 35
Errors of Commission: 30

Adaptive

Vineland Adaptive Behavior Scales
Communication Domain: 77 ± 8
Daily Living Skills Domain: 57 ± 8
Socialization Domain: 65 ± 11
Adaptive Behavior Composite: 70 ± 6

[a]*The first (whole) number refers to grade level (K = Kindergarten), and the second number (after the decimal) refers to the month of that grade level (with 0–9 months possible).*

formance, and should be considered in interpretation of her performance on these tasks.

Linguistic ability was monitored throughout the evaluation. Melissa's rate of speech was normal, but her pronunciation of words was poor intermittently. She occasionally reversed words within sentences (e.g., "I going am to scream"). Her performance on the Aphasia Screening Exam from the Reitan–Indiana battery revealed deficits in academic performance (reading, spelling, and writing), visuomotor, and spatial performance (constructional dyspraxia, right–left confusion, and body dysgnosia).

Adaptive functioning was on a level commensurate with her intellectual ability and reflected relatively poor socialization and daily living skills compared with communication ability.

Perhaps the most significant findings of the current evaluation related to Melissa's behavioral functioning and symptoms of hyperactivity, impulsivity, and distractibility. Melissa meets criteria in the *Diagnostic and Statistical Manual of Mental Disorders*, fourth edition (*DSM-IV*, American Psychiatric Association, 1994) for severe ADHD-combined type according to both parent and teacher reports. Examination of age-normed behavioral checklists (Conners Questionnaire and Achenbach Child Behavior Checklist) revealed clinically significant concerns by parents and teacher regarding hyperactivity and conduct. Performance on the CPTs (Gordon Diagnostic System) supports this pattern of behavior, as well as the diagnosis of ADHD. Melissa also meets criteria for a significant oppositional defiant disorder characterized by defiant, oppositional, and argumentative behavior; deliberately annoying others; blaming others for her own mistakes; lying; taking things from others; and physical aggression. Melissa exhibits extremely low frustration tolerance and poor ability to inhibit impulsive behavior. When confronted with challenging or stressful situations, she typically acts out in an oppositional or aggressive manner. Projective drawings suggested feelings of insecurity and inadequacy, and low self-esteem.

Summary. Melissa is a 7-year-old girl of American Indian heritage with a history of fetal exposure to alcohol. Current intellectual and academic performance are mildly depressed (in the borderline range), and it is apparent that she is not developing basic reading, spelling, and written expression skills at the rate needed to keep up with requirements of her grade placement. She is struggling with academic demands even though she has had consistent academic and developmental intervention since infancy. Neuropsychological functioning is variable, with strengths noted on visual discrimination and matching. Weaknesses are noted on tasks of visuospatial organization and perception, graphomotor ability, verbal syntactic and articulation abilities, cognitive flexibility, and memory. However, the most significant impairment is associated with her severe distractibility, hyperactivity, and impulsivity, which significantly impair her performance across all tasks. She also exhibits oppositional and aggressive behavior, especially in response to frustration. Despite intensive efforts by her adoptive family to participate in behavior management training, Melissa continues to be out of control at times and very difficult to manage behaviorally. Her behavioral and ADHD symptoms result in significant functional impairment, poor peer relationships, and difficulty adjusting to both the home and school environments. Recommendations have been made for continued behavioral intervention, along with special education services (under the classification "Other Health Impaired") to provide an individualized educational program to address the effects of her severe ADHD, oppositional behavior, and decreased intellectual and academic functioning.

Case 2

Referral question. Case 2 involves a family of four offspring of alcoholic parents and whose mother abused alcohol throughout her four pregnancies. Because alcohol was the only substance abused, this case history provides an opportunity to examine the relative effects of maternal alcohol abuse on the four siblings. All four boys were referred for evaluation because of their father's concern about their development, academic progress, and behavioral functioning.

Background. Family history revealed that the mother is of Eskimo descent and the father is American Indian. Mr. and Mrs. H. lived in a remote area of Alaska, accessible only by boat or plane, until all four children were born. The four children are Jess (age 11 years), Larry (age 10 years), Tom (age 7 years), and George (age 5 years). The family moved from Alaska to the lower United States when the youngest child was 3 years of age. While in Alaska, both parents abused alcohol regularly, often to the extent of passing out and leaving the children unattended. The father stopped drinking several years ago, but the mother continued abusing alcohol to the present time. She leaves the home periodically for days at a time to join her friends in drinking sprees and then returns to the home to live with her husband and children. The father provides child care and discipline for the children and takes great interest in their schooling. The four children were described as well mannered and well disciplined, and the father's concerns related primarily to their learning abilities and attention.

With regard to physical features suggestive of FAS, the four boys had minimal dysmorphic signs. Each had large ears with deep folds and "railroad track" markings but otherwise did not have physical features of FAS.

Evaluation. Evaluation consisted of full psychological, educational, speech–language, and medical evaluations on each of the four boys. Table 6 provides a summary of the test battery, test results, and physical features on each child. A brief summary of their evaluation findings follows. Essentially, the two middle children (10-year-old Larry and 7-year-old Tom) had no intellectual, academic, behavioral, or ADHD symptoms that were remarkable. Both of the boys had average intelligence with academic achievement in the average range. Receptive and expressive language skills were within normal limits, and their medical–neurological examinations were free of pathology. Larry was diagnosed as having a major depressive disorder related to his attachment relationship with his mother and his feelings of sadness and rejection related to her frequent absences.

The eldest child, 11-year-old Jess, had low average intellectual functioning, though with a significant discrepancy between his WISC-III Verbal IQ of 94 ± 7 and his Performance IQ of 79 ± 9. Perceptual organization abilities were relative weaknesses on the WISC-III (Perceptual Organization Index = 80 ± 10), along with delayed or depressed visuomotor integration skills. Neuropsychological functioning was not impaired, with the exception of significantly impaired attention or concentration and hyperactivity. Jess met *DSM-IV* criteria for ADHD-combined type.

The youngest child, 5-year-old George, appeared to be the most severely affected of the four siblings. George's intellectual functioning was within the low average to borderline range, with a WPPSI-R Verbal IQ of 79, Performance IQ of 87, and Full-Scale IQ of 81. George was attending a Head Start program at the time of evaluation, and his preacademic skills were more similar to those of a 4-year-old than a 5-year-old child. He was unable to recite any letters of the alphabet or to count by rote. He could state his first and last name but was unable to write his

TABLE 6

Neuropsychological Comparisons Among Four Brothers With Fetal Alcohol Effects

Measure	Jess (11 years, 6 months)	Larry (10 years, 4 months)	Tom (7 years, 9 months)	George (5 years, 1 month)
Intellectual				
Wechsler Intelligence Scale for Children–Third Edition[a]				
Full-Scale IQ	86	100	107	81
Verbal IQ	94	98	110	79
Performance IQ	79	103	103	87
Verbal Comprehension Index	96	99	103	—
Perceptual Organization Index	80	107	107	—
Freedom From Distractibility Index	96	109	115	—
Processing Speed Index	96	99	104	—
Information	10	8	15	5
Similarities	8	12	7	9
Arithmetic	8	9	16	6
Vocabulary	10	9	10	8
Comprehension	9	10	10	4
Digit Span	10	14	9	—
Picture Completion	7	15	12	10
Picture Arrangement	6	7	8	—
Block Design	6	11	14	5
Object Assembly	7	11	6	12
Coding	7	8	12	—
Symbol Search	11	11	13	—
Mazes	—	6	13	8
Geometric Design	—	—	—	6
Academic				
Woodcock–Johnson Psychoeducational Battery–Revised				
Broad Reading				
Standard score	100	115	124	—
Discrepancy	+4	+15	+20	—
Broad Math				
Standard score	108	120	116	—
Discrepancy	+12	+20	+12	—
Broad Written Language				
Standard score	91	111	112	—
Discrepancy	−5	+11	+8	—
Visuomotor integration				
Bender–Gestalt Test				
Percentile	13th	10th	60th	—
Age	8-6 to 8-11 yrs	7-6 to 7-11 yrs	8-0 to 8-5 yrs	
Beery Developmental Test of Visual–Motor Integration				
Standard score	79	—	88	85
Percentile	8th	—	21st	16th
Neuropsychological functioning				
Category test: Total errors	38 (50%)			31 (59%)
TPT				
Total time	6.8 min (30%)			Discontinued
Memory	5 (58%)			—
Location	3 (17%)			—

TABLE 6 (*Continued*)

Measure	Jess (11 years, 6 months)	Larry (10 years, 4 months)	Tom (7 years, 9 months)	George (5 years, 1 month)
Finger Tapping				
RH	37.6 (25%)			182 (63%)
LH	28.2 (4%)			144 (<1%)
Seashore Rhythm: RS	25 (Rank 6)			—
Speech Perception: Errors	7 (18%)			—
Trail-Making A	22 s (43%)			—
Trail-Making B	21 s (89%)			—
Sensory Perceptual Exam	No suppressions on bilateral stimulation			—
Finger number writing errors				
RH	4 (14%)			—
LH	2 (89%)			—
Finger identification errors				
RH	0			—
LH	0			—
Tactile form recognition errors				
RH	1			—
LH	0			—
Lateral Dominance Exam				
Hand	R 7, L 0			R 7, L 0
Eye	R 1, L 1			R 0, L 2
Foot	R 2, L 0			R 2, L 0
Name Writing Speed				
RH	5 s (90%)			—
LH	24 s (31%)			—
Grip Strength				
RH	22 kg (81%)			—
LH	19 kg (80%)			—
Aphasia Screening	WNL			—
Purdue Pegboard				
RH	60%			
LH	25%			
BH	<10%			
Criteria for fetal alcohol syndrome				
Positive history of maternal alcohol abuse	Yes	Yes	Yes	Yes
Prenatal/postnatal growth retardation:	No	No	No	No
Birth weight	6 lb, 8 oz	$6^1/_2$–7 lb	$5^1/_2$ lb	~6 lb
Gestation	Term	Term	Preterm (4 wks)	Term
Postnatal growth	Normal	Normal	Normal	Normal
Altered morphogenesis				
Facies				
Microcephaly	No	No	No	No
Short palpebral fissures	No	No	No	Yes
Flat midface	Yes	Yes	Yes	Yes
Indistinct philtrum	No	No	No	No
Thin upper lip	No	No	No	No
Epicanthal folds	No	No	No	No
Low nasal bridge	No	No	No	No
Ear anomalies	Yes	Yes	Yes	Yes
Short nose	No	No	No	No

(*continues*)

TABLE 6 (*Continued*)

Measure	Jess (11 years, 6 months)	Larry (10 years, 4 months)	Tom (7 years, 9 months)	George (5 years, 1 month)
Micrognathia	No	No	No	No
Other physical findings				
Cardiac Defects	No	No	No	No
Pectus excavatum	No	No	No	No
External genital anomalies	No	No	No	No
Aberrant palmar crease	No	Yes	No	No
Hemangiomas	No	No	No	No
Ptosis, strabismus	No	No	No	No
Posteriorly rotated ears	No	No	No	No
Prominent palatine ridge	No	Yes	Yes	Yes
Central nervous system involvement				
Microcephaly	No	No	No	No
Increased irritability (infancy)	?	?	?	?
Altered muscle tone (↓)	No	Yes	No	Yes
Poor fine/gross motor coordination	Yes	Yes	No	Yes
Hyperactivity	Yes	No	No	No
Lowered IQ	Yes	No	No	Yes
Lowered speech/ language	No	No	No	Yes
Clinical diagnoses	ADHD Dysthymia FAE	Major depressive disorder FAE	?FAE	FAE

Note: RH = right hand; LH = left hand; ADHD = attention deficit hyperactivity disorder; FAE = fetal alcohol effects. Dashes indicate that data were missing.
[a]Note that George was administered the Wechsler Preschool and Primary Scale of Intelligence.

name. He correctly identified 9 of 10 colors presented to him, and 4 of 6 shapes, reflecting the educational instruction that had been provided to him in recent months. His performance on a test of receptive vocabulary (Peabody Picture Vocabulary Test–Revised) was in the borderline range with a standard score of 71, and age equivalent of 3 years, 7 months. Expressive single word vocabulary (i.e., picture labeling) was average. However, more detailed speech–language evaluation revealed mildly to moderately depressed receptive and expressive language abilities overall, with significantly depressed articulation–phonological development for age. Intelligibility of speech was only fair. Adaptive functioning (Vineland scales), as reported by the father, was in the low-average-to-borderline range, with an overall composite score of 78 ± 7 (4 years, 2 months).

Neuropsychological evaluation was variable. Measures of visual discrimination and matching were within the average range, but tasks measuring visuomotor integration were significantly below average in both accuracy and speed. Several of the Reitan–Indiana Neuropsychological Battery tasks (e.g., Tactual Performance Test and Sensory Perceptual Exam) were unable to be administered because of his lack of understanding of the task requirements. Behavior was characterized by short attention span and increased activity level for age, which interfered with test performance. Emotionally,

George was viewed as a very emotionally fragile boy who easily became overwhelmed by situations and needed support in order to regain his composure. He was distressed by separation from his father and needed a great deal of support and reassurance to participate in the evaluation, although his three brothers were nearby. George also seemed to lack information in several areas associated with early developmental stimulation, such as knowledge of nursery rhymes and familiarity with developmental toys. This may reflect differences in cultural interest or environmental deprivation. Overall, George was felt to be at high risk for development of academic, behavioral, and emotional problems.

Summary. In this case example of four siblings of a mother who abused alcohol throughout her four pregnancies, the findings are remarkable for normal developmental functioning in two of the four siblings, and only mild impairment (ADHD) in the eldest. The youngest child appears to have the most significant risk for developmental problems, and there is some suggestion of potential cumulative risk following long-term abuse of alcohol throughout subsequent pregnancies. Interestingly, there is a relative absence of the dysmorphic physical features often found in children who have suffered fetal exposure to alcohol. In this family situation, the environmental risk is a potent factor because of the mother's continuing use of alcohol and her frequent absence from the home. The father, although providing a stable home environment and providing for the physical needs of the children, is not perceived by the children as being as warm and nurturing as their mother when she is present. This makes the absence of the mother and her erratic parenting behavior more detrimental and more painful to her children. At least two of the children are suffering effects of depression significant enough to warrant intervention.

TREATMENT AND FOLLOW-UP OF SUBSTANCE-EXPOSED CHILDREN

Intervention strategies for substance-exposed children should focus on helping each child grow and develop to his or her own best potential. Early medical and developmental evaluations, followed by a neuropsychological evaluation in the early school years, provides a baseline, allows practitioners to inform parents and school professionals of the child's strengths and potential problem areas, and assists in treatment planning. Follow-up evaluations throughout the school years are important, with the goal of providing an individualized educational plan, special education services, and tutoring as needed.

Even though significant improvement in intelligence usually is not found in children with FAS, many behavioral changes can be brought about with proper treatment and a supportive environment. Symptoms of ADHD, social interaction problems, and behavioral problems are common in children exposed to alcohol. Behavioral management techniques can be helpful in coping with hyperactivity and behavioral problems, which are often noted during the early preschool years. Early educational planning, including a structured preschool experience, can help compensate for the poor attentional skills often noted in children with FAS or FAE.

According to S. E. Shaywitz et al. (1980), even in the absence of a diagnosis of FAS, children born to alcohol-abusing mothers may be at risk for delayed development, educational problems, and learning disabilities, although their overall intellectual development may be within normal limits. Furthermore, continued maternal or parental substance abuse may contribute to environmental problems experienced by the child that require the coordinated intervention of educational, psychological, health care, and social welfare services.

CONCLUSION

The public education effort surrounding FAS since it was identified in 1973 has resulted in widespread public awareness of the syndrome. In a 1985 national survey about 84% of the respondents associated heavy drinking with increased risk of adverse pregnancy outcomes. At the same time, however, FAS or FAE is now costing millions of dollars a year to treat and is among the leading known causes of mental retardation in the Western world (U.S. Department of Health & Human Services, 1990).

Although it is important to continue investigations into the etiology and neuropathology of FAS or

FAE, it is imperative that the knowledge gained thus far is used to prevent any further loss of human potential as a result of prenatal alcohol exposure. The successful prevention of FAS or FAE may depend not only on individual motivation for behavior change but also on changes in existing medical and therapeutic support systems to increase accessibility and availability of appropriate programs and services for the pregnant substance abuser (I. E. Smith & Coles, 1991). Approaches to prevention and intervention need to encompass multisystem, multilevel strategies, including public and professional education, the development of appropriate and accessible treatment resources for pregnant substance abusers, the development of effective educational and therapeutic interventions with women who are at risk, and early identification and intervention with the substance-exposed child (I. E. Smith & Coles, 1991).

References

Abel, E. L. (1979). Prenatal effects of alcohol on adult learning in rats. *Pharmacology, Biochemistry, and Behavior, 10*, 239–243.

Abel, E. L. (1982). In utero alcohol exposure and developmental delay of response inhibition. *Alcoholism: Clinical and Experimental Research, 6*, 369–376.

Abel, E. L. (1984a). Factors affecting the outcome of maternal alcohol exposure: I. Parity. *Neurobehavioral Toxicology and Teratology, 6*, 373–377.

Abel, E. L. (1984b). *Fetal alcohol syndrome and fetal alcohol effects*. New York: Plenum.

Abel, E. L., & Dintcheff, B. A. (1978). Effects of prenatal alcohol exposure on growth and development in rats. *Journal of Pharmacology and Experimental Therapy, 207*, 916–921.

Abel, E. L., & Sokol, R. J. (1987). Incidence of fetal alcohol syndrome and economic impact of FAS-related anomalies. *Drug and Alcohol Dependence, 19*, 51–70.

Abidin, R. R. (1985). *Parenting Stress Index manual* (3rd ed.). Odessa, FL: Psychological Assessment Resources.

Achenbach, T. M., & Edelbrock, C. (1983). *Manual for the Child Behavior Checklist and Revised Child Behavior Profile*. Burlington: University of Vermont, Department of Psychiatry.

Alpern, G. D., Boll, T. J., & Shearer, M. S. (1980). *Developmental Profile II*. Aspen, CO: Psychological Development Publications.

American Psychiatric Association. (1994). *Diagnostic and statistical manual of mental disorders* (4th ed.). Washington, DC: Author.

Aronson, M., Kyllerman, M., Sabel, K. G., Sandin, B., & Olegard, R. (1985). Children of alcoholics. Developmental, perceptual and behavioral characteristics as compared to matched controls. *Acta Paediatrica Scandinavica, 74*, 27–35.

Barkley, R. A. (1990). *Attention Deficit Hyperactivity Disorder: A handbook for diagnosis and treatment*. New York: Guilford Press.

Barkley, R. A., DuPaul, G. J., & McMurray, M. B. (1991). Attention deficit disorder with and without hyperactivity: Clinical response to three dose levels of methylphenidate. *Pediatrics, 87*, 519–531.

Barkley, R. A., Fischer, M., Newby, R., & Breen, M. (1988). Development of a multi-method clinical protocol for assessing stimulant drug responses in ADHD children. *Journal of Clinical Child Psychology, 17*, 14–24.

Bayley, N. (1993). *Bayley Scales of Infant Development: Second edition manual*. New York: Psychological Corporation.

Beery, K. E. (1982). *Revised administration, scoring, and teaching manual for the Developmental Test of Visual–Motor Integration*. Cleveland, OH: Modern Curriculum Press.

Bond, N. E., & Digiusto, E. L. (1976). Effects of prenatal alcohol consumption on open-field behavior and alcohol preference in rats. *Psychopharmacology, 46*, 163–168.

Bonthius, D. J., & West, J. R. (1990). Alcohol-induced neuronal loss in developing rats: Increased brain damage with binge exposure. *Alcoholism, 14*, 107–118.

Boyd, T. A., Ernhart, C. B., Greene, T. H., Sokol, R. J., & Martier, S. (1991). Prenatal alcohol exposure and sustained attention in the preschool years. *Neurotoxicology and Teratology, 13*, 49–55.

Bracken, B. A. (1984). *Bracken Basic Concept Scale*. New York: Psychological Corporation.

Brigance, A. H. (1978). *Brigance Diagnostic Inventory of Early Development*. North Billerica, MA: Curriculum Associates.

Brown, R. T., Coles, C. D., Smith, I. E., Platzman, K. A., Silverstein, J., Erickson, S., & Falek, A. (1991). Effects of prenatal alcohol exposure at school age: II. Attention and behavior. *Neurotoxicology and Teratology, 13*, 369–376.

Bruininks, R. H. (1978). *Bruininks–Oseretsky Test of Motor Proficiency*. Circle Pines, MN: American Guidance Service.

Bruininks, R. H., Woodcock, R. W., Weatherman, R. F., & Hill, B. K. (1984). *Scales of Independent Behavior.* Allen, TX: DLM Teaching Resources.

Chandler, L. S., Andrews, M. S., & Swanson, M. W. (1980). *Movement assessment of infants: A manual.* Rolling Bay, WA: Author.

Chavez, G. F., Cordero, J. F., & Beccerra, J. E. (1988). Leading major congenital malformations among minority groups in the United States, 1981–1986. *Journal of the American Medical Association, 261,* 205–209.

Chernick, V., Childiaeva, R., & Joffe, S. (1983). Effects of maternal alcohol intake and smoking on the neonatal electroencephalogram and anthropometric measurements. *American Journal of Obstetrics and Gynecology, 146,* 41–47.

Children's Memory Test. (1993). Odessa, FL: Psychological Assessment Resources.

Church, M. W. (1987). Chronic in utero alcohol exposure affects auditory function in rats and humans. *Alcohol, 4,* 231–239.

Church, M. W., & Holloway, J. A. (1984). Effects of prenatal ethanol exposure on the postnatal development of the brainstem auditory evoked potential in the rat. *Alcoholism: Clinical and Experimental Research, 8,* 258–265.

Clarren, S. K. (1986). Neuropathology in fetal alcohol syndrome. In J. R. West (Ed.), *Alcohol and brain development* (pp. 158–166). New York: Oxford University Press.

Clarren, S. K., Alvord, E. C., & Sumi, S. M. (1978). Brain malformations related to prenatal exposure to ethanol. *Journal of Pediatrics, 92,* 64–67.

Clarren, S. K., & Smith, D. W. (1978). The fetal alcohol syndrome: A review of the world literature. *New England Journal of Medicine, 298,* 1063–1067.

Colarusso, R. P., & Hammill, D. D. (1972). *Motor-Free Visual Perception Test.* Novato, CA: Academic Therapy Publications.

Coles, C. D., Platman, K., & Smith, I. (1988). Infant status, maternal perception and 6 month development in alcohol exposed infants. *Alcoholism: Clinical and Experimental Research, 12,* 339.

Coles, C. D., Smith, I. E., & Falek, A. (1987). Prenatal alcohol exposure and infant behavior; immediate effects and implications for later development. Children of alcoholics. *Advance in Alcohol and Substance Abuse, 6,* 87–104.

Coles, C. D., Smith, I. E., Fernhoff, P. M., & Falek, A. (1984). Neonatal ethanol withdrawal: Characteristics in clinically normal, nondysmorphic neonates. *Journal of Pediatrics, 105,* 445–451.

Coles, C. D., Smith, I. E., Fernhoff, P. M., & Falek, A. (1985). Neonatal neurobehavioral characteristics as correlates of maternal alcohol use during gestation. *Alcoholism: Clinical and Experimental Research, 9,* 454–460.

Coles, C. D., Smith, I. E., Lancaster, J. S., & Falek, A. (1987). Persistence over the first month of neurobehavioral alterations in infants exposed to alcohol prenatally. *Infant Behavior and Development, 10,* 23–37.

Conners, C. K. (1989). *Manual for Conners' Rating Scales (Conners' Teacher Rating Scales, Conners' Parent Rating Scales).* North Tonawanda, NY: Multi-Health Systems.

Darby, B. L., Streissguth, A. P., & Smith, D. W. (1981). A preliminary follow-up of 8 children diagnosed fetal alcohol syndrome in infancy. *Neurobehavioral Toxicology and Teratology, 3,* 157–159.

DeBeukeler, M. M., Randall, C. L., & Stroud, D. R. (1977). Renal anomalies in the fetal alcohol syndrome. *Journal of Pediatrics, 91,* 759–760.

Delis, D. C., Kramer, J., Kaplan, E., & Ober, B. A. (1994). *California Verbal Learning Test for Children.* New York: Psychological Corporation.

Druse, M. J., & Paul, L. H. (1988). Effects of in utero ethanol exposure on serotonin uptake in cortical regions. *Alcohol, 5,* 455–459.

Dunn, L. M., & Dunn, L. M. (1981). *Peabody Picture Vocabulary Test–Revised.* Circle Pines, MN: American Guidance Service.

Ernhart, C. B. (1991). Clinical correlations between ethanol intake and fetal alcohol syndrome. In M. Galanter (Ed.), *Recent developments in alcoholism: Vol. 9. Children of alcoholics* (pp. 127–150). New York: Plenum.

Ernhart, C. B., Wolf, A. W., Linn, P. L., Sokol, R. J., Kennard, M. J., & Filipovich, M. A. (1985). Alcohol-related birth defects: Syndromal abnormalities, intrauterine growth retardation, and neonatal behavioral assessment. *Alcoholism: Clinical and Experimental Research, 9,* 447–453.

Eyberg, S. M., & Ross, A. W. (1978). Assessment of child behavior problems: The validation of a new inventory. *Journal of Clinical Child Psychology, 7,* 113–116.

Folio, M. R., & Fewell, R. R. (1983). *Manual for the Peabody Developmental Motor Scales and Activity Cards.* Allen, TX: DLM Teaching Resources.

Fried, P. A., Watkinson, B., Grant, A., & Knight, R. A. (1980). Changing patterns of soft drug use prior to and during pregnancy: A prospective study. *Drug and Alcohol Dependence, 6,* 323–348.

Gallant, D. M. (1991). Fetal alcohol syndrome. In M. Galanter (Ed.), *Recent developments in alcoholism: Vol. 9. Children of alcoholics* (pp. 89–94). New York: Plenum.

Golden, C. J. (1978). *Stroop Color and Word Test: A manual for clinical and experimental users.* Chicago: Stoelting.

Golden, N. L., Sokol, R. J., Kuhnert, B. R., & Bottoms, S. (1982). Maternal alcohol use and infant development. *Pediatrics, 70*, 931–934.

Goldstein, G., & Arulananthan, K. (1978). Neural tube defect and renal anomalies in a child with fetal alcohol syndrome. *Journal of Pediatrics, 93*, 636–637.

Gordon, M. (1983). *The Gordon Diagnostic System.* Boulder, CO: Clinical Diagnostic Systems.

Gordon, M., & Mettelman, B. B. (1988). The assessment of attention: I. Standardization and reliability of a behavior based measure. *Journal of Clinical Psychology, 44*, 682–690.

Gordon, M., Mettelman, B. B., & DiNiro, D. (1989, August). *Are continuous performance tests valid in the diagnosis of ADHD/hyperactivity?* Paper presented at the 97th Annual Convention of the American Psychological Association, New Orleans, LA.

Graham, J. M., Hanson, J. W., Darby, B. L., Barr, H. M., & Streissguth, A. P. (1988). Independent dysmorphology evaluations at birth and 4 years of age for children exposed to varying amounts of alcohol in utero. *Pediatrics, 81*, 772–778.

Grant, D. A., & Berg, E. A. (1948). A behavioral analysis of degree of reinforcement and ease of shifting to new responses in a Weigl-type card-sorting problem. *Journal of Experimental Psychology, 38*, 404–411.

Greene, T., Ernhart, C. B., Martier, S., Sokol, R., & Ager, J. (1990). Prenatal alcohol exposure and language development. *Alcoholism: Clinical and Experimental Research, 14*, 937–942.

Gusella, J., & Fried, P. (1984). Effects of maternal social drinking and smoking on offspring at 13 months. *Neurobehavioral Toxicology and Teratology, 6*, 13–17.

Hanson, J. W., Streissguth, A. P., & Smith, D. W. (1978). The effects of moderate alcohol consumption during pregnancy on fetal growth and morphogenesis. *Journal of Pediatrics, 92*, 457–460.

Heaton, R. K. (1981). *Wisconsin Card Sorting Test manual.* Los Angeles, CA: Western Psychological Services.

Hesselbrock, V., Bauer, L. O., Hesselbrock, M. N., & Gillen, R. (1991). Neuropsychological factors in individuals at high risk for alcoholism. In M. Galanter (Ed.), *Recent developments in alcoholism: Vol. 9. Children of alcoholics* (pp. 28–29). New York: Plenum.

Huer, M. B. (1988). *The Nonspeech Test for Receptive/Expressive Language–Revised.* Wauconda, IL: Don Johnston Developmental Equipment.

Iosub, S., Fuchs, M., Bingol, N., & Gromisch, D. S. (1981). Fetal alcohol syndrome revisted. *Pediatrics, 68*, 475–479.

Iosub, S., Fuchs, M., Bingol, N., Rich, H., Stone, R. K., Gromisch, D. S., & Wasserman, E. (1985). Familial fetal alcohol syndrome: Incidence in Blacks and hispanics. *Alcoholism: Clinical and Experimental Research, 9*, 185.

Joffe, S., & Chernick, V. (1988). Development of the EEG between 30 and 40 weeks gestation in normal and alcohol-exposed infants. *Developmental Medicine and Child Neurology, 30*, 797–807.

Joffe, S., Childiaeva, R., & Chernick, V. (1984). Prolonged effects of maternal alcohol ingestion on the neonate electroencephalogram. *Pediatrics, 74*, 330–335.

Jones, K. L., & Smith, D. W. (1973). Recognition of the fetal alcohol syndrome in early infancy. *Lancet, 2*, 999–1001.

Jones, K. L., Smith, D. W., Ulleland, C. N., & Streissguth, A. P. (1973). Pattern of malformation in offspring of chronic alcoholic mothers. *Lancet, 1*, 1267–1271.

Kaufman, A. S., & Kaufman, N. L. (1983). *Kaufman Assessment Battery for Children: Interpretive manual.* Circle Pines, MN: American Guidance Service.

Koppitz, E. M. (1975). *The Bender–Gestalt Test for Young Children* (Vol. 2). New York: Grune & Stratton.

Kotkoskie, L. A., & Norton, S. (1988). Prenatal brain malformations following acute ethanol exposure in the rat. *Alcoholism: Clinical and Experimental Research, 12*, 831–836.

Kyllerman, M., Aronson, M., Sabel, K.-G., Karlberg, E., & Olegard, R. (1985). Growth and motor performance compared to matched controls. *Acta Paediatrica Scandinavica, 74*, 20–26.

Lambert, N. M., Nihira, K., & Leland, H. (1993). *AAMR Adaptive Behavior Scales—School* (2nd ed.). Austin, TX: PRO-ED.

Landesman-Dwyer, S., Keller, S., & Streissguth, A. P. (1978). Naturalistic observations of newborns: Effects of maternal alcohol intake. *Alcoholism, 2*, 171–177.

Landesman-Dwyer, S., Ragozin, A. S., & Little, R. E. (1981). Behavioral correlates of prenatal alcohol exposure: A four-year follow-up study. *Neurobehavioral Toxicology and Teratology, 3*, 187–193.

Lee, M., & Leichter, J. (1980). Effect of litter size on the physical growth and motivation of the offspring of rats given alcohol during gestation. *Growth, 44*, 327–335.

Lemoine, P., Harousseau, H., Borteyru, J. P., & Menuet, J.-C. (1968). Les enfants de parents alcoholiques: Anomalies observees, a propos de 127 cas [The children of alcoholic parents: Anomalies observed in 127 cases]. *Ouest Medical, 21*, 477–482.

Lipson, A. A., Yu, J. S., & O'Halloran, N. T. (1981). Alcohol and phenylketonuria. *Lancet, 1*, 717–718.

Little, R. E., Asker, R. L., Sampson, P. D., & Renwick, J. H. (1986). Fetal growth and moderate drinking in early pregnancy. *American Journal of Epidemiology, 123*, 270–278.

Little, R. E., Graham, J. M., & Samson, H. H. (1982). Fetal alcohol effects in humans and animals. *Advances in Alcohol and Substance Abuse*, *1*, 103–125.

Little, R. E., & Streissguth, A. P. (1982). *Alcohol: Pregnancy and the fetal alcohol syndrome*. Seattle: University of Washington.

Lochry, E. A., & Riley, E. P. (1980). Retention of passive avoidance and T-maze escape in rats exposed to alcohol prenatally. *Neurobehavioral Toxicology*, *2*, 107–115.

Majewski, F. (1981). Alcohol embryopathy: Some facts and speculations about pathogenesis. *Neurobehavioral Toxicology and Teratology*, *3*, 129–144.

Marcus, J. C. (1987). Neurological findings in the fetal alcohol syndrome. *Neuropediatrics*, *18*, 158–160.

Martin, J. C., Martin, D. C., Sigman, G., & Radow, B. (1977). Offspring survival, development and operant performance following maternal ethanol consumption. *Developmental Psychobiology*, *10*, 435–446.

Martin, J. C., Martin, D. C., Sigman, P., & Radow, B. (1978). Maternal ethanol consumption and hyperactivity in cross-fostered offspring. *Physiological Psychology*, *6*, 362–365.

McCarthy, D. (1972). *McCarthy Scales of Childrens' Abilities*. New York: Psychological Corporation.

Miller, M. W. (1986). Effects of alcohol on the generation and migration of cerebral cortical neurons. *Science*, *233*, 1308–1311.

Miller, M. W. (1987). Effect of prenatal exposure to alcohol on the distribution and time of origin of corticospinal neurons in the rat. *Journal of Comparative Neurology*, *257*, 372–382.

Miller, M. W. (1988). Effect of prenatal exposure to ethanol on the development of cerebral cortex: I. Neuronal generation. *Alcoholism: Clinical and Experimental Research*, *12*, 440–449.

Miller, M. W., & Dow-Edwards, D. L. (1988). Structural and metabolic alterations in rat cerebral cortex induced by prenatal exposure to ethanol. *Brain Research*, *474*, 316–326.

Nanson, J. L., & Hiscock, M. (1990). Attention deficits in children exposed to alcohol prenatally. *Alcoholism: Clinical and Experimental Research*, *14*, 656–660.

Newborg, J., Stock, J. R., & Wnek, L. (1984). *Battelle Developmental Inventory*. Allen, TX: DLM Teaching Resources.

Newcomer, P. L., & Hammill, D. D. (1988). *Test of Language Development Primary* (2nd ed.). Austin, TX: PRO-ED.

Norton, S., & Kotkoskie, L. A. (1991). Basic animal research. In M. Galanter (Ed.), *Recent developments in alcoholism: Vol. 9. Children of alcoholics* (pp. 95–117). New York: Plenum.

Osborne, G. L., Caul, W. F., & Fernandez, K. (1980). Behavioral effects of prenatal ethanol exposure and differential early experience in rats. *Pharmacology, Biochemistry and Behavior*, *12*, 393–401.

Oulette, E. M., Rosett, H. L., Rosman, P., & Weiner, L. (1977). Adverse effects on offspring of maternal alcohol abuse during pregnancy. *New England Journal of Medicine*, *297*, 528–530.

Pfeiffer, J., Majewski, F., Fischbach, H., Bierich, J. R., & Volk, B. (1979). Alcohol embro- and fetopathy. *Journal of Neuroscience*, *41*, 125–137.

Reitan, R. M. (1979). *Manual for administration of neuropsychological test batteries for adults and children*. Tucson, AZ: Neuropsychological Laboratory.

Riley, E. P., Lochry, E. A., & Shapiro, N. R. (1979). Lack of response inhibition in rats prenatally exposed to alcohol. *Psychopharmacology*, *62*, 47–52.

Riley, E. P., Lochry, E. A., Shapiro, N. R., & Baldwin, J. (1979). Response perseveration in rats exposed to alcohol prenatally. *Psychopharmacology, Biochemistry, and Behavior*, *11*, 513–519.

Riley, E. P., Shapiro, N. R., Lochry, E. A., & Broide, J. P. (1980). Fixed-ratio performance and subsequent extinction in rats prenatally exposed to ethanol. *Physiological Psychology*, *8*, 47–50.

Robe, B. R., Gromisch, D. S., & Iosub, S. (1981). Symptoms of neonatal ethanol withdrawal. In M. Galenter (Ed.), *Currents of alcoholism* (Vol. 8, pp. 485–493). New York: Grune & Stratton.

Rosett, H. L. (1980). A clinical perspective of the fetal alcohol syndrome. *Alcoholism: Clinical and Experimental Research*, *4*, 119–122.

Rosett, H. L., Snyder, P., Sander, L. W., Lee, A., Cook, P., Weiner, L., & Gould, J. (1979). Effects of maternal drinking on neonate state regulation. *Developmental Medicine and Child Neurology*, *21*, 464–473.

Rosvold, H. E., Mirsky, A. F., Sarason, I., Bransome, E. D., & Beck, L. H. (1956). A continuous performance test of brain damage. *Journal of Consulting Psychology*, *20*, 343–350.

Russell, M. (1991). Clinical implications of recent research on the Fetal Alcohol Syndrome. *Bulletin of the New York Academy of Medicine*, *67*, 207–222.

Sampson, P. D., Streissguth, A. P., Barr, H. M., & Bookstein, F. L. (1989). Neurobehavioral effects of prenatal alcohol: Part II. Partial least squares analysis. *Neurotoxicology and Teratology*, *11*, 477–491.

Sander, L. W., Snyder, P., Rosett, H. L., Lee, A., Gould, J. B., & Ouellette, E. (1977). Effects of alcohol intake during pregancy on newborn state regulation: A progress report. *Alcoholism*, *1*, 233–241.

Sattler, J. M. (1988). *Assessment of children* (3rd ed.). San Diego, CA: Author.

Scher, M. S., Richardson, G. A., Coble, P. A., Day, N. L., & Stoffer, D. S. (1988). The effects of prenatal alcohol and marijuana exposure: Disturbance in neonatal sleep cycling and arousal. *Pediatric Research, 24,* 101–105.

Selz, M. (1981). Halstead–Reitan Neuropsychological Test Batteries for Children. In G. W. Hynd & J. E. Obrzut. (Eds.), *Neuropsychological assessment and the school-aged child* (pp. 195–235). New York: Grune & Stratton.

Semrud-Clikeman, M., & Hynd, G. W. (1993). Assessment of learning and cognitive dysfunction in young children. In J. L. Culbertson & D. J. Willis (Eds.), *Testing young children* (pp. 167–187). Austin, TX: PRO-ED.

Shaywitz, B. A., Griffieth, G. C., & Warshaw, J. B. (1979). Hyperactivity and cognitive deficits in developing rat pups born to alcoholic mothers: An expanded model of fetal alcohol syndrome. *Neurobehavioral Toxicology, 1,* 113–122.

Shaywitz, S. E., Cohen, D. J., & Shaywitz, B. A. (1980). Behavior and learning difficulties in children of normal intelligence born to alcoholic mothers. *Journal of Pediatrics, 96,* 978–982.

Sheslow, D., & Adams, W. (1990). *Wide Range Assessment of Memory and Learning administration manual.* Wilmington, DE: Jastak Associates.

Smith, I. E., & Coles, C. D. (1991). Multilevel intervention for prevention of fetal alcohol syndrome and effects of prenatal alcohol exposure. In M. Galanter (Ed.), *Recent developments in alcoholism: Vol. 9. Children of alcoholics* (pp. 165–180). New York: Plenum.

Smith, I. E., Lancaster, J. S., Moss-Wells, S., Coles, C. D., & Falek, A. (1987). Identifying high-risk pregnant drinkers: Biological and behavioral correlates of continuous heavy drinking during pregnancy. *Journal of Studies on Alcoholism, 48,* 304–309.

Smith, K. J., & Eckardt, M. J. (1991). The effects of prenatal alcohol on the central nervous system. In M. Galanter (Ed.), *Recent developments in alcoholism: Vol. 9. Children of alcoholics* (pp. 151–164). New York: Plenum.

Sokol, R. J., & Abel, E. L. (1988). Alcohol-related birth defects: Outlining current research opportunities. *Neurotoxicology and Teratology, 10,* 183–186.

Sokol, R. J., & Clarren, S. K. (1989). Guidelines for use of terminology describing the impact of prenatal alcohol on the offspring. *Alcoholism: Clinical and Experimental Research, 13,* 597–598.

Sokol, R. J., Miller, S. I., & Reed, G. (1980). Alcohol abuse during pregnancy: An epidemiological study. *Alcoholism: Clinical and Experimental Research, 4,* 135–145.

Sostek, A. J., Buchsbaum, M. S., & Rapoport, J. L. (1980). Effects of amphetamine on vigilance performance on normal and hyperactive children. *Journal of Abnormal Child Psychology, 8,* 491–500.

Sparrow, S. S., Balla, D. A., & Cicchetti, D. V. (1984). *Vineland Adaptive Behavior Scales.* Circle Pines, MN: American Guidance Service.

Spohr, H. L., & Steinhausen, H. C. (1984). Clinical, psychopathological and developmental aspects in children with fetal alcohol syndrome: A four year follow-up study. In M. O'Connor (Ed.), *CIBA Foundation Symposium No. 105: Mechanisms of alcohol damage in utero* (pp. 197–217). London: Pitman.

Stein, Z., & Kline, J. (1983). Smoking, alcohol and reproduction. *American Journal of Public Health, 73,* 1154–1156.

Streissguth, A. P., Aase, J. M., Clarren, S. K., Randels, S. P., LaDue, R. A., & Smith, D. F. (1991). Fetal alcohol syndrome in adolescents and adults. *Journal of the American Medical Association, 265,* 1961–1967.

Streissguth, A. P., Barr, H. M., Martin, D. C., & Herman, C. (1980). Effects of maternal alcohol, nicotine, and caffeine use during pregnancy on infant development at 8 months. *Alcoholism: Clinical and Experimental Research, 4,* 152–164.

Streissguth, A. P., Barr, H. M., & Sampson, P. D. (1990). Moderate prenatal alcohol exposure: Effects on child IQ and learning problems at age 7 1/2 years. *Alcoholism: Clinical and Experimental Research, 14,* 662–669.

Streissguth, A. P., Barr, H. M., Sampson, P. D., Darby, B. L., & Martin, D. C. (1989). IQ at age 4 in relation to maternal alcohol use and smoking during pregnancy. *Developmental Psychology, 25,* 3–11.

Streissguth, A. P., Barr, H. M., Sampson, P. D., Parrish-Johnson, J. C., Kirchner, G. L., & Martin, D. C. (1986). Attention, distraction and reaction time at age 7 years and prenatal alcohol exposure. *Neurobehavioral Toxicology and Teratology, 8,* 717–725.

Streissguth, A. P., Bookstein, F. L., Sampson, P. D., & Barr, H. M. (1989). Neurobehavioral effects of prenatal alcohol: Part III. PLS analyses of neuropsychologic tests. *Neurotoxicology and Teratology, 11,* 493–507.

Streissguth, A. P., Clarren, S. K., & Jones, K. L. (1985). Natural history of the fetal alcohol syndrome: A 10-year follow-up of eleven patients. *Lancet, 2,* 85–91.

Streissguth, A. P., Herman, C. S., & Smith, D. W. (1978a). Intelligence, behavior, and dysmorphogenesis in the fetal alcohol syndrome: A report on 20 patients. *Journal of Pediatrics, 92,* 363–367.

Streissguth, A. P., Herman, C. S., & Smith, D. W. (1978b). Stability of intelligence in the fetal alcohol syndrome: A preliminary report. *Alcoholism: Clinical and Experimental Research*, 2, 165–170.

Streissguth, A. P., LaDue, R. A., & Randels, S. P. (1988). *A manual on adolescents and adults with Fetal Alcohol Syndrome with special reference to American Indians* (2nd ed.). Seattle: University of Washington.

Streissguth, A. P., Martin, D. C., & Barr, H. M. (1977, August). *Neonatal Brazelton assessment and relationship to maternal alcohol intake*. Paper presented at the 85th Annual Convention of the American Psychological Association, San Francisco, CA.

Streissguth, A. P., Martin, D. C., Barr, H. M., Sandman, B. M., Kirchner, G. L., & Darby, B. L. (1984). Intrauterine alcohol and nicotine exposure: Attention and reaction time in four-year-old children. *Developmental Psychology*, *20*, 533–541.

Streissguth, A. P., Martin, D. C., Martin, J. C., & Barr, H. M. (1981). The Seattle longitudinal prospective study on alcohol and pregnancy. *Neurobehavioral Toxicology and Teratology*, *3*, 223–233.

Stromland, K. (1987). Ocular involvement in the fetal alcohol syndrome. *Surveys in Ophthalmology*, *31*, 277–284.

Tanaka, H., Arina, M., & Suzuki, N. (1981) The fetal alcohol syndrome in Japan. *Brain Development*, *3*, 305–311.

Thorndike, R. L., Hagen, E. P., & Sattler, J. M. (1986). *Guide for administering and scoring the Standford–Binet Intelligence Scale* (4th ed.). Chicago: Riverside.

Trites, R. L. (1977). *Neuropsychological test manual*. Ottawa, Ontario, Canada: Royal Ottawa Hospital. (Available from Lafayette Instrument Company, P. O. Box 5729, LaFayette, IN 47903.)

Trommer, B. L., Hoeppner, J. B., Lorber, R., & Armstrong, K. (1988). Pitfalls in the use of a continuous performance test as a diagnostic tool in attention deficit disorder. *Developmental and Behavioral Pediatrics*, *9*, 339–346.

U.S. Department of Health and Human Services. (1990). *Seventh special report to the U.S. Congress on alcohol and health* (DHHS Publication No. ADM 281880002). Washington, DC: U.S. Government Printing Office.

Warner, R. H., & Rosett, H. L. (1975). The effects of drinking on offspring: An historical survey of the American and British literature. *Journal of Studies of Alcoholism*, *36*, 1395–1420.

Wechsler, D. (1989). *Manual for the Wechsler Preschool and Primary Scales of Intelligence–Revised*. New York: Psychological Corporation.

Wechsler, D. (1990). *Wechsler Intelligence Scale for Children–Third edition manual*. New York: Psychological Corporation.

Wechsler Individual Achievement Test manual. (1992). New York: Psychological Corporation.

Weiner, L., & Morse, B. A. (1988). Clinical perspectives and prevention. In I. J. Chasnoff (Ed.), *Drugs, alcohol, pregnancy, and parenting* (pp. 127–148). Dordrecht: Kluwer.

Weiner, L., Rosett, H. L., Edelin, K. C., Alpert, J. J., & Zuckerman, B. (1983). Alcohol consumption by pregnant women. *Obstetrics and Gynecology*, *61*, 6–12.

West, J. R. (1987). Fetal alcohol-induced brain damage and the problem of determining temporal vulnerability: A review. *Alcohol and Drug Research*, *7*, 423–441.

West, J. R., & Pierce, D. R. (1986). Perinatal alcohol exposure and neuronal damage. In J. R. West (Ed.), *Alcohol and brain development* (p. 120). New York: Oxford University Press.

Wisniewski, K., Dambska, M., Sher, J. H., & Qazi, Q. (1983). A clinical neuropathological study of the fetal alcohol syndrome. *Neuropediatrics*, *14*, 197–201.

Woodcock, R. W., & Johnson, M. B. (1989). *Woodcock–Johnson Psychoeducational Battery–Revised: Tests of Achievement*. Allen, TX: DLM Teaching Resources.

Zimmerman, I. L., Steiner, V. G., & Pond, R. E. (1992). *Preschool Language Scale–3*. New York: Psychological Corporation.

Zuckerman, B. S., & Hingson, R. (1986). Alcohol consumption during pregnancy: A critical review. *Developmental Medicine and Child Neurology*, *28*, 649–661.

(Appendix follows)

APPENDIX

Achievement Readiness

Child's Name: ____________________________

Birthdate: __________________ Age: _____

UPPER CASE ALPHABET

	Matched	Identified	Wrote
A B C			
D E F			
G H I			
J K L			
M N O			
P Q R			
S T U			
V W X			
Y Z			

LOWER CASE ALPHABET

	Matched	Identified	Wrote
a b c			
d e f			
g h i			
j k l			
m n o			
p q r			
s t u			
v w x			
y z			

NUMBERS

	Matched	Identified	Wrote
1 2 3			
4 5 6			
7 8 9			
10 11 12			
13 14 15			
16 17 18			
19 20			

COLORS

	Matched	Identified
red blue green		
yellow pink white		
orange black brown		
purple gray		

SHAPES

	Matched	Identified
Circle Square		
Triangle Rectangle		
Diamond Other		

States Name: First _____ Last _____
Writes Name: First _____ Last _____
Knows Address: Street _____ City _____ State ____
Knows Phone Number: _____
Knows Parent's Name: Mother _____ Father _____

Recites: Alphabet _____ (Sings) _____
Counts by Rote: 1-20 _____
Number-Object Correspondence: 1-10 _____

Section III

ISSUES IN FORENSIC NEUROPSYCHOLOGY AND PSYCHOTHERAPY

CHAPTER 13

A PRACTICAL GUIDE TO FORENSIC NEUROPSYCHOLOGICAL EVALUATIONS AND TESTIMONY

Russell L. Adams and Eugene J. Rankin

A forensic neuropsychological evaluation is one that is completed in connection with legal proceedings. Clinical neuropsychologists are increasingly being asked to play the role of an evaluator during such proceedings (Doerr & Carlin, 1991).

Although neuropsychologists are involved in both civil and criminal cases, the focus of this chapter is on civil cases, because civil cases are much more likely to involve a neuropsychologist. Results of a recent survey (Putnam & DeLuca, 1990) obtained from 872 members of Division 40 (Clinical Neuropsychology) of the American Psychological Association (APA) indicated that approximately 22% of the respondents in private practice and 11% of the respondents in primary employment settings received civil case referrals involving personal injury. Far less common, however, were referrals involving criminal cases, which made up only 3.5% of the respondents. Other types of civil cases were received by approximately 4.5% of those responding.

OVERVIEW

In this chapter we first discuss why neuropsychologists are increasingly involved in forensic examinations, especially in cases involving traumatic brain injury. Typical referral issues are presented. A detailed discussion follows in which certain legal terms are defined and information concerning the burden of proof is presented. Suggestions for interacting actively with the referring attorney on initial contact are given. Suggestions for writing the neuropsychology report are presented, along with guidelines for presenting this information to the attorney either in person or on the phone.

We also explain the deposition and trial process, specifically outlining a discovery or trial deposition. Frequent questions asked of neuropsychologists are listed. Suggestions on how to respond to attorneys' questions on direct examination, cross-examination, redirect, and recross examination also are made. A description of the trial itself is then presented. Specific cross-examination ploys that opposing attorneys use are described, as well as some appropriate ways of dealing with such ploys. Different types of objections to testimony, such as irrelevant, immaterial, no foundation laid, form of the question, and so on, are presented.

Because integrity is probably the single most important characteristic of an expert witness, issues surrounding integrity in forensic testimony are presented, together with a detailed description of the APA Ethics Code as applied specifically to forensic cases. We then discuss the training and education a neuropsychologist should have to be properly credentialed to testify in court according to the guidelines of APA's Division 40. The vocational implications that neuropsychological findings can have in determining damages are then discussed. Finally, the

Special recognition and thanks are given to R.E.L. Richardson, a professor of mental health law at the University of Oklahoma, for his careful reading of this chapter and the suggestions he made.

issue of malingering in forensic examination is discussed, and suggestions for detecting dissimulation are offered.

Personal Injury Cases

Personal injury cases involving head injury caused by motor vehicle accidents probably make up the most common single type of case seen by neuropsychologists. The large numbers are due in part to the frequency of motor vehicle accident injuries entering the judicial system. In motor vehicle accidents, one party is usually characterized as the victim and the other as the responsible party. Neuropsychological measures of higher cortical functions can be critically important in answering a variety of questions, including the following: Is the client able to work at his or her previous job since the injury? Is the client capable of working at all? Is the client capable of returning to school or college? Has the client suffered a decrement in his or her ability to concentrate, pay attention, or solve problems? Is the client's planning and executive abilities impaired? Is the client's emotional functioning impaired? Is the client's personality different?

Although magnetic resonance (MR) imaging, computed tomography (CT) scanning, electroencephalography (EEG), and neurological examinations may or may not show "brain injury," the question that most concerns jurors is what the injury means relative to the patient's day-to-day functioning. A neuropsychological examination can translate deficits from the injury into concrete behaviors that the jury can understand (Sbordone, 1991). For example, some patients show anatomical changes of the brain and still are able to function at a high level. In our laboratory, we have evaluated medical students who had suffered brain injury documented by CT scans but were still able to successfully perform in medical school after rehabilitation. Other patients may show little or no damage on formal biomedical tests, yet are unable to function at the same level they performed before the accident. In the last case, the attorney would prefer a neuropsychological evaluation to a neurological evaluation or other biomedical testing because of the real-world implications gleaned from the neuropsychological evaluation.

The importance placed on neuropsychological evaluations in the legal arena is a relatively new development as the science and practice of neuropsychology become better known. The number of such referrals seems to have been increasing markedly in recent years as attorneys and others in the judicial system have become more aware of what neuropsychologists have to offer in such cases. Not only do attorneys seek the advice of neuropsychologists to support their particular positions, judges also seek neuropsychological counsel. Two reasons for this increase include the large normative samples used to compare patient performance across different participants of similar age and education and the ability to compare current performance with estimated premorbid performance within the same individual.

Data gathered within the context of a neuropsychological evaluation are frequently compared with large normative samples of patients of specified ages, educational levels, or both (Heaton, Grant, & Matthews, 1991). Being able to accurately estimate the expected performance of a client with a traumatic brain injury with normative comparisons results in less subjective interpretations. Although subjectivity is inevitable in the judicial system, objective data, such as normative comparisons, are more acceptable to the jury and the trier of fact. There are many neuropsychological measures with sound normative samples with which to compare one's findings, including the Halstead tests (Heaton et al., 1991), the Wechsler Adult Intelligence Scale–Revised (WAIS-R; Wechsler, 1981), the Wechsler Memory Scale–Revised (WMS-R; Wechsler, 1987), the Wide Range Achievement Test–Revised (Jastak & Wilkinson, 1984), and the Multilingual Aphasia Examination (Benton & Hamsher, 1989), to name a few.

In addition to normative comparisons, intraindividual comparisons of current performance with premorbid indexes are equally important when inferring a decline in cognitive functioning. For example, comparing neuropsychological test results with American College Test scores or Scholastic Aptitude Test scores can be helpful in quantifying the degree of change. American College Test scores, Scholastic Aptitude Test scores, or both are frequently available because one of these tests is usually required for admission to college. Granted, there are problems with such comparisons, but test-based comparisons are certainly more objective and thus more reliable than doing comparisons without formal neuropsychological tests. In addition, quantitative estimates of premorbid functioning can be obtained from demographic prediction formulas such as the Barona regression formula (Barona, Reynolds, & Chastain, 1984) or the National Adult Reading Test (Nelson, 1982). A recent suggestion of combining demographic predicting formulas with certain "hold tests" of the WAIS-R has been particularly promising (Krull, Scott, & Sherer, 1994). Finally, in certain instances, having the patient perform ecologically valid activities, such as telling time, using the telephone, balancing a checkbook, remembering a shopping list, and recognizing road signs can be helpful and easily communicated to a jury or trier of fact.

Typical Neuropsychological Referrals

The types of cases seen by neuropsychologists differ greatly, and no two cases are exactly alike. However, there are certain types of cases that are more frequently seen, and these are the ones in which neuropsychologists have more to offer (McMahon, 1983). The following are some examples of specific cases in certain categories referred to our neuropsychology laboratory. For the interested reader, a list can be found in Golden and Strider (1986).

1. Personal injury cases
   - Motor vehicle accidents in which the victim with a traumatic brain injury was a passenger, driver, or pedestrian
   - Falls or fights in which traumatic brain injury occurred or is suspected of having occurred
   - A severe head injury caused by a faulty piece of equipment
2. Product liability cases
   - Patients exposed to certain neurotoxic chemicals (e.g., perchlorethylene, trichloroethylene, hydrogen sulfide, solvents)
   - Carbon monoxide poisoning caused by a leaky heating system
   - Seatbelt or safety equipment malfunction resulting in brain injury
3. Medical malpractice suits
   - Inappropriate use of anesthesia
   - Brain injury suffered at birth
   - Problems occurring during the surgery itself that resulted in brain dysfunction (i.e., an otolaryngologist penetrating the roof of the ethmoid sinus during sinus surgery and creating an encephalocele involving the frontal lobe)
4. Workers' compensation cases
   - Client suffered a traumatic brain injury as a direct result of his or her employment
   - Chronic exposure to neurotoxic chemicals in the workplace
5. Social security determination and other disability assessment
   - Client suffered some presenile dementia and was claiming inability to be gainfully employed
   - Client claimed inability to work due to some type of brain injury
6. Inability to make a contract or will
   - Family members or other claimed that the patient was not competent to make a will or enter into a contract and an attempt to void a will in which he or she gave all of his or her assets to a nonfamily member
   - An elderly patient who was demented sold her house at a price well below market value.

Burden of Proof in a Lawsuit

The plaintiff is the party filing the lawsuit and the defendant is the party being sued. Because the plaintiff is bringing a matter to the attention of the court, the burden of proof rests with the plaintiff. *Burden of proof* simply means that the plaintiff must prove before the trier of fact that the defendant did something wrong and that the plaintiff was harmed because of it. *Damages* are the monetary cost of the wrong committed. In cases involving neuropsychological testimony, damages usually result from loss of wages, decreased ability to think clearly and solve problems, or decreased ability to interact with others or perform activities of daily living.

The burden of proof differs greatly in criminal cases and civil cases. In criminal cases (e.g., first degree murder), the state must prove the case beyond a reasonable doubt. In civil cases, the plaintiff must prove the case to a less strict standard. The standard used normally is "the preponderance of evidence." The preponderance of evidence standard means that a fact is more probably true than not true.

A crucial final question frequently asked of the clinical neuropsychologist during his or her testimony is stated by the examining attorney as follows: "Within a reasonable degree of neuropsychological certainty, what is your opinion of this case?" The term within a reasonable degree of neuropsychological certainty simply means that after weighing all the facts, the neuropsychologist believes that the issues at hand are true. Another way of saying this is that the neuropsychologist believes that most fully trained and experienced clinical neuropsychologists would state that the issue at hand is true. This, of course, leaves room for others who are equally trained to legitimately disagree.

SUGGESTED APPROACH TO FORENSIC NEUROPSYCHOLOGICAL EVALUATIONS

In this section we outline briefly various stages of involvement in neuropsychological forensic cases, beginning with the initial telephone contact, proceeding through preparation of the neuropsychological report, and concluding with telephone feedback to the attorney.[1] The following discussions are meant as guidelines that can and should be adapted depending on the case involved. Deviation from these suggestions in no way suggests errors by the individual conducting the examination.

Initial Telephone Contact

The attorney will call or personally visit the neuropsychologist to briefly describe the facts of the case and solicit the neuropsychologist's involvement. Note that even at this stage of involvement, the "facts" presented may not be a balanced picture. For ease of discussion in this section, the case involved is that of a traumatic brain injury caused by a motor vehicle accident. The neuropsychologist would likely obtain the following information from the attorney: (a) a brief description of the accident and the parties, dates, and vehicles involved; (b) periods of unconsciousness, if any; (c) involvement of emergency medical service or emergency room personnel; (d) summary of hospital records, including other neuropsychological evaluations that might have been completed; (e) depositions taken in the case to date; (f) the attorney's initial "theory of the case" if formulated; (g) any discovery deadlines (i.e., time limitations imposed by the court for completion of the neuropsychological evaluation and other information-gathering procedures); and (h) attorney asks the neuropsychologist whether a neuropsychological evaluation is necessary (the neuropsychologist occasionally might want to defer answering until the records are reviewed, although this depends on the case).

Information Discussed With the Attorney

If the case is appropriate and the neuropsychologist agrees to be involved, the following issues should be covered with the referring attorney:

1. The attorney should be informed about the nature of the neuropsychological evaluation and the time involved. If extensive testing time is required, this issue should be explained in advance to the employing attorney. Some patients are slow in completing testing and may require extra time, or testing may require several days to complete. This issue is particularly important if the referring attorney represents the defense in the case. On the other hand, the plaintiff's attorney can usually gain the patient's cooperation more easily and have the patient return for continued evaluation if needed.
2. The attorney should be told of the neuropsychologist's fee schedule for the evaluation, interviews of significant others, and review of medical and other records (including depositions if necessary). Deposition and trial testimony should be discussed at the outset to avoid confusion. Issues surrounding canceled appointments should also be discussed. Attorneys are notorious for scheduling patients and then the patient does not show up on the scheduled date. The financial ramifications of late cancella-

[1]The material presented in this section represents Russell L. Adams's own approach and opinions. Others may have somewhat different but equally valid approaches and opinions.

tions of evaluations or depositions need to be explained, and the amount of advance notice for the cancellations needs to be specified.

3. Attorneys should be informed that the neuropsychologist will keep precise records of the amount of time involved in the case and provide that information to the attorney.
4. Agreement should be reached on when bills will be submitted and paid. Cases can drag out for months or even years. If attorneys are aware of the neuropsychologist's policies prior to his or her involvement in the case, they are usually willing to follow the policies, especially if the policies are in writing.
5. The neuropsychologist's availability for testing and deposition in the near future should be discussed.
6. The attorney should be asked for all medical records, ambulance records, other neuropsychological records including the raw test data, and high school and college records.
7. If multiple attorneys are working together with the employing attorney, the neuropsychologist should find out which single attorney will coordinate contacts with him or her. Some legal cases can involve multiple attorneys, multiple parties, or both. The neuropsychologist, if he or she is not careful, can become involved in disputes among different parties, all of whom are presumably on the same side of the case.
8. The neuropsychologist should indicate to the attorney that he or she wants to talk with a significant other in the patient's life (spouse, parent, etc.), school officials, employers, or others as appropriate.
9. Scheduling of the patient is best done by the referring attorney's office as opposed to having the patient call the neuropsychologist's office. By using this approach, the attorney knows all the problems associated with scheduling and can coordinate with the opposing attorney if problems arise.
10. The specific referral question should be obtained from the attorney so that it can be addressed specifically in the neuropsychological report. The neuropsychologist might request (possibly at the conclusion of the conference) that the attorney specifically outline her or his particular needs or goals in a written memorandum to the neuropsychologist. This will help the attorney focus more particularly on his or her needs, and it will create better communication between the attorney and the neuropsychologist. The memorandum should also discuss the issue of the neuropsychologist's fees. The memorandum may be very important if the attorney does not like the neuropsychologist's findings, does not win the case, or drops the case.

Preparation for Neuropsychological Evaluation and the Neuropsychological Examination Itself

1. The neuropsychologist should read the relevant background information and medical records, as well as be aware of the facts of the case before the parties arrive.
2. The neuropsychologist should ask the patient his or her understanding of the reason for the evaluation and clarify any misunderstandings. Any limits to confidentiality should be explained. The neuropsychologist's role in the case should be explained. What will happen to the neuropsychological reports that are written and the fact that anything the patient says may appear in the neuropsychological report should be made clear.
3. Whenever possible, the patient and the patient's significant other should be interviewed as close in time as possible so that they cannot "compare notes." However, this arrangement is not always possible.
4. Behavioral observation of the patient by the neuropsychology technician, neuropsychologist, or both is especially important in forensic cases, particularly if malingering or less-than-candid responses is suspected. Writing down any inconsistencies, hesitancies of the patient, and so on, is important.
5. Test selection should be made with due consideration given to the previous tests given to the patient. If a patient has been given particular neuropsychological tests and the results are available to the neuropsychologist, current tests can be

used to plot changes in the patient's recovery. Issues such as practice effects need to be kept in mind. Normally, it is advisable in forensic cases to use well-standardized neuropsychological tests and test batteries containing appropriate age and education norms. This allows the opposing side to check the neuropsychologist's work with other knowledgeable neuropsychologists. Be careful to avoid short forms, shortcuts, or screening tests because time-saving measures may have to be defended in a deposition or court appearance. Defending shortcuts can be problematic even though they may sometimes be necessary. Record the patient's actual responses to test questions and interview questions as completely as possible. These notes can be crucial.

Neuropsychological Report

The neuropsychological report represents the neuropsychologist's assessment, conclusions, and answers to the referring attorney's question. Not only will the neuropsychological report be given to the employing attorney, but it also may be read by the opposing attorney, other expert witnesses, and the trier of fact. The neuropsychological report likely will be the basis for the majority of questions asked by the opposing side during the deposition or trial. Because attorneys do not normally understand the nuances of neuropsychological testing, they will usually concentrate the majority of their questions on the summary and conclusions section of the neuropsychological report.

The neuropsychological report should be balanced. Filtering out detrimental information to the employing attorney's case is specifically inappropriate. Of course, not all information collected during the course of the evaluation will end up in the report. At the same time, any systematic effort to present a lopsided argument diminishes the report's credibility.

Attorneys occasionally but infrequently ask a neuropsychologist to change a particular part of a finished report that is unfavorable to their case. To change a report under these circumstances (except when there are obvious mistakes of fact) would be inappropriate.

Vocational Implications of Neuropsychological Testing

Another issue concerns the vocational impact of a person's deficits. Frequently, there is a question about what impact the patient's neuropsychological deficits have on his or her job performance or on his or her ability to be employed. In addition, the safety of the patient in the workplace is another important question. For example, the patient may work around heavy equipment, climb ladders, or work on an assembly line.

Obtaining a formal job description is helpful in this regard. Questioning the patient about his or her specific job duties as well as talking to significant others or the employer directly may be necessary. Relating the patient's neuropsychological deficits directly to his job or her performance may need to be undertaken. Exhibit 1 gives an example of how this might be accomplished (Thomas, 1990).

Telephone Feedback to an Attorney

Telephone contact with the attorney after the neuropsychological evaluation is completed is helpful. The neuropsychologist can explain to the attorney any information in the report that was unclear. After seeing the report, the employing attorney may or may not want to use the report in the presentation of his or her case. If the neuropsychological report is not favorable to the attorney's client, the attorney will frequently not call the neuropsychologist as a witness in the deposition, court proceedings, or both. If the neuropsychologist is always called to testify after he or she evaluates a patient, one would question the objectivity of that neuropsychologist.

On receipt of the report, the attorney may ask the neuropsychologist to assist in developing a life care plan for that client. A life care plan delineates the projected care the patient would require for the rest of his or her life. Such care may include hospitalizations, day care, medical treatments, and so forth. Frequently, economists are asked to attach dollar figures to the cost of such a plan while factoring in the inflation of medical care cost and the cost of living. The assistance of physicians and other medical personnel may be needed to create such a plan.

EXHIBIT 1

Neuropsychological Variables Profile

Directions: This form was intended for use by personnel who will be planning rehabilitation activities. The neuropsychologist should be able to address the majority of the items on this list from his or her knowledge of the person. In cases in which a neuropsychologist is unable to complete this form, a rehabilitation specialist with access to neuropsychological information may be able to document the information requested.

Steps to Complete the Neuropsychological Variables Profile

1. Examine the list of variables and rate the degree of the problems or impairment that the variable causes. Note that this form provides for a simple means of determining the degree of limitations which exist.
   - 0 = **Within Normal Limits.** A variable is of no consequence, minor, is an infrequent occurrence, or the problem has been corrected by an aid or appliance such as glasses or a hearing aid. For informational purposes, the rater may wish to further indicate if the variable is at the high end (H) or low end (L) of the category "within normal limits." Note that in some cases this "H" or "L" rating will be irrelevant and unnecessary.
   - 1 = **Minor.** The variable is of some consequence and may conceivably affect vocational, social, or personal adjustment. As an example, the rater may wish to alert the rehabilitation counselor that a problem or a deficit exists, but it is questionable as to whether it will cause future problems. In some cases jobs may need to be modified to minimize problems.
   - 2 = **Notable.** Moderate-to-significant consequences are expected on vocational, social, or personal adjustment. Examples may include gross motor skill problems that are unlikely to be compensated.
2. After completing Column A, place a checkmark in Column B that indicates the source of the data (e.g., direct observation, examination, test results).
3. Complete Column C only if job goals are identified. Because the job goal will often determine whether an impairment or limitation will cause work-related problems, this part cannot be completed unless job goals are identified. Note that space for rating two separate job goals is provided.
4. Use the comment section between each category of variables to provide additional information if necessary, preceded by the item that you are addressing (e.g., "A-6: Range of motion is restricted in upper extremities, but contractures do not exist" or "A-2: Minor right sided weakness exists but continues to improve with therapy").

The Neuropsychological Variables Profile was developed as a means of identifying several areas of functioning that may affect the rehabilitation process of persons who have sustained a brain trauma injury. The variables listed on this form are not inclusive of all of the variables that may occur following a brain injury. This list, however, was developed from a research project that identified the types of variables that are most common and that tend to cause most of the problems in planning a return to the community and to employment following a brain injury. This form is intended to be used as an aid to rehabilitation planning, not as a replacement for a neuropsychological evaluation report.

(*continues*)

EXHIBIT 1 (*Continued*)

Person: ________ Primary job goal: ________ Secondary job goal: ________ Rater and job title: ________	A IMPAIRMENT OR FUNCTIONAL LIMITATIONS Circle the degree of impairment or functional limitation that exists			B	C LIKELIHOOD OF WORK-RELATED PROBLEMS IN AREA OF JOB GOAL Is it likely that the impairment or limitations will cause work problems?					
					Job Goal #1			Job Goal #2		
III. NEUROPSYCHOLOGICAL VARIABLES	Within normal limits	Minor problem	Notable problem	INFORMATION SOURCE	Yes	No	?	Yes	No	?
A. General cognitive functions										
1. Alertness and vigilance	0	1	2	____	__	__	__	__	__	__
2. Attention and concentration	0	1	2	____	__	__	__	__	__	__
3. Perseveration in speech or motor activities	0	1	2	____	__	__	__	__	__	__
4. Maintenance of problem-solving set	0	1	2	____	__	__	__	__	__	__
5. General fund of information	0	1	2	____	__	__	__	__	__	__
6. Abstraction skills	0	1	2	____	__	__	__	__	__	__
7. Arithmetic abilities	0	1	2	____	__	__	__	__	__	__
8. Hemispatial neglect	0	1	2	____	__	__	__	__	__	__
9. Insight	0	1	2	____	__	__	__	__	__	__
10. Decision-making ability	0	1	2	____	__	__	__	__	__	__
11. Judgment	0	1	2	____	__	__	__	__	__	__
12. Cognitive flexibility	0	1	2	____	__	__	__	__	__	__
13. Information-processing speed	0	1	2	____	__	__	__	__	__	__
14. Planning and carrying out activities	0	1	2	____	__	__	__	__	__	__
15. Self-regulation (ability to shift course)	0	1	2	____	__	__	__	__	__	__
16. Awareness of obvious limitations or deficits	0	1	2	____	__	__	__	__	__	__
17. Ability to learn new information	0	1	2	____	__	__	__	__	__	__

EXHIBIT 1 (*Continued*)

COMMENTS:

B. Memory (including immediate and delayed as appropriate)				
1. Auditory/verbal	0	1	2	_ _ _ _ _ _ _ _ _ _
2. Visual/nonverbal	0	1	2	_ _ _ _ _ _ _ _ _ _
3. Procedural/skill	0	1	2	_ _ _ _ _ _ _ _ _ _
4. Memory for designs or figures	0	1	2	_ _ _ _ _ _ _ _ _ _
5. Remote (historical)	0	1	2	_ _ _ _ _ _ _ _ _ _
6. Prospective	0	1	2	_ _ _ _ _ _ _ _ _ _

COMMENTS:

C. Communication skills				
1. Understand verbal commands	0	1	2	_ _ _ _ _ _ _ _ _ _
2. Writing skills	0	1	2	_ _ _ _ _ _ _ _ _ _
3. Stays on topic when speaking	0	1	2	_ _ _ _ _ _ _ _ _ _
4. Spontaneity and appropriateness of speech	0	1	2	_ _ _ _ _ _ _ _ _ _
5. Tangential/ circumstantial speech	0	1	2	_ _ _ _ _ _ _ _ _ _
6. Intelligibility of speech	0	1	2	_ _ _ _ _ _ _ _ _ _
7. Voice volume	0	1	2	_ _ _ _ _ _ _ _ _ _
8. Vocabulary	0	1	2	_ _ _ _ _ _ _ _ _ _

COMMENTS:

D. Psychomotor skills				
1. Simple assembly skills	0	1	2	_ _ _ _ _ _ _ _ _ _
2. Fine motor control	0	1	2	_ _ _ _ _ _ _ _ _ _
3. Gross motor control	0	1	2	_ _ _ _ _ _ _ _ _ _
4. Simple reaction time	0	1	2	_ _ _ _ _ _ _ _ _ _

(*continues*)

EXHIBIT 1 (*Continued*)

5. Simple drawing and assembly skills	0	1	2	__ __ __ __ __ __ __ __ __ __
6. Visual–spatial skills	0	1	2	__ __ __ __ __ __ __ __ __ __

COMMENTS:

E. Mental health issues				
1. Depression	0	1	2	__ __ __ __ __ __ __ __ __ __
2. Anxiety or panic states	0	1	2	__ __ __ __ __ __ __ __ __ __
3. Hypomanic or hyperactive	0	1	2	__ __ __ __ __ __ __ __ __ __
4. Suspiciousness or paranoid	0	1	2	__ __ __ __ __ __ __ __ __ __
5. Delusions	0	1	2	__ __ __ __ __ __ __ __ __ __
6. Auditory hallucinations	0	1	2	__ __ __ __ __ __ __ __ __ __
7. Visual hallucinations	0	1	2	__ __ __ __ __ __ __ __ __ __
8. Emotionally labile (mood swings)	0	1	2	__ __ __ __ __ __ __ __ __ __
9. Behavioral discontrol	0	1	2	__ __ __ __ __ __ __ __ __ __
10. Antisocial tendencies	0	1	2	__ __ __ __ __ __ __ __ __ __
11. Egocentric, self-centered, or childish	0	1	2	__ __ __ __ __ __ __ __ __ __
12. Disinhibition	0	1	2	__ __ __ __ __ __ __ __ __ __
13. Conceptual disorganization (tangential disconnected or confused thoughts processes)	0	1	2	__ __ __ __ __ __ __ __ __ __
14. Unusual content of thought	0	1	2	__ __ __ __ __ __ __ __ __ __

COMMENTS:

From Traumatic Brain Injury and Vocational Rehabilitation *by D. Corthell, 1990, pp. 267–272. Copyright 1990 by the University of Wisconsin. Adapted with permission.*

THE DEPOSITION

A discovery deposition is a formal information-gathering process in legal matters and is frequently requested by the opposing attorney sometime after the neuropsychological report is submitted. The length of time between submission of a report and the deposition can be 6 months to 1 year or longer.

The purpose of a deposition is to allow the opposing attorney the opportunity to discover what the neuropsychologist will say if he or she is called to court. The employing attorneys can find this out informally from the neuropsychologist, but the opposing attorney does not have this opportunity. The opposing attorney has not met personally with the neuropsychologist and does not know what the nature of his or her testimony will be except what appears in the neuropsychological report.

A second purpose of the discovery deposition is to allow attorneys from both sides the opportunity to assess the neuropsychologist's ability to testify, the clarity of the testimony, and the neuropsychologist's ability to respond under pressure and to respond when he or she is being attacked. Particularly damaging testimony to the opposing attorney also can be explored and any weaknesses in the testimony uncovered. The deposition is frequently used to help both attorneys decide whether the case should be settled out of court.

The deposition can take place in any office, but it normally occurs in the neuropsychologist's office. Those present at the deposition include the opposing attorney, the employing attorney, the court reporter, and the neuropsychologist. The opposing attorney occasionally may have another "expert" present to assist in formulating questions, although this is not normally done. The patient is normally not present. At the outset of the deposition, the court reporter will swear the neuropsychologist in, by asking the neuropsychologist to raise his or her right hand and swear to tell the truth, the whole truth, and nothing but the truth. Following the deposition, the court reporter will produce a written verbatim copy of the deposition and the neuropsychologist should request a copy. Objections to portions of the neuropsychologist's testimony are frequently made by attorneys at the time of the deposition to provide a record of these objections. (The types of objections are discussed later.) The neuropsychologist, however, is usually instructed by both parties to answer the question despite the objection, and the judge may decide later whether the objection is sustained.

A neuropsychologist should be careful about what he or she says at the deposition. Anything that is said to the opposing attorney before or after the deposition itself also can be used in court. If a neuropsychologist makes an offhand remark during a break, that information can be brought up at trial. The expert is cautioned against saying "uh-uh" or "uh-huh" or shaking his or her head "yes" or "no" in response to a question. Such information is not easily transcribed by the court reporter and can be misleading to the reader. Few questions are usually asked by the employing attorney at the actual deposition called by the opposing side because the employing attorney does not want to disclose his or her theory of the case.

Any written material brought to the deposition by the expert, such as interview notes, medical records, and so on, is subject to questions, and the opposing attorney will frequently ask for photocopies of all or portions of the material. The neuropsychological report likely will be made a formal exhibit and a copy of the exhibit given to the court reporter. An exhibit is usually written material used by the neuropsychologist in formulating his or her opinions about the case, although an exhibit could be any physical object relevant to the case.

A note of caution: If the opposing attorney contacts the clinical neuropsychologist directly and asks about his or her report, the clinical neuropsychologist should refuse to talk with the attorney unless it is approved by the employing attorney. To do so without permission would be a breach of confidentiality with the employing attorney. The employing attorney will seldom give permission to meetings with the opposing attorney without the employing attorney being present.

Videotaped Depositions

If the employing attorney does not think that the expert neuropsychologist's physical presence in court is needed or if the expert is unavailable for court, a videotaped deposition may be taken. The videotaped trial deposition will be used in court in lieu of a "live" court appearance. The videotaped trial deposition may be a completely different deposition than the discovery deposition. During the videotaped deposition, the court reporter usually transcribes the testimony. A videotape technician records the neuropsychologist's testimony. The expert should speak directly to and look at the videocamera because he or she is testifying "eye to eye" to the jury and the judge.

THE TRIAL ITSELF

The suit will sometimes go to trial. It has been our experience that less than 10% of cases actually go to trial because most cases are settled out of court or dropped. When a case does go to trial, not atypically there is a 6-month to 1-year delay between the deposition and the trial. Before the trial, the attorney and neuropsychologist typically meet to discuss the testimony. In fact, Brodsky (1991) stated that meeting with the attorney before the trial is essential.

At the trial itself, the plaintiff presents his or her side of the case first, followed by the defense. After the neuropsychologist is called to the stand and is sworn in, the direct examination begins by the employing attorney.

Direct Examination

In the direct examination, the employing attorney attempts to present as clearly as possible the portion of the clinical neuropsychologist's findings that he or she thinks support his or her case. The attorney wants to ensure that the facts are presented in a smooth, logical sequence that is understandable to the jury. Many legal authorities think that the best direct examination is one in which the expert serves as an educator or teacher of the jury about some issues involved in the case (Sbordone, 1991). The attorney obviously wants the jury to be attentive, engaged, and interested during the expert's testimony. Consequently, the use of visual aids is suggested whenever possible.

The first series of direct examination questions typically deal with qualifying the clinical neuropsychologist as an expert witness. The qualification process usually runs smoothly, with no major objections by the opposing attorney for a fully credentialed clinical neuropsychologist. At this stage, the employing attorney usually wants to present the expert neuropsychologist in the best possible light. For example, the attorney would highlight the expert's educational experiences, honors, and accomplishments (Sbordone, 1991). The attorney's goal, of course, is to present the expert as someone whom the jury should believe. Typical questions that the employing attorney might ask during the qualification process are as follows: What is your profession? Where do you work? What is your academic training? Are you board certified in your area? What is your educational background? What type of patients do you currently see? From where do you receive the majority of your referrals? What percentage of your patients are referred by the defense as opposed to the plaintiff? How many times have you given a deposition? How many times have you appeared in court? What do you charge for a neuropsychological evaluation? How many patients of the type involved in this case have you seen? What professional honors have you received? Do you have professional publications in this area? Have you held offices in professional associations? Have you ever served on a state board of psychological examiners?

During this qualifications stage, the opposing attorney may attempt to cast doubt on the neuropsychologist's credentials, motives, tests, and methods in his or her cross-examination. The opposing attorney's goal is to disparage the neuropsychologist's credibility and hence his or her testimony. For example, the opposing attorney may interrupt the qualification portion of the direct testimony and simply say that he or she acknowledges that the neuropsychologist is an expert. At this point, the employing attorney frequently will ask the judge to bear with him or her for a few moments because he or she wants to show that the expert has exceptional or superior qualifications.

Judicial appellate courts have held that the issue of whether a witness is qualified to render an expert opinion is left to the sole discretion of the trier of fact. Rule 702 of the *Federal Rules of Evidence* stipulates the following:

> *If scientific, technical, or other specialized knowledge will assist the trier of fact to understand the evidence or to determine a fact in issue, a witness qualified as an expert by knowledge, skill, experience, training, or education may testify thereto in the form of an opinion or otherwise.*
> *(Richardson & Adams, 1992, p. 298)*

Although there have been attempts to "prove" that neuropsychologists cannot testify about the presence of brain functioning, as indicated in Table 1, all jurisdictions reviewed at the time of the study indicated that neuropsychologists were allowed to testify

TABLE 1

Attitude of Jurisdictions on Using Neuropsychologists as Expert Witnesses

State	Qualified as to present brain dysfunction	Qualified as to cause of present brain dysfunction	Qualified as to future problems caused by brain dysfunction	Type of injury
Alabama[a]	Yes	Yes	Yes	Vehicle accident
Florida[b]	Yes	Yes	Yes	Respiratory distress/birth and vehicle accidents (both cases)
Georgia[c]	Yes	Yes	NA	Vehicle accident
Illinois[d]	Yes	Yes	NA	Vehicle accident
Louisiana[e]	Yes	Yes	NA	Vehicle accident
Massachusetts[f]	Yes	Yes	NA	Fight
Michigan[g]	Yes	Yes	NA	Vehicle accident
Nebraska[h]	Yes	Yes	NA	Vehicle accident
New York[i]	Yes	Yes	Yes	Industrial
North Carolina[j]	Yes	Yes	NA	Industrial
Virginia[k]	Yes	Yes	NA	Insecticide poisoning

Note: NA = not applicable (the issue was not discussed). From "Neuropsychologists as Expert Witnesses: Issues of Admissibility," by R. Richardson and R. Adams, 1992, *The Clinical Neuropsychologist*, 6, p. 297. Copyright 1992 by Swets & Zeitlinger. Adapted with permission.

[a]*Brannon v. Sharp*, 554 So.2d 951 (Ala. 1989); *Fabianke v. Weaver By and Through Weaver*, 527 So.2d 1253 (Ala. 1988).

[b]*GIW Southern Valve Co. v. Smith*, 471 So.2d 81 (Fla. App. 2 Dist. 1985); *Executive Car and Truck Leasing v. DeSerio*, 468 So.2d 1027 (Fla. App. 4 Dist. 1985). But see Section 490.003 (1989) of the Florida statutes.

[c]*Jacobs v. Pilgrim*, 367 S.E.2d 49 (Ga. App. 1988). See also *Chandler Exterminators, Inc.*, 409 S.E.2d 677 (Ga. App. 1991) and *Elbert County Bd. of Com'rs v. Burnett*, 498 S.E.2d 168 (Ga. App. 1991).

[d]*Valiulis v. Scheffels*, 547 N.E.2d 1289 (Ill. App. 2 Dist. 1989). See also *Barr v. Groll*, 576 N.E.2d 13 (Ill. App. 5 Dist. 1991).

[e]*Bourgeois v. Roudolfich*, 580 So.2d 699 (La. App. 5 Cir. 1991).

[f]*Commonwealth v. Monico*, 396 Mass. 793, 486 N.E.2d 1168 (1986).

[g]*Shaw v. Martin*, 399 N.W.2d 450 (Mich. App. 1986).

[h]*Sanchez v. Derby*, 433 N.W.2d 523 (Neb. 1989).

[i]*Baker v. Three Village Cent. School Dist.*, 546 N.Y.S.2d 490 (A.D. 3 Dept. 1989).

[j]*Horne v. Marvin L. Goodson Logging Co.*, 349 S.E.2d 293 (N.C. App. 1986).

[k]*Seneca Falls Greenhouse v. Layton*, 389 S.E.2d 84 (Va. App. 1990).

about the presence of brain dysfunction (Richardson & Adams, 1992).

In other words, the courts ruled that the neuropsychologist had expertise in assessing the neuropsychological consequences of brain injury and was competent to serve as an expert witness. However, just because a neuropsychologist can testify does not mean or imply that credibility is automatically assigned to that testimony. The credibility of any expert witness is always left to the trier of fact. As shown in Table 1, the neuropsychologist's testimony concerning the cause of brain dysfunction has generally been allowed in jurisdictions when the issue reached the appellate level. Although there are only a few cases concerning the issue of whether a neuropsychologist can testify about the prognosis of the patient after some type of brain dysfunction, jurisdictions have generally followed the same ruling as they did concerning causation (Richardson & Adams, 1992).

Once the employing attorney establishes the credibility of the neuropsychologist, the employing attorney then continues the direct examination by tracking the contact that the neuropsychologist has had with the patient. Questions such as the following are typically asked:

- When were you asked to see the patient?
- What were you asked to do?
- Did you write a neuropsychological report?

- Is this that report?
- What tests did you give to the patient?
- What do these tests measure?
- What were your findings?
- How much time did you spend testing the patient?
- Did you test the patient or did a technician perform the evaluations?[2]
- How long did you spend with the patient?
- Did you interview the patient?
- Did you interview significant others?
- Did you review other pertinent hospital records or documents?
- Did you review previous depositions?
- Have you worked with this employing attorney before?

In addition, the employing attorney may ask some specific questions about the difference among different professionals:

- How are the neuropsychologists trained?
- Are you a physician?
- How does a neuropsychologist differ from a neurologist, a psychiatrist, a neurosurgeon?

Finally, the employing attorney also may ask some general questions concerning the issue at hand in order to educate the jury. Assume, for example, that the plaintiff has a head injury. The attorney may ask questions such as the following:

- What is the normal recovery process for a person after a head injury?
- What is the relationship between neuropsychological tests and biomedical tests?
- What types of injuries can the brain endure (subdural hematoma, epidural hematoma)?
- Are there other factors that affect a patient's performance on neuropsychological tests other than brain damage per se?
- What is a coma?
- What is a postconcussion syndrome?
- What is a coup injury, a contrecoup injury?
- What is shearing and tearing effect?
- What are some of the major structures in the brain?

Toward the end of the testimony, the employing attorney will likely ask one or two very crucial questions, worded as follows: "With a reasonable degree of neuropsychological certainty, do you believe that this patient suffered brain dysfunction as a result of the motor vehicle accident?" and "With a reasonable degree of neuropsychological certainty, what do you expect the prognosis of this patient to be?" Occasionally, an attorney will mistakenly ask with a reasonable degree of "medical certainty." Obviously, this is a question the neuropsychologist cannot address because it is out of his or her area of expertise. Only physicians can have medical opinions. The neuropsychologist should caution the attorney to avoid the phrase "medical opinion" when examining the neuropsychologist in court.

Cross-Examination

After the direct examination has been completed by the employing attorney, the cross-examination begins by the opposing attorney. It is during the cross-examination process that the opposing attorney tries to discredit the neuropsychological testimony by pointing out things such as improper credentials, incomplete evaluation, inappropriate selection of tests, bias in interpretation, faulty conclusions, lack of validation data, and so forth. The cross-examination is usually the more confrontational portion of the testimony, in which the focus of the opposing attorney's examination is on the issues brought up during the direct examination by the employing attorney. In the direct examination, questions are usually open-ended and responses can be detailed and lengthy. In cross-examination, however, questions are frequently worded in such a way as to require yes or no responses such as "Isn't it true, Doctor, that you used the Category test in evaluating this patient?"

It is important to listen carefully to each and every question during the cross-examination. The

[2]The American Psychological Association's Division of Clinical Neuropsychology (Division 40) has ruled that either a clinical neuropsychologist or a trained neuropsychology technician are equally qualified to actually test the patient, but the interpretation is the responsibility of the clinical neuropsychologist (Report of the Division 40 Task Force on Education, Accreditation, and Credentialing, 1989).

opposing attorney sometimes will start off by getting the neuropsychologist to say yes over and over again to his or her questions. Then, seemingly out of nowhere, he or she throws a question requiring a "no" answer in an attempt to get the clinical neuropsychologist to agree with him or her and contradict what was said earlier. It also is important that the clinical neuropsychologist be highly critical of the questions that are heard and not to agree with anything that is not totally true. Usually, the expert can clarify his or her answer by explaining why he or she answered yes or no, although sometimes the expert is not allowed to do so by the opposing attorney. Although the total amount of time spent testifying in a case varies greatly, it can range from 1 to several hours.

Cross-Examination Ploys

Much has been written for attorneys about how to cross-examine witnesses in the behavioral sciences (Melton, Petrila, Poythress, & Slobogin, 1987). The following common cross-examination ploys were summarized by Melton et al. (1987) and are presented here. The ploys include the infallibility complex, the God-only-knows approach, yes–no questioning, bought-and-biased testimony, unreliable examination, subjective opinion, and the loaded-question ploy. These ploys represent just some of the more common approaches to cross examination, as there are literally hundreds which are used. These ploys are presented to give the clinical neuropsychologist some indication of what they may be up against during cross-examination. A more complete discussion can be found in Melton et al. (1987).

Infallibility complex. Using this approach, an attorney tries to get around the notion that the neuropsychologist is infallible. To do this, the attorney may pick some particular obscure study and ask the expert witness about it. The attorney hopes to have the neuropsychologist say that he or she does not know and thus decrease the neuropsychologist's credibility. The fact is, however, that no one knows all studies in the literature, and freely admitting so is a good counter to this ploy.

God-only-knows approach. In this approach, the attorney will ask a question that is literally unanswerable. The opposing attorney is trying to demonstrate that the knowledge base within neuropsychology, or for that matter any profession, is limited. An example of such questioning might be "How many brain cells did this patient lose as a result of his motor vehicle accident?"

Yes–no questioning. During cross-examination, yes–no questions are frequently used. Answering a question with a simple yes or no can be misleading, and, of course, a cunning attorney may use this misleading information to further his or her cause. An example of yes–no question is, "Doctor, are you always accurate in your assessment of patients?"

Bought-and-biased testimony. Using this approach, the lawyer is trying to portray the expert as a hired gun who is willing to testify no matter what the data may indicate in favor of the employing attorney. Questions include "How much are you being paid for your testimony?" and "How often have you testified for this particular attorney?"

Unreliable examination. Using this approach, the attorney will try to cast doubt on the reliability and validity of individual tests, the diagnosis, interview information, or information obtained from significant others. The attorney will try to point out inconsistencies in testimony or differences in opinion between different neuropsychologists seeing the patient.

Subjective opinion ploy. Using this approach, the attorney will try desperately to prove that the neuropsychologist's opinions are largely subjective and are based on the expert's own personal bias rather than on objective findings.

Loaded-question ploy. In this ploy, according to Melton et al. (1987), an attorney will misrepresent what the expert has said and then tack onto this information additional information the attorney may fabricate in order to support his or her case. For example, an expert previously might have testified to Points A, B, and C, and the attorney might later ask,

"Doctor, you testified earlier that A, B, C, and D were true. As a result, doesn't that imply that the following is true?" Here, the neuropsychologist actually never did admit to D and it may not be true.

Hypothetical Questions

A frequently used approach with expert neuropsychological witnesses is the use of hypothetical questions. In this approach, the expert is asked by the attorney to assume that certain facts are true and then render a requested opinion concerning the hypothetical case. For example, an attorney may say, "Doctor, let's assume that MR imaging demonstrated a right frontal hematoma in a patient and that the patient was in a coma for 3 days. Do you think that patient suffered significant brain injury that would render the patient incapable of working?" In making up the hypothetical case, Melton et al. (1987) stated that the lawyer may (a) omit evidence known to be true, (b) include facts that the neuropsychologist may be unaware of but that exist, and (c) may manufacture facts that are untrue. According to Melton et al. (1987), the opposing attorney may object to hypotheticals if manufactured information is included.

In this case, the hematoma might have been present 3 years ago and long since dissipated without the need for surgery. Moreover, the hematoma may have been small and was barely visualized on the MR image. The coma, which the attorney says the hypothetical patient had, may in fact not have been a coma at all but a short period of posttraumatic amnesia. For example, with the preceding case a response such as the following may be appropriate: "Not knowing the nature and extent of a hematoma or knowing what you mean by the use of the term *coma*, I would be hesitant to respond to this question. Different people mean different things by the use of the term *coma*." In other situations, it may be appropriate to respond more directly to a well-stated hypothetical question. Although the expert may answer hypothetical questions, they should do so cautiously and conservatively. Attorneys are adept at using hypothetical questions to support their case when the presumed facts are untrue.

Questions Concerning Learned Treatise

In the learned treatise approach, an attorney will select a textbook, research article, or clinical case study and ask the neuropsychologist if this is an authoritative learned treatise in a given area. The attorney will then select certain sections from the material and ask the expert if he or she agrees. The attorney will carefully select the material used to support his or her side of the case.

Several approaches have been recommended by experts concerning learned treatises (Melton et al., 1987). Admitting that the material is authoritative, if in fact it is, would clearly be appropriate. If the expert did not rely on the material for his or her case, the expert can so state. Also, the expert can ask to look at the material being quoted, especially if the expert feels that the information may have been taken out of context. The expert could also critically evaluate the material if the expert feels that improper methods were used or other errors were made.

Redirect and Re-Cross-Examination

After the opposing attorney's cross-examination is complete, the redirect examination by the employing attorney may occur. If a redirect examination occurs, the opposing attorney may recross and ask the neuropsychologist additional questions after the redirect. On redirect examination, the employing attorney will again have the opportunity to question the expert. Questioning on redirect can again be open-ended and is not limited to yes or no responses. Redirect examination is the employing attorney's opportunity to "rehabilitate" the neuropsychologist's testimony. In other words, points that may have been incompletely answered, misleading, or overemphasized can be addressed. By using yes–no responses in the cross-examination, the neuropsychologist may have been forced by the rules of cross-examination to admit certain information that, although true, may be misleading. For example, a question may have been asked on cross-examination by the plaintiff attorney trying to prove brain dysfunction concerning the Category test. The attorney may say something like, "Isn't it true, Doctor, that a given patient could have significant brain injury and not show any deficits on the Category test?" The answer, of course, is yes. On redirect, the employing attorney might say, "Doctor, how many tests did you give the patient? How many of these tests did the patient perform in the abnormal or impaired range? Does the fact that the patient performs within normal limits on the Category test, in and of itself, indicate the lack of brain dysfunction? Considering everything that you know about the patient, including his Category Test performance, do you feel the patient has brain dysfunction?" After redirect examination, a recross examination may begin.

Guidelines for Answering Direct and Cross-Examination Questions

The following guidelines were written by Benjamin and Kaszniak (1991) to assist the clinical neuropsychologist in his or her testimony:

> *1) Appear definite and reasonable by responding deliberately without qualifying or exaggerating phrases—hesitancies and uncertainty in the testimony may raise doubt in the fact finders' minds.*
> *2) Support all opinions with full descriptions of the data gathering techniques and the inferences drawn from the assessment results.*
> *3) Identify all vulnerable portions of the assessment process and analysis of results.*
> *4) Testify consistently with the earlier reports, interrogatory writings, or depositional statements. (p. 27)*

Other suggestions include the following:

1. Dress very conservatively.
2. Look at the jury whenever possible to help maintain their attention.
3. Have an attitude of confidence presenting the information you have and your opinions of the case based on your education, training, and experience. Other trained professionals obviously are entitled to their opinion based on their experience and assessment, and on occasion their opinion may differ from yours. If you are conducting a comprehensive evaluation and are confident of your results, do not feel intimidated that another professional may disagree.
4. Always testify within your area of expertise. Be wary of making medical as opposed to neuropsychological comments.
5. Be careful in responding to compound questions because they can be confusing to the jury. Any question that you do not understand fully, do not attempt to answer it. Ask for the question to be rephrased.
6. Remember that it is okay to say that you do not know or you have not formed an opinion on an issue.
7. Maintain a professional demeanor even when attacked.
8. Avoid arguments with opposing attorneys whenever possible.
9. Avoid making disparaging comments about colleagues or other professionals. Simply state what you feel is the truth even if others disagree.
10. Take sufficient time to answer a question. If you need to refer to your report, medical records, or other information, you are normally allowed to do so.
11. Avoid relying on any one piece of information as the sole basis of a major issue in the case.
12. An attorney may ask you to acknowledge that a particular article or book is a learned treatise on the subject at hand. You can acknowledge this if true, but state that you do not necessarily agree with every piece of information in the treatise.

Objections Raised During Expert Testimony

As stated earlier in this chapter, objections can be raised by the attorney on either side, and the validity of these objections is determined by the judge. The legal issue concerning objections are complicated and are not fully reviewed here. The primary reasons for objections is to keep irrelevant or immaterial information from being presented during testimony. As Benjamin and Kaszniak (1991) pointed out, the trier of fact must base his or her verdict solely on the evidence presented at the trial. One of the more common objections is "no foundation has been laid" for the expert to give his or her opinion. For example, the objecting attorney may feel that the neuropsychologist has omitted crucial facts in his or her review of this case and might have failed to review the appropriate medical records, depositions, and previous neuropsychological test results. The no-foundation objection can also be used when the expert is responding to a hypothetical question in which relevant facts have been omitted (Baum, 1984).

Another common objection is the "irrelevancy objection." This type of objection is raised when the objecting attorney thinks that the expert's testimony does not directly address the questions at hand. The opposing attorney may believe that the issue surrounding the question was not raised previously in the pretrial proceedings.

A third common objection is the "form of the question" (Benjamin & Kaszniak, 1991). This type of objection is usually designed to keep the expert from being attacked or badgered on the stand. An attorney may claim that a given question is "argumentative." A question may have already been "asked and answered." Here, the attorney simply does not want to go over the same material again and again. Finally, other common objections are that the question is "complex and confusing" or "cumulative."

Clearly, the neuropsychologist should stop testifying when an objection is made and should not interfere with the disagreement between the two attorneys. Let the attorneys fight it out. It is not the neuropsychologist's battle. During a trial, the judge will usually tell the expert neuropsychologist to proceed at the appropriate time.

INTEGRITY

Integrity is probably the most important characteristic of a neuropsychologist to a trier of fact. Above all, the believability of the neuropsychological testimony to the trier of fact is crucial. The neuropsychologist must not only adhere to the ethical standards of the APA, but he or she must also practice the highest personal and moral standards.

The jury or trier of fact will be listening to the neuropsychologist and asking themselves the question, "Can I trust this individual? Does he or she have ulterior motives in the case?" No matter how professionally qualified the clinical neuropsychologist may be, no matter how much experience he or she has, no matter how many publications he or she has, no matter how many professional organizations he or she belongs to, if the trier of fact has doubts about the expert's integrity, his or her testimony will be discounted. Maintaining integrity must be an ongoing effort on the part of the clinical neuropsychologist. When the direct or cross-examination of the neuropsychologist in court becomes heated, when personal or professional attacks are made on the clinical neuropsychologist, maintaining one's composure and truthfulness, although difficult, is imperative.

In the American adversarial judicial system, the role of the plaintiff attorney is to present strongly the plaintiff's position. Conversely, the role of the defendant is to present strongly the position of his or her client. Each side may present one-sided arguments and only information supporting that side's theory of the case. The attorney's role is to either agree or disagree with the neuropsychologist's testimony if it furthers the side's cause. If not, the attorney will vigorously oppose the neuropsychological testimony regardless of whether he or she personally agrees with the legitimacy of the neuropsychologist's position. As a result of the adversarial system, attorneys may overstate their case, fail to give the neuropsychologist all relevant information, or disparage the reputation of the neuropsychologist or the whole profession of neuropsychology. They may misquote information from previous depositions and take information out of context. Occasionally, attorneys will imply that they have information or facts that they do not have in order to confuse the neuropsychologist. Sometimes, attorneys will present the position they are taking as fact. Maintaining one's integrity and adhering to one's oath of "telling the truth and nothing but the truth" can be challenging to the neuropsychologist's skill under these circumstances.

For example, an opposing attorney may take the position that neuropsychologists are similar to astrologers, that there is no scientific basis for neuropsychology, that neuropsychological evaluations are based exclusively on subjective information rather than on fact. Opposing attorneys may imply that a neuropsychologist is an overpaid hired gun who is not presenting the truth in order to further the neuropsychologist's personal position. When attacked in this fashion, maintaining composure and presenting a balanced assessment is challenging, at the least. The neuropsychologist's natural inclination is to fight back vigorously when attacked, but this is not the expert's role. The expert's role is to tell the truth as he or she sees it. Even telling the truth at times can be difficult because an attorney may interrupt the expert as he or she tries to explain his or her answer and not allow the expert to do so.

The trier of fact is not naive and can usually see through the attorney's questions to the attorney's motives. Nevertheless, maintaining one's composure, professional decorum, and absolute truthfulness is necessary. Harry Truman's often-quoted statement is appropriate here: "If you can't stand the heat, get out of the kitchen."

Attorneys differ greatly in the degree that they use a negative confrontational approach in a case. The basic personality of the attorney, his or her theory of the case, and the presence of other evidence all have some bearing on the attorney's style. To be attacked vigorously by an attorney on one case and then having that same attorney consult with that same expert on another case supports the point that the attacks on an ethical neuropsychologist are seldom personal.

Application of APA Professional Ethics to Neuropsychological Evaluation in Civil Proceedings

In the Ethical Principles of Psychologists and Code of Conduct, there is a section pertaining to forensic activities (American Psychological Association [APA], 1992). In this section we discuss portions of the ethical guidelines and point out how they become important in conducting forensic evaluations. We also describe requisite training qualifications of psychologists calling themselves neuropsychologists.

For Standard 7.01, Professionalism, the code of ethics states that "in addition, psychologists base their forensic work on appropriate knowledge of and competence in the area underlying such work including specialized knowledge concerning special populations" (APA, 1992, p. 1610). Also under Principle A, Competence, the ethical principles read as follows: "They [psychologists] provide only those services and use only those techniques for which they are qualified by education, training, and experience" (APA, 1992, p. 1599).

Division 40 of the APA has defined what a clinical neuropsychologist is and has listed the education, training, and experience a neuropsychologist should have. The following statement represents the official definition of clinical neuropsychology by APA's Division 40:

> *A Clinical Neuropsychologist is a professional psychologist who applies principles of assessment and intervention based upon the scientific study of human behavior as it relates to normal and abnormal functioning of the central nervous system. The clinical neuropsychologist is a doctoral level psychology provider of diagnostic and intervention services who has demonstrated competence in the application of such principles for human welfare following: a) successful completion of systematic, didactic, and experiential training in neuropsychology and neurosciences at a reasonably accredited university, b) two or more years of appropriate supervised training applying neuropsychological services in a clinical setting, c) licensing and certification to provide psychological services to the public by the laws of the state or providence in which he or she practices, d) review by one's peers as a test of these competencies. Attainment of the ABCN–ABPP diplomate in clinical psychology is the clearest evidence of competence as a clinical neuropsychologist assuring that all these criteria have been met. This statement reflects the official position of the Division of Clinical Neuropsychology and should not be construed as either contrary to or subordinate to the policies of the APA at large (Adams & Rourke, 1992, p. 5).*

Education and training experiences of a clinical neuropsychologist. In the definition of clinical neuropsychology, the phrase "appropriate knowledge of and competence in clinical neuropsychology" is used. What is considered appropriate knowledge and competence? Division 40, in collaboration with the International Neuropsychology Society, has created formal guidelines for doctoral training in clinical neuropsychology. These guidelines delineate the minimum training requirements are for the independent practice of clinical neuropsychology, and are published by the International Neuropsychology Society–Division 40 Task Force on Education, Accreditation, and Credentialing (1987). Briefly stated, a clinical neuropsychologist should have a doctorate from a regionally accredited university in clinical neuropsychology or in a related specialty (e.g., clinical psychology), plus a full year's internship. In addition to the internship, 2-year, full-time formal postdoctoral training experience is required. This formal program should be directed by a clinical neuropsychologist having a diplomate in clinical neuropsychology.

As stated in the definition, the 2-year postdoctoral training should be associated with the hospital setting in which neurological and neurosurgery services are present in order to offer the necessary training background. Specifically, the following didactic training and experiential training are required (Adams & Rourke, 1992):

> Didactic Training
>
> A. *Training in neurological diagnosis.*
> B. *Training in consultation to neurological and neurosurgical services.*
> C. *Training in direct consultation to psychiatric, pediatric, or general medical services.*
> D. *Exposures to methods and practices of neurological and neurosurgical consultation (grand rounds, bed rounds, seminars, etc.).*
> E. *Training in neuropsychological techniques, examination, interpretation of test results, report writing.*
> F. *Training in consultation to patients and referral sources.*
> G. *Training in methods of intervention specific to clinical neuropsychology.*
>
> Experiential Training of a Clinical Neuropsychologist
>
> A. *Neuropsychological examination and evaluation of patients with actual and suspected neurological diseases and disorders.*
> B. *Neurological examination and evaluation of patients with psychiatric disorders and/or pediatric or general medical patients with neurobehavioral disorders.*
> C. *Participation in clinical activities with neurologists and neurosurgeons (bed rounds, grand rounds, etc.).*
> D. *Direct consultation to patients involving neuropsychological issues.*
> E. *Consultation to referral and treating professions (pp. 9–10).*

In summary, Satz (1988) stated that "psychologists (including clinical) who practice clinical neuropsychology outside these standards are operating in a violation of APA ethical and practice standards" (p. 99). This is a stern yet important reminder for individuals who are not thoroughly trained to cease their practice of neuropsychology until they obtain the proper formal training.

Case example: Testifying beyond one's area of competence. In the following case, some patient information has been changed. A clinical neuropsychologist was asked to see an inmate who was convicted of first degree murder and was in the penitentiary. Two years before the evaluation, the inmate was babysitting a child approximately 18 months old. The inmate was muscular and weighed more than 220 lb (99.8 kg). The baby apparently was crying and the man allegedly shook the baby and forcefully set the child down on the floor. The baby subsequently died of head injuries. The man was then convicted of first degree murder. Many months after he was convicted, prison personnel noted that he sat staring off into space. He was later medically evaluated and determined to have an extremely large meningioma occupying almost his whole left frontal lobe. The meningioma was removed. Later, a neuropsychologist was asked to evaluate the patient and discovered that he had little residual neuropsychological deficit at the time of the evaluation. Obviously, the inmate and others involved in the case wanted to reopen this case and have the neuropsychologist testify about the patient's brain functioning at the time of the alleged murder. Those involved in the case also wanted the neuropsychologist to testify, in effect, that the meningioma was slow growing and was present at the time of the injury. Although intriguing and certainly an important issue, the neuropsychologist thought that he could not comment on the status of the meningioma before the time the patient was actually evaluated; therefore, he refused to participate in this case. He did, however, give the referral source the names of certain other physicians, including a neuropathologist and neurologist.

To appropriately address the major issue in this case, a physician would have to track the development of the meningioma over time and state that the meningioma caused the patient to behave impulsively. This speculation would be beyond the capacity of a neuropsychologist or probably any professional regardless of discipline at this particular time. Such cases, although intriguing and certainly important, are currently beyond the scope of the science of neuropsychology. Although neuropsychologists may be allowed to testify in a case concerning causation, making such statements sometimes may be inappropriate. The acceptability of neuropsychological testimony depends on well-trained neuropsychologists testifying within their area of expertise and within the limits of their knowledge and skills.

PROBLEMS INHERENT TO CONDUCTING FORENSIC EVALUATIONS

Neuropsychologists get referrals from a variety of sources, including neurologists, internists, physiatrists, other psychologists, psychiatrists, neurosurgeons, and so on. Maintaining productive interpersonal relationships and a good reputation is extremely important in building and maintaining a neuropsychological practice. The adversarial judicial system, however, potentially can place a clinical neuropsychologist at odds with other professionals, perhaps even those who refer patients to him or her. A controversial case can put the neuropsychologist's testimony at odds with that of a potential referral source. After the case is over, the neuropsychologist will continue to have contacts with the other professionals, who may have had a different opinion on a case.

Some professionals, especially those who do few neuropsychological evaluations or little forensic work, may interpret disagreement with their opinions on a given case as a negative evaluation of them personally. Similarly, they may be reluctant to refer additional patients to the neuropsychologist for that reason. The problem is compounded because, typically, one does not know who will be on the other side of a case when one agrees to get involved in it. The best way to deal with these issues is simply to be honest and truthful. The truth usually wins in the long run, and if the expert has been scrupulously honest and thorough in his or her neuropsychological evaluations, the expert's relationships with other professionals are less likely to be harmed.

Another disadvantage to conducting forensic neuropsychological evaluations is that the neuropsychologist will lose some control over his or her schedule. Attorneys, like other professionals, frequently wait until the last minute to ask for an expert's involvement. A discovery deadline may be fast approaching when the expert is first asked to be involved in a case. Canceling other, less pressing neuropsychological assessments certainly does not help one's referral sources. Regularly scheduled psychotherapy patients may have to be canceled at the last moment. Depositions involve multiple parties, and 2 or more hours are usually needed. Scheduling depositions on short notice can be problematic, especially when the attorneys on both sides of the case are not willing to cooperate with each other.

Court appearances are especially difficult. Frequently, the case may be scheduled for a given date and then rescheduled at the last minute. Court appearances are routinely rescheduled several times. Further complicating the problem is that attorneys usually do not know precisely when a neuropsychologist will be called to testify. The attorney may say something like, "Well, it's on the docket for January 15, which is a Monday. Jury selection will likely take most of Monday. The opposing side will be put on the case on Tuesday and, to the best of my knowledge at this time, your testimony will be probably be on Wednesday afternoon. I'll keep you informed."

What does a busy clinical neuropsychologist to about such lack of control over his or her schedule? The approach we use is to respond to the attorney by saying, "Well, I'll be happy to set aside Wednesday afternoon for you and you can be assured I will be there. However, if I set aside that date, I must charge you for the time unless I am able to schedule a substitute patient on such short notice."

Even though this approach helps, the attorney may call on Wednesday morning and tell the expert that his or her testimony will be around 9:00 a.m. on Thursday. The attorney will sometimes give the expert only an hour's notice for a court appearance, especially if the expert's office is close to the court house. With these types of problems, a video deposition may be the best approach. However, the attorney may push for a court appearance because the expert's testimony may be crucial to the attorney's case. The most frustrating situation is to appear at the court house for one's testimony, wait an hour or so, and then be told later the testimony has been rescheduled.

Another disadvantage to conducting neuropsychological evaluations is the amount of time these cases can take. For example, one might have to go to the library to research an unfamiliar neuropsychological instrument used by the opposing side, or the neuropsychologist may need to conduct a literature review on the neurological problems associated with certain neurotoxic chemicals relevant to a case. A review of extensive medical records can itself take hours of time.

Unlike other neuropsychological evaluations, obtaining additional neuropsychological information from the patient after the day of the evaluation can be problematic. In defense work, the plaintiff may object to the neuropsychologist contacting the patient again, and legal maneuvers by the employing attorney may therefore be necessary. A significant other may not have been available for interview on the testing day and when the significant other is finally contacted and interviewed, issues may be brought up that may require obtaining additional information directly from the patient.

MALINGERING WITHIN THE CONTEXT OF A FORENSIC NEUROPSYCHOLOGICAL EVALUATION

In most nonforensic cases, the information a patient tells a neuropsychologist is usually true, at least from the patient's perspective. Memory problems may be present, but at least the patient is usually honest and forthright. Such honesty and forthrightness cannot be assumed automatically in forensic situations. For this reason, neuropsychologists should be alert to possible malingering, lack of candor, and overreporting or underreporting of symptoms. In this section, we discuss briefly the issue of malingering on symptom presentation and neuropsychological test performance on neuropsychological batteries and on individual tests. A sample of tests designed specifically to detect malingering is discussed.

Malingering is not a diagnosis. It is an accusation. Essentially, when someone is accused of malingering, he or she is accused of lying and misrepresentation. One's very motives are questioned. Because of the ramifications of such an accusation, great care should be taken before a person is accused of malingering. According to the fourth edition of the *Diagnostic and Statistical Manual of Mental Disorders* (*DSM–IV*; American Psychiatric Association, 1994), malingering is not a diagnosis in and of itself. Instead, it is classified as a condition not attributable to a mental disorder but a focus of attention or treatment. Malingering is defined as "the intentional production of false or grossly exaggerated physical or psychological symptoms, motivated by external incentives such as avoiding military duty, avoiding work, obtaining financial compensation, evading criminal prosecution, or obtaining drugs" (American Psychiatric Association, 1994, p. 683). Under some conditions, malingering may represent adaptive behavior (e.g., feigning illness while a captive of the enemy during wartime). Although no specific criteria are given for malingering in *DSM–IV*, malingering is strongly suspected if one of the following is noted:

> *1) Medicolegal context of presentation, e.g., the patient being referred by his or her attorney to the physician for examination;*

> *2) Marked discrepancy between the person's claimed stress or disability and the objective findings;*
> *3) Lack of cooperation during the diagnostic evaluation and in compliance with prescribed treatment regimen;*
> *4) The presence of Antisocial Personality Disorder. (American Psychiatric Association, 1994, p. 683)*

Malingering is different from a factitious disorder because there is the absence of external incentives in a factitious disorder. In other words, there is some internal need to maintain the sick role (American Psychiatric Association, 1994).

Clinical Assessment of Suspected Malingering on Interview and Medical Record Information

Binder (1992) stated that "the only sensible procedure for a clinician is to consider the possibility of malingering in each and every patient who has any monetary or external incentives for faking bad on a neuropsychological examination. Any other tactic is indefensible" (p. 355).

A thorough clinical interview can be helpful in detecting malingering. Here, we present a series of questions and issues to discuss with the patient. The patient's answers to the questions posed here may increase one's suspicion of malingering. One should not assume that a positive response to any question or issue necessarily means that the individual is malingering. One must consider all information and integrate it in a comprehensive fashion to reach a final conclusion.

Did the patient contact an attorney even before he or she consulted a physician about his or her injury? Are the ambulance records, emergency room records, and patient reports concerning loss of consciousness or other symptoms basically consistent? Did the patient report an atypical progression of symptoms for a head injury (e.g., initially no or few deficits and then an increase in symptoms over time)? On a symptom checklist given to the patient, did the patient subscribe to a whole list of symptoms having nothing to do with the head injury but still relate these symptoms directly to the head injury? Did a significant other's completion of an inventory such as the Cognitive Behavioral Rating Scale (Williams, 1987) indicate symptoms similar to those found during the interview and in formal testing?

During the interview, did the patient endorse outrageous symptoms? For example, neuropsychologists will sometimes ask the patient, "Do you sometimes see large, yellow lights in your visual field that vacillate between being small and large and later change to other colors such as red?" This is a good question to ask, especially when the patient answers yes to practically every symptom. Blau (1991) suggested inquiring about the following information:

> 1. *Change in glove or shoe size;*
> 2. *Sudden brittleness of nails;*
> 3. *Sudden change in hair thickness;*
> 4. *Increase/decrease in scalp oiliness;*
> 5. *Increase in colds and sore throats.*
>
> (p. 49)

Is there relative consistency between the patient's list of symptoms and the symptoms a significant other reports that the patient has experienced? A significant other will sometimes report to the neuropsychologist mostly symptoms of depression, whereas the malingering patient may emphasize memory problems and downplay signs of depression.

Does the patient report significant impairment of memory, concentration, attention, and so on, but on formal testing he or she performs normally on these tasks? Does the patient have a history of previous lawsuits or workers' compensation cases? Does the patient have a history of being in jail or prison? Obviously, having been in prison does not indicate that the patient is malingering, but it does increase suspicion. Is there a history of a severe alcohol or drug abuse? Is there a history of antisocial personality? Does the patient deny having previous problems such as learning disabilities, which are documented in his or her high school record?

In workers' compensation cases especially, one should look at the patient's employment history. Have there been long periods of unemployment? Was the patient working at the job where he or she was injured just a few weeks or months before the injury occurred?

Are there gross discrepancies between the nature of the patient's injury and the types of symptoms he or she reports? For example, a patient may have been in an accident, suffered no or little posttraumatic amnesia, yet reports significant problems in all areas of functioning, ostensibly rendering him or her unable to work.

Did the patient outright lie in any part of the interview or on the autobiographical data completed? For example, did the patient claim to have a college degree or state that he or she received excellent supervisory evaluations on the job but neither is true? Did the patient totally fabricate or exaggerate information such as having been involved in police work, having an outstanding combat record, or being involved in other types of activities?

In terms of behavioral observations, was the patient belligerent during the interview? Did the patient fail to keep scheduled appointments? Was he or she defensive in giving details or refuse to cooperate with the interviewer? Did he or she refuse to take certain tests?

Note that the presence of any one or combination of these does not necessarily in and of itself indicate fabrication, although one's level of suspicion is raised.

Malingering on neuropsychological testing. Given the large number of studies attempting to detect neuropsychological malingering, we summarize studies of malingering in terms of malingering on a common neuropsychological test batteries, malingering on single neuropsychological tests, and specialized malingering tests. For reviews of the malingering literature, see Nies and Sweet (1994), Rogers, Harrell, and Liff (1993), and Franzen, Iverson, and McCracken (1990).

Malingering on common neuropsychological test batteries. The Halstead–Reitan Neuropsychological Test Battery (HRNTB), which is probably the most commonly used forensic neuropsychological test battery, has been used frequently to detect malingering. Heaton, Smith, Lehman, and Vogt (1978) contrasted the performance of 16 nonlitigation patients with head injuries with 16 patients who were given a financial incentive to fake neuropsychological deficits of head injury. Malingering patients performed more poorly on the Speech Sounds Perception test, Tapping Test, Finger Agnosia, Digit Span, Suppression, and grip strength. Malingerers showed more pathology on the Minnesota Multiphasic Personality Inventory (MMPI) on Scales *F*, 1, 3, 7, 8, and 0. The patients with head injury, on the other hand, performed more poorly on the Category test, Trails B, and the memory and location scores of the Tactual Performance test (TPT). It is noteworthy that the patients with head injury tended to perform worse on tasks more sensitive to brain damage's effects on cognitive functions, whereas the malingering patient's performance was more impaired on tasks involving primarily motor functioning and sensory perceptual problems.

Two separate discriminant function analyses were later performed (Heaton et al., 1978), which yielded perfect prediction (100%) for both the malingering group and the patients with brain injury. A discriminant function analysis of MMPI performance revealed that the MMPI misclassified only one participant in each of the two groups. This discriminant function portion of their study, however, has been criticized for having too many variables and too few participants.

Goebel (1983) also used the HRNTB to distinguish 152 undergraduate volunteers who were asked to fake neuropsychological deficits attributable to head injury. The simulators were asked to simulate specific brain injury such as right-hemisphere, left-hemisphere, or diffuse dysfunction. Neuropsychological test results were compared with control undergraduates who took the HRNTB. Discriminant function analysis correctly classified 94.9–97.2% of the participants, depending on which base rate for malingering was used (Goebel, 1983). Like Heaton et al. (1978), Goebel, using a subjective analysis, found that the Category test, Trails B, TPT–Localization, and Halstead Impairment Index were most sensitive to faking. In his concluding remarks, Goebel stated that nonimpaired people cannot convincingly simulate traumatic brain injury on neuropsychological tests. Rogers et al. (1993) criticized Goebel's study because it involved a single examiner who had previous exposure to the cases involved.

Cullum, Heaton, and Grant (1991) presented an interesting approach to assessing malingering. Patients who had been given the HRNTB on two different occasions were investigated. In many forensic neuropsychological cases, two different neuropsychologists (employed by the plaintiff vs. the defense) may test the same patient independently. Cullum et al. examined their performance on each of the two administrations for patients whose symptoms presumably were static. The investigators then compared the results of the two testings to look for highly discrepant findings, given the fact that it would be difficult for a patient to consistently fake a whole day's worth of testing. Highly discrepant performance may indicate malingering when taking practice effect into consideration. Heaton is currently collecting data on a large normative sample of patients who have been tested twice (C. Cullum, personal communication, 1994). The final results of the study have not yet been published.

Malingering on single neuropsychological tests. When testing a patient who has either traumatic brain injury or is suspected of having traumatic brain injury, most neuropsychologists use a variety of testing instruments. Commonly used instruments also can be used to screen for malingering, and some specialized instruments designed specifically for detecting malingerers can be used. In other words, if common neuropsychological tests can differentiate malingerers from nonmalingerers, then these tests routinely can be given to patients as part of the standard battery and suspicious results can then be followed-up with other specialized testing.

Several common neuropsychological tests have been used for this purpose, including the Benton Visual Retention Test (Benton & Spreen, 1961; Spreen & Benton, 1963), the Bender–Gestalt Test (Bruhn & Reed, 1975), the Rey Auditory Verbal Learning Test (RAVLT; Bernard, 1991), the Recognition Memory Test (Millis, 1992), and the WMS-R (Mittenberg, Azrin, Millsaps, & Heilbronner, 1993).

The RAVLT (Rey, 1964) is a brief test that requires the patient to learn a series of 15 words presented over five trials. A series of studies have revealed that the RAVLT is sensitive to detecting patients who have suffered documented head injury (Bigler, Rosa, Schultz, Hall, & Harris, 1989).

Regarding faked deficits, Bernard (1991) gave the RAVLT to a group of patients with objectively verified closed head injury and a group of 57 undergraduates who were asked to simulate a head injury sustained in a motor vehicle accident. In addition, some of the simulators were given a financial incentive and some were not. The test also was given to a group of undergraduate students as a control. The results demonstrated that the simulators recalled fewer words from the first third of the word list than from the last third of the list, where the patients with closed head injury did not. Stated another way, the simulators showed a recency effect but did not show a primacy effect.

Two studies (Rawlings & Brook, 1990; Mittenberg et al., 1993) have investigated the WMS (Wechsler, 1945) or the WMS-R (Wechsler, 1987) as a test for simulators of head injury. Because the Wechsler Memory scales are the most frequently used neuropsychological tests of memory functioning (Guilmette, Faust, Hart, & Arkes, 1990; Hartlage, 1985; Sellers & Nadler, 1990), finding a particular pattern of neuropsychological test performance of malingerers on this test would be helpful to neuropsychologists in screening for possible malingering. If this pattern of performance is found in a given patient, additional specialized tests also could then be administered.

A well-designed study with cross-validation results, conducted by Mittenberg et al. (1993), illustrates this "pattern approach" with the WMS-R. In their study, 39 patients with documented head injury were compared with 39 age-matched control participants who were asked to malinger symptoms of head injury on the WMS-R. Malingering participants were given a brief description of an automobile accident in which the patient was reportedly unconscious for a while and woke up in the hospital. Malingerers were specifically warned not to produce memory deficits that would be obvious enough for detection. Patients in the head injury group represented a cross-section of patients with head injuries, involving brain contusions, hematomas, and cerebral edemas as well as different periods of unconsciousness. The median period of unconsciousness was 48 hr.

Mittenberg et al. (1993) investigated the pattern of performance on the WMS-R rather than the absolute level of performance on any given WMR index. The reason behind this approach is that, although most lay people realize that memory problems are common in head injury (Gouvier, Prestholdt, & Warner, 1988), most people probably do not know how to fake a given pattern of memory problems in head injury (Larrabee, 1991). For example, previous research has shown a characteristic postconcussion memory disturbance pattern on the WMS-R in which the Attention–Concentration Index is relatively higher than the General Memory Index (Boyer, 1991; Crossen & Wiens, 1988; Reid & Kelly, 1991; Wechsler, 1987).

Table 2 shows the characteristic pattern found by Mittenberg et al. (1993). Using a stepwise discriminant function analysis, Mittenberg et al. were able to correctly classify 91% of the participants in their study as either malingerers or patients with brain injury. Given the fact that this study had a 10:1 ratio of subjects to variables, cross-validation results would likely have limited shrinking. A jackknife discriminant analysis also was completed (Mosteller & Tukey, 1968), which resulted in only a slight reduction in the hit rate to 87%.

Table 2 shows that for patients with documented head injury, the General Memory Index was significantly lower than the Attention–Concentration Index ($p < .001$), whereas the opposite pattern was found for the malingering group ($p < .0001$).

A third discriminant function analysis was conducted by Mittenberg et al. (1993) in which the General Memory Index score minus the Attention–Concentration difference score was used as the independent variable. This analysis classified correctly 83% of the cases. This approach had a false-positive rate of 10% and a false-negative rate of 23%. Using this difference score between the General Memory Index and the Attention–Concentration Index, Mittenberg et al. constructed Table 3, which gives the probability of accurate malingering classifications for different decision-ruled scores. For example, if a given patient obtained a General Memory Index score of 100 and an Attention–Concentration Index score of 75, a difference between these two indexes of 25 would result (100 − 75 = 25). This difference in score of 25 would give that an 85% probability of being a malingerer (see Table 3). How a neuropsy-

TABLE 2

Summary Scores for the Wechsler Memory Scale–Revised (WMS-R) and Wechsler Adult Intelligence Scale–Revised (WAIS-R)

	Head trauma		Malingering	
Scale	***M***	***SD***	***M***	***SD***
Full-Scale IQ	91.59	11.26	87.54	15.15
Verbal IQ	95.59	13.22	90.62	15.05
Performance IQ	88.82	12.40	85.08	15.38
Verbal Memory Index (WMS-R)	86.26	12.24	88.10	14.07
Verbal Memory Index (WAIS-R)	90.82	18.94	86.72	16.16
General Memory Index	85.26	14.31	85.33	14.49
Attention–Concentration Index*	95.90	14.48	70.95	18.18
Delayed Recall Index	82.28	16.93	77.00	15.53

Note: From "Identification of Malingered Head Injury on the Wechsler Memory Scale–Revised," by W. Mittenberg, R. Azrin, C. Millsaps, and R. Heilbronner, 1993, *Psychological Assessment*, 5, p. 36. Copyright 1993 by the American Psychological Association. Adapted with permission of the author.
*$p < .001$.

TABLE 3

Probability of Accurate Malingering Classification for Different Decision Rule Scores

General Memory Index and Attention–Concentration Index difference score[a]	Discriminant function score[b]	Probability of malingering
35	1.94	.99
34	1.90	.98
—	1.86	.97
33	1.83	.96
32	1.79	.95
—	1.75	.94
31	1.71	.93
30	1.67	.92
29	1.63	.91
—	1.59	.90
25	1.39	.85
22	1.19	.80
19	0.99	.75
15	0.79	.70
12	0.60	.65
9	0.40	.60
5	0.20	.55
2	0.00	.50

Note: From "Identification of Malingered Head Injury on the Wechsler Memory Scale–Revised," by W. Mittenberg, R. Azrin, C. Millsaps, and R. Heilbronner, 1993, *Psychological Assessment*, 5, p. 37. Copyright 1993 by the American Psychological Association. Adapted with permission of the author.
[a]$p < .014871$ (difference score) + .472164. [b]$p = .252086$ (discriminant score) + .5.

chologist would use that information would depend on what confirmatory information was available.

Because clinical judgments concerning malingering must occur in a variety of different contexts, Mittenberg et al. (1993) stated that this table may be used in situations that require more or less stringent degree of confidence. The importance placed on a given difference score would have to be evaluated in light of the patient's history, other test results, and behavior during the examination itself.

In the Mittenberg et al. (1993) study, the average malingerer had a General Memory Index score that was 1 standard deviation below normal; however, malingerers had Attention–Concentration Index scores 2 *SD*s below normal. Mittenberg et al. stated that this does not make "neuropsychological sense." Attention capacity limits one's functioning so that the patient who is severely impaired in attention and concentration skills also should have near-equal impairment in general memory. This pattern approach on the WMS-R appears to have promise in screening for malingering. However, one limiting factor to studies such as that of Mittenberg et al. has to do with the use of individuals simulating malingering. The question arises as to whether an actual malingerer would simulate the same way as someone who was instructed to malinger. A simulated malingerer does not have large amounts of money that hinge on the accuracy of his or her efforts. However, obtaining a large group of actual malingerers is difficult to study because malingering involves deceit.

Specialized malingering tests. Basically, two primary approaches have been used in developing tests specifically designed to detect malingering. One approach has been referred to as the floor effect approach (Rogers et al., 1993) and the other approach as the forced-choice approach.

Floor effect malingering tests. In the floor effect test, the patient is presented with a task that seems, on the surface, to appear difficult but is actually simple. Some people attempting to fake head injury symptoms will perform very poorly on this test, thinking that it is difficult. What they do not know is that most patients with head injury, and even some patients with mental retardation, will perform adequately on this test. The test of this sort receiving the most attention has been the Rey 15-Item Test (Lezak, 1983). Numerous researchers have used the Rey 15-Item Test or other similarly constructed tests (Bernard & Fowler, 1990; Davidson, Suffield, Orenczuk, Nantau, & Mandel, 1991; Goldberg & Miller, 1986; Lee, Loring, & Martin, 1992; Schretlen, Brandt, Krafft, & Van Gorp, 1991).

In the Rey 15-Item Test (Rey, 1964; see Figure 1), the patient is presented with 15 items to remember. The 15 items are so easy to remember that even those with a brain injury, except those with the most severe brain injury, will remember most of them. Unfortunately, as a group, these studies had disap-

A	B	C
1	2	3
a	b	c
0	□	△
I	II	III

FIGURE 1. The Rey 15-Item Test (Rey, 1964). From *Neuropsychological Assessment* (p. 619), by M. D. Lezak, 1983, New York: Oxford University Press. Copyright 1983 by Oxford University Press. Adapted with permission.

pointing results. This test usually detects only a small percentage of malingerers, presumably because malingerers can see through the test to know that most patients with a brain injury would perform reasonably well on it. Rogers et al. (1993) stated that, at the least, the test can detect a few unsophisticated malingerers. It does, however, take only a short period of time to administer and will occasionally detect a malingerer. Its presence in a neuropsychological battery will depend partly on how much time one can allot to the detection of memory on their test battery.

Forced-choice malingering tests. The forced-choice test is the second method used to detect malingering. Using this approach, a patient is presented with one of two choices in a response to a given question. The questions are usually simple. The patient by chance would get 50% of the answers correct because there are only two choices. If a patient responded at a significantly below-chance level, then the probability is that patient must have been deliberately choosing the incorrect response. Binder (1992) stated that "performance significantly worse than chance results from the deliberate production of wrong answers. The probability of an explanation other than malingering is nil" (p. 357). The forced-choice technique has been applied in a variety of situations, including blindness (Grosz & Zimmerman, 1965; Pankratz, 1979), tactual sensory loss (Miller, 1986; Pankratz, Binder, & Wilcox, 1987), and memory deficits (Binder, 1990; Binder & Pankratz, 1987; Binder & Willis, 1991; Brandt, 1988; Hiscock & Hiscock, 1989; Pankratz, 1983, 1988).

An excellent study by Prigatano and Amin (1993) illustrates this forced-choice approach applied to a group of patients with unequivocal brain dysfunction and suspected malingers. We discuss this study in detail because it is one of the best examples in the literature. Participants in the study were 27 patients with cerebral dysfunction, 5 patients with postconcussion syndrome, 6 suspected malingerers, and 10 normal control individuals. Twenty patients with cerebral dysfunction had suffered traumatic structural brain injury documented by CT scanning, MR imaging, EEG, or all three.

Each participant was administered the Digit Memory Test (Hiscock & Hiscock, 1989). Participants were told they were being given a test measuring memory and concentration that people with memory problems had found to be difficult. In fact, the questions were simple and most patients with brain injury did well. Patients were then shown a five-digit number on a card for 5 s and then shown another card that contained two separate five-digit numbers, one of which had just been presented to them. The patients were asked to identify which digit sequence that they had just seen; hence, the term *forced choice*.

Participants were informed of the correctness of their responses after each trial. After Set A (24 trials), participants were told that they had done well and that the task would now become harder by increasing the delay to 10 s (Set B). After completing the 24 items in Set B and receiving feedback, the participants were told that because they had done so well, the delay would now be increased to 15 s. The whole test takes approximately 25 min to complete.

Except for extremely severe cases such as Alzheimer's disease or severe aphasia, repetition, and comprehension deficits, Hiscock and Hiscock (1989) found that patients with brain damage performed well on this task. Patients with the aforementioned disorders can be independently verified on other tests, and the Digit Memory Test should not be administered to them.

As shown in Table 4, patients in the cerebral dysfunction group, postconcussion group (nonmalingering patients), and control groups obtained an average of 99% of the items correct. However, the suspected malingering group obtained an average of only 74% of the items correct. Note that 74% is not

TABLE 4

Digit Memory Test Results

Group	*n*	Set A		Set B		Set C		% Correct	
		M	*SD*	*M*	*SD*	*M*	*SD*	*M*	*SD*
Control	10	24.0	0.00	23.9	0.32	23.9	0.32	99.7	0.59
Cerebral dysfunction	27	23.9	0.42	23.9	0.36	23.9	0.27	99.5	0.94
Postconcussional	5	24.0	0.00	23.8	0.45	23.8	0.45	99.4	0.76
Suspected malingerers	6	20.3	2.34	17.5	4.23	15.3	3.01	73.8	11.57

Note: From "Digit Memory Test: Unequivocal Cerebral Dysfunction and Suspected Malingering," by G. P. Prigatano and K. Amin, 1993, *Journal of Clinical and Experimental Neuropsychology, 15*, p. 542. Copyright 1993 by Swets & Zeitlinger. Adapted with permission.

below a 50% chance level of performance (i.e., 36 of 72 items correct). To be significantly below chance ($p < .05$), only 29 items would have to be correct. Prigatano and Amin (1993) concluded that the Digit Memory Test may be used to detect invalid test protocols even when a significant below-chance-level criterion is not met.

A multivariate analysis of variance completed across the four patient groups and the three sets yielded significant results. A significant Group × Set interaction was found. The data in Table 4 reveal that suspected malingerers performed worse as the sets were "supposed" to become more difficult, whereas the other groups did not. The investigators found that even patients with a history of Glascow Coma Scale scores between 3 and 8 performed at a near-perfect level.

An ethical note of caution was offered by Prigatano and Amin (1993). Patients were told that each set was progressively harder than the previous one. This would represent a type of deception by the neuropsychologist administering the test. To avoid this problem, Prigatano and Amin (1993) suggested that the following instructions be used:

> *I will show you some numbers and I would like you to look at them carefully. Later I will ask you to recall them. After a period of time, I will show you two sets of numbers and ask you to identify the one that you have just seen. (p. 545)*

After the patient has completed Set A, the participant should be instructed as follows:

> *The time interval between seeing the numbers and when you will be asked to recall them will now become longer. I want to see if you are still able to remember the numbers after a longer period of time. (p. 545)*

The use of the MMPI. The MMPI (Hathaway & McKinley, 1951) is perhaps the most commonly used personality instrument and is frequently used by clinical neuropsychologists in evaluating patients. Several specific scales have been developed to assess for malingering, including the *F* scale, $F - K$ Index, obvious/subtle ratios, dissimulation scale, among others. There are three recent reviews that summarize the extensive literature concerning the use of the MMPI to detect malingering: Berry, Baer, and Harris (1991), Franzen et al. (1990), and Schretlen (1988). Specific studies are not reviewed here. Basically, the MMPI has been used to detect malingering in a variety of groups ranging from prisoners, disability applicants, military personnel, psychiatric patients, and patients who have been instructed to malinger neuropsychological deficits.

In as major review of malingering studies, Berry et al. (1991) concluded that "the MMPI based scales for detecting faking are quite good at separating groups of subjects known or suspected of malingering from those completing the MMPI honestly" (p. 594). Similar conclusions were reached by Schretlen

(1988) and Franzen et al. (1990). A few studies were found in which the investigators used respondents who were instructed to malinger specific neuropsychological deficits. Care should be exercised when using the MMPI alone to detect malingering of suspected brain injury.

CONCLUSION

The testimony of clinical neuropsychologists is being increasingly used in the judicial system. Clinical neuropsychological evaluations are valuable because the tests are objectively based, are supported by normative data, and typically relate directly to the issues at hand. The issue at hand normally is the degree to which the patient's brain injury has affected his or her behavior. In the case of traumatic brain injury, the results are particularly helpful in quantifying and objectifying the degree of compromise of higher cortical functioning. The results can be used in computing the monetary value (i.e., damages) of the traumatic brain injury sustained by the patient. Neuropsychological findings are frequently more relevant than the results of biomedical tests such as an EEG or MR imaging because the neuropsychological findings are based on the patient's behavior and are directly relevant to how the injury affects the patient's life and livelihood.

Testimony itself consists of several stages, including qualification of the expert witness, direct examination, cross-examination, redirect examination, and recross examination. There are a number of frequently used questions that an attorney may ask. Knowledge of these questions and of court procedures helps the neuropsychologist understand the "rules" and keeps testimony within the bounds of those rules.

The clinical neuropsychologist must be aware that in certain instances, a patient may fake symptoms or overrepresent symptoms. Various sources of information, including medical records, interviews with the patient, interviews with significant others, and the patient's performance on common neuropsychological instruments and specialized instruments, can be useful. If neuropsychologists continue to use scientifically based information to evaluate forensic cases in a fair and impartial fashion, the legal system will continue to respect neuropsychologists' value in the courtroom. For attorneys reading this chapter, keep in mind the caution mentioned in the preface of this book. The information presented here are guidelines, and many competent clinical neuropsychologists can and do deviate markedly and still perform expert evaluations.

References

Adams, K. M., & Rourke, B. P. (Eds.). (1992). *The TCN guide to professional practice in clinical neuropsychology.* Lisse, The Netherlands: Swets & Zeitlinger.

American Psychiatric Association. (1994). *Diagnostic and statistical manual of mental disorders* (4th ed.). Washington, DC: American Psychiatric Association.

American Psychological Association. (1992). Ethical principles of psychologists and code of conduct. *American Psychologist, 47,* 1597–1611.

Barona, A., Reynolds, C. R., & Chastain, R. (1984). A demographically based index of premorbid intelligence for the WAIS-R. *Journal of Consulting and Clinical Psychology, 52,* 885–887.

Baum, D. B. (1984). Taking on the opposing expert. *Trial, 20,* 162–166.

Benjamin, G. A. H., & Kaszniak, A. (1991). The discovery process: Deposition, trial testimony, and hearing testimony. In H. O. Doerr & A. S. Carlin (Eds.), *Forensic neuropsychology: Legal and scientific bases* (pp. 17–32). New York: Guilford Press.

Benton, A. L., & Hamsher, K. deS. (1989). *Multilingual Aphasia Examination manual* (2nd ed.). Iowa City, IA: AJA Associates.

Benton, A. L., & Spreen, O. (1961). Visual Memory Test: The simulation of mental incompetence. *Archives of General Psychiatry, 4,* 79–83.

Bernard, L. C. (1991). The detection of faked deficits on the Rey Auditory Verbal Learning Test: The effect of serial position. *Archives of Clinical Neuropsychology, 6,* 81–88.

Bernard, L. C., & Fowler, W. (1990). Assessing the validity of memory complaints: Performance of brain damage and normal individuals on Rey's task to detect malingering. *Journal of Clinical Psychology, 46,* 432–436.

Berry, D., Baer, R. A., & Harris, M. J. (1991). Detection of malingering on the MMPI: A meta-analysis. *Clinical Psychology Review, 11,* 585–598.

Bigler, E. D., Rosa, L., Schultz, F., Hall, S., & Harris, J. (1989). Rey Auditory Verbal Learning Test and Rey–Osterreith Complex Figure Design performance in

Alzheimer's disease and closed head injury. *Journal of Clinical Psychology, 45,* 277–280.

Binder, L. M. (1990). Malingering following minor head trauma. *The Clinical Neuropsychologist, 4,* 25–36.

Binder, L. M. (1992). Deception and malingering. In A. E. Puente & R.J. McCaffrey (Eds.), *Handbook of neuropsychological assessment: A psychosocial perspective* (pp. 353–374). New York: Plenum.

Binder, L. M., & Pankratz, L. (1987). Neuropsychological evidence of factitious memory complaint. *Journal of Clinical and Experimental Neuropsychology, 9,* 167–171.

Binder, L. M., & Willis, S. C. (1991). Assessment of motivation after compensable minor head trauma. *Psychological Assessment: A Journal of Consulting and Clinical Psychology, 3,* 175–181.

Blau, T. (1991, November). *The neuropsychologist goes to court.* Workshop presented at the 11th Annual Meeting of the National Academy of Neuropsychology, Dallas, TX.

Boyer, C. L. (1991). Wechsler Memory Scale–Revised: Performance following severe closed head injury. *The Clinical Neuropsychologist, 5,* 262.

Brandt, J. (1988). Malingered amnesia. In R. Rogers (Ed.), *Clinical assessment of malingering and deception* (pp. 65–83). New York: Guilford Press.

Brodsky, S. L. (1991). *Testifying in court: Guidelines and maxims for the expert witness.* Washington, DC: American Psychological Association.

Bruhn, A. R., & Reed, M. R. (1975). Simulation of brain damage on the Bender–Gestalt Test by college subjects. *Journal of Personality Assessment, 39,* 244–255.

Corthell, D. (Ed.). (1990). *Traumatic brain injury and vocational rehabilitation.* Stout, WI: Research and Training Center Press.

Crossen, J. R., & Wiens, A. N. (1988). Residual neuropsychological deficits following head injury on the Wechsler Memory Scale–Revised. *The Clinical Neuropsychologist, 2,* 393–399.

Cullum, C., Heaton, R. K., & Grant, I. (1991). Psychogenic factors influencing neuropsychological performance: Somatoform disorders, factitious disorders, and malingering. In H. O. Doerr & A. S. Carlin (Eds.), *Forensic neuropsychology: Legal and scientific bases* (pp. 141–171). New York: Guilford Press.

Davidson, H., Suffield, B., Orenczuk, S., Nantau, K., & Mandel, A. (1991, February). *Screening for malingering using the memory for fifteen items test (MFIT).* Paper presented at the International Neuropsychological Society annual convention, San Antonio, TX.

Doerr, H. O., & Carlin, A. S. (Eds.). (1991). *Forensic neuropsychology: Legal and scientific bases.* New York: Guilford Press.

Franzen, M., Iverson, G., & McCracken, L. (1990). The detection of malingering in neuropsychological assessment. *Neuropsychology Review, 1,* 247–279.

Goebel, R. A. (1983). Detection of faking on the Halstead–Reitan test battery. *Journal of Clinical Psychology, 39,* 731–742.

Goldberg, J. O., & Miller, H. R. (1986). Performance on psychiatric inpatients and intellectually deficient individuals on a test that assesses the validity on memory complaints. *Journal of Clinical Psychology, 42,* 792–795.

Golden, C. J., & Strider, M. A. (1986). *Forensic neuropsychology.* New York: Plenum.

Gouvier, W. D., Prestholdt, P. H., & Warner, M. S. (1988). A survey of common misconceptions about head injury and recovery. *Archives of Clinical Neuropsychology, 3,* 331–343.

Grosz, H. J., & Zimmerman, J. (1965). Experimental analysis of hysterical blindness. *Archives of General Psychiatry, 13,* 256–260.

Guilmette, T. J., Faust, D., Hart, K., & Arkes, H. R. (1990). A national survey of psychologists who offer neuropsychological services. *Archives of Clinical Neuropsychology, 5,* 373–392.

Hartlage, L. C. (1985). Neuropsychology and the private practitioner. *Psychotherapy in Private Practice, 3,* 61–64.

Hathaway, S. R., & McKinley, J. C. (1951). *Minnesota Multiphasic Personality Inventory: Manual.* New York: Psychological Corporation.

Heaton, R. K., Grant, I., & Matthews, C. G. (1991). *Comprehensive norms for an expanded Halstead–Reitan Battery: Demographic corrections, research findings, and clinical applications.* Odessa, FL: Psychological Assessment Resources.

Heaton, R. K., Smith, H. H., Jr., Lehman, R. A. W., & Vogt, A. J. (1978). Prospects for faking believable deficits on neuropsychological testing. *Journal of Consulting and Clinical Psychology, 46,* 892–900.

Hiscock, M., & Hiscock, C. K. (1989). Refining the forced-choice method for the detection of malingering. *Journal of Clinical and Experimental Neuropsychology, 11,* 967–974.

International Neuropsychological Society, Division 40 Task Force on Education, Accreditation, and Credentialing. (1987). Guidelines for doctoral training programs, neuropsychology internships, and postdoctoral training in clinical neuropsychology. *The Clinical Neuropsychologist, 1,* 29–34.

Jastak, S., & Wilkinson, G. S. (1984). *Wide Range Achievement Test–Revised administration manual.* Wilmington, DE: Jastak Associates.

Krull, K. R., Scott, J. G., & Scherer, M. (1994). *Estimation of premorbid intelligence from combined performance and demographic variables.* Unpublished manuscript.

Larrabee, G. J. (1991). Cautions in the use of neuropsychological evaluation in legal settings: Neuropsychological tests can be failed for reasons other than brain damage. *Neuropsychology, 4,* 239–249.

Lee, G. P., Loring, D. W., & Martin, R. C. (1992). Rey's 15-item visual memory test for the detection of malingering: Normative considerations. *Psychological Assessment: A Journal of Consulting and Clinical Psychology, 4,* 43–46.

Lezak, M. D. (1983). *Neuropsychological assessment* (2nd ed.). New York: Oxford University Press.

McMahon, E. A. (1983). Forensic issues in clinical neuropsychology. In C.J. Golden & P.J. Vicente (Eds.), *Foundations of clinical neuropsychology* (pp. 401–427). New York: Plenum.

Melton, G. B., Petrila, J., Poythress, N. G., & Slobogin, C. (1987). *Psychological evaluations for the courts: A handbook for mental health professionals and lawyers.* Odessa, FL: Psychological Assessment Resources.

Miller, E. (1986). Detecting hysterical sensory symptoms: An elaboration of the forced choice technique. *British Journal of Clinical Psychology, 25,* 231–232.

Millis, S. (1992). The Recognition Memory Test in the detection of malingered and exaggerated memory deficits. *The Clinical Neuropsychologist, 6,* 406–414.

Mittenberg, W., Azrin, R., Millsaps, C., & Heilbronner, R. (1993). Identification of malingered head injury on the Wechsler Memory Scale–Revised. *Psychological Assessment, 5,* 34–40.

Mosteller, F., & Tukey, J. W. (1968). Data analysis including statistics. In G. Lindzey & E. Aronson (Eds.), *The handbook of social psychology* (Vol. 2, pp. 133–160). Reading, MA: Addison-Wesley.

Nelson, H. E. (1982). *The Nelson Adult Reading Test (NART) test manual.* Windsor, England: NFER–Nelson Publishing.

Nies, K. J., & Sweet, J. J. (1994). Neuropsychological assessment and malingering: A critical review of past and present strategies. *Archives of Clinical Neuropsychology, 9,* 501–552.

Pankratz, L. (1979). Symptom validity testing and symptom retraining: Procedures for the assessment and treatment of functional sensory deficits. *Journal of Consulting and Clinical Psychology, 47,* 409–410.

Pankratz, L. (1983). A new technique for the assessment and modification of feigned memory deficit. *Perceptual and Motor Skills, 57,* 367–372.

Pankratz, L. (1988). Malingering on intellectual and neuropsychological measures. In R. Rogers (Ed.), *Clinical assessment of malingering and deception* (pp. 169–192). New York: Guilford Press.

Pankratz, L., Binder, L. M., & Wilcox, L. M. (1987). Evaluation of an exaggerated somatosensory deficit with symptom validity testing. *Archives of Neurology, 44,* 787.

Prigatano, G. P., & Amin, K. (1993). Digit Memory Test: Unequivocal cerebral dysfunction and suspected malingering. *Journal of Clinical and Experimental Neuropsychology, 15,* 537–546.

Putnam, S. T., & DeLuca, J. W. (1990). The TCN Professional Practice Survey: Part 1. General practices of neuropsychologists in primary employment and private practice settings. *The Clinical Neuropsychologist, 4,* 199–244.

Rawlings, P., & Brooks, N. (1990). Simulation index: A method for detecting factitious errors on the WAIS-R and WMS. *Neuropsychology, 4,* 223–238.

Reid, D. B., & Kelly, M. (1991). A study of the Wechsler Memory Scale–Revised in closed head injury. *Journal of Clinical and Experimental Neuropsychology, 13,* 20.

Report of the Division 40 Task Force on Education, Accreditation, and Credentialing. (1989). Guidelines regarding the use of nondoctoral personnel in clinical neuropsychological assessment. *The Clinical Neuropsychologist, 3,* 23–24.

Rey, A. (1964). *L'examen clinique en psychologie* [The clinical examination in psychology]. Paris: Presses Universitaires de France.

Richardson, R. E. L., & Adams, R. L. (1992). Neuropsychologists as expert witnesses: Issues of admissibility. *The Clinical Neuropsychologist, 6,* 295–308.

Rogers, R., Harrell, E. H., & Liff, C. D. (1993). Feigning neuropsychological impairment: A critical review of methodological and clinical considerations. *Clinical Psychology Review, 13,* 255–274.

Satz, P. (1988). Neuropsychological testimony: Some emerging concerns. *The Clinical Neuropsychologist, 2,* 89–100.

Sbordone, R. J. (1991). *Neuropsychology for the attorney.* Orlando, FL: Paul M. Deutsch Press.

Schretlen, D. J. (1988). The use of psychological tests to identify malingered symptoms of mental disorder. *Clinical Psychology Review, 8,* 451–476.

Schretlen, D. J., Brandt, J., Krafft, L., & Van Gorp, W. (1991). Some caveats in using the Rey 15-item memory test to detect malingered amnesia. *Psychological Assessment: A Journal of Consulting and Clinical Psychology, 3,* 667–672.

Sellers, A. H., & Nadler, J. D. (1990, April). *A survey of current neuropsychological assessment procedures.* Paper presented at the meeting of the Southeastern Psychological Association, Atlanta, GA.

Spreen, O., & Benton, A. L. (1963). Simulation of mental deficiency on a visual memory test. *American Journal of Mental Deficiency, 67,* 909–913.

Thomas, D. F. (1990). Vocational evaluation of persons with traumatic head injury. In D. Corthell (Ed.), *Traumatic brain injury and vocational rehabilitation* (pp. 111–139). Memomonie: Research and Training Center, University of Wisconsin—Stout.

Wechsler, D. (1945). A standardized memory scale for clinical use. *Journal of Psychology, 19,* 87–95.

Wechsler, D. (1981). *WAIS-R manual: Wechsler Adult Intelligence Scale–Revised.* New York: Psychological Corporation.

Wechsler, D. (1987). *Wechsler Memory Scale–Revised manual.* New York: Psychological Corporation.

Williams, J. M. (1987). *Cognitive Behavioral Rating Scales manual: Research edition.* Odessa, FL: Psychological Assessment Resources.

CHAPTER 14

PSYCHOTHERAPY WITH CLIENTS WHO HAVE BRAIN INJURIES AND THEIR FAMILIES

William R. Leber and Michelle R. Jenkins

Neuropsychology has a long tradition in the study of brain–behavior relationships and the clinical assessment of people with brain impairment. Much of the research and development over the past 50 years has focused on assessment issues, especially in the cognitive area. Personality change and change in emotional functioning also have long been recognized as being the result of many types of brain impairment. Pioneers in the field, such as K. Goldstein (1973), recognized the importance of interventions aimed at helping people with brain injuries make adjustments to life. However, only within the past 15 years has literature begun to amass dealing with psychotherapeutic issues. In this chapter we introduce the therapist to the needs of survivors of traumatic brain injury and their families, as well as the issues involved in working with them. Ideas about individual and family therapy, which are based on the literature and our experience, also are presented.

Many articles have appeared that present various approaches and concepts relating to psychotherapy with patients with brain injuries. However, there are few if any true controlled outcome studies specifically aimed at demonstrating the efficacy of psychotherapeutic techniques. The best example we could find of an outcome study is that of Prigatano et al. (1984). Eighteen patients with closed head injury were treated in an intensive 6-month rehabilitation program, which included group, individual, and family interventions. These patients were compared with 17 control patients on a variety of cognitive and personality measures. Modest effects of treatment on neuropsychological functioning were found, and greater effects on emotional distress and interpersonal skills were noted. A later study (Prigatano et al., 1994) demonstrated that more patients with traumatic brain injuries who participated in a milieu program including both individual and group therapy were productive (employed or students) 40 months after injury than those who did not receive such treatment. Other authors have found that psychotherapeutic interventions have a positive effect. In the studies to date, the particular approaches and aspects of therapy that are most effective have not been delineated, and the reader must therefore determine their relative efficacy in his or her own practice. It is clear, however, that research is needed to delineate what techniques work best with which type of patient.

EPIDEMIOLOGY

Traumatic brain injuries have reached epidemic proportions in modern society (see chap. 1 in this book for detailed epidemiological data). Recent advances in acute medical care have increased the likelihood that people sustaining severe head injuries will survive with varying degrees of physical, cognitive, and emotional impairments that frequently place tremendous burdens on personal, social, and health care systems (Grimn & Bleiberg, 1986). Kaplan (1987) estimated that 400,000–500,000 people who sustain a traumatic head injury are admitted to hospitals every year. Of these, 40,000–50,000 have moderate-to-severe head injury causing significant, enduring disabilities (Kraus, 1987). The National Head Injury Foundation (1982) estimated that at least 50,000 people, most of whom are younger than 30 years of age, are left with disabilities that preclude resumption of a normal life. These individuals have a considerable life expectancy and must cope with a unique set of problems over their life span.

Because training with this special population is not a part of most training programs, therapists may not be as familiar with the special needs and issues of patients with brain injuries. In addition, many patients with postconcussion syndrome and their families seek psychological services believing that symptoms are reactive but do not know that they may have a neurological basis (Butler & Satz, 1988). Thus, it is important that the practicing clinician be aware of some of the common psychological manifestations of neurological damage and design interventions appropriately.

CONSEQUENCES OF HEAD TRAUMA

Until recently, it was assumed that mental disorders were the sequelae only of more severe brain trauma, typically involving coma, hospitalization, and posttraumatic amnesia lasting at least 14 days. However, Levin (1985) concluded that persistent residual mental dysfunction after mild head injury with only brief lapses of consciousness is relatively common.

Temporary or permanent mental disorders are common consequences of brain injury (Jennett & Teasdale, 1981). These disorders can be grouped loosely within the cognitive, emotional, and personality–behavior spheres. Cognitive sequelae of brain injury include retrograde and anterograde amnesias, intellectual ability deficits, dysphasias, and attention and information-processing abnormalities (Levin, Benton, & Grossman, 1982). The emotional problems that are common after a brain injury typically include poorer tolerance for frustration, greater dependence on others, and generally a more demanding attitude (Prigatano, 1986). Personality–behavioral sequelae of brain injury can include irritability, being unaware of one's personal impact on others, poor impulse control, initiation difficulties, affect disorders, and poor social restraint (Jennett & Teasdale, 1981; Prigatano, 1986). These cognitive, emotional, and personality–behavioral problems are frequently chronic and debilitating in terms of vocational, social, and interpersonal adjustment (Butler & Satz, 1988). Common psychosocial problems after brain injury include an inability to keep a job, loss of preinjury friendships and relationships, impaired body image, reduced self-esteem, and enhanced dependency on family and welfare systems (Prigatano, 1986).

BARRIERS TO TREATMENT

Despite the need for psychological services (Butler & Satz, 1988), emotional treatment for survivors of traumatic brain injury often have been limited. Interventions such as management with psychotropic medication, psychiatric hospitalization or nursing home placement, and behavior management (including token economies) have been used, but more general psychotherapy has been omitted (O'Hara & Harrell, 1991). The result for individual patients may be suboptimal treatment in private or public mental health sectors and welfare systems and marginal family adjustment at home.

According to Butler and Satz (1988), people with brain injuries are often considered inappropriate candidates for psychotherapy, except for behavior modification techniques. Prigatano (1991) pointed out that early contributors to the understanding of brain injury, such as Kurt Goldstein and Aleksandr Luria, generally did not describe a role for psychotherapy for this group. In his later writing, K. Goldstein (1973) stressed the importance of psychotherapy but provided little guidance for its implementation. Survivors of traumatic brain injury have been excluded from traditional insight-oriented or relationship psychotherapies and more structured cognitive–behavioral treatment. Prigatano (1991) suggested that this is because it is assumed that they could not benefit because of permanent cognitive, linguistic, and affective disturbances. The assumed practical effects of the deficits have been to interfere with the patient's understanding the purpose of psychotherapy, reduced concentration in sessions, poor memory for what occurred sequentially in sessions over time, and an inability to participate in a relationship that emphasizes verbal information processing.

O'Hara and Harrell (1991) suggested that the low expectation of the capacity of survivors of traumatic brain injuries to identify and meet their own emotional needs has limited many survivors from resuming what they termed *empowerment* and *equality*, *sensing survivorship*, and *redefining self*. They further stated that the absence of consistent psychotherapeutic services for survivors of traumatic brain injuries is a "systemwide omission" that extends into acute and postacute rehabilitation settings. Psychotherapeutic treatment is too often adjunctive, optional, or missing altogether. As a result, basic information on the client's own brain injury and its effects (i.e., emotional, interpersonal, phenomenological) is not yet being provided consistently to the client and to families (O'Hara & Harrell, 1991).

Individual psychotherapy may be contraindicated for some people with brain injuries and at some points in the recovery process. For example, when clients are confused or agitated, are globally aphasic, or have premorbid characterological factors that interfere with trust, it may be inappropriate to attempt direct psychotherapeutic interventions. However, many people with brain injuries, even those with severe cognitive and behavioral deficits, may profit from individual or group psychotherapy for support, alleviation of psychological symptoms, developing coping skills, understanding, and insight.

According to Prigatano (1986), the psychosocial adjustment problems of patients with brain injuries can frequently be substantially reduced, and psychotherapy, aimed at helping clients recognize, accept, and compensate for their deficits, is a vital component of any form of neuropsychologically oriented rehabilitation. Because of the efforts of neuropsychologists such as Prigatano (1986) and Ben-Yishay and Lakin (1989), the individual emotional needs and psychotherapeutic issues of survivors of brain injuries have received increased attention and clinical neuropsychologists are playing an increasingly important role in the rehabilitative process (Meier, Benton, & Diller, 1987).

Some head injury rehabilitation programs routinely provide individual psychotherapy as well as group, family, and marital therapies (Carberry & Burd, 1986). However, at the end of the typical rehabilitation program, which is usually brief (6 months or less), the patient still needs psychotherapeutic services (Butler & Satz, 1988) to assist in reintegration into the family and community. A referral is often made to a therapist in the community. Psychotherapists working with survivors of brain injury must be knowledgeable in the application of a broad range of psychotherapeutic theories, interventions, and strategies, selected not only to complement the individual client's personality but also the changing stages in emotional recovery, increasing sophistication and requests for information, emerging insight and self-awareness, and recapitulation of development and capacity for relationship (O'Hara & Harrell, 1991).

PRESENTING PROBLEMS

There are a variety of possible causes of the emotional and motivational problems that may be the impetus for a referral for psychotherapy. Brain trauma can precipitate an increase in preexisting psychopathology, bring about the emergence of previously unnoticed maladaptive tendencies, or even lead to decreases in psychological symptomatology (Prigatano, 1987).

As with other victims of trauma, people with brain trauma undergo a sudden, unexpected, environmentally induced change that may permanently alter their values, perceptions, and identities. Many experience symptoms of posttraumatic stress disorder, characterized by sleep disturbances, ruminations, hyperirritability, and social withdrawal. Intrusive recollections and flashbacks of their injuries and treatment are less common, particularly among those who lost consciousness at the time of the injury due to the common occurrence of retrograde or anterograde amnesia (O'Hara & Harrell, 1991).

Survivor guilt, however, may be an issue for some patients (O'Hara & Harrell, 1991). For example, the survivor might have sustained a head injury but his or her companion died in the accident. In addition to guilt, the patient may lack resolution of the death of the companion, who might have been buried while the patient was unconscious or hospitalized. The patient may need extensive time to deal with the permanent and total loss of the companion in order to move toward grieving for herself or himself, regenerating the desire or will to live, and opening up to new relationships. The task is even more difficult because the cognitive abilities and emotional resources have been altered by the injury.

Reactive depression after brain trauma is common and to be expected (Butler & Satz, 1988). Frequently, the patient's life has suffered a major disruption that, depending on the severity of the brain injury, can include loss of vocation and independence. Some symptoms, such as reduced motivation and anhedonia, are seen in major depressive disorders, but they are also common sequelae to brain damage (Butler & Satz, 1988). Problems associated with depression, impulse control, apathy, anxiety-related symptomatology, and psychosis are frequently observed in patients with brain damage (G. Goldstein & Ruthven, 1983).

Blumer and Benson (1975) described a syndrome labeled *pseudodepression*, which occurs after anterior or medial frontal lobe damage. A patient with brain trauma may appear depressed and manifest symptoms of memory dysfunction, psychomotor retardation, lack of initiation, apathy, and flat or blunted affect in the absence of a major depressive disorder. Accordingly, a patient with brain trauma who was indeed depressed may begin to improve in mood while his or her affect and behavior continue to appear dysfunctional (Butler & Satz, 1988).

Another personality syndrome found among patients with brain injury has been labeled *pseudopsychopathy* (Blumer & Benson, 1975). Such patients present with symptoms including disinhibition, facetiousness, sexual and personal hedonism, and a lack of concern for others. Full psychopathy in a patient with brain injury with good premorbid adjustment is relatively rare (Jennett & Teasdale, 1981). However, disinhibition, lack of concern, and self-defeating behaviors are common sequelae of a head injury. The therapist must avoid ascribing dynamic interpretations to behavioral symptoms that may have an organic cause (Butler & Satz, 1988). The premorbid history will assist the neuropsychologist in making differential diagnostic decisions. A history of head trauma coupled with adequate preinjury functioning suggest that psychopathic tendencies are a function of disinhibition rather than acting out. With such patients it is often necessary to arrange structured environmental and external controls, in addition to teaching the patient how to best use his or her own internal controls (Ben-Yishay, 1983).

INDIVIDUAL PSYCHOTHERAPY

The process of individual psychotherapy with a patient with brain injury can be slow and difficult. The degree and type of brain injury will greatly influence the therapy process (Prigatano, 1986), and a thorough neuropsychological evaluation (see chap. 1 in this book) will aid in planning therapy. Kay (1993) presented one way of integrating the results of an evaluation into treatment planning and pointed out that psychological difficulties will increase if primary neuropsychological deficits are not diagnosed and treated. Preexisting personality characteristics, preinjury life experiences, and the current family structure also affect the process; therefore, it is particularly crucial to gather thorough histories at intake (O'Hara & Harrell, 1991). Effective intervention requires attention to the psychological needs of the people who live with and care for patients with brain injuries as well as the patients themselves. Thus, psychotherapy after brain injury must be directed first to the patient who has suffered the injury and then to those who must interact with the patient (Prigatano, 1986).

The Treatment Alliance

Psychotherapy depends, to a great extent, on the development of a relationship between the therapist and patient. This relationship underlies any specific therapeutic techniques that are used. Common factors play an important role in the establishment of that relationship and thus help form a foundation for the therapy process (Garfield, 1980). Creation of a calm, deliberate, and reassuring environment, coupled with permission to ventilate one's fears and a future-oriented exploration of alternatives, appears to be helpful (Grimn & Bleiberg, 1986). Orlinsky and Howard (1986) suggested that the establishment of a good therapeutic bond should enhance the patient's willingness to engage in therapeutic interventions. Furthermore, they indicated that particular interventions, such as confrontation, interpretations, and exploration, may not be beneficial unless a reliable therapeutic bond is first established.

Factors such as warmth, support, empathic reelection, affective approximation, maintaining a nonjudgmental attitude, and expectancy for improvement are important to the therapeutic process and outcome. Therapists can rely on these factors to establish rapport, develop the therapeutic bond, and establish an atmosphere in which the therapist can implement other specific interventions as necessary.

As in all psychotherapeutic relationships, the patient may develop an emotional attachment to the therapist. Ellis (1989) summarized three types of maladaptive psychotherapy relationships that can emerge from the experiences of vulnerability and dependency of people with brain injury: hostile, dependent, and hostile–dependent. Because transference is considered an unconscious process, the client may not be aware of the psychodynamic factors contributing to his or her hostility toward or dependence on the therapist. The vulnerability provoked by trauma also may trigger re-creation of uncomfortable parent–child or perpetrator–victim roles. Personality characteristics or physical attributes may trigger an aversive or dependent response. The patient's hostile, dependent, or hostile–dependent response also may carry unrecognized sexual or romantic overtones, with accompanying inappropriate behavior. Misinterpretation of the relationship may be exaggerated by the patient's lengthy absence of sexual activity (through prolonged hospitalization or social isolation), diminished awareness of appropriate social boundaries, hypersexuality (Blackerby, 1988), or poor impulse control. Sensitivity, setting limits, and helping the patient identify suitable objects for romantic and sexual relationships should be helpful in working through transference (O'Hara & Harrell, 1991). As always, it is crucial that the therapist be aware of countertransference and to seek peer supervision in addressing its resolution.

Psychoeducation

Often, the most important early intervention is educational (Bennett, 1987). It might be assumed that someone else has already gone over the pertinent details. However, one would be amazed at how frequently patients and family members respond to information by saying, "Why didn't anyone ever tell me that?" It may be that earlier attempts at explanation were made but were lost in the events related to the acute recovery phase. Brief explanations of a patient's problems may spare the patient and family much confusion, anxiety, and inappropriate action based on inadequate or misinterpreted information. Patients and families benefit from understanding the symptoms and learning that these are normal consequences of brain injury. Additionally, there is an important existential component to education. When bad things happen, people need reasons. Knowledge also is a way to empower the patient and family.

A psychoeducational model is useful to help the patient and his or her family understand the meaning of brain injury in their lives (Prigatano & Klonoff, 1988). The psychotherapist must provide a model for understanding what has gone wrong that the person with a brain injury can handle. Knowledge of the neurological, neuropsychological, and psychological factors must be distilled and the essential message transmitted to the client in a noncondescending manner. The model must be simple, true, as best the facts are known, and relatively easy to remember. The explanation must explain much of what the patient experiences, irrespective of what he or she is able to verbalize (Prigatano, 1986).

We have found it helpful to use diagrams and a three-dimensional model of the brain to supplement verbal explanations. Additionally, listing the patient's strengths and deficits in functional terms often is beneficial and assists the patient in organizing, learning, and understanding the information. It may be necessary to encourage the patient to use nonverbal means, such as art or music, to express some ideas (Prigatano, 1991).

As an explanation of what has happened to the patient and as awareness of his or her deficits begins to unfold, there is usually the concomitant question, "Why has this happened to me?" Prigatano (1986) reported that there is much self-blaming as well as blaming others. The patient may see the tragedy as a punishment for sins or want to punish others for causing the brain injury. She or he requires help to achieve a sense of self-acceptance and forgiveness for himself or herself and others who caused the accident (Prigatano & Klonoff, 1988). Without these accomplishments, the patient may continue to spend a great deal of energy on these problems. Finally, fostering a sense of realistic hope is extremely important if therapists are to effectively work with these patients (Prigatano & Klonoff, 1988).

Prigatano and Klonoff (1988) described several useful approaches, including individual and group psychotherapy. Group pressure and group dynamics are powerful influences on behavior (Prigatano, 1986). As an educational technique, group feedback to patients can be invaluable because patients may accept suggestions and criticisms from peers more readily than from therapists. Group therapy also can be valuable in helping patients with behavioral problems become more sensitive to their negative social impact on others.

Dealing With Denial

Denial of deficits and a lack of awareness of deficits are common after brain injury (Rosen, 1986). Denial may be both a psychological defense mechanism and the result of deficits in self-awareness. O'Hara and Harrell (1991) defined self-awareness as "the recognition of how others perceive us, the ability to critique our own behavior, and the recognition of internal motivation, cognitive and emotional strengths and limitations, and change over time" (p. 394). Survivors of brain injury may experience partial losses in self-awareness; therefore, rebuilding self-awareness skills is an important therapeutic task. This can be accomplished through information gathering, audiotaped or videotaped feedback, psychological test review, and a comparison of the client's behavior with that of peers with brain injury.

Denial frequently may lead to failure to appreciate or acknowledge cognitive deficits in areas such as memory, planning and judgment, attention–concentration, speech, and general intellectual abilities (Caplan & Shechter, 1987). The patient also may deny personality changes and other psychological symptomatology (Butler & Satz, 1988). Direct confrontation often will result in hostility or a catastrophic reaction and is best avoided, at least initially. According to Butler and Satz, the best general method is to encourage graded, safe functional activities that will promote a more natural confrontational process. Specifically, the patient may profit from mistakes in real-life settings. However, as pointed out by Lezak (1988), the patient may not be able to independently learn from this experience. It is the therapist's role to provide a supportive but realistic environment in which this process can be productive, as illustrated in the following clinical example.

Case Example

A 40-year-old survivor of a brain injury insisted for some time that she could return to her old job as a paralegal, a job that involved a high degree of reasoning, planning and organizational skills, rapid cognitive processing, attention to detail, and at least average memory ability, even though her current level of impairment rendered such a prospect clearly out of the question. She adamantly refused to consider any other less demanding work, strenuously insisting that she had an excellent reputation in the legal community, that she had studied for years to prepare for that type of position, and that her employer had told her he would take her back now.

Initially, therapy focused on goal setting and establishing a series of subgoals related to the development of memory compensatory strategies (i.e., external memory aids, memory association strategies) that the patient could successfully accomplish. Additionally, we gradually focused on reality by using concrete feedback, checklists, structured self-monitoring inventories, and videotapes. By capitalizing on the patient's strong sense of pride in her reputation, we encouraged the substitution of a more negotiable defense, such as rationalization, for her outright denial. Gradually, she was able to embrace the idea that she had indeed "proved" herself to be an excellent paralegal who had worked hard and "paid her dues"; however, she had been forced to sacrifice time at home with her husband and daughter. Now she probably deserved time to take it easy and to improve the quality of her marital relationship and parenting skills. She could engage in part-time volunteer clerical activities at a volunteer lawyers program. This permitted her the psychological freedom and space to undertake tasks she could deal with more easily while continuing to improve her memory compensatory skills and gaining successes in the workplace and at home. By reframing the denial in a more ego-supportive context, she was empowered and able to acknowledge her cognitive deficits. Her insight improved and she attained enough skill using her memory book to be placed in a more challenging volunteer position. An added bonus was that her improved self-esteem led to marked reduction in conflict and stress at home.

Structure Within Therapy

According to O'Hara and Harrell (1991), the use of external structure within the psychotherapeutic relationship is extremely important, particularly early in treatment. It assists the client in establishing boundaries and expectations of her or his performance and participation, and it provides safety. The psychotherapist must be well versed in principles of cognitive and behavioral theory so that he or she can recognize when and how to alter such external structure as the client progresses.

One of the elements that is effective in defining boundaries and building the psychotherapeutic relationship is a written contract for participation in treatment (O'Hara & Harrell, 1991). Contracts emphasize the voluntary commitment to and negotiation of the psychotherapeutic alliance, the importance of the client's choice, and his or her equal participation. Providing the client with a copy of any contract allows the client to review his or her personal commitment to treatment (and circumvent absences caused by memory loss). Furthermore, the use of behavioral contracts has proved effective as an intervention in problems with impulse control, including aggressive and destructive behavior and suicidal ideation (O'Hara & Harrell, 1991). The following case illustrates these points.

Case Example

A 17-year-old survivor of a traumatic brain injury announced that he was tired of "people treating him like a baby." He loudly vented anger at his mother, who had insisted he enter treatment because of concerns about his destructive behavior, failing school performance, poor school attendance, and his "selfish attitude." The patient replied, "I am not going to come here for your reasons." We encouraged him to express his understanding of his mother's "reasons." Next, he was asked to discuss his opinions of the behaviors described and how the behaviors benefited him. The behaviors, his opinions, and the benefits were listed on the chalkboard. He was asked to discuss how these behaviors might make life more problematic for him, and these "cons" were listed on the board. At times he required help from the therapist to brainstorm and generate hypotheses. He was encouraged to discuss his personal goals and desires, and these were also listed on the board. Throughout the process he was consistently asked questions such as "How does your mother feel about this?" and "How do you feel when that happens?" in order to facilitate empathy and cognitive flexibility. The patient was asked to look at the board and prioritize his goals and desires. Next, he was asked to look at the board to see whether any of the behaviors listed would present obstacles to his achieving his goals. In this way he was able to concretely see the points his mother had been trying so desperately to make. However, by using this strategy, he was able to conclude that he needed to change these behaviors. This strategy helped him to analyze his own behaviors and choices and then to take on some of the responsibility of determining a treatment contract. The therapist and the patient negotiated a contract allowing him some choices while including some of his mother's concerns. The patient was asked to help write the contract agreement on paper and all parties signed it. The patient was given a copy of the contract to post on his wall at home. The patient consistently attended therapy sessions and completed all of the treatment objectives. He indicated that he appreciated being "treated like a regular real person."

The absence of such external structure or the presence of too much imposed structure (i.e., telling the client what he or she will do with no negotiation of choice) may contribute to the failure of traditional individual psychotherapy with survivors of brain injury. Open-ended, nondirective discussion of emotional distress results in many clients' cognitive confusion, sense of failure, absenteeism, and lack of clearly defined or attainable goals (O'Hara & Harrell, 1991), whereas an authoritarian approach may cause considerable open resistance.

Modification of Session Parameters

Clients with brain injury may be unable to acclimate to the traditional psychotherapy structure (i.e., the weekly hour) or variability in scheduling treatment. Table 1 outlines common problem areas and potentially useful methods for dealing with them. Shortened sessions may be necessitated by a client's limited attention span. Lengthened sessions can ac-

TABLE 1

Methods to Meet the Specific Needs of the Client

Problem	Method
Memory deficits	Increased frequency of sessions; consistent appointment times; periodic telephone reminders; use of audiovisual recordings; memory compensation strategies (e.g., memory log, mnemonics, calendars, pill organizers); present material in small chunks with rest periods in between; frequent repetition of material; present material both verbally and visually; client outlines sessions and takes notes for later review; client summarizes sessions at beginning, middle, and end; and enunciate words clearly.
Limited attention span	Shortened sessions; increased frequency of sessions; frequent breaks; repetition; present material in more than one modality; and use of client summarization and note taking.
Slowed information processing and speech	Lengthened sessions; allow extra time for formulation of responses; avoid answering for client; avoid inadvertent interruption of client; therapist must speak slowly and enunciate words clearly; repetition; and use of summarizing.
Self-awareness deficits	Audio- or videotaped feedback; psychological or neuropsychological test review; comparison of client's behavior with the literature on traumatic brain injury; and direct feedback by therapist.
Need for reinforcing external structure and information	Increased frequency of sessions; written contracts; consistent appointment times; and structured, directive therapy sessions.
Social skills deficits	Modeling by therapist; social skills training; role plays; audio- or videotaped feedback; and practice exercises.
Difficulty expressing ideas and feelings verbally	Use of symbolism, art, and music.
Alterations in sexual functioning	Permission giving; facilitating communication; providing information; and pleasuring exercises.

commodate slowed information processing and speech. An increased frequency of sessions assists the client who has short-term memory problems and is in need of reinforcement of external structure and information. Consistent appointment times and the availability of the therapist for crisis intervention also may be necessary. The following case illustrates some of these adaptations of the therapy session.

Case Example

A 47-year-old man with a brain injury was being treated for depression. Because of his severely limited attention span, profound memory impairment, and severely slowed processing speed, his sessions were uniquely structured. His sessions were scheduled at a consistent time in the morning in order to decrease the effects of fatigue on his cognitive functioning. He was asked to videotape all sessions and reviewed his tape during the week at regularly scheduled times noted on his calendar. Furthermore, he was encouraged to take "therapy notes" throughout each session in order to facilitate carryover from session to session and recall. The therapist used the chalkboard to help the patient outline the session and to note key ideas. Additionally, the hour-long session was divided into three 15-min segments, with two intervening 5-min breaks to facilitate attention, learning, and recall. The first segment of each session consisted of a "check-in" with the patient on his current mood and functioning and then a review of the previous session. A break allowed practice on relaxation breathing and stretching exercises and provided time for him to prepare for the second segment. The next 15-min segment consisted of the therapeutic work of the day followed by another 5-min break. In the final segment of the session, the patient and therapist reviewed and summarized the hour, with the patient completing a summary page in his therapy notebook for later review.

Within these modified sessions, the psychotherapist may need to alter his or her own behavior. When working with this population, it is important to speak slowly and enunciate one's words clearly. This is particularly important after significant brain injury, when patients may have difficulty with auditory comprehension, memory, and abstract reasoning.

Monitoring one's own social skills, strengths, and deficits as she or he becomes an important role model of appropriate social skills for a survivor of brain injury is also important. The therapist must exhibit self-control, particularly when the client is angry or anxious, and deal with misunderstandings or miscommunications objectively and nonpunitively. Furthermore, the therapist must be sensitive to the client's limitations (e.g., delayed cognitive processing and inadvertent social blunders). Extra time may need to be allowed for the client's formulation of responses to questions, and the therapist must avoid inadvertent interruptions or "answering" for the client. Finally, the therapist may need to edit her or his own tendencies toward storytelling and long-windedness with clients who may need to edit these same behaviors (O'Hara & Harrell, 1991).

EFFECTS OF COGNITIVE DEFICITS

Attention

In Ben-Yishay's (1983) model, one of the basic cognitive requirements to participate in treatment, including psychotherapy, is attention. The patient's attention span must be long enough to participate in at least brief (i.e., a few minutes) interactions. Distractibility also is a common problem and interventions that pique the client's interest and address his or her uniqueness will be more likely to maintain attention. Successful psychotherapy interventions must meet the client's emotional needs in a way that has personal meaning and cultural relevance, as illustrated in the following case.

> *A 23-year-old man with a traumatic brain injury had spent much of his time before the injury restoring automobiles. Although he was easily distracted from most tasks after the injury, he responded to the use of a metaphor in which each task was broken down into component parts, which were paired with the steps in the restoration process. He was subsequently able to use external cues to move through a sequence of tasks. Additionally, the restoration metaphor was used as a model for discussing and understanding his own rehabilitation.*

Memory Disturbances

Although each patient is different, a memory disturbance of varying severity is likely to be encountered, even in patients who have mild brain trauma. Butler and Satz (1988) recommended that all patients with brain trauma audiotape therapy sessions. This allows the patient to replay the session during the week in order to promote continuity in therapy, which is particularly vulnerable to the detrimental effects of a memory disturbance. Another helpful technique for some patients involves outlining the therapy session for the patient's later review. Butler and Satz pointed out that much of the patient's sense of self depends on intact memory. This process is disrupted in the patient with a head injury who has a memory disturbance. Even minor steps directed at preserving this continuity are important.

If lapses in memory create difficulties in keeping appointments, it is often best to initially assume a problem-solving approach (Butler & Satz, 1988). This can include memory compensation strategies, such as putting reminders in prominent places (e.g., a note on the bathroom mirror, a memory notebook or periodic telephone reminders). The therapist must differentiate between resistance and memory deficits as causes of late or missed appointments and failures to follow through on homework assignments (Small, 1973). If all attempts at problem solving fail and the patient is less than severely impaired, dynamic formulations become more attractive. Passive–aggressive behavior and memory deficits may coexist (Butler & Satz, 1988).

Other Deficits

In addition to difficulties related to memory, the therapist can expect other cognitive impairments to impinge on the therapeutic process (Butler & Satz, 1988). Mild forms of aphasia may persist for long periods and can cause difficulties in word finding and in expressive fluency, independent of memory. This can cause considerable anxiety and anger in the patient, which can then exacerbate symptoms. Impairment in planning ability can result in difficulties in organization, visual–spatial difficulties can result in patients becoming lost more easily, and attention–concentration impairment can cause a loss of train of thought with greater frequency. Frequently, language is affected and speech becomes digressive, circumstantial, and tangential (Jennett & Teasdale, 1981).

Even mild impairment in these areas can be exceedingly unsettling to patients, particularly those with high levels of premorbid functioning (Butler & Satz, 1988). Relaxation training is often highly effective in reducing self-fulfilling prophecies that result from a patient's excessive emotional reactions to brain-injury sequelae (Beck, Rush, Shaw, & Emery, 1979; Butler & Satz, 1988; Novack, Roth, & Boll, 1988; Stoyva, 1979). Patience, support, relaxation training, and teaching the clients ways in which they can structure their environment in order to minimize cognitive deficits is an important part of the therapeutic process with patients with brain injury (Butler & Satz, 1988).

Related Difficulties

Frequently, patients may experience difficulties with interpersonal functioning that are related to their becoming overwhelmed with tasks that are too difficult. This may cause feelings of anger, depression, or frustration, which may then be projected onto people in the environment, including family members, coworkers, and supervisors. When changes in behavior are explained to patients and their families, they often respond with a sense of relief because they then have a framework in which to interpret their behavior. For patients who have significant problems with judgment, reasoning, or reality, the therapist may act to help patients with decisions that they are genuinely unable to make independently (Werman, 1984). An example of this type of guiding approach is unrealistic work aspirations.

Next, guidance is needed to make realistic commitments to work, school, and interpersonal relationships. The patient also must be taught how to behave in different social situations to improve interpersonal competence. Behavioral techniques such as social skills training are useful here. Also, the patient needs to learn specific behavioral strategies when compensating for neuropsychological deficits. Survivors of traumatic brain injury need to learn decision-making, goal-setting, and troubleshooting skills. Another coping skill is the rehearsal of at least one strategy to handle emergencies. Survivors of traumatic brain injury frequently suffer from chronic pain (related to headaches and brain trauma as well as orthopedic injuries). Therefore, pain reduction and stress management skill-building strategies may need to be included (O'Hara & Harrell, 1991).

Existential Issues in Psychotherapy

Belief systems. The patient's beliefs about himself or herself in relation to the world play a major role in determining the patient's response to the many changes related to the injury. Butler and Satz (1988) stated that it is particularly important to determine the patients' preexisting attitudes toward people with brain injury. This often will provide information on how the patient currently views himself or herself. The therapist also can use this topic as a way to dispel myths and common misconceptions about people with brain injury.

Prigatano (1991) provided a useful conceptualization of the task confronting the patient with brain injury as a search for meaning or purpose for existence. He referred to the loss of sense of meaning as a "wounded soul." Some or all of the definitions of meaningfulness in life may no longer exist for the patient with a brain injury, as illustrated next.

> *A 19-year-old man who suffered a closed head injury in a car accident did not participate in physical therapy because he said he had been an award-winning athlete and would get well and be able to walk and run again. Hence, learning to walk with crutches was unnecessary. He and his family spoke as if life were meaningful only within the context of his former athletic prowess. Over the course of therapy, he and his family were helped to focus on and value other personal characteristics, and he eventually applied the same motivation to walking with crutches that he had previously used to run hurdles.*

Thus, establishing meaning in life often may involve paying attention to new aspects of life or applying old abilities in new ways.

Loss. Patients with brain injury are forced to cope with a unique sense of loss (Grzesiak, 1979). Specifically, they must cope with a loss of part of their self. Relatively few people will suffer a brain injury that results in a partial loss of self, which is qualitatively different from, and perhaps more threatening than, loss of people or things outside oneself. Once past the acute stage of recovery, the patient with brain injury becomes more and more aware of this, and such awareness may result in hostility and anger toward the therapist (Butler & Satz, 1988). Empathy by the therapist may be rebuffed.

Psychotherapists may help patients verbalize the breadth and depth of their losses. This allows therapists to join with clients in acknowledging multiple layers of loss. Psychotherapists can assist clients in interpreting anger and frustration as expressions of loss and grief and can make connections or associations to broaden their understanding of the specifics of their distress. Knowledge of previous losses patients may have experienced may be useful in helping them to acknowledge current losses and engage coping mechanisms.

The well-known model by Kubler-Ross (1969) describes stages of coping that occur in many individuals confronted with loss of life. These stages—denial, anger, bargaining, depression, and acceptance—appear equally appropriate in coping with the loss of self that can occur after a brain injury. By imposing structure on the onslaught of confusing emotions that patients may be feeling, and informing them that they are experiencing a normal reaction to their trauma, therapists can help patients to minimize catastrophic reactions and successfully adjust to their current situation.

According to Butler and Satz (1988), many patients with brain trauma struggle with issues concerning loss of self, which may become a major focus in therapy. One approach to restoring a sense of self involves identifying with those characteristics that have survived the brain injury (Margolis, 1993). For example, a 42-year-old woman with brain injury presented for therapy with symptoms of severe depression and low self-esteem. She indicated she felt "stupid" and "inferior." Structured self-observations, value clarification exercises, interest inventories, and self-esteem building exercises were used to assist her in identifying strengths and characteristics that had survived the brain injury. She was helped to develop and implement a plan to reestablish and develop some activities in which she could feel useful, successful, or both. These approaches facilitated her acceptance of her "new self" and resulted in a subsequent decrease in depressive symptomatology.

Vocational Issues

A number of factors influence the likelihood that a survivor of a brain injury will return to work, including age, premorbid adjustment, educational level, and severity of injury-related deficits. Although a high percentage of patients with the mildest head injuries may return to work within a year, those with more severe injuries may be unemployed for 2 years or longer (Dikmen et al., 1994, 1995). The client who is brain injured and suffering vocational disruption is at extremely high risk for adjustment difficulties related loss of self and low self-esteem (Butler & Satz, 1988). Even relatively mild head injuries can have devastating effects on vocational performance and result in an inability to continue in one's original employment. The therapist must be careful to fully appreciate not only the financial and other situational difficulties that this can entail, but also the loss of self-worth that is involved. Reestablishing some activities that are deemed useful by the patient and others is helpful. Such activities include limited household chores and child-care activities within the family. Another option is volunteer work in the health care rehabilitation setting, which might be specialized to the patient's ability, as well as supervised by staff. Later, volunteer work might include community agencies, churches, or work with children with disabilities, all of which may be able to adapt their needs to the survivor's ability level. Later in recovery, it may be that a return to at least part-time work is a reasonable goal.

FAMILY INTERVENTION

The survivor of a brain injury does not travel the road to recovery alone. Family members join their loved one in attempts to cope with the trauma and a family system that has changed. In the discussion that follows, a *family* is defined as the people with whom the patient has allegiance and defines as family. Nontraditional families may need extra support. Brain injury affects not only the patient but also the entire family and social system (Grimn & Bleiberg, 1986). Psychotherapy with patients with brain injury is less effective if there is not an ongoing working relationship with family members (Rollin, 1987).

Effects of Brain Injury on Family Functioning

The impact that a brain injury can have on a patient's family and marital relationships is devastating, although there are documented rare cases in which the family perceives the brain injury to have produced a positive outcome (Blyth, 1981). This may reflect the individual's poor premorbid adjustment. The family unit experiences major alterations in roles, rules, and internal responsibilities in its adjustment to a significantly different family member (Jones & Lorman, 1988). Ylvisaker, Szekeres, Henry, Sullivan, and Wheeler (1987), Klonoff and Prigatano (1987), Rosenthal and Muir (1983), and Brooks (1984) indicated that all aspects of family life can be affected by a head injury. Major changes in the structure and organization of the family can be anticipated. Brooks, McKinlay, Symington, Beattie, and Campsie (1987), Brooks, Campsie, Symington, Beattie, and McKinlay (1986), and Brooks (1984) reported that stress caused by changes in routine, social status, family health, and patient behaviors is a major factor in a family's inability to adjust to its different family member.

The families of patients with brain damage typically experience at least some social problems involving isolation, loss of emotional supports, restricted independence, and financial strain, as well as the psychological experiences of bewilderment, frustration, guilt, and depression (Lezak, 1988). It is essential that the psychotherapist working with these families identify and help them develop functional support patterns, within and outside the family.

The nature and severity of problems experienced by family members will differ from family to family, depending on premorbid cohesiveness, family attitudes about illness and responsibility, and financial and social supports (DePompei & Zarski, 1989; DePompei, Zarski, & Hall, 1988). It also will differ among family members, with the person who assumes the role of primary caretaker frequently carrying the greater part of the burden, whereas the severity of stress on other family members most typically varies according to their capacity for independence from the patient and the primary caretaker (Lezak, 1988).

Rosenthal and Muir (1983) indicated that there are three patterns of family functioning that can be considered to place families at high risk for becoming dysfunctional. They suggested that dysfunctional reactions will occur in families who exhibit any of the following: (a) a premorbid history of family problems such as marital stress or alcoholism; (b) an extended period of denial; and (c) persistent, severe cognitive or physical impairments of the patient with head injury.

Being alert to issues in the premorbid family history is particularly important. The families of many adult patients with head injury have a history of significant conflicts, which may involve spouse battering, child abuse, or alcoholism, among others. Such factors must be identified and their influences on the present system clarified. For example, a 50-year-old man, injured in a car accident while he was intoxicated, sustained a moderately severe brain injury. After 8 weeks of hospitalization, he returned home, but he and the family returned to the hospital for multiple outpatient therapy sessions to address physical and behavioral problems related to poor memory and judgment. Although his wife did not work outside the home, it became clear that she delegated responsibility for his care, as well as other family matters, to an adult daughter who lived nearby. All family members stated that they wanted the patient at home and indicated willingness to work with him, but they complained at every therapy session about his poor memory and impaired judgment. No homework assignments were carried out. The adult daughter was vehement in her complaints about her father. She eventually privately revealed to the therapist that she had been sexually abused by her father when she was a teenager. She was unwilling to deal with this in the context of the family therapy "because everyone is under too much stress," but she agreed that her brother should take the primary role with their father because "he is a man." After the brother became the responsible caretaker, there was some success in dealing with the patient's behavioral problems in the home. The daughter was referred for individual psychotherapy.

Additional stress affects the family when members begin to blame themselves or the member with brain injury for the turmoil and disruption of the family after the trauma (Prigatano & Klonoff, 1988). Blame is typically a function of how the family perceives the crisis and may indicate that the family sees the accident as unfair and beyond its ability to manage. Lezak (1978) reported that continued blaming or scapegoating may result in an older child's prematurely leaving home or in divorce, if the blame is focused on the marital unit.

Rationalization may be used by family members as a means for alleviating family distress associated with the crisis (Prigatano & Klonoff, 1988). Because feelings about the family member who is injured may be intense, family members may attempt to circumvent emotional conflicts by intellectualizing. Satir (1967) suggested that it is desirable to bring all significant members together to discuss the dynamics of their grieving and to validate family members' needs to express emotional pain.

Effects on Family Subsystems

Parents. Within the family sphere, the patient's parents frequently have caretaking responsibility thrust on them. This places considerable strain on family resources and confronts the patient and parents with dependency issues that may have been long dormant (Jennett & Teasdale, 1981). Although parental stresses differ somewhat according to whether the patient was a minor child or an independent adult when he or she became neurologically impaired, the core problems are similar. Not the least of these is dashed hopes, along with the realization that arrangements must be made for the lifelong care and well-being of that child. Marital conflicts may result as parents disagree over the care of the child, and often one parent feels neglected and the other feels overwhelmed with the demands of caretaking (Lezak, 1988).

Siblings. According to Lezak (1988), for most nonaffected children, brain impairment in a parent or sibling typically brings a sharp reduction in parental attention and an equally sharp increase in responsibilities. Shame and guilt are common reactions, which ultimately are compounded by frustration and anger at having a "different" family. Social activities are reduced because of shame or an inability to bring friends home, members may not participate in school or community activities requiring a parent because that parent is occupied with the patient's care, and there is an absence of parties and other kinds of good times the family had previously enjoyed. Older children and teenagers may react to stresses by running away, delinquency, truancy, dropping out of school, or getting pregnant (Lezak, 1988).

Marital relationships. Marital relationships are not impervious to disruption after a brain injury (Lezak, 1988). Role reversals may occur, and the significant other of the patient with brain injury may have to assume duties previously managed by the patient (Butler & Satz, 1988). Disharmony and maladjustment can result. The marital or significant other relationship, if present, needs close scrutiny and therapeutic intervention as necessary. One should always assess for the presence of depression or other reactive symptomatology in the partner, because his or her coping resources are likely to be challenged (Butler & Satz, 1988; Lezak, 1988). More often than not, the partner of the patient with brain injury will benefit from supportive psychotherapy, and this may be more true in nontraditional families.

Butler and Satz (1988) reported that one specific aspect of a couple's relationship that is often problematic after brain injury is sexual functioning. Apart from alterations in sexual functioning that are attributable to secondary depression in either partner, other issues may be involved. The patient's sexual behavior may change, depending on the nature of the brain injury. Damage to the frontal lobes may result in disinhibition, resulting in promiscuity, excessive sexual demands, or both. Symptoms such as a lack of initiation and inertia also can occur, which can lead to a decrease in sexual interest and behavior. Hormonal balances can be disrupted by brain injury, which also may result in alterations in sexual functioning.

Helping the patient and significant others to understand the origins of the behavioral changes is necessary, as is active therapeutic intervention (Butler & Satz, 1988). Frequently, the uninjured partner may feel uncomfortable having sex with the patient, particularly if the injury has resulted in relatively severe disabilities that have caused significant changes in functioning. In these cases, it is most important to help the partner to identify the specific reasons for his or her lack of sexual desire so that he or she can be examined and the problem addressed. Butler and Satz also commented on the importance of a predisability sexual functioning history in working with patients in rehabilitation and their partner. This history should include assessment of the level of sexual knowledge, past sexual experiences, and attitudes toward the acceptability of various sexual behaviors and feelings. Relatively straightforward interventions such as permission giving, facilitating communication, and providing information and specific suggestions can be helpful in maximizing the patient's and his or her partner's sexual adjustment after the trauma.

Stages of Family Adjustment

The various adjustment stages that families experience after a traumatic event have been well documented in the literature (Barry, 1984; Kubler-Ross, 1969; Lezak, 1978; Romano, 1974). The family has experienced a partial loss of the injured person. According to Rollin (1987), the adjustment process involves denial of the severity of the trauma that is caused by the brain injury. This denial may later be transferred to the survivor of the brain injury in an effort to deny the reality of the physical and cognitive impairments.

In another phase of adjustment, family members begin to recognize their helplessness and frustration. Expressions of anxiety, anger, bargaining, and depression replace denial (Prigatano & Klonoff, 1988). Family members may use one of many coping strategies during this period. These strategies may include (a) suppression, remaining distant from central issues (e.g., worrying about new clothes for the patient's return to school rather than about the educational problems likely to result from cognitive deficits); (b) avoidance, refusing to acknowledge the presence of problems; (c) projection, attributing negative feelings to other family members, including the patient; and (d) regression, using behaviors that might have been useful at an earlier time but are no longer appropriate or effective (e.g., talking to the survivor as if he or she were a child).

The final stage is the period of resolution (Prigatano & Klonoff, 1988). Ideally, at this stage, family members begin to accept the limitations of their injured family member and consider alternative ways to plan for the future of the family. Families may not move through these stages in any set pattern. Additionally, a different type of adjustment may accompany different problem areas. Each family's adjustment process is individualized, and there is no definitive time span that can be assigned or anticipated (Figley & McCubbin, 1983).

Rosenthal and Muir (1983) emphasized the importance of the family completing the mourning process, in that the family is never able to complete the ritual. In the case of brain injury, there is no burial, and the survivor remains with the family as a new and different individual. Therefore, the family must mourn the characteristics of the individual that have been lost while learning to respond to a person who behaves differently. It appears reasonable to assume that the patient also will experience incomplete mourning for the parts of himself or herself that were altered.

Comprehensive Family Intervention

A major task for the psychotherapist is to help the family comprehend the complex nature of brain injury and its sequelae. Prognosis and management strategies must be explained to the family in meaningful terms. As the families become better educated, they become more realistic and can manage the patient more effectively (Prigatano & Klonoff, 1988). This type of education can be provided through individual family meetings or in group counseling sessions (Diehl, 1983). Educational counseling can be viewed as a means to provide families with new information, to assist them to develop new skills, and to help them communicate. Another goal is to help families anticipate the inappropriate behaviors that their injured family member may exhibit in the future. Educating families in groups might begin with a series of meetings at which the general aspects of brain injury are discussed.

Rosenthal (1984) and Rollin (1987) described a four-part hierarchical approach to intervention with families of individuals with brain injury that consists of patient–family education, family counseling, family therapy, and family support groups. The type and amount of family involvement that are desirable depend on a variety of factors, including stage of recovery, family cohesiveness, prior family problems, type and severity of brain injury, and family responsiveness. Rollin (1987) suggested that families must be involved at their own pace and that it is best to plan the sharing of information according to their demonstrated and expressed readiness.

Support groups such as those that have been formed by the National Head Injury Foundation represent another means of providing educational information as well as peer support for family members. These support groups are helpful in a variety of ways, including the sharing of information and emotional support by others who have experienced a similar trauma in their families.

Inclusion of the family member with brain injury in educational sessions as soon as it is feasible aids in promoting family cohesiveness. Rosenthal and Muir (1983) pointed out that because of the emotional and cognitive demands placed on the family by family therapy, caution should be taken to avoid exposing the patient to family therapy before he or she is able to participate in a meaningful way. Education of the survivor of brain injury may be reinforced and verified with the patient in individual therapy sessions.

Videotapes of the patient with brain injury and of family interactions with him or her can be used to open discussion. Actively addressing the functional needs of the impaired member in the home and community also will stimulate frank discussion of altered capabilities and family expectations. Modeling by the therapist of desirable responses to the patient with brain injury also is helpful to families (Prigatano & Klonoff, 1988).

Lezak (1986) identified six general topics that should be discussed with most family members of the patient and, in order to be the most beneficial, be brought into discussion as early as possible:

1. Feelings of anger, frustration, and sorrow are natural emotions.
2. Caretakers must take care of themselves first.
3. Caretakers must rely on their own conscience and judgment when conflicts arise.
4. Role changes that may occur are distressing to all concerned.
5. Family members should not feel guilty because they are not helping or doing more.
6. When the welfare of dependent children is at stake, families must explore the issue of divided loyalties and weigh their responsibilities (Lezak, 1986).

When providing information to the patient and family, the therapist should adhere to several guidelines (Prigatano & Klonoff, 1988). First, the amount of information provided must be limited, and the therapist must allow time for the family to process the information. The therapist should be prepared to model correct responses for the family. Requesting that family members restate and rephrase what they have been told is often the most direct means of determining what they have learned. Asking one or two members to keep a journal of what goes on in each session, and then encouraging all others in the family to contribute additional information to it, also is helpful. Prognostic indications by the therapist must be offered with great caution. Until the patient's recovery process has reached some degree of stabilization, the patient and family will have great difficulty assimilating information about the multiple behavioral, communicative, and personality changes that are caused by a head injury.

When dysfunctional family patterns begin to emerge, counseling sessions can be directed at reframing the family's focus and reactions (DePompei et al., 1988). After several sessions, if the family seems unable to refocus its energies positively, more intensive family therapy may be indicated.

More traditional family therapy techniques can be initiated at any point in the recovery process. However, it appears that it is usually indicated later in the recovery process, after the person with brain injury has returned home and specific relationship problems have been identified (Rosenthal & Muir, 1983). Rosenthal (1978) and Rosenthal and Young

(1988) listed specific techniques that can be used in a family therapy session. They include (a) shifting responsibility for the impairment from the injured family member to the entire family system; (b) determining the positive aspects of the family system and emphasizing them; (c) identifying family conflicts and helping families to resolve them; and (d) prescribing homework for families to practice generalization of behaviors learned in therapy sessions.

SUMMARY

The deficits that occur after brain trauma are varied. Not only will the patient likely benefit from psychotherapy, but other therapies also may be required (Butler & Satz, 1988). The practitioner who treats patients with head injuries needs to maintain a referral network that includes clinical neuropsychologists, neurologists, speech pathologists, occupational therapists, physical therapists, and psychiatrists (Butler & Satz, 1988).

Individuals who are in active clinical practice must be aware of the special issues and techniques involved in psychotherapy with clients with brain injury. However, clinicians may build on their knowledge and use of common factors in establishing the therapeutic relationship and creating a foundation for the therapy process.

Given the large number of individuals who sustain traumatic brain injuries each year, and the number of patients in acute rehabilitation programs, psychology graduate training programs should include training in survivors' emotional needs as well as psychotherapy issues and approaches related to working with this population. Finally, more psychotherapy outcome research is needed in order to validate, develop, and refine effective psychotherapy techniques for use with people with brain injury.

References

Barry, P. (1984). *Family adjustment to head injury*. Framingham, MA: National Head Injury Foundation.

Beck, A. T., Rush, A. J., Shaw, B. F., & Emery, G. (1979). *Cognitive therapy of depression*. New York: Guilford Press.

Bennett, T. L. (1987). Neuropsychological counseling of the adult with minor head injury. *Cognitive Rehabilitation*, *5*, 10–16.

Ben-Yishay, Y. (1983). Working approaches to remediation of cognitive deficits in the damaged brain. *Supplement to the 11th Annual Workshop for rehabilitation professionals*. New York: New York University, Institute of Rehabilitation Medicine.

Ben-Yishay, Y., & Lakin, P. (1989). Structured group treatment for brain injury survivors. In D. Ellis & A. L. Christensen (Eds.), *Neuropsychological treatment after brain injury* (pp. 164–193). Norwell, MA: Kluwer Academic.

Blackerby, W. (1988). Head injury rehabilitation: Sexuality after TBI. *H. D. I. professional series on traumatic brain injury, Vol. 10* (7). Houston, TX: HDI.

Blumer, D., & Benson, D. F. (1975). Personality changes with frontal and temporal lobe lesions. In D. F. Benson & D. Blumer (Eds.), *Psychiatric aspects of neurologic disease* (Vol. 1, pp. 151–169). New York: Grune & Stratton.

Blyth, B. (1981). The outcome of severe head injuries. *New Zealand Medical Journal*, *93*, 267–269.

Brooks, N. (1984). Head injury and the family. In N. Brooks (Ed.), *Closed head injury: Psychological, social and family consequences*. New York: Oxford University Press.

Brooks, N., Campsie, L., Symington, C., Beattie, A., & McKinlay, W. (1986). The first year outcome of severe blunt head injury: A relative's view. *Journal of Neurology, Neurosurgery, and Psychiatry*, *49*, 765–770.

Brooks, N., McKinlay, W., Symington, C., Beattie, A., & Campsie, L. (1987). Return to work within the first seven years of severe head injury. *Brain Injury*, *1*, 5–19.

Butler, R. W., & Satz, P. (1988). Individual psychotherapy with head-injured adults: Clinical notes for the practitioner. *Professional Psychology: Research and Practice*, *19*, 536–541.

Caplan, B., & Shechter, J. (1987). Denial and depression in disabling illness. In B. Caplan (Ed.), *Rehabilitation psychology desk reference* (pp. 148–150). Rockville, MD: Aspen Publishers.

Carberry, H., & Burd, B. (1986). Individual psychotherapy with the brain injured adult. *Cognitive Rehabilitation*, *4*, 22–24.

DePompei, R., & Zarski, J. J. (1989). Families, head injury, and cognitive-communicative impairments: Issues for family counseling. *Topics in Language Disorders*, *9*, 78–79.

DePompei, R., Zarski, J. J., & Hall, D. E. (1988). Cognitive communicative impairments: A family focused viewpoint. *Head Trauma Rehabilitation*, *3*(2), 13–22.

Diehl, L. (1983). Patient-family education. In M. Rosenthal, E. R. Griffith, M. R. Bond, & J. D. Miller

(Eds.), *Rehabilitation of the head injured adult* (pp. 395–401). Philadelphia: F. A. Davis.

Dikmen, S. S., Machamer, J. E., Winn, H. R., & Temkin, N. R. (1995). Neuropsychological outcome at 1-year post head injury. *Neuropsychology, 9*, 80–90.

Dikmen, S. S., Temkin, N. R., Machamer, M. A., Holubkov, M. A., Fraser, R. T., & Winn, H. R. (1994). Employment following traumatic head injuries. *Archives of Neurology, 51*, 177–186.

Ellis, D. (1989). Neuropsychotherapy. In D. Ellis & A. L. Christensen (Eds.), *Neuropsychological treatment after brain injury* (pp. 249–266). Norwell, MA: Kluwer Academic.

Figley, C. R., & McCubbin, H. I. (1983). *Stress and the family: Vol. II. Coping with catastrophe*. New York: Brunner/Mazel.

Garfield, S. L. (1980). *Psychotherapy: An eclectic approach*. New York: Wiley.

Goldstein, G., & Ruthven, L. (1983). *Rehabilitation of the brain-damaged adult*. New York: Plenum.

Goldstein, K. (1973). Effect of brain damage on personality. In T. Millon (Ed.), *Theories of psychopathology and personality: Essays and critiques* (pp. 54–62). Philadelphia: W. B. Saunders.

Grimn, B. H., & Bleiberg, J. (1986). Psychological rehabilitation in traumatic brain injury. In S. B. Filskov & T. J. Boll (Eds.), *Handbook of clinical neuropsychology* (Vol. 2, pp. 495–547). New York: Wiley.

Grzesiak, R. C. (1979). Psychological services in rehabilitation medicine: Clinical aspects of rehabilitation psychology. *Professional Psychology, 10*, 511–520.

Jennett, B., & Teasdale, G. (1981). Mental sequelae. In *Management of head injuries* (pp. 289–299). Philadelphia: F. A. Davis.

Jones, C., & Lorman, J. (1988). *Head injury: A guide for the patient and family*. Stow, OH: Interactive Therapeutics.

Kaplan, E. (1987). Foreword. In B. Uzzell & Y. Gross (Eds.), *Clinical neuropsychology of intervention*. Dordrecht, the Netherlands: Martinus-Nijhoff.

Kay, T. (1993). Neuropsychological treatment of mild traumatic brain injury. *Journal of Head Trauma Rehabilitation, 8*, 74–85.

Klonoff, P., & Prigatano, G. P. (1987). Reactions of family members and clinical intervention after traumatic brain injury. In M. Ylvisaker & E. M. Gobble (Eds.), *Community reentry for head-injured adults*. Boston: College-Hill Press.

Kraus, F. G. (1987). Epidemiology of head injury. In P. R. Cooper (Ed.), *Head injury* (2nd ed., pp. 1–19). Baltimore: Williams & Wilkins.

Kubler-Ross, E. (1969). *On death and dying*. New York: Macmillan.

Levin, H. S. (1985). Neurobehavioral recovery. In D. P. Becker & J. T. Povlishock (Eds.), *Central nervous system trauma status report* (pp. 281–299). Washington, DC: National Institute of Neurological and Communication Disorders and Stroke/National Institutes of Health.

Levin, H. S., Benton, A. L., & Grossman, R. G. (1982). *Neurobehavioral consequences of closed head injury*. New York: Oxford University Press.

Lezak, M. D. (1978). Subtle sequelae of brain damage: Perplexity, distractibility and fatigue. *American Journal of Physical Medicine, 57*, 9–15.

Lezak, M. D.(1986). Psychological implications of traumatic brain damage for the patient's family. *Rehabilitation Psychology, 31*, 241–250.

Lezak, M. D. (1988). Brain damage is a family affair. *Journal of Clinical and Experimental Neuropsychology, 10*, 111–123.

Margolis, E. T. (1993, August). Individual psychotherapy with the brain-injured adult: A treatment for the soul? In W. R. Leber (Chair), *Psychotherapy for brain-damaged patients*. Symposium presented at the 101st Annual Convention of the American Psychological Association, Toronto.

Meier, M., Benton, A., & Diller, L. (Eds.). (1987). *Neuropsychological rehabilitation*. New York: Guilford Press.

National Head Injury Foundation. (1982). *The silent epidemic*. Framingham, MA: Author.

Novack, T. A., Roth, D. L., & Boll, T. J. (1988). Treatment alternatives following mild head injury. *Rehabilitation Counseling Bulletin, 31*, 313–324.

O'Hara, C. C., & Harrell, M. (1991). *Rehabilitation with brain injury survivors: An empowerment approach*. Rockville, MD: Aspen Publishers.

Orlinsky, D. E., & Howard, K. I. (1986). Process and outcome in psychotherapy. In S. L. Garfield & A. E. Bergin (Eds.), *Handbook of psychotherapy and behavior change*. New York: Wiley.

Prigatano, G. P. (1986). Psychotherapy after brain injury. In G. P. Prigatano, D. J. Fordyce, H. K. Zeiner, & J. R. Rouche (Eds.), *Neuropsychological rehabilitation after head injury*. Baltimore: Johns Hopkins University Press.

Prigatano, G. P. (1987). Personality and psychosocial consequences after brain injury. In M. Meier, A. Benton, & L. Diller (Eds.), *Neuropsychological rehabilitation* (pp. 335–378). New York: Guilford Press.

Prigatano, G. P. (1991). Disordered mind, wounded soul: The emerging role of psychotherapy in rehabilitation after brain injury. *Journal of Head Trauma Rehabilitation*, 6(4), 1–10.

Prigatano, G. P., Fordyce, D. J., Zeiner, H. K., Rouche, J. R., Pepping, M., & Wood, B. C. (1984). Neuropsychological rehabilitation after closed head injury. *Journal of Neurology, Neurosurgery, and Psychiatry*, 47, 505–513.

Prigatano, G. P., & Klonoff, P. S. (1988). Psychotherapy and neuropsychological assessment after brain injury. *Journal of Head Trauma Rehabilitation*, 3(1), 45–46.

Prigatano, G. P., Klonoff, P. S., O'Brien, K. P., Altman, I. M., Amin, K., Chiapello, D., Shepherd, J., Cunningham, M., & Mora, M. (1994). Productivity after neuropsychologically oriented milieu rehabilitation. *Journal of Head Trauma Rehabilitation*, 9(1), 91–102.

Rollin, W. (1987). *The psychology of communication disorders in individuals and their families*. Englewood Cliffs, NJ: Prentice Hall.

Romano, M. D. (1974). Family response to traumatic head injury. *Scandinavian Journal of Rehabilitative Medicine*, 6, 1–4.

Rosen, M. (1986). Denial and the head trauma patient: A developmental formulation and treatment plan. *Cognitive Rehabilitation*, 4, 20–22.

Rosenthal, M. (1978). *Family intervention strategies*. Paper presented at the Second Annual Conference on the Remediation of the Traumatic Brain Injured Adult, Williamsburg, VA.

Rosenthal, M. (1984). Strategies for family intervention. In B. Edelstein & E. Couture (Eds.), *Behavioral approaches to the traumatically brain injured* (pp. 227–246). New York: Plenum.

Rosenthal, M., & Muir, C. (1983). Methods of family intervention. In M. Rosenthal, E. Griffith, M. Bond, & J. D. Miller (Eds.), *Rehabilitation of the head injured adult*. Philadelphia: F. A. Davis.

Rosenthal, M., & Young, T. (1988). Effective family intervention after traumatic brain injury: Theory and practice. *Journal of Head Trauma Rehabilitation*, 3(4), 42–50.

Satir, V. (1967). *Conjoint family therapy*. Palo Alto, CA: Science and Behavior Books.

Small, L. (1973). *Neuropsychodiagnosis in psychotherapy*. New York: Brunner/Mazel.

Stoyva, J. M. (1979). Guidelines in the training of general relaxation. In J. V. Basmajean (Ed.), *Biofeedback: Principles and practice for clinicians*. Baltimore: Williams & Wilkins.

Werman, D. S. (1984). *The practice of supportive psychotherapy*. New York: Brunner/Mazel.

Ylvisaker, M., Szekeres, S. R., Henry, K., Sullivan, D., & Wheeler, P. (1987). Topics in cognitive rehabilitation therapy. In M. Ylvisaker & E. M. Gobble (Eds.), *Community re-entry for head-injured adults* (pp. 137–220). Boston: College-Hill Press.

Author Index

Numbers in italics refer to listings in reference sections.

Subject Index

About the Editors

Russell L. Adams is a professor at the University of Oklahoma Health Sciences Center. Also at the center, he is Director of the Adult Neuropsychological Laboratory (since 1978), Director of Postdoctoral Training in Neuropsychology, and Director of the Clinical Psychology Internship Program. Previously, he was Director of the Neuropsychology Laboratory at the University of Texas at San Antonio.

Adams holds diplomas in clinical neuropsychology as well as clinical psychology from the American Board of Professional Psychology (ABPP). He is on the Board of Directors of the American Board of Clinical Neuropsychology and is a Fellow of the Division of Clinical Neuropsychology (Division 40) and the Division of Clinical Psychology (Division 12) in the American Psychological Association (APA). He also holds Fellowship status in the National Academy of Neuropsychology.

Adams serves as a reviewer for many of the major journals in neuropsychology. He has over 25 years of experience in neuropsychology and has evaluated thousands of patients with neuropsychological problems in his career.

Oscar A. Parsons is George Lynn Cross Research Professor Emeritus in the Department of Psychiatry and Behavioral Sciences, University of Oklahoma Health Sciences Center, College of Medicine. He is an ABPP Diplomate in both clinical neuropsychology and clinical psychology. Parsons received his PhD in clinical psychology from Duke University in 1954. From 1954 to 1959, he was a faculty member of the Departments of Psychiatry and Psychology of Duke University. From 1959 to 1991, he served as Professor and Vice Chair of the Department of Psychiatry and Behavioral Sciences at the University of Oklahoma Health Sciences Center. He has also been President of the Oklahoma Psychological Association, the Southwestern Psychological Association, and Division 40 of the APA. He is a Fellow in APA Divisions 6, 12, 38, 40, and 50.

For many years, Parsons has conducted clinical training and research on the neuropsychology of alcoholism. He holds the Distinguished Scientific Contribution Award from Division 12 of APA, as well as the Distinguished Clinical Neuropsychologist Award from the National Academy of Neuropsychology.

Jan L. Culbertson is Associate Professor in the Department of Pediatrics and Director of Neuropsychology Services at the Child Study Center, University of Oklahoma Health Sciences Center. Previously, she directed the Pediatric Psychology Program in the Department of Pediatrics, Vanderbilt University School of Medicine. She is senior editor of the *Journal of Clinical Child Psychology* and past editor of *Child, Youth, and Family Services Quarterly* (the APA Division 37 journal). She has served as President of Division 37 (Child, Youth, and Family Services) and President of Division 12, Section 1 (Clinical Child Psychology) and has held numerous other offices and leadership positions within APA.

Culbertson has been senior editor of two other books—*Sudden Infant Death Syndrome: Medical Aspects and Psychological Management* (with Henry F. Krous and R. Debra Bendel), and *Testing Young Children* (with Diane J. Willis)—and has authored or coauthored several other publications. She has lectured widely and presented annual postdoctoral institutes for Division 12.

Sara Jo Nixon is Associate Professor in the Department of Psychiatry and Behavioral Sciences at the University of Oklahoma Health Sciences Center. She is also Associate Director for the Oklahoma Center for Alcohol and Drug-Related Studies and Director of the Cognitive Studies Laboratory at the University of Oklahoma Health Sciences Center. Her research focuses on identifying the underlying cognitive processes that may be compromised in various disorders. She has written extensively in the areas of neurocognitive changes in dementia and chronic substance abuse and has focused a component of her work on gender differences and the role of family history in predicting cognitive change. Her other research interests include investigating the interaction of behavioral and cognitive dysfunction in prisoner populations and examining the differential effects of substance use and abuse in specific psychiatric populations.